D1551869

THE UNITY OF LUKE-ACTS

BIBLIOTHECA EPHEMERIDUM THEOLOGICARUM LOVANIENSIUM

CXLII

THE UNITY OF LUKE-ACTS

EDITED BY

J. VERHEYDEN

LEUVEN
UNIVERSITY PRESS

UITGEVERIJ PEETERS
LEUVEN

1999

ISBN 90 6186 955 2 (Leuven University Press)
D/1999/1869/18
ISBN 90-429-0762-2 (Peeters Leuven)
D/1999/0602/51
ISBN 2-87723-448-7 (Peeters France)

Leuven University Press / Presses Universitaires de Louvain
Universitaire Pers Leuven
Blijde-Inkomststraat 5, B-3000 Leuven-Louvain (Belgium)

© 1999, Peeters, Bondgenotenlaan 153, B-3000 Leuven (Belgium)

PREFACE

The present volume comprises the papers read at the 47th *Colloquium Biblicum Lovaniense* (July 29-31, 1998). The general theme of the meeting was the unity of the Gospel of Luke and the Acts of the Apostles.

Part I contains fifteen "Main Papers" given by invited speakers. It includes contributions on the history of research (Verheyden), the methodology of reading Luke's work as a unity (Marguerat), textual criticism (Delobel), the relationship between God and his people in Lukan theology (Brawley), Luke's christology (Tuckett) and pneumatology (Fitzmyer), his characterization of the Jews (Rese) and the political authorities (Horn), narrative parallelism (Lindemann), themes from the social world of Lk-Acts (Denaux, Taylor), and studies of particular passages: the infancy narrative (Radl, Mainville), the stories of Paul's conversion (Kremer), and Lk 4,16-30 (Neirynck). Part II, "Offered Papers", includes twenty-four papers on various aspects of Luke's theology, the expansion of the Church, the genre of Lk-Acts, and the literary and stylistic means Luke used to make his work a unity. In total there are thirty-nine contributions by scholars from twelve countries: Germany (12), Belgium (7), USA (6), Austria (3), United Kingdom (3), Spain (2), and one each from Canada, Ireland, Israel, the Netherlands, Switzerland, and Zimbabwe.

About 150 participants enjoyed the warm and friendly welcome offered by the President and staff of the Pope Adrian VI College who excelled in practising the characteristically Lukan virtue of hospitality. Thanks are due also to the Secretary of the Faculty of Theology and his staff for their administrative support. The Colloquium was sponsored by the Katholieke Universiteit Leuven and the Université Catholique at Louvain-la-Neuve, and by the National Fund for Scientific Research (FWO / FNRS, Brussel).

I would like to express my gratitude to all who have helped me in many ways in preparing the Colloquium and the congress volume. I am grateful to the Committee of the Colloquium for electing me as President of the 1998 session. I especially wish to thank Professor Frans Neirynck for his guidance and advice in seeing this volume through completion.

The book is dedicated to the memory of Jacques Dupont (1915-1998).

Joseph VERHEYDEN

CONTENTS

INDEXES

INTRODUCTION

The 47th *Colloquium Biblicum Lovaniense*, held at the Leuven Faculty of Theology, July 29-31, 1998, was devoted to the study of "The Unity Luke–Acts". About 150 participants attended the meeting. The Gospel of Luke and the Acts of the Apostles had been the subject of the meetings of 1968 and 1977 respectively. But in this session the focus was on the whole of Luke's work as a unity. Here follows a presentation of the content of the main papers (in the order in which they appear in this volume).

The editor's paper (*The Unity of Luke–Acts: What Are We Up To?*) introduces the topic and surveys the research regarding different aspects of the unity of Luke's work. There may be an almost complete consensus on the view that Lk–Acts were written by the same author, but scholars otherwise use various models to designate the relationship between both volumes. While some refer to "Acts as the intended sequel to the Gospel" (I.H. Marshall), others will regard Acts as the continuation of a work that is already complete in itself (M.C. Parsons – R.I. Pervo). In my survey I pay special attention to the works of H.J. Cadbury and H. Conzelmann. Cadbury's famous definition of Lk–Acts as "a single continuous work" showed the way for studying Luke's double work as a narrative unity with a common purpose. His influence on subsequent research is illustrated with the discussion about the extent of the prologue in Lk 1,1-4 and possible indications in the Gospel that Luke was already looking forward to Acts. With Conzelmann, Luke became a theologian in his own right. His emphasis on the theological significance of Luke's work as a whole opened the discussion on what constitutes its distinctive theology and how to describe it. Is Luke's theology ruled by one central motive as some have thought? Or is it built according to one basic (theological) model, e.g., the apology or the model of announcement and fulfilment? This second model has proven to be very attractive in understanding the connexion between Lk and Acts and between Luke's work and Jewish tradition. Or should one look for coherency in Luke's thinking within a particular area (his christology or his pneumatology or ecclesiology)? The study of the genre and of the narrative unity of Luke's work and his artistry as a redactor and author bring in other aspects of the discussion. Luke masters a wide variety of narrative techniques that show up in both volumes of his work, some of which (such as his fondness for parallel stories) are fundamental for reading Lk–Acts as one continuous composition.

D. MARGUERAT (*Luc–Actes. Une unité à construire*) explores the limits of the hypothesis of the unity of Luke's work. Marguerat does not deny the literary and theological unity of Lk–Acts, but this unity is "a heuristic proposition" which is to be verified on the text and is realized in the act of reading. The reader must discover the signs the author has put in his text in order that his work should be read as a unity. In an initial section Marguerat first sums up some remarkable discontinuities (e.g., the change from a kerygma that is centered on the Kingdom in Lk to one that is basically christological in Acts). He then formulates the principles behind his own reading for which he is influenced by the work of G. Genette. Acts is a re–reading (*relecture*) of the Gospel. It is not a commentary of Lk, nor a repetition, but a continuation of the account in the Gospel which brings about a postponed re–reading of this latter (*une relecture en différé*). Marguerat analyzes three models of *relecture*, each of which contains specific text markers. The first one, which he calls "a re–reading by progressive elucidation", comprises such techniques as elliptic prolepsis, relocation of information from the Gospel to Acts, or the narrative chains Luke installs between different stories. The second one, *relecture par modélisation* in Marguerat's terminology, is perhaps better known as the old rhetorical technique of *synkrisis*. Luke models a story in Acts on a similar one from the Gospel and creates a comparison between the deeds (not the words) of his main characters, Jesus and Peter, Jesus and Paul, or also Peter and Paul. This parallelism is guided by the story of Jesus, but there always remains a difference between the initial act of Jesus and the imitation of it by the apostles. A more complex relation is found in the third model, the rereading by relocation, which focuses on themes for which there seems to exist a tension between the Gospel and Acts (e.g. regarding the Law or the Christian attitude towards wealth and property). Apparently Luke did not want to do away with these tensions. Marguerat distinguishes between Luke the theologian and Luke the historian, and emphasizes the function of both themes in establishing the Christian identity as Luke saw it.

J. DELOBEL surveys recent work on the text of Lk–Acts (*The Text of Luke–Acts. A Confrontation of Recent Theories*). The discussion on the relationship between the Alexandrian and the Western text in Lk–Acts, which seemed a foregone issue in Lukan studies, was reopened in the mid eighties. Taking as his starting point the survey of B. Aland (*ETL*,

1986), Delobel presents the works of É. Delebecque (1980-1986), M.-É. Boismard and A. Lamouille (1984), W.A. Strange (1992), C.-B. Amphoux (several contributions from 1986 on with special consideration for the Codex Bezae), J. Rius-Camps (esp. the series of articles on the Western recension in Acts), and P. Taverdon (1997) who continues in the line of Boismard. In a last section he formulates some observations on this revival of the interest in the Western text. One should realize, first, that those who are opposed to the consensus opinion do not constitute a homogeneous group. And second, a critique of the attempts at reassessing the value of the Western text should focus on the qualities of the methods that are proposed. Delobel makes nine observations in this regard which do not all apply to each and everyone of the proponents of the Western text. He is sceptical about the ease with which some authors go from the level of "tradition" to that of "written sources" that are no longer available to us. At the same time these authors have no problem with accepting the traditional ascription of Lk–Acts to a companion of Paul. Delobel further points out some of the risks and difficulties in using arguments based on the occurrence of doublets (do they always have to go back to different traditions?) or of "Lucanisms", and warns for too optimistic views on the possibility of reconstructing the Western text on the basis of Codex Bezae or other evidence. An important difficulty remains the lack of direct evidence from the second century, which is responsible for the widely diverging conclusions that are proposed regarding the date of the Western recension and of its nature. As a general observation, several of the attempts suffer from a lack of balanced text-critical method giving too much importance to internal criticism (e.g., Boismard-Lamouille).

R.L. BRAWLEY (*Abrahamic Covenant Traditions and the Characterization of God in Luke–Acts*) offers a reading of all the passages that refer to Abraham as a key towards a (partial) understanding of Luke's characterization of God. From the outset it is clear that the references to the Abrahamic covenant traditions stand along those to other OT figures as Moses and David. Thus Mary's interpretation in 1,37 of Gabriel's announcement, which echoes Davidic traditions (1,32-33), leads the reader beyond David to the scene in Gen 18,14 that proclaims the power of God to keep his promises. Zechariah's interpretation, on the other hand, is a synthesis of the two previous ones, though in such a way that God's promises to David are seen as the fulfilment of those that were given to Abraham. Brawley then discusses the other Abraham passages which together offer a double characterization of God as the One who keeps his promises and whose blessings are not bound to laws on religious praxis but include all the families of the earth (cf. Lk 3,8, where the negative qualification of the appeal to Abrahamic descent is balanced by the positive moment of revaluation by referring to the criterion of repentance; 13,10-17, with the expression "daughter of Abraham" that is reminiscent of 4 Macc 15,28 and the quotation of Gen 22,18 in Acts 3,25; 13,28-29, and also 16,19-31 and 19,1-10, all three again characterize God as He who blesses all people). Abraham plays a prominent role in the speech of Stephen who recalls the old promise about inheriting the land (7,3-5) which is followed by a reference in 7,16-17 to the fulfilment of God's promise to Abraham. Finally, the reference to Abraham in Paul's speech at Antioch is seen as in some sort summarizing God's promises to His people. Moreover, like Stephen, Paul synthesizes the covenant traditions about Abraham and David, subsuming the latter under the former. This is indeed Luke's way of understanding the significance of the promises originally made to Abraham. God has repeated them throughout history to Moses and David, and even if the Davidic and Mosaic covenants may have failed in some respect, it is the Abrahamic covenant that remains the touching stone.

C.M. TUCKETT deals with *The Christology of Luke–Acts*. Luke's christology is a central topic in current Lukan scholarship. By way of introduction Tuckett first reflects on what is meant by "the christology of Lk–Acts" (the christology of its historical as distinguished from that of its implied author). He then goes on to discuss the methodological problems involved in studying New Testament christology in general, in particular in determining the meaning and the relevance, besides other evidence, of the christological titles that were used by the early Christians to express their understanding of Jesus (and which remain the basis for any discussion). As a next step one has to ask whether Luke's writings contain evidence of a single christology or whether it would be more appropriate to speak of several Lukan christologies. It is striking, according to Tuckett, that Luke in his Gospel has taken over some of the identifications from his sources (Jesus as Son of Man, Jesus as a prophet of Wisdom or as a prophet like Moses) which he does not use again in other instances or in his other volume. Tuckett finds a basis for consensus in the conclusion that Luke's christology is before all a christology of the Exalted One, even though it remains debated what are the implications of such a statement. Several recent studies defend the view that Luke's writings represent a unified "high" christology of Jesus, as the Messiah-Servant (D.L. Bock), as the divine Lord of the Spirit equal to God (D. Buckwalter), or as the Davidic Messiah-Prophet (M.L. Strauss). None of these attempts have convinced Tuckett. A major argument is the

observation that Luke seems to have abandoned his christology at certain points in his narrative. E.g., the representation of Jesus as Lord does
not play a role in the christological debates in Acts about the Gentile
mission or the identity of Jesus (who is called the Christ, not the Lord,
in Acts 17,3; 18,5.28). This qualification, Jesus as the Christ, is the only
one, according to Tuckett, that could possibly fit a description of Luke's
christology as a consistent whole. But perhaps more typical is the variety of titles which are found in Lk–Acts and which lead to the conclusion that Luke is closely following his sources.

J.A. FITZMYER addresses another important topic in Lukan studies. His
paper on *The Role of the Spirit in Luke–Acts* comprises three sections. In
the first and second one he looks for the sources of Luke's references of
the Spirit in Graeco-Roman literature and in the LXX. In the third one
he goes through the relevant passages in Lk–Acts to present a general
description of Luke's understanding of the role of the Spirit in the life of
Jesus and of the early Church. Fitzmyer is sceptical of a possible Hellenistic influence. Though the concept of "inspiration" is well attested in
contemporary Greek literature, the specific interpretation of πνεῦμα that
is found in the texts of the NT is absent from it. Luke depends on the
LXX both for the vocabulary that he uses (e.g., πνεῦμα ἅγιον, πνεῦμα
κυρίου, or absolute πνεῦμα) and for its meaning. With one exception
(the "Spirit" of Jesus in Acts 16,7), πνεῦμα (ἅγιον or κυρίου) refers to
the Spirit of God and expresses God's presence to His people. This presence is especially experienced and mentioned at the beginning of each
period in Luke's conception of salvation history. It is the Spirit of God
who inaugurates a next development in that history. He is with Mary at
the conception (Lk 1,35), with Jesus at his baptism (Lk 3,22) and his
temptation by Satan (4,1.14), and with the apostles at the ascension
(Acts 1,9-11) and at the beginning of their ministry (2,4.36). This
emphasis on the presence of the Spirit at the beginning of a new era in
salvation history is in contrast with His absence later on, in the ministry
of Jesus (the Spirit plays no role in Jesus' miracles) or of his disciples
(no mention of the Spirit in Acts 17–18 or 22–27). On the other hand the
Spirit of God is mentioned again at certain crucial events in the history
of the Church, as in Acts 15 or in the account of Saul's conversion in
Acts 9. In Acts the Spirit also becomes personified at times. In some
passages, as in Acts 5,3-4, this personification adds an element of
dramatization. In the Old Testament or non-personified use, the Spirit is
spoken of as a gift, as something that falls or comes upon people who so
become filled with or full of the Spirit. This use is consistent in the
Gospel and in Acts and marks both volumes which are otherwise bound

together by such references to the Spirit as the quotations from Isa 61,1-2 and Joel 3,1-2 in Lk 4,18-19 and Acts 2,17-21. The reference to the Spirit in Jesus' and in Peter's opening discourse makes it clear to the reader that the Spirit that was given to Jesus at the beginning of his ministry is identical with the one that will be given later on to the whole of the community, indeed that the disciples in Acts 2 receive the Spirit of Jesus.

M. RESE deals with the crucial issue of the role of the Jews as the audience and opponents of Jesus and as addressees and characters of Luke's account (*The Jews in Luke–Acts. Some Second Thoughts*). Rese's "first" thoughts are found in an article he contributed to the FS G. Schneider in 1991. They are briefly summarized in the first part of his lecture and supplemented with a survey of the more recent literature. As before, current discussion centers around the question whether or not Luke, through the mouth of Paul, has "written off" the Jews (E. Haenchen). Rese is critical of J. Jervell's positive interpretation of Ἰουδαῖοι in the Gospel and Acts. Two aspects of the discussion that have received quite some attention in recent years are the identification of the God-fearers as Jews and the alleged Jewish origin of the author of Lk–Acts. Though he shows sympathy for some of the attempts proposed in this regard (e.g., by J.B. Tyson and D.L. Tiede), Rese also draws attention to the methodological difficulty of interpreting a text on the basis of presuppositions about the historical situation of Luke and his audience. In the second part of his lecture, Rese points out the difference there exists between the mention of οἱ Ἰουδαῖοι in the Gospel and in Acts and concluded with a study of the ending of Acts (28,17-31). From the significant difference in attestations of the plural in Lk (only 5 ×) and Acts (79 ×), he draws the double conclusion that Luke, on the one hand, emphatically distinguished between the literary genre of the Gospel and of Acts (a negative attitude to the Jews was understandable in an account of the growth of the Church out of Judaism, but less so in the Gospel) but, on the other hand, since Lk–Acts were intended as a unity, also could afford it to leave out the criticism from his first volume because he had planned to integrate it in the second one. As to Acts 28,17-31, Rese is sceptical of attempts to read the whole of Lk–Acts from its closing scene and to read it as an expression of hope that for Luke the fate of the Jews is not sealed. By way of conclusion he again points out (as he did already in 1991) that there remains a contrast between Paul's dealing with this topic in Acts 28,17-31 and in Rom 9–11.

Die Haltung des Lukas zum römischen Staat im Evangelium und in der Apostelgeschichte is the title of the article by F.W. HORN, who takes as his starting point the often formulated conclusion that for Luke it were the Jews who were opposed to Jesus and his followers, against the will of the Roman authorities who rather protected the Christians and saw no harm in their mission. In three parts Horn offers an exegetical study of the trial scenes of Jesus and Paul, a survey of recent contributions on the topic, and a proposal regarding Luke's intended audience on the basis of his dealing with the Herodian dynasty. Luke clearly puts the blame for the condemnation of Jesus and of Paul with the Jewish religious authorities. Pilate and his ally Herod Antipas in Lk, and the Roman military government in Acts, are not convinced of their guilt and, in the case of Paul, are rather more concerned about his safety (Acts 23,23). In the literature Luke's positive attitude towards the civil authorities is generally recognized, whatever one thinks that may have been the reason behind this apology. Herod Antipas and the other members of the dynasty are presented by Luke as reliable allies of Rome. They are his witnesses before his Roman audience that Christianity is not to be feared as a politically threatening movement. Those few passages that offer a different picture (Lk 13,31; 23,11; Acts 4,27-28) and put Herod and Pilate on the side of the opponents of Jesus, testify to what may have been historically the more probable situation and to the degree of Luke's efforts to discharge the Roman authorities and their allies of the accusation that they had any part in the death of Jesus.

A. LINDEMANN takes as his topic the parallelism between some of the speeches and between some of the miracle stories in Luke's writings (*Einheit und Vielfalt im lukanischen Doppelwerk. Beobachtungen zu Reden, Wundererzählungen und Mahlberichten*). He first compares Jesus' preaching in Nazareth (Lk 4,16-30) with Peter's speech at Jerusalem (Acts 2,14-42) and continues with a comparative analysis of the story of the healing of a paralytic in Lk 5,17-26 and similar stories about Peter and Paul in Acts (3,1-10; 9,32-35; 14,8-11), of the revivification stories in Lk 7,11-17 and Acts 9,36-42; 20,7-12, and of the summaries in Lk 4,40-41; 6,17-19 and in Acts 5,12-16. As an appendix he also briefly discusses Lk 22,14-20 and the passages referring to common meals in Acts. With regard to the speeches, Lindemann does not pass by the clear similarities there are between Lk 4,16-30 and Acts 2,14-42 (Jesus and Peter both heavily rely on and quote from the OT), but he gives special attention to the differences (length of the discourse, setting, and above all the contrast between the "disastrous" result of Jesus and the success of Peter). Similarly, with regard to the healing stories, it is the differences that are especially to be noted, not only between the Gospel and Acts, but also in the three accounts in Acts (Peter performs the healing in 9,32-35 as a means of converting the inhabitants of Lydda, whileas Paul's intervention serves to correct a misunderstanding from the side of his audience, and Peter's first miracle in 3,1-10 comes closer to the story in Lk 5,17-26 with its christological accentuation). The stories about the raising of a dead person likewise serve different purposes: while the account in Acts 9,36-42 can still be compared with the one in Lk 7,11-17 for its emphasis on the power of the miracle worker (in both cases it is Jesus) but also adds as a new element that it brought many to believe in the Lord, the raising of Eutychos in Acts 20,7-12 is performed in a Christian community and brings about relief and consolation.

A. DENAUX discusses *The Theme of Divine Visits and Human (In)hospitality in Luke–Acts. Its Old Testament and Graeco-Roman Antecedents.* He distinguishes four areas of application of the motif of hospitality. A first area is that of ethics, as in the parables of Lk 14,7-14 and 14,15-24 where Luke reflects on the essence of hospitality and presents a view that differs from the current appreciation of host-guest relations in his time. Luke also uses the motif in a christological sense to describe Jesus' earthly life and ministry in terms of a divine visit, of God who comes to earth and is received (or not) in an appropriate way as an honoured guest (sec esp. Lk 9,51–19,44). The missionary work of the disciples, as it is modeled after Jesus' ministry, forms a third field, in which hospitality is interpreted in an ecclesiological perspective (in the missionary discourses in Lk 9 and 10 and often in Acts in the stories about Paul). And finally hospitality is used by Luke as a metaphor for the Kingdom of God (the eschatological banquet of 13,22-30). In the second part of his paper Denaux further develops the christological or theological use of the motif arguing that Luke has taken over this theme of divine visit from Graeco-Roman literature (and also from the LXX). Among the former one should mention above all the story of Philemon and Baucis in Ovid's *Metamorphoses*; the clearest example in the Old Testament is undoubtedly the story of God's visit to Abraham in Gen 18. The motif occurs in Lk in the very beginning of the Gospel (the angelophanies in 1,5-25 and 1,26-38) and again in the Emmaus story. In the three passages Denaux discovers the same pattern. A verb that is frequently used by Luke in this connexion is ἐπισκέπτομαι (cf. 1,68.78; 7,16; Acts 15,14) which can have a positive (salvation) or a negative connotation (punishment) and can be translated as "visit" or as "look favorably upon" (in an eschatological perspective).

J. TAYLOR (*La fraction du pain en Luc–Actes*) argues that the custom among early Christians to break the bread (while nothing is said of the wine) is certainly not in all instances to be linked with the celebration of

the eucharist. His reasoning is based on the evidence from the New Testament (e.g., Acts 20,7.11) and on a detailed analysis of chapters 9 and
10 of the *Didache* which show that the rite could have different connotations. Among these is the interpretation of the breaking of the bread as
symbolizing the dispersion of the faithful. It was probably followed by
the positive act of reassembling the "pieces", a moment that is also
explicitly mentioned in the feeding narratives and for which Taylor finds
further evidence in such passages as Mk 13,19-20 and Jn 10,12-16;
11,50; 17,21-23, but also in Luke's version of the Last Supper. Defending the shorter reading at Lk 22,19-20, Taylor speculates about the possibility that the rite of breaking the bread could be a fragment of that
same pattern of negation (here the death of Jesus) and future restauration
(in the Kingdom of God). This would bring Luke's version very close to
Paul's interpretation in 1 Cor 11,23-26 and to *Didache* 9,4. In the
Emmaus story the mention of the breaking of the bread by Jesus in Lk
24,35 is to be understood in the same way as referring to the death of
Jesus and the hope of his resurrection (again, on the assumption that the
act was followed by one of assembling). Thus, the rite, as part of a double movement, could take different meanings, symbolizing as well the
death and resurrection of Jesus as the dispersion and future gathering of
God's people.

   In *Die Beziehungen der Vorgeschichte zur Apostelgeschichte,
dargestellt an Lk 2,22-39*, W. RADL examines how the Infancy narrative,
as the "prologue" to Luke's Gospel, and more specifically the narrative
of the presentation of Jesus in the Temple with the prophecies by
Simeon and Anna, also is related to Acts. In a first section Radl summarizes the results of his analysis of 2,22-39 as these are found in his recent
monograph. He draws attention to the contrast in genre and content
between the optimistic and universalistic perspective of the poetic
prophecy in vv. 29-32, which he attributes to Luke's redaction, and the
continuation in v. 34, which sounds more threatening and deals exclusively with the hopes and fate of Israel. He then compares some of the
core elements of the Simeon story with similar stories in Acts. The figure of the pious Jew who abides by the Law, goes up to the Temple, and
lives a life of prayer, fasting, and justice, in the expectation that the fulfilment of Israel's hope is near, is met time and again in Acts. Just as the
Spirit reveals to Simeon that he will "see" the Messiah (Lk 2,25-26), so
is Cornelius informed by an angel that he should invite Peter to his
house to receive his preaching (Acts 10,22), and Paul himself reports
about the vision of the Lord he was privileged to see in the Temple
(22,18). In his double prophecy Simeon calls Jesus τὸ σωτήριον but

also the σημεῖον ἀντιλεγόμενον. This means, for Radl, that, in Luke's view, both the Gentile mission and the rejection of the kerygma by the Jews were planned by God, and consequently that the former is not merely the result of the latter. But Simeon also speaks of the glory of Israel (Lk 2,32) and of the rising of many in Israel (2,34). The tension that is felt in these prophecies is found also in Acts where it is said, on the one hand, that many in Jerusalem were converted, and, on the other, that the Jews stubbornly went on rejecting Paul's preaching. It is inherent to Luke's story and reflects, according to Radl, the double perspective from which Luke was writing: as an historian, he looks back at how the separation of the synagogue gradually became irreversible; as a theologian, he interprets the rejection of the Christian mission and the re-establishment of the house of Israel as a house for Jews and Gentiles alike as the realization of God's plan that was foreseen by one of God's prophets.

O. MAINVILLE further develops the topic of her 1991 monograph in her contribution on *Le messianisme de Jésus. Le rapport annonce/ accomplissement entre Lc 1,35 et Ac 2,33.* Her thesis is that these two passages complement each other, the first one identifying the nature of Jesus' messianism as a "pneumatic messianism", while the second brings the confirmation of this promise. Against more common positions which place this event at Jesus' baptism or at his birth or conception, Mainville holds that Peter's speech at Pentecost is the demonstration that for Luke Jesus really was made the Messiah only at the resurrection. The quotation from Isa 42,1 in Lk 3,22 favours a prophetic understanding of God's words (contrary to the variant reading of the Western text which quotes here from Ps 2,7). In Acts 2,22-36 Peter places the decisive moment of Jesus' investiture as the Messiah at the resurrection and of this the disciples bear witness (2,32-33). Corroboration of this view is found in the speech of Paul at Antioch who follows the same pattern of argumentation (the witnesses in 13,33; use of the testimony of David in 13,35-37 as in 2,29-31.34). As Messiah Jesus is identified with the Spirit who will rule and direct the missionary life of the community. This qualification of Jesus' Messiahship is expressed in Acts 2,17-21 in the quotation of Joel 3,1-5 and in Acts 2,33 with its implicit reference to Isa 11,1-2. What was accomplished at the end of the Gospel and made known to the world by Peter at the beginning of Acts, was already announced at the very beginning of Luke's Gospel in the words the angel Gabriel spoke to Mary about the promise of the Spirit and of the birth of a holy child (1,35). Mainville argues that the reply of the angel in v. 35 does not provide the answer to the question that bothers Mary in

v. 34. In other words, v. 35 does not say that it is the Spirit who will engender Jesus. The role of the Spirit is to give "holiness" to the child that will be born (cf. "therefore..." in v. 35a). The angel already looks forth at what will happen in the Gospel. Mainville concludes by pointing out that such a pattern is consistent with Luke's theology and with his composition.

J. KREMER (*Die dreifache Wiedergabe des Damaskuserlebnisses Pauli in der Apostelgeschichte. Eine Hilfe für das rechte Verständnis der lukanischen Osterevangelien*) analyzes the threefold account of Paul's past as a persecutor and the decisive event of his conversion on the way to Damascus as a means towards a correct understanding of the encounters of the disciples with the Risen Lord in Lk 24. Kremer proceeds in four steps, offering first a synchronic and then a diachronic reading of the stories in Acts (9,3-22; 22,6-21; 26,12-20), a comparison with Lk 24, and finally formulating some conclusions about the fictional character, and the implications for our interpretation, of Luke's accounts. Luke and the author of the tradition of Saul's conversion are not interested in providing a historically reliable report of this event; they rather want to emphasize the divine initiative in the expansion of the early mission and to illustrate how God turns the former persecutor into one of his most important agents. The comparison with Lk 24 shows that Luke relied on earlier traditions which can (in 24,1-12 Luke depends on Mk 16,1-8) or cannot be identified (24,13-35.36-53 are thoroughly reworked by Luke), but which he has made his own. As an important characteristic of Luke's redaction Kremer points to the "novelistic" presentation and to his reshaping of the narratives, e.g. by turning a conversion story into a call story with a vision (Acts 22,17-22).

F. NEIRYNCK (*Luke 4,16-30 and the Unity of Luke–Acts*) examines the parallels with and allusions to Jesus' opening discourse in the Book of Acts. Similarities with Lk 4,16-30 can be found in the speeches of Paul: his synagogue preaching in Damascus (Acts 9,19b-25) and particularly his important speech at Antioch (13,14-52), in Peter's mission speeches (Acts 2,17-40; 3,11-26; and 10,34-43), and in the finale of Acts (28,17-31). Paul's inaugural preaching immediately after his conversion already follows the plan of his later missionary work and comes to the same negative results that are so frequently mentioned elsewhere in Acts (the public preaching in the synagogue ends in threats and attempts at the life of the missionary). This presentation is clearly influenced by the scene in Lk 4,16-30 and differs from Paul's own accounts of his mission in Gal 1,17 and 2 Cor 11,32-33. The introduction to the speech in Antioch in 13,14-52 (vv. 14-16a) can be compared with Lk 4,16 with regard to the vocabulary (going to the synagogue on Sabbath), but Neirynck is sceptical of readings that make use of the passage in Acts to interpret the scenery in Lk 4,16 (see also for the parallel κατὰ τὸ εἰωθός in 4,16 and Acts 17,2): one cannot simply transpose the description of Acts 17,2 and 13,15 to Lk 4,16 and suppose that Jesus had made it his habit of teaching in the synagogue on the Sabbath or that he was invited by the synagogue officials to take the floor as Paul is in 13,15. The reaction of the Jews (and the proselytes) in 13,43 and 13,45 is again comparable with that of Jesus' audience in Lk 4: initial openness to the preaching ends in hostility. The distinction that is often made with reference to v. 43, indicating that Paul succeeded in converting at least some members of his audience, may be not wholly correct since ἀκολουθέω is used here with a literal meaning. The final result of Paul's preaching is outright rejection on the part of the Jews and the firm announcement by Paul of his turning to the Gentiles. Here again the similarity with Lk 4 can be stressed, provided one is ready to read an allusion to the Gentile mission in the references to Elijah and Elisha in vv. 25-27. The references in 10,38 to Jesus being anointed by God with the Spirit and to Isa 61,1 (cf. Lk 4,18-19) constitute another kind of parallel with the opening discourse of Jesus: it looks as an explicit reference to the Gospel passage. In the discussion on the origin of the "mixed" Isaiah quotation in Lk 4,18-19 examples from Acts (1,20; 3,22-23) may be quoted in favour of its Lukan character. Similarly, Neirynck remains critical of the argument for assigning 4,18-19 to a pre-Lukan source because Jesus' power to perform miracles is there ascribed to the Spirit, while in Acts 10,38 this is regarded as the work of God. The explicit mention of ὁ θεὸς ἦν μετ' αὐτοῦ at the end of v. 38 does not rule out the emphasis on the effective presence of the Spirit in Jesus that is found in v. 38a. In the third and last part of his article Neirynck pays attention to the connexion with the end section of Acts. Lk 4,25-27 should be read in light of the later mission to the Gentiles.

It is impossible to present here in some detail the content of the twenty-four offered papers (Part II). As can be expected a whole range of topics is addressed. Special attention is given to the prologues and the genre of Lk–Acts (L. Alexander; D.P. Moessner; S. Walton; E. Plümacher); source criticism (T.L. Brodie); Luke and Paul (G. Carras; J. Pichler; G. Wasserberg); the geography of the Gospel and Acts (D. Béchard; G. Geiger; A. Puig i Tàrrech; B. Schwank); the relation with Judaism (P.J. Tomson; S. Van Den Eynde); christology (C. Focant); and themes from Luke's theology (H. Baarlink; M. Bachmann; A. del

Agua; G. Oegema; U. Schmid; N.H. Taylor; F. Wilk) and from his social world (B.J. Koet; V. Koperski).

The present collection of studies discusses several important issues regarding Luke's work and many topics that are crucial to Christian theology: Luke's and the early Christians' views on God, Christ and the Spirit, the message and the ministry of Jesus and of his disciples, and the struggles of the early Christian communities with their Jewish roots. The contributions in this volume focus on specific areas of Luke's theology, examine particular passages from Luke and Acts and particular aspects of Luke's redaction, and ask methodological questions about the exegetical interpretation of his work. Readers will find many opportunities to admire the strength and the depth of Luke's theology and the elegance of his artistry as a writer and narrator. Above all, the volume illustrates that these two impressive documents, Luke's Gospel and the Book of Acts, should be read and studied as the one great work by the same great author and theologian they were meant to be.

J. VERHEYDEN

MAIN PAPERS

THE UNITY OF LUKE–ACTS

WHAT ARE WE UP TO?

Thirty years ago, in 1968, the topic of the 19th Journées Bibliques was "L'évangile de Luc". The president was F. Neirynck[1]. It was not for the first time that the Colloquium Biblicum concentrated its attention on one book of the New Testament (the 8th meeting, in 1956, had dealt with the Gospel of John). But the meeting of 1968 on Luke was the first in a series on each of the canonical gospels. Matthew followed in 1970, Mark in 1971, and John in 1975. The next New Testament session, the 28th of 1977, under the presidency of J. Kremer, was on the Book of Acts[2]. Several of the contributors at the conferences of 1968 and 1977 discussed passages and themes from the Gospel of Luke or the Book of Acts with one eye on the other volume. But the specific and "unique phenomenon" (van Unnik) that one of the Gospel writers has composed his account as part of a larger work had not yet been dealt with as a separate topic at our Colloquium. So, this year's session, while taking us back in a certain sense into the history of the Journées Bibliques, also adds something new to it.

There is an almost complete consensus in Lukan studies today that Luke's work indeed constitutes a unity. For M. Rese this is even the one important development in Lukan studies in the first part of this century: "(es) hat nur an einem Punkt in der Auslegung des LkEv in der ersten Hälfte des 20. Jhdt. eine wichtige Verschiebung gegeben; dieser Punkt ist die Einsicht: LkEv und Apg sind als ein einheitliches Werk anzusehen, und man wird keinem der beiden Einzelteile dieses Werkes gerecht, wenn man es je für sich allein betrachtet"[3]. True as this may be, it is also

---

1. F. Neirynck (ed.), *L'évangile de Luc: Problèmes littéraires et théologiques* (BETL, 32), Gembloux–Leuven, 1973; revised and enlarged edition: *L'évangile de Luc – The Gospel of Luke* (BETL, 32), Leuven, 1989. The Journées of 1968 started tragically. A few days before, Prof. L. Cerfaux, one of its co-founders, had suddenly died. The congress volume was dedicated to his memory and included the text of the contribution he had prepared for that meeting (pp. 285-293: *L'utilisation de la Source Q par Luc. Introduction du séminaire*).

2. J. Kremer (ed.), *Les Actes des Apôtres. Traditions, rédaction, théologie* (BETL, 48), Gembloux–Leuven, 1979.

3. M. Rese, *Das Lukas-Evangelium. Ein Forschungsbericht*, in *ANRW* II.25.3, 1985, pp. 2258-2328, esp. 2298. See also W. Gasque, *A History of the Criticism of the Acts of the Apostles* (BGBE, 17), Tübingen, 1975, p. 309: "The primary gain of the recent criti-

a matter of fact that scholars use various words and models to designate the relationship between both volumes. It really makes a difference whether one labels Acts as an "afterthought" (Torrey) or regards Lk–Acts as "one single continuous work" (Cadbury). The qualification that is perhaps most frequently used for Acts is "sequel" ("Fortsetzung"). But here too there are nuances. I.H. Marshall calls Acts "the intended sequel to the Gospel of Luke"[4]. For G. Schneider, on the other hand, this is probably not the case: Acts is a "Fortsetzungswerk" (76), but it was written much later than the Gospel (120) and "wenn Lukas im Evangelium noch nicht auf die spätere Darstellung der Acta vorverweist, legt dies... die Vermutung nahe, daß die Fortsetzung der Evangelienschrift in einem zweiten 'Buch' nicht von Anfang an geplant war"[5]. M.C. Parsons and R.I. Pervo, in turn, use the same terminology ("Literarily, Acts is best characterized as a sequel") to argue that Lk and Acts each are complete in themselves and that "the relationships between these two books are relations *between two books*, not correspondences within a conveniently divided entirety"[6]. So, what are scholars talking about when they speak of the unity of Luke's work?

Marshall distinguishes four models to represent the relationship between Lk and Acts: (1) there is actually no connection since they were written by different authors; (2) the author who wrote Lk was also the one who produced Acts later on, but (a) these are autonomous works with their own topic and concerns, or (b) they somehow were assimilated in the process of writing; (3) one author planned and composed a work in two volumes as it is preserved in the Gospel and in Acts; (4) Lk–Acts were originally intended as one work which eventually became separated after it was finished, and this brought about some revision in the conclusion of the first and the introduction to the second volume[7].

cism of Luke–Acts has been the recognition that the Gospel according to Luke and the Book of Acts are really two volumes of one work which must be considered together"; rev. ed.: *A History of the Interpretation of the Acts of the Apostles*, Grand Rapids, MI, 1989, p. 309. Compare M. DUMAIS, *Les Actes des Apôtres. Bilan et orientation*, in M. GOURGUES – L. LABERGE (eds.), *"De bien des manières". La recherche biblique aux abords du XXIᵉ siècle* (LD, 163), Paris–Montréal, 1995, pp. 309-364, esp. 313-316 ("Acquis").

4. I.H. MARSHALL, *Luke: Historian and Theologian*, Carlisle, 1970; ³1988, p. 157. See also ID., *The Acts of the Apostles* (NT Guides), Sheffield, 1992, pp. 53-54; *Acts and the "Former Treatise"*, in B.W. WINTER – A.D. CLARKE (eds.), *The Book of Acts in Its Ancient Literary Setting* (BAFCS, 1), Grand Rapids, MI – Carlisle, 1993, pp. 163-182, esp. 163: "the prologues to the two books indicate that they are to be read as one connected story".

5. G. SCHNEIDER, *Apg*, I, 1980, p. 79. But see below, n. 67.

6. M.C. PARSONS – R.I. PERVO, *Rethinking the Unity of Luke and Acts*, Minneapolis, MN, 1993, p. 126; cf. pp. 117-118, n. 6 and p. 123.

7. MARSHALL, *"Former Treatise"* (n. 4), pp. 163-166.

Marshall remarks that his model no. 2b is closer to 3 than to 2a, since in both 2b and 3 the Gospel is thought to have been affected by the composition of its sequel. He further points out that the first and the last of the four proposals are no longer defended today (on the former, see below n. 13).

In addition some other marginal positions can be mentioned, such as the view that Acts was written first[8], that the Gospel and Acts are the first two volumes of a trilogy that was never completed[9], or that the composition of Lk–Acts extended over a longer period of time in which Luke subsequently wrote a first draft of his Gospel (Proto-Lk), Acts, and the final version of Lk[10]. Marshall sees some grounds for accepting this third suggestion arguing that if it was Luke who in a first move is responsible for bringing together the material from Q and from L, it is not impossible that "Luke could have been working on Acts at the same time" as he was revising his Gospel[11].

In their recent monograph Parsons and Pervo joined forces to "rethink" the unity of Lk and Acts[12]. They feel uneasy about the way many scholars tend to speak of unity without sufficiently clarifying their model, their arguments for it, or its implications. They list five levels on

    8. See H.G. RUSSELL, *Which Was Written First, Luke or Acts?*, in *HTR* 48 (1955) 167-174. This was also suggested by G. Bouwman arguing that Acts never refers back to the Gospel and has a more primitive theology. Cf. *De derde nachtwake. De wordingsgeschiedenis van het evangelie van Lukas*, Tielt – Den Haag, 1968; = *Das dritte Evangelium. Einübung in die formgeschichtliche Methode*, Düsseldorf, 1968, pp. 62-67. Bouwman returned to his hypothesis in 1989: *Le "premier livre" (Act., I,1) et la date des Actes des Apôtres*, in NEIRYNCK (ed.), *L'évangile de Luc* (n. 1), 1989, pp. 553-565. His arguments received some attention from Schneider though he was not convinced (*Apg*, pp. 78-79); see also MARSHALL, *"Former Treatise"* (n. 4), p. 166.
    9. References in W.G. KÜMMEL, *Einleitung in das Neue Testament*, Heidelberg, [21]1983, p. 127 n. 14, and in SCHNEIDER, *Apg*, p. 76 n. 1. See most recently, J. WINANDY, *La finale des Actes: Histoire ou théologie*, in *ETL* 73 (1997) 103-106, esp. p. 106. — A different discussion is the one about the Lukan authorship of the Pastoral Epistles: see the recent critical survey by J.-D. KAESTLI, *Luke–Acts and the Pastoral Epistles: The Thesis of a Common Authorship*, in C.M. TUCKETT (ed.), *Luke's Literary Achievement. Collected Essays* (JSNT SS, 116), Sheffield, 1995, pp. 110-126.
    10. Behind it is the concern to retain a date for Acts immediately after the death of Paul or even during his lifetime. See C.S.C. WILLIAMS, *The Date of Luke–Acts*, in *ExpT* 64 (1952-53) 283-284; ID., *Acts*, 1957, pp. 13-15; R. KOH, *The Writings of St. Luke*, Hongkong, 1953, pp. 31-35; P. PARKER, *The "Former Treatise" and the Date of Acts*, in *JBL* 84 (1965) 52-58. For discussion, cf. SCHNEIDER, *Apg*, p. 79 n. 20.
    11. *"Former Treatise"* (n. 4), p. 168; cf. 167 and 170.
    12. Cf. above n. 6. Their collaboration grew out of a paper Parsons read at the SBL meeting of 1988 and which was published afterwards as *The Unity of the Lukan Writings: Rethinking the Opinio Communis*, in N.H. KEATHLEY (ed.), *With Steadfast Purpose: Essays in Honor of Henry Jackson Flanders*, Waco, TX, 1990, pp. 29-53. On the book of Parsons and Pervo, see now J.B. GREEN, art. *Acts of the Apostles*, in R.P. MARTIN – P.H. DAVIDS (eds.), *Dictionary of the Later New Testament and Its Developments*, Downers Grove, IL – Leicester, 1997, pp. 7-24, esp. 12-13.

which the relationship has to be studied: the author and the canon (two issues which do not need a lot of discussion[13]), the genre, the narrative,

13. There is no undisputable manuscript or other external evidence that Lk and Acts were ever transmitted as one body of literature. Parsons and Pervo give some weight to this observation. However, it is far more common to regard the question of the canonization of Luke's work as a different one from that of its compositional or theological unity. It has to do with the reception of the early Christian writings by the Church. Concerns about preserving the original intended unity of Lk–Acts had to give way to other considerations of which the establishment of a Gospel canon may have been a most decisive one. It is really somewhat too easy to say that "the proposal that Acts became separated from Luke because of the four-gospel collection begs the question" (*Rethinking*, p. 42). Rather, it seemed "natural that the Gospel of Luke should be associated with other Gospels" (H.J. CADBURY, *The Book of Acts in History*, New York, 1955, p. 139). Canonical disunity may be no more than a regrettable accident: cf. M.A. POWELL, *Acts* (below n. 17), p. 6: "a fluke of mss arrangement".

The common authorship should not retain us too long either. It has been recognized from of old (Irenaeus and Jerome) and is supported by strong internal evidence. First, there is the explicit reference to the former treatise in Acts 1,1 which is briefly summarized and was addressed to the same (fictional) person. The remarkable similarities in the vocabulary and the style of both writings provide another weighty indication that Lk and Acts were written by the same author. At the beginning of this century A. Harnack had argued at length that nothing in Acts contradicts this view (*Lukas der Arzt*, pp. 86-102; vol. 3, pp. 199-205; vol. 4, pp. 21-62). The linguistic evidence for it was once more collected at that time by J.C. Hawkins (*Horae Synopticae*, 1899). The differences between the language of Lk and of Acts do not argue against it. For Hawkins they are to be taken as an indication that Acts was written long after the Gospel was finished, but they cannot invalidate the hypothesis of a single authorship. "These, however, are important in their way; for, while quite insufficient to throw doubt on the common authorship, they seem to suggest that a considerable time must have elapsed between the writing of the two books" (*ibid.*, p. 143/177). Cf. p. 146/180-81: "We have thus some internal evidence in favour of placing Luke at a considerably earlier date than Acts". The chronological interval serves also to explain the differences in the ascension narratives in Lk 24 and Acts 1 (p. 146/181 n. 1). Needless to add that Hawkins sees no reason to question Luke's authorship of Acts on the basis of the differences in vocabulary between Acts 1–12 and 13–28. Neither do the we-sections constitute a problem (pp. 146-149/182-188). — This aspect of the unity of Luke's work has not been seriously challenged again (for earlier criticism, see J.H. SCHOLTEN, *Is de derde evangelist de schrijver van het boek der Handelingen? Critisch onderzoek*, Leiden, 1873). The criticism of A.C. Clark, who took up the argument of the linguistic and stylistic differences between Lk and Acts, remained an exception. See *The Acts of the Apostles. A Critical Edition With Introduction and Notes on Selected Passages*, Oxford, 1933, pp. 393-408. See the reaction by W.L. KNOX, *The Acts of the Apostles*, Cambridge, 1948, pp. 1-15. Knox replied that Clark had neglected the influence of Luke's sources (which he himself greatly emphasized) and also pointed to the difference in purpose between the Gospel and Acts. Equally unsuccessful was A.W. Argyle's attempt to conclude, from the observation that the anonymous who wrote Acts prefers a synonym to certain words in Lk, that Acts was the work of another author: *The Greek of Luke and Acts*, in *NTS* 20 (1973-74) 441-445. In his response B.E. Beck criticized the accuracy of Argyle's list of synonyms and objected that the variation may in part be inspired by Luke's sources and that Luke makes use of synonyms also in his Gospel and in Acts taken separately; see *The Common Authorship of Luke and Acts*, in *NTS* 23 (1976-77) 346-352. — Today, the discussion on the common authorship of Lk and Acts, which is to be distinguished from that on the identity of the author, is closed. Of course, "resolution of this basic issue does not determine that the same author could

and the theology of the work. Parsons and Pervo regard the unity of Lk–Acts as an assumption of modern scholarship and as "a largely unexamined hypothesis"[14]. The two volumes are the work of the same author who produced, however, "very distinct narratives embodying different literary devices, generic conventions, and perhaps even theological concerns"[15]. When reading through their analysis of the various levels it appears, first, that their criticism is directed above all against one specific model (that proposed by Cadbury; see below), and second, that their own conclusions are sometimes rather ambiguous and in any case too general[16].

The quest for the purpose of Luke's work constitutes a third way to look at the relationship between Lk and Acts. R. Maddox in his monograph on *The Purpose of Luke–Acts* reviews seven theories which he divides in two groups according to whether Luke has in view an audience of co-believers or one that does not belong to the Church. In all seven Luke's purpose can be described to some degree in terms of apology or defence[17]. When it is assumed that Luke adresses non-Christians, he may have done so either in order (a) to propagate and spread the Gospel (F.F. Bruce), (b) to defend Paul in trial (A.J. Mattill), or (c) as an apology of Christianity before the Roman authorities to sollicitate their protection (B.S. Easton, E. Haenchen) or to refute rumours about alleged political aspirations of the Church. An inner-Church audience is intended when Lk–Acts is written (d) in defence of Paul and his heritage against fellow Christians who had criticized him as an apostate (J. Jervell), or to solve a theological problem, such as (e) the delay of the

not have written in different genres, employed different theological constructs in the two volumes, or used different narrators" (PARSONS–PERVO, *Rethinking*, p. 116). But it is a necessary condition to allow for a reflection on the way Luke has composed both writings.

14. *Rethinking*, p. 18.

15. *Ibid.*

16. See, e.g., p. 126: "As narratives they are independent yet interrelated works"; or p. 123: "There is little doubt that the theological unity of Luke and Acts is a good idea" (cf. again p. 126). One should also note that in discussing the narrative unity Parsons restricts himself to a narratological analysis (pp. 45-83) and that the chapter on the theological unity by Pervo is in fact a study of Luke's anthropological presuppositions in Acts (pp. 84-114).

17. R. MADDOX, *The Purpose of Luke–Acts* (FRLANT, 126), Göttingen, 1982; Edinburgh, 1982, pp. 20-23. For similar surveys, see, e.g., S. BROWN, *The Prologues of Luke–Acts in Their Relation to the Purpose of the Author*, in *SBL 1975 Seminar Papers*, 2, pp. 1-14: a rehabilitation of Paul; an apology of Christianity before the political authorities; evangelisation; a response to a theological problem; a polemic with heresies. M.A. POWELL, *What Are They Saying About Acts?*, New York – Mahwah, NJ, 1991, pp. 13-19, distinguishes six purposes: irenic (F.C. Baur); polemical (against heretics or Jewish-Christians); apologetic; evangelistic; pastoral (Maddox); and theological.

parousia (H. Conzelmann) or (f) the claims of people propagating Gnostic opinions on the resurrection and the experience of the Lord (C.H. Talbert), or else (g) to strenghten the faith of his Christian readers in light of developments that had recently taken place (W.C. van Unnik, R. Maddox). Maddox regards it as implausible that Luke was trying to convince a non-Christian audience, because of the shape and the content of his work that must have looked utterly strange to an (uninterested) outsider[18]. He thinks that Lk–Acts wants to support a Christian community that was shaken and disturbed in its expectation of the imminence of the parousia and unsure about its own identity as heirs of God's promise to the Jews after the separation from Judaism had become irreversible[19].

Such classifications as the three that I have mentioned are of course always somewhat artificial. For Maddox the question of the unity of Lk–Acts is preliminary to that of its purpose: only when it is agreed that Luke conceived his work as a two-volume unit "can we speak confidently of 'the purpose of Luke–Acts'"[20]. But one can also argue that discovering a common purpose (or for that reason, a set of purposes) in Lk and Acts is a primary factor in establishing this unity. The different models I just presented are also partially overlapping, but even then it appears that there exists a wide range of approaches and aspects to be dealt with.

It has been said and repeated many times: the flood of publications on Lk and on Acts is overwhelming. Fortunately, there is no lack of good bibliographies[21], important commentaries[22], and excellent surveys of

18. MADDOX, *Purpose*, p. 20. Cf. C.K. BARRETT, *Luke the Historian in Recent Study*, London, 1961, p. 63.

19. *Purpose*, pp. 180-187 and *passim*.

20. *Ibid.*, p. 4.

21. See, e.g., A.J. MATTILL – M.B. MATTILL, *A Classified Bibliography of Literature on the Acts of the Apostles* (NTTS, 7), Leiden, 1966. G. WAGNER, *An Exegetical Bibliography of the New Testament: Luke and Acts*, Macon, GA, 1985. W.E. MILLS, *A Bibliography of the Periodical Literature on the Acts of the Apostles 1962-1984* (NTSup, 58), Leiden, 1986. F. VAN SEGBROECK, *The Gospel of Luke: A Cumulative Bibliography (1973-1988)* (BETL, 88), Leuven, 1989 (a companion volume to the revised edition of *L'évangile de Luc*, 1989). J.B. GREEN – M.C. MCKEEVER, *Luke–Acts and New Testament Historiography* (IBR Bibliographies, 8), Grand Rapids, MI, 1994. W.E. MILLS, *The Gospel of Luke* (Bibliographies of Biblical Research. NT Series, 3), Lewiston, NJ – Queenston, Ont. – Lampeter, 1994. ID., *The Acts of the Apostles* (BBR, 5), 1996. — The *Elenchus* of *Biblica* and of *ETL* has a separate section on the "Opus lucanum" since 1979 and 1984 respectively.

22. The following list includes only the most important commentaries of the last 20 years. On Lk: I.H. Marshall, 1978; J.A. Fitzmyer, 1981-1985; C.H. Talbert, 1982; R.C. Tannehill, 1986 and 1996; D.L. Tiede, 1988; F.W. Danker, 1988; J. Nolland, 1989-1993; M.D. Goulder, 1989; C.F. Evans, 1990; L.T. Johnson, 1991; R.H. Stein, 1993; D.L. Bock, 1994-1996; J.B. Green, 1997. — G. Schneider, 1977; J. Ernst, 1977 (1993);

earlier and recent studies on the Gospel and on Acts[23]. Noteworthy is the great number of collective works on our topic, beginning with the 1966 FS for P. Schubert[24]. In recent years Lk–Acts also seems to be a

J. Jeremias, 1980; W. Schmithals, 1980; E. Schweizer, 1982; J. Kremer, 1988; W. Wiefel, 1988; F. Bovon, 1989 (FT 1991) and 1996 (9,51–14,35); H. Schürmann, 1994 (9,51–11,54). — R. Meynet, 1979 and 1988; L. Sabourin, 1985.
On Acts: I.H. Marshall, 1984; H. Conzelmann, 1987 (ET); F.F. Bruce, [3]1990; R.C. Tannehill, 1990; D.J. Williams, 1990; L.T. Johnson, 1992; J.B. Polhill, 1992; C.K. Barrett, 1994–1998; H.C. Kee, 1997; C.H. Talbert, 1997; B. Witherington, 1998; J.A. Fitzmyer, 1998. — G. Schneider, 1980-1982; J. Roloff, 1981; A. Weiser, 1981-1985; W. Schmithals, 1982; G. Schille, 1983; F. Mussner, 1984; R. Pesch, 1986; J. Zmijewski, 1994; J. Jervell, 1998. — M.-É. Boismard – A. Lamouille, 1990; Ph. Bossuyt – J. Rademakers, 1995; and J. Taylor, 1994-1996 (focuses on historical questions).
23. First to be mentioned for Lk is the monograph of F. Bovon, *Luc le théologien. Vingt-cinq ans de recherches (1950-1975)* (Le monde de la Bible), Neuchâtel–Paris, 1978, [2]1988; ET *Luke the Theologian. Thirty-three Years of Research (1950-1983)* (Pittsburgh Theological Monograph Series, 12), Allison Park, PA, 1987, including in appendix the translation of the author's *Chronique du côté de chez Luc*, in *RTP* 115 (1983) 175-189 (ET, 409-418); see also the introduction to Luke's writings in F. Bovon, *L'Évangile de Luc et Actes des Apôtres*, in J. Auneau (ed.), *Évangiles synoptiques et Actes des Apôtres*, Paris, 1981, pp. 195-283, and his *Studies in Luke–Acts. Retrospect and Prospect*, in *HTR* 85 (1992) 175-196, with FT in *RTP* 125 (1993) 113-135. Cf. also W. Radl, *Das Lukas-Evangelium* (Erträge der Forschung, 261), Darmstadt, 1988. A. Lindemann, *Literaturbericht zu den Synoptischen Evangelien 1978-1983*, in *TR* 49 (1984) 223-276, 311-371, esp. pp. 346-371; and the sequel for *1984-1991*, in *TR* 59 (1994) 41-100, 113-185, 252-284, esp. pp. 253-281; Lindemann continues the surveys by H. Conzelmann in *TR* 37 (1972) and 43 (1978) for the period 1963-1978. C.H. Talbert, *Shifting Sands. The Recent Study of the Gospel of Luke*, in *Int* 30 (1976) 381-395; repr. in J.L. Mays (ed.), *Interpreting the Gospels*, Philadelphia, PA, 1981, pp. 197-213. C.M. Tuckett, *Luke* (NT Guides), Sheffield, 1996. The surveys by Rese and Marshall were mentioned above (nn. 3 and 4); for Rese, see also *Neuere Lukas-Arbeiten. Bemerkungen zur gegenwärtigen Forschungslage*, in *TLZ* 106 (1981) 225-237. — M.A. Powell is the author of a double introduction to Lk and to Acts: *What Are They Saying About Luke?*, New York – Mahwah, NJ, 1989, and *What... About Acts?* (n. 17). Compare also R.J. Karris, *What Are They Saying About Luke and Acts? A Theology of the Faithful God*, New York, 1979.
For Acts, besides the introduction by Marshall (above n. 4), the survey by Dumais and the monograph of Gasque (both above n. 3), there is the important chronicle by E. Plümacher, *Acta Forschung 1974-1982*, in *TR* 48 (1983) 1-56 and 49 (1984) 105-169, which continues the surveys by E. Grässer in *TR* 26 (1960), 41 (1976), and 42 (1977). Cf. also J. Kremer, *Einführung in die Problematik heutiger Acta-Forschung anhand von Apg 17,10-13*, in Id. (ed.), *Les Actes des Apôtres* (n. 2), pp. 11-20. — Recent literature on Lk–Acts is reviewed by H. Giesen, *Im Dienst des Glaubens seiner Gemeinde. Zu neueren Arbeiten zum lukanischen Doppelwerk*, in *TGeg* 26 (1983) 199-208; G. Schneider, *Literatur zum lukanischen Doppelwerk*, in *TRev* 88 (1992) 1-18 (1990-91); cf. also his survey for Lk in *TRev* 86 (1990) 353-360 (for 1987-89). D.M. Sweetland, *Luke–Acts. An Overview*, in *BibTod* 35 (1997) 332-339. B. Corsani, *Bulletin d'études lucaniennes*, in *ETR* 73 (1998) 257-266.
24. L.E. Keck – J.L. Martyn (eds.), *Studies in Luke–Acts. Essays Presented in Honor of Paul Schubert*, Nashville, TN – New York, 1966, [2]1988. See also C.H. Talbert (ed.), *Perspectives on Luke–Acts* (Perspectives in Religious Studies, 5), Danville–Edinburgh, 1978. R.J. Cassidy – P.J. Scharper (eds.), *Political Issues in Luke–Acts*, Maryknoll, NY, 1983. C.H. Talbert (ed.), *Luke–Acts. New Perspectives from the Society of Biblical Lit-*

favourite subject for doctoral dissertations[25]. It is of course impossible, within the limits of this introduction, even to think of a more or less complete survey of the literature. My aim is a more modest one. I will call to mind some of the highlights of earlier research and sketch the state of affairs for various aspects of the topic that is addressed in this volume.

erature, New York, 1984. J.B. TYSON (ed.), *Luke–Acts and the Jewish People. Eight Critical Perspectives*, Minneapolis, MN, 1988. N.H. KEATHLEY (ed.), *With Steadfast Purpose*, 1990 (above n. 12). D.D. SYLVA (ed.), *Reimaging the Death of the Lukan Jesus* (BBB, 73), Frankfurt/M, 1990. E. RICHARD (ed.), *New Views on Luke and Acts*, Collegeville, MN, 1990. C. BUSSMANN – W. RADL (eds.), *Der Treue Gottes trauen. Beiträge zum Werk des Lukas. Für Gerhard Schneider*, Freiburg–Basel–Wien, 1991. P. LUOMANEN (ed.), *Luke–Acts. Scandinavian Perspectives* (Publications of the Finnish Exegetical Society, 54), Helsinki, 1991. G. MARCONI – G. O'COLLINS (eds.), *Luca–Atti. Studi in onore di P. Emilio Rasco nel suo 70° compleanno*, Assisi, 1991 (ET *Luke and Acts*, New York – Mahwah, NJ, 1993). J.H. NEYREY (ed.), *The Social World of Luke–Acts. Models for Interpretation*, Peabody, MA, 1991. P. SCHMIDT (ed.), *Één auteur, twee boeken. Lucas en de Handelingen van de Apostelen*, Leuven, 1992. C.A. EVANS – J.A. SANDERS, *Luke and Scripture: The Function of Sacred Tradition in Luke–Acts*, Minneapolis, MN, 1993. C.M. TUCKETT (ed.), *Luke's Literary Achievement* (above n. 9). B. WITHERINGTON (ed.), *History, Literature, and Society in the Book of Acts*, Cambridge, 1996. And most recently, R.P. THOMPSON – T.E. PHILLIPS (eds.), *Literary Studies in Luke–Acts. Essays in Honor of Joseph B. Tyson*, Macon, GA, 1998: with contributions by, among others, M.C. Parsons (on Jerusalem in Lk–Acts), R.L. Brawley (the God of promises and the Jews), and Phillips (subtlety as a literary technique in the characterization of the Jews).

The most famous and most prestigious achievement in Lukan studies in this regard remain no doubt the five volumes of *The Beginnings of Christianity* that were edited by F.J. Foakes Jackson and K. Lake between 1920 and 1933. Their approach was chiefly historical. The work has now been resumed by a team of historians and New Testament scholars "in the light of literary and theological studies" (I, p. XI) in the series *The Book of Acts in Its First Century Setting* (first volume published in 1993; six volumes until now).

Besides collective publications, one should also mention some collections of studies by distinguished Lukan scholars. See esp. J. DUPONT, *Études sur les Actes des Apôtres* (LD, 45), Paris, 1967 (partly translated as *The Salvation of the Gentiles. Studies in the Acts of the Apostles*, New York, 1979) and *Nouvelles études sur les Actes des Apôtres* (LD, 118), Paris, 1984; *Études sur les évangiles synoptiques* (BETL, 70B), Leuven, 1985, pp. 951-1181 ("Luc"). A. GEORGE, *Études sur l'œuvre de Luc* (Sources bibliques), Paris, 1978. J. JERVELL, *The Unknown Paul. Essays on Luke–Acts and Early Christian History*, Minneapolis, MN, 1984; cf. below, n. 139. G. SCHNEIDER, *Lukas, Theologe der Heilsgeschichte. Aufsätze zum lukanischen Doppelwerk* (BBB, 59), Bonn, 1985. F. BOVON, *Lukas in neuer Sicht. Gesammelte Aufsätze* (BTS, 8), Neukirchen, 1985; = *L'œuvre de Luc. Études d'exégèse et de théologie* (LD, 130), Paris, 1987.

25. See, e.g., in the series of JSNT SS, nos. 12 (D.L. Bock, below n. 172), 21 (M.C. Parsons, n. 96), 54 (R.P. Menzies, n. 190), 72 (S.M. Sheeley, n. 239), 106 (J.A. Weatherly, n. 151), 110 (M.L. Strauss, n. 197), 119 (D. Ravens, n. 139), 141 (R.I. Denova, n. 172), 144 (S.J. Roth, n. 146), 163 (J.A. Darr, n. 151); SBL DS, nos. 147 (W.H. Shepherd, n. 187), 155 (R.M. Price, n. 146), 158 (O.W. Allen, n. 151); SNTS MS, nos. 57 (P.F. Esler, n. 141), 76 (J.T. Squires, n. 159); 78 (L.C.A. Alexander, n. 68), 87 (P. Doble, n. 196), 89 (H.D. Buckwalter, n. 199), 99 (P. Böhlemann, n. 153); WUNT 2, nos. 32 (M. Klinghardt, n. 142), 49 (D.M. Crump, n. 144), 51 (M. Korn, n. 54), 89 (A. Prieur, n. 198).

I. H.J. CADBURY'S "SINGLE WORK"

A new dimension was given to the study of Luke's work by the publications of H.J. Cadbury. According to Cadbury, the uniformity in style and vocabulary of Lk and Acts, some variation notwithstanding, is proof that both are the work of the same author[26]. But "the recognition of the common authorship of Luke and Acts is not enough"[27]. One has to move beyond the level of authorial unity to that of the narrative itself. That is the topic of his book *The Making of Luke–Acts* (1927, repr. 1958).

Cadbury's interest is not so much in the facts that are related in Lk–Acts but in the factors which, in his view, determine the composition of Luke's work. There are four: the materials to which the author had access; his indebtedness to certain ways of formulating and expressing ideas that were currently accepted in his time; the author's personality: his views on secular, social, and religious matters, and his mastery of style and language; and finally, the purpose the author has set himself with his writings. These factors constitute the four parts of Cadbury's *Making*. Closer analysis reveals that the Gospel and Acts cannot be treated separately, but that Luke's writings are a unit. "They are not merely two independent writings from the same pen; they are a single continuous work. Acts is neither an appendix nor an afterthought. It is probably an integral part of the author's original plan and purpose"[28]. To express this insight Cadbury coined the hyphenated form "Luke–Acts"[29]. Here are three important conclusions of his work.

1. The evidence for his definition of Lk–Acts as a single work rests above all on his interpretation of the prologue in Lk 1,1-4. Cadbury had studied this passage in detail in one of his contributions to *The Beginnings*

---

26. "If anything can be proved by linguistic evidence, this fact is proved by it" (*The Making of Luke–Acts*, London, 1927, p. 8). Cadbury has greatly contributed to the study of Luke's style and vocabulary through various publications: see esp. *The Style and Literary Method of Luke*, I (HTS, 6), Cambridge, MA, 1920, his contributions to *The Beginnings of Christianity*, and his *Lexical Notes on Luke–Acts*, published in *JBL* 1925-1926, 1929, 1933, and 1962; full titles in the "Bibliography of H.J. Cadbury" compiled by B.R. Gaventa in M.C. PARSONS – J.B. TYSON (eds.), *Cadbury, Knox, and Talbert. American Contributions to the Study of Acts*, Atlanta, GA, 1992, pp. 45-51.

27. *Ibid.*, p. 8.

28. *Ibid.*, pp. 8-9.

29. He had already used the formula in the title of a series of articles on Lukan lexicography that had appeared in *JBL* in 1925-26, and exceptionally also in two of his contributions to *The Beginnings of Christianity* (*BC*). He formally introduced the expression and motivated his use of it in his 1927 monograph. See *BC* II, p. 364 and 510. These earlier occurrences are not always noticed (cf. POWELL, *What Are They Saying About Acts?*, p. 5). Parsons and Pervo draw attention to the articles in *JBL* but they do not mention the passages in *BC* (*Rethinking*, p. 4).

of Christianity. There he had argued that Lk 1,1-4 covers the content of the Gospel and of Acts[30]. When Luke describes the content of his work as διήγησιν περὶ τῶν πεπληροφορημένων ἐν ἡμῖν πραγμάτων (1,1) and concludes by stating that he writes to Theophilus ἵνα ἐπιγνῷς περὶ ὧν κατηχήθης λόγων τὴν ἀσφάλειαν (1,4), he has in mind both his Gospel and Acts. And what Luke says in the prologue about his predecessors[31], the eyewitnesses, and his own involvement in the events he will deal with[32], can equally be extended to include the account in the Book of Acts. In Cadbury's opinion, the preface in Acts does not argue against this interpretation. On the contrary, it rather proves it. Acts 1,1-2 is not a second but a secondary preface. It follows from the need to divide a longer work into individual books, each of which could be briefly introduced again. Such a phenomenon was well known in ancient literature and Luke's readers would never have had the impression that Acts 1,1-2 was the prologue to a new work. A reference to the preceding book (τὸν πρῶτον λόγον) and to its content (on ἤρξατο ὁ Ἰησοῦς ποιεῖν τε καὶ διδάσκειν) are typical of such prefaces[33], as is the repetition of the name of the addressee[34]. Usually there is also a summary of what is to follow. This is missing in Acts 1,1-2, which is remarkable but not unique (cf. Josephus' Ant. 13,1). It is no reason to speculate about possible corruptions in the text[35]. Lk 1,1-4 is "the real preface to Acts as well as to the Gospel, written by the author when he contemplated not merely one but both volumes"[36].

2. When Luke concludes his preface by addressing Theophilus in person and by expressing the wish ἵνα ἐπιγνῷς περὶ ὧν κατηχήθης λόγων τὴν ἀσφάλειαν, he also formulates the overall purpose of his work[37]. Lk–Acts is an apology of the Christian movement[38]. Cadbury is

30. *Commentary on the Preface of Luke*, in *BC* II, 1922, pp. 489-510. The suggestion had been made before by T. Zahn, E. Norden, and E. Meyer. Cadbury knew this and recognized his indebtedness to these authors (p. 492 n. 3), but he was the one who further developed it into a model for the interpretation of Lk and Acts.

31. Luke does not say that it is his intention to give a continuation to the story as it was told by others before him, but Cadbury reckons with that possibility (*Making*, pp. 331-332).

32. On this point and the meaning of παρηκολουθηκότι, see esp. also his *The Knowledge Claimed in Luke's Preface*, in *Exp* 8/24 (1922) 401-420.

33. Cf. *Commentary*, p. 491 n. 1.

34. *Making*, p. 201.

35. "Possibly the author himself is responsible for the anacoluthon" (*Making*, p. 199).

36. *Commentary*, p. 492.

37. Luke was not writing to strenghten the faith of someone who had already been instructed about the message of Christ. Theophilus is addressed not as a Christian but "as a man of influence liable to entertain a hostile view towards Christianity": *The Purpose Expressed in Luke's Preface*, in *Exp* 8/21 (1921) 431-441, p. 432.

38. It is v. 4 "which specially suggests that the author's avowed purpose in Luke–Acts is the defence of Christianity" (*Commentary*, p. 510; cf. 492). A similar

aware of the fact that if an apologetic purpose can be accepted for Acts "on the basis of its content"[39], the case might be less evident for the Gospel[40]. But this is not much of a problem to him. It might even be an argument for his position. Luke may have had subsidiary purposes in view[41], but in the preface he chose to concentrate on the one that would be most relevant with regard to the addressee. That this purpose is best realized in the second volume but nevertheless is emphatically mentioned in the preface to the Gospel, makes it "quite likely that the preface belongs to the work as a whole and not merely to the πρῶτος λόγος"[42]. Lk 1,4 may contain a clue as to when the preface was composed. If it was written after Acts was finished, it was but natural that Luke in formulating the main purpose of his work in 1,4 was still very much influenced by what is most characteristic of Acts, especially of the latter part of it[43].

3. Lk–Acts cannot be captured under one genre. Luke made use of the language and literary forms of his time[44], but his work cannot be classified under the headings biography or history[45]. However, this does not argue against the unity of Luke's work. It contains features of these genres, but is not merely identical with one of them[46]. Luke's chief aim is to transmit received, "non-literary" tradition[47]. His literary aspirations are

phrase occurs again, with some nuance, in *Making*, at the end of the section on "the object of Luke–Acts": "It is quite probable that Luke's avowed purpose so far as his preface expresses it... is to correct misinformation about Christianity" (*Making*, p. 315). In what precedes Cadbury had expanded the perspective of this apologetic of the legitimacy of Christianity to Jews and Gentiles alike (see esp. pp. 306-308).

39. *Purpose*, p. 439. See esp. the defence speeches of Stephen and Paul.

40. An apologetic purpose of Acts (in addition to a didactic one) was accepted by Foakes Jackson and Lake ("The Editors") in their contribution on *The Internal Evidence of Acts*, in *BC* II, pp. 121-204, esp. 177-180. They are even more affirmative in discovering the same purpose also in the Gospel. See the section on "The Gospel as an Apology" (pp. 180-187), which analyzes the Gospel and Acts from this perspective.

41. This is esp. stressed in *Making*, pp. 299-306.

42. *Purpose*, p. 439.

43. "Its associations in diction and style are much closer to the last chapters of Acts" (*Purpose*, p. 440).

44. See esp. *Making*, pp. 113-209.

45. "That Luke's gospel should not be counted a formal biography is further confirmed when one recalls that it is merely part of a longer work, and that its sequel, though full of biographical incident, is even less concerned with sketching the full career of its principal characters" (*Making*, p. 132). And Cadbury continues on the next page: "It is evident that the same objection can be made to other formal classification[s]".

46. "The comparison which we hoped to make with Luke–Acts cannot be made with them as a whole but in parts" (*Making*, p. 134). Maybe Luke, not unlike some of his contemporaries, was not interested in an exact technical definition of his work, – in Acts 1,1 he calls it a λόγος (*ibid.*, pp. 136-137).

47. Cadbury acknowledges the influence of the work of K.L. Schmidt on this point (cf. *Making*, p. 129 and 134).

restricted by the material on which he has to work, "but the literary aspects are unmistakable and are fully in accord, as far as they go, with contemporary prose writings"[48]. It is not the common genre, it is the literary effort of the author that unifies the work. The factual disunity of Luke and Acts in the textual tradition is not a objection either. The division into two volumes of a long work such as Lk–Acts, for matters of "physical convenience"[49], resulted in a more radical and definitive separation later on. A two-volume work such as Lk–Acts was not exceptional in ancient literature. But it was something new and unique in the Christian communities. Luke had innovated the emerging Christian literature but the world was not ready to accept it. The first volume showed strong similarities with other such writings. The second one remained an isolated case within Christian literature of the first century. So, "it is easy to understand how the early separation of the volumes took place"[50].

Cadbury showed the way for studying Lk and Acts as a narrative unity with a common purpose[51]. Many of his observations, as well as the model he proposed, continue to be of influence until today[52]. Thus, e.g., the view that the preface was meant to be the introduction to the Gospel and to Acts alike, that Luke's plan to write a two-volume work must have left its marks on the redaction of the first volume, and that the final chapter of the Gospel has a key function in the whole of the composition of Luke's work.

1. First, there is the question of the extent of the prologue. Cadbury's conclusion had been endorsed by J. Dupont in his survey of research on the sources of Acts[53]. In his commentary on Lk, J.A. Fitzmyer notes that

---

48. *Ibid.*, 139.
49. *Ibid.*, p. 9.
50. *Ibid.*, p. 10.
51. On the influence of Cadbury on Lukan studies, see, e.g., B.R. GAVENTA, *The Peril of Modernizing Henry Joel Cadbury*, in PARSONS–TYSON (eds.), *Cadbury, Knox, and Talbert* (n. 26), pp. 7-26, with a response by R.I. PERVO, *"On Perilous Things"*, pp. 37-43; D.L. JONES, *The Legacy of Henry Joel Cadbury*, pp. 27-36.
52. "Luke–Acts" is not found in *BC* outside the articles of Cadbury (see still V, 365). But when Lake speaks of "a two-volume work" that became separated (*BC* II, p. 159; IV, p. 1), he clearly follows Cadbury. — For recent "eulogies" of his model for understanding Lk–Acts, see PARSONS–PERVO, *Rethinking* (n. 6), pp. 2-3. Compare MADDOX, *Purpose* (n. 17), pp. 4-6: "the Gospel of Luke was written with Acts very much in mind: it was never intended to stand independently of its companion-volume. By far the simpler explanation of this is that the two-volume work was planned as a unity from the beginning" (p. 6).
53. J. DUPONT, *Les sources du Livre des Actes. État de la question*, Brugge, 1960, pp. 99-109, esp. 102-105; ET *The Sources of Acts. The Present Position*, London, 1964, pp. 101-112 (105-107).

"it is generally recognized among commentators today" that Lk 1,1-4 applies to the whole of Luke's work[54]. In his detailed analysis M. Korn does not accept Cadbury's understanding of παρακολουθέω as a reference to Luke's involvement in the affairs he will be telling[55], but he finds evidence in ἐν ἡμῖν that Luke wants to extend his account to his own time, which brings the demonstration of the fulfilment of the events that have been told about Jesus and in the mean time receives its legitimation from its connection with the time of Jesus[56]. "Lukas (hatte) in seinem Prolog schon das ganze Doppelwerk im Auge"[57].

Among those who challenged this opinion were H. Conzelmann and E. Haenchen (see also H. Schürmann)[58]. Dupont thought their critique was "pas fort éclairant" and even "surprenant"[59]. Most others who have expressed scepticism are rather reserved. É. Samain is not convinced by Cadbury's understanding of παρακολουθέω and by the distinction between ἀπ᾽ ἀρχῆς and ἄνωθεν ("since long")[60], and concludes that οἱ ἀπ᾽ ἀρχῆς αὐτόπται directs the preface "avant tout" to the events that are related in the Gospel. However, he approves of the suggestion of G. Klein[61] that with πᾶσιν Luke may have had in mind both volumes[62] and that καθεξῆς refers to the succession of the stories about Jesus and about the Church[63]. S. Brown sees a "primary objection" in the fact that, if Lk 1,1-4 includes Acts, Luke apparently acknowledges to have had predecessors also for the account in the second volume, "something that few contemporary critics would be prepared to admit"[64], but he recog-

54. *Lk*, p. 9. See also MARSHALL, *Lk*, pp. 39-40. Cf. M. KORN, *Die Geschichte Jesu in veränderter Zeit. Studien zur bleibenden Bedeutung Jesu im lukanischen Doppelwerk* (WUNT, 2/51), Tübingen, 1993, pp. 6-32. F. Ó FEARGHAIL, *The Introduction to Luke–Acts. A Study of the Role of Lk 1,1–4,44 in the Composition of Luke's Two-Volume Work* (AnBib, 126), Rome, 1991, pp. 85-116, esp. 96-102.

55. KORN, *Die Geschichte Jesu*, p. 25.

56. "Aber die Befestigung des im Lk über Jesus Erzählten durch die Schilderung der Erfüllung in der Apg ist nur die eine Seite. Es geht andererseits auch darum, daß die Apg durch den Aufweis ihrer Kontinuität zum Jesusgeschehen legitimiert wird" (*ibid.*, pp. 30-31).

57. *Ibid.*, p. 31.

58. H. CONZELMANN, *Die Mitte der Zeit. Studien zur Theologie des Lukas* (BHT, 17), Tübingen, ⁵1964, p. 7 n. 1. E. HAENCHEN, *Apg*, p. 105 n. 3.

59. *Sources* (n. 53), p. 106 n. 3 and 107 n. 2. H. SCHÜRMANN, *Evangelienschrift und kirchliche Unterweisung. Die repräsentative Funktion der Schrift nach Lk 1,1 4*, in *Miscellanea Erfordiana* (ETS, 12), Leipzig, 1962, pp. 48-73 (repr. 1968, pp. 251-271).

60. É. SAMAIN, *La notion de ἀρχή dans l'œuvre lucanienne*, in NEIRYNCK (ed.), *L'évangile de Luc* (n. 1), pp. 299-328, here 324 (= 1989, 209-238, 234).

61. G. KLEIN, *Lukas 1,1-4 als theologisches Programm*, in E. DINKLER (ed.), *Zeit und Geschichte. Dankesgabe an R. Bultmann*, Tübingen, 1964, pp. 193-216, esp. 209-210.

62. SAMAIN, *La notion*, p. 324 (234): "peut s'appliquer a '*tout*' le récit (Ev. et Ac.)".

63. SAMAIN, *La notion*, p. 324 n. 94; cf. KLEIN, *Lukas 1,1-4*, p. 211.

64. S. BROWN, *The Role of the Prologues in Determining the Purpose of Luke–Acts*, in TALBERT (ed.), *Perspectives* (n. 24), pp. 99-111, here 101.

nizes that it may not be a decisive one, since πολλοὶ ἐπεχείρησαν also may refer only to earlier attempts at writing a gospel account (so Klein).

G. Schneider regards the similarities in vocabulary between Acts and Lk 1,1-4 as an indication that the preface may have been written after Luke had finished his whole work, a possibility that had already been suggested by Cadbury (see above). In its present form, the prologue applies to both volumes, but it does not mean that Luke envisaged from the start to write a single two-volume work[65]. However, Schneider thinks it is also possible that the prologue was composed before Luke began writing Acts. He emphasizes the "Geschlossenheit" throughout Luke's treatment of what are the two central topics of his work, eschatology and the future of Israel[66]. He further points out that when Luke in 1,4 states that he will illustrate the trustworthiness of the words in which Theophilus has been instructed, he committed himself to relating also how the story of Jesus found its continuation into the preaching of his own time. Lk 1,1-4 contains a promise to the reader that goes beyond the account he finds in the Gospel. Luke must have had a second volume in mind when he wrote v. 4[67].

In her recent monograph on the prologue L.C.A. Alexander sets out working under the assumption that Lk and Acts are "two parts of a single work"[68]. At the end of her analysis, however, she casts doubts on this "axiomatic" position[69]. There are no clear hints in the preface that Luke was also thinking of Acts. Therefore, she reckons with the "possibility that Luke did not have the narrative of Acts immediately in mind when he wrote Luke 1.1-4"[70]. But note the "not immediately"[71].

65. G. SCHNEIDER, *Der Zweck des lukanischen Doppelwerks*, in *BZ* 21 (1977) 45-66, p. 52; repr. in *Lukas, Theologe der Heilsgeschichte* (n. 24), pp. 9-30, here 16.

66. *Zweck*, p. 56 (20).

67. "Da diese Kontinuität und sachliche Übereinstimmung aufzuweisen war, mußte wahrscheinlich von vornherein – falls Lk 1,1-4 *vor* Abfassung der Acta geschrieben wurde – der 'zweite Band' geplant gewesen sein" (*Zweck*, p. 54/18). Note the similarity in expression but the change in opinion in the Commentary (above n. 5). R.J. Dillon situates himself in the line of Schneider arguing that there is no proof in the Gospel that Luke intended to bring a continuation in Acts, but at the same time admitting that "the concept of Luke's two-volume opus might well be contained within the objective stated by the Gospel's prologue". Cf. *Previewing Luke's Project from His Prologue (Luke 1:1-4)*, in *CBQ* 43 (1981) 205-227, p. 225; comp. p. 218 n. 37.

68. L.C.A. ALEXANDER, *The Preface to Luke's Gospel. Literary Convention and Social Context in Luke 1.1-4 and Acts 1.1* (SNTS MS, 78), Cambridge, 1993, p. 2 n. 1.

69. Παρακολουθέω means "being familiar with" (an account or an event) rather than "having participated in it", as Cadbury would have it. And ἀσφάλεια might be overestimated as a clue for discovering Luke's purpose; it could simply refer to the higher degree of certainty that is gained when oral instruction is replaced with a written record (*ibid.*, pp. 140-141).

70. *Ibid.*, p. 146.

71. Cf. also p. 142: "applies much more directly to the Gospel than to Acts". See the comment by MARSHALL, *"Former Treatise"* (n. 4), pp. 173-174.

2. If Luke had already in mind a continuation of his Gospel from the start, it is utterly highly plausible that this has left its marks on the redaction of his first volume. So, one should find in the Gospel indications that Luke is looking forward to Acts. For Schneider this could be "ein eindeutiger Beweis" that Cadbury's hypothesis is correct, but, in his opinion, none of the passages that are usually quoted in this respect are conclusive[72]. For R. Pesch and C.K. Barrett, as for others[73], the evidence is convincing. In his commentary on Acts (1986), Pesch defines Acts as "'zweites Buch' des luk. Doppelwerkes". Luke had planned from the beginning to write a work that comprised both volumes[74]. This can be demonstrated, according to Pesch, by the many instances in which Luke has redacted Mark in view of his second volume[75]. However, the adaptations to the Gospel are not the result of Luke's free redaction of Mark. They show that some of his material occurred in the gospel tradition and also in the traditions on which he relied for writing Acts, "daß der Verfasser also traditionsgebundener arbeitete, als häufig angenommen wurde" (25), and that in some cases Luke preferred the wording or the context of Acts[76].

Barrett has collected 41 instances from all over the Gospel which may demonstrate that Luke was already preparing for Acts when writing his Gospel[77]. Not all of these are equally important and Barrett uses a variety of expressions to describe how Luke may have intended to establish the connection. It is said that Luke wants "to prepare" his readers for Acts[78], so that they will not be "surprised" when reading certain pas-

72. *Zweck* (n. 65), p. 52 (16). He refers to Lk 2,32 – Acts 13,47; Lk 6,40 and the picture of Paul in Acts; Lk 6,12-16 and the role of the apostles in Acts. The "transposition" of the temple saying from the Gospel to Acts 6,14-15 is not a proof that Luke deliberately postponed material from his Gospel sources to the second volume. And the promises that are made by the Risen Lord in Lk 24,44-49 about the Gentile mission and the Spirit retain their force even if Luke had originally not the intention also to relate their fulfilment (pp. 52-53/16-17).

73. See, e.g., W. ÜBELACKER, *Das Verhältnis von Lk/Apg zum Markusevangelium*, in LUOMANEN (ed.), *Scandinavian Perspectives* (n. 24), pp. 157-194, esp. 160-162 and 185-187.

74. "Der Arbeiter (hat) den beiden Büchern als Doppelwerk gleichzeitig konzipiert und (zumindest teilweise) ausgearbeitet" (R. PESCH, *Apg*, p. 24).

75. The majority of these are minor changes (e.g., the addition of "prison" in Lk 21,12 takes already into account the stories of the emprisonment of several of the disciples in Acts), but a few are more elaborate, as in the case of the omission of chapter 7 of Mark, a discussion which Luke postpones until Acts 10,1–11,18.

76. E.g., in Lk 21,27 Luke would have changed Mark's "in clouds" (13,26) into the singular in accordance with Acts 1,9 (cf. n. 24 and 72).

77. C.K. BARRETT, *The Third Gospel As a Preface to Acts? Some Reflections*, in F. VAN SEGBROECK, *et al.* (eds.), *The Four Gospels 1992*. FS F. Neirynck (BETL, 100), Leuven, 1992, II, pp. 1454-1466. Comp. also *The First New Testament?*, in *NT* 38 (1996) 94-104.

78. See, e.g., his comment on the Infancy Narratives and on the addition to Lk 3,6 (p. 1455).

sages in Acts[79]. Luke must "have had in mind" certain topics that will appear again in Acts[80], or he "makes space" for a continuation in Acts[81]. Even the lack of parallels may be instructive: with the exception of v. 11 (cf. Acts 13,51), the description of the mission of the seventy-two in Lk 10,1-12 differs from the picture in Acts, because Luke wants to distinguish between the pre- and the post-Easter mission of the disciples[82]. Among the most significant cases are the parable in Lk 14,15-24, which in Luke's version contains a clear reference to the Gentile mission, the section on persecution in Lk 21,12-19, and the conclusion of the Gospel, which may have been written as an introduction to or a summary of what Luke was going to bring "in a new and much expanded form" in Acts[83]. The preface covers both volumes and may have been written between the first and the second part of Luke's work[84]. All of this means that Luke had the firm intention to tell not only the story of Jesus but also what this story did to his witnesses. Paraphrasing van Unnik's "confirmation" (below), Barrett speaks of Acts as "the guarantee that what followed was the intended and valid outcome of what had been narrated in the first (volume)". Because Lk–Acts contains material about Jesus and about the apostles, he even suggests to call it "the first New Testament", with Lk as "the preface" to Acts[85].

This last expression is taken up by Fitzmyer in his commentary on Acts[86]. For Fitzmyer, the double prologue addressing the same person, together with the stylistic and the narrative unity (in which the parallelism between the major characters is most remarkable, though, in his opinion, at times somewhat overdrawn), and the theological unity, implies that Lk–Acts was written by the same author, who combined historiographical aspirations (the story of the spread of the church) with doctrinal and pastoral purposes, assuring "Theophilus and other Gentile–Christian readers like him that what the church of his day was teach-

79. *Ibid.*, p. 1454 and 1458 (on Lk 9,52-56).

80. Among others, the concern for the Gentile mission in Lk 4,16-30 (p. 1455); see also on Lk 13,22-30 (p. 1459).

81. On Lk 21,7-11 (p. 1460).

82. *Ibid.*, p. 1458. For a different view, see now T.J. Lane who argues that Luke's redaction of 10,1-20 is dominated by his presentation of the Gentile mission in Acts: T.J. LANE, *Luke and the Gentile Mission. Gospel Anticipates Acts* (EHS, 23/571), Frankfurt, 1996. Lane regards Lk 1,1-4 as the prooemium and 1,5-4,44 as the prologue to Lk–Acts. Compare on this Ó FEARGHAIL, *The Introduction to Luke–Acts* (n. 54), pp. 9-38 and 117-154.

83. *Preface*, p. 1461.

84. *Ibid.*, p. 1463.

85. *The First New Testament*, pp. 102-104. See now also *A Critical and Exegetical Commentary on the Acts of the Apostles*, 2 (ICC), Edinburgh, 1998, p. XLIII and LXVIII.

86. J.A. FITZMYER, *The Acts of the Apostles* (AB, 31), New York, 1998, p. 55.

ing and practising was rooted in the Period of Jesus, in the teaching of Jesus himself"[87]. J. Jervell, on the other hand, argues that the Gospel and the Book of Acts were written with an interval of some years, and that one should not expect Luke to have had already one eye on Acts when writing his Gospel. The double prologue characterizes Lk–Acts as "zwei Werke von demselben Verfasser, und nicht zwei Teile eines Buches"[88].

G. Wasserberg starts from the hypothesis that Luke has created a narrative unit. This means, "seine kohärente Anlage... erlaubt, Lk–Act auch synchron, als von vornherein einheitlich konzipiertes Erzählwerk zu lesen und zu interpretieren"[89]. Consequently, Wasserberg begins his analysis of Luke's interpretation of the reaction of the Jewish audience to the Christian preaching with Acts 28,16–31 ("am Anfang das Ende")[90]. The quotation from Isa in 28,26–27 marks the climax of the whole history of the opposition of the Jews to Jesus and to Paul (115: "jetzt reicht's"): it is now that Paul comes to realize ("die neue Erkenntnis, die der lk Paulus in Rom gewinnt!") that such is God's will ("aufgrund *göttlicher Verstockung*").

3. Lk looks forward to Acts. This is certainly true for the last chapter which has strong links with the second volume as J. Dupont has shown in his contributions to the Journées of 1968 and 1977. In the latter he studied the conclusion of Acts in its relation to Lk and especially also to Lk 24. In 1968 he analyzed Peter's speeches in Acts 1-5 demonstrating how the stories of the resurrection, the teaching of the Risen Lord, and his ascension have influenced the missionary discourses of the early Church[91]. Particularly striking is the fact that Luke begins his second

---

87. *Ibid.*, p. 59; cf. p. 49.
88. J. JERVELL, *Die Apostelgeschichte* (KEK, 3), Göttingen, 1998, p. 57 n. 23.
89. G. WASSERBERG, *Aus Israels Mitte – Heil für die Welt. Eine narrativ-exegetische Studie zur Theologie des Lukas* (BZNW, 92), Berlin – New York, 1998, pp. 31-32. One should note, however, that he somewhat relativizes his own position when he adds that Lk and Acts can also be understood for and from themselves: "Sie sind sowohl zwei Werke wie auch eins" (31 n. 5).
90. *Ibid.*, pp. 71-115.
91. J. DUPONT, *Les discours de Pierre dans les Actes et le chapitre XXIV de l'évangile de Luc*, in NEIRYNCK (ed.), *L'évangile de Luc*, pp. 329-374 (= 1989, 239-284; 328-330); *La conclusion des Actes et son rapport à l'ensemble de l'ouvrage de Luc*, in KREMER (ed.), *Les Actes des Apôtres* (n. 2), pp. 359-404. Both articles are reprinted in his *Nouvelles études* (n. 24), pp. 58-111 and 457-511. See also *La portée christologique de l'évangélisation des nations d'après Luc 24,47*, in J. GNILKA (ed.), *Neues Testament und Kirche. Für Rudolf Schnackenburg*, Freiburg–Basel–Wien, 1974, pp. 125-143 (repr. 37-57) and *La Mission de Paul d'après Actes 26,16-23 et la Mission des Apôtres d'après Luc 24,44-49 et Actes 1,8*, in M.D. HOOKER – S.G. WILSON (eds.), *Paul and Paulinism. Essays in Honour of C.K. Barrett*, London, 1982, pp. 290-299 (repr. 446-456). — Cf. also C.M. MARTINI, *L'apparizione agli Apostoli in Lc 24,36-43 nel complesso dell' opera lucana*, in É. DHANIS (ed.), *Resurrexit*, Rome, 1974, pp. 230-245. — In this volume J.

volume with the same story with which he had ended the first one. Cadbury saw no difficulty for his understanding of the relation between Lk
and Acts in the double version of the ascension narrative in Lk 24,50-53
and Acts 1,6-11[92]. He also argued that there is no need to suspect the
authenticity of Acts 1,1-5[93]. In the last volume of *The Beginnings of
Christianity*, K. Lake suggested that Lk 24,50-53 was added to assimilate the ending of Luke's Gospel to that of the other gospels[94]. Others
went one step further still and argued that Acts 1,6-11 might have been
the continuation of Lk 24,49 and that both Lk 24,50-53 (as a summary
of Acts 1,6-11) and Acts 1,1-5 were interpolations resulting from the
subdivision of Luke's work in the second century. Originally, Lk–Acts
was not a two- but a one-volume work[95].

Today it is still commonly accepted, e.g., in the recent monographs of
M.C. Parsons and A.W. Zwiep, that the two versions are an integral part
of Lk–Acts[96]. From his diachronic and synchronic analysis of Lk and of
Acts, Parsons concludes that the differences should not be explained
away by interpolation theories. They are due to the specific literary function of each narrative[97]. Luke's source in 24,50-53 is no longer recover-

Kremer illustrates the key function of this chapter from the stories of the conversion of
Paul in Acts (below pp. 329-355).

92. The differences between the two accounts "permit of other explanations and do
not seem to counterbalance the probability that we have here the usual two-volume work
with a single general preface" (*Making*, p. 9 n. 3).

93. *Ibid.*, p. 198. For a different opinion, see, e.g., Harnack, Norden, and Bauernfeind
(references in SCHNEIDER, *Apg*, p. 77 n. 6). See also E. MEYER, *Ursprung* I, pp. 34-45
(Acts 1,3-12 is an interpolation).

94. K. LAKE, *The Preface to Acts and the Composition of Acts*, in *BC* V, pp. 1-7, esp. 3-4.

95. See H. SAHLIN, *Der Messias und das Gottesvolk. Studien zur protolukanischen
Theologie* (ASNU, 15), Uppsala, 1945, pp. 11-18 and 343-347 (on the forty days). Ph.
MENOUD, *Remarques sur les textes de l'ascension dans Luc-Actes*, in *Neutestamentliche
Studien für Rudolf Bultmann*, Berlin, 1954, [2]1957, pp. 148-156, esp. 154; retracted in ID.,
"Pendant quarante jours" (Actes I, 3), in *Neotestamentica et Patristica*. FS O. Cullmann
(NTSup, 6), Leiden, 1962, pp. 148-156, p. 155; both articles are reprinted in ID., *Jésus-
Christ et la foi. Recherches néotestamentaires* (Bibliothèque théologique),
Neuchâtel–Paris, 1975, pp. 76-84 and 110-118. É. TROCMÉ, *Le "Livre des Actes" et l'his-
toire* (Études d'histoire et de philosophie religieuses, 45), Paris, 1957, pp. 31-35. CONZEL-
MANN, *Die Mitte der Zeit*, [5]1964, p. 86 and 189 n. 4, regarded only Lk 24,50-53 as an
interpolation. For criticism, see KÜMMEL, *Einleitung*, p. 126; HAENCHEN, *Apg*[7], p. 109
n. 2; SCHNEIDER, *Apg*, p. 77 n. 7. — It is sometimes said that Lake also defended the secondary character of Acts 1,1-5, but this is not true. Lake admits that the text of the prologue of Acts has "obviously suffered in transmission" (*BC* V, p. 1), but he does not
regard Acts 1,1-5 as an interpolation. The error seems to go back to Menoud (*Remarques*,
p. 151 n. 14) and is found also in Schneider (*Apg*, p. 77 n. 7).

96. M.C. PARSONS, *The Departure of Jesus in Luke–Acts. The Ascension Narratives in
Context* (JSNT SS, 21), Sheffield, 1987. A.W. ZWIEP, *The Ascension of the Messiah in Lukan
Christology* (NTSup, 87), Leiden, 1997 (with a Bibliography 1900-96 on pp. 200-215).

97. PARSONS, *The Departure of Jesus*, pp. 191-198.

able but he may have taken up a traditional ascension story which he condensed into the departure narrative of Lk 24,50-53 and turned into the assumption narrative of Acts 1,9-11[98]. Parsons is particularly interested in the literary devices that help characterize the function of the narratives. In Lk 24,50-53 Luke looks back ("circularity") to the very beginning of his Gospel in chapters 1-2 (see Lk 1,23 and 24,51; 2,45 and 24,52) and brings the story to an end in such a way that "there is no temporal gap between the body of the narrative and its conclusion"[99], but at the same time the reader will be aware that not all the promises that had been made about the salvation of Israel in Lk 1–2, or about Jesus' assumption in 9,51, have been fulfilled (the device of incompletion)[100]. In Acts 1,1-11, too, there is circularity, now from the beginning to the end (Acts 28,23-31), and there are links to the preceding, to Lk 24 and to Lk 9. Lk 24,50-53 is best described as the completion of the farewell address in Lk 22, with which it forms an inclusion around the passion narrative, through the actual departure of Jesus[101]. The close-up ending of 24,50-53 helps to emphasize the connection between passion, resurrection, and ascension. In Acts 1,1-11, on the other hand, Luke has another concern. The ascension concludes a period of forty days in which the disciples are instructed (see esp. the mention of the Kingdom in v. 3) to become the witnesses of Jesus, and it also confirms that this instruction is now completed[102].

A.W. Zwiep studies the Lukan ascension narratives within the larger context of the Jewish tradition (in particular Moses, Elijah, Enoch), of early Christianity (Mk 16,19 and the Gospel of John), and of other texts in Lk–Acts[103]. Unlike Parsons, Zwiep defends the longer reading at 24,51[104], and he is also less interested in a narrative-critical interpretation, but he agrees with Parsons that there is no need to suspect an interpolation in the first verses of Acts. Working from elements which may

98. "It is plausible that... Luke shaped an ascension story inherited from primitive tradition into a final departure scene in Luke 24,50-53 and a heavenly-assumption story in Acts 1" (p. 63); cf. p. 150.

99. *Ibid.*, p. 96 ("a close-up ending").

100. Parsons defends the shorter reading at 24,51. Ἀνελήμφθη in Acts 1,2 on the other hand is authentic and was removed only to assimilate with the shorter text of 24,51.

101. *Ibid.*, p. 58.

102. *Ibid.*, p. 195.

103. Lk 9,51; 22,69; 23,42-43; 24,26; Acts 1,21-22; 2,33-36; 3,19-21; 5,31; 13,30-37.

104. *The Text of the Ascension Narrative (Luke 24.50-3; Acts 1.1-2,9-11)*, in *NTS* 42 (1996) 219-244. See also E.J. EPP, *The Ascension in the Textual Tradition of Luke–Acts*, in ID. – G.D. FEE (eds.), *New Testament Textual Criticism. Its Significance for Exegesis*. FS B.M. Metzger, Oxford, 1981, pp. 131-145.

have their origin in a post-Easter appearance tradition, Luke has created the ascension narratives to explain the prolonged though temporal absence of the Lord. The narratives have a similar but not a completely identical function in Lk 24,50-53 and in Acts 1,9-11. In Lk 24 the story "rounds off an era in salvation history" (171); in Acts a new element is added with the motif of the forty days as the preparation for the beginning of a new era[105].

II. Luke the Theologian

Cadbury was interested above all in Luke as "an artist"[106]. The rise of redaction criticism brought about a major shift in emphasis in Lukan studies. Lk–Acts now came to be regarded and appreciated primarily as the work of a theologian.

In reaction to such critics who looked very negatively upon Luke's decision to give a continuation to the Gospel[107], Ph. Vielhauer first formulated the suggestion that his work was to be read as a well thought-out answer to a crisis in early Christianity. For Vielhauer, the very existence of the Book of Acts, along with Luke's reworking of Mark's story in his Gospel, is proof that for Luke the Christian kerygma is above all about salvation in history rather than about eschatology[108].

This view was further developed some years later by H. Conzelmann who introduced a new approach to Lukan studies and indeed also a new understanding of the relationship between the Gospel and Acts. As time went by Jesus' original promise of his imminent return was increasingly challenged. Ultimately the delay of the parousia would mean the denial of Jesus' message. History had forced its way into the kerygma. Luke responded to this challenge by making this factor into the dominant viewpoint from which to look at the kerygma: history is salvation history[109]. In the introduction to *Die Mitte der Zeit*, Conzelmann points out

105. ZWIEP, *The Ascension of the Messiah*, p. 116; cf. pp. 99, 171-175, and 187.

106. *Commentary*, in *BC* II, p. 490.

107. Probably the most famous statement is F. Overbeck's "Es ist das eine Takt-losigkeit von welthistorischen Dimensionen" (*Christentum und Kultur*, ed. C.A. BERNOUILLI, 1919, p. 78).

108. Ph. VIELHAUER, *Zum "Paulinismus" der Apostelgeschichte*, in *EvT* 10 (1950-51) 1-15, p. 13: "Wie uneschatologisch Lukas denkt, geht nicht nur aus dem Inhalt, sondern vor allem aus dem Faktum der AG. hervor"; ET *On the "Paulinism" of Acts*, in KECK–MARTYN (eds.), *Studies in Luke–Acts* (n. 24), pp. 33-50, here 47.

109. H. CONZELMANN, *Apg*, p. 9. Cf. VIELHAUER, *Zum "Paulinismus"*, p. 13. E. HAENCHEN, *Tradition und Komposition in der Apostelgeschichte*, in *ZTK* 52 (1955) 205-225, p. 225 n. 1; repr. in ID., *Gott und Mensch. Gesammelte Aufsätze*, Tübingen, 1965, pp. 206-226 (226 n. 1). — On salvation history as the core of Luke's work, see,

two important consequences. First, the narrative is no longer merely identical with the kerygma, as this was still the case for Mark. Rather, it informs us about the development of the kerygma in history[110]. Second, the development of time turns the earthly ministry of Jesus into an event of the past. This insight leads Conzelmann to his famous division of salvation history. The time of Jesus is to be separated from what preceded it, the period of Israel that came to an end with the death of John the Baptist, and from what followed after it, the time of the Church that understands its existence from the past. "Aber erst bei Lukas wird diese Grenze, wird der *Unterschied* von damals und heute, Jesuszeit und Zeit der Kirche, damaligen und heutigen Problemen, in vollem Anfang *bewußt*. Die Zeit *Jesu* und die Zeit der *Kirche* werden als verschiedene Epochen eines umfassenden heilsgeschichtlichen Ablaufes dargestellt, die jeweils durch ihre besonderen Charakteristica unterschieden werden" (p. 5; ET 13). The Gospel tells the history of Jesus' ministry, of the "middle period". The history of the third period is the subject of a separate volume. This leads to two further questions.

1. Is Luke an historian? According to Conzelmann he is not. He is concerned with history, but only in a specific way. The composition of Lk–Acts is no longer to be addressed in terms of the reliability of the reports. Luke is a theologian who reflects upon the meaning of history and he was the first Christian author to realize that the kerygma develops itself within history.

2. How has one to understand the connection between both volumes of Luke's work? When the story of Jesus is seen in light of salvation history one can no longer afford not also to tell its continuation. But Luke has done this without disrupting the Gospel form that he took over from Mark. Acts is the necessary complement to the Gospel, but it is to be distinguished from it by its content and form[111]. The two volumes cannot be fully understood when they are studied for themselves. Both have an identity of their own, but they are also essentially interconnected with each other. Together they constitute a unity based on a theological

---

e.g., J. JERVELL, *The Future of the Past. Luke's Vision of Salvation History and Its Bearing on His Writing of History*, in WITHERINGTON (ed.), *History, Literature, and Society* (n. 24), pp. 104-127 (on Acts).

110. "Mit diesem Auseinandertreten von Kerygma und Erzählung ist die Möglichkeit gegeben, daß sich beide als je eigene Größe entfalten" (*Die Mitte der Zeit*, ⁵1964, p. 3; ET *The Theology of St Luke*, London, 1960, p. 11).

111. "So ergibt sich Zusammengehörigkeit wie Abgrenzung der beiden lukanischen Bücher: aus der Kontinuität der Heilsgeschichte einerseits, ihrer Gliederung andererseits" (*ibid.*, p. 10; ET 17). It is not correct, then, to say that Conzelmann actually has given up the unity of Luke's composition. So, e.g., MADDOX, *Purpose* (n. 17), p. 4.

insight: Luke's understanding of the real dimensions of the eschatological perspective in Jesus' message and of the real importance of the growth and development of a Christian community. This insight has determined and shaped the composition and the structure of Lk–Acts.

In *Die Mitte der Zeit* Conzelmann had limited his analysis to Luke's account of the "middle period". The "epoch of the Church" was treated some years later in his commentary on Acts (1963). But already in 1956 E. Haenchen had developed an interpretation of Acts which was essentially in line with that of Conzelmann[112]. For Haenchen, as for Conzelmann, Luke belongs to a different world from that of Mark. "Lukas teilt die Naherwartung des Endes nicht mehr"[113]. Haenchen has maintained this position throughout the revisions and subsequent editions of his commentary[114]. But from the outset he also introduced important nuances. He is more interested in the internal unity of Lk–Acts and the periodisation of salvation history receives increasingly less emphasis. In the Gospel Luke describes how God has brought salvation in Jesus, and Acts is the continuation and completion of the Gospel[115]. Haenchen is reluctant to speak of "periods". Acts tells the story of the growth of the Word of God in the world during the apostolic age. It is an account not of a human enterprise, but of the will of God[116]. In the revised edition the concept of "the Word of God", which at first was the characteristic feature of the story of Acts, becomes the unifying element ("die Klammer") of the Gospel and Acts[117]. Though formally maintained, the division into "periods" is almost dissolved in the last edition, when it is said that Luke regards salvation history "als eine grosse Einheit bis zur Parusie"[118]. Accordingly, Luke's decision to divide his work into two volumes in the way he did was perhaps less the result of his understanding of the development of salvation history but rather forced upon him

112. See the preface of Conzelmann. Haenchen points out that the first draft of his commentary was finished in the autumn of 1946 (*Apg*, 1956, p. 5*).

113. *Apg*, 1956, p. 89.

114. From the first revised edition on he formulates it even more strongly: "Die Stellung, die Lukas zum eschatologischen Problem einnimmt, macht erst seine Geschichtsschreibung innerlich möglich" (*Apg*, [3]1959, p. 85 = [7]1977, p. 106).

115. *Apg*, 1956, p. 92: "(die) Fortsetzung und Ergänzung des Evangeliums".

116. "Das besagt aber: aufs Letzte gesehen ist nicht der Mensch das Subjekt dieses Geschehens, sondern Gott selbst" (*Apg*, 1956, p. 92; cf. 93).

117. "Dieses 'Wort Gottes' verbindet die Zeit nach Jesus mit der Jesuszeit; ist es doch die Botschaft von Jesus, an den zu glauben Vergebung der Sünden und Rettung im Gericht bringt. Damit ist die Klammer gefunden, welche die beiden Epochen zusammenhält, und so die Fortsetzung des ersten Buches... in einem zweiten Buch erlaubt, ja fordert: das erschienene Heil muß allen Völkern gepredigt werden" (*Apg*, [3]1959, pp. 87-88 = [7]1977, pp. 108-109).

118. *Apg*, [7]1977, p. 107.

because the Gospel existed already as a separate genre. Luke could not possibly have envisaged to write a one-volume work[119].

Conzelmann and Haenchen asked for the theological significance of Luke's work as a whole, while downplaying the relevance of Acts as an historical account. Though in both these respects the influence of M. Dibelius is undeniable (and also fully acknowledged by them), this was revolutionary[120]. Lk–Acts is not poor historiography but the highly innovating work of a theologian interpreting the Christian message for the situation of the Church of his time[121].

The work of Conzelmann (and Haenchen) brought "new life" to the study of Lk–Acts (so P. Schubert in the 1954 FS Bultmann), or, as others have said, turned it into "a storm center" in exegesis for many years (van Unnik in the FS Schubert). E. Grässer is prominent among those who further elaborated the hypothesis of Conzelmann for the Gospel and for Acts[122]. Critics took issue with Conzelmann's understanding of the aim of Luke's work, his interpretation of eschatology, his periodisation of salvation history, and his presentation of salvation history as the focus of Luke's theology. The discussion has its own history which has often been reviewed[123]. At the colloquium on Luke in 1968, W.G. Kümmel presented his famous assessment of the development of Lukan studies since Conzelmann. He was not convinced that Luke had ruled out or substantially weakened the original eschatological perspective of the kerygma arguing that Luke did not replace eschatological expectation with a history of salvation but that salvation history itself is an eschato-

---

119. *Apg*, [3]1959, p. 88 n. 8 = [7]1977, p. 109 n. 2.

120. See esp. M. DIBELIUS, *Aufsätze zur Apostelgeschichte*, ed. H. Greeven (FRLANT, 60), Göttingen, 1951, [4]1961 (ET 1956).

121. This is an important difference between Conzelmann and E. Käsemann who judged much more negatively on Luke's theological achievement; see, e.g., RESE, *Lukas-Evangelium* (n. 3), pp. 2301-2302. — On the relation between theology and historiography in Lk–Acts in general, see M. HENGEL, *Zur urchristlichen Geschichtsschreibung*, Stuttgart, 1979, [2]1984, pp. 54-61. V. FUSCO, *Progetto storiografico e progetto teologico nell'opera lucana*, in *La Storiografia nella Bibbia* (ABI Atti della XXVIII settimana biblica), Bologna, 1986, pp. 123-152. J.A. JAUREGUI, *Historiografía y teología en Hechos*, in *EstBib* 53 (1995) 97-123 (survey since 1980).

122. E. GRÄSSER, *Das Problem der Parusieverzögerung in den synoptischen Evangelien und in der Apostelgeschichte* (BZNW, 22), Berlin, 1957, [3]1977, pp. 178-215; ID., *Die Parusieerwartung in der Apostelgeschichte*, in KREMER (ed.), *Les Actes des Apôtres* (n. 2), pp. 99-127. – On Luke's understanding of the delay of the parousia in its relationship to the history of the rejection of the Christian mission by the majority of the Jewish people, see now M. WOLTER, *Israels Zukunft und die Parusieverzögerung bei Lukas*, in M. EVANG – H. MERKLEIN – M. WOLTER (eds.), *Eschatologie und Schöpfung*. FS E. Grässer (BZNW, 89), Berlin – New York, 1997, pp. 405-426.

123. See esp. BOVON, *Luc le théologien* (n. 23), pp. 11-84. MADDOX, *Purpose* (n. 17), pp. 100-157.

logical event[124]. At the same meeting E.E. Ellis pointed out that the proclamation of the Kingdom of God as partially realized and yet also still to be expected implies that Luke defended a two-step eschatology[125]. J. Dupont found indications in the Gospel and in Acts that for Luke eschatology had an individual aspect, whileas G. Schneider saw a shift in emphasis in Luke's Gospel from the imminence to the suddenness of the parousia which functions as an exhortatory device in many of his parables[126]. Others argued for a radically opposite view to that of Conzelmann by denying that Luke and his community had given up the hope that the Lord was soon to return[127].

A different path was taken by those authors who thought that Luke's struggle with the expectations of the Early Church might not be the dominating factor in his theology. While recognizing that the "'discovery' of Luke the theologian seems to me the great gain of the present phase"[128], W.C. van Unnik argued that the central concept in Lk–Acts is not salvation history but the proclamation of salvation[129]. In the Gospel Luke described how God offers salvation to the world through Jesus. Acts illustrates how this salvation is witnessed and preached by the disciples, and brings the confirmation of the message of the Gospel in order that its readers might be strenghtened in their faith. Acts is "a legitimate sequel and complement to Luke's gospel because it formed its confirmation"[130]. Others have followed van Unnik's suggestion that Lk–Acts

124. W.G. KÜMMEL, *Luc en accusation dans la théologie contemporaine*, in *ETL* 46 (1970) 265-281; repr. in NEIRYNCK (ed.), *L'évangile de Luc* (n. 1), pp. 93-109 (= 1989, 3-19; see the bibliographical note on p. 295 for translations).

125. E.E. ELLIS, *La fonction de l'eschatologie dans l'évangile de Luc*, in NEIRYNCK (ed.), *L'évangile de Luc*, pp. 141-155 (= 1989, 51-65 and add. note, pp. 296-303).

126. J. DUPONT, *L'eschatologie individuelle dans l'œuvre de Luc*, in P. HOFFMANN – N. BROX – W. PESCH (eds.), *Orientierung and Jesus. Zur Theologie der Synoptiker. Für J. Schmid*, Freiburg, 1973, pp. 37-47 (repr. *Études*, 2, pp. 1066-1075). G. SCHNEIDER, *Parusiegleichnisse im Lukas-Evangelium* (SBS, 74), Stuttgart, 1975. Cf., in line with Schneider, J.T. CARROLL, *Response to the End of History. Eschatology and Situation in Luke–Acts* (SBL DS, 92), Atlanta, GA, 1988. — For A.E. Nielsen it is rather the certainty of the parousia that is emphasized by Luke: *The Purpose of the Lucan Writings with Particular Reference to Eschatology*, in LUOMANEN (ed.), *Scandinavian Perspectives* (n. 24), pp. 76-93.

127. Cf. R.H. HIERS, *The Problem of the Delay of the Parousia in Luke–Acts*, in *NTS* 20 (1973-74) 145-155. A.J. MATTILL, *Luke and the Last Things. A Perspective for the Understanding of Lukan Thought*, Dillsboro, NC, 1979.

128. W.C. VAN UNNIK, *Luke–Acts, a Storm Center in Contemporary Scholarship*, in KECK–MARTYN (eds.), *Studies in Luke–Acts* (n. 24), pp. 15-32, here 24; repr. in ID., *Sparsa Collecta*, I (NTSup, 29), Leiden, 1973, pp. 92-110.

129. *The "Book of Acts" – The Confirmation of the Gospel*, in *NT* 4 (1960) 26-59, p. 53 (= 1973, 340-373, p. 367): "σωτηρία is the determining and decisive factor".

130. *Ibid.*, p. 59 (= 373); see already *Remarks on the Purpose of Luke's Historical Writing (Luke I,1-4)*, in *Sparsa Collecta*, pp. 6-15, here 13-15; Dutch original in *NTT* 9 (1955) 323-331.

is about God's salvation. Marshall finds in it "the key to the theology of Luke. Not salvation-history but salvation itself is the theme which occupied the mind of Luke in both parts of his work"[131]. Marshall then brings a survey of Luke's teaching on salvation and examines how it relates to other aspects of his theology[132].

With this second approach we touch upon the central question what exactly is meant by "the theological unity" of Luke's work. Since Conzelmann it has gradually become accepted that it is appropriate to ask for Luke's distinctive theology. And scholars also readily continue to speak of the theological unity of Luke's work. But it remains a complex issue to describe its content and also to determine in what sense Luke's theology constitutes a unity.

Parsons and Pervo introduce their chapter on Luke's theology by observing that "the existence of the two volumes is evidence that the problem of the theological unity of Luke and Acts is first and foremost the problem of continuity, of the relation of the life and activity of the Church to the 'Christ-event'"[133]. But they point out several areas where this criterion, in their opinion, seems to be lacking, and they conclude that "the theological unity of Luke and Acts is not a foregone conclusion"[134]. H. Hübner, in a section on "die lukanischen Schriften als theologische Einheit", defines it this way: "Die beiden lukanischen Schriften erschließen sich einem theologischen Verstehen nur, wenn sie als *theologische Einheit* gesehen werden. Das *Lukas-Evangelium* ist in seiner theologischen Aussage ganz auf seine Fortsetzung in der *Apostelgeschichte* ausgerichtet. Und diese Schrift offenbart sich in ihrer eigentlichen theologischen Intention nur, wenn ihre Fundierung im Lk berücksichtigt wird"[135].

There are probably many who can agree with this last description, even though one continues to write separate volumes on the theology of

131. MARSHALL, *Luke: Historian and Theologian* (n. 4), p. 92 (with reference to van Unnik on the next page).

132. He greatly emphasizes that for Luke salvation is not an abstract notion. It has taken the form of a concrete historical figure. What Luke tells us in the Gospel about Jesus, his ministry, his proclamation of the Kingdom, and his passion and resurrection is the account of how salvation is realized through Jesus (see esp. pp. 116-156, the chapter on "To Save the Lost"). In Acts Luke shows that this goes on in the preaching of Jesus as Lord, Saviour, and Christ by the disciples (see esp. pp. 157-188: "The Word of This Salvation").

133. PARSONS–PERVO, *Rethinking* (n. 6), p. 86.

134. *Ibid.*, p. 89. Comp. the contribution of D. Marguerat in this volume (below, pp. 57-81).

135. H. HÜBNER, *Biblische Theologie des Neuen Testaments*, 3, Göttingen, 1995, p. 122 (pp. 120-151: Lk–Acts).

Lk[136] and on the theology of Acts[137]. But one will also have to admit that
with this definition there are still a lot of opportunities to defend very
divergent interpretations of what is Luke's intention and theology in a
particular field. One could even get the impression that to ask for the
unifying factor(s) in Luke's writings is a moot question since scholars
have increasingly become aware of the fact that there hardly seems to be
a topic that Luke has not addressed, and there is a tendency in recent literature to fragmentarisation and to concentrate on one or another of the
many subjects that figure in Lk and in Acts. I give two examples.

There is, e.g., the whole area of studies on "Luke and the Jews". This
is a complex matter, first, because the data in Lk–Acts seem to support
differing, even outright opposite, interpretations, and second, because it
involves a wide array of questions. The central one is of course that of the
Gentile mission and the salvation of the Jewish people. But scholars have
also focused on side-topics such as Luke's presentation of the social (the
crowds[138]) and religious classes (the Jewish leaders[139], the Pharisees[140])

136. See, e.g., J. ERNST, *Lukas, ein theologisches Portrait*, Düsseldorf, 1985, ²1991
(though with a section on political apologetics and on poverty/wealth in Acts).
J.B. GREEN, *The Theology of the Gospel of Luke* (New Testament Theology), Cambridge,
1995.
137. Cf. J. JERVELL, *The Theology of the Acts of the Apostles* (New Testament Theology), Cambridge, 1996. I.H. MARSHALL – D. PETERSON (eds.), *Witness to the Gospel: The
Theology of Acts*, Grand Rapids, MI, 1998. – On the project of writing a "theology of
Acts", see now also Jervell's commentary: "(es) geht aber um zwei Werke [Lk–Acts],
die in zwei verschiedenen Zeitpunkten, in verschiedenen Situationen und aus verschiedenen Anlass verfasst worden sind. So muss auch die Theologie der Apg zunächst vom
Evangelium getrennt behandelt werden" (p. 91).
138. J.B. TYSON, *The Jewish Public in Luke–Acts*, in *NTS* 30 (1984) 574-583 (revised
in ID., *The Death of Jesus in Luke–Acts*, Columbia, SC, 1986, pp. 29-47).
139. Cf. J.T. SANDERS, *The Jews in Luke–Acts*, London, 1987, pp. 3-23. M.A. POW-
ELL, *The Religious Leaders in Luke: A Literary-Critical Study*, in *JBL* 109 (1990) 93-110.
See also A.J. SALDARINI, *Pharisees, Scribes and Sadducees. A Sociological Approach*,
Wilmington, DE, 1988, pp. 174-187. — On the Samaritans, cf. J. JERVELL, *The Lost
Sheep of the House of Israel. The Understanding of the Samaritans in Luke–Acts*, in ID.,
Luke and the People of God. A New Look at Luke–Acts, Minneapolis, MN, 1972, pp. 113-
132. J.T. SANDERS (see this note), pp. 142-150. D. RAVENS, *Luke and the Restoration of
Israel* (JSNT SS, 119), Sheffield, 1995, pp. 72-106.
140. J.A. ZIESLER, *Luke and the Pharisees*, in *NTS* 25 (1978-79) 146-157.
J.T. SANDERS, *The Pharisees in Luke–Acts*, in D.E. GROH – R. JEWETT (eds.), *The Living
Text. Essays in Honor of Ernest W. Saunders*, Lanham, MD – New York – London, 1985,
pp. 141-188 (repr. in *The Jews in Luke–Acts*, pp. 84-131). J.T. CARROLL, *Luke's Portrayal
of the Pharisees*, in *CBQ* 50 (1988) 604-621. D.B. GOWLER, *Host, Guest, Enemy, and
Friend. Portraits of the Pharisees in Luke and Acts* (Emory Studies in Early Christianity,
2), New York, 1991. J.D. KINGSBURY, *The Pharisees in Luke–Acts*, in F. VAN SEGBROECK,
et al. (eds.), *The Four Gospels 1992* (n. 77), 2, pp. 1497-1512. H. KAYAMA, *Believers
Who Belonged to the Sect of the Pharisees (Acts 15:5). Towards an Understanding of
Luke's Picture of the Pharisees*, in *AJBI* 22 (1996) 86-109. — Kingsbury challenges the
common view that Luke depicts the Pharisees more positively than the other gospel writ-

in first-century Judaism and of its institutions (the Temple[141], or the Law[142]).

My second example comes from a different field. It has long been observed that Luke's work is a treasure for our knowledge of the life of

ers and in some respect as objective allies of Jesus and the disciples. He calls for a "radical assessment" of the evidence and argues that Luke in his Gospel has not the intention to exonerate the Pharisees of their responsibility in the trial of Jesus, that Paul's reference to his Pharisaic background in Acts is linked to his history as a persecutor of Christianity, and that it is not the Pharisees, who are no better than other adversaries of Jesus and of the Church, but God himself who in Luke's eyes legitimates the Christian movement. But, with all the criticism, even Kingsbury admits that Luke's portrayal of the Pharisees is a fairly consistent, be it a negative one.

141. K. BALTZER, *The Meaning of the Temple in the Lukan Writings*, in *HTR* 58 (1965) 263-277. F.D. WEINERT, *The Meaning of the Temple in Luke–Acts*, in *BTB* 11 (1981) 85-89; ID., *Luke, Stephen, and the Temple in Luke–Acts*, in *BTB* 17 (1989) 88-90. A. CASALEGNO, *Gesù e il Tempio. Studio redazionale di Luca–Atti*, Brescia, 1984. TYSON, *The Death of Jesus* (n. 138), pp. 84-113. P.F. ESLER, *Community and Gospel in Luke–Acts. The Social and Political Motivations of Lucan Theology* (SNTS MS, 57), Cambridge, 1987, pp. 131-163. J.B. CHANCE, *Jerusalem, the Temple, and the New Age in Luke–Acts*, Macon, GA, 1988. A.G. VAN AARDE, *The Relativity of the Metaphor "Temple" in Luke–Acts*, in *Neotestamentica* 26 (1991) 51-64. See below n. 144 (J.H. Elliott). — On the meaning of synagogue: R.E. OSTER, *Supposed Anachronism in Luke–Acts' Use of συναγωγή*, in *NTS* 39 (1993) 178-208.

Chance combines his understanding of the role of Jerusalem and the temple in Luke's writings with a critique of Conzelmann. Jerusalem and its temple are the place of fulfilment of the promise for both the Jewish people and the Gentiles. In the Gospel city and temple are the location of Jesus' ministry and of the future restoration of Israel. In Acts there is a shift of interpretation in so far that Luke, due to the course of history, cannot maintain that Jerusalem literaly was going to be the gathering place of all the nations, but the city (no longer its temple) is still depicted as the place from where salvation went out to the whole world.

142. Luke's understanding of the significance of the Law for Christians (it is commonly held that, for various reasons, he looks positively upon the Law) has been dealt with in the monographs of S.G. Wilson, M. Klinghardt, and K. Salo, who also gives a good survey of previous research, and in a series of studies and articles, most recently by H. Merkel and F. Bovon. According to Merkel Luke regards the Law as a means of legitimation in the encounter with Graeco-Roman culture, because it gives Christianity the aura of a long established religion. Bovon emphasizes the role that Luke attributes to the Law in holding together the Jewish-Christian and Gentile-Christian factions in the Church.

Cf. J. JERVELL, *The Law in Luke–Acts* (1971), in ID., *Luke and the People of God* (n. 139), pp. 133-151. S.G. WILSON, *Luke and the Law* (SNTS MS, 50), Cambridge, 1984. C.L. BLOMBERG, *The Law in Luke–Acts*, in *JSNT* 22 (1984) 53-80. F.G. DOWNING, *Freedom from the Law in Luke–Acts*, in *JSNT* 26 (1986) 49-52. ESLER, *Community and Gospel in Luke–Acts* (n. 141), pp. 110-130. M. KLINGHARDT, *Gesetz und Volk Gottes. Das lukanische Verständnis des Gesetzes nach Herkunft, Funktion und seinem Ort in der Geschichte des Urchristentums* (WUNT, 2/32), Tübingen, 1988. J.A. FITZMYER, *Luke the Theologian. Aspects of His Teaching*, New York – Mahwah, NJ, 1989, pp. 175-202. K. SALO, *Luke's Treatment of the Law. A Redaction-critical Investigation*, Helsinki, 1991. J.B. TYSON, *Torah and Prophets in Luke–Acts. Temporary or Permanent?*, in *SBL 1992 Seminar Papers*, pp. 539-548. H. MERKEL, *Das Gesetz im lukanischen Doppelwerk*, in K. BACKHAUS – F.G. UNTERGASSMAIR (eds.), *Schrift und Tradition. Festschrift für Josef Ernst zum 70. Geburtstag*, Paderborn, 1996, pp. 119-133. F. BOVON, *La Loi dans l'œuvre*

the Early Church and of the social world of first-century Christianity. There now exists an abundant literature on such topics as Luke's community (its setting and its social and moral values[143]), the religious and sacramental praxis of the earliest communities[144], Luke's dealing with social questions (the position of the women among the disciples[145], Christian ethics and Christian attitudes towards poverty and wealth and

---

de Luc, in C. FOCANT (ed.), *La Loi dans l'un et l'autre Testament* (LD, 168), Paris, 1997, pp. 206-225. — On the specific topic of the Sabbath, see M.M.B. TURNER, *The Sabbath, Sunday, and the Law in Luke–Acts*, in D. CARSON (ed.), *From Sabbath to Lord's Day*, Exeter, 1982, pp. 99-157. J.B. TYSON, *Scripture, Torah and Sabbath in Luke–Acts*, in E.P. SANDERS (ed.), *Jesus, the Gospels, and the Church. Essays in Honor of William R. Farmer*, Macon, GA, 1987, pp. 89-104.

143. See the collection of studies in J.H. NEYREY (ed.), *Social World* (above n. 24). Cf. further, M.A. MOSCATO, *Current Theories Regarding the Audience of Luke–Acts*, in *CurrThMiss* 3 (1976) 355-361. R.J. KARRIS, *The Lukan* Sitz im Leben. *Methodology and Prospects*, in *SBL 1976 Seminar Papers*, pp. 219-234; ID., *Missionary Communities. A New Paradigma for the Study of Luke–Acts*, in *CBQ* 41 (1979) 80-97; see also below n. 146 and n. 220. L.T. JOHNSON, *On Finding the Lukan Community. A Cautious Cautionary Essay*, in *SBL 1979 Seminar Papers*, pp. 87-100. D.C. ALLISON, *Was There a "Lukan Community"?*, in *IBS* 10 (1988) 62-70. P.J. BOTHA, *Community and Conviction in Luke–Acts*, in *Neotestamentica* 29 (1995) 145-165. F.G. DOWNING, *Theophilus' First Reading of Luke–Acts*, in TUCKETT (ed.), *Luke's Literary Achievement* (n. 9), pp. 91-109. — On social values, cf. B.J. MALINA – J.H. NEYREY, *Honor and Shame in Luke–Acts: Pivotal Values of the Mediterranean World*, in NEYREY (ed.), *Social World*, pp. 25-65. I. CZACHESZ, *Narrative Logic and Christology in Luke–Acts*, in *ComViat* 37 (1995) 93-106 (on honour).

144. See, e.g., on the relation between baptism and the gift of the Spirit, W. RUSSELL, *The Anointing with the Holy Spirit in Luke–Acts*, in *TrinJ* 7 (1986) 47-63. H.-S. KIM, *Die Geisttaufe des Messias. Eine kompositionsgeschichtliche Untersuchung zu einem Leitmotiv des lukanischen Doppelwerks. Ein Beitrag zur Theologie und Intention des Lukas* (Studien zur klassischen Philologie, 81), Frankfurt, 1993. The motif is most prominent in Acts: cf. M. QUESNEL, *Baptisés dans l'Esprit. Baptême et Esprit Saint dans les Actes des Apôtres* (LD, 120), Paris, 1985. J.C. O'NEILL, *The Connection between Baptism and the Gift of the Spirit in Acts*, in *JSNT* 63 (1996) 87-103. — On the practice of community meals and the eucharist: G. GHIBERTI, *L'eucaristia in Lc 24 e negli Atti degli Apostoli*, in *ParSpirV* 7 (1983) 159-173. J.H. ELLIOTT, *Temple versus Household in Luke–Acts: A Contrast in Social Institutions*, in NEYREY (ed.), *Social World* (n. 24), pp. 211-240, and ID., *Household and Meals vs. Temple Purity. Replication Patterns in Luke–Acts*, in *BTB* 21 (1991) 102-108. Cf. also the contribution by J. Taylor in this volume (below pp. 281-295). — On prayer: P.T. O'BRIEN, *Prayer in Luke–Acts*, in *TyndB* 24 (1973) 111-127. A.A. TRITES, *Some Aspects of Prayers in Luke–Acts*, in *SBL 1977 Seminar Papers*, pp. 59-78; = *The Prayer Motif in Luke–Acts*, in TALBERT (ed.), *Perspectives* (n. 24), pp. 168-186 (revised). J. SCHLOSSER, *Marie et la prière de l'Église d'après Lc 1,48 et Ac 1,14*, in *Études mariales* 39 (1982) 13-22. S.F. PLYMALE, *The Prayer Texts of Luke–Acts* (American University Studies, 7/118), New York, 1991. G. SCHILLE, *Grundzüge des Gebetes nach Lukas*, in BUSSMANN–RADL (ed.), *Der Treue Gottes trauen* (n. 24), pp. 215-228. D.M. CRUMP, *Jesus the Intercessor. Prayer and Christology in Luke–Acts* (WUNT, 2/49), Tübingen, 1992.

145. L. PORTEFAIX, *Sisters Rejoice. Paul's Letter to the Philippians and Luke–Acts as Received by First-Century Philippian Women* (ConBibNT, 20), Stockholm, 1988. M.R. D'ANGELO, *Women in Luke–Acts. A Redactional View*, in *JBL* 109 (1990) 441-461.

the care for the destitute[146]), the political agenda he may have had in mind[147], the essence of discipleship[148], and the missionary activi-

T.K. SEIM, *The Double Message: Patterns of Gender in Luke–Acts*, Edinburgh, 1994. J.M. ARLANDSON, *Women, Class, and Society in Early Christianity: Models from Luke–Acts*, Peabody, MA, 1997. S. BIEBERSTEIN, *Verschwiegene Jüngerinnen – vergessene Zeuginnen. Gebrochene Konzepte im Lukasevangelium* (NTOA, 38), Freiburg–Göttingen, 1998, pp. 14-23 and 262-278 (on the mention of the women in Lk 24 and their absence in Acts 1 with its concentration on the apostles). — Specifically in Acts: I. RICHTER REIMER, *Frauen in der Apostelgeschichte des Lukas. Eine feministisch-theologische Exegese*, Gütersloh, 1992 (ET 1995).

146. Lukan ethics are primarily social ethics according to F.W. HORN, *Glaube und Handeln in der Theologie des Lukas* (GTA, 26), Göttingen, 1983, ²1986, pp. 89-120. Cf. ESLER, *Community and Gospel in Luke–Acts* (n. 141), pp. 164-200. See the survey of research in G. SEGALLA, *L'etica narrativa di Luca-Atti*, in *Teologia* 20 (1995) 34-74. The common view on Luke's interest in social ethics is now critically assessed by M.T. SPECKMAN, *Beggars and Gospel in Luke–Acts: Preliminary Observations on an Emerging Model in the Light of Recent Developmental Theories*, in *Neotestamentica* 31 (1997) 309-337. — See further L.T. JOHNSON, *The Literary Function of Possessions in Luke–Acts* (SBL DS, 39), Missoula, MT, 1977 and ID., *The Social Dimensions of Soteria in Luke–Acts and Paul*, in *SBL 1993 Seminar Papers*, pp. 520-536. W.E. PILGRIM, *Good News to the Poor. Wealth and Poverty in Luke–Acts*, Minneapolis, MN, 1981. D. SECCOMBE, *Possessions and the Poor in Luke–Acts* (SNTU, B/6), Linz, 1982. D.B. KRAYBILL – D.M. SWEETLAND, *Possessions in Luke–Acts. A Sociological Perspective*, in *PerspRelSt* 10 (1983) 215-239. J.R. DONAHUE, *Two Decades of Research on the Rich and the Poor in Luke–Acts*, in D.A. KNIGHT – P.J. PARIS (eds.), *Justice and the Holy. Essays in Honor of Walter Harrelson*, Atlanta, GA, 1989, pp. 129-144. R.J. KARRIS, *Poor and Rich. The Lukan Sitz im Leben*, in TALBERT (ed.), *Perspectives* (n. 24), pp. 112-125. J. GILLMAN, *Possessions and the Life of Faith. A Reading of Luke–Acts* (Zachaeus Studies NT), Collegeville, MN, 1991. R.F. O'TOOLE, *Poverty and Wealth in Luke–Acts*, in *Chicago Studies* 16 (1991) 29-41. D.L. BALCH, *Rich and Poor, Proud and Humble in Luke–Acts*, in L.M. WHITE – O. YARBROUGH (eds.), *The Social World of the First Christians. Essays in Honor of W.A. Meeks*, Augsburg, MN, 1995, pp. 214-233. J.P. GÉRARD, *Les riches dans la communauté lucanienne*, in *ETL* 71 (1995) 71-106 (esp. on Lk). S.J. ROTH, *The Blind, the Lame, and the Poor. Character Types in Luke–Acts* (JSNT SS, 144), Sheffield, 1997 (a literary-critical / reader-response approach). — Specifically on theme of the widows, see, e.g., F.S. SPENCER, *Neglected Widows in Acts 6,1-7*, in *CBQ* 56 (1994) 715-733. R.M. PRICE, *The Widow Traditions in Luke–Acts. A Feminist-Critical Scrutiny* (SBL DS, 155), Atlanta, GA, 1997.

147. See, e.g., the collection of studies in CASSIDY–SCHARPER (eds.), *Political Issues in Luke–Acts* (above n. 24) and Cassidy's *Jesus, Politics, and Society. A Study of Luke's Gospel*, Maryknoll, NY, 1978 and *Society and Politics in the Acts of the Apostles*, Maryknoll, NY, 1987. Cf. further ESLER, *Community and Gospel in Luke–Acts* (n. 141). T. HOSAKA, *Lukas und das Imperium Romanum. Unter besonderer Berücksichtigung der literarischen Funktion des Furchtmotives*, in *AJBI* 14 (1988) 82-134. J.A.H. REEVES, *Apology, Threat, or a New "Way". The Socio-Political Perspective of Luke–Acts*, in *Proceedings of the Eastern Great Lakes and Midwest Biblical Societies*, 10 (1990) 223–235. A. BRENT, *Luke–Acts and the Imperial Cult in Asia Minor*, in *JTS* 48 (1997) 411-438.

148. On Luke's portrayal of the role of the disciples: E. NELLESSEN, *Zeugnis für Jesus und das Wort. Exegetische Untersuchungen zum lukanischen Zeugnisbegriff* (BBB, 43), Köln, 1976. L.E. MURPHY, *The Concept of the Twelve in Luke–Acts as a Key to the Lukan Perspective on the Restoration of Israel*, diss. Louisville, KY, 1988. K. HAACKER, *Verwendung und Vermeidung des Apostelbegriffs im lukanischen Werk*, in *NT* 30 (1988) 9-38. G. LEONARDI, *"I dodici" e "gli apostoli" nei Vangeli sinottici e Atti. Problemi e*

ties[149] through which Jesus and the disciples after him are confronted with other cultures[150], suffer persecution[151], or realize the expansion of

prospettive, in *Studia Patavina* 42 (1995) 163-195. — On discipleship according to Luke: J. JERVELL, *The Twelve on Israel's Thrones: Luke's Understanding of the Apostolate*, in ID., *Luke and the People of God* (n. 139), pp. 75-112. C.H. TALBERT, *Discipleship in Luke–Acts*, in F. SEGOVIA (ed.), *Discipleship in the New Testament*, Philadelphia, PA, 1985, pp. 62-75. W.S. KURZ, *Narrative Models for Imitation in Luke–Acts*, in D.L. BALCH – E. FERGUSON – W.A. MEEKS (eds.), *Greeks, Romans, and Christians. Essays in Honor of Abraham J. Malherbe*, Minneapolis, MN, 1990, pp. 171-189. FITZMYER, *Luke the Theologian* (n. 142), pp. 117-145. D.M. SWEETLAND, *Our Journey with Jesus. Discipleship according to Luke–Acts* (Good News Studies, 30), Collegeville, MN, 1990. A. CASALEGNO, *O discípulo e a metáfora da luz nos escritos lucanos*, in *PerspTeol* 28 (1996) 65-81. R.N. LONGENECKER, *Taking Up the Cross Daily: Discipleship in Luke–Acts*, in ID. (ed.), *Patterns of Discipleship in the New Testament*, Grand Rapids, MI – Cambridge, 1996, pp. 51-76.

149. On Luke's concept of mission: F. PRAST, *Presbyter und Evangelium in nachapostolischer Zeit. Die Abschiedsrede des Paulus in Milet (Apg. 20,17-38) im Rahmen der lukanischen Konzeption der Evangeliumsverkündigung* (FzB, 29), Stuttgart, 1979. J. KREMER, *Weltweiter Zeugnis für Christus in der Kraft des Geistes. Zur lukanischen Sicht der Mission*, in K. KERTELGE (ed.), *Mission im Neuen Testament* (QDisp, 93), Freiburg, 1982, pp. 145-163. D. SENIOR – C. STUHLMUELLER, *The Biblical Foundations for Mission*, London, 1983, pp. 255-279. G. FRIZZI, *La "missione" in Luca–Atti. Semantica, critica e apologia lucana*, in *RivBib* 32 (1984) 395-423. — On the missionaries' travels and Luke's interest in geography: G. BOUWMAN, *Samaria im lukanischen Doppelwerk*, in *SNTU* 2 (1976) 118-141. G. MORALES GOMEZ, *Jerusalen – Jerosolima en el vocabulario y la geografia de Lucas*, in *RCT* 7 (1982) 131-186. E. ASANTE, *The Theological Jerusalem of Luke–Acts*, in *AfrTJ* 15 (1986) 172-182. J. REUMANN, *The "Itinerary" as a Form in Classical Literature and the Acts of the Apostles*, in M.P. HORGAN – P.J. KOBELSKI (eds.), *To Touch the Text. Biblical and Related Studies in Honor of Joseph A. Fitzmyer*, New York, 1989, pp. 335-357. D. MARGUERAT, *Voyages et voyageurs dans le livre des Actes et la culture gréco-romaine*, in *RHPR* 78 (1998) 33-59. — On the role of miracles in the ministry of the disciples in imitation of Jesus: see esp. P.J. ACHTEMEIER, *The Lucan Perspective on the Miracles of Jesus: A Preliminary Sketch*, in *JBL* 94 (1975) 547-562 (= TALBERT, *Perspectives*, pp. 153-167). U. BUSSE, *Die Wunder des Propheten Jesus. Die Rezeption, Komposition und Interpretation der Wundertradition im Evangelium des Lukas* (FzB, 24), Stuttgart, 1977. F. NEIRYNCK, *The Miracle Stories* (infra, n. 248). W. KIRCHSCHLÄGER, *Jesu exorzistisches Wirken aus der Sicht des Lukas. Ein Beitrag zur lukanischen Redaktion* (ÖBS, 3), Klosterneuburg, 1981. L. O'REILLY, *Word and Sign in the Acts of the Apostles. A Study of Lucan Theology* (AnGreg, 243), Rome, 1987. J.J. PILCH, *Sickness and Healing in Luke–Acts*, in NEYREY (ed.), *Social World* (n. 24), pp. 181-210. In the Hellenistic context: E. PLÜMACHER, *ΤΕΡΑΤΕΙΑ. Fiktion und Wunder in der hellenistisch-römischen Geschichtsschreibung und in der Apostelgeschichte*, in *ZNW* 89 (1998) 66-90.

150. On the "culture-shock" with Graeco-Roman paganism (esp. in Acts): B. WILDHABER, *Paganisme populaire et prédication apostolique d'après l'exégèse de quelques séquences des Actes. Éléments pour une théologie lucanienne* (Le monde de la Bible), Genève, 1987. H.E. DOLLAR, *A Biblical-Missiological Exploration of the Cross-Cultural Dimension in Luke–Acts*, San Francisco, CA, 1993. — J.A. FITZMYER, *Luke the Theologian* (n. 142), pp. 146-174 ("Satan and demons"). S.R. GARRETT, *The Demise of the Devil. Magic and Demonic in Luke's Writings*, Minneapolis, MN, 1989. H.-J. KLAUCK, *Magie und Heidentum in der Apostelgeschichte des Lukas* (SBS, 167), Stuttgart, 1996.

151. See B. DEHANDSCHUTTER, *La persécution des chrétiens dans les Actes des Apôtres*, in KREMER (ed.), *Les Actes des Apôtres* (n. 2), pp. 541-546 (also on Lk 21,12-

the community[152] and enjoy the success of new conversions[153] and the hospitality of fellow Christians and others[154]. All these topics occur in Lk and in Acts and of course they all have a theological meaning for Luke.

However, this proliferation of studies on a variety of specific subjects should not discourage us. Rather it may help to demonstrate to what a degree the Gospel and Acts are interconnected. It appears that even topics that are deemed less prominent show up in both of Luke's volumes. But there are also other indications. In the following I will briefly present three modes of dealing with this issue which can be found in current literature.

19). C.H. TALBERT, *Martyrdom in Luke–Acts and the Lukan Social Ethic*, in CASSIDY–SCHARPER (eds.), *Political Issues* (n. 147), pp. 99-110. S. CUNNINGHAM, *"Through Many Tribulations"*. *The Theology of Persecution in Luke–Acts* (JSNT SS, 142), Sheffield, 1997. B.J. MALINA – J.H. NEYREY, *Conflict in Luke–Acts: Labelling and Deviance Theory*, in NEYREY (ed.), *Social World* (n. 24), pp. 97-122. W. STEGEMANN, *Zwischen Synagoge und Obrigkeit. Zur historischen Situation der lukanischen Christen* (FRLANT, 152), Göttingen, 1991, pp. 91-146 (persecution in the synagogues) and 187-267 (conflict involving the political authorities). T. SELAND, *Establishment Violence in Philo and Luke. A Study of Non-Conformity to the Torah and Jewish Vigilante Reactions* (Biblical Interpretation Series, 15), Leiden, 1995, pp. 183-221 and 223-303 (Acts). See above n. 148 (on discipleship). — A side-aspect in Luke's interest is the "fate" of the persecutors (Paul, the Jews, Herod): see, e.g., J.A. WEATHERLY, *Jewish Responsibility for the Death of Jesus in Luke–Acts* (JSNT SS, 106), Sheffield, 1994. O.W. ALLEN, *The Death of Herod. The Narrative and Theological Function of Retribution in Luke–Acts* (SBL DS, 158), Atlanta, GA, 1997. J.A. DARR, *Herod the Fox. Audience Criticism and Lukan Characterization* (JSNT SS, 163), Sheffield, 1998, pp. 137-172 (Lk 3 to 9) and 173-212 (Lk 13,31-35; 23,6-12; Acts 4,23-31; 13,1).

152. On the theological significance of Luke's emphasis on the expansion of the Church for his ecclesiology, see G. LOHFINK, *Die Sammlung Israels. Eine Untersuchung zur lukanischen Ekklesiologie* (SANT, 39), München, 1975. K.N. GILES, *Luke's Use of the Term* ἐκκλησία, in *NTS* 31 (1985) 135-142. W. REINHARDT, *Das Wachstum des Gottesvolkes. Untersuchungen zum Gemeindewachstum im lukanischen Doppelwerk auf dem Hintergrund des Alten Testaments*, Göttingen, 1995.

153. On repentance, faith, and conversion: J.W. TAEGER, *Der Mensch und sein Heil. Studien zum Bild des Menschen und zur Sicht der Bekehrung bei Lukas* (SNT, 14), Gütersloh, 1982. D.-L. MATSON, *Household Conversion Narratives in Acts. Pattern and Interpretation* (JSNT SS, 123), Sheffield, 1996 (also on Lk 10,5-7; 19,1-10). P. BÖHLEMANN, *Jesus und der Täufer. Schlüssel zur Theologie und Ethik des Lukas* (SNTS MS, 99), Cambridge, 1997, pp. 96-123. — On faith (as related to conversion), W. SCHENK, *Glaube im lukanischen Doppelwerk*, in F. HAHN – H. KLEIN (eds.), *Glaube im Neuen Testament. Studien zu Ehren von Hermann Binder anläßlich seines 70. Geburtstag* (BTS, 7), Neukirchen-Vluyn, 1982, pp. 69-92.

154. Apart from numerous articles in *SBL Seminar Papers* of the last years (most of them on Lk only), see ESLER, *Community and Gospel in Luke–Acts* (n. 141), pp. 71-109. J.H. NEYREY, *Ceremonies in Luke–Acts: The Case of Meals and Table-Fellowship*, in ID. (ed.), *Social World* (n. 24), pp. 361-387. J. ASHWORTH, *Hospitality in Luke–Acts*, in *BibTod* 35 (1997) 300-304. The "classic" article is that by H.J. CADBURY, *Lexical Notes on Luke–Acts. Luke's Interest in Lodging*, in *JBL* 14 (1926) 305-322. — See now also the contribution by A. Denaux, below pp. 255-279.

1. A first approach is to write a synthesis of Luke's theology (as was done, e.g., by J.A. Fitzmyer in his commentary on Lk, and most recently by P. Pokorný, but these are rather exceptional undertakings[155]), or to look for the one overarching theme or perspective that dominates, explains, and holds together the whole of Luke's work. Conzelmann found such a theme in the concept of salvation history. Van Unnik defined it as salvation. Salvation is the central theme of Lk–Acts also for R.F. O'Toole[156]. It is the gift of God and He is the real protagonist of the story. The Scriptures, Jesus, the Spirit, and the disciples together realize and testify to the universality of God's salvific will[157]. For D. Juel, too, Lk–Acts deals primarily with God. Luke teaches his audience of Jewish Christians to put their faith in God[158]. According to J.T. Squires, Luke's work is ruled by the motif of God's providence that is also found in

155. In his commentary on Lk, J.A. Fitzmyer noted "the rarity of synthetic presentations of Lucan theology" (*Lk*, I, p. 143). Since then, the situation has not really changed. Fitzmyer's own "sketch" of Luke's theology is probably still the best and most complete survey (*ibid.*, pp. 143-283). In nine sections he examines the content of the Christian kerygma according to Luke and Luke's understanding of kerygma as proclamation, the structure of his Gospel, the geographical framework, the historical perspective, salvation history, Luke's christology and soteriology, the Spirit, eschatology, discipleship, and the Lukan portrait of Jesus. In *Luke the Theologian* (n. 142), Fitzmyer studies several other aspects: the authorship of Lk–Acts, the infancy narrative, the role of Mary and of John the Baptist, Luke's demonology, the fate of the Jewish people, and again discipleship. – Among the few other works that could be mentioned is P. Pokorný's recent *Theologie der lukanischen Schriften* (FRLANT, 174), Göttingen, 1998, which deals with Luke's christology and soteriology, with salvation history, and further also with his ecclesiology and with the ethical teaching in Luke's work. — A selection of significant theological themes in Lk–Acts is studied in the monographs by, e.g., E. RASCO, *La teologia de Lucas. Origen, desarollo, orientaciones* (AnGreg, 201), Rome, 1976 (survey of research, structure of Lk–Acts, Jesus, the Spirit and the Church, Luke and Paul). M. DÖMER, *Das Heil Gottes. Studien zur Theologie des lukanischen Doppelwerkes* (BBB, 51), Köln–Bonn, 1978 (John the Baptist, Jesus the Christ, the passion, the appearance and ascension narratives, the gift of the Spirit in Acts 2, and the mission to the Gentiles). KORN, *Die Geschichte Jesu* (n. 54): Lk 1–2; the Nazareth pericope; the central section in Lk; Lk 24; the beginning of Acts; the mission discourses in Acts; the Jesus story in Acts. Compare also ESLER, *Community and Gospel in Luke–Acts* (n. 141), who discusses the following topics: Luke's community, Christianity as a sectarian movement, table-fellowship, the Law and the Temple, the poor and the rich, and Luke's Roman readers.

156. R.F. O'TOOLE, *The Unity of Luke's Theology: An Analysis of Luke–Acts* (Good News Studies, 9), Wilmington, DE, 1984.

157. *Ibid.*, pp. 267-268. On salvation as a central concept of Luke's theology, see also, e.g., N.M. FLANAGAN, *The What and How of Salvation in Luke–Acts*, in D. DURKEN (ed.), *Sin, Salvation, and the Spirit*, Collegeville, MN, 1979, pp. 203-213. K.N. GILES, *Salvation in Lukan Theology*, in *RTR* 42 (1983) 10-16.

158. D. JUEL, *Luke–Acts*, Louisville, KY, 1983 (FT, 1984). — On Luke's theo-centrism, see also L. DOOHAN, *Images of God in Luke–Acts*, in *Milltown Studies* 13 (1984) 17-35. A. BARBI, *Il Dio di Gesù nell'opera lucana*, in *SC* 117 (1989) 167-195. C.W. WIBB, *The Characterization of God in the Opening Scenes of Luke and Acts*, in *Proceedings of the Eastern Great Lakes and Midwest Biblical Societies* 13 (1993) 275-292.

ancient historiography. History is to be read as the development of
God's plan to which the Christians contribute[159]. In this approach, the
question for the theological unity of Lk–Acts is that for "the unity of
Luke's theology" (O'Toole).

2. Another way to examine the unity of Luke's theology is to look for
the theological model(s) he may have used to structure his work. One
such model, though by itself not a theological one, is the apology. In this
view Lk–Acts are studied as an attempt at defending the legitimacy of
the Christian message and of the Christian preaching before fellow
Christians or, in the more common version, before external instances,
e.g., the political authorities. It is a theological model in so far as it uses
arguments and claims that are based on such categories as divine purpose and divine will. In recent years it received a lot of attention, e.g.,
through the monograph of P.F. Esler[160].

Esler is convinced that Luke wrote for a Christian audience. He is
critical, however, of the "extreme" positions of, on the one hand, R.J.
Cassidy, who argues that Luke portrays Jesus as a revolutionary with an
essentially political message that was strongly directed against the establishment[161], and, on the other, P.W. Walaskay, who reads Lk–Acts as an
apology "pro imperio" to counter anti-Roman sentiments in certain
Christian circles[162]. In either of these views Luke's work would be a failure. Luke's portrait of the attitude of the Roman authorities to Jesus and
to the Church is much too positive to accept Cassidy's position and not
positive enough to side with the opposite one[163]. According to Esler
Luke wrote for a mixed community of Jewish and Gentile (Roman)
Christians who both, to different degrees, faced the same problem of
integrating their conversion into their former way of life. Luke focuses
especially on the second group. Lk–Acts is a legitimation[164] of his

159. J.T. SQUIRES, *The Plan of God in Luke–Acts* (SNTS MS, 76), Cambridge, 1993,
and also *Fate and Free Will in Hellenistic Histories and Luke–Acts*, in T.W. HILLARD *et
al.* (eds.), *Ancient History in a Modern University*. FS E.A. Judge, Grand Rapids, MI –
Cambridge, 1998, 2, pp. 131-137 (summary of ch. 7 of his book). Cf. C.H. COSGROVE,
*The Divine δεῖ in Luke–Acts. Investigation into the Lukan Understanding of God's Prov-
idence*, in NT 26 (1984) 168-190. D. PETERSON, *The Motif of Fulfilment and the Purpose
of Luke–Acts*, in WINTER–CLARKE (eds.), *The Book of Acts*, pp. 83-104, esp. 100-104 (on
Squires). D.P. MOESSNER, *The "Script" of the Scriptures in Acts: Suffering as God's
"Plan" (βουλή) for the World for the "Release of Sins"*, in WITHERINGTON (ed.), *History, Literature and Society* (n. 24), pp. 218-250 (on Acts only).
160. ESLER, *Community and Gospel in Luke–Acts* (n. 141).
161. See the monographs by Cassidy in n. 147.
162. P.W. WALASKAY, *"And So We Came to Rome": The Political Perspective of
St Luke* (SNTS MS, 49), Cambridge, 1983.
163. ESLER, *Community and Gospel in Luke–Acts*, pp. 207-209.
164. Esler (p. 218) prefers this term over apology but the distinction is not so useful.

Roman audience. To achieve this Luke does not invoke the "religio licita" theory, as many have thought. Besides the lack of evidence that there ever was such an official Roman policy based on a "theory", the central objection against this hypothesis is the same as for the two that were mentioned before: it simply would not work as an argument. It was of no use to emphasize the connections with Judaism in a time when being a Jew was not really advantageous (after 70) and for a community that consisted (mainly) of non-Jewish Christians[165]. On the other hand, Luke did make use of an element that had great importance in the Roman way of dealing with foreign religions: the respect for the ancestral tradition, which shines through in his interest for the tradition "from of old" in the Gospel (Lk 4,36; 5,39) and for the ancestral law and customs in Acts. If Luke could convince his Roman converts that their religious practices were no novelties and constituted no danger to the Roman state of which they were citizens, Christianity could become as acceptable as any other religion. Unfortunately, in the opinion of Esler, the effort would fail and from the second century on the tension between Rome and Christianity would increase. Lk–Acts became a work that was written for "a particular community at a particular point in its history"[166].

Another model, which also includes apologetics and which is widely regarded as fundamental for reading Lk–Acts as one unity is that of "promise/announcement and fulfilment". It functions in two ways since it connects Lk and Acts with each other and also relates both Lk and Acts to the Old Testament[167].

---

165. *Ibid.*, p. 213.
166. *Ibid.*, p. 219. On Luke's policy towards the Roman authorities and their representatives in Palestine, see in this volume the article by F.W. Horn (below, pp. 203-224).
167. Luke's dealing with the Old Testament has been studied from different perspectives: see, e.g. EVANS–SANDERS, *Luke and Scripture* (n. 24): Luke as an expert in Biblical exegesis. C.K. BARRETT, *Luke/Acts*, in D.A. CARSON – H.G.M. WILLIAMSON (eds.), *It is Written: Scripture Citing Scripture: Essays in Honour of Barnabas Lindars*, Cambridge, 1988, pp. 231-244 and J.A. FITZMYER, *The Use of the Old Testament in Luke–Acts*, in *SBL 1992 Seminar Papers*, pp. 524-538 (literal quotations and citation formulas). H. RINGGREN, *Luke's Use of the Old Testament*, in *HTR* 79 (1986) 227-235. W.J.C. WEREN, *Psalm 2 in Luke–Acts. An Intertextual Study*, in S. DRAISMA (ed.), *Intertextuality in Biblical Writings. Essays in Honour of Bas van Iersel*, Kampen, 1989, pp. 189-203. W.S. KURZ, *Intertextual Use of Sirach 48.1-16 in Plotting Luke–Acts*, in C.A. EVANS – W.R. STEGNER (eds.), *The Gospels and the Scriptures of Israel* (JSNT SS, 104), Sheffield, 1994, pp. 308-324. T.L. BRODIE, *Luke the Literary Interpreter. Luke–Acts as a Systematic Rewriting and Updating of the Elijah-Elisha Narrative in 1 and 2 Kings*, Rome, 1987; ID., *Greco-Roman Imitation of Texts as a Partial Guide to Luke's Use of Sources*, in TALBERT (ed.), *New Perspectives* (n. 24), pp. 91-103 (the model of literary imitation). — See esp. the survey by A. DENAUX, *Old Testament Models for the Lukan Travel Narrative: A Critical Survey*, in C.M. TUCKETT (ed.), *The Scriptures in the Gospels* (BETL, 131), Leuven, 1997, pp. 271-305.

In his contribution on Lk 24 for the 1954 FS Bultmann, P. Schubert argued that Luke's use of Scripture was led by the purpose to demonstrate that Jesus is the Messiah. In Lk–Acts OT quotations function as "proof from prophecy" serving an apologetic messianic exegesis. Schubert examined how this model, which he considered as an original feature of Luke's work, is present throughout the first part of the Gospel (up to 9,51) and in the closing chapters of Lk and of Acts[168]. In the FS Schubert, N.A. Dahl studied the references and allusions to Abraham in Lk–Acts and found there "the confirmation that 'proof-from-prophecy' is a main theological and literary device of the work"[169]. The role of the Abrahamic covenant traditions for Luke's characterization of God is dealt with by R.L. Brawley[170]. The significance, if not the existence, of such a scheme was disputed by, among others, M. Rese. At the 1977 Leuven colloquium Rese took up the theme of his 1969 monograph on the function of the OT quotations in Luke's christology, repeating his thesis that "proof from prophecy" represents only part of the explanation and that Luke displays a far more diversified use of these quotations[171]. In turn, D.L. Bock proposed a modification. He argued, in particular on the basis of Acts 2,33-36, that the purpose of the quotations

168. P. SCHUBERT, *The Structure and Significance of Luke 24*, in *Neutestamentliche Studien für R. Bultmann*, pp. 165-186. Compare the article by J. Dupont on *L'utilisation apologétique de l'Ancien Testament dans les discours des Actes*, in *ETL* 29 (1953) 289-327; repr. in *Études* (n. 24), pp. 245-282 and ET in *The Salvation of the Gentiles*, pp. 129-159.

169. N.A. DAHL, *The Story of Abraham in Luke–Acts*, in KECK–MARTYN, *Studies in Luke–Acts* (n. 24), pp. 139-158, esp. 152; repr. in ID., *Jesus in the Memory of the Early Church*, Minneapolis, MN, 1976, pp. 66-86, esp. 83. In a later publication Dahl extended his investigation to Luke's portrayal of Jesus as the new David and the new Moses: cf. *The Purpose of Luke–Acts*, in ID., *Memory*, pp. 87-98, esp. 91. — See also J. JERVELL, *Die Mitte der Schrift. Zum lukanischen Verständnis des Alten Testaments*, in U. LUZ – H. WEDER (eds.), *Die Mitte des Neuen Testaments. Einheit und Vielfalt neutestamentlicher Theologie. FS E. Schweizer*, Göttingen, 1983, pp. 79-96; ET in *The Unknown Paul* (n. 24), pp. 122-137. J.T. SANDERS, *The Prophetic Use of the Scriptures in Luke–Acts*, in C.A. EVANS – W.G. STINESPRING (eds.), *Early Jewish and Christian Exegesis: Studies in Memory of W.H. Brownlee*, Atlanta, GA, 1987, pp. 191-198.

170. See his *The Blessing of All the Families of the Earth. Jesus and Covenant Traditions in Luke–Acts*, in *SBL 1994 Seminar Papers*, pp. 252-268; cf. *CurrTMiss* 22 (1995) 18-26, and in this volume, pp. 109-132. Brawley approaches the same topic from a different perspective in *Offspring and Parent. A Lucan Prolegomena to Ethics*, in *SBL 1998 Seminar Papers*, pp. 807–830 (the image of parent and child and God as Father in Lk–Acts).

171. Cf. M. RESE, *Alttestamentliche Motive in der Christologie des Lukas* (SNT, 1), Gütersloh, 1969, esp. pp. 37-42; *Die Funktion der alttestamentlichen Zitate und Anspielungen in den Reden der Apostelgeschichte*, in KREMER (ed.), *Les Actes des Apôtres* (n. 2), pp. 61-79, esp. 72. Rese's criticism was supported by C.H. Talbert in his survey of the discussion: C.H. TALBERT, *Promise and Fulfillment in Lucan Theology*, in ID. (ed.), *New Perspectives* (n. 24), pp. 91-103.

from the OT in Lk–Acts is to present Jesus not only as the Messiah but as the Lord who is to be preached to the whole of the world. Luke's use of Scripture for christology cannot be cast merely in terms of "proof from prophecy", which is still too closely bound up with apologetics, but is rather a "proclamation from prophecy and pattern", for it includes the proclamation of Jesus as Lord and Saviour. And so it remains true that "promise and fulfilment play a major role in Luke's use of the OT"[172].

The model of promise and fulfilment also functions within the framework of Lk–Acts itself. O. Mainville has analyzed how the promise of the Spirit in Lk 1,35, which signifies Jesus as the Messiah, finds its culmination in Acts 2,33, where Peter refers to the Spirit of the exalted Jesus which has been passed on to the disciples[173]. Another crucial passage in this respect is the prophecy of Simeon in Lk 2,29-34[174]. In general, scholars agree that Luke regards the decision to preach to the Gentiles as the realization of God's plan that is formulated at the very beginning of the Gospel (2,32) and is restated as a commandment of the Lord at the end of it and in the first verses of Acts (Lk 24,47; Acts 1,8)[175]. The motif of the conversion of the Gentiles is present and runs

172. D.L. BOCK, *Proclamation from Prophecy and Pattern. Lucan Old Testament Christology* (JSNT SS, 12), Sheffield, 1987, p. 275. Also ID., *Proclamation from Prophecy and Pattern: Luke's Use of the Old Testament for Christology and Mission*, in EVANS–STEGNER (eds.), *The Gospels and the Scriptures of Israel* (n. 167), pp. 280-307 (cf. *SBL 1990 Seminar Papers*, pp. 494-511). — Most recently the theme of fulfilment of prophecy has been studied from a narrative-critical perspective by R.I. Denova who comes to the surprising conclusion that, since its author is thoroughly acquainted with Jewish interpretation of Scripture, Lk–Acts must be the work of a Jew writing to convince a Jewish audience that the OT prophecies on the coming of the Messiah have been fulfilled in Jesus. Cf. R.I. DENOVA, *The Things Accomplished Among Us. Prophetic Tradition in the Structural Pattern of Luke–Acts* (JSNT SS, 141), Sheffield, 1997, esp. pp. 11-40 and 87-92.

173. *L'Esprit dans l'œuvre de Luc* (Héritage et projet, 45), Montréal, 1991, pp. 49-86 (Acts 2,33) and 168-188 (Lk 1,32-35). Compare in this volume, below pp. 313-327. Another prophecy in Lk concerning the Spirit that is fulfilled in Acts is studied in *Le péché contre l'Esprit annoncé en Lc 12.10, commis en Ac 4.16–18: une illustration de l'unité de Luc et Actes*, in NTS 45 (1999) 38–50.

174. Cf. the contribution by W. Radl in this volume (below, pp. 297-312), and see already *Der Ursprung Jesu. Traditionsgeschichtliche Untersuchungen zu Lukas 1–2* (HBS, 7), Freiburg, 1996, esp. pp. 203-242, with an outlook on Acts on pp. 237-242 (see, e.g., 240: "Was Lukas dem greisen Simeon in den Mund legt, ist also nichts Geringeres als das Programm, das er in seinem zweiteiligen Werk verwirklicht"). On Radl's tradition-critical analysis, see T. KAUT, review in *ComViat* 39 (1997) 60-94. — On the role of Luke's Infancy narratives in the whole of his work, see U. BUSSE, *Das "Evangelium" des Lukas. Die Funktion der Vorgeschichte im lukanischen Doppelwerk*, in BUSSMANN–RADL (eds.), *Der Treue Gottes trauen* (n. 24), pp. 161-179. A.J. MCNICOL, *Rebuilding the House of David: The Function of the Benedictus in Luke–Acts*, in RestQ 40 (1998) 25-38.

175. See W. STEGEMANN, *"Licht der Völker" bei Lukas*, in BUSSMANN–RADL (eds.),

throughout Luke's work, even though it becomes more acute only in the
second part. It is likewise agreed that in Lk 2,34 Simeon alludes to troubles with the mission to the Jews. These, too, have been foretold and
they are illustrated in Acts. Discussion continues, however, on the meaning that should be given to these "announcements" in their relation to
the account in Acts. In the traditional view, Luke is said to tell the story
of the transfert of God's promise of salvation from the Jews to a new
people[176]. This interpretation has been challenged from different sides.

J. Jervell argues that at the end of Acts the mission to the Jews is def-
initely discontinued, though Luke did not regard it as a complete failure,
and further that the objective of the mission to the Gentiles has been
misunderstood[177]. The early Christian mission is addressed to the synagogue and to those who sympathize with Judaism. For Luke, those who
belong to the Church are the same as those who formerly belonged to
the synagogue: the people of God is made up of Jews and Godfearers[178].
Others defend an even more positive interpretation. Acts 28 may well be
the end of Luke's story but not of God's story. As a matter of fact, Luke
has not told the most important part[179]. The Gentile mission, however
legitimate, is primarily an incentive or, if you wish, a reproach to unre-
pented Israel, but God's offer of salvation for his people remains valid
forever[180]. A radical opposite view is taken by those who read Lk–Acts

Der Treue Gottes trauen (n. 24), pp. 81-97 (Lk 2,32). G. BETORI, *Luke 24:47: Jerusalem
and the Beginning of the Preaching to the Pagans in the Acts of the Apostles*, in
G. O'COLLINS – M.J. O'CONNELL (eds.), *Luke and Acts* (n. 24), pp. 103-120.

176. See, e.g., among many others, E. HAENCHEN, *The Book of Acts as Source Material for the History of Early Christianity*, in KECK–MARTYN (eds.), *Studies in Luke–Acts*
(n. 24), pp. 258-278 (with the famous "Luke has written the Jews off"); German in *Die
Bibel und wir. Gesammelte Aufsätze*, Tübingen, 1968, pp. 312-337, here 337. Cf. also his
Judentum und Christentum in der Apostelgeschichte (1963), in *ibid.*, pp. 338-374,
esp. 370-373.

177. Among the many publications of Jervell, see esp. his *The Divided People of God.
The Restoration of Israel and Salvation for the Gentiles*, in *Studia Theologica* 19 (1965);
repr. in ID., *Luke and the People of God* (n. 139), pp. 41-74. And further, *The Church of
Jews and Godfearers*, in TYSON (ed.), *Jewish People* (n. 24), pp. 11-20. *Gottes Treue zum
untreuen Volk*, in BUSSMANN–RADL (eds.), *Die Treue Gottes trauen* (n. 24), pp. 15-27.
Retrospect and Prospect in Luke–Acts Interpretation, in *SBL 1991 Seminar Papers*,
pp. 383-404. *The Lucan Interpretation of Jesus as Biblical Theology*, in S. PEDERSEN
(ed.), *New Directions in Biblical Theology* (NTSup, 76), Leiden, 1994, pp. 77-92 (on the
reception of his work).

178. On the Godfearers in Luke's work, see now M.C. DE BOER, *God-Fearers in
Luke–Acts*, in TUCKETT (ed.), *Luke's Literary Achievement* (n. 9), pp. 50-71. Cf. n. 183.

179. Cf. D.L. TIEDE, *"Glory to They People Israel": Luke–Acts and the Jews*, in
TYSON (ed.), *Jewish People* (n. 24), pp. 21-34, esp. 23: "The fundamental tension of the
plot still awaits a final resolution" (cf. *SBL 1986 Seminar Papers*, pp. 142-151).

180. See, among others, D.L. TIEDE, *Prophecy and History in Luke–Acts*, Philadelphia, PA, 1980, esp. pp. 103-118. *The Death of Jesus and the Trial of Israel in Luke–Acts*,

as the history of the rejection of the Jewish people. According to J.T. Sanders, the Jewish leaders and the crowds at first seem to have some sympathy (Acts 1-5), a reaction which was prepared for by the sometime neutral attitude of the crowds in the passion narrative. The death of Stephen marks a turning point. From now on they resolutely opt for the hostile stand of the early days of Jesus' ministry (as already in Lk 4,16-30)[181]. Sanders sees no reason to call Luke's presentation a tragedy, as does R.C. Tannehill, for this would imply that Luke showed some "sympathetic pity" for the decline of the Jewish people[182]. Less radical is J.B. Tyson who, while agreeing that Luke leaves no hope at the end of Acts that the failed mission to the Jews will ever be resumed, nevertheless points out that Luke does report the conversion of individuals in the Jewish communities, but these results do not outweigh the negative conclusion that the Jews, as God's people, have not repented or accepted the message[183]. The discussion of the 70s and the 80s on this topic was critically reviewed by M. Rese in the FS G. Schneider (1991)[184].

in *SBL 1990 Seminar Papers*, pp. 158-164 (cf. *The Beginnings of Christianity*. FS H. Koester, 1991, pp. 301-308). *Fighting Against God. Luke's Interpretation of Jewish Rejection of the Messiah Jesus*, in C.A. EVANS, *et al.* (eds.), *Anti-Semitism and Early Christianity*, Minneapolis, MN, 1993, pp. 102-112. R.L. BRAWLEY, *Luke–Acts and the Jews. Conflict, Apology, and Conciliation* (SBL MS, 33), Atlanta, GA, 1987. B.J. KOET, *Simeons Worte (Lk 2,29-32.34c-35) und Israels Geschick*, in F. VAN SEGBROECK, *et al.*, *The Four Gospels 1992* (n. 77), 2, pp. 1549-1569. — For a reaction to Tiede, see D.P. MOESSNER, *The Ironic Fulfillment of Israel's Glory*, in TYSON (ed.), *Jewish People* (n. 24), pp. 35-50.
    181. J.T. SANDERS, *The Jews in Luke–Acts* (n. 139), esp. pp. 37-83 (revised version of an article that was first published in *SBL 1986 Seminar Papers*, pp. 110-129 and again in TYSON, *Jewish People*, pp. 51-75). Cf. also *The Salvation of the Jews in Luke–Acts*, in *SBL 1982 Seminar Papers*, pp. 467-483; = TALBERT (ed.), *New Perspectives* (n. 24), pp. 104-128. *Who is a Jew and Who is a Gentile in the Book of Acts?*, in *NTS* 37 (1991) 434-455. In the same line, M.J. COOK, *The Mission to the Jews in Acts: Unraveling Luke's "Myth of the 'Myriads'"*, in TYSON (ed.), *Jewish People* (n. 24), pp. 102-123.
    182. Cf. R.C. TANNEHILL, *Israel in Luke–Acts. A Tragic Story*, in *JBL* 104 (1985) 69-85. *Rejection by Jews and Turning to Gentiles. The Pattern of Paul's Mission in Acts*, in *SBL 1986 Seminar Papers*, pp. 130-141 (= TYSON, *Jewish People*, pp. 83-101).
    183. *The Death of Jesus in Luke–Acts* (n. 138), pp. 29-47 and 48-83. *The Problem of Jewish Rejection in Acts*, in ID., *Jewish People* (n. 24), pp. 124-137. *The Gentile Mission and the Authority of Scripture in Acts*, in *NTS* 33 (1987) 619-631. *Images of Judaism in Luke–Acts*, Columbia, SC, 1992. *Jews and Judaism in Luke–Acts: Reading as a God-fearer*, in *NTS* 41 (1995) 19-38.
    184. M. RESE, *"Die Juden" im lukanischen Doppelwerk. Ein Bericht über eine längst nötige "neuere" Diskussion*, in BUSSMANN–RADL (eds.), *Der Treue Gottes trauen* (n. 24), pp. 61-79 (with additional bibliography); see now also his "second thoughts" in this volume (below, pp. 185-201). The FS Schneider contains still other articles on the same topic: cf. W. RADL, *Rettung in Israel*, pp. 43-60 (on Acts), C.H. TALBERT, *Once Again: The Gentile Mission in Luke–Acts*, pp. 99-109, and J. Jervell (above n. 177). See further: D.P. MOESSNER, *The "Leaven of the Pharisees" and "This Generation": Israel's Rejection of Jesus according to Luke*, in *JSNT* 34 (1988) 21-46; repr. in SYLVA (ed.), *Reimag-*

3. A third way of addressing the issue of the theological unity is to look for the coherency of Luke's theology in a specific area. Again I give two illustrations. Luke's pneumatology was one of the first aspects of his theology that came to be studied for itself[185]. More than any other New Testament author Luke speaks of the Spirit of God and it is commonly observed that the Spirit is "the connecting thread which runs through both parts" of his work[186], or the "unifying force throughout Luke's narrative"[187]. Discussion has concentrated to a large measure on two questions: the identity and the role Luke assigns to the Spirit[188]. The former of these may not yet have been solved and scholars continue to debate whether Luke is an heir of the OT tradition in which the Spirit of God is an impersonal force (Lampe), or whether he already anticipates later developments and sees the Spirit as a person (Hull), or, in line with early Christian tradition, understands it both as a person and as a force (e.g., Bultmann). On the other question there is consensus to accept that Luke thinks of the Spirit as the Spirit of prophecy who inspires human

---

ing (n. 24), pp. 79-107, 190-194). F. Ó FEARGHAIL, *Israel in Luke–Acts*, in *PIBA* 11 (1988) 24-43. J.A. WEATHERLY, *The Jews in Luke–Acts*, in *TyndB* 40 (1989) 107-117 and his monograph (above n. 151). C.A. EVANS, *Is Luke's View of the Jewish Rejection of Jesus Anti-Semitic?*, in SYLVA (ed.), *Reimaging*, pp. 29-56, 174-184. H. RÄISÄNEN, *The Redemption of Israel. A Salvation-Historical Problem in Luke–Acts*, in LUOMANEN (ed.), *Scandinavian Perspectives* (n. 24), pp. 94-114. R.F. O'TOOLE, *Reflections on Luke's Treatment of the Jews in Luke–Acts*, in *Bib* 74 (1993) 529-555. D. MARGUERAT, *Juifs et chrétiens selon Luc–Actes*, in *Bib* 75 (1994) 126-146, repr. in ID. (ed.), *Le déchirement. Juifs et chrétiens au premier siècle* (Le monde de la Bible, 32), Genève, 1996, pp. 151-178, and GT *Juden und Christen im lukanischen Doppelwerk*, in *EvT* 54 (1994) 241-261. H. MERKEL, *Israel im lukanischen Werk*, in *NTS* 40 (1994) 371-398. D. RAVENS, *Luke and the Restoration of Israel* (n. 139). V. FUSCO, *Luke–Acts and the Future of Israel*, in *NT* 38 (1996) 1-17.

In recent years the discussion is pursued much along the same lines, with, e.g., Fusco arguing that Luke was sensitive of the "tragedy" of the fate of the Jews and still awaited the fulfilment of Israel's redemption (p. 8), though Marguerat proposes an interpretation that is said to transcend the impasse: the unresolved tension at the end of Acts reflects the essence of Luke's understanding of Christianity "à l'intersection de la continuité et de la rupture avec Israel" (p. 144). See now again D. MARGUERAT, *Luc–Actes entre Jérusalem et Rome. Un procédé lucanien de double signification*, in *NTS* 45 (1999) 70-87: Luke constantly works within a double framework (Jewish and Graeco-Roman), and this is even a rhetorical characteristic of his writing.

185. Cf. H. VON BAER, *Der Heilige Geist in den Lukasschriften*, Stuttgart, 1926. See A. GEORGE, *L'Esprit Saint dans l'œuvre de Luc*, in *RB* 85 (1978) 500-542 and the research survey by M.M.B. TURNER, *The Significance of Receiving the Spirit in Luke–Acts. A Survey of Modern Scholarship*, in *TrinJ* 2 (1981) 131-158.

186. G.W.H. LAMPE, *The Holy Spirit in the Writings of St. Luke*, in D.E. NINEHAM (ed.), *Studies in the Gospels. Essays in Memory of R.H. Lightfoot*, Oxford, 1955, pp. 159-200, here 159.

187. W.H. SHEPHERD, *The Narrative Function of the Holy Spirit as a Character in Luke–Acts* (SBL DS, 147), Atlanta, GA, 1994, p. 13.

188. See, e.g., SHEPHERD, *Narrative Function*, pp. 3-23.

speech[189]. But there is no agreement on whether this is the Spirit's only
task according to Luke. R.P. Menzies thinks it is[190]. Others argue that
the Spirit for Luke also has a soteriological function and that it is the gift
of the Spirit that realizes the conversion of new believers[191]. M. Turner
extends the role of the Spirit to include also other aspects of the ministry
of Jesus and of the missionary activity of the disciples, e.g., with regard
to the working of miracles[192].

From the perspective that interests us here, the discussion on the role
of the Spirit comes down to whether or not Luke ascribes (a) new func-
tion(s) to the Spirit in Acts and, if so, in how far this affects the unity of
his thinking and of his work. In his commentary on Lk, J.A. Fitzmyer
pointed out that the Spirit is emphatically mentioned by Luke at the
beginning of his Gospel and of Acts. In line with von Baer and Conzelmann, Fitzmyer connects the role of the Spirit in Lk–Acts with the salvation-historical perspective in Luke's work. It is the Spirit who initiates
both the era of Jesus and that of the Church. And it is "the same Spirit"
who, as the dynamic force behind Jesus' ministry, also energizes the disciples after Pentecost, even though in Acts the Spirit can assume "a new
role" and become "a substitute for the risen Christ himself"[193]. M.
Turner, on the other hand, gives more emphasis to the difference in the
way the Spirit is experienced by Jesus at his baptism and by the disciples
at Pentecost[194]. But this is not a reason for Turner to deny the literary or
theological unity, or to conclude that this marks a fundamental shift in

189. *Ibid.*, p. 22.
190. R.P. MENZIES, *The Development of Early Christian Pneumatology. With Special
Reference to Luke–Acts* (JSNT SS, 54), Sheffield, 1991, esp. pp. 114-279: "The prophetic
pneumatology of Luke"; revised as *Empowered for Witness. The Spirit in Luke–Acts*
(JPT SS, 6), Sheffield, 1994.
191. Thus, e.g., J.D.G. DUNN, *Baptism in the Holy Spirit: A Re-Examination of the
New Testament Teaching on the Gift of the Spirit in Relation to Pentecostalism Today*
(Studies in Biblical Theology, 2/15), London, 1970 and *Jesus and the Spirit: A Study of
the Religious and Charismatic Experience of Jesus and the First Christians as Reflected
in the New Testament*, Philadelphia, PA, 1975. But see W. ATKINSON, *Pentecostal
Responses to Dunn's* Baptism in the Holy Spirit: *Luke–Acts*, in *JPT* 6 (1995) 87-131.
192. M.M.B. TURNER, *Jesus and the Spirit in Lucan Perspective*, in *TyndBull* 32
(1981) 3-42; FT in *Hokhma* 26 (1984) 18-46. ID., *Spirit-Endowment in Luke–Acts. Some
Linguistic Considerations*, in *Vox Evangelica* 12 (1981) 45-63 and *Power from on High.
The Spirit in Israel's Restoration and Witness in Luke–Acts* (JPT SS, 9), Sheffield, 1996.
See also the discussion with Menzies: M. TURNER, *The Spirit and the Power of Jesus'
Miracles in the Lucan Conception*, in *NT* 33 (1991) 124-152. R.P. MENZIES, *Spirit and
Power in Luke–Acts. A Response to M. Turner*, in *JSNT* 49 (1993) 11-20. M. TURNER, *The
Spirit in Luke–Acts*, in *Vox Evangelica* 27 (1997) 75-101. Cf. also J.M. PENNEY, *The Mis-
sionary Emphasis of Luke's Pneumatology* (JPT SS, 12), Sheffield, 1997.
193. FITZMYER, *Lk*, pp. 228 and 230. See also in this volume, pp. 165-183.
194. Cf. *Jesus and the Spirit* (n. 192), pp. 28-33.

Luke's understanding which "necessitates" the separation into two volumes as Parsons and Pervo are ready to believe[195].

My second illustration is taken from christology. Again one could mention a wealth of studies that deal with several aspects of Luke's christology, e.g., the relation to soteriology, his theology of the cross (if he has one)[196], the christological titles that occur in Lk–Acts[197], or

195. *Rethinking* (n. 6), p. 113.

196. On christology and soteriology in Lk–Acts, see, e.g., G. Frizzi, *La soteriologia nell'opera lucana*, in *RivBib* 23 (1975) 113-146. K.P. Donfried, *Attempt at Understanding the Purpose of Luke–Acts. Christology and Salvation of the Gentiles*, in R.F. Berkey – S.A. Edwards (eds.), *Christological Perspectives*. FS H.K. McArthur, New York, 1982, pp. 112-122. Pokorný, *Theologie* (n. 155), pp. 110-176. — On Luke's theology of the death of Jesus: E. Schweizer, *Zur lukanischen Christologie*, in E. Jüngel, *et al.*, *Verifikationen*. FS G. Ebeling, Tübingen, 1982, pp. 43-65, esp. 52-58. D.P. Moessner, *"The Christ Must Suffer", the Church Must Suffer: Rethinking the Theology of the Cross in Luke–Acts*, in *SBL 1990 Seminar Papers*, pp. 165-195. J.B. Green, *The Death of Jesus, God's Servant*, in Sylva (ed.), *Reimaging* (n. 24), pp. 1-28, and the contributions by R.J. Karris (pp. 68-78: on Lk 23,47), J.T. Carroll (pp. 108-124: the crucifixion), E. Richard (pp. 125-152: the passion and death of Jesus in Acts) in the same volume. See also J.T. Carroll – J.B. Green, *The Death of Jesus in Early Christianity*, Peabody, MA, 1995, pp. 60-81 (on Lk). Ravens, *Luke and the Restoration of Israel* (n. 139), pp. 139-169. P. Doble, *The Paradox of Salvation. Luke's Theology of the Cross* (SNTS MS, 87), Cambridge, 1996 (on Lk 23,46-47 and the motif of the δίκαιος in Lk–Acts). — On Lk 22,19-20: B.D. Ehrman, *The Cup, the Bread, and the Salvific Effect of Jesus' Death in Luke–Acts*, in *SBL 1991 Seminar Papers*, pp. 576-591. I.J. du Plessis, *The Saving Significance of Jesus and His Death on the Cross in Luke's Gospel – Focussing on Lk 22:19b-20*, in *Neotestamentica* 28 (1994) 523-540.

197. See, e.g., Ravens, *Luke and the Restoration of Israel* (n. 139), pp. 110-138. D.L. Jones, *The Title κύριος in Luke–Acts*, in *SBL 1974 Seminar Papers*, pp. 85-101 and *The Title παῖς in Luke–Acts*, in *SBL 1982 Seminar Papers*, pp. 217-226 (cf. Talbert, *New Perspectives*, pp. 148-165). B. Witherington, *The Many Faces of the Christ. The Christologies of the New Testament and Beyond*, New York, 1998, pp. 153–168 ("Lord and Savior. The Christology of Luke–Acts"). — On Son of God: J. Kremer, *"Dieser ist der Sohn Gottes" (Apg 9,20). Bibeltheologische Erwägungen zur Bedeutung von "Sohn Gottes" im lukanischen Doppelwerk*, in Bussmann–Radl (eds.), *Der Treue Gottes trauen* (n. 24), pp. 137-158. — On the Son of man in Lk–Acts: G. Schneider, *"Der Menschensohn" in der lukanischen Christologie* (1975), in Id., *Lukas, Theologe der Heilsgeschichte* (n. 24), pp. 98-113. F.F. Bruce, *The Davidic Messiah in Luke–Acts*, in G.A. Tuttle (ed.), *Biblical and Near Eastern Studies*. FS W. LaSor, Grand Rapids, MI, 1978, pp. 1-17. M. Sabbe, *The Son of Man Saying in Acts 7,56*, in Kremer (ed.), *Les Actes des Apôtres* (n. 2), pp. 241-279, esp. 260-277 (Acts 7,56 and Lk 22,69); repr. in M. Sabbe, *Studia neotestamentica* (BETL, 98), Leuven, 1991, pp. 137-178 (156-173). M.L. Strauss, *The Davidic Messiah in Luke–Acts. The Promise and Its Fulfilment in Lukan Christology* (JSNT SS, 110), Sheffield, 1995. C.M. Tuckett, *The Lukan Son of Man*, in Id. (ed.), *Luke's Literary Achievement* (n. 9), pp. 198-217 (Lk). — On Jesus as Prophet: G. Nebe, *Prophetische Züge im Bilde Jesu bei Lukas* (BWANT, 127), Stuttgart, 1989. M. McVann, *Rituals of Status Transformation in Luke–Acts: The Case of Jesus the Prophet*, in Neyrey (ed.), *Social World* (n. 24), pp. 333-360. — On Jesus as miracle-worker: J.T. Carroll, *Jesus as Healer in Luke–Acts*, in *SBL 1994 Seminar Papers*, pp. 269-285. — A more peculiar approach is found in the monograph by C.H.T. Fletcher–Louis, *Luke–Acts. Angels, Christology and Soteriology* (WUNT, 2/94), Tübingen, 1997, who

Luke's interpretation of Jesus' preaching of the Kingdom[198]. Of more
importance perhaps is the observation that there is hardly an area of
Luke's theology in which scholars have done more to demonstrate the
consistency of his thought. In his recent monograph, H.D. Buckwalter
distinguishes no less than eighteen proposals of "controlling christologies"[199], as he calls them, which he divides into four categories according to whether the emphasis is on Jesus' humanity[200], his subordination
to the Father[201], his function as Saviour[202], or his authority[203]. Of course,
not all of these bear equal weight, but the situation may seem pretty des-

studies the possible influences of post-Biblical Jewish beliefs about angels and divine
identity upon early Christian thought and representations of the Risen Jesus.

198. Cf. V. Fusco, *Chiesa e Regno nella prospettiva lucana*, in G. Lorizio –
V. Scippa (eds.), *Ecclesiae Sacramentum*. FS A. Marranzini, Rome, 1986, pp. 113-135.
M. Wolter, *"Reich Gottes" bei Lukas*, in *NTS* 41 (1995) 541-563. A. Prieur, *Die
Verkündigung der Gottesherrschaft. Exegetische Studien zum lukanischen Verständnis
von* βασιλεία τοῦ θεοῦ (WUNT, 2/89), Tübingen, 1996.

199. H.D. Buckwalter, *The Character and Purpose of Luke's Christology* (SNTS
MS, 89), Cambridge, 1996, esp. pp. 6-31.

200. As, e.g., in C.H. Talbert's anti-gnostic christology or G.W.H. Lampe's suggestion that Luke develops his portrait of Jesus in view of the disciples who are to imitate his
life and teaching. Cf. C.H. Talbert, *An Anti-Gnostic Tendency in Lucan Christology*, in
NTS 14 (1967-68) 259-271; G.W.H. Lampe, *The Lucan Portrait of Christ*, in *NTS* 2
(1955-56) 160-175.

201. Buckwalter refers, among others, to H. Conzelmann (*Die Mitte der Zeit*), who
emphasized the instrumental role of Jesus in God's plan, and to E. Kränkel who linked
this role with a prophetic servant christology. Cf. E. Kränkel, *Jesus der Knecht Gottes.
Die heilsgeschichtliche Stellung Jesu in den Reden der Apostelgeschichte* (BU, 8),
Regensburg, 1972.

202. This is stressed, e.g., by I.H. Marshall and receives different qualifications in the
works of A.J. Hultgren (Jesus as the redeemer through his suffering *and* his glorification),
F. Schütz (Luke interprets the perils his community is living through in light of the
salvific effect of Jesus' passion), and J.B. Green (Jesus as the Suffering Servant of Isaiah
whose life and death make God's plan come true). See A.J. Hultgren, *Christ and His
Benefits. Christology and Redemption in the New Testament*, Philadelphia, PA, 1987;
F. Schütz, *Der leidende Christus. Die angefochtene Gemeinde und das Christuskerygma
der lukanischen Schriften* (BWANT, 89), Stuttgart, 1969; J.B. Green, *The Death of
Jesus, God's Servant*, in Sylva (ed.), *Reimaging* (n. 24), pp. 1–28.

203. Under this heading Buckwalter brings together various attempts to understand
Luke's christology from such christological titles as Messiah (E.E. Ellis, *Lk*), King
(A.R.C. Leaney, *Lk*), Lord (D.L. Bock; cf. above), or Son of God (G. Voss), from his
(presumed) typological reading of the OT (D.P. Moessner: Jesus as the Mosaic prophet),
from the hellenistic milieu (F.W. Danker's benefactor-hero), or even from an implied pre-
existence christology (in J. Roloff's *Apg*, interpretation of Acts 2,21). See G. Voss, *Die
Christologie der lukanischen Schriften in Grundzügen* (Studia neotestamentica, 2),
Brugge–Paris, 1965. D.P. Moessner, *Lord of the Banquet. The Literary and Theological
Significance of the Lukan Travel Narrative*, Minneapolis, MN, 1989. F.W. Danker, *Jesus
and the New Age: A Commentary of St. Luke's Gospel*, Philadelphia, PA, ²1988; also
Graeco-Roman Cultural Accomodation in the Christology of Luke–Acts, in *SBL 1983
Seminar Papers*, pp. 391-414, and again in *Imaged through Beneficence*, in Sylva (ed.),
Reimaging (n. 24), pp. 57-67.

perate and it is not surprising that some have resigned as, e.g., S.G. Wilson who thinks that it is a wrong question to ask for Luke's christology, since he is only the "somewhat indiscriminating collector of christological traditions"[204]. Buckwalter, however, is convinced that the question remains valid and he formulates some principles that should direct any further investigation. A synthesis should search for a model that is in agreement with Luke's writing purpose, explains his redaction, smooths out tensions, and takes into account all the available material. Buckwalter reads Lk–Acts as a call to perseverance. To encourage his troubled community Luke has developed a "humiliation-exaltation christology" in which he presents Jesus as "a model of servanthood for discipleship" by emphasizing the exemplary character of his life which Christians like Paul have imaged, but also as the Risen Lord who protects his people and divinely rules world history. To some this may seem an almost too perfect model in which all elements can be explained within the framework of Luke's redactional purpose, but it is one illustration of the importance and the role of methodological considerations in this discussion[205].

III. One Work – One Genre?

Cadbury delighted in studying every aspect of Luke's work, but he saw "no profit" in searching for the genre of Lk–Acts as a whole[206]. Conzelmann suggested in passing that Lk–Acts comes closest to the historical monograph, a genre which allowed for quite some flexibility and which he thought was well known in Greco-Roman literature[207]. E. Plümacher developed this suggestion of Conzelmann in a series of publications. At first he did so only with regard to Acts[208]. But later on he became increasingly more convinced that Luke's Gospel and the Book of Acts belonged to the same genre. What was still "kaum möglich" in

---

204. S.G. WILSON, *Luke and the Pastoral Epistles*, London, 1979, p. 80. Buckwalter (*Luke's Christology*, p. 6) regards this as a regression to the pre-redaction-critical period.

205. See BUCKWALTER, *Luke's Christology*, pp. 31 and 275 (on the "single overriding concern" behind Luke's christology). On this and similar proposals, see C.M. Tuckett (below, pp. 133-164).

206. *Making* (n. 26), p. 137: "There is a danger of 'fighting about words to no profit'".

207. *Die Mitte der Zeit* (n. 58), p. 15 n. 1 (ET 7 n. 1); *Apg*, pp. 6 and 20. The historical monograph is a systematic and autonomous treatment (it is not a part of a larger work), preferably, but not necessarily, of a topic from military or political history.

208. E. PLÜMACHER, *Lukas als hellenistischer Schriftsteller. Studien zur Apostelgeschichte* (SUNT, 9), Göttingen, 1972.

1974 is "wesentlich schwerer" but no longer impossible in 1978, and in
1979 Plümacher considers it as "durchaus möglich, die literarische Form
der Apostelgeschichte wie darüber hinaus auch des ganzen lukanischen
Werkes im Rahmen seinerzeit gängiger Formen zu bestimmen"[209]. Lk
and Acts remain relatively independent because of their content but they
are both "historische Monographien"[210].

In 1974 C.H. Talbert proposed an alternative: it is ancient biography
instead of historiography that provides the closest parallel[211]. Talbert
compared Luke's work with the *Lives of Eminent Philosophers* of the
early third-century author Diogenes Laertius which in his opinion contains remarkable similarities in content, form, and function. In both
works the reader finds reliable information about the founder of a school
or movement, his teachings or doctrines, and his disciples. And this was
precisely what was at stake in Lk–Acts, for Luke was involved in a dispute about the identity of the true successors and the content of the tradition they perpetuated. The specific type of biography of the Lives was
"a ready-made vehicle" for what Luke had in mind[212].

Over the past two decades the discussion on the genre of Lk–Acts has
developed mainly in two directions. Scholars have further explored the

209. *Apostelgeschichte*, in *TRE* 3, 1978, pp. 483-515, csp. 515, and *Die Apostelgeschichte als historische Monographie*, in Kremer (ed.), *Les Actes des Apôtres* (n. 2),
pp. 457-466, here 457. In the revised version of this article which appeared in the same
year as *Neues Testament und hellenistische Form. Zur literarischen Gattung der lukanischen Schriften*, in *TViat* 14 (1979) 109-123, Plümacher speaks of "die literarische Form
des lukanischen Werkes" (p. 112); see also p. 110: "die Frage nach der Form des
lukanischen Geschichtswerkes als ganzcm".

210. *Monographie*, p. 466; cf. *Apostelgeschichte*, p. 515. — On this genre, see now
also D.W. Palmer, *Acts and the Ancient Historical Monograph*, in Winter–Clarke
(eds.), *The Book of Acts* (n. 4), pp. 1-29 (cf. *TyndB* 43, 1992, 373-388). L.C.A. Alexander, *The Preface to Acts and the Historians*, in Witherington (ed.), *History, Literature,
and Society* (n. 24), pp. 73-103. See also the following note.

211. C.H. Talbert, *Literary Patterns, Theological Themes, and the Genre of
Luke–Acts* (SBL MS, 20), Missoula, MT, 1974, esp. pp. 125-140. Talbert has come back
to his suggestion in several contributions: see, e.g., *Prophecies of Future Greatness. The
Contribution of Greco-Roman Biographies to an Understanding of Luke 1:5–4:15*, in
J.L. Crenshaw – S. Sandmel (eds.), *The Divine Helmsman. Studies on God's Control of
Human Events Presented to Lou H. Silberman*, New York, 1980, pp. 129-141. *The Acts
of the Apostles: Monograph or "Bios"?*, in Witherington (ed.), *History, Literature,
and Society* (n. 24), pp. 58-72. C.H. Talbert – P.L. Stepp, *Succession in Mediterranean
Antiquity*, in *SBL 1998 Seminar Papers*, pp. 148-179 (in two parts). — For discussion, cf.
D.L. Barr, *The Conventions of Classical Biography and the Genre of Luke–Acts. A Preliminary Study*, in Talbert (ed.), *New Perspectives* (n. 24), pp. 63-98, L.C.A. Alexander, *Acts and Ancient Intellectual Biography*, in Winter–Clarke (eds.), *The Book of
Acts* (n. 4), pp. 31-64, and the articles by M.C. Parsons, J.B. Chance, and D.P. Moessner,
and Talbert's response in Parsons–Tyson (eds.), *Cadbury, Knox, and Talbert* (n. 26),
pp. 133-240.

212. *Literary Patterns*, p. 135.

affinities of Luke's work with ancient historiography[213]. In particular, it was asked which kind of historical work Luke has written. Indeed, "die antike Geschichtsschreibung hat viele Gesichter"[214], and the historical monograph represents but one type among others. According to D.E. Aune, Lk–Acts belongs to the subgenre "general history" which describes the history of a "nation" (in Lk–Acts, the Christian "nation") from its (mythic) origins to the author's own time. For Aune, the unity of genre is not something that would add proof to the assumption of the unity of Luke's work but it is the logical consequence from it. Because it constitutes a unity, Lk–Acts "*must* be treated as affiliated with *one* genre"[215]. But there are several other proposals. G.E. Sterling defines Lk–Acts as "apologetic historiography", a subgenre that narrates the history of a particular group, written by one of their own, in order to give the group an identity in a world that only recently has heard of it[216]. C.K. Barrett calls it "a popular history" with apologetic tendencies[217]. D.L. Balch argues that Luke "imitates and dramatically revises" the genre of political historiography, but was also influenced by ancient biography[218]. For H. Cancik Lk–Acts is "institutional history"[219]. Still others have invented a genus mixtum such as "historical novel"[220].

213. This was the subject of the contribution of van Unnik to the colloquium of 1977: W.C. VAN UNNIK, *Luke's Second Book and the Rules of Hellenistic Historiography*, in KREMER (ed.), *Les Actes des Apôtres* (n. 2), pp. 37-60. Cf. also ID., *Éléments artistiques dans l'évangile de Luc*, in NEIRYNCK (ed.), *L'évangile de Luc* (n. 1), pp. 129-140 (= 1989, 39-50). Cf. T. CALLAN, *The Preface of Luke–Acts and Historiography*, in *NTS* 31 (1985) 576-581.

214. PLÜMACHER, *Acta-Forschung* (n. 23), p. 150.

215. D.E. AUNE, *The New Testament in Its Literary Environment* (Library of Early Christianity, 8), Philadelphia, PA, 1987, pp. 77-115, here 80. This leads to the conclusion that, though the Gospel taken separately "could be classified as a type of ancient biography", it is not, because "Acts cannot be forced into a biographical mold" (77).

216. G.E. STERLING, *Historiography and Self-Definition. Josephos, Luke–Acts and Apologetic Historiography* (NTSup, 64), Leiden, 1992, pp. 17 and 311-389; cf. also *SBL 1989 Seminar Papers*, pp. 326-342.

217. BARRETT, *The First New Testament?* (n. 77), p. 101; *Acts* (n. 85), 2, p. LI: Acts provides the Church leaders of Luke's time with "a set of Christian ideals which would show them what their own Christian life should be"; but see below n. 228.

218. D.L. BALCH, *Comments on the Genre and a Political Theme of Luke–Acts. A Preliminary Comparison of Two Hellenistic Historians*, in *SBL 1989 Seminar Papers*, pp. 343-361, esp. 360-361 (Luke compared with Dionysius of Halicarnassus). Cf. also *The Genre of Luke–Acts: Individual Biography, Adventure Novel, or Political History?*, in *Southwestern Journal of Theology* 33 (1990) 5-19.

219. H. CANCIK, *The History of Culture, Religion, and Institutions in Ancient Historiography: Philological Observations Concerning Luke's History*, in *JBL* 116 (1997) 673-695.

220. R.J. KARRIS, *Windows and Mirrors: Literary Criticism and Luke's Sitz im Leben*, in *SBL 1979 Seminar Papers*, pp. 47-58, here 53.

A second tendency is to compare Lk–Acts with other genres besides historiography. V.K. Robbins, in line with Talbert, regards it, because of its purpose, as a "didactic biography"[221]. S. Praeder classifies Luke's work as a Christian adaptation of the ancient novel[222]. The qualification is essential: the work was not written to entertain but to communicate a theological message of salvation. Praeder insists that "in generic study as in theological study, Acts cannot be considered apart from its companion volume Luke"[223]. On this point she radically differs from R.I. Pervo who argues that the category of the novel is most appropriate to study the Book of Acts, but only Acts. Horace's "profit with delight" expresses its essence: Acts is an "edifying historical novel"[224]. It is impossible, however, to press both Lk and Acts into the same genre[225]. Most recently, L.C.A. Alexander has proposed yet another candidate. From her analysis of Luke's prefaces, which more closely resemble those of scientific treatises than of historiographical writings, she concludes that Lk–Acts was written "from within a Christian social context which is in significant respects like that of the hellenistic schools themselves"[226].

The search through ancient literature for the one genre that fits both the Gospel and Acts is probably not ended, but appears to be frustrating. It is no wonder, then, that some are inclined to conclude that it is an impossible, or better, an inadequate project[227]. But this does not have to mean that Lk–Acts do belong to different genres. "The whole work demonstrates affinities both to historical monographs and to biographies, but it appears to represent a new type of work, of which it is the only example"[228].

221. V.K. ROBBINS, *Prefaces in Greco-Roman Biography and Luke–Acts*, in *SBL 1978 Seminar Papers*, pp. 193-207, here 193; = *PerspRelSt* 6 (1979) 94-108.

222. S. PRAEDER, *Luke–Acts and the Ancient Novel*, in *SBL 1981 Seminar Papers*, pp. 269-292, esp. 289.

223. *Ibid.*, p. 283.

224. R.I. PERVO, *Profit With Delight. The Literary Genre of the Acts of the Apostles*, Philadelphia, PA, 1987, p. 137.

225. Compare the contrast he makes in the preface between the "popular" Acts and "Luke's serious theological program" which is supposedly found in the Gospel only (p. xii). See also *Must Luke and Acts Belong to the Same Genre?*, in *SBL 1989 Seminar Papers*, pp. 309-316.

226. ALEXANDER, *Preface* (n. 68), p. 211. In a more recent publication she rather emphasizes that the boundaries between fact and fiction are less clearly marked in Acts than is usually assumed and that Luke, in a sense, plays a dangerous game with his audience: *Fact, Fiction and the Genre of Acts*, in *NTS* 44 (1998) 380-399, esp. pp. 397-398.

227. See, e.g., KÜMMEL, *Einleitung*, p. 132.

228. MARSHALL, *"Former Treatise"* (n. 4), p. 180. Cf. C.J. HEMER, *The Book of Acts in the Setting of Hellenistic History*, ed. C.H. Gempf (WUNT, 49), Tübingen, 1989, pp. 33-43 and 63-100. BARRETT, *Acts* (n. 85), 2, p. LXXIX.

IV. The Composition of Lk–Acts

Luke made use of written sources in his Gospel and maybe also in Acts, though as it is well known this is a much more difficult question[229], but only exceptionally has it been argued that the material of Acts and that of the Gospel had in one way or another already been brought together in writing in his tradition. The assumption of P. Feine that Luke relied on a source that covered part of his Gospel and of Acts is an aspect of the Proto-Lk hypothesis that did not find wide acceptance later on[230], though it seems it has never completely been given up (see the recent publications by M.-É. Boismard and T.L. Brodie[231]). In their

229. For the renewed interest in source criticism and in the traditions that Luke has integrated in Acts, see G. Lüdemann, *Das frühe Christentum nach den Traditionen der Apostelgeschichte. Ein Kommentar*, Göttingen, 1987 (ET *Early Christianity according to the Traditions in Acts*, Minneapolis, MN, 1989) and C.J. Hemer, *The Book of Acts* (n. 228), esp. pp. 335-364 (sources in Acts) and 312-335 (the "We-passages"), who both emphasize that a reconstruction of such sources or traditions is very much hindered by the impact of Luke's redaction on his material. Cf. also the series of *The Book of Acts in Its First Century Setting* (above n. 24). — For studies of specific passages, see, e.g., J. Wehnert, *Die Wir-Passagen der Apostelgeschichte. Ein lukanisches Stilmittel aus jüdischer Tradition* (GTA, 40), Göttingen, 1989, esp. pp. 125-180. C.-J. Thornton, *Der Zeuge des Zeugen. Lukas als Historiker der Paulusreisen* (WUNT, 56), Tübingen, 1991, esp. 84-367 ("die Wir-Erzählungen"). J. Pichler, *Paulusrezeption in der Apostelgeschichte* (Innsbrucker theologische Studien, 50), Innsbruck, 1997. P.L. Dickerson, *The Sources of the Account of the Mission to Samaria in Acts 8:5-25*, in *NT* 39 (1997) 210-234: "Luke joined three sources" and not two as C.K. Barrett had suggested earlier in *Light on the Holy Spirit from Simon Magus (Acts 8,4-25)*, in Kremer (ed.), *Les Actes des Apôtres* (n. 2), pp. 281-295, here 284. Cf. also above n. 121 and below n. 231. — The source–critical problem of the Book of Acts constitutes an important section in the commentaries of Barrett, Fitzmyer, and Jervell. According to Jervell (*Apg*, pp. 61-72) Luke made use of many oral sources throughout Acts, and of more extensive written sources in Acts 13–20 (his own notes on Paul's mission) and in Acts 21–28 (not the acts of the process itself but an elogy of Paul's courageous attitude before the authorities); the "Itinerar" hypothesis is less certain (p. 64). Fitzmyer, in line with P. Benoit, also remains convinced that Luke must have had access to substantial source material, esp. concerning Paul and his missionary journeys (see the references to the "Pauline source" on pp. 85-88), but he admits that source criticism of Acts is "largely a speculative question" (p. 80) and recognizes that Luke's redactional treatment of his material has made the reconstruction of these sources an almost impossible task.

230. Cf. P. Feine, *Eine vorkanonische Überlieferung des Lukas in Evangelium und Apostelgeschichte. Eine Untersuchung*, Gotha, 1891, esp. pp. 236-252 (here 236). See also Sahlin, *Der Messias und das Gottesvolk* (n. 95), pp. 11-18. Compare with the "classic" presentation of the hypothesis by B.H. Streeter in which the source is limited to the Gospel: B.H. Streeter, *The Four Gospels. A Study of Origins*, London, 1924, pp. 199-222, esp. 214-217 ("The reconstruction of Proto-Luke") and 222; on Lk and Acts, cf. pp. 529-562.

231. M.-É. Boismard – A. Lamouille, *Les Actes des deux Apôtres*, I (ÉB, 20), Paris, 1990, esp. pp. 3-5 and 26-30. Cf. the review by J. Taylor, *The Making of Acts: A New Account*, in *RB* 97 (1990) 504-524. Taylor is currently publishing an historical commen-

reconstruction of the history of composition of Acts, M.-É. Boismard and A. Lamouille single out an early stage "Act I" in which Acts was not yet separated from the Gospel (Proto-Luke). In his recent study of the sources of the Gospel, Boismard also distinguishes three stages (L or Proto-Luc, Luc, l'ultime Rédacteur) which have a counterpart in the composition of Acts. "Proto-Luc" was written before 70 and reworked ("Luc – Act II") by the "historical Luke", the companion of Paul; a disciple of Luke was responsible for the final redaction[232].

For the large majority of scholars, however, the narrative unity of Lk–Acts is essentially the result of Luke's redaction. An important indication for this can be found in the coherency of the vocabulary and style of Lk–Acts, though for J. Jeremias, e.g., Luke in this respect remains also largely indebted to his tradition, whereas J.M. Dawsey points out that the evidence should not obscure the fact that there are instances that need further investigation[233]. A contribution from an unexpected corner

tary on Acts building on Boismard's literary-critical analysis: *Les Actes des deux Apôtres*, V (ÉB, 23), Paris, 1994 (Acts 9–18,22) and VI (ÉB, 30), 1996 (18,23–28,31). See also *The Book of Acts and History*, in *ScriptBull* 25 (1995) 66-76. — Among the publications of T.L. BRODIE, note esp. *Reopening the Quest for Proto-Luke: The Systematic Use of Judges 6–12 in Luke 16:1–18:8*, in *Journal of Higher Criticism* 2 (1995) 68-101 and *Intertextuality and Its Use in Tracing Q and Proto-Luke*, in TUCKETT (ed.), *The Scriptures in the Gospels* (n. 167), pp. 469-477 (with an outline of Proto-Lk on p. 473). See below, pp. 627-638.

    232. Cf. M.-É. BOISMARD, *En quête du Proto-Luc* (ÉB, 37), Paris, 1997, pp. 124, 333, and 341-342. A crucial text in the reconstruction and the dating of "Proto-Luc" is the apocalyptic discourse in Lk 21 (see the analysis on pp. 40-62); for a survey of earlier research, see J. VERHEYDEN, *The Source(s) of Luke 21*, in NEIRYNCK (ed.), *L'évangile de Luc* (n. 1), 1989, pp. 491-516.

    233. J. JEREMIAS, *Die Sprache des Lukasevangeliums. Redaktion und Tradition im Nicht-Markusstoff des dritten Evangeliums* (KEK, Sb), Göttingen, 1980. J.M. DAWSEY, *The Literary Unity of Luke–Acts: Questions of Style – a Task for Literary Critics*, in *NTS* 35 (1989) 48-66.

    A special topic in this respect which has received less attention in past years is that of the semitisms. F. Horton, who surveys previous research, is critical of earlier attempts to regard all of them as evidence that Luke is translating semitic sources (C.C. Torrey) or as consequent imitations of the LXX (H.F.D. Sparks) and argues that they reflect the kind of "Jewish Greek" which flourished as "the religious vernacular of the synagogue" (cf. M. Black). J.M. Watt's sociolinguistic approach leads him to the conclusion that Luke was raised in a multilingual environment and probably was competent in Greek and in Aramaic (p. 91). See F.L. HORTON, *Reflections on the Semitisms of Luke–Acts*, in TALBERT (ed.), *Perspectives* (n. 24), pp. 1-23. J.M. WATT, *Code-Switching in Luke and Acts* (Berkeley Insights in Linguistics and Semiotics, 31), New York, 1997.

    For some other aspects of Luke's vocabulary and style in recent studies taking into account Lk and Acts, see, e.g., A. DAUER, *Beobachtungen zur literarischen Arbeitstechnik des Lukas* (BBB, 79), Frankfurt, 1990: an analysis of passages in which Luke introduces information for which the reader has not yet been prepared ("Ergänzungen" or "Nachträge"); Dauer's article in the 1989 FS for J. Gnilka is integrated in this book. G. MUSSIES, *Variation in the Book of Acts*, in *Filologia neotestamentaria* 4 (1991) 165-

is the long list of Lukan style characteristics which was drawn up by M.-É. Boismard and A. Lamouille in their work on the text of Acts to demonstrate that both the Western recension (in its primitive form) and the Alexandrian (or rather the original or "pre-Alexandrian") recension of Acts as they are reconstructed by Boismard and Lamouille are two authentically Lukan compositions, representing respectively Luke's first edition of Acts and his revision of this work[234]. The list was discussed and corrected by F. Neirynck who also compared it with similar surveys of the characteristic vocabulary of Luke's Gospel and of Acts[235]. The Lukan idioms in the Western text of Lk–Acts have become a major interest in text-critical studies in recent years. The question received some attention at the Acts colloquium of 1977[236]. Subsequent research is surveyed by, among others, J. Delobel[237].

The structure and composition of Lk–Acts and Luke's narrative techniques are the central focus in the many narrative- or literary-critical studies of Luke's work, of which that of R.C. Tannehill is the most elaborate one[238], though it must be said that these analyses on important

182, esp. pp. 175-180 (Lk 24,51-53 par. Acts 1,2-14). D.L. MEALAND, *Luke–Acts and the Verbs of Dionysius of Halicarnassus*, in *JSNT* 63 (1996) 63-86. — Luke's rhetorical skills are studied by R. MORGENTHALER, *Lukas und Quintillian. Rhetorik als Erzählkunst*, Zürich, 1992 (the section on Acts is by H. Steichele), who takes up some of the perspectives of his monograph on *Die lukanische Geschichtsschreibung als Zeugnis* (1948) with the interest in the motif of (the disciples as) "double witness" (pp. 363-385) and who emphasizes the literary role of geography in Luke's work (pp. 341-355). See also W.S. KURZ, *Hellenistic Rhetoric in the Christological Proof of Luke–Acts*, in *CBQ* 42 (1980) 171-195 and F. SIEGERT, *Communication de masse et rythmes de prose dans Luc/Actes*, in *RHPR* 74 (1994) 113-127 (ET 1993).

234. M.-É. BOISMARD – A. LAMOUILLE, *Le texte Occidental des Actes des Apôtres. Reconstitution et réhabilitation*, 2 vols., Paris, 1984 (esp. II, pp. 195-335: "Index des caractéristiques stylistiques"). See also the adapted list for the Gospel in BOISMARD, *Proto-Luc* (n. 232), pp. 15-39.

235. F. NEIRYNCK, *Le texte des Actes des Apôtres et les caractéristiques stylistiques lucaniennes*, in *ETL* 61 (1985) 304-339 (esp. pp. 315-332); repr. in ID., *Evangelica* II (BETL, 99), Leuven, 1991, pp. 243-278 (esp. 254-271).

236. Cf. C.M. MARTINI, *La tradition textuelle des Actes des Apôtres et les tendances de l'Église ancienne* and M. WILCOX, *Luke and the Bezan Text of Acts*, in KREMER (ed.), *Les Actes des Apôtres* (n. 2), pp. 21-35 and 447-455 resp.

237. J. DELOBEL, *Focus on the "Western" Text in Recent Studies*, in *ETL* 73 (1997) 401-410; see now also below, pp. 83-107. Other surveys by P.M. HEAD, *Acts and the Problem of Its Texts*, in WINTER–CLARKE (eds.), *The Book of Acts* (n. 4), pp. 415-444, and by W.A. STRANGE, *The Problem of the Text of Acts* (SNTS MS, 71), Cambridge, 1992, pp. 1-34 (with an analysis of three test cases on pp. 57-106).

238. R.C. TANNEHILL, *The Narrative Unity of Luke–Acts. A Literary Interpretation*. Vol. 1: *The Gospel according to Luke*, Philadelphia, PA, 1986; vol. 2: *The Acts of the Apostles*, Minneapolis, MN, 1990. Tannehill has a thematical arrangement in the first volume (the birth narrative, the beginning of the ministry of John and of Jesus, Jesus as preacher and healer, the ministry to the oppressed, the crowds, the confrontation with the authorities, the disciples, the risen Lord) but for Acts he follows the structure of the book.

points often only seem to confirm to a large degree the results of sound redaction-critical investigations. Among the many narrative techniques which have been examined in Lk–Acts, including parentheses[239], chiasm as a major structuring principle[240], the device of irony[241], or the way Luke presents particular characters and introduces new characters into his narrative[242], two are of special importance because they are characteristic of Luke and because they express the intended unity of the narrative in a specific way.

The first of these is Luke's fondness of parallels. This feature of his composition was intensively studied in the seventies by C.H. Talbert, W. Radl, G. Muhlack, and F. Neirynck. C.H. Talbert drew a list of such correspondences in the narratives of the Gospel and of the Book of Acts and came to the "irresistible" conclusion that "this architectonic pattern which has Gospel and Acts correspond in content and in sequence at many points is due to deliberate editorial activity by the author of Luke–Acts"[243]. W. Radl studied the parallelism between Jesus and Paul, esp. in the passion narrative of the Gospel and the trial stories in Acts, and likewise argued that this composition is the result of "eine bewusste

---

— See also KARRIS, *Windows and Mirrors* (above n. 220). W.S. KURZ, *Narrative Approaches to Luke–Acts*, in *Bib* 68 (1987) 195 220 and *Reading Luke–Acts. Dynamics of Biblical Narrative*, Louisville, KY, 1993, who pays great attention to the narrators in Lk and in Acts (pp. 39-131) and to the device of implicit commentary (pp. 135-155), and has a section on canonical criticism to which he now returned in *The Open-ended Nature of Luke and Acts as Inviting Canonical Actualisation*, in *Neotestamentica* 31 (1997) 289-308. R.L. BRAWLEY, *Centering on God. Method and Message in Luke–Acts* (Literary Currents in Biblical Interpretation), Louisville, KY, 1990. K. SYREENI, *The Gospel in Paradigms: A Study in the Hermeneutical Space of Luke–Acts*, in LUOMANEN (ed.), *Scandinavian Perspectives* (n. 24), pp. 36-57 (on the paradigmatic function of certain scenes and characters). J.A. DARR, *On Character Building. The Reader and the Rhetoric of Characterization in Luke–Acts* (Literary Currents in Biblical Interpretation), Louisville, KY, 1992; *Herod the Fox* (n. 151), pp. 64-91; and his articles in *SBL 1992 Seminar Papers*, pp. 255-265 and in *Semeia* 63 (1993) 43-60. F.S. SPENCER, *Acts and Modern Literary Approaches*, in WINTER–CLARKE (eds.), *The Book of Acts* (n. 4), pp. 381-414. A. DEL AGUA, *La interprétación del "relato" en la doble obra lucana*, in *EE* 71 (1996) 169-214. J.-N. ALETTI, *Quand Luc raconte. Le récit comme théologie* (Lire la Bible, 115), Paris, 1998.

239. S.M. SHEELEY, *Narrative Asides in Luke–Acts* (JSNT SS, 72), Sheffield, 1992.
240. Cf. TALBERT, *Literary Patterns* (n. 211), pp. 51-58.
241. J.L. RAY, *Narrative Irony in Luke–Acts. The Paradoxical Interaction of Prophetic Fulfillment and Jewish Rejection* (Mellen Biblical Press Series, 28), Lewiston, Ont., 1996. Cf. above, n. 180 (Moessner) and 184 (Talbert). — On irony in the Gospel: J.M. DAWSEY, *The Lukan Voice. Confusion and Irony in the Gospel of Luke*, Macon, GA, 1986, esp. pp. 123-156.
242. Cf. R.S. ASCOUGH, *Narrative Technique and Generic Designation. Crowd Scenes in Luke–Acts and in Chariton*, in *CBQ* 58 (1996) 69-81. P.L. DICKERSON, *The New Character Narrative in Luke–Acts and the Synoptic Problem*, in *JBL* 116 (1997) 291-312.
243. *Literary Patterns* (n. 211), pp. 15-23 (quotation from 23).

Parallelisierung durch Lukas"[244]. Luke takes up a procedure ("Synkrisis") that was known to him from the Hellenistic biographical tradition[245], and uses it to undergird his understanding of salvation history and of the role of the Church in its relation to the ministry of Jesus[246]. For G. Muhlack, who analyzed a selection of passages from the miracle stories, the community life, and the missionary speeches, the parallelism exemplifies how the life and preaching of the disciples, like that of Jesus, is ruled by the Spirit and contributes to the realization of the Kingdom. "Um den Weg des Evangeliums darzustellen, schildert Lukas Ausschnitte aus dem Leben der Apostel. Sie zeigen, dass christliches Leben zum Gottesreich hinführt"[247]. At the 1977 colloquium on Acts, F. Neirynck offered a comprehensive study of the miracle stories in Acts in which he included a rich documentation of earlier research on the Jesus – Peter/Paul parallels[248]. The parallelism between Jesus and the disciples was also the subject of an article by R.F. O'Toole[249]. A parallelism that is primarily found in the Gospel is that between Jesus and John the Baptist, but according to P. Böhlemann this parallel extends into Acts, and he even regards it as an hermeneutical key to Luke's theology and to his writing of Lk–Acts[250].

---

244. W. RADL, *Paulus und Jesus im lukanischen Doppelwerk. Untersuchungen zu Parallelmotiven im Lukasevangelium und in der Apostelgeschichte* (EHS, 23/49), Bern–Frankfurt, 1975, p. 230.

245. Radl did not yet know the work of Talbert and compared Lk–Acts with Plutarch's *Vitae parallelae* (pp. 352-354).

246. "Die Voraussetzung der Parallelisierung bei Lukas ist die Grundüberzeugung, dass der Ablauf der Heilsgeschichte Gottes Plan entspricht" (p. 376; cf. 369-395: "Die theologische Bedeutung der Parallelisierung").

247. G. MUHLACK, *Die Parallelen von Lukas-Evangelium und Apostelgeschichte* (Theologie und Wirklichkeit, 8), Frankfurt–Bern, 1979, p. 144.

248. F. NEIRYNCK, *The Miracle Stories in the Acts of the Apostles. An Introduction*, in KREMER (ed.), *Actes des Apôtres* (n. 2), pp. 169-213, esp. 182-188 (= *Evangelica*, 1982, pp. 835-879, 848-854). See also A.J. MATTILL, *The Jesus–Paul Parallels and the Purpose of Luke–Acts: H.H. Evans Reconsidered*, in *NT* 17 (1975) 15-46. D.P. MOESSNER, *The Christ Must Suffer. New Light on the Jesus–Peter, Stephen–Paul Parables in Luke–Acts*, in *NT* 28 (1986) 220-256. For a survey of recent research, see S. PRAEDER, *Jesus–Paul, Peter–Paul, and Jesus–Peter Parallelisms in Luke–Acts. A History of Reader Response*, in *SBL 1984 Seminar Papers*, pp. 23-39.

249. R.F. O'TOOLE, *Parallels between Jesus and His Disciples in Luke–Acts. A Further Study*, in *BZ* 27 (1983) 195-212; cf. ID., *The Unity of Luke's Theology* (n. 156), pp. 62-94.

250. Cf. BÖHLEMANN, *Jesus und der Täufer* (n. 153): "Es liesse sich nur mit Hilfe der 'Täuferstellen' eine plausible Gliederung des gesamten lukanischen Doppelwerkes erstellen" (p. 313). Böhlemann, a student of A. Lindemann, studies the John–Jesus parallels with regard to christology (pp. 213-274) and various aspects of Luke's ethical teaching (cf. above n. 153). See also the contribution on narrative parallelism in Lk–Acts by Lindemann in this volume (below, pp. 225-253).

It is obvious that Luke used the technique not only to draw out similarities between individual stories[251], but also to structure larger units in
his work[252]. It is even one of the basic formal principles in the composition of Lk–Acts[253]. Amidst this consensus, J.B. Green's "the existence
of parallels does not itself prove compositional unity" sounds like a dis-
sonant, but appears to be a view which he does not share himself as he
then goes on arguing that narrative parallelism is Luke's means of representing, not what actually happened, but "reality as he understood
it"[254].

The second "marker" that needs to be mentioned here is the discourse
of Lk 4,16-30. For the second edition of the congress volume on Luke
(1989), C. Schreck reviewed the incredible amount of literature on the
Nazareth pericope that had appeared between 1973 and 1988[255]. He dis-

251. See, e.g., W. KIRCHSCHLÄGER, *Fieberheilung in Apg 28 und Lk 4*, in KREMER
(ed.), *Les Actes des Apôtres* (n. 2), pp. 509-521. T.Y. MULLINS, *New Testament Commission Forms, Especially in Luke–Acts*, in *JBL* 95 (1976) 603-614, pp. 609-613 and
B.J. HUBBARD, *Commissioning Stories in Luke–Acts. A Study of Their Antecedents, Form
and Content*, in *Semeia* 8 (1977) 103-126. R.F. O'TOOLE, *"You Did Not Lie to Us
(Human Beings) but to God" (Acts 5,4c)*, in *Bib* 76 (1995) 182-209, esp. pp. 204-207
(Lk 4,1-13; the Judas Story in Lk 22). — See also the comparison between Acts 8,26-40
and the Emmaus story in Lk 24,13-35 which is often mentioned: J.M. GIBBS, *Luke 24:13-
33 and Acts 8:26-39. The Emmaus Incident and the Eunuch's Baptism as Parallel Stories*, in *Bangalore Theol. Forum* 7 (1975) 17-30. C.H. LINDIJER, *Two Creative Encounters
in the Work of Luke. Luke xxiv,13-35 and Acts viii,26-40*, in T. BAARDA, et al. (eds.), *Mis-
cellanea neotestamentica* 2 (NTSup, 48), Leiden, 1978, pp. 77-85. É. CHARPENTIER,
L'officier éthiopien (Ac 8,26-40) et les disciples d'Emmaus (Lc 24,13-35), in *La Pâque du
Christ. Mystère du Salut. Mélanges F.-X. Durrwell* (LD, 112), Paris, 1982, 197-201.
B.P. ROBINSON, *The Place of the Emmaus Story in Luke–Acts*, in *NTS* 30 (1984) 481-497.
S. SCHREIBER, *"Verstehst du denn, was du liest?". Beobachtungen zur Begegnung von
Philippus und dem äthiopischen Eunuchen (Apg 8,26-40)*, in *SNTU* 21 (1996) 42-72, esp.
pp. 53-55 (Lk 24,13-35).
252. Cf. D.R. MIESNER, *The Missionary Journeys Narrative. Patterns and Implications*, in TALBERT (ed.), *Perspectives* (n. 24), pp. 199-214; also *the Circumferential
Speeches of Luke–Acts. Patterns and Purpose*, in *SBL 1978 Seminar Papers*, 2, pp. 223-
238. MOESSNER, *Lord of the Banquet*, pp. 294-307 (the travel narrative in Lk and Acts).
253. Thus, e.g., P. ROLLAND, *L'organisation du Livre des Actes et de l'ensemble de
l'œuvre de Luc*, in *Bib* 65 (1984) 81-86 (with Jerusalem as the focus). Ó FEARGHAIL, *The
Introduction to Luke–Acts* (n. 54), pp. 39-84. See now also T. BERGHOLZ, *Der Aufbau des
lukanischen Doppelwerkes. Untersuchungen zum formalliterarischen Charakter von
Lukas-Evangelium und Apostelgeschichte* (EHS, 23/545), Frankfurt, 1995: parallelism is
the literary expression of the theological purpose of Luke to emphasize for his readers
their responsibility to continue in the lines of Jesus and of his disciples.
254. J.B. GREEN, *Internal Repetition in Luke–Acts: Contemporary Narratology and
Lucan Historiography*, in WITHERINGTON (ed.), *History, Literature, and Society* (n. 24),
pp. 283-299, esp. 284 and 299.
255. C. SCHRECK, *The Nazareth Pericope: Luke 4,16-30 in Recent Study*, in NEIRYNCK
(ed.), *L'évangile de Luc* (n. 1), 1989, pp. 399-471. Another survey was published at the same
time by S.J. NOORDA, *Historia vitae magistra. Een beoordeling van de geschiedenis van de
uitleg van Lucas 4,16-30 als bijdrage aan de hermeneutische discussie*, Utrecht, 1989.

tinguishes three major areas of interest in the discussion on 4,16-30: source criticism[256]; the internal coherency of the passage; and its signif-icance as a "programmatic discourse" within the composition of Lk–Acts, in portraying Jesus as prophet and/or Messiah[257], and in announcing two of the key motifs of the Book of Acts, Israel's rejection of Jesus and the mission to the Gentiles that results from it (4,25-27), and the social dimension of the Christian message (4,18-19). But, as Schreck points out, scholars "still fiercely disagree on the nature of the program"[258], which can even result in scepticism about the program-matic status of the discourse. Thus, the prevailing view that Lk 4,16-30 is a model for or a prefiguration of the development of the Christian mis-sion in Acts[259] was challenged in the late eighties by authors who either stressed that Luke in 4,25-27 depicts the universalism and conciliatory intent of Jesus' mission (in line with that of the OT prophets Elijah and Elisha)[260], or simply denied that the Gentile mission was already at stake in Luke's opening discourse[261]. In the former of these interpretations, the

256. Of course the text was on the programme of the 1968 colloquium where J. Delo-bel critically examined H. Schürmann's so-called "Bericht vom Anfang" that had been incorporated in Luke's Q-text and argued that the introductory summary of 4,14-16a is best understood as the result of Luke's redaction of Mk. Cf. J. DELOBEL, La rédaction de Lc. iv,14-16a et le "Bericht vom Anfang", in NEIRYNCK (ed.), L'évangile de Luc (n. 1), pp. 203-223 (= 1989, 113-133 and add. note 306-312). Lk 4,16-30 made its reappearance in the 1982 meeting on the sayings material in the Gospels in a contribution by C.M. Tuckett who, in an adaptation of Schürmann's suggestion, ascribed vv. 16-21.23.25-27 to Q, and opposed Luke's redaction in Acts 10,38 to his use of Is 61,1 in Lk 4,18 and 7,22 (Q), a contrast which to F. Neirynck seemed "bien artificiel". Cf. C.M. TUCKETT, Luke 4, Isaiah and Q, in J. DELOBEL (ed.), Logia. Les Paroles de Jésus – The Sayings of Jesus (BETL, 59), Leuven, 1982, pp. 343-354 (rev. in C.M. TUCKETT, Q and the History of Early Christianity. Studies on Q, Edinburgh, 1996, pp. 226-237). F. NEIRYNCK, Actes 10,36-43 et l'Évangile, in ETL 60 (1984) 109-117, here 117 (= Evangelica II, pp. 227-236).
257. See, e.g., STRAUSS, The Davidic Messiah in Luke–Acts (n. 198), pp. 199-260. R.F. O'TOOLE, Does Luke Also Portray Jesus as the Christ in Luke 4,16-30?, in Bib 76 (1995) 498-522. O'Toole argues that Luke on the basis of Isa 61,1-2 presents Jesus not only as a prophet or as the Servant of the Lord but also as the Christ and the Anointed One, in line with Lk 3,15-17; 2,25-35; 7,18-23 and Acts 4,27 and 10,38.
258. The Nazareth Pericope (n. 255), p. 399.
259. See the references in SCHRECK, The Nazareth Pericope, pp. 443-444. Cf. now also J.S. SIKER, "First to the Gentiles": A Literary Analysis of Luke 4.16-30, in JBL 111 (1992) 73-90. KORN, Die Geschichte Jesu (n. 54), pp. 56-85.
260. Schreck mentions B.J. KOET, "Today This Scripture Has Been Fulfilled in Your Ears". Jesus' Explanation of Scripture in Luke 4,16-30, in Bijdragen 47 (1986) 368-394, esp. pp. 384-390, = Five Studies on Interpretation of Scripture in Luke–Acts (SNTA, 14), Leuven, 1989, pp. 24-55 (here 44-50) and R.L. BRAWLEY, Luke–Acts and the Jews (n. 180), pp. 4-12. See also DENOVA, The Things Accomplished Among Us (n. 172), pp. 126-154.
261. Thus, R.J. MILLER, Elijah, John, and Jesus in the Gospel of Luke, in NTS 34 (1988) 611-622, esp. 615. W. WIEFEL, Lk, 1988, p. 107.

Nazareth pericope – though no longer foreshadowing a dramatic evolution – still retains a programmatic function which should also direct our understanding of Luke's description of the mission of the disciples in Acts; in the latter view, however, the passage has greatly lost its significance as a structuring component of Luke's narrative[262].

CONCLUSION

It was not my intention (and I quote once more from Cadbury) to "repeat all that has been well said before, nor to refute all that has been ill said"[263]. I have paid special attention to the works of Cadbury and Conzelmann, who remain the cornerstones of all subsequent research on Lk–Acts. I also reviewed some of the literature of the last two or three decades to illustrate somewhat the diversity and the complexity of the issue. And I have sketched some of the major developments and indicated some of the problems and of the areas in which discussion involving the unity of Luke's work has been going on. It appeared that the large majority of scholars still holds to the view that Luke intended to write a work that covered both the story of Jesus and that of his disciples, and that he has composed this work in such a way that what is said about the history of Jesus contains all that which was regarded as important for continuing that history by the community that had committed itself to Jesus. This means that the Gospel is the introduction to Acts and the basis upon which Acts is built, but also that the Gospel, in a sense, needs Acts and calls for the continuation in which its message is realized in the world, and consequently that Lk and Acts together constitute one work.

A. Thiérylaan 32   Joseph VERHEYDEN
B-3001 Leuven

---

262. The significance of the discourse in 4,16-30 for the whole of Luke's work is studied in this volume by F. Neirynck (below, pp. 357-395).
263. *Commentary on the Preface of Luke* (n. 30), p. 489.

LUC-ACTES: UNE UNITÉ À CONSTRUIRE

En 1977, à l'occasion du 28ᵉ *Colloquium Biblicum* de Louvain consacré aux Actes des apôtres, Jacques Dupont tenait une conférence sur «La
conclusion des Actes et son rapport à l'ensemble de l'ouvrage de Luc»[1].
Ce grand exégète, à qui la recherche sur les Actes est immensément
redevable, savait allier la minutie de l'analyse littéraire à l'ampleur du
questionnement théologique. En l'occurrence, il anticipait sans le savoir
un axiome de l'analyse narrative, qui est le principe téléologique: l'intention d'une œuvre se dévoile à partir de sa fin. Jacques Dupont poin-
tait à l'époque sur la conclusion du livre des Actes (28,16-31), où il per-
cevait l'aboutissement du programme théologique lucanien sur
l'ouverture du salut aux nations; mais surtout, de proche en proche,
Dupont remontait en amont dans le récit, pour identifier l'esquisse de ce
programme au seuil de la mission paulinienne (Ac 13,13-51: Antioche
de Pisidie), et plus en amont encore, dans les discours de Pierre à Jérusalem (2,38s; 3,22s), puis en Lc 24, et enfin dans la prédication inaugu-
rale de Jésus à Nazareth (Lc 4,17-27). «Nazareth, Antioche de Pisidie,
Rome: trois jalons d'une même histoire, trois situations permettant des
variations sur le même thème: le salut passe des Juifs aux Gentils.…
Implicitement posé dès le début de l'évangile, explicité à la charnière de
l'évangile et des Actes, ce problème passe au premier plan avec l'histoire des missions pauliniennes»[2].
Je ne discuterai pas ici la conclusion théologique de J. Dupont, qui mérite
nuance[3], mais je retiens sa perception d'un thème qui au long du récit lucanien est «implicitement posé», puis «explicité», puis «passe au premier

---

1. Contribution publiée dans J. KREMER (éd.), *Les Actes des Apôtres. Traditions,
rédaction, théologie* (BETL, 48), Gembloux, Duculot – Leuven, University Press, 1979,
p. 359-404; reprise dans J. DUPONT, *Nouvelles études sur les Actes des Apôtres* (LD,
118), Paris, Cerf, 1984, p. 457-511. Cette étude développait et prolongeait une réflexion
amorcée sous le titre *Le salut des gentils et la signification théologique du livre des Actes*,
in *NTS* 6 (1959-60) 132-155 et reprise dans *Études sur les Actes des Apôtres* (LD, 45),
Paris, Cerf, 1967, p. 393-419.
2. *La conclusion des Actes*, p. 508s.
3. L'ouverture aux nations ne se substitue pas au rapport avec le judaïsme dans
l'œuvre de Luc; Israël demeure pour le christianisme le lieu de l'origine, une origine per-
due, objet d'une rupture indésirée, mais dont la mémoire est indispensable à l'identité
chrétienne. J'ai étudié cette question dans *Juifs et chrétiens selon Luc-Actes*, in D. MAR-
GUERAT (éd.), *Le déchirement. Juifs et chrétiens au premier siècle* (Le Monde de la Bible,
32), Genève, Labor et Fides, 1996, p. 151-178.

plan». On voit ici mis en œuvre, remarquablement, ce que Henry Joel Cadbury a appelé en 1927 «the making of Luke-Acts»[4], i.e. la construction narrative de Lc-Ac. L'exégète américain est en effet le premier à avoir gratifié l'œuvre *ad Theophilum* de l'appellation «Luc-Actes»[5].

Il est vrai que ce label a dû attendre la critique rédactionnelle (*Redaktionsgeschichte*) pour être reçu dans la recherche; mais après Conzelmann[6], il s'est imposé (presque) sans réserve. Si l'unité d'auteur de l'évangile de Luc et des Actes, affirmée par l'Église ancienne[7], n'a jamais été sérieusement mise en doute, la recherche doit à Cadbury, puis à Martin Dibelius, l'impulsion à explorer au plan littéraire et théologique l'unité du diptyque lucanien. Depuis les années 1960, considérer dans l'évangile de Lc et le livre des Ac l'œuvre du même écrivain et la cristallisation d'une même théologie s'est imposé comme le cadre incontournable de toute recherche lucanienne. Dans son récent état de la recherche, Marcel Dumais le considère comme le premier «acquis» de l'exégèse des Actes[8]. Acquis ou proposition heuristique? J'y reviendrai. Force est de reconnaître, à tout le moins, que «Luc-Actes» représente une entité très récente dans l'histoire bi-millénaire de la lecture du Nouveau Testament.

En adoptant le concept littéraire «Luc-Actes», les exégètes sanctionnaient deux décisions de poids. La première, méthodologique, désavoue le dispositif canonique et soutient qu'une correcte lecture de l'œuvre lucanienne doit unir ce que le canon néotestamentaire a désuni. Cette mesure heuristique, disons-le, a été d'une incontestable fécondité; elle a permis de prendre la mesure, au travers de son œuvre, du Luc historien, du Luc écrivain et du Luc théologien. La seconde décision sanctionnée est celle de l'auteur anonyme de l'écrit à Théophile, que nous appelons Luc: l'«unité Luc-Actes» est un *hapax*, non seulement néotestamentaire mais chrétien, puisqu'aucun auteur après Luc n'osera appendre à l'histoire de Jésus celle des premiers chrétiens. À la différence de l'auteur du *Protévangile de Jacques*, Luc ne sacralise pas le passé, mais sanctifie la suite de l'évangile, le temps postpascal. Décision d'une envergure théologique considérable: elle fait de Luc le premier à avoir formulé le fondement de la foi chrétienne en termes d'εὐαγγέλιον καὶ ἀποστολικόν,

---

4. H.J. CADBURY, *The Making of Luke-Acts,* London, Macmillan, 1927.
5. Voir la contribution de J. Verheyden (*supra*, p. 3-56).
6. H. CONZELMANN, *Die Mitte der Zeit. Studien zur Theologie des Lukas* (BHT, 17), Tübingen, Mohr, [5]1964.
7. E. JACQUIER, *Les Actes des apôtres* (ÉB), Paris, Gabalda, 1926, p. LVI-LVII.
8. M. DUMAIS, *Les Actes des Apôtres. Bilan et orientations,* in ACEBAC, *«De bien des manières». La recherche biblique aux abords du XXIe siècle* (LD, 163), Montréal, Fides – Paris, Cerf, 1995, p. 313.

l'Évangile et l'Apôtre, ou, pour le dire avec les mots de C. K. Barrett qui ne craint pas l'anachronisme, «Luke-Acts is the first New Testament»[9].

Mais ici guettent les malentendus. Car, qu'appelle-t-on «unité» en narrativité? Si l'unité de pensée dans la correspondance paulinienne peut se déduire d'une permanence de vocabulaire, d'un emploi homogène des outils conceptuels, d'une cohérence dans les scénarios argumentatifs, qu'en est-il en régime narratif? Les mêmes signaux sont-ils décelables? À l'évidence, non. Un narrateur n'expose pas systématiquement ses vues comme on le fait en régime argumentatif; il les transmet obliquement *via* ses personnages, ou les distille au gré de ses commentaires (implicites ou explicites). Un conteur comme Luc ne livre pas toujours clairement ce qu'il pense. Bref, même si la narrativité n'exclut nullement la cohérence d'un système de pensée chez l'auteur, celle-ci se dérobe à une logique de type argumentatif. Je reprends la question: comment se repère l'unité de pensée en narrativité?

Des tensions internes à l'œuvre

Des voix se sont élevées récemment pour inviter à «repenser l'unité de Luc et Actes» (c'est le titre du livre de Parsons et Pervo)[10]. Ces deux auteurs font valoir des tensions internes à l'œuvre, dont je signale les principales.

L'évangile et les Actes relèvent de deux genres littéraires différents, le premier de type biographique, le second de type historiographique[11].
Évangile et Actes se distinguent par un traitement différencié des sources (Dibelius en 1923 attirait déjà l'attention sur ce point[12]); du point de vue stylis-

---

9. C.K. BARRETT, *The Third Gospel as a Preface to Acts? Some Reflections*, in *The Four Gospels 1992*. FS F. Neirynck, II (BETL, 100), Leuven, University Press – Peeters, 1992, p. 1462; ID., *The First New Testament?*, in *NT* 38 (1996) 94-104, surtout p. 102s.

10. M.C. PARSONS et R.I. PERVO, *Rethinking the Unity of Luke and Acts*, Minneapolis, Fortress, 1993. Voir aussi: J.M. DAWSEY, *The Literary Unity of Luke-Acts: Questions of Style – a Task for Literary Critics*, in *NTS* 35 (1989) 48-66. M.C. PARSONS, *The Unity of Lukan Writings: Rethinking the Opinio Communis*, in *With Steadfast Purpose. Essays in Honor of H.J. Flanders*, Waco, Baylor University, 1990, p. 29-53. Bien auparavant: A.C. CLARK, *The Acts of the Apostles*, Oxford, Clarendon, 1933, p. 393-405.

11. Pour tenter de sortir de l'impasse où se trouve plongée l'identification d'un même genre littéraire pour Lc et Ac, R.I. Pervo a lancé en 1989 un pavé dans la mare: faut-il vraiment affilier les deux écrits au même genre littéraire? *Must Luke and Acts Belong to the Same Genre?*, in *SBL SP* 1989, p. 309-316. Voir aussi M.C. PARSONS et R.I. PERVO, *Rethinking the Unity of Luke and Acts*, p. 20-44.

12. M. DIBELIUS, *Stilkritisches zur Apostelgeschichte* (1923), in *Aufsätze zur Apostelgeschichte* (FRLANT, 60), Göttingen, Vandenhoeck und Ruprecht, [5]1968, p. 9-28. Dibelius en concluait que la tradition kérygmatique primitive excluait tout récit sur les apôtres, ce qu'a contesté avec raison J. JERVELL *Zur Frage der Traditionsgrundlage der Apostelgeschichte*, in *ST* 16 (1962) 25-41, traduit dans *Luke and the People of God*, Minneapolis, Augsburg, 1972, p. 19-39.

tique, le morcellement narratif de l'évangile n'offre aucun équivalent aux grands discours des Actes ou aux séquences narratives de grande amplitude (Ac 3–5; 10–11; 13–14; 21–26).
Le lecteur passe d'une thématique centrée sur la βασιλεία τοῦ θεοῦ (Lc) à un kérygme foncièrement christologique (Ac).
La dualité justes / pécheurs (δίκαιος / ἁμαρτωλός), décisive dans l'évangile (Lc 5,32; 7,34s.39; 15,1-17; 18,9-14; 19,6-10), disparaît dans les Actes.
L'autorité de la Torah est maintenue dans son intégralité en Lc 16,17; pourtant, elle ne régit plus la sotériologie des Actes (cf. 15,10.28s!).
Le discours acéré du Jésus lucanien contre les riches (Lc 6,24s; 12,13-21; 20,47) et sur les dangers de la richesse (Lc 12,33s; 16,19-31; 18,18-30) a disparu dans les Actes, au profit d'une éthique du partage (Ac 2,42-45; 4,32-37) et d'une fixation sur les personnes fortunées et de haut rang (Ac 8,27; 9,36; 16,14; 17,34; 18,7; etc.).

Prenant appui sur ces disparités, Parsons et Pervo appellent à découpler Lc et Ac, dont ils ne contestent pas l'unité d'auteur, mais l'homogénéité tant littéraire que générique ou théologique. Sans plaider le divorce des deux livres, ils invitent à repenser le rapport de l'un à l'autre. «Les relations entre ces deux livres sont des relations *entre deux livres*, et non des correspondances à l'intérieur d'un tout séparé en deux pour des raisons de commodité»[13]. La remarque est bonne. Elle nous alerte sur le risque qu'entraîne le statut axiomatique conféré dans la recherche à l'entité Lc-Ac; ce risque est d'attribuer à l'auteur *ad Theophilum* une pensée massifiée, que l'on retrouve distribuée au gré des épisodes du macro-récit (c'est ainsi que j'appelle le grand récit de Lc 1 à Ac 28), sans égard aux discordances[14]. Mais si la proposition de découpler Lc et Ac est suspecte d'exacerber leurs tensions internes au détriment de leur unité, comment rendre compte du rapport entre deux livres? Dans une perspective narratologique, on se demandera si malgré ses tensions internes, le macro-récit provoque un effet d'unité à l'intention du lecteur, et par quels moyens.

Deux thèses sur l'unité du récit

Je défends la thèse suivante: le récit de Lc-Ac vise effectivement à provoquer un effet d'unité au plan théologique; mais cette unité n'est pas énoncée dans le texte, elle est donnée à construire dans la lecture comme une tâche dévolue au lecteur. Le seul métadiscours que Luc pré-

13. *Rethinking the Unity of Luke and Acts*, p. 126.
14. Les monographies de Robert O'TOOLE, *The Unity of Luke's Theology: An Analysis of Luke-Acts* (GNS, 9), Wilmington, Michael Glazier, 1984, et de Donald JUEL, *La promesse de l'histoire* (Lire la Bible, 80), Paris, Cerf, 1987, ne sont pas exemptes de ce risque.

sente sur son récit (Lc 1,1-4; Ac 1,1s) induit que l'auteur a conçu son œuvre en deux parties, puisqu'il taxe l'évangile de «première parole» (πρῶτος λόγος, Ac 1,1a); en revanche, cette articulation ne tranche pas sur la cohérence. La question de l'unité doit être résolue au niveau de la stratégie narrative mise en œuvre. Or, l'écriture d'un double récit «Jésus+apôtres» ne prévoit pas que la lecture se déroule *ad libitum*: en vertu de la disposition linéaire du récit, la lecture des Actes présuppose l'information contenue dans l'évangile. D'autre part, le principe téléologique de la lecture implique que le sens (et l'unité) d'une œuvre sont perceptibles à sa fin, au moment où l'œuvre apparaît en sa totalité. C'est donc par un jeu d'échos entre l'amont et l'aval du récit que le narrateur provoquera le lecteur à construire l'unité de la narration. Pratiquement, la tâche consiste à inventorier les indicateurs visant à unifier le monde du récit, et à s'assurer que la fin du récit corrobore la visée unificatrice.

Je défends une seconde thèse: la recherche d'unité dans un récit doit intégrer la présence de tensions et de ruptures inhérente au phénomène narratif. Stephen Moore a soutenu avec raison que tensions et déplacements sont intrinsèques à la narrativité, qui répugne à la systématisation du discours argumentatif[15]; on ajoutera que ce trait est encore plus vrai de la narration historique, car le récit historique est assigné à rendre compte d'une évolution, d'une histoire qui avance, d'un projet qui se déplace. Symptomatique de ce type d'écarts: la pneumatologie lucanienne, distribuée différemment selon qu'il s'agit de l'histoire d'Israël (les prophètes), de l'évangile (Jésus) ou des Actes (les apôtres, puis les croyants)[16]. La question devient alors: comment, dans un récit assigné à enregistrer des déplacements, le narrateur joue-t-il la continuité dans l'écart?

Il importe également de se demander comment le narrateur signale dans son récit les faits qui provoquent un rebondissement. À cet égard, le rôle joué par le tournant de Pâques (c'est justement la charnière sur laquelle tourne le diptyque lucanien) ne doit pas être sous-estimé. De toutes les variations stylistiques et terminologiques soigneusement observées entre l'évangile et les Actes par Albert Clark et James Dawsey[17], certaines sont explicables par la présence de sources; beaucoup sont redevables au tournant pascal. Il en est ainsi de l'emploi de μαθητής (qualifié par un pronom possessif dans l'évangile, absolu dans les

---

15. S. MOORE, *Are the Gospels Unified Narratives?*, in *SBL SP* 1987, p. 443-458.
16. J'ai étudié sous cet aspect la pneumatologie lucanienne dans mon livre *La première histoire du christianisme (Actes des apôtres)* (LD, 180), Paris, Cerf, 1999.
17. Voir les références à la n. 10.

Actes)[18] ou de la gestion différente des titres christologiques entre Luc (usage différencié) et les Actes (usage cumulatif)[19].

Dès lors, ma démarche opérera en trois temps. En premier lieu, je m'interrogerai sur les indices littéraires signalant que le narrateur compte avec une entité narrative Lc-Ac. Dans un deuxième temps, je présenterai trois modalités par lesquelles est induite chez le lecteur l'unification du monde narratif de Lc-Ac: la prolepse, la chaîne narrative et la modélisation. En troisième lieu, on s'attachera à deux déplacements théologiques remarqués au sein de l'œuvre à Théophile: le changement du statut de la Loi entre l'évangile et les Actes, d'une part, l'éthique économique lucanienne d'autre part; je voudrais montrer, sur ces cas d'espèce, de quelle façon Luc maintient l'unité de son œuvre tout en enregistrant le déplacement fort qu'entraîne l'événement christologique.

I. Luc-Actes, une entité narrative

Rétention d'information

Quels signes donnent à entendre *littérairement* que l'auteur a conçu comme un tout les 52 chapitres de Lc-Ac? De façon inattendue, la première indication vient de la critique des sources. À plus d'une reprise, l'examen des parallèles synoptiques fait voir en effet que le narrateur a délibérément retenu un motif de l'évangile pour le déplacer en direction des Actes. À chaque fois, la raison de ce transfert est de ménager un effet en aval du récit.

Lors du procès de Jésus au sanhédrin, le motif marcien du faux-témoignage sur la destruction du sanctuaire et sa reconstruction en trois jours (Mc 14,58) est sauté par Luc (cf. 22,66), qui le réinvestit avec Étienne (Ac 6,14). Luc aurait-il ignoré la présence d'une critique du Temple dans la tradition de Jésus? Un détail du libellé d'Ac 6,14 nous prouve le contraire, car subtilement, l'accusation contre Étienne invoque non une parole directe, mais une parole rapportée: «Nous l'avons entendu dire que ce Jésus le Nazoréen détruira ce lieu et changera les coutumes que nous a transmises Moïse». Luc ne méconnaît donc pas l'origine de la critique, mais la transfère du Maître au disciple. Pourquoi ce déplace-

---

18. Alors que dans l'évangile, μαθητής est le plus souvent déterminé par un pronom possessif (généralement οἱ μαθηταὶ αὐτοῦ), le terme apparaît au sens absolu dans les Actes où il figure comme une désignation ecclésiologique équivalente à οἱ πιστεύοντες (exception: Ac 9,1.25).

19. L'évangile de Luc atteste une gestion des titres christologiques (κύριος, διδάσκαλος, ἐπιστάτης, υἱὸς τοῦ ἀνθρώπου, χριστός) différenciée selon les personnages du récit. Les discours des Actes pratiquent l'accumulation des titres, reflet d'une concentration kérygmatique postpascale (voir par ex. Ac 3,13-21).

ment? La raison la plus proche est que le rôle joué par le Temple en Ac 1–5 n'aurait pas supporté la dégradation eschatologique que lui fait subir le logion de Marc.

Dans le même sens, la suspension de la Torah de pureté que statue Mc 7,1-23 n'a pas sa place avant la vision de Pierre en Ac 10; Luc la biffe, pour ne pas anticiper la levée de la barrière entre le pur et l'impur signifiée à l'apôtre (Ac 10,15 «Ce que Dieu a rendu pur, tu ne vas pas, toi, le déclarer immonde!»)[20]. Encore un exemple: le poids donné par le narrateur à la question du refus d'Israël, à la fin du macro-récit (Ac 28,16-31), l'a conduit à réduire au plus bref la citation d'Is 6,9s dans l'enseignement en paraboles (Lc 8,10b; diff. Mc 4,12 et Mt 13,14s); le but est de réserver à ses derniers versets la version intégrale, et par là le poids intégral, du texte prophétique (Ac 28,26s).

Décelée à trois reprises, cette rétention d'information dénote à tout le moins que le narrateur compte avec une intrigue dont l'achèvement est posé en Ac 28 plutôt qu'en Lc 24. Observer le procédé rhétorique de l'inclusion permettra de faire un pas de plus.

Des inclusions signifiantes

L'inclusion, qui rappelle en finale un motif initial, est un procédé rhétorique connu des narrateurs comme des orateurs pour faire apparaître l'unité du propos. On peut le considérer comme une opération de bouclage du récit.

En l'occurrence, chacun des volets du diptyque lucanien est cerclé par une inclusion signifiante. L'évangile va du Temple, où est annoncée la venue du Sauveur (Lc 1,5-25), au Temple où les disciples attendent la venue de l'Esprit (Lc 24,53); le récit est ainsi ancré dans la présence de Dieu à son peuple, à laquelle renvoie le lieu symbolique du Temple. Le livre des Actes se déploie entre la prédication du Ressuscité sur la βασιλεία τοῦ θεοῦ (Ac 1,3) et la prédication de Paul sur la βασιλεία τοῦ θεοῦ (Ac 28,31); la continuité essentielle du message est posée, mais complétée pour Paul par la mention d'un enseignement «sur ce qui concerne le Seigneur Jésus Christ» (continuité *et* déplacement).

L'ensemble de l'œuvre est surplombé à son tour par l'arc narratif que dessinent entre elles les deux références lucaniennes au «salut de Dieu»[21]: le salut de Dieu prédit par le Baptiste avec les mots d'Is 40,5 (Lc 3,6 καὶ ὄψεται πᾶσα σὰρξ τὸ σωτήριον τοῦ θεοῦ) et l'offre du

20. Bien vu par C.K. BARRETT, *The Third Gospel as a Preface to Acts?* (n. 9), p. 1456s.
21. La formule τὸ σωτήριον τοῦ θεοῦ n'apparaît pas ailleurs dans Lc-Ac. La troisième occurrence de σωτήριον dans l'œuvre de Luc est Lc 2,30 («mes yeux ont vu ton salut»).

salut de Dieu aux nations (Ac 28,28 τοῖς ἔθνεσιν ἀπεστάλη τοῦτο τὸ σωτήριον τοῦ θεοῦ), qui suit la longue citation d'Is 6,9s. Entre ces bornes narratives s'installe une circularité du récit, permettant au lecteur de vérifier quelle est la visée de la narration lucanienne[22]: elle se cristallise dans une histoire de salut, un salut prédit, incarné, annoncé, refusé par la majorité des juifs, offert finalement aux païens «qui l'écouteront, eux» (Ac 28,28b).

Que ce soit par la voie négative (rétention d'information) ou par la voie positive (bouclage du récit par inclusion), il est apparu que l'œuvre à Théophile se donne à lire comme une entité narrative. De plus, son unité doit affecter sa visée. Pratiquement, de quels moyens l'auteur dispose-t-il pour induire l'unité de son histoire de salut?

II. TROIS PROCÉDURES UNIFICATRICES

Commençons par la prolepse, qui est une projection vers le futur de l'histoire racontée. Le livre des Actes s'ouvre par la gigantesque prolepse que représente la promesse du Ressuscité aux Onze: «Vous recevrez une puissance, le Saint-Esprit venant sur vous, et vous serez mes témoins aussi bien à Jérusalem que dans toute la Judée et la Samarie et jusqu'à l'extrémité de la terre» (1,8). La place de cet énoncé, au seuil des Actes, lui confère une valeur de programme narratif, débordant même Ac 28 (Rome n'est pas encore l'extrémité de la terre). Plus que de fournir au lecteur le plan du récit, 1,8 énonce l'engendrement christologique de l'histoire qui va suivre: au travers des heurs (et surtout malheurs) des envoyés, c'est l'histoire d'une promesse qui devient féconde. L'anticipation d'Ac 1,8 fonctionne donc très clairement comme une clef de lecture pour l'ensemble du récit. Mais l'auteur à Théophile affectionne de donner à ses prolepses[23] une tournure moins claire, *plus elliptique*; j'en donne quelques exemples.

22. J. Dupont (*La conclusion des Actes*, p. 457-511) a été très attentif à l'importance du procédé d'inclusion dans la construction de l'œuvre lucanienne, notamment à partir de la conclusion des Actes; il voit se condenser en 28,16-31 l'écho du procès de Paul (Ac 21–28), mais aussi du discours d'Antioche de Pisidie (Ac 13), de la prédication de Jésus à Nazareth (Lc 4) et de l'Évangile de l'enfance (Lc 1).
23. Épluchant l'évangile à la recherche d'indicateurs pointant en direction des Actes, C.K. Barrett inventorie 41 références possibles (*The Third Gospel as a Preface to Acts?* p. 1453-1461). De cet inventaire, je retiens une potentialité proleptique pour les références suivantes: Lc 3,6 (mission païenne); 4,16-30 (mission païenne); 7,1-10 (Ac 10–11); 9,52-56 et 17,11-19 (Ac 8); 10,11 (Ac 13,51); 10,19 (Ac 28,6); 11,49 (les apôtres); 12,8 (Ac 7,56); 12,11s (la souffrance des missionnaires); 19,45s (rôle du Temple); 21,12-19 (la souffrance des missionnaires); 22,15-20 et 24,30s.35 (fraction du pain); 23,6-12 (Ac 4,27); 23,34-46 (Ac 7); 23,47 (titre christologique δίκαιος); 24,49 (Ac 2).

Prolepses elliptiques

Au cœur de l'Évangile de l'enfance, l'oracle de Syméon conjoint à la bénédiction des parents de Jésus (Lc 2,34a) une annonce à Marie dont l'ombre plane sur la suite du récit: «Voici, celui-ci est placé pour la chute et le relèvement de nombreux en Israël, et pour être signe de contradiction; et toi-même, un glaive te transpercera l'âme» (Lc 2,34b-35a). Ce choc entre la paix célébrée par Syméon (2,29) et la souffrance annoncée laisse totalement imprécise la prédiction: en quoi consisteront la chute et le relèvement? à quel moment Marie sera-t-elle transpercée? Le lecteur ne le découvrira qu'en avançant dans la lecture.

Plus loin, en Lc 9,51, la grande itinérance du Jésus lucanien est introduite par un commentaire du narrateur sur lequel butent régulièrement les exégètes: «Et il advint, comme s'accomplissaient les jours de son enlèvement (τὰς ἡμέρας τῆς ἀναλήμψεως αὐτοῦ), que lui aussi durcit sa face pour marcher vers Jérusalem». Les commentateurs s'interrogent sur le sens d'ἀναλήμψις, *hapaxlegomenon* dans la forme substantivée, mais attesté en *TestLev* 18,3 et *PsSal* 4,18[24]. Le terme désigne-t-il ici l'Ascension de Jésus (ce qu'appuierait Ac 1,2.11.22)? Se réfère-t-il plus généralement à la montée de Jésus à Jérusalem, donc à la Passion (ce qu'appuierait l'usage d'ἀναλαμβάνω en Ac 7,43; 10,16; 20,13s; 23,31)[25]? Le pluriel τὰς ἡμέρας incline plutôt vers ce dernier sens, plus extensif (cf. le singulier ἕως τῆς ἡμέρας ἧς ἀνελήμφθη en Ac 2,21). Mais la connotation ascensionnelle n'est pas absente pour autant, si bien que la décision sémantique reste ouverte pour le lecteur; seuls les événements narrés à la jointure des deux parties de l'œuvre (Lc 24 / Ac 1) élucideront l'accomplissement de cette ἀναλήμψις qui, en l'état, demeure elliptique. L'écriture lucanienne, on le voit, use de l'ambivalence du terme pour laisser ouverte la décision du lecteur en Lc 9,51[26]; l'avancement du récit jusqu'à l'exaltation de Jésus conduit non seulement à réduire le flottement sémantique, mais aussi (et surtout) à enraciner le scénario Passion-résurrection dans la résolution de Jésus, «durcissant sa face» pour assumer un destin où s'accomplit la volonté du Père[27].

---

24. G. DELLING, art. ἀναλαμβάνω, in *TWNT*, 4, p. 8s. G. FRIEDRICH, *Lk 9,51 und die Entrückungschristologie des Lukas*, in *Orientierung an Jesus*. FS J. Schmid, Freiburg-Basel, Herder, 1973, p. 48-77.

25. Débat exégétique présenté par G. Friedrich (p. 70-74); l'auteur tranche en faveur d'une référence à la Passion.

26. Je m'appuie ici sur les fines remarques de F. BOVON, *Effet de réel et flou prophétique dans l'œuvre de Luc*, in *Révélations et Écritures* (Le Monde de la Bible, 26), Genève, Labor et Fides, 1993, p. 65-74, surtout p. 71; cf. aussi *L'Évangile selon saint Luc 9,51–14,35* (CNT, 3b), Genève, Labor et Fides, 1996, p. 33.

27. Le même procédé d'ambivalence, lors de la Transfiguration, a conduit le narrateur à faire parler Moïse et Élie (9,31) de «l'exode» (ἔξοδος) de Jésus plutôt que de son

Je perçois un même effet de flottement délibéré du sens en Lc 12,49s, dans la déclaration de Jésus sur le «feu» qu'il est venu jeter sur la terre et le «baptême» dont il doit être baptisé. Chercher la signification exacte de cette prolepse précipite dans l'embarras. Le feu est en effet une métaphore courante dans le judaïsme pour le jugement eschatologique, ce que le lecteur sait pertinemment depuis Lc 3,9.17; 9,54. Mais le parallélisme synonymique entre πῦρ et βάπτισμα appelle une référence à l'Esprit saint; les propos du Baptiste en 3,16 sollicitent déjà dans ce sens. C'est parvenu au récit de la Pentecôte que le lecteur pourra relire la déclaration de Jésus et y déceler *a posteriori* une prédiction de la venue de l'Esprit. Celle-ci est d'ailleurs formulée en des termes inhabituels, puisque sur les lèvres du Ressuscité, la promesse aux disciples n'est pas de recevoir l'Esprit, mais d'être «revêtus d'une puissance d'en-haut» (Lc 24,49 ἐνδύσησθε ἐξ ὕψους δύναμιν; cf. Ac 1,8). Une fois encore, le récit contient en amont ses propres clefs de lecture: l'usage de δύναμις comme métaphore de l'Esprit est un septantisme pratiqué par l'auteur de Lc-Ac (Lc 1,17.35; 4,14; Ac 8,10; 10,38)[28].

D'autres prolepses, tout aussi elliptiques, jalonnent la destinée de Paul dans le livre des Actes. Ac 9,15: «je lui montrerai moi-même tout ce qu'il lui faudra souffrir pour mon Nom». Ac 13,2: «Mettez à part pour moi Barnabé et Saul en vue de l'œuvre (ἔργον) à laquelle je les ai appelés». Ac 21,11: «L'homme à qui appartient la ceinture, ainsi à Jérusalem les juifs le lieront et le livreront aux mains des païens». Dans les trois cas, le lecteur est condamné à l'incertitude jusqu'au moment où le récit livre réponse à ses questions: que devra souffrir Paul pour le nom de Jésus? quel est l'ἔργον auquel sont appelés Barnabé et Saul? comment les juifs s'empareront-ils de Paul à Jérusalem?

On est en droit de se demander pourquoi Luc n'annonce pas plus directement les choses. Pourquoi éviter de parler clair? Nous touchons là un procédé d'écriture typique de notre auteur: l'ambivalence sémantique[29]. En l'occurrence, le potentiel de sens dégagé par l'ambiguïté laisse dans l'indécision une prédiction dont le récit, plus tard, présentera la réalisation. Narratologiquement, le fonctionnement est le suivant: le flou sémantique ouvre dans le récit un lieu d'indécision, qui frustre le

---

départ vers Jérusalem, en vue de pourvoir la montée vers la Passion d'une connotation exodiale. P. Doble y voit la reprise d'un motif sapiential: P. DOBLE, *The Paradox of Salvation. Luke's Theology of the Cross* (SNTS MS, 87), Cambridge, University Press, 1996, p. 210-214.

28. Sur l'équivalence δύναμις/πνεῦμα, voir Lc 1,35; 24,49; Ac 1,8; 10,38.

29. La question de l'ambivalence sémantique chez Luc est analysée dans mon article *Luc-Actes entre Jérusalem et Rome. Un procédé lucanien de double signification*, in *NTS* 45 (1999) 70-87.

lecteur en omettant ou voilant un élément nécessaire à la compréhension; le lecteur va donc chercher dans la suite du récit ce qui comble ce vide informatif. Une tournure elliptique ou ambiguë peut donc être (mais elle n'est pas toujours!) le résultat d'une stratégie narrative visant à exciter la quête de vérification chez le lecteur.

La tournure elliptique n'est pas le résultat d'une impéritie de l'écrivain Luc, mais une pratique consciemment appliquée, qui met à distance l'annonce et la réalisation. Ce procédé est d'une importance capitale, car il implique que le schéma annonce/réalisation, autrement dit promesse/accomplissement, se déploie au sein même du diptyque lucanien[30]. Avancer dans le macro-récit conduit ainsi le lecteur à vérifier la fiabilité des promesses, et par là, à déceler la logique unificatrice de la narration. Parce qu'il amène le lecteur à constater après coup la réalisation des prédictions énoncées, le récit fonctionne comme un lieu de véridiction des promesses divines.

Des chaînes narratives

Deuxième procédure d'unification du récit: la «chaîne narrative». J'appelle de ce nom les lignes tissées par l'auteur entre les deux parties de son diptyque, et dont le repérage permet au lecteur de mesurer la continuité et la progression du récit.

Une chaîne très visible est la *chaîne des centurions*. Trois centurions interviennent à des moments-clefs du récit lucanien: le centurion de Capharnaüm (Lc 7,1-10) est le premier non-juif à implorer une guérison de Jésus; un centurion confesse sa foi au pied de la croix (Lc 23,47); c'est aussi avec un centurion, Corneille, que Pierre expérimente l'octroi du salut aux païens (Ac 10–11; 15,7-11). Cette chaîne des centurions n'est pas anecdotique; elle relie trois hommes dont la foi est à chaque fois exemplaire: le centurion de Capharnaüm indique à Jésus le moyen de sauver son esclave malade en franchissant par la parole l'insurmontable distance séparant le juif du païen; l'exemplarité de sa foi est expressément soulignée par Jésus: «Je vous dis, même en Israël je n'ai pas trouvé une telle foi» (Lc 7,9b). Sous la croix, la déclaration de foi du soldat est unique (Lc 23,47). Quant au centurion Corneille, dont la piété est abondamment soulignée (pieux, craignant-Dieu, généreux en

---

30. Sans adopter la perspective narratologique que nous développons ici, F. BOVON, *Effet de réel et flou prophétique* (n. 26), parvient au même résultat: «Les exégètes ont trop peu remarqué que, conditionnée par le motif de l'accomplissement de l'Ancien Testament, la structure de Luc-Actes était aussi dominée par *un jeu de promesses et de réalisations internes*. Ils n'ont pas remarqué non plus que le jeu fonctionnait *grâce à des prophéties volontairement floues*» (p. 70; je souligne).

aumônes et constamment en prière: Ac 10,2), la grâce qui lui est accordée *via* Pierre est explicitement motivée par ce message de l'ange: «Tes prières et tes aumônes sont montées en mémorial devant Dieu» (10,4b). Entre ces trois militaires, le narrateur a tissé la continuité d'une grâce surprenante accordée à la foi; cet enchaînement est plus que nécessaire, puisque le narrateur doit préparer la rupture que représente, entre Pierre et Corneille, l'écroulement de la barrière entre le pur et l'impur (Ac 10,9-16). La chaîne des centurions exerce trois effets au plan du récit: a) elle fait continuité entre la rencontre de Pierre et Corneille et un geste de Jésus; b) elle légitime le regard favorable de Dieu sur Corneille par la construction positive du personnage «centurion»[31]; c) elle prépare le choc de l'ouverture du salut aux païens.

On sait la place que reçoit dans les Actes l'événement du chemin de Damas, relaté par le narrateur (Ac 9,1-19a), puis re-raconté par Paul devant le peuple de Jérusalem (22,1-21) et devant Agrippa (26,1-29). Or cette *chaîne de la conversion de Saul* est amorcée, et préparée, en amont dans l'évangile. La déclaration du Christ en Ac 9,15 («cet homme est un instrument d'élection pour moi en vue de porter mon Nom devant des nations et des rois (ἐνώπιον ἐθνῶν τε καὶ βασιλέων) et des fils d'Israël») est un écho direct de la prédiction de Jésus à ses disciples: «ils vous traîneront devant des rois et des gouverneurs (ἐπὶ βασιλεῖς καὶ ἡγεμόνας) à cause de mon Nom» (Lc 21,12). Plus en amont dans le récit, le Jésus lucanien avait avisé ses disciples de la nécessité de défendre leur foi: «Quand ils vous amèneront devant les synagogues et les chefs et les autorités, ne vous inquiétez pas de savoir comment vous défendre et que dire; car le Saint-Esprit vous enseignera à l'heure même ce qu'il faut dire» (Lc 12,11s). Luc a accordé au retournement de Saul une importance foncière: il assure à la mission hors judaïsme sa légitimité dans la continuité de l'histoire des pères. Mais, en ancrant la destinée de Paul en-deçà d'Ac 9, dans les paroles de Jésus préparant ses disciples au témoignage et à la souffrance, le narrateur imprime sur la mission de Paul la marque du *continuum*.

Troisième chaîne. Entre les paraboles de Lc 15 et la rencontre de Jésus avec Zachée (Lc 19,1-10), Jean-Noël Aletti a relevé un intéressant jeu d'échos par reprise d'un même scénario: a) contestation de l'accueil des pécheurs (15,2) ou de Zachée (19,5); b) déclaration sotériologique (15,7.10.24.32; 19,9); c) manifestation de joie (15,6s.10.23.32; 19,6)[32].

---

31. La positivité du personnage ἑκατοντάρχης rejaillira sur les centurions qui jalonneront le martyre de Paul dès le chapitre 21 des Actes, jouant constamment le rôle de protecteurs de l'apôtre menacé: 21,32; 22,25s; 23,17.23; 24,23; 27,1.6.11.31.43; 28,16.

32. J.-N. ALETTI, *Quand Luc raconte. Le récit comme théologie* (Lire la Bible, 115), Paris, Cerf, 1998, p. 260-263.

Ce report de scénario de Lc 15 à Lc 19 fait entendre qu'avec Zachée, l'affirmation parabolique trouve à la fois sa concrétisation et sa confirmation: le salut vient aux pécheurs malgré les protestations des justes. Le lecteur est évidemment attentif à cette récurrence lorsque réapparaît cette chaîne «grâce *versus* Torah rituelle», mais déplacée, à l'occasion de l'assemblée de Jérusalem (Ac 15). La mise en situation de cette rencontre au sommet réduplique de manière fascinante la situation de Lc 15: des croyants de Judée protestent qu'on ne peut être sauvé sans la circoncision (v. 1) alors que le récit de la conversion des païens par Paul et Barnabé cause «une grande joie à tous les frères» (v. 3). Le front de la contestation s'est donc déplacé à l'intérieur même de l'Église. Message induit par la répétition du scénario: la même grâce l'emportera. Le discours de Jacques confirme: «Dieu *dès le début* a pris soin de choisir parmi les nations païennes un peuple à son nom» (15,14)[33].

Mentionnons aussi une *chaîne pentecostale*, qui conduit le lecteur de la prédiction du feu imminent dont nous avons parlé (Lc 12,49), aux langues de feu de la Pentecôte (Ac 2,1-13), et aux irruptions collectives de l'Esprit en Ac 10,44-46 et 19,6. L'essor de l'Église se trouve ainsi jalonné par les interventions surprenantes de Dieu, bousculant son Église pour l'ouvrir au monde.

La présence des chaînes narratives signale que Luc travaille avec l'effet de redondance. Il serait intéressant, mais ce n'est pas ici le propos, d'observer les variations qu'introduit l'écrivain d'un récit à l'autre[34]. Car comme tout conteur, Luc évite de lasser. Mais ce qui m'intéresse est de noter l'effet des chaînes narratives sur la lecture de Lc-Ac. J'en note trois.

1. Le phénomène de redondance narrative a un premier effet qui est d'aider à la mémorisation et de structurer la compréhension. Les traversées qu'organisent les chaînes narratives au travers d'un macro-récit foisonnant ouvrent des axes de lecture; elles balisent des chemins; elles signalent les points-clefs. Vus à partir des Actes, les motifs mis en évidence sont l'ouverture aux païens, l'appel au témoignage, le don de l'Esprit et la suréminence de la grâce sur la Loi.

---

33. Nous repérons ici un autre type de rapport entre les Actes et l'évangile: il incombe au récit des Actes de verbaliser des attitudes qui se nouent dans l'évangile entre Jésus et ses interlocuteurs (ici: Jésus, Zachée, les foules). Zachée devient le prototype d'une grâce offerte et d'un accueil que viennent défendre à Jérusalem les tenants de la mission d'Antioche.

34. Les trois récits de la conversion de Saul (Ac 9; 22; 26) constituent un champ privilégié pour l'examen des variations introduites par le narrateur; je renvoie pour cela le lecteur à ma contribution *Saul's Conversion (Acts 9-22-26) and the Multiplication of Narrative in Acts*, in C.M. TUCKETT (éd.), *Luke's Literary Achievement* (JSNT SS, 116), Sheffield, Academic Press, 1995, p. 127-155.

2. Plus on avance dans le macro-récit, plus abondent les redon-
dances; elles se multiplient à partir d'Ac 10[35]. Ces retours plus fréquents
du récit sur lui-même signalent, de la part de Luc, la volonté de favori-
ser chez ses lecteurs une lecture globale, où progressivement s'appro-
fondit la signification des événements rapportés. Le cas le plus impres-
sionnant est la quadruple relecture que Pierre présente de sa conversion
– car Ac 10,9-29 peut à bon droit être appelé la «conversion de Pierre».
L'apôtre commence par transposer sa vision extatique sur le plan *éthique*
(«Dieu m'a montré de n'appeler immonde ou impur aucun homme»
10,28); puis il en déduit l'impartialité de Dieu (10,34 οὐκ ἔστιν
προσωπολήμπτης ὁ θεός), qu'il fonde *christologiquement* (10,36-43);
une lecture *pneumatologique* vient ensuite: si Dieu envoie son Esprit,
c'est qu'il accorde sa grâce (11,16); enfin, à Jérusalem, les conséquences *sotériologiques* sont tirées (15,9s): si Dieu a purifié leurs cœurs
par la foi, pourquoi leur imposer la Loi[36]? De l'éthique à la sotériologie
en passant par l'image de Dieu, la christologie et la pneumatologie: ce
chemin d'approfondissement du sens auquel invite la chaîne narrative
est un véritable parcours dogmatique.

3. Dans l'histoire du salut, Dieu ne se répète pas plus que Luc. Le jeu
d'échos que met en place la chaîne narrative signe d'une part la continuité d'une présence de Dieu aux siens, d'autre part les différentes
modalités de cette présence entre Jésus et ses messagers. Sans exception,
la clef herméneutique de la chaîne narrative réside dans une parole de
Jésus (Lc 7,9; 12,49; 15,7.10.32; 19,9; 21,12; Ac 11,16). La chaîne
construit ainsi une continuité foncière des Actes, non pas avec le
judaïsme[37], mais avec l'agir de Dieu en Jésus Christ, la continuité avec
la tradition juive passant par le truchement de celui-ci.

Une procédure de modélisation: la *syncrisis*

Redondance narrative et jeux d'échos sont de subtils instruments
d'appel à la mémoire, que Luc prise particulièrement. Il les met à l'hon-

---

35. La redondance narrative affecte les passages suivantes: 11,1-18; 15,7-11; 20,18-
35; 22,1-21; 25,10-21; 26,2-27; 28,17-20.
36. L'étude inégalée sur la construction de la séquence de 10,1 à 11,18, avec ses multiples effets de retour du récit sur lui-même, est celle de Louis MARIN, *Essai d'analyse
structurale d'Actes 10,1–11,18*, in R. BARTHES, *et al.*, *Exégèse et herméneutique* (Parole
de Dieu), Paris, Seuil, 1971, p. 213-238. Sur le phénomène de redondance en Ac 10–11,
voir aussi R. WITHERUP, *Cornelius Over and Over and Over Again*: «*Functional Redundancy» in the Acts of the Apostles*, in *JSNT* 49 (1993) 45-66 et W.S. KURZ, *Effects of
Variant Narrators in Acts 10–11*, in *NTS* 43 (1997) 570-586.
37. Contre l'opinion de J. JERVELL, *The Future of the Past: Luke's Vision of Salvation
History and its Bearing on his Writing of History*, in B. WITHERINGTON (éd.), *History,
Literature, and Society in the Book of Acts*, Cambridge, University Press, 1996, p. 125.

neur dans un autre procédé de relecture où il excelle: la modélisation, autrement appelée *syncrisis*. *Syncrisis* est le nom donné à une technique rhétorique de la plus haute antiquité, et qui consiste à modeler la présentation d'un personnage sur un autre en vue de les comparer, ou à tout le moins, d'établir entre eux une corrélation[38]. La *syncrisis* crée un réseau d'intertextualité interne à l'œuvre lucanienne[39]. Elle rapproche deux figures du récit à l'enseigne d'un événement analogue (comme le martyre de Jésus et d'Étienne: Lc 23,34-46 et Ac 7,55-60) ou par le biais d'un même scénario narratif (comme la rencontre d'Emmaüs et la conversion de l'Éthiopien: Lc 24,13-35 et Ac 8,26-40)[40].

L'exemple le plus achevé de la *syncrisis* lucanienne est la mise en parallèle Jésus–Pierre–Paul. La démonstration de ces rapprochements ayant été faite maintes fois, je n'éprouve pas le besoin de répéter ici des arguments connus[41]. Pour le dire en bref: Pierre et Paul guérissent comme Jésus a guéri (ex.: Lc 5,18-25; Ac 3,1-8; 14,8-10); comme Jésus lors de son baptême, Pierre et Paul bénéficient d'une vision extatique au moment-clef de leur ministère (Ac 9,3-9; 10,10-16); comme Jésus, ils prêchent et endurent l'hostilité des juifs; comme leur Maître, ils souffrent et sont menacés de mort; Paul est en procès à la manière dont Jésus l'a été (Ac 21–26); et comme Lui, Pierre et Paul sont à la fin de leur vie l'objet d'une miraculeuse délivrance (Ac 12,6-17; 24,27–28,6). De ce procédé, je ne retiens que l'aspect qui m'intéresse

38. A. George a consacré une belle étude à l'imposante *syncrisis* Jean-Baptiste/Jésus autour de laquelle Luc a construit son Évangile de l'enfance: A. GEORGE, *Le parallèle entre Jean-Baptiste et Jésus en Luc 1–2*, in *Études sur l'œuvre de Luc* (Sources bibliques), Paris, Gabalda, 1986, p. 43-65. J.-N. Aletti a voué aux *syncrisis* lucaniennes la plus grande partie de son livre *Quand Luc raconte* (n. 32), voir en particulier les p. 69-166.

39. Sur l'intertextualité interne à Lc-Ac, voir les remarques suggestives de J.B. Green, qui met en parallèle l'inscription de l'histoire de l'Église dans celle de Jésus et l'inscription de l'histoire de Jésus et de l'Église dans celle d'Israël: J.B. GREEN, *Internal Repetition in Luke-Acts: Contemporary Narratology and Lucan Historiography*, in B. WITHERINGTON (éd.), *History* (n. 37), p. 293-295.

40. Autres exemples: la mise en corrélation de la conversion de Saul (Ac 9,3-19a) avec la rencontre Pierre-Corneille (10,1-23), ou encore de la délivrance de prison de Pierre (Ac 12,12-17) avec les récits d'apparitions pascales (Lc 24,5-36).

41. On consultera dans la littérature récente sur le sujet: J. DUPONT, *Pierre et Paul dans les Actes*, in *Études sur les Actes des apôtres* (LD, 45), Paris, Cerf, 1967, p. 173-184. C.H. TALBERT, *Literary Patterns. Theological Themes, and the Genre of Luke-Acts* (SBL MS, 20), Missoula, Scholars Press, 1974, p. 15-23. W. RADL, *Paulus und Jesus im lukanischen Doppelwerk. Untersuchungen zu Parallelmotiven im Lukasevangelium und in der Apostelgeschichte* (EHS, 23/49), Bern, Lang, 1975. R.F. O'TOOLE, *Parallels between Jesus and His Disciples in Luke-Acts. A Further Study*, in *BZ* 27 (1983) 195-212. S.M. PRAEDER, *Jesus-Paul, Peter-Paul, and Jesus-Peter Parallelisms in Luke-Acts: A History of Reader Response*, in *SBL SP* 1984, p. 23-39. D.P. MOESSNER, *«The Christ Must Suffer»: New Light on the Jesus-Peter, Stephen, Paul Parallels in Luke-Acts*, in *NT* 28 (1986) 220-256. J.-N. ALETTI, *Quand Luc raconte* (n. 32), p. 84-103.

ici, à savoir les effets recherchés par le narrateur sur la lecture de son
œuvre. J'en discerne trois.

Je relève tout d'abord que la modélisation des disciples sur le Maître
touche les actions (l'agir et le souffrir), mais non le dire: la parole des
témoins ne se substitue pas à celle de Jésus, ni ne l'imite, mais renvoie
au kérygme christologique (Ac 2,22-36; 3,13-26; 4,10-12; 7,52; 10,37-
43; 13,26-39; etc.). L'évangile est le présupposé obligé de la lecture des
discours dans les Actes, mais étonnamment, jamais les acteurs du récit
ne citent l'évangile: des deux énoncés attribués à Jésus dans les Actes
(11,16 et 20,35), le premier remonte à Ac 1,5, le second est inconnu de
l'évangile. Résultat: la relation des Actes à l'évangile n'est pas de
l'ordre du commentaire, mais de la relecture par continuation; dans les
catégories de Genette, on parlerait d'hypertextualité plutôt que de méta-
textualité[42]. Les Actes ne sont pas un *pesher* de l'évangile; ils en obser-
vent les séquelles dans l'histoire.

Je relève en deuxième lieu que Luc a fixé le point de départ de la *syncrisis* dans un agir du Christ qui pallie l'impuissance des apôtres. La
technique de modélisation surgit en effet pour la première fois lors de la
guérison du boiteux à la Belle Porte du Temple (Ac 3,1-10)[43]. Observons
comment ce récit d'Ac 3 se greffe sur le modèle christologique de Lc 5.
À Pierre et Jean qui montent au Temple pour la prière de la neuvième
heure, le boiteux demande l'aumône (3,3). Pierre le fixe du regard et
déclare: «Argent et or ne sont pas à ma disposition, mais ce que j'ai, je
te le donne: dans le nom de Jésus Christ (ἐν τῷ ὀνόματι Ἰησοῦ Χριστοῦ) le Nazoréen, marche!» (3,6). À ce moment du récit débutent les
indices de corrélation, c'est-à-dire à l'instant précis où les apôtres signalent un manque. Ce manque est d'argent; il signale une impuissance des
témoins à subvenir au besoin exprimé par le boiteux. Comblant leur

---

42. G. Genette distingue ces deux variantes d'intertextualité en parlant d'*hypertextualité*
lorsqu'un texte se greffe sur un autre par référence ou allusion, réservant l'appellation *méta-
textualité* au commentaire explicite d'une premier texte par un second (exemple: le *pesher*):
G. GENETTE, *Palimpsestes. La littérature au second degré*, Paris, Seuil, 1982, p. 7-12.

43. Pour ce qui suit, j'emprunte à l'analyse de G. MUHLACK, *Die Parallelen von
Lukas-Evangelium und Apostelgeschichte*, Frankfurt, Lang, 1979, p. 27-36. Dans le texte
d'Ac 3,1-10, quelques signaux linguistiques appellent à la mémoire du lecteur la guérison
du paralysé de Lc 5,17-26: περιπάτει (ἔγειρε καί est textuellement secondaire) v. 6, cf.
Lc 5,23; παραχρῆμα v. 7, cf. Lc 5,25a; ἔστη v. 8, cf. Lc 5,25a ἀναστάς; αἰνῶν τὸν
θεόν v. 8s, cf. Lc 5,25s δοξάζων/ἐδόξαζον τὸν θεόν; πᾶς ὁ λαός v. 9, cf. Lc 5,26a
ἅπαντας; ἔκστασις, θάμβος v. 10, cf. Lc 5,26 ἔκστασις, φόβος. D'autres signaux, plus
nombreux et plus insistants, induisent une corrélation entre notre récit et la guérison par
Paul du paralysé de Lystre (Ac 14,8-11): τις ἀνὴρ... χωλὸς ἐκ κοιλίας μητρὸς αὐτοῦ
v. 2, cf. Ac 14,8; ἀτενίσας... εἶπεν v. 4, cf. Ac 14,9s; ἐξαλλόμενος ἔστη καὶ περιεπά-
τει v. 8a, cf. Ac 14,10b ἥλατο καὶ περιέπατει v. 10; εἶδεν πᾶς ὁ λαός v. 9a, cf. Ac
14,11b οἱ ὄχλοι ἰδόντες.

incapacité, l'ὄνομα Ἰησοῦ Χριστοῦ devient l'agent opérateur du miracle, par le truchement d'une parole calquée (partiellement) sur celle du Maître: «marche!» (περιπάτει 3,6). Le commentaire qu'en livre Pierre dans son discours est sans ambiguïté: «*son nom* l'a fortifié et la foi qui vient de Lui lui a donné toute sa santé» (3,16). Les indices de corrélation viennent donc ratifier littérairement le discours sur l'action du «nom de Jésus Christ»: le Ressuscité confirme et poursuit son action thérapeutique par la médiation des apôtres. Cadre, lieu et protagonistes ont changé; le lecteur des Actes est appelé à une mémoire d'évangile pour saisir que la guérison à la Belle Porte n'innove pas, mais se réclame d'un précédent christologique qui lui donne sens.

En troisième lieu, j'insiste sur le fait que la technique littéraire de Luc échappe aux qualifications schématiques. On a relevé la discrétion des indices de corrélation entre Ac 3 et Lc 5. Également, la destinée souffrante de Pierre et de Paul évoque la Passion de Jésus *sans la rejoindre*. C'est pourquoi j'hésite à parler, même sur un registre typologique, d'une «résurrection de Pierre» (Ac 12) ou d'une «Passion-résurrection de Paul» (Ac 27,9–28,6)[44]. La mort des deux héros est très précisément escamotée par le narrateur (Ac 12,17; 28,30s)[45], comme s'il ne fallait pas porter ombrage à la seule mort salvatrice, celle de Jésus. La *syncrisis* n'est pas un décalque; elle rapproche sur fond de différenciation. Il est remarquable que sur le chemin de l'identification du Christ et de l'apôtre, Luc n'ait pas franchi le seuil que les Actes apocryphes d'apôtres n'ont pas hésité à passer; le Christ apparaît sous les traits de Paul dans les *Actes de Paul et Thècle* (3,21) et prend le visage de Thomas dans les *Actes de Thomas* 151-153 et 154s.

La théologie lucanienne se tient en-deçà: la modélisation n'induit ni imitation ni confusion, mais intègre toujours le facteur de la différence. Elle signale une conformité à un modèle fondateur et une permanence de l'assistance divine aux témoins malmenés. Elle correspond en définitive à un rebondissement de la typologie vétérotestamentaire qui marque l'évangile: de même que la christologie de l'évangile se construit à

---

44. M.D. GOULDER, *Type and History in Acts*, London, S.P.C.K., 1964, p. 62s, a soutenu fortement cette lecture typologique, suivi par W. RADL, *Paulus und Jesus im lukanischen Doppelwerk* (n. 41), p. 222-251 et J.-N. ALETTI, *Quand Luc raconte* (n. 32), p. 69-103.

45. Nonobstant une brève réapparition à l'occasion de l'assemblée de Jérusalem (Ac 15,7-11), où il opère une lecture sotériologique de sa rencontre avec Corneille, Pierre disparaît du récit en 12,17 sur un commentaire sibyllin (et lourdement métaphorique!) du narrateur: καὶ ἐξελθὼν ἐπορεύθη εἰς ἕτερον τόπον («et sortant, il s'en alla vers une autre destination»). Quant à l'énigme classique du silence lucanien sur la mort de Paul (28,30s), voir mon étude: *The End of Acts (28,16-31) and the Rhetoric of Silence*, in S.E. PORTER et T.H. OLBRICHT (éds.), *Rhetoric and the New Testament. Essays from the 1992 Heidelberg Conference* (JSNT SS, 90), Sheffield, Academic Press, 1993, p. 74-89.

l'aide de modèles typologiques (Élie-Élisée et Moïse), la destinée des
témoins s'inscrit en Ac dans une typologie christologique qui conforme
la vie des témoins au message qu'ils annoncent.

Bilan. Trois procédures sont apparues jusqu'ici dénoter une volonté
auctoriale de faire découvrir au lecteur la logique de la conduite divine
de l'histoire: la prolepse elliptique, la chaîne narrative, la *syncrisis.* Ces
procédures ont un effet en commun: elles poussent le lecteur/auditeur à
parcourir les deux volets du diptyque lucanien, à circuler dans le récit
d'aval en amont et d'amont en aval. Elles conduisent à lire les Actes à
partir de l'évangile et à relire l'évangile du point de vue de l'avancement
de l'histoire notifié par les Actes. Ces procédures narratives suggèrent
plus qu'elles n'imposent. Elles évoquent une précédence christologique
plus qu'elles ne la désignent. Invitant le lecteur à découvrir la logique du
plan divin de salut, elles le poussent à tisser des liens d'un bout à l'autre
de l'écrit, bref, *elles le sollicitent à faire l'unité de Luc-Actes.*

III. LES DÉPLACEMENTS AU SEIN DE L'ŒUVRE LUCANIENNE

J'ai dit plus haut que tensions et rebondissements ne menaçaient en rien
l'unité d'intrigue d'un récit; une narration captivante les réclame au
contraire. Il nous reste à mettre cette affirmation à l'épreuve de la position
de l'auteur *ad Theophilum* sur la Torah et de son éthique économique.

Permanence et suspension de la Loi

La cohérence de la position lucanienne sur la Torah[46], lorsqu'on passe
de l'évangile aux Actes, n'apparaît pas avec clarté. Vu depuis l'évangile,
le statut de la Loi ne souffre d'aucune ambiguïté: «Il est plus facile au
ciel et à la terre de passer qu'à une seule virgule de la Loi de tomber»
(Lc 16,17). Même s'il est «partisan lui-même d'une concentration spirituelle de la Loi»[47], Luc ne fait aucunement l'impasse sur sa composante

---

46. Les derniers à s'être penchés sur la question de la Loi dans Lc-Ac sont F.G. Dow-
NING, *Freedom from the Law in Luke-Acts,* in *JSNT* 22 (1984) 53-80. M. KLINGHARDT,
*Gesetz und Volk Gottes. Das lukanische Verständnis des Gesetzes nach Herkunft, Funk-
tion und seinem Ort in der Geschichte des Urchristentums* (WUNT, 2/32), Tübingen,
Mohr, 1988. J.A. FITZMYER, *Luke the Theologian. Aspects of His Teaching,* New York,
Paulist Press, 1989, p. 175-202. K. SALO, *Luke's Treatment of the Law: A Redaction-
Critical Investigation* (AnASU, 57), Helsinki, Suomalainen Tiedeakatemia, 1991.
H. MERKEL, *Das Gesetz im lukanischen Doppelwerk,* in *Schrift und Tradition.* FS
J. Ernst, Paderborn, Schöningh, 1996, p. 119-133. F. BOVON, *La Loi dans l'œuvre de
Luc,* in C. FOCANT (éd.), *La Loi dans l'un et l'autre Testament* (LD, 168), Paris, Cerf,
1997, p. 206-225.
47. F. BOVON, *La Loi dans l'œuvre de Luc* (n. 46), p. 208.

rituelle. Au seuil de l'évangile, la mère de Jésus respecte la prescription mosaïque relative à la purification et offre le sacrifice requis (Lc 2,22-24). Luc reprend sans l'affaiblir le logion de Q reprochant aux Pharisiens de verser la dîme sur les herbes du jardin au lieu de pratiquer la justice et l'amour de Dieu, et qui ajoute: «c'est ceci qu'il fallait faire et ne pas négliger cela» (Lc 11,42). Le Jésus lucanien commente la Torah (6,27-42), renvoie un légiste au résumé de la Loi pour recevoir la vie éternelle (10,25-28), et répond par un condensé du Décalogue à la demande de l'homme riche (18,18-20). La Loi reste en vigueur dans son intégralité.

Qu'en est-il lorsqu'on passe au second tome de l'œuvre de Luc? Le résultat de l'analyse est double: observance et rejet. Ici comme ailleurs, Luc différencie. Je profile les deux positions. D'un côté, l'extase de Pierre a *ouvert la brèche*: si Dieu abat la séparation millénaire du pur et de l'impur (10,10-16.28), il invalide du coup la Torah rituelle. Sur la lancée, Pierre à l'assemblée de Jérusalem pousse à l'extrême: «Pourquoi éprouver Dieu en imposant un joug sur la nuque des disciples que ni nos pères, ni nous n'avons eu la force de porter?» (15,10). Auparavant, Étienne avait parlé de «la Loi que vous avez reçue promulguée par des anges et que vous n'avez pas observée» (7,53), et Paul prêchant à la synagogue d'Antioche de Pisidie avait annoncé détenir «la rémission des péchés et la justification que vous n'avez pas pu trouver dans la Loi de Moïse» (13,38). Pierre et Paul – notons le rassemblement d'autorités sur le sujet! – statuent une double impuissance sur la question de la Loi: elle n'a pas été respectée par Israël; elle n'est pas en mesure d'octroyer le pardon.

D'un autre côté, la Loi rituelle *dicte toujours la coutume*. Le Paul des Actes circoncit Timothée au moment d'en faire son collaborateur (16,3). Devant le sanhédrin, il s'écrie «moi je suis Pharisien» (23,6) – et le lecteur doit apprécier le poids du présent ἐγὼ Φαρισαῖός εἰμι. Face à la députation juive de Rome, sa ligne de défense se ramasse dans une formule cinglante: «n'ayant rien fait contre le peuple ou les coutumes des pères» (28,17 οὐδὲν ἐναντίον ποιήσας τῷ λαῷ ἢ τοῖς ἔθεσι τοῖς πατρῴοις). Il est remarquable que pas plus dans les Actes que dans l'Évangile de l'enfance (Lc 1–2), l'auteur n'élève quelque critique que ce soit face aux rituels juifs.

Faut-il en conclure qu'aux yeux de Luc, la Torah a perdu sa raison d'être pour les chrétiens d'origine non-juive, tandis qu'elle garderait son autorité, ritualité incluse, pour les judéochrétiens? Un commentaire du narrateur irait dans ce sens: Paul circoncit Timothée «à cause des juifs qui se trouvaient dans ces lieux, car ils savaient tous que son père était grec» (16,3b). La circoncision vient ici sceller la filiation juive de Timo-thée, le métis (juif de mère, grec de père), qui à l'image de la chrétienté issue de la mission paulinienne est mixte d'origine. Mais cette solution bi-partite n'est pas la solution lucanienne. À preuve le décret apostolique d'Ac 15,29, qui impose aux paganochrétiens des prescriptions rituelles.

L'aspect sotériologique et l'aspect historique

La position lucanienne est plus subtile, ou pour dire les choses plus adéquatement, Luc cumule sur la question de la Loi deux points de vue qu'il ne relie pas systématiquement: *l'aspect sotériologique et l'aspect historique*. D'un point de vue sotériologique, l'événement christologique met un point d'arrêt à la Loi: non parce que Dieu l'aurait désavouée, mais parce qu'elle s'est avérée incapable d'accorder le pardon des péchés; Pierre (10,43) et Paul (22,16) s'accordent là-dessus. En regard du salut, la Loi est caduque, et Luc trouve pour le dire – n'en déplaise à Vielhauer[48] – des accents très pauliniens: «c'est en lui [Jésus] que tout croyant est justifié (πᾶς ὁ πιστεύων δικαιοῦται)» (13,39).

Mais l'historien parle aussi en Luc, et c'est un historien de la conti-nuité, qui sauvegarde tout ce qui peut l'être. La Loi a régi le temps d'Is-raël, et même si le peuple ne l'a pas respectée, elle reste ces «oracles vivants (λόγια ζῶντα)» (7,38) reçus de Dieu. À la différence de Paul, Luc ne découple pas la Loi de la promesse. Parce que cette fonction de définir le peuple de Dieu (cette fonction identitaire comme dit Jacob Jer-vell[49]) demeure attachée à la Loi, Luc ne se sent pas plus que Paul le droit de la résilier. Elle continuera donc à marquer de son empreinte les gestes de Paul (la circoncision: 16,3; le rite de purification: 21,20-26), certifiant son irréfragable judaïté.

---

48. Dans un article célèbre et fracassant, P. Vielhauer a dénié à l'auteur des Actes tout certificat de paulinisme authentique: P. VIELHAUER, *Zum «Paulinismus» der Apostelge-schichte* (1950-51), in *Aufsätze zum Neuen Testament* (TB, 31), München, Kaiser, 1965, p. 9-27, citation p. 26: «Es findet sich bei ihm kein einziger spezifisch paulinischer Gedanke». Ce constat (correct) des déplacements théologiques entre le Paul des épîtres et le Paul des Actes doit être aujourd'hui replacé dans un paradigme historique comptant avec la réception de la tradition paulinienne et le phénomène d'école. Autrement dit: ces-sons de ressasser que Luc fut un (mauvais) élève de l'apôtre des Gentils, et demandons-nous pourquoi et comment la figure missionnaire de Paul a été reçue sur une ligne narra-tive (Lc-Ac; *Actes de Paul et Thècle*), la dimension pastorale et institutionnelle étant retenue sur une ligne argumentative (épîtres deutéropauliniennes; Pastorales; *Correspon-dance de Paul et Sénèque*).

49. J. JERVELL, *Luke and the People of God*, Minneapolis, Augsburg, 1972, p. 141-143. Toutefois, en affirmant que la Loi est marque identitaire de l'Église parce qu'elle est «character *indelebilis*» d'Israël, Jervell sous-estime le tournant christologique de l'his-toire du salut.

L'argument de continuité et la fonction identitaire jouent aussi pour l'Église composée de judéochrétiens et de paganochrétiens que Luc a en vue: la Torah demeure, mais spiritualisée, ramassée sur ses prescriptions morales: double commandement d'amour (Lc 10,27) et seconde table du Décalogue (Lc 18,20). Ce sont ces valeurs que Luc admire chez Corneille, le craignant-Dieu de Césarée: «Tes prières et tes aumônes sont montées en mémorial devant Dieu» (10,4). Prière et aumône, amour de Dieu et souci d'autrui sont les deux mamelles d'une Loi qui ne meurt pas; pour Luc, la reconnaissance de cette Torah morale dessine les contours d'un peuple qui se recrute aussi hors judaïsme. Ce peuple se reconnaît à la «purification du cœur» (15,9) dont parle Pierre, une purification que Dieu accorde par la foi en Jésus. On notera aussi que le fameux décret apostolique (15,28s) adopté au cours de l'assemblée de Jérusalem impose ses quatre continences non pas au nom de la Torah, mais au nom de l'Esprit saint et des apôtres: «Il a paru bon à l'Esprit saint et à nous...». C'est dire qu'en régime chrétien, le décret reçoit autorité non en tant que substrat de la Loi, mais en tant que *didachè* des apôtres.

Ce que fait découvrir un parcours sur la Loi au travers de l'œuvre à Théophile, c'est que Luc le théologien et Luc l'historien ne tiennent pas toujours le même discours. Le théologien repère la continuité de l'agir de Dieu dans l'histoire, tandis que l'historien est conscient que l'histoire évolue. Nous retrouvons la difficulté notée au début de cet article: la cohérence est plus difficile à saisir, puisque la pensée de l'auteur ne se dit pas en systématisation mais en narrativité. Faut-il penser avec Matthias Klinghardt[50] que la solution réside dans la diversité du lectorat visé par l'auteur, l'œuvre de Luc s'offrant à deux publics (judéo- et paganochrétien) dont chacun choisit sa piste prioritaire? Ou faut-il plutôt se dire que la rupture achevée entre la chrétienté lucanienne et la Synagogue ne confère qu'une valeur de légitimation à l'attachement que le Paul des Actes manifeste à la Torah rituelle? Cette seconde position me paraît plus conforme à la dimension historiographique de l'œuvre *ad Theophilum*.

Du «Malheur aux riches» aux femmes de la bonne société

L'éthique lucanienne sur le rapport aux biens pose un identique problème: comment, après les imprécations du Jésus de Luc contre les riches (6,24 «Malheur à vous, les riches, car vous tenez votre consolation»), comprendre l'intérêt complaisant de l'auteur pour la conversion

---

50. M. KLINGHARDT, *Gesetz und Volk Gottes* (n. 46), voir notamment les p. 306-309.

des «femmes de la bonne société» gréco-romaine (Ac 17,4.12)? L'analyse narrative se refuse à réduire la contradiction par des arguments littéraires (le rédacteur ne souscrirait pas à ses sources évangéliques); elle observe les moyens mis en œuvre par le narrateur pour déplacer le lecteur de l'idéal prescriptif de l'évangile (que jamais le récit n'invalide) à la réalité vécue dans les Actes, très précisément de l'impératif évangélique de dépouillement (Lc 12,13-21; 18,18-30) au modèle de partage des biens (Ac 2,42-45; 4,32-37) et à la prise en compte de la présence de riches dans la communauté (Ac 16,14s; 17,4.12; etc.).

Je me cantonnerai, ici encore, à la question qui nous occupe: de quels moyens s'est doté Luc pour que l'unité de son œuvre se fasse au niveau du rapport à l'argent?

La difficulté de répondre se mesure à l'hésitation de la recherche. On a proposé une solution historicisante: les imprécations évangéliques relèvent de la tradition, sans revêtir de pertinence pour l'auteur[51]. On a proposé une solution littéraire: la pauvreté deviendrait un motif littéraire équivalent à l'acceptation de Jésus[52]. On a proposé une solution sociologique: un clivage riches/pauvres dans la chrétienté lucanienne conduirait Luc à devenir l'évangéliste des riches[53] ou le vengeur des pauvres[54]. Une solution éthique a été également suggérée: Luc défend une éthique graduelle allant de l'invitation à l'aumône à l'exigence de pauvreté[55].

D'un point de vue strictement narratologique, le parcours des textes concernés (Lc 3,11; 4,18; 6,24s; 9,3; 12,13-21.33s; 16,13.19-31; 18,18-30; 20,47; 21,1-4; Ac 2,44s; 3,6; 4,32–5,11; 8,18-23; 16,16-24; 17,4.12; 19,18s; 28,10) permet de faire trois constats.

Premièrement: contrairement à la question de la Loi, explicitement reprise dans les Ac, les paroles de Jésus contre les riches (Lc 6,24s; 12,16-21) et l'appel au renoncement des biens (Lc 12,33s; 18,18-30) ne

---

51. F.W. HORN, *Glaube und Handeln in der Theologie des Lukas* (GTA, 26), Göttingen, Vandenhoeck und Ruprecht, 1983.

52. L.T. JOHNSON, *The Literary Function of Possessions in Luke-Acts* (SBL DS, 39), Missoula, Scholars Press, 1977.

53. W. STEGEMANN, *Nachfolge Jesu als solidarische Gemeinschaft der reichen und angesehenen Christen mit den bedürftigen und verachteten Christen – Das Lukasevangelium*, in L. SCHOTTROFF – W. STEGEMANN (éds.), *Jesus von Nazareth – Hoffnung der Armen* (UB, 639), Stuttgart, Kohlhammer, ²1981, p. 89-153. T. KATO, *La pensée sociale de Luc-Actes* (EHPR, 76), Paris, PUF, 1997.

54. P.F. ESLER, *Community and Gospel in Luke-Acts* (SNTS MS, 57), Cambridge, University Press, 1987.

55. H.J. DEGENHARDT, *Lukas – Evangelist der Armen. Besitz und Besitzverzicht in den lukanischen Schriften*, Stuttgart, KBW, 1965. H.J. KLAUCK, *Die Armut der Jünger in der Sicht des Lukas*, in ID., *Gemeinde–Amt–Sakrament. Neutestamentliche Perspektiven*, Würzburg, Echter, 1989, p. 160-194

sont jamais problématisés dans l'œuvre de Luc. Entre ces propos et l'image de la chrétienté dans les Ac, entre le dépouillement exigé des Douze (Lc 9,3) et l'assistance généreusement accordée aux missionnaires dans les Ac[56], gît une tension que l'auteur ne résout pas.

Deuxièmement: le renoncement n'est pas le seul modèle éthique de rapport à l'argent non confirmé dans la suite du récit; un autre modèle, la communion des biens (Ac 2,44s; 4,32-37), disparaît aussi sans être invalidé. Leur apparition temporaire n'induit pas l'idée qu'ils seraient réservés à une élite de croyants, mais plutôt qu'ils sont liés à une période de l'histoire du salut.

Troisièmement: l'argent demeure en permanence pour Luc un point crucial, qui ne touche pas seulement à la morale, mais à l'identité chrétienne. Que ce soit face aux juifs (Ac 2,44s; 4,32-37) ou face au monde religieux gréco-romain avec ses pratiques magiques et oraculaires (Ac 8,18-23; 16,16-19; 19,18s), la foi chrétienne affirme sa spécificité par un souci de partage et un refus de la vénalité. Le comportement chrétien face aux biens représente d'ailleurs dans les Actes un facteur important de croissance de la communauté[57].

Luc historien et Luc théologien

Comment expliquer cette tension? Pourquoi le narrateur a-t-il tenu à ce que l'auditeur/lecteur parvenu en fin de l'œuvre se trouve à la fois sous le coup des «Malheur!» de Jésus, et à la fois installé dans une situation économique vraisemblablement plus proche de la sienne? Je pense que la dualité du Luc historien et du Luc théologien nous aide à comprendre.

L'historien Luc rattache aux périodes historiques adéquates les modèles de rapport à l'argent que lui livrent ses sources. Il n'entend pas faire d'anachronisme; c'est pourquoi il ne parera pas, par exemple, la figure de Paul d'un idéal de pauvreté qui ne correspond pas à ce qu'il sait.

Le théologien Luc veut transmettre l'idée que la question des biens doit être pour le chrétien un souci identitaire. C'est pourquoi les invectives de Jésus ne sont pas seulement consignées, mais rédactionnellement accentuées; elles surplombent le macro-récit comme une instance critique, comme une parole tranchante qu'aucun épisode ultérieur ne

---

56. Lydie héberge Paul et Silas à Philippes (Ac 16,15); les Maltais pourvoient aux besoins de Paul et de ses compagnons (28,10 ἐπέθεντο τὰ πρὸς τὰς χρείας).

57. Cette observation n'a pas échappé à W. REINHARDT, *Das Wachstum des Gottesvolkes. Untersuchungen zum Gemeindewachstum im lukanischen Doppelwerk auf dem Hintergrund des Alten Testaments*, Göttingen, Vandenhoeck und Ruprecht, 1995, p. 171-180.

viendra émousser. L'avancement de l'histoire (et du récit) amèneront le déplacement vers d'autres modèles (la communion des biens, l'assistance aux démunis); mais cette relecture en différé de la parole sur le danger des richesses, cette adaptation aux conditions changeantes, ne vient jamais éteindre l'incandescence de l'invective originaire. Nul ne s'étonnera dès lors que le premier miracle du Nom du Christ au travers des apôtres intervienne sur fond de manque d'argent (3,6), ni que la première crise de la communauté – le péché originel en Église – soit un délit d'argent; je veux parler d'Ananias et Saphira (Ac 5,1-11)[58].

CONCLUSION: LUC-ACTES, UN DIPTYQUE

À partir d'une observation du statut de la Loi et du cas de l'éthique économique dans l'œuvre de Luc, il s'avère les Actes succèdent à l'évangile à la façon d'une histoire continuée, avec ses nécessaires déplacements. Le terme «diptyque» convient bien à l'entité Lc-Ac, si l'on a à l'esprit deux tableaux articulés sur une charnière centrale (Lc 24 / Ac 1: l'exaltation de Jésus). J'ai voulu montrer que les tensions et les écarts perceptibles entre évangile et Actes ne militent pas en soi contre la thèse d'une entité littéraire et théologique, ces facteurs étant inhérents à la narration historique. Par contre, je plaide pour que l'«unité» Lc-Ac ne quitte pas le statut d'une proposition heuristique, le chercheur étant à chaque fois assigné à montrer comment s'opère cette unité et à vérifier si le texte s'y prête ou non.

Plutôt que d'attribuer à Luc une pensée théologique massifiée qu'il distribuerait au gré des épisodes du récit, considérer les Actes comme une suite[59], ou mieux comme un effet de l'évangile, ménage d'un récit à l'autre un jeu de miroir, avec ses nécessaires reprises, déplacements et recompositions. Le va et vient de l'évangile aux Actes et des Actes à l'évangile, qu'appelle ce jeu de miroir, est le travail de la lecture; de ce travail naît l'unité de Lc-Ac.

La thèse défendue dans cet article est précisément que l'unité de l'œuvre à Théophile ne gît pas dans le texte, mais s'événementie dans

---

58. Sur la lecture d'Ac 5,1-11 comme récit de péché originel en Église, voir D. MARGUERAT, *La mort d'Ananias et Saphira (Ac 5,1-11) dans la stratégie narrative de Luc*, in *NTS* 39 (1993) 209-226, surtout p. 222-225.

59. M.C. PARSONS et R.I. PERVO, *Rethinking the Unity of Luke and Acts* (n. 10), p. 126: «Literarily, Acts is best characterized as a sequel». Ce terme est préférable à considérer Ac comme une «confirmation of the Gospel»: W.C. VAN UNNIK, *The «Book of Acts», the Confirmation of the Gospel*, in *NT* 4 (1960) 26-59, ou Lc comme «a preface to Acts»: C.K. BARRETT, *The Third Gospel as a Preface to Acts?* (n. 9).

l'acte de lecture. Elle est l'œuvre du lecteur, guidé par une série d'indicateurs mis en place par le narrateur à son intention: inclusions, prolepses, chaînes narratives et *syncrisis*. Parce qu'il fait constamment appel à sa mémoire, parce qu'il l'oblige à balayer les deux parties du diptyque lucanien, ce dispositif narratif conduit le lecteur à relire l'évangile à partir des Actes pour y chercher les clefs herméneutiques du récit, et à déceler dans les Actes la réalisation des prédictions de l'évangile. La précédence christologique à laquelle s'adosse la destinée des apôtres est constamment évoquée, plutôt que désignée, par le récit des Actes; elle sollicite une mémoire d'évangile qui convoque le lecteur à *faire* l'unité de Lc-Ac. Les Actes des apôtres s'offrent ainsi au lecteur comme un champ de vérification des promesses de l'évangile: l'auteur, dans sa préface, n'a-t-il pas averti le très honorable Théophile que son récit lui permettrait de vérifier «la sûreté (ἀσφάλεια) des enseignements» reçus (Lc 1,4)?

18 ch. de la Cocarde   Daniel MARGUERAT
CH-1024 Ecublens

THE TEXT OF LUKE-ACTS

A CONFRONTATION OF RECENT THEORIES

Until about fifteen years ago, one could have had the impression that the classical question concerning the relationship between the Alexandrian and the so-called "Western" text of Luke and Acts was settled, if not in theory, at least in practice. Apart from a few stubborn "heretics", most editors and exegetes during the preceding decades had based their text-critical decisions on the explicit or silent assumption that the "Western" text is the result of some form of corruption of the original text, which is more faithfully represented by the Alexandrian text-tradition. Everything seemed to be "quiet on the Western front". But all of a sudden, the hostilities started again. Before finishing her remarkable study published in *Ephemerides Theologicae Lovanienses* in 1986, Professor Barbara Aland had to include, unexpectedly, an additional passage. I quote: "Als ich diese methodischen Grundsätze niederschrieb, ging ich davon aus, die Ansicht, daß der sogenannte westliche text eine spätere Bearbeitung der Apostelgeschichte sei, habe sich – mit Variationen im einzelnen – allgemein durchgesetzt. Dem ist aber nicht so"[1]. The reason for her surprise and for the additional passage was the publication of the impressive study on the *Texte Occidental des Actes des Apôtres* by Marie-Émile Boismard and Arnauld Lamouille[2]. And this publication was only the beginning of a series of studies by these and other authors, as we will see, in which the convenient (though only apparent) consensus was dramatically shaken[3].

It was also usual, in text-critical publications as well as in commentaries, to discuss the textual problems in Luke and Acts separately. On the one hand, the study of the "Western" text in Luke concentrated mainly on the so-called "Western non-interpolations", a discussion which was considered virtually closed since the discovery of $\mathfrak{P}^{75}$. On the

---

1. B. ALAND, *Entstehung, Charakter und Herkunft des sog. westlichen Textes untersucht an der Apostelgeschichte*, in *ETL* 62 (1986) 5-65.
2. M.-É. BOISMARD & A. LAMOUILLE, *Le texte Occidental des Actes des Apôtres. Reconstitution et réhabilitation*, 2 vol., Paris, Éditions Recherche sur les Civilisations, 1984.
3. See also J. DELOBEL, *Focus on the "Western" Text in Recent Studies*, in *ETL* 73 (1997) 401-410; ID., *The "Apostolic Decree" in Recent Research*, in *EΠI TO AYTO*. FS P. Pokorny, Prague, Universita Karlova, 1998, pp. 67-81.

other hand, heavy emphasis was laid on the exceptional situation of the "Western" text of Acts with its numerous longer and shorter additions. Some recent studies suggest the unity of Luke-Acts, also in so far as their textual tradition is concerned.

Although the recent studies on the text of Acts and Luke are radically opposed to the relative consensus which dominated the scene for the last fifty years, and although most of them plead for the rehabilitation of the "Western" text as the most ancient textual tradition available, their theories, methods and arguments display an astonishing variety. Indeed, one can say that "l'histoire se répète", because the first wave of comprehensive theories concerning the origin and the value of the "Western" text, at the end of the nineteenth and in the first decades of this century, was also characterised by a series of contradictory theories.

After a brief survey of these older studies (I), I will try to describe the recent theories (II), in view of a confrontation and a more personal evaluation (III). I do not have the ambition to present a new solution to the problem, remembering that it has been called "the Waterloo" of so many authors[4]. Leuven is too close to Waterloo to ever forget this warning.

I. EARLY COMPREHENSIVE THEORIES
A SHORT HISTORY OF THE RESEARCH[5]

A glance at A.F.J Klijn's epoch-making dissertation[6] reminds us that the problem has occupied exegetes and editors since in the sixteenth century Theodore Beza acquired the famous bilingual codex which has been named after him. But the presentation of a comprehensive solution, based on an overall study, especially for the book of Acts, is credited to Blaß, Clark and Ropes.

---

4. Cf. B.H. STREETER, *Codices 157, 1071 and the Caesarean Text*, in R.P. CASEY & S. LAKE (eds.), *Quantulacumque*. FS K. Lake, London, Christophers, 1937, p. 150.

5. For a more extensive historical survey of the research on the text of Acts, see: B.M. METZGER, *A Textual Commentary on the Greek New Testament*, Stuttgart, United Bible Societies, 1971, pp. 259-272; BOISMARD & LAMOUILLE, *Texte Occidental*, I, pp. 3-8; W.A. STRANGE, *The Problem of the Text of Acts* (SNTS MS, 71), Cambridge, University Press, 1992, pp. 1-34; P. TAVARDON, *Le texte alexandrin et le texte occidental des Actes des Apôtres. Doublets et variantes de structure* (Cahiers de la Revue biblique, 37), Paris, Gabalda, 1997, pp. 1-41. Among the ancient studies, see also H. COPPIETERS, *De Historia Textus Actorum Apostolorum* (diss.), Leuven, Van Linthout, 1902.

6. A.F.J. KLIJN, *A Survey of the Researches into the Western Text of the Gospels and Acts*, Utrecht, Kemink, 1949; Part Two (NTSup, 21), Leiden, Brill, 1969.

1. In line with an earlier suggestion made by Johannes Clericus (Jean Leclerc)[7] and in accordance with the preference of Joseph B. Lightfoot[8], Friedrich Blaß[9] tried to prove, in 1895, that Luke produced two subsequent editions of Acts: a first draft, the "Western" text, for the Roman church, and a later, more polished edition, the Alexandrian text, for his friend Theophilus. Blaß's hypothesis has come back, in various forms, throughout this century, and remains to some degree the background of the recent revival of the preference for the "Western" tradition.

2. A few years later, in 1900, August Pott[10] proposed a slightly different solution, though also in favour of the priority of the "Western" text. Luke would have limited his work to the *Acta Pauli*, and this document, which survived in the "Western" text, would have been combined with another source, the result being the Alexandrian text.

3. Taking up a suggestion put forward by Friedrich A. Bornemann[11], Albert C. Clark[12] supported the priority of the "Western" text with a rather surprising hypothesis: a clumsy scribe had left out several lines by accident, due to the writing *per cola et commata*. The hypothesis, which was inspired by an analogous phenomenon in the transmission of classical texts, was unsuccessful, and some twenty years later, Clark presented an extensive analysis in which he turned his hypothesis of "accidental" changes into "intentional" changes. But the resultant shorter text of Acts was still the Alexandrian tradition.

4. In 1926, John H. Ropes[13] proposed a detailed argumentation in favour of the opposite hypothesis. The Alexandrian text represents the

---

7. J. CLERICUS, *Sentiments de quelques théologiens d'Hollande*, Amsterdam, Henri Desbordes, 1685, p. 451. The author suggests this as a mere possibility, which he *immediately* rejects himself. It is, therefore, somewhat misleading to write: "The first to make this suggestion appears to have been Jean Leclerc, who, however, *later* [italics mine] rejected his own hypothesis": cf. METZGER, *Commentary* (n. 5), p. 260.

8. J.B. LIGHTFOOT, *On a Fresh Revision of the English New Testament*, London, Macmillan, 1871, p. 29; ³1891, p. 32.

9. F. BLASS, *Acta apostolorum sive Lucae ad Theophilum liber alter. Editio philologica*, Göttingen, Vandenhoeck & Ruprecht, 1895; *Über die verschiedenen Textformen in den Schriften des Lukas*, in *NKZ* 6 (1895) 712-725; *Acta apostolorum sive Lucae ad Theophilum liber alter, secundum formam qua videtur Romanam*, Leipzig, Teubner, 1896; *Zu den zwei Textformen der Apostelgeschichte*, in *TSK* 73 (1900) 5-28.

10. A. POTT, *Der abendländische Text der Apostelgeschichte und die Wir-Quelle*, Leipzig, Hinrichs, 1900.

11. F.A. BORNEMANN, *Acta Apostolorum ab Sancto Luca conscripta ad Codicis Cantabrigiensis fidem recensuit*, Grossenhain – London, 1848.

12. A.C. CLARK, *The Primitive Text of the Gospels and Acts*, Oxford, Clarendon Press, 1914; *The Acts of the Apostles, a Critical Edition with Introduction and Notes on Selected Passages*, Oxford, Clarendon Press, 1933; ⁹1970.

13. J.H. ROPES, *The Text of Acts*, in F.J. FOAKES JACKSON & K. LAKE, *The Beginnings of Christianity. Part I. The Acts of the Apostles*, Vol. III, London, Macmillan, 1926.

most ancient text-form. By adding numerous glosses, the "Western" text attempts to improve the earlier tradition.

5. A few years before the Second World War, the peaceful "battle" about the text of Acts ended, though the outcome was still undecided. During the subsequent "armistice" among exegetes, which lasted for about fifty years and during which no one ventured a new comprehensive hypothesis, New Testament scholars practised a somewhat ambiguous eclectic method. "Eclectic" because, in view of the lack of a consensus on any comprehensive theory, exegetes, including the UBS-committee, proclaimed that, in principle, every variant reading had an equal claim to be original and, therefore, an equal right to be preferred[14]. "Ambiguous", because, in fact, most authors manifested a silent preference for the Alexandrian text, as appears from the dominance of this text-type in the leading text editions and the commentaries. Although the results of the eclectic approach were far from unanimous[15], one could have expected that this would become an (ever) lasting approach. "Dem ist aber nicht so...". A fresh look at some aspects of the "Western" text in the sixties and seventies awoke the somewhat "sleeping" topic and encouraged several scholars to engage in new overall research in view of proposing a new (or a revived) comprehensive theory.

II. The Text of Luke-Acts: A Storm Centre in Recent Research

In the sixties, Eldon Jay Epp's[16] much appreciated and much debated search for a theological tendency in Codex Bezae again focused the

---

14. Cf. Metzger, *Commentary*, pp. 271-272: "Since no hypothesis thus far proposed to explain the relation of the Western and the Alexandrian texts of Acts has gained anything like general assent, in its work on that book the Bible Society's Committee proceeded in an eclectic fashion, holding that neither the Alexandrian not the Western group of witnesses always preserves the original text, but that in order to attain the earliest text one must compare the two divergent traditions point by point and in each case select a reading which commends itself in the light of transcriptional and intrinsic probabilities". As a result of this sound method, one needs a magnifying-glass to discover "Western" readings which managed to emerge from the critical apparatus and to creep into the text.

15. Cf. the somewhat cynical comment by A.F.J. Klijn, *In Search of the Original Text of Acts*, in L.E. Keck & J.L. Martyn (eds.), *Studies in Luke-Acts.* FS P. Schubert, Nashville, TN, Abingdon Press, 1966, pp. 103-110, esp. 104: "Yet, those who, by way of the eclectic method, try to restore the original text have reached markedly disparate results. The eclectic method seems to be the only adequate method to regain the original text, but it also appears to lead us into complete chaos".

16. E.J. Epp, *The "Ignorance Motif" in Acts and Anti-Judaic Tendencies in Codex Bezae,* in *HTR* 55 (1962) 51-62; *The Theological Tendency of Codex Bezae Cantabrigiensis in Acts* (SNTS MS, 3), Cambridge, University Press, 1966. See also the reaction by C.K. Barrett, *Is There a Theological Tendency in Codex Bezae?* in E. Best & R.McL. Wilson (eds.), *Text and Interpretation. Studies in the New Testament.* FS M. Black, Cambridge, University Press, 1979, pp. 15-28.

attention of several scholars on the "Western" text. Carlo MARTINI's[17] and Max WILCOX's[18] contributions to the Leuven *Colloquium* in 1977 reinforced this renewed interest.

1. In the careful study in *ETL* mentioned above[19], Barbara ALAND strongly defended the priority of the Alexandrian text. In her opinion, an overall solution can only be expected when one takes into account *all* the major aspects of the problem[20] and when a balanced text-critical method, including both external and internal criticism, is applied. She started from text-samples in the oldest direct (though very fragmentary) evidence, $\mathfrak{P}^{38.48}$, and confronted these with the parallel passages in Codex Bezae, minuscule 614 and the Harklean Syriac. Her conclusions are, to some degree, parallel with the nuanced proposal of Ernst HAENCHEN in his commentary on Acts[21].   ·

She distinguishes three stages in the complex development of (or rather: towards) the "Western" text.

a. From the early second century on, she finds evidence of the (relatively free) creation of a series of readings mainly of a paraphrasing nature, which pave the way for the *later* "Western" text.

b. At some point, early in the third century, a copyist, using a manuscript of the type just mentioned (similar to the later minuscule 614) and acting as a real redactor, produced what she calls, the "Western" *Hauptredaktion*, not in order to create a radically new text, but in an attempt to faithfully transmit the text by making it "deutlicher, klarer und konsequenter".

c. In the later textual transmission of this type of text, a.o. in $\mathfrak{P}^{38.48}$, cod. D, Syr[hmg], further paraphrase may have been introduced, reinforcing this tendency of the "Western tradition".

The *Hauptredaktion* would have been produced in Syria, after Irenaeus, but before the third-century papyri. The main argument for this date is that the typically "Western" longer readings are absent from Irenaeus[22], but

17. C.M. MARTINI, *La tradition textuelle des Actes des Apôtres et les tendances de l'église ancienne,* in J. KREMER, *Les Actes des Apôtres. Traditions, rédaction, théologie* (BETL, 48), Gembloux, J. Duculot – Leuven, University Press, 1979, pp. 21-35.

18. M. WILCOX, *Luke and the Bezan Text of Acts* (*ibid.,* pp. 447-455).

19. B. ALAND, *Entstehung* (n. 1).

20. B. Aland distinguishes three main aspects: 1. "Die Tendenz der Änderungen..."; 2. "die jeweiligen Mitzeugen und deren Text bzw. die Entwicklung von deren Text zu D..."; 3. "das Phänomen des 'westlichen' Textes... in der Gesamtheit der neutestamentlichen Überlieferung...".

21. E. HAENCHEN, *Die Apostelgeschichte* (KEK, 3), Göttingen, Vandenhoeck & Ruprecht, [12]1959; [16]1977 (ed. E. Gräßer), pp. 64ff.

22. According to B. Aland, the few longer readings in Irenaeus' quotations of Acts do not belong to the "Western" tradition.

present in the third-century papyri. The main argument for the localisation is the concentration of early and diverse evidence of the "Western"
text related to that region[23].

2. From 1980 on, the classical scholar Édouard DELEBECQUE has published an extensive series of detailed linguistic and textual analyses of
individual passages of Acts, before collecting them in a comprehensive
study in 1986[24]. His rather particular theory has been determined by two
elements of a different nature: on the one hand, a careful philological
investigation of Lucan vocabulary and style, and, on the other hand, a
very traditional view on date and authorship of various New Testament
books, including the deutero-Pauline writings. He opines that both the
"Western" and the Alexandrian text are due to the same author, Luke
the "beloved physician", mentioned in Col 4,14. The Alexandrian text is
the first draft, written about A.D. 62. Only a few years later, about A.D.
67, Luke sought to improve his work by producing a second extended
edition, the "Western" text. In considering the Alexandrian text as the
earliest form of the text, Delebecque shares the points of view of Ropes
and Aland. In ascribing the "Western" text to the same author and dating it in the first century, he joins Blaß and anticipates some of the
recent scholars whom I will mention now.

3. For Marie-Émile BOISMARD's faithful readers the impressive studies on Acts, most of them published in collaboration with A. LA-
MOUILLE[25], should not have been a complete surprise. For more than half
a century now, Boismard has maintained his basic methodological principles. Firstly, in the field of textual criticism he always pays particular
attention to indirect evidence (Diatessaron, ancient versions, and patristic quotations), and gives special weight to a series of remote witnesses,
which are usually not very highly appreciated[26]. At the same time, he

23. Cf. B. ALAND, *Entstehung*, pp. 57-65. Her hypothesis is based on detailed studies
of the Syriac text and more particularly on her own view of the relationship between the
Philoxenian and Harklean Syriac.

24. É. DELEBECQUE, *Les deux Actes des Apôtres* (Études bibliques, n.s., 6) Paris,
Gabalda, 1986.

25. M.-É. BOISMARD, *The Text of Acts: A Problem of Literary Criticism?* in E.J. EPP
& G.D. FEE (eds.), *New Testament Textual Criticism. Its Significance for Exegesis*. FS
B.M. Metzger, Oxford, Clarendon Press, 1981, pp. 147-157; BOISMARD & LAMOUILLE,
Texte Occidental (n. 2), 1984; *Le texte Occidental des Actes des Apôtres. À propos
d'Actes 27,1-13*, in *ETL* 63 (1987) 48-58; *Les Actes des deux Apôtres*. I. *Introduction –
Textes*. II. *Le sens des récits*. III. *Analyses littéraires* (Études bibliques, n.s., 12-14), Paris,
Gabalda, 1990; M.-É. BOISMARD, *Le Codex de Bèze et le texte occidental des Actes*, in
D.C. PARKER & C.-B. AMPHOUX (eds.), *Codex Bezae. Studies from the Lunel Colloquium,
June 1994* (NTTS, 22), Leiden, Brill, 1996, pp. 257-270.

26. He himself calls them: "les petits, les obscurs, les sans grade…" (cf. *Texte Occidental*, I, p. 9). The choice has not been made at random, cf. *Les Actes*, I, p. 58: "Ces

puts a special emphasis on internal criticism. Secondly, in the area of
source criticism, apparently not sharing the philosophical principle:
"entia non sunt multiplicanda", he is not afraid of proposing various
hypothetical source-documents and several redactional stages. Because
of the unity and the continuity in his research, his conclusions concerning the Synoptics, John and Acts hold together, and there is also a close
relationship between textual criticism, source and redaction criticism.
This makes it practically impossible to isolate one aspect of his all-
encompassing theory and rather difficult to summarise it briefly as well
as faithfully.

a. Schematically, Boismard-Lamouille's theory concerning the text of
Acts can be presented as follows[27].

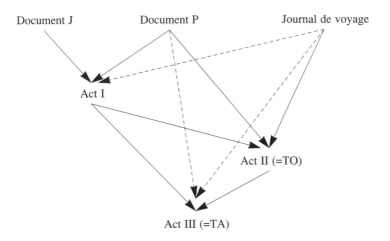

On the basis of three ancient documents – *Document P* about Peter, *Le
Journal de voyage* probably written by Silas, and *Document J* from the
circle of the disciples of the Baptist – three redactional levels are to be
distinguished: an (unknown) Jewish-Christian author wrote a first draft
about 60-62: it is referred to by the siglum Act I; Luke, Paul's companion and the author of the third Gospel, reworked this first draft about 80:
Act II; an unknown author brought the finishing touch, writing for Gen-

témoins secondaires, grecs, latins, syriaques, coptes, éthiopiens n'ont pas été choisis au
hasard. Nous avons pris un certain nombre de leçons longues du TO, les plus caractéristiques et dont l'appartenance au TO ne saurait être mise en doute, et nous avons noté
quels étaient les témoins qui les soutenaient, en dehors des quatre témoins majeurs".

27. See *Les Actes*, I, p. 5. The full lines mean full use of the source, the dotted lines
mean occasional use. I added the sigla TO and TA to indicate the relationship between
source-criticism and textual criticism.

tile Christians, perhaps in Rome in the last decade of the first century: Act III. In their opinion, Act II corresponds with the original form of the "Western" text, "Texte Occidental" (TO), whereas Act III represents the original form of the Alexandrian text, "Texte Alexandrin" (TA). In principle, TA is later than TO, except when Act III depends directly on the sources of Act II, rather than on Act II itself.

Source criticism of Acts has often come to a dead end for the obvious reason that there is only one book of Acts, and a direct comparison with parallel material, as in the case of the synoptic Gospels, is excluded. Boismard-Lamouille use the method which is available in this case: the only way to discover (possible) *sources* is the search for thematic unity (e.g. about Peter) and traces of a combination of diverse materials, like doublets, "seams" and transitional passages; the best, if not the only safe way to identify Lucan *redaction* is the study of Luke's procedure in handling the Marcan material. But because Boismard-Lamouille consider TO and TA as the result of two redactional stages, they feel entitled to use the textual evidence in their redaction-critical approach. In textual criticism, an extensive study of Lucan vocabulary and style, one of the most remarkable features of their publication[28], is a basic tool for their reconstruction of the original TO. This is an unavoidable task since the extant witnesses bear the signs of later corruption (TO[2]). An important argument in favour of the more primitive character of the TO is its brevity. Despite its reputation of being the "longer text", because of the numerous and well-known longer readings, the authors characterise it as "un texte court", and apply the text-critical canon "Lectio brevior potior"[29].

It appears from this summary that the theories of Aland and Boismard concerning the origin and nature of the "Western" text of Acts, are diametrically opposed. Aland situates it in the early *third* century (in line with a paraphrasing tendency in the second century), Boismard in the second half of the *first* century (followed by a growing corruption in later centuries). One could almost say that, according to Aland, the story

---

28. See *Texte Occidental*, II, pp. 195-349. A critical evaluation is given by F. NEIRYNCK & F. VAN SEGBROECK, *Le texte des Actes des Apôtres et les caractéristiques stylistiques lucaniennes,* in *ETL* 61 (1985) 304-339. Boismard and Lamouille have been inspired by de studies of Martini and Wilcox at the Leuven Colloquium mentioned above and by earlier authors, but they have tried to present an exhaustive list of the characteristics.

29. Cf. *Texte Occidental*, I, pp. 104-111, esp. 104: "Mais qu'arrive-t-il lorsque le TO offre un texte parallèle à celui du TA? Presque toujours il est alors plus court que le TA. C'est cet aspect si peu connu du TO que nous voudrions souligner maintenant; il contribue à faire de lui un texte excellent".

of the "Western" text begins there, where Boismard thinks that it ends. In Aland's opinion, the "Western" text is a corruption of the original text whereas the Alexandrian tradition remained much closer to the autographs. On the contrary, in Boismard's opinion, this last tradition is a later stage as a result of the reworking of the original "Western" text.

b. In the last few years, Boismard has published an analogous source- and redaction-critical theory concerning the Gospel of Luke, explicitly relating it to his former studies on Acts[30]. On the basis of ancient documents, he distinguishes, once more, three redactional levels: L (=Proto-Luke), Luke and a final Redactor, and he emphasises their relationship with the three redactional levels in Acts[31]. He rejects a purely redactional explanation of the *Sondergut* and joins the Proto-Luke hypothesis: Luke's basic document was an early gospel, composed of Q and L. Luke integrated Markan material into this primary source. In these studies about Luke, Boismard does not explicitly study the textual problem. But the parallelism between the redactional levels of Luke and Acts seems to suggest that the solution of the textual problem of Luke would be very close to Boismard-Lamouille's theory concerning the text of Acts[32].

4. The thesis of W.A. STRANGE[33] is, again, completely different, both in its approach and its results, although, like in Boismard-Lamouille's theory, "lucanisms" play an important role in the argument. Starting from certain established procedures in the process of writing and editing books in antiquity, and from the impression that most of the longer "Western" readings are narrative or theological comments, Strange comes to the following comprehensive theory concerning the two forms of the text of Acts. Luke wrote a "rough draft", to which he added, at some later point, marginal and interlinear notes. He did not edit his work

---

30. M.-É. BOISMARD, *L'Évangile de l'enfance (Luc 1-2) selon le Proto-Luc* (Études bibliques, n.s., 35), Paris, Gabalda, 1997; *En quête du Proto-Luc* (Études bibliques, n.s., 37), Paris, Gabalda, 1997.

31. Cf. *En quête*, p. 333: "Il est logique d'en conclure qu'il doit y avoir une identité entre le document L de l'évangile et notre Act I des Actes, entre Luc et notre Act II, enfin entre le Rédacteur final et Act III. La correspondance entre les deux niveaux fondamentaux de l'évangile et des Actes est confirmée par une certaine unité de style qui court tout au long de l'évangile de Luc et des Actes".

32. See also a remark on the problem of the "Western" text of the Gospels in M.-É. BOISMARD avec la collaboration de A. LAMOUILLE, *Le Diatessaron de Tatien* (Études bibliques, n.s., 15), Paris, Gabalda, 1992, p. 157: "C'est aussi tout le problème du texte dit 'Occidental' des évangiles qui pourrait ainsi trouver partiellement sa solution si, comme nous le croyons, les variantes de ce texte 'Occidental' ne sont que des échos des harmonies primitives, soit l'harmonie/Justin, soit l'harmonie syro-latine, soit le Diatessaron de Tatien". In his opinion, the "harmonie de Pepys" is particularly important for the reconstruction of the oldest harmony, the one which Justin would have known.

33. W.A. STRANGE, *The Problem of the Text of Acts* (n. 5).

himself, but it was published posthumously in two different forms. The first editor introduced the notes into the text, though not necessarily in a harmonious way: the resultant form was the "Western" text. The second editor inserted only a few of the marginal notes, limiting himself to an occasional clarification of obscure passages: the resultant (shorter) form was the Alexandrian text. Accordingly, both forms are basically Lucan in origin, as appears also from the lucanisms in vocabulary, style and theology in both textual traditions. One could say that the "Western" text conserves even more Lucan material, because the editor of the Alexandrian text left out most of the marginal notes.

5. Christian-Bernard AMPHOUX has not yet tackled the problem of Acts as such, but his numerous studies on the text of the gospels in Codex Bezae, indirectly concern the text of Acts as well[34]. The author has been impressed by the emphasis of his predecessor, Jean DUPLACY, on the possible critical value of the "Western" readings[35], but his own theory, especially in its more recent form[36], goes much further[37].

34. L. VAGANAY, *Initiation à la critique textuelle du Nouveau Testament,* Paris, Cerf, [2]1986; *An Introduction to New Testament Textual Criticism,* Cambridge, University Press, [2]1991 (amplified and updated by C.-B. Amphoux and J. Heimerdinger); C.-B. AMPHOUX, *Le chapitre 24 de Luc et l'origine de la tradition textuelle du Codex de Bèze (D.05 du NT),* in *Filología Neotestamentaria* 4 (1991) 21-49; *Les premières éditions de Luc.* I. *Le texte de Luc,* in *ETL* 67 (1991) 312-327; II. *L'histoire du texte au IIe siècle,* in *ETL* 68 (1992) 38-48; *Les premières versions de Luc 5 et leur contribution à l'histoire du texte,* in R. GRYSON (ed.), *Philologia Sacra. Biblische und patristische Studien. FS H.J. Frede & W. Thiele,* 2 vol., Freiburg, Herder, 1993, I, pp. 193-221; & J. MARGAIN (ed.), *Les premières traditions de la Bible* (Histoire du texte biblique, 2), Lausanne, Éditions du Zèbre, 1996; *Le texte* (Responses and Conclusions), in D.C. PARKER, & C.-B. AMPHOUX (eds.), *Codex Bezae* (n. 25), pp. 337-354; *L'Évangile selon Matthieu. Codex de Bèze,* Paris, Le bois d'Orion, 1996.

35. In the conclusions of the Lunel Colloquium of 1994, which he chaired together with D.C. Parker, Amphoux situates his researches concerning the second-century variant readings in the gospel text "dans la continuité de celles du regretté Jean Duplacy". He refers to Duplacy's contribution at the *Colloquium Biblicum Lovaniense* on Luke in 1968: cf. J. DUPLACY, $\mathfrak{P}^{75}(Pap.$ *Bodmer XIV-XV) et les formes les plus anciennes du texte de Luc,* in F. NEIRYNCK (ed.), *L'évangile de Luc. Problèmes littéraires et théologiques. Mémorial Lucien Cerfaux* (BETL, 32), Gembloux, Duculot, 1973, pp. 111-128 (revised and enlarged edition, 1989, pp. 21-38); repr. in J. DUPLACY, *Études de critique textuelle du Nouveau Testament,* ed. J. DELOBEL (BETL, 78), Leuven, Peeters – University Press, 1987, pp. 151-168; I quote from the first edition, p. 128: "Du point de vue de l'histoire du texte, il n'y a actuellement aucune raison valable de situer avec assurance cette 'apparition' [of the $\mathfrak{P}^{75}$-B-text] très haut dans le IIe siècle et, de ce point de vue, le 'texte occidental' garde l'avantage sur 'P^{75}-B'".

36. In his revision of Vaganay's *Introduction,* the presentation of Amphoux's theory on the development of the gospel-text can be regarded as a "first draft" which has been developed in his more recent and more personal publications. Cf. *Initiation,* pp. 135ff. In that earlier publication, Amphoux opined that the "Western" text largely corresponds with "le texte courant primitif" which is still close to the oral tradition, as is evident from its "style oral". This oral style was not suitable for widespread distribution, and thus an

a. From A.D. 110 to 138: "the edition of Smyrna". Amphoux distinguishes specific features in the gospels of Codex D, which point to "un projet d'évangélisation" in line with a suggestion in the letters of Ignatius[38]. This allows him to date this early edition of the D-text[39] in the first quarter of the second century. The sequence of the gospels is Mt-Jn-Lk-Mk. The *terminus a quo* is Ignatius, i.e., after A.D. 110. The *terminus ante quem* is Marcion, because this author appears to have known this type of text. Presumably, the edition is the work of Ignatius' collaborator and successor at Smyrna, Polycarp, perhaps together with Papias, about A.D. 120. It is a careful construction, in which the original text is already "méconnaissable", because the editor had a particular theological purpose. It is a masterpiece of rhetorical skill, a sophisticated kind of coded writing, not suitable for general circulation, because the broader audience was unable to grasp the hidden meaning. Amphoux discovers these "codes" within the pericopes, within the chapters, within the gospels as a whole and even throughout the four gospels taken together as a *corpus*[40]. In view of the fact that this oldest accessible text is itself already an artificial construction by an editor, any attempt to reconstruct the original text of the gospels seems to be an illusion[41].

actualisation took place, which we find in the Alexandrian text. The year A.D. 135, with the fall of Bar Kohba, may have been the starting point for this reworking, as it was the starting point for a new type of literature in the Jewish community. This theory is confirmed by the "Western" readings in second-century authors like Marcion, Justin, Tatian, Valentinus a.o. In a note from the English translator (J. Heimerdinger) of the *Initiation*, published in 1991, a new theory is announced and briefly summarised, which, in the opinion of the translator, will necessitate a revision of several pages in the *Introduction*: "If this suggested schema is ever confirmed, there would need to be a re-organisation of the paragraphs which follow here concerning the first, great recensions, for the Gospels at least, and perhaps for the New Testament overall" (*Introduction*, p. 98).

37. He is convinced that the history of the text of the gospels has never been described in a serious way. Cf. *L'Évangile selon Matthieu. Codex de Bèze*, p. 11: "Ce n'est pas que les informations nous manquent, mais les Évangiles sont avant tout l'affaire des théologiens, et ceux qui seraient compétents pour écrire l'histoire de leur texte ne s'y sont guère risqué jusqu'ici". With this warning in mind, we shall try to summarise his bold reconstruction of the textual history in the second century.

38. Cf. Ignatius in his letter to the Ephesians (ch. 19): "I hope to write you a further letter – if, in answer to your prayers, Jesus Christ allows it, and God so wills – in which *I will continue this preliminary account* for you of God's design for the New Man, Jesus Christ. It is a design which provides for faith in Him and love for Him, and comprehends His Passion and His Resurrection".

39. It is Amphoux' conviction that the fifth-century codex D, apart from a series of manifest scribal changes, both intentional and unintentional, is a rather faithful witness to the text of the gospels (and, may we suppose, of Acts?) in the early second century.

40. See, e.g., the conclusions of the Lunel Colloquium, pp. 343ff.: "le genre littéraire des Évangiles dans le Codex de Bèze".

41. Cf. *Les premières éditions de Luc* (n. 34), p. 47: "Le démon du 'texte primitif' n'est pas mort. (...) La belle poésie que la recherche des *ipsissima verba*".

b. From A.D. 138 to 172: "the Roman revisions". Because of the rather sophisticated nature of the above-mentioned edition, the need of a more simple form for a broader audience was felt. Several revisions were made in Rome. Marcion reworked the gospel of Luke. Although his text is closer to $\mathfrak{P}^{75}$-B, and despite the differences in content from the D-type, Amphoux maintains that Marcion used the D-type as the basis for his revision, because it appears that Marcion knew "les images chargées de symboles et la composition soucieuse d'une progression dans l'enseignement théologique"[42]. Tatian's Diatessaron is also based on the D-text. Valentinus has revised John.

c. From A.D. 172 to 178: "an edition in Alexandria". These "Roman" revisions paved the way for a new edition in the last quarter of the second century. The *terminus a quo* is Tatian's departure from Rome (A.D. 172) because the Diatessaron was not published before that date, and the *terminus ante quem* is the Platonic philosopher Celsus' allusion to several "revisions" of the gospels in A.D. 178[43]. The oldest witnesses, the papyri and Clement of Alexandria point to Egypt as its place of origin. The editor may have been Pantaenus, the founder of the school at Alexandria. This text-type is best represented by $\mathfrak{P}^{75}$-B. It is based on the revisions of the gospel texts by Marcion, Tatian, Valentinus and others, without, however, sharing their heterodox views. The sequence of the gospels is Mt-Mk-Lk-Jn, and this order is maintained from now on, as is already the case in Muratori's canon. The nature of this Alexandrian edition is described by Amphoux as follows: "Cette deuxième édition a la qualité essentielle qui manquait à la précédente: elle est plus simple, plus anecdotique, les images, moins liées entre elles, sont plus faciles a mémoriser. Les *Évangiles* ont trouvé le genre littéraire qui leur convenait, ils n'en changeront plus"[44].

In a nutshell: according to Amphoux, the "Western" text of the gospels is the most anciently accessible form of the text. Because of its editorial nature and sophisticated genre, it clearly does not allow the

---

42. *Le chapitre 24 de Luc* (n. 34), p. 41.

43. See, Origen, *Contra Celsum*, ed. H. CHADWICK, Cambridge, University Press, 1953, pp. 90-91: "After this he [Celsus] says that some believers, as though from a drinking bout, go so far as to oppose themselves and alter the original text of the gospel three or several times ever, and they change its character to enable them to deny difficulties in face of criticism. I do not know of people who have altered the gospel apart from the Marcionites and Valentinians, and I think also the followers of Lucan. But this statement is not a criticism of Christianity, but only of those who dared lightly to falsify the gospels". Chadwick's comment: "Celsus' meaning is uncertain. (...) Origen, however, may well be right, in view of Celsus' knowledge of Marcion, in taking him to refer to Marcion's alteration of the text" (p. 90, n. 2).

44. *Le chapitre 24 de Luc*, p. 46.

reconstruction of the original text of the gospels. The Alexandrian text, on the other hand, is the result of editorial work, about A.D. 175, based on several earlier revisions of the D-text. As a consequence, the Alexandrian text is even further removed from the origin than the "Western" text. If this is true, it is an illusion to think that our critical editions, which prefer the Alexandrian text-type, bring us close to the original text of the gospels.

6. The more primitive character of the "Western" text is also defended by Josep RIUS-CAMPS who is publishing a commentary on Acts in Catalan[45] and a continuing series of articles on sections of Acts in Spanish[46], and who is in the process of collecting the results of his research into a comprehensive commentary in English[47]. Textual criticism and exegesis are closely related in his approach. His preference for the originality of the "Western" text is related to his personal view on the aim of the author of Luke-Acts. Luke does not give his own idealised view on the beginnings of the church, but he describes how the disciples arrived step by step, by trial and error, at a better understanding of the meaning and the intention of Jesus. The particular readings of the "Western" text, even some of the smallest variants, betray this gradual development and Codex Bezae is a rather faithful witness ("de typo probablemente prerrecensional"[48]) of this most ancient textual tradition.

7. Finally, Paul TAVARDON[49] has tried to confirm and refine Boismard's text-critical and source-critical theory by a detailed investigation of selected passages from the first half of Acts. The combination of literary and textual criticism by Boismard-Lamouille is positively evaluated as a means to arrive at "un texte modèle". It is an illusion, in his opinion, to seek to reconstruct the "real" text. He investigates what he calls "doublets" and "variantes de structure", and comes to the conclu-

---

45. J. RIUS-CAMPS, *Comentari als Fets dels Apòstols.* Vol. I: *"Jerusalem" : configuració de l'església judeocreient (Ac 1,1–5,42)* (Collectània Sant Pacià, 14), Barcelona, Facultat de teologia de Catalunya, 1991; Vol. II: *"Judea i Samaria" : Gènesi de l'església cristiana a Antioquia (Ac 6,1–12,25)* (Collectània, 47), 1993; Vol. III: *"Fins als confins de la terra" : Primera i segona fases de la missió al paganisme (Ac 13,1–18,23)* (Collectània, 54), 1995.

46. J. RIUS-CAMPS, *Las variantes de la Recensión Occidental de los Hechos de los Apostóles.* I (Hch 1,1-3), in *Filología Neotestamentaria* 6 (1993) 59-68; II (Hch 1,4-14), 6 (1993) 219-229; III (Hch 1,25-26), 7 (1994) 53-64; IV (Hch 2,1-13), 7 (1994) 197-207; V (Hch 2,14-40), 8 (1995) 63-78; VI (Hch 2,41-47), 8 (1995) 199-208; VII (Hch 3,1-26), 9 (1996) 61-76; VIII (Hch 4,1-22), 9 (1996) 201-216.

47. See the announcement by J. HEIMERDINGER in *Filología Neotestamentaria* 9 (1996) 76-80.

48. *Las variantes,* I, p. 59.

49. P. TAVARDON, *Le texte alexandrin et le texte occidental des Actes des Apôtres* (n. 5).

sion that these literary phenomena are due to a combination of source-documents by a redactor: the result is the "Western" text (TO). Because these doublets were problematic for the readers, a reviser has tried to simplify the text by eliminating a series of doublets: the result is the Alexandrian text (TA). Again, in this theory, the "Western" text is more primitive than the Alexandrian.

III. CONFRONTATION AND EVALUATION

The surprisingly large number of recent studies on the text of Luke-Acts has led to a bewildering result. A glance at a schematic confrontation of some of these theories illustrates the confused situation (cf. the Table on p. 97). The diametrical opposition between defenders of the Alexandrian and partisans of the "Western" text at the beginning of this century has been "reanimated" and even reinforced. It is obvious that the majority of recent studies promote the rehabilitation of the "Western" text, and this concern goes often hand in hand with a renewed interest in, and in some cases a high esteem for, Codex Bezae[50]. It almost looks like a conspiracy against the dominant critical text, but the unanimity of the "Western camp" is only apparent, because the methods, theories, arguments and results are often completely irreconcilable.

How is it possible that the same textual data, the identical starting point for every scholar, can lead to such a paradoxical variety of theories? I see at least three causes.

The first cause is the virtual absence of any *direct* evidence from the second century, the period during which the text may be supposed to have enjoyed most freedom and to have suffered most corruption. For

50. The renewed interest in Codex Bezae also appears in several recent publications: J.N. BIRDSALL, *The Geographical and Cultural Origin of the Codex Bezae Cantabrigiensis: A Survey of the* status quaestionis, *Mainly from the Palaeographical Standpoint*, in W. SCHRAGE (ed.), *Studien zum Text und zur Ethik des Neuen Testaments*. FS H. Greeven (BZNW, 47), Berlin – New York, de Gruyter, 1986, pp. 102-114; D.C. PARKER, *A "Dictation Theory" of Codex Bezae*, in *JSNT* 15 (1982) 97-112; ID., *Codex Bezae: An Early Christian Manuscript and Its Text*, Cambridge, University Press, 1992; J.N. BIRDSALL, *After Three Centuries of the Study of Codex Bezae: The Status Quaestionis*; PARKER - AMPHOUX, *Codex Bezae* (n. 25), pp. XIX-XXX; A. AMMASSARI, *Bezae Codex Cantabrigiensis*, Città del Vaticano, Libreria Editrice Vaticano, 1996 (this is an new edition of the greco-latin text of the Codex, which takes into account the "struttura letteraria" and the "punteggiatura"); ID., *Il Vangelo di Matteo nella colonna latina del Bezae Codex Cantabrigiensis*, Città del Vaticano, 1996 (idem for *Marco, Luca, Giovanni*). Although these authors, and those mentioned in the survey in this contribution, share a common interest in the intriguing Codex Bezae, their evaluation of its reliability is far from being unanimous.

The origin of the "Western" text of Acts in some recent theories

Textual evidence of Acts	B. Aland	Boismard - Lamouille	W.A. Strange	C.-B. Amphoux (concerning the Gospels!)
Ic. direct indirect	Alexandrian text	Doc. P; Doc. J; Journal de voyage ca. 62 Act I ca. 80 Act II = TO ca. 90 Act III = TA	"rough draft" by Luke + marginal and interlinear notes, also by Luke	text not yet fixed
IIc. Vetus Latina Irenaeus	A series of minor (and major) changes (esp. paraphrase) paving the way for the "Western" text	corruption of TO = TO^2 corruption of TA = TA^2	- Alexandrian edition by a scribe with limited insertion of marginal notes - "Western" edition by a scribe, who inserted most of the Lucan notes Marcion: Luke	110: Ignatius: project 120: Smyrna: Polycarp: D-text (Mt-Jn-Mk-Lk) 130-172: Roman revisions: Tatian: Diatessaron Valentinus: John 172-178: Pantaenus: Alexandrian text (cf. P[75])
IIIc. Fathers P[45] P[38.48] 0171	"Western" *Hauptredaktion* minor and major variants in the genuine "Western" witnesses depending on the *Hauptredaktion*			

that reason, every theory can only be hypothetical, and imaginative constructions are to be welcomed. But there must be something wrong with the process involved in producing these hypotheses, because utterly divergent theories cannot all be equally right, and contradictory theories can hardly be complementary.

The second cause, in my opinion, is the inconspicuous and perhaps sometimes inadvertent transition from hypothesis to fact. Indeed, it often happens that a construction which is purely hypothetical at the outset, as a mere possibility among several other explanations which are equally possible, becomes the basis for the next step(s) and is gradually considered, presented and treated as a fact. This is not necessarily an unfair procedure on the part of the author, because one cannot constantly remind the reader of the hypothetical nature of the premises, but the result is that the reader, if not the author himself, runs the risk of forgetting that the foundation of the building is a pure hypothesis, and that the building is no stronger than its basement.

The third and most important cause of the paradoxical appreciation of the "Western" text in recent literature is the methodological approach. The quality of the method is, of course, crucial for the reliability of the results.

In this last part, I would like to confront the various theories, although there is little or no dialogue among the authors themselves. It is, of course, impossible to give an all-round critique of these often very detailed studies. I limit my critical approach to an evaluation of different aspects of the methodology as I find them used in these investigations, in order to highlight both their strength and their possible "Achilles-heel".

1. Source and Redaction Criticism of Acts and of the Lucan *Sondergut*

I already mentioned the main reason why source criticism of Acts is a problematic enterprise which, in spite of a century of research, has not led to any form of consensus. On the other hand, one can doubt as well the reliability of a redaction-critical approach, which consciously ignores the question of the sources. Redaction is not creation "ex nihilo". So, every endeavour in that field is praiseworthy, but one wonders whether the transition from "tradition" to "written source" in Boismard-Lamouille's theory is sufficiently founded. None of their three source-documents and none of their three redactional documents is, as such, available today[51]. Are we not confronted here with an overly bold accumulation of hypothe-

---

51. This is obvious as far as the source-documents are concerned, but even true for the redactional documents, albeit to a lesser degree. Indeed, although Act II is identified as

ses? "Entia non sunt multiplicanda" may be a sound principle in this respect after all. The very existence of any written documents in the earliest period of Christianity remains doubtful. Indeed, as many commentators have put forward, one wonders why the early generations, which were interested in the words and deeds of Jesus and expected his imminent parousia, would have written down their own history. Though being purely hypothetical as well, these remarks are valuable in my opinion. As far as the Lucan *Sondergut* is concerned, I would plead in favour of a redactional explanation that goes as far as it reasonably can go, taking fully into account the Lucan redactional procedures and the possible inspiration from Mk and Q (and oral tradition), and not passing too easily from *Sondergut* to *Sonderquelle*. It often appears then that hardly any peculiar pre-Lucan material remains, or that, what remains neither needs nor even allows its ascription to a written source.

2. The Attribution of Luke-Acts to Luke, the Companion of Paul

There is a growing tendency among some of the above-mentioned authors to come back to the traditional ascription of the Third Gospel and the book of Acts to the "beloved physician" of Col 4,14. One should not underestimate the consequences of this option. It is obvious that the author of Acts has a lot of information about Paul, but the traditional objections against the authorship of a historical companion of Paul (Boismard-Lamouille)[52], possibly related to a rather early date of Acts (Delebecque), are not to be overlooked: a.o. the chronological contradictions and theological differences between Acts and the Pauline Epistles, the divergent picture of the figure of Paul, and the absence of any reference to Paul's literary activity in Acts.

3. The Argument of Doublets

A real doublet can point to a combination of parallel traditions or even written sources. But the definition of a "doublet" is delicate and easily

TO and Act III as TA, and although the reconstruction of these texts is carefully based on the evidence in Greek manuscripts and ancient versions, TO and TA are to be purified, at least in some places, from later corruption (TO^2 and TA^2).

52. Concerning the Lukan authorship, there is a certain development in the views of Boismard and Lamouille. In *Texte Occidental*, pp. 8-9, Luke is said to have been the author of both TO and TA. In *Les Actes*, pp. 42 and 50, Act II (= TO) is attributed to Luke, whereas Act III (= TA) is the work of an anonymous author. In *En quête*, p. 15, "l'auteur du document L et celui que nous appelons Luc appartiendraient à une même école"; pp. 340-341: Proto-Luke (comp. Act I) is perhaps the work of Silas (presumably the author of "le Journal de voyage"); "Luke" (comp. Act II) is attributed to Luke, Paul's companion; the final redactor (comp. Act III), whose intervention is at times "assez maladroite" (p. 209), is not identified.

subjective. The mere (real or apparent) repetition of a motif is not yet a doublet betraying different sources. One has to check in the first place whether that sort of repetition is not simply typical for the author of Luke-Acts. And further: one cannot speak of a real doublet when several details within the alleged "doublet" are actually different, and when each element plays its own role in the passage[53]. The apparent "repetition" may be, in some cases, an intentional reinforcement of a literary or theological motif, a *Steigerung*, which has a narrative function in the development of the story[54].

4. The Argument of "Lucanism"

Several scholars, mentioned above, use the argument of "lucanism" to prove their ascription of both the Alexandrian and the "Western" text to one and the same author. Martini and Wilcox at the 1977 Colloquium in Leuven had been "forerunners" in pointing to the Lucan character of many "Western" passages, though they had been prudent in their conclusions[55]. It is true that certain passages in the "Western" text display a very Lucan outlook[56]. Yet, the reliability of this argument has been heavily criticised on several grounds[57]. "Lucanism" is a tricky argument indeed.

a. The basic question is: what is the criterion to determine a "lucanism"? Thomas C. Geer deplores the absence of a (clear) definition in Boismard-Lamouille[58] and the vagueness of R. Sheldon MacKenzie's

53. Several "doublets" proposed by P. Tavardon should be checked according to these principles.

54. See my explanation of the alleged "doublets" in Acts 15,1.5 in *The "Apostolic Decree"* (n. 3).

55. Cf. C.M. MARTINI, *La tradition* (n. 17), p. 33, attributes the Lucan character to the work of an interpolator (cf. Hanson) belonging to an environment with "un grand respect non seulement pour la langue et pour la substance doctrinale du texte, mais aussi pour son vocabulaire"; M. WILCOX, *Luke and the Bezan Text* (n. 18), p. 455, is closer to Blaß's theory, without, however, accepting it: "We are not proposing to resurrect the 'Double-edition' theory of Blaß, although that theory may now seem to have a slightly greater degree of plausibility".

56. See Boismard-Lamouille and Strange on Acts 11,1-2, but compare the critical remarks of T.C. GEER, *The Presence and Significance of Lucanisms in the 'Western Text' of Acts,* in *JSNT* 39 (1990) 59-76, esp. pp. 62-63.

57. Cf. T.C. GEER, *Lucanisms.* See also R.S. MACKENZIE, *The Western Text of Acts: Some Lukanisms in Selected Sermons,* in *JBL* 104 (1985) 637-650, and the reaction by R.F. HULL, *"Lucanisms" in the Western Text of Acts? A Reappraisal,* in *JBL* 107 (1988) 695-707.

58. It is not Boismard-Lamouille's intention to determine what exactly is a "lucanism". They provide a statistical survey of stylistic characteristics, leaving it to the reader to decide which of them can be considered as distinctively Lucan. Cf. *Texte Occidental,* II, p. 195: "Nous avons gardé le nom de 'caractéristique stilistique' bien qu'il ne soit pas très juste. Il est difficile de déterminer à partir de quelle fréquence l'emploi d'un terme ou d'une expression devient 'caractéristique' du style de tel ou tel auteur. Pour éviter toute

definition[59]. In his own opinion, one cannot claim Lucan origin when the term or the expression is also present elsewhere in the NT, in the LXX and in classical Greek. In that case, the word simply belongs to the general vocabulary of Greek authors and is not distinctive enough to identify with certainty the specific terminology of a particular author. Any ancient author may have used that terminology. Though this is true, the extreme consequence of Geer's reasoning would be that a "lucanism" ought to be exclusive to Luke as his own linguistic creation, completely absent from the other books of the NT, the LXX and the entire Greek literature! Geer cannot have intended this absurdity. Rather, one should draw two useful conclusions from his critical remarks: first, one should try to give a clearer definition of "lucanism"[60]; second, the argument of "lucanism" should be used prudently because a linguistic feature as such[61] is never a *proof*, but at best an (important) indication for the *probability* of Lucan redaction.

b. It is hard to determine how far a copyist, a reviser, a redactor can go in imitating the vocabulary and style of his model, spontaneously or intentionally. Even an accumulation of Lucan characteristics may be due to imitation. What is the criterion to conclude that the Lucan style of certain passages of the "Western" text "cannot possibly be the work of a skilful imitator of Luke's style"[62]? In the hypothesis of a deliberate revision, it would not be far-fetched to suppose that the *Hauptredaktor* has both the concern and the skill to imitate the style of the original work. It cannot be excluded that the imitator, in his effort to write in the "Lucan" manner, is now and then even more Lucan than the original author himself[63], whereas, on the other hand, a formulation by this original author may at times be "unlukanisch"[64]. The accumulation of "lucanisms" in a

décision arbitraire, nous avons fait un relevé matériel de *toutes* les fréquences dépassant une certaine proportion. À chacun de juger dans quelle mesure cette proportion devient 'caractéristique'".

59. Cf. R.S. MACKENZIE, *The Western Text of Acts*, p. 637.

60. An explicitation of the implicit definition of lucanism, which forms the background of Boismard-Lamouille's list, in the footsteps of Hawkins and Cadbury, could contribute to clarify the discussion.

61. Vocabulary and stylistic features *as such* are only one element in the process of identifying Lucan redaction, e.g., in the study of the Lucan *Sondergut*, next to context, literary genre, theological themes, etc.

62. Cf. M.-É. BOISMARD, *The Text of Acts* (n. 25), p. 148.

63. Comp. T.C. GEER, *Lucanisms* (n. 56), p. 61: "does not Bezae's 'extra-Lucan' flavor more likely suggest the work of a scribe who was concerned to add elements to his text of Acts, and to do it in as Lucan a manner as possible?". A more frequent use of a particular "Lucan" term in the "Western" text may also be due to a personal linguistic preference of the reviser, even without the intention to enhance the Lucan character of the text.

64. Cf. B. ALAND, *Entstehung* (n. 1), p. 9.

few "Western" passages (e.g., Acts 11,2; 19,1) obviously asks for an explanation: Lucan redaction or scribal imitation? Because of the subjective element in the appreciation, a reconciliation of the defenders and the opponents of the imitation-theory is not to be expected. But, whatever the real origin may be, these rather exceptional passages are not representative for the "Western" text as a whole.

c. The need for a reconstruction of the "Western" text from very diverse and corrupt documents implies the risk that the choice between variant readings is based itself on a (possibly inadvertent) prejudice in favour of the most Lucan among them: but would that not be a circular reasoning[65]? That brings us to the following item.

5. The Reconstruction of the "Western" Text

Even the strongest defender of the codex Bezae, as reliable representative of the "Western" text, will recognise that a series of intentional changes and scribal blunders have crept into the text. Everybody agrees that the "Western" text has to be reconstructed in some way. According to Boismard-Lamouille, D is even a rather bad witness[66] and we have to reconstruct the TO on the basis of direct and indirect evidence. According to Aland, the result of the *Hauptredaktion* has not been conserved in a pure way by any of the available witnesses. So, in every hypothesis concerning the origin and nature of the "Western" text, the need for a reconstruction is felt. But how to achieve it? I just mentioned the risk of using the criterion of "lucanism". The danger is that the result is sort of patchwork, composed of bits and pieces, a text which does not exist, as such, anywhere and probably has never existed[67]. Of course, every criti-

65. Comp. T.C. GEER, *Lucanisms*, p. 69: "Certainly the level of Lucanisms in the Egyptian tradition would be different if one were free to pick and choose among the different representatives of that tradition at each point of variation as Boismard does with the 'Western' tradition".

66. Cf. *Texte Occidental*, I, p. 11: "Le codex Bezae reste notre principal témoin du texte occidental des Actes; mais c'est un témoin très abâtardi de ce texte".

67. See the severe remark of T.C. GEER, *Lucanisms*, p. 69: "The first, and perhaps major, challenge for Boismard and others is to demonstrate convincingly that there was a 'Western' text rather than as it appears to be in his presentation, simply a collection of readings now pulled together by Boismard into some sort of running text". Again, on pp. 73-74, he calls Boismard-Lamouille's reconstruction "a manufactured text". B. ALAND, *Entstehung*, p. 8, warns us for a circular reasoning: "Das hier ein Zirkelschluß vorliegt ist offensichtlich". Comp. also G. SCHNEIDER, *Zum "westlichen Text" der Apostelgeschichte*, in *BZ* 30 (1986) 138-144, esp. p. 143: "Der von Boismard/Lamouille rekonstruierte 'westlicher Text' ist aus verschiedenen Gründen unzulänglich. Ganz abgesehen davon, daß es *diesen* Text wohl nie gegeben hat, muß man bezweifeln, ob es *den* 'westlichen Text' jemals gab". C.-B. AMPHOUX, recension of *Texte Occidental,* in *Bib* 67 (1986) 410-414, esp. 413: "le TO, tel qu'il est présenté, est plus théorique que réel (…) À la vérité, le lecteur ne peut être que sceptique devant la possibilité qu'une telle diver-

cal text, including that of most contemporary editions, which are mainly based on Alexandrian witnesses, is a scholarly construction, which, *as a whole*, does not exist in any manuscript. But the difference is obvious: larger parts, as well as numerous particular readings of the text of our critical editions, are indeed attested by many witnesses[68].

6. The Reconstruction of the Second-Century Situation

The absence of any direct evidence from the second century (*in casu* for Luke-Acts) is one of the major handicaps in textual criticism. The earliest papyrus for Luke dates from about 200 ($\mathfrak{P}^{75}$), the earliest papyri for Acts are from the third century ($\mathfrak{P}^{38.48}$). The earliest ecclesiastical authors do not faithfully quote the NT. Amphoux's "Roman revisers" do not tell us anything about Acts, and one has to rely on later documentary evidence for a partial and doubtful reconstruction of their gospel text. Irenaeus' book is only preserved in a Latin translation, though a faithful one. The oldest Vetus Latina manuscripts are dated in the fourth and fifth centuries and vary among each other. So, a hypothetical reconstruction is needed anyway, and some imagination is welcome. But it should be kept under control, and the hypothetical nature of the reconstruction should remain constantly in the mind of the author and the reader. Amphoux's reconstruction of the historical background of the development of the gospel text in the second century is astonishing. One may wonder which stones of the impressive building are based on the firm ground of a strong critical argument[69]. In my opinion, Aland's contribution is an example of a prudent and nuanced procedure, giving precise historical and/or documentary arguments for each supposition, and repeatedly underlining its hypothetical character. One of her conclusions is that the alleged universal circulation of the "Western"

sité de témoins permette de reconstituer un texte ayant réellement existé! (...) le TO risque d'être un amalgame ininterprétable, tant en exégèse qu'en histoire du texte". J.K. ELLIOTT, review of *Texte Occidental*, in *NT* 29 (1987) 285-288, esp. p. 286: "It may be claimed by many readers that B+L produced a maverick text".

68. Boismard-Lamouille are aware of the hypothetical nature of their reconstruction and they are open to suggestions for correction; see *Texte Occidental*: "libre à chacun de redonner au TO ce que nous avons cru devoir mettre au compte de TO²" (I, p. x and 118); "Nous ne prétendons donc pas offrir aux lecteurs 'le' texte Occidental des Actes, mais un texte comportant un grand nombre de variantes à débattre encore entre spécialistes" (p. 9). On the other hand, the authors use their reconstruction of the TO with confidence as the basis for their source- and redaction-critical theory.

69. Although his suggestions could make sense (Ignatius' "projet d'évangélisation", Polycarp's composition of the earliest D-text, its localisation at Smyrna, the D-text as basis for Marcion in spite of the fact that his text is closer to $\mathfrak{P}^{75}$-B, the interpretation of Celsus' statement, the ascription of the Alexandrian tradition to Pantaenus...), one wonders whether we are entitled to use them as a firm basis for the next step(s) of a reliable historical reconstruction.

text in the early period – a widespread opinion among scholars – is not confirmed by the rather meagre attestation of many of its readings.

7. The Date of the "Western" Text

The divergences among the conclusions of the authors mentioned above concerning the date of the "Western" text are bewildering. Boismard-Lamouille date the original TO in the second half of the first century, Amphoux (for the gospels) sometime in the early second century, Strange "relatively late in the second century, perhaps in the third quarter"[70]. Aland's *Hauptredaktion* is situated in the first part of the third century. Aland's thesis has the advantage that it can integrate various phenomena from different periods: the "beginnings" through the freely paraphrasing activity of second-century scribes, the edition by the *Hauptredaktor* in the third century, the further "westernisation" in third and subsequent centuries. The suggested date for the *Hauptredaktion* may be vulnerable: are the longer readings in Irenaeus really not typically "Western" in origin? And would a thorough check of all (indirect) second-century evidence confirm the claim that no typical "Western" readings are to be found in that early period? However, even if such research, or newly discovered evidence, would contradict this conclusion, it would only need a (somewhat) earlier dating of the *Hauptredaktion*, not the rejection of the theory as such.

8. The Nature of the "Western" Readings

A major objection to the theories concerning the priority of the "Western" text is, in my opinion, the *prima facie* impression concerning the secondary character of many of its longer readings[71]. I agree with

70. Cf. STRANGE, *The Problem* (n. 5), p. 182. As far as Strange's point of view is concerned, one should distinguish between the date of the marginal and interlinear "comments" added by the original author in the first century, and the date of their integration into a running ("Western") text by an editor late in the second century. According to Strange, the readings themselves cannot belong originally to the second century because they do not betray the interests and concerns of the Christian community of that period; cf. pp. 52-56, esp. 54: "There is little evidence in the Western Text of Acts of concern with the known problems of the second-century church, particularly Gnosticism in its various forms".

71. A century ago, we already find that conclusion at the end of a detailed investigation by T.E. PAGE, *Blaß' Edition of the Acts*, in *Classical Review* 11 (1897) 317-320, esp. p. 320: "The whole of them (i.e. the different groups of D-variants) bear traces of being subsequent corrections of the text by a second-rate hand; that they were Luke's original version is incredible". This is also the impression of G. SCHNEIDER, *Zum "westlichen Text"* (n. 67), p. 143: "Für eine zeitliche Priorität der alexandrinischen Textform spricht vor allem das 'Gefälle' der jeweiligen differierenden Lesarten: Die 'westlichen' erweisen sich, gerade wenn man die eklektische Methode praktiziert, auf der ganzen Linie als 'secundär'. Der 'westliche Text' ist aber in mancher Hinsicht 'besser' als der alexan-

Aland when she opines that the "Western" redactor wants to make the text "deutlicher, klarer und konsequenter". In the same line, Strange is correct, in my opinion, when he characterises the typically "Western" readings as (narrative or theological) commentary. This does not necessarily imply that these "comments" have been added by the author of the original draft and in the form of marginal or interlinear notes. Though attractive, this is a mere possibility, not supported by any documentary (biblical) evidence. But the idea of "notes and comments" rightly underlines the secondary nature of these passages.

9. A Balanced Text-Critical Method

The main strength of Aland's approach and the Achilles-heel of some of the alternative theories are, respectively, the presence or absence of a balanced text-critical method: the careful application of both external and internal criticism. Aland points to the "Eingleisigkeit der angewandten Methode" of Boismard-Lamouille[72]. As I indicated above, their method is almost exclusively confined to internal criticism. Their effort to collect evidence in all possible areas, ages and languages, which has impressively enriched the critical apparatus of Acts, ultimately serves to collect readings. This evidence plays hardly any role on the level of external criticism, which takes into account date and geographical distribution of readings, and weight and relationship of manuscripts. Although external criticism can never have the final say in the matter, it has its proper and essential role to play in the text-critical process. The very fact that the loss of numerous manuscripts and the difficulty in localising and dating the extant evidence do not allow a complete

---

drinische, was der Nicht-Theologe unter den Autoren [Delebecque] auf den ersten Blick erkannt". Of course, an impression is not yet a proof. Some authors have the opposite feeling and defend the secondary nature of the Alexandrian text. Cf. T.C. PETERSEN, *An Early Coptic Manuscript of Acts. An Unrevised Version of the Ancient So-called Western Text*, in *CBQ* 26 (1964) 225-241, esp. p. 228: "During the third century the time arrived when (...) the plain and artless pattern of the apostolic writings which had met the tastes and requirements of the Judaean Christian community of Palestine no longer fully satisfied the literary demands of the well-educated Hellenistic Christian community at Alexandria. Men trained at the famous school of Christian theology and bible studies, directed by Pantaenus, Clement, and Origen, recognised the need of freeing the sacred writings of the New Testament of their Aramaic phraseology, their repetitiousness and crudity and their grammatical and syntactical irregularities (...). The result of their labours was the Alexandrian recension". See also M. BLACK, *The Holy Spirit in the Western Text of Acts,* in EPP – FEE (eds.), *New Testament Textual Criticism* (n. 25), pp. 159-170, esp. 170: "It would seem *not improbable* that, at more than one point in the textual tradition, this 'spiritual' gospel has been pressed into the Procrustean bed of a pro-Jewish and anti-Montanist Alexandrian scholasticism".

72. B. ALAND, *Entstehung* (n. 1), p. 7.

stemma codicum, should not lead to complete agnosticism and radical eclecticism. Internal study of the documents refines our judgement of the critical value of manuscripts, groups and families, and this ever-growing knowledge can be used as a trustworthy argument in external criticism[73], sometimes even to correct the conclusions of internal criticism, which could be biased by exegetical preferences. Exegesis has a real role to play on the level of internal criticism but it should play its own specific role[74], and it may not become the only voice in the discussion.

CONCLUSION

It is not an exaggeration to pretend that the "Western" text is the most complicated matter in the field of New Testament textual criticism. The renewed interest in the problem and the impressive number and confusing variety of attempts at presenting an overall solution to this centuries-old riddle leave the reader somewhat perplexed. My critical remarks should not be misunderstood. I do appreciate most of these detailed studies, both for the courage of the endeavour and for the wealth of imaginative perspectives and fine analytical remarks. However, the consensus is further away than ever. Philip MENOUD's words, written in 1951, can still be applied to the present situation: "This problem remains, now as ever, 'a thorn in the flesh' for every student of the third Gospel and the book of Acts"[75].

Through the apparent comfort of the eclectic approach, the problem of the "Western" text had fallen asleep. The "sleeping beauty" did not have to wait hundred years before a prince tried to wake her up. Some fifty years after Ropes and Clark, more than one prince has knocked at the door of the castle. The future will teach us if one of them is the

73. Cf. B. ALAND, *Entstehung*, p. 7, n. 6, where she provides, in a nutshell, a clear and convincing plea for a balanced method, taking into account the knowledge of the "Textwert einer Handschrift".

74. See also J. DELOBEL, *Textual Criticism and Exegesis: Siamese Twins?*, in B. ALAND & J. DELOBEL (eds.), *New Testament Textual Criticism, Exegesis and Church History. A Discussion of Methods* (CBET, 7), Kampen, Kok Pharos, 1994, pp. 98-117. That the relationship between textual criticism and exegesis is delicate, is illustrated by the remarks of T.C. GEER, *Lucanisms* (n. 56), p. 73, who warns against "those who develop literary theories and then attempt to find support for them in textual criticism", and R.F. HULL, *"Lucanisms"* (n. 57), p. 707, who protests against the opposite procedure: "I question the validity of invoking a hypothetical source in support of a text-critical decision".

75. Cf. P.H. MENOUD, *The Western Text and the Theology of Acts*, in *SNTS Bulletin* 2 (1951) 19-32, esp. p. 19.

prince of her dreams. Others can take their chance. They should be encouraged to do so, provided that they realise that the castle of this sleeping beauty stands in Waterloo.

Naamsestraat 68/3   Joël DELOBEL
B-3000 Leuven

ABRAHAMIC COVENANT TRADITIONS
AND THE CHARACTERIZATION OF GOD IN LUKE-ACTS

INTRODUCTION

Abraham enters Luke-Acts intermittently. Mary, Zechariah, John the Baptist, and the narrator mention him in the first three chapters. He appears in Jesus' interpretations of his encounters with the woman bent double and Zacchaeus (13,16; 19,9). Luke 13,28 groups him with the patriarchs and prophets to give substance and quality to the eschatological kingdom of God. In the parable of the rich man and Lazarus (16,19-31), Abraham becomes an actor in a metadiegetic[1] narrative. In a controversy with Sadducees, Jesus alludes to Exod 3,6 where God's relationship with the patriarchs distinguishes the God who encounters Moses from all others (Luke 20,37). This evaluative characterization also differentiates God as the God of the living, and hence attests the resurrection[2].

In three cases in Acts the relationship between God and Abraham functions as evaluative characterization to differentiate God (3,13; 7,2; 7,32). Stephen begins his speech with God's appearance to Abraham and outlines Abraham's story from the promise of land as an inheritance through Abraham's circumcision (7,3-8). He returns to Abraham in 7,16-17. Paul mentions Abraham in what first appears to be a casual characterization of his audience in Pisidian Antioch as offspring of Abraham (13,26).

In addition to these overt references, there are covert allusions that make Abraham significant beyond the appearances of his name. The covert allusions constitute a form of intertextuality inasmuch as they draw on a cultural repertoire. This means that the more informed readers are of

---

1. A narrative embedded in another narrative often as an explanatory variant (G. GENETTE, *Narrative Discourse. An Essay in Method,* Ithaca, NY, Cornell University Press, 1980, pp. 228-232).
2. Are the patriarchs already raised, or is their future resurrection assured? E. ELLIS, *Jesus, the Sadducees and Qumran,* in *NTS* 10 (1963-64) 274-279, argues for the assured future resurrection. J. KILGALLEN, *The Sadducees and Resurrection from the Dead. Luke 20,27-40,* in *Bib* 67 (1986) 478-495, suggests that the love of God does not allow the children of God to remain dead. In any case Abraham is here an eschatological figure. Cf. N. DAHL, *The Story of Abraham in Luke-Acts,* in ID., *Jesus in the Memory of the Early Church,* Minneapolis, MN, Augsburg, 1976, p. 69.

the cultural repertoire, the more aware they are of the allusions. Thus my discussion alternates between features of the narrative and profiles from the cultural repertoire as the latter are implicated in the narrative.

Characterization is syntagmatic and composite. Readers encounter clues to characterization in sequential order and construe them in holistic patterns to build characters. But characterization is not merely cumulative in that the sequential discovery of what is true in the narrative world may redirect and revise as well as reinforce. Further, though sequential, characterization involves retrospection. The narrative unity of Luke-Acts is significant for both sequence and retrospection. The sequence continues from the first volume through the second, and retrospection involves material from both volumes.

I basically follow a sequential development of the characterization of God in relation to Abrahamic traditions in Luke-Acts. But I immediately violate my sequential reading with retrospection from Acts, because Acts provides readers clear evidence of the primary significance of the Abrahamic covenant in the narrative world. In his explanation of the healing of the lame man at the Temple, Peter epitomizes God's covenant with Abraham: "And in your seed all the families of the earth will be blessed" (Acts 3,25). The thesis is that God's promise to bless all the families of the earth is fundamental for the characterization of God[3].

GOD AND ABRAHAM

God slips into Luke-Acts in the divine passive πεπληροφορημένων (1,1). "Fulfillment" reaches back to a God of the cultural repertoire who anticipates the present (ἐν ἡμῖν), but also forward to what such a God will yet bring to fruition[4]. The prologue anticipates narrative unity in

3. U. Busse correctly maintains that all of Luke-Acts is fulfillment of the promises to the forebears: cf. Das "Evangelium" des Lukas. Die Funktion der Vorgeschichte im lukanischen Doppelwerk, in C. BUSSMANN and W. RADL (eds.), Der Treue Gottes trauen. Beiträge zum Werk des Lukas. FS Gerhard Schneider, Freiburg, Herder, 1991, pp. 175-176. T. SEIM, The Double Message. Patterns of Gender in Luke-Acts, Nashville, TN, Abingdon, 1994, p. 49, claims that liberation is the central motif for Abrahamic traditions in Luke 1,52-53.73-75; Acts 7,6-7. Though the blessing may be in the form of liberation, in a holistic reading the blessing of all the families of the earth is dominant. J. JERVELL, The Unknown Paul. Essays on Luke-Acts and Early Christian History, Minneapolis, MN, Augsburg, 1984, pp. 146-157, overemphasizes the needy in Israel as the issue in the Abrahamic heritage.

4. On anticipation of fulfillment see G. KLEIN, Lukas 1,1-4 als theologisches Programm, in E. DINKLER (ed.), Zeit und Geschichte. Dankesgabe an Rudolf Bultmann zum 80. Geburtstag, Tübingen, Mohr, 1964, pp. 196-199; R.J. DILLON, Previewing Luke's Project from His Prologue (Luke 1,1-4), in CBQ 43 (1981), p. 212; L. ALEXANDER, The

that the point of view toward the fulfillment is that of an obtrusive narrator who identifies with at least the second generation[5], and if the narrator identifies with things being fulfilled in the sequel to Theophilus, this warrants narrative unity[6]. From the perspective of narrative unity, however, the narrator's point of view is from the third generation[7], because the narrator looks in retrospect toward the story of Luke-Acts up to Paul's imprisonment in Rome.

At the first explicit reference, God is the God of commandments and righteous decrees whom Zechariah serves not only in the Temple but also, with his wife, in private. That is, God enters Luke-Acts as the God of Israel according to Luke's view of the God of Israel. Correspondingly, God turns attention to an Israelite couple and to the children of Israel (Luke 1,5.16)[8]. The reciprocal relationship between God and Israel is foundational for the characterization of God in Luke-Acts, and covenant traditions are pivotal for this relationship.

Covenant traditions surface with Gabriel's allusions to the Davidic covenant (1,32-33). The throne of Jesus' ancestor David, his rule over the house of Jacob forever, and his kingdom without end are patently a

Preface to Luke's Gospel. Literary Conventions and Social Context in Luke 1,1-4 and Acts 1 (SNTS MS, 78), Cambridge, University Press, 1993, p. 113. The prologue prepares and guides readers. BUSSE, *Evangelium* (n. 3), p. 165; R. DILLMANN, *Das Lukasevangelium als Tendenzschrift*, in *BZ* 38 (1994) 86-93.

5. F. BOVON, *Das Evangelium nach Lukas* (EKK, 3/1), Zürich, Benziger, 1989, vol. 1, p. 35. On the basis of parallels in Josephus, D. Moessner suggests that Luke claims either to be an actively informed contemporary of the eyewitnesses and ministers of the word or has immediate grasp of the significance of his sources. Cf. D. MOESSNER *'Eyewitnesses', 'Informed Contemporaries', and 'Unknowing Inquirers'. Josephus' Criteria for Authentic Historiography and the Meaning of* παρακολουθέω, in *NT* 38 (1996) 105-122. Moessner demonstrates the fallacy of using Josephus to indicate that Luke engages in historical investigation. But the narrator distinguishes himself from an earlier generation by associating ἀπ' ἀρχῆς only with the eyewitnesses and ministers of the word and by employing παραδίδωμι as a term for passing on tradition.

6. Conzelmann's thesis on the discontinuity between Luke 1–2 and the remainder of the work is problematic also for narrative coherence. On the coherence see P. MINEAR, *Luke's Use of the Birth Stories*, in L. KECK and J. MARTYN (eds.), *Studies in Luke-Acts*, Philadelphia, PA, Fortress, 1980, pp. 111-130; R. TANNEHILL, *The Narrative Unity of Luke-Acts*, Philadelphia, PA – Minneapolis, MN, Fortress, 1986-1990, vol. 1, pp. xiii, 1-9; BUSSE, *Evangelium* (n. 3), pp. 161-179; B. KAHL, *Lukas gegen Lukas lesen*, in *Bibel und Kirche* 50 (1995) 222-229.

7. W. MICHAELIS, *Einleitung in das Neue Testament. Die Entstehung, Sammlung, und Überlieferung der Schriften des Neuen Testaments*, Bern, Haller, 1954, pp. 14-15; J. FITZMYER, *The Gospel According to Luke* (AB, 28-28A), Garden City, NY, Doubleday, 1981-1985, vol. 1, p. 289.

8. The double focus on the people and the couple is also indicated by the correlation of the prayers of the people in 1,10 with the prayers of Zechariah in 1,13. See BUSSE, *Evangelium* (n. 3), p. 173; J. GREEN, *The Gospel of Luke* (NICNT), Grand Rapids, Eerdmans, 1997, p. 73.

rereading of 2 Kings 7,16[9]. Moreover, the rereading takes σπέρμα (7,12) as a literal singular. Rather than the collective Davidic dynasty, Jesus is the one σπέρμα of David who will rule forever. Ambiguity in the LXX invites such a rereading. Though neuter, σπέρμα is the antecedent of the masculine pronoun αὐτός in 7,13. Significantly, this masculine descendant stands in a relationship with God as a son to a father (7,14), as does Jesus in Luke 1,32[10].

But readers soon encounter a revision of royal theology. Though Gabriel interprets the annunciation and the birth of Jesus as fulfillment of the Davidic covenant, Mary interprets the same events as fulfillment of the Abrahamic covenant[11]. In fact, an Abrahamic allusion already slips into Gabriel's speech. His declaration, "Anything is not impossible with God" (1,37), echoes Gen 18,14 which affirms God's power to keep Abrahamic promises alive[12]. For her part, Mary grounds her song in God, namely, in God's attentive observation (1,48) and memory (1,54)[13] – memory of the Abrahamic covenant. What happens through Mary is in accord with God's promise πρὸς τοὺς πατέρας, to Abraham and to *his* σπέρμα forever. If readers have been lured into taking the Davidic σπέρμα as singular, it is possible for them to take the Abrahamic σπέρμα also as singular. But in Luke 1,54, Israel is personified collectively as God's παῖς, and "to Abraham and to his seed" in 1,55 is

---

9. So FITZMYER, *Luke* (n. 7), 1, p. 338; BOVON, *Lukas* (n. 5), 1, p. 75; F. MUSSNER, *Das "semantische Universum" der Verkündigungsperikope (Lk 1,26-38)*, in *Catholica* 46 (1992), p. 230; TANNEHILL, *Narrative Unity* (n. 6), 1, p. 25. 2 Sam 7,14 may be mediated through other traditions such as 1 Chron 22,8-10; Isa 9,6-7; Psalms 2 and 110. J. ERNST, *Das Evangelium nach Lukas. Übersetzt und erklärt* (RNT), Regensburg, Pustet, 1993, p. 61.

10. The annunciation is theocentric. So MUSSNER, *Das "semantische Universum"* (n. 9), pp. 231, 236-37. Cf. the christocentric and mariological emphasis of H. SCHÜRMANN, *Das Lukasevangelium* (HTKNT, 3), Freiburg, Herder, 1969, vol. 1, p. 40, and ERNST, *Lukas* (n. 9), pp. 60-61.

11. On Mary's prophetic role see B. GAVENTA, *Mary. Glimpses of the Mother of Jesus*, Columbia, SC, University of South Carolina Press, 1995, pp. 58, 73. On parallels between Mary's faith and Abraham's faith see F. MUSSNER, *Der Glaube Mariens im Lichte des Römerbriefs*, in *Catholica* 18 (1964) 258-268; ID., *Das "semantische Universum"* (n. 9), p. 238.

12. See MUSSNER, *Das "semantische Universum"* (n. 9), pp. 231-32.

13. On the emphasis on God and God's observation and memory see BOVON, *Lukas* (n. 5), pp. 88, 93. God's observation and memory are as significant as God's mercy and power, only the latter of which Tannehill accents for the characterization of God in the Magnificat: *Narrative Unity* (n. 6), 1, p. 29, but see p. 32. For the theocentricity of the Magnificat see I.H. MARSHALL, *The Interpretation of the Magnificat. Luke 1,46-55*, in C. BUSSMANN & W. RADL (eds.), *Der Treue Gottes trauen* (n. 3), pp. 182, 188; MUSSNER, *Das "semantische Universum"* (n. 9), p. 231. Cf. the christocentric and mariological emphasis of SCHÜRMANN, *Lukasevangelium* (n. 10), 1, p. 40, and ERNST, *Lukas* (n. 9), p. 69.

clearly parallel to "to our forebears", implying the collective reading[14]. Also in the development of what is true in the narrative world, Zechariah makes a connection between God's promises and God's people, between God's acts and both the forebears and ἡμῖν (1,72-73). Further, the wider development of what is true in the narrative world associates the people of Israel and their children (Acts 2,39) with the Abrahamic covenant (3,25) so that, if not exclusively collective, σπέρμα at least carries simultaneously the double connotations of the singular (Jesus) and the collective plural (the descendants of Abraham).

Given the distinct perspectives of Gabriel and Mary, one option for readers is to synthesize the two interpretations. One such reader is Zechariah. Though an actor in the story, he interprets parts of the narrative in which he has not participated. Zechariah interprets not only the story but also the prophets, who are characterized as ἀπ' αἰῶνος, and therefore may be prophetic personages as much as prophetic scriptures. Zechariah reinforces Mary's characterization of God as the one who attentively observes God's people (1,68) and remembers (1,72). But Zechariah also overlays David with Abraham. After mentioning David, he defines the covenant as God's memory of an oath that God swore to Abraham (1,72-73). Further, Zechariah indicates that the purpose of the Davidic covenant is to liberate the recipients of the promise from enemies so that they can serve God in consecration and righteousness.

God's promise is explicitly Abrahamic, and serving God in consecration and righteousness is implicitly also Abrahamic. The cultural repertoire provides evidence that readers could construe the ὁσιότης καὶ δικαιοσύνη that Zechariah anticipates as Abrahamic[15]. If God reckons Abraham's faith as δικαιοσύνη, what option do readers who recall Gen 15,6 LXX have but to reckon likewise? *Pseudo-Jubilees* records Abraham's fidelity to God in an apparent reference to the *Aqedah* but also with overtones of Gen 15,6[16]. Abraham is also πιστός in Sir 44,20. Even the fragmentary historians Berossus and Eupolemus consider Abraham to be δίκαιος and pleasing to God in εὐσέβεια[17]. Thus, when Zechariah

14. This weighs against H.-J. Klauck's suggestion that if σπέρμα is taken christologically, then τοῖς φοβουμένοις in Luke 1,50 anticipates the godfearers of Acts: *Gottesfürchtige im Magnificat?*, in *NTS* 43 (1997) 134-139.

15. Dahl's discernment of a common background for Luke-Acts and Greek-speaking Judaism indicates something of the cultural repertoire: cf. *Abraham* (n. 2), pp. 70-71.

16. 4Q 226 7,1. On the *Aqedah* and the test of Abraham's fidelity see also 4Q 225 2i,9-ii,10. 4Q 378 22i,1-5 associates the righteousness that Moses passed on to Joshua with the covenant God made with Abraham.

17. Eusebius cites Berossus and Eupolemus (according to Polyhistor) respectively in *Praepar. Evang.* 9.16.2 and 9.17.3. Abraham is a character of εὐσέβεια and πίστις in, e.g., Philo, *Migrat.* 132; *Abra.* 60; 208.

prophesies Davidic liberation so that the people can serve God in consecration and righteousness, the fulfillment of the Davidic covenant is a
particular way God also fulfills the Abrahamic covenant.

Synthesizing covenant traditions was one of the options open in
debates over covenant traditions in the Second Temple period. The
search for historical Israel has tended to place conditional covenantal
promises in competition with unconditional promises. But a tendency to
synthesize them appears already in the Pentateuch, the Prophets, and the
Psalms[18].

Phuichun Richard Choi surveys Palestinian traditions about Abraham
in the period of the Second Temple[19]. He locates Abrahamic traditions
on a continuum between two poles representing exclusivism at one
extreme and universalism at the other. In between there is room for synthesis, as in Sirach. But for Choi, a synthesis is incapable of harmoniz-
ing disparate Abrahamic traditions.

Choi makes a helpful correlation between creation theology and universalism on the one hand, and election theology and exclusivism on the
other. But even if aporias make harmony impossible, it does not mean
that no one made the effort. According to Choi, Sirach lists covenant traditions side by side without trying to correlate them. But he apparently
overlooks κληρονομία and its cognates[20]. In Sir 24, Israel's heritage is
spiritualized as Wisdom and, correspondingly the law. In fact, in 24,8
Israel is Wisdom's inheritance. In the same context, Jerusalem (in parallel with the people) is God's inheritance (24,11-12). In 24,20 the inheri-

---

18. Deuteronomy synthesizes the oath to the patriarchs and Sinai. N. LOHFINK, *Die
Landverheissung als Eid. Eine Studie zu Gn 15* (SBS, 28), Stuttgart, Katholisches Bibelwerk, 1967, p. 7; J. L'HOUR, *Die Ethik der Bundestradition im Alten Testament* (SBS,
14), Stuttgart, Katholisches Bibelwerk, 1967, pp. 18-19. L. PERLITT, *Bundestheologie im
Alten Testament* (WMANT, 36), Neukirchen-Vluyn, Neukirchener, 1969, p. 34, claims
that Deuteronomy relativizes the promise of the land through law. But a synthesis relativizes both components. Cf. G. VON RAD, *Old Testament Theology*, New York, Harper &
Row, 1962-1965, vol. 1, p. 199; ID., *Verheissenes Land und Jahwehsland im Hexateuch*,
in *Gesammelte Studien zum Alten Testament*, München, Kaiser, 1971, pp. 97-100; R.
CLEMENTS, *Abraham and David. Genesis XV and Its Meaning for Israelite Tradition*,
Napierville, IL, Allenson, 1967, pp. 47-60, 75-78, 81-82. On tensions between Abrahamic
and Mosaic covenant traditions and a synthesis of them already in Deuteronomy see
R. POLZIN, *Moses and the Deuteronomist. A Literary Study of the Deuteronomic History*.
Part 1. *Deuteronomy, Joshua, Judges*, New York, Seabury, 1980, pp. 53-54, 67-68.

19. P. CHOI, *Abraham Our Father. Paul's Voice in the Covenantal Debate of the Second Temple Period*, PhD dissertation, Fuller Theological Seminary (Ann Arbor, MI, University Microfilms), 1997. Choi confines himself to Greek sources and does not use QL.

20. Apocryphal Joseph 4Q 372 3,9 distinguishes Israel by its inheritance (נחלה) from
the Gentiles who received no portion (חק). Lacunae make it impossible to say precisely
that the Abrahamic covenant is mentioned, but the text reads: "... Abraham which he cut
with Jacob".

tance of Wisdom surpasses honey and the honeycomb, and in 24,23 the book of the covenant, the law that Moses commanded, is the inheritance for the congregations of Jacob. Sirach also spiritualizes the inheritance into the future. One who is wise among the people will inherit πίστις (37,26). Significantly, however, Sirach envisions an eschatological act of God in the gathering of all the tribes of Jacob so that they might receive their inheritance as a recapitulation of the beginning (36,10 LXX). Sirach does not leave readers in doubt that this future inheritance includes the land. In fact, 46,8 uses the formula "a land flowing with milk and honey" to define the inheritance of the land at the time of the conquest, and 44,21 describes the land as the inheritance promised to Abraham, the father of a multitude of nations, who kept the commandments of God and entered into a covenant with God. God swore an oath to him to *bless* the nations through his σπέρμα. Σπέρμα is here unambiguously collective as the related pronoun αὐτούς shows. The promise to Abraham is that God will *give* the descendants of Abraham an inheritance from sea to sea and from the river to the ends of the earth (44,19-21). What ties the Mosaic and Abrahamic covenants together is that the Mosaic covenant is a part of God's promise of *blessing* and of an *inheritance* for Abraham's descendants. Further, Sirach also enfolds the Davidic covenant in the notion of κληρονομία. On the one hand, God's covenant is the inheritance of kingship for one man. On the other, it is the inheritance of Aaron for all his seed (45,25). Similarly in Luke-Acts, Zechariah, as an interpreter of the annunciation and the Magnificat, synthesizes Davidic and Abrahamic covenant traditions.

Luke-Acts characteristically appeals to scripture rather than to literature of the Second Temple period. But appeals to scripture are mediated through traditions of the Second Temple period. When Simeon is waiting for the παράκλησις of Israel and Anna for the λύτρωσις of Jerusalem, the παράκλησις and the λύτρωσις enter Luke-Acts from a cultural repertoire. Thus Simeon mediates the Isaianic light for revelation to the Gentiles and for the glory of the people of Israel (Isa 42,6; 49,6) through Second Temple expectations of παράκλησις. Simeon then predicts a future division in Israel focused on Jesus (2,25-38). He is able to predict such a division in the future because it already existed. As Choi has demonstrated, debates between universalists at one extreme and exclusivists at the other populated the cultural repertoire.

John the Baptist also draws Abrahamic covenant traditions out of a cultural repertoire that includes debates about how one qualifies as an offspring of Abraham. In simplistic terms, the pre-Lucan debate ranged from physical descent from Abraham at one extreme to following in his footsteps at the other. The two poles represent appeals to exclusivism on the one hand and universality on the other. *PssSol* 9,9-11 claims divine election for Israel as the σπέρμα ’Aβραάμ above the Gentiles through a divine covenant with the ancestors. The *Damascus Document* is strongly exclusivistic in its presentation of Abraham but includes gentile household slaves in the Abrahamic covenant (CD 12,11). *Jub.* 22,16-18 appeals to keeping the commandments of Abraham the ancestor in tandem with an exhortation to be separate from the Gentiles. Similarly, 4 Macc 6,17-22 appeals to οἱ ’Aβραὰμ παῖδες in the course of resisting Hellenism[21] and exhorts its readers to follow, implicitly, Abraham’s εὐσέβεια.

But from a universalist perspective physical descent from Abraham could include Gentiles. *1 Enoch*, in allegorical language, makes Abraham a kind of Adamic ancestor of all nations and Jacob the ancestor of Israel and finally envisions a universal gathering of Gentiles by the God of Israel (90,33). Further, if we lay aside the perspective of a Pauline deprecation of Hagar and Ishmael (Gal 4,21-31), scripture itself holds a positive view of Abrahamic promises through Hagar and Ishmael. In continuity with promises to Abraham, God promises numerous descendants to Hagar and Ishmael (Gen 16,10; 21,13)[22]. Ishmael is Abraham’s legitimate son to whom Abrahamic promises of blessing for all the families of the earth (12,3) also pertain. These are promises of blessing precisely for those outside Israel who are also descendants of Abraham[23]. God’s covenant with Abraham in 17,4 is that he will be ancestor of many nations with specific promises of blessing and progeny for Ishmael (17,20), and Ishmael is circumcised as a sign of his participation in this covenant (17,23). *Jub.* 22,1-4 portrays Isaac and Ishmael in positive relationships with each other at the feast of Shebuot, and in 22,9 Abraham prays for God’s blessing on the seed of his *sons* that they might become an elect people and an inheritance from all the nations of the earth. Thus, *Jub.* 15,6 understands Abraham not only as the channel of

---

21. J. GOLDSTEIN contends that Judaism did not resist Hellenism as such but only such things as polytheism and abuses: *Jewish Acceptance and Rejection of Hellenism*, in E. SANDERS (ed.), *Jewish and Christian Self-Definition*. Vol. 2. *Aspects of Judaism in the Greco-Roman Period*, Philadelphia, PA, Fortress, 1981, pp. 64-87. On conflict as well as assimilation see M. HENGEL, *Judaism and Hellenism. Studies in Their Encounter in Palestine during the Early Hellenistic Period*, Philadelphia, PA, Fortress, 1974, esp. vol. 1, pp. 138-153, 224-254.

22. T. NAUMANN, *Ismael. Theologische und erzählanalytische Studien zu einem biblischen Konzept der Selbstwahrnehmung Israels im Kreis der Völker aus der Nachkommenschaft Abrahams*, Habilitationsschrift Universität Bern, 1996, pp. 40-44, 214-216.

23. NAUMANN, *Ismael*, pp. 75, 81.

blessing for the nations, but as the father of many nations[24]. Further, Ishmael and the sons of Keturah become in some traditions the ancestors of nations in the Mediterranean world[25].

It is not the interest of the Baptizer, however, to focus on imitation of Abraham. One can easily deduce from texts such as 4 Maccabees and *Pseudo-Philo* that appeals to Abraham constitute an ethic of imitation. 4 Macc 6,19 exhorts its readers to set an ethical παράδειγμα for their children in a context where the readers are identified as the children of Abraham. But the Baptizer stands in a line of thematic development in Luke-Acts where appeals to covenant traditions function principally to characterize God. Gabriel's announcement to Mary is a theocentric proclamation about Jesus' relationship with God as God's son, and about God's action to establish Jesus on the Davidic throne. The birth of Jesus will take place because of the power of God. The conclusion of this scene is a repetition of Gen 18,14, with slight variations: οὐκ ἀδυνατήσει παρὰ τοῦ θεοῦ πᾶν ῥῆμα (Luke 1,37).

The Magnificat is a very theocentric hymn, and reference to the Abrahamic covenant serves to identify God's action as commensurate with God's ancient promises. At the auspicious birth of John the Baptist, the neighbors question: "What will this child be?" (1,66a). The narrator makes the neighbors theocentric. They raise their question "because the hand of the Lord was with him" (1,66b). Correspondingly, Zechariah's hymnic response is constituted as a blessing of God. So also programmatically John's message is the word of God (3,2)[26]. What P. Bonnard says with respect to Abraham in Galatians holds also for the characteri-

---

24. *Midr. Gen. Rab.* 47 to Gen 17,19-21 presents an argument from lesser to greater that if God's promise to bless Ishmael produced twelve tribes (princes), all the more God will establish the covenant with Isaac. *B. Sanh.* 89b preserves a tradition about Abraham's love for both sons. When God commands Abraham to sacrifice his son, he replies, "[But] I have two sons!". God responds, "Thine only one". Abraham says, "Each is the only one of his mother!". God says, "Whom thou lovest!". Abraham responds, "I love them both!". Whereupon God specifies, "Isaac!".

25. 1 Macc 12,21 claims that the Spartans are descendants of Abraham. See Josephus *Ant.* 12 §§ 225-26. Josephus claims that Abraham's sons through Keturah founded colonies in Troglodytis, Arabia, and Libya, and citing Polyhistor, who is citing Cleodemus Malchus, claims that Abraham's sons by Keturah were the eponymous ancestors of Assyria and Africa (*Ant.* 1 §§ 238-41). Ishmael's twelve sons gave their names to Arabian tribes (*Ant.* 1 §§ 220-21). Similarly, Eusebius citing Polyhistor, who cites from Cleodemus Malchus and Demetrius, derives the Assyrians, Africans, the people of Carthage, and Moses' wife Zipporah from Abraham through Keturah (*Praepar. Evang.* 9.20; 9.29.1-3).

26. On the continuity between John and Jesus (Luke 16,16), and on John as part of the proclamation of God's kingdom (Luke 3,18), see M. BACHMANN, *Johannes der Täufer bei Lukas. Nachzügler oder Vorläufer?*, in W. HAUBECK and M. BACHMANN (eds.), *Wort in der Zeit*. Festschrift K. H. Rengstorf, Leiden, Brill, 1980, pp. 123-155; BUSSE, *Evangelium* (n. 3), pp. 166-169.

zation of God in Luke-Acts: "La figure d'Abraham servira donc à révéler aux Galates la volonté actuelle de Dieu pour eux: il ne s'agira pas d'imiter Abraham, mais de se laisser instruire par lui des intentions permanentes de Dieu à l'égard de son peuple"[27].

John refers to the offspring of Abraham only in a negative fashion. He warns against appealing to Abraham as ancestor and claims that God can raise up offspring to Abraham from stones. John's negative reference, however, has the possibility of functioning in two ways. Readers can take it as devaluing the Abrahamic heritage or revaluing it[28]. John himself gives one criterion for revaluation – bearing fruits worthy of repentance.

Nevertheless, Jesus' genealogy indicates that Abrahamic ancestry has value in the narrative world. On the basis of the text alone, Abraham has no more standing in the genealogy than do Addi, Cosam, and Elmadam (3,28). But against the cultural repertoire, Abraham and David are significant beyond others in the genealogy[29]. Joachim Jeremias exaggerates but nevertheless gives evidence for the tracing of Davidic ancestry in New Testament times[30]. On the other hand, the genealogy is theocentric in tracing a divine origin of the ancestry from which Abraham, David, Addi, Cosam, Elmadam, and Jesus descend (3,38). This is to say that given the origin of the human race in God, Luke-Acts has an optimistic anthropology[31]. But in this case one may take over for Luke-Acts, *mutatis mutandis*, Bultmann's dictum: "[Paul's] theology is, at the same time, anthropology"[32].

27. P. Bonnard, *L'Épître de saint Paul aux Galates* (CNT, 9), Neuchâtel, Delachaux & Niestlé, 1953, p. 65.

28. God's work over against the conventional claim to be offspring of Abraham offers both a devaluation of physical descent and a revaluation of God's creative power. See Bovon, *Lukas* (n. 5), 1, p. 172; Schürmann, *Lukas* (n. 10), 1, p. 165; J. Siker, *Disinheriting the Jews. Abraham in Early Christian Controversy*, Louisville, KY, Westminster – John Knox, 1991, p. 109. *Pseudo-Philo* 33,5, likely contemporaneous with Luke-Acts, holds a position that has the ring of Luke 3,8: "Therefore do not hope in your fathers. For they will not profit you at all unless you be found like them".

29. See Fitzmyer, *Luke* (n. 7), 1, p. 490.

30. J. Jeremias, *Jerusalem zur Zeit Jesu. Eine kulturgeschichtliche Untersuchung zur neutestamentlichen Zeitgeschichte*, Göttingen, Vandenhoeck & Ruprecht, 1969, pp. 257, 309. Subtly the grouping of generations in patterns of 3 x 7 and 2 x 7 may imply emphasis on Abraham and David: Schürmann, *Lukas* (n. 10), 1, p. 202; Ernst, *Lukas* (n. 9), pp. 121-122. Tannehill notes that ὡς ἐνομίζετο relativizes descent from David, Abraham, and Adam: *Narrative Unity* (n. 6), 1, p. 55 n. 18.

31. Cf. Acts 17,28; Philo, *Virt.* 204-205. See M. Parsons and R. Pervo, *Rethinking the Unity of Luke and Acts*, Minneapolis, MN, Fortress, 1993, p. 108.

32. R. Bultmann, *Theology of the New Testament*, New York, Scribner's, 1951, vol. 1, p. 191.

The next overt reference to Abraham occurs in the healing of the woman bent double. Through Jesus, God heals this woman who for eighteen years was unable to stand up straight (13,10-17). The incident precipitates a conflict in which the ruler of the synagogue directs his objections not to Jesus or the woman but to the crowd. Thus, his challenge is a social challenge. If his challenge is successful, the crowd will give the verdict against healing on the sabbath. Jesus' riposte contains three elements – two kinds of labeling stand on either side of a lesser to greater analogy. First, Jesus follows the ruler in addressing the crowd and labels them "hypocrites" (13,15). The taxonomy of labeling and deviance theory anticipates attempts of a social regulator to enlist agents who will subject someone with deviant social status to a ritual of degradation[33]. Jesus labels the crowd deviant but also attempts to enlist them as agents. Second, he attempts to persuade them by comparing the healing of the woman with caring for animals on the sabbath. The analogy entails not merely a comparison between human behavior toward animals and human behavior toward the woman, but also a comparison between human work and divine work on the sabbath. The opponents in fact read this healing anthropocentrically as if it is human work, and fail to discern God's action on the sabbath[34]. The woman, however, interprets the incident theocentrically. She praises God (13,13). Third, Jesus follows his analogy with positive labeling: "This woman who is a daughter of Abraham" (13,16)[35].

The levels of appeal in labeling the woman a daughter of Abraham are multiple. First, Jesus personalizes the woman. She is no longer a woman whom the narrator introduces, nor the woman whom Jesus addresses, but a daughter who evokes maternal and paternal instincts. Further, to name her a daughter of Abraham before children of Abraham in the synagogue evokes the maternal and paternal instincts of this crowd for this daughter.

33. B. MALINA and J. NEYREY, *Calling Jesus Names. The Social Value of Labels in Matthew*, Sonoma, CA, Polebridge, 1988, pp. 35-65, 96-97.

34. BOVON, *Lukas* (n. 5), 2, pp. 402-403; E. SCHÜSSLER FIORENZA, *Liberation, Unity and Equality in Community. A New Testament Case Study*, in *Beyond Unity-in-Tension. Unity, Renewal and the Community of Women and Men*, Geneva, WCC Publications, 1988, p. 59. R. O'TOOLE, *Some Exegetical Reflections on Luke 13,10-17*, in *Bib* 73 (1992), pp. 94-97, reads the incident with anthropocentric interests in the woman as an example of imitation and as a symbol for all Israel. But the focus is on Jesus rather than the woman. See also H. SAHLIN, *Die Perikope vom gerasenischen Besessenen und der Plan des Marcusevangeliums*, in *ST* 18 (1964), p. 161.

35. On labeling someone prominent see MALINA and NEYREY, *Calling Jesus Names* (n. 33), pp. 54-65, 99-102. The woman *is* a daughter of Abraham, a premise rather than a consequence of the healing: cf. SEIM, *Double Message* (n. 3), p. 48.

Labeling the woman a daughter of Abraham may recall another woman from the cultural repertoire. In 4 Macc 15,28, the mother of the seven sons is called a daughter not directly of Abraham but of Abraham's steadfastness and fear of God[36]. But if readers recall the mother of the seven through Jesus' labeling, they will experience a revision of the meaning of a daughter of Abraham. In 4 Maccabees, Eleazar urges Jews to die for their religion (εὐσέβεια), which in this case means the refusal to violate dietary laws (6,22). He and the seven undergo torture and death for the sake of the law. The mother of the seven loves her sons, and (in some resemblance to Jesus' argument) 4 Maccabees employs a lesser to greater analogy of the love of animals for their offspring (14,14-19). But the mother loves religion, manifest in the purity laws, more than she loves her sons (15,1-32). In the case of Luke 13, love for a daughter – ultimately God's love for a daughter of Abraham – surpasses religion as it is manifest in sabbath laws.

A third level of appeal for readers, however, has to do with a retrospect on the daughter of Abraham through the lens of Acts 3,25. In the Abrahamic covenant, God promises to bless all the families of the earth. Though Mary and Zechariah already claim God's mercy to the σπέρμα of Abraham in Luke 1, when readers are informed by Acts 3,25, they can construe the healing of the daughter of Abraham as a concrete case of God's promise to bless all the families of the earth. The crowd in the synagogue understands it also as a concrete case of God's blessing. In the honor/shame contest, Jesus' opponents are dishonored, and all the crowd gives a public verdict in favor of Jesus' healing of a daughter of Abraham on the sabbath (Luke 13,17). If Jesus

---

36. JERVELL, *Unknown Paul* (n. 3), p. 148, alleges that "daughter of Abraham" is unknown in the literature of the time. But 4 Maccabees comes close. S. SANDMEL, *Philo's Place in Judaism. A Study of Conceptions of Abraham in Jewish Literature,* New York, KTAV, 1971, p. 58, makes the mother of the seven sons directly the daughter of Abraham. But in 4 Macc 15,28 she is the daughter of Abraham's perseverance. English (NRSV) and German (H.-J. Klauck) versions translate 4 Macc 18,20 as "daughter" and "Tochter" of Abraham. But the LXX refers to the mother of the seven sons in the genitive as τῆς ᾿Αβρααμίτιδος, the only occurrence of the term in pre-Christian literature. A. Dupont-Sommer's French translation has "l'Abramitide". On analogy with the same ending in the LXX, such as Χανανίτιδος (Gen 46,10; 1 Chron 2,3), ᾿Ισραηλίτιδος (Lev 24,10), Μωαβίτιδος (Ruth 4,5; Isa 15,1; Jer 31,33), Σαμαρίτιδος (1 Macc 10,30; 11,34), and ἰσοπολίτιδος (4 Macc 13,9), ᾿Αβρααμίτις obviously designates ethnic identity. The attachment to the person of Abraham appears strong, however, in comparison with the geographical dimension of the vast majority of analogous endings. On the general geographical connotation of the ending see R. KÜHNER and F. BLASS, *Ausführliche Grammatik der griechischen Sprache,* Darmstadt, Wissenschaftliche Buchgesellschaft, 1966, part 1, vol. 2, p. 284; H. SMYTH, *Greek Grammar,* Cambridge, MA, Harvard University Press, 1980, p. 235.

has been persuasive, perhaps all the crowd includes even the opponents[37].

Jesus gives an ambiguous response to a question about numbers of people who will be saved, a question that is biased in the direction of the salvation of only a few (13,23). Initially, Jesus appears to confirm that few will be saved. This door is narrow – too narrow to accommodate the press of many struggling to enter. Moreover, the narrow door closes, and the master neither knows the crowd outside nor opens the door for them. In 13,28, the only inhabitants visible in God's kingdom are the patriarchs and the prophets. At this point, Jesus' hearers, including the one who asked the question, can only see themselves on the outside, weeping and grinding their teeth. On the other hand, in 13,29 people come in from all directions, and Jesus' hearers have the possibility of seeing themselves at the banquet in God's kingdom with Abraham, Isaac, Jacob, and the prophets[38]. For exclusivists anticipating a few, the kingdom is for very few – only the patriarchs and the prophets to the exclusion of the exclusivists themselves. But for those anticipating many, the kingdom is open from every direction. By implication and in retrospect from Acts 3,25, Abraham is again part of the characterization of God as the one who promises to bless all the families of the earth.

In Luke 13,28 Jesus predicts that his hearers will see Abraham, Isaac, Jacob, and the prophets in God's kingdom from the outside. On one level, this is an external prolepsis reaching beyond the temporal limits of Luke-Acts. But on another level, readers soon do see Abraham in God's kingdom from the outside (16,19-31). As a parabler, Jesus embeds a story in the narrator's story – a metadiegetic narrative in G. Genette's terminology[39]. Through Jesus' story, readers see Lazarus reclining in

---

37. FITZMYER, *Luke* (n. 7), 2, p. 1014. BOVON, *Lukas* (n. 5), 2, p. 404, plays the crowd off against the opponents who were put to shame. But if readers trace continuity among "people", "hypocrites", "opponents", and "all the people", then the crowd at the end includes the opponents.

38. J. Dupont ignores Luke 13,29 when he claims that 13,28 excludes descendants of Abraham from the kingdom: *Le riche publicain est aussi un fils d'Abraham (Luc 19,1-10)*, in C. BUSSMANN and W. RADL (eds.), *Der Treue Gottes trauen* (n. 3), p. 270. E. SCHÜSSLER FIORENZA, *But She Said. Feminist Practices of Biblical Interpretation*, Boston, Beacon, 1992, p. 207, claims that readers know that Jesus' call to repentance will meet rejection. But readers who differentiate among Jesus' opponents to the extent that Luke-Acts differentiates cannot identify these opponents with those who ultimately reject. Moreover, those exhorted to enter the narrow door are Judeans. FITZMYER, *Luke* (n. 7), p. 1023.

39. See note 1. L. DÄLLENBACH, *The Mirror in the Text*, Chicago, University of Chicago Press, 1989, pp. 51 and 53, makes a distinction between metadiegesis and meta-narrative, the latter designating cases in which an internal narrator takes over temporarily from the narrator.

Abraham's lap. The posture at least suggests reclining at a banquet in God's kingdom as in 13,29[40].

Significantly, not only do readers see Abraham, they also hear him in dialogue with the rich man. Abraham gives an obvious recommendation for living so as to be with Abraham after death – listen to Moses and the prophets. So interpreters quite correctly have turned to Moses and the prophets to uncover the motivation for the reversal of status in the parable. Deut 15,7-11 has proved to be fruitful in establishing scriptural warrants for the rich to help the poor: "You shall not harden your heart or shut your hand against your poor brother, but you shall open your hand to him, and lend him sufficient for his need, whatever it may be"[41]. But interpreters have generally overlooked the overtones of Abrahamic covenant traditions in both Deuteronomy and Luke-Acts.

From the beginning Deuteronomy synthesizes Abrahamic and Mosaic covenant traditions. In Deut 1,8 possession of the land is fulfillment of God's promise to the forebears, and 1,10-11 alludes to God's promise to multiply Abraham's descendants. Deut 4,31 reinforces God's memory of the Abrahamic covenant. Repeatedly, possession of the land is both the Abrahamic inheritance and the basis for Mosaic exhortations. Thus, Deut 15,4 recalls the inheritance of the land (ἐν κλήρῳ κατακληρονομῆσαι αὐτήν) and God's promise to bless (εὐλογῶν εὐλογήσει σε κύριος ὁ θεός σου) as correlates of the command to help the poor. Helping the poor is part of the way God blesses in the land God gives as an inheritance.

Overtones of the Abrahamic covenant also reverberate in Luke-Acts. To recapitulate, the reversal of status of the rich and the hungry in the Magnificat is correlated with God's memory of mercy promised to Abraham and his σπέρμα (Luke 1,54-55). The salvation that Zechariah anticipates is grounded in God's memory of the covenant God swore to Abraham. Further, in retrospect from Acts 3,25, readers know that in the covenant God promises to bless all the families of the earth. In the parable of the rich man and Lazarus, the Abraham who advises listening to Moses and the prophets is the Abraham whom the rich man repeatedly calls "father" and who calls the rich man "child". In the cultural repertoire, this parent-child relationship is nothing other than the covenantal line of promise, though in keeping with Luke 3,8 Abrahamic covenant relationships are being revised beyond merely physical descent.

40. So ERNST, *Lukas* (n. 9), p. 356.
41. B. SCOTT, *Hear Then the Parable. A Commentary on the Parables of Jesus*, Minneapolis, MN, Fortress, 1989, p. 158.

Unfortunately, a great chasm that cannot be crossed separates the rich man from Abraham and Lazarus. In a surprising case of sibling non-rivalry, the rich man asks for someone to be sent from the dead to his brothers. From a retrospective point of view outside the narrative, what the rich man requests has already come in Jesus[42]. Inside the narrative world, the siblings have Moses and the prophets, and the parable suspends on whether they will listen or not[43]. Readers soon encounter another rich man who fills the role of a sibling. In grief over his possessions, he apparently separates himself from God's kingdom (18,18-25). Like the chasm that the rich man of the parable cannot traverse, this rich ruler is a camel who cannot negotiate the eye of a needle. So who is able to be saved (18,26)? Two performances in the development of narrative schemata[44] respond to this question. One is a direct answer from Jesus that is a forceful characterization of God: "Impossibilities with human beings are possibilities with God" (18,27; cf. 1,37). The other is another narrative about a rich man who also plays the role of a sibling inasmuch as he, like the rich man of the parable, is also a child of Abraham (19,1-10).

As both the cultural repertoire and the murmuring crowd show[45], Zacchaeus has an impassible chasm to cross, and he is a camel who must pass through the eye of a needle. The narrative is sparse. Particularly, motivations are missing. But Jesus' social relationship with Zacchaeus is the point of objection for Jesus' detractors and evidently the point of attraction for Zacchaeus. Jesus' violation of cultural boundaries for his sake is then the causative factor in his decision to give half of his wealth to the poor and to repay those whom he has defrauded fourfold[46].

---

42. V. TANGHE, *Abraham, son fils et son envoyé (Luc 16,19-31)*, in *RB* 91 (1984), p. 577.

43. See D. BOCK, *Luke*, Grand Rapids, MI, Baker, 1994-1996, vol. 2, p. 1377; GREEN, *Luke* (n. 8), p. 517. L. JOHNSON, *The Gospel of Luke* (Sacra Pagina, 3), Collegeville, MN, Liturgical Press, 1991, p. 256, overlooks the conditional form in 16,31 to "seal [the five siblings'] rejection". The suspended ending obviates O. Glombitza's interpretation that it is too late for the synagogue that has overlooked Jesus: cf. *Der reiche Mann und der arme Lazarus. Luk. xvi 19-31. Zur Frage nach der Botschaft des Textes*, in *NT* 12 (1970), pp. 173-179 and Tanghe's view that the parable opposes Jewish refusal to repent: *Abraham* (n. 42), p. 577.

44. See A. GREIMAS and J. CORTÉS, art. *"Narrative Schema"*, *"Program, Narrative"*, in *Semiotics and Language. An Analytical Dictionary*, Bloomington, IN, Indiana University Press, 1982.

45. O. MICHEL, τελώνης, in *TDNT*, vol. 8, pp. 93-105; J. DONAHUE, *Tax Collectors and Sinners. An Attempt at Identification*, in *CBQ* 33 (1971) 39-61; W. WALKER, *Jesus and the Tax Collectors*, in *JBL* 97 (1978) 221-238.

46. FITZMYER, *Luke* (n. 7), 2, pp. 1221 and 1225, holds that Zacchaeus speaks in an iterative present as a claim that he already gives his money to the poor and restores to

Καθότι in 19,9 is ambiguous. Readers cannot distinguish between purpose and result. On the one hand, Zacchaeus, in parallel with the woman bent double in Luke 13, is of enough value for Jesus to violate cultural barriers because as an offspring of Abraham, he is a recipient of Abrahamic promises. On the other hand, Zacchaeus's decision to give to the poor and to restore his fraud fourfold manifests the heart of the Abrahamic heritage (e.g., Deut 15,7-11). In either instance, Zacchaeus is a concrete case of God's promise to bless all the families of the earth[47]. God is characterized by the crossing of an impassible chasm and by a camel that has passed through the eye of a needle. "Impossibilities with human beings are possibilities with God" (18,27).

Although the transition from Luke to Acts is not altogether smooth[48], the Gospel ends and Acts begins with emphasis on a promise from the God who is characterized as a parental God of promises. Robert Tannehill has demonstrated the narrative logic of reading Acts 1,4 as a flashback to Luke 11,13[49] rather than as an anticipation of Acts 1,5[50]. The father of Luke 11,13 has promised to give the holy spirit to those who ask. But the promise of the spirit is embedded in a larger promise, namely, God's promise to Abraham (Luke 1,55.73; Acts 3,25)[51]. Thus, the coming of the spirit on Pentecost occasions the invocation of another promise. After his explanation of the events of Pentecost as the fulfillment of the promise of the spirit (Acts 2,33), Peter reminds his hearers:

those who are defrauded fourfold. But against this, ἐσυκοφάντησα characterizes Zacchaeus from his own mouth as someone who has defrauded, and σήμερον implies that a change (σωτηρία) has come upon Zacchaeus.

47. In agreement and reading retrospectively from Acts 3,25, see also Dupont, *Riche publicain* (n. 38), pp. 271-272.

48. K. Lake, *The Beginnings of Christianity*. Part 1, *The Acts of the Apostles*, London, Macmillan, 1933, vol. 3, pp. 256-261; vol. 5, pp. 1-7; H. Conzelmann, *The Theology of St. Luke*, New York, Harper & Row, 1961, p. 15 n. 1 and p. 94; P. Menoud, *Remarques sur les textes de l'ascension dans Luc-Actes*, in W. Eltester (ed.), *Neutestamentliche Studien für Rudolf Bultmann*, Berlin, Töpelmann, 1954, pp. 148-156; M. Parsons, *The Departure of Jesus in Luke-Acts. The Ascension Narratives in Context* (JSNT SS, 21), Sheffield, Academic Press, 1987; Tannehill, *Narrative Unity* (n. 6), 1, pp. 299-300; 2, p. 11.

49. Tannehill, *Narrative Unity*, p. 12; also R. Pesch, *Die Apostelgeschichte* (EKK), Zürich, Benziger, 1986, 1, pp. 66-67. See C.K. Barrett, *A Critical and Exegetical Commentary on the Acts of the Apostles* (ICC), Edinburgh, T & T Clark, 1994, 1, p. 73.

50. E. Haenchen, *The Acts of the Apostles. A Commentary*, Philadelphia, Westminster, 1971, p. 142, takes Acts 1,5 as a reformulation of a saying from John the Baptist into a saying of Jesus. So also H. Conzelmann, *Acts of the Apostles. A Commentary on the Acts of the Apostles* (Hermeneia), Philadelphia, Fortress, 1987, p. 6; G. Schneider, *Die Apostelgeschichte* (HTKNT, 5), Freiburg, Herder, 1980, 1, pp. 200-201.

51. So also L. Johnson, *The Acts of the Apostles* (Sacra Pagina, 5), Collegeville, MN, Liturgical Press, 1992, p. 25.

"For the promise is to you and to your children and to all that are far off, every one whom the Lord our God calls to him"(2,39).

According to Haenchen, Peter refers back to the promise from Joel: "Whoever calls on the name of the Lord will be saved" (2,22)[52]. True, Acts 2,39 resumes an allusion to Joel 3,5 (LXX) just at the point where Peter's citation of Joel in Acts 2,21 breaks off ("whomever the Lord our God will call"). But in the context Haenchen is shortsighted. Peter specifies that the promise is "to you and to your children, and to everyone who is far off". The context in Joel 3,2 (4,5 LXX) leaves the heritage of parents to children out of the picture. With a retrospective reading from Acts 3,25, however, the promise for parents and children and those who are far off is God's promise to Abraham to bless all the families of the earth[53]. The gift of the spirit at Pentecost is a particular way God moves toward blessing all the families of the earth.

On the heels of Pentecost, the healing of a lame man at the Temple gate is a concrete case of God's bestowal of Abrahamic blessings (3,1-10)[54]. As an Abrahamic blessing, the restoration of this man aligns with the woman bent double and Zacchaeus. Peter's speech interprets the healing. His explanation is vital because, as 3,12 and 4,9 show, the source of the healing is debatable[55]. The close relationship between God's promise to Moses to raise up a prophet like Moses (3,22) and God's promise to Abraham to bless all the families of the earth (3,25) is another indication that Luke-Acts synthesizes the two covenants[56]. As Gabriel, Mary, and Zechariah fold the Davidic and Abrahamic covenants together, so Peter fuses the Mosaic and Abrahamic Covenants. Not only the Davidic messiah but also the prophet like Moses is a particular way God moves the Abrahamic covenant toward its term.

52. HAENCHEN, *Acts* (n. 50), p. 184; so also CONZELMANN, *Acts* (n. 50), p. 22; PESCH, *Apostelgeschichte* (n. 49), 1, p. 125; SCHNEIDER, *Apostelgeschichte* (n. 50), 1, p. 278. O. BAUERNFEIND finds here an allusion to Isa 57,19: *Kommentar und Studien zur Apostelgeschichte* (WUNT, 22), Tübingen, Mohr, 1980, p. 53.

53. So also JOHNSON, *Acts* (n. 51), p. 52. On the integrity of the context see CONZELMANN, *Acts*, p. 27; F. HAHN, *Das Problem alter christologischer Überlieferung in der Apostelgeschichte unter besonderer Berücksichtigung von Act 3,19-21*, in J. KREMER (ed.), *Les Actes des Apôtres. Traditions, rédaction, théologie* (BETL, 48), Gembloux, Duculot, 1979, pp. 137-138; R. DILLON, *The Prophecy of Christ and His Witnesses according to the Discourse of Acts*, in *NTS* 32 (1986), pp. 544, 552 n. 3; J. ROLOFF, *Die Apostelgeschichte* (NTD, 5), Göttingen, Vandenhoeck & Ruprecht, 1981, p. 71.

54. Beyond the events of Pentecost, the healing of the lame man is the first of the marvels and signs anticipated by Peter's citation of Joel in Acts 2,19. See A. WEISER, *Die Apostelgeschichte. Kapitel 1-12* (ÖTKNT, 5/1), Gütersloh, Mohn, 1981, p. 107.

55. On Peter's speech as an interpretation of the healing see ROLOFF, *Apostelgeschichte* (n. 53), p. 71.

56. BAUERNFEIND, *Kommentar und Studien* (n. 52), p. 67. Against BARRETT, *Acts* (n. 49), p. 212, there is no covenant renewal or new covenant here.

After the first part of Peter's speech, it is easy for readers to lose sight of the man who is healed[57]. But the narrative does not. The healed man is still present in 4,7-10 and is on the lips of both Peter and the council. Thus, the healing of the lame man brackets the reference to the Abrahamic covenant in 3,25 in such a fashion that it is a concrete instance of the times of refreshing and of the blessing of all the families of the earth (3,19-20.25)[58]. Moreover, he is a concrete case of the blessing available to all the people[59]. Peter's attempt to reverse the negative connotations of Jesus' crucifixion is integral to his speech. In playing out a cultural drama of honor and shame, the crucifixion is a forceful ritual declaration that Jesus is a detriment to the people[60]. Peter, however, portrays Jesus as a benefactor to the people. What is evident in the healing of the lame man is in fact available to all the people according to God's promise to Abraham to bless all the families of the earth[61].

57. On formcritical grounds Bauernfeind makes the healing an end in itself and separates it from the context: *Kommentar und Studien* (n. 52), p. 5. So also SCHNEIDER, *Apostelgeschichte* (n. 50), 1, p. 297. Further, Schneider labels the section 3,1–4,31 as the first persecution rather than a blessing (p. 295).

58. Acts 3,24 establishes that the present is the messianic age. Many interpreters distinguish between the times of refreshment in 3,20 and the times of restoration in 3,21. E.g., U. WILCKENS, *Die Missionsreden der Apostelgeschichte. Form und traditionsgeschichtliche Untersuchungen* (WMANT, 5), Neukirchen-Vluyn, Neukirchener Verlag, ³1974, p. 43; C.K. BARRETT, *Faith and Eschatology in Acts 3*, in E. GRÄSSER and O. MERK (eds.), *Glaube und Eschatologie. FS W.G. Kümmel*, Tübingen, Mohr, 1985, pp. 10-16. But Acts 3,24 establishes that the times of refreshment are the times of restoration on the way toward their term. So CONZELMANN, *Acts* (n. 50), p. 29; SCHNEIDER, *Apostelgeschichte* (n. 50), 1, pp. 326-327; A. OEPKE, ἀποκατάστασις, in *TDNT*, 1, p. 390. F. MUSSNER, *Die Idee der Apokatastasis in der Apostelgeschichte*, in *Gesammelte Studien zu Fragen und Themen des Neuen Testaments*, Düsseldorf, Patmos, 1967, p. 224. On the basis of the naming of Abraham in 3,13, Bauernfeind suggests a possible relationship to the Abrahamic covenant (*Kommentar und Studien*, p. 67).

59. Acts 3,25 uses πατριαί rather than φυλαί (Gen 12,3) or ἔθνη (22,18) in formulating the Abrahamic covenant. This makes the Abrahamic covenant more applicable to the Jewish audience. Cf. ROLOFF, *Apostelgeschichte* (n. 53), p. 78.

60. On social detriment and benefaction, see MALINA and NEYREY, *Calling Jesus Names* (n. 33), pp. 35-36, 54-65, 99-102; R. WEBER, *"Why Were the Heathen so Arrogant"? The Socio-Rhetorical Strategy of Acts 3–4*, in *BTB* 22 (1992) 19-25.

61. Commentators have generally not recognized the fulfillment of Abrahamic promises in the healing of the lame man. F. BRUCE, *Commentary on the Book of Acts. The English Text with Introduction, Exposition, and Notes* (NICNT), Grand Rapids, MI, Eerdmans, 1956, p. 85, relates the healing to the messianic age but not to the Abrahamic covenant. Bauernfeind recognizes that the healing pertains to every Israelite but connects the fulfillment of the Abrahamic covenant rather with the prophet like Moses. He also takes σπέρμα in 3,25 as a literal singular rather than as collective (*Kommentar und Studien*, pp. 63, 67, 70, but see 71). It is possible to take σπέρμα in Acts 3,25 as a literal singular. So PESCH, *Apostelgeschichte* (n. 49), 1, p. 157; SCHNEIDER, *Apostelgeschichte* (n. 50), 1, pp. 329-330. I argue similarly with respect to the σπέρμα of David implied in Luke 1,32-33. It is also possible to affirm both. SIKER, *Disinheriting* (n. 28), pp. 119-120. But the connection of the Abrahamic promise to Peter's audience in 2,39 implies rather the collective meaning.

Though Luke-Acts disproportionately emphasizes God's promise to bless in the Abrahamic covenant, it does not forget that the promises in Genesis are multiple. In Acts 7 Stephen recalls God's promise of land as an inheritance (7,3.5 ἡ γῆ is ἡ κληρονομία)[62]. Stephen makes a subtle distinction between the status of his auditors and Abraham's status. The auditors live in the land of the inheritance whereas God did not give Abraham as much as a footstep in the land. Thus the presence of the auditors in the land is confirmation of God's fidelity to the promise. An allusion to God's prediction of the Egyptian sojourn in Gen 15,13-16 follows (Acts 7,6-7), but because it flows so quickly into the stories of Isaac, Jacob, and Joseph, it appears at first glance to have little significance.

Abraham's name in 7,16 introduces a more significant reference to the promise (7,16-17). When 7,17 speaks of the drawing near of the time of promise that God made with Abraham, it is patent that the story that follows is the fulfillment of that promise. But how far forward does the notion of fulfillment carry? The overt presence of an allusion to Gen 15,13-16 in the near context means that the time of the drawing near of the promise to Abraham includes not merely the multiplication of Abraham's descendants but also Moses, the exodus, Sinai, and the entrance into the land[63]. Though Acts 7,32 is dependent on Exod 3,6 and though it serves as an evaluative characterization of God, it also keeps overtones of the Abrahamic covenant alive. Stephen, like other characters in Luke-Acts, synthesizes covenant traditions by making the exodus, Sinai, and the possession of the land particular ways God fulfills the promises to Abraham.

But two additional lines of development tie Stephen's story together. One is Moses' prediction of a prophet like himself, the other is the tent of witness. Moses has two essential functions in Stephen's speech. He leads the people out of Egypt, which in light of the allusion to Gen 15,13-16 is a particular way God fulfills the Abrahamic covenant. Second, Moses announces a prophet like himself. Thus accepting the prophet like Moses has priority over keeping the law as a criterion for obeying Moses, and this line of thought continues through the betrayal and murder of the righteous one in 7,52.

---

62. Stephen's speech is emphatically theocentric. Nevertheless, anthropocentric readings that center on Israel's unbelief (rather than the unbelief of Stephen's opponents) are common. One development of Israel's traditions took God's promise of ארץ or γῆ to Abraham as a promise of the whole world. So Sir 44,19-21; *Jub.* 17,3; 19,21; 22,14; 32,18-19; Rom 4,13; 1 Cor 6,2; Heb 2,5; cf. Jas 2,5; Philo, *Vit. Moses* 1.155; *Mek.* Exod 14,31. According to *Sifre* on Deut 34,1-4, on Mt. Nebo God showed Moses the whole earth.

63. On the embedding of Moses' story in the story of the patriarchs, see BAUERN-FEIND, *Kommentar und Studien* (n. 52), p. 111.

The second line of development that ties Stephen's story together has to do with the tent of witness. The tent in the wilderness stands in direct connection with David's desire to build a temple and Solomon's completion of the task. Contrary to conventional interpretations, Stephen raises no objection to the Temple[64]. What is problematic is the relationship of the people both to the tent in the wilderness and to the Temple in Jerusalem. Just as taking up the tent of Moloch stands over against the tent of witness, so also confining God to the Temple misconstrues what was originally given to Moses. Both the wrong Temple theology and the rejection of the prophet are failure to obey Moses.

In short, Stephen's speech is quite unified under the canopy of God's promises to Abraham[65]. Moses, the exodus, the announcement of the prophet like Moses, Sinai, the tent of witness, the Temple, and the coming of the righteous one are particular ways God moves promises to Abraham toward their term. Like Zechariah, Stephen synthesizes covenant traditions under the umbrella of the Abrahamic covenant[66].

Paul's speech at Pisidian Antioch also encompasses successive episodes in Israel's history under God's fidelity to promises to Abraham: the multiplication of the people, the sojourn in Egypt, the exodus, the wilderness wandering, the entrance into the land, the judges, the Davidic monarchy[67], and Jesus as savior. Paul accomplishes this, how-

---

64. For the view that the Temple should never have replaced the tent of testimony see BAUERNFEIND, *Kommentar und Studien*, p. 118. But ultimately Bauernfeind lodges the problem in the tendency of the people to make the Temple idolatrous. PESCH, *Apostelgeschichte* (n. 49), p. 245, takes the Temple made with human hands as a reiteration of the making of a golden calf with human hands and therefore idolatrous. But this would apply also to the tent of witness which Moses makes (7,44 ποιῆσαι αὐτήν). According to Stephen's speech, Solomon's temple is built for God (7,47 αὐτῷ) but is not God's dwelling place in agreement with Solomon in 1 Kings 8,27. SCHNEIDER, *Apostelgeschichte* (n. 50), 1, p. 467; J. DUPONT, *La structure oratoire du discours d'Étienne (Actes 7)*, in *Bib* 66 (1985), pp. 159-160. On God's transcendence of the Temple in Acts 7 see D. SYLVA, *The Meaning and Function of Acts 7:46-50*, in *JBL* 106 (1987), pp. 262, 270-272. See F. WEINERT, *Luke, Stephen, and the Temple in Luke-Acts*, in *BTB* 17 (1987) 88-90; J. KILGALLEN, *The Function of Stephen's Speech (Acts 7,2-53)*, in *Bib* 70 (1989) 175-193.

65. See TANNEHILL, *Narrative Unity* (n. 6), 2, p. 88-93. DAHL, *Abraham* (n. 2), pp. 72-73, 78, is correct that Stephen's speech foregrounds the history of Abraham's posterity and fulfillment of God's promise to Abraham. But against his emphasis on the fulfillment of prophecy as such, God's promise is fulfilled. On the theocentric nature of the speech see JOHNSON, *Acts* (n. 51), pp. 121, 135. BARRETT, *Acts* (n. 49), p. 337: "[The speech] teaches that God is constantly at work in the history of his people, and that his activity follows a recurring pattern in which good is brought out of evil. This recurring action is the working out of a covenant made between God and Abraham".

66. See TANNEHILL, *Narrative Unity* (n. 6), 2, p. 91.

67. The period of 450 years (different from Acts 7,6) may be a clue to how the events hang together. The period of time embraces a number of events, either from the time of

ever, without initially naming Abraham (Acts 13,17-23). Four particular details imply the Abrahamic covenant long before Abraham's name appears in 13,26. (1) Paul grounds his appeal in God's action to elect the patriarchs, to which covenant promises are integral (13,17)[68]. (2) Like Stephen, Paul follows Gen 15,13-16 as a summary of God's promise to Abraham (Acts 13,17-19). (3) Paul refers to the entrance into the land with the catchword κατακληρονομέω, an allusion to the Abrahamic heritage. (4) Paul brackets his summary with the identification of his audience as Israelites and godfearers at the beginning and as offspring of Abraham and godfearers at the end (13,16.26). This matches the motif of the promise to the people of Israel, to their children, and to all who are far off (2,39) and the construal of the Abrahamic covenant as God's promise to bless all the families of the earth (3,25).

As in the case of Stephen, Paul also subsumes the Davidic covenant under the Abrahamic. As I have already noted, Paul construes the Davidic monarchy as part of the summary of Israel's history in Gen 15,13-16. In Acts 13,23 he also identifies Jesus as the σπέρμα of David, as Gabriel does implicitly in Luke 1,32. Paul's allusion to the Davidic covenant reiterates the play on σπέρμα in 2 Kingdoms 7,12 as a literal singular over against the collective. The development of this motif in Luke 1 through Mary and Zechariah already establishes the synthesis of the Abrahamic and Davidic covenants in the narrative world. Further, Paul claims that he and Barnabas are proclaiming the good news that the promise to the forebears has taken place in the resurrection of Jesus (Acts 13,32-33). Not only is the promise to the forebears a striking echo of the Abrahamic covenant so also is its fulfillment to τοῖς τέκνοις [αὐτῶν] ἡμῖν (text uncertain) – the promise to Abraham and his σπέρμα.

But in close proximity to the reference to the promise to the forebears, Paul quotes a portion of Isa 55,3: τὰ ὅσια Δαυὶδ τὰ πιστά (Acts 13,34). Conzelmann takes this citation to be so fragmentary that it cannot be understood apart from its connection with Ps 15,10 LXX, which fol-

the election of the patriarchs or from the time of the sojourn in Egypt: SCHNEIDER, *Apostelgeschichte* (n. 50), 2, p. 132.

68. The speech is theocentric. God is the subject of Acts 13,17-24, and God's election of the forebears is thematic. SCHNEIDER, *Apostelgeschichte* (n. 50), 2, p. 131; JOHNSON, *Acts* (n. 51), p. 236.

69. CONZELMANN, *Acts* (n. 50), p. 105. See also BAUERNFEIND, *Kommentar und Studien* (n. 52), p. 176; HAENCHEN, *Acts* (n. 50), p. 412; M. RESE, *Alttestamentliche Motive in der Christologie des Lukas* (SNT, 1), Gütersloh, Mohn, 1969, pp. 87-89, suggests a possible pre-Lucan tradition as the basis for the omission of a reference to the covenant in Paul's citation of Isa 55,3. ROLOFF, *Apostelgeschichte* (n. 69), p. 207, construes τὰ

lows[69]. It is fragmentary, but it is a fragment to be construed intertextually with its original context in Isa 55,3 rather than with Ps 15,10 LXX from which it is explicitly set apart by καὶ ἐν ἑτέρῳ. Readers who know Isa 55,3 as a part of the cultural repertoire can fill in the gap with the first part of the sentence that Paul quotes: καὶ διαθήσομαι ὑμῖν διαθήκην αἰώνιον, τὰ ὅσια Δαυὶδ τὰ πιστά. The prominence of the Davidic covenant along with covert allusions to the Abrahamic indicates that the Davidic covenant has not lost its meaning in the narrative world. Rather, the Abrahamic and Davidic covenants are synthesized[70].

CONCLUSION

This is a restricted venture with limited results. A thorough investigation would need to extend consideration to (1) texts that appeal to the God of promises (e.g., Luke 24,49), to the God of the forebears (e.g., Acts 24,14), and to God's promises to the forebears (e.g., 26,6); (2) texts that allude subtly to the Abrahamic covenant, such as the devil's promise to give Jesus πάσας τὰς βασιλείας τῆς οἰκουμένης (Luke 4,5)[71]; and (3) the entire scope of the characterization of God and the relationship of God's promises to Abraham to the larger portrait of God, a larger portrait that presumes the characterization of God from a cultural repertoire (largely scripture) as Luke-Acts understands that characterization. Consequently, the results of this inquiry are partial.

Nevertheless, I present firm evidence that Abrahamic traditions are indispensable for the characterization of God. God's promises to Abraham are conspicuous at narrative beginnings (Mary, Zechariah, the Bap-

πιστά as establishing the reliability of David's words from Ps 15,10 LXX that follow. M. BUSS, *Die Missionspredigt des Apostels Paulus im pisidischen Antiochen; Analyse von Apg 13,16-41 im Hinblick auf die literarische und thematische Einheit der Paulusrede* (FzB, 38), Stuttgart, Katholisches Bibelwerk, 1980, p. 102, claims that the original Davidic covenant connotations in Isa 55,3 give way to the Abrahamic covenant.

70. E. PLÜMACHER, *Die Missionsreden der Apostelgeschichte und Dionys von Halikarnass*, in *NTS* 39 (1993) 161-177, reads the speech as a turning away from the Jews and a legitimation of a gentile church. Such a reading appears to me to neglect the content of the speech. O. Glombitza states that Paul's sermon is without success because Israel (*sic*), in contrast to Paul, interprets its tradition apocalyptically internal to its own world: see *Akta xiii.15-41. Analyse einer lukanischer Predigt vor Juden. Ein Beitrag zum Problem der Reden in Akta*, in *NTS* 5 (1958-59), p. 317. According to Acts 13,43, the sermon did have a measure of success among Jews in Pisidian Antioch. Against a rejection of a Jewish mission see PESCH, *Apostelgeschichte* (n. 49), 2, p. 47; BARRETT, *Acts* (n. 49), p. 657.

71. For a detailed account of the second temptation as an allusion to the Abrahamic covenant, see R. BRAWLEY, *Text to Text Pours Forth Speech. Voices of Scripture in Luke-Acts* (Indiana Studies in Biblical Literature), Bloomington, IN, Indiana University Press, 1995, pp. 20-22.

tizer) and foreshadow the mission of Jesus. The healing of the woman bent double and the salvation of Zacchaeus as instances of Abrahamic heritage are reiterated features of Jesus' profile. God's acts to fulfill Abrahamic promises are also foundational for new beginnings in Acts. Pentecost and the healing of a lame man are manifestations of God's promise to bless all the families of the earth. Healing and wholeness are manifestations of God's fidelity in particular instances, but they are also pledges of God's universal promise to bless all the families of the earth. Stephen and Paul interpret history, both Israel's history and ultimately universal history, in terms of God's promise to Abraham. In their characterization of God with respect to history, other momentous events such as the exodus, Sinai, the inheritance of the land, the Davidic monarchy, and the Christ event are instances of God's fidelity to ancient promises to Abraham. Though Abraham is implicated in the promises of God in Luke 24,49 and Acts 26,6, he is conspicuously inconspicuous at narrative endings. But he is present in endings of another order. He is an eschatological figure who distinguishes the God of the future and confers substance and quality on God's kingdom.

Choi specifies three particular ways that covenant traditions are synthesized in the Second Temple period: (1) subordination of the Abrahamic covenant to the Mosaic; (2) subordination of Mosaic to Abrahamic; and (3) a synthesis by coordinating the covenants without establishing relationships among them[72]. Luke-Acts, however, synthesizes covenant traditions in yet another way. The Abrahamic covenant is a characterization of God with respect to history. God promises to bless all the families of the earth at canonical narrative beginnings (Gen 12,1-3). Davidic and Mosaic covenants are related to the Abrahamic covenant as part of a sequence. They are particular ways God moves the promises toward their term. For Luke-Acts, Mosaic, Davidic, and Abrahamic

---

72. CHOI, *Abraham our Father* (n. 19), pp. 52, 104, 105, 108, 113, 154, 160, 227. Choi acknowledges that Sirach subsumes the Davidic under the Mosaic (p. 54). Though Choi works with Palestianian sources, Philo is an obvious example of the subordinaation of the Abrahamic covenant to the Mosaic. According to Philo, Abraham kept all the law, though it was unwritten, by nature, and the written law is a copy of the archetypal law that Abraham observed: *Migra. Abra.* 130; *Abra.* 3, 275; the subtitle of *Abra.* is *The Unwritten Laws.* The *Damascus Document* implies the subordination of the Abrahamic covenant to the Mosaic when in a discussion of the Mosaic covenant it gives the example of Abraham's circumcision "on the day of his knowing" (CD 16.6 ביום דתו). 4Q 225 1,4 also refers to Abraham's circumcision. 4Q 378 22i,1-5 may imply the subordination of the Abrahamic covenant to the Mosaic when it associates the righteousness that Moses passed on to Joshua with the Abrahamic covenant. In a swift survey of Israel's story, the *Damascus Document* ddistinguishes between those who walked perfectly in God's ways (CD 2.15-16) or after wantonness of their hearts (2.17-18). In this context, Abraham is a lover (presumably of God) because he kept God's ordinances (3.2 מצות).

covenants do not compete with each other but function properly when they play their role in a holistic program. There is a degree of failure attached to the Davidic and Mosaic covenants. The Davidic covenant was manifestly no longer a political reality after the demise of the monarchy, and so in Luke-Acts a risen Jesus sits on the throne of his ancestor David. Further, Acts indicates (1) an inability of the people to understand or to obey Moses (Acts 13,27) and (2) a deficiency in the efficacy of the Mosaic law to set free (13,39). But God's promise to bless all the families of the earth is frustrated in history as well, and its incompleteness makes space in Luke-Acts for Jesus as God's messiah and ultimately for eschatological hope.

McCormick Theological Seminary   Robert L. BRAWLEY
Chicago, IL
USA

THE CHRISTOLOGY OF LUKE-ACTS

The theme of this Colloquium is the Lukan writings, with the focus very much on the question of their unity: how far do Luke's gospel and Acts speak with the same voice and present a unified viewpoint? Over thirty years ago, W.C. van Unnik famously wrote his contribution to the Festschrift of Paul Schubert under the provocative title "Luke-Acts, A Storm Center in Contemporary Scholarship"[1]. Perhaps one could say that, some thirty years later within Lukan scholarship, the issue of Lukan Christology has become something of a mini-storm centre. For the last few years have seen four major full-length monographs on Lukan Christology, and a number of other major works on the topic have appeared only slightly less recently[2].

First I offer some brief methodological, or terminological, reflections.

I. What is "the Christology of Luke-Acts"?

What do we mean when we talk of "Luke's Christology", "Lukan Christology", "the Christology of Luke's gospel", "The Christology of Acts", or (as here) "the Christology of Luke-Acts"? I suspect that most people, if they talk of "Luke's Christology", or "the Christology of Luke", probably mean the Christology, or the views about the nature of

---

1. W.C. van Unnik, *Luke-Acts, A Storm Center in Contemporary Scholarship*, in L.E. Keck & J.L. Martyn (eds.), *Studies in Luke-Acts*. FS P. Schubert, London, 1968, pp. 15-32.

2. See P. Doble, *The Paradox of Salvation. Luke's Theology of the Cross* (SNTS MS, 87), Cambridge, 1996; M.L. Strauss, *The Davidic Messiah in Luke-Acts. The Promise and Its Fulfillment in Lukan Christology* (JSNT SS, 110), Sheffield, 1995; H.D. Buckwalter, *The Character and Purpose of Luke's Christology* (SNTS MS, 89), Cambridge, 1996; C.H.T. Fletcher-Louis, *Luke-Acts: Angels, Christology and Soteriology* (WUNT, 2/94), Tübingen, 1997. In the slightly more recent past, see D.L. Bock, *Proclamation from Prophecy and Pattern. Lucan Old Testament Christology* (JSNT SS, 12), Sheffield, 1987; D.P. Moessner, *Lord of the Banquet. The Literary and Theological Significance of the Lukan Travel Narrative*, Minneapolis, MN, 1989; Harrisburg, PA, ²1998. The books of Bock, Strauss and Buckwalter all originated as theses written at the University of Aberdeen: one is almost tempted to think of an "Aberdeen school" in relation to the topic! It has not been possible in the course of this essay to cover all the varied theories proposed in these recent studies: in particular, the theories of Doble and Fletcher-Louis have had to remain for the most part unexamined.

Jesus' person or identity, as held by the historical figure of "Luke" himself, i.e. the author of the two-volume work Luke-Acts[3].

One major difficulty with any attempt to discover such a Christology is that this Luke is not directly accessible to us. Of course no figure of antiquity is directly available for us to be able to question him or her directly. With Luke, as with so many other figures from the past, we have access through his writings which have survived. And in the case of Luke, as with most other figures of early Christianity attested in the New Testament, that is virtually the only access we have[4]. Further, with regard to Christology, the subject is not one that Luke ever writes about explicitly. He never writes an essay or a doctrinal treatise on his own understanding of the person of Jesus.

The preceding paragraph could have been written with "Paul" substituted for "Luke" throughout. Paul's Christology is only available to us indirectly through his writings, none of which fully and comprehensively deals with his understanding of the person of Jesus. (Indeed one could argue that Paul rarely if ever addresses the question directly.) Yet in the case of Paul, some kind of theologising does take place, albeit mostly (if not always) in a very ad hoc manner. In the case of Luke, no such theologising by the author himself is ever presented explicitly in the Lukan writings. Luke's genre is to tell a story (or many stories), at times presenting the "theologising" of characters in the story[5].

For our purposes, one key question is how far can/should the ideas of the characters in the story Luke tells be identified with the ideas of the author himself? We can perhaps attempt to discover "the Christology of the Lukan writings" (though even here, as we shall see, the task is by no means straightforward)[6]. Thus we might be able to discover the Christology of the "implied author". But is this then to be equated with the Christology of the real author? Is the Christology which emerges from

3. I assume here without discussion the common authorship of Luke-Acts, and refer to the author as "Luke", though without presupposing anything further about his identity, e.g. his relationship to Paul.

4. The only possible qualification to this would be if one wished to identify Luke with the Luke mentioned in the Pauline corpus at three places (Col 4,14; Phlm 24; 2 Tim 4,11) and/or to take note of patristic testimony about Luke. Yet even this would add little, if anything, of substance to our knowledge of Luke's views about Jesus.

5. Cf. E. HAENCHEN, *The Acts of the Apostles*, Oxford, 1971, p. 91: "Luke is no systematic theologian. He does not seek to develop any unified doctrine, the product of thorough reflection.... he does not proceed by the systematic discussion of dogmatic themes: these are rather, directly or indirectly, suggested to the reader in his historical presentation by means of vivid scenes".

6. I shall use the singular "Christology", rather than plural "Christologies", for the moment.

the story to be identified with the Christology of Luke himself? It is presumably the Christology which Luke chooses to preserve and to present through the medium of his story. Presumably too he chooses to preserve and present things of which he approves and about which he is (in very broad terms) positive. At least some characters in his story are "reliable" in that their "point of view" coincides with that of the author (or at least the implied author)[7]. Other characters are not and presumably their views are clearly not accepted. Thus Jesus or God in the gospel, or the Holy Spirit or Paul in Acts, are presumably for Luke "reliable" characters; Pilate, Felix and the sons of Sceva are not, and anything they say is not to be trusted[8].

However, "approval" and absolute agreement are not necessarily identical. It could be, for example, that Luke approves of some things simply because they are part of a revered tradition which he is anxious to preserve and to hand on. But this does not necessarily mean that he agrees with it entirely as fully reflecting his own views without any qualification. This applies at many levels. It seems quite clear that characters in Luke's story sometimes say things or do things in such a way that Luke clearly approves of their actions and/or words; but either the rest of the story, or some very basic considerations, make it very clear that these things are *not* simply blueprints which Luke thinks can be repeated exactly in his own day. For example, Luke preserves and hands on, or perhaps even creates, stories of pious Jews in the Temple (Luke 1–2) who provide the start of the Christian story about John the Baptist and Jesus. Further, it is quite clear that this activity of Temple-centred piety is regarded approvingly by Luke: it is an integral part of his thoroughly positive presentation of the start of the Christian story and finds an echo in the similar Temple-centred piety of the early Jerusalem church in Acts. Yet presumably Luke does not expect Christians in his own day to repeat such activity precisely. The very fact that he is (almost certainly) writing after 70 CE, and for Christians not living in or near Jerusalem, means that any Temple-centred activity is a physical impossibility. We can of course seek to get "behind" the stories and argue that there is a more indirect truth that Luke is trying to express (e.g. to show the positive links, and the continuity between the Christian

7. For characters as "reliable", cf. R.C. TANNEHILL, *The Narrative Unity of Luke-Acts. A Literary Interpretation*. Vol. 1. *The Gospel according to Luke*, Philadelphia, 1986, pp. 7-8. For "point of view", see N. PETERSEN, *'Point of View' in Mark's Narrative*, in *Semeia* 12 (1978) 97-121.

8. This is of course not to deny the possibility of irony, whereby characters in the story are unwittingly made to say things that are true. However, even the statement in the text above may have to be qualified, e.g. in relation to Jesus (see below).

story and "the Jewish tradition"). My point is simply that this represents a measure of abstraction and deduction.

Similarly, it seems clear that much of the teaching which Luke preserves – often expressed by characters in the story who are clearly "reliable" – is regarded by him as important, but *not* simply as teaching to be repeated in his own day verbatim. Jesus' teaching on riches, poverty and the necessity for would-be disciples to give up *all* their possessions is apparently not regarded as applicable in the post-Easter situation: in Acts there are clearly a number of Christians who do not give up everything and whose "failure" to do so seems to elicit no adverse comment from Luke in any way[9]. Presumably Luke regards Jesus as a thoroughly reliable character in his story. Yet Jesus' teaching is implicitly qualified later in Luke's own story. On a similar theme, the instructions about the "ascetic" lifestyle to be adopted by Jesus' own followers on mission during his ministry are cancelled by the Lukan Jesus himself (Lk 22,35; cf. Lk 10,4-7)[10].

Luke is above all a historian and he seems genuinely aware of the fact that the story he is recounting lies in the historical past. He is thus aware of the pastness of the past in a way that other NT writers, and other gospel writers, may not be[11]. Hence we cannot necessarily simply repeat the words of characters in the story and see them as a direct reflection of Luke's own views. Luke's views may differ slightly, or more than slightly, from what he puts on the lips of even his most revered characters in the story he tells.

We should perhaps also raise the question of whether it is even appropriate to think of Luke as having "a Christology" at all. His chosen

9. See my *Luke*, Sheffield, 1996, ch. 5, pp. 94-110, for details. For followers of Jesus as giving up everything, cf. Lk 5,11 (cf. Mk 1,20); Lk 5,28 (Levi leaves "everything", LkR of Mk 2,17); Lk 18,22 (the rich young man is to leave "everything", LkR of Mk 10,21); above all Lk 14,33: "None of you can become my disciple if you do not give up all your possessions". The issue is also discussed in the essay of D. MARGUERAT in this volume (above, pp. 57-81).

10. Even though Luke confuses the 12 and the 70! The same may well apply in relation to a number of other issues, e.g. Torah observance (is Jesus' saying on the abiding validity of the Law in Lk 16,17 really meant as a statement implying that all Christians in Luke's day must obey the whole Jewish Law?), or eschatology (cf. the well known difference between the teaching of Jesus in the gospel as in Lk 12,39-46; 17,23-37 and the almost total silence on futurist eschatology in Acts). See further my *Luke*, especially the "Concluding Hermeneutical Reflections", pp. 111-117. Also S.G. WILSON, *Related Strangers. Jews and Christians 70-170 CE*, Minneapolis, 1995, p. 61, on the dangers of "slid(ing) too easily between the Lucan narrative and the Lucan community", and the section on pp. 59-63 on Luke and the Law, as well as Marguerat's essay here and the distinction he draws between Luke the historian and Luke the theologian.

11. Cf. H. CONZELMANN, *The Theology of St Luke*, London, 1960, p. 170, and the whole of his Part 4, pp. 170-206.

genre is that of a story, not a doctrinal treatise. Recent study has made it very clear to many (myself included) that Luke has a definite agenda in writing, that he has a "point of view". But whether he has a "theology", or "a Christology", is perhaps another matter. One's answer depends of course to a certain extent on how one defines "theology". But insofar as theology (and Christology as a subset of the broader category of theology) represents a second order attempt to stand back from the primary first order evidence, or phenomena, or formulations of belief, and to seek to rationalise and synthesise such data into a coherent whole, then it is not at all clear that Luke ever makes this attempt[12]. It is arguable if Paul ever does so. In the case of Luke we have to say that if he did so, it has not come down to us directly. All we have is his story.

There are thus very real problems in seeking to determine the Christology of Luke from the Christology of Luke-Acts. The Lukan writings might give us access to "the Christology of Luke-Acts", i.e. the Christology of the implied author (if indeed that is recoverable). But we must then be fully aware of the very real problems involved in trying to get back from that to the possible Christology of Luke himself[13].

II. METHODOLOGY IN STUDY OF NEW TESTAMENT CHRISTOLOGY

Before discussing the Lukan writings in particular, we should perhaps consider briefly the wider question of how to approach the general topic of Christology in relation to the NT writings and early Christianity.

The older, traditional way to approach the topic of the Christology of a NT writer was via the use of specific Christological titles such as Lord, Christ, Son of God, Son of Man etc. Such investigations focused on these titles separately and sought to analyze how far they were significant and what might have been meant by them[14]. Such an approach has come under fire in recent years[15], with a number of criticisms raised.

---

12. Cf. Haenchen's comment cited in n. 5 above: "Luke is no systematic theologian".
13. Cf. too STRAUSS, *Davidic Messiah*, pp. 34, 349-350, distinguishing between Luke's own Christology and what Strauss calls his "Christological purpose" in writing.
14. Cf. the classic studies of O. CULLMANN, *The Christology of the New Testament*, London, 1959; R.H. FULLER, *The Foundations of New Testament Christology*, London, 1965; F. HAHN, *The Titles of Jesus in Christology*, London, 1969.
15. See especially L.E. KECK, *Toward the Renewal of New Testament Christology*, in *NTS* 32 (1986) 362-377, repr. in M.C. DE BOER (ed.), *From Jesus to John. Essays on Jesus and New Testament Christology in Honour of Marinus de Jonge* (JSNT SS, 84), Sheffield, 1993, pp. 321-340; cf. also E. RICHARD, *Jesus: One and Many. The Christological Concepts of New Testament Authors*, Wilmington, DE, 1988, pp. 64-65, with further literature.

Firstly, it has been pointed out that the titles which were applied to Jesus may not have been univocal in meaning within either Judaism or Greco-Roman thinking at the time. Secondly, it has been said that the exclusive focus on titles tends to ignore other evidence which may be just as, if not more, important for determining the significance which early Christians may have attributed to Jesus, e.g. the evidence of hymnody, the use of OT texts, the application of categories and factors other than the use of an (inevitably) small number of allegedly key terms such as Lord etc.

The first of these objections is not insuperable. The fact that titles were not univocal in meaning within non-Christian circles simply means that we have to have greater sensitivity in our analysis in seeing how Christians used such terms when they applied them to Jesus. Instead of simply assuming that one key term (e.g. Christ) had a single meaning and network of associated overtones, we have to reckon with the fact that terms had a range of possible meanings, and that we need some care to determine where within this range the Christian application of the term to Jesus is to be located[16].

The second objection is more real, and NT exegetes today are probably far more sensitive than in the past to parts of the evidence from a text like Luke-Acts which may be highly relevant in relation to assessments of the person of Jesus but which do not use "standard" Christological titles. For example, much has been made recently of the reference to "the Spirit of Jesus" in Acts 16,7 (see below), even though the phrase itself uses no "title" for Jesus at all but only his proper name. In similar vein, the Christological significance of the worship of Jesus has been emphasized by several scholars in recent years[17]. So too, Thiselton has pointed out that, from the point of view of speech act theory, many things predicated of Jesus in Luke's story presuppose a prior state of affairs for what is said to have validity[18]. Thus the saying of Jesus "My son, your sins are forgiven" (Lk 5,20) depends on a logically prior state of affairs regarding Jesus' status and authority as being valid for the saying to be accepted (as Luke does) as having any validity and actually achieving something[19].

---

16. Such a procedure has of course long been practised in relation to a term like κύριος.

17. See especially R.J. BAUCKHAM, *The Worship of Jesus in Apocalyptic Christianity*, in *NTS* 27 (1980-81) 322-341; L. HURTADO, *One God, One Lord. Early Christian Devotion and Ancient Jewish Monotheism*, Philadelphia, PA, 1988.

18. A.C. THISELTON, *Christology in Luke, Speech Act Theory, and the Problem of Dualism in Christology after Kant*, in J.B. GREEN & M. TURNER (eds.), *Jesus of Nazareth, Lord and Christ. Essays on the Historical Jesus and New Testament Christology*. FS I.H. Marshall, Carlisle, 1994, pp. 453-473.

19. *Ibid.*, p. 461.

Nevertheless, despite the undoubted significance of many such features in relation to Christology, one cannot ignore the more traditional approach entirely. The fact remains that certain key "titles" or terms were used by early Christians to refer to Jesus in a potentially significant way means that these terms do provide an important part of the evidence for seeking to uncover Christological ideas of early Christians. Thus whilst mindful of other evidence which must be given its full weight, we cannot ignore the evidence provided by the use of titles themselves. Indeed in the case of Luke-Acts, this is even more necessary, given the way in which at times titles are quite deliberately and explicitly predicated of Jesus with attempts made to justify their usage in this context[20].

III. LUKE-ACTS: A SINGLE CHRISTOLOGY?

I return then to Luke-Acts. A key question raised by the general theme of this Colloquium is whether it is right to talk of "the" Christology of Luke-Acts. Is there a single overriding Christology emerging from the Lukan writings as the Christology of the implied author (if not of the real author)? In relation to either of Luke's two books separately, such a question would be a real one. In relation to Luke-Acts considered as a unity, the question is even more pressing. Would it not be better to speak of at least the Christology of Luke's gospel and the Christology of Acts? Or are there not even Christologies (plural) within Acts itself? And perhaps within Luke's gospel?

There is no doubt that a strong case can be built up for the view that Luke-Acts does not present a single Christology but rather a whole variety of Christologies[21]. The reason for this variety may be two-fold. Firstly, Luke may be dependent on sources, and fidelity to his source material may be part of the reason for what appear as slightly discordant voices speaking through his writings. Secondly, it is striking that Luke seems to take care to make his characters say things that he thinks are appropriate for the occasion. Lucian's statement (*How to Write History*, 56), on how historians should put words on to the lips of their characters making speeches, is often cited in this context:

---

20. Cf. the sustained argument in the speech in Acts 2 to justify the use of the terms Lord and Christ of Jesus (the conclusion in Acts 2,36); cf. too Luke's notes that various Christians sought to show that Jesus was the Christ (Acts 9,22; 17,3; 18,5.28).

21. Virtually all the relevant evidence has been noted by others before and what is presented here can make no attempt to be startlingly original. See especially the important essay of C.F.D. MOULE, *The Christology of Acts*, in L.E. KECK & J.L. MARTYN (eds.), *Studies in Luke-Acts* (above, n. 1), pp. 159-185.

If you must introduce at a certain point a character who makes a speech, let his language before all things be adapted to his personality (εἰκότα τῷ προσώπῳ) and to his object.

So too there is the even more famous statement of Thucydides about his own procedure:

As to the speeches that were made by different men, either when they were about to begin the war or when they were already engaged therein, it has been difficult to recall with strict accuracy the words actually spoken, both for me as regards that which I myself heard, and for those who from various other sources have brought me reports. Therefore, the speeches are given in the language in which, as it seemed to me, the several speakers would express, on the subjects under consideration, the sentiments most befitting the occasion, though at the same time I have adhered as closely as possible to the general sense of what was actually said[22].

The precise meaning of what is said here, and the possible relevance to the study of Luke-Acts, has been frequently discussed[23]. We do not know the nature or extent of Luke's source material in relation to the speeches in Acts. Nevertheless, it may be significant that it is exclusively in words on the lips of Paul in Acts that Jesus is referred to as Son of God (Acts 9,22; 13,33). In similar vein, it is Paul, and only Paul, in Acts who refers in any way to Jesus' death as in some sense vicarious (Acts 20,28, even if the language is rather garbled and the precise sense obscure)[24]. At the very least, one can perhaps say that Paul is made to sound more "Pauline" than other characters in the narrative. In similar vein, it is Peter who refers to Jesus as the "servant" (Acts 3,13.26), probably referring to the Isaianic servant of Isa 53[25]. Admittedly Peter is not alone in this respect in Acts (cf. Acts 8); but it may be significant that one of the relatively few other references to Jesus as the servant figure of Isa 53 occurs in a work attributed to Peter, viz. 1 Pet 2,22-25. This is in no way intended as an argument for either the historical reliability of Peter's speech in Acts 3, or for the authenticity of 1 Peter. But it may show that Luke was aware of some link between the apostle Peter and ideas associating Jesus with the servant figure of Isa 53; and being per-

---

22. Thucydides, 1.22 (Loeb translation).

23. The secondary literature is enormous. Cf. recently W.J. McCoy, *In the Shadow of Thucydides*, in B. Witherington (ed.), *History, Literature and Society in the Book of Acts*, Cambridge, 1996, pp. 3-23, with an Addendum by the Editor, pp. 23-32.

24. See all the commentaries on Acts at this point. So too, it is Paul, and no one else, who is made to say something about the law, being justified and faith (Acts 13,39), again in an admittedly rather garbled way. But perhaps Luke is not a great theologian!

25. Cf. the reference to "glorifying" in v. 13 (cf. Isa 52,13). The reference to Jesus as παῖς in Acts 4,27.30 is almost certainly more of a royal idea: see Moule, *Christology of Acts*, p. 169.

haps aware of such a link, Luke has Peter then say what he thinks is appropriate. The same may also be implied by the rejected stone testimonium using Ps 118 which is referred to in Peter's speech in Acts 4,11 and also in 1 Pet 2,7[26].

Luke may thus be sensitive in writing his story in that he has his characters say things that he thinks are appropriate both to themselves as individuals and to the contexts in which they are speaking[27]. And this may make it all the harder to determine Luke's own view: for example, the speech in Acts 2 placed on Peter's lips may not tell us so much about Luke's own views, but more about what Luke thought were the kinds of things that Peter said, or should have said, in the context in which the speech is now placed within the story[28].

Within Luke's gospel, one can point to a number of Christological themes or ideas which show again either Luke's sensitivity to his story or his fidelity to his source material (or both). Certainly it is striking how far some of these ideas are confined to the gospel almost exclusively. If, as some have argued, Luke's own hand is more likely to be evident in Acts, and his own ideas are most likely to emerge in the speeches in Acts where he may have had less direct information available from his sources[29], then it is all the more striking that Luke's gospel is full of Christological motifs that are absent from Acts, and vice versa.

The case for this was argued strongly by Moule in his essay on the Christology of Acts in relation to the use of κύριος, arguing that Luke

26. The evidence is noted by MOULE, *Christology of Acts,* p. 173, who points out that, while Paul and 1 Peter also use other "stone" texts (from Isa 8 and Isa 28, cf. Rom 9,33; 1 Pet 2,6.8), only 1 Peter alludes to Ps 118 in this context. For an attempt to relate more of what is said by Luke's Peter to what is said in 1 Peter, see S.S. SMALLEY, *The Christology of Acts Again,* in B. LINDARS – S.S. SMALLEY (eds.), *Christ and Spirit in the New Testament.* FS C.F.D. Moule, Cambridge, 1973, pp. 79-96.

27. For the latter, cf. how Luke subtly alters the way in which Paul recounts the story of his own conversion later in Acts 22 and 26 in such a way as to be appropriate for the audiences he is addressing. See, for example, D. MARGUERAT, *Saul's Conversion (Acts 9, 22, 26) and the Multiplication of Narrative in Acts,* in C.M. TUCKETT (ed.), *Luke's Literary Achievement* (JSNT SS, 116), Sheffield, 1995, pp. 127-155, with further literature. Possibly relevant too may be the references to Christians showing that Jesus was the Christ (Acts 9,22; 17,3; 18,5.28), which are all located in synagogue discussions: see WILSON, *Related Strangers,* p. 74.

28. Cf. the widespread view that the Christology implied at the end of the speech in v. 36 may be pre-Lukan and not Luke's own: see C.K. BARRETT, *The Acts of the Apostles* 1 (ICC), Edinburgh, 1994, p. 152; HAENCHEN, *Acts,* p. 187.

29. The view that Luke had considerable creative input into the speeches is widespread: see M. DIBELIUS, *Studies in the Acts of the Apostles,* London, 1956; E. SCHWEIZER, *Concerning the Speeches in Acts,* in L.E. KECK & J.L. MARTYN (eds.), *Studies in Luke-Acts* (above, n. 1), pp. 208-206. For recent study of the speeches, see M. SOARDS, *The Speeches in Acts: Their Content, Context and Concerns,* Louisville, KY, 1994.

reserves the absolute use of ὁ κύριος for Jesus on the lips of human characters in the story for the narrative in Acts; in Luke's gospel, it is generally only the narrator who uses this, the vocative κύριε being Christologically less significant as just a polite form of address[30]. This aspect of Moule's essay has been criticised as not quite doing justice to the evidence[31]. Besides the slightly embarrassing exception (to prove the rule?!) of Lk 1,43 (recognised by Moule), there is the fact the Luke does sometimes juxtapose references to Jesus as ὁ κύριος with an address to him by characters in the story as κύριε (cf. Lk 12,41.42; 17,5.6; 19,8a.8b), thus suggesting that the use of the vocative may be more than simply a polite address: the one addressed as κύριε *is* ὁ κύριος. Nevertheless, Moule's general point can I think stand by referring to other examples (some of which were noted by Moule himself).

I have discussed Luke's use of the term Son of Man (SM) elsewhere[32]. Suffice it to note here that Luke uses the term freely in his gospel: indeed, arguably he expands the SM sayings in his sources (Mark and Q) with a number of other sayings which may be due to LkR. But even if these extra sayings are all from "L" tradition(s), the same overall picture emerges: Luke is happy to preserve and hand on a firmly established tradition whereby Jesus talked of himself as SM; but in Acts, in the post-resurrection era, all talk of Jesus as SM disappears almost completely. The one exception is of course the saying of the dying Stephen in Acts 7,56, but even this cannot wholly hide the otherwise deafening silence of Acts in relation to the term SM. This even covers instances where SM terminology would have been entirely appropriate, e.g. Acts 17,31 and the reference to judgement of the world "through a man", a context where SM language would have been very apt (cf. Lk 17,23-30; 21,36 etc.). It seems that Luke is aware of the fact that SM may have been a significant term on the lips of Jesus and during Jesus' own lifetime; after the resurrection, it was not apparently a category used by most of the earliest Christians, and Luke does not use it in Acts.

Similar arguments may apply to a group of other categories often associated with Q in Luke's gospel. The category of Wisdom, and perhaps Jesus as one of Wisdom's prophetic envoys, is a well known feature of Q's Christology[33]. The prime evidence for this comes from

30. See MOULE, *Christology of Acts*, pp. 160-161.
31. See E. FRANKLIN, *Christ the Lord. A Study in the Purpose and Theology of Luke-Acts*, London, 1975, pp. 49-53; also S.G. WILSON, *Luke and the Pastoral Epistles*, London, 1979, pp. 72-73.
32. C.M. TUCKETT, *The Lukan Son of Man*, in ID. (ed.), *Luke's Literary Achievement* (above, n. 27), pp. 198-217. See too MOULE, *Christology of Acts*, pp. 163-164.
33. See my *Q and the History of Early Christianity*, Edinburgh, 1996, pp. 218-221.

Lukan texts with their Lukan wordings, notably Lk 7,35; 11,49[34]. Yet this Wisdom Christology reappears nowhere else in Luke-Acts. Nowhere else does Luke redact Mark to introduce such an idea and it is absent from Acts. As such, this is often taken as a characteristic feature of Q, firmly distinguished from the Lukan viewpoint(s). But in this context, it is then all the more striking that it appears in Luke's writings at all. It may be due to Luke's sensitivity; it may be due to Luke's respect for his sources. But whatever the reason, Luke here seems to preserve an element with Christological significance that does not appear to be at all characteristic of the rest of the Lukan writings or of Luke himself.

I have argued elsewhere that a similar phenomenon may occur in the case of the quotation of Isa 61,1-2, cited in Lk 4,18-19[35]. This is often taken as a programmatic summary of Luke's whole two-volume story[36]. Yet it is remarkable how little the ideas expressed here either reflect, or even influence, the details of the story that follows. The Isa 61 reference is probably reflected in two later passages in Luke's gospel, viz. the opening beatitudes (Lk 6,20-21) and the reply of Jesus to John the Baptist's messengers (Lk 7,22). Yet it may be significant that both are Q passages, i.e. part of Luke's source material. Further, it is notable that Luke, unlike Matthew, does not alter the beatitude about the mourners to reflect the language of Isa 61,2. It may well be that Matthew's version represents Q more accurately, in which case Luke's different version here represents a redactional move away from the language of Isa 61[37].

The tasks set out in the Isa 61 citation do not correspond closely to the activity of either Jesus or the early Christians as described in Acts. Preaching good news to the poor is perhaps the one element which does find a positive echo elsewhere in Luke-Acts[38]. However, "release for the

34. Matthew regularly "upgrades" the Christological schema to identify Jesus with the person of Wisdom; see M.J. SUGGS, *Wisdom, Christology and Law in Matthew's Gospel*, Cambridge, MA, 1970.

35. See my *Luke 4, Isaiah and Q*, in J. DELOBEL (ed.), *Logia. Les Paroles de Jésus – The Sayings of Jesus* (BETL, 59), Leuven, 1982, pp. 343-354; and my *Q and the History*, pp. 226-237.

36. J.T. SANDERS, *The Jews in Luke-Acts*, London, 1987, p. 165: "The scene is 'programmatic' in Luke-Acts, as one grows almost tired of reading in the literature on the passage".

37. See my *The Beatitudes: A Source-Critical Study*, in *NT* 25 (1983) 193-207; also *Q and the History*, pp. 223-226; however, for an alternative view, see F. NEIRYNCK, *Q 6,20b.21; 7,22 and Isaiah 61*, in C.M. TUCKETT (ed.), *The Scriptures in the Gospels* (BETL, 131), Leuven, 1997, pp. 27-64, esp. 33-45, for the allusion to Isa 61,2 in Matt 5,4 being due to MattR (with further references to other secondary literature). See too his paper in this volume for further discussion of the Lk 4 material (below, pp. 357-395).

38. Though see J.B. GREEN, *Good News to Whom? Jesus and the "Poor" in the Gospel of Luke*, in J.B. GREEN & M. TURNER (eds.), *Jesus of Nazareth, Lord and Christ*

captives" in the normal sense is rare, as is "release for those crushed"[39]; and recovery of sight for the blind is scarcely a very prominent element in the miracles Luke records. The idea of the Spirit being "on" Jesus is also notorious by its absence in the subsequent Lukan story. It is true that, prior to this, Luke has the account of the Spirit coming on Jesus at his baptism (Lk 3,21) and he also has Jesus being driven into the wilderness by the Spirit for the temptations (Lk 4,1). But after the Nazareth scene, Jesus never appears specifically as Spirit-possessed[40]; rather, Luke seems to reserve the gift of the Spirit for the post-Easter situation and, moreover, presents it as sometimes a gift *by* Jesus, rather than a gift in which both Jesus and the disciples share as (equal) recipients (cf. Lk 24,49; Acts 2,33).

It is true that Isa 61 and (probably) the use of this text in Lk 4 are reflected once in Acts in the speech of Peter in Acts 10,38. Indeed this seems to give Luke's own interpretation of the Isa 61 quotation: the "oppressed" are now interpreted as "those oppressed by the devil", apparently referring to (all?) those who are sick (cf. the reference to "healing"). But again one has to say that such ideas are not prominent elsewhere in Luke's writings: illness is only rarely attributed to demonic influence (only Lk 13,16). It can be argued that Luke has slightly redacted the stories immediately following the Nazareth scene in Luke 4

(above, n. 18), pp. 59-74, who finds enough of a mismatch between the standard interpretation of the "poor" here as meaning the economically destitute and the rest of Luke-Acts to force a reinterpretation of the "poor" here (as meaning the socially excluded as much as the economically destitute).

39. In slightly different vein, Lemcio points out that the ἄφεσις which seems to be promised here is quite different from the ἄφεσις which is actually offered later in the story, especially in Acts, where it is always the ἄφεσις ἁμαρτιῶν, i.e. forgiveness rather than "release". See E.E. LEMCIO, *The Past of Jesus in the Gospels* (SNTS MS, 68), Cambridge, 1991, p. 81: "Proclaiming release to captives has little or nothing to do in an obvious sense with announcing repentance that leads to forgiveness. So, when it comes to describing what lay at the heart of Jesus' and the church's mission, Luke refuses to justify the Christian blueprint by making it a carbon copy of Jesus' sense of calling". Perhaps though I would add that release for captives also has little in any clear sense to do with what actually happens in Luke's account of the ministry of Jesus himself! Further, it is the Greek word ἄφεσις which is the key word linking the two texts from Isa 61,1 and 58,6 which form the mixed citation here: thus the originator of the mixed citation evidently laid great store by this kind of ἄφεσις brought by Jesus. Given that the use of the word here shows little contact with Luke's own prominent use of the word elsewhere in Luke-Acts, it seems unlikely that Luke is responsible for the mixed citation here.

40. As one way to try to solve the problem, see R.L. BRAWLEY, *Luke-Acts and the Jews. Conflict, Apology, and Conciliation* (SBL MS, 33), Atlanta, GA, 1987, p. 19: "Because Luke so strongly establishes the identity of Jesus as one anointed with the Spirit at the beginning of Jesus' ministry, he is able to assume it through the rest of his gospel with little need for additional references". But this rather begs the question and assumes, rather than demonstrates, a "narrative unity" in Luke-Acts.

to make them more exorcistic[41]; but again this is hardly a dominant theme in Luke-Acts and does not last much beyond Lk 4 itself. By the time one gets to ch. 5, Luke seems to have forgotten about it. Thereafter, exorcisms are not very prominent and, with the exception of the woman in Lk 13, physical illness is not attributed to demonic possession. Thus once again Luke seems to show either a "sensitivity" to his material[42] or a fidelity to source material that may not entirely chime in with his own views (or perhaps both).

Something of the same idea *may* be also the case in the idea of Jesus as a prophet. Luke's gospel in particular has often been interpreted as having a very prominent prophetic Christology[43]; and, for example, David Moessner has argued very strongly that the idea of a "prophet like Moses" is an important overarching motif linking different parts of the Lukan writings, especially the Travel Narrative[44]. However, it is not always so clear that the prophetic category is regarded positively by Luke. It is true that in Lk 4,24 Jesus himself compares his role with that of a prophet, as also in Lk 13,33. But in Lk 7,16 it is the reaction of a crowd which says that Jesus is a prophet (cf. Lk 7,39; 9,19), and it may be that Luke regards this as slightly inadequate: the next section of the gospel seems to be dominated by the question of who Jesus really is, and culminates in Peter's confession of Jesus as the Χριστός (9,20) and/or the declaration of God himself at the Transfiguration that Jesus is his Son (9,35)[45]. Further, the theory that a Mosaic-like prophet typology governs Luke's travel narrative has been searchingly examined by others and found to be not entirely convincing[46].

41. For details, see my *Luke 4, Isaiah and Q*, p. 349: in Lk 4,38 Luke has Jesus rebuke the fever of Peter's mother-in-law (LkR of Mark); and in Lk 4,40, in redacting the general summary in Mk 1,32-34, Luke focuses solely on the exorcisms, omitting the general healings mentioned by Mark as well.

42. Cf. LEMCIO, *Past of Jesus*, stressing the difference between Luke and Acts.

43. See G.W.H. LAMPE, *The Lucan Portrait of Christ*, in *NTS* 2 (1956) 160-175; U. BUSSE, *Die Wunder des Propheten Jesus*, Stuttgart, 1977; L.T. JOHNSON, *The Literary Function of Possessions in Luke-Acts* (SBL DS, 39), Missoula, MT, 1977; further literature in STRAUSS, *Davidic Messiah*, pp. 196-197 n. 2; also J.D. KINGSBURY, *Jesus as the "Prophetic Messiah" in Luke's Gospel*, in A.J. MALHERBE – W.A. MEEKS (eds.), *The Future of Christology*. FS L.E. Keck, Minneapolis, MN, 1993, pp. 29-42, on p. 30 n. 9.

44. MOESSNER, *Lord of the Banquet*; cf. earlier C.F. EVANS, *The Central Section of St Luke's Gospel*, in D.E. NINEHAM (ed.), *Studies in the Gospels. Essays in Memory of R.H. Lightfoot*, Oxford, 1955, pp. 37-53.

45. See A.J. McNICOL, D.L. DUNGAN, D.B. PEABODY, *Beyond the Q Impasse – Luke's Use of Matthew*, Valley Forge, PA, 1997, pp. 111ff.; also J.B. GREEN, *The Theology of the Gospel of Luke*, Cambridge, 1995, pp. 61-62; KINGSBURY, *Jesus as the "Prophetic Messiah"*, pp. 35-41.

46. See A. DENAUX, *Old Testament Models for the Lukan Travel Narrative*, in C.M. TUCKETT (ed.), *The Scriptures in the Gospels* (above, n. 37), pp. 271-305, esp. 281-285;

What is also striking is the way in which the prophetic category recedes sharply in Acts. It is true that the idea of Jesus as the prophet like Moses does surface on two occasions in speeches in Acts (Acts 3,22; 7,37); but it is only on these two occasions and never comes out anywhere else. It has been argued that even this shows a sharp distinction between the gospel and Acts: Jesus in the gospel is *a* prophet, whereas in Acts he is *the* prophet (like Moses)[47]. This may press things too far; but the fact remains that the prophetic category is one that recedes sharply in Acts when compared to the gospel. Could this then be another example of Lukan "sensitivity" and/or fidelity to his sources? Luke is maybe aware that prophetic ideas were predicated of Jesus in his ministry and in the earliest days of the Christian movement; but they died out later and do not reflect Luke's own views.

Connected with the "Wisdom Christology" (cf. above) and the SM texts is the fact that Wisdom terminology and SM references are often correlated in contexts which imply hostility, rejection and suffering. Again the passages are almost exclusively Q texts (Lk 6,22; 7,35; 9,58; 11,49) and may well represent a distinctive Q theologoumenon[48]. But once again the striking thing is that Luke has preserved the pattern, and yet does not develop it or exploit it at all outside these Q passages. Luke apparently feels constrained by his source material. Similarly, Luke takes over from Mark all the three Markan passion predictions which relate Jesus' passion to himself qua SM. Luke does redact some details of the predictions, notably rewriting the third prediction to bring in the notion of the fulfilment of scripture (Lk 18,31, cf. Mk 10,33); but he does not change the consistent Markan pattern whereby it is in his capacity/role as SM that Jesus must suffer. Again, however, Luke never develops or uses these ideas in Acts. Moreover, on occasions Luke does seek to have characters in the later (= post-Easter) story try to deal with the question of why Jesus had to suffer. But on such occasions, Luke has them all say consistently that it is in his capacity/role as the Χριστός, not SM, that Jesus had to suffer (cf. the risen Jesus himself in Lk 24,26.46, Peter in Acts 3,18, Paul in Acts 17,3; 26,23). The language of Luke's story seems to be of a suffering Christ after Easter, a suffering SM or a suffering prophet before Easter[49].

STRAUSS, *Davidic Messiah*, pp. 278-285. See too J.A. FITZMYER, *The Gospel according to Luke I-IX* (AB, 28), New York, 1981, p. 793: "Jesus as a new Moses is not a strong motif in the Lucan gospel.... If it is present here [in the Transfiguration story], it is inherited from the tradition and finds little development of it (*sic*) in the rest of the Lucan writings".
47. See MOULE, *Christology of Acts*, p. 162.
48. See my *Q and the History*, pp. 166-207, 253-276.
49. The point is also noted by LEMCIO, *Past of Jesus*, pp. 76-77.

Some of all these various pieces of disparate data might be reconcilable within a single broader Christological schema if one postulated the idea that, for Luke, Jesus' "anointing" was conceived of as an anointing with the Spirit (cf. Luke 4,18; Acts 10,38) to be primarily a *prophetic* figure: thus Jesus qua anointed, i.e. qua Messiah/Christ, is a prophet. Jesus the Christ is thus an anointed prophet. Such an idea would then encompass the idea of Jesus as a prophet, as the one who must suffer as one of Wisdom's envoys (who are the prophets, cf. 11,49), who is then by virtue of this the Χριστός[50].

That there is an element of truth in this is undeniable. It is clear that Luke does see Jesus' anointing as an anointing with the Spirit, and Luke does once correlate the "anointing" of Jesus with the fact that he is the Χριστός (see Acts 4,26-27). Moreover, such a link does seem to be peculiar to Luke[51]. Yet whether Luke then connects this with the idea of a prophet, especially that of a suffering prophet, seems more uncertain. Elsewhere in the Lukan writings, Luke seems to tie the Χριστός terminology very closely to Davidic and royal ideas. This comes out very firmly in the birth narratives, where Davidic (not prophetic) ideas about Jesus are very much to the fore, and also in some of the speeches in Acts, notably Peter's Pentecost speech in Acts 2 (cf. the appeal to the Davidic promises in Ps 16) and in Paul's speech at Pisidian Antioch in Acts 13. And in Acts 4,26-27, reference to Jesus as the Χριστός whom God "anointed" is set firmly in the context of a clear parallel to David[52].

50. Cf. HAHN, *Titles*, p. 381; I. DE LA POTTERIE, *L'onction du Christ*, in *NRT* 80 (1958) 225-252; also W.C. VAN UNNIK, *Jesus the Christ*, in *NTS* 8 (1962) 101-116, for the connection between messiahship and anointing with the Spirit (though he argues more at the level of Jesus than of Luke). For Lk 4 as implying a prophetic anointing, see FITZMYER, *Luke I-IX*, pp. 527-528. KINGSBURY, *Jesus as "Prophetic Messiah"*, sees Jesus in Luke as both prophet and Messiah, though with the emphasis very much on the latter, and he does not relate Jesus' ("messianic") anointing to his prophetic role.

51. See M. DE JONGE, *Christology in Context. The Earliest Christian Response to Jesus*, Philadelphia, PA, 1988, p. 100. Yet it is not at all clear how important this is for Luke. If it were, it is surprising that the idea of Jesus as the one endowed with the Spirit receives so little explicit mention in the gospel (unless one can take it as read on the basis of Lk 4,18: cf. n. 40 above and the discussion there). In Peter's speech in Acts 2, where there is an explicit argument to justify the term Χριστός being applied to Jesus, the basis of the argument is the resurrection of Jesus (coupled with an appeal to Ps 16), not a reference to Jesus' being anointed with the Spirit; similarly, in Paul's speech in Acts 13, Jesus "fulfils" the Davidic promises by virtue of the resurrection, not by virtue of being endowed with the Spirit. The passing reference in Acts 4 (which mentions the "anointing" but not explicitly the Spirit) remains the only place where Luke relates the term Χριστός to Jesus' being "anointed".

52. MOULE, *Christology of Acts*, p. 169, points to the parallel in the reference in v. 27 to Jesus as God's holy "servant" and the reference to David as God's "servant" in v. 25. Cf. too n. 25 above: παῖς here does not imply any idea of a suffering figure, let alone that of suffering servant of Isa 53 – rather, it is part of a royal typology.

As Strauss has argued, it would be hard if not impossible to divorce ideas of messiahship from Davidic/royal ideas[53], and it is all but impossible to find any idea of a suffering messiah figure in non-Christian texts prior to the New Testament[54].

All these considerations give strength to the widely held view that "Luke's Christology" may be all but irrecoverable. Thus Buckwalter cites S.G. Wilson's statement as representative of a broad consensus:

> Luke has used diverse, and often ancient, christological traditions without integrating them into any particular scheme. This leads to a certain lack of uniformity, a disjunction between different strands of material which stand side by side.... The use of christological titles is somewhat haphazard. They represent the terminology of Luke's day but, in many cases, the belief of the early Church as well. Some may have had an archaic ring and were for that reason deemed appropriate to the sermons of the early Church[55].
>
> Luke, it appears, was a somewhat indiscriminating collector of christological traditions who transmits a variety of traditional terms and concepts without reflecting upon them individually or in conjunction with each other[56].

Insofar as there is a unity to Luke's Christology, few would probably quarrel with the statement of Wilson that "the consensus is that the christology of Luke-Acts is fundamentally an exaltation christology"[57]. The great stress laid on the fact that Jesus has been exalted in the resurrection/ascension is both strongly anticipated in Luke's gospel (cf. Lk 4,16-30; 9,31.51) and also amply attested in the speeches in Acts. But what the precise significance of this fact is for Luke remains rather less clear. So too it is not agreed what capacity the risen and exalted Jesus occupies for Luke. Many have argued that, insofar as Luke's views can be discerned, the picture is fundamentally a "subordinationist" one:

53. See STRAUSS, *Davidic Messiah*, and also below for more on the Davidic/royal theme.

54. FITZMYER, *Luke I-IX*, p. 200, refers to the link between messiahship and suffering in Luke as "a peculiarly Lukan theologoumenon".

55. WILSON, *Luke and the Pastoral Epistles*, p. 79.

56. *Ibid.*, p. 80. Cf. LAMPE, *Lucan Portrait of Christ*, p. 160: "Even if we could readily isolate Luke's own theological outlook from that of his sources which he was using, the fact remains that the thought of the Lucan writings is seldom clear-cut. The author does not follow any one line of interpretation to the exclusion of all others; on the contrary, he prefers to make a synthesis... He prefers to hold a large number of threads in his hand at once, introducing first one and then another in a somewhat untidy and ill-defined pattern, without allowing any one of them so to predominate over the rest as to give unity and coherence to the whole. This tendency is perhaps especially marked in his presentation of the Person and work of Christ".

57. WILSON, *Luke and the Pastoral Epistles*, p. 69; cf. also FRANKLIN, *Christ the Lord*, passim.

Jesus is presented as above all a human being who is subordinate to God[58].

IV. LUKE-ACTS: A "HIGH" CHRISTOLOGY? JESUS AS LORD

Such a view has however been strongly challenged in recent years, above all in the books of Bock and Buckwalter (and also, from a very different perspective, that of Fletcher-Louis). Further, both Bock and Buckwalter would claim that a unified Lukan view can be discerned; moreover, this view represents a very "high" Christology, not a "low" one (to use what is admittedly rather anachronistic terminology). I take first the monograph of Bock[59].

BOCK's general thesis is that Luke develops one Christological schema in his gospel, viz. that of Jesus as a Messiah-Servant figure[60]. However, toward the end of the gospel, he starts to introduce elements which show some tension with this and begin to hint that such a Christology may be somewhat inadequate. Thus Lk 20,42-43 begins to hint that, on the basis of Ps 110, the category of Son of David may be an insufficient description for Jesus. So too the reference in Lk 21,27 to Jesus as SM, with its clear allusion to Dan 7, indicates the same. Hence hints emerge that Jesus is "more than Messiah". This comes out even more sharply in the trial narratives (cf. Lk 22,67.69) where the use of Ps 110 shows Jesus' authority to be able to go directly to God's presence and sit with him in heaven.

This tension is then resolved in Acts, especially in the speeches in the first half of Acts, where Luke develops the κύριος Christology as well as a Christology of Messiahship (Acts 2,21.34-36). As a result of his exaltation, Jesus is at God's right hand as Lord and can now mediate salvation as co-regent. He takes over divine prerogatives and shares the divine name of Lord. The scheme is developed in the subsequent speeches in Acts, so that by chapter 10,

> there is little doubt that Jesus as the Messiah-Servant is actually more than a regal messianic figure. He is Lord of all as he uniquely exercises many

---

58. See CONZELMANN, *Theology of St Luke*, pp. 173-184; WILSON, *Luke and the Pastoral Epistles*, p. 77; HAENCHEN, *Acts*, p. 92; cf. too H. BRAUN, *Zur Terminologie der Acta von der Auferstehung*, in *TLZ* 77 (1952) 533-536; U. WILCKENS, *Die Missionsreden der Apostelgeschichte* (WMANT, 5), Neukirchen, 1961, pp. 137-140.

59. BOCK, *Proclamation from Prophecy* (above, n. 2).

60. In itself this is of course something of a composite synthesis. Bock's view is, however, similar in this respect to that of Strauss (though Strauss extends the synthesis by including the idea of Jesus as the Mosaic prophet). On this, see the discussion below.

divine prerogatives with God, functioning as mediator of His salvation in His presence at His right hand. Lord is the supreme christological concept for Luke. This emphasis in Acts reflects Luke's conscious presentation of christology from the OT as he shifts the focus from regal Messiah-Servant to Lord[61].

By chapter 13 of Acts, there is no doubt about Jesus' true status as Lord of all. As such he can offer salvation to all, and the justification from the OT for Jesus' status can cease. Thus the story thereafter no longer focuses on Jesus' position but can develop by recounting the Gentile mission under the Lordship of Jesus.

Bock does address the real variations, both between Luke's two books and also within each book (or at least within Acts), and seeks to provide an overarching explanation. Thus the distinction between Luke and Acts is squarely faced, as is also the (rather less often noted) difference between the first half of Acts and the second half, where explicit Christological statements fall away very considerably. Nevertheless, Bock's theory is open to criticism at a number of points.

Although at one level having the whole of Luke's work in view, Bock's theory has the effect of making Luke-Acts into something of an enormous exercise in Christological self-correction. Luke's gospel apparently represents for the most part a Christology that is in some sense inadequate and inappropriate for Luke himself. Yet much of the material here, and the peculiar slant it receives, is presumably due to Luke himself (cf. the birth narratives, the Nazareth sermon etc.)[62]. Why then does Luke write a whole gospel with at times Jesus himself articulating what would appear to be an inadequate Christology? The idea of a corrective Christology has long been in vogue in Markan studies[63]. Yet a stock critique of such a theory is that it implies a degree of sophistication on the part of both Mark and his readers that is hard to conceive; it also has some characters in the story, whom one would otherwise regard as having impeccable credentials as reliable in what they say (e.g. God in Mk 1,11), become the mouthpieces for what the author apparently wants to correct[64].

Bock's theory could perhaps be rescued by claiming that the distinction between Messiah-Servant and Lord is not necessarily one of either-

61. BOCK, *Proclamation from Prophecy*, p. 265.
62. For Bock, much of this material is also authentic; but this is perhaps something of a red herring in his book. Cf. the review of M.C. PARSONS, in *JBL* 108 (1989) 348-350.
63. Following the work of T.J. WEEDEN, *Mark – Traditions in Conflict*, Philadelphia, PA, 1971, and others.
64. See H. RÄISÄNEN, *The Messianic Secret in Mark's Gospel*, Edinburgh, 1990; J.D. KINGSBURY, *The Christology of Mark's Gospel*, Philadelphia, PA, 1983.

or but of both-and: Jesus *is* Messiah-Servant: but he is also Lord of all. Nevertheless, it seems rather odd that Luke should spend so much time in his gospel story developing a view of Jesus (and at times making Jesus himself be the articulator of such a view!) which he then seeks to change substantially in his second volume.

Secondly, nowhere in Acts does Luke hint at the idea that Χριστός is in some way less adequate a term than κύριος to apply to Jesus. The speech in Acts 2 suggests no contrast at all: κύριος and Χριστός are placed alongside each other (Acts 2,36) with no indication at all that κύριος is the dominant partner in this duo. And the OT background is mined equally to seek to show that Jesus is *both* κύριος (via Ps 110) *and* Χριστός (via Ps 16). So too the two terms stand side by side already in Luke 2,11[65].

Similarly, Luke nowhere gives any explicit hint that Χριστός itself is inadequate as a term for Jesus. Indeed the speech in Acts 13 is still dominated by the theme of the *Davidic* promises which are not fulfilled in Jesus. It is thus still the royal idea which is to the fore here, and yet this comes *after* the alleged "trumping" of the royal/Davidic idea by the Lordship theme and the claim that Jesus is πάντων κύριος (10,36)[66].

Thirdly, in the later parts of Acts, at the (relatively few) places where any Christological question is raised, it is never discussed in relation to whether Jesus can or should appropriately be styled as κύριος. Rather, it is in terms of whether he is the Χριστός (Acts 17,3; 18,5.28; cf. 9,22); alternatively, the discussion is about the reason for the suffering of Jesus and again the terminology is that of Jesus as the Χριστός: Paul seeks to show from the scriptures that *the Christ* should suffer (Acts 17,3; 26,23; cf. 3,18; Lk 24,26.46): it is never in terms of the κύριος having to suffer.

Further, it is well known that κύριος is widely used by Luke, especially in Acts; but its function is usually simply as a way of denoting Jesus ("the Lord" as the subject of verbs, or "the Lord Jesus", or "the Lord Jesus Christ"). It is hardly ever used as a predicate (Jesus is the Lord: only really 2,36; 10,36), nor is it used in any confessional statement.

Fourthly, it is rather doubtful how far Luke regards the Gentile mission as in any way specifically grounded in a κύριος Christology. This

65. Cf. STRAUSS, *Davidic Messiah*, p. 29. Bock claims that κύριος is the title here that is not explained in terms of its OT background, and hence its true significance is only made apparent later in the story (*Proclamation*, p. 266). But this seems rather weak.

66. See STRAUSS, *Davidic Messiah*, p. 30. The point about Davidic messiahship dominating the speech in Acts 13 is noted by BOCK, *Proclamation*, p. 265, though the significance of the fact that this comes after the speech in Acts 10 and the alleged definitive establishment of Jesus' universal Lordship is not.

may be at one level the force of the argument in Acts 10: Jesus is Lord *of all* and this justifies salvation being made available to Gentiles[67]. But in Acts 15, James' justification for the Gentile mission makes no clear allusion to the explicit fact that Jesus is "Lord". Insofar as there is any Christological claim here, it is more in terms of the fulfilment of Davidic promises again[68]. But the dominant actor in the inauguration of the Gentile mission is primarily God, rather than the Lord Jesus, in Luke's account in Acts 15[69]. Certainly the Gentile mission has been clearly adumbrated in the Samaritan mission of Acts 8 and in the call and commissioning of Paul in ch. 9 before the claim of 10,36 that Jesus as "Lord" is "Lord of all"[70].

Bock claims that his theory can relate to Luke's overall purpose in writing which he outlines thus:

> Luke writes for anyone in the church suffering doubt and who, as a struggling believer, sees in the persecution of the church the possible judgement of God either for attributing to Jesus a position that is not rightfully his or for extending the offer of salvation directly to those who formerly were regarded as outside the promise of God[71].

In the second half of Acts, the issues of Gentile rights, and of Jew-Gentile relationships within the Christian community, are clearly important. But the position of Jesus, and Christian claims about Jesus, very

---

67. However, the phrase seems much more like a parenthesis in the course of the logical flow of the sentence: see BARRETT, *Acts 1*, p. 522.

68. See STRAUSS, *Davidic Messiah*, pp. 180-192, on the use of Amos 9,11-12 and the reference to σκηνή here (see the options discussed on pp. 188-189, though the Christological interpretation is only one amongst various others)

69. Thus Paul and Barnabas relate what God has done with them (Acts 15,4); Peter refers to the Cornelius episode, saying that "God made choice" (v. 7), and "made no distinction" (v. 9). Any opposition to the Gentile mission is regarded as "testing God" (v. 10) for God gave them the Holy Spirit (v. 8). Barnabas and Paul rehearse what God has done through them (v. 12) and James' speech notes how God has visited the Gentiles (v. 14). The account is entirely theological (in the strict sense of the word), not Christological. Cf. J.T. SQUIRES, *The Plan of God in Luke-Acts* (SNTS MS, 76), Cambridge, 1993, p. 61. More generally, see RICHARD, *Jesus*, p. 182.

70. It is probably adumbrated already in Lk 4,25-27, but there in terms of Jesus as a *prophetic* figure, similar to Elijah and Elisha and, like them, going outside their own home territory to bring God's salvation to others. The justification for the Gentile mission is thus via a prophetic typology, rather than based on any claims about Jesus' universal Lordship. I remain convinced that Lk 4,25-27 does function within the Lukan narrative, at least for Luke, to prefigure the Gentiles mission, despite the questioning of this by some in recent years: cf. B.J. KOET, *"Today This Scripture Has Been Fulfilled in Your Ears" : Jesus' Explanation of Scripture in Luke 4,16-30*, in *Five Studies on Interpretation of Scripture in Luke-Acts* (SNTA, 14), Leuven, 1989, pp. 24-55, here 42-52; also D.R. CATCHPOLE, *The Anointed One in Nazareth*, in M.C. DE BOER (ed.), *From Jesus to John* (above, n. 15), pp. 231-251, on pp. 244-250.

71. *Proclamation*, p. 277.

rarely surface as a contentious issue. When they do, it is solely in a context of synagogue discussions with Jews, and the claims made about resurrection (often in very general terms, i.e. not specifically in relation to Jesus: it is a matter of the more general belief in resurrection as such, claimed by Luke as standard Pharisaic belief), or about Jesus as the Christ and his sufferings as the Christ (see above). It is not about Jesus' status as κύριος.

What though does Jesus' status as κύριος imply for Luke? The issue is also raised by Buckwalter and in this respect Bock and Buckwalter present very similar conclusions. I turn therefore to a brief consideration of Buckwalter's thesis.

BUCKWALTER claims to be able to discern a distinct Lukan Christology that underlies the whole of Luke-Acts. Indeed he makes it an important part of his discussion about methodology that any approach to Luke's Christology must be a "synthetic" one, taking note of all the evidence of the Lukan writings[72]. For the present purposes, the central part of Buckwalter's book can be taken as his chapters 8 and 9, where he discusses the relationship in Luke between Jesus and God and between Jesus and the Spirit. Overall, Buckwalter claims that Luke present an extremely "high" Christology, with Jesus as fully divine, co-equal with the Father; similarly Jesus is the giver and Lord of the Spirit.

Jesus shares the name κύριος with God. In Acts 2,21 the salvation available to all who "call upon the name of the Lord" (citing Joel 3,5 LXX where the reference is to Yahweh) is reapplied to Jesus as Lord. Contra Moule, Buckwalter claims that Luke does not present an "absentee Christology"[73]: rather, just as in the OT Yahweh can be distant and yet immanent, e.g. through his Spirit, so too Jesus is also present with his church. Buckwalter points to Acts 2,33: Jesus himself dispenses the Spirit at Pentecost, and Acts 16,7 says that the Spirit is now the Spirit *of Jesus*. "Certainly Acts 2:33 and 16:7 indicate for Luke that the Spirit represents, if not mediates, the exalted Jesus' continued presence and activity" (p. 180). Buckwalter notes that references to the Spirit tend to die away in the second half of Acts, but this is simply because now Jesus takes over as the empowering agent in the story of the church (cf. Acts 18,9-10; 23,11). Since the Spirit mediates the presence of God himself, Luke's story suggests that "Luke thought of the work of Jesus and the Spirit as a coherent unity, paralleling that of Yahweh and his Spirit in the OT" (p. 182). Similarly the appearances of the risen Jesus and the

---

72. BUCKWALTER, *Character and Purpose* (above, n. 2), pp. 25-27.
73. Cf. MOULE, *Christology of Acts*, pp. 179-180.

references to the salvific power of Jesus' "name" imply "the personal, active presence of *transcendent deity* among his people" (p. 183 my italics), and the name of Jesus (cf. 2,21) and the name of God are so close that "the two are virtually indistinguishable" (p. 183). Buckwalter thus argues that Jesus for Luke is "Yahweh's co-equal", shown above all by Jesus' designation as κύριος in Acts 2,21 where what is said of Yahweh is now transferred to Jesus. So too his session at God's right hand implies a "shared divine dignity between Jesus and the Father" (p. 186, citing W. Foerster)[74]. Perhaps even the difficulty of distinguishing who is meant by κύριος in Acts is deliberate ambiguity on Luke's part. Further, contrary to many others, Buckwalter argues strongly that the terminology of Acts 2,36 ("God has *made* him Lord...") should not be read in any "adoptionist" way. Rather, "Acts presents a messianic unveiling of what was announced in Luke's Gospel right from the start" (p. 189)[75]. Thus the parallels between Jesus and God in relation to the Spirit (cf. Acts 2,21.33; 16,7) imply that "Luke believed Jesus' Lordship to represent a 'status equal to Yahweh'" (p. 188)[76].

The importance of the references to the Spirit is stressed in chapter 9 of Buckwalter's book, with particular reference again to the idea that Jesus is the giver of the Spirit: in Judaism this the exclusive activity of God alone[77], and hence the implications of Acts 2,33 and the reference in 16,7 to the Spirit of Jesus are clear. Similarly, there is a striking parallel in Luke's gospel between Lk 12,11-12 and Lk 21,14-15: in 12,11-12 the Spirit is the power who will assist Christians on trial; in 21,14-15 it is Jesus himself. This kind of functional parallel between Jesus and the Spirit thus again supports the theory that for Luke Jesus is Yahweh's co-equal.

Buckwalter's general argument leads to a number of comments. First, despite his claim of the need for a synthetic approach, the weight of his argument falls on a very small amount of evidence, virtually all in Acts[78]. Thus a great deal is made of texts such as Acts 2,21.33.36; 16,7,

---

74. W. FOERSTER, Κύριος, in *TWNT*, 3, p. 1089.

75. The use of the term "messianic" here is rather odd!

76. Buckwalter here cites J.A. FITZMYER, *Jesus in the Early Church through the Eyes of Luke-Acts*, in *Scripture Bulletin* 17 (1987) 26-35, on p. 33; repr. in *To Advance the Gospel*, Grand Rapids, MI, ²1998, pp. 249-264, on p. 260.

77. Cf. too the essays of M. TURNER, *The Spirit of Christ and Christology*, in H.H. ROWDON (ed.), *Christ the Lord. Studies in Christology Presented to Donald Guthrie*, Leicester, 1982, pp. 168-190; also his *The Spirit of Christ and Divine Christology*, in J.B. GREEN & M. TURNER (eds.), *Jesus of Nazareth Lord and Christ* (above, n. 18), pp. 413-436.

78. Cf. FLETCHER-LOUIS, *Luke-Acts* (above, n. 2), p. 27 n. 1: "Buckwalter's comprehensive title belies a narrower emphasis on Acts" (commenting on the earlier version of

but less consideration is given (at least in these chapters) to the evidence of Luke's gospel or large parts of other sections of Acts.

Second, some of the evidence adduced is of rather uncertain value. For example, in relation to Luke's use of κύριος and especially the use of Joel 3 in Acts 2,21, it is by no means clear that Luke has quite such a high Christology in mind. Thus Barrett writes on this verse *and* its sequel in v. 22:

> The *name of the Lord* (v. 21) is Jesus of Nazareth... The first proposition made about Jesus of Nazareth is that he was a man, ἀνήρ. It is from this starting point that the Christology of Acts proceeds, not from the notion of a divine being who by some kind of incarnation or kenosis accommodated himself to the human world[79].

So too Acts 2,36 is more naturally taken in some "adoptionist" sense (though the use of such a term is inevitably anachronistic and hence probably misleading): God has made Jesus into something he was not before[80].

A similar overpresssing of the language used by Luke is probably implied in the frequent references in Buckwalter's book to the phrase "the Spirit of Jesus" in Acts 16,7 and the relationship between Jesus and the Spirit. The uniqueness of Jesus as the giver of the Spirit is stressed frequently, with the correlative claim that elsewhere in Judaism God is uniquely the giver of the Spirit. There is in fact one possible counter-example to this, viz. Sus 44-45 OG where an angel apparently gives Susanna the spirit of understanding[81], which may then be a partial exception to the "rule". But in any case, Casey has shown very well how mediatorial figures in Judaism can and do take over a wide range of "divine" functions, without ever suggesting that such figures are in any sense "divine", or "co-equal with Yahweh"[82]. Notwithstanding Turner's protest, it is hard to see why the bestowal of the Spirit is to be seen as qualitatively different from e.g. the dispensing of divine judgement (by Abel in *TestAbr* 13)[83]. Even if there are not many (if any) exact

---

the work as a doctoral thesis). Buckwalter does have three chapters considering Luke's use of Mark, but these do not establish the theory of such a high Christology in quite the same way as the later chapters.

79. BARRETT, *Acts* 1, pp. 139-140.
80. BARRETT, *Acts* 1, p. 151, though he then says that this must mean that the verse is pre-Lukan, cf. too HAENCHEN, *Acts*, p. 187, and see above.
81. Cited by FLETCHER-LOUIS, *Luke-Acts*, p. 22. Theodotion has "God aroused the holy spirit of a young lad named Daniel" which may then be not so far from Acts 16,7!
82. M. CASEY, *From Jewish Prophet to Gentile God. The Origins and Development of New Testament Christology*, Cambridge, 1991, pp. 78-96.
83. TURNER, *Spirit of Christ*, p. 423.

parallels to intermediary figures in Judaism dispensing the Spirit, this
may simply reflect the peculiarity of the Christian experience of, and
claims about, the Spirit.

So too the appeal to Acts 16,7 may be pressed too far. The precise
force of the genitive in the phrase "the Spirit of Jesus" is by no means
clear. It could perhaps be regarded as parallel to the "Spirit of Elijah"
(cf. 2 Kings 2,9.15; also Lk 1,17)[84], or even the "holy spirit of the young
man Daniel" in Sus 45 Θ'. Given what is said elsewhere about the Spirit
and Jesus in Acts, it could be claimed as just as Lukan to postulate a
model of Jesus as the one on whom the Spirit came (cf. Luke 3,22; 4,18;
Acts 10,36 etc.). "The Spirit of Jesus" could then mean simply "the
Spirit, i.e. the same Spirit as rested on Jesus".

The theory that Jesus is seen as an omnipresent, powerful, guiding
figure in the church's mission may also push the evidence of Luke too
hard. Moule's case for Luke as presenting an "absentee Christology"
(see above) still has some considerable force. To counter this, Buckwalter cites a number of texts to try to show Jesus as the empowering agent
of the whole mission, referring to Acts 18,9-10; 22,7-10.17-21; 23,11;
26,14-18.23, cf. 7,55-56; 9,4-5.10-17[85]. But all the references in chs. 22
and 26 are effective repetitions of ch. 9, the single story of Paul's conversion[86]; and 18,9-10 and 23,11, as noted by Moule, are examples of
special visionary experiences. The one possible exception might be the
promise of the risen Jesus to Paul in 18,10 "I am with you", yet even
here the "you" is in the individual Paul (σοῦ singular), not the whole
Christian community (in contrast to Paul's "in Christ" language). In any
case, the strengthening power and help in ch. 27 is an angel of God, with
no Christological reference at all (Acts 27,23).

The linguistic parallel between Jesus κύριος and Yahweh κύριος also
may be pressed too far by Buckwalter (and in a similar way by Bock). It
is well known that the Greek word κύριος itself covers a very wide
range of possible meanings and referents. Thus whilst it is very probable
that Greek-speaking Jews referred to Yahweh as κύριος[87], one cannot

---

84. Cf. J.D.G. DUNN, *The Partings of the Ways between Christianity and Judaism and
Their Significance for the Character of Christianity*, London, 1991, p. 201.

85. BUCKWALTER, *Character and Purpose*, p. 182. The activity of the risen Jesus is
also stressed by R.F. O'TOOLE, *Activity of the Risen Jesus in Luke-Acts*, in *Bib* 61 (1981)
471-498, though without explicitly deducing that Luke had such a "high" Christology as
Buckwalter claims.

86. The differences between the three accounts do not affect the issue here.

87. The locus classicus is now the essay of J.A. FITZMYER, *The Semitic Background of*

simply reverse this and say that any reference to someone else as a κύριος figure was implicitly equating that person with Yahweh. The very use of Ps 110 itself in Greek ensures that Luke could distinguish between two people, both of whom could be appropriately referred to as κύριος, albeit with different nuances, without necessarily any confusion of their identities or characteristics[88]. So too, to claim that the difficulty modern interpreters might have in deciding whether ὁ κύριος is God or Jesus reflects a deliberate ambiguity on Luke's part and a conscious intermingling of the two is very dubious[89]. Just because we have difficulty deciding does not mean that Luke intended us to have that difficulty! The argument of the speech of Acts 2, which seeks to justify the epithet κύριος being applied to Jesus, is based on the use of Ps 110; and there it is very clear that the LXX Psalm text, whose meaning is clearly followed by Luke, is referring to different people by the same word. Thereafter it is striking that the use of κύριος to refer to Jesus is never felt to require justification or argument. This is the case even in 10,36 where the phrase "Lord of all" forms something of a parenthesis in the sentence (see n. 67 above) and (perhaps strikingly) can sit quite happily alongside v. 38 which implies a rather "low" Christology of God as the real power helping alongside Jesus[90]. Elsewhere, as already noted, ὁ κύριος is simply Jesus' name and description which is mostly assumed as self-evident. It is never defended, argued about, or even asserted explicitly, unlike Χριστός (cf. above).

The attempt to justify such a "high" Christology on the basis of the use of κύριος must therefore be seen as not entirely convincing.

---

the New Testament Kyrios-Title, in *A Wandering Aramean: Collected Aramaic Essays*, Missoula, MT, 1979, pp. 115-142.

88. BARRETT, *Acts* 1, p. 152; more generally, for Luke's readiness to vary the referent of κύριος quite freely between God and Jesus, see J.D.G. DUNN, ΚΥΡΙΟΣ *in Acts Again*, in C. LANDMESSER, H.-J. ECKSTEIN, H. LICHTENBERGER (eds.), *Jesus Christus als die Mitte der Schrift. Studien zur Hermeneutik des Evangeliums*. FS O. Hofius (BZNW, 86), Berlin, 1997, pp. 363-378; repr. in DUNN, *The Christ and the Spirit*. Vol. 1. *Christology*, Grand Rapids – Edinburgh, 1998, pp. 241-253.

89. For the case that there is no confusion between the two, see G. SCHNEIDER, *Gott und Christus als* κύριος *nach der Apostelgeschichte*, in J. ZMIJEWSKI – E. NELLESSEN (eds.), *Begegnung mit dem Wort*. FS H. Zimmermann (BBB, 53), Bonn, 1980, pp. 161-173. It is undeniable that Jesus qua κύριος in Acts takes over *some* of the activity of Yahweh κύριος (cf. Acts 2,21); but this is very far from ascribing to Jesus a "status equal to Yahweh" or thinking of Jesus as a "transcendent deity".

90. Cf. BARRETT, *Acts* 1, p. 525: "'God was with him' represents in itself a minimal Christology; it claims no more than that Jesus was a man whom God accompanied and aided as he might have been said, and was said, to have accompanied and aided e.g. Abraham, Moses or David".

V. JESUS AS MESSIAH – SERVANT – PROPHET

Part of the weakness of Bock's and Buckwalter's theses is their effective downplaying of the importance of the term Χριστός for Lukan Christology in favour of κύριος. This is all the more problematic given the importance of the former term in the latter part of Acts and also the way in which the two terms can apparently co-exist side by side quite happily in a text like Acts 2,36.

Thus the alternative thesis of M.L. STRAUSS which emphasises the importance of messiahship for Luke has an initial attractiveness and plausibility. Strauss makes a powerful case for the existence of a reasonably well defined "messianic" expectation in first century Judaism, focusing on a hope for a Davidic royal figure. He then shows well how this hope has profoundly affected Luke's narrative at many points. This is particularly the case in the birth narratives, where Davidic messianic expectations are repeatedly referred to and claimed to be fulfilled in the Christian story: the child Jesus will reign on the throne of David (Lk 1,32-33), he is the Lord's Christ (2,26) or Christ the Lord (2,11), the horn of salvation from David's house (1,69). Moreover, the Davidic ancestry of Jesus, his parents and his birthplace, are emphasized by Luke as the narrator (Lk 1,27.32.69; 2,4.11). The stress on Jesus as the fulfiller of Davidic promises is also emphasised in two important speeches in Acts: Peter's Pentecost speech in Acts 2 and Paul's speech at Pisidian Antioch in Acts 13.

Strauss concedes that Davidic royal ideas are by no means as prominent elsewhere in Luke's story. He argues however that this may be due to Luke's having formed a synthesis so that Jesus, as the royal Messiah, is seen also as fulfilling the roles of the Isaianic servant of Isa 40–55, and also that of the prophet like Moses, leading his people in a new Exodus[91]. Strauss argues that Luke could have formed such a synthesis on the basis of a holistic reading of the book of Isaiah: here Davidic promises in chs. 9 and 11 exist side by side with the role of the servant in chs. 40–55, where also the motif of a new Exodus is very prominent. It is then this Isaianic influence on Luke which produces the rounded synthesis of Jesus which appears in the gospel and Acts. "Luke links the Jesus event particularly to the Isaianic portrait of eschatological salvation, where the messianic deliverer is at the same time prophet, servant and king"[92].

---

91. Cf. Bock's similar theory that, in Luke's gospel at least, Jesus is presented as a Messiah figure who also combines the characteristics of the Servant of Deutero-Isaiah.
92. STRAUSS, *Davidic Messiah* (above, n. 2), p. 343.

Strauss makes a strong case for the importance of a Davidic royal Christology as a key theme in Luke-Acts. There is not enough time or space here to engage with all the detailed arguments of his book, though there are a number of questions to raise.

Strauss readily concedes that Davidic royal ideas as such are not very much to the fore in Luke's gospel after the introductory narratives[93], but seeks to explain this by reference to the alleged holistic reading of Isaiah. A number of points arise from this. First, would any first century reader have read the book of Isaiah in this way? Most Jewish exegesis was far more atomistic[94]. The whole question of how far those citing, or referring to, a text of OT scripture had in mind, and/or expected their hearers/readers also to have in mind, the wider context from which the allusion is taken is a much debated issue. Yet even if one granted this in general terms, there would be a question about how far in the wider context it might be reasonable to go. It might be one thing to expect the reader of Acts 8, hearing some verses cited from Isa 53, to recall the immediate context of the rest of the description of the servant figure in Isa 53 itself and perhaps bring in some idea of the vicarious nature of the suffering described[95]. But it seems quite a different order of magnitude to correlate what is said about one possible figure at one end of the book of Isaiah with what is said about a (different?) figure some 40 chapters earlier in chapters 9 and 11. Given too that one is presumably at a time when scrolls, rather than codices, were in use, the possibility of quickly flipping over a few pages to relate one passage to the other would not have been an open one.

Second, Strauss' alleged "holistic" reading of Isaiah by Luke has to assume that Luke chose to ignore the clear statements at many points in Isa 40–55 that equate the "servant" with the nation Israel (see Isa 41,8.9; 44,1; 45,4; 49,3 etc.)[96].

93. Strauss makes a good case for seeing the declaration of Jesus as God's Son at the baptism as primarily a royal term in Luke (pp. 199-208); he also seeks to argue that the use of Isa 61,1-2 in Luke 4,18-19 could also be seen as royal-messianic (pp. 219-250), but the arguments are rather general and not altogether convincing.

94. Cf. the review by D. JUEL, in *JBL* 116 (1997) 370-372; see also more generally his *Messianic Exegesis. Christological Exegesis of the Old Testament in Early Christianity*, Philadelphia, PA, 1988.

95. I am not necessarily arguing for this!

96. Strauss says: "In reading Isaiah as a unity Luke is unlikely to have distinguished the servant songs from their wider contexts" (p. 242 n. 4), and "The early Christians surely did not anticipate Duhm in 1892 by isolating these songs from their larger Isaianic contexts" (p. 239 n. 3); but then he seems to backtrack on this almost immediately, by continuing: "On the other hand, in view of the individual description of the 'servant' in these passages, it is likely they would have viewed this individual as distinct from Israel – as Luke clearly does". He deals with one of the references to the servant as Israel on

Third, one has to say that, quite apart from arguments about detailed
points, Strauss' thesis, like Bock's, has the effect at times of Luke presenting what is virtually a corrective Christology. Strauss himself points
to the way in which the discussions of the risen Jesus in Lk 24 about the
necessity of *the Christ* to suffer represent something of a change from
the earlier narrative where it was always as SM (Lk 9,22.44; 18,31-34;
22,22) or as prophet (Lk 4,24; 13,33-34) that Jesus was to suffer. "This
gives the narrative of ch. 24 a sense of surprise and revelation"[97]. But
why then has Luke spent 23 chapters of a narrative investing in ideas
which he eventually feels the need to alter radically in ch. 24?

Nor is it quite the case that the suffering of Jesus is explained by Luke
in terms of Jesus as the servant figure of Isa 40–55, or for that matter as
the Mosaic prophet inaugurating a new Exodus. References to the suffering servant figure of Isaiah are notoriously thin, even in Luke. (The
fact remains that the only explicit reference in the gospel to Isa 53 is Lk
22,37; references in Acts are also not frequent: perhaps Acts 3 and Acts
8, but rarely elsewhere explicitly[98].) Luke does have an idea of prophetic
suffering (cf. 4,24; 13,33-34), but it is not clear that this is due to his
reading of Isaiah specifically. A much more likely background is the
widespread motif of the violence suffered by the prophets[99]; but the
background for this in Jewish scripture is scarcely the book of Isaiah[100].
Related to this is probably the motif of Wisdom and the (Q?) tradition
linking themes of rejected Wisdom and the suffering prophets to produce the hybrid scheme of Wisdom as the sender of the prophets, all of
whom suffer violence (Lk 11,49). Again the background for this may be
scriptural, but is barely Isaianic[101]. Strauss himself also refers in this
context in passing to the suffering of Jesus as SM. But again, the background is not Isaianic. The precise background is hotly debated, though,
if a scriptural background is admitted, the only real candidate is Dan 7.
It seems then that the background from which the Lukan text draws to

p. 241 n. 3: "most commentators consider 'Israel' in 49.3 to be an interpretive gloss". But
was this gloss *not* read by Luke? Was it a gloss not added until after the first century CE?

97. STRAUSS, *Davidic Messiah*, p. 342; cf. also pp. 256-257. Cf. also above on Lemcio (above, n. 39).

98. For the view that Luke is strongly influenced by the story of the righteous sufferer
in Wis 2–5 in his presentation of Jesus' passion, see DOBLE, *Paradox of Salvation* (above,
n. 2). Isa 53 *may* have influenced the account in Wis 2–5 in the latter's earlier tradition
history; but whether Luke was aware of that is quite another matter.

99. See O.H. STECK, *Israel und das gewaltsame Geschick der Propheten* (WMANT,
23), Neukirchen-Vluyn, 1967.

100. See rather Neh 9,26; 1 Kings 18,4.13; 19,10; 2 Kings 17,7-41; 2 Chron 36,16.

101. For rejected Wisdom, cf. Prov 1 (developed more in non-biblical texts such as 1
Enoch 42).

"explain" Jesus' suffering is much wider than Strauss admits. And this means that it is not so easy to encompass all the Luke says about Jesus into the synthesis of the Messiah-servant-Mosaic prophet mould.

Finally, one may note that, if the new David/new Exodus motif is so central for Luke, it is surprising to say the least that it seems to peter out in Acts. Strauss says that it would be an interesting focus for future research[102], but this rather begs the question of why the new Exodus motif is not more obvious, e.g. in the second half of Acts. Why too does the category of Jesus as the servant, or Jesus as the Mosaic prophet, disappear from view? Part of the role of Jesus as servant, it could be argued, may be taken over by Paul (cf. Acts 26,18); but nothing more is said about suffering (of Jesus or others) in this context: as already noted on several occasions, it is exclusively as the Christ that Jesus' sufferings are explained in the second half of Acts.

VI. CONCLUSIONS – JESUS AS THE CHRIST

I find myself drive (somewhat unwillingly!) to the view I recently tried to articulate of Luke as something of a "conservative redactor"[103]. If one wishes to try to pin Luke down to a single Christological title, then probably Jesus as the Χριστός would have to be the most likely candidate[104]. As Strauss has shown, it is the royal messianic category that dominates the birth narratives, and these narratives are now widely regarded as occupying a key role in Luke's story as a whole[105]. So too, insofar as the last half of Acts is at all Christological (and in some ways it is surprisingly *un*christological: the key issues are much more belief in resurrection in general, or the claims that Christians do not violate Jew-

---

102. STRAUSS, *Davidic Messiah*, p. 356.

103. See my *Lukan Son of Man* (above, n. 32), p. 211.

104. See FITZMYER, *Luke I-IX*, p. 197: "Though not the most frequently used title for Jesus in the Lucan writings, *christos* has to be regarded as the most important". Also C.F. EVANS, *Saint Luke*, London, 1990, p. 73: "For Luke, it [= Christ] was perhaps the most important appellation of all". RICHARD, *Jesus*, p. 181. Cf. too STRAUSS, *Davidic Messiah*, p. 114. Pace FRANKLIN, *Christ the Lord*, pp. 55-56, and others. It is of course inappropriate in one way to restrict Luke's Christology to a single title, as if Luke's Christology can be encompassed in one word. One must also bear in mind all the strictures made earlier about the dangers of a titular-based approach to NT Christology. On the other hand, Luke's decision to seek to press so much into (or on to) the term Χριστός, including the somewhat forced attempt to predicate suffering of the Χριστός (cf. n. 54 above), makes it not inappropriate to see this as a central term for Luke in some sense.

105. See STRAUSS, *Davidic Messiah*, pp. 76-87, for the congruence between the birth narratives and the rest of Luke's story. Also P.S. MINEAR, *Luke's Use of the Birth Stories*, in L.E. KECK & J.L. MARTYN (eds.), *Studies in Luke-Acts* (above, n. 1), pp. 111-128.

ish Law, and are not a threat to the Roman political system), the Christology is one that focuses almost exclusively on Jesus as the Χριστός, and showing that Jesus' sufferings can fit this by arguing (from scripture) that "the Christ must suffer".

Yet this cannot hide the fact that much else in Luke-Acts, especially in Luke's gospel, points in different directions Christologically, as everyone who has read some of the secondary literature on Luke-Acts will be aware. Thus Jesus is presented as a prophet, and/or the prophet like Moses, Son of Man, in the line of Wisdom's envoys etc. It is hard not to believe that some of these are primarily due to Luke's source material. Thus Jesus as SM comes from Mark and Q; Jesus as Wisdom's envoy comes from Q. Luke is happy to take these over, and at times to develop them (cf. SM). But he seems also to respect some of the limitations he sees as inherent in some of these titles. Luke had no compunction about expanding the scope of some terms (cf. above on attributing suffering to the Χριστός); but other terms Luke seems to realise have only a limited application, or are appropriately used only in a limited time-span. Thus SM is all but once confined to the lips of Jesus, and is used by Luke in contexts determined by his sources Mark and Q. Wisdom ideas are not developed outside the gospel. Prophetic ideas develop a little, but seem to die away. Luke thus constrains himself to follow his sources and does not give himself free rein.

One further point must however be made about Luke's use of the term Χριστός. The claim that the Davidic promises are fulfilled in Jesus involve a redefinition of almost every aspect of those promises[106]. The "messianic" expectation of a new Davidic ruler was essentially a hope for a political, this-worldly restoration of the fortunes of the Jewish people and the re-establishment of the monarchy. The Christian claims about Jesus involve changing almost every element in the nature of this hope. Thus Jesus is a "royal" figure, but not in any political sense at all and his reigning has absolutely no consequences for the political status quo, either in Jewish political life or in the wider Roman Empire. Jesus sits on a "throne", but that throne is in heaven, not on earth. Any "peace" brought by the arrival of Jesus as king is in heaven (Lk 19,38, LkR of Mk 11,10), not apparently on earth[107]. Others had hoped that Jesus' coming might lead to liberation for Israel (cf. Lk 24,21); but such

---

106. Cf. H. RÄISÄNEN, *The Redemption of Israel: A Salvation-Historical Problem in Luke-Acts*, in P. LUOMANEN (ed.), *Luke-Acts: Scandinavian Perspectives*, Helsinki & Göttingen, 1991, pp. 94-114; repr. in *Marcion, Muhammed and the Mahatma*, London, 1997, pp. 49-63.

107. See STRAUSS, *Davidic Messiah*, p. 315; also E.E. ELLIS, *The Gospel of Luke*, London, 1974, p. 225.

expectations are firmly quashed by the risen Jesus himself: if they had only read the scriptures "properly" (i.e. in the way of the Lukan Jesus!), they would have realised that such hopes are entirely inappropriate. Jesus is thus the royal Messiah, but the nature of his reign, the place of his throne, and any consequences of his arrival in terms of political realities, are all radically altered in the process of adaptation of the network of ideas as appropriated by the Lukan Jesus and the Christian preachers in Acts[108]. Luke's Jesus seems to be at most a Christ figure in name alone. Almost everything else associated with a Χριστός figure, apart from the name itself, is implicitly denied to Jesus in the Lukan story.

In one sense, of course, Luke is no different from the rest of the NT and the whole of early Christianity. The use of the term Χριστός to refer to Jesus involves the adoption of the name but virtually none of the expectations or ideas associated with the name. Yet it seems to be Luke above all who consciously goes out of his way to emphasize the "messianic" identity of Jesus[109].

At the very least, it would seem that this must have some implications about Luke's readership and his purpose in writing. For it seems impossible to conceive of Luke addressing any real non-Christian Jews in any meaningful way at all. For Luke to say: Jesus is your expected king, but is quite unlike any king you may have been expecting, would simply make any meaningful dialogue all but impossible right from the outset[110].

Luke is thus almost certainly writing for a Christian (or just possibly a Gentile non-Christian) audience. The claims about the messianic nature of Jesus' life and death are thus more likely to be part of an agenda Luke is addressing to a Christian audience rather than part of any apology for non-Christian Jews. As such, the claims no doubt serve in part the function of legitimation for the Christian community, seeking to anchor the new Christian movement within the broader context of ancient Judaism[111].

---

108. This is recognised in part by STRAUSS, *Davidic Messiah*, p. 323, on the "irony" of Jesus' kingship, and pp. 256-257, 342, on the "surprising element" that the king must suffer. Cf. too p. 115: "Jesus fulfills the promised role of the Christ in a surprising and unexpected way" (also pp. 311, 343). The overturning of all previous expectations is more strongly seen by R.L. BRAWLEY, *Scripture Resisting the Carnivalesque in the Lucan Passion*, in C.M. TUCKETT (ed.), *The Scriptures in the Gospels* (above, n. 37), pp. 591-595 (at least in relation to kingship language in the passion narrative). The one possible positive link between messiahship and the Jesus story might be the claim that Jesus was "anointed with the Spirit" (cf. VAN UNNIK, *Jesus the Christ*, p. 114); but it must remain doubtful how significant this was for Luke himself (see n. 51 above).

109. The same might be true of, say, Mark, though the relative importance of Jesus' "messianic" identity (strictly speaking) for Markan Christology is debated. There is not time or space to discuss that issue here.

110. Though cf. the similar problems in relation to Justin's *Dialogue with Trypho*. See the discussion in WILSON, *Related Strangers*, ch. 9.

111. See STRAUSS, *Davidic Messiah*. For the importance of "legitimation" in the

Yet if this is the case, one wonders how significant the term Χριστός will have been for Luke himself. In other words, although a "messianic" Christology may have been a key feature in the Christology of Luke-Acts, it is not so clear that it was very important for the Christology of Luke. The very fact that, in the course of appropriating the term Χριστός for Jesus, virtually every association linked with the terms has had to be changed suggests that the ideas associated with the term had little significance for Luke (or if they did, they were regarded as largely negative, since they all had to be changed). Jesus is a Christ figure only in name. The fact that he is such expresses for Luke something of vital importance about the roots of the Christian movement within Judaism. But in and of itself, the term "Christ" appears to have no significance beyond that: the significance which Luke attaches to the term Messiah derives almost entirely from the Jesus story itself and *not* vice versa. It is Jesus who determines what messiahship means; it is *not* messiahship that determines who Jesus is.

In all this we see clearly a prominent aspect of the Christology of Luke-Acts: Jesus is the Messiah figure of Jewish expectation, fulfilling all the messianic expectations albeit in a highly unusual and distinctive way, i.e. via his exaltation to God's right hand in heaven where his "true" throne is to be located. In this then we see an important feature of the Christology of the implied author of Luke-Acts. But whether this is so important for the Christology of the real author is much more doubtful.

As with so many things, Luke does *not* present his own views, or even himself, on a plate for us to be able to gaze at them. Rather, he is content to hide behind his story. He presents us with a Christology, or several Christologies, from what is for him (and us) the past. How that is to be related to the present – to Luke's present or ours – is a task which Luke leaves tantalisingly open[112].

Theology Faculty Centre   Christopher M. TUCKETT
41 St Giles
Oxford OX1 3LW

Lukan writings more generally, see P.F. ESLER, *Community and Gospel in Luke-Acts* (SNTS MS, 57), Cambridge, 1987.

112. I am grateful to those who were present at the seminar in Leuven for a lively and enjoyable discussion, especially to David Moessner who gave an initial prepared Response. Since the paper is already rather long, I have left it largely unaltered with only minor changes, and I have not tried to respond to all the points made in the seminar.

THE ROLE OF THE SPIRIT IN LUKE-ACTS

In any discussion about the unity of the Lucan Gospel and the Acts of the Apostles, the role of the holy Spirit is an important element. Other New Testament writers have described the work of the Spirit in the early Christian community, but the unique character of the Lucan writings, which comprise almost a quarter of the New Testament, is seen partly in the way the Spirit is depicted both in the Third Gospel and in the sequel to the Jesus story that only Luke among the evangelists has bequeathed to us in the Acts of the Apostles.

I shall not regale you with reasons why I consider the author of Luke-Acts to be the Syrian, Antiochene Luke of ecclesiastical tradition[1], or with much detail about the purpose or goal of the Lucan story in the Gospel and Acts. Suffice it to say that I consider Luke's aim to have been a retelling of the Jesus story both in the form of a Hellenistic historical monograph, in which he has sought to continue biblical and historical accounts of old in such writings as Chronicles and Maccabees[2], and in an account in which he sought to connect the life and activity of the Christian church to the life and ministry of Jesus of Nazareth. Where Luke differs from such Old Testament models is found partly in the Jesus story, which he has inherited from the early Christian tradition enshrined in the Marcan Gospel and "Q", and in what he has learned about the sequel to that story, and partly in the way he has conceived his historical and literary task as a Hellenistic writer.

My remarks about the way Luke has described the role of the Spirit in his Gospel and in Acts will be made under three headings: (1) The influence of the Hellenistic understanding of πνεῦμα on the Lucan account? (2) The influence of the Septuagint on Luke's depiction of the Spirit; and (3) Luke's description of the Spirit's role[3].

---

1. See my commentary, *The Gospel according to Luke* (AB, 28-28A), Garden City, NY, Doubleday, 1981, 1985, pp. 35-53; also my commentary, *The Acts of the Apostles* (AB, 31), New York, NY, Doubleday, 1998.

2. This means that I assign far more historical value to Acts than does R.I. PERVO in *Profit with Delight*, Philadelphia, PA, Fortress, 1987. I borrow the term "historical monograph" from M. HENGEL, *Acts and the History of Earliest Christianity*, Philadelphia, PA, Fortress, 1980, p. 36. See also C.J. HEMER, *The Book of Acts in the Setting of Hellenistic History*, ed. C.H. GEMPF, Winona Lake, IN, Eisenbrauns, 1990, pp. 63-100.

3. See further H. VON BAER, *Der heilige Geist in den Lukasschriften* (BWANT, 39), Stuttgart, Kohlhammer, 1926; *Der heilige Geist in den Lukasschriften*, in G. BRAUMANN

I. THE INFLUENCE OF THE HELLENISTIC UNDERSTANDING OF *ΠΝΕΥΜΑ*
ON THE LUCAN ACCOUNT?

Although Luke was, in my opinion, an *incola* of Syria and a non-Jewish Semite, he was well schooled in the Greek language and in Hellenistic literary writing. Jerome said of him, *inter omnes evangelistas graeci sermonis eruditissimus fuit*, "among all the evangelists he was the most skilled writer of Greek"[4]. It has always been a puzzle, however, why Luke never used the noun εὐαγγέλιον in his Gospel[5], despite the notable occurrences of it in the Marcan Gospel[6], on which he otherwise depended, and used a technical Hellenistic literary term to characterize

(ed.), *Das Lukas-Evangelium: Die redaktions- und kompositionsgeschichtliche Forschung* (Wege der Forschung, 280), Darmstadt, Wissenschaftliche Buchgesellschaft, 1974, pp. 1-6; C.K. BARRETT, *The Holy Spirit and the Gospel Tradition*, London, SPCK, 1947 (reprinted 1954); G.R. BEASLEY-MURRAY, *Jesus and the Spirit*, in A. DESCAMPS and A. DE HALLEUX (eds.), *Mélanges bibliques en hommage au R. P. Béda Rigaux*, Gembloux, Duculot, 1970, pp. 463-478; F. BOVON, *Luc le théologien: Vingt-cinq ans de recherches (1950-1975)*, Neuchâtel-Paris, Delachaux et Niestlé, 1978, pp. 211-254; H.E. DANA, *The Holy Spirit in Acts*, Kansas City, KS, Central Seminary Press, ²1943; J.H.E. HULL, *The Holy Spirit in the Acts of the Apostles*, London: Lutterworth; Cleveland, OH, World, 1967; M.-A. CHEVALLIER, *Luc et l'Esprit Saint*, in *RevSR* 56 (1982) 1-16; A. GEORGE, *L'Esprit Saint dans l'oeuvre de Luc*, in *RB* 85 (1978) 500-542; J. GUILLET, *Saint Esprit*: II/I. Dans les *Evangiles Synoptiques*; II. *Dans les Actes des Apôtres*, in *DBS* 11 (1991) 172-191; G. HAYA-PRATS, *L'Esprit, force de l'église: Sa nature et son activité d'après les Actes des Apôtres* (Lectio Divina, 81), Paris, Cerf, 1975; J. JERVELL, *The Unknown Paul: Essays on Luke-Acts and Early Christian History*, Minneapolis, MN, Augsburg, 1984, pp. 96-121; C.S. KEENER, *The Spirit in the Gospels and Acts: Divine Purity and Power*, Peabody, MA, Hendrickson, 1997; J. KREMER, Πνεῦμα, -ατος, τό, in *EDNT*, 3, pp. 117-122; G.W.H. LAMPE, *The Holy Spirit in the Writings of St. Luke*, in D.E. NINEHAM (ed.), *Studies in the Gospels: Essays in Memory of R.H. Lightfoot*, Oxford, Blackwell, 1957, pp. 159-200; O. MAINVILLE, *L'Esprit dans l'œuvre de Luc* (Héritage et projet, 45), Montréal, Éditions Fides, 1991; *Jésus et l'Esprit dans l'œuvre de Luc: Éclairage à partir d'Ac 2, 33*, in *SE* 42 (1990) 193-208; G. MARCONI, *Lo Spirito di Dio nella vita interiore: L'opera di Luca, Vangelo dello Spirito* (Quaderni di Camaldoli. Meditazioni, 6), Bologna, Dehoniane, 1997; P. SAMAIN, *L'Esprit et le royaume de Dieu d'après saint Luc*, in *Revue diocésaine de Tournai* 2 (1947) 481-492; E. SCHWEIZER, Πνεῦμα, in *TDNT* 6 (1968) 332-455, esp. pp. 404-415; S.S. SMALLEY, *Spirit, Kingdom and Prayer in Luke-Acts*, in *NT* 15 (1973) 59-71; K. STALDER, *Der Heilige Geist in der lukanischen Ekklesiologie*, in *Una sancta* 30 (1975) 287-293; R. STRONSTAD, *The Charismatic Theology of St. Luke*, Peabody, MA, Hendrickson, 1984, pp. 13-27, 75-82; W.B. TATUM, *The Epoch of Israel: Luke i-ii and the Theological Plan of Luke-Acts*, in *NTS* 13 (1966-67) 184-195; É. TROCMÉ, *L'Esprit-Saint et l'Église*, Paris, Fayard, 1969, pp. 19-44; M. TURNER, *Power from on High: The Spirit in Israel's Restoration and Witness in Luke-Acts* (Journal of Pentecostal Theology SS, 9), Sheffield, Academic Press, 1996; *Spirit Endowment in Luke-Acts: Some Linguistic Considerations*, in *Vox evangelica* 12 (1981) 45-63.

    4. *Ep. ad Damasum 20* 4,4 (*CSEL*, 54, 108).
    5. It occurs only twice in Acts, once on the lips of Peter (15,7) and once on the lips of Paul (20,24).
    6. Mark 1,1.14.15; 8,35; 10,29; 13,10; 14,9; [16,15].

the *opus* that he was writing, διήγησις, "a narrative account". That term, along with the double prologue of Luke 1,1-4 and Acts 1,1-2, sufficiently relate his two-volume work to contemporary Greek literary writing.

If, then, Luke has produced a Hellenistic historical monograph in writing his form of the Jesus story with its sequel in Acts, does his treatment of (τὸ) πνεῦμα ἅγιον or simply τὸ πνεῦμα reveal traces of the contemporary Greek understanding of πνεῦμα in his double work?

The Greco-Roman world of that time was rife with ideas about "inspiration". That was normally expressed, however, by terms denoting "breath", such as πνοιά, πνοή, ἐπίπνοια, ἐπίπνευσις, or by μανία, ἐνθουσιασμός (and their Latin equivalents). These were sometimes modified by the adjective θεῖος (*divinus*) or the genitive θεοῦ, when expressing oracular, mantic, or poetic inspiration. On occasion, one finds in secular Greek texts πνεῦμα ἱερόν, especially in the sense of the life-begetting "breath" of Zeus[7], or when gods were considered the mantic inspirers of poets, orators, and the Pythian or Delphic oracles[8]. Divine spirits or θεῖα πνεύματα were those that endowed basic knowledge of nature, and divinized cosmic forces were so named in Stoic philosophy[9]. Hypostatized preternatural beings also populated the world of magic, often called δαίμονες or πνεύματα[10], sometimes good, sometimes evil[11]. But, as H. Kleinknecht has noted,

---

7. Diodorus Siculus, *Bibl. Hist.* 1.12.1-2. Cf. Aeschylus, *Suppliants* 18-19, 584-85 (κἀξ ἐπιπνοίας Διός); Plutarch, *Is. et Osir.* 36 365d).

8. Strabo, *Geogr.* 9.3.5 (πνεῦμα ἐνθουσιαστικόν, used of priestess of the Pythian oracle); Plutarch, *Def. Orac.* 42 (433d: τὸ μαντικὸν πνεῦμα); 51 (438a: πρὸς τὴν τοῦ πνεύματος ὥσπερ φαρμάκου κρᾶσιν); 51 (438b: ἀλάλου καὶ κακοῦ πνεύματος οὖσα πλήρης); 51 (438c: ἡ τοῦ πνεύματος δύναμις); *De exilio* 605a (τὸ δὲ ἱερὸν καὶ δαιμόνιον ἐν μούσαις πνεῦμα); Plato, *Ion* 533d, 534c (θεῖα μοίρα, δύναμις); Ps.-Plato, *Axiochos* 370c (τὶ θεῖον ὄντος ἐνῆν πνεῦμα τῇ ψυχῇ). In the Roman world Cicero speaks of *poetam... quasi divino quodam spiritu inflari* (*Pro Archia* 8.18); cf. Horace, *Carm.* 4.6.29; Lucan, *De bello civili* 5.65. Cf. E. WILL, *Sur la nature du pneuma delphique*, in *BCH* 66-67 (1942-43) 161-175; P. AMANDRY, *La mantique apollinienne à Delphes: Essai sur le fonctionnement de l'oracle* (Bibliothèque des Écoles Françaises d'Athènes et de Rome, 170), Paris, E. de Boccard, 1950, pp. 215-244.

Πνεῦμα ἱερόν used in such texts has at times been employed to explain the Greek background of the reception of the Spirit in Acts 2,4 and the subsequent speaking "in other tongues" that Luke recounts in his story of the first Christian Pentecost. See H. KLEINKNECHT, Πνεῦμα, πνεύματος, κτλ., in *TDNT*, 6, 334-359, esp. p. 346; cf. H. SAAKE, *Pneuma*, in *PWSup* 14 (1974) 387-412.

9. Ps.-Aristotle, *De Mundo* 394b.10; cf. Philo, *De Spec. leg.* 1,1 §6.

10. *IG* XIV.872.3; cf. J. MASPERO, *Papyrus grecs d'époque byzantine* (Catalogue général des antiquités égyptiennes du Musée du Caire), Cairo, 1911-1916; reprinted, Osnabrück, Zeller, 1973, §188.3.

11. See H. KLEINKNECHT, Πνεῦμα (n. 8), pp. 334-359.

there is as yet no instance of the concept of a πνεῦμα ἅγιον in secular Gk. Here biblical Gk. has coined a new and distinctive expression for the very different, suprasensual, supraterrestrial and in part personal character and content which πνεῦμα has in Judaism and Christianity[12].

That seems, then, to be the answer to the question posed above.

Nevertheless, Luke does use πνεῦμα at times, especially in miracle stories, when he refers to πνεῦμα δαιμονίου ἀκαθάρτου (Luke 4,33), to πνεῦμα ἀκάθαρτον (Luke 4,36; 6,18; 8,29; 9,42; 11,24.26; Acts 5,16; 8,7), or to πνεῦμα πονηρόν (Luke 7,21; 8,2; Acts 19,12.13.15.16), and even once to πνεῦμα πύθων (Acts 16,16). One might be tempted to think that such terms were part of the Greco-Roman world in which he lived, but it is not easy to find the exact equivalents of such phrases in secular Greek writings.

Πνεύματα πονηρά is found in the extant Greek version of *1 Enoch* 99,7; *Testaments of the Twelve Patriarchs* (*T. Simeon* 4,9; 6,6; *T. Judah* 16,1); and Josephus, *Ant.* 6.11.2 §211 (cf. 6.11.3 §214; *J.W.* 7.6.3 §185); ἀκάθαρτα πνεύματα occurs in *T. Benj.* 5,2. Such writings, however, are scarcely representative of secular Greek composition and undoubtedly owe much to Jewish conceptions. They should be considered rather in the second part of this paper.

II. THE INFLUENCE OF THE SEPTUAGINT ON LUKE'S DEPICTION OF THE SPIRIT

If Luke has been influenced by earlier Greek writings in his treatment of the role of the Spirit, it is clearly the world of the Greek Bible that has exerted most of the influence, and not only on Luke, but on all of early Christian tradition, to which Luke was indeed tributary. This is not surprising, since Luke's dependence on the Greek Old Testament, especially in the form that we call the Septuagint (LXX), has long since been shown.

In the LXX one finds the exact counterpart of the Lucan terms, πνεῦμα ἀκάθαρτον (Zech 13,2) and πνεῦμα πονηρόν (Judg 9,23; 1 Sam 16,14-16.23[bis]; 18,10; 19,9; Hos 12,2; Tob 6,8 [MSS S, B, A])[13]. From such passages, the same expressions employed in the intertestamental Jewish Greek writings mentioned above have also been derived. Here one encounters a Greek-speaking world and culture, but one in which the Jewish belief in intermediate beings such as angels and spir-

12. *Ibid.*, p. 338.
13. In the Greek of Tob 3,8.17 one finds a related expression, δαιμόνιον πονηρόν.

its, especially in postexilic period, has clearly modified the Hellenistic understanding of πνεύματα. Hence, if the Lucan references to "unclean" or "evil spirits" are related to Hellenism, they are related to it via the LXX.

More important for my topic, however, is the association of πνεῦμα with the monotheistic belief of ancient Israel in the Greek translation of the Hebrew Scriptures, for the Lucan idea of the holy Spirit owes much to the Old Testament conceptions of the "Spirit". Here one must consider six expressions that occur in the LXX:

(1) Πνεῦμα Θεοῦ: This phrase is found frequently enough in the LXX (Gen 1,2; 8,1; 41,38; Num 23,6; 24,2; 1 Sam 10,10; 19,20.23; 2 Chron 24,20; Isa 11,2; Ezek 11,24b)[14], but Luke never picks it up.

(2) Πνεῦμα ἅγιον: This occurs in the LXX with the article in Ps 51,13 [50,13]; 143,10 [MSS S, B, A]; Isa 63,10.11; Wis 9,17, and always with the possessive pronoun σοῦ or αὐτοῦ. Luke uses this term about forty times, sometimes with the article, sometimes without it, but never with the possessive pronoun.

(3) Πνεῦμα Κυρίου: This phrase occurs regularly in the LXX (Judg 3,10; 11,29; 13,25; 14,6.19; 15,14; 1 Sam 10,6; 11,6; 16,13.14; 2 Sam 23,2; 1 Kings 18,12; 22,24; 2 Kings 2,16; 2 Chron 15,1; 18,23; 20,14; Wis 1,7; Micah 2,7; 3,8; Isa 61,1; Ezek 11,5), and Luke employs it, not only when he quotes Isaiah in the programmatic scene in his Gospel, in the Nazareth synagogue (Luke 4,18), but also when he composes freely, as in Acts 5,9; 8,39.

(4) Πνεῦμα θεῖον: This is found only in the Book of Job (27,3; 33,4) and in some MSS (A, B², R) of Exod 31,3 (πνεῦμα θεῖον σοφίας), but it is never utilized by Luke.

(5) Πνεῦμα alone, but with a genitive possessive pronoun referring to God, αὐτοῦ, σοῦ, or μοῦ: πνεῦμα αὐτοῦ (Isa 48,16; Zech 7,12); πνεῦμά σου (Neh 9,20.30; Jdt 16,14; Ps 104,30; 139,7); and πνεῦμά μου (Gen 6,3; Joel 3,1-2; Hag 2,5; Isa 42,1; 44,3; 59,21; Ezek 36,27; 37,6.14). Of these only the last mentioned is used by Luke, πνεῦμά μου, and only in an Old Testament quotation (Joel cited in Acts 2,17-18).

(6) Πνεῦμα alone: When referring to God's influence on human beings or the world, (τὸ) πνεῦμα alone is not too common. It is found on occasion in the Book of Ezekiel (1,12.20; 2,2; 3,12.14.24; 8,3;

14. The Theodotion text of Dan 5,14 speaks of πνεῦμα Θεοῦ being in Daniel; see also LXX of Dan 5,12; Susanna 45.

11,1.24a; 43,5)[15]. This mode of expression is often used by Luke, in both the Gospel and Acts.

Such uses of πνεῦμα in the LXX obviously influenced the thinking of early Christians in general, as the occurrence of πνεῦμα ἅγιον in other New Testament writings attest. So the Lucan usage of πνεῦμα is directly influenced by this early Christian tradition, and indirectly by some Septuagintal expressions.

When the Old Testament thus speaks about God's Spirit, it is usually a way of expressing God's dynamic presence to the created world or to His Chosen People: a breath or forceful wind that reveals the activity of the divine presence (Gen 1,2; Ps 139,7). It expresses that presence as creative (Ps 33,6; Jdt 16,14), as inspiring prophecy (Num 24,2; Hos 9,7; 1 Sam 11,6), as raising up leaders (Judg 6,34; 11,29; Isa 11,1-5), or as renovating the earth (Ps 104,30). Such ideas associated with πνεῦμα Θεοῦ in the world of the Jewish monotheism thus brought significant Semitic nuances to the understanding of πνεῦμα in the Greek world of the last pre-Christian centuries.

It is not surprising that these Semitic nuances also found their way into the meaning of πνεῦμα in the compositions of Philo, Josephus, and various intertestamental Jewish Greek writers. Most frequently Philo speaks of πνεῦμα θεῖον[16], a phrase that he has derived from Exod 31,3, where God tells Moses that he has called Bezalel, son of Uri, and filled him with πνεῦμα θεῖον σοφίας καὶ συνέσεως καὶ ἐπιστήμης, "with a divine spirit of wisdom, understanding, and knowledge". Philo quotes this very verse[17]. Josephus too speaks of θεῖον πνεῦμα influencing Balaam or his ass[18], David and Daniel[19], and armed men who are thus made to prophesy[20]. Here too belong those Jewish intertestamental writings mentioned above in the last paragraph of part I, because they are influenced by the Greek biblical tradition.

---

15. Πνεῦμα alone is found in other senses (e.g. Num 11,16-17, and even in the Book of Ezekiel).

16. E.g., *Op. Mundi* 46 §135 (breathed in a human being, with Gen 2,7 quoted); *Leg. Alleg.* 1,13 § 33-34 (as one of the ἀγαθά given to humanity); *Gig.* 6 § 27 (given to Moses to instruct others); *De plantatione* 6 §24 (infused into the mind of the real philosopher); *Quis rer. div. heres* 11 § 55 (dominant part of soul breathed in by God [Gen 2,7]); 12 § 57; 53 § 265; *De vita Mosis* 2,48 § 265 (guides Moses to the truth); *De fuga et inven.* 33 § 186 (τὸ θεῖον . . . καὶ προφητικὸν πνεῦμα bestowed on the seventy elders of Num 11,16); cf. 24 § 134.

17. See *Quaestiones in Genesim* 1,90.

18. See *Ant.* 4.6.3 § 108; 4.6.5 § 118-19.

19. *Ant.* 6.8.2 § 166 (David); 10.11.3 § 239 (Daniel).

20. *Ant.* 6.11.5 § 222; cf. 8.4.3 § 114; 8.15.4 § 408.

III. LUKE'S DESCRIPTION OF THE ROLE OF THE SPIRIT

In his two-volume work Luke uses πνεῦμα thirty-six times in his Gospel and seventy times in Acts[21]. In all, these one hundred and six instances represent 28% of the New Testament occurrences of the word. Of these one hundred and six instances, the word refers to unclean or evil spirits twenty times (twelve times in the Gospel and eight times in Acts)[22], and in fifteen instances "spirit" is employed in some generic sense[23]. Hence Luke employs the divine πνεῦμα seventy-one times[24], significantly more than any of the other evangelists[25].

At times, the Lucan meaning of Spirit differs little from the Old Testament way of expressing God's dynamic presence to His people or the created world. Luke employs (τὸ) πνεῦμα ἅγιον (fifty-three times) or πνεῦμα Κυρίου (three times), πνεῦμά μου (of God, twice), or simply πνεῦμα (thirteen times), and it is his way of ascribing divine presence and activity among the people of Israel or among early Christians. Only once does Luke speak of "the Spirit of Jesus" (Acts 16,7); otherwise the Spirit is always that of ὁ Θεός, even if he never takes over the Septuagintism, πνεῦμα Θεοῦ.

Luke depicts the Spirit active in all the periods of salvation history. I have normally gone along with H. Conzelmann's division of that history into three periods: the Period of Israel, the Period of Jesus, and the Period of the Church under Stress (or *ecclesia pressa*). In my opinion, that best suits the Lucan view of things[26].

In the Period of Israel, Luke portrays the holy Spirit speaking beforehand "by the mouth of David" concerning Judas (Acts 1,16), or as he tells about Jerusalem Christians at prayer (Acts 4,25), or as having spoken "through Isaiah the prophet to the fathers" of the Jews of Rome, when he narrates their reluctance to accept Paul's message (Acts 28,25).

---

21. These statistics are taken from R. MORGENTHALER, *Statistik des neutestamentlichen Wortschatzes*, Zurich - Frankfurt am M., Gotthelf Verlag, 1958, p. 133; and K. ALAND *et al.* (eds.), *Vollständige Konkordanz zum griechischen Neuen Testament*, 2 vols., Berlin - New York, de Gruyter, 1975-83, 2, 1978, pp. 224-225.

22. Luke 4,33.36; 6,18; 7,21; 8,2.29; 9,39.42; 10,20; 11,24.26; 13,11; Acts 5,16; 8,7; 16,16.18; 19,12.13.15.16.

23. See Luke 1,7.47.80; 8,55; 9,55; 23,46; 24,37.39; Acts 6,10(?); 7,59; 17,16; 18,25; 19,21; 23,8.9.

24. He also uses it once of "Jesus" in Acts 16,7 (probably in the sense of the risen Christ).

25. Matthew uses it eleven times of God's Spirit; Mark six times; and John fourteen times.

26. See H. CONZELMANN, *The Theology of St Luke*, New York, NY, Harper & Bros., 1960, pp. 12-17; cf. J.A. FITZMYER, *The Gospel according to Luke* (n. 1), pp. 181-187.

This depiction of the Spirit as active in David or Isaiah enables Luke to relate the story that he is writing to the Period of Israel of old.

Similarly, in the infancy narrative Luke describes the Spirit active in the lives of pious Jews shortly before the birth of Jesus: promising the conception of John the Baptist (Luke 1,15), inspiring Elizabeth's blessing of Mary (1,41), moving Zechariah to prophesy about his son (1,67), and enabling Mary's conception (1,35). Once Jesus is born, the Spirit is further active in Simeon, moving him to foretell the future of the child brought to the Temple (2,25.27). All of this, of course, is preparatory, foreshadowing the work of the same Spirit in the two coming periods of salvation history. For it is important for Luke that it be the same Spirit.

I differ with Conzelmann in understanding the role of John the Baptist. He is in my opinion the precursor of Jesus in the Lucan Gospel. John is, indeed, the term of the Period of Israel, as Conzelmann has maintained, but he is also a transitional figure. In John's active ministry, the Period of Israel not only comes to an end (Luke 16,16), but John also introduces the Period of Jesus. That is why Luke supplies the significant dates, not for the start of Jesus' ministry, but for that of John (Luke 3,12). Immediately afterwards Jesus appears on the scene. Moreover, he depicts John comparing his own baptism "of water" with the baptism of "the mightier One", who will "baptize you with the holy Spirit and with fire" (3,16). In this way, John's words take on a nuance in the Lucan Gospel that they do not have in the earlier Marcan Gospel. For Luke joins to the Marcan account material from "Q", which associates "fire" with the role of the Spirit in the Period of Jesus.

Moreover, in the Period of Jesus itself, as Jesus begins his ministry, Luke recounts his baptism, and "the holy Spirit descends on him as a dove in bodily form" (3,22). Thus the Spirit becomes the *inaugurator* of Jesus' public ministry. This idea is stressed again, as Jesus returns from the Jordan "full of the holy Spirit" and "is led by the Spirit into the wilderness" (4,1), where he is to be tested. At the end of it Luke describes Jesus returning again from the wilderness to Galilee "under the power of the Spirit" (4,14). In the programmatic scene in the Nazareth synagogue, Jesus quotes Isa 61,1, "The Spirit of the Lord is upon me, for he has anointed me" (i.e., in the baptism) "to proclaim the kingdom of God," and this becomes the very purpose for which he has been sent (4,43)[27].

---

27. The only one said to have been "anointed" by the Spirit in Luke-Acts is Jesus (Luke 4,18, quoting Isa 61,1). See Acts 10,38: "How God anointed Jesus of Nazareth with a holy Spirit and with power", as Luke interprets the baptism of Jesus in Acts. Cf. Acts 4,27. See further W. RUSSELL, *The Anointing of the Holy Spirit in Luke-Acts*, in *TrinJ* 7 (1986) 47-63.

Strikingly enough, none of Jesus' miracles in the Lucan Gospel are associated with the Spirit, as has been recognized by E. Schweizer[28]. The other times, however, when we hear about the Spirit's influence during Jesus' ministry are isolated and unrelated. The first is found when Jesus "found delight in the holy Spirit" and uttered his famous prayer of thanks to his heavenly Father (10,21). Here Luke depicts Jesus praying to his Father in the Spirit. The second is the Lucan form of Jesus' saying about petitionary prayer. It is unique in the gospel tradition in that it ends with the comparison, "If you, then, evil as you are, know how to give your children good gifts, how much more surely will the heavenly Father give the holy Spirit to those who ask him?" (11,13)[29]. Unfortunately, the Lucan Jesus never explains this heavenly gift further; so we are left to speculate about the nature of this bounty. The third is a warning that Jesus utters, "Anyone who reviles the holy Spirit will not be forgiven" (12,10), i.e., by God, because such persons put themselves in an impossible situation of rejecting the very source (God or His Spirit), from which the forgiveness might come. The last is the instruction that the Lucan Jesus gives to his followers: they are not to be anxious about what they should say when they are haled into synagogues, and before rulers and authorities, because "the holy Spirit will teach you at that very moment what you must say" (12,12). In these sayings of Jesus about the Spirit's influence, one learns how his followers are to pray to the heavenly Father and await His bounty or instruction, which will come with the aid of the divine Spirit. Certain of these instructive sayings of Jesus find an echo in Acts, as the Spirit guides the conduct of early Christians there.

What is strange in the Lucan Gospel is that there is no further mention of the holy Spirit in the latter part of Luke's account of the Period of

---

28. See *TDNT*, 6, p. 407: "Though the miracles are important for Luke, they are never ascribed to the Spirit. Healing power is associated with the name of Jesus, with faith in Jesus, with Jesus Himself, with prayer, with bodily contact through the disciple, his shadow or his handkerchief, or more simply with the δύναμις of Jesus". I should not, however, limit Luke's understanding of the Spirit as "essentially the Spirit of prophecy", as Schweizer does (p. 409); it is certainly more than that. Even when Luke says that God anointed Jesus with the "holy Spirit and power" (Acts 10,38), that does not necessarily mean that the healings mentioned in v. 39 were directly caused by the power of the Spirit. Perhaps one might have to echo some of the criticism of Schweizer that M. Turner engages in *The Spirit and the Power of Jesus' Miracles in the Lucan Conception*, in *NT* 33 (1991) 124-152. See Luke 4,14, where the Spirit is related to Jesus' teaching. In 4,36 Jesus' "power" over unclean spirits is his own. In Luke 5,17 "the power of the Lord was with him to heal", but here one can debate the meaning of Κυρίου. It is most likely an allusion to God the Father; it is highly unlikely that Luke would be using Κύριος in the sense of the Spirit, as in 2 Cor 3,17. Again, in Luke 9,1, the "power" given to the Twelve "over all demons and to cure sicknesses" hardly means the power of the Spirit. It is rather Jesus' own power that he is passing on to his Apostles.

29. Compare Matt 7,11, where ἀγαθά occurs instead of πνεῦμα ἅγιον.

Jesus. After chap. 13 of the Gospel the word πνεῦμα occurs only three times, and only in a generic sense; they have nothing to do with the Spirit of God. This means that God's Spirit is not depicted as operative in the Lucan passion narrative or resurrection narrative. Jesus' passion, death, and burial are recounted without any involvement of the holy Spirit. Moreover, the stories of the discovery of the empty tomb and of the appearance of the risen Christ to his disciples are similarly told, without any mention of the holy Spirit. The next time the Spirit appears in the Lucan διήγησις is in the sequel to the Gospel, in the story of the Period of the Church under Stress. Even in Luke 24,49, where the risen Christ instructs the Eleven and those with them to remain in Jerusalem until he sends upon them "what my Father has promised", there is no explanation of what that promise is. For that one must wait until Acts 1,4-5.

As the account of the Period of the Church begins in Acts 1, one notes the prominence of the holy Spirit as its *inaugurator*. Not only does the risen Christ now charge the apostles "through the holy Spirit" (Acts 1,2) and instruct them about their coming baptism "with the holy Spirit" (1,5), but the programmatic verse of Acts itself tells how they "will receive power, when the holy Spirit comes upon" them, making them witnesses to him "in Jerusalem, in all Judea and Samaria, even to the end of the earth" (1,8). Thus the third period of salvation is begun, initiated by the Spirit in conjunction with the ascension of Christ (1,9-11)[30]. The power that the Spirit will endow will inaugurate apostolic testimony to the risen Christ and his gospel.

The Lucan story in Acts 2 tells how the first Christians "were all filled with the holy Spirit and began to speak in other tongues, as the Spirit gave them to utter" (2,4). That is an important description of the inaugurating work of the Spirit in this period of salvation history; but more important than the speaking in other tongues is the effect of testimony that the Spirit thus begins. For the Spirit enables Peter to stand up with the Eleven, confront the Jews gathered in Jerusalem for their feast

---

30. Even though Conzelmann never drew a clear line of demarcation between the Period of Jesus and the Period of the Church, I take the double account of the ascension (at the end of the Gospel, 24,50-52, and in Acts 1,9-11) to be the caesura. An important indicator of this caesura is Acts 1,6, where the apostles ask the risen Christ whether he would "at this time restore the kingdom to Israel". The phrase "at this time" indicates that it differs from the time that preceded, viz. the Period of Jesus, the period of his earthly ministry. On the heels of Jesus' answer to the query of the apostles comes the second account of the ascension. Hence the function of the ascension as the caesura between the two Periods.

of "Assembly"[31], and proclaim to "all the house of Israel" that "God has made him both Lord and Messiah, this Jesus whom you crucified" (2,36). In this way the Spirit instigates the very testimony of the apostles, about which the risen Christ spoke in Luke 24,47-48 and in Acts 1,8. The Spirit's influence is, indeed, the "power from on high" (Luke 24,49) and the "power" (Acts 1,8) that they were to await in Jerusalem. Moreover, the instruction given to the apostles by the risen Christ both at the end of the Lucan Gospel and at the beginning of Acts unites the two volumes and concentrates their attention on the effect of the Spirit active in them.

Peter's speech on Pentecost, on the first great Jewish feast after Passover, when Jesus had been crucified, not only proclaims God's good news to the assembled Jews of the twelve tribes of Israel, but relates his proclamation to the work of the Spirit. Peter quotes Joel 3,1-5 about the outpouring of God's Spirit on all flesh[32] and associates that outpouring explicitly with the activity of the risen and ascended Christ. Of him Peter announces, "Exalted to God's right hand, he has received from the Father the promised holy Spirit and poured it forth. This is what you now [both] see and hear" (2,33). This verse of Acts has been called "la clé d'interprétation de la pneumatologie lucanienne"[33]. For the Spirit, related in Joel's prophecy to the Day of Yahweh, becomes in Acts 2,17 the sign of the arrival of the *eschaton*, as Luke adds to the prophet's words ἐν ταῖς ἐσχάταις ἡμέραις.

Then when some of Peter's audience ask what they must do in light of all that has happened, he further proclaims, "Reform your lives and be baptized, every one of you, in the name of Jesus the Messiah for the forgiveness of your sins, and you will receive the gift of the holy Spirit" (2,38). In this way, the Spirit inaugurates the first Jewish Christian church of Jerusalem and gives a new, ecclesiastical meaning to the *eschaton*. Even though ἐκκλησία is not used in Acts 2, Luke records that "some three thousand persons" (2,41) were baptized that day, and that chapter ends with a summary that says, "Day by day the Lord added to the total those who were being saved" (2,47). In time, that total will be called "church" (5,11; 8,1). So the Period of the Church is officially inaugurated under the eschatological guidance of the Spirit in the Lucan

---

31. When Josephus speaks of Pentecost (*Ant.* 3.10.6 §252), he says, τῇ πεντηκοστῇ, ἣν Ἑβραῖοι ἀσαρθὰ καλοῦσι, "on the fiftieth day, which the Jews call *Asartha*", i.e. the Aramaic עצרתא, related to Hebrew עצרת, "assembly".

32. See P. BUIS, *Joël annonce l'effusion de l'Esprit*, in *Spiritus* 2 (1961) 145-152.

33. See O. MAINVILLE, *L'Esprit dans l'œuvre de Luc* (n. 3), p. 15.

story. Later on, the evangelist records, "So the church was at peace throughout all Judea, Galilee, and Samaria. It was gradually being built up and advanced in the fear of the Lord. With the encouragement of the holy Spirit, it grew in numbers" (9,31). The causes for this growth of the Christian church were the fear of the Lord and the encouragement (παράκλησις) of the Spirit. The first is a good Old Testament motif (יראת יהוה, Prov 1,7; 9,10; Job 28,28; Ps 19,10; Sir 1,14), but the second is a Lucan innovation. Another ecclesial role of the Spirit will be mentioned in time, for the Spirit will be said to put "overseers" in the church to care for God's flock (20,28).

The activity of the Spirit thus continues in the Lucan sequel to his Jesus story, in the account of the early church, the like of which no other evangelist has left us. Diverse effects of this activity are recounted in 4,31; 8,17-18; 9,17; 10,44; 11,15; 15,8; 19,16. Strangely enough, however, there is no mention of the holy Spirit in chaps. 3, 12, 14, 17, 18, 22–27, i.e. in much of the story of Paul's missionary endeavors[34]. At the very end Luke does introduce the Spirit, as Paul quotes Isa 6,9-10 against the Jews of Rome, who have come to visit him and are departing without accepting his message. This means that the effect of the holy Spirit is absent from much of the Lucan story about Paul, even though the beginning of his ministry is clearly marked by the Spirit's influence.

Ananias of Damascus tells Saul, "The Lord Jesus, who appeared to you on the road as you were coming here, has sent me that you might recover your sight and be filled with the holy Spirit" (9,17). The Spirit is not only portrayed as involved in the conversion and call of Saul, but also in a special way in the inauguration of his missionary journeys. The Spirit tells the church at Antioch, while they were at worship and were fasting, to set apart Barnabas and Saul "for the work to which I have called them" (13,2). The Lucan account continues, "Sent forth thus by the holy Spirit, these two went down to Seleucia and set sail from there" (13,4; cf. 13,9.52). As the Spirit inaugurated the testimony of Peter on Pentecost, so now the Spirit initiates the missionary journeys of Pauline testimony.

In Acts 15 Luke recounts the story of the "Council" of Jerusalem. It is an important, but complicated chapter, in which Luke has telescoped or joined together accounts of two decisions made at different times in

---

34. The Spirit appears, however, in Paul's speech to the presbyters of Ephesus at Miletus. In Acts 20,22-23 Paul admits that the Spirit has been warning him in many cities about what he is to face in Jerusalem; cf. Acts 21,4.11. In Acts 20,28, Paul also mentions that Spirit, but not as exercising influence on himself. The Spirit is rather to assist the presbyters in being good ἐπισκόπους of God's flock.

Jerusalem[35]. In the "Council" meeting itself, Peter recalls for his audience that "God, who reads the heart, has given testimony, granting to them [Gentiles] the holy Spirit, just as He did to us" (15,8). Peter insists that uncircumcised Gentiles, like Cornelius and his household, could be recipients of God's Spirit.

Later in the same chapter Luke quotes the letter that was sent by James, the apostles, and the presbyters of Jerusalem to the local churches of Antioch, Syria, and Cilicia: "It is the decision of the holy Spirit, and ours too, not to lay on you any burden beyond what is strictly necessary" (15,28)[36]. Thus the authority of the Spirit is invoked to regulate minor matters in mixed churches of the Gentile world.

In his narrative about the early church, one sees how Luke depicts the Spirit above all as its *inaugurator*. Just as the Spirit initiated the Period of Jesus, now it initiates that of the Church. Again, as in the Gospel, Luke recounts at times some of the follow-up of the Spirit's activity in the ministry of Peter and Paul, but the follow-up does not continue to the very end of his account. Moreover, the Spirit seems to be more active in the Lucan narrative of the early church than in the story of Jesus. That is undoubtedly because Luke, in telling the Jesus story, was more restricted, being dependent on sources (the Marcan Gospel and "Q"). If it seems likely that Luke made use of some sources in the composition of Acts, he clearly felt freer to introduce the Spirit's activity more often in this part of his writing[37].

There is, however, one aspect of the Spirit that needs further elaboration, viz. the way Luke has at times personified the Spirit. Earlier I admitted that Luke basically understands the "Spirit" as it was presented in the Greek Old Testament, as a way of expressing God's dynamic presence to His people or the created world. Nevertheless, an important difference is also seen at times in that Luke personifies πνεῦμα. For instance, he speaks of the Spirit actively "communicating" with Simeon (χρηματίζειν, Luke 2,25), "saying" to Philip, Peter, and Agabus (εἶπεν, λέγειν, Acts 8,29; 10,19; 11,12; 21,11)[38], "predicting" through David (προεῖπεν, Acts 1,16), "speaking" through Isaiah (λαλεῖν, Acts

35. See my commentary on Acts; consult the treatment in R. E. BROWN *et al.* (eds.), *The Jerome Biblical Commentary*, Englewood Cliffs, NJ, Prentice Hall, 1968, pp. 194-196 (art. 45, §72-77) and pp. 219-220 (art. 46, §28-34).

36. The Spirit is mentioned again in v. 29 in some MSS, but it is not part of the Alexandrian Text used in N-A[27].

37. See Acts 11,28, where even Agabus "predicts" through the Spirit. Compare Acts 15,29, where MS D reads εὖ πράξατε φερόμενοι ἐν τῷ ἁγίῳ πνεύματι. Compare also Acts 19,2.

38. And to Paul in MS D of 19,1.

28,25), "testifying" to Paul (διαμαρτύρεσθαι, Acts 20,23)[39], "teaching" Jesus' followers (διδάσκειν, Luke 12,12; cf. Acts 2,4b), "leading" Jesus (ἄγειν, Luke 4,1), "snatching" Philip (ἁρπάζειν, Acts 8,39), "sending out" Barnabas and Saul (ἐκπέμπειν, Acts 13,4), "making" presbyters overseers (τίθεσθαι, Acts 20,28), and "preventing" Paul and Silas (κωλύειν, Acts 16,6)[40].

Moreover, Luke makes the Spirit the object of several verbs, which similarly imply personification: "lying to, deceiving" the Spirit (ψεύδεσθαι, Acts 5,5), "testing, tempting" the Spirit (πειράζειν, Acts 5,9), "resisting" the Spirit (ἀντιπίπτειν, Acts 7,51), and "reviling" the Spirit (βλασφημεῖν, Luke 12,10).

In all these instances of personification of πνεῦμα, the article remains neuter (τό)[41], so that one cannot say for sure that Luke is thinking of the Spirit as a person, as in the later full-blown trinitarian teaching of the patristic period[42]. F.F. Bruce once claimed that "one recognizable difference... is that in the Qumran texts the 'holy spirit' can hardly be said to be personal, whereas his personality is clearly to be discerned in Acts (as elsewhere in the New Testament)"[43]. I doubt, however, that that is the way to put the matter; I prefer to speak of personification in the Lucan writings. Nor would I agree with Bruce that ἄγγελος Κυρίου (Acts 8,26) is not to be distinguished from πνεῦμα (8,29) or from πνεῦμα Κυρίου (9,39)[44].

An important Lucan passage for the development of the doctrine about the Spirit, which ensues in later times, is the account of Ananias and Sapphira. There Peter asks Ananias, "Why have you let Satan so fill your heart that you would lie to the holy Spirit?" (Acts 5,3). Later on Peter comments, "You have lied not to human beings, but to God" (5,4b). Here "holy Spirit" and "God" are juxtaposed and put on the same level.

39. Compare Acts 5,32, where the Spirit's testimony is compared with that of the apostles, Peter and John.

40. See also Acts 20,22, where Paul is said to be "bound" or "compelled" by the Spirit (δεδεμένος). Compare 21,4.

41. Contrast Eph 1,13-14, τῷ πνεύματι τῆς ἐπαγγελίας τῷ ἁγίῳ, ὅς ἐστιν ἀρραβὼν τῆς κληρονομίας ἡμῶν, as the words are read in MSS ℵ, D, Ψ, 33 and the Koine text-tradition. Is this a case of attraction of the relative pronoun to the gender of the predicate? Or the influence of patristic theology on the copyists?

42. To be noted is the absence in the Lucan writings of any term like πρόσωπον or ὑπόστασις, used of the Spirit, which would insure the meaning "person".

43. F.F. BRUCE, The Holy Spirit in the Acts of the Apostles, in Interpretation 27 (1973) 166-183, esp. p. 173. Bruce compares the Lucan mode of expression with 1QS 4,20-21; 9,3-4; CD 7,3-4. Similarly J.H.E. HULL, The Holy Spirit (n. 3), pp. 173-175.

44. The Acts of the Apostles: The Greek Text with Introduction and Commentary, Grand Rapids, MI, Eerdmans, 1951, p. 190.

Such Lucan passages, found in both the Gospel and Acts, stand apart from the way Luke speaks of the Spirit in what I might call the Old Testament way, the nonpersonified activity of the Spirit. These would include such expressions as "being filled with" or "full of" the holy Spirit; or as the Spirit "coming upon", "falling upon", "descending", "being poured out", or even as the Spirit being "promised" or "received", where πνεῦμα is sometimes to be understood symbolically in its more etymological sense of "breath, wind". In such expressions the Lucan usage does not move beyond the conception of the Old Testament, as it does, indeed, in the Lucan instances of personification.

In order to bring out the pertinence of some of these Lucan passages dealing with the Spirit to the question of the unity of Luke-Acts, I single out the following factors[45]. First, most frequently those who are considered favored with God's dynamic presence are said to be "filled with" (πιμπλάναι) or "full of" (πλήρης) the Spirit. This is found in both the Gospel (1,15 John the Baptist; 1,41 Elizabeth; 1,67 Zechariah; 4,1 Jesus) and in Acts (2,4a the assembled Christians on Pentecost; 4,8 Peter; 4,31 the Christians who pray at Peter's release from prison; 6,3 the Seven; 6,5 and 7,55 Stephen; 9,17 and 13,9 Saul; 11,24 Barnabas; and 13,52 disciples). The people who are so filled are either Jews or Jewish Christians, save in the last instance where μαθηταί is also used of Gentile Christians[46]. This idea of people being "filled with" the Spirit seems to be borrowed from the LXX of Sir 48,12, where the best Greek MSS say about Elisha ἐνεπλήσθη πνεύματος αὐτοῦ, "he was filled with his spirit," i.e. Elijah's spirit (an allusion to 2 Kings 2,9.13), but where MS A reads ἁγίου instead of αὐτοῦ[47]. Because the expression, "filled with the holy Spirit," does not occur as such in the LXX, its frequency is then significant as a Lucanism common to the two volumes and is a factor that contributes to the unity of Luke-Acts. It is an expression that serves to endow the persons so affected with the wherewithal to become agents of God's activity in human history, either in conversion, prophecy, or testimony.

Second, Luke depicts the Spirit "falling upon" (ἐπιπίπτειν), "coming upon" (ἐπέρχεσθαι), or "coming down" (καταβαίνειν) upon people in both the Gospel and Acts: on Mary (Luke 1,35), on Jesus (3,22), on Cornelius and his household (Acts 10,44; 11,15), on the "disciples"

---

45. See also R.F. O'TOOLE, *The Unity of Luke's Theology: An Analysis of Luke-Acts* (Good News Studies, 9), Wilmington, DE, Glazier, 1984, pp. 28-30 and 47-49.

46. This too is the only place where Luke uses πληροῦν with πνεῦμα, a usage that may depend on Wis 1,7, πνεῦμα Κυρίου πεπλήρωκεν τὴν οἰκουμένην, "the Spirit of the Lord has filled the universe".

of Ephesus baptized by Paul (Acts 19,6), or promised to the Eleven (Acts 1,8)[48]. Again, the common use of such verbs with πνεῦμα in the Gospel and Acts may be influenced by the LXX, for in Isa 32,15 one reads, ἕως ἂν ἐπέλθῃ ἐφ᾽ ὑμᾶς πνεῦμα ἀφ᾽ ὑψηλοῦ, "until a spirit from on high comes upon you", but ἐπιπίπτειν does not otherwise occur with "spirit" in the LXX.

Third, in all of this matter it is noteworthy how Luke speaks of the "gift" of the Spirit. The Lucan Jesus proclaims, "The heavenly Father will give the holy Spirit to those who ask him" (Luke 11,13), and Peter on Pentecost proclaims the same gift to those Jews in Jerusalem who ask what they must do: "Reform your lives and be baptized, everyone of you, in the name of Jesus the Messiah for the forgiveness of your sins, and you will receive the gift of the holy Spirit" (Acts 2,38). Implied in Peter's statement is that the gift comes from God. Compare too Acts 5,32; 8,18; 11,15; 15,8. Jewish Christians are even said to be bewildered that "the gift of the holy Spirit has been poured out on Gentiles too" (Acts 10,45). This gift may come from God or the Father, but it comes through the risen Christ.

Fourth, two passages about the Spirit in the Old Testament have influenced Luke in particular: Isa 61,1-2, which he quotes in his Gospel (4,18-19), and Joel 3,1-2 (2,28-29), which is cited in Acts (2,17-21). Each of them plays an important role in an early part of the two Lucan volumes, at the beginning of the public ministry of Jesus and at the beginning of formation of the Christian church. As G.W.H. Lampe has put it, "the connecting thread which runs through both parts [of the Lucan *opus*] is the theme of the operation of the Spirit of God"[49].

Conzelmann may be somewhat right in thinking that the Spirit in Luke-Acts is no longer regarded as God's gift at the eschaton, as Joel 3,1-2 might suggest, but has rather become a solution for the problem of the delayed parousia[50], "the substitute in the meantime for the posses-

47. The words πλησθήσεται πνεύματος are found in the LXX of Prov 15,4, but in an entirely different sense, having nothing to do with God's Spirit. Moreover, its Hebrew *Vorlage* is quite different.
48. Related to these expressions is εἶναι ἐπ᾽ αὐτόν (Luke 1,25), said of Simeon, to whom the Spirit communicates a message.
49. *The Holy Spirit in the Writings of St. Luke* (n. 3), p. 159. Cf. W.B. TATUM, *The Epoch of Israel* (n. 3), p. 185; H. VON BAER, *Der heilige Geist* (n. 3), pp. 43-112, esp. p. 43: "eines der Leitmotive im Aufbau des lukanischen Doppelwerkes". Von Baer is the one from whom Conzelmann derived his threefold division of Lucan salvation history: he speaks of the Spirit as (a) promised in the old covenant; (b) active in Jesus' public ministry; and (c) spread abroad in the church (pp. 111-112).
50. *The Theology of St Luke* (n. 26), p. 136.

sion of ultimate salvation"[51]. In reality, however, "what the Father has promised" (Luke 24,49) has already become in the Period of the Church the source of power for Christian missionary endeavor and endurance in the face of problems and persecution, but one can scarcely reduce the Lucan notion of the Spirit to that. Tatum has done well to insist on the Lucan portrayal of the role of the Spirit even in the Period of Israel, as the "period of preparation." This he does to correct Conzelmann's neglect of the infancy narrative in the study of Lucan theology. One must emphasize that in the Lucan writings it is the same Spirit that is promised for the *eschaton*, now inaugurated in the Period of the Church (Acts 1,4; 2,4.17)[52], which is active in the infancy narrative, the end of the Period of Israel, and at the inception of the public ministry, of the Period of Jesus. By referring to the Spirit twice as "the promise of my Father" (Acts 1,4; cf. Luke 24,49), and by relating the outpouring of it on Pentecost to the prophecy of Joel 3,1-2, Luke implies a distinct relation of the Spirit to the Old Testament, to Yahweh, precisely as Jesus' Father, and even to Jesus himself[53]. The relation of the Spirit to the Father is not further explained, except that in Acts 2,33 Luke makes Peter proclaim that Jesus, "exalted to God's right hand, has received from the Father the promised holy Spirit and poured it forth". This means that the Spirit is poured out anew. Although Luke may never appeal to a passage like Ezek 36,26, which promises a "new spirit" to be put within Israel, he seems to be thinking in this way. Hence Luke's use of Joel and his depiction of the Spirit operative in Israel and in the different periods of salvation history[54]. At the beginning of Acts the role of the Spirit is no longer seen as limited to an effect on John the Baptist or Jesus; all Israel is to be reconstituted anew through the outpouring of God's Spirit, which will also be poured out on Gentiles as they become part of reconstituted Israel.

To such a use of Joel in Acts one must relate that of Isa 61,1-2 in the Lucan Gospel. For one of the ways in which the Nazareth synagogue scene is programmatic for the Lucan two-volume work is the role that the Spirit plays as the public ministry of Jesus is initiated: "The Spirit of the Lord is upon me, for he has anointed me" (Isa 61,1). What Trito-Isa-

51. *Ibid.*, p. 95.

52. Recall the Lucan addition of ἐν ταῖς ἐσχάταις ἡμέραις to Joel's words in Acts 2,17.

53. See G. Stählin, τὸ πνεῦμα Ἰησοῦ (*Apostelgeschichte 16:7*), in B. Lindars and S.S. Smalley (eds.), *Christ and Spirit in the New Testament: In Honour of Charles Francis Digby Moule*, Cambridge, UK, University Press, 1973, pp. 229-252; R. Penna, *Lo 'Spirito di Gesù' in Atti 16: Analisi letteraria e teologica*, in *RivBib* 20 (1972) 241-261.

54. See further *The Gospel according to Luke* (n. 1), pp. 228-229.

iah spoke about centuries before now sees fulfillment in a new sense
"today" (Luke 4,21). Thus the start of Jesus' entire ministry is put under
the aegis of the Spirit of Yahweh.

The Spirit is thus seen not only as the creative and consoling presence
of God in Acts (9,31), but also as that of Jesus himself. The Spirit is not
merely "a solution to the problem of the delayed parousia", but the substitute for the risen Christ himself, when he is no longer physically present to his followers (Acts 16,7). Having taken his final leave from them
in the ascension, Christ will henceforth be "recognized" as present
among them in "the breaking of the bread" (Luke 24,35) and in "the
promise of my Father", poured out among them (Acts 1,4-5; 2,32-33).
Through the Spirit the risen Christ is present and active to his church
and thus carries his work forward.

An important aspect of the Spirit's role is presented in Acts, when it
is made clear that the Spirit is given only when the Twelve are present,
or a member of the Twelve, or one of their delegates is on the scene. For
the conferral of τὸ πνεῦμα makes the church a Spirit-guided Christian
community. The reconstitution of the Twelve (Acts 1,15-26) was a necessary preparation for the outpouring of the Spirit (2,1-4): the Twelve
not only had to confront the twelve tribes of Israel with their new proclamation and testimony, but as those on whom God's Spirit has been
poured out. They must also see to its further outpouring. This explains
why Philip, one of the Seven appointed to serve tables (Acts 6,2-6), may
evangelize Samaria and baptize there (8,5-13), but Peter and John have
to be sent to Samaria before the people there receive the Spirit (8,17).
Simon of Samaria explicitly notes that the Spirit was conferred by the
laying on of the apostles' hands (8,18). Similarly, only when Paul, indirectly a delegate of the Twelve (see 11,22.25-26; 13,2-4), arrives in
Ephesus, are "some disciples" (i.e. neophyte Christians) baptized "in
the name of the Lord Jesus" and receive the Spirit through the laying on
of his hands (19,1-6). The only exception to such a bestowal of the Spirit
is the case of Paul himself, who is baptized by Ananias of Damascus and
receives the Spirit through the laying on of his hands (9,17-18). This
obvious exception is made in Luke's narrative to stress the extraordinary
grace given to Paul[55]. He thereby becomes heaven's "chosen instrument" (or "vessel of election") to carry Jesus' name to Gentiles, kings,
and the children of Israel (9,15) and even Luke's hero in the second half
of Acts.

---

55. Recall that Paul is the only one to whom a post-pentecostal vision of the risen
Christ is accorded (Acts 9,4-6). This is true not only of the Lucan account, but even of
Paul's own letters (1 Cor 15,8).

Finally, we may note the effect of the Spirit on individual Christians in Acts. The reconstituted Twelve speak "in other tongues" (2,4.11), but others too experience something similar (10,45-46; 19,6). Individuals are emboldened by the Spirit to speak out forthrightly (4,31; 6,10). The Spirit's influence is related at times to "faith" of individuals (Stephen, 6,5; Barnabas, 11,23)[56], their "joy" (13,52), and "consolation" or "encouragement" (9,31). That influence is given to those who are baptized (2,38; 19,2)[57].

This description of the Spirit's role in the Gospel and Acts thus reveals how (τὸ) πνεῦμα ἅγιον is a major factor in the stress that must be given to the unity of Luke-Acts. In their book, M. C. Parsons and R. I. Pervo have reconsidered the unity of Luke-Acts under various aspects[58]. One of these aspects is the "theological unity", discussed in chap. 4. The "theology", however, quickly becomes "Lukan anthropology"; it is "no doubt a more subtle and possibly a less intentional component of Lukan theology than salvation history"[59]. Although Parsons and Pervo give some consideration to the Spirit, they are clearly more interested in the theological disunity of Luke and Acts in the way the Gospel depicts "the earthly Jesus" as "a human being, admittedly extraordinary. By virtue of his exaltation the Spirit that endowed him became available to all. This shift marks the fundamental demarcation and necessitates two separate volumes"[60]. Even if I were to agree with the difference in christology and anthropology that is involved in such a depiction, I would find it hard to see all this as a mark of *disunity*. Hence the stress that I have tried to put on the Spirit in this description of its role in the two-volume Lucan *opus*. I fail to see in Luke's treatment of the Spirit a sign of theological disunity.

Department of Biblical Studies   Joseph A. Fitzmyer
Catholic University of America
Washington, DC 20064
USA

---

56. Here one would have to consider Acts 19,2, where Paul asks Ephesian "disciples" whether they had received the holy Spirit when they "became believers" (πιστεύσαντες). Their answer, that they had not so much as heard that there was "a holy Spirit", creates a *crux interpretum*. The least one can say is that it is a Lucan way of emphasizing the role of the Spirit in Christian life and its relation to belief or faith.

57. See E. Schweizer, *The Holy Spirit*, Philadelphia, PA, Fortress, 1980, pp. 407-408.

58. *Rethinking the Unity of Luke and Acts*, Minneapolis, MN, Fortress, 1993.

59. *Ibid.*, pp. 89-90.

60. *Ibid.*, p. 113.

THE JEWS IN LUKE-ACTS

SOME SECOND THOUGHTS

Let me begin with a personal note: In all the years in which I have tried to work in the field of New Testament studies I have always kept a certain interest in Luke-Acts, i.e. in those two books of the New Testament, whose unity is the theme of this 47th Colloquium Biblicum Lovaniense. This interest is easy to explain. At the beginning of the 1960's Philipp Vielhauer was my "Doktorvater". His essay "On the 'Paulinism' of Acts" from 1950[1] had been the starting-point of a discussion on Luke's theology[2] that made the two volumes of Luke and Acts to "one of the great storm-centers of New Testament scholarship" (van Unnik) in the third quarter of this century (1950-1975)[3]. From the end of the sixties until his death in 1975 Ernst Haenchen took me as one of his discussion-partners. He called me up nearly every day for at least an hour, and we talked about the problems of interpreting Luke-Acts and the gospel of John. As you all know, Ernst Haenchen wrote one of the outstanding commentaries on Acts in this century[4]. His successor in the "Meyer-Kommentar" series, Jacob Jervell – his commentary was published just two months ago – has named it "the most comprehensive and important work of the critical German post-World War II research on

---

* My thanks go to all who reacted critically to my paper in Leuven, especially to Professor William C. Robinson, who took the trouble of formulating his criticism in a long letter and of correcting and improving the English of my text. For doing the latter, too, and expressing clearer some of my thoughts I thank my doctoral student Martin Dorn.

1. P. VIELHAUER, Zum "Paulinismus" der Apostelgeschichte (1950), in ID., Aufsätze zum Neuen Testament (TB, 31), München, Chr. Kaiser, 1965, pp. 9-27; in English in L.E. KECK – J.L. MARTYN (eds.), Studies in Luke Acts. Essays presented in honor of Paul Schubert, Nashville – New York, Abingdon, 1966, pp. 33-50.

2. From himself I know that VIELHAUER was quite surprised at the discussion his "little article" had stirred up. Cf. M. RESE, Zur Lukas-Diskussion seit 1950, in WuD 9 (1967) 62-67.

3. W.C. VAN UNNIK, Luke-Acts, A Storm Center in Contemporary Scholarship, in FS P. Schubert (n. 1), 15-32, 16. It is an entirely wrong picture of the history of New Testament research, which MERKEL, Israel (n. 13) assumes when stating that "for more than 40 years Luke-Acts has been a storm-center of New Testament research" (p. 371). SANDERS, Can Anything (n. 12), says of Merkel that he shies away from and "twist(s) the meaning of those statements in Luke-Acts that are hostile and defamatory toward Jews" (p. 309).

4. E. HAENCHEN, Die Apostelgeschichte (KEK, 3), Göttingen, Vandenhoeck & Ruprecht, 1956, ⁷1977; in English: E. HAENCHEN, The Acts of the Apostles. A Commentary, Oxford, Blackwell, 1971.

Acts, for which the names of Martin Dibelius, Philipp Vielhauer, Hans Conzelmann, and Ernst Käsemann stand"[5]. Nowadays many of those working on Acts consider the so-called "Dibelius-Haenchen-Conzelmann point of view"[6] as outdated – I do not, although I have never agreed with all of its judgements and results.

This is the background for my second thoughts on the theme "The Jews in Luke-Acts", which I will present in the following order. In the first part (I) of my paper there will be some repetition of my first thoughts on the theme (1) and a look at the further discussion of it within the last eight years (2). The second part (II) will move to the text of Luke-Acts and treat the difference between the Gospel of Luke and the Acts of the Apostles in mentioning the Jews (1) and the much discussed interpretation of Acts 28,17-31 (2). Finally (III) I shall draw some conclusions.

I

1. Some Repetition of My First Thoughts on "The Jews in Luke-Acts"

More than ten years have passed since I noticed that in Anglo-Saxon New Testament research there was quite some discussion going on about the Jews in Luke-Acts. In 1991 I reported on this discussion in the

---

5. J. JERVELL, *Die Apostelgeschichte* (KEK, 3), Göttingen, Vandenhoeck & Ruprecht, 1998: "das umfassendste und bedeutendste Werk der vor allem durch die Namen MARTIN DIBELIUS, PHILIPP VIELHAUER, HANS CONZELMANN und ERNST KÄSEMANN repräsentierten kritischen deutschen Nachkriegserforschung und -beurteilung der Apostelgeschichte" (p. 49). – At the same time JERVELL emphasizes that his own commentary represents "a decidedly different position over against that of its... predecessor" (p. 49), and on pages 50-51 he gives a convenient summary of this position. It is that well-known position, which JERVELL has consequently been taking and developing since 1965: J. JERVELL, *Das gespaltene Israel und die Heidenvölker. Zur Motivierung der Heidenmission in der Apostelgeschichte*, in *ST* 19 (1965) 68-96; = *The Divided People of God. The Restoration of Israel and Salvation for the Gentiles*, in ID., *Luke and the People of God. A New Look at Luke-Acts*, Minneapolis, MN, Augsburg Publishing House, 1972, 41-74; ID., *The Unknown Paul. Essay on Luke-Acts and Early Christian History*, Minneapolis, MN, Augsburg Publishing House, 1984; ID., *The Theology of the Acts of the Apostles*, Cambridge, University Press, 1996. JERVELL's new commentary is quite conservative as is shown by all the statements in which the historicity of events and speeches is explicitly stated, e.g.: "indeed there was a byelection of a Matthias as the twelfth apostle" (p. 130); "well, at Pentecost there was obviously a speech of Peter" (p. 153); "but the kernel of the narrative (sc. Acts 4,1-22) is certainly historical" (p. 183); "it is impossible to get rid of the story (sc. Acts 5,1-11) as unhistorical" (p. 199).

6. W. GASQUE, *A History of the Criticism of the Acts of the Apostles* (BGBE, 17), Tübingen, Mohr–Grand Rapids, MI, Eerdmans, 1975 (Peabody, MA, Hendrickson, ²1989), p. 250. Cf. the review by M. RESE in *TRev* 72 (1976) 375-377.

Festschrift for Gerhard Schneider under the titel "'The Jews' in Luke-Acts. A report on a long needed 'newer' discussion"[7]. Already the formulation of the title and subtitle gives some hints at the points I wanted to make with my report:

(1) By enclosing the plural "the Jews" within quotation marks I indicated that it was especially the use of this plural in Luke-Acts (5x in Luke, 79x in Acts, which quantitatively has its only parallel in John: 71x), which was incisively discussed and interested me, and not so much the question of the meaning of Israel in Luke-Acts. Both terms, "the Jews" and "Israel", are related to each other, of course, but they are not identical[8].

(2) Naming the discussion "a long needed" served to express two points, a) that the use of the plural "the Jews" had indeed not found much interest in the discussion about Luke's theology in 1950-1975, and b) that necessarily this lacuna had to be filled for any serious study of Luke-Acts.

(3) By bracketing the word "newer", attention should be called to the fact that at least some of those who worked in the field of the New Testament in the 19th century (the "Tendenzkritiker") had been aware of the problem of the use of the plural "the Jews" in Luke-Acts. Especially Franz Overbeck treated it in a way that, in my opinion, is still today worthwhile to be taken notice of[9].

I do not want to trouble you now by repeating the contents of my earlier report. Yet I should like to recall three of my conclusions:

(1) While the older interest in the use of the plural "the Jews" in Luke-Acts was related to the question of the purpose of Luke-Acts, apparently one of the most important incentives of the newer discussion was the broader question, if traces of antijudaism are to be found in

7. M. RESE, *"Die Juden" im lukanischen Doppelwerk. Ein Bericht über eine längst nötige "neuere" Diskussion*, in C. BUSSMANN – W. RADL (eds.), *Der Treue Gottes trauen. Beiträge zum Werk des Lukas. Für Gerhard Schneider,* Freiburg-Basel-Wien, Herder, 1991, pp. 61-79.

8. Cf. how cautiously this topic has been treated by P. RICHARDSON, *Israel in the Apostolic Church* (SNTS MS, 10), Cambridge, University Press, 1969, pp. 1-8. For a detailed discussion, see the monograph by G. HARVEY, *The True Israel. Uses of the Names Jew, Hebrew and Israel in Ancient Jewish and Early Christian Literature* (AGAJU, 35), Leiden – New York, Brill, 1996, and the review by D. SÄNGER in *TLZ* 123 (1998) 737-740.

9. By this point I did not want to claim that in the more recent discussion this fact was not noticed. Over against quite a number of the contributors one of the protagonists of the debate has been very well aware of it, i.e. J. T. SANDERS, *The Jews in Luke-Acts*, London, SCM Press, 1987.

the New Testament, a question placed in the context of the debate about the Christian roots of modern antisemitism.

(2) When dealing with the question of the purpose of Luke-Acts or of any other of the New Testament writings it is quite normal to take into consideration the intention and the situation of the author on the one hand, and on the other hand the needs and the situation of the addressees. In the newer discussion on "the Jews" in Luke-Acts it was different. Nearly everyone who took part in that discussion argued mainly out of the needs and the situation of the addressees, apparently convinced they were well-informed about them. In my opinion our knowledge of the needs and the situation of Luke's readers is purely hypothetical. Thus I pointed out that it would be much better to concentrate on the intention and situation of the author. Here all assumptions could be verified or falsified by looking at the text of Luke-Acts, at least to a certain degree. To emphasize my argument I quoted Overbeck's dictum that "to explain the problems of Acts by the needs of the readers of the book means to illuminate darkness by means of darkness"[10].

(3) Most of Luke's instances of the plural οἱ Ἰουδαῖοι are to be found in the context of Luke's description of Paul's mission in Acts. For assessing Luke's picture of "the Jews" theologically I recommended comparing it with Paul's own position as it is formulated in Romans 9–11, and I emphasized my recommendation by quoting Overbeck once again: "In the end the historical Paul can see himself as an apostle to the Jews, since for him the Gentiles are a means of converting the Jews, and thus even in his apostolate to the Gentiles the unforfeitable privileges of his people have been maintained. For Acts the Jews have been a means of converting the Gentiles, and Acts is essentially interested in proving that the privileges of the Jews have been forfeited by themselves. Hence in Acts the apology of Paul has been founded on an argument, by which Paul himself could never have argued, and the declarations in Acts 13,46f.; 18,6; 28,26ff. are of a harshness that would be unthinkable in the mouth of the author

---

10. W.M.L. DE WETTE, *Kurze Erklärung der Apostelgeschichte*, vierte Auflage bearbeitet und stark erweitert von F. OVERBECK, Leipzig, S. Hirzel, 1870: "Das Problem des Inhalts der AG. erklären mit den Bedürfnissen der Leser des Buchs… heisst Dunkles mit Dunklem zu erhellen" (p. XXVII); cf. RESE, *"Die Juden"* (n. 7), p. 77 n. 43. M.L. SOARDS, *The Speeches in Acts. Their Content, Context, and Concerns*, Louisville, KY, Westminster – John Knox, 1994, p. 207 n. 51 has rightly corrected my wrong page-number (XVII).

of Romans 9–11, while at the same time they expose the author of Stephen's speech all the more"[11].

2. A Look at the Discussion on "The Jews in Luke-Acts" in 1990-1998

There has been some further discussion in the last years, yet somehow there is more stagnation than progress, and not much has been left of the fierceness of the debate in the last decade. As then, the discussion has gone on mainly in English[12], even if there have been some publications

---

11. OVERBECK (n. 10): "Der histor(ische) Paul(us) kann sich daher im letzten Grunde als Judenapostel betrachten, sofern ihm die Heiden als Mittel zur Bekehrung der Juden gelten und er damit auch in seinem Heidenapostolat die unverwirkbaren Vorrechte seines Volkes gewahrt sieht. Der AG. sind die Juden Mittel zur Heidenbekehrung, und sie ist durchaus auf den Nachweis aus, dass die Vorrechte der Juden von ihnen selbst *verwirkt* sind. Die AG. gründet daher die Apologie des Paul(us) auf ein Moment, auf welches es dieser selbst nie gründen konnte, und die Erklärungen AG. 13,46f. 18,6. 28,26ff. sind von einer im Munde des Verf. von Röm. C(ap). 9-11 undenkbaren, den Verf. der Stephanusrede aber um so deutlicher verrathenden Härte" (p. 210 n. *); quoted by RESE, *"Die Juden"* (n. 7), pp. 71-72 n. 27.

12. For a well readable review of most of the questions of this discussion see C.M. TUCKETT, *Luke* (New Testament Guides), Sheffield, Academic Press, 1996, ch. 3: "Jews, Gentiles and Judaism" (pp. 51-71). See also F. BOVON, *Studies in Luke-Acts: Retrospect and Prospect*, in *HTR* 85 (1992) 175-196, pp. 186-190. — Publications in English from 1990-1998: R.A. BRAWLEY, *The God of Promises and the Jews in Luke-Acts*, in R.P. THOMPSON – T.E. PHILLIPS (eds.), *Literary Studies in Luke-Acts. Essays in Honor of Joseph B. Tyson*, Macon, GA, Mercer University Press, 1998, pp. 279-296; C.A. EVANS, *Is Luke's View of the Jewish Rejection of Jesus Anti-Semitic?* in D.D. SYLVA (ed.), *Reimaging the Death of the Lukan Jesus* (BBB, 73), Frankfurt a.M., Anton Hain, 1990, pp. 29-56 and 174-183; ID., *Introduction. Faith and Polemic. The New Testament and First-century Judaism*, in C.A. EVANS – D.A. HAGNER (eds.), *Anti-Semitism and Early Christianity. Issues of Polemic and Faith*, Minneapolis, MN, Fortress, 1993, pp. 1-17; V. FUSCO, *Luke-Acts and the Future of Israel*, in *NT* 38 (1996) 1-17; D.B. GOWLER, *Host, Guest, Enemy and Friend. Portraits of the Pharisees in Luke and Acts* (Emory Studies in Early Christianity, 2), New York, Peter Lang, 1991; J.D. KINGSBURY, *The Pharisees in Luke-Acts*, in F. VAN SEGBROECK – C.M. TUCKETT – G. VAN BELLE – J. VERHEYDEN (eds.), *The Four Gospels 1992. Festschrift Frans Neirynck* (BETL, 100), Leuven, University Press – Peeters, 1992, pp. 1497-1512; R.F. O'TOOLE, *Reflections on Luke's Treatment of the Jews in Luke-Acts*, in *Bib* 74 (1993) 529-555; T. E. PHILLIPS, *Subtlety as a Literary Technique in Luke's Characterization of Jews and Judaism*, in FS J.B. Tyson (see BRAWLEY), pp. 313-326; M.A. POWELL, *The Religious Leaders in Luke. A Literary-Critical Study*, in *JBL* 109 (1990) 93-110; H. RÄISÄNEN, *The Redemption of Israel. A Salvation-Historical Problem in Luke-Acts*, in P. LUOMANEN (ed.), *Luke-Acts. Scandinavian Perspectives*, Helsinki – Göttingen, 1991, pp. 94-114; D. RAVENS, *Luke and the Restoration of Israel* (JSNT SS, 119), Sheffield, Academic Press, 1995; J.T. SANDERS, *Who is a Jew and Who is a Gentile in the Book of Acts?*, in *NTS* 37 (1991) 434-455; ID., *Can Anything Bad Come Out of Nazareth, or Did Luke Think That History Moved in a Line or in a Circle?*, in FS J.B. Tyson (see BRAWLEY), pp. 297-312; R.P. THOMPSON, *Believers and Religious Leaders in Jerusalem: Contrasting Portraits of Jews in Acts 1-7*, in FS J.B. Tyson (see BRAWLEY), pp. 327-344; D.L. TIEDE, *"Fighting against God": Luke's Interpretation of Jewish Rejection of the Messiah Jesus*, in EVANS – HAGNER (eds.),

in German[13] and French[14]. Although some new methodological approaches ("reader-response criticism", etc.) have been tried, the contributions to the recent discussion still move in a circle around the interpretation of the Jews in Luke-Acts given by Ernst Haenchen and Jack T. Sanders. From Haenchen had come the harsh judgement: "For Luke the Jews are 'written off'", since in Acts "three times over – before the Jews of Asia Minor (13.46), Greece (18.6) and Rome (28.28) – it is explained that the Jewish people (λαός 28,26!) has forfeited its salvation"[15]. J.T. Sanders had sharpened Haenchen's interpretation and spoken of Luke's "antisemitism"[16]. To avoid too much repetition I will take up only those contributions which, in my opinion, are of importance for the discussion.

a. There are those who never had any problems with Luke's use of the plural "οἱ Ἰουδαῖοι". For Jervell the 84 occurrences of this plural in Luke-Acts (out of "192 occurrences... in the New Testament") are "mostly in a positive sense", "the rest" of the occurrences are "in John, and there to a great extent in a negative sense"[17]. Regarding Jervell's evaluation of the evidence in John nearly everybody will agree, yet his evaluation of the evidence in Luke-Acts is rather vague and open to criticism. To some degree it is to be understood on the background of Jervell's opinion that in Acts "from the beginning the mission to Jews was very successful, so that a significant portion of the people was con-

Anti-Semitism, 1993, pp. 102-112; J.B. TYSON, *Images of Judaism in Luke-Acts*, Columbia, SC, University of South Carolina Press, 1992; ID., *Jews and Judaism in Luke-Acts: Reading as a Godfearer*, in *NTS* 41 (1995) 19-38; J.A. WEATHERLY, *Jewish Responsibility for the Death of Jesus in Luke-Acts* (JSNT SS, 106), Sheffield, JSOT Press, 1994: cf. the review by M. RESE in *TLZ* 120 (1995) 1081-1082; L.M. WILLS, *The Depiction of the Jews in Acts*, in *JBL* 110 (1991) 631-654.

13. B.J. KOET, *Simeons Worte (Lk 2,29-32.34c-35) und Israels Geschick*, in F. VAN SEGBROECK, *et al.* (eds.), *The Four Gospels 1992* (n. 12), 1992, pp. 1549-1562; D. MARGUERAT, *Juden und Christen im lukanischen Doppelwerk*, in *EvT* 54 (1994) 241-264; = ID., *Juifs et chrétiens selon Luc-Actes. Surmonter le conflit des lectures*, in *Bib* 75 (1994) 126-146; H. MERKEL, *Israel im lukanischen Werk*, in *NTS* 40 (1994) 371-398; F. MUSSNER, *Die Erzählintention des Lukas in der Apostelgeschichte*, in ID., *Dieses Geschlecht wird nicht vergehen. Judentum und Kirche*, Freiburg – Basel – Wien, Herder, 1991, pp. 101-114 (= in FS G. Schneider, pp. 29-41); P. POKORNÝ, *Theologie der lukanischen Schriften* (FRLANT, 174), Göttingen, Vandenhoeck & Ruprecht, 1998, pp. 58-59; W. RADL, *Rettung in Israel*, in FS G. Schneider (n. 7), pp. 43-60; G. WASSERBERG, *Aus Israels Mitte – Heil für die Welt. Eine narrativ-exegetische Studie zur Theologie des Lukas* (BZNW, 92), Berlin – New York, de Gruyter, 1998.

14. MARGUERAT, *Juifs* (n. 12); A. VANHOYE, *Les Juifs selon les Actes des Apôtres et les Épîtres du Nouveau Testament*, in *Bib* 72 (1991) 70-89.

15. HAENCHEN, *Acts* (n. 5), p. 128.

16. SANDERS, *Jews* (n. 9), pp. XVI-XVII.

17. JERVELL, *Theology* (n. 6), p. 35 and n. 53.

verted... The church is a church primarily of Jews and for the Jews";
regarding the "Gentiles, non-Jews, in the church" Jervell maintains:
"The Gentiles of the church are God-fearers", and "Paul is a missionary
first to Jews, and only in addition to that and combined with this mission
does he turn to Gentiles", and "these Gentiles are the God-fearers,
whom Paul meets in the synagogues"[18].

   b. When J.T. Sanders contributed to the discussion about the Jews in
Luke-Acts once again in 1991, he sorted out two positions for criticism,
the equation of the Gentiles in the church with the "Godfearers" by
Jervell (and others), and the opinion of Salmon (and others) that "the
author of Acts, himself a Jewish-Christian, ... cannot condemn Jews
generally, since he knows himself to be a Jew", i.e. that Acts should be
seen "as an 'insider' document, as a family argument, so to speak"[19].
Against Jervell's presupposition, that Luke could understand τὰ ἔθνη
in a number of cases as "Godfearers", Sanders shows that there is not
"any precedent for such a use of the term by the author of Acts", neither by Paul, nor in other parts of the New Testament, nor in the Septuagint, nor by Josephus. In the opinion of Sanders this fact has also not
been refuted by Jervell's combination of the conversion of the God-
fearer Cornelius with Acts 11,18 ("So also to the Gentiles God has
given repentance unto life") and Acts 15,14 ("God has looked at getting from among the Gentiles a people for his name"), and therefore
Sanders happily affirms, "that the Gentiles in Acts are indeed Gentiles
and not God-fearers"[20]. As regards Salmon's argument based on the
Jewishness of the author of Acts Sanders demands at first that the
author should at least be "self-consciously Jewish", otherwise the argument would not work, and then he tries to prove in detail that the author

---

18. JERVELL, *Theology* (n. 6), p. 37.39.85. Cf. J. JERVELL, *The Church of Jews and
Godfearers*, in J.B. TYSON (ed.), *Luke-Acts and the Jewish People. Eight Critical Perspectives*, Minneapolis, MI, Augsburg Publishing House, 1988, pp. 11-20 and 138-140:
"The types of Gentiles who, according to Luke, belong to the church are exclusively
those who may be called Jewish Gentiles. That means proselytes, whom Luke does not
often mention and, above all, the socalled Godfearers or worshipers of God, that is, people with strong ties to Israel and the Law, who are members of the synagogue but are not
circumcised" (p. 12).
19. SANDERS, *Who is a Jew* (n. 12), p. 438. Sanders' criticism is directed against
Jervell (the article mentioned in n. 18) and M. SALMON, *Insider or Outsider? Luke's Relationship with Judaism*, in TYSON (ed.), *Luke-Acts*, pp. 76-83 and 149-150. As the title of
her article already indicates, Salmon works with the difference between insiders and outsiders: "Outsiders form opinions of people collectively, as a whole, what they are in their
essence, whether it is 'the Jews' or 'the Blacks' or 'Catholics' or 'women'. But that is not
the perspective of an insider... Spoken from the outside, harsh words are condemning;
from the inside, the same words are prophetic" (p. 77).
20. SANDERS, *Who is a Jew* (n. 12), pp. 442-443.447.455.

is not "self-consciously Jewish", but "understands himself to be a Gentile Christian"[21]. May I add that in my first report I already criticized the inner logic of the argument based on the Jewishness of the author of Acts, which assumes a postulated fundamental ontological difference between the language of insiders and that of outsiders. It seems to me to be contrary to logic and reality, if judgements about a group are only classified and assessed on account of the position of the judging person within or outside of that group, and the contents of the judgements are not taken into account[22]. Bad words and harsh judgements about a group remain bad words and harsh judgements, whoever makes use of them, an insider or an outsider.

Certainly Sanders has picked out two important positions for criticism. Both the "Godfearers" and the postulated Jewishness of the author do play quite a major part in the further discussion about the Jews in Luke-Acts, although with quite different accentuations.

c. With regard to the "Godfearers" the first one who should be mentioned is Joseph B. Tyson. His book "Images of Judaism in Luke-Acts" appeared in 1992; he abbreviated and summarized it in an article in 1995[23]. For Tyson "the implied reader in our texts is similar to those characters in Acts that are called 'Godfearers'"; he is generally characterized in Acts 10,35 ("in every people anyone who fears him [God] and does righteousness is acceptable to him" [my translation]), and the centurion in Luke 7 and the centurion Cornelius in Acts 10–11 are his "intratextual representation"[24]. For understanding the images of the Jews in Luke-Acts, and especially for answering the difficult question, how Luke-Acts "can be both pro-Jewish and anti-Jewish", Tyson suggests the following reading of the text: "The treatment of Jewish religion and people forms part of the rhetorical strategy used by the implied author in addressing the implied reader [the Godfearer]. Positive images of Judaism [in Luke 1–2; the scriptures; the reception of the preaching of Peter; the depiction of Paul as a faithful Jew] are consistent with the assumed attitudes of a Godfearer as he is first addressed. But negative images [Jews, who oppose Paul's mission; Acts 28,28 as the "final proclamation of the termination of the Pauline mission to the Jews"], which show the inferiority of Judaism to Christianity and help to explain Jewish rejection of the Christian message, urge the Godfearer to abandon the philo-Judaism with which he began...(and) to make a positive

21. *Ibid.*, pp. 438.451-454.455.
22. RESE, *"Die Juden"* (n. 7), p. 75.
23. TYSON, *Images* (n. 12); ID., *Jews* (n. 12).
24. ID., *Jews*, p. 25.

commitment about Jesus"[25]. For Tyson "the images [of Judaism] that seem more powerful are the negative ones", and the ending of Acts "leaves the reader with a memorable portrait of the Jewish people as obstinately imperceptive and unheeding"[26]. Tyson closes his article with the following statement: "Tragically, many flesh-and-blood readers have... found in these texts a justification not only for anti-Jewish polemic but even for oppressive and violent forms of anti-Semitism"[27].

Tyson's interpretation has two advantages: (1) It is done in close contact with the texts, and Tyson does not lose himself in historical speculations about the author or the addressees. (2) Tyson is well aware of the fact that New Testament texts have had and have a history of being read and used by Christians ("Wirkungsgeschichte"). But besides these positive comments I shall have to make a critical remark on Tyson's defining the Godfearer as implied reader. I shall leave aside the much discussed question, if the Godfearers are Lukan fiction or reality[28], and start by noting that there are others, who have tried to isolate the implied reader, and they have identified him differently. With the help of these different descriptions of the implied reader I shall formulate my criticism. For John A. Darr "it is an intimate knowledge of the Jewish scriptures in Greek [the Septuagint]", that "most clearly distinguishes Luke's reader from the vast majority of Greco-Roman readers in the late first century", and therefore he infers "that Luke-Acts is intended for a highly hellenized audience within the broad stream of Jewish tradition (Jews, whether Christian or non-Christian, 'god-fearers', and Gentile Christians)"[29]; by the way, I wonder how the "Gentile Christians" fit into "the broad stream of Jewish tradition". Expressly against Tyson's definition, Günter Wasserberg has pointed out, rightly, I think, that according to Luke 1,3-4 "every person who... has a Christian orientation comes into question as an implied reader"[30]. Nevertheless, I should like to add at once that my earlier mentioned reservations about speculating on the situation and the needs of the readers are relevant to the implied reader just as well.

25. ID., *Jews* (n. 12), pp. 37-38.

26. ID., *Images* (n. 12), p. 188.

27. ID., *Jews* (n. 12), p. 38.

28. For this question see J. MURPHY-O'CONNOR, *Lots of God-fearers: Theosebeis in the Aphrodisias Inscription*, in *RB* 99 (1992) 418-424, and WASSERBERG, *Aus Israels Mitte* (n. 13), pp. 44-54.

29. J.A. DARR, *On Character Building. The Reader and the Rhetoric of Characterization in Luke-Acts*, Louisville, KY, Westminster – John Knox, 1992, p. 28.

30. WASSERBERG, *Aus Israels Mitte* (n. 13): "Jeder, der im wörtlichen Sinne *christlich orientiert* ist, kommt als impliziter Leser in Betracht" (p. 66). On p. 67 n. 86 he notes his consent with Darr.

d. In the discussion about the Jews in Luke-Acts the argument of the Jewishness of its author has not often been used. The somewhat related, but different question, whether or not his thinking and arguing are Jewish, has always found much more interest, even among the growing number of those who think that the author of Luke-Acts was a Jewish Christian[31]. There is a good example of this situation in an article by David L. Tiede from 1993, published in a volume on "Anti-Semitism and Early Christianity"[32]. In 1980 Tiede had claimed that the author of Luke-Acts is a Jewish Christian, but more important for him was, that "the polemics... in Luke-Acts are part of an *intra-family* struggle that, in the wake of the destruction of the temple, is deteriorating into a fight over who is really the faithful 'Israel'"; the Gentiles were another problem, and here "Luke-Acts presents the contested case that in accepting the Gentiles *as Gentiles*, the church is nevertheless faithful to 'Moses and the Prophets'", yet "in the face of Israel's common plight, the rift between the synagogue and the church was probably unavoidable"[33]. In the following years Tiede has stressed and developed his understanding of the "intra-family struggle" in several articles[34], but neither in them nor in his article of 1993 does the presupposed Jewish Christian authorship of Acts play any role. In 1993, as before, Tiede has no doubt that Luke-Acts has to be "viewed... in its historical setting" towards the end of the first century. This does not mean, he emphasizes, a comparison of Luke-Acts to Paul or Mark. That would be "too narrow a base for determining whether or how Luke's narrative may be anti-Jewish [my proposal to compare Paul's attitude to the Jews in Acts with Romans 9-11 falls under this verdict]. Comparisons with other late first-century literature are more productive", and thus it is possible to show that Luke-Acts cannot be "anti-Jewish, at least not anti-Jewish in the way it will later be used by a dominant culture of gentile Christianity"[35].

In order to evaluate Tiede's contribution to the discussion on the Jews in Luke-Acts the positive remark I want to make is that Tiede like Tyson has been aware of what has happened to New Testament texts in the his-

31. Cf. the names referred to in my former report: RESE, *"Die Juden"* (n. 7), p. 75 n. 37; p. 76 n. 40. Add U. BUSSE, *Das "Evangelium" des Lukas. Die Funktion der Vorgeschichte im lukanischen Doppelwerk*, in FS G. Schneider (n. 7), pp. 161-179: Behind "Luke" one has to assume a "Diaspora-Jew" (p. 162 n. 6).

32. Cf. n. 12.

33. D.L. TIEDE, *Prophecy and History in Luke-Acts*, Philadelphia, Fortress, 1980, pp. 10.7.50.131.

34. Of these articles I mention only one: D.L. TIEDE, *"Glory to Thy People Israel" : Luke-Acts and the Jews*, in TYSON (ed.), *Luke-Acts* (n. 18), pp. 21-34 and 140-142; cf. my critical review in RESE, *"Die Juden"* (n. 7), pp. 72-73.

35. TIEDE, *"Fighting"* (n. 12), pp. 104-106.

tory of Christianity, and that he, when looking at the later history, speaks freely about the anti-Jewish use of New Testament texts. It remains open, however, how much Tiede's awareness informs his interpretation of the New Testament. As regards Tiede's classification of the polemics against the Jews in Luke-Acts as part of an "intra-family struggle", I want to emphasize that he was not the first to use this argument, and not the last[36]. I shall only pick out the use made of it in the volume "Anti-Semitism and Early Christianity", in which Tiede's article from 1993 appeared. In the editors' preface to this volume it is stated against Samuel Sandmel's and others' (e.g. J.T. Sanders) conclusion, that the New Testament is "permeated" by antisemitism[37]: "It is our con-tention..., that this conclusion is erroneous and rests upon a failure to appreciate the historical context of religious conflict and polemic within Judaism of the first century. The New Testament is... a collection of writings that reflect a primarily *Jewish intramural struggle* [my empha-sis]. New Testament polemic, we believe, parallels to a large degree the polemic that existed among various competing religious groups within Judaism"[38]. And as if this statement were not clear enough, one of the editors of the volume, Craig A. Evans, writes in his programmatic intro-duction: "In my judgment viewing the New Testament and the first two generations of early Christianity as anti-Semitic is hopelessly anachro-nistic... (and) fundamentally erroneous", since such a view is not aware of the historical fact that "early Christianity was one Jewish sect among several". Moreover, there exists *"confusion and faulty exegesis...* Exe-gesis, if it is truly exegesis, must be securely anchored in *history*. By 'history' I mean a given document's full context – the meaning of its language as seen against social, historical, religious, and traditional fac-tors... exegesis in in context must be *comparative*. Herein lies the prob-lem with the recent study... by Jack Sanders", for he "has not placed Luke's polemic and self-understanding in full context", but only offered "a close reading of the text... (and) never studied (it) in the light of con-temporary texts left behind by writers struggling with the same questions and issues"[39].

---

36. It had already been used by G. BAUM, *The Jews and the Gospel*, London 1961. Later Baum retracted this argument in his introduction to R.R. RUETHER, *Faith and Frat-ricide. The Theological Roots of Antisemitism*, New York, Seabury Press, 1974. Nowa-days this argument has become so widespread that it does not make much sense to name all those who use it.

37. S. SANDMEL, *Anti-Semitism in the New Testament?*, Philadephia, Fortress, 1978, p. 160.

38. EVANS – HAGNER (eds.), *Anti-Semitism* (n. 12), p. XIX.

39. EVANS, *Introduction. Faith and Polemic* (n. 12), pp. 11.16-17 (all italics my

This last quotation makes clear, for what the whole argument of a
"Jewish intramural struggle" stands. Historical facts or facts assumed to
be historical are taken up for attacking text-interpretations of other
exegetes and for defending one's own. This in itself is not a bad thing.
We all do it. What concerns me here is the very polemical attempt to
condemn other interpretations, an attempt based on a historical presupposition which is, at best, conjecture. As regards the relations between
Christians and Jews in the first century, the "Jewish intramural struggle"
is an open historical question which is misused here as a basis for intol-
erance. Moreover, in my opinion, "historicism", i.e. the excessive
regard for historical facts, has taken over in this kind of New Testament
exegesis.

II

1. The Difference Between the Gospel of Luke and the Acts of the Apostles in Mentioning the Jews

Statistics bring out the most obvious difference. Even if we all know
that statistics do not always tell the truth, yet at least they might indicate
some points of which one should take notice. The simple and important
fact is: While the term Jew(s) ('Ιουδαῖος / 'Ιουδαῖοι) is found in Acts
79x, it appears in Luke only 5x. This enormous difference in quantity is
all the more telling, if one takes into account that the relatively few
occurrences of 'Ιουδαῖοι in the Gospel of Luke do correspond with the
frequency of 'Ιουδαῖοι in the two other synoptic gospels (Mt 5x, Mk
6x), and that the great number of occurrences of the term Jew(s) in Acts
has only one parallel within the New Testament, the gospel of John
(71x). The one thing that surprises me is that Mikeal C. Parsons and
Richard I. Pervo did not take up as an argument this striking difference
between Luke and Acts when they tried "to underscore the division
between Luke and Acts" and proposed to replace Cadbury's hyphenated
Luke-Acts with "a far from superfluous 'and'"[40]. This astonishing oversight has not been caused by the rather general character of most of their

emphasis). How such a comparative exegesis looks like, EVANS had already shown by
criticizing Sanders in his article from 1990 (*Luke's View* [n. 12]). In his response to that
article SANDERS, *Can Anything* (n. 12), asks, "what help is it to introduce comparative
polemic in defence of Luke's polemic? 'Everyone else is doing it' is always the self-jus-
tification for everything from speeding on the highway to evading taxes to selling dope.
Is that the morality to which Evans wants to hold the New Testament?" (p. 307).
    40. M.C. PARSONS – R.I. PERVO, *Rethinking the Unity of Luke and Acts*, Minneapolis,
MN, Fortress, 1993, pp. v and 127.

arguments; instead, I think, the reason might be, that "proper names" had been omitted in John C. Hawkins' lists "on the linguistic relations between Luke's Gospel and Acts"[41] – and Parsons and Pervo know of these lists[42]. Apparently they did not notice that Hawkins had indicated in a foot-note to the list "Words and phrases rarely occurring in Luke, but frequently in Acts", that on a different page there is a note "on the use of Ἰουδαῖοι"[43]. However, more important than pointing to Parsons' and Pervo's oversight is to look for an explanation of the remarkable difference between Luke's and Acts' use of Ἰουδαῖοι, assuming, of course, that the two works do indeed belong together.

As far as I know, this difference has not yet played an important role in the discussion about the Jews in Luke-Acts. Other groups in Luke-Acts find much more interest, first and foremost the Pharisees[44], then "Israel", "the religious leaders"[45], or ὄχλος and λαός[46]. I shall leave aside these groups and concentrate on the difference between Luke's and Acts' use of Ἰουδαῖοι. The first thing to notice is that this difference is not just one of quantity, but also one of quality. In none of the five occurrences of Ἰουδαῖοι in Luke is the term used in a negative sense. Rather one can speak of a neutral use: in Lk 7,3 "elders of the Jews" of Capernaum are sent by a centurion to Jesus, in Lk 23,3.37.38 Jesus is named ὁ βασιλεὺς τῶν Ἰουδαίων, and in Lk 23,51 Arimathea is "a town of the Jews". As regards the 79 occurrences of Ἰουδαῖοι in Acts even Jervell would concede that in some of them the term has a negative meaning[47]. Already Acts 9,23 does not speak of "some Jews" of Damascus, who plotted to kill Paul, but of οἱ Ἰουδαῖοι. In Acts 12,3 Herod proceeds to arrest Peter, since it pleased "the Jews" that he had killed James the brother of John, and in Acts 12,11 Peter recognizes that God had sent his angel to rescue Peter from Herod and from all that the people of "the Jews" had been expecting. In Acts 13,43 many of the Jews

41. J.C. HAWKINS, *Horae Synopticae. Contributions to the Study of the Synoptic Problem*, Oxford, Clarendon Press, ²1909 (Reprint Oxford University Press, 1968), p. 175 n. 1.

42. Cf. PARSONS – PERVO, *Rethinking*, p. 53 and n. 34.

43. HAWKINS, *Horae*, p. 179 n. 1.

44. See, e.g., PARSONS – PERVO, *Rethinking*: "In Luke the Pharisees are willing to entertain and to listen to Jesus on occasion, but receive harsh criticism for their attitudes and practices. In Acts, however they are often supportive of the movement" (pp. 39-40). Parsons and Pervo have here taken up the opinio communis, which has lately been fully developed by GOWLER, *Host* (n. 12) and which has been fiercely attacked by DARR, *Character* (n. 29), ch. 4: "Observers Observed: The Pharisees and the Rhetoric of Perception" (pp. 85-126).

45. POWELL, *Religious Leaders* (n. 12).

46. MARGUERAT, *Juden* (n. 13), pp. 253-256.

47. This I infer from Jervell's "mostly in a positive sense" (see p. 190).

and of the devout proselytes still followed Paul after he had spoken to
them, but in Acts 13,45 suddenly there are "the Jews" who are filled
with jealousy and contradict the preaching of Paul. Also in Acts 13,50
"the Jews" incite the devout women of high standing and the chief men
of the city and stir up a persecution against Paul and Barnabas. And so
it goes on through all the mission of Paul.

What causes this difference between the use of Ἰουδαῖοι in Luke and
in Acts? My proposal is to explain this difference by taking account of
the different literary genres of Luke (gospel!) and Acts (religious narrative). The names for the genres are not significant; important is only the
fact that Luke and Acts do not belong to the same genre. It seems as if
it is impossible to depreciate the Jews in a gospel about Jesus, the "king
of the Jews" (ὁ βασιλεὺς τῶν Ἰουδαίων)[48], but possible in a narrative
of events and developments in post-Easter Christianity. I have to admit
that my proposal has an Achilles' heel and that it might invite wrong
conclusions about the unity of Luke-Acts. As regards the Achilles' heel:
There are gospels in which οἱ Ἰουδαῖοι is used negatively, namely the
gospel of John, with its well-known depreciation of "the Jews", and the
gospel of Mark, with its seldom noticed deprecatory πάντες οἱ
Ἰουδαῖοι in Mk 7,3. The latter instance does not carry so much weight
on account of its singularity in Mark, but what about John? My answer
sounds simple: John is not Luke! As everybody knows who has done
some work on the gospel of John, John differs from the three other
gospels in more than one regard. In whatever manner the peculiarity of
John is explained, most of the interpreters of John would agree on this
one point that in the gospel of John a theological understanding of Jesus
is more strongly fused with a theological understanding of the church
and of Christian existence than in the other gospels. John wrote only one
book and not two, and that makes all the difference. However, there is
also the gospel of Luke, and to this gospel there exists a sequel, the Acts
of the Apostles. Luke wrote two books, one about the "time of Jesus"
and another one about the "time of the church" – here I have taken up
Conzelmann's denotations quite consciously. In his two books Luke
could use the term Ἰουδαῖοι differently, perhaps because for him the
Jews had played different roles in the "time of Jesus" and in the "time
of the church". Even if this last assumption would have to be proved in
detail, nevertheless the difference between the use of the term Ἰουδαῖοι
in Luke and in Acts cannot be employed for doubting the unity of Luke-

48. It is this term that occurs in Mt 27,11 / Mk 15,2 / Lk 23,3; Mt 27,37 / Mk 15,26 /
Lk 23,38; Mt 27,29 / Mk 15,18; Mk 9,12; Lk 23,37.

Acts. On the contrary, this unity has been presupposed in the whole argument. Since Luke knew that he would be writing a sequel to his gospel, so I assume, he could withhold his criticism of "the Jews" in his first book, the gospel, in order to bring it up in his second book, Acts.

2. The Much Discussed Interpretation of Acts 28,17-31

Mussner has seen in the ending of Acts "a hermeneutical key for 'understanding' Acts"[49], and Wasserberg has even claimed that it functions as a key for understanding Luke-Acts on the whole[50]. That seems to me to be a "wee bit" exaggerated (judging a literary product from its end might apply to a detective story), and I prefer Tyson's view that "the ending of Acts, like narrative endings generally, functions to ease the reader out of the narrative and back into the real world"[51]. To be interested in the literary function in this way means that there is no need to worry about the much discussed question that the ending of Acts does not mention the end of Paul's trial or his martyrdom[52]. Rather one can concentrate on the question, what importance does the ending in Acts 28,17-31 have for Acts' picture of the Jews. I have already quoted Haenchen's conclusion based on Acts 28,28 ("Be it known to you now that this salvation of God has been sent to the Gentiles; they will listen"): "For Luke the Jews are 'written off'" (see p. 190). In the further discussion on the Jews in Acts three topics have found special attention.

a. In Acts 28,25 Paul states: "Rightly did the holy spirit speak to your fathers through the prophet Isaiah". The distancing "your fathers" is quite a change over against the inclusive "our fathers", which Paul had used in his first sermon to Israelites and Godfearers in Acts 13,17. This change has been noticed for a long time, and from this change, the Isaiah quotation (6,9-10) in Acts 28,26-27 and Paul's declaration in Acts 28,28, it has been inferred (to use the formulation of Peter Richardson): "Luke seems to seal Jewish rejection of the gospel"[53], and thus, in the words of Haenchen, "bases the justification of the Gentile mission on the refusal of the Jews"[54], as he had done more than once after Acts 13,46. – There are basically two arguments against this interpretation,

---

49. MUSSNER, Erzählintention (n. 13), pp. 105-132.
50. WASSERBERG, Aus Israels Mitte (n. 13), p. 71.
51. TYSON, Images (n. 12), p. 188.
52. For an informative review see HAENCHEN, Acts (n. 5), pp. 724-726 n. 3.
53. RICHARDSON, Israel (n. 8), p. 160. In n. 5 he points out that already R.B. Rackham noted the use of "your fathers". More recently it was used as an argument by TYSON, Images, 176; ID., Jews, p. 34 (wrongly comparing Acts 28,25 with Acts 28,17 and not with Acts 13,17).
54. HAENCHEN, Acts (n. 5), p. 730.

the last two words of the Isaiah quotation in Acts 28,27 and the term πάντες in Acts 28,30.

b. For François Bovon "there remains only one uncertainty", and he asks: "Is there a slight hope for the salvation of Israel expressed in the last phrase of the quotation, if one can read it in the future tense [ἰάσομαι instead of ἰάσωμαι], 'and I shall heal them'?". Bovon answers "this question positively"[55]. Marguerat follows him, as does Brawley[56]. Merkel is uncertain; on the one hand he emphasizes that for Paul God's hardening is not final (Rom 11,25-32), while Luke "does not speak directly" about this question; on the other hand he points out that the future tense of ἰάσομαι is the wording of the Septuagint[57]. By this latter he has outdone Bovon's "slight hope", and I do not know of any reason to revive it.

c. The πάντες in Acts 28,30, so Haenchen, "does not mean... 'Jews and Greeks', but rather... the unrestricted reception of all visitors, who are now to be considered as Gentiles"[58]. This interpretation has often been contradicted, mainly with the argument that the mission of Paul never excluded the Jews. After Acts 13,46 Paul started again to preach in the synagogue of Iconium (Acts 14,1), and in this way did all of his mission work take place. Why should it be different in Rome? Thus Marguerat writes: "With regard to the Jews this πάντες sounds more like opening a door than closing it"[59]. Yet I should like to ask, what will happen, when the door is opened? Nothing else than what has been happening all the time: The Jews would be expected to listen to Paul's preaching on the fulfillment of the scriptures in Jesus Christ and to obey; in short, the Jews would be expected to become Christians.

At the end of this section on Acts 28 it seems to me appropiate to lead your attention once again (after having done it above; see p. 188) to the

---

55. BOVON, *Studies in Luke-Acts* (n. 12), pp. 189-190. Cf. his article from 1984: *"Schön hat der heilige Geist durch den Propheten Jesaja zu euren Vätern gesprochen" (Act 28,25)*, in ZNW 75 (1984) 226-232: "Lukas hat uns nämlich nicht verboten, die Worte καὶ ἰάσομαι αὐτούς und vielleicht auch καὶ ἐπιστρέψωσιν, wo oft auch καὶ ἐπιστρέψουσιν gelesen wird (die Verwechslung zwischen ω und ου ist wohlbekannt), unabhängig von μήποτε (v. 27) *positiv* als Ausdruck einer letzten Hoffnung für Israel aufzufassen" (p. 230).

56. MARGUERAT, *Juden* (n. 13), p. 261; BRAWLEY, *God of Promises* (n. 12), p. 294. Already KOET, *Simeons Worte* (n. 13) had declared, that "gerade der LXX-Text doch die Tür für eine Bekehrungsmöglichkeit offen(hält).... In der LXX bleibt Gott, trotz der Haltung des Volkes, bereit, es dennoch zu retten ('und ich werde sie heilen')" (p. 1554).

57. MERKEL, *Israel* (n. 13), p. 396 and n. 88. For the details of the text and grammar of the Isaiah quotation, see in this volume W. RADL, *Die Beziehungen der Vorgeschichte zur Apostelgeschichte, dargestellt an Lk 2,22-39* (below, pp. 297-312).

58. HAENCHEN, *Acts* (n. 5), p. 726.

59. MARGUERAT, *Juden* (n. 13), p. 261.

difference between Romans 9–11 and Acts 28,17-31. While in Romans 9–11 Paul himself thinks and writes about God's salvation for the unbelieving Jews, the last word spoken by the Paul of Acts is a condemnation of "the Jews", and in the last chapter of Acts there is not the slightest trace of an interest in the fate of the unbelieving Jews.

III

To conclude my second thoughts on the Jews in Luke-Acts I shall stress two points which have to do with the role of history in exegesis and which have been repeatedly indicated in my paper.

1. It has troubled me quite a bit how little awareness there is of what in German is called "Wirkungsgeschichte", which means the fact that the text of the New Testament has been and will be used by Christians and non-Christians. This use had and has results, intended ones and others. New Testament scholars should know of that use and of these results and try to judge them and to find out to what degree the old texts of the New Testament have been misused or have been themselves the cause of the effects in later use.

2. Although the increasing spread of historicism in New Testament exegesis has not surprised me[60], I cannot see anything good in this manner of scholarship. I admit that there are serious and diligent women and men at work. But in my opinion apologetics which attempt to protect the innocence of the Christian faith and Bible play too big a role in this type of research and interpretation, and many of the results are simply twisted. As scholars we need to be a little more self-critical – of our own shortcomings and of the problems in the material we are researching. More than two hundred years ago Lessing spoke about the accidental truths of history that never can prove the truths of revelation. Why should we not take this warning seriously, especially those of us, who do their New Testament research as theologians? I for my part shall try to give heed to this warning.

Rudolf-Harbig-Weg 23   Martin RESE
D-48149 Münster/Westf.

---

60. Already in 1982 I raised this point when critically evaluating the programmatic booklet by M. HENGEL, *Zur urchristlichen Geschichtsschreibung*, Stuttgart, Calwer Verlag, 1979; see M. RESE, *Zur Geschichte des frühen Christentums – ein kritischer Bericht über drei neue Bücher*, in *TZ* 38 (1982) 98-110, esp. pp. 100-101.

DIE HALTUNG DES LUKAS ZUM RÖMISCHEN STAAT
IM EVANGELIUM UND IN DER APOSTELGESCHICHTE

Eine Einheit von Evangelium und Apostelgeschichte des Lukas fällt bei der Betrachtung der Haltung ihres Verfassers zum römischen Staat schon bei oberflächlicher Lektüre mehrfach und prononciert auf. In beiden Werken steht eine Verhandlung vor römischen und ihnen zuge-ordneten jüdischen Behörden an exponierter Stelle: einerseits das Ver-hör Jesu (Lk 22,1–23,56), andererseits das langwierige Prozeßverfah-ren gegen Paulus, angefangen von der Festnahme in Jerusalem bis zur Ankunft in Rom (Apg 21,15–28,31). In beiden Gerichtsszenen wird die Anklage von jüdischer Seite erhoben, von römischer Seite hinge-gen betont die Unschuld der Angeklagten festgestellt. Zugleich erscheinen in beiden Werken die Jesusbewegung und die apostolische Mission an keiner Stelle als eine ernsthafte Gefährdung für den römi-schen Staat, da der unpolitische Anspruch mehrfach festgehalten wird. Wenn Aufruhr, στάσις/*seditio* (Lk 23,19.25; Apg 19,40; 24,5) oder θόρυβος/*tumultus* (Apg 20,1; 21,34; 24,18), in den Blick kommt, dann geht er in der Regel von jüdischer, nicht von christlicher Seite aus. Der römische Staat andererseits, vertreten durch seine Behörden vor Ort, nimmt das Christentum in Schutz, und die Apg beschließt den Prozeß des Paulus, der unter dem vertrauensvollen Ausblick auf die Appellation an den römischen Kaiser steht (Apg 25,11), mit einem Hinweis auf den in Rom ungehindert verkündigenden Apostel (Apg 23,11; 28,30-31).

Diese Tendenz innerhalb des Doppelwerks wurde von dem Göttinger Gelehrten Christoph August Heumann 1721 auf den Begriff gebracht[1]. Sie hat sich seitdem als lukanische Apologetik in der Einleitungswissen-schaft festgesetzt, wenngleich dieser Begriff nicht allein auf die politi-sche Zielsetzung zu begrenzen ist, sondern literaturwissenschaftlich in einen weiteren Kontext einzuordnen ist. Die redaktionsgeschichtliche Analyse des lukanischen Doppelwerks durch Hans Conzelmann hat den Begriff der lukanischen Apologetik aufgenommen und von ihr als einem nicht zufälligen, sondern aus grundsätzlicher Besinnung resultierenden

---

1. C.A. HEUMANN, *Dissertatio de Theophilo, cui Lucas historiam sacram inscripsit*, (Bibliotheca Historico-Philologica-Theologica, Class. IV), 1721, pp. 483-505. Dieser Hinweis findet sich bei W. GASQUE, *A History of the Criticism of the Acts of the Apostles* (BGBE, 17), Tübingen, Mohr, 1975, pp. 21-22.

Element gesprochen². Allerdings hat die jüngere Forschung gezeigt, daß Lukas unbeschadet dieser grundsätzlichen Tendenz doch auch um Differenzierungen bemüht ist³.

Nicht in der Grundtendenz, aber doch an ihren historischen Rändern und literarischen Zielsetzungen stellt sich die Erklärung der lukanischen Apologetik uneinheitlich dar. Bietet Lukas eine Apologie der Kirche vor dem römischen Staat oder eine Apologie des römischen Staates vor der Kirche? Wer sind seine Leser, welche impliziten und potentiellen Leser hat er vor Augen? Schreibt Lukas auch für heidnische, römische Leser? Will er sie zu einer bestimmten Einstellung bewegen? Ist seine Darstellung von aktuellen Gemeindeerfahrungen geleitet, etwa einer akuten Verfolgungssituation der christlichen Gemeinde durch römische Behörden? Weshalb diese ausführliche Darstellung des Prozesses des Paulus mit der Einführung seines römischen Bürgerrechts, ohne über den Ausgang dieses Prozesses zu berichten? Ist dies gerade die Spitze der apologetischen Ausrichtung in dem Sinne, daß an Paulus paradigmatisch eine Klärung der christlichen politischen Einstellung herbeigeführt und aus lukanischer Sicht abwegige Meinungen abgewiesen werden sollen? Verfolgt er überhaupt mit der Apologetik ein klar erkennbares politisches Ziel, oder handelt es sich, wie Conzelmann sagt, um eine »grundsätzliche Besinnung heilsgeschichtlicher Art«⁴?

Es ist im folgenden zunächst der wesentliche exegetische Befund festzuhalten⁵, sodann sind Beiträge aus der exegetischen Diskussion vorzu-

---

2. H. CONZELMANN, *Die Mitte der Zeit. Studien zur Theologie des Lukas* (BHT, 17), Tübingen, Mohr, ⁵1964, p. 139; aber auch schon R. BULTMANN, *Die Geschichte der synoptischen Tradition* (FRLANT, 29), Göttingen, Vandenhoeck & Ruprecht, ⁸1970, p. 392, in dem Abschnitt der Behandlung der Redaktion des Traditionsstoffes.

3. Vgl. etwa zuletzt L. BORMANN, *Die Verrechtlichung der frühesten christlichen Überlieferung im lukanischen Schrifttum*, in L. BORMANN – K. DEL TREDICI – A. STANDHARTINGER (eds.), *Religious Propaganda and Missionary Competition in the New Testament World. Essays Honoring Dieter Georgi* (NTSup, 74), Leiden, Brill, 1994, pp. 283-311; W. STEGEMANN, *Zwischen Synagoge und Obrigkeit. Zur historischen Situation der lukanischen Christen* (FRLANT, 152), Göttingen, Vandenhoeck & Ruprecht, 1991; H.W. TAJRA, *The Trial of St. Paul. A Juridical Exegesis of the second Half of the Acts of the Apostles* (WUNT, 2/35), Tübingen, Mohr, 1989; ID., *The Martyrdom of St. Paul* (WUNT, 2/67), Tübingen, Mohr, 1994; B. RAPSKE, *The Book of Acts and Paul in Roman Custody* (The Book of Acts in Its First Century Setting, 3), Grand Rapids, MI, Eerdmans – Carlisle, Paternoster Press, 1994. — Exakt am 30.7.1998, an dem Tag also, an dem ich diesen Vortrag in Löwen hielt, erschien in der an eben diesem Tag überreichten Festschrift für W. Schrage der Beitrag von M. WOLTER, *Die Juden und die Obrigkeit bei Lukas*, in K. WENGST und G. SASS (eds.), *Ja und nein. Christliche Theologie im Angesicht Israels. Festschrift zum 70. Geburtstag von Wolfgang Schrage*, Neukirchen, Neukirchener Verlag, 1998, pp. 277-290, auf den ich hier nur noch verweisen kann.

4. CONZELMANN, *Mitte* (n. 2), p. 139.

5. Vgl. etwa die Zusammenstellung bei CONZELMANN, *Mitte*, pp. 128-135; W. SCHRAGE, *Ethik des Neuen Testaments* (GNT, 4), Göttingen, Vandenhoeck & Ruprecht, ²1989, pp. 162-164.

stellen, schließlich soll die eigene Sicht dargelegt werden. Für sie spielt die Darstellung der Herodesfamilie im lukanischen Doppelwerk eine wesentliche Rolle.

I. Der exegetische Befund

Die apologetische Tendenz ist nicht auf die beiden Prozeßberichte reduziert, sondern durchgehend zu finden[6]. Es können hier aber nicht alle Belege im Doppelwerk ausführlich gewürdigt werden. Eine gewisse Beschränkung auf zentrale Aussagen, eben auf die Prozeßberichte, ist zunächst – auch im Sinne der Fragestellung nach der Einheit von Evangelium und Apostelgeschichte – unumgänglich[7].

1. Das Verhör Jesu

Nach dem Verhör vor dem Hohen Rat (Lk 22,63-71) wird Jesus Pilatus vorgeführt (Lk 23,1-25). Die von den Synhedristen vorgebrachte Anklage »wir haben gefunden, daß dieser unser Volk aufhetzt und verbietet, dem Kaiser Steuern zu geben, und spricht, er sei ein gesalbter König« (Lk 23,2) kann vom Leser, was die Steuerfrage betrifft, leicht als Lüge erkannt werden. In Lk 20,22-26 hat Jesus die Kaisersteuer bejaht. Dieser konkrete Vorwurf spielt im Verhör keine Rolle mehr. Pilatus orientiert sich an der dreimal erwähnten Anklage subversiven Verhaltens, die Jesus in die Nähe des Zelotismus stellt (Lk 23,2: διαστρέφοντα τὸ ἔθνος ἡμῶν; Lk 23,5: ὅτι ἀνασείει τὸν λαόν; Lk 23,14: ἀποστρέφοντα τὸν λαόν)[8], um nun und im folgenden insgesamt dreimal die Schuldlosigkeit Jesu festzustellen (23,4.14.22 diff Mk).

Ausschließlich Lk berichtet im Zusammenhang der Urteilsfindung über die Begegnung Jesu mit Herodes Antipas, die gleichfalls mit der Erklärung der Schuldlosigkeit Jesu schließt (23,15). Wiederum dreimal

---

6. Grundlegende jüngere Arbeiten zum Thema haben die Belege im Doppelwerk umfassend analysiert: P.W. WALASKAY, 'And So We Came to Rome'. The Political Perspective of St. Luke (SNTS MS, 49), Cambridge, University Press, 1983; R.J. CASSIDY, Society and Politics in the Acts of the Apostles, Maryknoll – New York, Orbis, 1987; ID., Jesus, Politics, and Society: a Study of Luke's Gospel, Maryknoll – New York, Orbis, 1978; P.F. ESLER, Community and Gospel in Luke-Acts. The Social and Political Motivations of Lucan Theology (SNTS MS, 57), Cambridge, University Press, 1987.
7. In weitgehender Parallelität werden hier nacheinander berichtet: a) Verhör vor dem Synhedrium (Lk 22,26/Apg 23,1-11); b) vor dem römischen Beamten Pilatus (Lk 23,1-5) bzw. Felix/Festus (Apg 24,1-21; 25,1-12); c) vor Antipas (Lk 23,6-12) bzw. Agrippa (Apg 25,13–26,32); und d) Unschuldserklärung der Beteiligten (Lk 23,13-16/Apg 26,31f).
8. Darauf deuten hin: a) die Verweigerung der Kaisersteuer war zentraler Bestandteil der Verkündigung des Judas Galiläus (vgl. Josephus, Bell 2,118); b) das Auftreten Jesu wird in Lk 23,5 betont an seinen galiläischen Ausgangspunkt angebunden; die Wurzeln der jüdischen Widerstandskämpfer liegen in Galiläa; c) Jesus wird von Pilatus als messianischer Thronprätendent angesprochen (Lk 23,3).

kündigt Pilatus seine Absicht, Jesus freizulassen, an (23,16.20.22 diff
Mk), läßt sich aber durch das Geschrei der Synhedristen und des Volks
von seinem Plan abbringen. In der lk Darstellung des Verhörs Jesu voll-
zieht sich daher die Einwilligung des Pilatus in den Wunsch der Juden
(Lk 23,24) und die Übergabe Jesu an sie (Lk 23,25 diff Mk: τὸν δὲ
Ἰησοῦν παρέδωκεν τῷ θελήματι αὐτῶν). Nach Pilatus und Herodes
Antipas stellt schließlich der Verbrecher am Kreuz die Unschuld Jesu
fest (Lk 23,41 diff Mk: οὐδὲν ἄτοπον ἔπραξεν), und der römische
Hauptmann betont in Lk 23,47 diff Mk: ὁ ἄνθρωπος οὗτος δίκαιος
ἦν.

Innerhalb der lk Passionsgeschichte wird also derjenige, der wegen
στάσις und φόνος (Lk 23,19) gefangengenommen wurde, auf das Drän-
gen der Juden hin freigelassen, und derjenige, dessen Unschuld Pilatus,
Herodes, der Hauptmann und der Verbrecher bestätigt haben, verurteilt.
Die Tötungsabsicht bringt die Hohenpriester und Schriftgelehrten
schließlich nicht nur in einen Gegensatz zu den Genannten, sondern
auch zu einem großen Teil des jüdischen Volks (Lk 22,2 diff Mk 14,2;
Lk 23,27.48)[9].

Die Verse Lk 23,2.4f.6-12.13-16.22.27-32.39-43.48, Textteile also, in denen
sich diese Überlieferung findet, haben bekanntlich keine Entsprechung in der
mk Passionsgeschichte. Dies berührt die Frage, ob Lukas innerhalb der Passionsgeschichte auf eine von Mk unabhängige Passionsgeschichte, zumindest aber
auf einen größeren Komplex schriftlichen Sonderguts zurückgreifen konnte. Ein
Blick auf die Kompositionstechnik innerhalb der Apg legt m.E. nahe, daß Lukas
auch in seiner Passionsgeschichte unter theologischen Zielsetzungen kompo-
niert, dabei traditionelles Einzelmaterial einarbeiten kann, nicht aber einer
nebenmarkinischen Quelle folgt[10].

Für die Annahme, daß die in dieser Überlieferung zum Ausdruck
kommende Apologetik ein redaktionelles Interesse wiedergibt[11], spricht
die entsprechende Bearbeitung der Markusvorlage innerhalb der Passi-

9. Zum Thema: R.L. BRAWLEY, *Luke-Acts and the Jews. Conflict, Apology and Conciliation* (SBL MS, 33), Atlanta, GA, Scholars Press, 1987.
10. Zur Diskussion grundsätzlich: W. RADL, *Das Lukas-Evangelium* (EdF, 261),
Darmstadt, Wissenschaftliche Buchgesellschaft, 1988, pp. 28-41; zuvor bereits *Paulus
und Jesus im lukanischen Doppelwerk. Untersuchungen zu Parallelmotiven im Lukas-
evangelium und in der Apostelgeschichte* (EHS, 23/49), Frankfurt-Bern, Peter Lang,
1975. Zu Lk 23,1-25: F.J. MATERA, *Jesus Before Pilate, Herod, and Israel*, in F.
NEIRYNCK (ed.), *L'Évangile de Luc. The Gospel of Luke* (BETL, 32), Leuven, University
Press – Peeters, 1989, pp. 535-551.
11. Die Entlastung der Römer und die Belastung der Juden kennzeichnet die Redaktion in jedem Evangelium, und sie wird in jedem Fall mit sog. Sondergut vorgetragen;
vgl. auch Mt 27,19.24f; Joh 19,11. Man muß vermuten, daß diese christliche Geschichts-
perspektive durch die Folgen und die Deutungen des jüdischen Kriegs eine erhebliche
Verstärkung erfuhr.

onsgeschichte. Lukas streicht die Anklage der falschen Zeugen (Mk 14,57f) und die hierauf blickende Verspottung Jesu mit dem Tempelwort (Mk 15,29f), nimmt in der Verarbeitung dieses Logions in Apg 6,14 auch nicht mehr Bezug auf die politisch zumindest mißverständliche Ansage, Jesus wolle einen neuen Tempel bauen[12]. Die Verspottung Jesu durch die römischen Soldaten (Mk 15,16-20a) entfällt bei Lukas, was zur Entlastung der Römer beiträgt. Gleichfalls wird die durch Pilatus vollzogene Züchtigung mit παιδεύσας (Lk 23,16) gegenüber φραγελλώσας (Mk 15,15/Mt 27,26) verharmlosend beschrieben.

Innerhalb des Verhörs kommt es nur in der lukanischen Darstellung zu einer Begegnung Jesu mit Herodes Antipas, dem Tetrarch von Galiläa und Peräa und dem Landesherrn Jesu. Pilatus arrangiert dieses Treffen, schaltet also die zuständige Instanz mit ein, nachdem er erfahren hat, daß Jesus Galiläer ist. Präzisere Motive nennt Lukas nicht. Die Begegnung trägt für die Urteilsfindung nichts aus. Herodes Antipas erwartet von Jesus, dem Magier, ein Zeichen, was ihm nicht gewährt wird. Alle Fragen des Tetrarchen bleiben unbeantwortet[13]. Die Begegnung schließt mit einer Verspottung und Rücksendung Jesu zu Pilatus, was in Lk 23,15 als Entlastung Jesu durch Herodes Antipas interpretiert wird.

Da Herodes Antipas sich an Festtagen in Jerusalem aufhielt, kann man historisch die Möglichkeit einer Begegnung mit Jesus nicht ausschließen (vgl. auch Apg 4,27f). Es entspricht allerdings in keiner Weise der römischen Rechtspraxis, das Urteil durch einen Klientelfürsten aus einer anderen Provinz sprechen zu lassen[14]. Pilatus hätte allenfalls die Angelegenheit ganz abgeben können. Will Lukas Pilatus als korrekt und verantwortlich handelnden, der Wahrheitsfindung verpflichteten Beamten darstellen[15]? Die lukanische Darstellung hält sich, was den Fortgang

12. In Apg 6,14 beziehen sich die Falschzeugen, die Stephanus verklagen, nicht auf Jesu Ansage des Tempelneubaus, sondern auf seine Änderung der Ordnungen, die Mose gegeben hat. Man kann fragen, ob Jesu Ansage eines neuen Tempels, wenige Jahre nach dem in dem Logion angesagten, in Wirklichkeit ja von römischen Soldaten ausgeführten Falls des herodianischen Tempels, politische Brisanz hatte. — Nach B. KINMAN, *Jesus' Entry into Jerusalem in the Context of Lukan Theology and the Politics of His Day* (AGAJU, 28), Leiden, Brill, 1995, p. 177, verkürzt Lukas die Tempelreinigung aus apologetischen Gründen, um Jesus von den Zeloten zu distanzieren.
13. Die Verweigerung einer Antwort vor Herodes, nicht aber vor Pilatus (diff Mk 15,5), dient nach G. SCHNEIDER, *Das Evangelium nach Lukas* (ÖTK, 3/2), Gütersloh, Gütersloher Verlagshaus, 1977, p. 475, »dem Anliegen politischer Apologie des Christentums vor dem Urteil Roms«.
14. Vgl. J. BLINZLER, *Der Prozeß Jesu*, Regensburg, Pustet, ⁴1969, p. 285.
15. So BORMANN, *Verrechtlichung* (n. 3), p. 302: »Das juristische Interesse des Lukas führt zur Aufnahme der Sonderüberlieferung in Lk 23,4-16, die ein korrektes polizeiliches Verhör, die Einschaltung der zuständigen Instanzen (Herodes, weil Jesus Galiläer ist) und als Ergebnis dieser Untersuchung die Unschuldsvermutung des Pilatus bringt (V. 14-16)«.

des Verhörs betrifft, sehr bedeckt, zielt aber auf die Bemerkung, daß
Pilatus und Herodes Antipas an diesem Tag Freunde wurden[16].

Was aber will Lukas letztlich mit dieser Begegnung Herodes/Jesus
andeuten? Es wird der jüdische Tetrarch, der aus Roms Gnaden regiert,
betont von den Hohenpriestern und Schriftgelehrten abgesetzt (Lk
23,10.15). Er stimmt nicht ihrem Urteil, sondern dem des Pilatus zu,
klagt nicht Jesus an, sondern entlastet, wenngleich Lukas an keiner
Stelle das Verhalten des Herodes Antipas gegenüber Jesus verharmlost
oder beschönigt. Die Freundschaft zwischen Pilatus und Herodes Antipas, so muß der Leser annehmen, wird begründet durch die Übereinstimmung in einer politischen Angelegenheit. Die lukanische Apologetik
umgreift alle, die auf Roms Seite stehen. Natürlich ist es bedeutsam, daß
ein weiterer Zeuge auftritt, um Jesu politische Unschuld zu betonen.
Wesentlich für die lukanische Zielsetzung ist aber wohl die zuerst
genannte, nämlich Rom entlastende Funktion.

Im Zusammenhang der Gesamtkonzeption des lukanischen Doppelwerks verdienen zwei weitere Aspekte synchroner Textbetrachtung Aufmerksamkeit.
Zum einen hat allein Lukas Herodes Antipas zuvor im Evangelium so eingeführt, daß der Leser eine Begegnung Jesu mit Herodes Antipas geradezu erwartet. Nach Lk 9,9 (diff Mk 6,16) begehrt Herodes, Jesus zu sehen, nach Lk 13,31,
erneut einem Text des lukanischen Sonderguts, trachtet Herodes nach dem
Leben Jesu. Dieser aber läßt Herodes ausrichten, ein Prophet müsse in Jerusalem umkommen (Lk 13,33). Lukas schließt hieran aus der Logienquelle die
Wehklage über Jerusalem unmittelbar an (Lk 13,34-35/Mt 23,37-39). Im
Zusammenhang der heilsgeschichtlichen Linienführung ist deutlich, daß Herodes zwar feindliche Gesinnung gegenüber Jesus haben kann, aber niemals als
derjenige auftreten wird, der Jesus zum Tode verurteilen wird. Die Stadt Jerusalem, nach Lk 23,10 ihre Hohenpriester und Schriftgelehrten, ist verantwortlich
für seinen Tod[17].

16. Es wurde also diese Freundschaft durch das Verhör Jesu begründet. Die Suche
nach einem historischen Haftpunkt der vorhergehenden Entzweiung läßt BLINZLER, *Prozeß* (n. 14), p. 291, daran denken, daß das Verhältnis der beiden Machthaber möglicherweise durch die Aufstellung von Weiheschilden im Palast durch Pilatus und durch die nur
von Lk berichtete, von Pilatus veranlaßte Ermordung von Galiläern im Jerusalemer Tempel (Lk 13,1-5) belastet war. Da andererseits Herodes Antipas mit Kaiser Tiberius nach
Josephus, *Ant* 18,36 eng befreundet war, wäre die von Lukas berichtete Begegnung des
Herodes Antipas mit Jesus letztlich auch Dokument einer von Pilatus gesuchten Aussöh-
nung mit Herodes Antipas. BLINZLER, *Prozeß*, p. 286, vermutet an anderer Stelle, Pilatus
habe »offensichtlich die lästige Rechtssache loswerden« wollen. U. WILCKENS, *Die Missionsreden der Apostelgeschichte. Form- und traditionsgeschichtliche Untersuchungen*
(WMANT, 5), Neukirchen, Neukirchener Verlag, [3]1974, pp. 230f erkennt in Lk 23,12
(und Apg 4,25-27) ein traditionelles Motiv. Hier sei Lukas eine passionsgeschichtliche
Deutung von Ps 2,1f wahrscheinlich vorgegeben. Für den traditionellen Charakter von Lk
23,12 spreche gerade Lk 23,15, wo Pilatus und Herodes als Verfechter der Unschuld Jesu
auftreten. Auf der redaktionellen, lukanischen Textebene ist daher wohl wichtig, daß
diese Freundschaft eben an diesem Tag des Verhörs Jesu begründet wurde.

17. Herodes Antipas steht folglich in einer gewissen Ambivalenz. Neben offener Geg-

Zum anderen kann die m.E. redaktionelle Einführung der Herodes Antipas-Szene im Verhör Jesu nicht ohne Ausblick auf den Prozeß des Paulus verstanden werden. Es treten in Apg 25,13–26,32 König Agrippa II. und Berenike, die zum Antrittsbesuch bei Festus nach Cäsarea gekommen sind, gemeinsam mit dem Statthalter Festus auf, um die Unschuld des Paulus festzustellen. Auch hier entsprechen sich die Koalitionen und ihr Verhalten: hier der römische Statthalter in Verbindung mit dem jüdischen König (Apg 25,13), dort die Hohenpriester und die Angesehensten der Juden (Apg 25,2). Beide Szenen müssen in Beziehung zueinander interpretiert werden. Da Lk 23,6-12 wohl keinen historischen Anhalt am Prozeß Jesu hat und auch nicht durch eine Sonderüberlieferung vorgegeben ist, verdient die Vermutung von Frank J. Matera eine ernsthafte Überprüfung, daß Lukas das Verhör vor Herodes Antipas nach dem Verhör des Paulus vor Agrippa II. gestaltet hat[18].

2. Der Prozeß des Paulus

Der Versuch einer Lynchjustiz an Paulus durch jüdische Einwohner der Stadt Jerusalem wird durch den römischen Oberst, seine Hauptleute und Soldaten verhindert (Apg 21,31-33). Weitere jüdische Mordanschläge auf Paulus erwähnt Lukas in Apg 23,12-15; 25,3. Wohl als Schutzhaft vor dem drängenden Volk bringt der Oberst Paulus in die Burg (Apg 22,24; vgl. ebenso in Apg 23,10). Was oder wer Paulus aus römischer Sicht nicht ist, wird gleich zu Beginn des Prozesses durch ein Mißverständnismotiv festgehalten (Apg 21,38). Paulus ist nicht einer der zelotischen Führer, die große Menschenmengen hinter sich bringen und für Aufruhr (ἀναστατόω) sorgen, deren Verhalten, wie der Gamalielratschlag in Bezug auf Theudas und Judas den Galiläer gezeigt hat (Apg 5,38f), keinen heilsgeschichtlichen Bestand hat. Paulus hingegen ist römischer Bürger. Die Berufung auf das römische Bürgerrecht läßt den Oberst von Gewaltmaßnahmen zur Erpressung eines Geständnisses absehen (Apg 22,25). Um Paulus vor dem Mordanschlag der mehr als vierzig Juden zu schützen, läßt der Oberst Paulus in der denkwürdigen Begleitung[19] von 200 Soldaten, 70 Reitern und 200 Schützen nachts, wohl um absoluten Schutz zu gewähren, nach Caesarea zum Statthalter Felix bringen (Apg 23,23). In dem Begleitbrief an Felix erwähnt der

---

nerschaft zum Täufer und Jesus (Lk 3,19f; 13,31f; 23,11; Apg 4,27) steht herzliches Interesse an Jesus (Lk 9,7-9; 23,8). Lukas nennt Herodes Antipas außerdem im Synchronismus (Lk 3,1) und in Lk 8,3; Apg 13,1, insofern eine Nähe der Jesusbewegung und der frühen Mission zum Hof des Herodes Antipas bestand. Lukas streicht in Lk 12,1 diff Mk 8,15 ζύμη Ἡρῴδου. Auch wird der Bericht über das durch Herodes verursachte Ende des Täufers aus Mk 6,14-29 in Lk 3,19f; 9,9 auf das Äußerste reduziert, indem nur noch die Enthauptung als Faktum erwähnt wird. Andererseits aber spricht ausschließlich Lk 13,32 von Herodes Antipas als von einem ἀλώπηξ, also von einem verschlagenen Menschen.

18. MATERA, *Luke 23,1-25* (n. 10), p. 546.
19. H. J. HOLTZMANN, *Die Apostelgeschichte* (HCNT, 1/2), Tübingen-Leipzig, Mohr, ³1901, p. 139: »woher und wozu so viele?«.

Oberst, daß nach seiner Erkundung gegen Paulus nichts vorliegt, was Todesstrafe oder Gefängnis rechtfertigt (Apg 23,29).

Der römische Oberst Lysias erwähnt in seinem Begleitbrief ausdrücklich, daß ausschließlich Anklagen περὶ ζητημάτων τοῦ νόμου αὐτῶν erhoben wurden (Apg 23,29). Die von jüdischer Seite vorgebrachten Beschuldigungen gehen allerdings erheblich darüber hinaus. Apg 21,28 bleibt zunächst ausschließlich dem religiösen Aspekt der Anklage verpflichtet. Es sprechen Juden aus der Provinz Asia in der Meinung, Paulus habe den Tempel entweiht: οὗτός ἐστιν ὁ ἄνθρωπος ὁ κατὰ τοῦ λαοῦ καὶ τοῦ νόμου καὶ τοῦ τόπου τούτου πάντας πανταχῇ διδάσκων. Der Anwalt Tertullus erweitert bereits den religiösen Aspekt um einen politischen Vorwurf: εὑρόντες γὰρ τὸν ἄνδρα τοῦτον λοιμὸν καὶ κινοῦντα στάσεις πᾶσιν τοῖς Ἰουδαίοις τοῖς κατὰ τὴν οἰκουμένην πρωτοστάτην τε τῆς τῶν Ναζωραίων αἱρέσεως (Apg 24,5)[20]. Nach Apg 25,8 muß die von den aus Jerusalem zu Festus gekommenen Juden vorgebrachte Anklage noch deutlicher zum politischen Vorwurf (Majestätsbeleidigung) hin formuliert worden sein, da Paulus betont, er habe sich weder gegen das Gesetz der Juden, noch gegen den Tempel, noch gegen den Kaiser versündigt.

Die von einer jüdischen Delegation vor Felix vorgebrachte Anklage verläuft ergebnislos. Nach Apg 24,22-27 gewährt Felix Paulus zwar leichte Haftbedingungen, erweist sich im übrigen jedoch als korrupter Beamter. Er verzögert den Prozeß, weil er die Aussage des Oberst Lysias (Apg 24,22) hören will, erscheint zugleich aber bestechlich, da er von Paulus Geld erhofft, will zugleich der jüdischen Delegation einen Gefallen bieten, da Paulus gefangen gehalten wird.

Sein Nachfolger Festus hingegen kann Paulus zunächst ein weiteres Mal vor einem Mordanschlag (Apg 25,3) bewahren, indem er Paulus nicht, wie vom Synhedrium gewünscht, sogleich nach seinem Amtsantritt nach Jerusalem überführt, sondern ihn in Caesarea in einer Schutzhaft hält (Apg 25,1-8.21). Apg 25,9 mutet sodann wie ein Kompromißvorschlag an, dessen Konsequenz allerdings undeutlich ist: Soll Paulus in Jerusalem von Festus oder in Jerusalem im Beisein des Festus vom Synhedrium verurteilt werden? Erst durch den Einwand des Paulus, vor des Kaisers Gericht (in der Person des Festus) zu stehen, und durch die Appellation an den Kaiser (Apg 25,10-12), verlagert sich der Prozeß endgültig von einem Religionsprozeß vor jüdischen Behörden zu einem politischen Prozeß vor kaiserlichen Behörden. Festus hat erkannt, daß von jüdischer Seite in Wahrheit keine politischen (Apg 25,18), sondern ausschließlich religiöse Anklagen vorliegen, die allerdings entweder nicht bewiesen werden können (Apg 25,7) oder eben nicht in seine Zuständigkeit fallen (Apg 25,19f).

---

20. Στάσις in der Diasporajudenschaft bedeutete, was Rom vielfach erfahren mußte, zugleich Unruhe für den Staat.

Das Gespräch mit Herodes Agrippa steht hinsichtlich der Position des Festus unter der Absicht, zusätzliche Informationen über Paulus zu gewinnen, die dem Begleitbrief an den Kaiser beigefügt werden sollen, obwohl Festus die Unschuld des Paulus bereits jetzt mehrfach festgestellt und bestätigt hat (Apg 25,10.18.25-26). Festus befindet sich in der mißlichen Lage, ein Begleitschreiben nicht formulieren zu können: Eine Appellation an den Kaiser ohne vorausgehende Verurteilung entspricht keiner Rechtspraxis, eine Appellation ohne Anklagepunkte wäre völlig absurd. Die Unterredung zwischen Herodes Agrippa, Berenike und Festus schließt mit der Einsicht: ὅτι οὐδὲν θανάτου ἢ δεσμῶν ἄξιόν τι πράσσει ὁ ἄνθρωπος οὗτος (Apg 26,31b). Paulus könnte mithin freigelassen werden, wenn er nicht an den Kaiser appelliert hätte (Apg 26,32).

Bis hierhin hat der Leser erkannt: die Festnahme des Paulus in Jerusalem gründet auf der irrigen Meinung einiger Juden aus der Provinz Asia, Paulus habe den Tempel entweiht. Alle religiösen Vorwürfe gegen Paulus sind entweder unbegründet oder für den Statthalter uninteressant. Alle politischen Vorwürfe gegen Paulus sind haltlos und führen zu der Feststellung, daß keine Schuld vorliegt. Weshalb hat er überhaupt an den Kaiser appellieren müssen, da weder eine politische Schuld noch ein Urteil eines Verfahrens vorliegt? Nach dem Gang der Darstellung ist zu vermuten, daß Paulus in der Situation einer sich abzeichnenden Übertragung seines Falls durch Festus an das Jerusalemer Synhedrium (Apg 25,9) diesen Schritt wählt. Der Leser weiß nach dem bisher Berichteten freilich, daß diese Übertragung an das Synhedrium für Paulus tödlich enden würde.

Die apologetische Tendenz der 'Entlastung der Römer und Belastung der jüdischen religiösen Führer' in den beiden Prozeßverfahren wurde bislang in einem synchronen Überblick aufgezeigt. Sie kann aber ebenso, wie an zwei Beispielen belegt werden soll, in Detailbeobachtungen wahrgenommen werden.

Nach Apg 23,27; 26,21 ist Paulus von den Juden verhaftet worden. Das hier von Lukas verwendete Verb συλλαμβάνειν dient wie in Lk 22,54; Apg 1,16; 12,3; Jos, bell 2,292; ant 15,124 u.ö. zur Beschreibung einer behördlichen Festnahme (daneben auch κρατεῖν Apg 24,6). Auch ἐπέβαλον ἐπ᾿ αὐτὸν τὰς χεῖρας (Apg 21,27) muß im Vergleich mit der Verwendung in Apg 12,1 geradezu als amtliche Wendung verstanden werden, obwohl der Übergriff der asiatischen Juden auf Paulus dies nun wirklich nicht war. Demgegenüber beschreibt Lukas die Festnahme des Paulus durch Lysias in Apg 21,33 mit ἐπελάβετο αὐτοῦ, was hier im Sinne einer Schutzhaft vor der Tötungsabsicht der Stadt Jerusalem interpretiert werden kann[21]. Egger erkennt hierin eine »unter-

---

21. In Apg 21,30 verwendet Lk das Verb für den Übergriff der Jerusalemer auf Paulus (vgl zu solchem Gebrauch auch Apg 16,19; 18,17).

schwellige Umkehrung der historischen Vorgänge«, welche »mit Kalkül« geschieht[22].

Über das historisch Wahrscheinliche geht die Stärke der Eskorte hinaus, die Paulus von Jerusalem nach Caesarea bringen soll (Apg 23,23).
Immerhin handelt es sich um die Hälfte der Gesamtstärke der römischen
Truppe in Jerusalem. Natürlich wird damit für den Leser, sieht man von
der Dramaturgie des nächtlichen Geschehens einmal ab, auch die Bedeutung des Gefangenen Paulus und die Gefahr der Feinde in der Stadt Jerusalem unterstrichen, die ja bereits mehrfach einen Mordanschlag auf
Paulus geplant hatten (Apg 23,12.21; vgl. auch Apg 21,31; 22,22) und
vor deren Angriff Paulus jetzt mit Hilfe der Römer gerettet, bewahrt
werden muß (Apg 23,24 διασώσωσι). Es wird aber auch gezeigt, daß
der römische Oberst mehr für die Sicherheit und die Bequemlichkeit des
Reiseweges (κτήνη τε παραστῆσαι) des Paulus unternimmt als üblich
ist.

II. ASPEKTE DER FORSCHUNGSGESCHICHTE

Eine ausführliche Forschungsgeschichte zum Thema kann hier nicht
geboten werden, da das Thema in seiner Vielschichtigkeit einer diffe-
renzierten ausführlichen Aufarbeitung bedürfte. Es sollen daher nur
einige Aspekte aufgezählt werden. Daß die Apologetik nicht einen peri-
pheren Aspekt, sondern ein zentrales Thema des Doppelwerks darstellt,
betonen 1897 Johannes Weiß (»eine Apologie der christl. Religion vor
Heiden gegen die Anklage der Juden«) und 1901 Heinrich Julius Holtzmann bereits deutlich[23]. Die möglichst präzise Voraussetzung dieser
Apologetik, ihre Zielsetzung und Ausführung im Doppelwerk wurde
allerdings hier wie in der Folgezeit recht unterschiedlich bestimmt. Die
Aufzählung aller Nuancen würde ein Thema für sich sein. Lukas stellt,

---

22. W. EGGER, »*Crucifixus sub Pontio Pilato*«. *Das »crimen« Jesu von Nazareth im
Spannungsfeld römischer und jüdischer Verwaltungs- und Rechtsstrukturen* (NTAbh, 32),
Münster, Aschendorff, 1997, pp. 94-95 n. 279.

23. J. WEISS, *Absicht und literarischer Charakter der Apostelgeschichte*, Göttingen,
Vandenhoeck & Ruprecht, 1897, p. 56. HOLTZMANN, *Apostelgeschichte* (n. 19), p. 3 ver-
weist seinerseits auf die Vorarbeiten von J.W. STRAATMAN, *Paulus de Apostel van Jezus
Christus*, Amsterdam, Loman, 1874, und O. PFLEIDERER, *Das Urchristenthum*, Berlin,
Georg Reimer, 1887. Straatman entdeckt nach Holtzmann eine »auf ein heidenchristl.
Publikum berechnete... Apologie des in Pls als 'römischem Bürger' vertretenen Chri-
stenthums«. Vgl. auch die Ausführungen von Th. ZAHN, *Einleitung in das Neue Testament. Mit einer Einführung von* R. Riesner, Wuppertal-Zürich, Brockhaus, 1994 (Nachdruck der 3. Aufl. 1906/1907), II, p. 399 und die Auseinandersetzung mit M.
SCHNECKENBURGER, *Über den Zweck der Apostelgeschichte*, Bern, Chr. Fischer, 1841, der
die Apg als eine Apologie des Paulus betrachtet.

darin besteht immerhin weitgehende Übereinstimmung, keinesfalls das Christentum als wahre jüdische Religion dar, um nun für das Christentum die durch Caesar gewährten jüdischen Privilegien[24] in Anspruch nehmen zu können[25].

Die Apologetik wird gegenwärtig häufig abgeleitet aus konkreten, aktuellen Ereignissen. Sie sind zum einen endogener, d.h. innerchristlicher Herkunft. So bemüht sich Lukas nach A.J. Mattill[26], Paulus vor den Judenchristen in Rom zu verteidigen, nach Donald A. Carson[27] hingegen, den römischen Konvertiten das Verhältnis Rom – Kirche positiv nahezubringen, andererseits das Christentum als harmlose Religion darzustellen, da Rom Angst vor östlichen Religionen habe. Als exogener Anlaß der Apologetik wird zum anderen oft eine Verfolgungssituation (jüdischer oder römischer Herkunft; das hängt auch mit der zeitlichen Ansetzung der Apg zusammen) benannt[28].

Demgegenüber verweisen neuere, vorwiegend sozialgeschichtlich orientierte Arbeiten auf das allgemeine politische Klima, beschreiben also die Voraussetzung der Apologetik. Wolfgang Stegemann nennt einerseits »die Distanzierung von (sic!) Diasporasynagogen von den Christen«[29]. Auch Bruce W. Winter vermutet, ausgehend von Apg 18, daß die jüdischen Diasporagemeinden eine Konfrontation zwischen den Christen und dem römischen Staat betrieben hätten, da diese sich am Kaiserkult nicht beteiligt hätten[30]. In diese Richtung der Kriminalisierung der Christen als Voraussetzung der Apologetik argumentieren auch Ekkehard W. und Wolfgang Stegemann. Lukas reflektiere Erfahrungen

24. Vgl. E. SCHÜRER, *The History of the Jewish People in the Age of Jesu Christ (175 B.C.-A.D. 135)*. A new English Version revised and edited by G. Vermes & F. Millar, Vol. I, Edinburgh, T.&T. Clark, 1993, pp. 267-280.

25. Vgl. H. CONZELMANN, *Die Apostelgeschichte* (HNT, 7), Tübingen, Mohr, ²1972, p. 12; E. PLÜMACHER, Art. *Apostelgeschichte*, in TRE 3 (1978), p. 518. M. WOLTER, *TLZ* 120 (1995) 1005-1007, muß in einer Rezension gegenüber B.W. WINTER, *The Imperial Cult*, in D.W.J. GILL and C. GEMPF (eds.), *The Book of Acts in its First Century Setting*, 2, Grand Rapids MI, Eerdmans – Carlisle, Paternoster Press, 1994, pp. 93-103, diesen Forschungsstand erneut einklagen.

26. A.J. MATTILL, *The Purpose of Acts: Schneckenburger reconsidered*, in W.W. GASQUE and R.P. MARTIN (eds.), *Apostolic History and the Gospel: Biblical and Historical Essays Presented to F.F. Bruce*, Grand Rapids, MI, Eerdmans, 1970, pp. 108-122.

27. D.A. CARSON – D.J. MOO – L. MORRIS, *An Introduction to the New Testament*, Grand Rapids MI, Zondervan, 1992, p. 197.

28. W. SCHMITHALS, *Lukas – Evangelist der Armen*, in TViat 12 (1975) 153-167; vgl. zur Kritik der These einer akuten Verfolgungssituation: F.W. HORN, *Glaube und Handeln in der Theologie des Lukas* (GTA, 26), Göttingen, Vandenhoeck & Ruprecht, ²1986, pp. 216-220.

29. STEGEMANN, *Synagoge* (n. 3), p. 36.

30. WINTER, *Imperial Cult* (n. 25), p. 99.

nach 70. Sie laufen auf den Vorwurf der Asebie und *perduellio* (Hochverrat) hinaus[31].

Vernon Robbins zeichnet eine von Lukas intendierte Perspektive der positiven Symbiose von Christentum und römischem Staat, deren Ziele kongruent seien[32]. In dieser Linie liegt auch die Arbeit von Paul Walaskay: »Far from supporting the view that Luke was defending the church to a Roman magistrate, the evidence points us in the other direction. Throughout his writings Luke has carefully, consistently, and consciously presented an *apologia pro imperio* to his church«[33].

Donald Guthrie erneuert die alte These, Lukas wolle Paulus vor offiziellen Behörden in Rom in Schutz nehmen, gleichsam eine Verteidigungsschrift bieten[34].

Gerhard Schneider spricht die Erwartung aus, daß nach Lukas die römischen Behörden zur Zeit des Lukas die Sache Jesu gleichermaßen beurteilen wie seinerzeit die Statthalter im Prozeß des Paulus. Zusätzlich verweist er auf die missionarisch – werbenden Intentionen[35]. Dies setzt voraus, was in unterschiedlicher Form vielfach angenommen wird, daß Lukas heidnische römische Leser, gegebenenfalls auch Behörden, als

---

31. E.W. STEGEMANN – W. STEGEMANN, *Urchristliche Sozialgeschichte. Die Anfänge im Judentum und die Christusgemeinden in der mediterranen Welt*, Stuttgart, Kohlhammer, 1995, pp. 272-305; vgl. jetzt auch G. HOLTZ, *Der Herrscher und der Weise im Gespräch. Studien zu Form, Funktion und Situation der neutestamentlichen Verhörgespräche und der Gespräche zwischen jüdischen Weisen und Fremdherrschern* (ANTZ, 6), Berlin, Institut Kirche und Judentum, 1996, pp. 162-166. M. DIBELIUS, *Aufsätze zur Apostelgeschichte*, ed. H. GREEVEN (FRLANT, 60), Göttingen, Vandenhoeck & Ruprecht, ⁵1961, las den Prozeßbericht des Paulus im Sinne einer Instandsetzung des christlichen Lesers zur Apologie; vgl. pp. 179-180: »Wenn Paulus in den fünf hier untersuchten Verhörszenen immer wieder das gleiche zu seiner Verteidigung sagt, so will der Verfasser damit den Christen seiner Zeit den Rat geben, dieselben Gedanken zu ihrer Verteidigung zu gebrauchen«.
32. V.K. ROBBINS, *Luke-Acts: A Mixed Population Seeks a Home in the Roman Empire*, in L. ALEXANDER (ed.), *Images of Empire* (JSOT, 122), Sheffield, Academic Press, 1991, pp. 202-221, esp. 202: »This means that Christianity functions in the domain of the Roman Empire, and this empire is good because it works symbiotically with Christianity. Roman law, correctly applied, grants Christians the right to pursue the project started by Jesus, and the goals of Christianity, rightly understood, work congruently with the goals of the Roman empire«.
33. WALASKAY, '*And So We Came to Rome*' (n. 6), p. 54. Entsprechend formuliert auch J. ROLOFF, *Die Kirche im Neuen Testament* (GNT, 10), Göttingen, Vandenhoeck & Ruprecht, 1993, p. 211. In dieser Linie bewegten sich bereits die Ausführungen von E. HAENCHEN, *Die Apostelgeschichte* (KEK, 3), Göttingen, Vandenhoeck & Ruprecht, ¹⁴1965, p. 619. Zustimmend auch RADL, *Lukas-Evangelium* (n. 10), p. 127. CONZELMANN, *Apostelgeschichte* (n. 25), p. 135 nennt als eindrucksvolle Zielvorstellung das Vertrauen auf die Gerechtigkeit des Kaisers.
34. D. GUTHRIE, *New Testament Introduction*, Leicester, Apollos, ⁴1990, p. 369.
35. G. SCHNEIDER, *Verleugnung, Verspottung und Verhör Jesu nach Lukas 22,54-71*, München, Kösel, 1969, p. 194; zustimmend J. ERNST, *Das Evangelium nach Lukas*

potentielle Leser im Blick hat.

Takaya Hosaka deutet eine Perspektive an, nach der Lukas erwartet, daß der Weltherr Rom sich durch die christlichen Lehren immer mehr beeinflussen läßt und sich selbst zu fürchten anfängt[36].

Freilich finden sich auch gelegentlich noch Stimmen, denen zufolge Rom in einer ausschließlich negativen Sicht behandelt wird[37]. Hier kann von einer apologetischen Tendenz keine Rede sein. Richard J. Cassidy betont die staatskritischen Elemente im lukanischen Doppelwerk, um so auch die apologetische Absicht in Frage stellen zu können[38].

III. LUKAS UND DIE HERODESFAMILIE

Die jüngere Forschungsgeschichte hat alternativ diskutiert, ob Lukas sich primär an die christliche Gemeinde oder an einen römischen Leserkreis wendet, und ob er hier bei den Christen um Vertrauen in den römischen Staat werben oder eben diesem die politische Ungefährlichkeit des Christentums aufzeigen will. Mit Walter Radl meine ich, daß Lukas in diesen Fragen keine Gegensätze aufbaut, sondern beides je im Blick hat[39]. Ein grundsätzliches, immer noch offen diskutiertes Problem ist etwa, ob das von Lukas für Paulus reklamierte römische Bürgerrecht (Apg 22,25)[40] und die gleichfalls nur von ihm erwähnte Appellation an

---

(RNT, 3), Regensburg, Pustet, 1977, p. 647. S. SCHULZ, *Neutestamentliche Ethik*, Zürich, TVZ, 1987, p. 480, spricht sogar von dem »Ziel, Christentum und Staat dauerhaft auszusöhnen«.

36. T. HOSAKA, *Lukas und das Imperium Romanum. Unter besonderer Berücksichtigung der literarischen Funktion des Furchtmotivs*, in *AJBI* 14 (1988) 82-134. Hosaka betont, daß in der lukanischen Darstellung mit Hilfe des Furchtmotivs den römischen Beamten gegenüber Paulus eine tiefrangige Stellung zugewiesen wird.

37. J.M. SCOTT, *Luke's Geographical Horizon*, in D.W.J. GILL and C. GEMPF (eds.), *The Book of Acts* (n. 25), p. 524, zeichnet den römischen Staat in der apokalyptischen Folge der vier Reiche des Buches Daniel.

38. CASSIDY, *Society and Politics* (n. 6), kritisiert die Hauptthesen der sog. politisch-apologetischen Positionen: a) Lukas stellt die Christen als harmlos und gesetzeskonform dar; b) Lukas zeichnet Paulus als idealen römischen Bürger; c) Lukas stellt das römische System günstig dar.

39. RADL, *Lukas-Evangelium* (n. 10), p. 127.

40. Die Historizität des römischen Bürgerrechts des Paulus wird in neuerer Zeit bestritten von W. STEGEMANN, *War der Apostel Paulus ein römischer Bürger?*, in *ZNW* 78 (1987) 200-229. Für W. SCHMITHALS, *Die Apostelgeschichte* (ZBK, 3/2), Zürich, TVZ, 1982, p. 153, ist der Hinweis auf das römische Bürgerrecht »ein massiv herausgestelltes Motiv des Schriftstellers Lukas« und »der Hinweis auf dies Bürgerrecht des Christen Paulus gehört in den Rahmen der apologetischen Tendenz des Schriftstellers Lukas, der auf diesem Wege mit großem Nachdruck die politische Unschuld der Missionare offenkundig macht«. Dagegen gegenwärtig M. HENGEL, *Der vorchristliche Paulus*, in ID. und U. HECKEL, *Paulus und das Judentum* (WUNT, 58), Tübingen, Mohr, 1991, pp. 177-291, esp. 193-208.

den Kaiser (Apg 25,11) eine historische Grundlage haben, oder ob sie als redaktionelle Aussagen gerade die Spitze der apologetischen Aus-richtung darstellen. Ich lasse diese Fragen hier bewußt offen, um einen weiteren, m.E. zu wenig berücksichtigten Aspekt zur Frage des lukani-schen Verhältnisses zum römischen Staat zu wählen. Man kann in der Beantwortung dieser Frage zu einer recht eindeutigen Position kommen, wenn man betrachtet, wie ausschließlich Lukas in seinem Doppelwerk gezielt Hinweise auf die Herodesfamilie gibt und wenn man zugleich die politische Funktion dieser Hinweise bestimmt. Zum ihrem Verständnis und zu ihrer Einordnung will ich zunächst zwei literaturgeschichtliche Verständnishilfen in Erinnerung rufen.

Eckhard Plümacher hat in diesem Jahr, seine früheren Arbeiten[41] auf-nehmend, weiterführend und präzisierend, zur Geschichtsschreibung des Lukas ausgeführt: »Zu jener Geschichtsschreibung indes, die einer der Hauptströme der hellenistisch-römischen Historiographie gewesen ist, möchte ich Lukas unbedingt zählen: zur tragisch-pathetischen Historio-graphie, die man allerdings, Klaus Meister und Otto Lendle folgend, besser als mimetische oder sensationalistische Geschichtsschreibung bezeichnen sollte«[42]. Zu deren Wesen gehört nach Plümacher auch unabdingbar, »auf Wirkung bedacht zu sein und es deshalb mit der historischen Wahrheit nicht sonderlich genau zu nehmen, wenn die Gestaltung einer fiktiven Wirklichkeit der emotionalen Beteiligung des Lesers förderlicher zu sein schien als ein Bericht nur des tatsächlich Geschehenen«[43]. Plümacher verweist in diesem Zusammenhang auch auf die lukanische Darstellung des Prozesses des Paulus: »die Erzählung vom Jerusalemer Komplott der Juden gegen Paulus und dessen Rettung durch die zu diesem Zweck die Hälfte ihrer Jerusalemer Garnison auf-bietenden Römer – all dies verrät sich durch das bewußt Spektakuläre der Darstellung als gleichfalls dem Bereich der τερατεία zugehörig«[44]. Es steht für Eckhard Plümacher allerdings außer Frage, daß Lukas sich mit dieser mimetischen Historiographie den »breiteren, auf der sozialen Stufenleiter eher in der Mitte oder sogar noch darunter anzusiedelnden Bevölkerungsschichten«[45] zuwendet, von denjenigen aber, die über

---

41. E. PLÜMACHER, *Lukas als hellenistischer Schriftsteller. Studien zur Apostelge-schichte* (SUNT, 9), Göttingen, Vandenhoeck & Ruprecht, 1972; ID., Art. *Apostelge-schichte*, in *TRE* 3 (1978), pp. 483-528.
42. E. PLÜMACHER, *TEPATEIA. Fiktion und Wunder in der hellenistisch-römischen Geschichtsschreibung und in der Apostelgeschichte*, in *ZNW* 89 (1998) 66-90, esp. p. 67.
43. *Ibid.*, p. 72.
44. *Ibid.*, p. 83.
45. *Ibid.*, p. 89.

literarische Bildung besaßen, verachtet werden muß. Lukas finde Gefallen an dieser Geschichtsschreibung, weil er ein »Geschichtsbild mit deutlich apologetischen Zügen« besitzt[46].

Lukas Bormann hat den Begriff der »Verrechtlichung im lukanischen Schrifttum« ins Gespräch gebracht, auch um von dem allgemeinen Schlagwort des »apologetischen Interesses« wegzukommen. Er bezieht diesen Begriff auf »die Tendenz eines Autors, Überlieferungen mit rechtlichen Details anzureichern, Vorgänge innerhalb juristischer Kategorien zu interpretieren und juristische Problemstellungen in den Erzählablauf zu integrieren«[47]. Damit kommt Lukas vordergründig den Leserinteressen – »Gerichtsszenen sind ein im antiken Roman häufig eingesetztes Mittel zur Erzeugung von Spannung«[48] – entgegen.

Im einzelnen kann Bormann u.a. auf folgende Sachverhalte in Apg verweisen: a) die Vielzahl rechtlich relevanter Situationen (Apg 4,1-23; 5,17-41; 6,12–7,60; 12,1-19; 16,19-39; 17,6-9; 18,12-17; 19,35-40; 21,27-40; 22,24–23,11; 24–26; 28,16); b) die Einführung des Bürgerrechts des Paulus bringt eine entscheidende Wende in die Behandlung durch die Behörden und strukturiert ab Apg 22,25 den Prozeß; c) es werden die rechtlichen Beziehungen des Paulus zu Tarsus und Rom zunächst angedeutet, im Verlauf der Darstellung geklärt; d) nach dem Stephanusmartyrium findet kein Jesusanhänger mehr den Tod[49] und nach der Philippiepisode findet keine polizeiliche Bestrafung mehr statt.

Bormann verweist nun auf das Engagement der jüdischen Apologetik in politischen Fragen über den Weg der diplomatischen und juristischen Auseinandersetzung mit ihrer jeweiligen Umwelt, an die Lukas anknüpfe. Zwar habe dieser nicht die Möglichkeiten der hohen Diplomatie, versuche aber, diesen Nachteil »durch die Verrechtlichung seiner Quellen, durch die erzählerische Bearbeitung rechtlich relevanter Themen und durch die Einordnung ihm bekannter Vorgänge in juristisch-prozessuale Ereignisfolgen«[50] auszugleichen. Hierbei betone er den aus römischer Sicht unschuldigen Status der beiden Protagonisten. Bormann unterscheidet betont die von ihm analysierte *Tendenz* der Verrechtlichung von der mit ihr verbundenen *Intention*, die freilich nur, auch wenn Bormann hier eine klare Antwort schuldig bleibt, in der Tendenz der

---

46. *Ibid.*, p. 90.
47. BORMANN, *Verrechtlichung* (n. 3), p. 287.
48. Bormann (p. 304) verweist zum Unterhaltungswert der Gerichtsszenen in der Apg vor allem auf R.I. PERVO, *Profit with Delight: The Literary Genre of the Acts of the Apostles*, Philadelphia, Fortress, 1987, pp. 42-48.
49. Hat Lukas in Apg 12,1-3 die Umstände um die Ermordung des Zebedaiden Jakobus derart verharmlosend dargestellt, daß Bormann diesen Sachverhalt nach dem Stephanusmartyrium übersehen hat?
50. BORMANN, *Verrechtlichung*, p. 310.

jüdischen Apologetik liegen kann: »Der mit diesem Begriff (Verrechtlichung; F.W. H.) erfaßte Vorgang der Neubestimmung von Traditionen
angesichts neuer rechtlicher Kontexte ist eine Antwort auf die Ausbreitung und Festigung römischer Herrschaft und römischen Rechtes in der
Mittelmeerwelt und greift auf Erfahrungen und Traditionen der jüdischen Apologetik in der hellenistisch-römischen Welt zurück«[51].

Beide Hinweise bestärken darin, nach den Hintergründen und der
lukanischen Absicht zu fragen, die in der Einführung der Herodesfamilie zum Ausdruck kommen. Es sind dies Herodes Antipas im Verhör
Jesu, Herodes Agrippa II. und Berenike im Prozeß des Paulus, sodann
sind die kurzen Hinweise auf die Mißhandlung der Gemeinde, das Ende
des Zebedaiden Jakobus unter Herodes Agrippa I. und auf die Verfolgung des Petrus in Apg 12,1-3.17 zu bedenken, sowie der Hinweis auf
Johanna, die Frau des Chuza, des Verwalters des Herodes Antipas (Lk
8,3) und derjenige auf den antiochenischen Propheten und Lehrer
Manaen, der zusammen mit Herodes Antipas erzogen worden war (Apg
13,1). Schließlich ist die lukanische Bearbeitung der markinischen Aussagen zu Herodes zu bedenken.

In der Erwähnung der Herodesfamilie, speziell im Auftreten des
Herodes Agrippa II. und der Berenike muß einerseits das erkannt werden, was Plümacher als »Sensationshistorie«[52] beschrieben hat. Es wird,
kurz vor der Überfahrt nach Rom, in Apg 25–26 eine Prunkszene mit
den höchsten Repräsentanten inszeniert. Das Auditorium, das Paulus
betritt, stellen das jüdische Herrscherpaar mit ihrem Hofstaat, Berenike,
eine auch in Rom bekannte femme fatale, die Tribunen der in Caesarea
stationierten Kohorten, die vornehmsten Männer und der römische Pro-
kurator Festus dar. Da andererseits aber der Herodesfamilie sowohl in
der Zuordnung zu jüdischer Tempelgemeinde als auch als Vasallenköni-
gen zu Rom eine spezifische politische Funktion zukommt, ist nach ihrer
möglichen, von Lukas in Anspruch genommenen Rolle im Kontext der
Verrechtlichung der Überlieferung zu fragen.

Auch wenn die doppelte Tendenz – Belastung der Juden und Entlastung der Römer – durchgängig zu greifen ist, so bezeugt Lukas an anderer Stelle, daß es eben eine von ihm der Tradition und dem Wissen um
die historischen Umstände aufgepfropfte Sicht ist. Nach Apg 4,27f ver-

---

51. *Ibid.*, pp. 310-311. Bereits ERNST, *Evangelium nach Lukas* (n. 35), p. 647, sieht
das Bestreben der jungen Missionskirche, sich mit der römischen Verwaltung zu arran-
gieren, und CONZELMANN, *Apostelgeschichte* (n. 25), p. 129, erkennt den Versuch, mit
dem Staat ins Gespräch zu kommen, um eine Dauerregelung zu erzielen.
52. PLÜMACHER, *TEPATEIA* (n. 42), p. 73, in Aufnahme einer Einschätzung von K.
MEISTER, *Historische Kritik bei Polybios* (Palingenesia, 9), Wiesbaden, Steiner, 1975,
pp. 109-126, esp. 125.

sammeln sich Herodes Antipas und Pontius Pilatus mit den Heiden und den Stämmen Israels gemeinsam in Jerusalem gegen Jesus. Sie führen gemeinsam aus, wozu der Ratschluß Gottes sie zuvor bestimmt hat. In dieser Linie liegen gleichfalls die Tötungsabsicht des Herodes Antipas (Lk 13,31) und die Verspottung Jesu durch die herodianischen Soldaten (Lk 23,11).

Dennoch überwiegt deutlich die gegenläufige, nämlich die die Herodesfamilie entlastende Tendenz. Da vieles dafürspricht, daß die in Apg 4,27f zum Ausdruck kommende Sicht nicht spezifisch lukanisch, sondern eher gemeinchristlich ist[53], muß in der die Herodesfamilie entlastenden Tendenz das spezifisch Lukanische gefunden werden. Weil aber das christliche Gemeinwissen um das dem Christentum entgegenstehende Verhalten der Herodesfamilie weiß (in Bezug auf den Täufer in Mk 6,14-29; auf Jesus in Apg 4,27f), wird sich das im Doppelwerk beschriebene, das Christentum in Schutz nehmende Verhalten der Herodesfamilie nicht an Christen richten, sondern an potentielle heidnisch-römische Leser, deren Kenntnisse über die Vorgänge um die Anfänge des Christentums begrenzt waren.

Die Frage des Leserkreises kann als Problem hier nur angesprochen werden. Sie wurde klassischerweise oft mit der Einschätzung der Apg als einer Verteidigungsschrift des Paulus vor römischen Behörden verbunden[54]. Da aber Lukas deutlich nach dem Tod des Paulus (in Apg 20,17-35 vorausgesetzt) schreibt, ist diese These abwegig. Diese Frage müßte natürlich in einem umfassenderen Rahmen behandelt werden. In älteren einleitungswissenschaftlichen Stellungnahmen wird potentielle heidnische Leserschaft selbstverständlich vorausgesetzt. Für Theodor Zahn ist die Ausrichtung an Heiden schon wegen der Widmung im Prolog selbstverständlich[55]. Heinrich Julius Holtzmann verbindet die lukanische Apologetik mit einer nichtchristlichen Adressierung[56].

Wenn Lukas daran gelegen ist, gegenüber potentiellen römischen Lesern das Christentum als eine politisch unverdächtige, den Staat nicht gefährdende Religion auszugeben, dann ist für ihn die Herodesfamilie der ideale Zeuge. Ihr Interesse und ihre Kenntnisse des jüdischen und

---

53. CONZELMANN, *Apostelgeschichte* (n. 25), p. 43. WILCKENS, *Die Missionsreden der Apostelgeschichte* (n. 16), pp. 230f hat in diesem Nachtrag ausführlich die in der Erstauflage vertretene Position, Apg 4,25-31 sei einschließlich 4,25-27 lukanische Bildung, revidiert und die Deutung von 4,25-27 als Tradition ausführlich begründet.

54. Dazu ZAHN, *Einleitung*, II (n. 23), p. 399; R. PESCH, *Die Apostelgeschichte* (EKK, 5/1), Neukirchen, Neukirchener Verlag, 1986, p. 29. Diese These wird jetzt wieder vertreten von GUTHRIE, *New Testament Introduction* (n. 34), p. 369.

55. ZAHN, *Einleitung*, II, p. 400.

56. HOLTZMANN, *Apostelgeschichte* (n. 19), p. 11 betont die »Aehnlichkeit mit der Taktik der Apologeten; gleich ihren Schutzreden scheint auch Act an eine nichtchristl. Adresse gerichtet«.

christlichen Glaubens werden eigens attestiert (vgl. das offenkundige
Interesse des Herodes Antipas in Lk 23,8f und die *captatio benevolen-
tiae* gegenüber Herodes Agrippa II. in Apg 26,2f.26). Zu ihrem Hof
bestanden in der Jesusbewegung (Lk 8,1-3) und in der antiochenischen
Gemeinde (Apg 13,1) persönliche Kontakte. Zugleich aber waren sie als
römische Bürger[57] und als von Rom eingesetzte Machthaber in den
Tetrarchien politisch relativ unbedenkliche Gewährsmänner. Dies will
nicht besagen, daß Herodes Antipas, Agrippa I. und Agrippa II. historisch nicht ohne Spannung zum römischen Kaiser und seinen Prokuratoren gestanden hätten. In der Retrospektive nach dem jüdischen Krieg
jedoch war deutlich, daß vor allem Agrippa II. als letzter der Herodesfamilie eindeutig auf Roms Seite gekämpft hatte.

Wir wissen aus vielen Indizien, daß aus römischer Perspektive, sofern
sie aus frühen Quellen gewonnen werden kann, keine deutlichen Vorstellungen vom Christentum in seiner Differenz zum Judentum gegeben
sind, wohl aber neue Vereinsgründungen mit Sorge beobachtet wurden[58]. Die Frage, ob Jesus (Lk 23,2), Paulus (Apg 21,38) und die Urgemeinde (Apg 5,34-42 wählt als Vergleichspunkt zur christlichen
Gemeinde das Auftreten des Judas des Galiläers und des Theudas) in
einer Nähe zur zelotischen Bewegung stehen bzw. gestanden haben, mag
durchaus römische Verdächtigungen wiedergeben. Auch wird die Stellung der christlichen Bewegung zum Judentum klärungsbedürftig gewesen sein. Die Abschwächung des römischen Anteils an den Verfahren
gegen Jesus und Paulus erklärt sich auch aus der Sorge, in den Augen
der Römer als Staatsfeinde zu gelten[59]. Daß darüber hinaus der bestän-
dige Kontakt der Herodesfamilie mit den Anfängen des Christentums
dieses wiederum politisch aufwertet, ja Agrippa II. kurz vor einer Konversion zum Christentum steht (Apg 26,28), ist gleichfalls Teil der apologetischen Zielsetzung.

Halten wir kurz wesentliche biographische, in Rom bekannte Fakten
zu der von Lukas eingeführten Herodesfamilie fest, um ihre positive
Zuordnung zu Rom zu verdeutlichen[60]. Herodes Antipas, mit seinem
Bruder Archelaos in Rom erzogen, nannte die von ihm erbaute Hauptstadt Tiberias nach dem Namen des römischen Kaisers, der Stadt Betha-

57. Caesar hatte Antipater, damit der herodianischen Familie, im Jahr 47 v. Chr. das
römische Bürgerrecht verliehen (Josephus, *Bell* 1,188; *Ant* 14,8,3; OGIS 428); dazu A.
SCHALIT, *König Herodes. Der Mann und sein Werk*, Berlin, de Gruyter, 1969, pp. 36-40.
58. H.-J. KLAUCK, *Die religiöse Umwelt des Urchristentums. I. Stadt- und Hausreli-
gion, Mysterienkulte, Volksglaube* (Kohlhammer-Studienbücher Theologie, 19), Stuttgart,
Kohlhammer, 1995, p. 52.
59. BLINZLER, *Prozeß* (n. 14), p. 62 n. 91.
60. Vgl. zum folgenden vor allem: SCHÜRER, *History* (n. 24), pp. 340-483.

ramphtha gab er den Namen der Frau des Kaisers, Livias, später umbenannt in Julias. Daß Herodes Antipas sich an der Klage gegen Pilatus
wegen der Aufstellung der Weiheschilde im Jerusalemer Palast (Philo,
Leg. ad Gaium 38,299-305) beteiligte, und er zuletzt wegen einer
Anklage durch Agrippa verbannt wurde, schmälert nicht seine grundsätzlich prorömische Einstellung. Herodes Agrippa I., gleichfalls in Rom
und in großer Nähe zum Kaiserhaus aufgewachsen, erhält durch Cali-
gula im Jahr 37 n. Chr. die Tetrarchie des Philippus und diejenige des
Lysanias, zusätzlich den Königstitel und durch den römischen Senat die
Ehrenrechte eines Prätors (Philo, in Flaccum 6,40). Agrippa I. hatte die
Erhebung des Claudius in Rom gefördert, der ihm als Gegenleistung
zusätzlich die Gebiete Judäa und Samaria überträgt. Die Schenkungsur-
kunde wird auf dem Capitol in Rom aufgestellt. Drusilla, die Schwester
Agrippas I., war seit 53 n. Chr. mit Statthalter Felix verheiratet (Josephus, *Ant* 20,148; Apg 24,24f). Agrippa II. hatte vielfache Gebietszu-
weisungen von Rom erhalten, war jedoch gegenüber seinen Vorgängern
im herodäischen Königshaus weitaus schwächer. Caesarea Philippi wird
in seiner Zeit zu Neronias umbenannt. Er stand im jüdischen Krieg deutlich auf Roms Seite (vgl. die von Josephus nachempfundene Rede, *Bell*
2,345-401). Seine Schwester Berenike war zeitweise Geliebte des Titus
und hoffte, dessen Ehefrau zu werden. Agrippa II. und sein Vater
Agrippa I. werden auf Inschriften βασιλεὺς μέγας φιλόκαισαρ
εὐσεβὴς καὶ φιλορώμαιος[61] genannt.

Die in der Exegese häufig verhandelte historische Frage, ob nämlich
ein Kontakt Jesu mit Antipas bzw. des Paulus mit Agrippa II. vorstellbar
sei, übersieht die lukanische Zielsetzung. Die inszenierten Gerichtsssze-
nen dienen dem Aufweis der von oberster politischer jüdischer Seite
festgehaltenen Schuldlosigkeit des Christentums. Bestehende jüdische
Anklagen, Lukas weist sie den religiösen, nicht politischen Führern des
Volkes zu, werden als haltlos und unaufrichtig befunden. Herodes Antipas schickt Jesus zu Pilatus zurück, was als Bestätigung der Schuldlosigkeit aufgenommen wird (Lk 23,15). Herodes Agrippa II. sagt zu
Festus: Dieser Mensch könnte freigelassen werden, wenn er sich nicht
auf den Kaiser berufen hätte (Apg 26,31).

Im Lichte dieses Urteils über die Herodesfamilie gewinnen weitere,
nur bei Lukas bezeugte Textpassagen gleichfalls eine Funktion im Rahmen der apologetischen, das Christentum als politisch unverdächtig dar-
stellenden Zielsetzung. Lukas erwähnt beiläufig, daß schon eine Frau
eines Verwalters des Herodeshofes Kontakt zur Jesusbewegung hatte

---

61. *Ibid.*, p. 452 und n. 42.

(Lk 8,1-3) und daß einer der ersten Apostel, Manaen, mit Herodes Antipas aufgewachsen war (Apg 13,1). Diesem Benennen von im Grunde nichtssagenden biographischen Notizen entspricht das Verschweigen der unübersehbaren Konflikte der Jesusbewegung und des frühen Christentums mit dem Herodeshaus[62]. Auf die gegenüber Markus äußerste Reduktion der Hinrichtung des Täufers (Lk 3,19f; 9,9) wurde bereits verwiesen. Daß die feindliche Absicht in einer Anfrage der Pharisäer und Herodianer zum Ausdruck kommt, verschweigt Lk 20,20 gegenüber Mk 12,13; Mt 22,16. Schwerer wiegt, daß die Hinrichtung des Zebedaiden Jakobus, die Gefangennahme des Petrus und die christenfeindliche Einstellung durch Herodes Agrippa I. in Apg 12,1-3 nur mit wenigen Worten erwähnt werden. Unter Herodes Agrippa I. (41-44 n. Chr.) wurde durch den Tod des Jakobus und Petrus' Weggang aus Jerusalem (Apg 12,17) die bisherige Leitung der Urgemeinde beseitigt. Es ist unvorstellbar, daß Lukas nicht mehr Informationen über diesen Einschnitt hat, als er in Apg 12,1-3 preisgibt[63]. Freilich muß auch gesehen werden, daß Apg 12,3 eine partielle Entschuldigung des Herodes insofern vorbringt, als sein Verhalten als Entgegenkommen an die Juden gewertet wird. Ebenso spricht Apg 12,11 nicht allein von der Errettung aus der Hand des Herodes, sondern auch aus den feindlichen Erwartungen der Juden. Allein über den Tod des Herodes Agrippa I. berichtet Lukas ausführlicher, befindet sich hier allerdings auch in einer weitreichenden sachlichen und hinsichtlich der Wertung des Geschehens inhaltlichen Übereinstimmung mit Josephus (*Ant* 8,343-352), der im übrigen wahrlich prorömisch schreibt[64].

62. Gegenüber Mk 3,6 entfällt bei den Seitenreferenten die dort geschilderte Absicht der Tötung Jesu durch die Herodianer. Es handelt sich aber um ein minor agreement, so daß nicht sicher davon ausgegangen werden kann, daß Lukas diesen markinischen Text auch gelesen hat.

63. Lukas scheint weitergehende Kenntnisse zu haben. Nach Lk 18,34 übernimmt er nicht aus der mk Abfolge das Wort über das Martyrium der beiden Zebedaiden (Mk 10,39), was doch wohl darauf hindeutet, daß das Schicksal des Johannes von dem des Jakobus gegen Mk 10,39 zu unterscheiden ist. R. RIESNER, *Die Frühzeit des Apostels Paulus. Studien zur Chronologie, Missionsstrategie und Theologie* (WUNT, 71), Tübingen, Mohr, 1994, pp. 109-110 erkennt in Agrippa einen Herrscher mit messiasähnlichen Ansprüchen. Seine Verfolgungsmaßnahmen beziehen sich auf τινας τῶν ἀπὸ τῆς ἐκκλησίας (Apg 12,1). Riesner setzt diese τινας in Beziehung zur Stephanusgruppe (vgl. auch Apg 8,1-3). Die Maßnahme des Agrippa hätte sowohl den sadduzäischen als auch den zelotischen Teil der jüdischen Gemeinde beeindrucken können. Aber stehen Petrus und Jakobus in einer Nähe zu dieser Gruppierung? Sind sie, so Riesner, aufgeschlossen für die beschneidungsfreie Heidenmission? Ausschließlich politische Gründe für die Verfolgung der Christen nennt D.R. SCHWARTZ, *Agrippa I. The Last King of Judea* (TSAJ, 23), Tübingen, Mohr, 1990.

64. Vgl. dazu jetzt O. Wesley ALLEN, *The Death of Herod. The Narrative and Theo-*

Die Beobachtungen zu der Herodesfamilie modifizieren nicht die grundsätzliche Einschätzung der lukanischen Apologetik, sie bestätigen sie vielmehr. Allerdings wird die Darstellung der Herodesfamilie als in Religionsfragen kenntnisreiche und politisch verläßliche Zeugen primär für potentielle römische Leser gedacht sein: das Rom verbundene jüdische Königshaus[65] tritt gegen die eigenen religiösen Führer in den Rechtsfällen der Protagonisten Jesus und Paulus zum Schutz des Christentums auf. Freilich weiß der christliche Leser, daß beide Protagonisten durch römische Strafe gestorben sind. Ihm wird die lukanische Darstellung als Ausdruck des mittlerweile gewonnenen allgemein christlichen Bewußtseins erscheinen, daß Rom nämlich so, wie es sich verhalten hat, nur durch die religiösen Führer Israels gedrängt wurde. Was an negativer Konnotation zum Christentum besteht, das kam durch ungerechtfertigte Vorwürfe vom Judentum, von seinen religiösen Führern her. Es ist ein notwendiger Nebeneffekt dieser Darstellung, um Vertrauen in den römischen Staat zu werben. Dem potentiellen römischen Leser gegenüber allerdings, der eventuell um die römischen Strafen der Protagonisten Jesus und Paulus und das hierin zum Ausdruck kommende Urteil über die für ihn undeutliche Gruppierung der Christen weiß, wird erklärt, daß kein strafwürdiges Verhalten vorlag, daß diese Gruppierung von den diversen zelotischen Aktivitäten zu unterscheiden ist und daß eben mit der Herodesfamilie zuverlässige Zeugen aufgetreten sind, die in Gerichtsverfahren die politische und religiöse[66] Unbedenklichkeit des Christentums attestiert haben. Der ausführlichen Darstellung des Verfahrens des Paulus kommt sicherlich grundsätzlich exemplarische Funktion für die positive Zuordnung zum römischen Staat zu.

Allerdings treten die Mitglieder der Herodesfamilie nicht nur als Zeugen für die Christen auf, da sie zugleich von der Mehrheit des jüdischen

---

logical Function of Retribution in Luke-Acts (SBL DS, 158), Atlanta, GA, Scholars Press, 1997. In diesem Zusammenhang sei noch darauf verwiesen, daß Herodes Agrippa II. den Hohenpriester Ananus, der für die Hinrichtung des Herrenbruders Jakobus 62 n. Chr. maßgeblich verantwortlich war, absetzte. Da Josephus, *Ant* 20,197-203, über den Sachverhalt berichtet, kann Lukas dieses prochristliche Verhalten von Herodes Agrippa II. gegen den jüdischen Hohenpriester wohl auch als in Rom bekannt voraussetzen.

65. Paulus redet Agrippa in Apg 26,3.8 (παρ' ὑμῖν).27 betont als jüdischen König an.

66. Die römischen Beamten attestieren durchweg die Unzuständigkeit in religiösen Fragen und betrachten Streitigkeiten zwischen Juden und Christen als innerjüdischen Konflikt. Da aber sowohl Herodes Antipas (Lk 23,8) als auch Herodes Agrippa II. (Apg 25,22) zustimmend einer Begegnung mit Jesus bzw. Paulus entgegengehen, ja Agrippa als religiös Kundiger bei der Predigt des Paulus kurz vor einer Konversion steht (Apg 26,26), weckt Lukas über die Herodesfamilie sogar Interesse für den christlichen Glauben.

Volkes, vor allem seinen religiösen Führern, abzuheben sind. Da wir aus verschiedenen neutestamentlichen und frühchristlichen Schriften im Ausgang des 1. Jh. und Anfang des 2. Jh. um die Absetzbewegung des Judentums vom Christentum und des Christentums vom Judentum wissen, fungiert das Zeugnis der Herodesfamilie zugleich als politische Unbedenklichkeitsaussage gegen mögliche Beschuldigungen der Christen durch Juden vor römischen Behörden[67]. Die Herodesfamilie ist in dieser Doppelstrategie gegenüber römischen Verdächtigungen und jüdischen Angriffen des Christentums der ideale Zeuge für eine Apologie des Christentums.

Evangelische Theologie   Friedrich W. HORN
Johannes-Gutenberg-Universität
D-55099 Mainz

67. Vgl. etwa Lk 6,22f; Joh 9,22; 12,42; 16,2; Justin, *Dial* 16,4; 93,4; 95,4; 96,2; 133,6. STEGEMANN, *Synagoge* (n. 3), p. 36: »daß Lukas die heilsgeschichtliche Kontinuität der christlichen Gemeinschaft mit Israel … *unter den Bedingungen der Distanzierungserfahrung formuliert*«.

EINHEIT UND VIELFALT IM LUKANISCHEN DOPPELWERK

BEOBACHTUNGEN ZU REDEN, WUNDERERZÄHLUNGEN UND MAHLBERICHTEN[1]

I. JESU ANTRITTSREDE IN NAZARETH UND DIE PFINGSTPREDIGT DES PETRUS IN JERUSALEM

Die Frage nach Form und insbesondere Funktion der Reden in der Apostelgeschichte des Lukas ist in der Forschung oft gestellt und seit Martin Dibelius[2] im ganzen wohl auch sachgemäß (wenn auch natürlich im einzelnen auf unterschiedliche Weise) beantwortet worden[3]. Im Blick auf das Evangelium des Lukas kann man dagegen von »Reden« im eigentlichen Sinne kaum sprechen[4], ganz anders als etwa beim Matthäusevangelium. Der einzige explizit als Rede eingeleitete Textabschnitt ist die weitgehend unverändert aus der Logienquelle Q übernommene »Feldrede« (Lk 6,20-49)[5]; sie ist aber, im Unterschied zur Bergpredigt

---

1. Überarbeitete und ergänzte Fassung des für das deutschsprachige Seminar vorgelegten Diskussionspapiers. Die von den Teilnehmern des Seminars vorgetragenen kritischen Anfragen und Gegenvorschläge, insbesondere die von Dietrich-Alex Koch in seinem 'response-paper' gegebenen Hinweise, wurden bei der Neufassung des Textes berücksichtigt.
2. M. DIBELIUS, *Die Reden der Apostelgeschichte und die antike Geschichtsschreibung*, in DERS., *Aufsätze zur Apostelgeschichte*, ed. H. GREEVEN (FRLANT, 60), Göttingen, Vandenhoeck & Ruprecht, 1951, pp. 120-162. Es kam Dibelius entscheidend auf die Feststellung an, daß die Reden der Apg als Werk des *Schriftstellers* Lukas aufzufassen sind.
3. Vgl. die Zusammenfassung der Ergebnisse bei U. WILCKENS, *Die Missionsreden der Apostelgeschichte. Form- und traditionsgeschichtliche Untersuchungen* (WMANT, 5), Neukirchen-Vluyn, Neukirchener, ³1974, vor allem 187-189, ferner M.L. SOARDS, *The Speeches in Acts. Their Content, Context, and Concerns*, Louisville, KY, Westminster – John Knox Press, 1994, pp. 182-208.
4. Eine ähnliche Beobachtung läßt sich bei einer anderen Erzählgattung machen: Während Lukas im Evangelium mehrfach von Gastmahlgesprächen Jesu berichtet (5,27-39; 7,36-50; 11,37-54; 14,1-24; 22,14-38), fehlt diese Form in der Apostelgeschichte vollständig (Hinweis von D.-A. Koch).
5. Die »Feldrede« stammt offenbar nicht nur nach ihrem Wortlaut, sondern auch nach dem Kontext aus Q; denn der in Lk 7,1 erkennbare redaktionelle Übergang vom Schluß der Rede (6,49) hin zur Erzählung vom Hauptmann von Kapharnaum (7,2-10) entspricht Mt 7,28, was den Schluß zuläßt, daß beide Texte schon in Q aufeinander folgten und dabei redaktionell miteinander verknüpft waren. Vgl. dazu die knappe Skizze bei D. LÜHRMANN, *Die Redaktion der Logienquelle. Anhang: Zur weiteren Über-*

bei Matthäus und vielleicht auch anders als in Q selbst, von Lukas jedenfalls nicht als eine »programmatische« Rede gedacht, wie schon ihre vergleichsweise späte Stellung im Aufriß des Lk erkennen läßt[6]. Im lukanischen Reisebericht (9,51–18,14) gibt es zwar längere Abschnitte, in denen Jesus redet; aber hier handelt es sich schon angesichts des größeren Zusammenhangs nicht wirklich um »Reden«, da sich Jesus ja beständig »auf dem Wege« befindet. So dient beispielsweise die »Aussendungsrede« in Lk 10,2-16 lediglich dazu, Jesu Besuche in den nächsten Städten vorzubereiten (vgl. V. 1 ἀπέστειλεν αὐτοὺς ἀνὰ δύο [δύο] πρὸ προσώπου αὐτοῦ εἰς πᾶσαν πόλιν καὶ τόπον οὗ ἤμελλεν αὐτὸς ἔρχεσθαι); auch die in Lk 11 und 12 vorhandenen längeren Redestücke haben offenbar nicht die Funktion von Reden im literarischen bzw. rhetorischen Sinne, denn sie werden im Gegenteil durch dialogische Elemente unterbrochen – man könnte geradezu sagen: aufgelockert[7]. Am ehesten scheint noch der mehrere Gleichnisse enthaltende Abschnitt Lk 15–16 der Gattung »Rede« zu entsprechen; doch auch hier wird durch kleine eingestreute Hinweise angezeigt, daß Jesu Worte im Sinne des Evangelisten nicht als rhetorisch geschlossene Rede aufzufassen sind[8]. Ähnliches gilt für die lukanische Aufnahme sowohl der Q-Apokalypse in 17,22-37 als auch der Mk-Apokalypse in 21,5-36[9]. Angesichts des in den beiden Teilen des lukanischen Werkes derart dif-

lieferung der Logienquelle (WMANT, 33), Neukirchen-Vluyn, Neukirchener, 1969, pp. 53-56.

6. Lukas hat die Feldrede erst im Anschluß an Mk 3,19 in den Mk-Faden eingefügt; nach dem dann in Lk 7,1–8,3 verarbeiteten Q- und Sondergutmaterial nimmt er von Lk 8,4-8 an den Mk-Faden (4,1-9) – mit einigen kleineren Umstellungen – wieder auf. Bei Mt dagegen steht die Bergpredigt (Mt 5–7) im Aufriß des Mk-Fadens schon hinter Mk 1,39, wobei überdies die Erzählungen aus Mk 1,21-28 entweder ganz ausgelassen oder hinter die Bergpredigt verschoben wurden.

7. Auffällig ist etwa die Stellung des Vaterunser-Gebets, das in Lk 11,2-4 als *Antwort* auf eine entsprechende Bitte der Jünger gelehrt wird, während es innerhalb der Bergpredigt eine sehr herausgehobene Stellung besitzt. In dem in Lk 11 dann folgenden Text (V. 5-54) gibt es zwar nahezu keine Handlung; aber der redende Jesus wird immer wieder kurz unterbrochen (11,14.27.29a.37.38.45). Ähnliches läßt sich auch in Lk 12 beobachten, wo der Evangelist geradezu gezielt den Redefluß Jesu durch knappe Zwischenbemerkungen unterbricht (12,13.16.22.41.54).

8. Vgl. 15,11; 16,1. In 16,14 ist offenbar bewußt ein dialogisches Element eingefügt worden (ἤκουον δὲ ταῦτα πάντα οἱ Φαρισαῖοι φιλάργυροι ὑπάρχοντες καὶ ἐξεμυκτήριζον αὐτόν). Vor allem ist auch zu beachten, daß 15,1-3 nicht als Einleitung einer längeren »Rede« erscheint und daß umgekehrt am Ende jeder Hinweis auf einen »Redeschluß« fehlt (vgl. 17,1.5f.).

9. Am Ende (17,37a) wird die apokalyptische Rede als »Gespräch« erwiesen; ebenso findet sich in der Übernahme der Mk-Apokalypse in 21,29 ein Neueinsatz (καὶ εἶπεν αὐτοῖς), für den es in der Mk-Parallele kein Vorbild gibt (vgl. Mk 13,28).

ferierenden Befundes kann man die Frage stellen, ob die literarische Gattung »Rede« von Lukas womöglich bewußt der nachösterlichen Situation zugewiesen wird, weil sie für ihn im wesentlichen für »Missionspredigt« steht.

Eine Ausnahme von der Regel bildet im Evangelium die Szene der »Antrittspredigt« Jesu in Nazareth (Lk 4,16-30)[10]. Zwar wird man auch diesen Text kaum als eine Rede im eigentlichen Sinne bezeichnen können; aber im Kontext des Evangeliums ist doch deutlich, daß Lukas die von Jesus gesprochenen Worte sehr wohl als eine Rede Jesu verstanden wissen will; das wird schon durch ihre programmatische Stellung zu Beginn des öffentlichen Auftretens Jesu sichtbar[11], insbesondere auch dadurch, daß der ganze Abschnitt Lk 4,14-30 eine Umarbeitung der Vorlage Mk 1,14f. darstellt[12]. Lukas übernimmt in 4,14 zunächst aus Mk 1,14a die Ortsangabe 'Galiläa' und aus Mk 1,14b den Hinweis auf Jesu Verkündigungstätigkeit; die knappe markinische Notiz, die den »Wortlaut« der ersten Predigt Jesu in Galiläa wiedergibt (Mk 1,15), ersetzt er dagegen durch die breit erzählte Gottesdienst-Szene 4,16-30, für die es bei Mk in dieser Form kein Vorbild gibt[13]. Angesichts der Tatsache, daß auch in der Apostelgeschichte mit der Pfingstpredigt des Petrus in Jerusalem eine Redeszene am Anfang des öffentlichen Wirkens der christlichen Apostel steht (2,14-41), dürfte es sich lohnen, beide Texte trotz ihrer Unterschiedlichkeit miteinander zu vergleichen[14].

---

10. Vgl. zu diesem Text die eingehende Studie von U. Busse, *Das Nazareth-Manifest Jesu. Eine Einführung in das lukanische Jesusbild nach Lk 4,16-30* (SBS, 91), Stuttgart, Katholisches Bibelwerk, 1977. Ferner M. Korn, *Die Geschichte Jesu in veränderter Zeit. Studien zur bleibenden Bedeutung Jesu im lukanischen Doppelwerk* (WUNT, 2/51), Tübingen, Mohr, 1993, pp. 56-85. Zur Forschungsgeschichte C.J. Schreck, *The Nazareth Pericope: Luke 4,16-30 in Recent Study*, in F. Neirynck (ed.), *L'Évangile de Luc. The Gospel of Luke* (BETL, 32), Leuven, University Press – Peeters, ²1989, pp. 399-471.

11. Vgl. Busse, *Nazareth-Manifest* (s. die vorige Anm.), vor allem pp. 47-54.

12. Vgl. vor allem J. Delobel, *La rédaction de Lc., IV, 14-16a et le »Bericht vom Anfang«*, in F. Neirynck (ed.), *L'Évangile de Luc* (s. Anm. 10), pp. 113-133. 306-312.

13. Natürlich berührt sich Lk 4,16-30 mit Mk 6,1-6a: s. dazu Busse, *Nazareth-Manifest* (s. Anm. 10), pp. 62-67; aber die mk Überlieferung von der Verwerfung Jesu in Nazareth hat bei Lk eine so tiefgreifende Veränderung erfahren, daß man von einer »Parallele« nicht mehr sprechen kann.

14. Vgl. dazu G. Muhlack, *Die Parallelen von Lukas-Evangelium und Apostelgeschichte* (Theologie und Wirklichkeit, 8), Frankfurt am Main, Peter Lang, 1979, pp. 117-139. Sie bezieht dann auch die »Antrittspredigt« des Paulus im pisidischen Antiochia (Apg 13,16-41.46f.) in den Vergleich mit ein.

Lk 4,16-30		Apg 2,14-41 (42)	
4,16	Orts- und Situationsangabe	2,1-13	Orts- und Situationsangabe
		2,14.15	Situationsbezogene Redeeröffnung
4,17	Einleitung der Leseszene	2,16	Einleitung des Bibelzitats
4,18.19	Bibelzitat(e) Jes 61 (58)	2,17-21	Bibelzitat Joel 3,1-5 LXX
4,20	Ausleitung der Leseszene		
4,21a	Predigteinleitung		
4,21b	Predigt	2,22-24	Christuskerygma des Petrus
		2,25-28	Bibelzitat Ps 15,8-11 LXX
		2,29-31	Auslegung des Zitats
		2,32.33	Christuskerygma
		2,34.35	Bibelzitat Ps 109,1 LXX
		2,36	Anklage des Petrus gegen die Hörer
4,22	Reaktion der Hörenden	2,37	Reaktion der Hörenden
4,23-27	Jesu Antwort	2,38.39	Antwort des Petrus: Buße und Taufe
4,25-27	Biblische Beispiele	2,40	Wiederholung der Predigt
4,28-30	Jesu Vertreibung aus Nazareth	2,41.42	Massentaufe. Gemeindeleben

Der erste Vergleich zwischen beiden Texten ist ernüchternd: Sieht
man genau hin, so erweist sich die in Nazareth gehaltene Rede, die Jesu
öffentliches Auftreten einleitet, als aus nur einem einzigen Satz beste-
hend (V. 21b), während die Pfingstpredigt des Petrus in Jerusalem zu
den längsten Reden in der Apostelgeschichte gehört, vergleichbar der
(Antritts-)Rede des Paulus in Antiochia Pisidiae (13,6-41)[15]. Der Vergleich im einzelnen läßt dann freilich neben erheblichen Unterschieden
vor allem auch auffällige Strukturanalogien erkennen.

1. Die Eröffnung der Nazareth-Szene (Lk 4,16-21)

Nach Lk 4,16a kommt Jesus während seiner als überaus erfolgreich
dargestellten, im einzelnen aber nicht geschilderten Lehrtätigkeit in den
Synagogen Galiläas (4,14.15) nach Nazareth, seiner Vaterstadt (2,4.51),
wo er »nach seiner Gewohnheit« in die Synagoge geht (4,16b). Lukas
beschreibt nun zunächst Elemente eines synagogalen Gottesdienstes[16],
bei dem Jesus die Gelegenheit wahrnimmt, einen biblischen Text zu ver-
lesen (4,16c)[17]. Die am Anfang stehende Orts- und Situationsangabe ist
also vergleichsweise ausführlich.

---

15. Nur die Stephanusrede in Apg 7 ist deutlich länger.

16. S. dazu, insbesondere auch zu den historischen Problemen des Gottesdienst-
ablaufs, BUSSE, *Nazareth-Manifest* (s. Anm. 10), pp. 107-112.

17. An den näheren »liturgischen« Einzelheiten ist Lukas hier nicht interessiert. Vgl.
in der Sache den Exkurs »Der altjüdische Synagogengottesdienst« bei H.L. STRACK – P.
BILLERBECK, *Kommentar zum Neuen Testament aus Talmud und Midrasch*, IV/1, München, C.H. Beck, [5]1969, pp. 153-188.

Auch die Einleitung der sich anschließenden eigentlichen Leseszene ist sorgfältig gestaltet (V. 17): Man reicht Jesus das »Buch« des Propheten Jesaja, das er »aufrollt«[18] und in dem er eine bestimmte Textstelle »findet«[19], die dann in V. 18.19 zitiert wird (Jes 61,1f.; 58,6). Das Zitat nach LXX ist im Wortlaut fast korrekt: Zwar ist aus Jes 61,1 die Zeile ἰάσασθαι τοὺς συντετριμμένους τῇ καρδίᾳ entfallen[20], und als vorletzte Zeile ist ein (leicht variierter) Satz aus Jes 58,6 eingefügt, bevor das Zitat mit Jes 61,2a abgeschlossen wird; aber Lukas setzt durch die Art seiner Darstellung voraus, daß jedenfalls die Leser annehmen sollen, es handele sich bei dem verlesenen Prophetenwort wirklich um *eine* Textstelle und nicht um ein Mischzitat, das Jesus in dieser Form gar nicht hätte »finden« können[21]. Daß Jesus das Schriftwort (τὸ γεγραμμένον) auch tatsächlich verliest, wird nicht gesagt, ist aber wohl doch vorausgesetzt; wichtig ist allerdings die Beobachtung, daß sich durch die Art der Zitierweise der biblische Text als unmittelbare Anrede an die Leser des Evangeliums erweist[22].

Mit V. 20a wird die Leseszene ausgeleitet: Jesus rollt das Buch zusammen, gibt es dem Synagogendiener und setzt sich. Die Wendung ἐκάθισεν signalisiert bereits (was durch V. 20b dann bestätigt wird), daß Jesus »lehren« will, daß er also den Text auszulegen beabsichtigt[23]. Alle Anwesenden blicken gespannt (V. 20b) auf ihn[24], und Jesus spricht sie an (V. 21a)[25]: »Heute ist dieses Schriftwort (ἡ γραφή) erfüllt in

18. ἀναπτύσσω »öffnen (sc. einer Buchrolle)« ist im NT nur hier gebraucht, ebenso in V. 20 dann πτύσσω.

19. Die Überlegung von F. BOVON, *Das Evangelium nach Lukas. 1. Teilband: Lk 1,1–9,50* (EKK, 3/1), Zürich, Benziger – Neukirchen-Vluyn, Neukirchener, 1989, p. 211, es sei »auch möglich, daß sie [sc. die Textstelle] für diesen Tag vorgesehen war oder daß sie Jesus durch das Los zugeteilt wurde«, geht m.E. an der Zielrichtung des lk Textes vorbei.

20. In den Codices A Θ Ψ sowie in den Handschriften des Mehrheitstextes sind diese Worte nachgetragen.

21. Zur Frage der traditionsgeschichtlichen Herkunft dieser Textfassung vgl. R. ALBERTZ, *Die »Antrittspredigt« Jesu im Lukasevangelium auf ihrem alttestamentlichen Hintergrund*, in ZNW 74 (1983) 182-206.

22. Zur Interpretation vgl. P.F. ESLER, *Community and Gospel in Luke-Acts. The Social and Political Motivations of Lucan Theology* (SNTS MS, 57), Cambridge, University Press, 1987, ²1996, pp. 180-182.

23. Vgl. Lk 5,3 καθίσας ... ἐδίδασκεν. Vgl. auch Mt 5,1 (Jesus »hält« die Bergpredigt im Sitzen) und vor allem Mt 23,2. Es fällt auf, daß Lukas die Verwendung des Verbs διδάσκειν an dieser Stelle vermeidet, obwohl er es sonst häufig verwendet (zuletzt 4,13). Zum »sitzenden Lehren« vgl. BILLERBECK, *Kommentar*, I (s. Anm. 17), p. 997.

24. Das Verb ἀτενίζω ist im Lk-Evangelium nur noch 22,56 belegt (die Magd im Hof des Hohenpriesters »blickt gespannt« auf Petrus), oft aber in der Apg. Die Wendung πάντων οἱ ὀφθαλμοί könnte bewußt »biblische Sprache« sein, vgl. Ps 144,15 LXX.

25. Die Wendung ἤρξατο (δὲ) λέγειν (πρὸς αὐτούς) ist bei Lk nicht selten (Lk 7,24.49; 11,29 u.ö.).

euren Ohren«, d.h. es ist Realität geworden im Augenblick des gegenwärtigen Hörens (V. 21b)[26]. Damit ist Jesu »Rede« aber auch schon
abgeschlossen, denn in V. 22 folgt bereits die Schilderung der Reaktion
der Hörenden. Offenbar meint Lukas, daß mit V. 21b alles Notwendige
gesagt ist.

2. *Die Eröffnung der Jerusalem-Szene (Apg 2,14-36)*

Der Vergleich des Berichts über die »Rede« Jesu (Lk 4,16-21a.21b)
mit dem Bericht von der ersten Predigt des Petrus in Jerusalem (Apg
2,14-41) zeigt als erstes, daß in Apg 2,1-13 eine für das Verständnis des
folgenden wichtige Orts- und Situationsangabe vorangeht, die sehr viel
ausführlicher gestaltet ist als die entsprechende Angabe in Lk 4,16: Am
Tag der πεντεκόστη[27] haben sich »alle«, d.h. die in 1,13f. genannten
Mitglieder der Jesus-Gruppe, versammelt; sie erfahren die Ausgießung
des πνεῦμα ἅγιον (2,2-4) entsprechend der in 1,8 ausgesprochenen Verheißung Jesu. Dabei sind auch zahlreiche Bewohner Jerusalems anwe-
send (2,5f.), die das Geschehen gegensätzlich interpretieren (V. 7-12
einerseits, V. 13 andererseits). Angesichts dessen beginnt Petrus zu
reden (V. 14a); er *steht* dazu *auf* (σταθείς), wodurch deutlich wird, daß
das Folgende nicht als »Lehre«, sondern als »öffentliche Rede« zu verstehen ist[28]. Die dann zur eigentlichen Rede hinführende Einleitungs-
wendung ist im übrigen recht umständlich gestaltet[29].

Die Rede selbst wird in V. 14bα mit einer ausdrücklichen Anrede an
das Publikum eingeleitet, wobei Petrus auf die zuvor in V. 5 geschilderte
Situation Bezug nimmt. In V. 14bβ folgt eine feierliche Redeeröffnung:
Die Wendung γνωστὸν (ὑμῖν) ἔστω reflektiert biblische Sprache und
ist so oder ähnlich in der Apg des öfteren belegt[30]; ἐνωτίζομαι ist zwar
im NT hapax legomenon, wird aber in LXX, auch als Impt. mit τὰ

---

26. Es ist wenig wahrscheinlich, daß sich die Aussage auf die Taufszene Lk 3,22
bezieht. Da Lukas Jesus von Anfang an mit dem Geist in Verbindung bringt (vgl. 1,35;
2,26f.; 4,14), denkt er wohl auch in 4,21b nicht an einen gesonderten Akt der »Geistverleihung« an Jesus.

27. Zur biblischen Sprache in Apg 2,1 vgl. H. CONZELMANN, *Die Apostelgeschichte*
(HNT, 7), Tübingen, Mohr, ²1972, p. 30.

28. Vgl. die entsprechende Angabe in Apg 17,22; 21,40.

29. Zu ἐπαίρειν τὴν φωνήν vgl. Apg 14,11; 22,22. Auch das Verb ἀποφθέγγεσθαι
wird im NT nur in der Apg gebraucht.

30. Die Wendung wird in der Apg offenbar vor allem dann eingesetzt, wenn eine
besonders wichtige »Botschaft« ausgesprochen werden soll; vgl. 4,10 (Petrus wendet
sich an das Synedrium), 13,38 (Rechtfertigungsbotschaft des Paulus am Ende seiner Rede
in Antiochia Pisidiae) und 28,28 (Paulus an die Juden in Rom). Zur »biblischen Sprache«
vgl. Ez 36,32 LXX: λέγει κύριος κύριος, γνωστὸν ἔσται ὑμῖν, αἰσχύνθητε καὶ
ἐντράπητε ἐκ τῶν ὁδῶν ὑμῶν, οἶκος Ἰσραηλ.

ῥήματά μου, häufiger gebraucht[31]. Auch der zweite Teil der Eröffnung der Rede (V. 15) nimmt sehr konkret auf die Situation Bezug: Petrus verweist auf die frühe Stunde und sieht darin ein Argument gegen den in V. 13 ausgesprochenen Trunkenheitsvorwurf. Da die eigentliche Rede bis dahin aber noch gar nicht begonnen hat, kann man sagen, daß im Grunde der ganze Abschnitt Apg 2,1-15 einerseits und Lk 4,16 andererseits einander entsprechen.

Das Redecorpus wird in 2,16 eröffnet mit der Hinführung zu dem langen Schriftzitat in V. 17-21; insofern liegt eine Entsprechung zwischen Apg 2,16 und Lk 4,17 vor, auch wenn es sich dort um eine vom Erzähler geschilderte Szene, hier dagegen um einen Teil der Rede handelt. Ein wesentlicher Unterschied liegt natürlich von vornherein darin, daß in Apg 2 das Schriftwort nicht »gefunden« zu werden braucht, da die »Erfüllung« ja als bereits geschehen dem Zitat vorangegangen war – man könnte geradezu von einem »Erfüllungszitat« sprechen. Wird in Lk 4,17, der Gottesdienstszene entsprechend, der biblische Text als *das Geschriebene* (τὸ γεγραμμένον) bezeichnet (vgl. 4,21b ἡ γραφή), so heißt die biblische Überlieferung in Apg 2,16 *das Gesprochene* (τὸ εἰρημένον), wobei der Prophet als das »Medium« erscheint, durch das Gott spricht (διὰ τοῦ προφήτου[32]; vgl. V. 17 λέγει ὁ θεός). Lukas setzt voraus, daß der aus Joel 3,1-5 LXX übernommene Text in Apg 2,17-21 als korrektes Zitat zu gelten hat[33]. Beide Redeszenen sind also in starkem Maße durch die Bibel bestimmt. Dabei setzt die Rede Jesu ein mit dem gleichsam »vorgegebenen« Wort, das der Deutung bedarf; in der Rede des Petrus dagegen dient das vom Propheten gesagte Gotteswort dazu, ein bereits geschehenes Ereignis sachgemäß zu interpretieren.

Eine Entsprechung zu Lk 4,20.21a gibt es in Apg 2 nicht. Vielmehr schließt sich an das Schriftwort sogleich der zweite Teil der Petruspredigt an, der 2,22-36 umfaßt und der eigentlichen »Rede« Jesu in Lk 4,21b entspricht. Dieser Teil der Rede ist in sich klar gegliedert. Petrus »erzählt« in dem in besonderer Weise durch die Anrede ἄνδρες Ἰσραηλῖται eingeleiteten Redeabschnitt V. 22-28 zunächst in kerygmatischer Form vom Christusgeschehen (V. 22-24)[34] und fügt zur Interpre-

---

31. Vgl. z.B. Gen 4,23; Hiob 32,11; Ps 5,1 u.ö.
32. Vgl. Apg 3,18.21 u.ö.
33. Die Änderung zu Beginn (V. 17: ἐν ταῖς ἐσχάταις ἡμέραις statt μετὰ ταῦτα) berücksichtigt, daß der ursprüngliche Kontext nicht mitzitiert ist, und sie ist sachlich insofern durchaus korrekt; der ausdrückliche Hinweis, daß Gott redet (λέγει ὁ θεός), entspricht der Tatsache, daß der zitierte Text Joel 3 Teil einer längeren Gottesrede ist. Reine Präzisierungen ohne inhaltliche Änderung sind die Ergänzungen καὶ προφητεύσουσιν in V. 18fin sowie die Einfügungen von ἄνω, σημεῖα und κάτω in V. 19.
34. Vgl. dazu KORN, *Geschichte* (s. Anm. 10), pp. 234-236.

tation das Zitat aus Ps 15,8-11 LXX an[35]; es liegt also grundsätzlich dasselbe Verfahren vor wie zuvor in V. 1-13 und in V. 14-21. Das Zitat
wird aber nun seinerseits interpretiert (V. 29-31): Es zeige, sagt Petrus,
daß der »Patriarch« David als Prophet die ἀνάστασις Jesu vorhergese-
hen habe (V. 31). Sachlich ist hier bemerkenswert, daß der lukanische
Petrus zwar das Grab Davids erwähnt, daß er aber nicht auf das (leere)
Grab Jesu hinweist, obwohl das von der geschilderten Situation her doch
unmittelbar nahegelegen hätte; Lukas setzt offenbar voraus, daß für die
Osterverkündigung in Jerusalem die Frage des (leeren) Grabes bedeu-
tungslos war[36].

Nach dem Zitat und seiner Auslegung folgt in Apg 2,32.33 abermals
eine kerygmatische, zu V. 22-24 parallele Aussage; dabei nehmen V. 32
und V. 33b die Oster- und Himmelfahrtserzählung aus Lk 24 bzw. Apg
1 sowie den Beginn der Pfingsterzählung Apg 2 auf, wobei der jetzt ausdrücklich eingeführte Zeugenbegriff an Apg 1,8 anknüpft; die Aussage
in V. 33a, daß Christus »zur Rechten Gottes erhöht« worden sei, ist
dagegen aus den zuvor und anschließend zitierten Schriftworten (V. 25
und 34) gewonnen. In V. 33b erwähnt Petrus dann mit direkter Hinwendung zu den Hörern erneut das Pfingstgeschehen. In Apg 2,34.35
schließt sich ein drittes ausdrücklich eingeleitetes Schriftzitat an (Ps
109,1 LXX)[37], das vorab bereits dadurch kommentiert wird, daß gesagt
wird, David selber sei nicht der in den Himmel Hinaufgestiegene.
Schließlich folgt in 2,36 als Höhepunkt und Abschluß die direkte Botschaft an die Adressaten, daß der Jesus, den »ihr« gekreuzigt habt, von
Gott zum κύριος und zum χριστός gemacht wurde, und daß »das ganze
Haus Israel« dies erkennen solle[38]. Zu all dem gibt es in Lk 4 verständ-
licherweise keine Parallele; denn das Zitat aus Jes 61 ist ja in der Person
Jesu selber umfassend »erfüllt«, und einer näheren Explikation bedarf
es deshalb also nicht.

3. Die Reaktion der Hörer in Nazareth (Lk 4,22-30) und in Jerusalem (Apg 2,37-41)

In der Nazareth-Szene Lk 4 schließt sich an Jesu kurze Rede V. 21b
unmittelbar der Bericht von der Reaktion der Hörer an (Lk 4,22), auf die

---

35. Das Zitat folgt korrekt LXX, nur die letzte Zeile ist nicht übernommen.
36. Das ist m.E. auch der historisch wahrscheinlichste Befund.
37. Dies Psalmwort wird im NT überaus häufig zitiert, in der Apg aber nur hier (vgl.
Lk 20,42f. in der Parallele zu Mk 12,36).
38. Die Unterscheidung zwischen πᾶς οἶκος Ἰσραήλ und »ihr« (ὑμεῖς ἐσταυρώ-
σατε) zeigt übrigens, daß nach Lukas nicht »die Juden«, sondern die Bewohner Jerusalems für Jesu Kreuzigung verantwortlich waren.

eine überaus kritische Antwort Jesu erfolgt (V. 23.24-27). Die Auslegung des »Dialogs« V. 22f. bereitet Schwierigkeiten. Ulrich Busse meint, Lukas schildere in V. 22 »die im Grunde positive, aber in gewisser Hinsicht auch zweideutige und oberflächliche Reaktion der Zuhörer«[39]. Dann aber erscheint Jesu Antwort als durchaus unangemessen[40]. Will man diese Annahme vermeiden, so spricht alles dafür, daß Lukas von vornherein eine negative Reaktion der Bewohner Nazareths beschreiben will. Dementsprechend ist schon die einleitende Wendung πάντες ἐμαρτύρουν αὐτῷ καὶ ἐθαύμαζον im Sinne des Lukas offenbar nicht »positiv« gemeint, sondern im Sinne eines ungläubigen Staunens zu verstehen, entsprechend der (empörten) Frage: »Wie kann der Sohn Josephs [!] *so* von sich reden?«[41]. Ganz anders sieht dagegen die Reaktion der Hörer der Pfingstpredigt in Apg 2,37 aus: Ihre Antwort auf die Predigt des Petrus ist nicht ungläubige Skepsis, sondern sie fragen τί ποιήσωμεν[42]. Die Jerusalemer Hörer des Petrus verstehen also, im Gegensatz zu den Hörern Jesu in Nazareth, daß die Botschaft, die sie vernommen haben, nicht in den ihnen (scheinbar) längst bekannten Erfahrungshorizont eingeordnet werden kann, sondern daß diese Botschaft etwas von ihnen fordert, nämlich ein Tun, und das meint: ein gegenüber ihrem bisherigen Handeln *verändertes* Tun, nach dem sie wirklich *fragen* müssen. Die Hörer in Jesu Vaterstadt Nazareth dagegen meinen, sie wüßten längst, wer Jesus ist, und sie wüßten also auch, daß er keineswegs dazu berechtigt ist, das verlesene Schriftwort auf sich selbst zu beziehen.

Dementsprechend fallen die Antworten, die Jesus und Petrus jeweils geben, sehr unterschiedlich aus: Jesus übt Kritik an seinen Hörern (Lk

---

39. BUSSE, *Nazareth-Manifest* (s. Anm. 10), p. 37. Für diese Auslegung spreche auch die »eindeutige Wortwahl« mit den positiven Begriffen μαρτυρεῖν und θαυμάζειν. Ähnlich BOVON, *Evangelium nach Lukas I* (s. Anm. 19), p. 213.

40. Das sieht auch BUSSE, *Nazareth-Manifest*, p. 38: »Die Erwiderung Jesu ist nach dem eben noch gespendeten Beifall auf den ersten Blick merkwürdig brüsk«.

41. μαρτυρεῖν meint dann nicht »Beifall spenden«, sondern einfach »bezeugen«; und θαυμάζειν drückt die kritische Verwunderung und keineswegs Zustimmung aus. Die zweifellos positive Wendung ἐπὶ τοῖς λόγοις τῆς χάριτος τοῖς ἐκπορευομένοις ἐκ τοῦ στόματος αὐτοῦ gibt nicht die Worte der Bewohner Nazareths wieder, sondern mit ihnen charakterisiert Lukas selber das von Jesus Gesagte. Das μαρτυρεῖν καὶ θαυμάζειν der Nazarener äußert sich dagegen in ihrer Feststellung, er sei (nur) der Sohn Josephs.

42. T. BERGHOLZ, *Der Aufbau des lukanischen Doppelwerkes. Untersuchungen zum formalliterarischen Charakter von Lukas-Evangelium und Apostelgeschichte* (EHS, 23/545), Frankfurt am Main, Peter Lang, p. 85, sieht die Parallele zu Lk 4,22b in Apg 2,7: »In beiden Fällen werden die Redenden ihrer Herkunft nach erkannt, mit der impliziten Folgerung: so jemand *kann* nicht solche Worte sprechen«. Diese Auslegung übersieht die unmittelbare Fortsetzung der wörtlichen Rede in Apg 2,8-11; Apg 2,7 steht überdies im Kontext an einer ganz anderen Stelle als Lk 4,22b.

4,23f.), eben weil ihre Reaktion auf seine Rede ihre (letztlich dem Prophetenwort widersprechende!) Skepsis beweist. Dabei weist er sie darauf hin, daß es für die soeben wieder bestätigte Regel, wonach der Prophet nichts gilt in seiner πατρίς, biblische Vorbilder bzw. Belege gibt; Jesus zitiert diese Belege zwar nicht, er weist auf sie aber in V. 25-27 referierend hin. Im übrigen erklärt er, in Nazareth, anders als in Kapharnaum, kein Wunder zu tun[43]. Dagegen nimmt Petrus in seiner Antwort (Apg 2,38f.) die Frage der Hörer »Was sollen wir tun?« positiv auf: Die Adressaten haben alle Chancen zur Umkehr und zur Vergebung der Sünden, denn sie sind es ja, denen die Verheißung gilt. Lukas ergänzt die wörtliche Rede des Petrus durch den referierenden Hinweis (V. 40a), Petrus habe den Hörern gegenüber auch noch auf andere Weise Zeugnis abgelegt; abschließend läßt er nochmals in wörtlicher Rede (V. 40b) die Aufforderung zum Ergreifen der Rettungschance folgen (σώθητε).

Die Jesus-Szene in Nazareth endet mit einer Niederlage Jesu, nämlich seiner Vertreibung aus der Stadt (V. 28-30); allenfalls mag es als ein »Wunder« gedeutet werden, daß Jesus dem Anschlag souverän entgeht und er διὰ μέσου αὐτῶν davonschreitet[44]. Die Petrus-Szene in Jerusalem dagegen endet mit einem grandiosen Triumph des Redners: An einem einzigen Tag nimmt eine große Zahl von Menschen seine Botschaft an, läßt sich taufen und wird (sc. zur Jesus-Gruppe) »hinzugetan« (προσετέθησαν) – und zwar sind es, wie mit schönem Achtergewicht gesagt wird, »etwa dreitausend Seelen« (2,41).

4. Ergebnis des Vergleichs

Die beiden Redeszenen in Lk 4 und in Apg 2 sind von Lukas offensichtlich bewußt parallel gestaltet worden: Beide leiten das öffentliche Auftreten der im folgenden dargestellten Hauptpersonen ein; in beiden Reden geht es darum, das geschilderte Geschehen und die damit verbundenen Personen umfassend zu deuten; beide Reden beziehen sich auf

---

43. Daß schon an dieser Stelle Taten in Kapharnaum erwähnt werden, widerspricht der Textfolge; denn Jesus wird erst in 4,31 in diese Stadt kommen und dann dort erstmals ein (Heilungs-)Wunder tun.

44. Vgl. zu diesem Motiv Joh 8,59 und vor allem Apg 14,19f. BUSSE, *Nazareth-Manifest* (s. Anm. 10), p. 46 meint, V. 30 stelle »einen großartigen Ausklang« dar: »Wie Lukas die durch den Schlußteil der Rede aufgestaute Wut in szenische Aktion umsetzt, so dramatisch läßt er Jesus ohne Schaden, ja vielmehr ebenso souverän, wie er aufgetreten ist, Nazareth verlassen.« Dagegen verweist KORN, *Geschichte* (s. Anm. 10), p. 83f. zutreffend darauf, daß »von der Errettung Jesu nur ganz allgemein erzählt« wird; vgl. R.C. TANNEHILL, *The Mission of Jesus according to Luke IV, 16-30*, in E. GRÄSSER u.a. (eds.), *Jesus in Nazareth* (BZNW, 40), Berlin, de Gruyter, 1972, pp. 51-75, hier: 61.

das Wirken des göttlichen Geistes. Beide Reden lassen sich auch hinsichtlich ihrer Stellung im Kontext miteinander vergleichen, denn sowohl in Lk 4 als auch in Apg 2 folgt auf die Rede ein Summar. Im Evangelium handelt es sich um die aus Mk 1,21f. übernommene knappe Einleitung zur ersten Exorzismus-Erzählung (4,31f.); Lukas will dabei im Unterschied zu Mk die Notiz über Jesu Lehren ἐν τοῖς σάββασιν nicht als Einleitung zur folgenden Wundererzählung verstanden wissen, sondern er formuliert offenbar gezielt eine grundsätzliche Aussage über Jesu andauernde – und offenbar erfolgreiche – Predigttätigkeit in Kapharnaum[45]. In der Apostelgeschichte dient das der Predigtszene folgende Summar in ähnlicher Weise dazu, grundsätzlich die Lebenswirklichkeit der auf wunderbare Weise so groß angewachsenen Gemeinde zu beschreiben; Lukas will hier deutlich machen, daß sich gegenüber der in 1,14 geschilderten Situation in der Praxis der gemeindlichen Lehr- und Lebensformen nichts ändert[46]. Ein Unterschied zwischen beiden Texten liegt natürlich darin, daß im Evangelium das Summar mit einer präzisen Angabe über Jesu (nach V. 30 verständliche) Wanderung nach Kapharnaum eingeleitet wird (ἐπορεύετο καὶ καθῆλθεν εἰς Καφαρναοὺμ πόλιν τῆς Γαλιλαίας), während in der Apostelgeschichte natürlich kein Ortswechsel stattfindet.

Die zu diskutierende Frage lautet: Warum läßt Lukas Jesu öffentliches Wirken mit einem derartigen Fehlschlag beginnen, das nachösterliche öffentliche Wirken des Petrus (bzw. der Jünger Jesu überhaupt) dagegen mit einem so überaus großen Erfolg? Die Feststellung, Lukas habe sich einfach an die Nazareth-Überlieferung gehalten, wie er sie in Mk 6,1-6a vorfand, reicht als Antwort keinesfalls aus. Denn zum einen hätte Lukas zweifellos die Freiheit gehabt, seine Vorlage an dieser Stelle zu korrigieren bzw. gar nicht erst zu übernehmen, wenn sie nicht in sein Konzept gepaßt hätte. Und zum andern ist zu beachten, daß Lukas sich ja nicht darauf beschränkt hat, Mk 6,1-6a mit allenfalls geringen Veränderungen zu »übernehmen«; er hat vielmehr die dortige Szene erheblich ausgebaut. Er hat ihr insbesondere auch durch ihre neue Plazierung zu

45. Diese Veränderung gegenüber der Mk-Vorlage kommt durch verhältnismäßig einfache schriftstellerische Mittel zustande: Statt εὐθὺς ... ἐδίδασκεν (Mk 1,21) heißt es in Lk 4,31 ἦν διδάσκων; das Erstaunen der Hörenden (ἐξεπλήσσοντο) bezieht sich nicht mehr auf die aktuelle Verkündigung Jesu in der Synagoge, sondern darauf, daß »sein Wort« ἐν ἐξουσίᾳ erging (Lk 4,32 diff. Mk 1,22).
46. Das Summar Apg 2,42.43-47 knüpft bewußt an die Beschreibung der ursprünglich kleinen Gruppe aus 1,14 an (ἦσαν προσκαρτεροῦντες ...). Vgl. A. LINDEMANN, *The Beginnings of Christian Life in Jerusalem According to the Summaries in the Acts of the Apostles*, in J.V. HILLS (ed.), *Common Life in the Early Church*. FS Graydon Snyder, Downers Grove, IL, Trinity Press International, 1998, pp. 202-218.

Beginn (!) der Darstellung des öffentlichen Wirkens Jesu einen besonders prominenten Platz im Aufriß des Evangeliums gegeben[47].

Wie schon erwähnt, reagieren die Zuhörer sowohl in Lk 4 (V. 22) als auch in Apg 2 (V. 37) auf das Gehörte mit einer Frage. Im Evangelium handelt es sich dabei um eine rein rhetorische Frage, die tatsächlich (scheinbares) »Wissen« anzeigt: Der »Sohn Josephs«[48] *kann* doch gar nicht die Erfüllung der prophetischen Verheißung sein. Dementsprechend vertreiben die Bewohner Nazareths Jesus aus ihrer Stadt und versuchen sogar, ihn hinzurichten (V. 29). Damit verweist die Reaktion der Hörer Jesu also bereits auf das Ende der im Evangelium erzählten (Lebens-)Geschichte Jesu – die künftige Katastrophe ist bereits vorgezeichnet[49]. In der Apostelgeschichte dagegen zeigt die von den Zuhörern gestellte Frage deren existentielle Sorge; und dementsprechend wird die Antwort, die sie von Petrus erhalten, von ihnen auch sofort in die Tat umgesetzt. Auch dies ist zu verstehen als Vorausverweis auf den Fortgang der im zweiten Teil des lukanischen Werkes erzählten Geschichte: Die Gruppe derer, die die von den Aposteln verkündigte Botschaft hören und glaubend annehmen, wird beständig wachsen – unaufhaltsam und ohne überhaupt an ein definitives Ziel zu gelangen[50]

Mit der Beobachtung, daß die ganze Szene in Nazareth – und zwar sowohl das biblische Zitat als auch dessen Auslegung in Jesu »Rede« wie auch die Reaktion der Hörer und Jesu Antwort darauf – als vorwegnehmende Beschreibung des weiteren irdischen Wirkens Jesu verstanden werden kann, ist deren Funktion im Rahmen des lukanischen Doppelwerks im ganzen aber noch nicht vollständig erfaßt. Die in Lk 4,16-30

47. Zum Verhältnis von Lk 4,14-44 und Mk 6,1-6 vgl. BUSSE, *Nazareth-Manifest* (s. Anm. 10), pp. 62-67.

48. Das ist möglicherweise der Grund, weshalb Nazareth ausdrücklich als die πατρίς Jesu bezeichnet wird: Die Bewohner dieser Stadt »wissen« natürlich, wessen Sohn Jesus ist.

49. So auch KORN, *Geschichte* (s. Anm. 10), p. 83: »Die Steigerung der Ablehnung bis zur Tötungsabsicht ist wohl das Werk des Lukas, um der Ablehnung Jesu durch die Menschen in der Synagoge von Nazareth typische Bedeutung zu geben. Umgekehrt wird von hier aus die Passion Jesu als Verwerfung des durch ihn repräsentierten Heils gedeutet«. Unzutreffend scheint mir freilich die Erwägung zu sein, diese Verwerfung des Evangeliums setze sich in der Apostelgeschichte fort.

50. Der von Lukas in der Apostelgeschichte erzählte Missionserfolg und also die Geschichte der Kirche wird im Gegensatz zur Geschichte des irdischen Jesus, keinen wirklichen »Abschluß« und also kein erzählbares Ende haben. Das berühmte Schlußwort der Apostelgeschichte (ἀκωλύτως) signalisiert, daß die Mission gar nicht behindert werden kann; vgl. M. WOLTER, *Die Juden und die Obrigkeit bei Lukas* in K. WENGST – G. SASS (eds.), *Ja und nein. Christliche Theologie im Angesicht Israels*. FS W. Schrage, Neukirchen-Vluyn, Neukirchener Verlag, 1998, pp. 277-290, vor allem 280.289. Wolter meint, das ἀκωλύτως beziehe sich auf die Juden als Gegenüber, nicht auf den römischen »Staat«.

beschriebene Szene enthält vielmehr auch schon einen Vorausverweis auf die Geschichte der nachösterlichen Kirche: Zwar werden sich die in 4,18-19 zitierten Verheißungen aus Jes 61 schon in dem einen Jahr des Auftretens Jesu[51] erfüllen; aber der in den in 4,25-27 referierten biblischen Beispielen betonte Akzent, daß durch das Jesusgeschehen das Heil den *Fremden* zukommt[52], wird erst in der Apostelgeschichte verwirklicht werden. Wenn Jesus die Bewohner Nazareths auf die Wundererzählungen von Elia (1 Kön 17) und Elisa (2 Kön 4) hinweist, dann stellt er dabei nicht das Wunder in den Mittelpunkt, sondern er spricht von der Herkunft derer, denen durch das Wunder geholfen wurde: Elia wurde während der Hungersnot im Lande zu niemandem geschickt außer allein zu einer Witwe aus dem »in der Gegend von Sidon gelegenen Sarepta«; Elisa heilte unter allen Aussätzingen in Israel »niemanden außer Naeman, den Syrer«. Berücksichtigt man, daß Lukas die Überlieferung von der Syro-Phönizierin (Mk 7,24-30) nicht übernommen hat, dann läßt sich das in Lk 4,25-27 Gesagte nicht anders denn als ein gezielter Vorausverweis auf die erst in der Apostelgeschichte dargestellte Entwicklung verstehen[53].

Will Lukas nur aus einem lediglich »biographischen« Interesse heraus berichten, daß Jesus in seiner πατρίς erfolglos gewesen sei? Das ist ebenso unwahrscheinlich wie die Annahme, Lukas habe den Bericht in Apg 2 allein aus »historischem« Interesse geschrieben. Vielmehr ist anzunehmen, daß Lukas mit den beiden Szenen »theologisch« sagen will, zwar habe Jesu irdisches Wirken ebenso begonnen, wie es dann endete, nämlich mit einer Katastrophe, das Wirken der durch den von Jesus verheißenen Geist geleiteten Kirche hingegen sei von Anfang an in höchstem Maße erfolgreich gewesen.

II. WUNDERERZÄHLUNGEN UND WUNDERSUMMARIEN

Der Vergleich zwischen den im Evangelium des Lukas und den in der Apostelgeschichte erzählten Wundergeschichten soll sich auf wenige

---

51. Mit der Übernahme der Wendung κηρύξαι ἐνιαυτὸν κυρίου δεκτόν in V. 19 scheint Lukas anzudeuten, daß er sich Jesu Auftreten als ein Jahr dauernd vorstellt.

52. Vgl. dazu ESLER, *Community* (s. Anm. 22), pp. 34f.

53. Anders BUSSE, *Nazareth-Manifest* (s. Anm. 10), pp. 43f., der meint, diese Auslegung nähere sich »bedenklich einer Überinterpretation«. Wenig später stellt Busse dann fest: »Die Elias- und Elischatypologie des Lukas im Sinne einer umfassenden heilsuniversalistischen Aussage schließt zwar die kommende Heidenmission der Kirche mit ein, aber der Evangelist stellt hier letzteres noch nicht in den Mittelpunkt, weil es seinen Gedankengang stören, der möglichen Entwicklung vorgreifen und sie frühzeitig präjudizieren würde«. Die Schlußbemerkungen gehen über das im Text Erkennbare hinaus.

Texte beschränken, wobei das Auswahlkriterium ganz äußerlich die Übereinstimmung der Motive ist: In beiden Teilen des lukanischen Werkes wird von Gelähmtenheilungen und von Totenerweckungen erzählt. Ein knapper Vergleich der in beiden Teilen des lukanischen Werkes enthaltenen Wundersummarien schließt sich an[54].

1. Gelähmtenheilungen durch Jesus (Lk 5,17-26), durch Petrus (Apg 3,1-10; 9,32-35) und durch Paulus (Apg 14,8-13)[55]

a. Die Erzählung Lk 5,17-26[56] entspricht im ganzen der Vorlage Mk 2,1-12, einschließlich des Kontexts; vorausgeht die Heilung des Aussätzigen (Lk 5,12-16 / Mk 1,40-45), es folgen die Berufung des Levi und das Zöllnergastmahl (Lk 5,27-32 / Mk 2,13-17). Zu den auffallendsten lukanischen Änderungen gehört, daß die »Gegner« Jesu schon gleich zu Beginn erwähnt werden (V. 17)[57] und nicht erst dort, wo sie aktiv in das Geschehen eingreifen (V. 21 diff. Mk 2,6). Die sehr ungewöhnliche Art der Annäherung des Gelähmten erfolgt dagegen nahezu unverändert entsprechend der Mk-Vorlage[58]. Auch der durch das Sündenvergebungswort Jesu ausgelöste Konflikt mit den »Gegnern« wird in fast gleicher Weise wie bei Mk geschildert. Die Art der einleitenden Frage in V. 21b ist gegenüber Mk 2,7 allerdings signifikant verändert: Die – jetzt ausgesprochene und nicht nur ἐν ταῖς καρδίαις αὐτῶν gedachte – kritische Frage lautet bei Lukas τίς ἐστιν οὗτος; sie zielt damit bewußt auf die *Person* Jesu, während sich die entsprechende Überlegung bei Mk (τί

---

54. Zur Quellenfrage und zu formgeschichtlichen Problemen s. F. NEIRYNCK, *The Miracle Stories in the Acts of the Apostles*, in DERS., *Evangelica. Gospel Studies – Études d'Évangile. Collected Essays*, ed. F. VAN SEGBROECK (BETL, 60), Leuven, Peeters – University Press, 1982, pp. 835-880. Vgl. auch A. GEORGE, *Les récits de miracles. Caractéristiques lucaniennes*, in DERS., *Études sur l'œuvre de Luc* (Sources bibliques), Paris, Gabalda, 1978, pp. 67-84.

55. Vgl. zum folgenden MUHLACK, *Parallelen* (s. Anm. 14), pp. 15-36.

56. Vgl. dazu U. BUSSE, *Die Wunder des Propheten Jesus. Die Rezeption, Komposition und Interpretation der Wundertradition im Evangelium des Lukas* (FzB, 24), Stuttgart, Katholisches Bibelwerk, 1977, pp. 115-134.

57. Die Pharisäer und die νομοδιδάσκαλοι (dagegen Mk 2,6: τινὲς τῶν γραμματέων) werden sehr eingehend vorgestellt; Lukas will offenbar betonen, daß man »überall« an Jesus interessiert ist. Der Hinweis auf die Jesu Heiltätigkeit ermöglichende δύναμις κυρίου soll offenbar unter der Perspektive gelesen werden, daß auch die Gegner Jesu diese »Kraft« wahrnehmen.

58. Lukas hat den etwas umständlichen mk Bericht über das durch »Aufgraben« erfolgende Abdecken des Daches (ἀπεστέγασαν τὴν στέγην ... ἐξορύξαντες) durch den knappen Hinweis auf die »Ziegel« (διὰ τῶν κεράμων) ersetzt. Ob er damit tatsächlich eine »Anpassung der Erzählung an das griechisch-römische Lokalkolorit« beabsichtigte (so BUSSE, *Wunder*, pp. 133f.), oder die Aussage lediglich vereinfachen wollte, läßt sich kaum sagen; jedenfalls hat Matthäus diesen Teil seiner Mk-Vorlage ersatzlos gestrichen (vgl. 9,2).

οὗτος οὕτως λαλεῖ;) auf Jesu *Handeln* bzw. *Sprechen* bezog. Der folgende Abschnitt V. 21b-24 entspricht nahezu wörtlich der Vorlage Mk 2,7b-11. Dagegen ist die »Demonstration« des Wunders (V. 25) gegenüber Mk 2,12a umformuliert worden, zum einen durch das von Lukas gern gebrauchte Adverb παραχρῆμα und zum andern vor allem dadurch, daß zunächst der »in sein Haus«[59] gehende Geheilte selber Gott preist. Der »Chorschluß«, in dem »alle« das Gotteslob wiederholen (V. 26), entspricht dann mit einigen Erweiterungen[60] im wesentlichen wieder der Mk-Vorlage (2,12b).

b. Vergleicht man mit dieser von Lukas aus dem Markusevangelium übernommenen Erzählung von einer Gelähmtenheilung die drei (!) entsprechenden Erzählungen in der Apostelgeschichte, so zeigen sich einerseits signifikante Analogien, andererseits aber auch bemerkenswerte Differenzen (s. die Übersicht auf der folgenden Seite):

1. In der von einer Wundertat des Petrus[61] am Jerusalemer Tempel sprechenden Erzählung *Apg 3,1-10* wird die Person des Gelähmten sehr breit eingeführt; im Grunde spricht Lukas in V. 2-5, mit Ausnahme von V. 4, ausschließlich von ihm. Er wird ausführlich vorgestellt mit Informationen, die über das auf der Erzählebene Wahrnehmbare weit hinausgehen (V. 2). Er ist es dann auch, der die Handlung eröffnet (V. 3); und der Erzähler weiß sogar, was der Gelähmte angesichts der Aufforderung des Petrus (V. 4 βλέψον εἰς ἡμᾶς) »erwartet« (V. 5 προσδοκῶν ... λαβεῖν), auch wenn sich dies dann sogleich als Mißverständnis erweist (vgl. die Aussage des Petrus in V. 6a). Erst in V. 6 wird eindeutig Petrus der Handelnde. Sein Wort wird in V. 6a bewußt mit δίδωμι eingeleitet, als Kontrast zum zweimaligen λαβεῖν in V. 3.5. Der Gelähmte »empfängt« von Petrus nicht Silber oder Gold, sondern der Apostel »gibt« ihm etwas ganz anderes ἐν τῷ ὀνόματι Ἰησοῦ Χριστοῦ; erst dann folgt das eigentliche Heilungswort (V. 6b)[62]. Die Heilung geschieht

---

59. In der Wendung ἀπῆλθεν εἰς τὸν οἶκον αὐτοῦ in 5,25b liegt ein »minor agreement« mit Mt 9,7 vor; nach Jesu vorangegangenem Befehl ὕπαγε (Lk πορεύου) εἰς τὸν οἶκόν σου lag diese Korrektur gegen Mk aber nahe.

60. Bemerkenswert ist vor allem das Stichwort παράδοξα, das sonst im NT nicht begegnet. Vgl. BUSSE, *Wunder* (s. Anm. 56), pp. 123f.

61. Neben Petrus wird auch Johannes erwähnt (V. 1.3.4); der aber an der eigentlichen Handlung nicht beteiligt ist (vgl. vor allem V. 4). Möglicherweise handelt es sich um eine von Lukas nachträglich vorgenommene Ergänzung einer ursprünglich nur von *einem* Wundertäter sprechenden Erzählung. Vgl. CONZELMANN, *Apostelgeschichte* (s. Anm. 27), p. 39.

62. Ob im Heilungswort V. 6b die Worte ἔγειρε καί zu lesen sind oder nicht, läßt sich kaum sagen. Das Fehlen in den Codices ℵ B D wiegt schwer, aber da zur Schilderung der Heilungshandlung in V. 7 auch die Formulierung ἤγειρεν folgt, wird man es doch wohl zu lesen haben.

Lk 5,17-26		Apg 3,1-10		Apg 9,32-35		Apg 14,8-13	
5,17	Situation	3,1	Situation	9,32	Situation		
5,18.19	Exposition	3,2	Exposition	9,33	Exposition	14,8	Exposition
5,20	Reaktion Jesu: Sündenvergebungswort	3,3	Handeln des Bettlers				
5,21-24	Diskussion mit den Gegnern (V. 17a)	3,4-6a	»Mißverständnis«	9,34a	Hinweis auf Christus	14,9	Stummer »Dialog«:
5,24b	Heilungswort	3,6b 3,7a	Heilungswort Heilungsgeste	9,34b	Heilungswort	14,10a	Heilungswort
5,25	Demonstration	3,7b.8	Demonstration	9,34c	Demonstration	14,10b	Demonstration
5,26	Chorschluß. Reaktion des Publikums: Gotteslob	3,9.10	Chorschluß: Reaktion des Publikums	9,35	Reaktion der Stadtbewohner: Bekehrung	14,11-13	Reaktion des Publikums: »Vergottung«

nicht allein durch das Wort des Petrus, sondern zusätzlich durch eine helfende Handlung (V. 7a). In der anschließenden Demonstration der Heilung (V. 7b.8a) verwendet Lukas wie in Lk 5,25 das Adverb παραχρῆμα; und es findet sich dabei vor allem auch wieder der Topos des ausdrücklichen Gotteslobs durch den Geheilten[63]. Bemerkenswert ist der ungewöhnlich breite »Chorschluß« (V. 9f.): Da πᾶς ὁ λαός die in V. 2 geschilderten Verhältnisse ja genau kannte (V. 10a), haben θαμβός und ἔκστασις jetzt besonderes Gewicht (V. 10b).

2. Die Heilung des Gelähmten in Lydda ebenfalls durch Petrus (*Apg 9,32-35*) wird völlig anders erzählt: Petrus kommt im Verlauf seiner Reisen[64] nach Lydda, wo bereits Christen (ἅγιοι) wohnen. Er »findet« dort einen Mann, der seit acht Jahren unter einer Lähmung leidet und »bettlägerig« ist[65]. Anders als in den Wundererzählungen meist üblich, wird der Gelähmte jetzt mit seinem Namen eingeführt (V. 33 Aeneas) und dann auch entsprechend von Petrus angeredet (V. 34). Die das wunderwirkende Wort des Petrus einleitende Aussage ἰᾶταί σε Ἰησοῦς Χριστός (V. 34a) ist ohne jede Parallele; dagegen ist das in V. 34b folgende eigentliche Heilungswort (ἀνάστηθι) jedenfalls nicht ungewöhnlich[66], und dem entspricht dann die Schilderung der Demonstration (V. 34c εὐθέως ἀνέστη). Durch die Wendung καὶ εἶδαν αὐτὸν πάντες οἱ κατοικοῦντες (V. 35a) wird ähnlich wie in Apg 3,10a angezeigt, daß Aeneas und also auch sein Schicksal in der Stadt bekannt ist; anders als in Jerusalem wird aber jetzt das Wunder Anlaß zur Bekehrung »aller« in der Stadt Lydda und in der Saron-Ebene Wohnenden (V. 35b)[67].

3. Die Erzählung von der Heilung des Gelähmten durch Paulus in Lystra (*Apg 14,8-13*) scheint demgegenüber von Lukas offenbar bewußt als eine Art Kurzfassung der Erzählung von Apg 3,1-10 gestaltet wor-

---

63. Die Wendung αἰνῶν τὸν θεόν (das Verb αἰνέω begegnet im NT ganz überwiegend bei Lukas) paßt zur erzählten Szene; der Geheilte begleitet Petrus und Johannes nun auf deren Weg in den Tempel (V. 8, vgl. V. 1).

64. Die Reisennotiz διερχόμενον διὰ πάντων (9,32a) bezieht sich offenbar auf die in 9,31 genannten Gebiete Judäa, Galiläa und Samaria, in denen die Kirche (nach der Bekehrung des Paulus) »Frieden« hatte.

65. Lukas verwendet hier (9,33) das Wort κράβαττος, das er in der Parallele zu Mk 2,1-12 gerade vermieden und durch κλίνη bzw. κλινίδιον ersetzt hatte; im Wundersummar Apg 5,15 (s.u.) spricht er von Kranken, die ἐπὶ κλιναρίων καὶ κραβάττων lagen.

66. Ἀνιστάναι ist in Wundererzählungen häufig gebraucht (Mk 5,42; 9,27; Lk 17,19 u.ö.); die impt. Wendung ἀνάστηθι ist dabei aber selten, vgl. Apg 14,10 (s.u.). Zu στρῶσον ἑαυτῷ vgl. CONZELMANN, *Apostelgeschichte* (s. Anm. 27), p. 68: Das Wort dient schon als solches der (bevorstehenden) Demonstration; der seit acht Jahren im Bett Liegende soll selber sein Bett in Ordnung bringen.

67. Ἐπιστρέφειν εἰς τὸν κύριον ist als Reaktion des Publikums sonst nicht belegt, so daß man von einer »stilgemäßen« Wirkung eigentlich nicht sprechen kann (zu CONZELMANN, *Apostelgeschichte*, p. 68).

den zu sein[68]. Zwar geht jetzt die Situations- und Ortsangabe der eigentlichen Erzählung voraus (nach 14,6b.7 befinden sich Paulus und Barnabas nach ihrer Flucht aus Ikonion in Lystra); aber die Exposition (V. 8) entspricht dann weithin derjenigen in 3,2[69]. Vor allem fällt auf, daß in 14,9, ähnlich wie in 3,3-5, die »Initiative« von dem Gelähmten ausgeht: Er hört Paulus reden (V. 9a), der dann seinerseits den Gelähmten »sieht«. Die hiervon in V. 9b gegebene Beschreibung (ἀτενίσας [αὐτῷ] καὶ ἰδὼν κτλ.) entspricht zwar nicht inhaltlich, wohl aber im Duktus der Erzählung im wesentlichen der Schilderung in 3,4, insofern die Leser erfahren, was die Beteiligten jeweils »denken«[70]. Das nun unmittelbar folgende Heilungswort 14,10a entspricht dem Kontext[71]. Wenn ausdrücklich gesagt wird, Paulus habe μεγάλη φωνῇ gesprochen, so könnte diese Kennzeichnung den Sinn haben, das folgende Geschehen (14,11-13) von vornherein als besonders absurd erscheinen zu lassen: Paulus spricht sein wunderwirkendes Wort mit *lauter* Stimme und also jedenfalls nicht etwa in »geheimnisvoller« Weise; und dennoch meinen die Lystrer, sie hätten es mit Göttern zu tun[72]. Dementsprechend fallen die »Chorschlüsse« gegensätzlich aus: Während das Volk am Tempel in Jerusalem (ebenso wie in die Volksmenge in Kapharnaum) Gott ob des Wunders des Petrus (bzw. Jesu) preist (Apg 3,9f.; Lk 5,26) und die Bewohner von Lydda und Saron sich sogar »zum Herrn« bekehren (Apg 9,35), mißverstehen die Menschen in Lystra und insbesondere der Priester des Zeus das Wunder auf groteske Weise, so daß Paulus und Barnabas viel rhetorisches Geschick aufbieten müssen (14,14-18), um die Lystrer allmählich von ihrem Opferwahn abzubringen[73]. Die Wundererzählung in Apg 14,8-13(18) enthält also ein starkes Element der Verspottung derer, in deren Mitte das Wunder geschah.

68. Anders CONZELMANN, *Apostelgeschichte* (s. Anm. 27), p. 87, der unter Verweis auf Dibelius meint, es handele sich um eine »Einzelgeschichte«, und »die Ähnlichkeit beider Vorgänge« ergebe sich »durch den durchschnittlichen Stil der Wundergeschichte«.
69. Neben der Wiederholung der Ortsangabe ἐν Λύστροις findet sich in V. 8 die, z.T. etwas umständlich formulierte, Information darüber, daß der Mann von Geburt an gelähmt ist.
70. Die Wendung ἔχει πίστιν τοῦ σωθῆναι ist offenbar bewußt doppeldeutig gemeint: Der Gelähmte hat den »Glauben gerettet zu werden« (bzw. das »Vertrauen, geheilt zu werden«). Vielleicht will Lukas auf diese Weise sagen, daß sich beides nicht voneinander trennen lasse.
71. Zu ἀνάστηθι vgl. 9,34b (s.o. Anm. 66).
72. Denkbar wäre, daß Lukas die Lykaonier als des Griechischen nicht mächtig erscheinen lassen will; darauf könnte V. 11 hindeuten. Die Worte der »Apostel Barnabas und Paulus« in V. 15-17 scheinen von ihnen dann aber doch verstanden zu werden.
73. Ein ähnlicher Zug findet sich auch in Apg 28,6, dort jedoch ohne eine derart explizit kritisch-ironische Tendenz.

2. *Totenerweckungserzählungen: Der Jüngling zu Nain (Lk 7,11-17),*
Tabitha in Joppe (Apg 9,36-42), Eutychos in Troas (Apg 20,7-12)[74]

a. Die nur im lukanischen Sondergut überlieferte Erzählung von der
Auferweckung des Jünglings zu Nain durch Jesus (*Lk 7,11-17*) ist der
einzige Text in der synoptischen Tradition, der eindeutig als Totenerweckungserzählung bezeichnet werden kann. Denn bei der in Mk
5,22-24.35-43 überlieferten und sowohl von Matthäus (9,18f.23-26) wie
auch von Lukas (8,40-42.49-56) übernommenen Erzählung von der
»Auferweckung« der Tochter des Jairus bleibt offen, ob das Mädchen
wirklich tot ist, wie die aus dem Hause des Jairus entsandten Boten und
dann auch die dort anwesenden Trauernden sagen[75], oder ob sie – wie
Jesus sagt – schläft[76]. Zwar heißt es in Lk 8,53b anders als bei Mk im
Zusammenhang der Verspottung Jesu (κατεγέλων αὐτοῦ) ausdrücklich,
die Trauernden hätten »gewußt, daß sie gestorben war« (εἰδότες ὅτι
ἀπέθανεν); aber damit scheint auch bei Lukas nicht eine »objektive«
Tatsache, sondern lediglich ein subjektives »Wissen« der Anwesenden
ausgesagt zu sein, dem das Wort Jesu (οὐκ ἀπέθανεν) entgegensteht[77].
Demgegenüber ist die Erzählung Lk 7,11-17 ohne Zweifel als Totenerweckungserzählung zu lesen[78].

Die Erzählung beginnt in V. 11 mit einer sehr genauen Situations-
schilderung: Jesus befindet sich nach seinem mit einem Heilungswunder
(7,1-10) verbundenen Aufenthalt bei Kapharnaum[79] auf dem Wege in
die sonst in der Jesus-Überlieferung nicht erwähnte Stadt Nain; man
erfährt ausdrücklich, daß er von einer größeren Anzahl (ἱκανοί) seiner
Jünger sowie einem ὄχλος πολύς begleitet wird (V. 11b). Als sie sich

---

74. Vgl. zum folgenden MUHLACK, *Parallelen* (s. Anm. 14), pp. 55-71.

75. In Mk 5,35 wird der Tod der Tochter mitgeteilt, was Lk (8,49) übernommen hat,
im Unterschied zu Mt, der die Erzählung aber ohnehin erheblich gekürzt hat. Die Trau-
erszene im Hause (Mk 5,38b) findet sich sowohl bei Mt als auch bei Lk nahezu unverändert.

76. Der »Dialog« zwischen Jesus und der Menge (οὐκ ἀπέθανεν ἀλλὰ καθεύδει.
καὶ κατεγέλων αὐτοῦ) wird von Lukas und von Matthäus wörtlich aus Mk 5,39b.40b
übernommen (in Mt 9,24 sind lediglich die Worte γάρ und τὸ κοράσιον eingefügt).

77. Vgl. dazu A. LINDEMANN, *Die Erzählung der Machttaten Jesu in Markus 4,35-*
6,6a. Erwägungen zum formgeschichtlichen und zum hermeneutischen Problem, in C.
BREYTENBACH & H. PAULSEN (eds.), *Anfänge der Christologie*, FS F. Hahn, Göttingen,
Vandenhoeck & Ruprecht, 1991, pp. 185-207, hier 200-202.

78. Zur Analyse vgl. BUSSE, *Wunder* (s. Anm. 56), pp. 161-175.

79. Es ist bemerkenswert, daß Lukas in 7,11 die beiden Szenen miteinander verknüpft
durch die Wendung ἐν τῷ ἑξῆς, die an das programmatische καθεξῆς des Prologs (1,3)
erinnert, in einem wirklich »chronologischen« Zusammenhang aber nur selten gebraucht
wird (Lk 9,37 τῇ ἑξῆς ἡμέρᾳ; in Apg 21,1; 25,17; 27,18 hat die Angabe keine besondere Bedeutung). Zu dem im ganzen fünfmal bei Lk/Apg belegten καθεξῆς vgl. vor
allem Lk 8,1.

»dem Stadttor«[80] nähern, begegnet ihnen ein Leichenzug (V. 12a). Der Erzähler informiert die Leser darüber, daß der Verstorbene der einzige Sohn seiner verwitweten Mutter gewesen sei (V. 12b), und er hebt hervor, daß auch sie, ähnlich wie Jesus, von einem ὄχλος ἱκανός begleitet wird (V. 12c). Die Erzählung betont in der Exposition also die Anwesenheit einer überaus großen Menschenmenge als »Öffentlichkeit«; und die ausdrückliche Erwähnung der Mutter des Toten deutet offenbar schon darauf hin, daß sie im Fortgang der Erzählung eine wichtige Rolle spielen wird. Als Jesus, vom Erzähler als ὁ κύριος eingeführt, die Mutter sieht, hat er Mitleid mit ihr und spricht sie an: μὴ κλαῖε (V. 13). Das ist im Duktus der Erzählung geradezu als ein Verzögerungselement aufzufassen, weil der Sinn der Aufforderung zunächst offen bleibt[81]. Jesus geht dann näher heran und berührt die Totenbahre[82]; erst jetzt (V. 14) spricht er den Toten an: νεανίσκε, σοὶ λέγω, ἐγέρθητι. Der Gestus der Berührung und vor allem das wunderwirkende Wort entsprechen der Schilderung und teilweise sogar der Formulierung in Mk 5,41[83]. Ein grundlegender Unterschied besteht allerdings darin, daß Jesus in Mk 5,41 / Lk 8,54 die Hand des Kindes ergreift, während er in Lk 7,14 nicht den Leichnam, sondern lediglich die Bahre berührt. Ungewöhnlich ist in V. 15 die Demonstration: Der Tote (ὁ νεκρός) richtet sich auf und beginnt zu reden. Der Erzähler spielt dann offensichtlich bewußt auf die Elia-Erzählung von der Auferweckung des Sohnes der Witwe von Sarepta (1 Kön 17) an[84]; denn es heißt ausdrücklich, daß Jesus ihn seiner Mutter »gab«[85]. Im Chorschluß (V. 16) wird – jedenfalls aus der Perspektive des Evangelisten – zunächst insofern nicht ganz sachgemäß von Jesus gesprochen, als dieser von der Menge (nur) als προφήτης

---

80. Die Erwähnung dieses Details ist in der Überlieferung ohne Parallele; ein Stadttor wird im NT sonst nur noch in Apg 9,24 im Zusammenhang der Gefährdung des Paulus in Damaskus erwähnt.

81. Dieser Zug erinnert an die oft als Parallele zitierte Szene bei Philostrat *VitApoll* IV 45: Apollonius begegnet einem Leichenzug und kündigt den Trauernden an, er wolle ihre Tränen trocknen; dort heißt es dann aber, die Menge habe angesichts dieser Ankündigung eine tröstende Ansprache erwartet. Vgl. B. KOLLMANN, *Jesus und die Christen als Wundertäter. Studien zu Magie, Medizin und Schamanismus in Antike und Christentum* (FRLANT, 170), Göttingen, Vandenhoeck & Ruprecht, 1996, pp. 266-268.

82. Die erst an dieser Stelle verspätet eingeschobene Bemerkung, die Träger seien stehengeblieben, stellt ein weiteres Verzögerungsmoment dar.

83. In Mk 5,41 heißt es κρατήσας τῆς χειρὸς τοῦ παιδίου (ebenso Lk 8,54), Jesu Anrede an das Mädchen (τὸ κοράσιον, σοὶ λέγω, ἔγειρε) hat Lukas in seiner Textfassung geändert (Lk 8,54 ἡ παῖς, ἔγειρε).

84. Ein Bezug zu dieser Erzählung war bereits in der Nazareth-Szene (Lk 4,25f.) hergestellt worden, freilich nur zum ersten Teil (Hungersnot im Lande, V. 1-16) und gerade nicht zum zweiten Teil (V. 17-24).

85. 3 Regn 17,23 καὶ κατήγαγεν αὐτὸν ἀπὸ τοῦ ὑπερῴου εἰς τὸν οἶκον καὶ ἔδωκεν αὐτὸν τῇ μητρὶ αὐτοῦ, καὶ εἶπεν Ηλιου Βλέπε, ζῇ ὁ υἱός σου.

μέγας apostrophiert wird[86]; dann aber sprechen die Menschen in biblischer Sprache vom ἐπισκέπτειν Gottes über sein Volk[87]. Abschließend (V. 17) heißt es auffälligerweise, die Kunde davon[88] sei »in ganz Judäa« ergangen, obwohl Nain in Galiläa liegt[89]. Die Totenerweckungserzählung in Lk 7,11-17 hat also zum einen die Funktion, zu erklären, daß und auf welche Weise Jesu Ruhm gemehrt wurde; zum andern aber ist durch die relativ enge Bindung an 1 Kön 17 ein starker biblischer Bezug erkennbar, der mit dazu beiträgt, daß die für Lukas auch sonst charakteristische »soziale« Komponente[90] in besonderer Weise unterstrichen wird.

b. In der Apostelgeschichte überliefert Lukas zwei Totenerweckungserzählungen[91]. Die erste Erzählung (*Apg 9,36-42*)[92] beginnt mit einer Personalnotiz über eine in der Stadt Joppe lebende Jüngerin[93] namens Tabitha[94] (V. 36a); die Leser erfahren von ihrem »sozialen« Handeln, das hohes Lob erhält (V. 36b). Die eigentliche Erzählhandlung beginnt damit, daß berichtet wird, sie sei »in jenen Tagen« krank geworden, gestorben und im »Obergemach« aufgebahrt worden (V. 37). Nun ruft man Petrus, der sich in der »nahegelegenen«[95] Stadt Lydda aufhält; er solle unverzüglich nach Joppe kommen (V. 38). Daß sich mit diesem Ruf eine bestimmte Absicht verbindet, sagt die Erzählung nicht. Petrus ist zwar als Wundertäter in der Apostelgeschichte bereits bekannt, nicht zuletzt durch die unmittelbar vorangegangene Heilung des gelähmten

86. Vgl. dazu Bovon, *Evangelium nach Lukas I* (s. Anm. 19), pp. 364f. (mit Anm. 61).

87. Vgl. Ruth 1,6 LXX: Während der Hungersnot kehren Naemi und ihre beiden Schwiegertöchter aus Moab »in das Land« zurück, weil sie erfahren hatten ἐν ἀγρῷ Μωαβ, ὅτι ἐπέσκεπται κύριος τὸν λαὸν αὐτοῦ δοῦναι αὐτοῖς ἄρτους. Vgl. im übrigen Bovon, *Evangelium nach Lukas I*, p. 104 (zu Lk 1,68).

88. Zu λόγος οὗτος in solchem Zusammenhang vgl. Lk 4,36.

89. Nach H. Conzelmann, *Die Mitte der Zeit. Studien zur Theologie des Lukas* (BHT, 17), Tübingen, Mohr, ⁵1964, p. 35 Anm. 1 zeigt sich hier die lk Unkenntnis der geographischen Gegebenheiten Palästinas. Dem widerspricht Bovon, *Evangelium nach Lukas I*, p. 365 mit der These, Ἰουδαία meine bei Lukas »ganz Palästina«. Dagegen sprechen aber die Aussagen in Lk 2,4 und 5,17. Erwähnt wird in 7,17 neben Judäa, freilich ohne nähere Spezifizierung, die »ganze Umgebung« (πάσῃ τῇ περιχώρῳ).

90. Vgl. dazu G. Stählin, Art. χήρα, in *TWNT*, 9, 1973, pp. 428-454, hier 439.

91. Zum Vergleich der Erzählungen s. Bovon, *Evangelium nach Lukas I* (s. Anm. 19), p. 357.

92. Diese Erzählung weist sehr deutliche Parallelen zu 1 Kön 17,17-24 bzw. 2 Kön 4,19f.30-37 auf; vgl. die Übersicht bei A. Weiser, *Die Apostelgeschichte. Kapitel 1-12* (ÖTK, 5/1), Gütersloh, Gütersloher – Würzburg, Echter Verlag, 1981, p. 238.

93. Das Wort μαθήτρια ist im NT nur hier belegt.

94. Die griech. Übersetzung des hebr. Namens wird hinzugefügt (»Gazelle«); vgl. dazu Conzelmann, *Apostelgeschichte* (s. Anm. 27), p. 68.

95. Die Entfernung zwischen beiden Orten beträgt ca. 13 km, etwa drei Wegstunden; vgl. Conzelmann, *Apostelgeschichte*, p. 69.

Aeneas (9,32-35); aber daß er die Fähigkeit besitzt, Tote zu erwecken, ist kaum zu erwarten[96]. Der Fortgang der Ereignisse (V. 39) steht dann in einem eigenartigen Kontrast zur anfänglich geschilderten »Eile« (V. 38): Zwar wird Petrus sogleich nach seiner Ankunft in Joppe in den Raum geführt, wo die tote Tabitha aufgebahrt liegt; aber es ergeht nicht etwa die Bitte um ein Wunder, sondern man zeigt ihm Kleidungsstücke, die Tabitha hergestellt hatte[97]. Insofern paßt die in V. 39 geschilderte Szene weniger zur Exposition einer Wundererzählung als vielmehr zum Bericht von einem Beileidsbesuch, in dessen Verlauf der Besucher erfährt, *warum* gerade in diesem Fall der Tod so besonders schmerzlich ist. Erst in V. 40a kommt es zur Wunderhandlung: Nachdem Petrus alle Anwesenden aus dem Raum geschickt hat[98], kniet er nieder und betet; danach spricht er unter Hinwendung zu dem Leichnam das wunderwirkende Wort aus (Ταβιθά, ἀνάστηθι). Die Differenz zu der in Lk 7,14 beschriebenen Handlung Jesu ist deutlich: Jesus sprach sein Wort ἐγέρθητι aus eigener Vollmacht (vgl. V. 13 ὁ κύριος ἐσπλαγχνίσθη); Petrus dagegen betet zunächst, d.h. er bittet Gott um dessen Beistand, bevor er die tote Tabitha anredet. Die anschließende Demonstration (V. 40b.41) ist vergleichsweise breit ausgestaltet: Zunächst wird der eigentliche Vorgang der Erweckung sehr viel deutlicher nachgezeichnet, als das in Lk 7 der Fall gewesen war[99], und dann wird auch das Publikum nochmals sehr betont erwähnt (V. 41b). Einen »Chorschluß« im eigentlichen Sinne gibt es zwar nicht; es wird aber berichtet (V. 42), daß das Geschehen in ganz Joppe bekannt geworden sei, und hier heißt es nun ausdrücklich, »viele« seien zum Glauben an den κύριος gekommen[100]. Lukas will offensichtlich betonen, daß das von Petrus vollbrachte Wunder nicht etwa dessen Ruhm gedient, sondern im Gegenteil die »Ehre« des κύριος gemehrt habe.

---

96. Selbst in Joh 11 wird Jesus zum kranken Lazarus gerufen, während dieser noch lebt, und dasselbe gilt für die kranke Tochter des Jairus; Tabitha dagegen ist bereits gestorben, als Petrus gerufen wird.

97. Durch V. 39b wird also die eingangs in V. 36b gegebene Charakterisierung der Tabitha näher illustriert.

98. Die Wendung ἐκβαλὼν δὲ ἔξω πάντας entspricht beinahe wörtlich Mk 5,40; in der Parallele dazu rückt Lukas aber diesen Topos an eine andere Stelle und nimmt vor allem sprachlich eine deutliche Veränderung vor (Lk 8,51 οὐκ ἀφῆκεν εἰσελθεῖν τινα ... εἰ μὴ κτλ.).

99. Das »Aufwachen« der Tabitha wird zunächst »objektiv« (ἤνοιξεν τοὺς ὀφθαλμοὺς αὐτῆς) und dann nochmals aus ihrer Perspektive (ἰδοῦσα τὸν Πέτρον) geschildert, wozu Lk 7,15 gar keine Parallele bietet, identisch aber ist die abschließende »objektiv« wichtige Notiz ἀνεκάθισεν. In V. 41a wird die Schilderung noch ein Stück fortgesetzt.

100. Vgl. schon unmittelbar zuvor 9,35b. Daß ein Wunder Glauben ausgelöst habe, wird auch im Anschluß an die Auferweckung des Lazarus gesagt (Joh 11,45), während dieser Zug in der synoptischen Überlieferung nirgends begegnet.

Lukas erzählt von einer weiteren Auferweckung, die in Troas lokalisiert ist (*Apg 20,7-12*). In dieser Erzählung wird zu Beginn die Situation außerordentlich breit geschildert (V. 7-9): Der Erzähler beschreibt einen in einem »Obergemach«[101] stattfindenden Gottesdienst, der durch eine lange Predigt des Paulus zeitlich sehr ausgedehnt wird. Ein νεανίας namens Eutychos fällt in tiefen Schlaf, stürzt aus dem Fenster und wird »tot aufgehoben« (ἤρθη νεκρός). Auch die Fortsetzung ist ungewöhnlich: Paulus geht hinab, »legt sich auf ihn«[102] und stellt, beinahe wie ein Arzt, fest, daß ἡ ψυχὴ αὐτοῦ in dem Jüngling ist (V. 10). Dann geht er wieder hinauf, wo der Gottesdienst bis zum Morgengrauen fortgesetzt wird. Anschließend verläßt Paulus die Stadt (V. 11), ohne sich um das Schicksal des Eutychos noch weiter zu kümmern[103], d.h. er setzt voraus, daß die Auferweckung des Eutychos selbstverständlich eintritt. Daß im Sinne der Erzählung Eutychos nach seinem Sturz tatsächlich tot und nicht etwa scheintot oder nur betäubt ist, kann – anders als im Fall der Jairus-Tochter – nicht bezweifelt werden: Das νεκρός-Sein wird in V. 9 vom Erzähler konstatiert und nicht wie in Mk 5,35.38-40 / Lk 8,49.52f. lediglich von den in der Erzählung auftretenden Personen behauptet; und auch die Verwendung des Begriffes ψυχή spricht dafür, daß vom »Leben« (und nicht etwa nur vom Bewußtsein) des Eutychos die Rede ist[104]. Dementsprechend hat die »Diagnose« des Paulus ἡ γὰρ ψυχὴ αὐτοῦ ἐν αὐτῷ ἐστιν in 20,10 eine andere Funktion als das Wort Jesu οὐκ ἀπέθανεν ἀλλὰ καθεύδει in Mk 5,39 / Lk 8,52: Paulus spricht damit faktisch bereits das wunderwirkende Wort aus, dem ein weiteres infolgedessen nicht zu folgen braucht. Die Demonstration erfolgt dann aber zeitlich versetzt (V. 12), was den Effekt im Grunde sogar noch steigert; die Erzählung hat es als geradezu selbstverständlich vorausgesetzt, daß sich der tote Jüngling entsprechend dem Wort des Paulus als lebendig (ἤγαγον ζῶντα) erweisen wird.

Das Wunder von Troas führt, anders als das Wunder in Joppe, nicht zum Glauben – schon deshalb nicht, weil ja alle Anwesenden Gläubige sind. Wohl aber führt es dazu, daß sie getröstet werden οὐ μετρίως[105]. Diese Schlußbemerkung ersetzt den »Chorschluß«; dieser kann fehlen, weil nach dem von Paulus bereits gesprochenen wunderwirkenden Wort

---

101. Vgl. dazu Apg 1,13.

102. Zu ἐπέπεσεν αὐτῷ vgl. abermals die Elia-Erzählung in 1 Kön 17 (V. 21 LXX καὶ ἐνεφύσησεν τῷ παιδαρίῳ τρὶς καὶ ἐπεκαλέσατο τὸν κύριον καὶ εἶπεν Κύριε ὁ θεός μου, ἐπιστραφήτω δὴ ἡ ψυχὴ τοῦ παιδαρίου τούτου εἰς αὐτόν).

103. In V. 12.13 heißt es mit deutlicher Unterscheidung: »*Sie* brachten den παῖς lebendig und wurden getröstet« (V. 12), »*wir* dagegen reisten ab« (V. 13).

104. Vgl. den in Anm 102 zitierten Text.

105. Es ist erzählerisch sehr geschickt, daß Lukas diese Notiz ganz an den Schluß stellt (V.12b) und sie nicht etwa schon auf die »beruhigenden« Worte des Paulus in V. 10 folgen läßt.

angesichts des παῖς ζῶν ein Anlaß zum Erstaunen oder auch nur zu einem besonderen Gotteslob gar nicht mehr besteht.

Der Vergleich der im ganzen drei Totenerweckungserzählungen im lukanischen Doppelwerk ergibt also, daß sie nach Form und Erzählzweck erheblich differieren. Auffällig ist aber die ihnen allen gemeinsame starke Bindung an die biblische Überlieferung von Elia und Elisa; diese verdankt sich möglicherweise der lukanischen Redaktion und entspricht jedenfalls den Interessen der Theologie des Lukas, ohne daß man deshalb schon annehmen müßte, daß eine dieser Erzählungen überhaupt als »redaktionell« von Lukas geschaffen zu gelten hätte.

3. Wundersummarien

Sowohl im Evangelium als auch in der Apostelgeschichte finden sich Summarien, in denen der Erzähler mehr oder weniger »pauschal« von der Wundertätigkeit Jesu bzw. dann der Apostel berichtet. Bei der Anwendung dieses Stilmittels folgt Lukas dem im Markusevangelium vorgegebenen Verfahren. Sowohl in Lk 4,40f. als auch in Lk 6,17-19 übernimmt er die Summarien aus seiner Mk-Vorlage; in der Apostelgeschichte setzt er das im Evangelium begonnene literarische Vorgehen fort.

a. Die Stellung des ersten Summars im Evangelium (*Lk 4,40f.*) entspricht im Aufriß ganz der Stellung des entsprechenden Summars in Mk 1,32-34[106]. Auch im Duktus der Darstellung gibt es keine gravierenden Änderungen[107]: Es wird gesagt, daß Jesus *Kranke heilte* (entsprechend der Heilungserzählung Lk 4,38f.) und daß aus vielen Menschen *Dämonen ausfuhren* (entsprechend der Exorzismuserzählung Lk 4,31-37). Die Bemerkung, die δαιμόνια hätten geschrien σὺ εἶ ὁ υἱὸς τοῦ θεοῦ (V. 41a), hat Lukas offensichtlich aus dem zweiten Mk-Summar (3,11) nach vorn gezogen[108]; das von Jesus ausgesprochene Sprechverbot entspricht dann aber wieder fast wörtlich der unmittelbaren Parallele Mk 1,34b. Überraschend ist die Einfügung des Elements der Handauflegung (V. 40b)[109]; denn diesen

---

106. Die Erzählung von der Heilung der Schwiegermutter des Simon geht voran (Lk 4,38f. / Mk 1,29-31), und es folgen der Aufbruch aus Kapharnaum und der knappe Bericht von der Predigttätigkeit Jesu in Galiläa (Lk 4,42-44 / Mk 1,35-39) sowie die Erzählung von der Heilung des Aussätzigen (Lk 5,12-16 / Mk 1,40-45); lediglich in 5,1-11 ist die Berufung des Simon eingefügt, die *nach* 4,38f. eigentlich merkwürdig »deplaziert« ist.

107. Abgesehen von einigen sprachlichen Korrekturen ist die stärkste Veränderung die Streichung von Mk 1,33; dem entspricht dann auch, daß auch in Lk 5,17 der Hinweis auf die Tür (Mk 2,2) fehlt.

108. In der vorausgegangenen Exorzismus-Erzählung Lk 4,31-37 hatte der Dämon, ebenso wie bei Mk, von Jesus als dem ἅγιος τοῦ θεοῦ gesprochen.

109. Es heißt ausdrücklich, Jesus habe »jedem einzelnen von ihnen« die Hände aufgelegt und sie so geheilt.

Heilgestus hatte Lukas in den vorangegangenen Wundererzählungen *nicht* erwähnt; man kann fragen, ob hier ein Vorgriff auf Mk 6,5 vorliegt[110].

b. Das zweite Summar des Evangeliums (*Lk 6,17-19*) steht in der Textfolge ebenfalls an derselben Stelle wie bei Mk (3,7-12), mit dem Unterschied allerdings, daß die Berufung der Zwölf nach der Darstellung des Markus erst *nach* dem Summar erfolgte (3,13-19), nach Lukas dagegen vorher (Lk 6,12-16). Dieses zweite Summar hat im Lukasevangelium zugleich die Funktion, zur »Feldrede« hinzuführen (6,20-49)[111], denn Lukas hebt betont bevor, die »große Volksmenge« sei gekommen, um ihn zu *hören*[112] und um sich von Krankheiten (Lk 6,18a / Mk 3,10) und von unreinen Geistern heilen zu lassen (Lk 6,18b / Mk 3,11). Nicht zufällig scheint zu sein, daß Lukas den Schluß des Summars umgestaltet hat: Während bei Mk zum Abschluß (3,12) die Aussage wiederholt wird, Jesus habe den Dämonen befohlen, ihn nicht »offenbar« zu machen, ist in Lk 6,19 betont davon die Rede, daß Jesus *alle* geheilt habe.

c. In der Apostelgeschichte sind die Wundersummarien, vor allem Apg 5,12-16; 19,11.12, verglichen mit den Summarien im Evangelium in ihrer Wirkung erheblich gesteigert. Am auffälligsten ist, daß sie vor allem im Blick auf das mirakulöse Element durchgängig über das zuvor in den Einzelüberlieferungen Erzählte hinausgehen. Sie haben offensichtlich nicht nur die Funktion, bereits Erzähltes gleichsam zu »multiplizieren«; sie dienen vielmehr darüber hinaus auch dazu, das in den vorangegangenen Erzählungen sichtbar gewordene »Wunderbare« noch zusätzlich zu steigern. So heißt es innerhalb des Summars Apg 5,12-16, man habe Kranke auf die Straße gebracht, damit der *Schatten* des Petrus auf sie falle (V. 15)[113]. Und abschließend wird dann festgestellt, es seien aus den rings um Jerusalem liegenden Städten Kranke und von unreinen Geistern Besessene gebracht worden, die *alle* geheilt wurden (V. 16). Ein vergleichbares Element enthält das kurze Paulus betreffende Summar in Apg 19,11f., wenn gesagt wird, daß dessen σουδάρια und σιμι-

---

110. Der Topos ist in Mk 6,5 in der summarischen Schlußnotiz über Jesu Aufenthalt in Nazareth ausdrücklich verwendet worden (εἰ μὴ ὀλίγοις ἀρρώστοις ἐπιθεὶς τὰς χεῖρας ἐθεράπευσεν); in der lk Fassung der Nazareth-Perikope ist dies natürlich ganz entfallen.

111. Auch bei Mt geht der Bergpredigt ein Summar unmittelbar voran (4,23-25 entsprechend Mk 1,39).

112. Lukas erreicht diese gegenüber Mk inhaltlich erhebliche Korrektur durch eine minimale Textänderung. Statt πλῆθος πολὺ ἀκούοντες ὅσα ἐποίει ἦλθον πρὸς αὐτόν (Mk 3,8) heißt es in Lk 6,18 οἳ ἦλθον ἀκοῦσαι αὐτοῦ καὶ ἰαθῆναι ἀπὸ τῶν νόσων αὐτῶν.

113. Die Codices D und E (sowie ein Teil der lateinischen Überlieferung) fügen – mit unterschiedlichem Wortlaut – hinzu, daß die Betreffenden dann auch tatsächlich geheilt wurden; der ursprüngliche Text sagt dies nicht ausdrücklich, setzt es aber natürlich voraus.

κίνϑια heilkräftig gewesen seien[114]. Die »summarischen« Notizen über die Wunder des Stephanus (6,8)[115] und über die Wundertätigkeit des Philippus in Samaria (8,6-8 bzw. 8,13)[116] haben überhaupt keinen Anhalt an einer Einzelüberlieferung. Dagegen hat die kurze Barnabas und Paulus betreffende Notiz in 14,3 (Gott habe bewirkt, daß σημεῖα καὶ τέρατα γίνεσϑαι διὰ τῶν χειρῶν αὐτῶν) die für ein Summar übliche Funktion; es läßt sich allerdings kaum entscheiden, ob die Aussage im Rückgriff auf die Erzählung von der Begegnung des Paulus mit Bar-Jesus auf Zypern (13,6-12) formuliert ist oder ob sie der Vorbereitung der Erzählung von der Gelähmtenheilung in Lystra (14,8-13) dient. Die Notiz über die Heilungswunder des Paulus auf der Insel Melite (28,9) schließt sich unmittelbar an die (äußerst knapp erzählte) Wunderüberlieferung von 28,8 an[117].

Die Wundersummarien der Apostelgeschichte haben offensichtlich ein eigenes Gewicht: Die ausführlich erzählten Einzelgeschichten sollen nicht nur verallgemeinert, sondern sie sollen darüber hinaus auch inhaltlich ergänzt werden. Da es um das Ansehen der vom Geist Gottes geleiteten kirchlichen Verkündigung geht, ist das Mirakelhafte sowohl im Vergleich zur Überlieferung im Evangelium wie auch im Vergleich zu den in der Apg überlieferten Einzelerzählungen bewußt und nachdrücklich gesteigert. Zugleich aber wird immer wieder betont, daß die Apostel die Wunder nicht aus eigener Kraft vollbracht hätten, sondern daß es im Grunde Gott selber ist, der »durch ihre Hand« geheilt hat.

III. ABENDMAHL UND MAHLGEMEINSCHAFT IM LUKASEVANGELIUM UND IN DER APOSTELGESCHICHTE

Die Untersuchung der Mahlüberlieferungen im lukanischen Doppelwerk führt vor ein auffälliges Problem: Das in der Apostelgeschichte an

---

114. Auch in den Summarien findet sich der Aspekt, daß die Wunder »durch die Hände« der Apostel bzw. des Paulus geschehen, daß also nicht sie selber die eigentlichen »Wundertäter« sind (5,12 διὰ δὲ τῶν χειρῶν τῶν ἀποστόλων ἐγίνετο σημεῖα καὶ τέρατα πολλὰ ἐν τῷ λαῷ; 14,3 σημεῖα καὶ τέρατα γίνεσϑαι διὰ τῶν χειρῶν αὐτῶν; 19,11 δυνάμεις τε οὐ τὰς τυχούσας ὁ ϑεὸς ἐποίει διὰ τῶν χειρῶν Παύλου).
115. Apg 6,8 Στέφανος δὲ πλήρης χάριτος καὶ δυνάμεως ἐποίει τέρατα καὶ σημεῖα μεγάλα ἐν τῷ λαῷ.
116. Vgl. Apg 8,6f. βλέπειν τὰ σημεῖα ἃ ἐποίει. πολλοὶ γὰρ τῶν ἐχόντων πνεύματα ἀκάϑαρτα βοῶντα φωνῇ μεγάλῃ ἐξήρχοντο, πολλοὶ δὲ παραλελυμένοι καὶ χωλοὶ ἐθεραπεύϑησαν; 8,13 Der »Zauberer« Simon »sieht« τε σημεῖα καὶ δυνάμεις μεγάλας γινομένας. Vgl. dazu D.-A. KOCH, Geistbesitz, Geistverleihung und Wundermacht. Erwägungen zur Tradition und zur lukanischen Redaktion in Act 8,5-25, in ZNW 77 (1986) 64-82.
117. Diese Erzählung erinnert ihrerseits an das Summar Lk 4,38f. (vgl. Mk 1,29-31).

einigen Stellen (2,42.46; 20,7.11) erwähnte für die christliche Gemeinde charakteristische Mahl wird stets mit dem Begriff »Brotbrechen« (κλάσις τοῦ ἄρτου bzw. das verbale κλᾶν ἄρτον) bezeichnet. Welche Handlung will Lukas damit bezeichnen? Liegt eine Kurzbezeichnung für das Abendmahl (Eucharistie) vor, und setzt Lukas also voraus, daß das von ihm erwähnte »Brot(brechen)« neben dem Essen des Brotes auch den Kelchgenuß mitumfaßt, ohne daß dies ausdrücklich erwähnt zu werden braucht? Oder handelt es sich bei der κλάσις τοῦ ἄρτου gar nicht um das »Abendmahl« im kultischen Sinne, d.h. denkt Lukas möglicherweise an ein bloßes Gemeinschaftsmahl, in dessen Verlauf die Teilnehmenden dann zwar sicherlich auch etwas tranken, der »Kelch« jedoch eine eigene, ausdrücklich zu erwähnende Bedeutung nicht besaß?

Möglicherweise kommt man einer Antwort auf diese Frage näher, wenn man die Wiedererkennungsszene in der Emmaus-Erzählung Lk 24,13-35 mit einbezieht. Dort wird berichtet, daß die beiden Jünger den auferstandenen Jesus erst erkennen, als er sich mit ihnen zur Mahlzeit niederläßt, das Brot bricht, ein Gotteslob ausspricht und ihnen dann das Brot gibt (V. 30f., vgl. V. 35). Man könnte zunächst meinen, Lukas wolle hier eine Szene schildern, die sich an den Bericht vom Abendmahl (Lk 22,14-23) anschließt[118]. Es darf aber nicht übersehen werden, daß in Lk 24,30 im Zusammenhang des Mahlgebets vom »Lobpreis« Gottes gesprochen ist (εὐλόγησεν), Lukas aber in seiner Fassung der Abendmahlsworte in 22,17.19 gerade nicht das Verb εὐλογεῖν, sondern das Verb εὐχαριστεῖν verwendet, und zwar abweichend von Mk 14,22[119]. Man kann angesichts dieses Befundes zumindest Zweifel haben, ob Lukas wirklich meint, die Szene in 24,30 sei als Anspielung auf das Abendmahl (22,14-20) zu lesen[120].

Näher liegt deshalb die Annahme, daß ein Zusammenhang besteht zwischen der Emmaus-Szene und der lukanischen Fassung der Erzäh-

---

118. Vgl. W. WIEFEL, *Das Evangelium nach Lukas* (THNT, 3), Berlin, 1988, p. 411, der zunächst eine enge Anlehnung an Lk 9,16 feststellt, dann jedoch die Erwägung anschließt: »Vielleicht ist aber auch an eine Neuaufnahme des eucharistischen Mahles (vgl. 22,19) gedacht, das im Brotbrechen beim Gemeinschaftsmahl der Apostelzeit seine Fortsetzung findet«. Anders W. SCHMITHALS, *Das Evangelium nach Lukas* (ZBK NT, 3/1), Zürich, Theologischer Verlag, 1980, p. 235: »Ein spezifischer Bezug zum Abendmahl (von Wein ist keine Rede) oder zum eschatologischen Mahl (vgl. 13,28f.; Off. 3,20) dürfte dabei (auch bei Lukas) nicht intendiert sein (vgl. V. 35)«.

119. Dagegen steht in der von Paulus überlieferten Fassung der Mahlworte in 1 Kor 11,24 ebenso wie in Lk 22,19 εὐχαριστήσας. Auch in Apg 27,35 schreibt Lukas εὐχαρίστησε; dort ist allerdings von einer gewöhnlichen Mahlzeit die Rede.

120. Gegen einen Bezug zum Abendmahl spricht auch, daß die beiden »Emmaus-Jünger« offenbar nicht zu den ἀπόστολοι gehören, die sich nach Lk 22,14 mit Jesus zum Mahl versammelt hatten; freilich nennt Lukas sie δύο ἐξ αὐτῶν (24,13), d.h. ihr genauer Status wird von ihm nicht festgelegt.

lung von der Speisung der Fünftausend. Lukas hat von den beiden Spei-
sungserzählungen Mk 6,30-44 und Mk 8,1-10 nur die erste in seine Darstellung übernommen (Lk 9,12-17) und dort in 9,16 entsprechend der
Vorlage Mk 6,41 ebenso wie in 24,30 εὐλόγησεν verwendet. Angesichts dessen legt sich die Folgerung nahe, daß die Wiedererkennungsszene Lk 24,30 an das Speisungswunder anknüpft und nicht an das
Abendmahl[121]. Dann aber kann man es ebenso für möglich und vielleicht
sogar für wahrscheinlich halten, daß sich auch die für die Apostelgeschichte typische Rede vom »Brotbrechen« gar nicht auf ein an Lk 22
anknüpfendes Abendmahl (Eucharistie) bezieht, sondern Lukas auch
hier an die Fortsetzung jener Mahlgemeinschaft denkt, die in der Spei-
sungserzählung symbolisch vorabgebildet worden war. Der Kelch des
Letzten Mahls Jesu würde dann bei der Beschreibung der gemeindlichen
Mahlhandlung weder »fehlen« noch läge eine »verkürzte« Redeweise
vor; vielmehr würde gelten, daß bei dem hier gemeinten Mahl der Kelch
gar nicht im eigentlichen Sinne als Teil des Mahlvollzugs zu verstehen
ist.

Nun ist es ja für die lukanische Darstellung des letzten Mahls Jesu mit
seinen Jüngern in Lk 22 besonders charakteristisch, daß hier eine Form
vorliegt, die sich sowohl von der bei Paulus wie auch von der bei Markus anzutreffenden Überlieferung deutlich unterscheidet: Nach dem −
sicher ursprünglichen − »Langtext«[122] nimmt Jesus zuerst den Kelch
(22,17f.), bricht dann das Brot (22,19) und läßt μετὰ τὸ δειπνῆσαι
nochmals einen Kelch folgen. Durch diesen vorangestellten (zweiten
bzw. »ersten«) Kelch ist die Form des letzten Mahls Jesu dem Passamahl etwas angenähert, allerdings ohne daß es dadurch wirklich zu
einem Passamahl geworden wäre[123]. Nun ist es aber für die hier disku-
tierte Frage von erheblicher Bedeutung, daß die lukanische Fassung des
Mahlberichts ebenso wie die von Paulus überlieferte Fassung zwar einen
Wiederholungsbefehl enthält mit derselben Formulierung, die sich auch
in 1 Kor 11,24.25 findet (τοῦτο ποιεῖτε εἰς τὴν ἐμὴν ἀνάμνησιν), daß
dieser Befehl bei Lukas aber *nur das Brot* betrifft (22,19), nicht jedoch
einen (oder gar beide) Becher, während die von Paulus zitierte ver-

---

121. Vgl. WIEFEL, *Evangelium nach Lukas* (s. Anm. 118), p. 411.
122. Zum Problem s. H. FELD, *Das Verständnis des Abendmahls* (EdF, 50), Darmstadt, Wiss. Buchgesellschaft, 1976, pp. 18-21; ferner ausführlich J. JEREMIAS, *Die
Abendmahlsworte Jesu*, Göttingen, Vandenhoeck & Ruprecht, ³1960, pp. 133-153.
123. Der schon in Mk 14,14.16 hergestellte Bezug zum Passamahl ist von Lukas in
22,15 noch zusätzlich verstärkt worden, und dem entspricht dann auch der zweite Kelch;
bei einem Passamahl werden allerdings vier Becher getrunken.

wandte Fassung sowohl beim Brot als auch beim Kelch einen Wiederholungsbefehl enthält[124].

Daraus ergibt sich die Frage: Meint Lukas möglicherweise, daß die in
Lk 22,14-20 erzählte Handlung Jesu als ein *einmaliger* und durchaus
nicht als ein in dieser Form kultisch zu *wiederholender* Vorgang anzusehen ist? Dann wäre, wie es in 22,19 explizit gesagt wird, tatsächlich
nur »das Brotbrechen« die nach Jesu Weisung kultisch zu vollziehende
Handlung – und so geschieht es nach der Darstellung der Apostelgeschichte dann ja auch tatsächlich. Das in Lk 22,14-20 geschilderte
Geschehen würde dagegen im Sinne des Lukas durchaus nicht als »Stiftung« einer regelmäßig zu wiederholenden Handlung aufzufassen sein,
sondern es bliebe ein in jeder Hinsicht singuläres Ereignis.   ·

Eine ergänzende Erwägung spricht für die Wahrscheinlichkeit dieser
Vermutung: Es wäre im Grunde ja höchst erstaunlich, wenn Lukas
einerseits im Evangelium von einer im übrigen analogielosen Form der
Stiftung der christlichen Mahlfeier berichtet haben sollte, dieser Aspekt
dann andererseits aber in den Hinweisen der Apostelgeschichte auf die
entsprechende gemeindliche Feier gänzlich übergangen worden wäre[125].

Das in Lk 22,14-20 geschilderte Mahl ist nach der lukanischen Darstellung offensichtlich als einmalig und unwiederholbar gedacht; nur bei
der κλάσις τοῦ ἄρτου hat Jesus ausdrücklich eine Wiederholung angeordnet. Dementsprechend ist mit den in der Apostelgeschichte erwähnten Mahlzeiten, bei denen das »Brot gebrochen« wird, offenbar nicht
eine lediglich »abgekürzt« bezeichnete kultische Wiederholung des letzten Abendmahls Jesu gemeint und auch nicht eine *communio sub una*;
vielmehr denkt Lukas an jene – bewußt vom Geschehen beim letzten
Mahl mit den Jüngern abweichende – Form der Mahlfeier, wie sie Jesus
mit seinem Wiederholungsbefehl in Lk 22,19 selber angeordnet hatte.
Diese Mahlfeier ist in der Speisung der Fünftausend vorweggenommen
und dann beim österlichen Mahl mit den beiden Emmaus-Jüngern erstmals begangen worden.

An der Rehwiese 38   Andreas LINDEMANN
D-33617 Bielefeld

---

124. In der in Mk 14,22-24 überlieferten Fassung der Abendmahlsworte fehlt jeder
Wiederholungsbefehl.

125. Das würde gelten, wenn Lukas die in 22,14-20 geschaffene Form redaktionell
selber geschaffen haben sollte (so FELD, *Verständnis* [s. Anm. 122], p. 30), aber auch
dann, wenn er sie aus einer im übrigen unbekannten Tradition übernommen hätte (so
JEREMIAS, *Abendmahlsworte* [s. Anm. 122], p. 148).

THE THEME OF DIVINE VISITS
AND HUMAN (IN)HOSPITALITY IN LUKE-ACTS

ITS OLD TESTAMENT AND GRAECO-ROMAN ANTECEDENTS

In his classic work, "The Making of Luke-Acts" (1927), Henry J. Cadbury has pointed to some "secular interests" of Luke, one of them being his attention to the matter of lodging, hospitality, and table-fellowship[1]. A year before, in a Lexical Note on Luke-Acts published in *JBL*, Cadbury called Luke's interest in lodging "a minor personal interest of the third evangelist"[2]. Although "hospitality" is quite a distinctive feature of Luke's work, it is indeed sometimes understood as only one of the sub-themes woven together with Luke's primary intentions[3]. As John Koenig rightly remarks, however, "the sheer quantity of evidence for our author's regular accentuation of guest and host roles in his two-volume work suggests that the whole matter is more than peripherical to his concerns"[4]. As a matter of fact, even a quick reading of Luke-Acts shows the frequent and varied use of the theme.

I. THE HOSPITALITY THEME IN LUKE-ACTS

In what follows we will first give a short description of what we mean by "hospitality". Second, we will make a survey of the texts in Luke-Acts which deal with hospitality. The main focus of our contribution will then turn to Luke's theological and christological use of the theme of hospitality and its possible antecedents in the Old Testament and in Graeco-Roman literature[5].

---

1. H.J. CADBURY, *The Making of Luke-Acts*, New York, 1927; London, [2]1961, pp. 249-253.

2. H.J. CADBURY, *Lexical Notes on Luke-Acts: Luke's Interest in Lodging*, in *JBL* 14 (1926) 305-322, esp. p. 305.

3. Cf. D. RIDDLE, *Early Christian Hospitality: A Factor in the Gospel Transmission*, in *JBL* 57 (1938) 141-153, esp. pp. 151-153; A.J. MALHERBE, *Social Aspects of Early Christianity*, Philadelphia, [2]1983, esp. pp. 66-67; D. JUEL, *Luke-Acts: The Promise of History*, Atlanta, 1983, pp. 88-90.

4. J. KOENIG, *New Testament Hospitality: Partnership with Strangers as Promise and Mission*, Philadelphia, 1985, pp. 85-86.

5. Our primary source for the Graeco-Roman world will be Homer's *Iliad* and *Odyssey*, since these works were part of the general culture and were compulsory reading in education. We use the editions of A.T. MURRAY, *Homer. The Iliad, with an English*

What Is "Hospitality" and How Is It Expressed in Greek?

In common language, being hospitable means "offering or affording welcome and entertainment to strangers; extending a generous hospitality to guests and visitors", and hospitality means "the act or practice of being hospitable; the reception and entertainment of guests or strangers with liberality and goodwill"[6]. Hospitality normally implies offering lodging and/or food, so that table fellowship, meals or even symposia constitute a part thereof. According to Malina, in the Mediterranean world hospitality might be defined as "the process by means of which an outsider's status is exchanged from stranger to guest... it differs from entertaining family and friends"[7]. Given the human tendency to treat outsiders as simply non-human, which eventually forms the basis for torture, racism, genocide, etc., this process is crucial: strangers are "received", or shown hospitality, instead of being eliminated, either physically or socially. Every stranger is a potential enemy. By the offer of hospitality, he "must be transformed from being a potential threat to becoming ally"[8]. Malina certainly points to an important dimension of hospitality, but his definition may be too narrow when he says that receiving family and friends has nothing to do with the idea of hospitality. It is our belief that "hospitality" primarily designates the benevolent and receiving attitude one takes towards "outsiders" coming along or on a visit, i.e. persons belonging to a group other than the reference group[9]. Given that the reference group can be understood in various ways and

Translation, 2 vols. (The Loeb Classical Library, 170-171), London – Cambridge, MA, 1965-1967; and A.T. MURRAY & G.E. DIMOCK, *Homer. The Odyssey*, 2 vols. (The Loeb Classical Library, 104-105), Cambridge, MA – London, 1995. Thanks are due to Inge Van Wiele, for her indispensable assistance in collecting the materials from the Graeco-Roman world. For a more general treatment of hospitality in the Graeco-Roman world, see L.J. BOLCHAZY, *Hospitality in Early Rome. Livy's Concept of its Humanizing Force*, Chicago, 1977; H. BOLKESTEIN, *Wohltätigkeit und Armenpflege im vorchristlichen Altertum. Ein Beitrag zum Problem "Moral und Gesellschaft"*, Utrecht, 1939.

6. *The Shorter Oxford English Dictionary*, Vol. I, Oxford, ³1973, p. 988.

7. B.J. MALINA, *The Received View and What It Cannot Do: III. John and Hospitality*, in *Semeia* 35 (1986) 171-189, p. 181; = ID., *The Social World of Jesus and the Gospels*, London – New York, 1996, pp. 217-241.

8. V.H. MATTHEWS, *Hospitality and Hostility in Judges 4*, in *BTB* 21 (1991) 13-21, p. 14.

9. J.P. LOUW & E.A. NIDA, *Greek-English Lexicon of the Greek New Testament Based on Semantic Domains*, Vol. 1, New York, 1988, p. 121, divide the semantic domain "groups and classes of persons" into five sub-domains: general, socio-religious, socio-political, ethnic-cultural, philosophical, and on p. 132 they state: "Terms for 'stranger' or 'foreigner' are often based upon geographical differences or upon lack of previous knowledge. For example, 'I was a stranger' may be rendered as 'I came from another country' or 'I was not known to any of you'".

can point to such different things as family, kinship, members of the household, social group, city, country, race, religion, culture, accordingly the notions of "outsider" and of "hospitality" can have a more or less strict meaning. The outsider can be known or unknown, a friend, a family member or a stranger[10]. He may be an invited or an unexpected guest. Moreover, even when one might perhaps speak of a transcultural law of hospitality, the code of hospitality differs from time to time and from region to region[11].

According to Johannes P. Louw and Eugene A. Nida, the notions of "visit", "welcome, receive" and "show hospitality" belong to the semantic domain of "Association"[12]. The meaning of "visit" can be expressed by words such as ὁράω[d], θεάομαι[b], ἐπισκέπτομαι[b] (Lk 1,68.78; 7,16; Acts 7,23; 15,36), ἐπισκοπή (Lk 19,41) and ἱστορέω. The notion of "welcome, receive" can be expressed by verbal signs like προσλαμβάνομαι[e], παρα[d]- and ἀπολαμβάνω[d], δέχομαι[b] and seven of its compounds, δεκτός[b], ἀσπάζομαι[c], and εἴσοδος[b]. Finally, the meaning "show hospitality" is designated by the terms ξενίζω (Acts 10,6.18.23.32; 21,16; 28,7), ξενοδοχέω (1 Tim 5,10), φιλοξενία (Rom 12,13), ξενία[b] (Phlm 22), φιλόξενος (1 Pet 4,9), πόδας νίπτω (1 Tim 5,10), ξένος[b] (Rom 16,23), and καταλύω[e] (Lk 9,12; 19,7)[13].

---

10. Louw & Nida (*ibid.*) assign the notion of "stranger" to the socio-political subdivision of semantic domain 11 referring to "Groups and Classes of Persons and Members of Such Groups and Classes". The meaning of stranger/foreigner is expressed by verbal signs such as ξένος[a], ἀλλότριος[b], ἀπαλλοτριόομαι, ἀλλογενής, πάροικος and παρεπίδημος (11.73-77, pp. 132-133). M. CHIN, *A Heavenly Home for the Homeless. Aliens and Strangers in 1 Peter*, in *TyndB* 42 (1991) 96-112, notes that in the MT four general terms are used to designate the 'outsider': *ger, tosab, nokri* and *zar*. He tabulates their translations and occurrences in the LXX as follows: *ger* 92x = προσήλυτος, πάροικος; *tosab* 13x = πάροικος, παρεπίδημος; *nokri* 45x = ἀλλότριος, ἀλλογενής, ξένος; *zar* 71x = ἀλλότριος, ἀλλογενής (p. 98). He summarises his lexical observations as follows: ξένος means 'a mere passing stranger', πάροικος and παρεπίδημος point to sojourners, strangers who dwell transitorily, whereas in contrast κάτοικος means a permanent dweller (pp. 99-100).

11. Cf. J. PITT-STENGERS, *The Stranger, the Guest, and the Hostile Host: Introduction to the Study of the Laws of Hospitality*, in J.G. PERISTIANY (ed.), *Contributions to Mediterranean Sociology*, Paris, 1968, pp. 13-30; V.H. MATTHEWS, *Judges 4* (n. 8); ID., *Hospitality and Hostility in Genesis 19 and Judges 19*, in *BTB* 22 (1992) 3-11; and B.J. MALINA, *Received View* (n. 7), pp. 217-241. These authors all try to describe the protocol of hospitality customs in the Ancient Near East or in Mediterranean societies. Maybe the text basis on which they construct this protocol is too small. See our footnote 34 and T.R. HOBBS, *Man, Woman, and Hospitality – 2 Kings 4:8-36*, in *BTB* 23 (1993) 91-100.

12. LOUW & NIDA, *Lexicon* (n. 9), I, 446.

13. LOUW & NIDA, *Lexicon* (n. 9), I, 453-455. We have added references to Luke-Acts.

Fields of Application of the Hospitality Motif

Going through Luke-Acts, one notes that the theme of hospitality is not treated in itself nor is it the object of explicit reflection. Indeed, it is difficult to find even one pericope where hospitality is really at the centre of Luke's interest. In this sense, hospitality is but a sub-theme of Luke-Acts. Nevertheless, hospitality sometimes forms the very framework of a story (e.g. Lk 10,38-42), or it becomes an eloquent means to develop the real purpose of the Gospel, namely to show the readers how, through the mission of Jesus, Israel's God brings salvation to his own people and, with the help of Jesus' disciples, even to the Gentiles (e.g. Lk 19,1-10; 24,46-48; Acts 1,8). Moreover, one has the impression that the author feels it impossible to tell the history of salvation without making use of the hospitality theme. For Luke, hospitality is a key to understanding and describing reality; it is an integral part of human life and of the way God cares for his people and Jesus deals with men and women. That this is the case is shown by the fact that many aspects of his message are explained by means of hospitality. Let us describe the four main fields of application.

a. The first field is of ethical nature. In Lk 14,1-24, which takes the form of a symposium (cf. Lk 5,29-39; 7,36-50; 11,37-54; 15,31-32; 19,1-27)[14], Jesus addresses a parable to both guests and hosts. Guests should take the lowest places instead of the places of honour (vv. 7-10). Hosts should not invite friends, brothers, relatives or wealthy neighbours, "lest they also invite you in return, and you be repaid" (μήποτε καὶ αὐτοὶ ἀντικαλέσωσίν σε καὶ γένηται ἀνταπόδομά σοι); they should rather invite poor, crippled, lame and blind people, "because they cannot repay you" (οὐκ ἔχουσιν ἀνταποδοῦναί σοι; vv. 12-13). In other words, real hospitality has nothing to do with seeking honour; moreover, it does not belong to the realm of reciprocity. Jesus behaves here like a wisdom teacher (cf. Prov 25,6-7)[15], reminding his audience about what authentic hospitality is like. This parable, which is peculiar

14. For the literary genre of the symposium, see J. DELOBEL, *L'onction par la pécheresse. La composition littéraire de Lc., VII,36-50*, in *ETL* 42 (1966) 414-475, esp. pp. 458-464; D.E. SMITH, *Table Fellowship as a Literary Motif in the Gospel of Luke*, in *JBL* 106 (1987) 613-638.

15. Cf. the commentary on Prov 25,7 in *Midrash Rabbah Leviticus* 1,5: "R. Akiba taught in the name of R. Simeon b. 'Azzai: Go two or three seats lower and take your seat, until they say to you, 'Come up', rather than that you should go up and they should say to you, 'Go down'. Better that people say to you 'come up, come up', and not say to you, 'go down, go down'; and so used Hillel to say: 'My self-abasement is my exaltation, my self-exaltation is my abasement'" (*The Midrash Rabbah*, ed. H. FREEDMAN & M. SIMON, Vol. 2, London – Jerusalem – New York, 1977, p. 9).

to Luke, is one of the rare texts reflecting on the essence of hospitality. Jesus' moral teaching concerns human behaviour and points to the ethical dimension of hospitality. His view on hospitality remarkably runs counter to conceptions held in Graeco-Roman culture. While receiving a guest was considered to be an honour for the host[16], guests were also shown honour when they were invited[17]. The Lucan Jesus, however, rebukes guests seeking honour. Moreover, in the Graeco-Roman world hosts often offered hospitality to somebody because they had once had the same positive experience[18] or because they hoped to receive it in return[19]. In Luke, Jesus reacts against this ethics of reciprocity, just as he

16. Cf. *Od.* 7,333: when Alcinous, king of the Phaeacians and Odysseus's host, has promised to help him in going back home, Odysseus prays: "Father Zeus, grant that Alcinous may bring to pass all that he has said. So shall his fame (κλέος) be unquenchable over the earth, the giver of grain, and I shall reach my native land"; 11,338: Arete, the wife of Alcinous, says to the Phaeacians about Odysseus: "And moreover he is my guest (ξεῖνος), though each of you has a share in this honour (τιμή)"; 15,78-79: Menelaus, king of Sparta and Odysseus's host says: "It is a double boon – honour and glory it brings, and profit too (κῦδός τε καὶ ἀγλαίη καὶ ὄνειαρ) – that the traveler should dine before he goes off over the wide and boundless earth". The hosts offer gifts to their guest so that they may always be remembered, which in fact is also a kind of honour: *Od.* 1,313: Telemachus, son of Odysseus, says to the goddess Athena, whom he received as guest in the form of Mentes, king of the Taphians: "a gift costly and very beautiful, which shall be to you an heirloom (κειμήλιον) from me, such a gift as dear friends give to guest-friends (ξεῖνοι ξείνουσι διδοῦσι)"; 4,592: Menelaus says to Telemachus, his guest: "I will give you a beautiful cup, that you may pour libations to the immortal gods, and remember me all days" (ἐμέθεν μεμνημένος ἤματα πάντα); 8,430-432: Alcinous says to his wife Arete about Odysseus: "And I will give him this beautiful cup of mine, wrought in gold, that he may remember me all his days as he pours libations in his halls to Zeus and to the other gods"; 15,54: "For a guest remembers (ξεῖνος μιμνήσκεται) all his days the host (ἀνδρὸς ξεινοδόκου) who shows him kindness"; 15,125-126: Helen, Menelaus' wife, gives a robe to Telemachus with the words: "This gift, dear child, I too give you, a remembrace of the hands of Helen (μνῆμ' Ἑλένης χειρῶν), against the day of your longed for marriage, for your bride to wear".

17. Cf. *Od.* 5,36: "the Phaeacians... shall heartily show him (= Odysseus) all honour (τιμήσουσιν), as if he were a god"; 19,280: "the Phaeacians... showed him (= Odysseus) all honour (τιμήσαντο), as if he were a god, and gave him many gifts, and were glad themselves to send him home unscathed"; 23,339: "Then how he came after many toils to the Phaeacians, who heartily showed him all honour, as if he were a god (τιμήσαντο)". The guests sometimes receive gifts which bring them honour: cf. *Od.* 4,614; 8,393; 15,114.

18. *Od.* 4,33-34: Menelaus says to his squire Eteoneus concerning two strangers: "Surely we two many times ate the hospitable cheer of other men on our way here, hoping that Zeus would some day grant us respite from pain. No, unyoke the strangers' horses, and bring the men in, that they may feast". In the Old Testament, members of the Jewish people are asked not to oppress strangers nor to treat them differently because they have been strangers themselves: Exod 22,20; 23,9; Lev 19,34; Deut 10,19; 23,8.

19. *Il.* 6,212-236 (Glaucus and Diomedes); 17,149-153 (Glaucus says to Hector: "How art thou like to save a meaner man amid the press of battle, thou heartless one, when Sarpedon, that was at once thy guest and thy comrade [ἄμα ξεῖνον καὶ ἑταῖρον], thou didst leave to the Argives to be their prey and spoil!- one that full often proved a

does in the Sermon on the plain (Lk 6,32-35)[20]. Jesus' lesson to guest and host in Lk 14,7-14 thus primarily provides ethical wisdom: it pleads for a reversal of the common human behaviour concerning hospitality. At the same time, however, his lesson also has an eschatological connotation: it motivates this "conversion" by looking forward to the eschatological reward for genuine hospitality (v. 14: ἀνταποδοθήσεται γάρ σοι ἐν τῇ ἀναστάσει τῶν δικαίων)[21].

b. Another domain in which Luke uses the hospitality theme is that of theology and christology. Luke certainly knows the Hellenistic pattern

boon to thee, to thy city and thine own self, while yet he lived; whereas now thou hadst not the courage to ward from him the dogs"); 21,42-45: "For that time he [=Achilles] sold him [=Lycaon] into well-built Lemnos, bearing him thither on his ships, and the son of Jason had given a price for him – but from thence a guest-friend (ξεῖνος) had ransomed him – and a great price he gave – even Eetion of Imbros"; Od. 1,314-318: "Then the goddess, flashing-eyed Athene, answered him (= Telemachus): 'Keep me no longer, when I am eager to be gone, and whatever gift your heart bids you give me, give it when I come back, to bear to my home, choosing a very beautiful one; it shall bring you its worth in return (σοὶ δ' ἄξιον ἔσται ἀμοιβῆς)'"; 21,34-35: Odysseus as the guest of Iphitus gives him a bow coming from his father, "And to Iphitus Odysseus gave a sharp sword and a stout spear, as the beginning of a loving friendship (ἀρχὴν ξεινοσύνης προσκηδέος)"; 24,283-286: Laertes, speaking to his son Odysseus thinking he is a guest-friend of Odysseus who has died: "And all in vain did you bestow those gifts, the countless gifts you gave. For if you had found him still alive in the land of Ithaca, then would he have sent you on your way with ample requital of gifts and good entertainment; for that is the due of him who begins the kindness (τῷ κέν σ'εὖ δώροισιν ἀμειψάμενος ἀπέπεμψε καὶ ξενίῃ ἀγαθῇ ἢ γὰρ θέμις, ὅς τις ὑπάρξῃ)"; 24,314 Odysseus speaks: "Our hearts hoped that we should yet meet as host and guest and give one another glorious gifts (θυμὸς δ' ἔτι νῶϊν ἐώλπει μίξεσθαι ξενίῃ ἠδ' ἀγλαὰ δῶρα διδώσειν)". M. FINLEY, The World of Odysseus, London, ²1977, speaks about an "exchange mechanism" which is the basic organising mechanism among many primitive peoples (p. 64); "No single detail in the life of the heroes receives so much attention in the Iliad and the Odyssey as gift-giving, and always there is a frank reference to adequacy, appropriateness, recompense" (p. 65); "The word 'gift' is not to be misconstrued. It may be stated as a flat rule of both primitive and archaic society that no one ever gave anything, whether goods or services or honours, without proper recompense, real or wishful, immediate or years away, to himself or his kin. The act of giving was, therefore, in an essential sense always the first half of a reciprocal action, the other half of which was a counter-gift" (p. 64).

20. Cf. W.C. van Unnik, Die Motivierung der Feindesliebe in Lukas VI 32-35, in NT 8 (1966) 284-300: "Lukas hat hier formell hellenisiert, aber zugleich die griechische Moral aufs schärfste kritisiert. Er hat die Worte in ein griechisches Gewand gekleidet, aber damit die Substanz von Jesus' Predigt nicht geändert, sonder sie gut übersetzt, für seine griechischen Leser pointierter ausgedrückt, aktualisiert und die Nutzanwendung dieser Predigt gegeben".

21. The idea of divine reward or retribution is also well known in Homer. Zeus and the other gods reward (normally spoken) hospitality and punish violation of the rights of the guest: Od. 1,318 (reward by a divine guest); 3,58.62 (reward by a divine guest [Poseidon as well as Athena]); 9,275-277 (punishment); 13,213-214 (punishment); 14,53-54 (reward).284 (punishment).300 (punishment); 9,475-479 (punishment); 17,475-476 (punishment); 21,26-29 (punishment).

of gods visiting the earth in human form and receiving/or being refused hospitality by human beings (Acts 14,8-18; 28,6). He is also acquainted with the Old Testament stories telling of God's coming down to earth in the form of angels, messengers or prophets. The divine visit leads to blessings when God is received in a hospitable way (Gen 18), or to punishments when the laws of hospitality are disregarded (Gen 19). One has the impression that Luke is making use of this fundamental scheme when he tells the story of Jesus' life. Jesus is God's messenger and prophet, or even more, his own son, wandering around and visiting God's people in order to offer them salvation. "The salvation which Jesus brings is often associated in Luke's Gospel with meals, table fellowship and hospitality"[22]. Jesus is a stranger on earth, a πάροικος dwelling transitorily in the city of men (Lk 24,18), having nowhere to lay his head (Lk 9,58), and dependent on the hospitality of others. Through him, God himself visits his people (Lk 1,68.78; 7,16). His own town folk (Lk 4,16-30), the religious leaders (Lk 5,21; 7,44-46; 9,21; 11,37ff.), and/or Jerusalem, however, refuse to receive him in a proper way (Lk 13,33; 19,12.14.39.41-44; 20,9-19). Jesus is the journeying guest bearing God's dynamic presence, who is often not received (Lk 9,51–19,44), and is finally rejected in Jerusalem (Lk 19,45–23,49)[23]. God's revenge, therefore, will come over them, because they did not recognize the "time of their visitation" (Lk 19,27.44). On the other hand, the people who offer him genuine hospitality, will receive God's blessing and salvation (Lk 7,36-50; 10,38-41; 19,1-10; 24,28-32). We will deal more fully with this aspect in the second part of our paper.

c. A third area in which the hospitality motif plays a considerable role is the reality of mission and ecclesiology[24]. Luke may have thought that, because Jesus himself was a wandering prophet messiah, his disciples must also have experienced an existence resembling that of wandering prophets. In the stories of the commissioning of the Twelve (Lk 9,1-6) and of the Seventy (Lk 10,1-16), which Luke received from his sources

---

22. D. McBRIDE, *Emmaus. The Gracious Visit of God According to Luke*, Dublin, 1991, p. 50; see the whole chapter: "The Saving Visit of God in Luke's Gospel" (pp. 30-56).

23. Cf. D.P. MOESSNER, *Lord of the Banquet. The Literary and Theological Significance of the Lukan Travel Narrative*, Minneapolis, MN, 1987, pp. 132-186.

24. Cf. R.J. DILLON, *From Eye-Witnesses to Ministers of the Word: Tradition and Composition in Luke 24* (AnBib, 82), Rome, 1978, pp. 228-249; J. KOENIG, *New Testament Hospitality: Partnership with Strangers as Promise and Mission*, Philadelphia, 1985, pp. 85-123 (Chapter 4): "Guest and Hosts, Together in Mission (Luke)"; H. RUSCHE, *Gastfreundschaft in der Verkündigung des Neuen Testaments und ihr Verhältnis zur Mission* (Veröffentlichungen des Instituts für Missionswissenschaft der Westfälischen Wilhelms-Universität Münster Westfalen, 7), Münster, 1957.

(resp. Mk and Q), the mission to proclaim the kingdom of God and to heal (9,2) is to be fulfilled in the context of hospitality and table fellowship. The messengers should take nothing for their journey (9,3; 10,4). This implies that, as foreign visitors, they are totally dependent on the hospitality of the towns and houses they pass through. The instructions envisage two possible responses from the side of the people addressed: either they are well received (9,4; 10,6-9), or they are refused hospitality (9,5; 10,10-11). In accordance with the way people react, the messengers either have to stay where they are (9,4; 10,7), enjoying the table fellowship offered to them (10,7), and bring the blessings of the kingdom (peace, healings: 9,6; 10,6a.9), or they have to leave the place and testify against the city (9,5; 10,10b-11). Jesus even threatens the inhospitable cities (Chorazin, Bethlehem, Capernaum) with an eschatological punishment. Their destiny will be worse than that of the citizens of Sodom, who violated the laws of hospitality in trying to 'know' the two angels of Yahweh who were the guests of Lot (Gen 19) (Lk 10,12-15). The messengers are clearly identified with their commissioner, Jesus, and finally with God, who sent Jesus (Lk 10,16 par. Mt 10,40). Their coming is the human way God visits the cities and offers them salvation. What is done to them, is done to Jesus, even to God himself. The final retribution therefore comes from God and is eschatological in nature.

In the Book of Acts the Early Christian mission is often performed within a network of hospitality: evangelists wandering about in Mediterranean areas receive hospitality in local churches (Acts 21,4; 10,48; 18,20; 21,7.17; 28,14) or with persons mentioned by name (e.g. Acts 9,43; 10,6.23b-28.32; 16,13-15.33-34; 17,6-7; 18,1-4.26; 21,8.10.16; 28,7); prosperous Christians place their houses at the disposal of the local churches for their meetings (the so-called house churches in Acts 2,1.44-47; 4,23.31; 5,42; 12,12; 16,40; 20,7-8). Perhaps for Luke, this feature of the early Church is not without relation to the experience of the people of God in the past. When Stephen is giving a survey of the history of the salvation God brought to his people, he links this history to the forefathers who lived as strangers in a foreign land where they received some kind of hospitality: Abraham in Haran, Joseph in Egypt, Moses in Midian (Acts 7,2ff.).

On occasion, the Apostle Paul seems to make an exception to the rule of hospitality in the Early Church. On his missionary journeys, he does not always make use of his right to maintenance and works for his lodging (Acts 18,3; cf. 1 Cor 9,3-6), although at other times, he enjoys the hospitality of the disciples (Acts 21,16). After his arrival in Rome, he is allowed to stay by himself, albeit under the guardianship of a soldier.

For two years he lives there at his own expense. As a real host he receives people all day, testifying to the kingdom of God and trying to convince them about Jesus (Acts 28,16.23.25.30).

d. Finally, in Luke's Gospel, hospitality functions as a metaphor to describe the Kingdom of God. In the parable of the narrow door (Lk 13,22-30), which Luke has redacted on the basis of a cluster of logia found in Q, the reality of the Kingdom is described as an eschatological Banquet, entry to which is not easy to achieve. The Lord Jesus will open the door for Abraham, Isaac, Jacob, all the prophets and people coming from every corner of the earth, but the door will remain closed for Jews who ate and drank with him, who heard his teachings but nevertheless were evildoers. The earthly Jesus will in the future be the Lord/host who offers or refuses hospitality and table-fellowship in the guest-room of God's eschatological kingdom. Within the framework of the symposium we mentioned already, Jesus tells another parable about the great banquet that symbolises the kingdom of God (Lk 14,15-24). Those who were invited first make all kind of excuses, whereas the poor, the crippled, the blind and the lame, and even the people wandering along the roads and lanes are compelled to enter the Master's room. There is a similar shift from the first candidates for the kingdom to those who, according to normal expectations, have no chance ever to enter the divine guest-room.

II. THEOLOGICAL AND CHRISTOLOGICAL APPLICATIONS OF THE HOSPITALITY THEME

We would like to focus now on the second aspect which we mentioned above, namely the theological and christological use of the hospitality theme in Luke-Acts. The thesis we would like to propose here is that Luke, as a Hellenistic author writing for Greek readers, was well acquainted with a very common pattern in Graeco-Roman literature, that of divine beings visiting human beings on earth. It also occurs in the Septuagint, albeit in a different context of monotheistic faith. This pattern forms the framework for Luke's presentation of Jesus' mission as a visit of God to his people.

Graeco-Roman Antecedents

In Acts 14,8-18 Luke tells the story of Paul and Barnabas healing a lame man in the city of Lystra. Seeing this, the crowds shout out (in Lycaonian dialect): "The gods have come down to us in human form" (οἱ θεοὶ ὁμοιωθέντες ἀνθρώποις κατέβησαν πρὸς ἡμᾶς; v. 11). They identify Barnabas with Zeus and Paul with Hermes. Paul and Barnabas have to do everything possible to prevent the crowds, presided over by the priest of "Zeus before the City", from offering sacrifice to them. A similar story is told in Acts 28,1-6. The natives of the island Malta kindly offer hospitality to Paul and his companions after they have escaped from a shipwreck (v. 2: οἵ τε βάρβαροι παρεῖχον οὐ τὴν τυχοῦσαν φιλανθρωπίαν ἡμῖν ... προσελάβοντο πάντας ἡμᾶς). When a viper bites Paul's hand, they first think he is a murderer. When they see he does not suffer any harm, however, they change their minds and begin to say that he is a god (ἔλεγον αὐτὸν εἶναι θεόν).

These two texts (and probably also Acts 10,25-26) unmistakably show Luke's knowledge of a widely spread feature of Graeco-Roman religiosity: "the conviction that the membrane separating the realms of the human and the divine was a permeable one, with traffic possible in both directions. Not by accident is Ovid's great compendium of Greco-Roman mythology called simply *Metamorphoses* ('The Changing of Forms', see for example 1:390-779; 2:466-495)"[25]. L.T. Johnson, from whom this quotation comes, points to several texts illustrating this fact[26], but a more specific set of parallels could be selected which illustrate the idea of gods descending to the earth, disguised in human form and visiting mortals[27]. Most commentators on Acts 14,8-18 only refer to the text of the story of Philemon and Baucis in Ovid's *Metamorphoses* 8,611-724, which indeed shows a striking parallel[28]. Ovid tells a tale about

25. Cf. L.T. JOHNSON, *The Acts of the Apostles* (Sacra Pagina, 5), Collegeville, MN, 1992, p. 248.

26. Chariton of Aphrodisias, *Chaereas and Callirhoe* 1,1,16; 1,14,1; 3,2,15-17; Heliodorus, *The Ethiopians* 1,2,1; Ovid, *Metamorphoses*, 1,390-799; 2,466-495; 8,611-724; Xenophon, *The Ephesians* 1,12,1

27. For the Greek world, see e.g. Homer, *Il.* 3,385; 6,128-129; 13,43-45; 24,338ff.; *Od.* 1,105; 2,382-383.399-401; 3,13-24; 7,19-20.199-200; 17,484-487; cf. J.H. ROSE, *Divine Disguisings*, in *HTR* 49 (1956) 63-72; S. MURNAGHAN, *Disguise and Recognition in the Odyssey*, Princeton, NJ, 1987. For the Latin world, see e.g. Ovid, *Metamorphoses* 1,35.213; 4,231; 7,125.642; 8,181.626; 11,203; *Fasti* 5,495-504; F. BÖMER, *P. Ovidius Naso. Metamorphosen. Kommentar. Buch VIII-IX*, Heidelberg, 1977, p. 198 offers even further parallels. For parallels in texts from the Ancient Near East, see D. IRVIN, *Mytharion. The Comparison of Tales from the Old Testament and the Ancient Near East* (Alter Orient und Altes Testament, 32), Kevelaer – Neukirchen-Vluyn, 1978, p. 137. Cf. S. THOMPSON, *Motif-Index of Folk Literature*, 6 vols., Copenhagen-Bloomington, IN, 1955-1958: Motif D 42 (God in guise of a mortal); and K 1811 (Gods in disguise visit mortals).

28. Cf. F.F. BRUCE, *Acts*, London, 1954, p. 291; E. HAENCHEN, *Apostelgeschichte* (KEK), Göttingen, 1965, p. 367-68; R. PESCH, *Apostelgeschichte (Apg 13–28)* (EKK, 5/2), Neukirchen, 1986, p. 55; G. SCHILLE, *Apostelgeschichte* (THNT, 5), Berlin, 1983, p. 305; A. WEISER, *Apostelgeschichte. Kapitel 13-28* (ÖTK, 5/2), Gütersloh-Würzburg, 1985, p. 350; J. ZMIJEWSKI, *Die Apostelgeschichte* (RNT), Regensburg, 1994, p. 530.

Jupiter and Mercurius, the Roman counterparts of the Greek Gods Zeus and Hermes, coming down in human form and seeking hospitality with the poor and aged couple Philemon and Baucis. The couple kindly welcomes them in their humble cottage "in the Phrygian hills"[29]. As a reward for their hospitality they are made priests of a temple of Jupiter. Moreover, Ovid's story of Philemon and Baucis is also remarkably parallel with Gen 18–19. There are indeed a lot of striking agreements between both stories[30]. There cannot be much doubt that Ovid, in telling this marvellous story, was in one or another way dependent on Greek tradition (e.g. Homer, Kallimachos) and one may even ask whether he was not dependent also on Gen 18–19, since he clearly had knowledge of other parts of the Jewish tradition[31]. It is too farfetched to think that both Luke and Ovid, two authors who lived almost within the same century, might sometimes have found their inspiration in the same streams of tradition?

That Luke had read the Latin author Ovid is, of course, very unlikely. His knowledge of the Hellenistic theme of gods visiting men and being received by them must have its origin elsewhere. When we make a – reasonable – supposition that Luke, as one of the most literate authors of the New Testament, had received a good Hellenistic education, we may take for granted that Homer's *Iliad* and *Odyssey* were part of his

---

29. Some authors point to a local tradition, e.g., A. WEISER, *Apostelgeschichte* (n. 28), p. 350; J. ZMIJEWSKI, *Apostelgeschichte* (n. 28), p. 530: "Es lässt sich dafür vielmehr auch die Tatsache ins Feld führen, dass sich das hier szenisch ausgestaltete Motiv der in Menschengestalt erscheinenden Götter gerade in den bodenständigen Überlieferungen Phrygiens und Lykaoniens findet. Wenn das Motiv, wie die griech. Götternamen Zeus und Hermes zu erkennen geben, hier [wie bei Ovid, Metam VIII 611-724] in *hellenistischer* Fassung erscheint, dann spricht dies noch keineswegs für eine Abfassung der Szene durch Lukas"; he refers to L. MALTEN, *Motivgeschichtliche Untersuchungen zur Sagenforschung. I. Philemon und Baucis*, in *Hermes* 74 (1939) 176-206, esp. p. 182; and *II. Noch einmal Philemon und Baucis*, in *Hermes* 75 (1940) 168-176, esp. p. 171; see also M. BELLER, *Philemon und Baucis in der europäischen Literatur. Stoffgeschichte und Analyse* (Studien zum Fortwirken der Antike, 3), Heidelberg, 1967, p. 15; F. BÖMER, *Metamorphosen* (n. 27), pp. 190-191.

30. M. BELLER, *Philemon und Baucis* (n. 29), pp. 22-26 gives a list of parallels; F. BÖMER, *Metamorphosen* (n. 27), pp. 190-91; J. FONTENROSE, *Philemon, Lot and Lycaon*, in *Classical Philology* 13/4 (1945) 93-120.

31. Cf. F. BÖMER, *Metamorphosen* (n. 27), p. 190-193, esp. p. 191: "Es ist nicht ausgeschlossen, dass Ovid hier, in welcher Weise im einzelnen auch immer, auf jüdische Traditionen zurückgeht, zumal es als sicher gelten darf, dass er und seine Zeit, Traditionen dieser Herkunft auch in anderen Fällen gekannt haben: I 76ff S. 42. VIII 6ff. S. 12f. (Scylla und das Samson-und-Dalila-Motiv). fast. IV 679ff. und 901ff. Die Füchse im Philisterlande"; and p. 192: "die hellenistische Zeit hatte die Hauptmotive, das Idyll der pietas der Armen, den Besuch der Götter und die Bestrafung der Gottlosen, in ihren eigenen Raum gestellt, allen voran und als vielbeachtetes Vorbild für die Folgezeit, Kallimachos".

schooltime readings and of his general culture. The French historian Henri-Irénée Marrou has shown convincingly that Homer was the most important classical author read in 'secondary school' during the Hellenistic period[32]. When one re-reads the two Homerian classics one is struck by the fact that the theme of gods visiting men and of men receiving them is frequently present.

Let us first look at the way Homer describes divine visits, whereby it must be noted that divine visits do not necessarily imply a hospitable reception. A divine visit means a spacial displacement of a god(dess). He or she goes to other gods or to human beings, either in recognizable divine appearance, or in the form of a human being, an animal, or something else. The purpose of the visit is to bring a message, to intervene in human affairs (e.g. to put to the test, to bring salvation or disaster, to attend a festival meal or for other reasons). The pattern of a "divine visit" consists of several motifs[33]:

(1) a descent (κατάβασις) or an ascension (when the gods come from Hades or out of the water), and/or a wandering;
(2) a transfiguration or a disguise of the divine;
(3) an appearance of the god(dess) and/or a being seen through human beings;
(4) the (potential) host offers hospitality or refuses it;
(5) the divine guest brings in turn salvation or disaster;
(6) disappearance of the divine visitor (in a normal or an extraordinary way); an ascension into heaven (ἀνάβασις), or a descent (when the gods go back to Hades or into the water).
(7) sometimes at that moment (or before the disappearance) the gods are recognized by the host.

The first chapter of the *Odyssey* has all the topoi of a divine visit. It tells the story of the visit of the flashing-eyed goddess Athene to

---

32. Cf. H.-I. MARROU, *A History of Education in Antiquity*, London, 1956, pp. 160-175 ("Part Two, Chapter VII: Literary Studies at Secondary School Standard"), esp. p. 162: "In the forefront, of course, and dominating all the rest, stands Homer. Throughout the Hellenistic period his popularity never wavered. There is abundant proof of this". Marrou points *inter alia* to the huge number of papyri containing fragments of Homer's work. This observation has been confirmed recently by the computer research programme set up by a team of K.U. Leuven classical scholars under the direction of J. Clarysse. They try to measure the popularity of ancient authors on the basis of the extant numbers of papyri. From their findings, it is obvious that Homer was the most popular writer of Antiquity: cf. W. CLARYSSE – K. VANDORPE, *Boeken en bibliotheken in de Oudheid, op basis van een tentoonstelling door Odette Bouqiaux-Sion*, Leuven, 1996, pp. 69-71.

33. The scheme we present here is a reworking of earlier proposals made by D. FLÜCKIGER-GUGGENHEIM, *Göttliche Gäste. Die Einkehr von Götter und Heroen in der griechischen Mythologie* (EHS, 3/237), Bern – Frankfurt – New York, 1984, pp. 11-17 and M. LANDAU, *Die Erdenwanderungen der Himmlischen und die Wünsche der Menschen*, in *Zeitschrift für vergleichende Literaturgeschichte* 14 (1901) 1-41, esp. p. 5.

Telemachus, Odysseus's son, who lives in Ithaca with his mother Pene-
lope amidst the suitors who try to win her heart and her properties in the
absence of Odysseus and are constantly violating the laws of hospitality.

(1) Athene descends from the Olympos (βῆ δὲ κατ' Οὐλύμποιο:
1,102) to the palace of Odysseus in Ithaca.

(2) She comes in the appearance of a male stranger (εἰδομένη
ξείνῳ: 1,105), namely Mentes, the leader of the Thaphians.

(3) There is a meal going on, but the suitors do not pay attention to
the stranger, whereas Telemachus is the first to see her (πρῶτος ἴδε
Τηλέμαχος: 1,113; εἴσιδ᾽ Ἀθήνην: 1,118).

(4) He kindly offers her hospitality. This implies different things. He
"goes quickly to the outer door (βῆ δ᾽ ἰθὺς προθύροιο)" to meet her,
because "in his heart he counted it shame that a stranger (ξεῖνος) should
stand long at the gates" (1,120-21). He clasps her right hand (χεῖρ᾽ ἕλε
δεξιτερήν), takes from her the spear of bronze and addresses her with
the following welcome words: "Hail, stranger (χαῖρε, ξεῖνε), in our
house you shall find entertainment, and then, when you have tasted food
(δείπνου πασσάμενος), you will tell what you need" (1,124-25). He
leads her into the house and invites her to sit in a beautiful chair with a
footstool for her feet. A handmaid brings water to wash her hands. At a
polished table he offers her a copious meal. Then Telemachus asks
where his guest is coming from and whether he is a guest-friend of his
father's house (ἦ καὶ πατρώιός ἐσσι ξεῖνος:1,175-76)[34]. The goddess
tells her own story and says that their fathers were friends from of old
(ξεῖνοι δ᾽ ἀλλήλων πατρώιοι εὐχόμεθ᾽ εἶναι ἐξ ἀρχῆς: 1,187-88).

(5) Then the guest asks the host about his identity ("declare it truly,
whether indeed, tall as you are, you are the son of Odysseus himself":
1,206-07) and about the situation in the house. After Telemachus' explanation, Athene counsels him on what to do. She brings hope in assuring

---

34. According to V. Matthews' view on the hospitality protocol in the Ancient Middle East (*Judges 4* [n. 8]), p. 15), "The host must not ask personal questions of the guest.
These matters can only be volunteered by the guest". This view must be relativised, at
least for Greece and for the Hellenistic period, in the light of the data in Homer. In the
Odyssey it is indeed not allowed to ask questions to the guest as long as he has not yet
taken the guest-meal. Only thereafter comes the "ritual" moment to ask questions about
the identity and the origin of the guest (cf. *Od.* 3,69-74; 4,60-61: "Take of the food, and
be glad, and then when you have supped, we will ask you who among men you are". 138-
139; 7,215: "But as for me, suffer me now to eat, despite my grief".237-239; 8,548-586)
and also about the reason for the visit (cf. *Od.* 1,123-124: "Hail, stranger; in our house
you will find entertainment, and then, when you have tasted food, you will tell us what
you need"; 5,95-97: "So he drank and ate, the messenger Argeïphontes. But when he had
dined and satisfied his soul with food, then he answered, and addressed her, saying: 'You,
a goddess, does question me, a god, upon my coming'"); cf. *Od.* 21,35-36: οὐδὲ
τραπέζῃ γνώτην ἀλλήλων ("the meal had not yet made them known to each other").

that Odysseus is still alive and may come back; she suggests that Telemachus get more information about his father from his former fellow-fighters (salvation); she foresees a harsh punishment for the suitors, through Telemachus' hands (punishment).

Although the guest is eager to go, Telemachus asks her to stay a bit longer in order to have a bath and another meal and then to receive a gift (1,309-13). The goddess replies that she would like to leave immediately but that one day she will come back to receive his gift, which will bring him its worth in return (1,314-18).

(6) Then comes the departure of the divine guest: "So spoke the goddess, flashing-eyed Athene, and departed, flying upward as a bird" (ἀπέβη γλαυκῶπις Ἀθήνη, ὄρνις δ' ὣς ἀνόπαια διέπτατο: 1,319-20).

(7) The departure is followed by Telemachus' recognition of the true identity of the stranger: "And in his mind he marked her and marvelled, for he deemed that she was a god" (ὀΐσατο γὰρ θεὸν εἶναι: 1,322-23).

The story of the goddess Athene in the *Odyssey* (ch. 1), is not exceptional. Anne P. Burnett remarks that Gracco-Roman epic and folk tales tell of many such divinities. "Gods often wandered on earth incognito (cf. *Od.* 17,485-87)... Sometimes they took service with mortals; sometimes they were in exile; sometimes they were engaged in quests or on general tours of inspection, but the pattern of their adventures was always roughly the same. Seeking aid or acceptance or hospitality, they were either rejected or received, and in response they visited those who refused them with flood, plague, or other natural disaster (like the exemplary earthquake of the *Bacchae*), while they rescued their hosts and rewarded them with plenty (crops, marriage, children, victory)"[35].

Old Testament Models

It is quite obvious that Luke was familiar with the Graeco-Roman theme of divine visits to human beings on earth although it is difficult to tell which specific story he had read. What we do know for certain is that he knew the Septuagint, and more specifically the double narrative of Gen 18–19 which is the story *par excellence* of how God visits indi-

---

35. Cf. A.P. BURNETT, *Pentheus and Dionysos. Host and Guest*, in *Classical Philology* 65 (1970) 15-29, p. 24-25, and the references in footnotes 8 and 9. A number of the motifs constituting the pattern occur in Ovid, *Metam.* 1,211-241 (visit of Jupiter to Lycaon); *Fasti* 4,507ff (Ceres is received by Celeus, Metanira and their daughter); 5,495-536 (Jupiter, his brother, and Mercury visit Hyrieus).

viduals or cities and how that visit can end with salvation or disaster according to the way people receive him[36].

The story of God's visit to Abraham (Gen 18) shows a number of similarities and differences with the scheme we have observed in the *Odyssey*, ch. 1. The opening words of Gen 18 clearly announce a divine visit: ὤφθη δὲ αὐτῷ ὁ θεός.

(1) The way God comes from heaven to earth is not explicitly stated, but that He comes from above could be implicitly suggested by Abraham's "looking up" (ἀναβλέψας: v. 2), by the suggestion that God's presence is unexpected (εἱστήκεισαν ἐπάνω αὐτοῦ: v. 2; cf. Lk 24,36), and by the use of the verb παρέρχομαι ("to pass along": vv. 3.5) which elsewhere is a terminus technicus for a theophany (cf. Exod 33,19.22; 34,5 [καὶ κατέβη κύριος].6 [καὶ παρῆλθεν κύριος]; 1 Kings 19,11; Job 9,11; Ezek 16,6.8; Hos 10,11; Mk 6,48).

(2) The text does not speak of a transfiguration or a disguisement. But God is not seen face to face, which in Old Testament terms would simply be impossible. What is remarkable here, is that the visit of the one God is realised by a group of "three men" (τρεῖς ἄνδρες: v. 2), who later on are addressed as one Lord (κύριε: v. 3). When "the two angels" of Gen 19,1 are refering back to the story of Gen 18, we may conlude that two of the three men of Gen 18,2 are understood to be angels, whereas the third is Yahweh, thus appearing in human form. The constant switching between plural and singular in Gen 18–19 functions as a subtle indication by the narrator of the divine character of the visitors.

(3) The visit is presented as an appearance of God (ὤφθη δὲ αὐτῷ ὁ θεός: v. 1). At the same time much stress is laid on the "seeing" of Abraham (ἀναβλέψας, καὶ ἰδού, καὶ ἰδών: v. 2).

(4) Abraham behaves like a perfect host. His generous hospitality is described in detail. Like Telemachus, he is in haste to meet them (προσέδραμεν εἰς συνάντησιν αὐτοῖς: v. 2) and bows down. There is also a welcome address: "Lord, if I have found favor before you, do not pass your servant". Instead of the guests asking a favour of the host, it

---

36. Nestle-Aland (27th ed.) points to the following "loci citati vel allegati" (p. 771): Gen 18,4 (Lk 7,44); Gen 18,11 (Lk 1,7.18); Gen 18,14 (Lk 1,37); Gen 18,18 (Acts 3,25); Gen 18,20s. (Lk 17,28); Gen 19,15 (Lk 17,29); Gen 19,17 (Lk 9,62; 17,31); Gen 19,19 (Lk 1,58); Gen 19,24s. (Lk 17,29); Gen 19,26 (Lk 9,62; 17,31). On the idea of divine visitation in both Gen 18 and 19 based on recognition (Abraham) and non-recognition (Lot), see B. DOYLE, *The Sin of Sodom: yāḏaʿ, yāḏaʿ, yāḏaʿ? A Reading of the Mamre-Sodom Narrative in Genesis 18-19*, in *Theology and Sexuality* 9 (1998) 94-100. See also J.A. LOADER, *A Tale of Two Cities: Sodom and Gomorrah in the Old Testament, Early Jewish and Early Christian Traditions* (CBET, 1), Kampen, 1990; J. H. SAILHAMER, *The Pentateuch as Narrative*, Grand Rapids, 1992, pp. 160-174.

is as if the host is asking a favour of the guests. Water is brought so that the visitors may wash their feet while a cool resting place is offered (under the tree), and a copious meal is served (vv. 4-8).

(5) The divine guests bring salvation to the host's house: they promise that Abraham and Sarah will have a child despite their advanced age (v. 9-15). Moreover, they hold out the prospect of punishment for Sodom and Gomorrah (vv. 16-32).

(6) The divine visitors (οἱ ἄνδρες) stand up to leave (ἐξαναστάντες δὲ ἐκεῖθεν) and Abraham walks along with them to see them on their way (v. 16). After the Lord has revealed the reason for his coming to Abraham (v. 20-21), there seems to be a division of the three visitors, because "the (two?) men turned away and went toward Sodom; and Abraham was still standing before the Lord" (v. 22). After a long discussion (between Abraham and the Lord), when the Lord has finished speaking with Abraham, he leaves (ἀπῆλθεν δὲ κύριος), and Abraham returns home (v. 33).

(7) It is not said explicitly that Abraham recognizes the one God in the three visitors or at what point he recognizes that. Nevertheless the story seems to imply that Abraham is aware of their divine identity. This is suggested in the way Abraham approaches (προσεκύνησεν in v. 2; "ἑστηκὼς ἔναντίον κυρίου: standing before the Lord": v. 22) and addresses (at least one of) them (e.g. the question of v. 3: κύριε, εἰ ἄρα εὗρον χάριν ἐναντίον σου; cf. κύριε in vv. 30, 31, 32).

Gen 19 forms, at least in part, the counterpart of the preceding chapter in the sense that we have to do with a clear example of inhospitality. At the same time, the specific features of the divine visit are also present in this story.

(1) The descent is already anticipated in the preceding story, where the narrator remarks that the men (οἱ ἄνδρες) "looked down toward Sodom and Gommorah (18,16 κατέβλεψαν ἐπὶ πρόσωπον Σοδομων καὶ Γομορρας), and that the Lord has come down to see (καταβὰς οὖν ὄψομαι) if what they have done is as bad as the outcry that has reached him (18,21). One could object that Gen 18,16.21 speak of a descent on earth, from the place where Abraham lives to the cities Sodom and Gommorah which lie below in the plain. It is not impossible, however, that the author has also the descent of Yahweh from heaven in mind and that his text is consciously ambiguous[37]. The men then turn away and go toward Sodom (18,22) and arrive there in the evening (19,1 ἦλθον δὲ

37. This is especially the case in Gen 18,21, where the aorist participle (καταβὰς) could refer to God's descent from heaven before visiting Abraham. See B. DOYLE, *The Sin of Sodom* (n. 36), p. 98, n. 19.

... εἰς Σοδομα ἑσπέρας). The Lord himself does not go to Sodom, since He has already departed in 18,33.

(2) Nevertheless He visits the cities through the two angels (19,1 οἱ δύο ἄγγελοι). That Gen 19 in the author's mind really describes a divine visit, becomes clear from the fact the author first says that the Lord has sent the angels to destroy the place (ἀπέστειλεν ἡμᾶς κύριος ἐκτρῖψαι αὐτήν: 19,13), and then that it is God himself who destroys the city (ἐκτρίβει κύριος τὴν πόλιν: 19,14.29). Again, the constant switching between the plural and the singular is a suggestive indication of this (cf. 19,13-14.16.18).

(3) The two angels obviously come in visible form because Lot, who is sitting in the gateway of the city, "sees" them (ἰδὼν δὲ Λωτ: 19,1).

(4) Lot behaves like a perfect host (19,1b-3), although he is but an alien dwelling transitorily in the city (εἷς ἦλθες παροικεῖν: 19,9). The native citizens intend to violate the laws of hospitality in the most agressive way possible, although they do not succeed (19,4-9).

(5) The divine guests save Lot and his family from the threat of his fellow-citizens (19,10-11) and from the destruction the Lord brings over the cities (19,12-26).

(6) The disappearance of the angels is not mentioned explicitly.

(7) At their first encounter, it would appear that Lot does not recognise the status of his visitors, whom he adresses as κύριοι (19,2: pl.). Accordingly, his greeting (προσεκύνησεν ἐπὶ τὴν γῆν: 19,1) is but a simple gesture of reverence. Only in 19,13 the visitors reveal their identity as messengers from God, after which Lot expresses recognition of their divine status in the way he addresses them: εἶπεν δὲ Λωτ πρὸς αὐτούς (pl.) Δέομαι, κύριε (sg.) (19,18). He can now speak (19,19) with words similar to those of Abraham (18,3): "If I/your servant have/has found favour in your eyes" (ἐπειδὴ εὗρεν ὁ παῖς σου ἔλεος ἐναντίον σου).

The stories of Abraham and Lot in Gen 18 and 19 serve as narrative illustrations of the broader Old Testament theme of God's visitation ("Heimsuchung"). The theme is often linked with the use of the word-group פקד/פקדה with God as the subject, which in the LXX is usually translated by the word-group ἐπισκέπτομαι, ἐπισκοπή[38]. "This visita-

---

38. In secular Greek ἐπισκέπτομαι is derived from ἐπισκοπέω, which has the meanings 1. look upon or at, inspect, observe; 2. visit; 3. of a general: inspect, review; 4. consider, reflect, meditate; 5. exercise the office of ἐπίσκοπος (cf. H.G. LIDDELL & R. SCOTT, A Greek-English Lexicon, Oxford, 1961, p. 657). For the OT, see H.W. BEYER, ἐπισκέπτομαι, ἐπισκοπέω, in TDNT 2, 1964, pp. 599-608, esp. 602: In the LXX the verb has a religious content when God is the subject of the action. "It combines the various senses of 'to visit, to look upon, to investigate, to inspect, to test, to be concerned

tion takes place when God draws near to His people in its sin and distress, and shows Himself to be the Lord of history. It may entail the judgment executed by Him. But it may also consist in an act of mercy. The point is that He manifestly enters history. The word 'to visit' may signify a visitation of both judgment and grace in the same sentence"[39]. Examples of the use of the verb ἐπισκέπτομαι for God's visitation in a positive, salvific sense are Gen 21,1[40]; 50,24.25; Exod 4,31; 13,19; Ps 8,5; 79(80),15; Jer 36(29),10; Zeph 2,7; Zech 10,3; for a negative sense, see Job 35,15; Ps 88(89),32; Isa 10,12; Jer 36,32; 37(30),20; 43(36),31; Lam 4,22. The corresponding noun ἐπισκοπή is accordingly used in a positive sense in Wis 3,7 (ἐν καιρῷ ἐπισκοπῆς).9; 4,15 (with χάρις and ἔλεος) (?); Sir 18,20 (ἐν ὥρᾳ ἐπισκοπῆς); Isa 23,17, and in the negative sense of ἐκδίκησις in Wis 3,7 (καιρῷ); 14,11; 19,15[41]; Sir 23,24; Isa 10,3 (ἡμέρᾳ); 24,22; 29,6; Jer 6,15 (καιρῷ); 10,15 (καιρῷ); 11,23 (ἐνιαυτῷ).

God's Visitation Through Jesus in Luke

When Luke gives a picture of Jesus' mission towards Israel he seems to consistently bear this larger Graeco-Roman and Old Testament context of divine visitations in mind. At the same time, he presupposes that his Hellenistic readers are also familiar with the theme in question and with the narrative development thereof.

a. First, Luke may have fashioned some of his *narratives* after the Graeco-Roman-Septuagintal pattern of divine visitations. His Infancy Narrative starts with two angelophanies (Lk 1,5-25.26-38) which are generally recognized as a Lukan mixture of three different literary genres occuring in the Old Testament, namely apocalypse, birth announce-

---

about, to care for', in description of the act in which the Lord in a special incursion into the course of life of individuals or of a people, mostly Israel, makes known to them His will either in judgment or in grace. It is worth noting that this sense does not occur in secular Greek but only in the context of the OT history of salvation, from which it passes into the NT"; H.S. GEHMAN, Ἐπισκέπτομαι, ἐπίσκεψις, ἐπίσκοπος, and ἐπισκοπή in the Septuagint in Relation to פקד and other Hebrew Roots – a Case of Semantic Development Similar to that of Hebrew, in VT 22 (1972) 197-207; W. SCHOTTROFF, פקד pqd heimsuchen, in E. JENNI & C. WESTERMANN (eds.), Theologisches Handwörterbuch zum Alten Testament, Vol. 2, München – Zürich, 1976, pp. 466-486.

39. H.W. BEYER, Ἐπισκέπτομαι (n. 38), p. 602.

40. God's gracious looking down on Sarah (καὶ κύριος ἐπισκέψατο τὴν Σαρραν) in Gen 21,1 is the fulfilment of God's promise given to her during his visit narrated in Gen 18.

41. In Wis 19,15, the notion of ἐπισκοπή (judgment in the negative sense) is linked with inhospitable behaviour towards strangers: "There is indeed judgment awaiting those who treated foreigners as enemies" (ἐπισκοπὴ ἔσται αὐτῶν, ἐπεὶ ἀπεχθῶς προσεδέχοντο τοὺς ἀλλοτρίους).

ment, and vocation narrative[42]. One wonders, in the light of what has been said above, whether Luke did not understand these announcement stories primarily as divine visits through the mediation of God's angel[43]. Let us look primarily at Lk 1,26-38, comparing this annunciation story when necessary with the announcement to Zechariah in Lk 1,5-25. Two observations could support our hypothesis. First, the story fits rather well within the pattern of the divine visit narrative, although there are also differences: (1) the descent of the angel is suggested by the words ἀπεστάλη ὁ ἄγγελος Γαβριὴλ ἀπὸ τοῦ θεοῦ εἰς πόλιν ... καὶ εἰσελθὼν πρὸς αὐτήν (1,26); (2) while there is no transfiguration or a disguisement, there is a "representation": the angel stands for God; (3) in the announcement to Zechariah the visual dimension of the appearance is explicitly stressed (1,11-12 ὤφθη δὲ αὐτῷ ἄγγελος κυρίου ... Ζαχαρίας ἰδών); in the announcement to Mary our entire attention is drawn to the verbal aspect of the communication (1,28-29 εἶπεν ... ἡ δὲ ἐπὶ τῷ λόγῳ διεταράχθη καὶ διελογίζετο ποταπὸς εἴη ὁ ἀσπασμὸς οὗτος); (5) the divine visitor brings a positive message: God promises a child to a barren woman (1,7.13; cf. Gen 18,11) or to a virgin (1,27.34); the child will fulfil a role of salvation for the people; (4-5) the motif of hospitality is not at stake here[44], but there is an analogous problem of reception, not of the person, but of the message; the reception is twofold, on the one hand a reaction of unbelief (1,18.20), on the other a reaction of belief (1,34.38.45); Zechariah is punished for his unbelief (1,20); Mary is blessed for her belief (1,45); (6) the disappearence of the angel is mentioned in Lk 1,38 (καὶ ἀπῆλθεν ἀπ' αὐτῆς ὁ ἄγγελος); (7) in 1,19 the angel Gabriel reveals his identity to Zechariah, which is not the case in the annunciation to Mary; the reaction of the visionaries shows that they recognize the divine origin of the appearing angel (1,12 and 29). The words of the angel are the words of God: the reaction to his

---

42. Cf. R.E. BROWN, *The Birth of the Messiah. A Commentary on the Infancy Narratives in Matthew and Luke*, Garden City, NY, 1977; Rev. ed., 1993, pp. 270-271.292-298.

43. Cf. M. LANDAU, *Erdenwanderungen* (n. 33), p. 2: "So finden wir denn in vielen Mythen, Sagen und Legenden die 'Wanderung der Götter' unter den Menschen. Doch vertritt bei den zu monotheistischen Religionen bekennenden Völkern gewohnlich ein Engel oder Heiliger, Christus in menschlicher Gestalt, ein Apostel, manchmal sogar eine Fee, ein Dämon oder ein Abgeschiedener die Stelle Gottes"; see esp. P. HOFRICHTER, *Parallelen zum 24. Gesang der Ilias in den Engelerscheinungen des lukanischen Doppelwerkes*, in *Protokolle zur Bibel* 2 (1993) 60-76: Luke has probably read and imitated the Homeric Ilias: Lk 1–2 has a parallel in *Il.* 24,143-193 (Iris as ἄγγελος); Acts 12,7-10 is also parallel to *Il.* 24,77-100.

44. Divine visit stories do not necessarily have the topos of a hospitable reception, as is clear from Judges 6,11-24 (God's angel visits Gideon) and 13,2-23 (God's angel visits Manoah and his wife), texts which could have influenced Lk 1,26-38.

words is in fact a deed of disobedience or obedience to God himself. A second observation that corroborates our view is the fact that in Lk 1,26-38 there are two verbal agreements with Gen 18: first, the expression "to find favour with God" in Lk 1,30 (εὗρες γὰρ χάριν παρὰ τῷ θεῷ) reminds us of Gen 18,3 "If I have found favour in your eyes, my Lord" (εἰ ἄρα εὗρον χάριν ἐναντίον σου[45]), and second, Lk 1,37, "no word shall be impossible with God" (οὐκ ἀδυνατήσει παρὰ τοῦ θεοῦ πᾶν ῥῆμα) is almost certainly a quotation of Gen 18,14, "a word shall not be impossible with God" (μὴ ἀδυνατήσει παρὰ τοῦ θεοῦ ῥῆμα). It is to this divine word that Mary expresses faithful obedience, in contrast to Sarah who cannot believe that God's word to her is possible.

The pericope of the disciples of Emmaus (Lk 24,13-35) shows even more agreements with the scheme we expounded above, because the motifs of hospitality and of recognition are clearly part of the story. Let us look at the seven topoi.

(1) While there is no question of a descent in the text, the story starts with the motif of wandering: two disciples are walking on the road to Emmaus (24,13 πορευόμενοι; 24,17 περιπατοῦντες) and the risen Jesus comes near and goes along with them (24,15 ἐγγίσας συνεπορεύετο αὐτοῖς).

(2) While there is no description of a transfiguration or a disguisement, Luke tells us that Jesus joins the disciples on their way to Emmaus as a "stranger" (24,18 παροικεῖς).

(3) Obviously the risen Lord appears to them in human form and they can see him in a visible way, "but *their eyes* were prevented from recognizing him" (24,16 οἱ δὲ ὀφθαλμοὶ αὐτῶν ἐκρατοῦντο τοῦ μὴ ἐπιγνῶναι αὐτόν). So they do not perceive the heavenly identity of the stranger.

(4) After a dialogue during which the stranger tries to clarify the situation by reference to the Scriptures, the walkers approach the village and the disciples urge the stranger to accept their offer of hospitality (24,29 καὶ παρεβιάσαντο αὐτὸν λέγοντες, Μεῖνον μεθ᾽ ἡμῶν; cf. Lot in Gen 19,3 καὶ κατεβιάζετο αὐτούς). The guest stays with them (24,29 καὶ εἰσῆλθεν τοῦ μεῖναι σὺν αὐτοῖς) and is offered a meal (24,30 ἐν τῷ κατακλιθῆναι αὐτὸν μετ᾽ αὐτῶν).

(5) The guest brings salvation to the hosts: he behaves like a host and offers them the broken bread (symbol of his life given for others?) and brings them to faith in the risen Jesus and to the joy of understanding the Scriptures (24,32).

---

45. It must be admitted that, while the expression occurs several times in the Old Testament and does not prove a conscious allusion to Gen, in the light of the second reference it becomes at least possible.

(6) The sudden disappearence of the divine visitor is mentioned explicitly: he vanishes from their side (24,31b καὶ αὐτὸς ἄφαντος ἐγένετο ἀπ' αὐτῶν).

(7) The disappearance takes place at the moment of recognition from the side of the disciples: "Their eyes were opened and they recognized him" (24,31a αὐτῶν δὲ διηνοίχθησαν οἱ ὀφθαλμοὶ καὶ ἐπέγνωσαν αὐτόν). The recognition is linked to and provoked by the breaking of the bread (24,35 ἐγνώσθη αὐτοῖς ἐν τῇ κλάσει τοῦ ἄρτου).

b. Next to these agreements with respect to the narrative pattern of divine visitations, Luke has also made use of the *terminology* of ἐπισκέπτομαι, ἐπισκοπή connected with this theme. As is the case in the LXX, the N.T. and especially Luke also use the word-group to describe God's visitation in history either in a positive sense (salvation) or in a negative sense (punishment)[46]. For Luke, however, God's visitation takes place through the mission of his prophet Jesus.

In the canticle of Zechariah, the reality of God's redemptive and gracious visitation is mentioned two times, once with respect to the past, and once with respect to the future. In Lk 1,68 the Lord, the God of Israel is praised because in the past "he has visited and accomplished redemption for his people" (ὅτι ἐπεσκέψατο καὶ ἐποίησεν λύτρωσιν τῷ λαῷ αὐτοῦ). The content thereof is developed in 1,69-75. In Lk 1,76-78 Zechariah looks to the future and to the preparatory role John will fulfill with respect to Jesus. The hymn does not yet mention the names of the two protagonists. John is indicated as "my child" and as "the prophet of the Most High", who will prepare the way of "the Lord". The title "the Lord" is transfered here from God to his Messiah. The coming messiah is further described in an allusive, metaphorical way: he is called the "Sunrise from on high". His future mission is summarised in the notion of "visit" (1,78b ἐπισκέψεται ἡμᾶς ἀνατολὴ ἐξ ὕψους). The qualification "from on high" has a spacial connotation and

---

46. For the N.T., see W. BAUER – K. ALAND, *Griechisch-deutsches Wörterbuch zu den Schriften des Neuen Testaments und der übrigen urchristlichen Literatur*, Berlin – New York, 1988, pp. 603-606; LOUW & NIDA, *Lexicon*, 2 (n. 9), p. 101: ἐπισκέπτομαι means (a) select carefully, (b) visit, (c) take care of, and (d) be present; ἐπισκοπή means (a) visitation, (b) office of Church leader, and (c) position of responsibility; J. ROHDE, *EDNT* 2, 1991, pp. 33-35, distinguishes three different meanings of the verb ἐπισκέπτομαι: (a) to visit, with the related meaning care for: Mt 25,36.43; Acts 7,23; 15,36; Heb 2,6 (= Ps 8,5); Jas 1,27; (b) seek out/look out (for): Acts 6,3; 15,14; (c) with God as subject, graciously visit: Lk 1,68.78; 7,16. The noun ἐπισκοπή means either (a) gracious visitation: Lk 19,44; 1 Pet 2,12 or (b) office: Acts 1,20; 1 Tim 3,1. For the theological notion of "Heimsuchung" (divine visitation) in Luke, see W.C. ROBINSON, *Der Weg des Herrn. Studien zur Geschichte und Eschatologie im Lukas-Evangelium* (Theologische Forschung, 36), Hamburg-Bergstedt, 1964, pp. 50-59.

reminds us of the "descent" (κατάβασις) of the visitation stories[47]. This means that God's gracious visit will from now on be realised through the mission of Jesus. Through this mission God reveals once again his tender mercy which has been present from of old (1,78a διὰ σπλάγχνα ἐλέους θεοῦ ἡμῶν, ἐν οἷς; cf. 1,72).

The reaction of the citizens of Nain after Jesus raised a widow's son from the dead is another suggestive text (Lk 7,11-17). The reaction of the people (7,16) shows that they experience God's presence in Jesus's action: "Fear seized them all" (ἔλαβεν δὲ φόβος πάντας). Moreover, their reaction is addressed directly to God, not to Jesus: "they glorified God" (ἐδόξαζον τὸν θεόν). Further, they glorify God in saying who Jesus is and what God is doing in him. The people give an interpretation of Jesus' action which encompasses in a sense his whole mission and which has a christological and theological aspect. Through his deed, Jesus is recognised as a "great prophet" (of God) who "has arisen among us" (προφήτης μέγας ἠγέρθη ἐν ἡμῖν). At the same time, his prophetic mission is perceived as a concrete realisation of God's visit to his people (ἐπεσκέψατο ὁ θεὸς τὸν λαὸν αὐτοῦ). He is indeed the "coming one" (ὁ ἐρχόμενος) (7,19). Thus the verbal act of glorification shows a kind of telescoping of Jesus' prophetic activities and God's gracious visitation of his people.

Finally, the dramatic episode of Jesus nearing the city of Jerusalem and weeping over it (Lk 19,41-44), throws retrospective light on Jesus' journey towards Jerusalem (Lk 9,51-19,27 or 44), the refusal by the citizens (19,14) and the religious leaders (19,39) to receive God's prophet and Davidic king (Lk 19,14), in contrast to Jesus' disciples who recognize him as the king who comes in the name of the Lord (19,37-38 ὁ ἐρχόμενος ὁ βασιλεὺς ἐν ὀνόματι κυρίου). Luke interprets the journey as God's visit to the city Jerusalem through his prophet Jesus, which ends in a tragic failure because the city refuses to receive God's mes-

---

47. The qualification ἐξ ὕψους in Lk 1,78 reminds us of similar spacial images with which the conception through the virgin Mary is evoked: πνεῦμα ἅγιον ἐπελεύσεται ἐπὶ σέ, καὶ δύναμις ὑψίστου ἐπισκιάσει σοι (Lk 1,35). One wonders whether Luke has consciously made a link between this "descent" (Lk 1,78) and the "ascension" at the end of Jesus' mission (Lk 9,51 ἀνάλημψις; 24,51 ἀνεφέρετο; Acts 1,2.11.22 ἀναλαμβάνεσθαι), which is specific to Luke in the NT. That Luke knew the motif of the divine κατάβασις in bodily or human form (cf. Il. 1,43.194-95; 4,73-88; 6,128-129; 7,17-22; 8,41-50; 11,181-184) is clear from texts such as Lk 3,22 (καὶ καταβῆναι τὸ πνεῦμα τὸ ἅγιον σωματικῷ εἴδει) and Acts 14,11 (οἱ θεοὶ ὁμοιωθέντες ἀνθρώποις κατέβησαν πρὸς ἡμᾶς). Luke's subtle application of the descensus/ascensus imagery to Jesus may have implications for his christology: does he, by doing this, somehow suggest Jesus' divine origin? If this is the case, Luke's christology would form an intermediate stage between the christologies of Mark and John.

senger. From 9,51 on Jesus has decided to go up to Jerusalem to offer the city God's salvation and peace (19,42 εἰ ἔγνως ἐν τῇ ἡμέρᾳ ταύτῃ καὶ σὺ τὰ πρὸς εἰρήνην; cf. 2,11.14). The city, however, does not recognize the importance of the moment of God's "visit" in Jesus (19,44 οὐκ ἔγνως τὸν καιρὸν τῆς ἐπισκοπῆς σου). It does what it has always done: kill the prophets and stone God's messengers (Lk 13,34; 22–23). Instead of the salvation God was eager to offer, therefore, his punishment will come over the city: Jerusalem will be destroyed by the armies of the (Roman) enemy (Lk 19,43-44).

There is of course a question which may be asked concerning our interpretation and translation of the word-group ἐπισκέπτομαι, ἐπισκοπή. Is "to visit/visit" the only possible translation in the texts concerned? A survey shows that translators do not agree about the answer to be given: they hesitate between "visit" and "look favorably upon"[48]. The notion "visit" implies a spacial movement from the place where one normally lives to the place where the visited person finds himself. One can visit other people for different reasons, to inspect or to judge (visitation), to take care of (e.g. in the case of a visit to prisoners or to the sick). The notion "look favourably upon" can, but does not necessarily imply the notion of "visit" in this spacial sense. Etymologically, the word-group ἐπισκέπτομαι, ἐπισκοπή certainly indicates the meaning of "look upon" in a favourable or pejorative sense. In some cases, the context proves or suggests that the notion of "visit" (in the spatial sense) is also connoted: see, e.g., Exod 32,34; Num 16,5; Ps 16(17),3; 79(80),15; 1 En 25,3[49]; TLevi 4,4[50]; 16,5 [?]; TJos 1,6 [?];

48. Lk 1,68 εὐλογητὸς κύριος ὁ θεὸς τοῦ Ἰσραήλ, ὅτι ἐπεσκέψατο καὶ ἐποίησεν λύτρωσιν τῷ λαῷ αὐτοῦ: he has visited: KJV; NASB; NAB; RNT; RSV; he has come: AB; NIV; he has looked favourably on: NRSV; he has turned to his people: NEB. Lk 1,78 διὰ σπλάγχνα ἐλέους θεοῦ ἡμῶν, ἐν οἷς ἐπισκέψεται ἡμᾶς ἀνατολὴ ἐξ ὕψους: has visited: KJV; RNT; shall/will visit us: ASV; NASB; NAB; RV; shall/will dawn upon us *and* visit [us]: AB; RSV; will come to us: NIV; the dawn from on high *will break upon* us: NRSB; the morning sun from heaven *will rise upon* us: NEB. Lk 7,16 ἐπεσκέψατο ὁ θεὸς τὸν λαὸν αὐτοῦ: God has visited his people: AB; ASV; KJV; NASB; NAB; RNT; RSV; RV; God has come to help his people: NIV; God has looked favourably on his people: NRSV; God has shown care for his people: NEB. Lk 19,44 ἀνθ᾽ ὧν οὐκ ἔγνως τὸν καιρὸν τῆς ἐπισκοπῆς σου: the time of thy/your visitation (from God): AB; ASV; KJV; NAB; NASB; NRSV; RNT; RSV; the time of God's coming to you: NIV; God's moment when it came: NEB. See also note 46.

49. 1 En 25,3: "He answered saying: 'This tall mountain which you saw whose summit resembles the throne of God is (indeed) his throne, on which the Holy and Great Lord of Glory, the Eternal King, will sit when he descends to visit the earth with goodness (ὅταν καταβῇ ἐπισκέψεσθαι τὴν γῆν ἐπ᾽ ἀγαθῷ)" (Transl. E. Isaac in *The Old Testament Pseudepigrapha*, ed. J.H. Charlesworth, London, 1985, I, 26).

50. TLevi 4,4: "Blessing shall be given to you and to all your posterity until through his son's compassion the Lord shall visit all the nations forever (ἕως ἐπισκέψηται

TAsh 7,3[51]; PssSol 15,12[52]: with God as subject; TBenj 9,2[53]; TJob 28,2[54]; Mt 25,36.43: with a human being as subject. The question then is to establish whether the word-group also bears both meanings of "visit" and "look favorably upon" in Luke. It seems to us that this is the case. Two arguments may support this understanding. First, in 7,16 and 19,44, the immediate context qualifies Jesus as the ἐρχόμενος (7,19.20 and 19,38). Second, the expression καιρὸς ἐπισκοπῆς (Lk 19,44) has eschatological connotations. It refers to the day of judgement when God comes down to judge the earth. These are just some aspects of the problem which call for more thorough investigation.

CONCLUSION

Let us formulate the main conclusions emerging from the analysis given in this paper. First, as a Hellenistic author writing for Hellenistic readers, Luke has, in his description of Jesus' mission, made use of the pattern of "divine visits on earth" which was widespread in Graeco-Roman literature and present in the Septuagint[55]. Through the prophet-

κύριος πάντα τὰ ἔθνη ἐν σπλάγχνοις υἱοῦ ἕως αἰῶνος), [although your sons will lay hands on him in order to impale him]" (Transl. H.C. Kee in OTP I, 789).

51. TAsh 7,1-3: "Do not become like Sodom, which did not recognize the Lord's angels and perished forever. For I know that you will sin and be delivered into the hands of your enemies; your land shall be made desolate and your sanctuary wholly polluted. You will be scattered to four corners of the earth; in the despersion you shall be regarded as worthless, like useless water, until such time as the Most High visits the earth (ἕως οὗ ὕψιστος ἐπισκέψηται τὴν γῆν). [He shall come as a man eating and drinking with human beings,] crushing the dragon's head in the water. He will save Israel and all the nations, [God speaking like a man]" (Transl. H.C. Kee in OTP I, 789).

52. PssSol 15,12: "And sinners shall perish forever in the day of the Lord's judgment (ἐν ἡμέρᾳ κρίσεως κυρίου), when God oversees the earth at his judgment (ὅταν ἐπισκέπτηται ὁ θεὸς τὴν γῆν ἐν κρίματι αὐτοῦ) [13] But those who fear the Lord shall find mercy in it and shall live by their God's mercy; but sinners shall perish for all time" (Transl. R.B. Wright in OTP II, 147); ἐπισκέπτηται could also be translated by "visits" in stead of "oversees". See also PssSol 10,4; and 11,1.6 ("supervision").

53. TBenj 9,2: "But in your allotted place will be the temple of God, and the latter temple will exceed the former in glory. The twelve tribes shall be gathered there and all the nations, until such time as the Most High shall send forth his salvation through the ministration of the unique prophet (ἕως οὗ ὁ ὕψιστος ἀποστείλῃ τὸ σωτήριον αὐτοῦ ἐν ἐπισκοπῇ μονογενοῦς προφήτου" (Transl. H.C. Kee in OTP I, 827). Here also, ἐπισκοπῇ may be better translated by "visitation".

54. TJob 28,1-2: "After I had spent twenty years under the plague, the kings also heard about what happened to me. They arose and came to me, each from his own country, so that they might encourage me by a visit (ἀναστάντες ἦλθον πρός με ἕκαστος ἐκ τῆς ἰδίας χώρας ὅπως ἐπισκεψάμενοι παραμυθήσονται με)" (Transl. R.P. Spittler in OTP I, 852).

55. The influence of the LXX (esp. Gen 18 and 19) on Luke-Acts with respect to the theme of divine visits on earth can be established on the basis of clear literary evidence.

guest Jesus, more than through any other messenger, the one "God, who made the world and everything in it, being Lord of heaven and earth" (Acts 17,24), has visited humankind and made himself known to all human beings[56]. Moreover, in the light of the larger context of Luke's vision on the history of salvation and on the meaning of Jesus' mission, it seems justified to propose the following hypothesis: Luke has developed the traditional motif of Jesus' going up to Jerusalem (Mk 10,32; 11,1) into an extended "journey to Jerusalem", which covers one third of his Gospel (Lk 9,51–19,44). One of the reasons for this thorough rewriting of the tradition might lie in the fact that the author also understood Jesus' journey to Jerusalem against the background of the Hellenistic pattern of divine visits and human (in)hospitality which he also read in the LXX. The Lukan Travel Narrative can thus be understood as a narrative dramatisation of a traditional motif with the help of a Hellenistic-Septuagintal pattern.

Tiensestraat 112   Adelbert DENAUX
B-3000 Leuven

Luke's knowledge of Graeco-Roman variants of the theme is evident from Acts 14,8-18 and 28,1-6, although it is difficult to be more precise which concrete examples Luke had in mind. It is not a question of either/or: both streams of tradition have played a role in Luke's philosophical outlook and editorial work. The question as to primary which tradition has exerted the influence should be placed whithin a larger context: all themes and motifs borrowed from the secular Graeco-Roman culture were remoulded whithin the context of the monotheistic and christological convictions of the Jewish-Christian tradition in which the author of Luke-Acts stands.

56. The christological implications of the use of this theme could be further explored. For Luke, standing in a monotheistic tradition, the pattern seems no longer applicable to human beings, even when they are apostles like Paul and Barnabas (cf. Acts 14,8-18). In this, he takes his distance from an easy confusion between gods and human beings in the Graeco-Roman culture. On the contrary, when applying the pattern in an exclusive or excellent way to the life of Jesus, Luke might once again be suggesting his divinity in a subtle way (cf. n. 47). Jesus is more than just a human representative of the one God: in Jesus' mission on earth, God himself is really visiting his people.

LA FRACTION DU PAIN EN LUC-ACTES

Le geste de la fraction du pain est nommé en Luc-Actes mais il est clairement attesté dans presque tout le NT et ailleurs. Dans cette conférence je veux montrer qu'il s'agit d'un rite pratiqué par Jésus et ses disciples. Ce rite structure un certain nombre de passages, et d'autres encore le supposent. Rite symbolique mais polyvalent, il se prêtait à plusieurs significations que nous pourrons repérer dans les textes que nous allons étudier.

1. Commençons par relever les termes apparentés: 'rompre' / 'fraction' / 'fragment' – (κατα)κλάω / κλάσις / κλάσμα. Voici leurs occurrences dans le NT:

a. La (les) multiplication(s) des pains et des poissons: (κατα)κλάω Mt 14,19; 15,36; Mc 6,41 (κατακλάω); 8,6.19; Lc 9,16 (κατακλάω). Le verbe lui-même ne se lit jamais chez Jean. κλάσμα (toujours au pluriel) Mt 14,20; 15,37; Mc 6,43; 8,8; 8,19-20 (deux fois); Lc 9,17; Jn 6,12-13 (deux fois).

b. Le dernier repas: κλάω Mt 26,26; Mc 14,22; Lc 22,19; 1 Co 11,24 (deux fois dans certains mss).

c. Le souper à Emmaüs: κλάω Lc 24,30; κλάσις Lc 24,35.

d. La pratique de l'Église: κλάω: Ac 2,46 (en général); Ac 20,7.11 (la nuit à Troas); Ac 27,35 (Paul en mer); 1 Co 10,16 (en général); κλάσις: Ac 2,42 (en général).

À ces occurrences tirées du NT, ajoutons-en deux autres qui se lisent dans la littérature chrétienne ancienne:

Didachè 9,3 (περὶ δὲ τῆς εὐχαριστίας...) Περὶ δὲ τοῦ κλάσματος; 9,4 Ὥσπερ ἦν τοῦτο τὸ κλάσμα; 14,1 κατὰ κυριακὴν δὲ κυρίου συναχϑέντες κλάσατε ἄρτον καὶ εὐχαριστήσατε...
Ignace, *Ad Eph.* 20,2 συνέρχεσϑε ἐν μιᾷ πίστει καὶ ἐν Ἰησοῦ Χριστῷ ἕνα ἄρτον κλῶντες.

2. Nous constatons d'abord que, dans le NT, ces expressions ne sont utilisées qu'en référence à la fraction du pain; mais il est clair qu'en grec classique, selon les dictionnaires usuels, l'utilisation de ces mots n'est pas aussi restreinte.

Nous remarquons également une certaine insistance sur 'la fraction du pain', au point que ce geste donne son nom à toute la cérémonie: Ac 2,42, et cf. 2,46; peut-être Lc 24,35. Étant donné ce fait, on peut penser qu'il y a plus qu'une simple référence à l'acte qu'il faut faire pour partager un morceau de pain entre plusieurs personnes, mais qu'une importance particulière était attachée au geste lui-même[1]. L'expression précise 'la fraction du pain' (ἡ κλάσις τοῦ ἄρτου) est propre à Luc, mais le geste auquel elle fait allusion est clairement attesté dans presque tout le NT – Synoptiques, Jean, Actes, Paul – et dans la *Didachè* et chez Ignace d'Antioche. En conséquence, pour expliquer le sens de ses expressions en Luc-Actes et pour souligner la signification particulière qu'elles y revêtent, nous allons avoir à étudier un bon nombre d'autres passages.

Quel est le point de référence commun à tous les textes du NT qui parlent de 'rompre' (le pain)? Bien entendu, on répond souvent que c'est la dernière Cène au cours de laquelle Jésus rompit du pain … et dit à ses disciples: «Faites ceci en mémoire de moi». On pourrait en effet penser que ce geste hautement significatif reviendrait naturellement dans d'autres passages du NT: il aurait été anticipé dans les récits de multiplication des pains et évoqué ultérieurement dans des scènes où, nous pouvons le supposer, les disciples de Jésus exécutaient son commandement.

Cette explication, toutefois, n'est pas entièrement satisfaisante. Dans les récits de la dernière Cène, l'ordre donné par Jésus de répéter son geste ne se lit ni chez Matthieu, ni chez Marc, ni dans le texte court de Luc (texte occidental)[2]. L'origine des gestes et des paroles eucharistiques de Jésus à la dernière Cène est encore sujet à discussion[3]. De toute façon, il est difficile de voir comment un rite qui avait pour origine la répétition de ces gestes et de ces paroles ait pu prendre le nom de 'fraction du pain'. Pourquoi spécialement 'la fraction du pain', qui semble donner une importance injustifiée à un seul des éléments, tandis que l'autre, la coupe, tient une importance égale dans les récits du NT (sauf, bien entendu, dans la recension courte de Luc)?

---

1. Les exégètes ont discuté pour savoir si le geste de Jésus rompant le pain à la dernière Cène avait intentionnellement une valeur symbolique, ou s'il n'était là que pour préparer la distribution du pain; voir le bref relevé des opinions fait par A.R. WINNETT, *The Breaking of the Bread: Does It Symbolize the Passion?*, in *ExpT* 88 (1976-77) 181-182.
2. Ce texte omet tout ce qui suit «Ceci est mon corps» au verset 19 et l'ensemble du verset 20, soit l'action et les paroles de Jésus sur la coupe, après le pain. Pour l'adoption de ce texte court, voir les arguments donnés par É. NODET et J. TAYLOR, *Essai sur les origines du christianisme*, Paris, Cerf, 1998, p. 17s., malgré l'opinion contraire de M.-É. BOISMARD, *En quête du proto-Luc* (ÉB, n.s. 37), Paris, Gabalda, 1997, pp. 76-78.
3. Voir NODET-TAYLOR, *Essai*, pp. 86-115.

En fait, dans le NT, les autres occurrences de l'expression 'rompre le pain' sont indépendantes de toute référence à la dernière Cène. Ainsi, les récits de multiplication des pains et des poissons peuvent se comprendre dans la seule perspective de Jésus nourrissant ceux qui le suivent, matériellement comme spirituellement. Notons d'ailleurs comment certains de ces récits sont liés au thème de Jésus qui enseigne: Mc 6,34; Lc 9,11 (les contextes des autres montrent plutôt Jésus comme un guérisseur). Même les passages postérieurs à la dernière Cène n'exigent pas, pour être compris, une référence implicite à cette Cène. Prenons d'abord le souper à Emmaüs; il est pertinent de se demander pourquoi les disciples auraient reconnu Jésus ressuscité 'à la fraction du pain', comme nous le lisons en Lc 24,35. Il n'existe aucune raison de supposer qu'ils furent présents à la dernière Cène. Il n'est pas pertinent non plus de dire que Jésus aurait eu une façon à lui de rompre le pain durant les repas, geste grâce auquel on aurait pu le reconnaître; même dans ce cas, d'ailleurs, la réponse ferait appel à des repas autres que la dernière Cène.

Un cas spécialement instructif est celui de la fraction du pain durant la nuit, à Troas, en Ac 20,7-12. Notons d'abord que, dans le récit, ce geste est étroitement lié à la 'mort' et à la 'résurrection' d'Eutychus (que l'on admette ou non que le jeune homme ait été réellement mort). La structure du récit suppose un moment négatif suivi d'un moment positif. Nous notons aussi l'imagerie de la nuit et de l'aurore, liée respectivement au moment négatif et au moment positif. Ajoutons une remarque: d'après le verset 7, il est clair que les gens qui participent au repas ont l'habitude de s'assembler pour rompre le pain durant la nuit du premier jour de la semaine. Il ne faudrait pas supposer trop vite qu'ils avaient adopté récemment cette coutume en référence à la dernière Cène ou à la résurrection de Jésus: on n'en a aucune mention ou aucune référence dans le récit. Bien mieux, le nom de Jésus n'y apparaît nulle part, et Eutychus est le seul qui meure et se relève[4].

Il faut donc, semble-t-il, envisager sérieusement la possibilité que l'on se trouve en présence d'un rite qui n'aurait pas son origine dans la dernière Cène. Après tout, dans les mots 'Faites ceci en mémoire de moi' (qui d'ailleurs ne se lisent pas dans tous les récits, comme nous l'avons vu), l'insistance n'est pas dans 'faites ceci' mais dans 'en mémoire de moi'. Le 'ceci' qu'ils doivent 'faire' à partir de maintenant 'en mémoire de' Jésus peut fort bien être quelque chose qu'ils ont déjà l'habitude d'accomplir[5].

4. Voir la discussion de cet événement dans J. TAYLOR, *Les Actes des deux apôtres*, 6 (ÉB, n.s. 30), Paris, Gabalda, 1996, pp. 83-92; NODET-TAYLOR, *Essai*, pp. 44-50.
5. Par «rite», nous entendons un geste qui est habituel, et reconnu, et capable d'évo-

3. À ce point de notre exposé, commençons une analyse détaillée de *Did.* 9–10. Voici ses parties principales: 9,1-3 «action de grâces» (εὐχαριστία) sur la coupe, puis sur le «fragment» (κλάσμα)[6]; 9,4 prière pour le rassemblement de l'église; 9,5 rubrique interdisant l'accès aux non-baptisés; 10,1-4 «actions de grâces» après avoir mangé tout son content; 10,5 prière pour le rassemblement de l'église, analogue à celle de 9,4.

Nous pouvons noter tout d'abord une ressemblance générale avec les rites et les prières de la table juive en usage aujourd'hui: (a) l'ordre des «actions de grâces» en *Did.* 9,1-3 est le même que celui de la «bénédiction» en usage la veille du sabbat et des fêtes, à savoir: le *qiddush* (propre à chaque occasion) sur la coupe et sur le jour (cf. *MBerak,* 8,1); la *birkat ha-motsi* (commune à tout repas comportant du pain) sur le pain *rompu*; (b) les actions de grâces après avoir mangé, en 10,1-4, correspondent à la rabbinique *birkat ha-mazon* récitée après le repas.

Arrêtons-nous un instant pour noter que nous avons le même ordre – coupe, pain – dans ce rite rabbinique, dans la *Didachè*, en Lc et en 1 Co 10,16[7]. Le rite rabbinique lui-même semble composite puisque c'est seulement la veille du sabbat et des fêtes que la bénédiction sur le pain, par laquelle commencent les repas ordinaires, est précédée par la bénédiction sur la coupe[8]. Nous trouvons des variantes instructives dans les récits de l'institution: selon Mt et Mc, l'action de grâces sur la coupe suit immédiatement après la bénédiction sur le pain, laquelle se fait pendant que les disciples mangent, tandis qu'en 1 Co 11, Jésus rend grâces pour le pain au début du repas et pour la coupe après qu'ils ont mangé; chez Lc y a-t-il une seule coupe avant le pain (texte court), ou deux, avec des significations différentes, l'une avant le pain et l'autre à la fin du repas (texte long)[9]? En 1 Co, le fait que, à quelques pages d'inter-

quer une signification; comme tel, c'est un élément constitutif de la communauté qui le pratique. Nous supposerons que les rites tendent à être stables, même si leur signification change.

6. Les textes parallèles (voir plus loin) ont «pain», et nombre de commentateurs supposent que l'expression κλάσμα ici est secondaire; ainsi A. Vööbus, *Liturgical Traditions in the Didache,* Stockholm, Etse, 1968, pp. 87-89, à la suite notamment d'E. Peterson. L. Cerfaux, *La multiplication des pains dans la liturgie de la Didachè (Did. IX,4),* in *Bib* 40 (1959) 943-958, propose de prendre κλάσμα non pas dans le sens de «morceau» mais de «(pain) rompu», c'est-à-dire comme le résultat de l'action de κλάσις (p. 953, n. 3).

7. À Qumrân, en revanche, selon 1 QS 6.4-6 et surtout 1 QSa 2.17-22, le prêtre qui préside fait la double bénédiction sur les prémisses du pain et du *tirôsh* (en cet ordre) au commencement du repas.

8. Voir Nodet-Taylor, *Essai,* pp. 86-87.

9. Au lieu de vouloir harmoniser toutes ces variantes en supposant un seul substrat, il vaut mieux y reconnaître les traces de différentes traditions narratives et coutumes liturgiques.

valle, la coupe soit mentionnée, d'abord avant, puis après le pain, fait penser aussi que sa place n'était pas fixée, et donc que les rites concernant la coupe et le pain n'ont pas forcément été toujours liés. Nous en avons un autre témoignage en Mc 14,23, où nous lisons: «Et ayant pris une coupe, il rendit grâces et (la) leur donna et ils en burent tous». C'est seulement au verset suivant, donc après qu'ils eurent bu, que Jésus prononce les «paroles de l'institution»; cette incohérence fait penser que les mots sur la coupe furent ajoutés au récit qui, primitivement, ne les contenait pas[10]. En d'autres termes, tandis que l'on a toujours le pain (à vrai dire la fraction du pain), la coupe de vin peut manquer.

On dit d'ordinaire que *Did.* 9,1-3 n'est qu'une spiritualisation, ou une christianisation, des prières que les Juifs récitaient d'ordinaire à table, prières que l'on suppose avoir été déjà d'usage courant à cette époque[11]. Cette explication, toutefois, n'est pas très satisfaisante. Il est vrai que *Did.* 9,1-3 a été christianisé par la double insertion des mots «que tu nous fis connaître par ton serviteur Jésus» (ἧς ἐγνώρισας ἡμῖν διὰ Ἰησοῦ τοῦ παιδός σου)[12]. Mais, même sans cette phrase, la bénédiction sur la coupe rend grâces à Dieu pour la «sainte vigne de David», une expression qui est encore symbolique et hautement spiritualisée, bien que purement juive; et elle ne correspond pas à la bénédiction rabbinique concernant Dieu «qui a créé le fruit de la vigne». Dans la bénédiction sur le «fragment», si nous écartons l'expression «de la connaissance»[13] qui n'est pas attestée dans le parallèle des *Constitutions Apostoliques* 7,25,2[14], il ne reste plus qu'une action de grâces pour la «vie». Même si nous prenons ce mot en son sens premier, de la vie humaine (sans tenir compte de sa connotation spirituelle), ce n'est toujours pas le texte de la rabbinique *birkat ha-motsi* qui bénit Dieu «qui a fait venir le pain de la terre». Finalement, on ne peut pas supposer que le fait de bénir le Créateur pour ses dons constituerait l'«eucharistie» juive primitive dont toutes les autres dériveraient, y compris les gestes et les paroles de Jésus lors de la dernière Cène: les actuels *qiddush* et *birkat ha-motsi* pourraient bien être le résultat d'un développement de

---

10. Comparer M.-É. BOISMARD, *L'évangile de Marc, sa préhistoire* (ÉB, n.s. 26), Paris, Gabalda, 1994, p. 199s., qui cite dans le même sens d'autres auteurs.

11. Ainsi l'édition standard de W. RORDORF et A. TUILIER dans les *Sources Chrétiennes*, 248, Paris, Cerf, 1978, pp. 176, n. 4 et 177, n. 7, citant *BBerak.* 35a.

12. Notons en passant que David et Jésus sont tous les deux dits παῖς θεοῦ, comme en Ac 4,25.27.

13. Cette variante montre l'influence d'une interprétation sapientielle du rite telle que nous la verrons aussi en Luc et en Jean (plus loin).

14. Sans parler du remplacement par «résurrection» dans le parallèle du traité *De Virginitate*, 13 (voir la note 17 plus loin).

formes primitives, introduisant une insistance sur les moyens prévus par le Créateur en vue de la subsistance de l'espèce humaine, peut-être pour éviter d'autres interprétations (par exemple messianiques) du rite.

La *Didachè* présente un problème embarrassant bien connu: elle ne contient aucune référence à la dernière Cène (ni à la mort et à la résurrection de Jésus). Diverses hypothèses ont été proposées pour expliquer cette apparente lacune; elles supposent que le récit de l'institution devait toujours avoir fait partie de l'«eucharistie»[15]. Nous n'avons pas à discuter ce problème, nous contentant de faire remarquer qu'il n'y a aucune nécessité de supposer que le rite prescrit en *Did.* 9–10 ne serait pas complet.

Voici les conclusions préliminaires que nous pouvons établir à ce point de notre exposé. Tous les textes que nous avons étudiés semblent supposer un rite familier de «fraction du pain» qui peut avoir plus d'une signification. En quoi consiste le rite en question? On pourrait imaginer le simple fait de séparer des morceaux de la miche, en les rompant, comme dans les rites rabbiniques du repas à table et dans l'«Artoklisia» de l'église grecque. Toutefois, il y a des indices permettant de penser qu'au moins certains de ces textes supposent un rite plus spécifique.

4. Regardons de plus près la *Didachè*, en particulier la 'prière pour le rassemblement' en 9,4: «Comme ce fragment (κλάσμα) fut dispersé sur les montagnes et, ayant été rassemblé, est devenu un, de même rassemble ton église des coins de la terre dans ton royaume». Par son intention générale et en partie par son vocabulaire, cette prière, comme la prière analogue de 10,5, ressemble à la dixième des Dix-huit Bénédictions juives: «Fais que le grand *shofar* sonne pour notre liberté, et hisse la bannière pour réunir nos dispersés. Rassemble-nous des coins de la terre dans notre terre». Toutefois, la prière de *Did.* 9,4 contient un détail important qui a suscité bien des commentaires: Ὥσπερ ἦν τοῦτο τὸ κλάσμα διεσκορπισμένον ἐπάνω τῶν ὀρέων καὶ συναχθὲν ἐγένετο ἕν: «Et comme ce fragment fut dispersé sur les montagnes et, ayant été rassemblé, est devenu un». On interprète habituellement l'image exprimée ici comme se référant aux grains qui ont été dispersés lors des semailles, puis rassemblés lors de la moisson pour devenir un pain unique. C'est l'image que donne explicitement Cyprien, *Ep.* 63,13: «… comme beaucoup de grains rassemblés en un, et moulus ensemble, et mêlés ensemble font un» (*quemadmodum grana multa in unum collecta*

15. Voir la revue de la discussion dans VÖÖBUS, *Liturgical Traditions*, pp. 63-65, et très récemment W. RORDORF, *Die Mahlgebete in Didache Kap. 9–10. Ein neuer* Status Quaestionis, in *Vigiliae Christianae* 51 (1997) 229-246.

et commolita et commista unum faciunt)[16]. Toutefois, le texte de la *Didachè* n'a pas «grains», mais «fragment» (et les textes parallèles ont «pain»). Et pourquoi «sur les montagnes»? Ce détail n'a jamais été suffisamment expliqué, même si l'on en a conclu que la *Didachè* avait été composée en Syrie-Palestine et non en Égypte.

On peut proposer une ligne de pensée tout à fait différente en regardant de plus près l'image de «dispersé sur les montagnes», suivie par «rassembler des coins de la terre dans ton royaume». En fait, elles rappellent plutôt clairement Ez 34 LXX, spécialement les versets suivants:

5 mes brebis ont été dispersées parce qu'il n'y avait pas de pasteurs
(διεσπάρη τὰ πρόβατά μου διὰ τὸ μὴ εἶναι ποιμένας)
6 mes brebis ont été dispersées sur toute montagne
(διεσπάρη μου τὰ πρόβατα ἐν παντὶ ὄρει)
12 ainsi, je rechercherai mes brebis
(οὕτως ἐκζητήσω τὰ πρόβατά μου)
13 et je les ferai sortir de toutes les nations et je les rassemblerai des pays
(étrangers) et je les ferai entrer dans leur propre pays
(καὶ ἐξάξω αὐτοὺς ἐκ τῶν ἐθνῶν καὶ συνάξω αὐτοὺς ἀπὸ τῶν χωρῶν, καὶ εἰσάξω αὐτοὺς εἰς τὴν γῆν αὐτῶν)
14 je les ferai paître dans un bon pâturage, dans la montagne élevée d'Israël
(ἐν νομῇ ἀγαθῇ βοσκήσω αὐτούς, ἐν τῷ ὄρει τῷ ὑψηλῷ Ἰσραήλ)
23 et je ferai lever sur eux un seul pasteur et il les paîtra, mon serviteur David
(καὶ ἀναστήσω ἐπ᾽ αὐτοὺς ποιμένα ἕνα καὶ ποιμαίνει αὐτούς, τὸν δοῦλόν μου Δαυίδ).

Nous pouvons remarquer ici les contacts étroits de thème et de vocabulaire avec la *Didachè*, en particulier entre les vv. 6, 12, 13 et la «prière de rassemblement» de *Did.* 9,4; de même, au v. 23, la référence à «mon serviteur David» a son écho en *Did.* 9,2: Δαυὶδ τοῦ παιδός σου.

On trouve ailleurs des parallèles au texte de *Did.* 9,4, dont deux ont déjà été mentionnés. Celui qui se lit dans les *Constitutions Apostoliques* (7,24,3) omet la clause ἐπάνω τῶν ὀρέων; et celui du *De Virginitate* 13[17] a ἐπάνω τῆς τραπέζης. Ce dernier ouvrage, qui est attribué à St. Athanase, offre, quant à son contenu, une ressemblance générale avec la *Didachè* et d'autres documents canonico-liturgiques – bien qu'adapté

16. Ainsi, par exemple, Vööbus, *Liturgical Traditions*, pp. 141-144. Cette interprétation a été contestée, et notamment par Cerfaux, *La multiplication des pains*, qui voit dans la prière de la *Didachè* une allusion à l'action d'enlever ou de rassembler les fragments qui restaient après que la foule s'est rassasiée des pains multipliés par Jésus.

17. Édité par E. von der Goltz, in *Texte und Untersuchungen*, 14/2, Leipzig, Hinrichs, 1905. Nous lisons ce texte avec les corrections proposées par K. Lake et R.P. Casey, *The Text of the* De Virginitate *of Athanasius*, in *HTR* 19 (1926) 173-180, lesquelles d'ailleurs ne sont pas importantes pour notre argument.

pour former une règle de vie pour les vierges – sans toutefois qu'il y ait une dépendance littéraire avec elle, comme c'est le cas du livre 7 des *Constitutions Apostoliques*. La prière qui nous concerne a cette forme: «Et tout comme ce pain fut (ὑπῆρχεν) dispersé *sur la table*, et, ayant été rassemblé, est devenu un, etc.». Cette formulation implique claire-ment que le pain est d'abord rompu ou coupé, puis que les fragments sont ré-assemblés pour re-former l'unité primitive du pain. Un tel geste est un symbole efficace du fait de rassembler l'Église des quatre coins de la terre dans le royaume de Dieu. La variante que contient le *De Vir-ginitate* explicite l'analogie impliquée dans le premier élément de la «prière de rassemblement» de la *Didachè*: «Tout comme ce fragment fut dispersé *sur la table, ainsi le peuple de Dieu fut dispersé* sur les montagnes».

La formulation de *Did.* 9,4 apparaît ainsi être elliptique. Sous sa forme complète, on aurait eu: «Tout comme ce fragment fut dispersé sur la table, ainsi ton peuple fut dispersé sur les montagnes; et tout comme ce fragment, ayant été rassemblé, est devenu un, ainsi rassemble ton Église des coins de la terre dans ton royaume». Rappelons l'insistance de Paul sur l'unité: un seul pain (εἷς ἄρτος), un seul corps (ἓν σῶμα). Si cette interprétation de la prière de la *Didachè* est correcte, cela sup-poserait qu'ici aussi le geste de rompre le pain était suivi par un autre selon lequel les fragments rompus étaient ré-assemblés pour former à nouveau le pain unique, afin de symboliser le rassemblement de l'Église.

Un tel geste, à savoir rassembler les morceaux de pain rompus pour reformer un pain unique, peut trouver son écho dans l'insistance que les récits de la multiplication des pain mettent sur le fait de «enlever (αἴρω) les fragments (κλάσματα)», spécialement en Jn 6,12-13 qui utilise le verbe «rassembler» (συναγάγετε τὰ περισσεύσαντα κλάσματα). Il semble que ceci implique plus que le simple souci de nettoyer l'endroit où la foule vient d'être nourrie, ou même de démontrer l'abondance miraculeuse de la nourriture. Il est vrai que ce second élément était déjà contenu en 2 R 4,42-44, cet épisode selon lequel Élie nourrit ses dis-ciples et dont s'inspirent les récits du NT; mais le détail de «enlever» ou de «rassembler» les fragments est nouveau dans le NT où il est spécia-lement souligné.

5. Le texte de *Did.* 9,4, et celui de Ez 34 dont il est l'écho, compor-tent un moment négatif (dispersion) suivi par un moment positif (ras-semblement). Nous avons déjà noté cette structure dans le bref récit de la nuit de Paul à Troas, en Ac 20. On la trouve encore, avec un vocabu-laire analogue, dans d'autres textes significatifs qui parlent de la disper-

sion et du rassemblement eschatologique du peuple de Dieu. Tout d'abord Za 13,7: «Je frapperai le pasteur et les brebis du troupeau seront dispersées» (πατάξω τὸν ποιμένα καὶ διασκορπισθήσονται τὰ πρόβατα τῆς ποίμνης). Ce texte est cité par Jésus avant sa passion en Mt 26,31 et Mc 14,27, qui le font suivre de ces mots: «mais après que je serai ressuscité, je vous précéderai en Galilée» (ἀλλὰ μετὰ τὸ ἐγερθῆναί με προάξω ὑμᾶς εἰς τὴν Γαλιλαίαν). Sous sa forme complète, cette parole de Jésus comporte un moment négatif (le pasteur est frappé, le troupeau est dispersé), suivi d'un moment positif (la résurrection de Jésus, sa promesse de «précéder» ses disciples). Ces paroles sont éclairées par le texte de Ez 34,23: «Et je susciterai sur eux un pasteur unique et il les paîtra, mon serviteur David» (καὶ ἀναστήσω ἐπ᾽ αὐτοὺς ποιμένα ἕνα καὶ ποιμαίνει αὐτούς, τὸν δοῦλόν μου Δαυείδ). Ici, le verbe ἀναστήσω, comme ailleurs dans le NT (cf. Ac 3,22, citant Dt 18,15-22 LXX), se prête à évoquer la résurrection de Jésus. Et si nous nous rappelons que c'était la coutume du pasteur de «précéder» son troupeau, l'allusion faite par Jésus en Mt 26,31 et Mc 14,27 devient claire. Cette citation et cette promesse ne se lisent pas chez Luc, ce qui répond à l'absence de toute référence à Ez 34 dans son récit de la multiplication des pains et des poissons, comme nous allons le voir[18].

Mais c'est chez Jean que nous trouvons peut-être la moisson la plus riche de références du thème de ré-unifier ceux qui ont été dispersés ou du moins séparés. En Jn 11,50, le grand prêtre Caïphe déclare que «il vaut mieux qu'un seul homme meure pour le peuple plutôt que toute la nation périsse», et l'évangéliste tient cette parole pour une prophétie: Jésus devait mourir «afin qu'il rassemble dans l'unité les enfants de Dieu qui ont été dispersés» (ἵνα καὶ τὰ τέκνα τοῦ θεοῦ τὰ διεσκορπισμένα συναγάγῃ εἰς ἕν). Dans ce texte, les thèmes de la dispersion (au passé), de la mort (dans le proche futur) et du rassemblement (futur éloigné) sont exprimés en termes qui rappellent Ez 34 comme aussi la *Didachè*.

En Jn 10,12, Jésus avertit ses auditeurs que «le loup saisira (le troupeau) et les dispersera» (ὁ λύκος ἁρπάζει (τὰ πρόβατα) καὶ σκορπίζει). Puis il conclut, au v. 16: «Et je les conduirai (les brebis qui ne sont pas de ce troupeau) ... et il y aura un seul troupeau et un seul pasteur»

---

18. Le «discours eschatologique» de Mc 13 comporte aussi un moment négatif, à savoir la «détresse» (vv. 19-20, θλῖψις) qui va s'abattre sur le monde, suivi par un moment positif qui est exprimé en terme de «rassemblement» (v. 27): «Et alors il enverra ses anges et il rassemblera (ἐπισυνάξει) les élus des quatre vents, de l'extrémité de la terre à l'extrémité du ciel». Les mots ne sont pas identiques à ceux qui se lisent en *Did.* 9,4 mais ils les rappellent, et l'idée est celle du rassemblement des élus dans le royaume de Dieu, conçu comme devant se réaliser sur la terre.

(κἀκεῖνα δεῖ με ἀγαγεῖν ... καὶ γενήσονται μία ποίμνη, εἷς ποιμήν). Ici encore, il y a une «dispersion» suivie d'un «rassemblement»; cette fois, le texte fait écho plutôt à Ez 37,24, qui prophétise la réunification finale des deux royaumes divisés «sous mon serviteur David... et il y aura un seul pasteur pour tous» (καὶ ὁ δοῦλός μου Δαυεὶδ ἄρχων ἐν μέσῳ αὐτῶν ἔσται ποιμὴν εἷς πάντων).

L'unité, bien que sans référence explicite à une dispersion précédente, forme le thème de Jn 17,21-23. Jésus y prie, en termes qui rappellent ceux de Paul et de la *Didachè*, «afin que tous soient un» (ἵνα πάντες ἐν ὦσιν). Cette unité sera accomplie, selon la même «prière sacerdotale», par la présence ou l'habitation mutuelle du Père et du Fils et des croyants. Mais justement, cette mutuelle présence, et donc aussi l'unité, sont obtenues par ceux qui «mangent ma chair et boivent mon sang», selon Jn 6,55-56. Le contexte de ces paroles est un repas, mais non la dernière Cène, ce qui nous ramène une fois de plus à notre point de départ.

6. En tenant compte de tous ces développements, nous pouvons reprendre les principaux textes du NT qui se réfèrent à la «fraction du pain».

a. La multiplication des pains et des poissons.

Le thème principal de ces récits est que Jésus nourrit ceux qui le suivent. Mais il comporte deux variantes, l'une eschatologique et l'autre sapientielle. Selon la première, Jésus est le pasteur royal (David) qui nourrit son peuple en accomplissement de la promesse divine. La référence la plus obvie est à Ez 34,14: «Je les ferai paître dans un bon pâturage, sur la montagne élevée d'Israël» (ἐν νομῇ ἀγαθῇ βοσκήσω αὐτούς, ἐν τῷ ὄρει τῷ ὑψηλῷ Ἰσραήλ). Dans les récits de multiplication des pains, plusieurs détails semblent faire écho à ce chapitre d'Ézéchiel. On lit par exemple en Ez 34,5 «mes brebis ont été dispersées car il n'y avait pas de pasteurs» (διεσπάρη τὰ πρόβατά μου διὰ τὸ μὴ εἶναι ποιμένας); ce texte est cité en Mc 6,34 (ὡς πρόβατα μὴ ἔχοντα ποιμένα) avant que Jésus, ému de compassion, n'enseigne la foule et ne la nourrisse (la même citation précède le récit de Mt 9,36 dans lequel Jésus envoie les Douze). De même, Jésus se trouve sur une montagne avant de nourrir le peuple en Jn 6,3 et avant la seconde multiplication des pains en Mt 15,29. En Jn 6,15, ceux qui ont été nourris veulent s'emparer de Jésus pour le faire roi: ils le tiennent pour le pasteur, «mon serviteur David», que Dieu a promis de leur susciter (cf. Ez 34,23; 37,24).

Ces allusions sont absentes de Luc (9,12-17). Sa version de l'événement n'offre aucun lien explicite avec Ézéchiel. Toutefois, selon lui, Jésus vient de donner un enseignement sur le royaume de Dieu (v. 11), un thème qui n'est pas sans lien avec Ez 34. Il faut cependant reconnaître que la présentation lucanienne de la multiplication des pains est plus proche du thème de la Sagesse qui nourrit ses enfants; Jésus est le Maître qui fournit la nourriture à l'ensemble de l'humanité.

Jn 6,26ss va même plus loin: Jésus n'est pas seulement celui qui nourrit ceux qui le suivent, mais il déclare: «Je suis le pain de vie». La suite de cette parole contient des allusions au thème de la Sagesse qui nourrit ses disciples de sa propre substance (Sg 9,1-6; Si 15,3; 24,19-22 [26-30])[19].

Si l'insistance principale de ces récits est sur la distribution et la manducation des pains, rappelons que les Synoptiques mentionnent explicitement la fraction du pain, et tous insistent sur le fait de ramasser les fragments, bien entendu après que la foule s'est rassasiée. Si Jean ne mentionne pas la «fraction» du pain, il termine son récit (6,12) en insistant sur le rassemblement des fragments, «afin que rien ne se perde»; ce détail évoque le thème qu'il précisera en 11,52: Jésus doit mourir afin de rassembler dans l'unité les enfants de Dieu qui ont été dispersés. C'est à dire que chez Jean on trouve le deuxième volet de la double comparaison qui, selon nos explications données plus haut, serait implicite dans *Did.* 9,4.

Il semble donc que ces récits ont été structurés selon un rite de «fraction du pain» qui peut avoir compris aussi le rassemblement des fragments pour re-former le morceau unique. Ils reflètent deux significations symboliques différentes attachées au rite: le rassemblement eschatologique du peuple de Dieu dispersé; mais aussi la Sagesse considérée comme le pain de vie. Dans ce dernier cas, le symbolisme porte seulement sur la fraction et la distribution du pain; dans le premier cas, il porte aussi sur le rassemblement des fragments[20].

b. La dernière Cène.

Les récits de la dernière Cène sont beaucoup plus complexes et, sous leur forme actuelle, ils sont le résultat d'une pratique liturgique et d'une réflexion théologique, plutôt que leur point de départ.

19. Voir encore M.-É. BOISMARD et A. LAMOUILLE, *L'évangile de Jean* (Synopse des quatre évangiles en français, 3), Paris, Cerf, 1977, p. 197 s.
20. Cette conclusion est cohérente avec l'évolution remarquée dans l'iconographie de la multiplication: évoquant au début un repas, qui est facilement assimilé à l'eucharistie, la représentation veut ensuite y introduire le Christ en personne, puis elle met de plus en plus l'accent sur l'aspect miraculeux du geste et sur la scène racontée dans les évangiles; comparer CERFAUX, *La multiplication des pains*, p. 957, n. 1.

En Mt 26,26 et Mc 14,22, comme dans le texte occidental court de Lc 22,19, la déclaration de Jésus: «Ceci est mon corps» (i.e. «Ceci, c'est moi»), ferait penser au même motif sapientiel que nous avons vu à propos des récits de la multiplication des pains: Jésus, la Sagesse de Dieu, nourrit ses disciples de sa propre personne[21]. Ce thème est encore plus marqué dans le texte court de Luc où, à l'inverse de ce qui se lit dans Matthieu et dans Marc (au moins sous leur forme actuelle), il manque la déclaration de Jésus sur la coupe: «Ceci est mon sang…».

Par ailleurs, dans les trois Synoptiques, les gestes et les paroles de Jésus sont situés dans le contexte d'un repas pascal qui doit être son dernier repas; en 1 Co 11, pareillement, le contexte est «la nuit où il fut livré»[22]. Étant donné ces circonstances, ses gestes et ses paroles peuvent porter d'autres significations symboliques, et notamment celle de sa mort. En effet la transition du thème de la Sagesse nourrissant ses enfants à celle de l'autosacrifice jusqu'à la mort n'est pas trop étrange, spécialement quand la nourriture est identifiée avec celui qui la procure. Le geste même de rompre le pain exprime facilement le prix sacrificiel que coûte le fait de procurer cette nourriture.

En Lc 22,15-18, Jésus déclare qu'il a beaucoup désiré manger la Pâque avec ses disciples avant de mourir, et il ajoute qu'il ne la mangera plus avant qu'elle ne soit accomplie dans le royaume de Dieu. Puis il «rend grâces» sur la coupe et il ordonne aux disciples de la prendre et de la partager, ajoutant qu'il ne boira plus du fruit de la vigne jusqu'à ce que vienne le royaume de Dieu[23]. Ensuite il romp le pain. Dans le texte standard de Lc 22,19, le rite est lié encore plus explicitement à la passion de Jésus: ici la déclaration sur le pain, plus longue, contient les mots «(ce corps) qui est donné pour vous», et elle continue, comme chez Paul, par le commandement de répéter l'action «en mémoire de lui».

En d'autres termes, la Pâque qui va se célébrer va se trouver interrompue par la passion de Jésus mais sera accomplie dans le royaume de Dieu[24]: entre ces deux moments se situe la «fraction du pain». Nous ne sommes pas loin de le conclusion de Paul en 1 Co 11,26, où le fait de

---

21. Voir M.-É. BOISMARD, *Jésus un homme de Nazareth, raconté par Marc l'évangéliste*, Paris, Cerf, 1996, pp. 151-154.

22. Ceci explique pourquoi il n'y a pas, dans Matthieu, Marc et Luc (TO), d'ordre donné par Jésus de répéter cette cène; le NT ne comporte aucune idée de répéter le repas pascal comme tel; par ailleurs, en 1 Co 11, il n'y a aucune référence explicite à la Pâque, de telle sorte que l'ordre de répéter la cène n'offre aucune ambiguïté. Luc (TA) est influencé par 1 Co pour ce qui est la présence, et le redoublement, du commandement de répéter la cène.

23. Cette dernière prédiction se lit aussi en Mt 26,29 et Mc 14,25.

24. La référence implicite est à la célébration de la Pâque faite par Josué après l'entrée en terre promise (Jos 5,10-12).

manger le pain (rompu) et de boire la coupe proclame la mort de Jésus et en même temps anticipe son retour. Nous ne sommes pas loin non plus de la *Didachè* qui, bien qu'elle ne fasse pas allusion à la mort de Jésus, se réfère à la dispersion du peuple de Dieu et envisage ensuite la venue du royaume. De toute façon, au niveau de la signification symbolique, un moment négatif (dans le passé ou dans le proche futur) va être suivi par un moment positif (dans un futur plus éloigné). Cette dernière signification serait encore plus claire si le rite symbolique comprenait aussi le rassemblement des fragments séparés.

c. Le souper à Emmaüs (Lc 24,13-35).

Dans la dernière partie de ce récit, Jésus ressuscité a ouvert le sens des Écritures aux deux disciples déçus, leur montrant qu'il était nécessaire que le Christ mourût pour entrer dans sa gloire. Rendus dans leur maison, il accomplit le rite de rompre le pain. À la lumière de ce que nous avons montré nous pouvons comprendre comment les disciples furent capables de le reconnaître «à la fraction du pain», i.e. grâce au rite lui-même, un rite qui leur était familier. En d'autres termes, ils ont pu percevoir que le rite, maintenant, symbolise la mort de Jésus (moment négatif), suivi par sa résurrection (moment positif). Ce double symbolisme devait être fortement suggéré si le rite en question était articulé par les deux gestes de rompre, puis de rassembler les fragments de pain. Que le symbolisme de la mort, et du retour à la vie ait pu déjà être perçu dans le rite, même indépendamment de la passion de Jésus, nous avons pour signe l'histoire d'Eutychus en Ac 20 (voir plus haut).

Pour apprécier l'eschatologie de Luc, il est important de noter que, au niveau de la signification symbolique, le moment positif n'est pas le retour de Jésus lors de la venue du royaume, attendue pour l'avenir (comme dans certains passages analogues du NT et de la *Didachè*), mais il est la présence actuelle, avec ses disciples, de Jésus ressuscité. Notons aussi le mouvement de la scène: d'abord éloignés de Jérusalem et des autres qui ont suivi Jésus (moment négatif, dispersion), les deux disciples se retrouvent à Jérusalem où ils rejoignent les Onze et ceux qui sont avec eux, lesquels leur disent que «le Seigneur est ressuscité et est apparu à Simon» (moment positif, rassemblement).

d. Paul.

Pour Paul, le pain rompu symbolise avant tout l'unité de ceux qui le partagent. Il traite ce thème à deux reprises, avec à chaque fois une nuance légèrement différente. En 1 Co 10,16, la coupe «que nous bénissons» et le pain «que nous rompons» sont une communion au sang et au corps du Christ (excluant ainsi toute communion avec les démons, vv. 20-21). Il conclut au v. 17: «Parce qu'il y a un seul pain (εἷς ἄρτος), nous qui sommes multiples nous sommes un seul corps (ἓν σῶμα) car tous nous participons à ce pain unique (τοῦ ἑνὸς ἄρτου μετέχομεν)». Le vocabulaire, une fois de plus, est assez semblable à celui de la *Didachè* et il conviendrait bien si Paul avait dans l'esprit le geste de rassembler les fragments pour reformer un seul morceau de pain. Il connaît ce repas symbolique comme étant «la table du Seigneur» (v. 21 τραπέζης κυρίου μετέχειν).

En 1 Co 11,23-26, Paul rappelle que les gestes et les paroles de Jésus sur le pain et sur la coupe eurent lieu «la nuit où il fut livré». Mais même ici, c'est le thème de l'unité qui prédomine: Paul rapporte le récit traditionnel tandis qu'il s'efforce de corriger les abus dans la célébration du «repas du Seigneur» (v. 20), qui sont les signes de la désunion et contredisent ainsi la véritable signification du repas; un peu plus loin, il va parler du «corps» et de ses «parties» (12,12 ss). Ignace d'Antioche, *Ad Eph.* 20,2, met de même l'accent sur l'unité du pain et de ceux qui se rassemblent pour le rompre.

7. Concluons. Il est ainsi possible d'expliquer les diverses sortes de symbolisme «eucharistique» que nous trouvons dans le NT. Nous supposons que Jésus et ses disciples (et d'autres groupes de même type) ont pratiqué un rite de rompre et de se partager du pain, et que c'était la coutume, au moins chez certains, de rassembler les fragments rompus avant de les distribuer. L'action était accompagnée d'une «bénédiction» ou «action de grâces» qui exprimait le symbolisme de ce geste, un symbolisme qui était articulé sur un moment négatif suivi d'un moment positif. Il n'est pas nécessaire de supposer que tous ceux qui pratiquaient ce rite familier lui donnaient une seule et même signification: il y avait toutes chances, d'un groupe à l'autre, ou même au sein d'un même groupe, pour que la signification du rite puisse varier et se transformer, et même pour que le rite lui-même puisse prendre des formes variées.

Un thème ainsi symbolisé était celui de la dispersion et du rassemblement eschatologique du peuple de Dieu, Israël, puis l'Église: ceci est exprimé en *Did.* 9,4 et en Jn 11 et était retenu dans la tradition liturgique chrétienne[25]. Celui qui nourrit son peuple (avec une harmonique eschatologique, comme aussi sapientielle) est le thème qui trouve son écho dans les récits de la multiplication des pains et aussi dans ceux de la der-

---

25. Par exemple, l'Anaphore de l'Euchologe de Sérapion (IVe siècle, de type alexandrin), où une prière quasi identique est insérée dans le récit habituel de l'institution de l'eucharistie, entre le pain et la coupe.

nière Cène. Le rite peut aussi symboliser la mort de Jésus et la venue du royaume, ou le retour de Jésus, comme dans les récits synoptiques de la dernière Cène et chez Paul; ou encore la mort et la résurrection (actuelle) de Jésus, comme à Emmaüs. Paul, quant à lui, insiste sur le thème de l'unité: parce qu'il y a un seul pain, il y a un seul corps.

École Biblique   Justin TAYLOR
P.O.B. 19053
Jérusalem

DIE BEZIEHUNGEN DER VORGESCHICHTE ZUR APOSTELGESCHICHTE

DARGESTELLT AN LK 2,22-39

Die Beziehungen der Vorgeschichte Lk 1,5–2,52 zur Apostelgeschichte sind anders geartet als die zwischen zwei beliebigen Kapiteln innerhalb Lk 3–24 oder Apg 1–28. Denn die Vorgeschichte ist nicht der erste Abschnitt einer längeren Linie, sondern dieser Linie vorangestellt. Obwohl sie die Anfänge des Lebens Jesu enthält, stellt sie eigentlich nicht das erste Stück seines Lebensweges dar. Daran ändern auch die summarischen Wachstumsnotizen 2,40 und 2,52 nichts. Sie erwecken zwar den Eindruck biographischer Überbrückungen, dienen aber der literarischen Verknüpfung. Die Vorgeschichte ist ein echter Prolog, sozusagen das Evangelium vor dem Evangelium[1].

Seine Beziehungen zu dem Werk, dem er voransteht, liegen auf verschiedenen Ebenen. Seine Texte üben unterschiedliche Funktionen aus. Teils wirken sie wie das Vorbild für Späteres, teils sind sie dessen Vorwegnahme, teils bieten sie die Vorschau darauf. So entspricht die Art, wie in Lk 1 die Mutter Jesu mit den Eltern des Johannes zusammengeführt wird, ähnlichen Vorgängen mit Hananias und Paulus (Apg 9) oder Petrus und Kornelius (Apg 10–11). Auch die Darstellung einer Einzelperson kann vorbildhaft sein, z.B. die der Maria als Gestalt des Glaubens. Das Auftreten Jesu im Tempel (2,41-51) – danach lebt er wieder zurückgezogen – nimmt sein späteres Lehren ebenso vorweg wie der Titel σωτήρ (2,11) das Christusbekenntnis der Kirche. Die Ankündigung der Umkehrpredigt des Johannes dagegen (1,16f) sagt einfach voraus, was geschehen wird. Abgesehen von anderen, z.B. stilistischen Beziehungen[2] finden sich die genannten auch in der Erzählung von Simeon und Hanna (Lk 2,22-39).

---

1. Cf. U. Busse, *Das »Evangelium« des Lukas. Die Funktion der Vorgeschichte im lukanischen Doppelwerk*, in C. Bussmann & W. Radl (eds.), *Der Treue Gottes trauen. Beiträge zum Werk des Lukas.* FS G. Schneider, Freiburg, Herder, 1991, pp. 161-179.

2. Dazu, aber auch zu den Unterschieden auf diesem Gebiet cf. J. Dawsey, *The Literary Unity of Luke-Acts: Questions of Style – a Task for Literary Critics*, in NTS 35 (1989) 48-66.

I. ANALYSE VON LK 2,22-39

Manche Autoren lassen unsere Erzählung schon mit v. 21 beginnen. Die beiden Aussagen v. 21 und vv. 22-24 scheinen zusammenzugehören, weil ihre Anfänge parallel formuliert sind und ihr Inhalt jeweils rituelle Dinge betrifft. Aber erzählerisch blickt v. 21 doch eher zurück; denn er bringt mit 2,1-20 die Erfüllung von 1,31. Als Eröffnung wird man 2,22-24 betrachten müssen. Der Leser erfährt, daß die Familie Jesu nach den Tagen der Reinigung nach Jerusalem zieht. Den Abschluß der Erzählung bildet v. 39, eine typische Rückkehrnotiz (cf. 1,56; 2,51), die die Familie wieder dorthin zurückführt, von wo sie nach Judäa aufgebrochen ist (2,4).

Die Rahmenverse beschreiben aber nicht nur die Bewegung zum Tempel und von dort zurück, sondern auch das Motiv des Tempelbesuchs. Der Erzähler betont mehrfach, daß die Eltern Jesu gesetzliche Verpflichtungen erfüllen (2,22.23.24.39; cf. v. 27). Im Verlauf dieses Geschehens kommt es zu einer doppelten Begegnung, die das rituelle Tun ganz in den Hintergrund drängt und vergessen läßt. Es treten nacheinander zwei Personen auf, Simeon und Hanna. Bisher unbekannt, werden sie beide vor allem in religiöser Hinsicht charakterisiert, Simeon als gerecht und gottesfürchtig, wartend auf den »Trost Israels« und mit dem Heiligen Geist begabt (v. 25), Hanna als Prophetin, die die meiste Zeit ihres Lebens als Witwe gelebt hat und bis in ihr hohes Alter nicht vom Tempel gewichen ist, sondern mit Fasten und Beten Tag und Nacht Gott dient (v. 36f). Auch sie lebt, wie zum Schluß indirekt gesagt wird (v. 38), in der Hoffnung auf Jerusalems Erlösung. Das Verbum προσδέχομαι (vv. 25 und 38) rahmt die ganze Erzählung. Simeon ist sogar offenbart worden, daß er den Gesalbten des Herrn noch »sehen« werde (v. 26).

Als nun Jesus in den Tempel gebracht wird, führt der Heilige Geist auch ihn dorthin, und so treffen sie durch die göttliche Regie aufeinander[3]. Mit dem Kind auf seinen Armen weissagt Simeon nun zweierlei. Zunächst sieht er, Gott dankend, in Jesus das Heil für alle Völker, für die Heiden ebenso wie für Israel (vv. 30-32), dann aber auch das Zeichen des Widerspruchs, an dem viele einmal zu Fall kommen werden (v. 34), was auch Maria nicht unberührt lassen wird (v. 35). Dann kommt Hanna

---

3. Vom »Spiel der himmlischen Regie mit ihren spezifischen Möglichkeiten, die Bewegungen von Figuren in Zeit und Raum zu koordinieren«, spricht K. LÖNING, *Das Geschichtswerk des Lukas. I. Israels Hoffnung und Gottes Geheimnisse* (Urban-Taschenbücher, 455), Stuttgart, Kohlhammer, 1997, p. 122.

hinzu. Auch sie preist Gott und spricht prophetisch über das Kind (v. 38).

Die Erzählung ist kein einheitlicher, geschlossener Text. Der Hauptteil besteht aus zwei ungleichen Abschnitten, einem langen über Simeon (vv. 25-35) und einem äußerst kurzen über Hanna (vv. 36-38). Das in den Rahmenversen betonte Thema der Gesetzeserfüllung spielt sonst keine Rolle mehr. Der Prosatext wird von dichterischen Zeilen (vv. 29-32) unterbrochen. Diese fallen inhaltlich dadurch auf, daß sie im Unterschied zur sonstigen Rede von der Hoffnung Jerusalems und Israels den Blick auf alle Völker ausweiten. Die hoffnungsfrohen, lichtvollen Aussagen des Dankliedes stehen auch in Spannung zu den düster klingenden Weissagungen in v. 34f.

Offenbar hat der Evangelist seine Tradition stark bearbeitet. Mit ihrer Rahmung hat er das Motiv der rituellen Gesetzeserfüllung eingebracht und neben das der Tempelfrömmigkeit gestellt. Von ihm stammt wohl auch die mehrmalige Erwähnung des Heiligen Geistes bei Simeon (vv. 25.26.27) und vielleicht die Vorstellung von dem unaufhörlichen Gottesdienst mit Fasten und Gebet bei Hanna (v. 37; cf. 5,33 diff Mk 2,18). Vor allem aber das »Nunc dimittis« vv. 29-32 scheint ein regelrechter Einschub zu sein. Ein (mit seiner literarischen Form vertrauter) hellenistischer Schriftsteller, wahrscheinlich Lukas selbst, hat dieses »Dankgebet eines Todgeweihten«[4] in die Erzähltradition von dem rätselhaften Orakel Simeons eingebracht. Die Sichtweise dieses Gebets unterscheidet sich nicht nur von der Konzentration auf Israel im Rest der Erzählung, sie deckt sich auch mit der weltweiten Perspektive im Korpus des Evangeliums und in der Apostelgeschichte[5].

II. Vergleich mit der Apostelgeschichte

Wie immer die Redaktion des Evangelisten im einzelnen einzugrenzen ist, de facto besteht eine Reihe von Bezügen zwischen unserer Erzählung und der Apostelgeschichte gerade in den genannten Punkten, angefangen von dem Charakter der Personen, über ihre Begegnung mit Jesus, bis zum Gegenstand der Weissagungen Simeons, dem strahlenden σωτήριον und dem überwiegend dunklen σημεῖον.

---

4. Zu dieser Gattungsbezeichnung s. K. BERGER, *Das Canticum Simeonis (Lk 2:29-32)*, in *NT* 27 (1985) 27-39.

5. Zum redaktionellen bzw. lukanischen Charakter des Gebets cf. W. RADL, *Der Ursprung Jesu. Traditionsgeschichtliche Untersuchungen zu Lukas 1–2* (HBS, 7), Freiburg, Herder, 1996, pp. 223f.

A. *Fromme Menschen*

Die Grundgegebenheit, die den Personenkreis unserer Erzählung mit vielen anderen im Werk des Lukas verbindet, ist die Frömmigkeit in der Treue zum *Gesetz*. Wie die Familie Jesu alles nach dem »Gesetz des Mose« bzw. nach dem »Gesetz des Herrn« vollzieht (2,22.23.24.27.39), so hält es noch die »Myriaden« zählende Christengemeinde in Jerusalem: Sie sind »Eiferer für das Gesetz« (Apg 21,20 ζηλωταὶ τοῦ νόμου). Auch Paulus, bei Gamaliel selbst »genau nach dem väterlichen Gesetz« (κατὰ ἀκρίβειαν τοῦ πατρῴου νόμου) erzogen (Apg 22,3) und von Hananias, einem »gesetzestreuen, frommen Mann« (εὐλαβὴς κατὰ τὸν νόμον), getauft (22,12), wandelt nach Lukas »in Beobachtung des Gesetzes« (21,24 φυλάσσων τὸν νόμον) und hat sich keine Verfehlung »gegen das Gesetz der Juden« vorzuwerfen (25,8). Er dient dem väterlichen Gott im Glauben an »alles, was das Gesetz bestimmt« (24,14 πᾶσι τοῖς κατὰ τὸν νόμον). Er beschneidet Timotheus (16,1-3) und beteiligt sich an der Auslösung einiger Nasiräer im Tempel (21,23f). Und selbst für die Heidenchristen bleibt nach dem Beschluß der Apostel und der Ältesten vom »Gesetz dcs Mose« (15,5) das gültig, was nach den Bestimmungen des Heiligkeitsgesetzes, wie sie seit alters in den Synagogen aller Städte verkündet werden (15,21), Heiden in Israel zu beachten haben (Lev 17–18; cf. Apg 15,20.29; 21,25).

Der Mittelpunkt der Religion Israels, der Ort des Kultes schlechthin, ist der *Tempel*. Er wird zum Schauplatz der Begegnung Jesu mit zwei Idealgestalten Israels. Für sie ist der Tempel nicht der Ort des Opfers, sondern der Erwartung und Hoffnung, des Fastens und Betens und schließlich der Offenbarung[6]. Wie Jesus bei seinem Einzug in Jerusalem als erstes dem Tempel zustrebt, ihn wieder zu einem »Haus des Gebetes« macht und dann tagaus, tagein dort das Volk lehrt (Lk 19,45-47; 21,37), so bleibt auch die Urgemeinde, wie deren Kern schon seit Jesu Himmelfahrt (24,53), dem Tempel verbunden. Täglich versammelt sie sich dort zum Gebet (Apg 2,46; 5,12). Auf dem Weg zum Gebet heilen Petrus und Johannes den Gelähmten an der Schönen Pforte des Tempels (3,1-10), um dann trotz des gerichtlichen Verbots auf himmlische Anweisung täglich im Tempel das Volk zu lehren (5,19-21.25.42). Beim Gebet im Tempel ist Paulus in einer Vision Jesu (ἰδεῖν αὐτόν) sein Missionsauftrag bei den Heiden offenbart worden (22,17-21); aber das Pfingstfest feiert er gern in der Stadt des Tempels (20,16).

---

6. Zum Tempel als »Ort von Lehre, Gebet und exemplarischer ... Gesetzeserfüllung« cf. M. KLINGHARDT, *Gesetz und Volk Gottes. Das lukanische Verständnis des Gesetzes nach Herkunft, Funktion und seinem Ort in der Geschichte des Urchristentums* (WUNT, 2/32), Tübingen, Mohr, 1988, p. 278.

Überhaupt ist das *Gebet* ein wesentlicher Zug des frommen Menschen, das ständige Beten ebenso wie das Gebet an Höhe- und Wendepunkten des Weges. Wie Hanna Tag und Nacht Gott damit dient (Lk 2,37), so verharrt der Jüngerkreis Jesu vor Pfingsten und die Urgemeinde nach dem Fest im Gebet (Apg 1,14; 2,42; cf. 4,31; 12,5). Wer betet, ist offen für Gott. Das Kennzeichen des taufwilligen Paulus besteht darin, daß er »betet« (9,11 προσεύχεται), und der Heide Kornelius ist für die Aufnahme des Evangeliums dadurch vorbereitet, daß er Almosen gibt und »beständig zu Gott betet« (10,2 δεόμενος τοῦ θεοῦ διὰ παντός; cf. 10,4.30.31).

Mit dem Gebet ist bei Hanna das *Fasten* verbunden (Lk 2,37), auch eine Weise, sich bereitzuhalten für Gottes Wort und Weisung. So wählt der Heilige Geist Paulus und Barnabas während Gottesdienst und Fasten zu Missionaren aus (Apg 13,2), und die Gemeinde entläßt sie mit Fasten, Gebet und Handauflegung (13,3). Das gleiche praktizieren sie selbst bei der Einsetzung der Ältesten in ihren Missionsgemeinden (14,23).

Für seine Frömmigkeit und Gesetzestreue erhält Simeon die Prädikate »*gerecht*« und »*gottesfürchtig*« (Lk 2,25 δίκαιος καὶ εὐλαβής). Δίκαιοι sind auch Zacharias und Elisabet (1,6). Ein ἀνὴρ ἀγαθὸς καὶ δίκαιος ist Josef von Arimathäa (23,50 diff Mk 15,43), ein ἀνὴρ εὐλαβὴς κατὰ τὸν νόμον Hananias (Apg 22,12), und beides, Gerechtigkeit und Gottesfurcht, verbindet, ähnlich Simeon, der Heide Kornelius als ἀνὴρ δίκαιος καὶ φοβούμενος τὸν θεόν (10,22; cf. 10,2 εὐσεβὴς καὶ φοβούμενος τὸν θεόν). Insgesamt sind es durch Gesetzestreue, Gebet, Fasten oder Almosen ausgezeichnete Fromme, denen Gott seine Offenbarung schenkt.

Den inneren Rahmen unserer Erzählung bildet das Motiv des *Wartens* mit dem Stichwort προσδέχομαι in den vv. 25 und 38[7]. Simeon und Hanna sind schon sehr alt und dem Tode nah. Sie halten schon lange Ausschau nach der Erlösung[8] und verkörpern damit die Erwartung Israels[9]. Diese »lange gegen den Tod behauptete Hoffnung«[10] ist es auch, die das Volk insgesamt ausharren läßt. Das »Zwölfstämmevolk« hofft ja nach den Worten des Paulus (Apg 26,6f), »in Beharrlichkeit Tag und Nacht Gott dienend« – exemplarisch dargestellt in der Prophetin Hanna

---

7. Cf. S.F. PLYMALE, *The Prayer Texts of Luke-Acts* (American University Studies, 118), New York – San Francisco – Bern, Lang, 1991, p. 39.

8. Zum »Trost (Israels)« cf. Jes 40,1; 49,13; 66,12f, zur »Erlösung (Jerusalems)« Jes 41,14; 43,14; 44,24, zu beiden Motiven Jes 52,9: »Der Herr tröstet sein Volk, er erlöst Jerusalem«.

9. Cf. R. LAURENTIN, *Struktur und Theologie der lukanischen Kindheitsgeschichte*, Stuttgart, KBW, 1967, p. 116.

10. K. LÖNING, *Geschichtswerk* (n. 3), p. 124.

»aus dem Stamme Ascher« (Lk 2,36)[11] –, die Erfüllung der den Vätern gegebenen Verheißung zu erleben. Er selbst steht wegen des Streits um diese Verheißung und ihr Eintreffen vor Gericht, »wegen der Hoffnung Israels«, wie er den römischen Juden sagen wird (28,20). Es ist die »Hoffnung« auf die Auferstehung, deren Erfüllung sie ebenso erwarten (προσδέχονται) wie er (24,15; cf. Lk 23,50)[12].

B. *Die Begegnung*

Die Begegnung mit dem Erwarteten ist bei Simeon vorbereitet. Dem »Gerechten und Gottesfürchtigen«, dem Mann der Hoffnung und des Heiligen Geistes (Lk 2,25), ist von diesem Geist »offenbart« worden (κεχρηματισμένον), er werde den Gesalbten des Herrn noch kommen sehen, »bevor er den Tod sehe« (v. 26). Und als die Stunde gekommen ist, da führt ihn der Heilige Geist in den Tempel. Ähnlich bereitet Gott die Begegnung des ersten Heiden mit dem Evangelium von Jesus vor. Kornelius, der »beim ganzen Volk der Juden in gutem Ruf stand, erhielt von einem heiligen Engel die Weisung (ἐχρηματίσθη)«, Petrus »in sein Haus kommen zu lassen« und seine Worte zu hören (Apg 10,22). Wie diesen selbst schon eine Vision dafür bereit gemacht hat (10,9-16), wird vor der Taufe des Paulus Hananias in einer Vision über das göttliche Vorhaben aufgeklärt und zu dem Bekehrten gesandt (9,10-16). Auch Paulus, dieses »auserwählte Werkzeug« (9,15 σκεῦος ἐκλογῆς), hat Gott schon im voraus dazu »bestimmt« (προεχειρίσατο), »den Gerechten zu sehen« (22,14).

Die Begegnung selbst erlebt Simeon dann im Tempel. Dort sehen seine Augen den Erwarteten (v. 30). Ihn darf auch Paulus im Tempel »sehen« (Apg 22,18). Die erste Bekanntschaft mit dem Evangelium macht Paulus allerdings in einem Wohnhaus, in dem ihn Hananias aufsucht, ebenso Kornelius, zu dem Petrus kommt. Aber bei allen dreien führt Gott die Begegnung herbei, wobei Simeon Jesus selbst begegnet, Paulus und Kornelius dagegen dem Evangelium von Jesus in seinen Boten (Apg 9,17f; 10,23-48). Den Akt der Aufnahme des Gekommenen,

---

11. Den Hinweis auf die Beziehung zwischen dem δωδεκάφυλον Apg 26,7 und der Angabe von Lk 2,36, Hanna stamme ἐκ φυλῆς Ἀσήρ, verdanke ich M. BACHMANN. Für ihn ist diese Korrespondenz »um so bemerkenswerter, als die Formulierung aus Lk 2,36, sofern sie die φυλή einer einzigen Person meint, im lukanischen Werk nahezu singulär ist«; so in *Jerusalem und der Tempel. Die geographisch-theologischen Elemente in der lukanischen Sicht des jüdischen Kultzentrums* (BWANT, 109), Stuttgart, Kohlhammer, 1980, pp. 337f n. 511.

12. Cf. R.C. TANNEHILL, *The Narrative Unity of Luke-Acts. A Literary Interpretation*. I. *The Gospel According to Luke* (Foundations and Facets), Philadelphia, PA, Fortress Press, 1986, p. 39.

Jesu selbst bzw. seines Evangeliums, bezeichnet jeweils das Verbum δέχομαι. Simeon nimmt das Kind in seine Arme (v. 28), die späteren Hörer nehmen das Wort Gottes an[13], einige Tausend in Jerusalem (Apg 2,41; hier ἀποδεξάμενοι), die Samariter (8,14), die Heiden in Cäsarea (11,1) und die Juden von Beröa (17,11).

C. *Die Prophetie*

Angesichts des Kindes auf seinen Armen stimmt Simeon zunächst einen Lobpreis an, der neben dem Dank für das Erleben dieser Stunde eine große Heilsprophetie enthält, um dann, der Mutter Jesu zugewandt, mit einer dunklen Weissagung über das Kind fortzufahren. Das strahlende σωτήριον wird in seinen Worten zum rätselhaften σημεῖον.

1. Jesus als σωτήριον

In Jesus sieht Simeon das »Heil«, das Gott »vor dem Angesicht aller Völker bereitet« hat (v. 30f). Mit den »Völkern« (λαοί) sind hier nicht die Stämme Israels gemeint, sondern die Nationen der ganzen Erde. Dagegen spricht auch nicht Apg 4,25.27[14]. Denn 4,25f zitiert mit Ps 2,1f einen doppelten synonymen Parallelismus, in dem ἔθνη und λαοί dasselbe bedeuten, ebenso βασιλεῖς und ἄρχοντες. Diesen Parallelismus hat Lukas (oder seine Tradition), auf das Stichwort λαοί hin – λαός bezeichnet sonst das Bundesvolk –, v. 27 entweder mißverstanden oder wissentlich falsch auf die Passion Jesu angewandt. Wie er Herodes und Pilatus die beiden Herrscherbegriffe βασιλεῖς und ἄρχοντες (parallel) zuordnet, so auch (chiastisch) ἔθνη und λαοί, das letztere freilich mit dem Zusatz Ἰσραήλ[15].

Mit diesem Wort Simeons reißt der Erzähler den bis dahin auf Israel beschränkten Horizont der endzeitlichen Erwartung[16] weltweit auf[17]. Die

---

13. Cf. Lk 8,13; 9,48; 10,8. Nichtannahme: Lk 9,5.53; 10,10, mit παραδέχομαι Apg 22,18.

14. Darauf berufen sich G.D. KILPATRICK, *Λαοί at Luke II.31 and Acts IV.25,27*, in *JTS* 16 (1965) 127, und W. STEGEMANN, *»Licht der Völker« bei Lukas*, in FS G. Schneider (n. 1), pp. 81-97, hier 89, die die kritisierte Deutung vertreten.

15. Ähnlich verfährt Joh 19,23f mit dem in 19,24 zitierten Psalmvers 21,19 LXX. Die beiden Zeilen, die eigentlich nicht zwei Vorgänge beschreiben, bezieht 19,23f auf verschiedene Handlungen und Gegenstände: die erste auf die Verteilung der Gewänder und die zweite auf die Verlosung des Leibrocks.

16. Cf. 1,14.16f.32.55.69.77; 2,10. Höchstens bei 2,14 denkt Lukas schon über die Grenzen Israels hinaus; cf. jedoch J.A. FITZMYER, *The Gospel According to Luke I* (AB, 28), Garden City, NY, Doubleday, 1981, p. 422.

17. Also nicht erst 24,47. Vielleicht ist gerade darin das Staunen der Eltern v. 33 begründet; cf. B. REICKE, *Jesus, Simeon, and Anna (Luke 2:21-41)*, in J.I. COOK (ed.), *Saved by Hope*. FS R.C. Oudersluys, Grand Rapids, MI, Eerdmans, 1978, pp. 96-108, 104.

universale Heilsankündigung in Verbindung mit dem Wort σωτήριον knüpft dabei an die LXX-Stellen Ps 97,2f und 66,3 sowie an Jes 40,5 und 52,10 (LXX σωτηρία) an. Σωτήριον, in Jes 40–66 noch häufiger zu finden, begegnet im Neuen Testament außerhalb der lukanischen Schriften nur noch Eph 6,17, bei Lukas jedoch an programmatischen Eckpunkten seines Werkes. Das Jesajazitat im Munde Johannes des Täufers, mit dem er das Korpus seines Evangeliums eröffnet, erweitert er bekanntlich bis zu jener Stelle, die »allem Fleisch« das Schauen (ὄψεται; cf. πρόσωπον in 2,31) des »göttlichen Heils« (σωτήριον τοῦ θεοῦ) verheißt (Lk 3,6 = Jes 40,5 LXX). Und von hier aus spannt sich ein Bogen bis zum Abschluß des Werkes in Apg 28,28, wo er nach der Ankunft des Paulus in Rom das Evangelium als σωτήριον τοῦ θεοῦ für die Heiden bezeichnet[18].

Der Engel der Weihnachtserzählung verkündet den Hirten die Geburt des Retters, des σωτήρ. Wenn Simeon statt dessen vom σωτήριον spricht, dann vielleicht nicht nur in Anlehnung an Jes 40,5, sondern auch um das zu benennen, was tatsächlich zu allen Völkern gelangen wird. Das ist nicht der Retter Jesus persönlich und leibhaftig, sondern die Kunde von ihm. Wie Simeon jetzt mit seinen »Augen« das Messiaskind sieht, wird auch das Volk Israel den »Heiland« selbst sehen und erleben; die Völkerwelt dagegen wird das von ihm ausgehende »Heil« erfahren. Dieses wird im Wort der Boten zu den Heiden gesandt (ἀπεστάλη), wie es Apg 28,28 heißt, und indem sie es »hören«, wird es ihnen zuteil. Nach Lk 3,6 wird zwar alle Welt das Heil Gottes »sehen«; aber ὁράω bedeutet neben der Wahrnehmung mit dem Sehorgan auch das Erleben und Erfahren einer Sache (cf. Lk 17,22; Joh 1,50; 3,36; Ps 88,49 LXX)[19].

Der Gedanke des universalen Heils steht programmatisch wieder am Anfang der Apostelgeschichte. Wie schon am Ende des Evangeliums (24,47f) erhalten die Apostel hier vom Auferstandenen den Auftrag zur Zeugenschaft bei allen Völkern, angefangen von Jerusalem, »bis an das Ende der Erde« (Apg 1,8; cf. Jes 49,6; 52,10). Und als am Pfingstfest »aus allen Völkern unter dem Himmel« stammende Diasporajuden in Jerusalem zusammenströmen und die Predigt des Petrus hören, da wirkt das wie die zeichenhafte Vorwegnahme der Jesusverkündigung in allen Teilen der Welt. Von da ab durchzieht die Dynamik des bis in die Welthauptstadt Rom strebenden Evangeliums die Apostelgeschichte.

18. Cf. R.C. TANNEHILL, *Unity* (n. 12), p. 40.
19. Cf. W. BAUER, *Wörterbuch*, col. 1172; W. MICHAELIS, in *TWNT*, 5, pp. 340-342; J. KREMER, in *EWNT*, 2, cols. 1288f.

Obwohl mit v. 30f eigentlich alles, auch das überraschend Neue, gesagt ist, daß nämlich Gottes Heil in Jesus allen Menschen zugedacht ist, greift v. 32 diesen Gedanken nochmals auf und differenziert ihn durch die Gegenüberstellung von Heiden und Israel, wobei die Heiden sogar zuerst genannt werden. Das Nebeneinander von Heiden und Israel (oder ἔθνη und λαός) kehrt in der Apostelgeschichte dort wieder, wo aus der Berufung des Paulus und seinem Rückblick auf die Mission zitiert wird. Zu Hananias spricht Christus vom Auftrag des Paulus »sowohl vor Heiden und Königen[20] als auch vor den Söhnen Israels« (Apg 9,15) und zu Paulus von seiner Erwählung »aus dem λαός und aus den ἔθνη« (26,17). Er selbst versteht sich als Missionar »für das ganze Judenland und die Heiden« (26,20) bzw. »für den λαός und die ἔθνη« (26,23). In den Berichten vom Fortgang der Mission wird allerdings regelmäßig ein anderes Begriffspaar gebraucht: Ἰουδαῖοι und Ἕλληνες (14,1; 16,1.3; 17,1-4; 18,4; 19,10.17; 20,21; cf. 17,10-12)[21]. An diesen Stellen erscheinen die Juden gegenüber dem Evangelium als neutrale bzw. positive Größe. Wo sie aber neben den ἔθνη genannt werden wie 13,45f; 13,48-50; 14,2 und 14,5, sind sie die Widerspenstigen, die vor allem Paulus bekämpfen, ebenso wie »die Juden« 12,3.11; 14,19; 17,5.13; 18,12; 19,13f; 20,3.19; 21,11 und 21,27–26,21[22].

Als das »Licht« hingegen empfangen Jesus bzw. das Wort von ihm die ἔθνη und der λαὸς Ἰσραήλ. Manche Autoren beziehen die Prophetie Simeons vom Licht – grammatisch möglich – nur auf die Heiden, möglicherweise wegen des Zitats vom φῶς ἐθνῶν Apg 13,47 (= Jes 49,6; vgl. 42,6). Dem φῶς entspricht dann δόξα als zweite Apposition zu σωτήριον, was sich vielleicht von der (allerdings nur auf Jerusalem bezogenen) Paarung φῶς und δόξα in Jes 60,1.19 (cf. v. 2f) her begründen läßt[23]. Aber nach Lukas ist Jesus gleichermaßen für die Heiden und

---

20. Die Könige sind keine dritte Gruppe, sondern Bestandteil der ersten, und wir haben im ersten Doppelausdruck nichts anderes als die aus der LXX geläufige Umschreibung der Völkerwelt; cf. Gen 17,16; 1 Chr 29,11; 1 Esr 6,32; Jes 60,12; EpJer 51; Jer 1,10 (v.l.); entsprechend Apg 4,25f (= Ps 2,1f); fast gleichbedeutend Num 21,18; 2 Esr 9,7; Hag 2,22; Jes 14,9.18.32: die Könige *der* Völker.

21. In Apg 11,19f stehen den »Juden« möglicherweise die »Hellenisten« gegenüber, obwohl Ἕλληνας (von P[74] א[2] A D*) nicht schlecht bezeugt ist.

22. Cf. A. GEORGE, *Israël*, in DERS., *Études sur l'œuvre de Luc* (Sources bibliques), Paris, Gabalda, ²1986, pp. 87-125: Für Lukas existiert Israel auf zwei Ebenen, als Volk wie andere Völker auch (»die Juden«) und als Volk Gottes (p. 122).

23. So J. NOLLAND, *Luke 1–9:20* (WBC, 35a), Dallas, TX, Word Books, 1989, p. 120; J.J. KILGALLEN, *Jesus, Savior, the Glory of Your People Israel*, in *Bib* 75 (1994) 305-328, pp. 305-307; cf. H. SCHÜRMANN, *Das Lukasevangelium. I. Kap. 1,1–9,50* (HTK, 3/1), Freiburg, Herder, ⁴1985, p. 126 n. 209. Anders R.E. BROWN, *The Birth of the Messiah. A Commentary on the Infancy Narratives in Matthew and Luke*, Garden City, NY, Doubleday, 1977, p. 440; W. STEGEMANN, »*Licht der Völker*« (n. 14), p. 90; B.J. KOET,

für Israel das Licht: Paulus, »aus dem λαός und den ἔθνη erwählt«, ist zu ihnen (εἰς οὕς) gesandt, »ihre Augen zu öffnen, sie von der Finsternis zum Licht (εἰς φῶς) zu bekehren« (26,17f), und Christus, »als erster von den Toten auferstanden«, verkündet »Licht sowohl dem Volk als auch den Heiden« (26,23 φῶς … τῷ τε λαῷ καὶ τοῖς ἔθνεσιν).

Das Licht wird zur Erleuchtung, zur Offenbarung (εἰς ἀποκάλυψιν) für die Heiden; und Israel, das ja Gott schon kennt[24], gereicht es zum Ruhm (εἰς δόξαν). Von der Offenbarung vor den Völkern spricht die Jes-Stelle, an die schon v. 30f erinnert hat: »Der Herr enthüllt (ἀποκαλύψει) seinen heiligen Arm vor den Augen aller Völker« (52,10). Und die Verbindung von Licht und Erleuchtung bieten Jes 42,6f (εἰς φῶς ἐθνῶν ἀνοῖξαι ὀφθαλμοὺς τυφλῶν) sowie 49,9 (λέγοντα … τοῖς ἐν τῷ σκότει ἀνακαλυφθῆναι). Für die Heiden wird Wirklichkeit, was Gott schon Jes 56,1 LXX angekündigt hat: »Genaht hat sich mein Heil (σωτήριον), um anzukommen, und mein Erbarmen (ἔλεος), um sich zu offenbaren (ἀποκαλυφθῆναι)«. Daß das Aufgehen des Lichts in Israel das Volk selbst im Ruhmesglanz erstrahlen läßt, drückt bcsonders schön Jes 60,1-9.19-22 aus. Ganz kurz sagt im Grunde das gleiche Jes 46,13: δέδωκα ἐν Σιὼν σωτηρίαν τῷ Ἰσραὴλ εἰς δόξασμα. »Es gibt kaum eine Aussage über Israel im Neuen Testament, die weiterreichend wäre als diese: Jesus ist gekommen, um Israel auf größtmögliche Weise an Gottes Doxa selbst teilnehmen zu lassen«[25].

Wenn das Heil Gottes von vornherein, wie Simeon sagt, vor allen Völkern, als Licht für die Heiden und für Israel, bereitet ist, dann ist der Weg des Evangeliums zu den Heiden nicht durch den in Israel und in der Diaspora vorkommenden jüdischen Unglauben veranlaßt. Das Heil für die Heiden ist von Anfang an geplant und wird dann in Erfüllung der Schrift (Lk 24,46f) und der Prophetie Simeons auf göttliche Weisung ins Werk gesetzt[26]. Christus selbst beauftragt damit seine Apostel (Apg 1,8) und macht aus dem Verfolger Saulus den späteren Heidenmissionar (9,15f). Den ersten Schritt tut dann nicht irgendein von Juden abgelehnter Missionar, sondern nach Gottes Plan und Führung der Sprecher der Apostel, Petrus höchstpersönlich, ein Vorgang, auf dessen theologische Bewältigung Lukas eineinhalb Kapitel verwendet (10,1–11,18). Freilich

Simeons Worte (Lk 2,29-32.34c-35) und Israels Geschick, in F. VAN SEGBROECK, *et al.* (eds.), *The Four Gospels 1992.* FS F. Neirynck (BETL, 100), Leuven, University Press – Peeters, 1992, II, pp. 1549-1569, 1551 n. 12.

24. Cf. K. BERGER, *Canticum* (n. 4), p. 36.

25. *Ibid.*

26. Wie sehr Lukas den Gedanken von Gottes Plan und Vorherbestimmung betont, zeigt C.H. TALBERT, *Once Again: The Gentile Mission in Luke-Acts*, in FS G. Schneider (n. 1), pp. 99-109, 101.

kommt es dann im pisidischen Antiochia zu jüdischem Widerstand, der die Missionare sich abwenden und zu den Heiden gehen läßt (13,46). Aber auch das ist nichts Überraschendes, weil es schon vorhergesagt ist. Paulus zitiert die entsprechende Warnung (13,41) und dann die Rechtfertigung für die Hinwendung zu den Heiden (13,47).

2. Jesus als σημεῖον

Nach seinem Dankgebet mit dem verheißungsvollen Ausblick auf eine neue Zeit für die Heiden und eine glorreiche Zukunft Israels wendet sich Simeon der Mutter Jesu zu, um mit einem geheimnisvollen, orakelhaften Wort die Bestimmung ihres Kindes zu beschreiben. Die Beziehungen zur Apostelgeschichte sind hier nicht so klar. Das ist auch nicht verwunderlich, wenn das Orakel tatsächlich zur traditionellen Erzählung gehört. Am ehesten zugänglich und als Konzentration des Ganzen zu verstehen ist vielleicht das Stichwort vom »Zeichen« (v. 34b σημεῖον). Dieses wird, wie unmittelbar hinzugefügt wird, Widerspruch auslösen, eine Spannung, die auch an Maria nicht spurlos vorübergehen wird (v. 35a). Der Widerspruch wird die innere Einstellung vieler Menschen verraten (v. 35b). Sie wird nämlich so sein, wie Simeon gleich als erstes sagt, daß viele zu Fall kommen werden. Aber das ist nicht das letzte Wort. Es gibt auch ein Aufstehen.

a. Der Widerspruch

Als sich in Antiochia »die ganze Stadt versammelt, um das Wort des Herrn zu hören« (Apg 13,44), werden die Juden von Eifersucht erfüllt und »widersprechen« (ἀντέλεγον) unter Lästerungen den Worten des Paulus (13,45). Damit beginnt der Widerstand der Diasporajuden gegen seine Predigt. Er setzt sich von Stadt zu Stadt fort, so daß am Ende die Juden in Rom, die davon gehört haben, sagen können, der Lehre des Paulus werde »überall widersprochen« (28,22 πανταχοῦ ἀντιλέγεται). Dieses Stichwort bezeichnet ein Merkmal der gesamten paulinischen Mission. Nicht umsonst rahmt es gewissermaßen den Paulusteil der Apostelgeschichte. Ja es rahmt im wesentlichen sogar das ganze Werk des Lukas; denn das ἀντιλέγεται von Apg 28,22 entspricht dem ἀντιλεγόμενον von Lk 2,34. Schon Jesus erfährt den Widerspruch, unter dem – so wird man v. 35a verstehen müssen – auch seine Mutter leidet. Lukas berichtet mehrmals von jüdischer Gegnerschaft (z.B. Lk 20,20). Aber gerade im Zusammenhang der Auseinandersetzung um die Auferstehung, die auch bei Paulus den Streitpunkt bildet (Apg 17,32; 23,6.8; 24,15.21), erwähnt er die gegensätzliche Auffassung der Sadduzäer (Lk 20,27 ἀντιλέγοντες, diff Mk 12,18 λέγουσιν). Wichtiger und entscheidend ist freilich die Ablehnung, die Jesus selbst als Person und auf andere Weise Paulus (Apg 28,19 ἀντιλεγόντων … τῶν Ἰουδαίων) erfährt, die bei Jesus zu seinem gewaltsamen Tod führt. Aber gerade so wird er, weil Gott ihn auferweckt, von neuem zum Zeichen, nämlich zum »Zeichen des Jona« (Lk 11,29). Es ist das einzige, das »diesem bösen Geschlecht« gegeben wird (*ibid.*). Und um dieses Zeichen, das die Erfüllung der Hoffnung auf die Auferstehung bedeutet, geht, wie gesagt, der Streit des Paulus mit den Juden.

Zerstritten sind die Juden auch unter sich. Immer wieder kommt es wegen der Predigt des Paulus zur Spaltung unter ihnen (Apg 13,45.50; 14,2.4; 17,4f; 19,9)[27], bis zur letzten Begegnung in Rom (28,24f). Dort lassen sich die einen von Paulus überzeugen, die anderen glauben ihm nicht. Untereinander uneinig, verlassen sie ihn.

Wie in anderen Städten vorher macht Paulus also auch in Rom die Erfahrung jüdischen Unglaubens und Streits. Hier nun faßt er sein Urteil darüber mit dem Jes-Zitat zusammen, das die blinden Augen, die tauben Ohren und das verschlossene Herz anprangert (28,26f = Jes 6,9f LXX): Das »Volk« hört, ohne zu begreifen, es sieht, ohne zu sehen, und ihr Herz kommt nicht zur Einsicht. So kommt es auch nicht zur Bekehrung und Heilung. Der Widerspruch ist konsequent[28]. Eine Umkehr der ungläubigen Juden ist in diesem Zusammenhang nicht angedeutet, auch nicht mit dem das Zitat abschließenden Futur ἰάσομαι αὐτούς. Dieses scheint sich von dem vorausgehenden μήποτε … ἐπιστρέψωσιν inhaltlich zu unterscheiden, als würde Gott in dem letzten Wort, mit einem καί adversativum, sein zukünftiges Eingreifen zum Heil des Volkes ankündigen: »… aber ich werde sie heilen«[29]. Aber in Wirklichkeit ist das Futur hier dem Konjunktiv Aorist gleichwertig[30] und ebenso wie dieser noch von μήποτε abhängig, wie auch sonst im hellenistischen Griechisch der Konjunktiv Aorist des Finalsatzes durch das Futur ersetzt

---

27. Der von den Aposteln ausgelöste Gegensatz (4,1-4.21; 5,12-17) betrifft das Volk und seine Führer in Jerusalem.

28. J. JERVELL, *Die Apostelgeschichte* (KEK, 3), Göttingen, Vandenhoeck & Ruprecht, 1998, p. 628: »Zum vierten Mal in der Apg wird jetzt das Urteil über das ungläubige Israel gespochen: 7,51-53, wo Jerusalem angesprochen ist; 13,46: Kleinasien, 18,6: Griechenland. In allen diesen Fällen geht es um bestimmte geographische Bezirke … Jetzt aber ist das Urteil über das gesamte unbussfertige Judentum endgültig«.

29. So die Vermutung bei F. BOVON, »*Schön hat der heilige Geist durch den Propheten Jesaja zu euren Vätern gesprochen« (Act 28,25)*, in *ZNW* 75 (1984) 226-232, p. 230; B.J. KOET, *Five Studies on Interpretation of Scripture in Luke-Acts* (SNTA, 14), Leuven, University Press – Peeters, 1989, p. 129; DERS., *Simeons Worte* (n. 23), p. 1554; H. VAN DE SANDT, *Acts 28:28: No Salvation for the People of Israel? An Answer in the Perspective of the LXX*, in *ETL* 70 (1994) 341-358, p. 357.

30. Dem entspricht die Variante in E 33 81 2464 usw.

werden kann[31]. Das letzte Wort des Paulus ist offenbar auch die endgül-
tige Stellungnahme des Lukas zu den Juden: Nach seinem Eindruck sind
sie hoffnungslos zerstritten[32]. Und wenn er ihnen abschließend kundtut,
daß »dieses Heil Gottes« zu den Heiden gesandt wurde und diese es
auch annehmen (28,28 »sie werden auch hören«), dann spricht daraus
das Mitglied einer Kirche, die sich nicht nur – zwangsläufig – vom Tempel verabschiedet, sondern auch von der Synagoge getrennt hat[33] und
hauptsächlich aus Heidenchristen besteht[34].

b. Die Offenbarung der Gedanken

Sowohl διαλογισμός als auch διαλογίζομαι fehlen in der Apostelgeschichte. Die Weissagung v. 35b scheint sich, jedenfalls dem Wortlaut
nach, nur auf das Evangelium zu beziehen. Hier haben das Substantiv
und das Verbum mit Ausnahme von 1,29 durchweg negative Bedeutung[35]. Sie bezeichnen die falsche Vermutung »in den Herzen« des
Volkes (3,15), die ehrgeizigen Gedanken im »Herzen« seiner Jünger
(9,46 par Mk; 9,47 diff Mk) wie auch die Zweifel in ihrem »Herzen«
(24,38), die törichten, gottvergessenen Überlegungen des reichen Korn-
bauern (12,17) sowie vor allem die von Jesus durchschauten Gedanken
in den »Herzen« seiner Kritiker (5,21.22 par Mk; cf. 6,8 diff Mk; 11,17
par Mt)[36] und die mörderischen Pläne der bösen Winzer (20,14 diff Mk).

Vom menschlichen Herzen spricht die Apostelgeschichte dagegen oft,
positiv und negativ. Was Simeon die Gedanken der Herzen nennt, könnten hier – neben der Falschheit von Hananias und Saphira (5,3.4) und
der Verkehrtheit des Zauberers Simon (8,21.22) – vor allem die Ver-

31. So M. ZERWICK, *Biblical Greek*, §§ 340-342; BLASS-DEBRUNNER, *Grammatik*,
§ 442,2d mit n. 8. Beispiele: Der Wechsel Konj. Aor. – Futur begegnet nach μήποτε
auch Lk 12,58 (cf. Mt 5,25); 14,8f; Herm s IX 7,6, nach ἵνα Eph 6,3 (Zitat aus Ex 20,12;
Dtn 5,16, wo aber jeweils zweimal ἵνα mit Konj. Aor. steht); Joh 15,8 v.l.; Offb 22,14
(in umgekehrter Reihenfolge); Barn 4,3, nach ὅπως ἄν Röm 3,4 (Zitat von Ps 50,6 LXX,
wo zweimal der Konj. Aor. steht), ohne Konjunktion Mk 6,37. Das Futur allein nach ἵνα
findet sich Lk 14,10; Apg 21,24 (zweimal); 1 Kor 13,3 v.l.
32. Cf. H. CONZELMANN, *Die Apostelgeschichte* (HNT, 7), Tübingen, Mohr, ²1972,
p. 159.
33. Daß sich noch einzelne Juden bekehren, ist damit nicht ausgeschlossen; cf.
D. MARGUERAT, *The End of Acts (28.16-31) and the Rhetoric of Silence*, in S.E. PORTER
& T.H. OLBRICHT (eds.), *Rhetoric and the New Testament* (JSNT SS, 90), Sheffield, JSOT
Press, 1993, pp. 74-89, hier 86f.
34. Cf. S.G. WILSON, *The Gentiles and the Gentile Mission in Luke-Acts* (SNTS MS,
23), Cambridge, University Press, 1973, p. 232.
35. Cf. J. WINANDY, *La prophétie de Syméon (Lc, II, 34-35)*, in *RB* 72 (1965) 321-
351, p. 327; R.C. TANNEHILL, *Unity* (n. 12), pp. 43f.69.
36. Auf diese Gedanken der Gegner Jesu bezieht G. WASSERBERG, *Aus Israels Mitte –
Heil für die Welt. Eine narrativ-exegetische Studie zur Theologie des Lukas* (BZNW, 92),
Berlin – New York, de Gruyter, 1998, pp. 182f, Lk 2,35b.

stocktheit und der Zorn gegenüber Stephanus (7,51.54) sowie die Verschlossenheit gegenüber Paulus (28,27) sein[37]. Dazu würden dann auch die Eifersucht der Juden (5,17; 13,45 ζῆλος), ihr Widerspruch, ihr Unglaube und ihre Zerstrittenheit gehören. Den erstarrten, undurchdringlichen Herzen der ungläubigen (28,27) stünden die »durchbohrten« Herzen (2,37 κατενύγησαν τὴν καρδίαν) der am Pfingstfest bekehrten Juden gegenüber. Und das Gegenbild zur Spaltung der Juden (28,25) wäre die Gemeinde der Getauften, die »ein Herz und eine Seele« ist (4,32).

c. Fall und Aufstehen

Noch rätselhafter ist der Anfang von Simeons Weissagung mit der Verbindung von »Fall und Aufstehen vieler«. Wer sind die Fallenden, wer die Aufstehenden? Sind es jeweils dieselben oder verschiedene? Oder ist es ganz Israel, das zu Fall kommt und dann wieder aufgerichtet wird[38]? Weniger schwierig erscheint die Rede vom Fall für sich genommen. Danach werden an Jesus viele zu Fall kommen. Aber wer sind die Vielen? Wenn Lukas sonst vom Fallen spricht, bezieht er das öfter auf ein Haus. Das Haus aber kann für das Volk stehen, für das Haus Israel. Ganz allgemein vergleicht Lukas das Hören des Wortes ohne nachfolgendes Handeln, also das Hören ohne Begreifen, mit dem Bau eines Hauses, das eines Tages in einem gewaltigen Fall zusammenstürzt (Lk 6,49 συνέπεσεν ... ῥῆγμα ... μέγα). Auch die Metapher vom gespaltenen Reich, das verwüstet wird, so daß »Haus über Haus fällt« (11,17 diff Mk/Mt), bezieht sich zwar auf Beelzebul und die Dämonen, läßt aber im Zusammenhang der Meinungsverschiedenheiten gegenüber Jesus (11,14-16) auch an Israel denken, zumal Jesus kurz darauf im Blick auf Jerusalem von der kommenden Verödung des Hauses spricht (13,35 par Mt 23,38). Die Zerstörung Jerusalems, bei der »kein Stein auf dem anderen« bleiben wird (19,44), begründet Jesus mit der Blindheit der Stadt: »Wenn du doch erkannt hättest, was dir zum Frieden dient; nun aber ist es vor deinen Augen verborgen« (19,42). Längst bevor Jerusalem zerstört wird, ist Israel durch die Ablehnung Jesu zu Fall gekommen.

---

37. Cf. H. RÄISÄNEN, *Die Mutter Jesu im Neuen Testament* (AASF, B 247), Helsinki, Academia Scientiarum Fennica, ²1989, p. 130.

38. So etwa B.J. KOET, *Simeons Worte* (n. 23), p. 1563, mit Verweis auf Jes 51,17-23. Cf. die kurze Diskussion der Problematik bei M. WOLTER, *Israels Zukunft und die Parusieverzögerung bei Lukas*, in M. EVANG, H. MERKLEIN & M. WOLTER (eds.), *Eschatologie und Schöpfung*. FS E. Gräßer (BZNW, 89), Berlin – New York, de Gruyter, 1997, pp. 405-426, vor allem 410f.

Der heillose Zustand Israels in dieser Stunde ist wahrscheinlich gemeint, wenn Lukas Apg 15,16 von der »gefallenen Wohnung Davids« spricht. Aber dieser Fall ist nicht das letzte Wort. Gott baut das Haus aus seinen Trümmern wieder auf (ἀναστρέψω καὶ ἀνοικοδομήσω τὴν σκηνὴν Δαυὶδ τὴν πεπτωκυῖαν καὶ τὰ κατεσκαμμένα αὐτῆς ἀνοικοδομήσω καὶ ἀνορθώσω αὐτήν)[39]. Israel, das aus Unwissenheit gehandelt hat und gefallen ist, bekehrt sich zu Tausenden (Apg 2,41; 4,4; 21,20) und steht mit Gottes Hilfe wieder auf. Er baut das Haus größer als vorher. Denn Israel bewohnt es nun nicht mehr allein. Gott hat die Heiden mit in das erneuerte Haus Israel geladen (cf. Lk 14,23; cf. Apg 14,27), »ein Volk für seinen Namen aus den Heiden« (Apg 15,14; cf. 18,10). Aber es bleibt das Haus Israel, in dem die Heiden das Heil finden (15,17), und das ist sein »Ruhm« vor allen Völkern, wie Simeon ihn geschaut hat.

III. Fragen zum Schluss

Mit den letzten Hinweisen schließt sich zwar der Kreis unserer Beobachtungen, und wir können an die großen Heilsweissagungen des Dankliedes anknüpfen; aber die Schwierigkeiten sind nicht ausgeräumt. Im Gegenteil, der Widerspruch ist noch deutlicher geworden.

In Jerusalem sind schließlich Zehntausende bekehrt (Apg 21,20), und doch wird Paulus dort von den Juden fast umgebracht (21,27-31). Auch in der Diaspora stehen sich jüdische Gefolgschaft und Verfolgung des Paulus gegenüber. Einerseits wird das Haus Davids glorreich wieder aufgerichtet, andererseits erscheint das Volk Gottes in heilloser Verstocktheit. Einerseits eröffnet Petrus feierlich nach Gottes Plan die Heidenmission, andererseits begibt sich Paulus mehrmals erst nach der Ablehnung bei den Juden, obwohl sich auch viele von ihnen bekehrt haben, auf den Weg zu den Heiden.

Lukas scheint sich auf zwei Ebenen zu bewegen, wobei er jeweils eine Perspektive absolut setzt, ohne bei seiner Wertung zu differenzieren[40]. Das eine wäre der Rückblick des Historikers auf den Verlauf des Jesusgeschehens und die Anfänge der Missionsgeschichte, wie sie vor

---

39. Dieser Text steht in der Mitte des Abschnitts 15,1-35 und des ganzen Buches. Zu seiner formalen Gestaltung mit Parallelismen und Chiasmen cf. W. RADL, *Rettung in Israel*, in FS G. Schneider (n. 1), pp. 43-60, hier 55.

40. Cf. G. WASSERBERG, *Aus Israels Mitte* (n. 36), pp. 94f: Lukas macht Apg 13 und 28 jeweils den jüdischen Widerspruch zum Thema und blendet das andere aus. So kann er Paulus mit dem Jes-Zitat in Kap. 28 seine ganze Erfahrung als Judenmissionar zusammenfassen lassen, und zwar an wichtiger Stelle, als letztes Wort (p. 93).

allem im Licht der zu seiner Zeit vollzogenen Trennung von der Synagoge erscheinen, verbunden mit einer scharfen Verurteilung des jüdischen Widerstands gegen die paulinische Mission, den auch Paulus
selbst bezeugt (1 Thess 2,15f). Das andere wäre das Bild des Theologen
Lukas, der den unglaublichen Vorgang der Erneuerung des Hauses Israel
und seiner Öffnung für die Heidenvölker als Gottes heilsgeschichtliches
Walten beschreibt und verherrlicht. Beide Sichtweisen sind bereits in der
Vision Simeons angelegt. Die letztere hat wahrscheinlich erst Lukas ein-
getragen.

Watzmannstraße 5   Walter RADL
D-86368 Gersthofen

LE MESSIANISME DE JÉSUS

LE RAPPORT ANNONCE/ACCOMPLISSEMENT ENTRE LC 1,35 ET AC 2,33

L'unité théologique de Luc et des Actes des Apôtres, voire leur complémentarité, est généralement reconnue dans le monde des études lucaniennes. En raison de cette unité/complémentarité, il convient d'aborder les grands axes de la théologie de Luc dans une perspective globale. Le thème du messianisme[1] de Jésus, un de ces grands axes, doit donc être appréhendé en tenant compte de la continuité entre les deux livres. L'objet du présent article est précisément d'examiner ce thème en faisant ressortir le rapport établi entre ses deux pôles d'expression, soit l'annonce du messianisme en Lc 1,35 et sa proclamation en Ac 2,33. On vérifiera, à cette fin, l'hypothèse suivante: Les deux énoncés contenus respectivement en Lc 1,35 et en Ac 2,33 s'inscrivent dans un rapport de complémentarité: le premier identifie la nature du messianisme de Jésus, en terme de messianisme pneumatique; le deuxième confirme cette identification. Voici les libellés de ces deux proclamations:

> Lc 1,35: L'Esprit Saint (sur)viendra sur toi et la puissance du Très-Haut te couvrira de son ombre; et c'est pourquoi le Saint qui doit naître (étant naissant) sera appelé fils de Dieu.
> Ac 2,33: Exalté à la droite de Dieu, il a donc reçu du Père l'Esprit Saint promis et il a répandu ce que, vous, vous voyez et vous entendez.

La démonstration de l'hypothèse adoptera un parcours en trois étapes: premièrement, elle fera ressortir, en recourant au texte d'Ac 2,22-36, que Jésus n'est fait Messie qu'à la résurrection; deuxièmement, elle établira, en observant l'expérience de la communauté primitive, que le type de messianisme exercé par Jésus est bien d'ordre pneumatique; troisièmement, elle montrera, en scrutant le texte du récit de l'Annonciation, que ce type de messianisme était déjà annoncé en Lc 1,35.

---

1. Dans cet article, le terme messianisme fait exclusivement référence à la fonction royale. À noter que J.J. COLLINS, *The Scepter and the Star. The Messiahs of the Dead Sea Scrolls and Other Ancient Literature*, New York, Doubleday, 1995, pp. 195-209, distingue quatre paradigmes messianiques dans le judaïsme au tournant de l'ère chrétienne: royal, sacerdotal, prophétique et céleste.

I. Jésus fait Messie à la résurrection

Le texte d'Ac 2,22-36 montre sans équivoque que, dans l'œuvre de Luc, l'investiture messianique de Jésus n'advient qu'à sa résurrection[2]. De nombreux auteurs continuent pourtant de la situer au baptême[3], ou même à la conception[4]. Nous reviendrons implicitement, dans la troisième partie de cet article, sur la dernière position. Quant à celle qui situe l'investiture au baptême, rappelons qu'elle s'appuie ordinairement sur le choix, en Lc 3,22, de la citation scripturaire favorisant le texte occidental, celle tirée du psaume messianique par excellence, le Ps 2,7: «Tu es mon fils, moi, aujourd'hui, je t'ai engendré»[5].

La parole céleste, selon le texte occidental ne laisse effectivement aucun doute quant à la nature messianique de l'investiture liée à l'événement du baptême. Par contre, l'option en faveur du texte oriental, qui adapte une citation d'Is 42,1 («Tu es mon fils; en toi je prends plaisir»)[6], ouvre la voie à une interprétation de type prophétique. Il faut toutefois préciser que cette version n'exclurait pas, elle non plus, la possibilité d'une lecture messianique si, comme plusieurs le prétendent, elle fusionnait une partie du Ps 2,7a («Tu es mon fils») et une partie d'Is 42,1b («en toi je prends plaisir»)[7]. Il est cependant loin d'être acquis que la tradition originale ait vraiment contenu cette fusion. Il se pourrait très bien, au contraire, qu'elle ait tout simplement cité Is 42,1: «Voici

2. Comp. J.A. Fitzmyer, *The Gospel According to Luke. A New Translation with Introduction and Commentary* (Anchor Bible, 28A), Garden City, NY, Doubleday, 1985, p. 485.

3. Entre autres, F. Bovon, *L'évangile selon saint Luc 1–9* (Commentaire du Nouveau Testament, 3a), Genève, Labor et Fides, 1991, p. 177; H. Cousin, *L'évangile selon saint Luc* (Commentaires), Paris, Centurion, 1993, p. 58; J.D.G. Dunn, *Baptism in the Holy Spirit. A Re-examination of the New Testament Teaching on the Gift of the Spirit in Relation to Pentecostalism Today*, London, SCM, 1973 (1970), p. 27; I.H. Marshall, *Commentary on Luke*, Grand Rapids, Eerdmans, 1986, p. 155; P.-G. Müller, *Lukas-Evangelium* (SKK, 3), Stuttgart, Katholisches Bibelwerk, 1986 (1984), p. 49; H. Schürmann, *Das Lukasevangelium. Kommentar zur Kap. 1,1–9,50* (HTK, 3/1), Freiburg, Herder, 1969, pp. 194-195; R.H. Stein, *Luke* (The New American Commentary, 24), Nashville, Broadman, 1992, p. 58; M.L. Strauss, *The Davidic Messiah in Luke-Acts. The Promise and its Fulfillment in Lukan Christology* (JSNT SS, 110), Sheffield, Academic Press, 1995, pp. 203-208.

4. Entre autres, L. Sabourin, *L'Évangile de Luc. Introduction et commentaire*, Roma, Editrice Pontificia Universita Gregoriana, 1985, pp. 120-121; A. Stöger, *L'évangile selon Luc*, Paris, Desclée, 1968, pp. 124-125.

5. Leçon appuyée par D, it, Ju, Meth, Hil, Aug.

6. Leçon appuyée par P[4], ℵ, A, B, W, f[1], f[13], 28, 33.

7. Parmi ceux-là, F. Bovon, *L'évangile selon Luc*, p. 177; I.H. Marshall, *Commentary on Luke*, p. 155. Par contre, J.A. Fitzmyer, *Luke*, pp. 485-486, conteste l'idée d'une telle fusion.

mon serviteur, en qui j'ai mis mon plaisir». Mais comme serviteur peut se dire παῖς ou δοῦλος et fils peut se dire παῖς ou υἱός, il est bien possible qu'au fil du développement de la christologie, on ait jugé plus convenable d'utiliser υἱός pour désigner Jésus, en considération de l'importance accordée à sa filiation divine. Le παῖς d'Isaïe[8] aurait alors été remplacé par le υἱός[9], que l'on retrouve dans la tradition synoptique sur le baptême[10]. La tradition originale aurait pu, dans ce cas, citer Is 42,1, avec l'intention de faire du baptême l'occasion de l'investiture prophétique de Jésus. Par contre, l'argument le plus solide en faveur de l'originalité de la leçon orientale, qui citerait exclusivement Is 42,1, tire son appui de l'organisation christologique du double ouvrage. Tout au long de son évangile, Luc a en effet clairement présenté un Jésus jouant le rôle de prophète durant son ministère terrestre[11]. Pour y arriver, il a dû s'adonner à un travail rédactionnel considérable comme en font foi les multiples remaniements, les ajouts et les omissions, ainsi que ses propres créations[12]. Des rétrospectives du livre des Actes sur la carrière terrestre de Jésus, dont celles de Ac 3,22-23 et 7,37, confirment d'ailleurs cette volonté de l'hagiographe de le présenter comme prophète:

> Moïse a dit, en effet: «Le Seigneur Dieu vous suscitera d'entre vos frères un prophète comme moi (…) Quiconque n'écoutera pas ce prophète sera retranché du peuple».
> C'est lui, Moïse, qui a dit aux Israélites: «Ce Dieu vous suscitera d'entre vos frères un prophète comme moi».

Une interprétation messianique de l'investiture au baptême irait donc à l'encontre de la critique interne tout autant que de la critique externe. Comment alors expliquer qu'une telle interprétation soit retenue par un aussi grand nombre d'auteurs? Serait-ce imputable à une lecture non révisée du troisième évangile où on a pris pour acquis que le messianisme de Jésus y était déjà affirmé? Ou bien à l'habitude encore tenace de lire le troisième évangile comme une entité indépendante du livre des Actes des Apôtres? Un passage probant des Actes ne laisse pourtant aucun doute quant au moment de l'accession de Jésus au trône messia-

---

8. Le texte de la Septante, en Is 42,1, utilise παῖς et non δοῦλος.

9. Voir à ce sujet F. GILS, *Jésus prophète d'après les évangiles synoptiques*, Louvain, Publications universitaires, 1957, pp. 56ss.

10. La substitution des titres avait probablement déjà eu lieu au niveau de la tradition orale.

11. J.A. FITZMYER, *Luke*, p. 486, croit, pour sa part, que la parole du baptême identifie Jésus au Serviteur de Yahvé et lui confère ce rôle.

12. En ce qui concerne ce travail rédactionnel de Luc en vue de faire ressortir le statut de Jésus prophète, voir O. MAINVILLE, *L'Esprit dans l'œuvre de Luc* (Héritage et projet, 45), Montréal, Fides, 1991, pp. 218-230.

nique: il s'agit de cet extrait, en Ac 2,22-36, du discours pentecostal de
Pierre à Jérusalem[13], comme le démontre ce qui suit.

Après avoir accusé les Israélites d'être responsables de la crucifixion
de Jésus en dépit de son accréditation par Dieu (vv. 22-23), Pierre
affirme que Dieu l'a ressuscité, le délivrant du pouvoir de la mort (v.
24). Il bâtit alors sa preuve sur la base de deux témoignages: le témoignage posthume de David et le témoignage direct des disciples eux-
mêmes. Le premier, qui se joue à deux niveaux, tire sa validation du statut de prophète (v. 30) reconnu ici à David. Tout d'abord, Pierre cite le
Ps 16,8-11, selon la version de la Septante, dans lequel David avait
exprimé sa confiance que Dieu n'abandonnerait pas son Saint à la
décomposition[14]. Mais l'ancêtre ne peut certainement pas avoir parlé à
son propre sujet, précise Pierre, puisque la présence de son tombeau est
justement un rappel de sa décomposition (v. 29). De cet argument éliminatoire à la défaveur de David surgit alors l'argument implicite à la
faveur de Jésus: David a donc parlé de Jésus. Or, si David a pu prédire
une telle chose au sujet de Jésus, c'est qu'il était prophète (v. 30). Mais
en plus d'être prophète, il savait que Dieu avait promis de faire asseoir
sur son trône quelqu'un de sa descendance. De ces deux dernières données – la science prophétique de David et la connaissance de la promesse de Dieu à l'égard de son trône – Pierre tire la conclusion qu'il a
vu d'avance la résurrection de Jésus (vv. 30-31). Ce syllogisme tronqué
nous apprend donc que, dans l'optique de David prophète, la résurrection était un préalable à la session sur le trône. Voilà la première partie
de la preuve appuyée sur le témoignage de David.

La deuxième partie s'appuiera sur le témoignage des disciples. Ces
derniers confirment non seulement la réalité de la résurrection (v. 32)
mais aussi celle de l'accession au trône (v. 33). À nouveau, Luc recourt
au même *pattern* rhétorique: Pierre évoque le témoignage de David en
citant le Ps 110,1 sur la session à la droite de Dieu (vv. 34-35); puis il
précise, une fois de plus, que David ne peut avoir parlé à son propre
sujet puisqu'il n'est pas monté au ciel (v. 34a), son tombeau en faisant
foi. Ainsi, le mouvement de la preuve va encore une fois de l'argument
éliminatoire à l'argument implicite. La péricope se termine enfin par une
proclamation solennelle de Pierre, et de la seigneurie et du messianisme
de Jésus (v. 36).

La trajectoire du texte va donc de l'affirmation de la résurrection de
Jésus à l'affirmation de son exaltation, sur la base du double témoignage

---

13. Voir en ce sens le commentaire de J.B. POLHILL, *Acts* (The New American Commentary, 26), Nashville, Broadman, 1992, pp. 111-116.
14. Le texte hébreu parlait de la «fosse» et non de la «décomposition».

de David, interprété par Pierre et confirmé par le témoignage même des disciples. La structure de la péricope vise clairement à faire ressortir la concomitance des événements de la résurrection et de l'intronisation de Jésus:

24 Attestation par Pierre de la résurrection de Jésus.

25-29 Témoignage de David anticipant la résurrection de Jésus.

30-31 Interprétation par Pierre du témoignage de David en terme d'annonce du moment de l'intronisation de Jésus.

32 Témoignage des disciples confirmant celui de David sur l'authenticité de la résurrection de Jésus[15].

33 Témoignage des disciples confirmant à l'avance celui de David sur l'exaltation de Jésus[16].

34a Interprétation anticipée par Pierre du témoignage de David sur l'exaltation de Jésus.

34b-35 Témoignage de David sur l'exaltation de Jésus

36 Proclamation solennelle par Pierre de l'exaltation de Jésus.

Pour la démonstration qu'il comptait faire, Luc a introduit un procédé qui lui est bien familier et qui consiste à mettre en scène des personnages qui témoignent en faveur d'un protagoniste et qui interprètent les révélations de Dieu à son sujet. Cette technique littéraire est évidente dans les deux premiers chapitres de son évangile où des personnages parlent et s'agitent autour de la naissance de Jésus. De la même manière, dans le discours de la Pentecôte, Pierre devient l'interprète des révélations de Dieu à l'endroit de Jésus. Mais l'astuce de Luc est, cette fois, remarquable: il amène sur la même scène le premier et le dernier de la dynastie, en l'occurrence David et Jésus, faisant témoigner le premier en faveur du dernier. Le statut de prophète de David cautionne la valeur de son témoignage. Mais comme le prophète Jean le Baptiste s'est effacé devant Jésus qui amorçait son ministère prophétique, le roi David s'efface à son tour devant le Christ qui amorce son règne.

Enfin, il est important de rappeler que le discours de Paul à Antioche (Ac 13,26-41) corrobore celui de Pierre à Jérusalem quant au moment de l'entrée en vigueur du messianisme de Jésus. Il adopte, de façon plus succincte, un parcours analogue à celui de Pierre: Jérusalem et ses chefs ont fait exécuter Jésus (vv. 27-29), mais Dieu l'a ressuscité (v. 30) comme le confirment ceux à qui il est apparu (v. 31). La promesse faite aux pères, celle comprise dans le Ps 2,7 (v. 33b), Dieu l'a accomplie en

---

15. La confirmation s'appuie, ici, sur ce qui a déjà été dit, dans les versets qui précèdent, au sujet du témoignage de David.

16. La confirmation anticipe, cette fois, ce qui va être dit, dans les versets qui suivent, au sujet du témoignage de David.

ressuscitant Jésus (v. 33a)[17], affirme Paul. À nouveau, l'orateur recourt au témoignage de David, en citant le passage du Ps 16,10, et en spécifiant qu'il ne peut s'appliquer à David, puisque celui-ci a connu la décomposition (v. 36), tandis que celui que Dieu a ressuscité n'a pas connu la décomposition (v. 37).

Les propos de Paul confirment donc ceux de Pierre quant au moment de l'intronisation royale de Jésus. Luc réitère au monde païen ce qu'il a d'abord adressé au monde juif, universalisant alors la portée de sa proclamation. Cette double attestation ne laisse donc aucun doute sur la volonté de Luc de situer l'avènement du messianisme de Jésus à sa résurrection. Mais comment Jésus exerce-t-il ce messianisme?

II. Un messianisme pneumatique

La proclamation de l'exaltation de Jésus, Christ, au sommet du premier discours de Pierre venait, en réalité, interpréter l'événement de clôture du troisième évangile (24,51-53), à nouveau relaté au début des Actes (1,9-11), celui de l'Ascension. Dans la cohérence cosmologique de l'époque, la session du Christ à la droite de Dieu présupposait, en effet, une montée. Luc n'a pas manqué d'en faire une description événementielle[18]. Ayant ainsi solidement attesté la seigneurie du Christ, il fallait ensuite rendre compte à la fois de la nature de son règne et de son mode d'exercice. La suite narrative du livre des Actes répond à cette double nécessité.

Le règne de Jésus, selon la perspective lucanienne, s'exerce à l'intérieur des frontières de la communauté ecclésiale; des frontières qui, cependant, ne cessent de s'élargir au rythme de la poussée missionnaire. Mais il s'agit d'un règne spirituel et universel qui dépasse les limites temporelles et politiques; ce qui, en conséquence, marque un décalage par rapport au règne traditionnel de la dynastie davidique. En effet, la communauté est essentiellement sous la motion de l'Esprit. Le messianisme de Jésus est à caractère pneumatique; une simple observation de la vie ecclésiale de la première communauté le démontre clairement.

17. L'ensemble du verset 33 se lit comme suit: «(La promesse faites à nos pères), Dieu l'a accomplie pour nous, leurs enfants, en ressuscitant Jésus, tout comme il est écrit au psaume second: Tu es mon fils, moi, aujourd'hui, je t'ai engendré». Le seul fait que Luc, par l'intermédiaire de Paul, cite le Ps 2,7 pour appuyer une promesse de Dieu, qui devait s'accomplir à la résurrection de Jésus et qui devait, par la même occasion, définir sa fonction devenant effective à ce moment-là, exclut la possibilité qu'il ait utilisé ce même psaume à son baptême où était alors définie sa fonction terrestre.

18. D'autres passages du Nouveau Testament font état de cette montée sans toutefois en faire une description événementielle: Jn 20,17; 1 P 3,22; Ep 4,10; 1 Tm 3,16.

En partant, le récit de la Pentecôte (Ac 2,1-4) vient identifier ce dynamisme qui donne le coup d'envoi à la communauté, soit celui de l'Esprit. Par la suite, tout se déroule sous l'égide de l'Esprit. En effet, l'Esprit cautionne le discours des croyants (2,14-36.38-39; 4,8-12.19-20; 4,31; 7,2-53; 9,17.19b-20); il collabore avec la communauté (5,32; 15,28); on ne doit cependant pas s'y opposer (5,3.9; 7,51); il conduit l'évangélisation au-delà des frontières juives, chez les Samaritains d'abord (8,15-17), puis chez Corneille, le craignant-Dieu (10,19.44-48; 11,15-17) et enfin, dans le vaste monde païen (13,2-4; 15,28; 16,6-7).

La gouverne est donc assumée par l'Esprit; mais il s'agit bien de l'Esprit de Jésus, Christ, comme le proclame sans équivoque Ac 2,33[19]. Ce passage renseigne d'ailleurs sur la condition du règne et son mode d'exercice. Il révèle, d'une part, que le don de l'Esprit au Ressuscité par Dieu est la condition *sine qua non* à l'exercice du règne (2,33a), et d'autre part, que l'exercice de ce règne se réalise par l'effusion de l'Esprit sur la communauté par le Ressuscité (2,33b).

On sait cependant, à la lumière des recherches contemporaines[20], que le fil narratif des Actes répond davantage à une préoccupation d'ordre théologique qu'historique. On ne saurait, en conséquence, attribuer une cote d'historicité absolue aux données de ce livre. On peut plutôt penser, considérant la date probable de sa rédaction (vers 85), que Luc a surtout cherché à expliquer une réalité, celle de l'expansion fulgurante de l'Église, «jusqu'aux extrémités de la terre» (Ac 1,8) au cours des quelques décennies qui ont suivi la résurrection du Christ; une réalité qui ne peut certes pas être imputable aux seuls mérites des missionnaires chrétiens. On l'attribue alors à la présence du Christ, agissant par la puissance de son Esprit. Pour parler de cette présence efficace du Ressuscité, Luc montrera que ses œuvres se prolongent dans la mission des disciples[21]. Or, comme cette puissance n'a cessé d'agir en eux et par eux depuis les tout débuts, force est de reconnaître que le Christ les a investis de son Esprit dès le départ. Le récit étiologique de la Pentecôte (Ac 2,1-21) rend compte de cette réalité. Ainsi, l'expérience de la puissance du Res-

---

19. Une seule occurrence des Actes (16,7), il est vrai, mentionne explicitement que l'Esprit est celui de Jésus; mais la clarté de la proclamation en Ac 2,33 ne requérait aucune attestation supplémentaire.

20. Surtout depuis le tournant marqué par le livre de H. CONZELMANN, *Die Mitte der Zeit. Studien zur Theologie des Lukas*, Tübingen, Mohr, 1953.

21. Tout comme Jésus a été baptisé dans l'Esprit (Lc 3,22), aussi le sont les disciples à la Pentecôte (Ac 2,1-4); tout comme le discours de Jésus à la synagogue (Lc 4,16ss) a été accrédité par un signe (Lc 4,33ss), aussi le discours de Pierre à la Pentecôte est-il suivi d'un signe (Ac 3,1-10), comme le sera également celui de Paul à Antioche (discours: Ac 13,17-41; signe: 14,8-11).

suscité à l'œuvre a donc amené les croyants à reconnaître en lui le Messie; mais à reconnaître aussi la forme tout à fait inattendue de l'exercice de son règne. Le parcours de foi de la communauté primitive est donc allé de l'expérience à la proclamation[22].

Il fallait toutefois inscrire l'expérience chrétienne dans le sillage de la tradition juive. Luc a alors trouvé, dans le langage du prophète Joël, les mots propres à traduire le phénomène pneumatique observé dans la communauté: «En ces jours-là, je répandrai mon Esprit sur toute chair. Alors vos fils et vos filles prophétiseront» (Jl 3,1 cité en Ac 2,17). Mais cette lecture était-elle légitime, considérant que la prophétie de Joël n'émanait pas d'un contexte messianique? Comment pouvait-elle, de quelque manière, être greffée à l'espérance davidique[23]? La prophétie d'Is 11,1-2[24], où le don de l'Esprit est clairement lié à l'avènement messianique, a très certainement servi à établir le pont nécessaire. Car même si Luc n'y réfère pas explicitement, elle est présupposée dans la proclamation d'Ac 2,33a. La deuxième partie du verset, Ac 2,33b, montre alors comment la condition pneumatique du Messie se prolonge au cœur de l'Église. Ainsi, la prophétie d'Is 11,1-2 répondait, du côté du Messie lui-même, à l'exigence posée par le caractère inédit du messianisme éprouvé, tandis que la prophétie de Jl 3,1 répondait à cette même exigence, mais du côté de la communauté. Par ailleurs, Luc ne pouvait faire autrement que de tenir compte de ce caractère inédit du messianisme quand il a anticipé celui de Jésus dans le récit de l'Annonciation.

III. DE L'ANNONCE À L'ACCOMPLISSEMENT: DE LC 1,35 À AC 2,33

Avant d'établir le rapport annonce/accomplissement entre Lc 1,35 et Ac 2,33, dans la cohérence globale de l'œuvre de Luc, il faut d'abord considérer la proclamation de Lc 1,35 dans son contexte littéraire immédiat du récit de l'Annonciation et, plus spécifiquement, au cœur de la révélation de l'ange, aux versets 31-35 de ce récit.

---

22. Voir à cet égard, O. MAINVILLE, *De l'expérience de l'Esprit au messianisme de Jésus*, in R. DAVID (éd.), *Faut-il attendre le Messie? Études sur le messianisme* (Sciences bibliques, 5), Montréal, Médiaspaul, 1998, pp. 95-109.

23. Même si on était loin de l'univocité, les divers modes d'expression des attentes messianiques juives regroupaient néanmoins quelques paramètres communs: par exemple, le messianisme devrait être de portée nationale; il devrait s'inscrire dans l'histoire d'Israël; il devrait aussi être lié à la fonction politique.

24. «Un rameau surgira de la souche de Jessé; un rejeton sortira de ses racines. Sur lui reposera mon Esprit».

La similitude terminologique de l'oracle contenu au verset 31 avec les oracles vétérotestamentaires de naissance, dont ceux de Gn 17,19[25], Jg 13,5[26] et Is 7,14, a été depuis longtemps observée. La parenté verbale avec Is 7,14 est particulièrement marquée, comme le démontre le parallélisme suivant:

Is 7,14	Lc 1,31
ἰδοὺ ἡ παρθένος ἐν γαστρὶ ἕξει καὶ τέξεται υἱὸν καὶ καλέσεις τὸ ὄνομα αὐτοῦ Εμμανουηλ.	καὶ ἰδοὺ συλλήμψῃ ἐν γαστρὶ καὶ τέξῃ υἱὸν καὶ καλέσεις τὸ ὄνομα αὐτοῦ Ἰησοῦν.
Voici que la jeune femme est enceinte et enfantera un fils et tu l'appelleras du nom d'Emmanuel.	Et voici que tu concevras et tu enfanteras un fils et tu l'appelleras du nom de Jésus.

L'option de Luc en faveur du modèle d'Is 7,14, à teneur messianique, est indicative de l'orientation théologique que Luc veut donner à la révélation. Il faut donc en tenir compte dans l'interprétation de la suite du contenu verbal aux versets 32-35, où l'ange dévoile la mission du personnage qui fait l'objet de la révélation. Son message se partage en deux temps bien distincts: vv. 32-33 et v. 35. La facture messianique de la première partie du message (vv. 32-33) est évidente, comme en font foi les rapprochements avec l'oracle de Nathan illustrés dans le tableau suivant[27]:

2 S 7,9-16	Lc 1,32-33
Je te donnerai un *grand* nom. Il sera pour moi un *fils*.	Il sera *grand* et sera appelé *Fils* du Très Haut.
J'affermirai *pour toujours* son *trône royal*.	Le Seigneur Dieu lui donnera le *trône* de son père David
Ta *maison* et ton *règne* sera affermi *pour toujours*.	Il régnera sur la *maison* de Jacob *pour toujours* et son *règne* sera *sans fin*.

La valeur fonctionnelle, en terme messianique, du titre *Fils du Très Haut*, au verset 32, est attestée par son association au trône de David.

---

25. Ἰδοὺ Σαρρα ἡ γυνή σου τέξεταί σοι υἱόν, καὶ καλέσεις τὸ ὄνομα αὐτοῦ Ισαακ – «Voilà que Sara, ta femme, t'enfantera un fils et tu l'appelleras du nom d'Isaac». Cette formulation est reprise dans l'annonce à Zacharie en Lc 1,13.

26. Ἰδοὺ σὺ ἐν γαστρὶ ἕξεις καὶ τέξῃ υἱόν – «Voici que tu vas concevoir et enfanter un fils».

27. Nous adaptons le tableau de L. LEGRAND, *L'Annonce à Marie* (LD, 106), Paris, Cerf, 1981, p. 56.

Cette association, d'une part, révèle la nature du rôle que l'Annoncé aura à exercer, en l'occurrence, un rôle messianique; d'autre part, elle place son règne futur dans la lignée historique de la dynastie davidique. Cependant, l'introduction, dans la troisième partie du parallélisme, de οὐκ ἔσται τέλος pointe vers l'importante distinction qui devra être faite entre le messianisme de Jésus et celui des autres successeurs de David. En effet, en 2 Samuel, c'est la dynastie de David qui durera toujours, alors qu'en Luc, c'est le règne de l'Annoncé qui sera sans fin. L'attention est donc déplacée de la pérennité de la dynastie de David à la pérennité du règne d'un seul de ses descendants, Jésus. Luc a ainsi tracé une ligne de démarcation, annonçant déjà l'inédit du règne anticipé. Mais il fallait absolument préciser la spécificité de ce règne. Luc répond à cet impératif dans le deuxième volet du message de l'ange.

Tout d'abord (v. 34), Marie réagit à l'annonce de l'ange: «Comment cela se fera-t-il puisque je ne connais pas d'homme?». À cela l'ange répond (v. 35):

Πνεῦμα ἅγιον ἐπελεύσεται ἐπὶ σὲ καὶ δύναμις ὑψίστου ἐπισκιάσει σοι· διὸ καὶ τὸ γεννώμενον ἅγιον κληθήσεται υἱὸς θεοῦ.

L'Esprit Saint (sur)viendra sur toi et la puissance du Très-Haut te couvrira de son ombre; et c'est pourquoi le Saint qui doit naître (étant naissant) sera appelé fils de Dieu[28].

Cette réponse de l'ange est tout à fait étonnante puisqu'elle transpose au plan théologique une question d'ordre biologique[29]. Autrement dit, elle n'apporte pas de solution au problème soulevé par Marie; ce qui fera dire à certains auteurs que cette question n'est rien de plus qu'un artifice littéraire en vue de paver la voie à l'annonce du verset suivant[30]. La réponse de l'ange n'a effectivement rien à voir avec la préoccupation d'engendrement véhiculée par la question de Marie, comme l'ont démontré les études antérieures. Une simple révision de la teneur terminologique de la première partie de cette réponse suffira.

---

28. La deuxième partie du verset est difficile à traduire; elle pourrait encore être rendue par: «celui qui va naître sera appelé saint et fils de Dieu»; «celui qui va naître sera saint et sera appelé Fils de Dieu»; «celui qui va naître sera appelé saint, fils de Dieu». Voir à ce sujet la discussion de R.E. BROWN, *The Birth of the Messiah. Commentary on the Infancy Narratives in Matthew and Luke*, Garden City, NY, Doubleday, 1977, pp. 291-292. Quant à notre choix de traduction, (le Saint), il s'éclaire à partir de l'usage que Luc fait de ce titre dans les Actes (infra).

29. Voir L. LEGRAND, *L'Annonce à Marie*, p. 24.

30. C'est l'opinion de J. GEWIESS, *Die Marienfrage Lk 1,34*, in *BZ* 5 (1961) 221-254; aussi R.E. BROWN, *The Birth of the Messiah*, p. 308 et J.A. FITZMYER, *Luke*, p. 348.

Les verbes ἐπέρχομαι ἐπί (survenir sur) et ἐπισκιάζω (couvrir de son ombre) ne revêtent, nulle part dans la Bible, de connotation d'engendrement. On retrouve le premier verbe à quelques reprises dans l'Ancien Testament. En Is 32,15, il est question du *souffle* de Dieu qui *viendra sur* Israël (ἕως ἂν ἐπέλθη ἐφ᾽ ὑμᾶς πνεῦμα ἀφ᾽ ὑψηλοῦ), ce qui est, ici, une intervention favorable de Dieu à l'endroit de son peuple. Il est cependant intéressant de noter que Dieu intervient par l'intermédiaire de son πνεῦμα[31]. En Luc et Actes, le verbe est employé six autres fois[32], mais sans jamais véhiculer l'idée d'engendrement. Une des occurrences, celle en Ac 1,8, est toutefois très signifiante puisqu'il est question de *l'Esprit Saint* qui *viendra sur* les disciples pour les rendre aptes à témoigner. Il vient donc sur eux en vue de la mission à accomplir, ou du rôle à jouer. Quant au deuxième verbe, ἐπισκιάζω, il évoque, dans l'Ancien Testament[33], la protection de Dieu à l'égard du peuple. Il n'est employé dans le Nouveau Testament que quatre autres fois: en Lc 9,34 (et les parallèles synoptiques dans le récit de la transfiguration) et en Ac 5,15 (pour désigner l'ombre de Pierre touchant les malades).

Il n'est pas nécessaire d'élaborer davantage sur la portée des verbes ἐπέρχομαι et ἐπισκιάζω puisque les auteurs reconnaissent unanimement qu'ils ne recèlent pas de connotation d'engendrement. Il semble donc avisé d'éclairer leur utilisation en Lc 1,35 à la lumière des indications sémantiques fournies par les Écritures. Conséquemment, il faut conclure en toute logique que l'Esprit Saint, en Lc 1,35, ne joue pas le rôle de géniteur. On peut ajouter, en corollaire, que l'objectif de Luc, en faisant intervenir l'Esprit, ne vise pas l'affirmation de la conception virginale[34]. Quel est donc le rôle de l'Esprit?

Notons tout d'abord la formulation du v. 35; elle est expressément voulue en deux temps:

1) l'énoncé d'un fait: «L'Esprit saint (sur)viendra sur toi et la puissance du Très Haut te couvrira de son ombre».
2) la conséquence de ce fait: «c'est pourquoi le Saint qui doit naître sera appelé Fils de Dieu».

31. Voir aussi Nb 5,4; Jb 1,19; 4,15.
32. Lc 11,22; 21,26; Ac 1,8; 8,24; 13,40; 14,19. On retrouve ce verbe deux autres fois dans le Nouveau Testament: Ep 2,7 et Ja 5,1.
33. Ex 25,20; 40,35; Nb 10,34; Dt 32,12; Ps 91,4.
34. L'étude du genre littéraire «annonce de naissance» a démontré que les données véhiculées par cette forme n'avaient pas valeur d'historicité. Les parallèles vétérotestamentaires et extra-bibliques montrent, en effet, que le recours à ce genre ainsi que l'évocation d'interventions divines dans la conception d'un enfant n'ont rien à dire sur la conception biologique elle-même, mais visent plutôt à glorifier la grandeur du personnage concerné et à définir le rôle qu'il aura à jouer dans l'histoire. C'est donc sous l'angle théologique qu'il faut aussi lire les récits entourant la naissance de Jésus.

Comme on peut l'observer, le rôle de l'Esprit ne se comprend qu'en lien avec le deuxième volet du verset, en raison du rapport de cause à effet établi par le διό (c'est pourquoi) placé à la charnière des deux parties du verset. En raison du διό effectivement, la proclamation contenue dans la deuxième partie est conséquente de l'intervention de l'Esprit attestée dans la première. Cette intervention a un impact direct et sur la condition et sur la fonction de celui qui va naître.

En ce qui concerne sa condition, il faut spécifier que Luc réserve le titre Saint, utilisé comme substantif et sans adjonction, au Christ ressuscité. En effet, c'est dans un déploiement christologique d'exaltation qu'il est utilisé, en Ac 2,27, dans le discours de Pierre et qu'il est repris, en Ac 13,35, dans le discours de Paul («Tu ne laisseras pas ton Saint connaître la décomposition»). On le retrouve à nouveau dans le deuxième discours de Pierre, en Ac 3,14, cette fois jumelé au titre Juste: «Vous avez rejeté le Saint et le Juste… Le Prince de la vie que vous avez fait mourir, Dieu l'a ressuscité». L'association du titre Saint au statut messianique de Jésus est, ici, explicite comme on peut le lire quelques versets plus loin (v. 18): «Dieu avait annoncé d'avance… que son Messie souffrirait». Enfin, en Ac 4,27 (aussi au v. 30), le titre est utilisé dans sa forme adjective: τὸν ἅγιον παῖδά σου Ἰησοῦν ὃν ἔχρισας[35]. Dans la cohérence de Luc, le titre Saint de Lc 1,35 oriente donc vers la condition future de celui qui va naître, celle qui adviendra après sa résurrection.

«Le Saint qui va naître sera appelé Fils de Dieu». Quelle est donc la teneur de ce dernier titre? Quelques auteurs l'interprètent encore sous l'angle ontologique[36]. N'est-ce pas appliquer au texte de Luc une lecture étrangère à la tradition biblique elle-même? Cette acception s'écarte, de plus, de l'intention habituelle véhiculée par le genre littéraire «annonce de naissance», qui vise à définir le rôle du protagoniste à l'intérieur du plan de Dieu. On ne voit donc pas pourquoi Luc aurait subitement introduit une notion qui serait en rupture avec la cohérence de son récit; car en toute logique, le deuxième volet de la péricope doit se lire dans le prolongement du premier, c'est-à-dire dans une perspective fonctionnelle, en l'occurrence messianique[37]. Le titre Fils de Dieu viendrait ren-

---

35. «Ton saint fils, Jésus, que tu avais oint». À noter que l'onction dont il est question ici renvoie à celle du baptême, soit une onction d'ordre prophétique, comme le confirme l'interprétation qui en est faite, en Lc 4,18-19, à l'aide de la citation d'Is 61,1 qui, elle, évoquait la consécration d'un prophète.

36. Entre autres, R. LAURENTIN, *Structure et théologie de Luc I-II*, Paris, Gabalda, 1957, pp.72ss; I.H. MARSHALL, *Luke*, p. 71.

37. De plus en plus d'auteurs reconnaissent la portée messianique du titre Fils de Dieu en Lc 1,35; parmi ceux-là, F. BOVON, *L'évangile selon saint Luc*, p. 78; R.H. STEIN, *Luke*, p. 86.

chérir le titre Fils du Très-Haut[38]. Mais ici encore, le livre des Actes offre bon un éclairage. En Ac 9,20, on apprend que Paul proclame dans les synagogues que Jésus est le Fils de Dieu; or, deux versets plus loin, on lit que Paul confondait les Juifs de Damas en prouvant que Jésus est bien le Messie. De même, en Ac 13,33, le titre Fils de Dieu est associé au messianisme de Jésus[39].

Deux données importantes émanent de ce qui précède: 1) les titres Saint et Fils de Dieu sont associés au messianisme de Jésus dans les Actes; 2) le titre Fils de Dieu est à caractère messianique en Lc 1,35. On peut donc comprendre que l'introduction du διό, en Lc 1,35, vient présenter la filiation messianique de Jésus comme un effet de l'intervention de l'Esprit[40]. En couvrant Marie de son ombre, l'Esprit Saint crée un environnement propre à protéger celui qui va naître et à le garder dans la sainteté. L'épreuve de la mort et la gloire de la résurrection révéleront qu'il est effectivement le Saint de Dieu, par conséquent, habilité à assumer la fonction messianique à titre de Fils de Dieu. L'intervention de l'Esprit a donc quelque chose à dire sur le messianisme de Jésus. D'une part, elle lui imprime son caractère inédit; d'autre part, elle le distingue de celui qui était attendu dans la tradition juive. Le messianisme attendu dans la tradition juive est selon la chair, comme en font état les versets 32-33[41]; celui de Jésus sera selon l'Esprit, comme en fait état le verset 35. Un messianisme qui adviendra quand l'Esprit saint lui sera donné par Dieu de façon définitive à la résurrection. C'est précisément ce qui se réalise selon le texte de Ac 2,33: «Exalté à la droite de Dieu, il a donc reçu l'Esprit Saint promis». En réalité, l'adjonction du verset 35 à l'annonce messianique des versets 32-33, en Lc 1, vient spécifier la nature du messianisme de Jésus, soit un messianisme pneumatique, ce que vient confirmer Ac 2,33.

---

38. Lc 22,67-70 offre un autre exemple où le titre Fils de Dieu vient supporter, voire approfondir, le titre de Messie.

39. Notons ici que certains auteurs traduisent la formule d'Ac 4,27 (τὸν ἅγιον παῖδά σου Ἰησοῦν; aussi au v. 30) par «ton saint fils, Jésus»: cf. H. CONZELMANN, *Acts of the Apostles* (Hermeneia), Philadelphia, Fortress, 1987, p. 34; E. HAENCHEN, *The Acts of the Apostles*, Oxford, Blackwell, 1971, p. 225. L.T. JOHNSON, *The Acts of the Apostles* (Sacra Pagina, 5), Collegeville, Michael Glazier Book, 1992, p. 82, pour sa part, traduit par «your holy child Jesus». Par contre, la *TOB*, la *BJ* et *Osty* traduisent par «ton saint serviteur Jésus». Conzelmann (p. 35) lit cette formule en lien avec le titre Oint au verset précédent (v. 26), auquel il accorde une portée messianique.

40. On pourrait objecter que l'Esprit intervient sur Marie et non sur Jésus; oui, mais l'effet porte sur celui qui va naître. D'ailleurs, l'hagiographe aura encore l'occasion de faire intervenir une mère à la place de son fils, cette fois Élisabeth à la place de Jean (Lc 1,41-45).

41. Comparer F. BOVON, *L'évangile selon saint Luc*, p. 78.

Cette lecture respecte non seulement la théologie de Luc, mais elle s'inscrit aussi dans la cohérence du développement christologique des débuts de la chrétienté, comme le démontre le rapprochement avec le credo ancien de Rm 1,3-4[42]. On retrouve effectivement, entre les deux volets de ce credo, la même progression qu'en Lc 1,32-33 et 35[43], soit un messianisme selon la chair et un messianisme selon l'Esprit Saint:

περὶ τοῦ υἱοῦ αὐτοῦ τοῦ γενομένου ἐκ σπέρματος Δαυὶδ κατὰ σάρκα,
τοῦ ὁρισθέντος υἱοῦ θεοῦ ἐν δυνάμει κατὰ πνεῦμα ἁγιωσύνης ἐξ
ἀναστάσεως νεκρῶν, Ἰησοῦ Χριστοῦ τοῦ κυρίου ἡμῶν

Concernant son fils issu de la semence de David selon la chair,
Établi fils de Dieu dans la puissance selon l'Esprit de sainteté, à partir de la résurrection des morts, Jésus Christ, notre Seigneur.

Les rapprochements entre Rm 1,3 et Lc 1,32-33, quant au messianisme selon la chair, et entre Rm 1,4 et Lc 1,35, quant au messianisme selon l'Esprit, sont tout à fait frappants. Il est tout aussi frappant de noter, en Rm 1,4, que selon Paul (ou selon une tradition encore plus ancienne), le messianisme n'advient aussi qu'à la résurrection et, encore une fois, par l'intervention de l'Esprit. On doit conclure que le caractère pneumatique du messianisme du Christ ressuscité est reconnu depuis longtemps. Luc a voulu en faire état en le présentant depuis son annonce (Lc 1,35) jusqu'à son accomplissement (Ac 2,33)[44].

42. Les auteurs sont d'avis que Paul utilise un credo ancien en Rm 1,3-4, mais la plupart croient que ce dernier y a apporté des ajouts. Il n'y a toutefois pas d'unanimité quant à la teneur exacte des soi-disant remaniements pauliniens. Voir l'étude de R. JEWETT, *The Redaction and Use of an Early Christian Confession in Romans 1:3-4*, in D. GROH & R. JEWETT (éds.), *The Living Text: Essays in Honor of Ernest W. Sanders*, Lanham, MD, University Press of America, 1985, pp. 99-122, qui a répertorié et analysé les diverses tentatives en vue d'isoler la formule crédale originale. Actuellement, la tendance est de ne retenir comme ajouts probables que les membres de phrase ἐν δυνάμει et ἐξ ἀναστάσεως νεκρῶν (Fitzmyer), bien que plusieurs, percevant dans ces expressions des indices d'ancienneté et les associant volontiers au langage de la première communauté, estiment qu'ils faisaient plutôt partie du credo reçu par Paul (Dunn): voir J.A. FITZMYER, *Romans. A New Translation with Introduction and Commentary* (Anchor Bible, 33), New York, Doubleday, 1993, pp. 235-236; J.D.G. DUNN, *Romans 1–8* (World Biblical Commentary, 38A), Dallas, Word Books, 1988, pp. 5-6. Face à ce manque de consensus quant aux possibles remaniements, on peut tout aussi bien croire que Rm 1,3-4 rend le credo dans son intégrité. Mais même si on admet que Paul est responsable de ces ajouts, on retrouve néanmoins une interprétation messianique qui précède de vingt ans la rédaction du troisième évangile.

43. Voir L. LEGRAND, *Fécondité virginale*, in NRT 84 (1962), p. 789.

44. Le rapport annonce/accomplissement entre le troisième évangile et les Actes est une technique littéraire constamment utilisée au fil du double ouvrage lucanien, dont voici quelques exemples: annonce du baptême dans l'Esprit Saint en Lc 3,16 et accomplissement en Ac 2,1-4; annonce du secours de l'Esprit Saint au temps de persécution en Lc 12,12 et accomplissement en Ac 4,8-20; annonce de l'aide d'une puissance (l'Esprit) en vue du témoignage des disciples en Lc 24,49 et accomplissement en Ac 2,1-36;

Conclusion

La proclamation d'Ac 2,33 informe donc que le messianisme de Jésus advient parce que, d'une part, Dieu lui a donné son Esprit au moment de sa résurrection et parce que, d'autre part, Jésus l'a, à son tour, répandu sur la communauté. On peut, dès lors, conclure que l'Esprit est l'agent qui, non seulement, confère à Jésus sa fonction messianique, mais aussi la rend efficace au sein de la communauté. Ainsi, ce messianisme est essentiellement d'ordre pneumatique. Il faut comprendre, en toute logique, que l'introduction du thème de l'Esprit au moment de l'annonce de ce messianisme, en Lc 1,35, visait nécessairement à marquer le caractère unique de ce messianisme. Par ailleurs, la vie de la première communauté, sous la motion de l'Esprit du Christ ressuscité, témoigne avec éloquence de la nature spécifique de ce messianisme. Il est donc tout à fait normal de prétendre que Luc ait voulu en faire état en créant son récit d'annonciation. Ainsi voyons-nous mieux le rapport d'annonce/ accomplissement entre Lc 1,35 et Ac 2,33.

Faculté de théologie   Odette Mainville
Université de Montréal
Montréal, Québec
Canada

annonce du don de l'Esprit comme réponse à la prière en Lc 11,13 et accomplissement en Ac 4,31. Les exemples retenus ici sont d'autant plus aptes à appuyer notre propos que, dans chaque cas, l'Esprit est l'agent responsable de l'accomplissement des choses annoncées.

DIE DREIFACHE WIEDERGABE DES
DAMASKUSERLEBNISSES PAULI IN DER APOSTELGESCHICHTE
EINE HILFE FÜR DAS RECHTE VERSTÄNDNIS DER LUKANISCHEN
OSTEREVANGELIEN

Im Rahmen des Tagungsthemas »Lukasevangelium und Apostelgeschichte« ist es angebracht, die dreifache Wiedergabe des Damaskuserlebnisses in der Apostelgeschichte im Hinblick auf seine Darstellungsweise mit den lukanischen Osterevangelien zu vergleichen. Dabei
erweist sich das Vorgehen des Verfassers in Apg 9; 22 und 26 als eine
Hilfe zum rechten Verständnis der lk Osterevangelien; denn diese werden heute noch in weiten Kreisen als protokollarische Berichte – Lk
24,36-49 sogar als »handfester Beweis« für die Wahrheit der Osterbotschaft – mißverstanden. Außerdem ist eine nähere Beschäftigung mit Lk
24 im Licht von Apg 9; 22; 26 höchst aufschlußreich für die neuerlich
durch G. Lüdemann wieder aufgegriffene Behauptung, alle Ostererfahrungen seien nur subjektive Visionen gewesen[1]. Die lk Darstellungsweise der Berufung des Paulus scheint dafür ja einen Beleg zu bieten;
im Unterschied zu Paulus selbst schildert nämlich der Verfasser der Apg
dessen Berufung als eine Vision unter anderen.

In diesem Referat werden die in Kommentaren, Monographien und
Artikeln oft untersuchten Texte von Apg 9; 22; 26 und Lk 24 nicht noch
einmal im einzelnen diskutiert. Ich versuche vielmehr, die Aussagen der
Apostelgeschichte im Hinblick auf die angegebene Fragestellung
zunächst synchron (1) und dann diachron (2) zu erhellen. Ein daran
anschließender Vergleich der Ergebnisse mit Lk 24 (3) ermöglicht es
sodann, daraus Folgerungen (4) für die fiktionale Darstellungsweise des
Verfassers von Lk/Apg und das damit gegebene Problem heutiger Vermittlung dieser Aussagen über die Ostererfahrungen bzw. die Berufung
des Paulus zu ziehen.

I. Synchrone Analyse von Apg 9; 22; 26

Die Eigenart der dreifachen Wiedergabe des Damaskuserlebnisses
wird schon ersichtlich, wenn wir Kontext und Struktur der drei Erzäh-

---

1. G. Lüdemann, *Die Auferstehung Jesu. Historie, Erfahrung, Theologie*, Göttingen,
1994.

lungen betrachten und diese Beobachtungen durch eine semantische Untersuchung ergänzen, auch wenn sich diese auf einige wichtige Aussagen beschränken muß.

1. Beobachtungen zu Kontext und Struktur

a. Der Abschnitt *Apg 9,3-22* bildet eine Texteinheit, die eingerahmt ist durch die kurze Angabe über die Verfolgertätigkeit des Paulus, die ihn bis nach Damaskus führt (V. 3a) und über die Predigt des Bekehrten in Damaskus (V. 19b-22). Im *Kontext* der Apg steht dieser Text nach den Berichten über die Christusverkündigung ausgehend von Jerusalem über Samaria (nach der Steinigung des Stephanus) bis hin zur Verkündigung in Caesarea (nach der Bekehrung des Kämmerers durch Philippus auf dem Weg nach Gaza). Auf unseren Text folgen kurze Angaben über Paulus (in Damaskus, in Jerusalem, in Tarsus), Informationen über den Aufenthalt des Petrus in Lydda bzw. Joppe und schließlich die breite Doppelerzählung über die Visionen des Cornelius und Petrus im Hinblick auf den Anfang der Heidenmission (Kap. 10–11). Die *Struktur* von Apg 9,3-22 ist – abgesehen von der schon erwähnten Rahmung (*inclusio*) im ersten Teil – geprägt durch den kurzen Erzählerbericht über ein unerwartetes Erlebnis (V. 3b-4b), den wiedergegebenen Dialog zwischen der Stimme und Paulus (V. 4c-6) und die Notiz über die Begleiter des Paulus und seine Blindheit (V. 7-9). Der zweite Teil beginnt mit einem kurzen Bericht über Hananias und dessen Vision (V. 10) und enthält einen breiten, wörtlich wiedergegebenen Dialog zwischen dem Herrn und Hananias über die Bestimmung des Paulus (V. 11-16). Als dritter Teil folgt der Bericht über den Gang des Hananias zu Paulus sowie dessen Heilung und Taufe (17-19a).

b. Der Abschnitt *Apg 22,6-21* weicht, bedingt durch den unterschiedlichen *Kontext,* teilweise stark von Apg 9,3-22 ab. Der Hauptbericht steht nämlich in der Verteidigungsrede des Paulus vor den Juden in Jerusalem nach der Erzählung über seine Gefangennahme im Tempel zu Jerusalem, die wegen seiner Missionstätigkeit bei den Heiden erfolgt (21,27–22,5). Pauli Selbstverteidigung wird nach der von ihm erwähnten Aussendung zu den Heiden (22,17-21) von empörten jüdischen Zuhörern abgebrochen, die seinen Tod fordern (22,22). Die *Struktur* dieses Abschnitts ist dadurch geprägt, daß in einem ersten Teil Paulus selbst über das Erlebnis auf dem Weg nach Damaskus berichtet (V. 6-7a) und den kurzen Dialog mit der Stimme wiedergibt (V. 7b-8). Nach einer Bemerkung über seine Begleiter (V. 9) referiert er dann noch einen zweiten Dialog (V. 10) und berichtet anschließend über seine Erblindung und Hinführung nach Damaskus (V. 11). Im zweiten Teil erzählt Paulus dann zuerst über den bei den Juden geschätzten Hananias, dessen Kommen zu ihm (V. 12-13a) und der mit einer Aufforderung (V. 13b) eingeleiteten Heilung von der Blindheit. Ausführlich gibt er dann die weiteren Worte des Hananias wieder (V. 14b-16). Im dritten Teil folgt der Bericht des Paulus über eine ekstatische Vision im Tempel zu Jerusalem (V. 17-18), wobei der Herr ihn in einem Dialog auffordert, Jerusalem zu verlassen und zu den Heiden in die Ferne zu gehen (V. 19-21). In Entsprechung zu der vorher geschilderten Gefangennahme schließt der Abschnitt, wie schon erwähnt, mit der Forderung seines Todes durch die darüber empörten Juden (V. 22).

c. Der Abschnitt *Apg 26,12-20* steht im *Kontext* der Haft des Paulus in Caesarea, wo ihm die Möglichkeit zu einer Verteidigungsrede vor dem hellenistisch gebildeten König Agrippa II. und seinem Gefolge gegeben wird. In dieser Rede geht er unmittelbar vor unserem Text auf sein Leben, seine mit den Vätern geteilte Hoffnung auf die Auferstehung der Toten und seine Verfolgung der Christen ein (26,9-11). Zum Abschluß unseres Textes und der gesamten Verteidigungsrede bekennt der Gefangene seinen Gehorsam gegenüber der himmlischen Erscheinung, seinen Glauben an die Auferstehung Christi (in Einklang mit den Worten der Propheten) und seine Predigttätigkeit (26,19-23).

Für die *Struktur* dieses Redeteils ist beachtenswert, daß Paulus nach dem Bericht über sein Erlebnis vor Damaskus (V. 12-14b) und dem damit verbundenen Dialog (V. 14c-15) eine unmittelbar anschließende, längere Rede des Erschienenen über seine Berufung und seine Sendung zu den Heiden wiedergibt (V. 16-18), ohne Hananias, Blindenheilung und Taufe zu erwähnen. Den Abschluß bildet der schon erwähnte Bericht des Paulus über seine Reaktion (V. 19-23).

2. Beobachtungen zur Semantik

Die Untersuchung des Kontextes und der Struktur der dreifachen Wiedergabe des Damaskuserlebnisses lassen schon beachtliche Unterschiede erkennen. Eine auf unsere Fragestellung konzentrierte semantische Analyse vermag diese weiter zu erhellen. Es ist dabei methodisch angebracht, zunächst die Aussagen zu Apg 9,3-20 ausführlicher auf ihre Bedeutung und Funktion hin zu untersuchen und dabei schon die beiden anderen Erzählungen mit zu berücksichtigen, soweit sie nicht eine gesonderte Untersuchung fordern.

a. Apg 9,3-20

9,3-4a: Das einleitende »es geschah« (ἐγένετο) weist auf ein Geschehen hin, das Paulus bei der Annäherung (fehlt 26,12) an Damaskus widerfuhr (22,6 »um die Mittagszeit«; 26,12 »mittags«): »Plötzlich« (fehlt 26,12) »umstrahlt ihn ein Licht vom Himmel« (22,6 »ein großes Licht«; 26,13 »ich sah ein Licht vom Himmel her, heller als der Glanz der Sonne, das mich und meine Begleiter umleuchtete«). In Reaktion darauf stürzt Paulus zu Boden (26,14 »wir alle«) und hört eine ihn anredende Stimme (26,14 »in hebräischer Sprache«). Daß in dem Licht eine redende Person zu sehen ist, wie der anschließende Dialog voraussetzt, wird nicht gesagt.

Als Parallele zu dieser Schilderung wird oft 2 Makk 3,23-40 herangezogen: Bei seinem Versuch, den Tempelschatz zu rauben, werden Heliodor und seine Begleiter durch »eine gewaltige Erscheinung« in Schrecken versetzt, und ihre Kräfte verlassen sie (V. 24). Nachdem andere erschienene Männer auf Heliodor einschlagen, »stürzte er zu Boden und es wurde ihm schwarz vor Augen« (V. 26f). Am Schluß verkündigt Heliodor als ein vom Himmel Gezüchtigter vor allen Menschen »die Taten des größten Gottes« (V. 34-36). Ungeachtet der vieldiskutierten Frage, ob unser Text von dieser Parallele abhängig sei, kann dieser trotz seiner beträchtlichen Differenzen zeigen, wie damals über die plötzliche Wandlung eines Feindes gesprochen werden konnte[2].

9,4b-6: Die aus dem Licht bzw. in Verbindung damit ergehende »Stimme« redet Paulus mit seinem aramäischen Namen »Saul, Saul« an (26,24 ausdrücklich als solcher erklärt) und nicht etwa in der gräzisierten Form Σαῦλος (vgl. Apg 8,1.13; 9,1.8.11 u. ö.) oder mit dem ihm von Kind an eigenen lateinischen Namen Παῦλος (so in der Apg regelmäßig ab 13,9 »Saulus aber, der auch Paulus heißt«). Eine Verdoppelung der Anrede findet sich im NT noch Lk 7,14 (*v.l.*); 8,24 »Meister, Meister«; 10,41 »Marta, Marta«; 22,31 »Simon, Simon«; sie ist auch belegt Gen 22,11 »Abraham, Abraham«; 46,2 »Jakob, Jakob«; Ex 3,4 »Mose, Mose«; 1 Sam 3,6 »Samuel, Samuel«. Die Frage: »Was verfolgst du mich?« besagt schlicht, daß die Ablehnung und Verfolgung der Anhänger Christi sich letztlich gegen Christus wendet (vgl. Lk 10,16 »Wer euch ablehnt, lehnt mich ab«)[3]. Die Gegenfrage des Paulus: »Wer bist du, Herr (κύριε)?« setzt voraus, daß er irgendwie in oder mit dem

---

2. Das gilt weniger für die ebenfalls mehrfach als Parallele bemühten Aussagen über die Konversion Aseneths in dem spätjüdischen Roman »Josef und Aseneth«.
3. Apg 26,14 ergänzt die Frage mit dem in der griechischen Literatur oft belegten Sprichwort: »Es ist dir hart (schwierig), gegen den Stachel auszuschlagen«, d. h. die Verfolgung (oder der Widerstand gegen die Bekehrung) wird dir nichts nützen.

Licht eine Person wahrgenommen hat, die er allerdings nicht identifizieren kann. Die Anrede »Herr« steht hier wohl im alltäglichen Sinn. In der Antwort stellt sich der Sprecher als »Jesus« (22,8 »Jesus, der Nazarener«) vor, gegen den sich die Verfolgung des Paulus richtet, und fordert den zu Boden Gestürzten auf, in die Stadt zu gehen, mit der Zusage, dort werde ihm gesagt werden, was er tun müsse. Damit ist die Bekehrung des Paulus schon vorausgesetzt[4]. Für ein solches Erscheinungsgespräch finden sich mehrere Parallelen im AT (z.B. Gen 22,1f; 31,11-13; 46,2f), in der jüdischen Literatur (z.B. Jub 18,1f; 44,5; 4 Esr 12,8-13) und im NT (Apg 10,3-5; vgl. Lk 1,13-20.28-38). Mit Recht kann es als »literarisches Stilmittel«[5] bewertet werden. Gemäß der Zwischenbemerkung des Verfasssers (9,7) standen die Begleiter (sozusagen als objektive Zeugen) »sprachlos« (ἐνεοί); sie hörten eine Stimme, sahen aber niemand[6]. Es heißt dann weiter (9,8f), daß Paulus von der Erde aufstand, beim Öffnen der Augen seine Erblindung (ein Grund dafür wird hier nicht genannt) konstatierte, an den Händen genommen, nach Damaskus geführt wurde (in Kontrast zu seiner Absicht, andere gefangen wegzuführen) und dort »drei Tage« (Zeit der großen Wende wie in den Auferstehungstexten) blind war, nichts aß und nichts trank, vermutlich als Ausdruck seiner Buße[7].

9,10-16: In der Einleitung zu dem neuen Abschnitt wird »ein Jünger in Damaskus mit Namen Hananias« genannt (9,10ab; nach 22,12 von allen dortigen Juden als gesetzesfromm geschätzt). Von ihm wird berichtet, daß »der Herr« (hier als Titel Christi) in einer »Vision« (ἐν ὁράματι) zu ihm sprach, und zwar in einem längeren Erscheinungsgespräch (9,10c-16; fehlt 22,12). Die einfache Anrede »Hananias« und die Entgegnung des Angesprochenen: »hier bin ich, Herr« (ähnlich wie in atl. Erscheinungsgesprächen) zeigen, daß hier ein Christ auf den Anruf des Herrn antwortet. In einem längeren Wechselgespräch erteilt »der Herr« dann Hananias mit präzisen Ortsangaben (Gerade Straße, Haus des Judas) den Auftrag, dort den »Saulus aus Tarsus« (dieselbe

---

4. Apg 22,10 wird das mit der Antwort auf eine Frage des Paulus uminterpretiert: »über alles, was dir zu tun (von Gott) aufgetragen ist«, d.h. als Hinweis auf eine besondere Sendung.

5. G. LOHFINK, *Paulus vor Damaskus. Arbeitsweisen der neueren Bibelwissenschaft dargestellt an den Texten Apg 9,1-19; 22,3-21; 26,9-18* (SBS, 4), Stuttgart, 1965. ID., *Eine alttestamentliche Darstellungsform für Gotteserscheinungen in den Damaskusberichten (Apg 9; 22; 26)*, in *BZ* 9 (1965) 246-257. ID., *Die Himmelfahrt Jesu* (SANT, 26), München, 1971. ID., *»Meinen Namen zu tragen...« (Apg 9,15)*, in ID., *Studien zum Neuen Testament* (SBAB, 5), Stuttgart, 1989, pp. 213-221.

6. Nach 22,7 sahen sie das Licht, hörten aber nicht die Stimme; ähnlich 26,14.

7. Nach 22,11 war seine Erblindung die Folge der Lichterscheinung; es fehlt dort aber die Zeitangabe sowie die Erwähnung des Fastens.

Angabe 21,39) zu suchen. Als Begründung fügt der Herr an: »Denn
siehe, er betet (bittet um Belehrung oder Hilfe) und hat in einer Vision
(ἐν ὁράματι, textkritisch unsicher) einen Mann mit Namen Hananias
gesehen, der zu ihm kommt und ihm die Hände auflegt, damit er wieder
sehe« (9,11f). Durch diese Zweckangabe (Heilung von der Blindheit)
unterscheidet sich diese Wiedergabe von der dem Paulus selbst angege-
benen (9,6), nämlich der Ankündigung dessen, was Paulus zu tun habe.
Im Stil eines auch in anderen Erscheinungsgesprächen belegten Einwan-
des (vgl. Lk 1,18.34) verweist Hananias auf die ihm bekannte Verfolgertätigkeit des Paulus in Jerusalem und dessen Vollmacht, auch hier die
Christen gefangen zu nehmen, die mit der alten Wendung bezeichnet
werden: »die den Namen des Herrn anrufen« (vgl. 1 Kor 1,2). Dennoch
wiederholt der Herr seinen Auftrag, indem er auf die Erwählung
(σκεῦος ἐκλογῆς) des Paulus verweist, damit er seinen Namen »trage
(βαστάσαι) vor (ἐνώπιον) Heiden, Königen und Söhnen Israels«, d.h.
ihn vor diesen drei Gruppen öffentlich unter Widerständen bekenne. Wie
das gemeint ist, geht aus dem Begründungssatz hervor: »denn ich werde
ihm zeigen, wie viel er für meinen Namen leiden muß«. Der Herr teilt
hier also dem Hananias nicht etwa die Berufung des Paulus zum Heidenapostel mit (ἐνώπιον steht im Sinne von »wo« und nicht von
»wohin«), sondern seine Erwählung zum Martyrium für Christus bei
Heiden und Juden anstelle der bisherigen Verfolgung von Christen (zu
den anders lautenden Parallelen 22,15.21 und 26,18 s.w.u.).

9,17-19a: In dem abschließenden Bericht wird erzählt, daß Hananias
den Auftrag ausführt: er legt Paulus die Hände auf – mit der Anrede
»Bruder Saul« – und begründet dies unter Berufung auf die Sendung
durch Jesus, der, wie er sagt, Paulus auf dem Wege erschienen ist, damit
er wieder sehe und erfüllt werde mit Heiligem Geist. Als Wirkung der
Handauflegung wird die sofortige Heilung in volkstümlicher Sprache
(»wie Schuppen von den Augen«, vgl. Tob 11,12) erzählt, sowie daß
der Geheilte aufstand, sich (ohne vorherige Unterweisung) taufen ließ
und durch die Nahrungsaufnahme wieder zu Kräften kam. Den
Abschluß der ganzen Erzählung bildet der Bericht über das Bleiben des
Bekehrten bei den »Jüngern« in Damaskus und seine dortige Verkündigung Christi in den Synagogen (9,19b-20).

b. Apg 22,6-21

Als Abweichung von der Schilderung in Kap. 9 fällt hier als erstes ins
Gewicht, was Hananias, ohne Beauftragung durch eine Vision, dem
durch ihn (22,13) von seiner Blindheit geheilten Saulus mitteilt: seine
Erwählung durch den »Gott der Väter«, um dessen Willen zu erkennen

(wohl die Berufung der Heiden) und den »Gerechten« zu sehen und zu hören (nach 22,17-21 bei der Vision in Jerusalem und wohl kaum auf das Damaskuserlebnis bezogen). Als Ziel wird angegeben: »damit du ihm Zeuge sein wirst vor allen Menschen von dem, was du gesehen und gehört hast« (22,15). Damit ist die Berufung zum Zeugen bei allen (also auch bei den Heiden) für die ihm anvertraute Botschaft ausgesprochen. Im Blick auf ein vorausgesetztes Zögern des Paulus (»und nun, was zögerst du?«) wird er aufgefordert (22,16), sich taufen und von den Sünden reinigen zu lassen, »anrufend seinen Namen« (vgl. 9,14 »die seinen Namen anrufen« und 9,16 »für seinen Namen«).

In dieser Verteidigungsrede erwähnt Paulus – ein zweiter Unterschied – überhaupt nicht seine anschließende Verkündigung in Damaskus (wie 9,19bf); statt dessen berichtet er (22,17-21) über ein unmittelbar sich anschließendes ekstatisches Erlebnis (vgl. 10,10; ähnlich 11,5; anders 2 Kor 12,1-4) im Tempel zu Jerusalem: Dort sah und hörte er (wie angekündigt) »ihn«, der ihn aufforderte, Jerusalem eilends zu verlassen, weil sie dort sein Zeugnis für Jesus nicht aufnehmen (vgl. Apg 28,26f; ähnlich Lk 14,16-24). Einem Erscheinungsgespräch entsprechend erhebt Paulus einen Einwand unter Hinweis auf sein bekanntes Wirken als Verfolger, u. a. beim Martyrium »seines Zeugen« Stephanus. Dieser Einwand dient hier dazu, dem Zeugnis des bekehrten Verfolgers eine besondere Überzeugungskraft zu verleihen. Die Wiedergabe der Rede des im Tempel zu Jerusalem Erschienenen beschließt Paulus mit den bisher so deutlich noch nicht ausgesprochenen Worten über seine Sendung zu den Heiden in der Ferne, was bei den jüdischen Zuhörern schärfsten Protest auslöst (22,22ff).

c. Apg 26,12-20

Von dem Erzählerbericht in Apg 9,3-20 und der Selbstverteidigung des Apostels in Apg 22,6-21 beträchtlich verschieden sind die Worte des Paulus in der Verteidigungsrede vor König Agrippa II. über seine Berufung durch den ihm vor Damaskus erschienenen Christus. Nach der Selbstvorstellung (26,15c) befiehlt ihm »der Herr« (in Abwandlung der Aufforderung 9,6): »Aber steh auf und stell dich auf deine Füße«[8]. Zur Begründung fügt er an, wozu er ihm erschienen sei (ὤφθην σοι): um ihn zum »Diener« (vgl. Lk 1,2; Apg 13,5; 1 Kor 4,1) und »Zeugen« (vgl. 22,15) dessen zu machen, »was du gesehen hast und ich dich werde sehen lassen«. Das nimmt hier Bezug auf das gegenwärtige Sehen

---

8. Fast gleichlautend mit der Einleitung der Prophetensendung Ez 2,1: »stell dich auf deine Füße, Menschensohn, ich will mit dir reden«.

vor Damaskus (vgl. V. 13 »ich sah« und V. 16b) und ein zukünftiges Sehen (vgl. 16,7-9; 18,9; 22,17-20; 23,11). Dabei darf Paulus sich der Hilfe (ἐξαιρούμενος, vgl. den Jer 1,7f LXX ausgesprochenen Beistand) gegen die Widerstände seitens seines Volkes und der Heiden, zu denen er gesendet wird, bewußt bleiben. Das Ziel der Sendung gibt der Erscheinende mit drei Infinitiven an: 1. ihre Augen zu öffnen (vgl. die Kap. 9 und 22 erzählte Blindenheilung, bes. aber Jes 42,7; 61,1; Eph 5,8; Kol 1,12f; 1 Petr 2,9); 2. sie zu bekehren von der Finsternis zum Licht und von der Macht Satans zu Gott (vgl. Apg 14,15; 15,19; 1 Thess 1,9; Kol 1,13); 3. ihnen Vergebung der Sünden und Anteil bei den Geheiligten durch den Glauben an ihn anzusagen (vgl. Apg 10,43; 22,16; Lk 24,47). Als Antwort auf diese ganz in der Sprache des Alten Testaments und der urkirchlichen Predigt formulierte Aussendungsrede nennt Paulus seinen Gehorsam gegenüber dem »himmlischen Gesicht« und sein anschließendes Wirken, das zu seiner Gefangennahme führt.

3. Erste Folgerungen

Die noch in mancher Hinsicht zu ergänzenden synchronen Beobachtungen zu Kontext, Struktur und Semantik der dreifachen Wiedergabe des Damaskuserlebnisses Pauli in der Apg lassen mehrere Schlußfolgerungen und ergänzende Bemerkungen betreffs der Eigenart dieser Texte zu:

a. Alle drei Texte handeln über ein und dasselbe Erlebnis des Paulus vor Damaskus (Lichterscheinung und Stimme). Gemeinsam ist allen Texten die Form einer fortlaufenden Erzählung (nicht etwa einer theoretischen Abhandlung), die Verwendung von Dialogen mit doppelter Anrede am Beginn und mit Einwänden, wie sie auch in anderen biblischen Erscheinungsgesprächen belegt sind. Gemeinsam sind ferner kurze Angaben über die Auswirkung auf den bzw. die Betroffenen (z.T. ähnlich wie in verwandten Erzählungen, etwa über die Bekehrung des Heliodor), vor allem im Blick auf die Bekehrung und das zukünftige Geschick der Hauptperson (statt Verfolgung nun Bezeugung bzw. Verkündigung des Verfolgten).

b. Im einzelnen weisen die Texte jedoch beachtliche Unterschiede auf, und zwar nicht bloß bei nebensächlichen Angaben (z.B. über die Begleiter: 9,7 hören, aber nicht sehen; 22,9 sehen, aber nicht hören; 26,13d alle vom Licht umleuchtet und zu Boden gestürzt), sondern vor allem hinsichtlich der Bedeutung des Geschehens selbst: 1. Heilung und Bekehrung des Paulus sowie Vermittlung des durch eine Vision dazu beauftragten Hananias, der Paulus seine mit Leiden verbundene Aufgabe als Zeuge kundtut (9,10-18); 2. Ankündigung der Erwählung des Paulus durch Hananias in Form eines Botenspruchs (ohne Vision), damit er den Willen Gottes erkenne (Berufung der Heiden) und Christus sehe sowie höre, um sein Zeuge zu sein bei allen Menschen; in Ergänzung dazu die (nach seiner Taufe) in Jerusalem erfolgende Aussendung zu den Heiden (22,14-21); 3. direkte Bestellung des Paulus durch den erschienenen Herrn (ohne Vermittlung des Hananias, ohne Angabe über Erblindung, Heilung und Taufe) zum »Diener« und »Zeugen« mit der dreifachen Angabe seiner prophetischen Sendung (26,16-18).

c. Beachtenswert ist außerdem, daß die drei Schilderungen in ihren übereinstimmenden und unterschiedlichen Angaben manche sprachliche und thematische Analogien aufweisen, die auf eine gewählte, kunstvolle Ausdrucksweise schließen lassen: Dazu gehören erstens die leichten Abwandlungen bei der Schilderung des auslösenden Ereignisses, z.B. »Licht« (9,3), »großes Licht« (22,6), »ein Licht, heller als der Glanz der Sonne« (26,12) und die Verdeutlichung der unbestimmten Lichterscheinung als »Vision« des Herrn (9,17; 26,13 »ich sah« und 26,16 »erschien«). Zweitens kann dazu gerechnet werden die nähere Bestimmung der Frage des Herrn mit der Angabe »in hebräischer Sprache« (vorher schon durch die Wiedergabe »Saul, Saul« angedeutet) und einem griechischen Sprichwort (26,14). Besonders charakteristisch ist drittens die Fortführung der Angabe über Erblindung und Heilung (9,3.9.12.17f; 22,11.12) in metaphorischer Bedeutung mit »zu öffnen ihre Augen« (26,18). Hierher gehört viertens auch die Verwendung von »den Namen des Herrn anrufen« als Bezeichnung für die Christen (9,14) bei der Taufe des Paulus (22,16) und als Grund seines Leidens (9,16). Schließlich ist fünftens noch zu erwähnen die Wiederaufnahme von »steh auf« (9,6.11 »um in die Stadt zu gehen«; ähnlich 22,10), sodann 22,16 vor der Taufe; und 26,16 »steh auf und stell dich auf deine Füße«.

d. Die zuletzt angeführten Besonderheiten deuten u.a. an, daß der Verfasser dieser Texte (bzw. dessen Garant), seine Aussagen zwar in der damals verbreiteten Sprache trifft, die Wörter und Sätze aber nicht bloß in ihrer alltäglichen Bedeutung, sondern z.T. in einem übertragenen bzw. für Metaphorik offenen Sinn verwendet (Licht, Erblindung, Heilung von Blindheit, öffnen). Sie zeigen an, daß es sich nach Auffassung des Schreibers in allen drei Erzählungen um ein und dasselbe Geschehen handelt. Dieses erzählt er in dreifacher, zum Teil steigernder und verdeutlichender Weise, die in Apg 22 und 26 rhetorisch geschickt (dama-

338 J. KREMER

liger Praxis gemäß[9]) auf die jeweils verschiedenen Zuhörer abgestimmt ist. Der Verfasser bedient sich dieser Rhetorik, um so überzeugend unterschiedliche Aspekte des einen Geschehens aufzuzeigen: als Bekehrungsgeschichte, als Erwählungsgeschichte mit der dazu gehörenden in Jerusalem erfolgten Aussendung zu den Heiden, als prophetische Berufung zum »Diener und Zeugen« bei den Heiden.

Die durch das neuzeitliche Geschichtsverständnis bedingte Frage, »wie es eigentlich gewesen ist«, interessiert den Verfasser dieser Texte nicht; ihm geht es um die dem oberflächlichen Blick des Historikers verborgene Bedeutung des Erzählten: daß die Bekehrung des Verfolgers auf ein Wirken des verfolgten Herrn zurückgeht, der den ehemaligen Verfolger durch Hananias in die Gemeinschaft der Glaubenden (die Kirche) aufnahm und zu seinem Zeugen machte, ihn in Einklang mit dem Glauben Israels zu den Heiden aussandte und ihm die ganz auf der Linie der Propheten liegende Botschaft des Auferstandenen anvertraute. Für den heutigen Leser stellt sich die Frage, wie es zu dieser dreifachen Wiedergabe des Damaskuserlebnisses gekommen ist und wie sich die Aussagen der Apg zu denen des Apostels selbst verhalten. Eine Antwort darauf versucht die diachrone Untersuchung.

II. DIACHRONE UNTERSUCHUNG

1. Redaktionskritische Beobachtungen

Eine Durchsicht der drei Texte zeigt, wie in vielen Arbeiten und Kommentaren schon dargelegt[10], eine Fülle von Anzeichen lk Diktion. Hier seien nur einzelne Beispiele angeführt:

In *9,3-19* die häufige Verwendung von δέ anstelle von καί, ferner 9,3 ἐγένετο, auch ἐν τῷ mit Infinitv, das Verb ἐγγίζω und außerdem »plötzlich« (im Kontext einer Theophanie nur noch Lk 2,13). Die vorliegende doppelte Anrede »Saul, Saul« (9,4) entspricht der lk Vorliebe für die Übernahme solcher Verdoppelungen aus dem AT; ebenso die Identifikation Christi mit denen, die um seinetwillen verfolgt werden (9,5; vgl. Lk 10,6; Apg 5,39). Als Vorzugsworte des Lukas gelten ἀνάστηθι, λαληθήσεται, δεῖ (9,6); ferner in V. 7 οἱ ἄνδρες (9,7). »Ein Jünger mit Namen Hananias« (9,10) entspricht »ein Priester mit Namen Zacharias« (Lk 1,5a). Die 22,10-16 vorliegende Entsprechung des Erscheinungsgesprächs Christus und Hananias mit dem vorher erzählten

---

9. D. MARGUERAT, *Saul's Conversion (Acts 9, 22, 26) and the Multiplication of Narrative in Acts*, in C.M. TUCKETT (ed.), *Luke's Literary Achievement. Collected Essays*, Sheffield, 1995, pp. 127-155.
10. Vgl. bes. S. SABUGAL, *La Conversione di S. Paolo. Esegesi, storia, teologia*, Rom, 1992.

Gespräch Christus und Paulus hat ihre Parallele in den Visionen des Cornelius in Apg 10,3-6 und des Petrus in Apg 10,10-16. Die Einwände im Erscheinungsgespräch V. 13 haben außer Gen 22,1-2; 1 Sam 3,4-6 Parallelen in den Einwänden von Zacharias und Maria in den Verkündigungsgeschichten Lk 1. Als lk gilt auch V. 15 der Imperativ πορεύου, das bei Mt und Mk völlig fehlende ἐνώπιον und die Wendung »für meinen Namen leiden« (9,16). Charakteristisch für Lukas ist schließlich »damit...du erfüllt wirst mit Heiligem Geist« (9,18), sowie die in Gegenüberstellung zu V. 9 gemachten Aussagen ἀνέβλεψεν (vgl. 9,12) und λαβὼν τροφὴν ἐνίσχυσεν (vgl. 2,46; 27,33.34).

Anzeichen lk Redaktion ist innerhalb von *22,6-21* die Schilderung der Blindenheilung 22,13 analog zu der Heilung des Blinden bei Jericho (Lk 18,43). Charakteristisch für Lukas ist auch καὶ νῦν τί μέλλεις sowie »anrufend den Namen des Herrn« (22,16). Viele Merkmale lk Stils finden sich in 22,17-21, angefangen von der einleitenden Partizipialkonstruktion »es geschah mir dem Zurückkehrenden nach Jerusalem und als ich betete (προσευχομένου μου) im Tempel...« (22,17) bis hin zu dem erwähnten typischen Einspruch in dem Erscheinungsgespräch (22,19; wie bei Zacharias, Maria, Hananias), der hier zudem die Steinigung des Stephanus mit den gleichen Worten wie Apg 7,58–8,1 (jetzt nur im Mund des Paulus) geltend macht.

In der dritten Wiedergabe des Damaskuserlebnisses *26,12-18* verraten die Verdeutlichungen (»ein Licht heller als die Sonne umleuchtet mich«; »in hebräischer Sprache«) und die Ergänzung durch das griechische Sprichwort die Handschrift des Verfassers. Das gilt auch für die analog zu 9,6 und in engster Anlehnung an Ez 2,1 wiedergegebene Aufforderung: »steh auf und stell dich auf die Füße; denn dazu bin ich dir erschienen« (22,16). Der Sprache des Lukas entspricht die Bestellung zum »Diener und Zeugen« (s.o.); auf ihn geht wohl auch die Ausweitung der Zeugenschaft über das »was du gesehen hast« hinaus auf »das, was ich dich werde sehen lassen« zurück (22,10; 26,16), wie auch die Formulierung »zu denen (den Heiden) ich dich sende« (26,17; vgl. 28,28). Außerdem entspricht die inhaltliche Bestimmung der Sendung in 26,18 der Sprache des Lukas: mit Worten aus Jes 42,7.16 (»blinde Augen zu öffnen...«; vgl. Lk 4,18) und der urkirchlichen Verkündigung über Erlangen der Sündenvergebung, Teilhabe an dem Los der Geheiligten durch den Glauben an Christus (ähnlich wie in Apg 5,31; 20,21.32; vgl. Lk 24,47).

Als allgemeines Charakteristikum lk Redaktion kann schließlich noch die Erzählweise insgesamt (hellenistischer Episodenstil[11]) mit der Vorliebe für Dialoge und dramatische Szenen angeführt werden.

2. Traditionskritische Beobachtungen

Es stellt sich die Frage: Lassen sich unter dieser lk Redaktionsdecke noch Anzeichen erkennen, die auf eine Vorlage oder Quelle für diese

---

11. Vgl. E. PLÜMACHER, *Lukas als hellenistischer Schriftsteller. Studien zur Apostelgeschichte* (SUNT, 9), Göttingen, 1972. ID., *Die Apostelgeschichte als historische Monographie*, in J. KREMER (ed), *Les Actes des Apôtres. Traditions, rédaction, théologie* (BETL, 48), Gembloux, 1979, pp. 457-466. ID., Art. *Apostelgeschichte*, in *TRE* 3 (1978), pp. 483-528.

Angaben verweisen und Rückschlüsse darauf und nicht zuletzt auf das Damaskuserlebnis selbst erlauben.

a. Indizien für vorlk Tradition

Mehrere Angaben in den drei Texten können als Spuren einer vom Redaktor benutzten Quelle bewertet werden (im Blick auf die Zielsetzung des Referates werden hier nur einige angeführt), das gilt besonders für 9,3-20:

(1) Die Ortsangabe Damaskus; die Angabe über die Verfolgertätigkeit des Paulus.

(2) Die Form »Saul« (der Verfasser verwendet sonst die griechische Form Σαῦλος: 7,58; 8,1-3; 9,1.8.11.24; 11,25.30; 13,1.2.7.9); das Verbum περιστράπτειν und die Wendung »ein Licht vom Himmel« (9,3); vermutlich auch der dreimal fast wörtlich wiederholte Dialog 9,4b.5.

(3) Die Angaben über eine Reaktion des Paulus und seiner Begleiter; dafür sprechen das Hapaxlegomenon ἐνεοί (9,7), die dreimalige Wiederholung dieser Angaben darüber (wie vielleicht auch über die Erblindung?).

(4) Der Name Hananias, dessen Begegnung mit Paulus in dem Haus eines »Judas« (mit der Ortsangabe »die Gerade Straße«) sowie dessen Beteiligung an der Taufe des Paulus. Inwieweit nach der Vorlage Hananias dem Paulus irgendeinen Auftrag (eine Sendung) mitteilte, ist kaum mehr unter der lk Redaktionsdecke zu erkennen.

Aufgrund dieser Beobachtungen legt sich die Hypothese nahe, daß der Verfasser der Apg eine Überlieferung (mündlich oder schriftlich) gekannt hat, die von einer Bekehrung des Paulus in Verbindung mit einem außergewöhnlichen, wunderbaren Erlebnis vor Damaskus erzählte[12]. Diese bildete die Grundlage seiner Darstellung in Apg 9,3-20, die er dann – vermutlich unter Benützung noch anderer Nachrichten – (z.B. über die Heidenmission des Paulus und andere Visionen des Apostels) redaktionell überarbeitet hat, bzw. zu Berufungserzählungen umgestaltet hat.

b. Herkunft der Vorlage (Saulustradition) und weiterer Quellen des Verfassers

(1) Auf die Existenz einer Tradition über die Bekehrung des Paulus verweist in Gal 1,22-24 die Angabe des Paulus: »Ich war persönlich in

---

12. Vgl. K. LÖNING, *Die Saulustradition in der Apostelgeschichte* (NTAbh, 9), Münster, 1973.

den christlichen Kirchen in Judäa unbekannt. Sie hatten aber nur gehört, daß derjenige, der uns einst verfolgte, jetzt den Glauben, den er früher zerstören wollte, verkündet, und sie lobten Gott um meinetwillen«. Nach dieser Aussage des Apostels war also den Gemeinden Judäas bekannt, daß der einstige Verfolger jetzt das Evangelium verkündete. Ob diesen Gemeinden auch die von Paulus Gal 1,16 später niedergeschriebene besondere Berufung zum Heidenapostel bekannt war, geht aus dem Text nicht hervor und ist eher unwahrscheinlich.

Die Verse von Gal 1,22-24 sagen nichts über ein besonderes Erlebnis des Paulus, das seine Umkehr bewirkte. Es liegt aber nahe, daß in den Gemeinden Judäas über den großen Wandel des ehemaligen Verfolgers gesprochen und dieser auf ein wunderbares Geschehen zurückgeführt wurde. Dabei konnten sich die Erzähler möglicherweise auf Angaben des Hananias oder der Begleiter des Paulus bei seinem Gang nach Damaskus berufen und diese entsprechend damaliger Auffassungen anschaulich schildern, ähnlich etwa wie die Bekehrung eines Heliodor und unter kreativer Gestaltung eines Erscheinungsgesprächs.

(2) Für die freie, dichterische Umgestaltung dieser Bekehrungsgeschichte in Apg 22 und 26 stand Lukas wohl kaum eine Vorlage zur Verfügung. Jedenfalls weisen die Texte keine eindeutigen Indizien dafür auf. Allerdings konnte Lukas diese Umgestaltung der Bekehrungsgeschichte zu Berufungsgeschichten nur leisten, weil er um die Bedeutung des Paulus für die Heidenmission wußte, wie die Schilderungen der Missionsreisen sowie der Gefangenschaft unmißverständlich belegen. Das Wissen darum kann in etwa als eine »zweite Quelle«, nicht aber als eine schriftliche Vorlage, angesehen werden. Inwieweit dazu auch Angaben über weitere Visionen und sogar eine solche in Jerusalem gehörten, ist kaum mehr zu eruieren[13]. Die eigenen Angaben des Paulus kommen dafür weniger in Frage, wie ein Vergleich seiner Aussagen mit denen in der Apg zeigt.

3. Vergleich mit den eigenen Aussagen des Paulus

Der Apostel Paulus hat in seinen Briefen zwar niemals sein Damaskuserlebnis geschildert, aber mehrfach darauf kurz Bezug genommen. Eine Betrachtung dieser Stellen ist für die Frage nach einer Vorlage von Apg 9 und deren redaktioneller Umgestaltung durch Lukas höchst aufschlußreich.

---

13. Betreffs der Vision in Jerusalem wird vereinzelt vermutet, daß Lukas eine diesbezügliche Sonderüberlieferung zur Verfügung gestanden habe. Näher liegt es jedoch, daß Lukas diese Vision frei gestaltet hat unter Auswertung der Nachrichten von einem Besuch Pauli in Jerusalem (vgl. 9,26; 15,4) und unter Rückgriff auf 7,58; 8,1.3.

a. Die eigenen Aussagen des Paulus

(1) *Gal 1,15-17*: Im 1. Kap. des Gal sieht Paulus sich gezwungen, seine Sendung als Apostel gegenüber deren Infragestellung durch die Gegner zu verteidigen. Dies tut er schon am Anfang des Briefes mit den Worten: »Paulus, Apostel, nicht von Menschen und durch Menschen, sondern durch Jesus Christus und Gott, den Vater, der ihn von den Toten auferweckt hat« (1,1). Er wiederholt dies kurz darauf (1,12), indem er nochmals betont, daß er das Evangelium »nicht von Menschen übernommen« habe, sondern »durch die Offenbarung Jesu Christi« (gen. obj.). Als Beleg dafür erinnert er an seinen Werdegang, nämlich den früheren Gesetzeseifer und seine Verfolgung der »Kirche Gottes« (1,13f), sodann seine Berufung. Dazu schreibt er: »Als es aber Gott gefiel, der mich vom Mutterschoß an aussonderte und durch seine Gnade berief, seinen Sohn mir (ἐν ἐμοί) zu offenbaren, damit ich ihn bei den Heiden verkünde« (1,15.16ab). Dieser Nebensatz ist hingeordnet auf den Hauptsatz: »Da wandte ich mich sofort nicht an Fleisch und Blut« (1,16c). Unter Hinweis auf seine Erwählung in der Sprache der Prophetenberufung (vgl. Jes 49,1) erwähnt er kurz die ihm von Gott geschenkte »Enthüllung« (ἀποκαλύψαι) seines Sohnes (des Gekreuzigten als Sohn Gottes) Die Bestimmung ἐν ἐμοί meint nicht unbedingt ein bloß inneres, sondern ein ihn existentiell ganz ergreifendes Geschehen. Es geht also nicht um die Offenbarung einer Wahrheit, sondern einer Person. Dies geschah mit dem Ziel (ἵνα), ihn bei den Heiden zu verkünden. In dem anschließenden Hauptsatz betont er dann, daß er sich unmittelbar darauf nicht an Menschen (Fleisch und Blut) wandte, auch nicht an die vor ihm zu Aposteln Berufenen in Jerusalem, sondern in die Arabia ging und wieder nach Damaskus zurückkehrte. Es kommt also Paulus hier darauf an, den Gegnern zu beweisen, daß er seine Berufung zum Apostel nicht Menschen verdankt, sondern einzig Gott. Er ist also kein zweitrangiger Apostel, auch wenn er nicht der Apg 1,21f genannten Voraussetzung für ein Apostelamt gerecht wird. Beachtenswert ist andererseits für einen Vergleich mit den Angaben der Apg, daß sich diese Offenbarung Christi offensichtlich in der Nähe oder in der Stadt Damaskus ereignete, wie die Notizen über seine Rückkehr dorthin (Gal 1,17) und über seine spätere Flucht von dort (2 Kor 11,32f) wahrscheinlich machen.

(2) *1 Kor 9,1*: In der Auseinandersetzung mit Gegnern in der Gemeinde von Korinth beruft sich Paulus zur Verteidigung seiner Freiheit auf die Berufung zum Apostel mit den Worten: »Bin ich nicht frei? Bin ich nicht ein Apostel? Habe ich nicht den Herrn gesehen?«. Damit meint Paulus eindeutig ein Sehen des Kyrios, des erhöhten Herrn, das den anderen Christen in Korinth nicht zuteil geworden ist. Durch das Perfekt ἑόρακα deutet er an, daß dieses Sehen nicht bloß ein einmaliges Konstatieren war, sondern eine bis jetzt andauernde Wirkung hat. Wie aber dieses »gesehen« zu verstehen ist, das führt Paulus hier nicht aus und kann nur aus anderen Texten irgendwie näher bestimmt werden.

(3) *1 Kor 15,8*: Im Rahmen seiner Verteidigung der Osterbotschaft zitiert Paulus hier eine alte, ihm schon vorgegebene Überlieferung (1 Kor 15,3-11), zu der auch eine Aufzählung derer gehört, denen wie Kephas und den Zwölf der Auferstandene »erschien« (ὤφθη). Am Ende der Aufzählung schreibt er: »Als letztem von allen, wie der Fehlgeburt, erschien er auch mir«. (Paulus übernimmt hier die vorgegebene Form ὤφθη). Dabei setzt er voraus, daß das Gal 1,15-17 und 1 Kor 9,1 erwähnte »Offenbaren« bzw. »Sehen« auf einer Ebene

liegt mit den einzigartigen Ostererfahrungen von Petrus und den anderen Aposteln. Mit der Angabe »als letztem von allen« (vgl. Mk 12,22) bezeichnet er sich nach der vorherigen Aufzählung (»dann... darauf«) als den, dem der Auferstandene zeitlich zuletzt erschien. Daß er »der geringste« (ἐλάχιστος) der Apostel ist (im Unterschied zu dem als ersten genannten Petrus oder den »drei Säulen« Gal 2,9), begründet er mit dem Hinweis auf seine Tätigkeit als Verfolger (V. 9). Die von 1 Kor 9,1 (ἑόρακα) und von Gal 1,16 (ἀποκαλύψαι) verschiedene Diktion setzt voraus, daß es sich um ein Geschehen handelt, das im Unterschied zu alltäglichen Begebenheiten als Wirken Gottes (»offenbaren«), als Handeln des Auferstandenen (»erschien«) und aus der Sicht des Betroffenen (in seiner eigenen Sprache) als »sehen« bezeichnet werden kann. Es fehlt hier jeder Hinweis auf ein ekstatisches Erlebnis (wie Apg 22,17; vgl. 2 Kor 12,1f), bzw. die Verbindung mit einer außergewöhnlichen Lichterscheinung (wie Apg 9,3; 22,6; 26,13). Beachtenswert ist, daß er unmittelbar anschließend auf seine Tätigkeit als Verfolger eingeht (15,9), die er auch im Kontext von Gal 1,15-17 erwähnt.

(4) *Phil 3,7f*: Paulus schreibt hier im Rahmen einer Selbstverteidigung (3,3-11) und nach Angaben über seinen Eifer als Pharisäer bei der Verfolgung der Kirche (3,6) über den Grund seiner Wende: »Aber was mir ein Gewinn war, dies habe ich um Christi willen für Schaden erachtet. Ja ich erachte alles für Schaden gegenüber der überragenden Erkenntnis (τὸ ὑπερέχον τῆς γνώσεως) Christi Jesu, meines Herrn, um dessentwillen ich alles für Schaden erachte, und ich erachte es als Dreck, damit ich Christus gewinne« (3,7-8). Maßgeblich für seine Wende war demnach eine einzigartige »Erkenntnis« Christi. Allerdings zeigt der Kontext, daß diese »Erkenntnis« noch hingeordnet ist auf ein entsprechendes Leben (»damit ich Christus gewinne«, 3,8) und ein weiteres Erkennen: »ihn zu erkennen und die Macht seiner Auferstehung und die Gemeinschaft seiner Leiden« (3,10). Das dem Apostel bei seiner Wende geschenkte einzigartige Erkennen Christi findet demnach in seiner Christusgemeinschaft und der damit verbundenen tieferen Erkenntnis Christi eine Weiterführung.

(5) *2 Kor 4,6*: Paulus verteidigt in 2 Kor 2,14–7,4 sein ihm durch Gottes Erbarmen verliehenes »Amt« (διακονία), mit dem eine unlautere Amtsführung, wie sie ihm unterstellt wird, unvereinbar ist (4,1-6). Als Verwurzelung seiner ihm anvertrauten Christusverkündigung führt er an: »Denn Gott, der sprach: aus der Finsternis soll Licht aufleuchten, er ist in unseren Herzen aufgeleuchtet zum Aufstrahlen der Erkenntnis der Herrlichkeit Gottes auf dem Antlitz Christi« (πρὸς φωτισμὸν τῆς γνώσεως τῆς δόξης τοῦ θεοῦ ἐν προσώπῳ Χριστοῦ). Diese in etwa für alle Hörer des Evangeliums geltende Aussage (vgl. V. 4) ist vom Kontext her auf eine besondere Erleuchtung des Apostels bezogen und somit eine Anspielung auf die ihm durch Gott geschenkte »Offenbarung Christi« (Gal 1,11.16), die ihm wie anderen Aposteln gewährte »Erscheinung« Christi (1 Kor 15,8) und das ihn vor anderen auszeichnende »Sehen« (1 Kor 9,1) und »Erkennen« (Phil 3,8) des Herrn Jesus Christus. Paulus betrachtet dies hier – über die anderen Aussagen hinausgehend – unter dem Aspekt, daß der Schöpfer des Lichts ihm in seinem Herzen aufleuchtete (in freier Wiedergabe von Gen 1,3; vgl. Jes 9,1) und dieses Licht (φωτισμόν) ihn dazu befähigte, den Anteil Christi an der Herrlichkeit Gottes, d.h. die göttliche Majestät Christi als »Bild Gottes« (4,5) und »Sohn Gottes« (vgl. Gal 1,16) zu erkennen.

b. Vergleich der Selbstaussagen mit Apg 9; 22; 26

Bei einem Vergleich dieser Selbstaussagen des Apostels Paulus mit den Erzählungen der Apg lassen sich mehrere Gemeinsamkeiten, aber auch viele Unterschiede feststellen:

(1) Gemeinsam: Die Erwähnung der Verfolgertätigkeit des Paulus (Gal 1,13; 1 Kor 15,9; Apg 9,1-2; 22,5; 26,12); die Angabe des Ortsnamens Damaskus (Gal 1,17; Apg 9,2.3.8.10; 22,6.10; 26,12); die Motive »Licht« (2 Kor 4,6; Apg 9,3; 22,6; 26,13) und »Sehen« (1 Kor 9,1; Apg 9,7 μηδένα; 22,9; 26,13); die Berufung zur Predigt bei den Heiden (Gal 1,16; Apg 22,21; 26,17.20).

(2) Verschieden: Es fehlt bei Paulus jede anschauliche Erzählung über eine außergewöhnliche Lichterscheinung und Stimme vom Himmel, über seine Begleiter und sein Erblinden, seine Heilung und Taufe sowie ein dreitägiges Fasten; es fehlt eine Wiedergabe von Dialogen in den Erscheinungsgesprächen und vor allem jeder Hinweis auf die Vermittlerrolle des Hananias; schließlich fehlen die Ankündigung über sein zukünftiges Leiden, über ein erst in Zukunft erfolgendes Sehen und Hören Christi bzw. über ein ekstatisches Erlebnis in Jerusalem.

(3) Unvereinbar mit den Aussagen des Paulus ist, ja in direktem Widerspruch dazu steht, daß in Apg 9 seine Berufung zur Verkündigung bei den Heiden nicht erwähnt wird (anders 26,16-18) und er nach Apg 22,17-21 erst bei einem ekstatischen Erlebnis im Tempel zu Jerusalem dazu ausgesandt wird. Unvereinbar ist auch mit Aussagen des Paulus, daß die einzigartige Christuserfahrung (die letzte Ostererfahrung) in der Apg zwar als »Sehen«, aber nach Art einer bloßen Vision, ja einer unter anderen geschildert wird.

Die angeführten Unterschiede und Widersprüche lassen kaum einen anderen Schluß zu, als daß Lukas sowie auch die Verfasser der ihm vorgegebenen Tradition (Saulustradition) die im Neuen Testament vorliegenden Selbstaussagen des Paulus so wohl nicht gekannt haben. Daraus folgt weiter: Lukas und die Verfasser seiner Vorlage haben das einzigartige Damaskuserlebnis des Paulus nicht einfach aufgrund zuverlässiger Nachrichten berichtet, sondern unter Auswertung von vorgegebenen Vorstellungen in erzählerischer Ausdeutung wiedergegeben. Dabei hat Lukas eine ihm vorgegebene Saulustradition, die am besten noch in Apg 9 zu erkennen ist, zumindest in Apg 22 und 26 dichterisch ausgestaltet, unter Berücksichtigung der ihm sonst noch bekannten Nachrichten über das Wirken des Paulus als Heidenapostel und der gegen ihn gerichteten Angriffe. Dabei ließ er sich nicht von einem neuzeitlichen oder auch damaligen Geschichtsinteresse leiten, sondern von der Absicht, das letztlich auf Gott und Jesus selbst zurückgehende Wirken des Apostels und seine Bedeutung für die Kirche zu verteidigen.

III. Vergleich von Apg 9; 22; 26 mit Lk 24

Die bei der synchronen und diachronen Untersuchung von Apg 9; 22; 26 festgestellte Eigenart des Umgangs mit vorgegebenen Überlieferungen lädt zu einem Vergleich dieser Texte mit den lk Osterevangelien ein. Im Blick auf die in der Einleitung genannte Zielsetzung beschränke ich mich darauf, auf einige Gemeinsamkeiten in der Darstellungsweise beider Textkomplexe aufmerksam zu machen.

1. Die Grabesgeschichte *Lk 24,1-12* beruht nicht auf einer Sonderüberlieferung (wie früher vertreten), sondern ist eine lk Redaktion von Mk 16,1-8[14]. Allenfalls für V. 12 rechnen manche Ausleger mit einer zusätzlichen, auch Joh 20,6-8 zugrundeliegenden Tradition. Voraus geht der Abschluß der Grabesgeschichte in Lk 23,55-56 (einer lk, szenischen Gestaltung der Angabe von Mk 15,47 »*sie sahen*«): die Frauen »*sahen*« das Grab Jesu, bereiteten nach ihrer Rückkehr wohlriechende Öle und Salben und »ruhten« während des Sabbats. Nach 24,1 kamen sie am Morgen des ersten Tages der Woche früh zum Grab mit den vorbereiteten wohlriechenden Ölen. Unter Auslassung der Frage, wer wohl den Stein wegwälzen werde (Mk 16,3), heißt es dann in einer sprachlich ausgewählten Diktion: »Sie *fanden* aber den Stein weggewälzt vom Grab, hineingehend aber *fanden* sie nicht den Leichnam des Herrn Jesus« (24,2; vgl. 24,23). Der Erzähler bemerkt darauf mit der für Lukas typischen Wendung ἐγένετο ἐν τῷ (so auch Apg 9,3): »Es geschah aber, als sie darüber ratlos waren, siehe, da traten zwei Männer in leuchtenden Gewändern zu ihnen«. Anstelle des Mk 16,5 erwähnten »jungen Mannes« sind es »zwei Männer« (ähnlich wie Apg 1,10, die nach jüdischer Auffassung als glaubwürdige Zeugen galten; vgl. Lk 24,13). Ihr Herantreten ruft bei den Frauen, die durch das Nicht-Finden des Leichnams schon verwirrt waren, nicht etwa bloß Entsetzen und Furcht hervor (so Mk 16,5), sondern läßt sie erschrocken »ihre Gesichter zu Boden neigen« (wohl angesichts der Betroffenheit durch diese »Erscheinung von Engeln«). Anders als Mk 16,6 reden die beiden himmlischen Boten

---

14. F. Neirynck, *Le récit du tombeau vide dans l'évangile de Luc (Lc 24,1-12)*, in Id., *Evangelica* (BETL, 60), Leuven, 1982, pp. 297-328. Id., *Luc 24,36-43. Un récit lucanien*, in Id., *Evangelica II 1982-1991* (BETL, 99), Leuven, 1991, pp. 205-226. Id., *Once more Luke 24,12*, in *ETL* 70 (1994) 319-340.

sie direkt mit einer Frage an, die einem Sprichwort ähnelt: »Was sucht
ihr den Lebenden bei den Toten?« (24,5c). Diese spricht plastisch die
Nutzlosigkeit ihres Suchens aus, so wie das Apg 26,14 zitierte Sprichwort die Nutzlosigkeit der Verfolgung bzw. des Widerstandes gegenüber
der Erwählung ausdrückt. Die Worte des Engels (nach Mk 16,6 »er ist
auferstanden; er ist nicht hier...«) gibt Lukas in umgestellter und ver-
kürzter Form wieder: »er ist nicht hier, er ist auferstanden« (24,9), wohl
nicht zuletzt in enger Anknüpfung an die sprichwortartige Frage, die von
dem Gesuchten als einem »Lebenden« sprach.

Ganz im Unterschied zu der Vorlage erzählt 24,6b-8 nicht eine Aussendung der Frauen zu den Jüngern und Petrus mit dem Auftrag, sie
mögen nach Galiläa gehen (Mk 16,7), sondern ihre Belehrung in Form
einer katechetischen Unterweisung. Durch diese werden die Frauen aufgefordert, sich an Jesu Worte in »Galiläa« zu erinnern. Damit wird die
Ortsangabe von Mk 16,7, die mit der lk Begrenzung aller Ostererscheinungen auf Jerusalem und Umgebung unvereinbar ist, auf kunstvolle
Weise beibehalten (wie bei der Renovierung eines Bauwerks ein guter
Konservator einen an seiner ursprünglichen Stelle nicht mehr gebrauch-
ten wertvollen Stein anderswo einfügt). Ausdrücklich bemerkt Lukas,
daß die Frauen sich wie gelehrige Schülerinnen an Jesu Ankündigung
seines Leidens und Auferstehens »erinnerten« (vgl. 22,61: »und Petrus
erinnerte sich...«), obwohl er diese nach Lk 9,22.43f; 17,22-25; 18,31-
33 nur an die Jünger richtete[15]. Die Frauen kehrten nach 24,9 zurück und
»berichteten dies alles den Elf und allen *übrigen*« (im Gegensatz zu Mk
16,8). Lukas führt die Frauen hier 24,10 namentlich an und erwähnt
auch »die *übrigen* Frauen bei ihnen«. Als sie das Erlebte den Aposteln
sagten, erschienen denen »diese Worte wie Geschwätz« und sie glaubten ihnen nicht. Die kunstvoll eingefügte Erinnerung der Frauen an die
Leidensankündigungen Jesu und die Notiz, daß ihr Bericht bei den Aposteln auf Unglauben stieß, dienen hier dazu, das Außergewöhnliche der
in Jesu eigenen Worten (nach 24,26 in den Schriften der Propheten)
schon verankerten Wahrheit der Osterbotschaft in Form einer Erzählung
zu betonen. Der in manchen Handschriften fehlende V. 12, der in letzter
Zeit mit Recht aber als authentisch bewertet wird, fügt noch an, daß
Petrus zum Grab lief, dort nur die Leinentücher sah und nach Hause ging
»staunend über das Geschehene«. Der Evangelist, der auch sonst die
Jünger entschuldigt (vgl. 22,45; Apg 12,14 sowie Lk 9,21 und die Auslassung von Mk 8,33), hat hier den Verweis auf Petrus in Mk 16,7 kunst-

---

15. Ein solches Desinteresse an logischer Übereinstimmung entspricht den unterschiedlichen Angaben über die Begleiter des Paulus in Apg 9; 22; 26.

voll aufgegriffen und als Vorbereitung auf die Wiedergabe der alten Tradition in Lk 24,34 (»dem Simon erschienen«) erzählerisch festgehalten. Durch diese Entsprechung (*inclusio*) zu 24,1 hat er zudem den Abschnitt abgerundet (wie Apg 9,3.19c). Sollte außer Mk 16,7 und Lk 24,34 noch eine weitere mit Joh 20,6-8 verwandte Vorlage bekannt gewesen sein, so wäre dies ein Anzeichen der auch sonst bei Lukas zu beobachtenden »gebundenen Redaktionsweise«.

Die hier in Kürze gebotene Durchsicht von Lk 24,1-12 zeigt, daß Lukas hier ähnlich wie Apg 9; 22; 26 eine ihm vorgegebene Tradition (hier Mk 16,1-8) in freier Weise und sprachlich kunstvoll wiedergegeben hat, nicht um eine exakte Berichterstattung zu bieten, sondern um den Leser von der Zuverlässigkeit der Lehre, in der sie unterwiesen sind (Lk 1,4), zu überzeugen, damit auch sie wie die Frauen und Petrus »staunen« und die unglaubwürdig klingende (vgl. 24,34: »wirklich«) Osterbotschaft im Licht der Worte Jesu sehen.

2. Die lange Ostergeschichte *Lk 24,13-35* über die Begegnung der Jünger mit dem Auferstandenen auf dem Weg nach Emmaus ist so deutlich durch die Sprache und Erzählweise des dritten Evangelisten geprägt, daß es kaum mehr möglich ist, eine zugrundeliegende Tradition im einzelnen zu erschließen[16]. Mehr noch als Apg 9; 22; 26 ist hier die kunstvolle Struktur und Erzählweise zu beobachten: z.B. von Jerusalem weg und nach Jerusalem zurück; Behinderung und Öffnung der Augen; drei Gespräche auf dem Weg; das Wortspiel »öffnen der Augen« und »öffnen der Schrift«. Die dramatische Gestaltung und die Fragen sowie Dialoge wecken ähnlich wie in Apg 9; 22; 26 das Interesse der Leser und beziehen sie in die Handlung mit ein. Die sympathische Schilderung der beiden Jünger leitet die Leser dazu an, sich mit ihnen und deren Fragen zu identifizieren, ähnlich wie dies die Einwände in den Erscheinungsgesprächen der Apg tun. Thematisch verwandt ist die Betonung des heilsgeschichtlichen »muß« (24,26; vgl. Apg 9,16; auch 14,26) sowie die Bezüge zum Alten Testament (Lk 24,27; Apg 22,14; 26,16-18.22), nicht aber zuletzt auch der Bezug auf Jerusalem (24,33; Apg 22,17f). Gemeinsam sind der Emmausgeschichte wie auch den Schilderungen in Apg 9; 22; 26 das Fehlen jeglichen Interesses an exakten Angaben, z.B. über die Lage von Emmaus und den zweiten Begleiter. Hierher gehören auch mehrere zumindest aus heutiger Sicht widersprüchliche Aussagen[17]

---

16. Vgl. J. WANKE, *Die Emmauserzählung. Eine redaktionsgeschichtliche Untersuchung zu Lk 24,13-35* (ETS, 31), Leipzig, 1973.
17. So z.B. die erwähnten Spannungen zwischen den Angaben von Lk 24,22-24 und 12; zwischen Lk 24,35 und 37.

sowie auch die chronologisch unrealistische Zeichnung, daß die erst spät (nach der Rückkehr des Petrus vom Grab) von Jerusalem weggegangenen Jünger nach dem Mahl beim Sonnenuntergang noch am selben Abend nach Jerusalem zurückkehren und dort die versammelte Gemeinde antreffen, die ihnen über die Erscheinung des Auferstandenen vor Simon Petrus (24,34) berichtet und der sie über ihr Erlebnis auf dem Weg und beim Brotbrechen erzählen.

Die oben zu Apg 9; 22; 26 gemachten Beobachtungen über die dichterische Erzählweise des Verfassers zwingen dazu, auch bei der Emmausgeschichte mit einer fiktionalen Darstellung zu rechnen, der es nicht um Information über der äußeren Ablauf, sondern um Hinführung zum Glauben an den Auferstandenen geht. Das trifft auch auf die – ohne Parallele in Apg 9; 22; 26 – dargebotenen Schilderungen von Schriftauslegung und »Brotbrechen«, den beiden Teilen urkirchlichen Gottesdienstes zu (vgl. 2,42.46; 20,7). Als Indizien für eine vorgegebene Überlieferung gelten die Namen Emmaus und Kleopas, das Motiv vom Wiedererkennen beim Mahl und das 24,34 zitierte Bekenntnis über die Erscheinung vor Simon. Vielleicht können auch mehrere Spannungen zum Kontext (z.B. zwischen 24,22-24 und 24,12; zwischen 24,35 und 24,37) als Anzeichen einer verwendeten Vorlage gewertet werden. Diese erlauben es allerdings ebenso wenig wie die zu Apg 9; 22; 26 angeführten Indizien, den Hergang des Erzählten im einzelnen zu bestimmen. Ein Vergleich mit der Apg bewahrt auch davor, aus der Emmausgeschichte zu folgern, daß der Auferstandene sozusagen »in anderer Gestalt« (vgl. Mk 16,12), auf diese Erde zurückgekehrt sei und mit den Jüngern wanderte wie solches in Mythen erzählt wird. So wie der Verfasser von Apg 9; 22; 26 die Leser in erzählerischer Form anleitete, über die wunderbare Berufung des Verfolgers Paulus zum Heidenapostel zu staunen und seine Botschaft anzunehmen, so werden die Leser von Lk 24,13-35 durch diese Erzählung angehalten, sich ähnlich wie die Emmausjünger durch die Besinnung auf die Schriften des Alten Bundes und durch das »Brotbrechen« zum Glauben an den Auferstandenen hinführen zu lassen.

3. Wie die beiden anderen lk Ostergeschichten weist auch *Lk 24,36-53* viele Merkmale einer kunstvollen Erzählung auf. Ein Vergleich mit der dreifachen Wiedergabe des Damaskusgeschehens ist bei diesem Text besonders hilfreich, da er schon von frühester Zeit an mißverstanden wurde und auch heute noch oft falsch interpretiert wird. Deshalb ist auf die einzelnen Teile dieses Osterevangeliums besonders einzugehen. In dem ersten Teil (24,36-43) schildert Lukas eine Erscheinung des Auferstandenen am Osterabend vor den in Jerusalem versammelten Jüngern

(parallel zu der von Joh 20,19-23), unmittelbar nach der Rückkehr der Emmausjünger und dem Bericht über die dem Simon wie ihnen zuteil gewordenen Erscheinungen des Auferstandenen (24,36). In Spannung dazu steht, daß Jesu Erscheinen bei ihnen Angst auslöste (24,37; anders als Joh 20,20). Ein Grund dafür, etwa die Betroffenheit durch ein leuchtendes Aussehen (vgl. 24,4), wird nicht genannt, wohl aber damit angedeutet, daß sie meinten, »einen Geist« (πνεῦμα, nach D φάντασμα) zu sehen (24,36; vgl. 39), den sie nicht mit ihrem Meister identifizieren konnten. Der Erschienene richtet daraufhin an die Betroffenen zwei Fragen (der auch Apg 9; 22; 26 beobachteten Vorliebe des Lukas entsprechend) nach dem Grund ihres Entsetzens und ihrer Zweifel (24,38). Er fordert sie dann (24,39) auf, seine Hände und Füße zu »sehen« und zu »betasten«, um sich davon zu überzeugen, daß er es ist und nicht ein Geist (πνεῦμα), dem Fleisch und Knochen fehlen. Möglicherweise liegt dieser Aufforderung die in Jerusalem weniger, aber Lukas (vgl. 10,4) bekannte griechisch-hellenistische Auffassung eines Unterschieds zwischen Leib und Seele zugrunde[18]. Der Evangelist erzählt nicht, daß die Jünger dieser Aufforderung folgten und die ihnen gezeigten Gliedmaßen (24,40 nach der besten Textüberlieferung; das Gesicht wird nicht erwähnt) kritisch anschauten oder sogar berührten; er hält hingegen fest, daß sie noch nicht glaubten und nur staunten (wie Petrus nach 24,12; vgl. 32). Ihren Unglauben entschuldigt er seinem oben erwähnten Interesse an einer Verteidigung der Seinigen gemäß mit dem Hinweis auf ihre Freude (24,41). Um sie daraufhin zum Glauben zu führen, fragt Jesus (wiederum der Vorliebe des Lukas für Fragen entsprechend) nach einer Speise und ißt den ihm dargereichten Teil eines gebratenen Fisches (nach jüngeren Handschriften: »und einer Honigwabe«) vor ihren Augen, sozusagen als stringenter Beweis dafür, daß er vor ihnen steht (nicht aber als Zeichen der Mahlgemeinschaft mit ihnen wie 24,30; Apg 10,40 und Joh 21,10, wie eine wohl jüngere Textvariante nahelegt: »und das Übriggebliebene gab er ihnen«). Auffallenderweise schreibt Lukas nichts darüber, ob die Jünger dadurch zum Glauben kamen, sondern führt unmittelbar anschließend (die Übersetzung »dann« EÜ verdeckt das) eine zusammenfassende Wiedergabe von Worten Jesu an.

Bei der Übersicht wurde schon angedeutet, daß diese anschauliche Schilderung viele Anzeichen lk Redaktion aufweist. Dazu gehören nicht bloß das lk Vokabular und die Vorliebe für Fragen, sondern vor allem die anschauliche, im einzelnen aber an dem Hergang nicht so sehr inter-

---

18. P. HOFFMANN, *Studien zur Frühgeschichte der Jesus-Bewegung* (SBAB, 17), Stuttgart, ²1995, pp. 188-256.

essierte Schilderung eines dreifach gesteigerten Beweises (sehen, berühren, essen) in dem für Lukas typischen Episodenstil, der vieles offen und unbestimmt läßt (z.B. keine Angabe über das Befolgen der Aufforderung zum Sehen und Berühren). Wie die dreifache Wiedergabe des Damaskuserlebnisses läßt diese lk Wiedergabe einer Erscheinung des Auferstandenen auch mehrere Indizien einer ihm vorgegebenen Tradition erkennen: (1) Die Erscheinung des Auferstandenen wohl am Osterabend (vgl. Joh 20,19-22), die in Spannung zu dem vorausgehenden Kontext steht (nach der Rückkehr der Emmausjünger und der erwarteten Freude über das Wiedersehen). (2) Das Motiv des Nicht-Erkennens bzw. Zweifels und Angebotes einer Hilfe zur Überwindung dieser Zweifel wie bei Thomas (Joh 20,25-29; vgl. Joh 21,4f). (3) Das abrupte Abbrechen dieser Szene ohne Angabe einer Reaktion der Jünger.

Die im zweiten Teil (24,44-49) ohne Überleitung angefügte Rede Jesu weist formal und zum Teil inhaltlich eine auffallende Verwandtschaft mit Apg 26,16-18 auf. Es geht hier zwar nicht direkt um die Aussendung eines Apostels zu den Heiden, sondern um eine ganz in der Sprache urkirchlicher Verkündigung vorliegende Zusammenfassung der Botschaft Jesu: dazu gehört erstens der Hinweis auf das heilsgeschichtliche »Muß« (24,44) der Erfüllung der alttestamentlichen Aussagen über Jesus (vgl. 24,7.26; Apg 2,23-28; 8,32-35; 13,27). Um dieses zu verstehen, so erklärt der Auferstandene, »öffnete« er ihnen den »Sinn« (24,45), d.h. ihr verschloßenes »Herz« (vgl. Apg 16,14) in einer Abwandlung der Metapher vom Öffnen der »Augen« (24,31; vgl. Apg 26,18) bzw. der »Schriften« (24,32). Nur so können sie seine Passion, seine Auferstehung und die in seinem Namen erfolgende Predigt der Umkehr bei allen Völkern, angefangen von Jerusalem (vgl. Apg 1,8), erkennen. Ausdrücklich heißt es weiters, wie auch Apg 22,15.18; 26,16, daß sie »Zeugen« dafür sein sollen und werden (24,48). Die hier verheißene Zusage der »Kraft aus der Höhe« darf in Analogie zu der Paulus nach Apg 9,17 in Verbindung mit seiner Blindenheilung und Taufe zugesagten Begabung mit dem »Heiligen Geist« gesehen werden. Es ist kaum zu bezweifeln, daß diese Worte des Auferstandenen von diesem so nicht am Osterabend gesprochen wurden. Die freie Wiedergabe seiner Botschaft bei der Schilderung der Berufung des Paulus vor Damaskus in Apg 26,16-18 kann als eine Bestätigung dafür dienen.

In dem dritten Teil (24,50-53) berichtet Lukas, ohne vorher eine Reaktion der Jünger auf die Worte Jesu zu erwähnen, daß der Auferstandene die Jünger nach Betanien führte und dort am Osterabend, während er sie in der Weise des Hohenpriesters segnete (vgl. Lev 9,22-24; Sir 50,20), in den Himmel aufgenommen wurde. Beachtenswert ist für diese geraffte, realistisch anmutende Schilderung, daß das Erzählte sich kaum mit der vorgerückten Stunde des Osterabends und erst recht nicht mit den Angaben von Apg 1,3.9-12 (nach 40 Tagen) vereinbaren läßt. Inwieweit Lukas für diese Erzählung (wie auch für Apg 1,9-14) die Überlieferung von einer »Aufnahme in den Himmel« (wie die des Elija) vorgegeben war, läßt sich nicht mehr mit Sicherheit feststellen. Jedenfalls unterstreicht die eindeutig fiktionale Schilderung der Vision im Tempel zu Jerusalem (Apg 22,17-21) die Vermutung, daß auch hier (wie Apg 1,9-13) eine fiktionale Erzählung vorliegt, die in narrativer Weise aufzeigen soll, daß die Ostererscheinungen ein Ende gefunden haben und somit einer vergangenen Epoche angehören. Die abschließende Notiz, daß die Jünger Jesus »anbeteten« (es ist die erste Angabe über ihre Reaktion in dieser Perikope) und mit großer »Freude« (vgl. 24,41) nach Jerusalem zurückkehrten, kann als eine Entsprechung (*inclusio*) zu Lk 24,33 (Rückkehr nach Jerusalem) und Lk 24,36f (Erschrecken der Jünger) gewertet werden, somit als ein weiteres Anzeichen für die kunstvolle Erzählweise des Evangelisten, wie sie auch Apg 9 bestimmt.

IV. Ergebnis und Folgerungen

1. Als erste Folgerung aus dem dargebotenen Vergleich von Apg 9; 22; 26 mit Lk 24 kann festgehalten werden: In den Texten liegt unverkennbar eine typisch lk Erzählweise vor. In beiden Fällen sind aber noch Indizien erkennbar, die dank der »gebundenen Redaktion« des Verfassers auf von ihm benützte Vorlagen bzw. Quellen verweisen, mögen diese auch im einzelnen nicht ganz zu rekonstruieren sein. Die untersuchten Texte sind also keineswegs völlig freie Bildungen, ohne jeglichen Anhalt in älteren Überlieferungen bzw. in der Geschichte, wie viele Dichtungen oder antike Mythen[19].

Als zweite und wohl wichtigere Folgerung ist festzuhalten, daß der Verfasser die ihm vorgegebenen Traditionen sehr eigenständig gestaltet hat. Charakteristisch dafür ist die novellistische, den Leser fesselnde Darstellungsweise, z.B. die Fragen, Dialoge (mit Einwänden), Illustrationen (z.B. Heilung von der Blindheit durch Hananias), die Umgestaltung der Bekehrungsgeschichte – je nach Kontext – zu einer Berufungsgeschichte mit der Vision im Tempel und der freigestalteten

---

19. Vgl. dem gegenüber die verwandte, aber völlig andere Schilderung bei Homer, Odyssee XXIII, 220-240: Begegnung von Athene und Odysseus; ähnlich Aeneis II, 268-294: Vision der Creusa.

Aussendungsrede. Ebenso hat Lukas – geleitet durch ein besonderes Interesse – die ihm vorgegebene Grabesgeschichte in seinem Evangelium fiktional umgestaltet, etwa durch Einfügung der sprichwortartigen Frage der beiden »Männer« (als zuverlässige Zeugen), durch ihre Aufforderung, sich an Jesu Voraussagen in Galiläa zu erinnern, und deren Folgeleistung durch die Frauen, weiters durch die Angabe, daß die Frauen die Jünger benachrichtigen, aber auf Unverständnis stoßen, den Petrus jedoch veranlassen, zum Grab zu eilen (in Abwandlung der vorgegebenen Erwähnung des Petrus und in Entsprechung zur Überlieferung von der ihm gewährten Christuserscheinung). Auf ähnliche Weise hat Lukas auch in der Emmausgeschichte die Überlieferung von der Christusbegegnung des Kleopas redaktionell umgestaltet: durch die Erscheinung vor zwei Männern (als glaubwürdigen Zeugen), ihre im Episodenstil geschilderte Belehrung durch den Auferstandenen über die Auslegung der Schriften und schließlich durch die *relecture* der Tradition vom urkirchlichen »Brotbrechen« in der knappen Schilderung eines Mahles in Emmaus. Wenn wir den freien Umgang des Lukas mit seiner Vorlage in Apg 9; 22; 26 berücksichtigen, kann auch die Schilderung über die Erscheinung des Auferstandenen am Osterabend nur als fiktionale *relecture* einer vorgegebenen Überlieferung bewertet werden, die dazu dient, den Osterglauben vor dem Verdacht der Illusion zu schützen. Das zeigt besonders der in der Apologetik oft mißverstandene dreifache Beweis der Leiblichkeit des Auferstandenen, aber auch die freie Wiedergabe der Worte Jesu. Als fiktionale Schilderung ist zudem die episodenartig erzählte Himmelfahrt am Osterabend zu bewerten, die den Abschluß der Ostererscheinungen veranschaulichen und die Bindung der Apostelpredigt an Jerusalem und den Tempel betonen soll. Dagegen sprechen nicht die alten Historisierungen[20].

2. Die festgestellte fiktionale Darstellungsweise bereitet nicht wenigen Lesern unserer Tage große Schwierigkeiten. Im Gefolge der neuzeitlichen, durch das Modell der Naturwissenschaften geprägten Sicht der Geschichte lesen sie die aus der Vergangenheit stammenden Texte unter der Fragestellung, »wie es eigentlich gewesen ist« (L. von Ranke), und erwarten aus den biblischen Erzählungen und Berichten eine entsprechende Antwort. Die freie, fast dichterisch anmutende und in Einzelheiten oft gegenüber anderen Texten divergierende Darstellung der Begegnung mit dem Auferstandenen in Lk 24 erweckt daher bei vielen

---

20. Ansatzweise schon Mk 16,14.19, deutlich in der Lokaltradition eines »Klein-Galiläa« auf dem Ölberg, die diese Angabe mit der Erscheinung in Galiläa nach Mt 28 zu harmonisieren sucht.

den Eindruck, sie sei »nicht wahr«. Demgegenüber regt die unterschiedliche, jeweils gesteigerte Wiedergabe ein und desselben Damaskusgeschehens in der Apg durch denselben Autor dazu an, auf die Eigenart und Textpragmatik der drei Schilderungen zu achten. Diese lassen nämlich bei näherer Betrachtung erkennen: Es geht ihrem Verfasser nicht um historisch exakte, protokollarische Geschichtsschreibung; vielmehr will er die Leser durch die unterschiedliche, rhetorisch geschickte Darbietung dazu anzuleiten, die einzigartige Wende im Leben des Verfolgers Paulus und sein Engagement für die Heidenmission als eine durch den auferstandenen Herrn bzw. durch Gott gewirkte Bekehrung und Berufung zu verstehen, und nicht etwa als Produkt von Überlegungen, Enttäuschungen oder anderen Ursachen.

Für den freien Umgang des Verfassers mit seiner Vorlage und eventuell auch anderen Quellen bietet die Kunst- und Musikgeschichte mehrere illustrative Beispiele. Ich erwähne nur die »Bekehrung des Paulus« von Pieter Bruegel d. Ä. († 1569; Wien, Kunsthistorisches Museum), die das Geschehen in eine felsige Landschaft verlegt, welche eine mächtige Truppe zur Umkehr zwingt, und den vom Pferd (vom hohen Roß) gestürzten Paulus ganz klein (und kaum sichtbar) in die monumentale Szenerie einbettet. Diese kunstvolle Interpretation der biblischen Texte regt den Betrachter zum Staunen und Nachsinnen an (mag sie auch mehr die Bekehrung als die Berufung in den Mittelpunkt stellen). Ähnlich gestaltet Felix Mendelsohn-Bartholdy († 1847) in seinem Oratorium »Paulus« die Bekehrung und Berufung nicht bloß durch musikalische Wiedergabe von Texten aus Apg 9, sondern vor allem durch eingestreute Choräle nach Worten von Jes 60,1-2; Röm 11,33.36; Offb 15,4 und Arien (z.B. die Gebete des Paulus) in Anlehnung an Ps 51,3.13.19 und Ps 76,12.13. Analog dazu bieten nicht wenige bildnerische Darstellungen der in Lk 24 wiedergegebenen Szenen eine Illustration der fiktionalen Ostergeschichten. So finden sich ebenso wie in Lk 24 mehrmals die dort erzählten Episoden alle auf einer Bildtafel zusammen (z.B. »Auferstehung Christi«, Westfälischer Meister, Aachener Privatbesitz, Ende des 15. Jahrhunderts). Solche Kunstwerke verlangen vom Zuhörer und Betrachter, das musikalisch Dargebotene und bildnerisch Dargestellte nicht unter dem Aspekt der historischen Abfolge und Treue, sondern nach Art von poetischen Liedern und Bildern zu betrachten. Ebenso sind die untersuchten biblischen Texte in einer Art »deuxième naivité« (P. Ricœur) zu lesen, ohne sich durch heutige kritische Rückfragen den Blick für das verstellen zu lassen, was der biblische Verfasser als Wort Gottes in der Sprache seiner Zeit uns damit verkündet.

3. Die Frage nach der geschichtlichen Verankerung der dreifachen Wiedergabe des Damaskuserlebnisses Pauli wie auch der lk Osterevangelien kann aus heutiger Sicht nur durch eine sehr differenzierte Beurteilung der vorliegenden Texte beantwortet werden. Dies ist m.E. das wichtigste Ergebnis der Untersuchung; denn ein aufmerksamer Vergleich von Apg 9; 22; 26 mit den eigenen Angaben des Apostel Paulus

zeigt, wie oben dargelegt: Der Verfasser der Apg hat die Berufung des Paulus zum Heidenmissionar sozusagen auf eine »Vision« des Verfolgers vor Damaskus (so nach Apg 26) bzw. in Jerusalem (nach Apg 22), und zwar eine Vision neben anderen (Apg 26,16), reduziert. Diese hat Lukas gewiß nicht wie liberale Theologen des letzten Jahrhunderts und neuerdings G. Lüdemann als rein subjektive, psychologisch oder tiefenpsychologisch erklärbare Vision aufgefaßt. Eine solche Betrachtungsweise lag ihm völlig fern. Allerdings unterscheidet sich diese lk Sicht wesentlich von der des Paulus; denn dieser wertete seine Berufung zum Apostel der Heiden als einzigartiges Geschehen, das er weder anschaulich schildert noch mit eindeutig klaren Begriffen definiert: als letzte Ostererscheinung (1 Kor 15,8), als ein anderen nicht zuteil gewordenes »Sehen« (1 Kor 9,1), ein einzigartiges »Erkennen« (Phil 3,7-8), das ihm durch eine Offenbarung Gottes (Gal 1,16) und eine damit verbundene innere »Erleuchtung« (2 Kor 4,6) zuteil wurde. Im Vergleich damit ist die Darstellungsweise in der Apg sehr unvollkommen, inadäquat und – buchstäblich aufgefaßt – sogar falsch. Sie hat ihre Berechtigung als Versuch, das unser »normales« Verstehen übersteigende Geschehen auf menschliche Weise verständlich zu machen, sie läuft aber Gefahr, Mißverständnisse zu produzieren. Um solche Mißverständnisse zu vermeiden, ist die alte hermeneutische Regel der Unterscheidung zwischen der Art und Weise (*modus quo*) einer Aussage und dem damit ausgedrückten Inhalt (*id quod*) zu beachten. Dasselbe gilt für die lk Schilderungen der Erscheinungen des Auferstandenen in Lk 24,13-35 und 36-52. Die durch diese Erzählungen nahegelegte Reduktion der Erscheinung des Auferstandenen auf ein innerweltliches, physisch greifbares Geschehen (vgl. KKK 643: »ein geschichtliches Faktum«, das »der physischen Ordnung angehört«) bedarf einer Korrektur durch den Leser. Eine solche wird schon durch den Text selbst nahegelegt, insofern in der Emmausgeschichte jegliche Beschreibung der Erscheinungsweise des Auferstandenen fehlt (im Unterschied zu Mk 16,12: »in anderer Gestalt«) und die Erzählung von der Erscheinung am Osterabend auf eine Angabe über das Berühren von Händen und Füßen sowie über eine dadurch bewirkte Glaubenszustimmung verzichtet. Die hier zutage tretenden Grenzen der lk Darstellungsweise gründen letztlich darin, daß das Erscheinen des Auferstandenen wie die Auferstehung selbst die Grenzen unseres irdischen Erkennens und Sprechens übersteigt. Wie über Gott und seinen Sohn können wir darüber immer nur mit einer *docta ignorantia* und (im Sinne ostkirchlicher Frömmigkeit) nur »apophatisch« (verneinend und anbetend) sprechen. Wer sich, wie G. Lüdemann, in einer positivistischen, nur an den Naturwissenschaften orientierten Einstellung dieser tieferen Dimension unserer Welt und Geschichte verschließt, verweigert sich damit dem Verständnis des in der Bibel bezeugten Wirkens Gottes im Leben des Paulus und der Urkirche.

Boltzmanngasse 9   Jacob KREMER
A-1090 Wien

LUKE 4,16-30 AND THE UNITY OF LUKE–ACTS

When the president of the Colloquium invited me to give this lecture he referred to the session on the Gospel of Luke I was given to preside in 1968[1]. We are now thirty years later and the president of this year is now at the age I was in 1968. But it soon became clear that he did not intend to speculate on coincidences in the number of years. His point was a more serious one, the unity of Luke–Acts, and what he so kindly suggested was in fact some sort of "amende honorable", the Gospel of Luke this time to be studied as part of Luke–Acts.

There are a number of good reasons to justify the choice of Lk 4,16-30, widely held to be programmatic for Luke–Acts. First, I can refer to the example of a great *alumnus Lovaniensis*: the Nazareth pericope was studied by J. Dupont in his SNTS paper of 1959 ("Le salut des Gentils et la signification théologique du Livre des Actes")[2], and again in 1978 as Part One of his essay "Jésus annonce la bonne nouvelle aux pauvres" (with a special section on "L'épisode de Nazareth dans le cadre de l'ouvrage de Luc")[3]. Secondly, I may refer to the second edition of the volume of the Colloquium on the Gospel of Luke which was published in 1989, enlarged with substantive supplements including a 73-page survey

1. F. NEIRYNCK (ed.), *L'Évangile de Luc. Problèmes littéraires et théologiques. Mémorial Lucien Cerfaux* (BETL, 32), Gembloux, 1973 (²1989, cf. n. 4); 19th Colloquium Biblicum Lovaniense, 1968.

2. J. DUPONT, *Le salut des Gentils et la signification théologique du Livre des Actes*, in *NTS* 6 (1959-60) 132-155, esp. 141-146 ("Discours de Nazareth et discours de la Pentecôte"); = ID., *Études sur les Actes de Apôtres* (LD, 45), Paris, 393-419, esp. 404-409; *The Salvation of the Gentiles. Essays on the Acts of the Apostles* (ET by J. Keating), New York, 1987, 11-33: *The Salvation of the Gentiles and the Theological Significance of Acts* (no footnotes included).

3. J. DUPONT, *Jésus annonce la bonne nouvelle aux pauvres*, in *Evangelizare pauperibus* (Atti della XXIV Settimana Biblica Italiana), Brescia, 1978, 127-189, esp. 129-164 (147-155); = ID., *Études sur les Évangiles synoptiques* (BETL, 70), Leuven, 1985, 23-85, esp. 25-60: "Jésus à Nazareth (*Lc.* 4,16-30)" (43-51: "L'épisode de Nazareth dans le cadre de l'ouvrage de Luc"). See also his *La conclusion des Actes et son rapport à l'ensemble de l'ouvrage de Luc*, in J. KREMER (ed.), *Les Actes des Apôtres: Traditions, rédaction, théologie* (BETL, 48), Gembloux, 1979, 359-404, esp. 396-401; = *Nouvelles études sur les Actes des Apôtres* (LD, 118), Paris, 1984, 457-511, esp. 502-508. Cited here as *Jésus* and *Conclusion*.

J. Dupont (°1915) died on September 10, 1998. Cf. F. NEIRYNCK, *L'exégèse catholique en deuil: R.E. Brown – J. Dupont*, in *ETL* 74 (1998) 506-516. Dupont served as the president of the 24th Colloquium Biblicum Lovaniense in 1973 ("Jésus aux origines de la christologie"). On his life and work, see B. STANDAERT, *"Au carrefour des Écritures": Le Père Jacques Dupont, moine exégète* (Cahiers de Clerlande, 6), Ottignies, 1998.

by C. Schreck: "The Nazareth Pericope: Luke 4,16-30 in Recent Study"[4]. The third reason is my friendly dispute with C.M. Tuckett on the presence of Q-material in Lk 4,16-30[5], a still ongoing debate, now revived and facilitated by the publication of the *Documenta Q* volume on the alleged Q fragment *Nazara* in Lk 4,16[6]. But it is quite obvious, my decisive reason is the fact that, more than for any other section in the Gospel of Luke, the parallels in Acts and the way these parallels are read play an important role in the interpretation of the Nazareth episode in Lk.

In accord with an almost universal consent today[7], the theory that the Book of Acts was written before the Gospel of Luke will not be consid-

4. C.J. SCHRECK, *The Nazareth Pericope: Luke 4,16-30 in Recent Study*, in F. NEIRYNCK (ed.), *L'Évangile de Luc – The Gospel of Luke* (BETL, 32), Leuven, [2]1989, 399-471 (456-471: "Studies on Luke 4,16-30, 1973-1989"); revised and enlarged in Chapter V of his unpublished dissertation, *Luke 4,16-30. The Nazareth Pericope in Modern Exegesis: A History of Interpretation*, Leuven, 1990, 333-421; with supplement on two 1989 dissertations: S.J. NOORDA, *Historia vitae magistra. Een beoordeling van de geschiedenis van de uitleg van Lucas 4,16-30 als bijdrage aan de hermeneutische discussie*, Amsterdam, 1989; G.K.-S. SHIN, *Die Ausrufung des entgültigen Jubeljahres durch Jesus in Nazareth. Eine historisch-kritische Studie zu Lk 4,16-30* (EHS, 23/378), Bern-Frankfurt, 1989 (423-438).

In the same volume (BETL, 32): J. DELOBEL, *La rédaction de Lc. IV, 14-16a et le "Bericht vom Anfang"*, [2]1989, 113-133 (= 1973, 203-223), reprinted with additional note, 306-312.

5. C.M. TUCKETT, *Luke 4,16-30: Isaiah and Q*, in J. DELOBEL (ed.), *Logia: Les paroles de Jésus – The Sayings of Jesus. Mémorial Joseph Coppens* (BETL, 59), Leuven, 1982, 343-354 (p. 354: 4,16-21.23.25-27 form a unit in the source used by Luke); *On the Relationship between Matthew and Luke*, in *NTS* 30 (1984) 130-142, p. 131 (Ναζαρά); *The Temptation Narrative in Q*, in F. VAN SEGBROECK, C.M. TUCKETT, G. VAN BELLE, J. VERHEYDEN (eds.), *The Four Gospels 1992*. FS F. Neirynck (BETL, 100), Leuven, 1992, 479-507, p. 501 n. 101; *The Lukan Son of Man*, in ID. (ed.), *Luke's Literary Achievement: Collected Essays* (JSNT SS, 116), Sheffield, 1995, 198-217, p. 217 n. 65; *Q and the History of Early Christianity: Studies on Q*, Edinburgh, 1996, 226-237 ("Luke 4:16ff."; also 124 and 428-431). See p. 227: "I remain persuaded…".

6. *Documenta Q: Q 4:1-13,16. The Temptations of Jesus. Nazara*, Leuven, 1996. The first and main part of the volume (1-389) treats "Q 4:1-4,9-12,5-8,13: The Temptations of Jesus"; cf. F. NEIRYNCK, *Note on Q 4,1-2*, in *ETL* 73 (1997) 94-102. The second part (391-462) is devoted to "Q 4:16,3̶1̶: Nazara"; cf. F. NEIRYNCK, *NAZAPA in Q: Pro and Con*, in *From Quest to Q*. FS J.M. Robinson (BETL, 146), 1999 (forthcoming).

7. C.M. TUCKETT, *Luke* (New Testament Guides), Sheffield, 1996, 14. Cf. J. JERVELL, *Die Apostelgeschichte* (KEK[17]), Göttingen, 1998, 85 (n. 194: Bowman, read Bouwman); B. WITHERINGTON, *The Acts of the Apostles. A Socio-Rhetorical Commentary*, Grand Rapids, MI / Cambridge, UK – Carlisle, 1998, 60; J.A. FITZMYER, *The Acts of the Apostles* (AB, 31), New York, 1998, 51: "most of the reasons suggested for such a view are highly speculative and unconvincing"; C.K. BARRETT, *The Acts of the Apostles* (ICC), vol. II, Edinburgh, 1998, XIX-CXVIII (Introduction), esp. LI. Cf. ID., *The Third Gospel as a Preface to Acts? Some Reflections*, in *The Four Gospels 1992* (n. 5), 1451-1466. On Lk 4,16-30: "Luke certainly was aware of the fact that the mission to Gentiles would be a major theme in any continuation that he wrote" (1455). — Special attention is given to the four commentaries on Acts that independently appeared in the course of 1998; here in the order: Jervell, Witherington, Fitzmyer, and Barrett (vol. I, 1994). For the commentaries, the abbreviation *Acts* or *Apg* will be used in the footnotes.

ered in this paper. Just one preliminary remark: for scholars who defend the priority of Acts, the parallel to the Nazareth pericope in Paul's first major speech in Ac 13,14-52 is part of their argument[8].

In my investigation Lk 4,16-30 will be treated as a Lukan composition relocating the story of the rejection of Jesus in his hometown (Mk 6,1-6a) and taking from Q 6,20-49 the function of Jesus' inaugural sermon.

I. Lk 4,16-30 and Paul's Synagogue Preaching

Acts 9,19b-25

19b   Ἐγένετο δὲ μετὰ τῶν ἐν Δαμασκῷ μαθητῶν ἡμέρας τινὰς
20   καὶ εὐθέως ἐν ταῖς συναγωγαῖς ἐκήρυσσεν τὸν Ἰησοῦν ὅτι
      οὗτός ἐστιν ὁ υἱὸς τοῦ θεοῦ.
21   ἐξίσταντο δὲ πάντες οἱ ἀκούοντες καὶ ἔλεγον·
      οὐχ οὗτός ἐστιν ὁ πορθήσας εἰς Ἰερουσαλὴμ τοὺς ἐπικαλουμέ-
      νους τὸ ὄνομα τοῦτο, καὶ ὧδε εἰς τοῦτο ἐληλύθει ἵνα δεδεμένους
      αὐτοὺς ἀγάγῃ ἐπὶ τοὺς ἀρχιερεῖς;
22   Σαῦλος δὲ μᾶλλον ἐνεδυναμοῦτο καὶ συνέχυννεν [τοὺς] Ἰουδαίους
      τοὺς κατοικοῦντας ἐν Δαμασκῷ συμβιβάζων ὅτι
      οὗτός ἐστιν ὁ χριστός.
23   Ὡς δὲ ἐπληροῦντο ἡμέραι ἱκαναί, συνεβουλεύσαντο οἱ Ἰουδαῖοι
      ἀνελεῖν αὐτόν·
24   ἐγνώσθη δὲ τῷ Σαύλῳ ἡ ἐπιβουλὴ αὐτῶν. παρετηροῦντο δὲ καὶ τὰς
      πύλας ἡμέρας τε καὶ νυκτὸς ὅπως αὐτὸν ἀνέλωσιν·
25   λαβόντες δὲ οἱ μαθηταὶ αὐτοῦ νυκτὸς διὰ τοῦ τείχους καθῆκαν αὐτὸν
      χαλάσαντες ἐν σπυρίδι.

To begin with, I cite P.F. Esler's summary presentation of the similarities between Lk 4,16-30 and Paul's preaching at Damascus[9]:

> 1. both Jesus and Paul enter a synagogue as the first public step in their ministry and deliver a message of salvation; 2. their respective audiences

---

8. See G. Bouwman, Le "premier livre" (Act., I,1) et la date des Actes des Apôtres, in L'Évangile de Luc – The Gospel of Luke, 1989 (above n. 4), 553-565, esp. 563; Id., De derde nachtwake. De wordingsgeschiedenis van het evangelie van Lucas, Tielt – Den Haag, 1968, 93-95 (= Das dritte Evangelium. Einübung in die formgeschichtliche Methode, Düsseldorf, 1968). See also among the more recent curiosa: J.L. Staley, "With the Power of the Spirit": Plotting the Program and Parallels of Luke 4:14-37 in Luke–Acts, in SBL 1993 Seminar Papers, 281-302, esp. 287-291 (Lk 4,16-30); = Narrative Structure (Self Structure) in Luke 4:14–9:62: The United States of Luke's Story World, in Semeia 72 (1995) 173-213, esp. 187-191 (see also 176 and 201: "it was not until after he had written Acts, that he could finally envision a way to revise Mark. The Lukan author then wrote a prequel to Acts, by putting back into his plot of the Jesus story his idealized, previously composed description of Paul's evangelistic program").

9. P.F. Esler, Community and Gospel in Luke–Acts (SNTS MS, 57), Cambridge, 1987, 235 n. 39; followed by B. Witherington, Acts, 1998 (n. 7), 320.

are astonished and also confused by the change of roles they observe in Jesus and Paul, with the Jews in Nazareth asking if this is not the son of Joseph and those in Damascus asking if this is not the man who has hitherto opposed Christianity; 3. there is an attempt to kill Jesus and a plot to kill Paul; 4. both Jesus and Paul escape.

The short story of "Paul at Damascus" (9,19b-25)[10] is the first example and in some sense the proto-type of the well-known pattern for Paul's preaching in Acts: "Luke is already following what he takes to have been Paul's regular plan of starting mission work in the synagogue"[11]. The preaching in the synagogues of the Jews is indeed a constant motif of Paul's missionary journeys: 13,5 (Salamis); 13,14 (Pisidian Antioch); 14,1 (Iconium); 17,1-2 (Thessalonica); 17,10 (Beroea); 17,17 (Athens); 18,4 (Corinth); 18,19 and 19,8 (Ephesus). The peculiarity of his preaching in the synagogues of Damascus is that it comes first[12] after Paul's conversion and hence for Paul, like the Nazareth pericope for Jesus, inaugurates his preaching ministry.

Paul's own parallel accounts exhibit significant differences. First, Gal 1,17... ἀπῆλθον εἰς Ἀραβίαν καὶ πάλιν ὑπέστρεψα εἰς Δαμασκόν. His return to Damascus may imply that he had been in Damascus before going to Arabia (cf. Ac 9,19b). But in Acts there is no mention at all of a trip to Arabia or of any interruption of his stay in Damascus. Second, 2 Cor 11,32-33: ἐν Δαμασκῷ ὁ ἐθνάρχης Ἀρέτα τοῦ βασιλέως ἐφρούρει τὴν πόλιν Δαμασκηνῶν πιάσαι με, [33] καὶ διὰ θυρίδος ἐν σαργάνῃ ἐχαλάσθην διὰ τοῦ τείχους καὶ ἐξέφυγον τὰς χεῖρας αὐτοῦ. The means of Paul's escape are the same in Ac 9,25 (ἐν σαργάνῃ/σπυρίδι ἐχαλάσθην/χαλάσαντες διὰ τοῦ τείχους), though the assistance of (his?)[13] disciples is not mentioned in Paul's own ver-

10. On the segment 9,19b-25 in the text of Ac 9,1-30(31), see Tischendorf, Wikenhauser, Dupont, Dillon, Bossuyt-Radermakers, Jervell, Fitzmyer. Contrast Westcott-Hort, Nestle, Nestle-Aland: three paragraphs (9,19b-22.23-25.26-30), in GNT entitled as: Saul preaches at Damascus, Saul escapes from the Jews, Saul at Jerusalem. Even more problematic is J.D.G. Dunn's proposal (*Acts*, 1996): The conversion of Paul (9,1-22) and The initial opposition to Paul (9,23-31). See D. MARGUERAT, *Saul's Conversion (Acts 9, 22, 26) and the Multiplication of Narrative in Acts*, in *Luke's Literary Achievement* (n. 5), 127-155: "a parallelism of motifs is to be detected between 9.19b-25 and 26-30, which function like twin narratives" (135 n. 23).

11. BARRETT, *Acts*, 464.

12. And without delay: εὐθέως. Compare εὐθέως after his conversion in Gal 1,16b. On this link between Paul's conversion and his preaching in Damascus, see Barnabas's declaration in 9,27: πῶς ἐν τῇ ὁδῷ ... καὶ πῶς ἐν Δαμασκῷ ἐπαρρησιάσατο ἐν τῷ ὀνόματι τοῦ Ἰησοῦ.

13. "The most satisfactory solution appears to be the conjecture that the oldest extant text arose through scribal inadvertence, when an original αὐτόν was taken as αὐτοῦ" (METZGER, *Textual Commentary*, 321-322). Cf. Conzelmann, Haenchen, *et al.* Jervell reads αὐτοῦ: "das zeigt die besondere Stellung des Paulus in der Kirche" (*Apg*, 286); cf.

sion. Neither the status of the ethnarch (Nabatean governor?)[14] nor the motive of his action (Paul's mission in Arabia?)[15] can be identified; and the incident of the escape is not associated with any particular period of Paul's life (the end of a second stay in Damascus?). In Ac 9 it is linked with Paul's post-conversion preaching: *the Jews* of Damascus were confounded by Paul's powerful preaching (v. 22), and "when some time had passed" *they* plotted to kill him (v. 23) and *they* were watching the gates (v. 24). Since it is hardly provable that the Nabatean king Aretas made common cause with the Jews, or that "Paul wanted to spare his own countrymen by not mentioning their participation in the persecution of Damascus"[16], it is most likely that it was Luke, responsible for the reworking of a tradition like 2 Cor 11,32-33, who introduced here the hostile action of the Jews[17].

"Paul and the Jews" is a major theme of the two- or three-stage theory in the volumes *Les Actes des deux apôtres*[18]:

Paulus in der Apostelgeschichte und die Geschichte des Urchristentums, in *NTS* 32 (1986) 378-392: "Lukas stellt wiederholt Ähnlichkeiten oder Parallelen zwischen Jesus und Paulus dar... Paulus ist ausser Jesus der einzige in Acta der Jünger hat, 9.25" (383, and 392 n. 29). Fitzmyer shows more reserve: "One can only ask who 'his disciples' might have been" (*Acts*, 436). — For some commentators of 2 Cor the passive voice ἐχαλάσθην indicates that Paul had assistance, "and this in accord with Acts 9:25" (V.P. Furnish, 522).

14. J. Taylor, *The Ethnarch of King Aretas at Damascus: A Note on 2 Cor 11,32-33*, in *RB* 99 (1992) 719-728.

15. R. Riesner, *Paul's Early Period: Chronology, Mission Strategy, Theology*, Grand Rapids, MI, 1998, 258-260: "It thus remains a possibility worthy of consideration that for some time... Paul lived in 'Arabia' somewhat reclusively" (260).

16. *Ibid.*, 89. Cf. 86-89: "The Circumstances of Paul's Flight".

17. M. Harding, *On the Historicity of Acts: Comparing Acts 9.23-25 with 2 Corinthians 11.32-3*, in *NTS* 39 (1993) 518-538, esp. 536; A. Weiser, *Apg*, 232: "(wahrscheinlich ist) die Nennung der Juden als Gegner des Saulus erst von Lukas eingeführt"; C. Burchard: "Zu fragen ist nur, ob erst Lukas 'die Juden' hereingebracht hat. Denkbar ist das; Lukas beschreibt immer wieder eben sie als Paulus' Gegner und hält sie auch eines Mordes durchaus für fähig" (152). See *Der dreizehnte Zeuge. Traditions- und kompositionsgeschichtliche Untersuchungen zu Lukas' Darstellung der Frühzeit des Paulus* (FRLANT, 103), Göttingen, 1970, 136-161 ("Der Beginn der paulinischen Wirksamkeit: Apg. 9,19b-30"): Ac 9,19b-25 is a Lukan composition, only vv. 24b-25 rely on "geformte Tradition" (153). See also L. Wehr, *Petrus und Paulus – Kontrahenten und Partner* (NTAbh, 30), Münster, 1996, 131 n. 25 (with reference to A. Lindemann, *Paulus im ältesten Christentum*, 1979, 169 n. 129).

18. In anticipation of the 'Cleopas question' (on the things that have happened in Jerusalem) I mention here the thesis propounded by M.-É. Boismard – A. Lamouille and J. Taylor: Ac 9,20.23.30* are from Proto–Luke (= Act I) and 9,19b.21-22.24-25 are added by Luke (= Act II); on v. 20c, see below n. 22. Cf. *Les Actes des deux apôtres*: M.-É. Boismard – A. Lamouille, vol. I-III (ÉB 12, 13, 14), Paris, 1990: vol. I. *Introduction – Textes*, 39, 98; vol. II. *Le sens des récits*, 120-121, 123-134 (Act I); 182, 185-186 (Act II); 211 (Act III); vol. III. *Analyses littéraires*, 133-137; vol. V: J. Taylor, *Commentaire historique (Act. 9,1–18,22)* (ÉB 23), 1994, 15-25. Two commentaries on

Pour Act I, Paul est avant tout celui qui, de ville en ville, entre dans les synagogues, y annonce aux Juifs le message chrétien, mais, malgré quelques succès, se heurte à une hostilité de plus en plus marquée, à une volonté de le mettre à mort...[19]

Act II évite de condamner en bloc "les Juifs"... Dans la geste de Paul, ce ne sont plus "les Juifs" (Act I) qui s'en prennent violemment à la prédication de l'évangile, mais seulement certains d'entre eux (17,5 TO; 18,6 TO; cf. 23,12).[20]

Mais dans ces cas, Act III abandonne les textes de Act II pour revenir à ceux de Act I... Cette tendance 'dure' se manifeste à l'égard des Juifs, alors que Act II voulait au contraire les innocenter.[21]

In the case of Ac 9,19b-25 the reconstruction of *Act I* (= Proto-Luke) includes nothing more than the two verses 9,20.23 (and 30ac). The hostility of the Jews is evident in v. 23: they conspired to murder him. It is less evident that the term οἱ Ἰουδαῖοι can be used as an argument for Proto-Luke. This is the first reference to οἱ Ἰουδαῖοι in *Act I* and without the preceding v. 22 it comes rather unprepared. In the text of *Act II* (= Luke) it resumes [τοὺς] Ἰουδαίους τοὺς κατοικοῦντας ἐν Δαμασκῷ (v. 22), not unlike οἱ μαθηταί in v. 25 (if read, with αὐτόν, as "the disciples") resumes μετὰ τῶν ἐν Δαμασκῷ μαθητῶν (v. 19b). Following the same theory, verses 24–25 were added to the source by Luke, but given the emphasis on the Jews' ἐπιβουλή and their activity (v. 24: παρετηροῦντο ... ὅπως αὐτὸν ἀνέλωσιν) one can hardly say: "Act II voulait les innocenter"[22]. — In Proto-Luke (the still undivided

Acts, both published in the second half of 1998 (above, n. 7), contain a summary presentation and brief evaluation of the theory: BARRETT, XXX-XXXI: "incapable of proof or of disproof, and therefore beyond serious discussion" (XXXI); FITZMYER, 84-85: "The major problem with it is the building of hypothesis on hypothesis, for the linking of hypotheses decreases the probability, the more one links them" (85). Fitzmyer prefers P. Benoit's less complicated source analysis. He assigns Ac 9,19b-25 to the Pauline source.

On Luke's direct use of Paul's Letters, in Ac 9,24-25 (cf. 2 Cor 11,32-33): "le propre récit de Paul est probablement la source de celui de Luc" (V, 21; cf. I, 38; II, 186: "L'allusion... est ici transparente"; III, 135; V, 21 n. 5: "les contacts littéraires... sont pourtant évidents"); see also Ac 9,21 ὁ πορθήσας, cf. Gal 1,13.23: "le contact littéraire est quasi certain"; 9,22 ἐνεδυναμοῦτο: "une influence paulinienne... probable" (II, 185). Contrast FITZMYER, 434: "There is no substantial evidence that Luke had ever read any of Paul's letters. Rather, the information that Luke has about Saul and his ministry has come to him from other sources, esp. his Pauline source".

19. *Les Actes*, vol. I, 26-27. Cf. vol. II, 123: "La réaction hostile des Juifs".

20. Vol. I, 33. Cf. II, 187: "Une perspective plus favorable aux Juifs".

21. Vol. I, 48, 49.

22. Note on ὁ υἱὸς τοῦ θεοῦ: added by Act II in 9,20c to replace ὁ χριστός (= Act 1), now in v. 22c (*Les Actes*, vol. III, 133-134; cf. II, 187). On the order in vv. 20 (the Son of God) and 22 (the Christ): "l'on aurait attendu l'inverse (cf. Lk 22,67.70)". No other parallel in Luke–Acts is cited. The decrescendo in Ac 9,20.22 has a parallel in Lk 4,41 (ὁ υἱὸς τοῦ θεοῦ, τὸν χριστόν). The observation on grammatical ambiguity seems to neglect that v. 22 repeats the parallel v. 20 (τὸν Ἰησοῦν ὅτι οὗτός ἐστιν).

L + Act I) the Nazareth section does not include Lk 4,22b-30[23]. The parallel between Jesus and Paul is thus restricted to the christological preaching in Lk 4,16-22a and Ac 9,20, and that is much less than the common pattern assigned to Act I[24]. Not even the question in Lk 4,22b and its parallel in Ac 9,21[25] are assumed to be part of Proto-Luke.

At this point I conclude with a quotation from J. Dupont[26]:

> Dans l'ensemble des Actes, la notice sur la première prédication de Paul dans les synagogues de Damas (9,20-25) n'est encore qu'un prélude. Déjà cependant, elle se déroule en deux temps... Pour saisir le rapport entre cette courte notice et les récits concernant Antioche de Pisidie et Rome, il faudrait tenir compte en même temps de l'épisode de Nazareth en Lc 4,16-30.

Acts 13,5

Paul's mission to Cyprus (13,4-12) is the initial episode of his first missionary journey: Barnabas and Saul sailed to Cyprus and "arriving at Salamis they proclaimed the word of God in the synagogues of the Jews" (κατήγγελλον τὸν λόγον τοῦ θεοῦ ἐν ταῖς συναγωγαῖς τῶν Ἰουδαίων). The reference in 13,5 is extremely brief; the story simply continues in v. 6: "They went through the whole island as far as Paphos". Two comments are in order: (1) The plural ἐν ταῖς συναγωγαῖς

---

23. M.-É. BOISMARD, *En quête du proto-Luc* (ÉB, 37), Paris, 1997, 190-194; cf. 264-266: Lk 4,14a.*16-22a*.42-43.15.14b. See my review in *ETL* 73 (1997) 453-455.

24. TAYLOR, vol. V, 20: "un schéma de récit". Cf. vol. II, 124.

25. See the commentaries: "der an Lk 4,22 erinnernde Vers" (Haenchen); "die Sachparallele Lk 4,22" (Schneider); "vgl. Lk 4,22; Apg 2,7.12" (Weiser). Compare:
Ac 9,21a ἐξίσταντο δὲ πάντες οἱ ἀκούοντες
      b καὶ ἔλεγον· οὐχ οὗτός ἐστιν ὁ πορθήσας;
Lk 4,22a καὶ πάντες ... καὶ ἐθαύμαζον...
      b καὶ ἔλεγον· οὐχὶ υἱός ἐστιν Ἰωσὴφ οὗτος;
Ac 2,7   ἐξίσταντο δὲ καὶ ἐθαύμαζον
      λέγοντες· οὐχ ἰδοὺ ἅπαντες οὗτοί εἰσιν οἱ λαλοῦντες Γαλιλαῖοι;
On Lk 4,22 / Ac 2,7, cf. É. SAMAIN, *Le récit de Pentecôte dans l'exégèse actuelle* (STL diss.), Leuven, 1964, 55: "un excellent parallèle tant au point de vue du sens que du vocabulaire employé"; cf. ID., *Le discours-programme de Jésus à la synagogue de Nazareth. Lc 4,16-30*, in *CBFV* 10 (1971) 25-43, here 41; C. BURCHARD, *Der dreizehnte Zeuge* (n. 17), 1970, 152: "die Strukturverwandtschaft von V. 20-22 mit Apg 2,7.12 und besonders mit Lk 4,22"; J. DUPONT, *Jésus*, 130 (= 24): "un excellent parallèle"; F. BOVON, *Lukas*, 1989, 213 n. 29 (*Luc*, 1991, 208); T. BERGHOLZ, *Der Aufbau des lukanischen Doppelwerkes. Untersuchungen zum formalliterarischen Charakter von Lukas-Evangelium und Apostelgeschichte* (EHS, 23/545), Frankfurt, 1995, (diss. Bonn, 1994), 85.

26. *Conclusion*, 383 (= 487), n. 68. Cf. *Le discours de l'Aréopage (Ac 17,22-31)*, in *Bib* 60 (1979) 530-546, here 532 (= 382): "chacun (des trois grands discours) avait été annoncé par une première ébauche: le thème de la prédication de Paul aux Juifs (13,16-41) est indiqué dès la notice de 9,20.22 sur son activité dans les synagogues de Damas".

is usually understood as suggesting the presence of a considerable Jewish population in Salamis, with more than one local synagogue (cf. 9,20: Damascus). But G. Schneider considers another possibility: "Oder sollte der Plural 'in den Synagogen' schon auf den Anfang von V 6 bezogen sein?" (i.e., throughout the island)[27]. (2) In contrast to the Damascus story there is here no mention of any reaction[28]. For Boismard this silence can be explained as follows:

> Act I ne mentionne aucune réaction favorable à leur prédication, seul cas dans les Actes... Act I nous fait comprendre, discrètement, que Barnabé et Saul n'eurent guère de succès dans leurs efforts pour implanter le christianisme à Chypre.[29]

Even the reason for their failure can be indicated:

> l'argument apologétique du miracle n'avait plus aucune valeur dans un milieu où les mages prodiguaient eux-mêmes de tels signes et de tels prodiges. D'où l'échec de la prédication de Barnabé et de Saul.[30]

In this solution, however, the continuation of the Cyprus episode in vv. 6-12, with the Jewish magician and the proconsul Sergius Paulus, is left out of consideration. If this story, ending with the conversion of the proconsul (v. 12b in *Act I*: ἐπίστευσεν ἐκπλησσόμενος ἐπὶ τῇ διδαχῇ τοῦ κυρίου)[31], is taken together with v. 5a, one can no longer, with regard to the preaching on Cyprus, employ general qualifications such as *insuccès*, *échec*, and *fiasco*. Contrast Fitzmyer: "... Cyprus, where he and Barnabas have some success... They convert even the proconsul..."[32], and Jervell:

> Nichts wird über den Erfolg der Verkündigung in den Synagogen gesagt, wahrscheinlich weil der grösste Erfolg die Bekehrung des gottesfürchtigen Prokonsul Sergius Paulus, V 12, ist.[33]

---

27. *Apg*, 120 n. 19. Cf. TAYLOR, vol. V, 134: "Le pluriel indiquerait plutôt que c'est durant leur trajet jusqu'à Paphos (cf. v. 6) qu'ils prêchaient dans les communautés juives réparties dans l'île" (n. 4: ctr. Haenchen). Cf. D.W.J. GILL, *Paul's Travels through Cyprus (Acts 13.4-12)*, in *TyndB* 46 (1995) 219-228.

28. HAENCHEN, 339 (= 381): "Über den Erfolg der Predigt sagt Lukas nichts"; G. SCHILLE, 287: "Er (Lukas) notiert nicht einmal den Erfolg in Salamis!"

29. Vol. II, 233: "Insuccès de la prédication de la Parole". See also TAYLOR: "Il semble que la mission n'eut aucun succès" (vol. V, 135).

30. Vol. II, 233 (slightly adapted).

31. Ἐκπλησσόμενος ἐπὶ τῇ διδαχῇ τοῦ κυρίου (Act I) is replaced with ἰδὼν τὸ γεγονός in Act II (vol. II, 267: "la force apologétique des miracles"), and both are combined in Act III (358: "il obtient ainsi un texte un peu boiteux"). But this combination can be Lukan: see Lk 4,36 and 32 (ἐξεπλήσσοντο ἐπὶ τῇ διδαχῇ αὐτοῦ).

32. *Acts*, 500.

33. *Apg*, 345. On the God-fearer: "Er gehört offenbar zu den Gottesfürchtigen" (346, and n. 422; 374 n. 574), contrast his *Retrospect and Prospect in Luke–Acts Interpretation*, in *SBL 1991 Seminar Papers*, 383-404: "where do we find 'pure' Gentiles without any connection to the synagogue? Perhaps Sergius Paulus is one" (391).

Jervell concludes with a comment on Lukan redaction, "vor allem" their being sent "by the Holy Spirit" (v. 4) and their preaching in the synagogues (v. 5)[34]. L.T. Johnson notes Luke's penchant for parallellism in Ac 13,1-3.4-12 (cf. Lk 3,21-22; 4,1-13): "empowerment by the Holy Spirit followed immediately by a confrontation with demonic powers. Such was the case with Jesus after his baptism with the Spirit"[35].

Acts 13,14-52

Paul and his company continued their journey from Paphos to Perga in Pamphylia and from Perga they came to Antioch of Pisidia. The long section on Pisidian Antioch characteristically articulates the synagogue setting and presents Paul's *first* speech (13,16-41) as a synagogue sermon. The similarities between Ac 13,14-52[36] and Lk 4,16-30 are generally recognized and W. Radl's survey[37] is a steadfast reference in the studies on the Nazareth pericope in Lk.

Ac 13,14-16a

14 Αὐτοὶ δὲ ... παρεγένοντο εἰς ᾿Αντιόχειαν τὴν Πισιδίαν, καὶ [εἰσ]ελθόντες εἰς τὴν συναγωγὴν τῇ ἡμέρᾳ τῶν σαββάτων ἐκάθισαν.

34. *Apg*, 349. For more detail, see A. WEISER, *Apg*, 1985, 312-314 ("Tradition und Redaktion"), esp. 313.

35. *Acts*, 1992, 226. See also 237 and 243, on "narrative mimesis" in Ac 13,13-41 and 42-52 (cf. Lk 4,22.23-27.28-29). On Johnson's parallel reading of Ac 13, see S. CUNNINGHAM, *'Through Many Tribulations'. The Theology of Persecution in Luke–Acts* (JSNT SS, 142), Sheffield, 1997, 244 n. 194.

36. On the three stages in Ac 13,14-52 according to Boismard-Lamouille-Taylor (n. 18), see *Les Actes*, vol. I, 113-117; vol. II, 237-240, 267-271, 358-359; vol. III, 184-188; vol. V, 150-165: Ac 13,14-16a|16b.17-22a^J.22b.23^J.24-25.26^J.27-31.32-34a.34b-35a.35b. 36-37.38.39.[40-41]|42.43.44-48.49-51.52. The Act I text (including J = Johannite source) is marked by underlining; verses within brackets are from Act III. – Ac 13,43 (= Act I) is replaced by v. 42 in Act II (v. 44: the next sabbath); both are combined in Act III. But see G. SCHILLE: the doublet is only "scheinbar" (*Apg*, 297: "Tatsächlich muß die Bitte um eine weitere Ausführung zum Gegenstand dem, was nach der Versammlung geschieht, vorausgehen").

For an analysis of Ac 13,14-52, see M.F.-J. BUSS, *Die Missionspredigt des Apostels Paulus in Pisidischen Antiochien. Analyse von Apg 13,16-41 im Hinblick auf die literarische und thematische Einheit der Paulusrede* (FzB, 38), Stuttgart, 1980; J. PICHLER, *Paulusrezeption in der Apostelgeschichte. Untersuchungen zur Rede im pisidischen Antiochien* (Innsbrucker theologische Studien, 50), Innsbruck-Wien, 1997 (88-92: "Apg 13 und Lk 4").

37. W. RADL, *Paulus und Jesus im lukanischen Doppelwerk. Untersuchungen zu Parallelmotiven im Lukasevangelium und in der Apostelgeschichte* (EHS, 23/49), Bern-Frankfurt, 1975, 82-100 ("Der Anfang: Apg 13,14-52 – Lk 4,16-30"). Cf. M. KORN, *Die Geschichte Jesu in veränderter Zeit. Studien zur bleibenden Bedeutung Jesu im lukanischen Doppelwerk* (WUNT, 2/51), Tübingen, 1993, 56-85: "Jesu Antrittspredigt in Nazareth als Programm des lukanischen Doppelwerks (Lk 4,16-30)", esp. 60. See also A. WEISER, *Apg*, 339-340.

15 μετὰ δὲ τὴν ἀνάγνωσιν τοῦ νόμου καὶ τῶν προφητῶν ἀπέστειλαν
οἱ ἀρχισυνάγωγοι πρὸς αὐτοὺς λέγοντες· ἄνδρες ἀδελφοί, εἴ τίς
ἐστιν ἐν ὑμῖν λόγος παρακλήσεως πρὸς τὸν λαόν, λέγετε. 16a
ἀναστὰς δὲ Παῦλος καὶ κατασείσας τῇ χειρὶ εἶπεν·

The mise-en-scene in Ac 13,14-16a can be compared with Lk 4,16:
Καὶ ἦλθεν εἰς Ναζαρά, οὗ ἦν τεθραμμένος, καὶ εἰσῆλθεν κατὰ τὸ
εἰωθὸς αὐτῷ ἐν τῇ ἡμέρᾳ τῶν σαββάτων εἰς τὴν συναγωγὴν καὶ
ἀνέστη ἀναγνῶναι. The phrase εἰσελθεῖν εἰς τὴν συναγωγήν (Lk
4,16, cf. Mk 1,21; Lk 6,6 = Mk 3,1) is a standard formula in Acts
(13,14; 14,1; 18,19; 19,8)[38]. The closest parallel is Ac 13,14, where it
is used in combination with the phrase ἐν τῇ ἡμέρᾳ τῶν σαββάτων
(om. ἐν)[39]. It is less likely that we can infer from Ac 13,15 that "Jesus
was invited by the president of the synagogue assembly to read and
expound a Scripture text"[40]. In Ac 13,15 Paul and Barnabas are present
as visitors at the sabbath service in Antioch (v. 14 ἐκάθισαν) and it is
after the reading of the Law and the Prophets[41] that they were invited to
address the congregation. Then Paul stood up (ctr. Lk 4,20 ἐκάθισεν,
after the reading) and with the gesture of an orator[42] he began to speak.
Here too some commentators think that "we must assume some previous conversation with the synagogue rulers"[43]. Lk 4,16c has καὶ
ἀνέστη ἀναγνῶναι and the Scripture text from Isaiah is quoted sur-

38. Cf. Ac 17,2 εἰσῆλθεν πρὸς αὐτούς (v. 1 συναγωγὴ τῶν Ἰουδαίων); 17,10 εἰς
τὴν συναγωγὴν τῶν Ἰουδαίων ἀπήεσαν.
39. See also Ac 16,13 τῇ τε ἡμέρᾳ τῶν σαββάτων ... (οὗ ἐνομίζομεν προσευχὴν
εἶναι). Cf. 20,7 ἐν δὲ τῇ μιᾷ τῶν σαββάτων. Lk 13,14.16 τῇ ἡμέρᾳ τοῦ σαββάτου (in
contrast to the ἓξ ἡμέραι in v. 14); 14,5 ἐν ἡμέρᾳ τοῦ σαββάτου. — Busse's emphasis
on the plural τῶν σαββάτων: "betont die Modelhaftigkeit des Ereignisses durch den
Plural 'am Tage *der Sabbate*'" is less convincing. See U. BUSSE, *Das Nazareth-Manifest
Jesu. Eine Einführung in das lukanische Jesusbild nach Lk 4,16-30* (SBS, 91), Stuttgart,
1978, 31. Cf. J. JEREMIAS, *Sprache*, 121: "formelhafte Septuagintawendung..., die Lukas
unbedenklich übernehmen konnte (Lk 4,16; Apg 13,14; 16,13), weil durch das vor-
angestellte τῇ ἡμέρᾳ die singularische Bedeutung von τὰ σάββατα klargestellt war".
40. FITZMYER, *Luke*, 531. Cf. J.D. KINGSBURY, *Conflict in Luke: Jesus, Authorities,
Disciples*, Minneapolis, MN, 1991, 44: "Invited by the leader of the synagogue to read
from scripture"; BOVON, *Lk*, 210: "sonst hätte er (Lukas) sicher die ungewöhnliche Initiative Jesu als solche signalisiert". Compare MARSHALL, *Luke*, 182: "Possibly Jesus had
informally requested permission to read before the service began, and Luke has not gone
into the details of the arrangement" (sic). Cf. below, n. 43.
41. Cf. 13,27 τὰς φωνὰς τῶν προφητῶν τὰς κατὰ πᾶν σάββατον ἀναγινωσκομέ-
νας and 15,21 Μωϋσῆς ... ἐν ταῖς συναγωγαῖς κατὰ πᾶν σάββατον ἀναγινωσκό-
μενος. It is of course not so that "he [Paul] reads from the Law and Prophets" (JOHNSON,
237).
42. Haenchen, Conzelmann, Schneider, Weiser, *et al.* Cf. WITHERINGTON, 407: "it is
probable that Luke intends to portray Paul in his first major discourse in Acts as a great
orator". Contrast Jervell: "zeigt nur, dass er zum Reden bereit ist" (353).
43. B. WITHERINGTON, 406. Cf. above, n. 40.

rounded with an artful chiastic structure from v. 16c (ἀνέστη) to v. 20a (ἐκάθισεν)[44]:

A   ἀνέστη ἀναγνῶναι.
B   καὶ ἐπεδόθη αὐτῷ βιβλίον τοῦ προφήτου Ἡσαΐου
C   καὶ ἀναπτύξας τὸ βιβλίον
D   εὗρεν τὸν τόπον οὗ ἦν γεγραμμένον· [ ]
C′   καὶ πτύξας τὸ βιβλίον
B′   ἀποδοὺς τῷ ὑπηρέτῃ
A′   ἐκάθισεν.

One may observe that Luke's account is elliptical and presupposes an intervention of the ruler of the synagogue, the lection of the Torah, and other elements of the synagogue worship, but the point Luke is making concerns the prophetic text he quotes from Isaiah.

In this connection mention should be made of the phrase (εἰσῆλθεν) κατὰ τὸ εἰωθὸς αὐτῷ in Lk 4,16 and its parallel in Ac 17,2: κατὰ δὲ τὸ εἰωθὸς τῷ Παύλῳ (εἰσῆλθεν). A few comments on Lk 4,16: "the parallel expression in Acts 17:2 suggests that here the reference is rather to his regular use of the synagogue for teaching (4:15)" (Marshall); "Luke's presentation indicates... that it was his habit to take the role of the one who read and expounded the Scriptures (cf. Acts 17:2)" (Green)[45]. Instead of reading Lk 4,16 in the light of Ac 17,2, as these commentators do, Boismard-Lamouille-Taylor propose a reverse relationship: "le texte de Act I renvoie implicitement à Lc 4,16"; "le récit est calqué sur celui de Jésus dans la synagogue de Nazareth"[46].

44. See, e.g., J.-N. ALETTI, *L'art de raconter Jésus-Christ. L'écriture narrative de l'évangile de Luc*, Paris, 1989, 39-61: "Récit et révélation. Lc 4,16-30" (esp. 41: "la disposition concentrique"); J.S. SIKER, *"First to the Gentiles" : A Literary Analysis of Luke 4:16-30*, in *JBL* 111 (1992) 73-90, esp. 77: "showing Luke's intention to highlight the Isaiah reading"; U. BUSSE, *Nazareth-Manifest* (n. 39), 32: "eine Ringkomposition, die... stilistisch die Bedeutung des Mischzitats unterstreichen soll". It is less appropriate to include, as does Siker (*et al.*: see below, n. 144; cf. N.W. Lund), vv. 16b καὶ εἰσῆλθεν ... εἰς τὴν συναγωγήν and 20b καὶ ... ἐν τῇ συναγωγῇ, or, as does Busse (esp. 49: *Ringkomposition* 4,17-20), to include v. 20b and not v. 16c. For a correct presentation of Luke's *procédé d'inclusion*, see J. DUPONT, *Jésus*, 130 (= 24); *Conclusion*, 398 (= 504). See also *ibid.* his description of this *procédé d'encadrement* in v. 4,20b-22:
    20b καὶ πάντων οἱ ὀφθαλμοὶ ἐν τῇ συναγωγῇ...
    21 Jesus' saying
    22 καὶ πάντες ἐμαρτύρουν αὐτῷ...
45. MARSHALL, *Luke*, 181; GREEN, *Luke*, 209. Cf. NOLLAND, 195: "It refers to Jesus' synagogue teaching habits".
46. *Les Actes*, I, 130; II, 243-244, 293, 365; III, 224; V, 269. See esp. II, 244 (Lc 4,16 / Ac 17,1b-2a): "La suite des deux récits offre des analogies évidentes: Jésus et Paul partent des Écritures pour montrer la légitimité de la mission de Jésus (Lc 4,17-21; Act 17,2b-3). La réaction des auditeurs est analogue; les uns sont favorables (Lc 4,22; Act 17,4) tandis que d'autres veulent lapider Jésus (Lc 4,29) ou suscitent une émeute contre Paul et son compagnon (Act 17,5). Mais Jésus (Lc 4,30) comme Paul et son compagnon

Lk 4,16	Ac 17,1b-2a
καὶ ἦλθεν εἰς Ναζαρά,	ἦλθον εἰς Θεσσαλονίκην
οὗ ἦν τεθραμμένος,	ὅπου ἦν συναγωγὴ τῶν Ἰουδαίων.
καὶ εἰσῆλθεν	
κατὰ τὸ εἰωθὸς αὐτῷ	κατὰ δὲ τὸ εἰωθὸς τῷ Παύλῳ
	εἰσῆλθεν πρὸς αὐτοὺς
ἐν τῇ ἡμέρᾳ τῶν σαββάτων	καὶ ἐπὶ σάββατα τρία...
εἰς τὴν συναγωγήν	

Taken by itself, Lk 4,16 allows us to read the phrase "as was his custom" not about Jesus' habitual synagogue teaching in Galilee (as exemplification of 4,15) but as referring to his regular synagogue attendance in Nazareth[47], and ἀνέστη ἀναγνῶναι as *erstmalig* in Nazareth and as Jesus' own initiative[48].

Ac 13,43: Jews and proselytes

The synagogue sermon in Ac 13 concludes with the positive reaction of πολλοὶ τῶν Ἰουδαίων καὶ τῶν σεβομένων προσηλύτων. Together with the addresses in vv. 16 (ἄνδρες Ἰσραηλῖται καὶ οἱ φοβούμενοι τὸν θεόν) and 26 (ἄνδρες ἀδελφοί, υἱοὶ γένους Ἀβραὰμ καὶ οἱ ἐν ὑμῖν φοβούμενοι τὸν θεόν), the phrase in v. 43, with a shift in the terminology from φοβούμενοι to σεβόμενοι[49], is one of the central data in the debate on the God-fearers in Acts[50]. It is now almost a common

(Act 17,10) échappent au danger qui les menace". Note however that the distinction "les uns... d'autres" (Ac 17,4.5) is not applicable in the case of Lk 4,22.29. — On Lk 4,22b-30 excluded from Boismard's reconstruction of Proto-Lk (L+Act I), see above, n. 23.

47. In connection with 4,16a Ναζαρά, οὗ ἦν τεθραμμένος. See E. KLOSTERMANN, 1919, 425 (²1929, 62): "die Gewohnheit scheint nur von dem sabbatlichen Synagogenbesuch ausgesagt zu sein, nicht von dem Lehren bei solcher Gelegenheit"; FITZMYER, 530: "stresses Jesus' habitual frequenting of the synagogue". Cf. J. ERNST, 169: "eine biographische Reminiszenz aus der Jugendzeit Jesu"; Bengel, Meyer, Godet, *et al.*

48. SCHÜRMANN, 227: "Jesus wird hier (anders als Apg 13,15) betont in Eigeninitiative geschildert". Cf. GRUNDMANN, 120: "Jesus ... der die Initiative ergreift"; REILING-SWELLENGREBEL, 198: "the fact that there is no hint at such an invitation seems to suggest that Jesus himself wanted to address the Nazarenes". See U. BUSSE, *Nazareth-Manifest* (n. 39), 33: "eine selbständige, auf die Sitte wenig Rücksicht nehmende Initiative (vgl. dagegen Apg 13,15)"; 50: "ohne Einladung ergreift er im Synagogengottesdienst die Initiative und liest die Haphthara".

49. Note οἱ φοβούμενοι τὸν θεόν in 13,16.26 (cf. 10,2.22.35) and σεβόμενοι in 13,43 (cf. 13,50; 16,14; 17,4.17; 18,7).

In the new Dutch translation (NBV, 1998): "die *de* God *van Israël* vereert" (italics F.N.). Cf. NBG: "vereerder van God / die God vereert"; NWV: "godvrezende". Note Ac 13,43: "vrome bekeerlingen"; compare RSV: "devout converts to Judaism". Why not "proselieten" (= 2,11; 6,5), and why the first addition ("van Israël") and not this last addition ("to Judaism")?

50. See the bibliography in FITZMYER, *Acts*, 450, including I. LEVINSKAYA, *The Book of Acts in Its Diaspora Setting* (BAFCS, 5), Grand Rapids, MI, 1996, ch. 7: "God-fearers: The Literary Evidence", 117-126 (for critical review, cf. R.S. ASCOUGH, in *Toronto*

assumption that the word προσηλύτων either can be dropped from the text as "eine alte Glosse" (Haenchen)[51] or as "sorglose Ausdrucks-weise" (Conzelmann)[52]. For K. Lake the meaning is "many of the Jews and the proselytes who were worshipping"[53]. At least one commentator of the post-Haenchen era reads τῶν σεβομένων προσηλύτων in v. 43 ("fromme Proselyten") and raises the further question: "Sind also die 'Gottesfürchtigen' von V 16b als Proselyten zu verstehen?"[54]. Barrett answers positively: "In the present verse [16], Paul (as represented by Luke) is probably addressing Jews and proselytes... It would be strange if, in v. 16, Paul ... ignored the proselytes completely. In fact we know that he did not ignore the proselytes for they are mentioned in v. 43... [In v. 26] it seems best to take οἱ φοβούμενοι to be not uncircumcised 'God-fearers' but proselytes. They are ἐν ὑμῖν, *among you...* they have joined your ranks. [And in v. 43] *Jews* will mean Jews by birth, *prose-lytes* Jews by conversion and adoption... *devout proselytes,* perhaps *worshipping proselytes,* that is, proselytes who had duly attended the Sabbath service in the synagogue". See also his comment on the 'God-fearer' term at Ac 10,2: "not so fully and universally technical in the description of Gentile adherents that they could not be used of Jews and

---

Journal of Theology 44, 1998, 268-169). Add the survey article M.C. DE BOER, *God-fear-ers in Luke–Acts,* in *Luke's Literary Achievement* (n. 5), 1995, 50-71 (esp. 53, for the 'consensus' on the God-fearers in Ac 13,16.26 as "Gentile sympathizers, such as Cor-nelius"; cf. Fitzmyer); B. WANDER, *Trennungsprozesse zwischen Frühem Christentum und Judentum im 1. Jahrhundert n. Chr.* (TANZ, 16), Tübingen-Basel, 1994, 173-185 ("Exkurz: 'Gottesfürchtig'"); ID., *Gottesfürchtige und Symphatisanten. Studien zum heidnischen Umfeld von Diasporasynagogen* (WUNT, 2/104), Tübingen, 1998; M. REISER, *Hat Paulus Heiden bekehrt?,* in *BZ* 39 (1995) 76-91; H.-J. KLAUCK, *Gottes-fürchtige im Magnificat?,* in *NTS* 43 (1997) 134-139. See also B. Witherington's excur-sus "Gentile God-fearers – The Case of Cornelius" (*Acts,* 1998, 341-344), esp. 343: "we can't be sure Luke isn't simply equating proselytes with God-fearers";
  51. *Apg,* at 13,43. See also J. ROLOFF ("vielleicht"); K.G. KUHN, in *TWNT* 6, 743: "eine Ungenauigkeit des Lukas oder eine alte Glosse"; H. KUHLI, in *EWNT* 3, 413; CAMERLYNCK – VANDER HEEREN, [7]1923, 255: "Non immerito forte supponeres textum primitivum de solis *colentibus* Deum egisse".
  52. *Apg,* at 13,43. See also n. 51. G. SCHILLE: "ungenaue Redeweise"; A. WEISER: "Der Ausdruck 'Proselyten' ist hier ungenau"; R. DILLON: "Does this not commingle separate groups: converts and nonconverts?" (*NJBC,* 750). Cf. BAUER-ALAND: "eine Vermischung beider Arten"; BAG: "a mixed expression". See TAYLOR, *Les Actes,* vol. V, 158-162 ("Les 'craignant-Dieu' à Antioche"), 159 n. 1: "plusieurs justifications". Cf. below, n. 55.
  53. K. LAKE, *Proselytes and God-fearers,* in *Beginnings,* vol. V, 1933, 74-96, 88. Cf. 86: "It should be noted... that a proselyte is in Jewish thought quite as much an Israelite as a born Jew". Compare G. WASSERBERG (cf. below, n. 55), 49: "ein Proselyt war Juden rechtlich gleichgestellt und verhielt sich kultisch-religiös wie ein geborener Jude".
  54. G. SCHNEIDER, *Apg* II, 131; see also 142 n. 141: "Doch ist auch denkbar, daß Lukas selbst im Hinblick auf 13,46f deutlich machen will, am ersterwähnten Sabbat habe es sich nur um geborene Juden und zum Judentum voll Übergetretene gehandelt".

full proselytes"[55]. In his speech at Antioch Paul speaks as a Jew to a Jewish audience, referring to "our fathers" in treating the history of "this people Israel" (13,17), and it would not be correct to call it simply a mixed audience of two groups, Jews and Gentiles[56]. On the following sabbath, Paul and Barnabas can declare to the Jews: "it was necessary that the word of God should be spoken *first* to you" (13,46).

The reaction of Jews-and-proselytes in v. 43 has been seen as comparable to the initial attitude of the people in the synagogue of Nazareth in Lk 4,22. Both will be followed by comparable reactions of hostility: ἐπλήσθησαν ζήλου... (the Jews in Ac 13,45) and ἐπλήσθησαν πάντες θυμοῦ... (in Lk 4,28). For not a few interpreters, however, there is a significant difference: in Ac 13,43 these πολλοί "have become Christians" and should not be included among those Jews filled with jealousy on the following sabbath. I quote J. Dupont: "Il est clair que ces convertis, qu'on invite à se montrer fidèles à la grâce de Dieu, ne sont pas inclus dans ce que le v. 45 dit de l'hostilité des 'Juifs'"[57]. Some commentators attenuate their expression: "οἱ Ἰουδαῖοι (in v. 45) can hardly refer to all the Jews, since some of them seem to have been *favourably*

---

55. *Acts*, 631, 630, 639, 654. See now also G. WASSERBERG, *Aus Israels Mitte – Heil für die Welt. Eine narrativ-exegetische Studie zur Theologie des Lukas* (BZNW, 92), Berlin – New York, 1998, 48-51: "Zur Crux interpretum οἱ σεβόμενοι προσήλυτοι (Act 13,43)". There is no mention of Barrett, *Acts* I (1994). He refers to Schneider (142 n. 141), though not to his text at 13,16b (131, quoted above), and so he states incorrectly that Schneider did not consider "die Konsequenzen, die sich daraus für die Deutung der 'Gott Fürchtenden' Act 13,16.26 ergeben müßten" (51 n. 59). — Wasserberg's own argument: "Da Lukas sowohl Juden (Lk 1,50) wie auch ἔθνη (Act 10,2.22) mit dem Etikett der Gottesfurcht behaften kann, muß folglich am Einzelfall entschieden werden, welcher ethnischen Herkunft die jeweils 'Gott Fürchtenden' sind. Wenn einmal das 'Vor-Urteil' beiseite gelassen wird, die von Lukas gekennzeichneten 'Gott Fürchtenden' seien selbstredend nichtjüdische Sympathisanten, so eröffnet sich auch ein neuer Zugang zur Deutung der Gottesfürchtigen in Act 13,16.26. Sie hat von Act 13,43 her zu erfolgen" (50); "Folglich besteht der Adressatenkreis ... für Lukas aus Juden und Proselyten (Act 13,43), nicht auch aus vermeintlichen 'Gottesfürchtigen'" (51). Cf. J. MURPHY-O'CONNOR, *Lot of God-fearers?* Theosebeis *in the Aphrodisias Inscription*, in *RB* 99 (1992) 418-424. The second list contains 52 names introduced as *kai hosoi theosebis*, but the Jewish group in the first list includes three names identified as proselytes and two others identified as *theosebis* (Emmonios and Antoninos). Note therefore Murphy-O'Connor's conclusion: "the fact that here it is used in two consciously differentiated senses in the same document makes it clear that the meaning of the term *must be determined in each instance from the context*" (424, italics F.N.).

56. BUSS, *Missionspredigt* (n. 36), 34-35, although he emphasizes "die gemeinsame Anrede von Israeliten und Proselyten" (35) and also notes that Paul "in Antiochien vor Juden situationsgerecht zunächst vom Schöpfer und Erhalter Israels (spricht)" (37). Cf. JERVELL, on Ac 13,16.26: "es (gibt) in der Synagoge zwei Gruppen, die voneinander getrennt sind" (353; cf. 357).

57. *Conclusion*, 384 (= 488). Cf. below, n. 140.

impressed by what Paul had said" (Barrett)[58]. Others, like Jervell, stress the notion of conversion (*Bekehrung*) and include Ac 13,43 in the list of Luke's characteristic reports of "mass conversions of God-fearers"[59]. But it has been rightly observed: v. 43 "spricht noch nicht von Bekehrungen"[60]. Ἀκολουθεῖν has its literal meaning: they 'followed' Paul and Barnabas[61]. The phrase προσμένειν τῇ χάριτι τοῦ θεοῦ has been compared to 11,23 (τὴν χάριν [τὴν] τοῦ θεοῦ ... προσμένειν τῷ κυρίῳ) and 14,22 (ἐμμένειν τῇ πίστει), but in both cases the context clearly indicates that the exhortation to remain faithful is addressed to Christians (cf. 11,21; 14,22a), whereas in ch. 13 an act of believing is not mentioned before v. 48 (ἐπίστευσαν).

The conclusion in Ac 13,43 (λυθείσης δὲ τῆς συναγωγῆς...) is preceded by an immediate reaction to Paul's speech: ἐξιόντων δὲ αὐτῶν παρεκάλουν εἰς τὸ μεταξὺ σάββατον λαληθῆναι αὐτοῖς τὰ ῥήματα ταῦτα (13,42)[62]. The verb παρεκάλουν has no expressed subject and can be translated: "*the people* urged them" (NRSV; Luther: "*die Leute*"). Some translators prefer to keep the indefinite "they" ("*man*"). In J. Roloff's understanding it refers to the synagogue officials (cf. 13,15) who invite Paul and Barnabas to speak again on the following sabbath. In v. 45 "die anfänglich freundliche Zurückhaltung der

---

58. *Acts*, 655 (italics mine). Moreover, see 624: "does Luke imply that those who at first were favourably impressed changed their minds?".

59. *Apg*, 362 (cf. 151, 524): "auch hier: *Einige* glauben" (italics F.N.). — Jervell's list (* = conversions of 'God-fearers'): Ac 2,41; 4,4; 5,14; 6,7; 9,42; 11,21*.24*.26; 12,24; 13,43*; 14,1*; 17,4*.12*; 18,8*.10; 21,20 (cf. 151, 297, 524; *Retrospect* [n. 33], 390-391). With regard to "God-fearers" and proselytes, Jervell (here, 362 n. 505, and again 389 n. 647) refers to M. KLINGHARDT, *Gesetz und Volk Gottes. Das lukanische Verständnis des Gesetzes nach Herkunft, Funktion und seinem Ort in der Geschichte des Urchristentums* (WUNT, 2/32), Tübingen, 1988, 183-184: "Die Verwendung der Bezeichnung Proselyt für den beschnittenen Konvertiten ist mE. keineswegs so eindeutig, wie dies aus den neueren Untersuchungen hervorzugehen scheint. Es ist denkbar, daß man – obwohl in aller Regel ein eindeutiger, technischer Sprachgebrauch vorliegt – bewußt oder unbewußt die Grenze zwischen beschnittenen Konvertiten und unbeschnittenen Gottesfürchtigen nicht so streng gezogen hat, zumal die Gottesfürchtigen sehr häufig Frauen waren, bei denen der Übertritt zum Judentum nicht so eindeutig war, da die Beschneidung fehlte". Klinghardt reads "proselytes" in Ac 13,43 as "eine Gruppe von Gottesfürchtigen, frommen Heiden also, die sich eng zur Synagoge hält"; he uses the term God-fearer without discussing its meaning, technical or descriptive.

60. BUSS, *Missionspredigt* (n. 36), 134. Cf. SCHNEIDER: "Daß sie gläubig geworden seien, sagt der Bericht nicht" (142). Ctr. G. Stählin, F. Mussner, A. Weiser, J. Jervell, B.J. Koet, *et al.*

61. Cf. WASSERBERG, *Aus Israels Mitte* (n. 55), 314. Ctr. MUSSNER, 82: "schließen sich... an, d.h. sie werden Christen"; WEISER, 337: "'Nachfolgen': Anschluß an den christlichen Glauben".

62. Cf. above, n. 36.

maßgeblichen jüdischen Kreise (schlägt um) in unverhohlene Ablehnung"[63]. Compare again Lk 4,22 and 28.

Ac 13,45: The jealousy of the Jews

The story of the second sabbath at Pisidian Antioch begins with the gathering of "almost the whole city" (v. 44) and the reaction of the Jews: ἰδόντες δὲ οἱ Ἰουδαῖοι τοὺς ὄχλους ἐπλήσθησαν ζήλου... (v. 45). The same phrase is used in the conflict of the high priest and the Sadducees with the apostles (5,17) and is usually translated: "they were filled with jealousy"[64]. The participle ζηλώσαντες, in the same meaning, occurs at 7,9 and 17,5. This motif in Ac 13,45 is not irrelevant in a study of the Nazareth pericope because of the parallel expression in Lk 4,28: ἐπλήσθησαν πάντες θυμοῦ (in reaction to 4,25-27)[65]. Moreover, jealousy is implied in the demand attributed to the people of Nazareth: "the things that we have heard you did at Capernaum do also here ἐν τῇ πατρίδι σου" (Lk 4,23)[66].

B. Koet has devoted a special study to Ac 13,45. I quote here his conclusion: "We cannot interpret the reaction of the Jews to what Paul has said as jealousy. Their attitude is based on zeal for their interpretation of the Law"[67]. The Jews in 13,45 react to Paul's pronouncement on the Law. They are not jealous but they show a certain zealousness and especially a zeal against the interpretation of the *Torah* as presented in Paul's speech, 13,38-41. Koet has to note that the use of ζῆλος in 5,17 "is not clearly related to zeal for the Law", but he stresses the parallel in 17,5, ζηλώσαντες δὲ οἱ Ἰουδαῖοι: the Jews in Thessalonica "are not jealous but they disagree with zeal against Paul's preaching of the Word of God to the Gentiles"[68].

63. *Apg*, 209.
64. EÜ: wurden eifersüchtig; BJ: furent remplis de jalousie; NWV: werden met jaloezie vervuld. — Compare the variation in NBG: naijver (5,17; 7,9), nijd (13,45), afgunst (17,5). See now NBV (1998): 5,17 vervuld van jaloezie; 7,9 (waren) jaloers; 13,45 werden jaloers; 17,5 werden vervuld van jaloezie. The inversion of 13,45 and 17,5 would be closer to the Greek: ἐπλήσθησαν ζήλου, and ζηλώσαντες (cf. NWV).
65. BJ: furent remplis de fureur; TOB: remplis de colère. — Note the TOB translation of ζῆλος in Ac 13,45: "furent pris de fureur" (5,17: remplis de fureur; 17,5: furieux)!
66. J. DUPONT, *Jésus*, 149 (= 45): "On peut se demander ici si le récit des Actes ne manifeste pas le sous-entendu de *Lc.* 4,23: les Nazaréens sont jaloux". Cf. R.C. TANNEHILL, *The Narrative Unity* (below, n. 74), 70: "the jealous possessiveness which is indicated by v. 23 and underscored by the angry reaction to vv. 25-27".
67. B.J. KOET, *Paul and Barnabas in Pisidian Antioch: A Disagreement over the Interpretation of the Scriptures (Acts 13,42-52)*, in ID., *Five Studies on Interpretation of Scripture in Luke–Acts* (SNTA, 14), Leuven, 1989, 97-118, 117.
68. *Ibid.*, 101, 105 n. 28, 104.

In 13,45 it is said that the Jews contradicted "what was spoken by Paul", ἀντέλεγον τοῖς ὑπὸ Παύλου λαλουμένοις. Does it mean that they particularly object to "Paul's pronouncement on the Law"? What Paul said in his synagogue preachings is time and again summarized by Luke: that Jesus is the χριστός (9,22)[69]. Thus, in 17,3 ὅτι οὗτός ἐστιν ὁ χριστὸς [ὁ] Ἰησοῦς and 18,5b διαμαρτυρόμενος τοῖς Ἰουδαίοις εἶναι τὸν χριστὸν Ἰησοῦν (cf. 18,28 Apollos), in each instance followed by the Jews' opposition. The christological theme is of course not absent in 13,38 on forgiveness of sins (διὰ τούτου) and in v. 39 on justification (ἐν τούτῳ). Is it not thinkable[70] that the λαλούμενα in 13,45 refer to a preaching of Paul on the second sabbath, not quoted but implied in the intention of the people of Antioch "to hear the word of the Lord"? Anyway in the text of Ac 13,45 "the immediate cause of the reaction of the Jews is their 'seeing the multitudes'" (Koet) and I see no urgent reason for changing here the usual translation of ζῆλος (and of ζηλώσαντες in 17,5)[71].

J.B. Tyson[72] has repeatedly studied the pattern of initial acceptance and final rejection:

> The narrative about Paul in Pisidian Antioch expresses this literary pattern in fullest fashion... In Acts 13 ... Paul speaks on two Sabbaths. After the first, many Jews and proselytes join with Paul and Barnabas, and Paul is invited to speak again. But on the second Sabbath there is nothing but opposition. 'But when the Jews saw the crowds, they were filled with jealousy; and blaspheming, they contradicted what was spoken by Paul' (13,45). As was the case with the sermon of Jesus in Luke 4, so here with Paul initial acceptance is followed by rejection, in a pattern that is familiar to readers of Luke–Acts.

> In terms of public response the pattern is clear: initial acceptance followed by rejection. Luke 4:16-30 anticipates the Jewish public response to Jesus

69. Cf. P. POKORNÝ, *Theologie der lukanischen Schriften* (FRLANT, 174), Göttingen, 1998, 112: "Der Satz, wonach 'dieser' (d.h. Jesus) der Sohn Gottes (d.h. auch Messias – Act 9,22) sei, ist nach Lukas die Zusammenfassung dessen, was Paulus in den Synagogen predigte (Act 9,20; 13,33)".

70. See E. PLÜMACHER, *Die Missionsreden der Apostelgeschichte und Dionys von Halikarnass*, in *NTS* 39 (1993) 161-177: "Da Lukas den Paulus das Missionskerygma wenige Verse zuvor schon ausführlich hat vortragen lassen und man aus V. 42 weiß, daß er es jetzt lediglich wiederholen wird, braucht Lukas es nicht abermals *verbaliter* zu präsentieren; der schlichte Hinweis auf die Tatsache, daß Paulus predigt, auf τὰ ὑπὸ Παύλου λαλούμενα, genügt" (165).

71. On Ac 13,45, see also WASSERBERG, *Aus Israels Mitte* (n. 55), 315-316. On Ac 17,5, cf. below, text at n. 80.

72. Cf. J.B. TYSON, *The Jewish Public in Luke–Acts*, in *NTS* 30 (1984) 574-583; = *The Death of Jesus in Luke–Acts*, Columbia, SC, 1986, 29-47 ("Acceptance and Rejection: Jesus and the Jewish Public"); *The Gentile Mission and the Authority of Scripture in Acts*, in *NTS* 33 (1987) 619-631 (esp. 622-624); *Jews and Judaism in Luke–Acts: Reading as a Godfearer*, in *NTS* 41 (1995) 19-38 (esp. 29-37).

that will be worked out in the rest of the Gospel (and Acts). It is significant that the rejection is associated with favourable treatment of Gentiles.[73]

Ac 13,46: Turning to the Gentiles

ὑμῖν ἦν ἀναγκαῖον πρῶτον λαληθῆναι τὸν λόγον τοῦ θεοῦ·
ἐπειδὴ ἀπωθεῖσθε αὐτὸν καὶ οὐκ ἀξίους κρίνετε ἑαυτοὺς τῆς αἰωνίου ζωῆς,
ἰδοὺ στρεφόμεθα εἰς τὰ ἔθνη.

Ac 13,46 is the first of three announcements that Paul is turning to the Gentiles (cf. 18,6; 28,28): "Rejection by Jews and turning to Gentiles, the pattern of Paul's mission in Acts"[74]. For those who accept the allusion to the Gentiles in Lk 4,25-27 (the Elijah and Elisha material) it is easy to make the link with Nazareth. Thus, for J. Dupont,

> Le récit d'Antioche de Pisidie nous est précieux, car c'est lui qui assure le pont entre l'épisode de Nazareth et celui de Rome... Les déclarations faites par Paul aux Juifs d'Antioche de Pisidie (13,46-47) et de Corinthe (18,6) [sont des] déclarations préparées de longue main par les précédents prophétiques auxquels Jésus se réfère à Nazareth, en Lc 4,25-27. Nazareth, Antioche de Pisidie, Rome: trois jalons d'une même histoire, trois situations permettant des variations sur le même thème: le salut passe des Juifs aux Gentils.[75]

The solemn announcement in 13,46(-47)[76] is followed by the joyful reaction of the Gentiles and, in v. 50, the final, and now more than verbal, aggression by the Jews of Antioch. Notice the phrase ἐξέβαλον αὐτοὺς ἀπὸ τῶν ὁρίων αὐτῶν and Lk 4,29 ἐξέβαλον αὐτὸν ἔξω τῆς πόλεως[77]. Note also 13,51...ἦλθον εἰς Ἰκόνιον, followed by a new synagogue scene in 14,1-7 (cf. Lk 4,30... ἐπορεύετο. 31 καὶ κατῆλθεν εἰς Καφαρναούμ...). The opening sentence in 14,1 makes clear that,

73. Quotations: 1995, 29-30; 1984, 578 (1986, 33: "and Acts", "connected").
74. R.C. TANNEHILL, *Rejection by Jews and Turning to the Gentiles*, in *SBL 1986 Seminar Papers*, 130-141 (= J.B. TYSON, ed., *Luke–Acts and the Jewish People*, Minneapolis, MN, 1988, 83-101); *The Narrative Unity of Luke–Acts: A Literary Interpretation*. I. *The Gospel according to Luke*, Minneapolis, MN, 1986 (esp. 60-73); II. *The Acts of the Apostles*, 1990 (esp. 164-175). Cf. *The Mission of Jesus according to Luke IV 16-30*, in W. ELTESTER (ed.), *Jesus in Nazareth* (BZNW, 40), Berlin – New York, 1972, 51-75.
75. *Conclusion*, 400-401 (= 507-508).
76. On the citation of Isa 49,6, interpreted as a direct command of the Lord (v. 47 οὕτως γὰρ ἐντέταλται ἡμῖν ὁ κύριος· τέθεικά σε εἰς φῶς ἐθνῶν τοῦ εἶναί σε εἰς σωτηρίαν ἕως ἐσχάτου τῆς γῆς), see B.J. KOET, *Paul and Barnabas* (n. 67), 106-114; H. VAN DE SANDT, *The Quotations in Acts 13,32-52 as a Reflection of Luke's LXX Interpretation*, in *Bib* 75 (1994) 26-58, esp. 50-54; G.J. STEYN, *Septuaginta Quotations in the Context of the Petrine and Pauline Speeches of the Acta Apostolorum* (CBET, 12), Kampen, 1995, 159-202 (Ac 13), esp. 196-201.
77. This parallel is heavily stressed by G. Muhlack, *Parallelen* (below, n. 83), 124 ("Die Parallele... reicht bis in die Ausdrucksweise"), 139. See also n. 80.

despite their turning to the Gentiles (v. 46), "they entered into the synagogue of the Jews κατὰ τὸ αὐτό"[78], i.e., *in the same way* as in Antioch
(emphasized in NRSV: "The same thing occurred in Iconium..."):

> The scene is almost a replay of that in Antioch, and its literary function is
> much the same. Luke is at great pains to show that the turn to the Gentiles
> was not because God rejected the Jews, but because some Jews rejected the
> gospel and prevented its being spread among them. Nothing will make the
> point more forcibly than such repetition of patterns.[79]

The three stations of Antioch, Iconium, and Lystra are marked by
growing Jewish opposition. In Antioch Paul and Barnabas are perse-
cuted and expelled from the district (13,50), in Iconium there is an
attempt to stone them (14,5), and in Lystra "Jews came there from Antioch and Iconium; and having persuaded the people, they stoned Paul
and dragged him out of the city" (14,19). Compare the repetition of the
pattern in Ac 17: Paul's successful preaching in Thessalonica (vv. 1-4)
is followed by opposition of "the Jews" who became jealous (v. 5) and
in Beroea "the Jews of Thessalonica... came there too, to stir up and
incite the crowds" (v. 13)[80].

II. Lk 4,16-30 and Peter's Mission Speeches

The sermon in the synagogue of Pisidian Antioch is Paul's inaugural
speech, the first of his three major speeches in Acts: 13,16-41

78. Κατὰ τὸ αὐτό = in the same way, *ebenso*: compare the plural κατὰ τὰ αὐτά in
Lk 6,23.26; 17,30 (cf. κατὰ τὸ εἰωθὸς τῷ Παύλῳ in Ac 17,2). The alternative translation: together, *zusammen* (Vulg. *simul*) reads the singular as a variant of ἐπὶ τὸ αὐτό
(Lake-Cadbury, Bauer *Wb*, REB, NAB; undecided: Conzelmann, Fitzmyer). More exceptional, and less convincing: "vers la même époque" (Delebecque, Bossuyt-Radermakers).
79. L.T. JOHNSON, *Acts*, 250. For a stylistic analysis of Ac 13,44-52 / 14,1-7, see C.
BREYTENBACH, *Paulus und Barnabas in der Provinz Galatien. Studien zu Apostelgeschichte 13f.; 16,6; 18,23 und den Adressaten des Galaterbriefes* (AGAJU, 38), Leiden, 1996, 24:

Interessierte Heiden	13,44	14,1d
Hindernis durch Juden	45	2
Rede	46-47	3
Überwindung	48-49	—
Steigerung des Konfliktes	50	4-5
Jüngerflucht	51	6-7
Missionserfolg	52	—

80. In connection with Ac 13,50 (n. 77) I note here the parallels between Lk 4,28-29
and the account of Stephen's death: Lk 4,28 ἀκούοντες ταῦτα, 29 καὶ ... ἐξέβαλον
αὐτὸν ἔξω τῆς πόλεως and Ac 7,54 ἀκούοντες δὲ ταῦτα, 58 καὶ ἐκβαλόντες ἔξω τῆς
πόλεως ἐλιθοβόλουν (cf. Ac 14,5 λιθοβολῆσαι). See also J. NOLLAND, *Luke*, 201:
"Both Stephen and Jesus accuse their hearers of rejecting God's prophets (Acts 7:52;
Luke 4:24) and identify them as outsiders to what God is presently doing (Acts 7:51;
Luke 4:25-27)".

(addressed to a Jewish audience); 17,22-31 (to Gentiles in Athens); 20,18-35 (to Christians in Miletus). In this second part I turn to Peter's three major mission speeches (2,17-40; 3,12-26; 10,34-43), beginning with his Pentecost sermon, the inaugural discourse in the Book of Acts.

Acts 2,17-40

C.H. Talbert describes the parallel with Lk 4,16-30 as follows: "each speech (1) opens a period of public ministry (Jesus' resp. the church's) and (2) gives the theme for what follows in that ministry, namely, fulfillment of prophecy and rejection of Jesus by many of the Jewish people"[81]. Compare D.L. Tiede: "Thus as the Isaiah prophecy in Luke 4 serves to articulate the program of the Spirit-anointed Jesus, so the direct citation of the Book of Joel identifies the new phase of the eschatological activity of God's Spirit which is being disclosed at Pentecost"[82]. The "Antrittspredigten" in Lk 4, Ac 2 (and Ac 13) are included in G. Muhlack's survey of *Parallelen*[83]. The parallelism between Lk 4,16-30 and Ac 2,14-40 is now examined anew in A. Lindemann's seminar paper[84]. At first glance his conclusion goes in the traditional line of previous studies[85]:

> Die beiden Redeszenen in Lk und in Apg 2 ... leiten das öffentliche Auftreten der im folgenden dargestellten Hauptpersonen ein; in beiden Reden geht es darum, das geschilderte Geschehen und die damit verbundenen Personen umfassend zu deuten; beide Reden beziehen sich auf das Wirken des göttlichen Geistes.

81. C.H. TALBERT, *Literary Patterns, Theological Themes, and the Genre of Luke–Acts*, Missoula, MT, 1974, 18-19, esp. 16.

82. D.L. TIEDE, *Acts 2:1-47*, in *Interpretation* 33 (1979) 62-67, here 63. Cf. J.-N. ALETTI, *Quand Luc raconte. Le récit comme théologie* (Lire la Bible, 114), Paris, 1998, 81: "Discours inaugural (insistant sur l'Esprit de prophétie)". See also in this volume: H. BAARLINK, *Die Bedeutung der Prophetenzitate in Lk 4,18f. und Apg 2,17-21 für das Doppelwerk des Lukas*, 483-491. His thesis: "die theologischen Eckdaten der Apostelgeschichte (haben) die Strukturierung und Darstellung in seinem Evangelium maßgeblich mitbestimmt" (491). Yet, the evidence he provides, the influence of Ac 2,17-21 (= Joel) upon Lk 8,1-3 and the man-woman pairs in Lk, is hardly convincing.

83. G. MUHLACK, *Die Parallelen von Lukas-Evangelium und Apostelgeschichte* (Theologie und Wirklichkeit, 8), Frankfurt, 1979, 117-139 ("Die Antrittspredigt in Lukas-Evangelium und Apostelgeschichte"), esp. 118, 125-131, 138 ("Die Pfingstpredigt des Petrus").

84. "Zu Form und Funktion von Reden und Wundererzählungen im Lukasevangelium und in der Apostelgeschichte. A. Reden im lukanischen Doppelwerk" (pp. 1-5; discussion paper available at the Colloquium). See now the slightly revised text, supplemented with footnotes, in this volume: *Einheit und Vielfalt im lukanischen Doppelwerk. Beobachtungen zu Reden, Wundererzählungen und Mahlberichten*, 225-253, esp. 225-237 ("I. Jesu Antrittsrede in Nazareth und die Pfingstpredigt des Petrus in Jerusalem").

85. *Ibid.*, 234 ("Ergebnis des Vergleichs"). Cf. BAARLINK (n. 82), 485.

Yet the words omitted in this quotation need further explication: "Beide sind von Lukas offensichtlich bewußt parallel gestaltet worden". Lindemann emphasizes the presence of structural analogies in the text and context of Lk 4,16-30 and Ac 2,14-41. Both speeches are followed by a narrative summary, Lk 4,31-32 and Ac 2,42.43-47. In both scenes he notes a two-part division: an opening section (*Eröffnung*), Lk 4,16-21 and Ac 2,14-36, and in a second part the reaction of the audience (*Reaktion der Hörer*), Lk 4,22-30 and Ac 2,37-41, both in the form of a question to the speaker. However, in his own interpretation, the question in Lk 4,22 is an expression of "ungläubige Skepsis"[86], while Peter's listeners were "cut to the heart" and they inquired, "What are we to do?" (Ac 2,37). The Nazareth scene ends with Jesus' failure (*Fehlschlag, Niederlage, Katastrophe*) in contrast to the success of Peter's speech ("endet mit einem grandiosen Triumph des Redners"). In Lk 4,30 a change of location forms the transition to the summary (4,31-32), while in Ac 2 there is no such *Ortswechsel*. The differences are even more striking in the so-called first part. Ac 2,14-36 is one continuous uninterrupted speech of Peter, with no other parallel than Jesus' *Predigt* in Lk 4,21b. The presentation of correspondences in a synoptic table[87] creates a misleading impression. The *Orts- und Situationsangabe* Lk 4,16 / Ac 2,1-13(15) as well as the *Einleitung* Lk 4,17 / Ac 2,16 are in reality hardly comparable parallels. The quotations in Lk 4,18-19 / Ac 2,17-21 are presented as parallels, but Lindemann's comment shows that there is "ein wesentlicher Unterschied" between Jesus' reading of the Isaiah text and Peter's use of Joel 3,1-5 as the correct interpretation of "ein bereits geschehenes Ereignis"[88].

Since Lindemann understands Lk 4,25-27 as "Vorausverweis auf die Apg"[89], it is rather amazing that he has no comment on Ac 2,39: ὑμῖν γάρ ἐστιν ἡ ἐπαγγελία καὶ τοῖς τέκνοις ὑμῶν καὶ πᾶσιν τοῖς εἰς μακράν, ὅσους ἂν προσκαλέσηται κύριος ὁ θεὸς ὑμῶν[90]. Cf. Dupont's *Le salut des Gentils*:

---

86. *Ibid.*, 233 (in confrontation with U. Busse, *Nazareth-Manifest*). Cf. below, n. 156.
87. *Ibid.*, 228.
88. *Ibid.*, 231.
89. In the revised text: "ein gezielter Vorausverweis auf die erst in der Apostelgeschichte dargestellte Entwicklung" (237), here too in dialogue with Busse (n. 53).
90. Two OT passages are alluded to: Joel 3,5d καὶ εὐαγγελιζόμενοι οὓς κύριος προσκέκληται (cf. 3,1-5a LXX, quoted in Ac 2,17-21) and Isa 57,19a εἰρήνην ἐπ' εἰρήνην τοῖς μακρὰν καὶ τοῖς ἐγγὺς οὖσιν (cf. Eph 2,17; Ac 22,21, the commission conferred on Paul: πορεύου, ὅτι ἐγὼ εἰς ἔθνη μακρὰν ἐξαποστελῶ σε). – "Per eos hic nonnulli intelligunt Gentes, tamquam quae Judaeis ut τοῖς ἐγγὺς opponi soleant. Ita olim Theophylactus…" (J.C. WOLFIUS, 1725, at Ac 2,39). H.H. Wendt calls it "die gewöhnliche Erklärung" (⁹1913, 96). Wendt himself opted for Diaspora Jews; see also Zahn, Roloff, Mussner, Witherington. Less likely: of time, "future generations" (BAUER, *Wb*, art. μακράν 1.b).

La conclusion du discours permet un rapprochement avec la conclusion de la prédication de Jésus à Nazareth... L'expression d'Ac 2,39 "tous ceux qui sont au loin", formant antithèse avec "vous et vos enfants", s'entend assez naturellement des Gentils, ou plus exactement de ceux qu'en grand nombre, parmi les Gentils, le Seigneur appellera.[91]

The promise is "even to 'those still far off'. So Luke foreshadows the carrying of Christian testimony to Gentiles, which will become the burden of his narrative in the later chapters of Acts" (Fitzmyer)[92]. One can agree with Lindemann's statement in reference to Lk 4,25-27: "wird erst in der Apostelgeschichte verwirklicht werden"[93], but it is still in the form of *Vorausverweis* that Peter alludes to the Gentiles in his Pentecost speech (Ac 2,39): "Luc ne pouvait pas prêter à Pierre au jour de la Pentecôte un universalisme explicite, qui aurait été anachronique"[94].

Acts 3,11-26

Peter's Temple discourse is mentioned here for two reasons. First, the contrast between the end of Lk 4,16-30 and the response to Peter's speech in Ac 2 ("in höchstem Maße erfolgreich")[95] can in some sense be mitigated if the reaction to Ac 3,11-26 in 4,1-3.5ff. is taken into consideration. Second, the allusion to the Gentiles in Ac 2,39 receives here confirmation: "die Analogie von 3,26 πρῶτον (spricht) für die gewöhnliche Beziehung auf die Heiden" (Holtzmann)[96]. I can refer again to J. Dupont:

Ce "d'abord" suppose un "ensuite"; le contexte indique clairement le sens: La bénédiction est d'abord pour Israël, ensuite pour toutes les nations de la terre... Les deux premiers discours missionnaires de Pierre se terminent donc par un élargissement des perspectives, élargissement qui fait prévoir l'évangélisation des Gentils.[97]

91. *Le salut des Gentils* (n. 2), 145 (= 408). Cf. *Jésus*, 148 (= 44); *Conclusion*, 392 (= 497). See also BOISMARD-LAMOUILLE, *Les Actes*, vol. II (n. 18), 1990, 148-150 ("L'universalisme"; Act II); H. VAN DE SANDT, *The Fate of the Gentiles in Joel and Acts 2: An Intertextual Study*, in *ETL* 66 (1990) 56-77, esp. 72-74 ("The Intertextual Functions of Isa 57,19a and Joel 3,5b.d in Act 2,39").
92. *Acts*, 265 (and 267). Cf. note on 22,21: "'Far away' is an allusion to Isa 57:19 and echoes Acts 2:39" (709). On "Lucan foreshadowing" at work in Acts, cf. his *Luke the Theologian: Aspects of His Teaching*, New York – Mahwah, NJ, 1989, 192.
93. *Einheit und Vielfalt*, 237.
94. DUPONT, *Conclusion*, 392 (= 497). See also 395 (= 500), on πᾶσαι αἱ πατριαὶ τῆς γῆς in Ac 3,25: "La citation parle de toutes les 'familles' de la terre...: est-ce parce qu'il serait prématuré de parler déjà des ἔθνη, dans leur opposition au peuple juif?". On this possibility, see also G.J. STEYN, *Quotations* (n. 76), 157: "because Luke could not refer explicitly to the Gentiles without a clear reference to the gentile mission, which at this stage in the story still lies in the future" (cf. Haenchen).
95. See Lindemann's conclusion (237).
96. *Apg*, 1889, 335.
97. *Le salut des Gentils* (n. 2), 146 (= 409).

Ac 3,26 ὑμῖν πρῶτον ἀναστήσας ὁ θεὸς τὸν παῖδα αὐτοῦ... The ὑμῖν are the Jewish people Peter is addressing in this call to conversion (εὐλογοῦντα ὑμᾶς ἐν τῷ ἀποστρέφειν ἕκαστον ἀπὸ τῶν πονηριῶν ὑμῶν). Apart from the debate on ἀναστήσας either referring to the earthly mission of Jesus or (more likely) to the resurrection, πρῶτον is qualifying ὑμῖν and "wird durch 13,46 erklärt" (Conzelmann)[98].

Acts 10,34-43

If already in the speeches to the Jews in Jerusalem Luke alludes to the Gentiles (2,39; 3,25-26), the turning point in Acts comes much later in the Cornelius episode with Peter's speech in Cornelius's house: 10,34-43. "After the speech, the narrative is resumed, and Peter's listeners are baptized and receive the Spirit. In effect, it recounts a 'Pentecost of the Gentiles'"[99].

Peter begins his speech in vv. 34-35 with a reference to God's impartiality and the statement that "in every nation (ἐν παντὶ ἔθνει) anyone who fears him and does what is right is acceptable to him" (v. 35), in correspondence to Peter's last words in v. 43: πάντα τὸν πιστεύοντα εἰς αὐτόν. Note also the universalistic πάντων in the parenthetical clause οὗτός ἐστιν πάντων κύριος (v. 36b) and οὗτός ἐστιν ... κριτὴς ζώντων καὶ νεκρῶν (v. 42).

Ac 10,42-43 shows a striking resemblance to Lk 24,47: καὶ κηρυχθῆναι ἐπὶ τῷ ὀνόματι αὐτοῦ μετάνοιαν εἰς ἄφεσιν ἁμαρτιῶν εἰς πάντα τὰ ἔθνη.... 48a ὑμεῖς μάρτυρες τούτων. Compare Ac 10,42 καὶ παρήγγειλεν ἡμῖν κηρύξαι... 43... μαρτυροῦσιν ἄφεσιν ἁμαρτιῶν λαβεῖν διὰ τοῦ ὀνόματος αὐτοῦ... G. Schneider's comment on this parallel is noteworthy[100]:

> Die Diskrepanz zwischen Lk 24,47 und Apg 10,34-43 hat Lukas wohl empfunden: Petrus hätte von der Ostererscheinung Jesu den Auftrag zur Heidenmission kennen müssen. Dennoch wird er Apg 10 erst von Gott zu den Heiden gewiesen.
> Möglicherweise hatte er [Lukas] beabsichtigt, daß man die beiden Schriften seines Doppelwerks auch unabhängig voneinander lesen konnte. Vielleicht hängt damit zusammen, daß Lk 24,47 die Heidenmission schon am Ostertag von Jesus angeordnet sein läßt.

98. A few more recent comments: "Nur mit einem Wort eröffnet Lukas vorsichtig eine weitere Perspective. Israel wird zuerst gesegnet, später kommen aber auch andere hinzu, die Heiden" (JERVELL, *Apg*, 171); "Here (v. 25) and in v. 26 the blessing of the Gentiles is clearly alluded to, but only in connection with Jews or after the Jews. Luke is masterfully preparing for later developments in his narrative" (WITHERINGTON, *Acts*, 188).

99. FITZMYER, *Acts*, 460.

100. *Petrusrede*, 1985 (below, n. 120), 278 n. 159, 279 and n. 161.

Thus the hints at Ac 2,39; 3,25-26 and the solemn inauguration of the Gentile mission in Ac 10 appear to be strangely parallel to the indirect allusion in Lk 4,25-27 on the one hand and the explicit command of the risen Christ in Lk 24 (and Ac 1,8) on the other.

More directly relevant for our study of the Nazareth pericope is the reminiscence of Lk 4,18 in Ac 10,38:

a Ἰησοῦν τὸν ἀπὸ Ναζαρέθ,
   ὡς ἔχρισεν αὐτὸν ὁ θεὸς πνεύματι ἁγίῳ καὶ δυνάμει,
b ὃς διῆλθεν εὐεργετῶν
   καὶ ἰώμενος πάντας τοὺς καταδυναστευομένους ὑπὸ τοῦ διαβόλου,
c ὅτι ὁ θεὸς ἦν μετ' αὐτοῦ.

Once more I can refer to J. Dupont's 1978 essay[101]:

> Dans l'état actuel de nos connaissances, *Act*. 10,38 et son exégèse d'*Is*.
> 61,1 doivent être lus comme une composition de Luc, relevant du même
> niveau littéraire que *Lc*. 4,16-22.

Lk 4,18-19

The Isaiah text quoted in Lk 4,18-19 corresponds to Isa 61,1-2a LXX:

18a πνεῦμα κυρίου ἐπ' ἐμέ, οὗ εἵνεκεν ἔχρισέν με·
  b εὐαγγελίσασθαι πτωχοῖς ἀπέσταλκέν με,
  c κηρύξαι αἰχμαλώτοις ἄφεσιν καὶ τυφλοῖς ἀνάβλεψιν,
  d ἀποστεῖλαι τεθραυσμένους ἐν ἀφέσει,
19 κηρύξαι ἐνιαυτὸν κυρίου δεκτόν.

Three differences (besides the omission of καὶ ἡμέραν ἀνταποδόσεως) are to be noted: the omission of ἰάσασθαι τοὺς συντετριμμένους τῇ καρδίᾳ / τὴν καρδίαν (before 18c); the insertion of 18d ἀποστεῖλαι τεθραυσμένους ἐν ἀφέσει from Isa 58,6d (ἀπόστελλε...); and in v. 19 κηρύξαι (for καλέσαι in Isa 61,2a). These divergences from the Septuagint are occasionally cited as an argument for dependence on a pre-Lukan source, either Q[102] or Proto-Luke[103] or some undefined source of Lk[104].

---

101. *Jésus*, 155 (= 51).
102. Cf. above, n. 5: TUCKETT, *Luke 4,16-30*, 1982, esp. 346-351; *Q*, 1996, esp. 229-236. For Tuckett, "the reference to Ναζαρά in v. 16a and the Isaiah quotation belong together. Thus if Ναζαρά derives from Q, the Isa 61 citation *may* also derive from Q" (1996, 229); cf. 1982, 345: "... *must* also derive from Q" (italics F.N.). On Ναζαρά in Q, cf. above, n. 6.
103. On Lk 4,16-22a in Proto-Luke, cf. above, n. 23 (M.-É. Boismard, 1997). See now also T.L. Brodie in this volume (627 n. 3): 4,16-22a (compare 1993: 4,16-30; 1997: 4,16-27).
104. See, e.g., M. TURNER, *Power from on High. The Spirit in Israel's Restoration and Witness in Luke–Acts* (Journal of Pentecostal Theology SS, 9), Sheffield, 1996, 220-

As indicated in an earlier paper, the allusion to Isa 61 in Q 7,22 (with πτωχοὶ εὐαγγελίζονται in final position) may have called forth the Isaiah text for quotation by Luke in his inaugural Nazareth section[105]. The redactional composition of Lk 7,21 in preparation of Q 7,22 clearly indicates that physical healing is regarded by Luke as the fulfilment of Isa 61,1:... καὶ τυφλοῖς πολλοῖς ἐχαρίσατο βλέπειν (in reference to τυφλοὶ ἀναβλέπουσιν which comes first in 7,22). In the light of this clause in 7,21 the objection that "curing blindness is not prominent among Luke's miracle stories"[106] has little force. Physical healing is so "prominent" in Lk's summaries (7,21 ἐθεράπευσεν πολλοὺς ἀπὸ νόσων καὶ μαστίγων καὶ πνευμάτων πονηρῶν, cf. 6,18 ... ἰαθῆναι ἀπὸ τῶν νόσων αὐτῶν· καὶ οἱ ἐνοχλούμενοι ἀπὸ πνευμάτων ἀκαθάρτων ἐθεραπεύοντο) that it can be assumed to explain Luke's deletion of ἰάσασθαι τοὺς συντετριμμένους τῇ καρδίᾳ / τὴν καρδίαν. In Luke–Acts, except Ac 28,27 (= Isa 6,10 ἰάσομαι αὐτούς), the verb ἰᾶσθαι is never used metaphorically, as it clearly is in Isa 61,1: "to 'heal' the broken-hearted"[107].

Lk 4,18d ἀποστεῖλαι τεθραυσμένους ἐν ἀφέσει (from Isa 58,6) is usually translated in English: "to let the oppressed go free" (NRSV).

226 (226: "The citation form in Lk. 4.18-19 belongs fundamentally to Luke's source, not to his own redactional activity"). This source of Luke is not Q (219: ctr. Tuckett). Cf. *The Spirit and the Power of Jesus' Miracles in the Lucan Conception*, in *NT* 33 (1991) 124-152, esp. 150-152; *The Spirit of Prophecy and the Power of Authoritative Preaching in Luke–Acts: A Question of Origins*, in *NTS* 38 (1992) 66-88.

105. *Q 6,20b-21; 7,22 and Isaiah 61*, in C.M. TUCKETT (ed.), *The Scriptures in the Gospels* (BETL, 131), Leuven, 1997, 27-64, esp. 63. On Q 6,20b, see *ibid.*, 44. On Lk 4,18-19 and 7,18-23, see M.D. HOOKER, *'Beginning with Moses and from all the Prophets'*, in M.C. DE BOER (ed.), *From Jesus to John*. FS M. de Jonge (JSNT SS, 84), Sheffield, 1993, 216-230, esp. 223.

106. TUCKETT, *Q*, 232 (= 1982, 348). Tuckett tries to minimize the evidence of Lk 7,21 (LkR): "the clause in 7:21 prepares for 7:22 which is more likely to be an allusion to Isa 35:5 (and in any case this is already in Q, not LkR)" (*ibid.*, n. 81). One can agree about the influence of Isa 35,5 on the Q-saying (cf. my *Q 6,20b-21; 7,22 and Isaiah 61*, 46-49), but the point is that Lk 7,21 testifies for Luke's redactional understanding of τυφλοὶ ἀναβλέπουσιν in Q.

107. Cf. J. DUPONT, *Les Béatitudes*, vol. II, Paris, 1969, 132 n. 1: "Luc entend le verbe 'guérir' au sens propre; cela le porte à omettre l'expression 'guérir les cœurs brisés' en *Lc* 4,18". See also D.R. CATCHPOLE, *The Anointed One in Nazareth*, in M.C. DE BOER (ed.), *From Jesus to John* (n. 105), 231-251, here 237: "the absence of the one element of the Isa. 58.6 text [read: 61.1] which has no counterpart in Isa. 61.1 [read 58.6], that is, τὴν καρδίαν ... serves to highlight the achievement of *physical* healing within the programme"; see 236: "The omission... is only partial"; συντρίβειν, cf. θραύειν in v. 18d; ἰάσασθαι, cf. the ἰατρός proverb in v. 23. — See also Catchpole's reply to Tuckett ("There is no good reason why Luke should omit the healing clause from Isaiah 61"): "the heavy emphasis on healings within vv. 18-19... makes the address ἰατρέ [v. 23a] appropriate and the omission of the healing clause from Isaiah 61 a mark of sophistication rather than a cause of surprise" (252, and n. 1).

'Απόστελλε (LXX) is changed to the syntax of Isa 61,1, the infinitive ἀποστεῖλαι, possibly in assimilation to κηρύξαι in v. 18c. Ἄφεσις may have been the link word: "release" for the prisoners and "release" for the oppressed. In M. Turner's opinion Isa 58,6 was possibly incorporated "to clarify that he [Jesus] does not merely announce messianic liberty (as the use of Isa. 61.1-2 alone might suggest) but also *effects* it. Luke ... has an interest in such a theme"[108].

One could argue that, in contrast to "the important Lukan theme" ἄφεσις ἁμαρτιῶν (Lk 1,77; 3,3 [= Mk]; 24,47; and five occurrences in Acts), the word ἄφεσις alone is "highly unusual in Luke"[109]. But the word is there, in the Isaiah text, following on εὐαγγελίσασθαι πτωχοῖς (which is accepted as congenial to Luke) and in parallel to τυφλοῖς ἀνάβλεψιν (the healing of the blind, stressed by Luke in 7,21). Such a context is not at all un-Lukan, and in this context the literal meaning of ἄφεσις (used with αἰχμαλώτοις), though unique in Luke–Acts, is hardly refutable. – It is amazing how word statistics are sometimes misinterpreted: the meaning "forgiveness of sins" of the stereotyped ἄφεσις ἁμαρτιῶν (eight times in Luke–Acts) is applied again and again in comments on the two instances of ἄφεσις (4,18c and d)[110].

---

108. *Power from on High*, 224 (= *Spirit*, 1991, 148). See also G.R. BEASLEY-MURRAY, in *Mélanges Bibliques*. FS B. Rigaux, Gembloux, 1970, 473. Cf. R. ALBERTZ, *Die "Antrittspredigt" Jesu im Lukasevangelium auf ihrem alttestamentlichen Hintergrund*, in *ZNW* 74 (1983) 182-206, esp. 198, on Luke's insertion of Isa 58,6: "Damit konkretisiert er die schwebende, übertragene Sprache von Jes 61,1f. in soziale Richtung"; cf. 197: "mit den τεθραυσμένοι (sind) eindeutig die wirtschaftlich Ruinierten gemeint".

On the catchword ἄφεσις: "The link appears to have been made via the Greek word ἄφεσις in both Isaianic texts and hence seems to depend on the LXX version of the two texts concerned (the MT has םישפה in Isa 58:6 and רורד in Isa 61:1)" (TUCKETT, *Q*, 232). Cf. B.J. KOET, *Five Studies* (n. 67), 29-30 (= 1986, 372-373), on the later rabbinic midrashic technique *gezerah shawah*. See now C.A. KIMBALL, *Jesus' Exposition of the Old Testament in Luke's Gospel* (JSNT SS, 94), Sheffield, 1994, 97-119 ("The Nazareth Sermon"): "In Jesus' day the *gezerah shawah* technique ... was frequently used" (107); "the unique text form caused by the insertion ... is evidence for the authenticity of the citation on the lips of Jesus" (109), though "the joining of these two texts was only possible on the basis of a Greek text" (107)!

109. TUCKETT, *Q*, 233, 234 n. 86 (= 1982, 348). Cf. TURNER, *Power from on High*, 223. On the use of Isa 61,1 (ἄφεσις) in Ac 10,43 (ἄφεσις ἁμαρτιῶν), suggested by Dupont, see my reply in *Ac 10,34-43* (below, n. 120), 113 (= 231): "La suggestion... n'a pas été faite à propos des autres discours (ἄφεσις ἁμαρτιῶν: Ac 2,38; 5,31; 10,43; 13,38; 26,18; cf. Lc 24,47)".

110. See, e.g., M. KORN, *Geschichte* (n. 37), esp. 75-78 (with reference to M. Rese, 1969; contrast U. Busse, 1978). See also B.J. KOET, *Five Studies* (n. 67), 24-55 ("Luke 4,16-30"), esp. 34 (with reference to J.J.A. Kahmann, 1975); and more recently, R. O'TOOLE, *Does Luke also Portray Jesus as the Christ in Luke 4,16-30?*, in *Bib* 76 (1995) 498-522, esp. 511-512 (cf. 511, on the metaphorical use of "open the eyes"); R.I. DENOVA, *The Things Accomplished Among Us: Prophetic Tradition in the Structural Pattern of Luke–Acts* (JSNT SS, 141), Sheffield, 1997, 133-138: ἄφεσις = forgiveness of sins in

The insertion of 4,18d from Isa 58,6d is part of the evidence mounted against assigning the Isaiah quotation in Lk 4,18-19 to Luke: "There is no other example of a similarly mixed citation in Luke–Acts"[111]. One may have some doubt about the relevance of this observation with regard to the Scripture text chosen by Luke for the opening of Jesus' public ministry. What is meant by "mixed" or "composite" citation, said to be unique in Luke–Acts, is not entirely clear. In Ac 1,20 there is a quotation from "the book of the Psalms" combining simply with καί Ps 68,26 and 108,8b LXX[112]. Another example, Ac 3,22-23 introduced with "Moses said": "ein Zitat von Dtn 18,15, das ergänzt ist durch ein Mischzitat aus Dtn 18,19 und Lev 23,29"[113]. Thus it is apparently not without certain analogies in Acts that the combination of Isa 61,1-2a and 58,6d in Lk 4,18-19 is introduced as one quotation taken from "the book of Isaiah" (v. 17).

There is still the change of καλέσαι (LXX) to κηρύξαι in Lk 4,19, which can be seen as an attempt "Jesu Verkündigung in das Jesajazitat einzutragen"[114].

The discussion of the divergences from the Septuagint should not obnubilate the basic conformity of Lk 4,18-19 to the Isaian text[115]. To a

4,18g (the oppressed) but not in 4,18e (the captives) (136-137); "sight to the blind": both metaphorical and literal (135). For emphasis on literalness and physicality of Jesus' announcements in Lk 4,18-19, see P.F. ESLER, *Community* (n. 9), 179-183.

111. TUCKETT, *Q*, 232 (= 1982, 347). Tuckett calls it "this *mixed* citation" (232 n. 79) or "the specific *composite* citation of Isa 61 + 58" (431). See also TURNER, *Power from on High*, 216: "Luke–Acts never elsewhere *sandwiches* one Old Testament quotation within another in this way" (cf. *Spirit*, 146; italics F.N.); C.A. KIMBALL, *Jesus' Exposition* (n. 108), 109: "The insertion of one text between another is not paralleled elsewhere in the Gospels or Acts"; D.R. CATCHPOLE, *Anointed One* (n. 107), 239: "the interpenetration of OT texts ... is not exactly typical of the writer of the Gospel (though, one might add, less untypical of the writer of Acts)".

112. The two quotations are introduced with a single formula (v. 20a) and are linked together with καί· (cf. text editions). However, this καί can be part of the second quotation text itself (LXX: καὶ τὴν...): see G.D. KILPATRICK, *Some Quotations in Acts*, in J. KREMER (ed.), *Les Actes des Apôtres*, 1979, 81-97, esp. 87; HAENCHEN, *Apg*, 124 n. 6 (= 163 n. 6). In G.J. Steyn's opinion both can be combined: καί part of the quoted text and connecting word. Cf. *Septuagint Quotations* (n. 76), 58. In any case, the two quoted texts "are presented as one single explicit quotation" (62).

113. SCHNEIDER, *Apg*, I, 328. See KILPATRICK, *Some Quotations*, 86: "Like Acts 15,16-18, Acts 3,22f is a composite quotation". Cf. FITZMYER, *The Use of the Old Testament in Luke–Acts*, in *SBL 1992 Seminar Papers*, 524-238: "In three instances (Luke 4:18-19; 19:46 [par. Mk]; Acts 3:22-23) he [Luke] combines two quotations" (526 n. 5).

114. M. KORN, *Geschichte* (n. 37), 74: Lk 4,19 "als Umschreibung der Verkündigung der Gegenwart des Reiches Gottes".

115. The "mixed" form of the citation does not allow to treat Lk 4,18-19 as "a free composition" which because of the centrality of ἄφεσις (supposed to be "*un*characteristic for Luke") cannot be due to LkR. Cf. TUCKETT, *Q*, 235 n. 86. See n. 87 (and 229 n. 68): "It is of course pre-Lukan in the sense of being words from Isaiah"!

certain degree it can be called conflation or composite citation, but *text* citation it certainly is, and, in my view, not so close to conflational compositions like 4Q521 as some now seem to suggest[116].

Ac 10,38

Lk 4,18 πνεῦμα κυρίου ἐπ᾽ ἐμὲ οὗ εἴνεκεν ἔχρισέν με. The Spirit of the Lord is upon Jesus by reason of his anointing. Fitzmyer's comment is concise: "In the baptism (3:22; cf. Acts 10:38)". In Lk 4 it is not said that the 'anointing' occurred at his baptism, and it is hard to maintain that, in the account of Jesus' baptism and the descent of the Spirit upon him (Lk 3,22), Luke changed Mk's εἰς αὐτόν to ἐπ᾽ αὐτόν precisely in view of ἐπ᾽ ἐμέ in 4,18 (Isa 61,1)[117]. In the prayer of the Christians at Ac 4,27-30, συνήχθησαν ... ἐπὶ τὸν ἅγιον παῖδά σου Ἰησοῦν ὃν ἔχρισας (4,27) is a word-for-word paraphrase of Ps 2,2 συνήχθησαν ... κατὰ τοῦ κυρίου καὶ κατὰ τοῦ χριστοῦ αὐτοῦ (quoted in v. 26)[118]. Nothing in this etymology of the χριστός title refers to the baptism of Jesus[119].

---

116. K.-W. NIEBUHR, *Die Werke des eschatologischen Freudenboten (4Q521) und die Jesusüberlieferung*, in C.M. TUCKETT (ed.), *The Scriptures in the Gospels* (n. 105), 637-646. He refers to "die freie, mosaikartige Rezeption biblischer Wendungen in frühjüdischen Texten" (644). It is noteworthy that 4Q521 connects Isa 61,1 with the Messiah. On the similarities with Q 7,22 (not a citation!), cf. above, n. 105.

117. Ctr. J. NOLLAND, *Lk*, 161: "The change ... anticipates Luke 4:18" (R.F. Collins, *TBT* 84 [1976] 824)"; KORN, *Geschichte* (n. 37), 65 n. 47 ("Daß Lukas die Beziehung des Taufberichts zu Lk 4,18a bewußt war,..."). J.M. Robinson's view on ἐπ᾽ αὐτόν shows a noteworthy 'trajectory' from LkR to Q. See his *The Sayings Gospel Q*, in *The Four Gospels 1992* (n. 5), 361-388, here 383, on the minor agreements diff. Mk 1,10: "notoriously inconclusive", with reference to J. Kloppenborg in n. 30: the use of ἐπί is preferred by Luke "in dependence on Isa 61,1-2 (quoted Lk 4,18)"; now in *The Matthean Trajectory from Q to Mark*, in A.Y. COLLINS (ed.), *Ancient and Modern Perspectives on the Bible and Culture*. FS H.D. Betz, Atlanta, GA, 1999, 122-154, here 131-132: Jesus' baptism is ascribed to Q, "where the minor agreements of Q using the Isa 61:1 LXX preposition ἐπ᾽ rather than Mark's εἰς for 'upon' is a tell-tale sign" (131 n. 13); contrast Lk 4,18 (not Q): "The ἔχρισέν με of Isa 61:1 is a christological point of departure not picked up explicitly either by Q or by Matthew" (132). But see Kloppenborg's argument in *The Formation of Q*, 1987, 85 n. 157: "assimilation to Isa 61:1-2 (= Luke 4:18) *and* [!] general Lucan usage (Acts 1:8; 2:17,18; 10:44,45; 11:15; 19:16)". Cf. my *The Minor Agreements and Q*, in R. PIPER (ed.), *The Gospel Behind the Gospels* (NTSup, 75), Leiden, 1995, 49-72, here 65.

On the relation between Lk 4,18-19 and Ac 10,38, see U. BUSSE, *Wunder* (below, n. 128), 369: "Lk 4,18f steht... zu Apg 10,38 wie die erste Verkündigung zur abschließenden Zusammenfassung, in der die Realisierung des angekündigten Auftrages bestätigt wird".

118. On ἐπί + acc. in hostile sense (for κατά + gen.), cf. J.A. WEATHERLY, *Jewish Responsibility for the Death of Jesus in Luke–Acts* (JSNT SS, 106), Sheffield, 1994, 92 (ctr. J.T. Sanders).

119. Ctr. JERVELL, *Apg*, 187: "ὃν ἔχρισας, d.h. er wurde bei der Taufe in das messianische Amt eingesetzt". Cf. WENDT, *Apg*, 116 ("Wahrscheinlich"); more hesitant: LAKE-CADBURY, *Acts*, 47; SCHILLE, *Apg*, 141.

An explicit reference to anointing and baptism is provided in Ac 10,38. Verse 38a is to be read, I think, in parallel with v. 37b:

37a   ὑμεῖς οἴδατε τὸ γενόμενον ῥῆμα καθ' ὅλης τῆς Ἰουδαίας,
37bᵃ   ἀρξάμενος ἀπὸ τῆς Γαλιλαίας
37bᵝ   μετὰ τὸ βάπτισμα ὃ ἐκήρυξεν Ἰωάννης,
38aᵃ   Ἰησοῦν τὸν ἀπὸ Ναζαρέθ,
38aᵝ   ὡς ἔχρισεν αὐτὸν ὁ θεὸς πνεύματι ἁγίῳ καὶ δυνάμει.

The beginning of Jesus' public ministry throughout Judea (cf. Lk 23,5) is described as starting from Galilee (par. Nazareth) after the baptism (par. anointing)[120]. Luke never uses the identification Ἰησοῦς ὁ ἀπὸ Ναζαρέθ for "Jesus of Nazareth"[121], and here in parallel to ἀπὸ τῆς Γαλιλαίας the preposition ἀπό may indicate "the point from where" Jesus' ministry began.

The first principle C.M. Tuckett applies in his approach to Lk 4,18-19 is his statement that "in Luke–Acts the Spirit is never the agent by which miracles occur"[122]. This leads to a rather strange comment on Ac 10,38. He admits that it is "probably referring explicitly to Luke 4:18-19", but:

> Acts 10:38 appears to avoid attributing this aspect of Jesus' work to the Spirit. Luke here says that Jesus was anointed with the Spirit 'and power'

120. On symmetric composition, parallel ἀπό (= from), and temporal ὡς (= when, after), see É. SAMAIN, *La notion de* APXH *dans l'œuvre lucanienne*, in F. NEIRYNCK (ed.), *L'Évangile de Luc*, 1973 (n. 1), 299-328; = ²1989, 209-238, esp. 218-220; with my additional note (327) on É. Samain (diss. 1965), J. Dupont, and G. Schneider. Cf. DUPONT, *Jésus*, 150-155 (= 46-51): "Is. 61,1-2 dans le discours de Césarée (Act. 10,34-43)". — On the Lukan composition of Ac 10,34-43, see my *Ac 10,36-43 et l'évangile*, in *ETL* 60 (1984) 109-117 (= *Evangelica II*, 227-235), and the additional note on A. Weiser and G. Schneider in *ETL* 62 (1986) 194-196 (= *Evangelica II*, 235-236). Cf. A. WEISER, *Tradition und lukanische Komposition in Apg 10,36-43*, in À *cause de l'évangile*. FS J. Dupont (LD, 123), Paris, 1985, 757-767; G. SCHNEIDER, *Die Petrusrede vor Kornelius. Das Verhältnis von Tradition und Komposition in Apg 10,34-43*, in ID., *Lukas, Theologe der Heilsgeschichte. Aufsätze zum lukanischen Doppelwerk* (BBB, 59), Königstein-Bonn, 1985, 253-279.

121. Ἰησοῦς ὁ Ναζαρηνός (Lk 4,34; 24,19); Ἰησοῦς ὁ Ναζωραῖος (Lk 18,37; Ac 2,22; 3,6; 4,10; 6,14; 22,8; 16,9). On Mt 21,11; Jn 1,45, cf. J.M. ROBINSON, in *The Four Gospels 1992* (n. 117), 377.

122. *Q*, 230 (= 1982, 347). Cf. 231: "miracles do not generally seem to be the work of the Spirit" (with reference to E. SCHWEIZER, art. πνεῦμα, in *TWNT* 6, 405; *TDNT* 6, 407). Tuckett interprets πνεῦμα in Luke–Acts in the line of E. Schweizer (the Spirit of prophecy), against those who, on the basis of "occurrences where πνεῦμα and δύναμις occur together, or possibly interchangeably", argue "that πνεῦμα for Luke can be the agency by which miracles occur" (230 n. 73; cf. 231 n. 74: Conzelmann, Busse, Neirynck, Turner). J. Jervell's recent commentary can be added to the list: "Er hat Jesus mit heiligem Geist und Kraft gesalbt. Das sind kaum zwei verschiedene Grössen, denn für Lukas ist der Geist vor allem mirakulöse Wunderkraft. Nicht nur Kraft, denn der Geist ist viel mehr...".

(δύναμις being often used by Luke to describe the agency by which miracles occur), and that Jesus heals 'because God was with him'.[123]

The addition (by Luke?) of the clause ὅτι ὁ θεὸς ἦν μετ᾽ αὐτοῦ is indicated without further comment (cf. Ac 7,9 Joseph). With regard to καὶ δυνάμει, it is noted that "Luke's tendency is always to use δύναμις language when referring to miracles" (Lk 4,36; 5,17; 6,19; 9,1; Ac 6,8; 10,38)[124]. In a separate list he cites the instances where δύναμις and πνεῦμα appear together or in parallel (Lk 1,35; 4,14; Ac 1,8; cf. too Lk 1,17; 24,49). Tuckett wishes not to argue for a rigid distinction: "δύναμις for Luke is clearly broader than that, as texts like Luke 4:14 show"[125]. However, his illustration is one-directional: "the immediate context in v. 15 speaks exclusively of Jesus' 'teaching' only"[126]. The context of Lk 4,14a deserves closer examination. In the broader context of Lk 3–4, the Lukan phrases in 4,1a πλήρης πνεύματος ἁγίου and 4,14a ἐν τῇ δυνάμει τοῦ πνεύματος (before and after the temptation ὑπὸ τοῦ διαβόλου) appear as stepping-stones from 3,22 to 4,18. The most immediate context of 4,14a, v. 14b καὶ φήμη ἐξῆλθεν καθ᾽ ὅλης τῆς περιχώρου περὶ αὐτοῦ, corresponds to 4,37 καὶ ἐξεπορεύετο ἦχος περὶ αὐτοῦ εἰς πάντα τόπον τῆς περιχώρου, both parallel to Mk 1,28. Like Lk 4,37 follows on the reaction to the exorcism in v. 36: ἐν ἐξουσίᾳ καὶ δυνάμει ('power' LkR), so Lk 4,14b follows on v. 14a, ἐν τῇ δυνάμει τοῦ πνεύματος. That Lk 4,15 mentions Jesus' teaching in their synagogues (generalizing Mk 1,21-22, cf. v. 39) is not a valid reason for making it the exclusive theme in 4,14. In v. 14a "the thought of power to do mighty works may be present" (Marshall: cf. 4,23). If in Lukan usage there is no disjunction between 'power' and 'Spirit', we can read πνεύματι ἁγίῳ and καὶ δυνάμει in Ac 10,38 without assigning them to separate levels, pre-Lukan tradition and Lukan redaction[127].

Tuckett's discussion with U. Busse on Ac 10,38 and Lk (1982, reprinted in 1996)[128] concentrates upon "healing all those oppressed by

123. Q, 234 (= 1982, 349).
124. Q, 231 n. 77 (and 230). I note here a corrigendum on Ac 6,8.10 ("Neirynck runs the two together..."). In fact my observation did concern the two "full of" phrases in Ac 6,5 πλήρης πίστεως καὶ πνεύματος ἁγίου, 8 πλήρης χάριτος καὶ δυνάμεως.
125. Q, 231 v. 77.
126. Ibid., n. 75.
127. This is, I think, what was suggested by Tuckett, although his description of "the earlier passage" (or "original passage") and "Luke's interpretation" (or "slight modification") could be understood as a distinction between 'Q' 4,18-19 (source) and Ac 10,38 (Luke).
128. Q, 230 n. 73; 235-236 n. 90 (= 1982, 347 n. 23; 349-350 n. 36). Cf. U. BUSSE, Die Wunder des Propheten Jesus. Die Rezeption, Komposition und Interpretation der Wundertradition im Evangelium des Lukas (FzB, 24), Stuttgart, 1977, 59-60; ID., Nazareth-Manifest (n. 39).

the devil". One can agree with Tuckett that in Lk not all healings are regarded as exorcisms and that the neutral words θεραπεύειν and ἰᾶσθαι are used for both, but Busse's reading of Ac 10,38 in the light of Lk 4 cannot be dismissed by stating that "there are no extra exorcism stories in the gospel"[129]. Lk 4,31-43 is a Markan sequence, but the "arrangement" is Lukan: the exorcism in 4,33-37 is distinguished from 4,31-32, in 4,38-39 Jesus rebukes the fever as one rebukes a demon, and in 4,40-41 demon possessions are treated as a higher or stronger form of illness.

Since it is undisputed that in Lk the use of ἰᾶσθαι in combination with δύναμις is redactional (5,17 καὶ δύναμις κυρίου ἦν εἰς τὸ ἰᾶσθαι αὐτόν, cf. 6,19; 8,46.47; 9,1.2), it is less certain that ἰώμενος in Ac 10,38 should be seen as part of the allusion to Isa 61,1 (ἰάσασθαι... omitted in Lk 4,18)[130]. As Tuckett wrote, "It may be that the 'oppressed' of Isa 58:6 in Luke 4:18 is seen by Luke as referring to oppression by Satan"[131].

Turning back to the text of Lk 4,18-19, the parallel in Ac 10,38a indicates that the punctuation of N-A, et al. (ἔχρισέν με εὐαγγελίσασθαι πτωχοῖς,) should be corrected by placing a stop after ἔχρισέν με (and not after πτωχοῖς)[132].

III. Lk 4,16-30 and the End of Acts

J. Dupont's essay *La conclusion des Actes* (which was delivered here at the Colloquium in 1977) is completed with a corollary on Lk 4,16-30:

> Pour montrer que la double rencontre de Paul avec les Juifs de Rome constitue bien la conclusion de l'ensemble de l'ouvrage de Luc, il semble que

129. *Q*, 235 (= 349).

130. The influence of Ps 106,20 LXX καὶ ἰάσατο αὐτούς (G.N. Stanton, P. Stuhlmacher, *et al.*) is even more doubtful: see my *Ac 10,36-43*, 115 (= 233); SCHNEIDER, *Petrusrede*, 275 n. 137; WEISER, *Tradition*, 762 n. 29; 764 n. 38: "Die relativ häufige Verwendung von *iasthai* im Werk des Lukas empfiehlt nicht die Annahme, daß Apg 10,38 von Ps 106,20 LXX beeinflußt ist". The case of Isa 61,1 is different because of the allusion to ἔχρισέν με in v. 38a. But given the indeed relatively frequent use of the verb in Luke–Acts, the influence of ἰάσασθαι remains uncertain because of its lacking in Lk 4,18 and the change of the complement of the verb from "the brokenhearted" to "all the oppressed by the devil". See my *Ac 10,36-43*, 115 (= 233): "si on continue de donner à ἄφεσις en Lc 4,18 son sens propre de délivrance des captifs et des opprimés (la bonne nouvelle aux pauvres), on peut y rattacher l'idée de 'guérir ceux qui sont au pouvoir du diable' (Ac 10,38)".

131. *Q*, 233 (= 349). On his objections, see above.

132. NOORDA, *Historia* (n. 4), 226; DUPONT, *Jésus*, 133 (= 27): "Il me paraît certain, quant à moi, que seule la seconde (ponctuation) correspond à la manière dont Luc a lu le texte"; cf. Lc 4,43; Ac 10,38. See Greeven's text, the commentaries by Marshall, Fitzmyer, Nolland, Johnson, Green and the translations REB (English), EÜ (German), Osty (French), NWV (Dutch).

nous pouvons concentrer notre attention sur un texte principal: celui par lequel Luc a voulu introduire toute l'histoire du ministère de Jésus... En esquissant le programme du ministère public de Jésus, cette page fait en même temps pressentir toute la suite du récit jusqu'à la conclusion que lui donne l'épisode de Rome.[133]

I may cite here one of R. Maddox's 1982 statements on the unity of Luke–Acts:

> More significant is the fact that the mission of Jesus begins with a scene in which the rejection of the message of salvation by the Jews and its acceptance by the Gentiles is anticipated, and the mission of Paul ends with a scene in which this is declared to be an established fact (Luke 4:16-30; Acts 28:17-28). This looks like a deliberate, structural element.[134]

Other authors like D.R. Miesner[135], A. Weiser[136], and J.T. Sanders[137] have provided more detailed descriptions of the parallels between Lk 4,16-30 and Ac 28,17-31. I quote here a passage taken from Sanders:

> This final scene of Paul's ministry is therefore a reprise of the first scene of Jesus. Do we have a synagogue sermon there? So we have here, with the adjustment for verisimilitude that Paul is a prisoner. Is the Book of Isaiah quoted there? So it is here. Is there at first a favorable and then a hostile response there? Similarly here the one response is mixed, part favorable and part unfavorable. And does Jesus there make it clear to his audience that they were never the intended recipients of God's salvation, which is a salvation for the Gentiles? So here as well. The issue was never in doubt.[138]

Ac 28,17-31

The section "Paul at Rome" in Ac 28,17-31 comprises two meetings with the leaders of the Jews in Rome (vv. 17-22 and 23-28) and a concluding summary (vv. 30-31). The double encounter shows striking similarities with Ac 13,14-43.44-52[139]. The first meeting upon invitation by

---

133. "La prédication de Jésus dans la synagogue de Nazareth", in *Conclusion*, 396-402 (= 502-508), here 396 (= 502).

134. R. MADDOX, *The Purpose of Luke–Acts* (FRLANT, 126), Göttingen, 1982, 2-6: "The Unity of Luke–Acts", here 5.

135. D.R. MIESNER, *The Circumferential Speeches of Luke–Acts: Patterns and Purpose*, in *SBL 1978 Seminar Papers*, 223-237, esp. 234 (table of twelve "Parallels at the Circumference", Lk 4,14-30 and Ac 28,17-31).

136. A. WEISER, *Apg* II, 1985, 678 ("enge Beziehungen zur *Nazaret-Perikope* Lk 4,16-30").

137. J.T. SANDERS, *The Jewish People in Luke–Acts*, in *SBL 1986 Seminar Papers*, 110-129, esp. 127 (with reference to Dupont's remark on "the three landmarks of the same history": see above, n. 75).

138. *Ibid.* This last issue, as stated by Sanders ("never ... intended"), is not undisputed. On the mixed response, cf. below, n. 140.

139. Cf. WEISER, 678: "hat inhaltlich und formal große Ähnlichkeiten mit der *Doppelszene am Anfang der ersten Missionsreise*" (cf. 679 on 28,17-31: "erst Lukas selbst

Paul is followed by a second meeting on a fixed day (28,23a; cf. 13,42: on the following sabbath); the Jews are present in larger numbers (πλείονες, cf. 13,44); Paul testifies to the kingdom of God and tries to convince them about Jesus; the reactions of the Jews are mixed: καὶ οἱ μὲν ἐπείθοντο τοῖς λεγομένοις, οἱ δὲ ἠπίστουν (28,24; cf. 13,43); but Paul's last speech is a quotation of Isa 6,9-10 with a concluding word on the salvation of the Gentiles: γνωστὸν οὖν ἔστω ὑμῖν ὅτι τοῖς ἔθνεσιν ἀπεστάλη τοῦτο τὸ σωτήριον τοῦ θεοῦ· αὐτοὶ καὶ ἀκούσονται (28,28; cf. 13,46.48).

> La seconde scène d'Antioche peut être considérée comme un développement de ce que la déclaration de 28,28 condense en quelques mots. L'essentiel est dit en 13,46... Il faut noter d'ailleurs que, pas plus que la déclaration de Rome, celle d'Antioche ne tient compte du fait que la prédication de Paul a convaincu un certain nombre de ses auditeurs juifs.[140]

Paul's speech at the first meeting in Ac 28,17b-20 is a more personal defense in view of his approaching trial: "he delivers an apologetical exposition in which the content of the preceding chapters in Acts is summed up and his innocence is affirmed"[141]. Likewise, within the lit-

---

hat diesen Abschluß geschaffen"). Contrast BARRETT, 1236-1237: "There seems little point however in an artificial repetition of this double scene; it would have been easy to compress the substance of vv. 17-28 into one event, and there is therefore some probability that there is some distinct traditional recollection of what took place". But the point is that Luke did not compress this substance into a one-day meeting. Cf. Ac 28,23: "Paul's (second) interview with the Jewish representatives lasted all day" (BARRETT, 1243). Moreover the content is different (see text).

140. DUPONT, *Conclusion*, 384 (= 488); cf. above, n. 57. See also 386 (= 490), in Corinth: "Le fait que certains parmi les Juifs se soient convertis ne change rien à la manière dont le tournant se prend" (Ac 18,6 ἀπὸ τοῦ νῦν εἰς τὰ ἔθνη πορεύσομαι). Notwithstanding their "part favorable and part unfavorable" reactions, the Jews in Ac 13,45 (οἱ Ἰουδαῖοι); 18,6 (αὐτῶν, cf. v. 5); 28,28 (ὑμῖν) are taken as one whole of unconverted Jews (compare Lk 4,28-29). "Jewish acceptance of Jesus and the early Christians has been either neglected or suppressed" (J.B. TYSON, *The Jewish Public*, 582; cf. n. 72).

This is one of the "inconsistencies" in Acts. But is it a reason to conclude that "das für Lk 4,22-30 gültige Schema in Apg nicht in gleicher Weise wiederkehrt"? Cf. M. MEISER, *Die Reaktion des Volkes auf Jesus. Eine redaktionskritische Untersuchung zu den synoptischen Evangelien* (BZNW, 96), Berlin – New York, 1998, 277 n. 74 (and 285 n. 115); with reference to R.S. ASCOUGH, *Rejection and Repentance: Peter and the People in Luke's Passion Narrative*, in *Bib* 74 (1993) 349-365, here 349. It is another "inconsistency" that, after the statements on turning to the Gentiles in 13,46 and 18,6, Paul returns to speak in Jewish synagogues. Neither is it consistent that Paul and Barnabas after the symbolic gesture in 13,51 return to Pisidian Antioch as if it were already evangelized (14,22-23).

141. H. VAN DE SANDT, *Acts 28,28: No Salvation for the People of Israel? An Answer in the Perspective of the LXX*, in *ETL* 70 (1994) 341-358, here 341. The author's conclusion: "the charge with obduracy of Isa 6,9-10 is extended and sharpened in Acts 28,25c-28 under the influence of Ezek 2,3-5 and 3,4-7" (357). On rephrasing of Ezek 3,6b in Ac 28,28 (*ibid.*), see now also FITZMYER, *Acts*, 796.

erary unit of Lk 4,16-30, one can distinguish two parts (4,16-22 and 23-30)[142], each with a speech of Jesus: first his personal self-presentation in vv. 18-19 and 21 and then the more polemic vv. 23-27, ending with a reference to Elijah and Elisha and to the benefits of their healing ministry outside Israel (vv. 25-27). Cf. Dupont's remark on the two-part division:

> Remarquons simplement le rapprochement qui peut être fait entre l'épisode de Nazareth et celui de Rome en raison de ce qu'ils sont divisés en deux temps l'un et l'autre, en raison aussi de ce que le premier temps doit permettre au personnage principal, Jésus ou Paul, de se présenter lui-même à ses compatriotes.[143]

More structural resemblances can be added. The Isaiah text quoted in Lk 4,18-19 is followed in v. 21 by the one-line commentary: σήμερον πεπλήρωται ἡ γραφὴ αὕτη ἐν τοῖς ὠσὶν ὑμῶν. Some analogy has been seen in Paul's quotation of Isa 6,9-10 in Ac 28,25-27 and the brief explicatory comment in v. 28[144].

Lk 4,30 αὐτὸς δὲ ... ἐπορεύετο concludes the Nazareth pericope (cf. 16a καὶ ἦλθεν εἰς Ναζαρά). It is clearly to be read in connection with v. 29 (διελθὼν διὰ μέσου αὐτῶν) and not a few interpreters refer to Johannine parallels (Jn 7,30.44; 8,59; 10,39)[145]. Some call it "a fitting prelude to the story which is to follow in Acts"[146]. J. Dupont compares

142. On the interpretation of Lk 4,22b, cf. below, 393-394.
143. *Conclusion*, 398 (= 504). See also *Jésus*, 148 (= 44): "Comme la scène de Nazareth, celle de Rome se divise en deux temps, caractérisés par deux attitudes différentes de la part des auditeurs juifs de Paul". Cf. above, n. 140.
144. DUPONT, *ibid.* On the parallel "quotation from Isaiah", see D.R. MIESNER, *Circumferential Speeches* (n. 135), 234. Miesner proposes for both Lk 4,18-19 and Ac 28,25-29 (v. 29 included!) a chiastic structure turning around "to give sight to the blind" and "blindness confirmed" (224, 230). — On Lk 4,18-19, see K.E. BAILEY, *Poet & Peasant*, Grand Rapids, MI, 1976 (= 1985), 68; D.L. TIEDE, *Prophecy and History in Luke–Acts*, Philadelphia, PA, 1980, 35. But see J.S. SIKER, *"First to the Gentiles"* (above, n. 44), 77 n. 13: "By structuring even the Isaiah citation chiastically, Tiede stretches the structure a bit further than it really goes". The same remark applies to J.-N. Aletti's suggestion. For criticism of R. Meynet (1979), cf. NOORDA, *Historia* (n. 4), 226-227. Cf. J.-N. Aletti's *L'art de raconter* (n. 44), 60 n. 28; *Jésus à Nazareth (Lc 4,16-30). Prophétie, Écriture et typologie*, in R. GANTOY (ed.), *À cause de l'Évangile*. FS J. Dupont (LD, 123), Paris, 1985, 431-451, esp. 439 n. 15: "Tous les commentateurs..." (sic). Lk 4,18b is not included: κυρίου κηρύξαι ἄφεσιν τυφλοῖς ἀφέσει κηρύξαι κυρίου. Cf. R.C. Tannehill: τυφλοῖς between the lines which refer to ἄφεσις.
145. See the commentaries on Lk by E. Klostermann, F. Hauck, W. Grundmann, W. Wiefel (Jn 10,39!), E.E. Ellis, *et al.*
146. J.M. Creed; cf. A. Loisy. See G. SCHNEIDER, 111: "Die Verfolgung von seiten der Israeliten behindert nicht nur nicht das Fortschreiten der Botschaft Jesu, es fördert dieses sogar (vgl. Apg 13,46; 18,6; 19,9; 28,24-28). Das ist ein feststehendes Schema zum Ausdruck der lukanischen Auffassung" (see also J.A. Fitzmyer). F. HAUCK: "Das Heil geht seinen Weg weiter (AG 28,28)" (65).

Lk 4,30 with the concluding summary in Ac 28,30-31 and notes "sa parenté profonde avec l'adverbe ἀκωλύτως qui termine les Actes"[147].

Lk 4,25-27

The salvation for the Gentiles is the prevailing theme in Ac 28 (v. 28c αὐτοὶ καὶ ἀκούσονται). Though not undisputed[148], it is widely held that the Gentile mission is foreshadowed in the references to Elijah and Elisha in Lk 4,25-27[149]:

25   ἐπ' ἀληθείας δὲ λέγω ὑμῖν,
      πολλαὶ χῆραι ἦσαν ἐν ταῖς ἡμέραις Ἡλίου ἐν τῷ Ἰσραήλ,
          ὅτε ἐκλείσθη ὁ οὐρανὸς ἐπὶ ἔτη τρία καὶ μῆνας ἕξ,
          ὡς ἐγένετο λιμὸς μέγας ἐπὶ πᾶσαν τὴν γῆν,
26   καὶ πρὸς οὐδεμίαν αὐτῶν ἐπέμφθη Ἡλίας
          εἰ μὴ εἰς Σάρεπτα τῆς Σιδωνίας πρὸς γυναῖκα χήραν.
27   καὶ πολλοὶ λεπροὶ ἦσαν ἐν τῷ Ἰσραὴλ ἐπὶ Ἐλισαίου τοῦ προφήτου,
          καὶ οὐδεὶς αὐτῶν ἐκαθαρίσθη
          εἰ μὴ Νααμὰν ὁ Σύρος.

In D. Catchpole's opinion, however, "the function of vv. 25-27 is more limited than some commentators suppose... Not even a sidelong glance is cast at any mission among Gentiles"[150]; and: "The principle is

147. *Conclusion*, 397 (= 503). See also M. KORN, *Geschichte* (n. 37), 84.

148. C.J. SCHRECK, *The Nazareth Pericope* (n. 4), 445-449: "vigorously challenged by B. Koet (1986), R.L. Brawley (1987), R.J. Miller (1988), and W. Wiefel (1988), respectively" (445). See now also D.R. CATCHPOLE, *Anointed One*, 1993 (n. 107), 244-250; J.A. WEATHERLY, *Jewish Responsibility* (n. 118), 127-128.

149. See Schreck's list, from 1973 (S.G. Wilson) to 1989 (G.N. Stanton), supplemented in his dissertation (402-404, and passim). See now also M. ÖHLER, *Elia im Neuen Testament. Untersuchungen zur Bedeutung des alttestamentlichen Propheten im frühen Christentum* (BZNW, 88), Berlin – New York, 1997, 175-184 ("Jesus in Nazareth: Lk 4,25-27"), here 182 n. 369 ("das Ziel des Lk (ist) hier die Heidenmission": some 30 scholars). His list of the opposite position ("... keinen Hinweis auf Mission") includes Brawley and Catchpole (but not Koet) and, more contestably, Tuckett and Nolland. Cf. Nolland's distinction between Lk 4,25-27 "in the immediate context" and "the wider Lukan context" in which "the blessed Gentiles adumbrate the universalism which is to be the basis of the Gentile mission (see already 2:32; 3:6)" (*Luke* I, 201 and 203); ID., *Salvation-History and Eschatology*, in I.H. MARSHALL – D. PETERSON (eds.), *Witness to the Gospel. The Theology of Acts*, Grand Rapids, MI – Cambridge, U.K., 1998, 63-81, here 77 ("in a later reading and in the context of the whole story of Luke–Acts..."). Compare Tuckett's distinction between Lk 4,25-27 in Q (1982, 352-353) and the Lukan redaction: cf. *Luke* (above, n. 7), 52 (and 54); *Q*, 277; and now his *Christology* (in this volume, 152 n. 70): "I remain convinced that Lk 4,25-27 does function within the Lukan narrative, at least for Luke, to prefigure the Gentile mission" (*contra* B.J. Koet and D.R. Catchpole). See also above, 377, n. 89 (A. Lindemann).

150. *Anointed One* (n. 107), 245, 249 (ctr. L.C. Crockett and P.F. Esler: neither Jew/Gentile table-fellowship nor the inclusion of God-fearers).
Cf. L.C. CROCKETT, *Luke 4,25-27 and Jewish-Gentile Relations in Luke–Acts*, in *JBL* 88 (1969) 177-183. Starting from v. 25bc (without counterpart in v. 27) he compares the

not that of 'Gentiles as well as Jews', which is the missionary programme of Acts, but 'Gentiles instead of Jews' in a very limited and
well defined context"[151]. Though not mentioned in Catchpole's essay
B.J. Koet and R.L. Brawley are not far away. The same volume includes
an article by M.D. Hooker on Luke's use of Old Testament quotations
and allusions. The Gospel of Luke, she writes, "contains very little
about salvation for the Gentiles", but "there are hints of that theme":
"The references to Elijah and Elisha... point forward to the mission to
the Gentiles which lies beyond Jesus' rejection, death and resurrection"
and "it is the promise of salvation for the Gentiles which stirs up his
countrymen's hostility"[152].

Like Catchpole, A. Vanhoye refers to C. Schreck's critical survey as
a challenge inciting him to a renewed study of Lk 4,16-30. He proposes
a two-stage reading ("il importe de bien distinguer les deux temps de
lecture"), comparable to that in Nolland's commentary. The possessive
attitude of the people of Nazareth is the theme of the first stage, in which
"l'épisode ne préfigure pas l'évangélisation des païens". But this first
stage seems to be only a theoretical possibility[153]:

clause on the famine in Elijah's time with Agabus' prediction in Ac 11,28 and regards the
Elijah-widow and Elisha-Naaman narratives, joined in Lk 4,25-27, as "models" for the
events narrated in Ac 10–11, "as a prolepsis ... of Jewish-gentile *reconciliation*" (183).
Catchpole's reply: the fact that the language in Lk 4,25c is traditional biblical "does not
help the suggestion that Luke intends to foreshadow Acts 11.28" (245). In addition, it is
not said in Lk 4,25-26 that Elijah is sent to the widow "in order to be fed there" and that
"the result is beneficial to both" (cf. Crockett, 179). Anyway the emphasis is not on
"reconciliation". — For P.F. Esler the reference in Lk 4,25-27 is "undoubtedly meant to
foreshadow a mission among non-Jews in the Christian period" (*Community*, 34; cf.
above, n. 9). It is less apparent that the poor widow and the army commander in Lk 4,25-
27 "pointed to the presence in Luke's community of representatives from either extreme
of the socio-economic spectrum" (183). On (Naaman and) the God-fearers in Luke–Acts
(33-45, esp. 37), see also R.I. DENOVA, *Things Accomplished* (n. 110), 149: "in Lk 4,25-
27, we have the origins of Luke's conception of God-fearers". Cf. above, n. 50.
    151. *Ibid.*, 248. These statements are extracted from an overall analysis of Lk 4,16-30.
Catchpole shows convincingly the exclusively Markan derivation of vv. 16, 22b, and 24;
he stresses the careful construction of the quotation in 4,18-19 ("a literary product", "the
creation of Luke") and the significance of physical healing (above, n. 107); he proposes
Lk 4,14 as "wholly adequate preparation" for v. 23b (243: the Capernaum crux). I discussed elsewhere his position on Mark's use of Q (234) and the Q-origin of Ναζαρά
(235; cf. above, n. 6).
    On the alleged Q-origin of 4,25-27 (Tuckett): "the extent to which this pair of Old
Testament-based arguments reflects the concerns of the Lucan gospel and connects up
with LukeR activity in 4,23, suggests that the evangelist is responsible for an imitation of
the approach of Q" (249). Compare BUSSE, *Nazareth-Manifest* (n. 39), 41-45 ("Lukas als
Verfasser des Doppelspruchs"); 43: "mit Hilfe von Lk 11,31f" (= Q). Lk 4,25-26.27 can
be added to H. Baarlink's list of man-woman pairs in Luke–Acts (in this volume, 489).
    152. M.D. HOOKER, *'Beginning with Moses and from all the Prophets'* (n. 105), here
218, 224 (n. 1: in reply to Koet).
    153. A. VANHOYE, *L'intérêt de Luc pour la prophétie en Lc 1,73; 4,16-30 et 22,60-65,*

... la portée prophétique de cet épisode inaugural s'étend beaucoup plus loin. Il préfigure, en effet, le sort de la prédication chrétienne, telle qu'elle est décrite dans les Actes.[154]

The important element in Vanhoye's approach remains that

l'attitude possessive des Nazaréens, qui *rend ambigu leur accueil favorable*, provoque donc une mise au point de la part de Jésus et ensuite, pour ce motif, un retournement complet de leur part. Ce schéma complexe se retrouve en Ac 13,43-45.50; 17,1-5; 22,17-22.... Comme dans le récit de Lc 4, ... *ils veulent garder leur Messie pour eux*.[155]

'Jealous possessiveness' (Tannehill) is suggested by Vanhoye as the factor of coherence in Lk 4,16-30, explaining the turn from initial acceptance to final rejection: following the reference to Elijah and Elisha's ministry among the Gentiles, "la tendance possessive provoque une amère déception et se mue en agressivité (Lc 4,28-29)"[156].

A more radical option for coherence is to eliminate from v. 22 all connotation of acceptance or approval and to read the entire verse in a hostile sense as witnessing against Jesus (J. Jeremias, H. Baarlink, *et al.*)[157]. In a more nuanced approach F. Ó Fearghail interprets ἐμαρτύρουν in a neutral sense but argues that ἐθαύμαζον indicates "astonishment coupled with criticism and rejection" and takes καὶ ἔλεγον as an explicative phrase: "And they all witnessed to him, and (= *but*) were astonished, and (= *for*) they said: Is not this Joseph's son?"[158]. Many others take (ἐμαρτύρουν and) ἐθαύμαζον in a positive sense while seeing the question in v. 22b as negative, (merely) Joseph's son: "der Einwand der Leute bereitet den *Umschwung* des Urteils vor (28)" (F. Hauck), and

in *The Four Gospels 1992* (n. 5), 1529-1548, esp. 1535-1543 ("Jésus prophète dans sa patrie. Lc 4,16-30"), here 1542 n. 43: "... pour un lecteur qui suit pas à pas le récit de Luc. Mais s'il s'agit d'un lecteur déjà catéchisé (Lc 1,4), ce premier stade n'est guère possible. Le lecteur voit tout de suite plus loin".

154. *Ibid.*, 1541; with reference to J. DUPONT, *Jésus*, 148-150 (= 44-46), on Ac 13,34-52.

155. *Ibid.*, 1541-1542 (italics F.N.). As for Ac 22,17-22, cf. J.-N. ALETTI, *Quand Luc raconte* (n. 82), 149-150: "Jésus à Nazareth (Lk 4,24.26) et Paul à Jérusalem (Ac 22,18.21), les deux discours finissent pratiquement de la même façon, sur l'envoi aux étrangers et sur le refus de croire des concitoyens" (150). Note, however, that the positive reaction (the initial acceptance in Lk 4,22) has no parallel in Ac 22. There is no mention of Ac 22 in A. VANHOYE, *Les Juifs selon les Actes des Apôtres et les Épîtres du Nouveau Testament*, in *Bib* 72 (1991) 70-89, esp. 75: the pattern in Ac 13,14-52 (complete: nos. 1-6); 14,1-7; 17,1-10; 17,10-15; 18,4-11; 19,8-10 (and 28,22.28).

156. *L'intérêt de Luc*, 1540.

157. Cf. SCHRECK, 427-436 ("Internal Coherence"); NOORDA, *Historia*, 155-160. See also above, n. 86 (A. Lindemann).

158. F. Ó FEARGHAIL, *Rejection in Nazareth: Lk 4,22*, in *ZNW* 75 (1984) 60-72; ID., *The Introduction to Luke–Acts: A Study of the Role of Lk 1,1–4,44 in the Composition of Luke's Two-Volume Work* (AnBib, 126), Rome, 1991, 31 n. 128.

less reservedly: "Die Stimmung der Zuhörer schlägt jedoch mit der Rückfrage V. 22 Ende um" (G. Petzke)[159]. Catchpole defends a quite different view on Lk 4,22: "the evangelist wants to underline with all possible firmness the positive reaction which is forthcoming from the audience in Nazareth". The witnessing (ἐμαρτύρουν αὐτῷ) is positive. The astonishment (ἐθαύμαζον ἐπί) is also positive. "And even the question (οὐχὶ υἱός ἐστιν Ἰωσὴφ οὗτος) is positive – just as positive as the questions which erupt in Lk. 4.36; 8.25"[160]. It is a more problematic suggestion that "the tone of the hypothetical request in v. 23 must be adjudged entirely positive"[161].

The discussion of the Nazarenes' initial reaction to Jesus concentrates on v. 22b, the question of Jesus' identity. Mark's "the son of Mary" (6,3 οὐχ οὗτός ἐστιν ... ὁ υἱὸς τῆς Μαρίας) is changed by Luke to "son of Joseph" in accordance with Lk 3,23 (ὢν υἱός, ὡς ἐνομίζετο Ἰωσήφ). I quote here Green's recent commentary:

> Luke has already informed us that people assumed that Jesus was son of Joseph (3:23) ... In this way, ... they respond to Jesus according to their own parochial understanding ... They claim Jesus as 'the son of one of our own' – indeed, as 'one of us'. Reading their response from within the narrative, we can understand that their response is positive, even expectant ...
> We (Luke's readers outside the narrative) know that their understanding of Jesus is erroneous, for we know that Jesus is Son of God, not son of Joseph.[162]
> [In 4,23] Jesus addresses the parochial version of his townspeople directly, countering their assumptions that, as Joseph's son, he will be especially for them a source of God's favor.[163]

The articulation of their unspoken thoughts in the words of Luke's Jesus in 4,23 may indicate the inadequacy of their understanding[164]; it does not imply that their reaction is not presented positively in v. 22[165]. "Der

---

159. G. PETZKE, *Das Sondergut des Evangeliums nach Lukas*, Zürich, 1990, 79. Cf. F. HAUCK, *Lk*, 64 (62: "sich an seiner geringen Herkunft stoßend"). Note Hauck's division of the pericope: a) *Die Bewunderung 16-22ᵃ*, b) *Das Ärgernis 22ᵇ-30*.

160. *Anointed One*, 239.

161. *Ibid.*, 240. Cf. 239: "the eminent reasonableness of the request 'physician, heal yourself'".

162. J.B. GREEN, *Luke*, 1997, 215.

163. *Ibid.*, 217.

164. G. WASSERBERG, *Aus Israels Mitte* (n. 55), 160: "ohne in ihm den Sohn Gottes zu sehen"; in that sense "(ist) der Satz 'Ist das nicht Josefs Sohn?' der Schlüssel zum Verständnis der lk Nazaretperikope" (*ibid.*). Cf. W. WIATER, *Komposition als Mittel der Interpretation im lukanischen Doppelwerk* (diss.), Bonn, 1972, 90-105 (Lk 4,16-30), here 101: "der Angelpunkt" in the composition of Lk 4,16-30.

165. See R.C. TANNEHILL, *Mission*, 1972, 53: "So the question of the Nazarenes indicates their failure to understand who Jesus is, ... but it is not an indication of hostility"; ID., *Narrative Unity*, 1984, 68 (cf. above, n. 74). Ctr. J.A. WEATHERLY, *Jewish Responsibility* (n. 118), 122-124.

Umschlag der Stimmung erfolgt erst in 4,28" (Wellhausen). The shift comes after 4,25-27 (v. 28 ἀκούοντες ταῦτα).

R.L. Brawley stresses the parallellism between 4,25-27 and v. 24: "The function of the allusions to Elijah and Elisha is to demonstrate that a prophet is not acceptable ἐν τῇ πατρίδι αὐτοῦ"[166]. But nothing in the text of Luke(!)[167] alludes to inacceptability of both prophets. The change from ἐν τῇ πατρίδι αὐτοῦ (v. 24) to ἐν τῷ Ἰσραήλ indicates that more is involved than an analogy to the Nazareth-Capernaum antithesis. Catchpole's comment stresses God's freedom of choice (cf. the divine passives ἐπέμφθη and ἐκαθαρίσθη) and a *Sitz im Leben* of Lk 4,25-27 which is "quite unmistakably mission in Israel"[168]. But the emphasis in Lk 4,25-27 is laid on Elijah and Elisha's work among non-Israelites in contrast to the πολλαί/πολλοὶ ἐν τῷ Ἰσραήλ and οὐδεμίαν/οὐδεὶς αὐτῶν:

> The emphasis on Elijah and Elisha's ministry among Gentiles rather than Jews foreshadows the development of the Gentile mission in Acts... This reference (to Gentiles) is not out of place when we view the scene from the larger Lukan perspective.[169]

Defenders of a proleptic allusion to Gentile mission in Lk 4,25-27 may refer to Simeon's announcement of universal salvation: φῶς εἰς ἀποκάλυψιν ἐθνῶν καὶ δόξαν λαοῦ σου Ἰσραήλ (2,32)[170]. Cf. Ac 13,47: τέθεικά σε εἰς φῶς ἐθνῶν (Isa 49,6). Although some commentators hesitate about the meaning of πάντες οἱ λαοί in v. 31[171], ὅτι εἶδον οἱ ὀφθαλμοί μου τὸ σωτήριόν σου (2,30) can be read in the light of 3,6: καὶ ὄψεται πᾶσα σάρξ τὸ σωτήριον τοῦ θεοῦ (Isa 40,5) and of Luke's third use of σωτήριον in Ac 28,28: γνωστὸν οὖν ἔστω ὑμῖν ὅτι τοῖς ἔθνεσιν ἀπεστάλη τοῦτο τὸ σωτήριον τοῦ θεοῦ· αὐτοὶ καὶ ἀκούσονται[172].

Tiensevest 27   Frans NEIRYNCK
B–3010 Leuven

166. *Luke–Acts and the Jews: Conflict, Apology, and Conciliation* (SBL MS, 33), Atlanta, GA, 1987, 11 (and passim: cf. 9, 16).
167. B.J. KOET notes that "Luke enlarges the contrast between the inhabitants of Israel and the Gentiles", but he reads Lk 4,25-27 in the light of 1-2 Kings as the prophet's task to incite people to conversion (*Five Studies*, 50).
168. *Anointed One* (n. 107), 248-249.
169. R.C. TANNEHILL, *Narrative Unity* (n. 74), 71.
170. Cf. B.J. KOET, *Simeons Worte (Lk 2,29-32.34c-35) und Israels Geschick*, in *The Four Gospels 1992* (above, n. 5), 1551-1569; on δόξαν in parallel with ἀποκάλυψιν, see 1551-1552 n. 12. See also G. WASSERBERG, *Aus Israels Mitte* (n. 55), 134-147 («Lk 2,29-35»), here 138 (note 13: read «1552, Anm. 12»).
171. Cf. G.D. KILPATRICK, *Λαοί at Luke ii.31 and Acts iv.25,27* (1965), in his Collected Essays (BETL, 96), Leuven, 1990, 312. See G. WASSERBERG, 139-140.
172. Cf. above, 389.

OFFERED PAPERS

THE LUKAN PROLOGUES
IN THE LIGHT OF ANCIENT NARRATIVE HERMENEUTICS
ΠΑΡΗΚΟΛΟΥΘΗΚΟΤΙ AND THE CREDENTIALED AUTHOR

Central to the quest for the unity of Luke's two books is a greater understanding of the specific content of each preface and the intertext thus created "between" Luke's two volumes[1]. Understandably one approach to the rhetorical import of each proemium and their interface is the pursuit of genre specific details which would lead readers to anticipate certain "matters"[2] to follow within each indicated literary type. What signal(s) does each prologue emit concerning the genre to follow? Some otherwise illuminating studies of the genre(s) of Luke and Acts, however, have gone awry in placing too much emphasis on parallels and formal adherence to Greco-Roman preface conventions. According to this approach, the prologues' perceived (in)compatibility of genre would seem to go a long way in determining the nature of the unity of the Lukan writings. For example, a difference in generic signals between the prefaces of Luke and Acts argues presumably against an organic narrative unity. Failing both generic and narrative unity, the cohesion of Luke and Acts, then, must be found elsewhere, perhaps at the literary functional level of some authorially intended use of the two books[3].

Any alleged discrepancies of genre that may be detected between the two prologues quickly dissipate, however, when we see that the Gospel prologue has very little to do with literary "type" but everything to do with commending the distinctive scope and sequence of Luke's διήγη-σις (Lk 1,1.3) vis-à-vis the "many" other accounts, as well as any oral

---

1. Acts 1,1: "The first volume (τὸν ... πρῶτον λόγον), O Theophilus, I composed concerning all of the matters which Jesus began to do and to teach until the day... he was taken up"; cf. Lk 1,1-4, esp. v. 3.

2. For "matters" (πράγματα) as the subject matter of both volumes, see the way πάντα (Acts 1,1) refers back to the πάντα of Lk 1,3 which, in turn, points to its antecedent as the πράγματα of Lk 1,1.

3. E.g., L.C.A. ALEXANDER, *The Preface to Acts and the Historians*, in B. WITH-ERINGON, (ed.), *History, Literature and Society in the Book of Acts*, Cambridge, University Press, 1996, pp. 73-103. Alexander concludes that the Gospel prologue points to the scientific or technical traditions and treatises, whereas the Acts prologue would seem to be introducing a continuation of the "first volume" as biography. This divergence of genre thus signals a unity which cannot be realistically predicated at either the narrative (plot) level or the generic level. But cf. p. 102: "There is sufficiently varied use of prefaces among Hellenistic Jewish writers to provide a literary context for Luke's".

reports, that are already at hand (Lk 1,1; cf. Theophilus' "instruction" in Lk 1,4). Luke is intent in his opening statements to explain why he should attempt yet another construal and why he especially – as neither eyewitness nor attendant from the beginning of these traditions – should present himself qualified to re-configure these traditions in a new narrative proposal. Rather than locate his writings within the formal boundaries of discrete genres, Luke uses his opening statement to place his work within the ambiance of current poetics debates concerning what constitutes "good" narrative. On the basis of those criteria, he presents his narrative as a worthy and legitimate re-configuration of the "many" other attempts.

The thesis of this paper, then, is that the specific content of the Gospel prologue can best be illuminated by contemporary Hellenistic writers' references to their own superior credentials in producing another version of specific traditions, themes, or periods of history, ostensibly already well represented in the current literature. Often justification for the new compilation includes – whether explicitly or implictly – criticism of others' narrative sequences as well as of their starting points and overall scope. The limited scope of this paper, however, permits comparisons of Greco-Roman poetics texts only with Luke's Gospel prologue and with only one of several key terms in Luke 1,1-4, viz. παρηκολουθηκότι in v. 3.

It is hard to overestimate the importance of this perfect participle which directly qualifies Luke as a composer of διήγησις and situates him vis-à-vis the "many others" and the tradents of oral λόγοι who have instructed the likes of Theophilus. L. Alexander in her ground-breaking *The Preface to Luke's Gospel* refers to this participle as bringing "some sort of epistemological claim about the status of the material presented"[4], while earlier in this century H.J. Cadbury had contended that the proper interpretation of the whole of the Prologue depended on the more precise meaning of παρηκολουθηκότι[5].

A. Possible Meanings of Παρακολουθέω

Παρηκολουθηκότι cannot mean one who has "followed up", "traced", "investigated", "informed himself about", "gone back and

---

4. L.C.A. ALEXANDER, *The Preface to Luke's Gospel. Literary Convention and Social Context in Luke 1.1-4 and Acts 1.1* (SNTS MS, 78), Cambridge, University Press, 1993, pp. 133-134.

5. See H.J. CADBURY, *The Knowledge Claimed in Luke's Preface*, in The *Expositor* 8 (1922) 401-420; cf. J.A. FITZMYER, *The Gospel According to Luke I-IX* (AB, 28), Garden City, NY, Doubleday, 1981, 1, p. 296: "It is the crucial word in the modern interpretation of the Lucan prologue".

familiarized himself with", etc. As Cadbury demonstrated in several articles, παρακολουθέω always has the sense of staying current or abreast of something or someone that is developing, increasing, or occurring over a period of time[6]. In the Festschrift for Prof. J. Smit Sibinga[7], I have shown that the usual appeal to Josephus' *Against Apion* I.53, in support of the current, almost 'orthodox' rendering of παρακολουθέω as "investigate" or "go back over something" (as in Bauer/many commentaries) has got it dead wrong; in fact, by παρ-ηκολουθηκότες in I.53, Josephus means something quite the opposite (see below). Παρακολουθέω can be profiled under three main senses:

(1) "One who has followed with the mind" a speech, a text[8] (through reading/hearing), a teaching[9] (hence approximates "observant", "adherent of"), a habit[10] (habitual behavior) or ritual[11] (as a religious observant), events, persons, movements of history[12].

(2) "A literal physical accompanying of a person(s)" at their side or in their entourage, or of "things alongside or accompanying other things", or a metaphorical use of "accompanying" or "attending" in the negative sense of "pestering", "insulting" someone[13]. Prior to the Papias fragment, no use of παρακολουθέω can be adduced in the positive sense of a disciple or student "physically accompanying/following" a teacher. In fact, before this reference to the disciples of the apostles "following them", no instance can be demonstrated of any positive physical accompaniment[14]; rather, as in the figurative use, the sense can

---

6. In addition to *The Knowledge Claimed* (n. 5), see *The Purpose Expressed in Luke's Preface*, in *The Expositor* 10 (1922) 431-441; *Commentary on the Preface of Luke*, in *The Beginnings of Christianity*, 2, pp. 489-510; *"We" and "I"Passages in Luke–Acts*, in *NTS* 3 (1956-57) 128-132.

7. D.P. MOESSNER, *'Eyewitnesses,' 'Informed Contemporaries,' and 'Unknowing Inquirers': Josephus' Criteria for Authentic Historiography and the Meaning of* παρακολουθέω, in *NT* 38 (1996) 105-122.

8. In addition to the passages treated in sections B and C below, see, esp. Dionysius of Halicarnassus, *de Thucydide* 9.

9. 1 Tim 4,6 or 2 Tim 3,10.

10. Josephus, *Against Apion* II.5; K.H. RENGSTORF (ed.), *A Complete Concordance to Flavius Josephus*, Leiden, Brill, 1973-1983, lists "habit" as a distinct referent for παρακολουθέω.

11. Josephus, *Antiquities* 12.259; cf. 2 Tim 3,10.

12. In addition to the passage treated in section C below, see, 2 Tim 3,10; Josephus, *Life* 357; Demosthenes, *de Corona* 53; *de Falsa Legatione* 257; *UPZ* 71,20; *PSI* IV.411.3.

13. E.g., Aristophanes, *The Ecclesiazusae* 725:10; Plato, *The Sophist* 266a; Demosthenes, *Oration (Against Meidias)* XXI.14.69; *de Corona* 162; Philemon 124; Aristotle, *Historia Animalium* 496A29; Josephus, *Antiquities* 14.438; *Jewish War* 1.455.

14. Eusebius, *Ecclesiastical History* III.39.4 (παρηκολουθηκὼς ... τοῖς πρεσ-

be negative, "dogging" someone or "accompanying with malevolent intent"[15].

(3) "Follow logically" in the intransitive sense of "result from"[16]. Since παρηκολουθηκότι in Luke 1,3 has πᾶσιν as its direct object, this third sense can be ruled out. Likewise, the second sense can be eliminated since:

a) Luke aligns himself with "us" (Lk 1,2 καθὼς παρέδοσαν ἡμῖν) who have received tradition delivered over by others. Moreover, this traditional material comes from those, unlike him, who were "eyewitnesses" or "attendants" of the traditions ἀπ' ἀρχῆς.

b) The credibility of πᾶσιν as masc. pl. (i.e., "all" the eyewitnesses and attendants as tradents of "the word") becomes stretched even if Luke is indicating that he has physically accompanied only "some" of the apostles and teachers. At best it produces a confused profile of his qualifications to compose διήγησις, particularly when Luke describes his narrative as concerning "events that have come to fruition in our midst" (Lk 1,1)[17].

c) The syntax and balanced period of the proemium in the last half (Lk 1,3-4) point to the author's understanding and management of the λόγοι that Theophilus has learned. Luke's credentials must therefore indicate how well he is qualified to re-order those traditions which have been delivered over by the eyewitnesses and attendants who have already set the standard concerning the integrity of their material. In order to accomplish his goal of giving Theophilus the "certainty" of understanding or "proper grasp" of these traditions' true significance (Lk 1,4 ἡ ἀσφάλεια), Luke finds it necessary to compose another narrative, not simply to correct the accuracy of individual traditions of the "many" or of the tradents of the "oral" word. Hence this requisite relation to the various traditions accords well with the common sense of ἀκριβῶς as "with understanding"[18]. Otherwise, ἀκριβῶς sits rather awkwardly with παρηκολουθηκότι as connoting physical accompaniment. In fact, neither Bauer nor L & S attest any physical following "closely" or "accurately"; on the other hand, both establish

βυτέροις); III.39.15 (παρηκολούθησεν αὐτῷ. [i.e., κυρίῳ]). Neither Bauer nor Liddell & Scott, for instance, attest this positive sense from among their many examples of "physical accompaniment".

15. See Josephus, *Jewish War* 6.251.

16. *PSI* III. 168.24; *PRein*.18.15.

17. The rather late appearance of "we" in Acts 16, in fact, becomes even more mysterious than it already is if Luke is claiming that he had physically accompanied several eyewitnesses "for some time back" or "from the top" (ἄνωθεν).

18. See esp. Dionysius of Halicarnassus, *de Thucydide* 9.

that ἀκριβῶς goes hand in hand with verbs of perception and cognition, sc., with the notion of παρακολουθέω as "following with the mind"[19].

d) Finally, the recurrence of πάντα in the Acts prologue as "all that Jesus began to do and teach" (Acts 1,1) reinforces its dynamic sense and referent in the Lukan prologue as "all" the events or matters (πράγματα) that have been delivered over to the "us" (Lk 1,2) including traditions/matters/reports that are circulating as sources of instruction (cf. λόγοι). The fact that "eyewitnesses" are linked to these πράγματα "from the beginning" in the Lukan prologue and that the opening of Acts takes great pains to define this "beginning" with respect to the apostles as eyewitnesses "from this beginning" points to a common πάντα as the material linking both volumes (Acts 1,5.22). The further fact that the closing πράγματα of the Gospel are repeated and re-figured as the opening πράγματα of Acts[20] is a graphic portrayal of this common πάντα of traditions.

Παρηκολουθηκότι in Luke 1,3 must therefore mean "one who has followed with the mind" all the traditions of the πράγματα that have been delivered over from those tradents of the word from the beginning. But what more precisely does this mean?

B. Παρακολουθέω in Prologues

Most instructive are the ways that ancient Greek authors of historiography, of philosophical essays, and of scientific or technical treatises employ παρακολουθέω in prefaces to provide a rationale for and/or legitimation of their undertaking[21].

1. Polybius, *The Histories* I.1-15.

In this first of two introductory books to his larger 40-volume history, Polybius is justifying the scale, the starting point, and the sequence of his composition for his readers. παρακολουθέω functions as a fulcrum to tie the reader to the nature, scope, and authorial intention for the work as a whole, on the one side, and to the author's special credentials, on the other.

---

19. See Bauer (ad loc.), who lists the verbs ἀκούειν, προσέχειν, γινώσκειν, κατανοεῖν, εἰδέναι, ἱστορῆσαι, ἐκτίθεσθαι, etc.; Liddell & Scott: εἰδέναι, ἐπίστασται, καθορᾶν, μαθεῖν.

20. Luke 3,21–24,53 cf. Acts 1,1-2; Lk 24,13-43 cf. Acts 1,3; Lk 24,36-49 cf. Acts 1,4-5; Lk 24,50-51 cf. Acts 1,6-11; Lk 24,52-53 cf. Acts 1,12-14; notice the special catena of Acts 1,5 – Lk 24,47 – Lk 3,16.

21. The relevant passages are quoted in the Appendix. All translations are from the Loeb Classical Library, unless otherwise indicated.

In order for the reader to gain an overall grasp (σύνοψις) of Rome's supremacy – i.e., the main purpose of Polybius' enterprise – they will have to follow (παρακολουθέω) the earlier events of Rome's rise by integrating them into the sequel (I.12.7-8 ἐν τοῖς ἑξῆς; cf. καθεξῆς in Lk 1,3): the reader must follow the sequence of Polybius' διήγησις. Only so will a clarity emerge (σαφέστερον κατανοεῖν; cf. Lk 1,4 ἐπιγινώσκειν ... ἀσφάλειαν) which Polybius argues is critical and which motivates him to write in the light of others accounts. The reason is as profound as it is obvious. Polybius writes an extended, multi-volume narrative which in effect is a mimesis of the workings of Fortune (τυχή) in the rise of Roman power. Polybius' narrative must "re-present" in its scope and its multiple narrative connections the grand sweep of Fortune in her multi-farious interconnecting performances. Both the whole and all of the parts of Polybius' narrative must reflect the total purpose (συντέλεια) and all of the particular operations that Polybius himself in his study of history has discerned as the master-orchestration of Fortune. It is not just the case that contemporary treatments of more recent wars are inadequate or mis-presenting the truth, as for instance in Josephus' *Against Apion*; rather, above and beyond that rationale, no reader is able to discover the greater truth of the grander purpose – not to mention the significance of the various events – without a "synoptic" view of all the events, including those extending back to a logically conceived beginning (ἀρχή). To say it another way, the poetics of Polybius' narrative are constitutive of his own "synopsis" of reality. Both the scope and the sequence of Roman ascendancy must be re-construed through a new narrative road which will "guide my readers... to a true notion (ἀλήθινα ἔννοια) of this war" (I.15.13).

It is already clear that παρακολουθέω also links the readers' "following" to the credentials of the author to "lead". A number of times throughout his forty volumes Polybius draws attention to his keen study of the rise of Rome both through his first-hand witness of many of the events themselves and through careful study or inquiry of government documents and earlier histories. We learn, for instance in III.4-5, that in the course of composing the history of Rome's rise from the Second Punic War to the end of the Third Macedonian War (220-168 B.C.E.) according to his original plan, Polybius learned especially through his own experiences of turbulent times following "the last conquest" of 168 that he must continue his narrative to describe the aftermath of Rome's rule as well as to have his readers follow (παρακολουθέω) back to the earlier "beginning" of 264 B.C.E. to bring this new state of affairs into proper perspective. Polybius' active engagement both as eyewitness and as an informed contemporary follower of the rise of Rome produced his special qualifications to compose a narrative. Polybius can lead his readers to follow his narrative construal precisely because of his "mind's own ability to follow" the rise of Rome's preeminence.

In sum, Polybius was an avid student of history. He also assumed that his readers would be so engaged. All the emphasis in Polybius' use of παρακολουθέω in his extended preface is upon the effective "following of the mind" into new vistas of understanding which will occur through following the distinctive scope and sequence of his narrative. Παρακολουθέω thus ties the readers' ability to follow to the author's peculiar competence to lead.

2. Theophrastus, *The Characters*, Proemium.

Though still some four times longer than the Gospel prologue, this concentrated preface contains some intriguing parallels with Luke 1,1-4: Like Lk (Lk 1,1), Theophrastus begins with a summary description of the content before proceeding immediately to his credentials; like Luke (Lk 1,3), he addresses his patron/dedicatee in the vocative (cf. esp. Acts 1,1 ὦ Θεόφιλε) by way of introducing his special qualifications: Careful observation (συνθεωρήσας; cf. Lk 1,3 παρηκολουθηκότι), for a long period of time (ἐκ πολλοῦ χρόνου; cf. Lk 1,3 ἄνωθεν), and with great carefulness/diligence (ἀκρίβεια; cf. Lk 1,3 ἀκριβῶς). Such qualifications are then expressly linked to the desired impact upon the reader: it is only as the reader follows the distinctive sequence of the author's composition that the attainment of the true understanding (i.e., the author's!) of the subject matter ensues. Again, tying the reader's competence and intended goal for the reader to the author's special competence and unparalleled literary result is παρακολουθέω. Unlike Luke and Polybius, however, Theophrastus does not mention any others' attempts and therefore does not have to provide legitimation for his own re-working of some conventional τόπος.

3. Strabo, *Geography* 1.1.14-15.22-23; 1.2.1.

In this extended proemium (I.1-2), Strabo delineates the scope and nature of his subject matter in order to justify the intended illumination of his readers. Unless his readers follow this scope through following (παρακολουθέω) the peculiar sequence of his treatise, they will not be able to attain a "clear exposition" (σαφῶς ἐξειπεῖν). Moreover, they will be in no position to judge whether his own undertaking – which both adds to the information of his predecessors and criticizes certain insights of these – has been worth the effort. For instance, it would be futile, he claims, to present a clear understanding of the ways that geography bears on the political life of the nations without also treating the influence of the celestial world upon these affairs. Without that critical component, the readers would not be able to follow (παρακολουθέω) his text so as to gain an accurate understanding (ἄπαντα ἀκριβοῦν) of the subject matter.

Once again, the pivotal term linking the scope and the author's intended purpose for his readers to the readers' experience of the author's special qualifications is παρακολουθέω. For as Strabo invites his readers to "follow", he stresses more than the previously cited authors the high level of education which is required of them, e.g., his primary reader, the person of public life or the statesman (τὸ πολιτικόν). Only such a reader who is schooled in "virtue" and "practical wisdom" will be able to appreciate the "additions" that Strabo makes to the "many" before him and to "follow" the criticisms of certain predecessors (including Polybius!) through their "following" (παρακολουθέω) the structured arrangement (σύνταξις) of his arguments. Hence, similar to Polybius and Theophrastus, παρακολουθέω again links the author's qualifications to expectations placed upon the readers. Only "schooled" readers will be able to follow with understanding the distinctive nature of the arguments that has motivated Strabo to put together a new, rhetorical sequence (ὑπόθεσις) in the first place. Thus both literary and material rationale are linked to παρακολουθέω.

4. Apollonius of Citium, *Commentary on the* De Articulis *of Hippocrates* I, Praef.

Prefaces in the scientific or technical prose traditions are generally much shorter and follow a standard sequence that L. Alexander outlines as follows[22]: (1) The authors's decision to write; (2) the subject and contents or scope of the book; (3) second-person address of dedication; (4) the nature of the subject matter; (5) others who have written on the subject, whether predecessors and/or rivals; (6) the author's qualifications; (7) general remarks on methodology[23].

---

22. ALEXANDER, *The Preface* (see n. 4), pp. 69-91.
23. The last two categories emerge in the late and post-Hellenistic period, and by the first century CE the "author's qualifications" "was well established in the scientific tradition" (p. 87). In her contribution to D.P. MOESSNER (ed.), *Luke the Interpreter of Israel. 1. Jesus and the Heritage of Israel*, Harrisburg, PA, Trinity Press International, forthcoming 1999, Alexander amends the 7-fold schema to 6 categories, subsuming the "subject and contents" as part of the "nature and sources" of the subject and changing "general methodological remarks" to "the intended effect of the book" on the reader.

Παρακολουθέω or its cognate εὐπαρακολουθέω is found in several of these prefaces, usually tying the author's distinctive credentials and literary product to the impact on the reader. In the example of Apollonius, both "hands-on" experience as well as faithfulness to a tradition mark him as distinctly qualified to lead the reader through the sequence of an easily-graspable path of understanding[24].

To sum up, παρακολουθέω (or εὐπαρακολουθέω) spans different genres (historiography, philosophical and moral treatises, scientific/technical prose) to link the author's distinctive credentials and rationale for writing to the specific goals the reader is to achieve through this "following" (παρακολουθέω). The verb occurs in a variety of socio-literary circumstances of the author with respect to others' writings on the same topic, whether in cases of inadequate rival versions (Polybius), or unprecedented (or perhaps alleged un-rivaled) undertakings (Theophrastus), or in supplementing and correcting only certain aspects of previous and/or rival treatments (Strabo)[25]. Strabo would appear, at first glance, to provide the closest parallel to Luke's usage in Lk 1,3. Strabo justifies his version by virtue of the supplemental and complementary material, while at points correcting certain impressions of those he otherwise follows rather closely. And yet Polybius' rationale would seem to be much closer. Like Polybius, Luke emphasizes the unique subject matter that consists of matters/events in history that have come to a certain τέλος[26] or "completion" (Lk 1,1 πεπληροφορημένων). And though Luke does not directly articulate the basis for this "fulfillment", as Polybius does in his references to "Fortune", throughout his two volumes Luke does refer to a "divine necessity" or "plan" as the source of coherence for the matters/events (Lk 1,1 πράγματα)[27]. Second, Luke refers to a "beginning" that is critical as a base point for the narrative and records his own credentials in relation to that ἀρχή: παρηκολουθηκότι ἄνωθεν. Yet nei-

---

24. ALEXANDER, *The Preface*, p. 96, also points to the following examples: εὐπαρακολούθητος: Hero of Alexandria, *Belopoeica* W 73.11 "so that the tradition may be easy to follow for all"; Dioscorides, *De Simplicibus*; παρακολουθέω: Diocles of Carystus, *Letter to Antigonus* "And you, if you are persuaded by what I say, will be able to understand their accuracy" (ἀκριβείᾳ).

25. With regard to the scientific texts, Alexander notes: "It is a particular feature of the post-Hellenistic prefaces regularly to place this theme at the beginning of their work and to make the work of others the explicit basis of the author's own decision to write. This basis is by no means always polemical" (p. 76).

26. *The Histories* I.3.4; but see also the many times Luke uses the τελε- word group and synonyms in what has come to be called his theology of "promise"/"prophecy" and "fulfillment".

27. Already, however, the passive voice of πεπληροφορημένα is suggestive! For "the plan (βουλή) of God", cf. Lk 7,30; Acts 2,23; 4,28; (5,38); 13,36; 20,27; (27,42-43).

ther Polybius nor Luke were eyewitnesses or engaged contemporaries of their "beginning point". And both trace events even further back so that the reader will gain a firmer perspective on the significance of the "beginning" for the rest of the narrative. Third, Luke ties his new narrative sequence, as well as its scope, to a deliberate enlightenment of his readers which includes a firmer grasp of the significance of individual events as they relate to a larger whole. Finally, unlike Polybius, Luke does not openly or explicitly challenge any other's account[28]. Yet the consistent linkage of scope and sequence which παρακολουθέω provides would seem to indicate that in Luke's mind all is not necessarily well with these "many" other accounts. It could well be that on this score also, Luke closely parallels Polybius[29].

Yet for all these similarities between Luke's use of παρακολουθέω and the multi-genred authors we have reviewed, the striking difference between Lk 1,3 and the other occurrences in prefaces is that παρηκολουθηκότι is predicated of Luke the author – and not of his readers – in claiming the ability to "follow"; and moreover, the perfect tense suggests some previous activity or ability on the part of Luke, the consequence of which has become crucial to his qualifications to tender yet another diegetic version, rather than his present ability "to follow with the mind" the sequence of his own account. Do not, in fact, these differences sever the linkage of παρακολουθέω in Greco-Roman prefaces with the œuvre of the author *ad Theophilum?*

First, it needs to be stated that Polybius' use of the aorist infinitive in I.12.7 (παρακολουθῆσαι) applies to any reader, including himself, since it is only through following through reading the specific "arrangement" (I.13.9 οἰκονομία) of the connected events in and through the narrative itself that any person can attain a sufficient point of viewing (I.4.1 σύνοψις) to bring intelligibility to the rise of Rome (see esp. I.13.9). Only the narrative in its multi-valent connections is epistemologically adequate to the task! To underscore this point Polybius repeats this argument with παρακολουθέω within the composition itself by "breaking frame" (III.32.2) in a "digression" (III.32, cf. παρέκβασις in III.33.1) against his detractors who contend his multi-volume "viewing" is too difficult to read (III.32.2 δυσανάγνωστον)[30].

---

28. See, e.g., Book XII, where Polybius challenges both the facts as well as the methods of other historians.

29. Ironically, more like Theophrastus' *Characters*, the resulting generic shape of Luke's two volumes has produced something "new", for which the church's separation of Acts from the Gospel in the New Testament canon is the most glaring evidence.

30. "How much easier it is to acquire and peruse forty Books, all as it were connected by one thread, and thus to follow clearly (III.32.2 παρακολουθῆσαι σαφῶς) events in

Even more importantly, however, Josephus uses the perfect participle, παρηκολουθήκοτες, of himself in arguing for his superior credentials and superior narrative over against rival accounts of the war with Rome. More than that, later in the same work, *Against Apion*, he employs the present infinitive to describe how he, similar to Polybius with Rome's past, could "follow" the "early" events hundreds or more years removed from his "following" of Israel's current events.

C. Παρακολουθέω in Josephus

1. *Against Apion* I.53-56

The cluster of παράδοσις, ἀκριβῶς, πράξεις, with the perf. ptc. of παρακολουθέω provides striking parallels to Lk 1,1-4. The context of Josephus' argument vis-à-vis the "others'" accounts is that Greek history writers show much less regard for historical records and historical accuracy than other peoples, but especially compared with the Jews and the long-standing tradition that has formed him as a writer. He expatiates at length on how he is a more qualified writer of the history of the war with Rome than others of late who have "never visited the sites nor were anywhere near the actions described" (I.46). Josephus, on the contrary, has "composed (ἐποιησάμην; cf. Acts 1,1) a veracious account", as "one present in person at all the events" (I.47 πράγμασιν αὐτὸς ἅπασι παρατυχών). So confident is he of his final narrative account of the events (I.50 ἐποιησάμην τῶν πράξεων τὴν παράδοσιν) that, in countering his critics, he can call as his witnesses (I.50 μάρτυρες; cf. Acts 1,8), if need be, no one less than Vespasian or Titus, commanders in chief of the war. Other notables who have read Josephus' *War* have already "born testimony" (I.52 ἐμαρτύρησαν) to its "safeguarding of the truth" (I.49-52).

The poignant parallels notwithstanding, Josephus' relationship to the "other" history writers would seem to be the very obverse of Luke's relation to the "many". Josephus makes "eyewitness" claims for "all" the events he recounts in his *War*, whereas Luke refers to another group of "eyewitnesses" upon whom he is dependent for his information. *Prima facie*, it would seem that Luke fits into Josephus' second category of writers who must "inquire" (I.54 πυνθάνομαι) from "those who know".

But what about the distant events of the *Antiquities*? Obviously Josephus could not make the same eyewitness claims and perforce would

Italy, Sicily... than to read or procure the works of those who treat of particular transactions".

have to include himself as an inquirer, those who must study and research (πυνθάνομαι) the ancient documents and other pertinent (re)sources[31]. But Josephus never concedes any inquiry stage. On the contrary, he applies his definition of "following" the relatively recent events of the *War* immediately to the ancient events of the *Antiquities* in justifying his credentials as an historian for that work! He has met his own criterion of providing a reliable (ἀκριβῶς) account of ancient events because he "translated our sacred scriptures" (I.54 ἐκ τῶν ἱερῶν γραμμάτων μεθηρμήνευκα). Accordingly in the same Book I of *Against Apion*, Josephus will use παρακολουθέω of an historian's ability to "follow" Israel's ancient scriptures, reminding us of Polybius' assertion concerning his knowledge of the early events of Rome's ascendancy. But how can his translation of Jewish scripture be deemed a "following" (παρακολουθέω) when he is hundreds of years removed from the events he "translates"? Josephus continues to provide an answer in I.54: "In my *Antiquities*, as I said, I have given a translation of our sacred books; being a priest and of priestly ancestry, I am well versed in the philosophy of those writings". Years of training and immersion (μετέχω) in Israel's texts have formed and informed Josephus into one supremely qualified to comprehend and "to follow" these scriptures when he reads them or translates them for a less informed audience. Josephus has superior credentials to follow (with his mind) the meaning of these texts since he, as he says in introducing his qualifications, by "instinct (σύμφυτον) with every Jew, from the day of his birth" has come to regard the Scriptures "as the decrees of God, to abide by them, and, if need be, cheerfully to die for them" (I.42).

2. *Against Apion* I.213-218

In his survey of historical accounts of the Jewish nation, Josephus mentions three historians who out of the best of intentions have studied

---

31. It is tempting to understand I.53-54 as a straightforward chiasm: a) "Following" events as they occur; b) "Inquiring" (after the event) from "those who knew/know them"; b') *Antiquities* is an "inquiry" of the Scriptures "from those [the authors, eyewitness sources, etc.] who knew them"; a') The *War* recounts the events by one who "followed" them as they occurred. Is this not the general sense of Josephus' claims? Yet neither in this passage nor in *Ant.* I.5 does Josephus speak of "inquiring" or "seeking information" (πυνθάνομαι) from the Scriptures. Rather, he "translates" them. That is to say, his means of presenting an accurate account of the ancient events "leaps over" the "inquiry" stage directly to the "following" stage. This leap is all the more striking given his usage in the opening of the treatise of the necessity of πυνθάνεσθαι τὴν ἀλήθειαν ("inquiring after the truth") through the means of studying the texts of the primeval histories of nations other than his own (*Against Apion* I.6). But this difference in referent between other nations', including Greek historiography, and Josephus' own saturation in the scriptural traditions of Israel's history illustrates precisely the distinction between πυνθάνομαι and παρακολουθέω.

Israel's scriptures but still evince "the inability to follow the meaning of our records with complete reliability/accuracy" (οὐ γὰρ ἐνῆν αὐτοῖς μετὰ πάσης ἀκριβείας τοῖς ἡμετέροις γράμμασι παρακολουθεῖν) when they read them (my translation).

He does not mean that their ability to read Hebrew was limited, since Josephus himself appears to rely heavily on an Alexandrian version of the Old Testament in his own "translation". And more to the point, as a priest from a line of priests, Josephus may "excuse" (I.218 οἷς συγγιγνώσκειν ἄξιον) a Demetrius or Eupolemus or Philo for their lack of "insider" knowledge since they do not have the long years of training of one "schooled" in the ideas and way of life of these sacred writings. However diligent and competent the three "exceptional" historians may be, compared with Josephus, their ability to "follow" (παρακολουθέω) Israel's scriptures obviously pales alongside this one who for many years had been steeped (I.54 μετεσχηκώς) in the meaning of those scriptures and thus did not need to "seek information" (I.53 πυνθάνομαι).

In sum for Josephus, παρακαλουθέω in *Against Apion* is a credentialing term which links the author's superior qualifications to the desired impact of his works upon his readers. It functions, therefore, in the same manner as παρακαλουθέω does in the prefaces surveyed above. Like the Greco-Roman authors reviewed there, Josephus legitimates his writing of history in part by the superior impact his unique works will have upon his readers. Just as Polybius stresses his ability to provide readers with the necessary perspective from which one must interpret the parts and the whole, Josephus for his *Antiquities* emphasizes his longstanding, deeply-rooted expertise in the texts and traditions of his nation, which therefore, better than any rival, qualifies him to lead his readers to and through those traditions. For both of Josephus' historiographical works, then, παρακολουθέω connotes a credentialed expert whose mastery of the subject effects fundamental confidence for the reader: whether that competence is exhibited by having stayed abreast of events as they occurred through active engagement over a longer period of time (the *War*), or by the ability to "comprehend immediately" the history of a nation through "following" their ancient texts and traditions and thereby leading others into new territories of knowledge through the superior structuring and sequencing of the (expert's) own account (the *Antiquities*).

Conclusions

Of the authors investigated, Josephus provides the greatest illumination for παρηκολουθηκότι in Lk 1,3.

(1) Similar to Josephus in *Against Apion* I.54 and 213ff., Luke is claiming the credentials of one "steeped" in the events, traditions, and reports that have come to fruition in his and his readers' "midst" (Lk 1,1) and one who has kept abreast of "all" of them "from farther back"[32] or "for a long time"[33]. Like Josephus who was able to "follow" (παρακολουθέω) the War with Rome through physical presence or through informants (i.e., oral reports) even when he was incarcerated by Titus, so Luke is able to "follow" (παρακολουθέω) oral accounts/ teachings (λόγοι) as he encounters them or the written διήγησεις (of the "many"!), and assess their reliability (ἀκριβῶς) in providing his readers a "firmer grasp" (ἡ ἀσφάλεια) of the significance of the events through his own distinctive diegetic sequence. In neither author is there the slightest suggestion that a "tracing back" or investigative research is included in their activity of "following". Rather, immediate comprehension, whether of oral or written material, is underscored by the "informed familiarity" that παρακολουθέω entails. Both writers are invoking a stock term from poetics discussions and possibly also rhetorical handbooks to assure their readers of their impeccable credentials.

(2) The literary-social setting is intriguingly parallel. Like Josephus for his *Antiquities*, Luke must distinguish his narrative from others' accounts when he himself could not claim eyewitness or informed contemporary status for the vast majority of the events he recounts. Moreover, like Josephus for his *War*, Luke is writing to a readership in which many could well have some experience or information about certain of the events (περὶ ... ἐν ἡμῖν; περὶ ὧν κατηχήθης). In the midst of competing accounts, Luke like Josephus, draws on παρακολουθέω to signal his superior credentials to write a more reliably construed, better composed narrative. Thus like Josephus for his *War*, Luke engages παρακολουθέω when grounding his diverging epistemological configuration of events upon the firm foundation of eyewitness evidence. Similar to Josephus in his appeals to the number of trustworthy witnesses standing behind his particular diegetic rendering, Luke already anticipates in the Gospel preface the development of witness (μάρτυς) and bearing testimony (μαρτυρ, -ειν/ουν) as a constitutive component of his distinctive enterprise (Lk 1,2). Later in the opening preface of his second volume, he will link those who were "from the beginning eyewitnesses and ministers" to the authoritative apostolic witness (Acts 1,1b-2.8 ὧν ἤρξατο ὁ Ἰησοῦς ... ἄχρι ἧς ἡμέρας ... τοῖς ἀποστόλοις ... οὓς

---

32. Liddell & Scott; they include also "from the beginning" with reference to "in narrative or inquiry", cited in conjunction with ἄρχεσθαι and ἐπιχειρεῖν!
33. Bauer lists Acts 26,5 and not Luke 1,3 under this definition.

ἐξελέξατο .... μάρτυρες) before he goes on in the second half of the sequel volume to introduce Paul as his chief ὑπηρέτης καὶ μάρτυς (Acts 26,16). In other words, in justifying his own beginning and ending points for his narrative, as well as for his diverging sequence, Luke is parading the confidence of eyewitness corroboration, especially vis-à-vis the sequel volume. As we have seen for the epistemological predicament of Josephus, invoking eyewitnesses is not an idiosyncratic ploy when other accounts are vying for a "following".

To sum up, Luke draws upon παρακολουθέω as a conventional term of Greek prefaces of the Hellenistic and Roman periods in presenting superior credentials to write yet another account of the fulfilled events. In conjunction with others' renditions and the terminology of narrative poetics, παρακολουθέω pinpoints, even as it broadcasts, Luke's claim to a most reliable account.

APPENDIX (cf. n. 21)

1. Polybius, *The Histories* I.1-15

1.1 Had previous chroniclers neglected to speak in praise of History in general, it might perhaps have been necessary for me to recommend everyone to choose for study and welcome such treatises as the present, since there is no more ready corrective of conduct than knowledge of the past. But all historians... have impressed on us that the soundest education and training for a life of active politics is the study of History... **1.5** For who is so worthless or indolent as not to wish to know by what means and under what system of polity the Romans in less than fifty-three years have succeeded in subjecting nearly the whole inhabited world to their sole government – a thing unique in history? Or who again is there so passionately devoted to other spectacles or studies as to regard anything as of greater moment than the acquisition of this knowledge?... **2.8** In the course of this work it will become more clearly intelligible by what steps this power was acquired, and it will also be seen how many and how great advantages accrue to the student from the systematic treatment of history. **3.1** The date from which I propose to begin (ἄρξει) is the 140th Olympiad... **3.4** ever since this date history has been an organic whole (σωματοειδῆ), and the affairs of Italy and Africa have been inter-linked with those of Greece and Asia, all leading up to one end (τέλος). And this is my reason for beginning (τὴν ἀρχήν) where I do... **4.1** For what gives my work its peculiar quality, and what is most remarkable in the present age, is this. Fortune having guided almost all the affairs (πράγματα) of the world in one direction and having forced them to incline toward one and the same end, a historian should bring before his readers under one synoptical view (σύνοψιν) the operations by which she has accomplished her general purpose (πρὸς τὴν τῶν ὅλων πραγμάτων συντέλειαν)... **4.3** I observe that while several modern writers deal with particular wars and certain matters connected with them, no one... has even attempted to inquire critically when and whence the general and comprehensive scheme of events originated and how it led up to the end. I therefore thought it quite necessary (ἡμᾶς εἰδέναι ... ἀναγκαῖον) not to leave unnoticed or allow to pass into oblivion this the finest and most beneficent of the performances of Fortune... **4.10** Special histories therefore contribute very little to the knowledge of the whole and conviction of its truth. It is only indeed by study of the interconnexion of all the particulars (τῆς ἁπάντων πρὸς ἄλληλα συμπλοκῆς)... that we are enabled at least to make a general survey, and thus derive both benefit and pleasure from history... **5.1** I shall adopt as the starting-point (ἀρχήν) of this book the first occasion on which the Romans crossed the sea from Italy... The starting-point must be an era generally agreed upon and recognized, and one self-apparent from the events (πράγμασι), even if this involves my going back a little in point of date and giving a summary of intervening occurrences. For if readers are ignorant or indeed in any doubt as to what are the facts from which the work opens, it is impossible that what follows (τῶν ἐξῆς) should meet with acceptance or credence... **12.5** Such then was the occasion and motive of this the first crossing of the Romans from Italy with an armed force, an event which I take to be the most natural starting-point (ἀρχήν) of this whole work. I have therefore made it my serious base, but went also somewhat further back in order to leave no possible obscurity in my statements of general causes. To follow (παρακολουθῆσαι) out this previous history... seems to me necessary for anyone who hopes to gain a proper general survey (συνόψεσθαι) of their present supremacy. My readers need not therefore be surprised if, in the further course of this work (ἐν τοῖς ἐξῆς), I occasionally give them in addition some of the earlier history of the most famous states; for I shall do so in order to establish such a fundamental view (ἀρχάς) as will make it clear (σαφῶς κατανοεῖν) in the sequel starting from what origins and how and when they severally reached their present position... **13.2** To take them in order (κατὰ τὴν τάξιν) we have first the incidents of the war between Rome and Carthage for Sicily. Next follows... **13.9** Thus there will be no break in the narrative (διηγήσεως) and it will be seen that I have been justified in touching on events which have been previously narrated by others, while this arrangement (οἰκονομίας) will render the approach to what follows intelligible and easy for students (τοῖς ... φιλομαθοῦσιν ... εὐμαθῆ καὶ ῥᾳδίαν)... **14.1** An equally powerful motive with me for paying particular attention to this war is that the truth (τὴν ἀλήθειαν) has not been adequately stated by those historians who are reputed to be the best authorities on it, Philinus and Fabius. I do not indeed accuse them of intentional falsehood, in view of their character and principles, but they seem to me to have been much in the case of lovers; for owing to his convictions and constant partiality Philinus will have it that the Carthaginians in every case acted wisely, well, and bravely, and the Romans otherwise, whilst Fabius takes the precisely opposite view... **14.5** but he who assumes the character of a historian must ignore everything of the sort, and often... speak good of his enemies... while criticizing and even reproaching roundly his closest friends, should the errors of their conduct impose this duty on him... **14.6** if History is stripped of her truth all that is left is but an idle tale... **14.8** We must therefore disregard the actors in our narrative and apply to the actions such terms and such criticism as they deserve... **15.13** Now that I have said what is fitting on the subject of this digression, I will return to facts (πράξεις) and attempt in a narrative that strictly follows the order of events to guide my readers by a short road to a true notion (ἀληϑινὰς ἐννοίας) of this war.

2. Theophrastus, *The Characters*, Proemium

I have often marvelled, when I have given the matter my attention... why it has come about that, albeit the whole of Greece lies in the same clime and all Greeks have a like upbringing, we have not the same constitution of character. I therefore, Polycles (ἐγὼ οὖν, ὦ Πολύκλεις), having observed (συνϑεωρήσας) human nature a long time (ἐκ πολλοῦ χρόνου)... and moreover had converse with all sorts of dispositions and compared them with great diligence (ἐξ ἀκριβείας πολλῆς), have thought it incumbent upon me to write in a book (ὑπέλαβον δεῖν συγγράψαι) the manner of each several kind of men both good and bad. And I will set down for you each in its place (κατὰ γένος; cf. Lk 1,3 καϑεξῆς) the behaviour proper to them and the fashion of their life; for I am persuaded, Polycles, that our sons will prove the better men if there be left them such memorials as will... make them choose the friendship and converse of the better sort, in the hope they may be as good as they. But now to my tale (λόγος; cf. Lk 1,2); and be it yours to follow with understanding (σὸν δὲ παρακολουϑῆσαί τε εὐμαϑῶς) and see if I speak true (εἰδῆσαι εἰ ὀρϑῶς λέγω; cf. Lk 1,4). First, then, I shall dispense with all preface and with the saying of much that is beside the mark (ἔξω τοῦ πράγματος) and treat of those (ποιήσομαι τὸν λόγον; cf. Acts 1,1) that have pursued the worser way of life, beginning with (ἄρξομαι πρῶτον; cf. Lk 1,1 and Acts 1,1) Dissembling and the definition of it... and thereafter I shall endeavour, as I purposed to do, to make clear (φανερὰ καϑιστάναι) the other affections each in its own place (κατὰ γένος).

3. Strabo, *Geography* 1.1.14-15.22-23; 1.2.1

1.1.14 So, if one is about to treat of the differences between countries, how can he discuss his subject correctly and adequately if he has paid no attention, even superficially, to any of these matters? For even if it be impossible in a treatise (ὑπόϑεσις) of this nature, because of its having a greater bearing on affairs of state, to make everything scientifically accurate (ἅπαντα ἀκριβοῦν), it will naturally be appropriate to do so, at least in so far as the man in public life is able to follow the thought (παρακολουϑεῖν). **1.1.15** Moreover, the man who has once thus lifted his thoughts to the heavens will surely not hold aloof from the earth as a whole; for it is obviously absurd, if a man who desired to give a clear exposition (σαφῶς ἐξειπεῖν) of the inhabited world had ventured to lay hold of the celestial bodies and to use them for the purposes of instruction, and yet had paid no attention to the earth as a whole... **1.1.22** In short, this book of mine should be generally useful – useful alike to the statesman (πολιτικόν) and to the public at large – as was my work on *History*. In this work, as in that, I mean by "statesman", not the man who is wholly uneducated, but the man who has taken the round of courses usual in the case of freemen or of students of philosophy. For the man who has given no thought to virtue and to practical wisdom, and to what has been written about them would not be able even to form a valid opinion either in censure or in praise; nor yet to pass judgment upon the matters of historical fact that are worthy of being recorded in this treatise. **1.1.23** And so, after I had written my *Historical Sketches,* which have been useful, I suppose for moral and political philosophy, I determined to write the present treatise (σύνταξις) also; for this work itself is based on the same plan, and is addressed to the same class of readers, and particularly to men of exalted stations in life... **1.2.1** If I, too, undertake (ἐπιχειροῦμεν) to write upon a subject that has been treated by many others (πολλοί) before me, I should not be blamed therefor, unless I prove to have discussed the subject in every respect (ἅπαντα) as have my predecessors. Although various predecessors have done excellent work in various fields of geography, yet I assume that a large portion of the work still remains to be done; and if I shall be able to make even small additions to what they have said, that must be regarded as a sufficient excuse for my undertaking... I therefore may have something more to say than my predecessors. This will become particularly apparent in what I shall have to say in criticism of my predecessors, but my criticism has less to do with the earliest geographers than with the successors of Eratosthenes and Eratosthenes himself... And if I shall, on occasion, be compelled to contradict the very men whom in all other respects I follow (ἐπακολουθοῦμεν) most closely, I beg to be pardoned... Indeed, to engage in philosophical discussion with everybody is umseemly, but it is honourable to do so with Eratosthenes, Hipparchus, Poseidonius, Polybius, and others of their type.

4. Apollonius of Citium, *Commentary on the* De Articulis *of Hippocrates* I

In order that every detail may be thoroughly easy for you to follow (εὐπαρα-κολούθητα), I shall set out the text... and methods of operation... some of which I have performed myself, while others I observed as a student of Zopyrus in Alexandria. And Posidonius, who studied with the same doctor, would testify with us that this man performed cures with the highest degree of fidelity to Hippocrates.

5. Josephus, *Against Apion* I.53-56

I.53 Nevertheless, certain despicable persons have essayed to malign my history, taking it for a prize composition such as is set to boys at school. What an extraordinary accusation and calumny! Surely they ought to recognize that it is the duty of one who promises to present his readers with actual facts (παρά-δοσιν πράξεων ἀληθινῶν) first to obtain an exact knowledge (ἐπίστασθαι ταύτας πρότερον ἀκριβῶς) of them himself, either through having been in close touch with the events (ἢ παρηκολουθηκότα τοῖς γεγονόσιν), or by inquiry from those who knew them (παρὰ τῶν εἰδότων πυνθανόμενον). **I.54** That duty (πραγματεία) I consider myself to have amply fulfilled in both my works. In my Antiquities, as I said, I have given a translation of our sacred books (ἐκ τῶν ἱερῶν γραμμάτων μεθηρμήνευκα); being a priest and of priestly ancestry, I am well versed in the philosophy of those writings (ἱερεὺς ἐκ γένους καὶ μετεσχηκὼς τῆς φιλοσοφίας τῆς ἐν ἐκείνοις τοῖς γράμ-μασι). **I.55** My qualification as historian of the war was that I had been an actor in many (πολλῶν μὲν αὐτουργὸς πράξεων), and an eyewitness of most, of the events (πλείστων δ᾽ αὐτόπτης γενόμενος); in short, nothing whatever was said or done of which I was ignorant. **I.56** Surely, then, one cannot but regard as audacious the attempt of these critics to challenge my veracity. Even if, as they assert, they have read the Commentaries of the imperial commanders, they at any rate had no first-hand acquaintance (παρέτυχον) with our position in the opposite camp.

6. Josephus, *Against Apion* I.213-218

I.213 That the omission of some historians to mention our nation was due, not to ignorance, but to envy or some other disingenuous reason, I think I am in a position to prove. Hieronymus... was a contemporary of Hecataeus... **I.214** Yet, whereas Hecataeus devoted a whole book to us, Hieronymus, although he had lived almost within our borders, has nowhere mentioned us in his history. So widely different were the views of these two men. One thought us deserving of serious notice; the eyes of the other, through an ill-natured disposition, were totally blind to the truth. **I.215** However, our antiquity is sufficiently established by the Egyptian, Chaldaean, and Phoenician records, not to mention the numerous Greek historians... **I.217** The majority of these authors have misrepresented the facts of our primitive history (ἐξ ἀρχῆς πραγμάτων διήμαρτον), because they have not read (μή ... ἐνέτυχον) our sacred books... **I.218** Demetrius Phalereus, the elder Philo, and Eupolemus are exceptional in their approximation to the truth (οὐ πολὺ τῆς ἀληθείας διήμαρτον), and [their errors] may be excused (οἷς συγγιγνώσκειν ἄξιον) on the ground of their inability to follow quite accurately the meaning of our records (οὐ γὰρ ἐνῆν αὐτοῖς μετὰ πάσης ἀκριβείας τοῖς ἡμετέροις γράμμασι παρακολουθεῖν).

2000 University Ave.
Dubuque, IA 52001
USA

David P. MOESSNER

READING LUKE-ACTS FROM BACK TO FRONT

In literary-critical terms, the ending of Acts is a notorious puzzle. Many readers would query (and have queried from earliest times) whether it even makes a fitting closure to Acts as a single volume[1]. After the drama of the repeated trial scenes in Jerusalem and Caesarea, it is odd to say the least that we never find out what happened to Paul. Why do we have no grand climactic trial before Caesar? Why, if Paul is being presented as a proto-martyr (as I believe in some sense he is[2]), do we not have the narrative of his death? The narrative of voyage and shipwreck (27,1–28,15) is conceived on the grand scale, but after this Paul's story seems in a curious way to meander to an unsatisfactory and provisional close, living "at his own expense" in a hired lodging, waiting for a denouement which never happens. The ending is equally unsatisfactory for Luke's presentation of Paul the missionary, for although in the final verses Paul is portrayed as preaching the Gospel "unhindered", he has lost the dynamic freedom of movement which so characterises his missionary voyages, and in any case Luke has made it clear that there is already a church in Rome before Paul arrives. More to the point, the emphasis in ch. 28 is not on missionary preaching but on community conflict: it is the disturbing encounter with the leaders of the Jewish community in Rome, with its harsh and menacing ending, which dominates the final chapter of Acts. My question here is, Is it possible that this puzzling ending actually makes as much sense – maybe even more sense – as an ending to Luke-Acts as a two-volume work? Is Acts ch. 28 actually intended to provide a closure for the longer story which began in Luke ch. 1? If so, that would give us a rather powerful argument in favour at least of a retrospective narrative coherence for Luke's two-volume composition. Whether this is sufficient to establish the "unity" of the two volumes is a different question, however: and that is the question with which I shall begin.

1. Cf. D. MARGUERAT, *"Et quand nous sommes entrés dans Rome" : L'énigme de la fin du livre des Actes (28,16-31)*, in *RHPR* 73 (1993) 1-21, esp. pp. 2-6, citing Chrysostom, *Hom. Act.* 15. L.T. JOHNSON, *The Acts of the Apostles* (Sacra Pagina, 5), Collegeville, MN, Liturgical Press, 1992, p. 474 traces this sense of unfinishedness back to the Muratorian canon.
2. L.C.A. ALEXANDER, *Acts and Ancient Intellectual Biography,* in B.W. WINTER – A.D. CLARKE (eds.), *The Book of Acts in Its First Century Setting. I. Ancient Literary Setting,* Grand Rapids MI, Eerdmans, 1993, pp. 31-63, esp. 62-63.

I. BEGINNINGS AND ENDINGS

In an earlier paper on the preface to Acts[3], I have suggested that there are two ways in which readers of Acts tend to approach the unity question. The first is prospective: we ask the question, Is the story of the apostles envisaged right from the start of Luke's Gospel? Gospel critics often ask this question in terms of the author's intention: Did Luke have the second volume in mind when he wrote the first? Was Acts part of Luke's conception from the outset? But it can just as well be asked from the point of view of the reader: Can the reader predict the end of the story (or at least its development in the second volume) from the beginning? This question in itself raises issues about the creation of suspense and the maintenance of narrative tension, to which we shall return.

The second question is retrospective, and likewise can be asked in terms of the readers as well as of the author. Does the second volume provide a coherent continuation to the first? Here we are on slightly firmer ground. We do know at least that the Gospel is part of the reading experience expected of the readers of Acts. Luke tells us so much in his opening verse (Acts 1,1): Acts is clearly intended to be read as a sequel to the Gospel story. But this does not of itself tell us the answer to the first question (a sequel may still be an afterthought); and the question of coherence still remains. Does Luke carry through his narrative programme in a coherent way? When we reach the end of volume two, do we feel that we have reached a proper closure to the work as a whole, or is it simply the end of a discrete episode within an ongoing series? Can we as readers spot connections which link the end of the story to its beginning, and if so are these connections contrived by the narrator, or are they simply the result of readerly hindsight? And either way, what is their function? What effect does it have on the reader if the entrance to the text is recalled just as she or he reaches the exit?

How many of these different types of coherence do we have to have in order to substantiate the claim to have discovered the "unity" of Luke-Acts? Writers do not always know exactly where they are going to end up when they begin their work: and without the benefit of the word-processor, they may not have either the inclination or the capacity to go back to the beginning and adjust their opening to fit their closing scene. What they may do instead is to write a sequel which contains a sufficient

---

3. L.C.A. ALEXANDER, *The Preface to Acts and the Historians*, in B. WITHERINGTON (ed.), *History, Literature and Society in the Book of Acts*, Cambridge, University Press, 1996, pp. 73-103.

number of retrospective connections to create a convincing sense of narrative coherence. This kind of coherence, *ex hypothesi,* would not have been envisaged at the start and could not be predicted from the start: but I see no reason in principle why it should not count as "unity". There is however one kind of indication which might allow us to move from this kind of retrospective coherence (readerly or authorial) to a prospective coherence planned by the author from the start of the work, and that is the significant omission or holding over of narrative detail from the first volume to the second. This of course takes us back into the sphere of redaction-critical analysis, and is only possible within the matrix of a broad consensus on the Synoptic Problem (something which it would be dangerous to assume). Nevertheless, it would be foolish for the literary critic to ignore this perspective, precisely because of its potential importance for the question of unity. I shall return to this point in my final section.

What signals were available to the ancient reader for determining the narrative unity of a sequence of texts? For modern authors, there is a whole barrage of extra-textual devices for giving the reader directions about sequence and coherence in a multi-volume narrative: this is one of the functions of what Genette calls the "paratexte", that is,

> titre, sous-titre, intertitres; préfaces, postfaces, avertissements, avant-propos, etc.; notes marginales, infrapaginales, terminales; épigraphes; illustrations; prière d'insérer, bande, jaquette, et bien d'autre types de signaux accessoires, autographes ou allographes, qui procurent au texte un entourage (variable) et parfois un commentaire, officiel ou officieux, dont le lecteur le plus puriste et le moins porté à l'érudition externe ne peut pas toujours disposer aussi facilement qu'il le voudrait et le prétend.

This "paratexte", Genette goes on, "est sans doute un des lieux privilégiés de la dimension pragmatique de l'œuvre, c'est-à-dire de son action sur le lecteur – lieu en particulier de ce qu'on nomme volontiers... le *contrat* (ou *pacte*) générique"[4]. An important aspect of this pragamatic function is to assist the reader's entry into and exit from the narrative world: that is, to facilitate the transitions between the readers' real world(s) and the world of the text[5].

---

4. G. GENETTE, *Palimpsestes: la littérature au second degré,* Paris, Seuil, 1982, p. 9; cf. *Seuils,* Paris, Seuil, 1987, pp. 376-377: "Le paratexte n'est qu'un auxiliaire, qu'un accessoire du texte. Et si le texte sans son paratexte est parfois comme un éléphant sans cornac, puissance infirme, le paratexte sans son texte est un cornac sans éléphant, parade inepte. Aussi le discours sur le paratexte doit-il ne jamais oublier qu'il porte sur un discours qui porte sur un discours, et que le sens de son objet tient à l'objet de ce sens, qui est encore un sens. Il n'est de seuil qu'à franchir".

5. "Le début d'une œuvre (comme sa fin d'ailleurs) veut assister (conduire) le lecteur

In the absence of the exterior apparatus available to modern authors (ancient books did not have bookjackets, spines, blurbs, or page headers, and titles were rudimentary and easily lost), ancient authors made extensive use of prefaces, transitional summaries, and epilogues for these purposes. In Genette's words, "une simple mention comme *Premier volume* ou *Tome I* a force de promesse – ou, comme dit Northrop Frye, de 'menace'"[6]. I could cite plentiful examples of clear and explicit authorial guidance to the reader from ancient authors (especially authors of technical handbooks) indicating exactly how one volume is related to another in a multi-volume work, and I have shown elsewhere how Luke's prefaces match the conventional language used in these recapitulatory prefaces[7]. However, the preface to the Gospel does not by itself contain sufficiently precise indications of content to decide the question of unity[8]. As it stands, it makes perfect sense either as the preface to the Gospel alone or as the preface to both volumes. The preface to Acts, by contrast, does give us a clear retrospective indication that there is some kind of link between the two volumes, i.e. that Acts is to be read as a sequel to the Gospel (Acts 1,1). But there are no further explicit authorial guideposts (that is, passages in which the author speaks in his own voice) either in transitional passages such as were common in ancient texts, or at the end of either volume[9]. This is one reason why we still have a debate about the unity of Luke-Acts, and why we have to look for

dans son passage du mode du texte au monde réel, l'aider à prendre position et à lire correctement le récit et veut programmer une réponse particulière de sa part": A. STEINER, *Le lien entre le prologue et le récit de l'Évangile de Marc,* Colloque de sciences bibliques Manchester-Lausanne 'Bible et intertextualité', May 1998 (forthcoming). Cf. M.C. PARSONS, *The Departure of Jesus in Luke-Acts* (JSNT SS, 21), Sheffield, JSOT Press, 1987, p. 173.

    6. GENETTE, *Seuils,* p. 16.

    7. Cf. L.C.A. ALEXANDER, *The Preface to Luke's Gospel* (SNTS MS, 78), Cambridge, University Press, 1993, esp. pp. 143-144; and further in *The Preface to Acts and the Historians* (n. 3 above).

    8. Cf. *The Preface to Acts and the Historians,* pp. 76-82. Presumably because of the uncertainties of roll-length (and of handwriting), most ancient authors do not indicate the precise distribution of contents between rolls at the beginning of the first volume, since it was not at that stage possible to determine exactly how much the first roll would hold. Precise description of the contents of a given roll is normally made retrospectively, at the beginning of the next: cf. Josephus, *C. Ap.* I,59, where the final topic promised in the opening volume actually spans the last section of the first roll and the first section of the second; the roll-break presumably could not have been predicted at the outset. Dioscorides, *De Simplicibus* I pref., speaks of τὰ βιβλία, but only in the second volume does he commit himself to "two books": ed. M. WELLMANN, *Dioscoridis Anazarbei De Materia Medica Libri V,* Berlin, Wiedmann, 1907-1914, vol. 3, pp. 151,13, and 242, 317.

    9. Cf. PARSONS, *The Departure of Jesus* (n. 5), p. 177: the authorial voice and the dedication help to manage the move from the real world to the story world, but neither reappears at the end.

more subtle narrative clues to the coherence of the composition as a whole.

But there are other means readers can use to determine the overall narrative coherence of a text. "Paratext" is not limited to formal, externally bounded prefaces of the type we find in Lk 1,1-4[10]. Some at least of the pragmatic functions associated with the authorial or editorial apparatus which constitutes the "peritext" of the modern book[11] can in antiquity be found in the narrative itself, especially in its opening and closing scenes. A number of recent studies have analysed the pragmatic functions of Gospel beginnings along these lines, and have stressed the importance of the interpretative framework provided by the narrative prologues and epilogues to the Gospels[12].

In this sense, we could look not to the authorial *preface* to Luke's work (Lk 1,1-4) but to its narrative *prologue,* by which I mean the first four chapters of the Gospel. In his important 1987 study of the Ascension narratives, Mikéal Parsons has explored the links between the ending of the Gospel and Luke's narrative prologue (Lk 1–4) in terms of Uspensky's analysis of the "framing" patterns created by the beginnings and endings of narratives[13]. Joseph B. Tyson also uses Uspensky's analysis to examine the relationship of the birth narratives (Luke 1–2) to the rest of the Gospel narrative[14]. Neither of these has attempted to read the end of Acts as a framing device in relation to the narrative prologue of the Gospel, however: most important in this respect is a study of J. Dupont[15], in which Dupont notes a number of links between

10. Even in antiquity, as GENETTE insists, "il n'existe pas, et... il n'a jamais existé, de texte sans paratexte" (*Seuils,* p. 9). Much of this "paratext" was supplied for ancient books by the social context in which they were encountered: L.C.A. ALEXANDER, *Ancient Book-Production and the Circulation of the Gospels,* in R.J. BAUCKHAM (ed.), *The Gospels for All Christians: Rethinking the Gospel Audiences,* Grand Rapids, MI, Eerdmans, 1997, pp. 71-111.
11. GENETTE, *Seuils,* p. 8.
12. Cf. the articles in D.E. SMITH (ed.), *How Gospels Begin,* in *Semeia* 52 (1991); F.J. MATERA, *The Prologue as the Interpretative Key to Mark's Gospel,* in *JSNT* 34 (1988) 3-20; A. STEINER, *Le lien* (n. 5).
13. PARSONS, *Departure* (n. 5), ch. 3. He also examines the links between the ending of Acts and Acts ch. 1, but notes that, while numerous, these links are "rather weak" (p. 159).
14. J.B. TYSON, *The Birth Narratives and the Beginning of Luke's Gospel,* in *How Gospels Begin* (n. 12), pp. 103-120.
15. J. DUPONT, *La conclusion des Actes et son rapport à l'ensemble de l'ouvrage de Luc,* in J. KREMER (ed.), *Les Actes des Apotres. Traditions, rédaction, théologie* (BETL, 48), Gembloux, Duculot – Leuven, University Press, 1978, pp. 359-404. Subsequent to the presentation of this paper I was alerted to the important study of G. WASSERBERG, *Aus Israels Mitte – Heil für die Welt. Eine narrativ-exegetische Studie zur Theologie des Lukas* (BZNW, 92), Berlin, de Gruyter, 1998. Wasserberg highlights the significance of

Acts 28 and Lk 3–4. I hope here to build on and extend Dupont's insightful analysis.

II. THE ENDING OF ACTS

Dupont supplies a detailed narrative analysis of the ending of Acts, and makes the following fundamental points: (a) Acts 28,30-31 should be treated as summary, not climax; (b) The core scene of ch. 28 runs from 28,17 to 28,28 and consists of a staged debate between Paul and the members of the Jewish community in Rome, ending with Paul's "last words" at 28,26-28; (c) 28,11-16 is a narrative link passage describing the final stages of the journey to Rome and introducing the dramatic location for the book's final scene.

I would argue in addition, however, that Acts 27,1–28,16 cannot be left out of account in any consideration of the ending of Acts. The shipwreck and Melita narrative is of course a substantial "scene" in its own right[16], and contains many significant narrative details which cannot be brought into consideration in this paper. However, it is above all else a journey *to Rome*, and as such adds to the decided effect of closure – not necessarily climax – which marks the ending of Acts. In this sense I would designate the whole of the last two chapters of Acts (27–28) as the book's narrative epilogue, culminating in a final scene in Rome (28,17-28) and topped off by a two-verse summary (28,30-31).

In this final scene of Acts, four obvious narrative features can be identified: its geographical location is Rome; its dramatic scenario is a debate within the Jewish community; its hermeneutical framework is provided by a long quotation from Isaiah; and it foregrounds the act of proclamation (witness) and the person of the proclaimer.

1. *The Geographical Location*

The geographical framework of Acts is one of its most striking features: the story ends in Rome, emphatically not where it started, either

---

Acts 28,16-31 "als hermeneutischer Schlüssel zum Gesamtverständnis von Lk-Act" (ch. IV), and notes hermeneutical links with Simeon's prophecy (ch. VI) and the Nazareth episode (ch. VII).

16. For the terminology, cf. T. HÄGG, *Narrative Technique in Ancient Greek Romances. Studies of Chariton, Xenophon Ephesius, and Achilles Tatius* (Acta Instituti Atheniensis Regni Sueciae, 8), Stockholm, Almqvist & Wiksell, 1971, ch. 2. Travel can either form a significant "scene" in its own right or function simply as a "summary" link between scenes in a narrative. The shipwreck of Acts 27–28 clearly falls into the former category.

in the Gospel or in Acts itself. The start of ch. 27 signals a distinctive new direction within the complex journeyings of Acts, marked by a formal decision (ἐκρίϑη), by the sudden reappearance of Paul's journeying companions (27,1 "we"), and by the solemn evocation of the nautical ceremonies of embarkation and coastal voyaging (27,2-5). The whole pace of the narrative changes as the cerebral cut and thrust of forensic drama is left behind and the narrator (and perforce the reader) becomes immersed in the slow details of cargoes and harbours, of wind-directions and sails, dinghies and anchors, and finally drawn into the nightmare of storm and shipwreck. Parsons notes how the final scene of Acts has "a static texture which may assist the reader in entering into and exiting from a story which is momentarily stationary"[17]; but Luke has been slowing his narrative down all through ch. 27, as Paul's ship tacks laboriously against the wind along the coast of Asia[18]. The original motivation for the voyage is almost forgotten in all this, except by Paul himself, who reports the assurance of an angelic vision to the effect that "you must stand before Caesar" (27,24).

This superbly (and realistically) detailed voyage description adds to a real sense of climax when the party finally, after a three-month delay in Melita, set out for the last stages of the journey to Rome (28,11). Once again the redundant detail of ships, winds, ports of call, and intermediate stages on the road (three days 28,12; two days 28,13; seven days 28,14) slows the narrative down and builds the tension. There is a real sense of arrival in 28,14-16, with the double announcement (28,14 "And that's how[19] we got to Rome"; 28,16 "When we entered Rome") separated by the emergence from the city of a church delegation which ceremoniously escorts Paul along the final stages of the Via Appia[20].

The narrative significance of this westward voyage is not always appreciated. Luke has been at pains up to this point to centre his story on Jerusalem even against the grain of his source-material (so far as we can conjecture). Jesus' story is given an additional Jerusalem focus in the opening chapters of the Gospel[21], and Luke's Paul visits Jerusalem more

17. PARSONS, *Departure* (n. 5), p. 159.
18. 27,4; cf. 27,7 βραδυπλοοῦντες ... μὴ προσεῶντος ἡμᾶς τοῦ ἀνέμου.
19. Note the emphatic (and summative) force of καὶ οὕτως in 28,14: not just "And so", but "And that's how...". Taken this way, there is no redundancy with Ὅτε δὲ εἰσήλϑομεν εἰς Ῥώμην in 28,16.
20. "'Απάντησις appears to have been a sort of technical term for the official welcome extended to a newly arrived dignitary by a deputation which went out from the city to greet him and escort him for the rest of his way": F. F. BRUCE, *The Acts of the Apostles: Greek Text with Introduction and Commentary*, Grand Rapids, MI, Eerdmans, ³1990, p. 536.
21. Lk 1,5-23; 2,22-38.41-51.

often than we would have expected from the Epistles[22]. Luke uses
Jerusalem to create a novel-like outward-and-return pattern to the journeys of Peter, Paul, and the other apostles in Acts, culminating in Paul's
long-drawn-out final journey to Jerusalem (Acts 20–21), which so strikingly parallels Jesus' final journey to Jerusalem to imprisonment and
death[23]. Structurally, then, the last two chapters of Acts form an odd,
almost anti-climactic coda to the narrative, an additional voyage outside
the expected *nostos*-pattern, and this gives the book an unexpectedly
open-ended structure. Luke has of course been at pains to stress that this
ending, though it might be unexpected to the reader, was by no means
unexpected to Paul – and, more importantly, that it was part of the
divine plan for the apostle[24].

But in what sense is Rome the proper ending for the narrative as a
whole? Many generations of exegetes[25] have taken the narrative's ending in Rome as a fulfilment of the task laid on the apostles at Acts 1,8:
though Rome can at best be only a representative symbol for "the end of
the earth", alongside the implied voyages of the Ethiopian of Acts 8 and
the other unnamed travellers of Acts 2. But does it make sense to regard
Rome as "the end of the earth" at all? Acts provides some evidence that
Luke is working, at least in part, with a mental map which entails a
reversal of the geographical perspectives of the Greco-Roman reader: cf.
especially Acts 2,9-11, where Rome is one of the most distant points on
the circumference of a Jerusalem-centred compass rose[26]. PsSol 8,16
suggests that for some first-century readers at least, Rome was at "the
end of the earth". In this sense the voyage of Acts 27 can be read within
the genre of exotic voyages, but with a reversal of the usual Greco-
Roman perspective which tends to locate the exotic in the east. It takes
Paul and his companions decisively away from Syria-Palestine and the

22. Cf. R. JEWETT, *Dating Paul's Life*, London, SCM, 1979, p. 86: "Luke's insertion
of extra Jerusalem journeys causes irreducible pressures.... the traditional compromises
between the ascertainable data and the Lukan framework of Jerusalem journeys are all
unworkable".
23. L.C.A. ALEXANDER, *"In journeyings often" : Voyaging in the Acts of the Apostles
and in Greek Romance*, in C.M. TUCKETT (ed.), *Luke's Literary Achievement: Collected
Essays*, Sheffield, Academic Press, 1995, pp. 17-49, esp. 23-24 and fig. 3.
24. Acts 19,21; 23,11.
25. Cf. BENGEL's representative comment, cited in BRUCE, *Acts* (n. 20), p. 543: "Vic-
toria Verbi Dei: Paulus Romae, apex evangelii, Actorum finis.... Hierosolymis coepit,
Romae desinit. Habes, Ecclesia, formam tuam: tuum est, servare eam, et depositum cus-
todire".
26. ALEXANDER, *"In journeyings often"* (n. 23), p. 30 and fig. 9; J. M. SCOTT, *Luke's
Geographical Horizon*, in D.W.J. GILL & C. GEMPF (eds.), *The Book of Acts in Its First
Century Setting*. II. *Graeco-Roman Setting*, Grand Rapids, MI, Eerdmans, 1994, pp. 483-
544, esp. 496-499.

coastlands of the Aegean, narrowly escaping the legendary terrors of Syrtis (27,17) and driven by the forces of nature across the stormy and chaotic wastes of the Ionian sea[27]. Landfall, after such a voyage, is predictably exotic: a bay, a beach, an island unrecognisable even to the experienced sailors (27,39). Given the symbolic significance of "the islands" in biblical geography, it is not unreasonable to suggest that readers might see this as a rather subtly-hinted fulfilment of the commission of Acts 1,8. This island turns out rather prosaically to have a name (28,1), but it is still peopled by "barbarians" (28,2: the only βάρ-βαροι in the whole of Acts), who, like the Lycaonians of 14,11, show a satisfying readiness to attribute divine status to the apostle (28,6).

But it is not so easy to be confident that the voyage's final destination, Rome, has this symbolic significance. After the romantic thrills of the shipwreck it is almost an anti-climax to find that Melita has a "first man" with the very Roman name of Publius (28,7) and that one can pick up an Alexandrian grain-ship wintering on the other side of the island (28,11). And the onward journey to Rome breathes an atmosphere which is progressively less, rather than more, exotic: "brothers" greet the party at Puteoli (28,14), more "brothers" come out to meet them from Rome, and the naming of the final, local stages of the road, Apii Forum and Tres Tabernae, has almost an air of homecoming (28,15)[28]. The names themselves (well known on the itineraries of the Roman road system) are a reminder that from a Roman perspective, Rome was not the end but the centre of the earth, with a central milepost from which all the roads of the empire radiated out[29].

2. The Central Dramatic Scenario of the Final Chapter of Acts: Not the City of Rome but the Divided Jewish Community

I have already noted Dupont's important distinction here between the two-verse "summary" of 28,30-31 and the carefully-constructed final

27. The fearsome reputation of this stretch of sea can be gauged from the novelists: cf. Chariton, *Callirhoe*, III.3.9-12; III.5.1-9; VIII.4.10; VIII.6.1; Xenophon of Ephesus, *Ephesiaca*, V.1.

28. Contrast Athens (Acts 17), where Paul visits the city like a tourist.

29. The Antonine Itinerary (107,3-4) lists *Tres Tabernae* and *Apii Forum* as the second and third stations on the *Via Appia*, working outwards from the city (O. CUNTZ, *Itineraria Romana*, I, Stuttgart, Teubner, 1990). There are other "Three Taverns" elsewhere in the system: cf. 318,3 and 329,9 (Macedonia); 617 (Gallia Cisalpina). Dio Cassius 54.8.4 records that a golden milestone was erected in the Forum in 20 B.C.E., symbolizing "[Rome's] position as centre of the world: it was engraved with the distances from the principal cities of the empire to the gates of Rome": M.T. GRIFFIN, *Urbs Roma, Plebs and Princeps*, in L.C.A. ALEXANDER (ed.), *Images of Empire* (JSOT SS, 122), Sheffield, Academic Press, 1991, pp. 19-46, here 20. SCOTT, *Luke's Geographical Horizon* (n. 26), p. 541, also argues that Rome is not "the end of the earth" for Luke.

"scene" of 28,16-28. These two elements point in different directions, one forward, one back.

The final summary of vv. 30-31 points forward to some unnarrated and undefined conclusion beyond the bounds set by the narrative. It leaves a number of questions unanswered: what happened after "the whole two years"? How long did Paul remain in the essentially transitional phase[30] implied by verse 30? How long did the lack of opposition (negatively construed: ἀκωλύτως) last? These unanswered questions create a forward-looking cluster in the reader's mind along with certain events anticipated in earlier stages of the narrative, like Paul's standing before Caesar (27,24) and his death (implied in 20,25 and 20,38). As unfulfilled prophecies, these are themselves an important factor in the open-ended effect of the conclusion of Acts. But the final summary is doubly open-ended in that it leaves the apostle, despite the uncertainties surrounding his personal future, engaged in "unhindered" evangelisation which implies (although it does not narrate) the future fulfilment of Paul's last prophecy in 28,28: "They will listen".

But the more substantial final scene which precedes this (28,17-28) is harder to configure as a climax to the career of Paul the missionary. Paul is certainly not a church-founder in this scene: Luke has taken pains to tell the readers (quite unnecessarily) that there are already "brothers"[31] in Italy, both in Puteoli and in Rome. The stress in ch. 28 is not so much on preaching the Gospel to the Romans (contrast the Athens scene of Acts 17) as on an ongoing debate within the divided Jewish community. This is the forum before which Paul presents his own last *apologia* and a final exposition of the Gospel message before turning his attention "to the Gentiles" (28,28). The dramatic scenario of the Jewish community is of course familiar throughout Acts, but it is formalised in an unusually careful and explicit manner in 28,17-22. Note especially the neutral, objective tones of the community leaders in 28,21-22: "But we desire to hear from you what your views are; for with regard to this sect, we know that everywhere it is spoken against". Paul's own relationship with this community is underlined in his own opening words (v. 17

30. Ἐν ἰδίῳ μισθώματι: Luke's choice of words here emphasizes that Paul's residence in Rome was "at his own expense", i.e. not in a public prison; but the noun (which normally means "contract", "hire", or "rent") also underlines the transitional nature of the residence.

31. Most commentators assume these were Christians, though Paul also addresses his fellow-Jews as "brothers" in 28,17 and elsewhere (see next note). More significant, I suspect, is that Luke takes no trouble to clarify the point: either it is not important, or perhaps better the ambivalence of the relationship between the Nazarene sect and the parent body is precisely what he needs to maintain at this stage in the book.

ἄνδρες ἀδελφοί), a formula which has occurred throughout Acts[32] and which also hints at the formal address to a civic assembly familiar from Greek rhetoric. Note also that the final state of the community which Luke chooses to highlight (using the classical οἱ μέν ... οἱ δέ formula, another classic device for describing tensions within the body politic) is not simply disbelief but division: "Some were convinced by what he said, while others disbelieved. So they departed, in a state of disharmony" (vv. 24-25 ἀσύμφωνοι δὲ ὄντες).

3. *The Hermeneutical Framework: The Extended Quotation from Isaiah ch. 6 (28,26-27)*

The foregrounding of this quotation in the final scene of Acts (where, significantly, it forms the core of Paul's last recorded words) is part of a coherent pattern throughout the two-volume work which establishes the Jewish Scriptures (Luke quotes the text here in its LXX-form) as the hermeneutical framework for understanding not only the Jesus-story itself (cf. Lk 24), but also the adventures of those who fulfil Jesus' command to act as "witnesses".

This particular text from Isaiah ch. 6 figures prominently in early Christian hermeneutics as a key to understanding the Gospel's lack of success within the Jewish community[33]. It is already firmly embedded in the synoptic tradition as part of what B. Lindars calls the "apologetic of response", and is quoted at some length in the interpretation of the Parable of the Sower at Mark 4,12 (par. Matt 13,14-15; Lk 8,10), more briefly at Mark 8,17-18 (applied to the disciples' failure to understand), and again in a more general context at John 12,39-40, where it is part of an extended editorial reflection on the unbelief of "the Jews". What is interesting for our purposes is that Luke, although he includes the citation in his Sower narrative (Lk 8,4-15) cuts it down to the briefest possible compass (unlike Matthew, who gives it in a longer form than Mark). Acts 28,25b, moreover, in Lindars' words, "bears a close similarity to the way Mark has introduced another quotation which is very relevant to the same issue (Mark 7.6)" (p. 165). In both cases it is not unreasonable to conclude (as Lindars does) that "Luke has been saving up this quotation as the climax to the repeated

---

32. Acts 1,16; 2,29.37; 7,2; 13,15.26.38; 15,7.13; 22,1; 23,1.6. The formula is used indiscriminately in address to audiences within the church and within the Jewish community.

33. B. LINDARS, *New Testament Apologetic. The Doctrinal Significance of the Old Testament Quotations*, London, SCM Press, 1961, *passim,* esp. pp. 159-167, 254-255.

theme that Paul was opposed by the Jews, but found a better hearing amongst the Gentiles"[34]. If it is the case that the citation has been "saved up" for the end of Acts (i.e. displaced from its synoptic context), we have a *prima facie* reason for taking very seriously the idea of a *prospective* unity for Luke's two volumes (authorial intent): though it should also be noted that, in Lindars' analysis, the Marcan application of the text to the parables is almost certainly the latest in the hermeneutical sequence, and Luke's use of the text in Acts corresponds to a logically earlier stage[35].

4. *The Act of Proclamation and the Proclaimer*

Although the implied focus of the debate (and of Paul's preaching) is Jesus and "the Kingdom of God" (28,23.31), the actual topic foregrounded in the text is the act of proclamation itself and the person of the proclaimer (28,17 ἐγώ). It is no accident, I believe, that Luke uses a variety of words to describe the content of Paul's preaching in ch. 28: "the kingdom of God" (28,23 and 28,31); "about Jesus from both the law of Moses and the prophets" (28,23); "the things to do with the Lord Jesus Christ" (28,31). These terms underline the catholicity of Paul's preaching, and also its continuity with the preaching of the Jerusalem apostles and of Jesus himself: cf. esp. Acts 1,3; Lk 24,27; 24,44. The verbs used are equally varied. Within the Jewish community, verbs of debate and persuasion are used (28,23 διαμαρτυρόμενος, πείθων), recalling the many scenes in Acts where the apostles (and especially Paul) have been depicted in argumentative mode: neither of these terms is used in an evangelistic sense in the Gospel[36]. In the final summary, however, κηρύσσων τὴν βασιλείαν τοῦ θεοῦ (28,31) takes us right back through Paul's own summary of his life's work (20,25) to the Gospel directives to the apostles (Lk 9,2; 24,47; cf. Acts 10,42) and

---

34. LINDARS, *Apologetic*, pp. 164, 166. Cf J. DUPONT, *Le salut des Gentils et la signification théologique du Livre des Actes*, in *NTS* 6 (1960) 132-155.

35. LINDARS, *Apologetic*, p. 18: "This example is especially instructive, because the sequence of interpretation is the direct opposite of the presumed order in which the books themselves were written. John preserves the oldest application, Acts the second, and Mark the latest! This does not mean that our estimate of the dates when these books were written must now be radically revised. But it does provide a warning not to evaluate a book by its date alone, for a later book may preserve more primitive ideas. The shift of application shows the logical sequence in the development of thought".

36. Διαμαρτυρόμενος: cf. Acts 2,40 (Peter); 8,25 (Peter and John); 10,42 (Peter and thy other apostles); 18,5 (Paul); 20,21.24 (Paul); 23,11 (Paul). The only occurrence of the verb in the Gospels is at Lk 16,28, where it is used of the brothers of Dives. – πείθων: cf. Acts 18,4; 19,8; 26,28. The passive (which has a wide semantic range) also occurs in the very Lucan parable of Dives and Lazarus (Lk 16,31).

behind them to the proclamation of the Baptist (Lk 3,3; Acts 10,37) and of Jesus himself (Lk 4,18-19; 8,1). Διδάσκων (28,31) also echoes terminology used earlier of Paul himself (often in a church or synagogue context), but even more of the activities of the Jerusalem apostles in the early part of Acts, and very characteristically of Jesus (cf. Acts 1,1)[37]. There seems to be a deliberately resumptive air about this terminology, drawing together the threads of the proclamation right back through Paul's argumentative career to the preaching of the apostles and ultimately to Jesus and the Baptist.

But although the last chapter of Acts tells us quite a lot about Paul's proclamation of Jesus, it does not show us much of that proclamation. Paul's recorded words in the final scene (there are none in the final summary) are not about Jesus but about the message and its reception (28,26-27) and about the messenger himself (28,17-20). It is Paul who is the focus of vv. 17-20, right from the opening ἐγώ: "I have done nothing against the people or the ancestral customs; I was handed over bound into the hands of the Romans; they judged me to have done nothing worthy of death; I was compelled to appeal to Caesar; I had no accusation to bring against my race; it is for the hope of Israel that I am bound like this". This is an extension of Paul's lengthy *apologia* before the bar of the Jewish community, an appendix to the debate which has occupied most of chs. 21–26: it is surely significant that this is the apologetic message Luke chooses to record in Rome, rather than an *apologia* before a Roman tribunal[38]. The reply of the community leaders has the same focus (περὶ σοῦ twice in v. 21; παρὰ σοῦ ἀκοῦσαι ἃ φρονεῖς in v. 22), and then moves on to the messenger's group affiliation: "for about this sect, it is known to us that it is spoken against everywhere" (v. 22). As in the forensic speeches, the messenger's self-defence slides neatly into an exposition of the message (v. 23); but what Luke foregrounds, by the direct speech he assigns to Paul's final "word" (v. 25 ῥῆμα ἕν) is not the discourse of salvation itself but a debate about that discourse and its reception. This is the phenomenon for which Paul invokes the authority of the Holy Spirit expressed in the words of the prophet (v. 25). It is not only the Jesus event that can be persuasively argued from Scripture (v. 23), but the events of its proclamation and

37. Διδάσκων: cf. Lk 4,15.31; 5,3.17; 6,6; 13,10.22.26; 20,1; Acts 4,2.18; 5,21.25.28.42. Missing in Acts 28 are the "gospel"-words common elsewhere in Acts (εὐαγγελίζομαι, εὐαγγέλιον: cf. 5,42; 8,4; 14,7; 17,18).
38. L.C.A. ALEXANDER, *The Acts of the Apostles as an Apologetic Text,* in M.J. EDWARDS, M. GOODMAN, C. ROWLAND (eds.), *Jewish and Christian Apologetic in the Graeco-Roman World*, Oxford, University Press, 1999, pp. 15-44, esp. 36-38.

reception: and this is the focus with which Luke chooses to close his two-volume work[39].

IV. The Prologue to the Gospel

All four of these features are foreshadowed in the extended narrative prologue with which Luke begins his Gospel (chs. 1–4).

1. *Rome as the Geographical Location for the Proclamation of the Word*

The introduction of the city of Rome as a geographical location is, as we have seen, a markedly new feature of the end of Acts, and in this sense signals a new theatre of action for the sect whose activities begin in Jerusalem (Acts 1) and which traces its origins back to the even more provincial setting of Galilee (Acts 1,11; 2,7; 10,37; 13,31). In a sense, Luke has already created a broader spatial frame for his story by highlighting the role of Jerusalem in the Gospel prologue (Lk 1,8; 2,22-39. 41-50; 4,9). But the importance of the Roman framework in which the whole narrative operates is also highlighted at the beginning of the Gospel. Not the city, but the empire and its interlocking hierarchies are foregrounded in the prologue, which includes the names of two reigning emperors: by contrast, only one reigning emperor is named in Acts[40]. This is seen most obviously in the formal multiple dating of Luke 3,1-2, which establishes a spatio-temporal location for the Gospel narrative by placing it within a series of Chinese boxes: the principate of Tiberius, the governorship of Pontius Pilate, the tetrarchates of Herod, Philip and Lysanias, and the highpriesthood of Annas and Caiaphas. It is worth noting that the event dignified with this ceremonial date – to which there is no parallel in Acts – is not (or not directly) the coming of Jesus but the coming of the prophetic Word: "the word of God came to John the son of Zechariah in the wilderness". But Luke has already (ironically, as I believe) created an imperial setting for the whole Jesus event by linking Jesus' birth with the empire-wide census of Augustus at 3,1ff. Note again that an awareness of regional and imperial hierarchies is assumed (3,2).

39. Cf. Dupont, *La conclusion* (n. 15), p. 371; Parsons, *Departure* (n. 5), p. 158: "Jesus is no longer the teacher, but the subject matter, no longer the proclaimer, but the proclaimed".

40. The Caesar to whom Paul appeals at 25,10-11 must be Nero, but he is never named. Claudius is named at 11,28 (prospectively) and at 18,2 (retrospectively): whatever chronological deductions we may make from these texts, neither sets out to provide a formal temporal framework for the narrative of Acts in the way that Lk 3,1-2 does for the Gospel.

2. *The Gospel Prologue*

The Gospel prologue already highlights the fact that the proclaimer of God's word may not find ready acceptance within the Jewish community. The Jewish community forms the dramatic scenario against which the whole action of Luke-Acts is played out: even on the "missionary voyages" in Acts, preaching to the Gentiles is subordinated to preaching and debates within the Jewish community. This element of internal dispute – the fact that the proclaimers of God's word may find themselves at odds with the leaders of God's people – is already foreshadowed in the narrative prologue to the Gospel. It is evident in the preaching of John the Baptist (more extensively reported in Luke than in Mark), which causes "debate" (3,15) and includes a warning against relying on descent from Abraham (3,7-9). It is evident again in the Nazareth scene (a Lucan creation: Lk 4,16-30), where Jesus incurs the wrath of his compatriots (and narrowly escapes death) by reminding them that God's word and God's healing power have in the past by-passed Israel and "been sent" (4,26) to Gentiles. For Dupont, who devotes several pages to an extensive analysis of this passage, "En esquissant le programme du ministère public de Jésus, cette page fait en même temps pressentir toute la suite du récit jusqu'à la conclusion que lui donne l'épisode de Rome"[41]. The crucial move here, as Dupont rightly notes, is the progression from Capernaum[42] as a potential object of local resentment in Lk 4,23 to the introduction of Naaman the Syrian and the widow of Sarepta as much more potent objects of patriotic resentment in vv. 25-27:

> Il est clair que ces versets font passer d'un horizon à un autre: d'une querelle de clocher, où les gens de Nazareth estiment que, comme πατρίς de Jésus, leur village a plus de droits que Capharnaüm, à la grosse question théologique de la situation privilégiée d'Israël par rapport aux nations païennes. Et on peut se demander si ce n'est pas précisément en raison de cette perspective plus large que Luc a voulu placer l'épisode de la synagogue de Nazareth au point de départ de la ministère de Jésus. Le texte-programme d'Is 61,1-2 aurait pu être cité dans n'importe quelle synagogue; mais c'est Nazareth qui fournissait l'occasion de jouer sur le double sens du mot πατρίς et de faire pressentir dans un incident local le sens d'un évolution dont le Livre des Actes racontera les grandes étapes[43].

The Nazareth episode can thus be read as a direct counterpoint to Paul's final word in Acts 28; and the echo is intensified by Paul's use of

---

41. Dupont, *La conclusion* (n. 15), pp. 396-402, here 396.
42. The introduction of Capernaum is itself an oddity, "une maladresse littéraire" (p. 397).
43. *Ibid.*, p. 400.
44. Other possible narrative echoes are Lk 4,30 and Acts 28,31 (Dupont, p. 397); Lk 4,17-18 and Acts 28,25 (linkage of Isaiah quotation with the Spirit).

"Israel" in 28,20[44]. But the striking phrase "the hope of Israel" has even stronger echoes in an earlier episode in the Lucan narrative prologue, bringing to mind the description of Simeon in Lk 2,25 as "waiting for the consolation of Israel". Even more clearly than the Nazareth episode, Simeon's song (Lk 2,29-32) prefigures the proclamation to the Gentiles.

There is no prediction here of final rejection: the hymns of Luke's first two chapters clearly configure the coming of Jesus in terms of "salvation" for "Israel" (both terms figure prominently in the hymns: cf. Lk 1,47.54.68-69.77; cf. also 24,21) and as a fulfilment of the promises to Abraham (1,55.73). Simeon holds out the hope that the light of God's salvation will produce the simultaneous effects of "revelation" for the Gentiles and "glory" for Israel. But there is a clear warning of pain and conflict to follow the revelation, both personal pain for Mary and conflict within the community ("Israel"). In this context it is surely significant, as Dupont observes, that the rare septuagintal word σωτήριον, which occurs only four times in the whole New Testament, turns up three times in the narrative prologue and epilogue to Luke-Acts: here in Simeon's song, in the extended Isaiah quotation at Lk 3,6 (see below), and again in Paul's final word at Acts 28,28.

3. *The Hermeneutical Framework*

The Gospel prologue, like the ending of Acts, is dominated by the hermeneutical framework provided by the Jewish Scriptures, and assigns a particularly important role to the prophet Isaiah. The link between the prophecies of Isaiah and the beginning of the Gospel goes back to Mark (Mark 1,2-3) and is clearly deeply embedded in the hermeneutical tradition of the early church[45]. Luke extends the use of this crucial intertext in two obvious ways in his Gospel prologue. In his account of the Baptist in ch. 3 he extends the Marcan quotation from Isaiah 40 to include the implicitly universalist promise, "All flesh shall see the salvation (τὸ σωτήριον) of our God" (Lk 3,6). He also introduces a further Isaiah quotation (Isaiah 61,1f) in the Nazareth scene at 4,18-19, in a position which assigns the prophecy a controlling role in the reader's interpretation of the Jesus event (see above). It thus comes as no surprise to find that an equally substantial quotation from Isaiah 6 (apparently "held over" from its Marcan context) is used to create an effective "last word" for Paul in Acts 28,27-28, completing the "framing" effect[46]. By using

45. Cf. K. STENDAHL, *The School of St. Matthew and Its Use of the Old Testament*, Lund, Gleerup, 1954, pp. 47-54.

46. Note that although there are other implicit allusions to Isaiah in Luke's work, the

this text here, in other words, Luke establishes a line of continuity which links Paul's activities in Rome right back to the Baptist's proclamation.

But the hermeneutical matrix which links the ending of Acts with the beginning of the Gospel is also established in more subtle ways. There are several significant lexical choices in Acts 28 which tie the final scene of Paul's life – despite its Roman setting – firmly into the framework of biblical history which has dominated Luke's narrative from the beginning. The link between Jesus and "Moses and the prophets" is stated explicitly at Acts 28,23 (echoing Lk 24); the importance of the prophets (cf. also 28,25) has been a consistent thread throughout the two-volume work. Paul's allusion to "the hope of Israel" (28,20) introduces an openly theological tone[47] which contrasts oddly with the studiedly neutral language of 28,17-22 (τῆς αἱρέσεως ταύτης). At one level, as I have argued, the use of "Israel" underlines Paul's links with the Jewish community; but as a political term (especially in Rome) it is anachronistic. "Israel" is essentially a theological term, tying Luke's story into biblical history: there is no place for it in the imperial hierarchies of Lk 3,1f. It is common, however, in the early chapters of Acts, and especially in the first four chapters of the Gospel, where it occurs nine times[48]; cf also 24,21, which underlines its hermeneutical role.

And there are also more subtle intertextual echoes, both with Isaiah and with other scriptural texts. Paul's use of the rare word τὸ σωτήριον at 28,28 sets up multiple intertextual links with a cluster of texts which speak of the "knowledge" of God's salvation "among the Gentiles" and at "all the bounds of the earth": cf. Ps 66,3 LXX and 97,3 LXX.

The citation of Isa 49,6 at Acts 13,47 reinforces the links between "salvation" (here σωτηρία) and "the end of the earth" with "light to the Gentiles" (φῶς ἐθνῶν). This latter is a key concept for the self-understanding of the apostle as it is presented in Acts: cf. especially 26,18, which picks up the theme of "light to the Gentiles" from Isaiah 42,7, where it is combined with the "eyes of the blind" motif (ἔδωκά σε εἰς διαθήκην γένους, εἰς φῶς ἐθνῶν ἀνοῖξαι ὀφθαλμοὺς τυφλῶν). But, as we have seen, both terms, "salvation" and "light to the Gentiles", are anticipated in the Gospel prologue in Simeon's song (Lk

only places where the prophet is named are at the end of Acts (Acts 28,25), in the Gospel prologue (Lk 3,4; 4,17), and in Acts 8,30.

47. For "hope", cf. esp. Acts 26,6-7: but is this really about resurrection? See also Lk 24,21. The noun does not occur in the Gospel.

48. Lk 1,16.54.68.80; 2,25.32.34; 4,25.27. All of these are Lucan uses without synoptic parallel, as is 24,21. The only occurrence of the term in Mk (apart from the scriptural quotation at 12,29) is at 15,32 (which Lk omits). Luke's other two uses are Q passages: Lk 7,9 par. Mt 8,10; Lk 22,30 par. Mt 19,28.

2,32)⁴⁹. In this context it is not without significance, I would suggest, that Luke stresses the perspicuity of Simeon's spiritual eyesight by the apparently redundant phrase οἱ ὀφθαλμοί μου in Lk 2,30. What after all would one use eyes for but to "see" (εἶδον)? This spiritual vision is something achieved by "all flesh" in Isa 40,5 (Lk 3,6) καὶ ὄψεται πᾶσα σὰρξ τὸ σωτήριον τοῦ θεοῦ. But the Isaiah 6 passage cited at the end of Acts makes it clear that it is possible to have "eyes" and yet fail to "see": and this is indeed the tragedy of the story Luke unfolds.

4. *The Proclaimer and the Proclaimed*

There is no question that Luke is committed to telling the story of Jesus at length and in detail in his two-volume work: even in Acts, the story is repeatedly retold in summary form in the apostolic witness. The bulk of Acts, though, focusses not so much on the story of Jesus as on the persons of the witnesses and on the act of witness itself, with all its dangers and internal contradictions. It is not difficult to read Luke-Acts as a diptych for which the Ascension narrative provides the hinge: before it comes the Gospel, predominantly devoted to Jesus; after it comes Acts, predominantly devoted to the apostles. This focus on the person of the proclaimer and the act of proclamation itself is, as we have seen, accentuated in the ending of Acts, where the overt focus of the text is very much on the person of Paul (vv. 17-22) and on the Gospel message itself and its reception (vv. 23-31).

But it is in many ways too simple to treat Luke-Acts as a diptych. If it is a diptych, it is at least a diptych with a substantial frame. We have already seen how Luke uses the prologue of the Gospel (partly building on Mark and Q, partly introducing his own material) to create a "framing narrative" for the whole two-volume story: and Acts' focus on the person of the proclaimer is in many ways foreshadowed here too. This is most obvious in the enhanced role given to John the Baptist in Lk 1–4. First of all, Luke concentrates his Baptist material in this section by moving back the story of John's imprisonment and telling it prospectively (but without explanation) before the baptism of Jesus (Lk 3,19-20). This creates some narrative oddities (e.g. Lk 9,7-9), but it allows Luke to telescope John's career and cast him as the "forerunner" to Jesus (Lk 7,28; 16,16) rather more effectively than the other evangelists: Luke's story implies that there is no overlap between the active career of John and that of Jesus. Yet it is hard to read this as a down-

---

49. Note also that ἄφεσιν ἁμαρτιῶν is echoed in Lk 1,77.

grading of John. Luke's Jesus gives him extensive coverage and warm commendation as "more than a prophet" (7,18-35; cf. 20,3-8); and the narrator adds his own comment, in words which imply that rejection of John's baptism is tantamount to rejecting "the purpose of God" (7,29-30). And although John's action of baptizing Jesus is downplayed in the baptism narrative itself (Lk 3,21), his preaching (dignified with the term εὐηγγελίζετο: 3,18) is given increased coverage in 3,7-18; and by juxtaposing this immediately with John's imprisonment (3,19-20), Luke creates another typological parallel between the witness of the forerunner and that of the apostles who suffer a similar fate.

Most remarkably of all, John has his own birth narrative in Lk, culminating in a hymn which highlights his role as "prophet" (1,76-79); and this prophetic role is emphasised by the full prophetic formula which marks the start of his ministry and begins the Gospel narrative proper: "The word of God came to John the son of Zechariah in the wilderness" (Lk 3,1-2). His status as proclaimer is authenticated by his miraculous birth (told in as much detail as the birth of Jesus: Lk 1,5-25. 57-80) and by an angelic announcement (Lk 1,13-17). It is also authenticated by the witness of the Holy Spirit, whose activity is prominent in these opening chapters but not elsewhere in the Gospel narrative. It is the Spirit who fills John "from his mother's womb" (Lk 1,15), and who inspires Elisabeth to recognise the nature of John's relationship with his cousin (Lk 1,41-45). It is the Spirit who inspires Zechariah to describe John's future role as forerunner (Lk 1,67-79).

John is not the only prophetic character in the prologue to Luke's Gospel. Zechariah and Elizabeth, Simeon and Anna are all in different ways singled out as inspired by the Holy Spirit (Lk 1,41.67; 2,25-26.36) to recognise and testify to the significance of Jesus' birth. These minor characters too can be seen as foreshadowing the prophetic witness to Jesus which is the main subject of Acts, and which receives its final vindication in Paul's last debate in Rome.

This focus on the messengers rather than the message is already hinted at in the Gospel preface (Lk 1,1-4). As I have noted elsewhere[50], it is remarkable how little Luke manages to convey, when speaking *in propria persona* in his explanatory peritext, about the subject-matter of his discourse. The name of Jesus is not mentioned in Luke's Gospel until 1,31 (contrast Mt 1,1 and Mk 1,1); the preface never speaks of God (contrast Jn 1,1). Instead we have the opaquely-coded phrase "the business fulfilled among us" (Lk 1,1), syntactically and pragmatically sub-

50. ALEXANDER, *Preface* (n. 7), pp. 113-114; *Preface to Acts* (n. 3), pp. 92-93.

ordinated to the activities of the "many" who have drawn up an account of this business (1,1 ἐπεχείρησαν ἀνατάξασθαι διήγησιν) and the "eyewitnesses and ministers of the word" who have passed it on in the form of tradition (1,2 παρέδοσαν). This second-order discourse ("un discours qui porte sur un discours", as Genette would put it; cf. above n. 4) is framed in its turn by a third-order discourse which foregrounds the activities of the observing and recording authorial self (1,3 παρ-ηκολουθηκότι, γράψαι) and of the inscribed reader (1,4 ἐπιγνῷς, κατηχήθης). None of this constitutes either a promise or a programme to narrate the story of the discourse alongside the discourse itself; but it does give us a hint that Luke has his attention fixed from the outset on the frame of Jesus' story (potentially, on its multiple frames!) as well as on the story itself.

IV. Conclusion
The Ending of Acts as Epilogue to Both Volumes

How should we assess the significance of these echoes? In particular, what do they mean for the question of unity? I would suggest four points for further consideration.

1. *Unity: Authorial and Prospective?*

Somewhat to my own surprise, this study has convinced me that a case can be made out for the proposition that Luke conceived his work from the outset as a two-volume set in which the Gospel story would be balanced and continued with stories of the apostles. I say, "at the outset" with reference purely to the sequence within the text as we have it: I do not pretend any privileged insight into the processes of composition, and would not presume to enter the debate about when and how the various parts of the narrative prologue to the Gospel assumed their present shape. It is not difficult to trace the development of this narrative pro-logue in reverse, as it were, working backwards from the core of the Marcan prologue which Luke expands into chs. 3–4, and then into the birth narratives – a development which makes sense as a logical pro-gression quite apart from any source-critical theories[51]. But what is important from my perspective – at least if I am right about the narrative echoes between the prologue and in the ending of Acts – is that the first four chapters of the Gospel have strong elements of narrative coherence

---

51. For a useful summary, cf. Tyson, *Birth Narratives* (n. 14), pp. 106-109.

with the ending of Acts, and that the two passages together may be thought of as a narrative frame, providing a prologue and epilogue to the whole two-volume work. If the prologue was added at a secondary stage in the composition of the Gospel, in other words, it was added with Acts in mind. But if these narrative links make any sense, we should also be prepared to allow the real possibility of strong *narrative* reasons for precisely some of the elements in the prologue which have been read as evidence for a source-critical view. This is especially true of the role of the Baptist, which I am arguing makes sense as a foreshadowing of the role of the proclaimers of the Gospel in Acts.

Whether we can move beyond the prologue to the Gospel as a whole is a different question. It is beyond the scope of this short paper to explore further links between Acts and the Gospel, and I have deliberately restricted myself in this study to trying to make sense of the beginning and ending of the two volumes. But, given the importance of beginnings and endings in narrative, it is worth remembering that the paratextual "threshold" (as Genette reminds us; cf. n. 4) is simply that, a point of no significance in itself except as the entry point to a narrative world: the more we can make unified sense of the narrative as it stands, the less need we have to resort to source criticism. In this context, the phenomenon of details which are apparently "held over" from the Gospel to Acts assumes a particular importance (though that can only be assessed fully in the context of a larger analysis of the phenomenon). The fact that Luke appears to have held over the full quotation of Isaiah 6 from Luke ch. 8 to the conclusion of Acts must at least be taken into consideration in that wider debate.

2. *Unity: Readerly and Retrospective?*

What is the effect of these narrative connections on the reader? Oddly enough, despite my (somewhat reluctant) conversion to authorial unity, I would argue that the nature of the echoes and foreshadowings I have identified precludes a strong view of *prospective* unity for the reader. There is no way the reader could *predict* the plot of the second volume from the prologue to the first as it stands: there are warnings of conflict and a hint of "light to the Gentiles", but these are slight indications in a complex narrative which is enthralling and colourful in its own right. The hints of conflict and tragedy in the prologue are hidden among its many prophetic utterances: they are there to be discovered with hindsight, but the prologue (like real life) is not constructed in such a deterministic way that the outcome could be predicted in advance.

Nevertheless, I would argue that there is sufficient *retrospective* narrative coherence to entitle us to speak of Luke's two-volume work as a unity from the reader's point of view. It is over-simple to equate coherence with predictability, especially within a complex literary narrative: we might in fact ascribe the greater literary art to a narrative whose outcome is not totally predictable in advance. In the ancient world, moreover (certainly with early Christian texts), we need to reckon with reading strategies rather more complex than that of the critic's "ideal reader", approaching the text *tabula rasa* and reading from front to back. The actual readers of Luke's work were almost certainly Christians themselves, reading in Greek, and knowing full well (whatever their own ethnic background) that the Gospel had in fact been preached to Gentiles as well as to Jews. Their prior knowledge of this state of affairs will inevitably rob the ending of Acts of some of its suspense: to paraphrase Acts 28,14, their reaction will be not so much, "So *that's* what happened in the end!" as "So *that's* how it happened!". The same prior knowledge may of course also account for Luke's failure to narrate what happened to Paul. The existence of such readers is in fact already presupposed by the preface, with its ambiguous ἡμῖν and its "retrospective" address to the already-instructed reader Theophilus[52]. Readers starting from this position are, we might say, already starting from the end of Acts: even without knowing the details of the story, they will read the beginning of the Gospel with the benefit of some kind of hindsight and may well therefore pick up some of Luke's hints at the outset.

The possibility of this kind of prior knowledge is, we might say, borrowing Genette's terminology, an aspect of the text's "epitext", now inaccessible to us but none the less real for that[53]. Its importance for the readers of ancient texts (who rarely expected the kind of detective-story suspense that is taken for granted by the readers of fiction today) has been underlined in a number of studies of classical and biblical texts[54].

52. A point made by B. USPENSKY, *A Poetics of Composition*, Berkeley, Univ. of California Press, 1973, p. 149 (cited from TYSON, *Birth Narratives*, pp. 110-111): "Temporal framing may be realized by the use at the beginning of a narrative of the retrospective point of view .... as an example we may cite the Gospel of Luke, which begins from a retrospective position with a direct address to Theophilus".

53. GENETTE, *Seuils* (n. 4), pp. 10-11, 316f: "Est épitexte tout élément paratextuel qui ne se trouve pas matériellement annexé au texte dans le même volume, mais qui circule en quelque sorte à l'air libre, dans un espace physique et sociale virtuellement illimité. Le lieu de l'épitexte est donc *anywhere out of the book,* n'importe où hors du livre".

54. Cf. MARGUERAT, *L'énigme* (n. 1), p. 4, n. 12; J. L. MAGNESS, *Sense and Absence. Structure and Suspension in the Ending of Mark's Gospel* (Semeia Studies), Atlanta, Scholar's Press, 1986. A similar point is made by E. Bowie on readers' knowledge of Apollonius of Tyana: E. BOWIE, *Philostratus: Writer of Fiction,* in J.R. MORGAN –

But there is another important aspect of retrospective narrative coherence which needs to be taken into account here, and that is the phenomenon of re-reading. "Most readers of the gospels," as Elizabeth Struthers Malbon points out, "are re-readers"; and (whether or not they are actually written last), this is one reason why beginnings as well as endings have a deeply retrospective nature: "The prologue represents a *Meta-reflexion,...* 'a deeply retrospective gesture', a 'postface'. Only from the perspective of the ending are the implications of the beginning fully understood – if they are ever fully understood"[55]. So for Matera, the privileged information given to the reader in the prologue to Mark's Gospel is still not sufficient by itself to unlock the mystery of Jesus' identity, but "must be supplemented by what is told in the rest of the narrative. Thus, by the end of the narrative the readers discover that they must integrate their knowledge of Jesus learned in the prologue with their knowledge of him learned in the light of the cross and resurrection"[56]. A more recent study of the Marcan prologue makes the point well:

> Le prologue de l'évangile de Marc se présente comme un pacte de lecture qui donne les moyens au lecteur[trice] de se situer dans la narration. Toutefois, le prologue et la suite de la narration entretiennent un rapport dynamique et doivent toujours à nouveau être relus l'un par l'autre.
> Ce système de renvoi semble comporter une forte dimension stratégique. Il invite à le lecteur[trice], dans une seconde lecture du texte, à porter une grande attention au jeu d'échos et d'annonces implicites que l'on peut percevoir entre le prologue et le corps du récit, et invite à l'interprétation[57].

The links between the prologue to Luke and the ending of Acts seem to work very much in this way: what we have here is not prediction, certainly not a "table of contents"[58], but the creation of a paratextual framework whose full significance will only emerge on re-reading.

3. *The Theological Script*

This invitation to re-read the prologue in the light of the ending of Acts – and vice-versa – has, it seems to me, potentially important implications for our reading of the theology of Luke's work, especially his view

R. Stoneman (eds.), *Greek Fiction: The Greek Novel in Context*, London, Routledge, 1994, pp. 181-199, esp. 193.
55. E.S. Malbon, *Ending at the Beginning: A Response*, in *How Gospels Begin* (n. 12), pp. 175-184, here 184, citing Kelber's essay in the same volume.
56. Matera, *Prologue* (n. 13), p. 4.
57. Steiner, *Le lien* (n. 5), p. 10.
58. *Ibid.*, p. 7 and n. 15.

of the theological relationship between Jew and Gentile at the end of Acts. I would concur with R. Tannehill's view that the tone in Acts 28 is properly understood as tragic rather than triumphalist[59]. If the reader is sent back from Acts 28 to re-read the Gospel prologue, it seems to me, this awareness of tragedy can only be enhanced. There is no hint there of triumphalism: even where Simeon's vision encompasses the prophecy of "revelation to the Gentiles", it is still paralleled with the promise of "glory to your people Israel". And what is the reader to make, on such a re-reading, of all the promises held out in Luke's opening chapters of "salvation" to Israel? Are these simply unfulfilled predictions? If so, it is to say the least inartistic of the narrator to redirect the reader's attention to them at the end of the story. I would suggest rather that Luke, writing in full awareness of the tragic dimension of the story of Israel's rejection of the Gospel, invites the reader both to contemplate the tragedy for what it is and to read it as a warning of the possibility of having eyes, yet failing to "see". There is also, perhaps, an invitation to do some theological reflection of the kind Paul undertakes in Romans 9–11: one solution to the problem of unfulfilled predictions may be to change the definition of God's people (cf. Rom 9,24-26)[60]. But Luke is writing narrative, not argument, and he does not present the reader with a single, unified solution to the problem. The mere fact that Luke's Paul, despite constant "last words" to "the Jews"[61], keeps going back to the Jewish community right up to the book's final scene, seems to dramatize the kind of ambivalence that Paul himself shows in Romans and elsewhere. A similar ambivalence is implicit in Luke's use of texts from Isaiah to provide a hermeneutical framework for the Gentile mission. And by redirecting the reader to the prologue, especially to the hymns of the infancy narrative (which are after all Lucan *Sondergut:* there was no traditional imperative to include this material), Luke seems deliberately to heighten the tension between the high hopes of his story's opening and the downbeat tragedy of its conclusion.

4. *Climax or Closure?*

To approach Luke's work, we have argued, the reader has to unwrap two successive layers of paratext: first the preface (Lk 1,1-4), then the lengthy and engrossing narrative prologue (Lk 1,5–4,30). One of the most important functions of paratext is to assist the passage of the reader

59. R. TANNEHILL, *Israel in Luke-Acts: A Tragic Story*, in *JBL* 104 (1985) 69-85.
60. J.T. SANDERS, *The Jews in Luke-Acts*, London, SCM, 1987, pp. 48-49.
61. Acts 13,45-48; 14,27; 18,6.

from the real world to the textual world at the beginning of the narrative, and back again to the real world at the end (cf. above, n. 5). The preface addresses this problem formally and directly: the author speaks in his own voice to the inscribed reader, using the conventions of academic prose to externalise his own project and describe it in neutral, objective third-order discourse. At Lk 1,5 he slips into the role of narrator, enveloping the Gospel story in thick swaddling-bands of biblical narrative style. The ἐγένετο ἐν ταῖς ἡμέραις Ἡρῴδου βασιλέως of Lk 1,5 is the equivalent of the "Once upon a time" of English folktale, a formal marker of the start of narrative time, while the multiple dating of Lk 3,1-2 marks a second beginning of a different kind, recalling the formulae used to tie the biblical prophecies into the events of world history. It is a slowly-paced opening which draws the reader gently into the narrative world of the Gospel, introducing a whole series of secondary characters who point up the significance of the main character well before he appears on the scene: only at 4,1 do we encounter the adult Jesus in person, and he does not speak until 4,4. But the effect of these preliminary encounters is similar to that of the Marcan prologue: before getting to the main text, the reader is forearmed with privileged information (much of it imparted with the divine sanction of vision, prophecy or angelic visitation) about the identity of the story's protagonist[62].

In what sense does the ending of Acts provide a counterpart to this framework, and how does Luke ease the reader's transition back to the world outside the text? The third-level discourse of the preface reappears briefly at the beginning of Acts, but it has no match at the end of either volume: in this sense (not unusually for ancient texts) the paratextual frame is incomplete. But if, as we have argued, the last two chapters of Acts form a kind of epilogue to the whole narrative, there is a complete narrative framework of prologue plus epilogue, and we should be able to identify in the ending of Acts similar transitional effects (either parallel or inverted) linking back into the real world of the reader.

In one way we might say that the whole of Acts forms a narrative bridge between the story of Jesus and the world of the reader. Acts begins on a mountain-top outside Jerusalem, with Jesus just departed into the clouds and two angels telling the disciples to turn their attention away from heaven (Acts 1,11) and (by implication) to get on with the earthly task they have been given (Acts 1,8). All the movement of the narrative from this point is downwards (from the mountain) and outwards (from Jerusalem), and whatever the timescale of the book's com-

62. TYSON, *Birth Narratives* (n. 14), pp. 107, 115-116.

position, the end point of Paul's journeys must be considerably closer to the time of the readers than its beginning. In strictly linear terms, of course, the beginning of the Gospel is even further away from the time of the readers (and the biblical style of the temporal markers at Lk 1,5 and 3,1-2 reinforces the impression of distance). In this sense the whole movement of Luke-Acts is from the unknown to the known, from the distant to the near: and this sense of temporal movement is strongly reinforced by the geographical movement of the book of Acts. The final chapters of the book, as we have seen, combine a strong outward movement with an odd sense of homecoming: outward, towards the periphery of the narrative map, crossing the uncharted and storm-tossed Ionian Sea to landfall on a barbarian island; and homecoming, back to familiar territory, as the party pick up the regular shipping lanes again and make their way up the Appian Way to be greeted by "brothers" in Rome. Whatever the actual location of Luke's readers, it seems likely that the book's final scenario in Rome is closer to their world than its opening scenes; and the bridging effect of this epilogue can only be aided by the ruthlessly pragmatic vocabulary of the final voyage[63].

The closest approach to the world of the reader, as I have argued above, comes in the preface, where the author addresses a representative reader directly and make it clear that what he narrates is tradition received (Lk 1,2). There is reassurance in this claim[64]: but there is also distancing, for Luke's words make it clear that he himself stands at one remove from the "business" he reports. Luke's story is mediated by tradents (reliable tradents, but tradents none the less), the "eyewitnesses and ministers of the word" who passed on the tradition to "us" (Lk 1,2). It is this intermediate group, the proclaimers, who form the subject of Acts: another bridge between the narrative world of the Jesus story and the world of the readers ("us"). This shift, as we have seen, is intensified in the final scene of Acts, and is foreshadowed in the prologue to the Gospel with the figure of the Baptist. But there is a difference. The Gospel prologue, like the prologue to Acts, is a place of vision, peopled with angels and open to direct revelation from God. In this sense too the movement of Acts is downward and outward, constantly further away from the mountain of revelation where Jesus speaks clearly and is visible (until the intervention of the cloud) to the disciples' eyes (Acts 1,9). It is,

---

63. Cf. further L.C.A. ALEXANDER, *Narrative Maps: Reflections on the Toponymy of Acts*, in M.D. CARROLL R. – D.J.A. CLINES – P.R. DAVIES (eds.), *The Bible in Human Society: Essays in Honour of John Rogerson* (JSOT SS, 200), Sheffield, Academic Press, 1995, pp. 17-57 esp. 43-45.
64. Cf. further ALEXANDER, *Preface* (n. 7), pp. 118-125.

as so often in biblical narrative, a movement from clarity to unclarity, from a moment of public vision to an ongoing journey into darkness. Here too the epilogue to Acts functions as a bridge back into the mundane realities of the readers' world: no angels, no heavenly voice, just the ongoing task of teaching and proclamation, and the tragedy of eyes and ears that fail to perceive the salvation sent by God (Acts 28,26-27). Paul invokes the authority of prophecy as a hermeneutical key to what is happening: but we have only Paul's word for it that the prophecy was inspired by the Holy Spirit (Acts 28,25), and no consoling angel or heavenly voice sounds out from behind the cloud to tell us whether he was right.

In this sense Acts is indeed an open-ended narrative, opening out into a world where even the words of apostles are the subject of doubt and debate. On the one hand, the attentive reader has already had sufficient reassurance from the previous chapter as to Paul's right to speak on the Spirit's behalf. Nothing in the shipwreck narrative, strictly speaking, is miraculous: storms, winds, waves and the behaviour of the ship's crew are all natural phenomena. Yet one character stands out clearly from the narrative as a man whose courage and vision are vindicated by events. Paul predicts the storm, keeps his nerve, and advises the ship's captain – all in obedience to his own angelic vision (27,23). This is still in the world of private vision, carefully contextualised for a pagan audience: but it cannot but impress us as readers, just as it impresses the characters, when everything turns out just as Paul predicts. To readers well-versed in the grammar of hellenistic shipwreck narratives, the moral is clear: this is a man unjustly accused, vindicated by the God whom he serves (28,4-6)[65]. To readers who can place Luke's story within its biblical matrix, the episode has another dimension. The only comparable sea-story in the Hebrew Bible is the story of Jonah, who runs away from God (and from his missionary vocation) and gets his ship into trouble as a result. Paul, travelling in obedience to his own missionary calling, has the opposite effect: the ship on which he is a passenger owes its salvation to him (27,24). So Paul's vindication, for all its naturalistic clothing, cannot really be in doubt; yet it is subordinated, in the final scene, to a Paul immersed once again (as his readers will be) in the entirely human and open-ended activities of debate and "persuasion". I conclude with a citation from Genette, the last words in fact, of

65. Cf. the plea of the pirate Theron in Chariton, *Callirhoe* III.4.9-10, "I alone was saved because never in my life have I done anything wrong"; or Lucian's shipwrecked sailors, "not only unfortunate but dear to the gods" (*On Salaried Posts in Great Houses*, 1).

his *Seuils*: "Aussi le discours sur le paratexte doit-il ne jamais oublier qu'il porte sur un discours qui porte sur un discours, et que le sens de son objet tient à l'objet de ce sens, qui est encore un sens. Il n'est de seuil qu'à franchir" (see above n. 4). Luke's paratext, I am now convinced, provides with the prologue a carefully constructed *entrée* into the narrative world, a world where prophets and angels are always on hand to point up the significance of the encounter with Jesus. But his epilogue suggests that he has taken equal care to negotiate the voyage back to the everyday world where the rest of us live, a world where prophets and angels have receded back into a mythical past, but where the more mundane and open-ended tasks of teaching and persuasion continue "unhindered".

Department of Biblical Studies   Loveday C.A. ALEXANDER
University of Sheffield
Sheffield S10 2TN, UK

WHERE DOES THE BEGINNING OF ACTS END?

There have been numerous proposals for delimiting the 'beginning' of Acts, by which I mean the section which is Luke's 'introduction' to the book. This paper outlines some representative proposals, identifies key themes in the first two chapters of Acts which echo emphases of Luke's Gospel and/or announce issues to be developed more fully in Acts, and considers the function of Acts 1–2 in the light of these discoveries.

1. *Proposals*

At least six different delimitations of Luke's introduction have been proposed in twentieth-century scholarship, namely 1,1-5; 1,1-8; 1,1-11; 1,1-14; 1,1-26; 1,1–2,41 and 1,1–2,47. We shall briefly examine the arguments of typical proponents of each view.

1,1-5 is often suggested as the "prologue" or "preface" to Acts[1]. Formally, these verses (or vv. 1-2) appear to be the "preface" of the whole book – although they lack a clear closure formula to indicate the end of the preface[2]. Marshall[3] argues that, since vv. 1-5 are largely recapitulation of the content of the Gospel and fresh material begins at v. 6, vv. 1-5 constitute Luke's introduction. However, v. 8 is recapitulation of the statement in Luke 24,47-49 concerning the church's mission being empowered by God, and vv. 9-11, which report Jesus' departure, are (at

---

1. R.B. RACKHAM, *The Acts of the Apostles* (WC), London, Methuen, 1904, p. cix; I.H. MARSHALL, *The Acts of the Apostles: An Introduction and Commentary* (TNTC), Leicester, IVP, 1980, p. 55; J. MUNCK, *The Acts of the Apostles* (AB), New York, Doubleday, 1967, pp. 4f; D.J. WILLIAMS, *Acts* (NIBC, 5), Peabody, MA, Hendrickson, 1990, p. 1 (with reservations); R.N. LONGENECKER, *Acts* (EBC), Grand Rapids, Zondervan, 1995, p. 48 (with reservations).

2. L.C.A. ALEXANDER, *The Preface to Acts and the Historians*, in B. WITHERINGTON (ed.), *History, Literature and Society in the Book of Acts*, Cambridge, University Press, 1996, pp. 73-103 (esp. pp. 82f), contrasts 2 Macc 2,19-32, which has the closure formula, "At this point therefore let us begin our narrative, without adding any more to what has already been said; for it would be foolish to lengthen the preface while cutting short the history itself". See further her discussion of the demarcation of other ancient prefaces in *The Preface to Luke's Gospel: Literary Convention and Social Context in Luke 1.1-4 and Acts 1.1* (SNTS MS, 78), Cambridge, University Press, 1993, pp. 30f, 93, 149, 152, 155, 158, 161f.

3. MARSHALL, *Acts* (n. 1), p. 55 in agreement with F.F. BRUCE, *The Acts of the Apostles*, Leicester, Apollos, 1990, p. 102.

least to some extent) recapitulation of Luke 24,50-53[4], and so Marshall's argument is not conclusive.

1,1-8 is favoured by Haenchen[5], who sees vv. 6-8 as going straight into the material contained in the new book, rather than providing an outline of what is to follow (which might be expected in the form of a δέ-clause to answer the opening μέν-clause in v. 1). He states that ancient writers could do this (although without citing any examples), and argues that in any case v. 8 provides an outline of the contents of the book which follows in the form of a promise by the risen Jesus. Further, vv. 6-8 have thematic links with vv. 2-5 (e.g. Jesus' presence with the disciples, the kingdom, the promise of the Spirit) and the construction μὲν οὖν (v. 6) is regularly used in Acts for a new section which is quite closely linked with the preceding section[6].

However, the separation of vv. 6-8 from vv. 9-11 seems artificial, since the disciples are gathered in v. 6 not only to have the question in v. 6b answered, but also to witness Jesus' ascension (vv. 9-11)[7]. The presence of the aorist participial phrase καὶ ταῦτα εἰπών followed by the present genitive absolute βλεπόντων αὐτῶν (v. 9) links the ascension scene very closely to the preceding dialogue – and it would be a little surprising to have an ascension account which contained no words by the departing person[8]. Tannehill[9] further observes that 1,8 does not actually give an outline of the whole of Acts (as is often asserted), but merely covers the mission until it reaches Samaria, and then goes beyond the end of Acts in its final phrase καὶ ἕως ἐσχάτου τῆς γῆς. Accordingly, some scholars favour seeing *1,1-11* as the opening section of Acts[10]. Johnson believes, "The reader … is meant to imagine the ges-

4. See especially M.C. PARSONS, *The Departure of Jesus in Luke-Acts: The Ascension Narratives in Context* (JSNT SS, 21), Sheffield, JSOT, 1987.

5. E. HAENCHEN, *The Acts of the Apostles*, Oxford, Blackwell, 1971, pp. 144-146.

6. It is used at 1,6.18; 2,41; 5,41; 8,4.25; 9,31; 11,19; 12,5; 13,4; 14,3; 15,3.30; 16,5; 17,12.17.30; 19,32.38; 23,18.22.31; 25,4.11; 26,4.9; 28,5: HAENCHEN, *Acts* (n. 5), p. 142 n. 6; F.J. FOAKES JACKSON – K. LAKE, *The Beginnings of Christianity, Part I*, London, Macmillan, 1920-33, vol. IV, p. 7. This collocation comes only 11 times in the NT outside the Lukan writings.

7. T. MORITZ – S. TRAVIS – M. TURNER, *Biblical Studies: New Testament: Luke-Acts: Part II. Acts*, Cheltenham, Open Theological College, 1995, p. 29.

8. Cf. Josephus, *Ant.* IV.8.48; 2 Kings 2,9-12. "Last words" are, of course, a standard feature of farewell scenes; see S.J. WALTON, *Paul in Acts and Epistles: The Miletus Speech and 1 Thessalonians as a Test Case*, unpublished PhD thesis, Sheffield University, 1997, pp. 69-74 and the literature discussed there (forthcoming in SNTS MS).

9. R.C. TANNEHILL, *The Narrative Unity of Luke-Acts: A Literary Interpretation. Vol. 2: The Acts of the Apostles*, Minneapolis, Fortress Press, 1990, pp. 17f.

10. R.P.C. HANSON, *The Acts* (New Clarendon Bible), Oxford, Clarendon, 1967, pp. 57f; R. PESCH, *Die Apostelgeschichte* (EKK, 5), Zürich-Neukirchen, Benziger Verlag,

tures and words in Acts 1:1-11 as an elaborate variant of those in Luke 24:36-53"[11], that is, that Luke is reworking material he has already used, but this time to form a transition to a new phase in his story.

Barrett considers that vv. 12-14 are "a further piece of stage-setting", and argues that it is only in vv. 15ff that Luke breaks new ground with the appointment of Matthias, whereas the contents of vv. 1-14 are paralleled in the Gospel[12]. He proposes: v. 1 summarises the ministry of Jesus; vv. 3-6 outline resurrection appearances and refer to John the Baptist's prediction of the gift of the Spirit; vv. 7f correspond to Luke 24,47-49; the account of the ascension proper (vv. 9-11) parallels Luke 24,51; the list of names in vv. 13f corresponds to Luke 6,14-16. Accordingly, he (in common with others[13]) prefers to see the introduction as *1,1-14*.

Barrett considers the possibility of seeing *1,1-26* as the introduction, "since it is necessary that we should know who the apostles are before their acts are recorded"[14], but rejects it (as we noted above). Dunn[15], however, opts for this view, seeing Acts 1 as paralleling Luke 1–2, in that both sections are preparation for the anointing with the Spirit of the main character(s) (Luke 3,21f; Acts 2,1ff). Pesch[16] similarly considers that 1,1-11 and 1,12-26 together form a prologue to the book.

Neil believes that 2,1-13 is the "real beginning of [Luke's] story in Acts"[17]. The missionary work of the church cannot begin until the Spirit has come to endow the church with power (cf. 1,8). In Longenecker's

---

1986, vol. 1, p. 59; F.S. SPENCER, *Acts* (Readings: A New Biblical Commentary), Sheffield, Academic Press, 1997, pp. 24-27; TANNEHILL, *Narrative Unity*, 2 (n. 9), pp. 9f, 18; MORITZ *et al.*, *Acts* (n. 7), pp. 2.2f, 2.9.

11. L.T. JOHNSON, *The Acts of the Apostles* (Sacra Pagina, 5), Collegeville, Liturgical Press, 1992, p. 28; cf. PARSONS, *Departure* (n. 4), p. 172; C.H. TALBERT, *Literary Patterns, Theological Themes, and the Genre of Luke-Acts* (SBL MS, 20), Missoula, Scholars, 1974, pp. 58-61.

12. C.K. BARRETT, *A Critical and Exegetical Commentary on the Acts of the Apostles. Vol. I: Preliminary Introduction and Commentary on Acts I-XIV* (ICC), Edinburgh, Clark, 1994, pp. 61f.

13. A.Q. MORTON – G.H.C. MACGREGOR, *The Structure of Luke and Acts*, London, Hodder & Stoughton, 1964, p. 44; B. WITHERINGTON, *The Acts of the Apostles: A Socio-Rhetorical Commentary*, Carlisle, Paternoster – Grand Rapids, Eerdmans, 1998, p. 105 n. 1; G. LÜDEMANN, *Early Christianity according to the Traditions in Acts: A Commentary* (ET of *Das frühe Christentum nach den Traditionen der Apostelgeschichte: Ein Kommentar*), London, SCM, 1989, pp. 25-27.

14. BARRETT, *Acts*, I (n. 12), p. 61.

15. J.D.G. DUNN, *The Acts of the Apostles* (Epworth Commentaries), London, Epworth, 1996, p. 3; so also BRUCE, *Acts* (n. 3), p. 97.

16. PESCH, *Die Apostelgeschichte*, 1 (n. 10), p. 41.

17. W. NEIL, *The Acts of the Apostles* (New Century Bible), London, Oliphants, 1973, p. 71.

view[18], 1,6-26 has prepared the way for 2,1-41, which is itself preparing the way for the heart of the book. Thus Longenecker sees *1,1–2,41* as setting the scene for the ministry of the church, a ministry which is outlined in the thematic paragraph 2,42-47 and then illustrated by a series of snapshots from 3,1 onwards.

A further step can be made, for, accepting Longenecker's view that 2,42-47 is a thematic statement, *1,1–2,47* can be seen as the introduction to the book. Looking back from the end of Acts 2: the departure of Jesus has happened after he has left instructions to his community (1,3-14); the symbolic number of twelve apostles has been restored, so that the church can be the true and renewed Israel (1,15-26; cf. Luke 22,30); the power of the Spirit has come upon the core of the renewed Israel (2,1-13) and the community of believers has become established (2,14-47). Now we are to see the initial mission of the church in Jerusalem (3,1–7,60) before movement into Judaea and Samaria (8,1).

Spencer[19] notes several thematic links between Acts 1 and 2, features which are spread through the whole of Acts 1–2: (1) unusual celestial phenomena (1,10f; 2,2); (2) prophecy (1,4f.8) and fulfilment (2,1-13.17f); (3) the Galilean origin of the first disciples (1,11; 2,7) who nevertheless play a leading role in events in Judaea (1,8; 2,14), combined with a universalistic emphasis (1,8; 2,5.39); (4) the emergence of the twelve as the main leaders of the early community in Jerusalem, with Peter as chief spokesman (1,2.13.15-26; 2,14.37.42f). Further, the involvement of the whole membership in its own life is important, including women (1,14.23-26; 2,17f.44f).

This material suggests that we may be right to think of Luke's "introduction" to Acts as being the whole of chapters 1 and 2, while at the same time believing that it may not be totally clear where the beginning ends and Acts 'proper' starts. This latter point fits with Luke's known propensity for not having crisp section boundaries in Acts, of which the lack of a clear closure formula at the end of the formal introduction is one example[20]. Our next step, then, is to examine the vocabulary and themes of Acts 1–2 to see how far they prepare for the rest of the book, as well as considering how far they recapitulate material in the Gospel[21].

18. LONGENECKER, *Acts* (n. 1), pp. 29, 48; he also observes that 1,1-15 should be seen as a resumptive preface to Acts.

19. SPENCER, *Acts* (n. 10), p. 23.

20. See above (n. 2) and MARSHALL, *Acts* (n. 1), p. 55; WITHERINGTON, *Acts* (n. 13), p. 106.

21. This method is similar to that developed in my doctoral dissertation, *Paul in Acts and Epistles* (n. 8), esp. ch. 2; see the summary in S. WALTON, *Leadership and Lifestyle: Luke's Paul, Luke's Jesus and the Paul of 1 Thessalonians*, in *TyndB* 48 (1997) 377-380.

2. The Themes of Acts 1–2 in Relation to Luke and Acts

The repetition of Jesus' departure implies that there is some link between Acts 1 and Luke 24, rather like the introduction to some TV programmes in which the story so far is reprised, often introduced by the words, "Previously on..." followed by the name of the TV series. The function of this feature is to assist continuity with preceding programmes, and to enable viewers to tune into the stage which the (often multi-layered) plot has reached. In this vein, for example, Parsons[22] has considered the repetition of the ascension in some detail. We note first some brief observations about the language of Acts 1–2 and then enumerate eight major themes of these chapters which reprise the contents of Luke's Gospel and/or anticipate themes to be developed in Acts. Space forbids full treatment of these themes, so we shall consider each only briefly – but we shall examine them sufficiently to see that Luke has taken a number of threads from his sewing basket and woven them into the fabric of the Gospel and Acts, while always running the path of the thread through Acts 1–2.

a. The Language of Acts 1–2

It is noticeable how Lukan the language of Acts 1–2 is. The following 33 verbs are characteristic Lukan vocabulary (rather than *distinctive* Lukan vocabulary[23]): ἀποφθέγγομαι (2,4.14[24]), ἀτενίζω (1,10), βαπτίζω (1,5; 2,38.41), δεῖ (1,16.21[25]), διαμαρτύρομαι (2,40), διαμερίζω (2,3.45), διδάσκω (1,1), ἐκλέγομαι (1,2.24), ἐξίστημι (2,7.12), ἐπαίρω (1,9; 2,14), ἐπέρχομαι (1,8), ἐπικαλέω (1,23; 2,14[26]), εὐφραίνω (2,26), θάπτω (2,29), κλάω + ἄρτος (2,46), μεταλαμβάνω (2,46), μετανοέω (2,38), ὁρίζω (2,23), παραγγέλλω (1,4), παρίστημι (1,3.10), παρακαλέω (2,40), πίμπλημι (2,4[27]), προσεύχομαι (1,24), προσκαλέομαι (2,39), προσκαρτερέω (1,14; 2,42.46), προστίθημι (2,41.47), σαλεύω (2,25), συγχέω (2,6), συλλαμβάνω (1,16), συμπληρόω (2,1), ὑπάρχω (2,30), ὑποστρέφω (1,12), φημί (2,39).

---

22. PARSONS, *Departure* (n. 4).
23. Cf. the lists of Lukan vocabulary – mostly distinctive Lukan vocabulary – in M.D. GOULDER, *Luke: A New Paradigm* (JSNT SS, 20), Sheffield, JSOT Press, 1989, pp. 800-809; J.C. HAWKINS, *Horae Synopticae: Contributions to the Study of the Synoptic Problem*, Oxford, Clarendon, 1899, pp. 13-24, 29-41, 140-143; S. KUBO, *A Reader's Greek-English Lexicon of the New Testament*, Leiden, Brill, 1971, pp. 49f, 99-101.
24. Only other NT use is Acts 26,25.
25. See C.H. COSGROVE, *The Divine δεῖ in Luke-Acts: Investigations into the Lukan Understanding of God's Providence*, in *NT* 26 (1984) 168-190.
26. Found 20 times in Acts, never in Luke, 30 times in NT in total.
27. Cf. D. PETERSON, *The Motif of Fulfilment and the Purpose of Luke-Acts*, in B.W. WINTER – A.D. CLARKE (eds.), *The Book of Acts in Its Ancient Literary Setting* (BAFCS, 1), Carlisle, Paternoster – Grand Rapids, Eerdmans, 1993, pp. 83-104.

Likewise, the following 42 nouns or noun-expressions are characteristic Lukan vocabulary: ἀνάστασις (1,22; 2,31), ἀνήρ (1,10.16.21; 2,5.14.22. 29.37), ἄφεσις (2,38[28]), βάπτισμα (1,2[29]), βουλή (2,23[30]), διὰ στόματος (1,16[31]), ἐλπίς (2,26[32]), ἡμέρα (1,2.3.5.15.22; 2,1.15.17.18.20.29.41.46.47), ἦχος (2,2[33]), Ἰερουσαλήμ (1,8.12.19; 2,5.14), Ἰσραηλίτης (2,22), κλάσις + ἄρτος (2,42[34]), κύριος[35] (1,6.21.24; 2,20.21.25.34.36.39.47), λόγος[36] (2,22. 40.41), διάλεκτος (1,19; 2,6.8[37]), ἐπαγγελία (1,4; 2,33.39[38]), κλῆρος (1,17.26), λαός (2,47[39]), μάρτυς (1,8.22; 2,32), ὁδός (1,12; 2,28), οἶκος (2,2.36.46[40]), ὄνομα (1,15; 2,21.38[41]), Παμφυλία (2,10[42]), πλῆθος (2,6), πνοή (2,2[43]), πούς (2,35), πρόγνωσις (2,23[44]), προσευχή (1,14; 2,42), προφήτης (2,16.30), Ῥωμαῖος (2,10[45]), Σαμάρεια (1,8), σημεῖον + τέρας (2,19.22.43[46]), τόπος (1,25 twice), ὑπερῷον (1,13[47]), Φίλιππος (1,13[48]), φόβος (2,43),

28. Always "forgiveness *of sins*" in Acts (2,38; 5,31; 10,43; 13,38; 26,18).

29. Mostly used of John's baptism in Acts (10,37; 13,24; 18,25; 19,3.4). The verb βαπτίζω is only used of John's baptism at Acts 19,3; other uses of the verb in Acts are for Christian baptism.

30. See J.T. SQUIRES, *The Plan of God in Luke-Acts* (SNTS MS, 76), Cambridge, University Press, 1993 and *The Plan of God in the Acts of the Apostles*, in I.H. MARSHALL – D. PETERSON (eds.), *Witness to the Gospel: The Theology of Acts*, Grand Rapids, Eerdmans, 1998, pp. 19-39.

31. Found in the NT only at Luke 1,70; Acts 1,16; 3,18.21; 4,25; 15,7; Matt 4,4.

32. Found only in Luke-Acts among the NT evangelists.

33. Only used in the NT at Luke 4,37; 21,25; Acts 2,2; Heb 12,19.

34. Only used elsewhere in the NT at Luke 24,35 – a significant echo.

35. Particularly as a description of Jesus after his resurrection; cf. C.F.D. MOULE, *The Christology of Acts*, in L.E. KECK – J.L. MARTYN (eds.), *Studies in Luke-Acts*, London, SPCK, 1968, pp. 159-185, p. 160; and now J.D.G. DUNN, *ΚΥΡΙΟΣ in Acts*, in J.D.G. DUNN, *The Christ and the Spirit: Collected Essays of James D. G. Dunn*. Vol. 1. *Christology*, Edinburgh, Clark – Grand Rapids, Eerdmans, 1998, pp. 241-253.

36. Especially the characterisation of the Christian message as ὁ λόγος, e.g. Acts 4,4.29.31; 6,2.4.7; 8,4.14.21.25; 10,36.44; 11,1.19; 12,24; 13,5.7.26.44.46.48.49; 14,3.25; 15,6.35.36; 16,6.32; 17,11.13; 18,5.11; 19,10.20; 20,32.

37. Found only in Acts in the NT.

38. Found only in Luke-Acts among the Evangelists.

39. Almost invariably meaning "the Jews" in Jewish settings in Acts (3,9.11.12.23; 4,1.2.8.10.17.21.25.27; 5,12.13.20.25.26.34.37; 6,8.12; 7,17.34; 10,2.41.42; 12,4.11; 13,15.17.24.31; 18,10; 19,4; 21,28.30.36.39.40; 23,5; 26,17.23; 28,17.26.27).

40. Here featuring a more literal use of a place (v. 2), a metaphorical use of the nation (v. 36) and the characteristic expression κατ' οἶκον (v. 46; cf. 5,42; 8,3; 20,20; Rom 16,5; 1 Cor 16,19; Col 4,15; Phlm 2), discussed in R.A. CAMPBELL, *The Elders: Seniority within Earliest Christianity*, Edinburgh, Clark, 1994, pp. 152f.

41. Particularly with Ἰησοῦς (Χριστός), e.g. Acts 4,10.18.30; 5,40; 8,12; 9,27; 10,48; 15,26; 16,18; 19,5.13.17; 21,13; 26,9.

42. The 5 uses in Acts (2,10; 13,13; 14,24; 15,38; 27,5) are the only NT uses.

43. This and Acts 17,25 are the only NT uses.

44. The only other NT use is 1 Pet 1,2; the verb προγινώσκω is used at 26,5.

45. Found 11 times in Acts; the only other NT use is John 11,48.

46. Found particularly in Acts in the Lukan expression σημεῖα καὶ τέρατα (or *vice versa*): 1,17.25; 4,30; 5,12; 6,8; 7,36; 14,3; 15,12.

47. Only used in Acts in the NT (1,13; 9,37.39; 20,8).

48. Cf. F.S. SPENCER, *The Portrait of Philip in Acts: A Study of Roles and Relations* (JSNT SS, 67), Sheffield, JSOT, 1992.

Φρυγία (2,10⁴⁹), φωνή (2,6.14), χάρις (2,47⁵⁰), χείρ (2,23), χρόνος (1,6.7.21), ψαλμός (1,20⁵¹).

Acts 1–2 also contains 21 NT *hapax legomena*, including: Ἄραψ (2,11), ἀφελότης (2,46), γλεῦκος (2,13), Ἐλαμίτης (2,9), ἐνύπνιον (2,17), ἐνωτίζομαι (2,14), ἔπαυλις (1,20), Ἰωήλ (2,16), καταμένω (1,13), κατανύσσομαι (2,37), καρταριθμέω (1,17), λακάω (1,18), Λιβύη (2,10), μεγαλεῖος (2,11), μεστόω (2,13), ὀπτάνομαι (1,3), Πάρθος (2,9), προσπήγνυμι (2,23), συγκαταψηφίζομαι (1,26⁵²), συναλίζομαι (1,4), τεκμήριον (1,3).

b. The Fulfilment of Scripture or God's Promises

The fulfilment of the Scriptures or God's promises⁵³ is a prominent idea in Acts 1–2, as it is in the whole of Luke-Acts. Barrett summarises judiciously⁵⁴:

> It is safe to say that there is no major concept in the two books that does not to some extent reflect the beliefs and theological vocabulary of the OT.

Luke is the only Evangelist to employ ἐπαγγελία; he uses it with reference to the promise of the Spirit in the only use in Luke (24,49) and in the early chapters of Acts (1,4; 2,33.39)⁵⁵. Luke can refer to the Scriptures in Acts 1–2 using both verbs and nouns of writing (γράφω, γραφή: 1,16.20) and of speaking (λέγω, λαλέω: 2,16.25.31.34), as he does in the rest of the Gospel and Acts⁵⁶. Luke speaks of "the Scriptures" as an entity (Luke 24,37.42.44.45) or refers to a particular passage as "the Scripture" (Acts 1,16; Luke 4,21), and he sees the OT as "standing written" (Acts 1,20)⁵⁷.

49. Found in the NT only at Acts 2,10; 16,6; 18,23.

50. While clearly a favourite word of Paul, it is used 17 times in Acts.

51. Only Luke-Acts in the NT names this OT book (Luke 20,42; 24,22; Acts 1,20; 13,33).

52. Luke-Acts contains three of the four NT examples of συγκατα- compound verbs (Luke 23,51; Acts 1,26; 25,5; 2 Cor 6,16), in line with Luke's general penchant for compounds: J.H. MOULTON – W.F. HOWARD, *A Grammar of New Testament Greek. Vol. II. Accidence and Word Formation*. Edinburgh, Clark, 1929, p. 11; P.K. NELSON, *Leadership and Discipleship: A Study of Luke 22:24-30* (SBL DS, 138), Atlanta, Scholars, 1994, 182f.

53. See D.L. BOCK, *Scripture and the Realisation of God's Promises*, in MARSHALL – PETERSON (eds.), *Witness to the Gospel* (n. 30), pp. 41-62; C.K. BARRETT, *Luke-Acts*, in D.A. CARSON – H.G.M. WILLIAMSON (eds.), *It is Written: Scripture Citing Scripture. Essays in Honour of Barnabas Lindars*, Cambridge, University Press, 1988, pp. 231-244.

54. BARRETT, *Luke-Acts* (n. 53), p. 231.

55. Later uses in Acts (13,23.32; 26,6) see the ministry, death and resurrection of Jesus as the fulfilment of God's promises.

56. E.g. γράφω, γραφή: Luke 2,23; 3,4; 4,4.8; 7,27; 10,26; 18,31; 19,46; 20,17; 22,37; 24,32.44.46; Acts 7.42; 8.32.35; 13,29.33; 15,15; 17,2.11; 18,24.27.28; 24,14; λέγω: Luke 4,12; Acts 13,40; λαλέω Luke 24,25; Acts 3,22.24; 28,25. See further BARRETT, *Luke-Acts* (n. 53), p. 242.

57. Using the perfect tense of γράφω, see Luke 2,23; 3,4; 4,4.8; 7,27; 10,26; 19,46; 24,44.46; Acts 7,42; 13,29.33; 15,15; 23,5;24,14.

For Luke, "In the Scriptures ... you ... find the Jesus story and what happens in the church"[58]. Luke is unusual among the NT authors in naming the OT author/book which he cites[59]. In regarding the OT writers as prophets (Acts 2,16.30) Luke is reiterating a theme from the post-resurrection period of the Gospel (Luke 24,25.27.44), where Jesus is seen as the reality of which the Scriptures speak[60]. Luke's Christology has thoroughly Jewish origins; Luke sees the person of Jesus through the lens of the Scriptures[61], and utilises scriptural categories to understand and identify him, such as "your holy one" (2,27; 3,14), παῖς (3,13.26) and, above all, Χριστός (2,31.36.38[62]). Luke also uses the verbs πληρόω and πίμπλημι to denote his understanding that "this is that" (e.g. Acts 1,16; Luke 4,21; 9,31; 24,44)[63].

c. God's Superintendence of History

Luke's view of Scripture spills over into the wider theme of God's superintendence of history, both in the past and in the time of Jesus and the early church. Luke's choice of two particular verbs in Acts 1–2 testifies to this belief, namely δεῖ (1,16.21) and ὁρίζω (2,23). The former is a particular feature of Luke's writings (Luke-Acts contains 40 of the 101 NT uses[64]) and expresses Luke's belief that God's purposes are ultimately unstoppable; things must be this way (e.g. Acts 1,16.21; Luke 9,22; 13,33; 17,25; 22,37; 24,7.26.44). The rare verb ὁρίζω[65] reinforces this view, and Luke's use of the passive voice of this verb suggests that it is God determining events[66].

58. J. JERVELL, *The Theology of the Acts of the Apostles*, Cambridge, University Press, 1996, pp. 74f.

59. In Acts 1–2, the Psalms (1,20), Joel (2,26ff) and David (1,16; 2,25-31.34f). In Acts subsequently Luke refers to the Psalms (13,33.35) and the prophets (7,42; 15,15).

60. See also Luke 1,70; 3,4; 4,17; 20,6, which regard events at the time of Jesus as fulfilling prophecy. The themes of the revival of prophecy surrounding the coming of Jesus (e.g. Luke 1,67.76; 2,36) and of Jesus as a prophet, prominent in Luke, are also relevant (Luke 4,24; 7,16; 9,19; 22,64); see further L.T. JOHNSON, *The Gospel of Luke* (Sacra Pagina, 3), Collegeville, Liturgical Press, 1992, pp. 15-21; JOHNSON, *Acts* (n. 11), pp. 12-14.

61. Cf. BARRETT, *Luke-Acts* (n. 53), p. 243; JERVELL, *Theology* (n. 58), pp. 26-31.

62. See Luke 2,11.26; 4,41; 9,20; 22,67; 23,2.35.39; 24,26.46; Acts 3,18.20; 4,26; 5,42; 8,5; 9,22; 17,3; 18,5.28; 26,23. It is noticeable that Luke does not represent Jesus as initiating direct discussion of his messiahship until after his resurrection.

63. See further PETERSON, *The Motif of Fulfilment* (n. 27), pp. 83-104; SQUIRES, *The Plan of God* (n. 30), pp. 143-145, 149-151.

64. See COSGROVE, *Divine δεῖ* (n. 25); SQUIRES, *The Plan of God* (n. 30), pp. 5-7, 167-169, 173f.

65. Of 8 NT uses, 6 are in Luke's writings (Luke 22,22; Acts 2,23; 10,42; 11,29; 17,26.31).

66. Using the perfect passive in Luke 22,22; Acts 2,23; 10,42. The aorist active in

d. The Teaching and Example of Jesus

The teaching and example of Jesus are highlighted in Acts 1–2. Two examples will illustrate this theme. First, Luke summarises the teaching of Jesus during the post-resurrection period as λέγων τὰ περὶ τῆς βασιλείας τοῦ θεοῦ (1,3). He thereby represents the post-resurrection Jesus as in continuity with the pre-resurrection Jesus, for the kingdom of God has been arguably the most prominent theme of Jesus' teaching in Luke's Gospel[67]. It will be developed in Acts, where 8,12; 19,8; and 28,23.31 use the same language to represent central characters in the apostolic church as preaching the same message as Jesus.

Second, the description of the successor to Judas is that he will be engaged in διακονία (1,17.25), repeating a theme from Jesus' own example and teaching (e.g. Luke 12,35-38; 22,26f[68]). This is a key to understanding Luke's view of church leaders, that they should serve in the same manner in which Jesus himself served. This theme is wide-spread in Acts (e.g. 6,4 in the context of 6,1-2; 11,29; 12,25; 19,22; 21,19), but it is particularly noticeable in the speech to the Ephesian elders (20,18-35). There Paul speaks of his διακονία (20,24) explicitly, but the whole speech mirrors the farewell by Jesus in Luke 22,14-38, especially vv. 24-30[69]. Paul models the servant leadership shown by Jesus, for he can speak of himself as "serving the Lord" (20,19, using δουλεύω), and he has exercised a ministry in ταπεινοφροσύνη (20,19), a quality central to the style of leadership commended by Jesus (Luke 22,26f). This servant ministry includes care for the weak (20,34f), show-ing that such leadership is for the benefit of those led rather than the leader. More than that, Paul commends this style of leadership to the elders (20,28), particularly by calling them to copy his provision for those in need (20,35). Tannehill, noticing that διακονία and διακονέω are used elsewhere of those who serve at table, finely observes[70]:

> The humble service that Jesus commended by including himself among the waiters and waitresses is now being carried out through Paul's dedicated service to the Lord and others in his mission.

Acts 17,26.31 is clearly God's determining, as the contexts make clear. See further SQUIRES, *The Plan of God* (n. 30), p. 171; *TDNT*, 5, pp. 452f; *EDNT*, 2, p 532.

67. Ἡ βασιλεία τοῦ θεοῦ is mentioned 33 times in Luke, notably in the summaries of 4,43; 8,1; 9,2.60; 10,9.11, where it is the central topic of Jesus' and the disciples' proclamation.

68. On the latter, see NELSON, *Leadership and Discipleship* (n. 52); WALTON, *Paul in Acts and Epistles* (n. 8), pp. 118-123.

69. See more fully WALTON, *Paul in Acts and Epistles* (n. 8), pp. 108-125; on this theme especially pp. 118-123.

70. TANNEHILL, *Narrative Unity, 2* (n. 9), p. 260.

e. Phenomena from the Ministry of Jesus

A number of phenomena from the ministry of Jesus are re-run or reca-
pitulated in Acts 1–2. Four particular examples are of interest.

First, the darkening of the sun (2,20, quoting Joel 3,4 LXX) echoes
the darkness surrounding the death of Jesus (Luke 23,44f, using both
ἥλιος and σκότος[71]; cf. 22,53 αὕτη ἐστὶν ὑμῶν ἡ ὥρα καὶ ἡ ἐξουσία
τοῦ σκότους) and the darkness warned of by Jesus in the eschatological
discourse (Luke 21,25). It also reminds the careful reader of the purpose
of the ministry of Jesus, to "bring light to those who sit in darkness"
(Luke 1,79). Acts 2,20 also prepares the way for Saul's rebuke of Ely-
mas, "And now listen – the hand of the Lord is against you, and you will
be blind for a while, unable to see *the sun*". Luke immediately records
that, "Immediately mist *and darkness* came over him" (Acts 13,11). A
further allusion may be seen to Paul's own account of his
conversion/call, in which he says that he saw a light "brighter than *the
sun*" (26,13) and describes his mission as enabling people "to turn *from
darkness* to light" (26,18). Through this web of references Luke is paint-
ing a picture of darkness as symbolic of the absence of God, a darkness
which Jesus himself experiences on the cross, but a darkness which is
banished in the presence of God.

The appearance of the two men in white clothes (1,10f ἐσθῆτα) is
described in similar terms to the (post-resurrection) appearance of two
men at the tomb (Luke 24,4) and the one who appears to Cornelius (Acts
10,30). It is no exaggeration to say that Luke-Acts is full of the presence
of angelic beings, markedly more so than the writings of the other Evangelists[72]. They appear at key moments to indicate that the other world is
breaking into this one: at the conception and birth of John (Luke 1,11-
20), at the coming of Jesus (Luke 1,26-38; 2,8-15.21), preparing Jesus
for the cross (Luke 22,43), at the empty tomb (Luke 24,4.23), to free
imprisoned Christians (Acts 5,19f; 12,6-11.15), to direct the mission of
the church (Acts 8,26; 10,3.7.22; 11,13), to punish those who oppose
God's work (Acts 12,23), and to reassure and protect God's servants
(Acts 27,23). Thus the appearance of the men in white, whom Luke
identifies as angels (Acts 10,3.22; 11,13), is part of the wider theme of

---

71. Echoing Luke 22,53. This understanding of Acts 2,20 is in agreement with BRUCE,
Acts (n. 3), p. 121; SPENCER, *Acts* (n. 10), p 35; J.B. GREEN, *The Gospel of Luke*
(NICNT), Grand Rapids, Eerdmans, 1997, p. 825; *contra* WITHERINGTON, *Acts* (n. 13),
pp. 142f.

72. The word ἄγγελος appears 25 times in Luke and 21 times in Acts; only Matthew
comes at all near to this (20 times; Mark 6 times; John 3 times); see further *NIDNTT*, 1,
pp. 103f. It is surprising that JERVELL, *Theology* (n. 58), hardly discusses angels.

God's ordering of the course of events both in the coming, ministry, death and resurrection of Jesus and also in the life of the first Christians.

Third, suffering is a keynote in Acts 1–2, reflecting a theme found more widely in Luke and Acts[73]. In Acts 1–2 Luke speaks of Jesus' appearances μετὰ τὸ παθεῖν αὐτόν (1,3), choosing a verb which he will use again in Acts to speak of Jesus' suffering (3,18; 17,3) and of the suffering of Paul (9,16), who reproduces the suffering of Jesus in his own life and ministry (Acts 20,19.22-24[74]). The suffering which Paul experiences is modelled on the suffering of Jesus, and the same verb is used in the Gospel at key points to describe Jesus' own destiny (Luke 9,22; 17,25; 22,15; 24,26.46; cf. Acts 26,23)[75]. I have summarised this point elsewhere as follows[76]:

> The suffering which Jesus and Paul experienced are an inevitable part of Christian leadership as Luke understands it (e.g. Luke 21,12-19.36; 22,28; Acts 20,19.23f.31), but should not be feared above God himself (e.g. Luke 12,4-7; Acts 20,24). For sure, such suffering and threats from false teachers (e.g. Luke 10,3; 21,8f; Acts 20,29f) call for watchfulness (e.g. Luke 12,1.5.37; 21,34; Acts 20,28.31), but in the end suffering and struggle lead purposefully to glory (e.g. Luke 13,32; Acts 20,22; Luke 22,16.29f; Acts 20,19).

Fourth, language about teaching is predicated of Jesus (Acts 1,1 διδάσκω) and the apostles (Acts 2,42 διδαχή) in our chapters, reflecting a theme prominent in the Gospel and Acts. Jesus' ministry is a teaching ministry (Luke 4,15.31f; 5,3.17; 6,6; 11,1; 13,10.22; 19,47; 20,1; 21,37; 23,5) – and almost all of these references to "teaching" are unique to Luke[77] (often coming in Lukan summary passages), showing that Luke makes a particular point of Jesus as a teacher. In Acts, too, Luke draws attention to teaching as a characteristic activity of the apostles (4,2.18; 5,21.25.28.42; 11,26; 13,12; 15,35; 17,19; 18,11.25; 20,20; 28,31), implying thereby that they continue the ministry of Jesus – and this connection is by the two references to teaching in Acts 1–2[78].

---

73. See D. PETERSON, *Luke's Theological Enterprise: Integration and Intent*, in MAR-SHALL – PETERSON (eds.), *Witness to the Gospel* (n. 30), pp. 534-537, 540-544.

74. More fully, in WALTON, *Paul in Acts and Epistles* (n. 8), pp. 101-103, 111-115, 131-133.

75. The Lukan verb συλλαμβάνω (7 times in Luke, 4 times in Acts, 16 times in total in the NT) is predicated of those who took Jesus both in the Gospel and early in Acts (Luke 22,54; Acts 1,16).

76. WALTON, *Paul in Acts and Epistles* (n. 8), p. 145.

77. The exception is 20,1, partially paralleled in Matt 21,23.

78. In agreement with JOHNSON, *Acts* (n. 11), p. 58; PARSONS, *Departure* (n. 4), p. 158. TANNEHILL, *Narrative Unity*, 2 (n. 9), p. 44 n. 4, suggests that Peter's speeches in Acts 2–5 are intended as examples of "the apostles' teaching".

f. The Resurrection, Exaltation and Authority of Jesus

From a large number of points in Acts 1–2 about the position of Jesus after the resurrection, we shall consider a sample.

The ζάω-word group is used twice in Acts 1–2, and is the tip of a large iceberg of references to the aliveness of Jesus. Jesus presented himself living to his disciples after his death (1,3) and David testifies that God would raise the Messiah from death (2,28, "You have made known to me the path of life" quoting Ps 16,8 LXX). The aliveness of Jesus is central to Peter's sermon (2,24.31-33, supported by scriptural testimonies in vv. 25-28.31.34).

This theme can be traced back into the Gospel, where Jesus has answered the Sadducees' question about the resurrection by asserting that God is the God of the living (20,38), and particularly by the testimony of angels to Jesus' aliveness (24,5.23). In Acts the resurrection is a major theme of the evangelistic and apologetic speeches, sometimes using ζάω-language (3,15; 5,20) – and notably in the summary of Paul's message, περί τινος Ἰησοῦ τεθνηκότος, ὃν ἔφασκεν ὁ Παῦλος ζῆν (25,19, cf. Luke 24,23).

The other word group used in such contexts is, of course, ἀνίστημι/ ἀνάστασις. It can be used simply of "standing up" or "setting out" (e.g. Luke 1,39; 4,16; Acts 1,15), but becomes almost a technical term when used of Jesus after his death. Thus in Peter's speech, he uses both the verb and the noun for God's action in relation to Jesus: ὃν ὁ θεὸς ἀνέστησεν λύσας τὰς ὠδῖνας τοῦ θανάτου (2,24); προϊδὼν ἐλάλησεν περὶ τῆς ἀναστάσεως τοῦ Χριστοῦ (2,31).

The Gospel has again prepared the way for this in the debate with the Sadducees (20,27ff) and the account of the post-resurrection period (24,7.46), where it is the scriptural necessity of Jesus' resurrection which is the focus in uses of this word group. The development of the theme in Acts is seen in the preachers asserting that Jesus was raised from the dead (4,2.33; 10,41; 13,33f; 17,3.18.31.32; 26,23), as well as in the accounts of the raisings of two dead people using this language (Dorcas, 9,36-42, esp. vv. 40f; Eutychus, 20,9-12, esp. the use of ζάω in v. 12). The latter point suggests that these stories are to be seen as miniature reproductions of the resurrection of Jesus.

Luke also uses the imagery of feet and footstools in the context of triumph over enemies. Acts 2,34f represents Peter using Ps 109,1 LXX to argue that the now-triumphant Jesus is the one of whom the Psalmist writes, and in doing this he echoes his Master, who produces precisely the same phrase from Ps 109,1 as his trump card in debate on the identity of the Messiah (Luke 20,41-44). Later in Acts we find the language of feet and footstools on the lips of Stephen (but this time quoting Isa 66,1), to argue that God does not live in temples (7,49), and the language of ἐχϑρός (in its only other use in Acts) of Simon Magus (13,10) – an enemy of God who is subdued by the power of the Spirit in a manner not dissimilar to Saul on the Damascus Road[79].

The fleshliness of the resurrection of Jesus is asserted in Acts 1–2 by the use of σάρξ (2,31[80]), repeating an assertion from Luke 24,39, in a scene where Jesus eats fish (24,41-43) in order to demonstrate the physicality of his body after the resurrection.

The exaltation of Jesus is seen most obviously in the story of the departure of Jesus (Acts 1,9-11; Luke 24,50-53). Peter's sermon can therefore assert that it is because of Jesus' exaltation that the Spirit has been poured out (Acts 2,33, using the relatively uncommon verb ὑψόω[81]). Jesus now sits at the right hand of God (2,34, quoting Ps 109,1 LXX), the place of authority and power – a claim made elsewhere in Luke-Acts (Luke 20,42; 22,69; Acts 5,31; 7,55.56).

The present authority of the exalted Jesus can be seen from the use of the phrase "the name of Jesus", a particular favourite of Luke in Acts[82]. In Peter's Pentecost sermon it is baptism ἐπὶ τῷ ὀνόματι Ἰησοῦ Χριστοῦ (2,38) which is mentioned, and baptism is a common context for the phrase elsewhere in Acts (8,16; 10,48; 19,5; and perhaps 8,12) – although it is at least possible that the use of 'the name' here denotes the candidate calling upon the name (that is, the authority) of Jesus[83]. Luke's wider use of the phrase is in contexts where it denotes the authority of Jesus quite explicitly, such as healing (3,6.16; 4,7.10.12), exorcism (16,18; 19,13 – where it goes wrong!), signs and wonders (4,30) or preaching (4,17f; 5,28.40; 8,12; 9,27)[84].

---

79. Cf. Acts 9,8; 22,11, using the verb χειραγωγέω, cognate to the noun χειραγωγός found in 13,11 but nowhere else in the NT.

80. Adapting Ps 15,10 LXX by adding the reference to σάρξ, also quoted at Acts 2,27; 13,35.

81. Found 6 times in Luke, 3 times in Acts, 3 times in Matthew, 5 times in John, and only 3 other times in the rest of the NT.

82. Found 17 times in Acts (2,38; 3,6; 4,10.18.30; 5,40; 8,12.16; 9,27; 10,48; 15,26; 16,18; 19,5.13.17; 21,13; 26,9) and never in the other NT Evangelists. Paul uses it four times in 1 Cor, once in Phil, Eph, Col and twice in 2 Thess (if the latter three are considered Pauline), and it is found once in 1 John. JERVELL, *Theology* (n. 58), p. 33 n. 49, records that Luke-Acts has 94 of the NT's 238 uses of ὄνομα (60 in Acts).

83. J.A. ZIESLER, *The Name of Jesus in the Acts of the Apostles*, in *JSNT* 4 (1974) 28-41 (esp. pp. 29-32), argues this at least in baptismal contexts where the preposition is ἐν or ἐπί, including Acts 2,38.

84. JOHNSON, *Acts* (n. 11), p. 57, suggests that "the name of Jesus" is used to indicate divine power and authorisation for apostolic activity. The older (and still common) view is that to be baptised "into the name of the Lord Jesus" implies becoming his property:

Most notably of all, Jesus is referred to as κύριος, both in Acts 1–2 and throughout the remainder of the book. It is noticeable that this term is used for both Jesus (1,6.21; 2,21 [?].34 [second use].36.47 [?]) and God (1,24; 2,20.25.34 [first use].39). Dunn sees this dual use of the term as indicating that Luke is recording "an unreflective stage in early christology, where both the belief in the supreme God was unquestioned and the belief that Jesus was Lord had become an established and distinctive Christian confession"[85]. Certainly the identification of Jesus by this term is a keynote of the Christology of the rest of the book (e.g. 4,33; 7,59f; 8,16; 9,10.11.13.15.17.27.28; 10,36; 11,16f; 15,11.26; 16,31; 19,5.13. 17; 20,21.24.35; 21,13; 22,8.10).

In the Gospel, Moule[86] has shown that κύριος is only very rarely used by human beings of Jesus prior to the resurrection (hence 24,34) with the exception of the vocative (which need be no more than a respectful title). Luke himself, as narrator, speaks of Jesus as κύριος (e.g. 7,13.19; 10,1.39.41; 11,39; 17,5f; 18,6; 19,8; 22,61), but this should be understood in the same way as a modern British person speaking of 'Queen Elizabeth II' when describing something which The Queen did before her accession in 1952. We may agree[87] that for Luke Jesus did not change his status or identity to *become* Lord at the resurrection, while maintaining that Luke's usage of κύριος shows that he believes that Jesus was *declared* to have the role of Lord by the resurrection (cf. Acts 2,36), and that he was not recognised as such beforehand[88].

g. Consequences of the Ministry, Death, Resurrection and Exaltation of Jesus

The consequences of the ministry, death and resurrection of Jesus are identified by three themes in Acts 1–2.

so BARRETT, *Acts*, I (n. 14), p. 154. See further the discussions in ZIESLER, *The Name of Jesus* (n. 83); L. HARTMAN, *'Into the Name of Jesus': A Suggestion Concerning the Earliest Meaning of the Phrase*, in *NTS* 20 (1973-74) 432-440 and now ID., *'Into the Name of the Lord Jesus': Baptism in the Early Church*, Edinburgh, Clark, 1997, esp. pp. 37-50, the latter asserting that the 'name' denotes the content of the baptism, i.e. that it is *Christian* baptism.

85. DUNN, *ΚΥΡΙΟΣ in Acts* (n. 35), pp. 241-253, p. 253; cf. JERVELL, *Theology* (n. 58), p. 29: "In using the title of both God and Jesus, Luke in some sense regarded Jesus as on a level with God".

86. MOULE, *The Christology of Acts* (n. 35), p 160, notes Luke 1,43.76; 19,31 as the only possible exceptions – and the latter two are debatable, since in 1,76 κύριος only refers to Jesus when read through Christian spectacles, and in 19,31 it is Jesus himself speaking. cf. WITHERINGTON, *Acts* (n. 13), pp 148f; J.A. FITZMYER, *Luke I-IX* (AB, 28), Garden City, NY, Doubleday, 1981, p. 203.

87. D.L. JONES, *The Title κύριος in Acts*, in *SBL 1974 Seminar Papers*, II, pp. 85-101 (esp. pp. 93, 96); E. FRANKLIN, *Christ the Lord*, London, SPCK, 1975, pp. 52-54.

88. LONGENECKER, *Acts* (n. 1), pp. 76f; cf. WITHERINGTON, *Acts* (n. 13), p. 149.

First, through Jesus' work people can receive ἄφεσις ἁμαρτιῶν (2,38)[89]. Ἄφεσις occurs three times in Luke's Gospel in this phrase (1,77; 3,3; 24,47), the last of which particularly anticipates the response for which Peter calls at the day of Pentecost[90]. Forgiving sins is also a marker of the ministry of Jesus (using the cognate verb ἀφίημι: Luke 5,20f.23f; 7,47-49; 11,4; 23,34). In Acts, ἄφεσις is only used in conjunction with ἁμαρτιῶν; forgiveness of sins is proclaimed as a key blessing which a believer receives (5,31; 10,43; 13,38; 26,18).

Another way in which Luke expresses what Jesus now offers is using the vocabulary of salvation[91]. In Acts 2, the result of responding to the preaching of Peter is to be saved (2,21.40.47), and this continues to be the case through the rest of the book (Acts 4,12; 5,31; 11,14; 13,23.26.47; 15,1.11; 16,17.30f; 28,28). The fact that 28,28 comes at the end of the book in a summary of Paul's message and ministry suggests that 'salvation' should be regarded as a key category for Luke[92]. But this is not an innovation in Acts; Luke has used the same language in the Gospel. God is the saviour for Luke (Luke 1,47), but this God has sent a saviour (Luke 1,69; 2,11). Salvation is a big category, bigger than the forgiveness of sins (for it can include healing, for example[93]), but it is always through Jesus that salvation is available.

Second, the blessings which accrue are for the people of Israel. Twice in Acts 1–2 Luke shows that it is Israel which is the first 'target audience' of the work of Jesus (1,6; 2,36) – and it is a Jewish audience to whom Peter speaks on the day of Pentecost. Luke has already shown that God's purposes are to restore Israel, not least in the early chapters of the Gospel[94] and most notably in Luke 2,32, where the parallel between blessing to Israel and the Gentiles is clear[95]. He also utilises

89. Cf. C. STENSCHKE, The Need for Salvation, in MARSHALL – PETERSON (eds.), Witness to the Gospel (n. 30), pp. 125-144, esp. 132-134.

90. The only other uses of ἄφεσις in Luke are in the quotation from Isa 61,1. This is not a verbatim reproduction of the LXX, for Luke introduces a second use of ἄφεσις into the quotation, probably drawn from Isa 58,6. GREEN, The Gospel of Luke (n. 71), p. 211, argues that these uses should be seen as alluding to the Jubilee of Lev 25, contra FITZMYER, Luke I-IX (n. 86), p 533, who understands these uses in the light of Luke's uniform usage elsewhere, in relation to forgiveness of sins.

91. In Luke 1,77 the relationship between salvation and forgiveness of sins is particularly close.

92. Cf. I.H. MARSHALL, Luke: Historian and Theologian Exeter, Paternoster, 1970, esp. pp. 92-102, 157-187, who regards 'salvation' as the centre of Luke's theology.

93. So B. WITHERINGTON, Salvation and Health in Christian Antiquity: The Soteriology of Luke-Acts in its First Century Setting, in MARSHALL – PETERSON (eds.), Witness to the Gospel (n. 30), pp. 145-166.

94. Luke 1,16.54.68; 2,25.32.34.

95. "The setting of Jews and Gentiles in parallel here corresponds to the pattern Luke develops in Acts where Jews and Gentiles are seen as parallel beneficiaries of that salva-

'the people' as a description of the Jewish people (Acts 2,47), invariably in Jewish settings and often portrayed as the beneficiaries of God's action in Jesus[96]. Another Jewish turn of phrase is found when preachers address Jewish audiences ἄνδρες ἀδελφοί (Acts 1,16; 2,29.37), highlighting the concern which Luke has to show that Jewish people heard and responded to the message about Jesus. This phrase is taken up in Acts 7,2; 13,26.28; 15,7.13; 22,1; 23,1.6; 28,17 – the latter verse coming in a location at the end of the book which suggests that Jewish people hear about Jesus throughout the story, rather than the book of Acts being the story of how the Jews gradually rejected Jesus[97].

Third, people from other nations will join the community of believers. Luke describes the crowd at Pentecost as coming from "every ἔθνος under heaven" (2,5). Much later use of ἔθνος in Acts comes in the context of Gentiles becoming believers in Jesus[98], and the programmatic-looking Luke 2,32[99] in combination with Luke 7,9; 24,47 (the latter forming a kind of *inclusio* with 2,32) suggests that we should hear Acts 2,5 as hinting at this later development. That impression is reinforced by the phrase πᾶσιν τοῖς εἰς μακράν (Acts 2,39), a phrase which is most naturally understood as referring to Gentiles[100]. More than that, the dedicatee of the two books is himself a Gentile (Luke 1,3f; Acts 1,1) – of equestrian rank if Luke is writing to an actual person[101] – and this in

tion which is offered in the name of Jesus...The Jews have priority, but salvation is there just as much for Gentile as for Jew". J. NOLLAND, *Luke 1–9:20* (WBC, 35A), Dallas, TX, Word Books, 1989, p. 120, in agreement with D.L. BOCK, *Luke. Vol. 1. 1:1–9:50* (BECNT, 3A), Grand Rapids, Baker Book House, 1994, pp. 244f.

96. Luke 20,1.6.19.26; 21,38; 22,2; Acts 3,9.11f.23; 4,8.10.21; 5,12f.20.25f.34; 6,8.12; 10,2.41f; 12,4; 13,15.31; 19,4; cf. Luke 2,10; 3,15.18; 18,43; 19,48; 23,5.27.35; 24,19.

97. In agreement with J. JERVELL, *Luke and the People of God*, Minneapolis, Augsburg, 1972, pp. 41-74.

98. E.g. 9,15; 10,35.45; 11,1.18; 13,46-48; 14,27; 15,3.7.12.14.17.19.23; 18,6; 21,19.25; 22,21; 26,17.20.23; 28,28. See further S.G. WILSON, *The Gentiles and the Gentile Mission in Luke-Acts* (SNTS MS, 23), Cambridge, University Press, 1973.

99. Alluding to Isa 49,6, as Acts 1,8 does: cf. NOLLAND, *Luke 1–9:20* (n. 95), p. 120; FITZMYER, *Luke I-IX* (n. 86), p 428; R.H. STEIN, *Luke* (NAC, 24), Nashville, Broadman Press, 1992, p. 116.

100. Cf. Acts 22,21; Isa 57,19 LXX; Eph 2,17 in agreement with JOHNSON, *Acts* (n. 11), p. 58; J.B. GREEN, *Salvation to the End of the Earth: God as the Saviour in the Acts of the Apostles*, in MARSHALL & PETERSON (eds.), *Witness to the Gospel* (n. 30), pp. 83-106, p. 92; BRUCE, *Acts* (n. 3), p 130; BARRETT, *Acts*, I (n. 12), pp. 155f; PESCH, *Die Apostelgeschichte*, 1 (n. 10), p. 125; *contra* WITHERINGTON, *Acts* (n. 13), pp. 155f; WILSON, *The Gentiles* (n. 98), p. 219.

101. This continues to be the likeliest understanding, since Theophilus is a common name: see C.J. HEMER, *The Book of Acts in the Setting of Hellenistic History* (WUNT, 49), Tübingen, Mohr, 1989, p. 221 n. 1. We lack clear ancient examples of a dedication to a fictional person; so most recently GREEN, *The Gospel of Luke* (n. 71), p. 44.

itself shows Luke's concern that the message about Jesus is for non-Jews as well as Jews. It is of interest that key new steps to mission among non-Jews are marked by a special work of the God of Israel, such as the apostles' visit to Samaria after Philip's initial evangelism (8,4-17), the conversion of the Ethiopian eunuch (8,26-40), and the conversion of Cornelius (10,1–11,18[102]).

In this context the programmatic-looking phrase ἕως ἐσχάτου τῆς γῆς (Acts 1,8) merits brief discussion. This verse has often been seen as providing the outline of Acts[103], although it is in reality extremely vague after Samaria[104], and it is puzzling that it does not mention Galilee at all[105]. The specific phrase comes elsewhere at Acts 13,47, quoted (as here) from Isa 49,6. Jervell[106] sees this phrase as primarily geographical: Rome is the "ends of the earth" – but in his view it does not specifically mean the Gentile mission; rather, it means a geographically widespread mission to Israel, an Israel that now can include Gentiles. Johnson[107] notes a number of possible parallel uses of the phrase in non-biblical and biblical use, proposing that the meaning of the phrase is contextually determined. LXX usage suggests "to the whole earth"[108], and Luke would be very unusual in the ancient world if here were not aware of a geographical horizon wider than Italy. Witherington[109] regards it as likely that the text should be read in the light of Luke 24,47 (and, we might add, Acts 24,5), and that this likelihood is reinforced by the open-endedness of the closing of Acts. We may agree with the consensus of these scholars that Luke has a worldwide mission which will include Gentiles in mind, and that Acts 1,8 should therefore be understood as setting an agenda which the remainder of the book addresses, while

102. Variously discussed in R.D. WITHERUP, *Cornelius Over and Over and Over Again: "Functional Redundancy" in the Acts of the Apostles*, in *JSNT* 49 (1993) 45-66; R.W. WALL, *Peter, "Son" of Jonah: The Conversion of Cornelius in the Context of the Canon*, in *JSNT* 29 (1987) 79-90; W.S. KURZ, *Effects of Variant Narrators in Acts 10–11*, in *NTS* 43 (1997) 570-586.

103. E.g. HAENCHEN, *Acts* (n. 5), p. 143 n. 9; BRUCE, *Acts* (n. 3), p. 103; JOHNSON, *Acts* (n. 11), p. 26.

104. TANNEHILL, *Narrative Unity*, 2 (n. 9), pp. 17f.

105. BARRETT, *Acts*, I (n. 12), pp. 80f.

106. JERVELL, *Theology* (n. 58), pp. 41, 105.

107. JOHNSON, *Acts* (n. 11), p. 26.

108. See esp. Isa 8,9; 14,22; 48,20; 49,6; 62,11; Jer 10,13; 28,16; 32,32; 38,8; 1 Macc 3,9 (all LXX references). Pss Sol 8,15 does refer to Pompey as "one from the end of the earth", which forms a possible parallel, but need not mean that Luke saw the world as the pseudepigraphic author did. BARRETT, *Acts*, I (n. 12), p. 80, takes the phrase to refer to Rome, but as representative of the whole world. DUNN, *Acts* (n. 15), p. 11, appears to concur.

109. WITHERINGTON, *Acts* (n. 13), pp. 110f.

being doubtful that Luke necessarily intended it as providing an outline, except in the sketchiest terms.

h. The Holy Spirit

It goes without saying that the Holy Spirit is a major theme in Acts 1–2 and in the remainder of Luke and Acts[110]. Here we focus on a number of phrases used in connection with the Spirit in Acts 1–2 which echo language from the Gospel and/or anticipate such use later in Acts.

Luke writes of the Spirit as "the promise of the Father" twice, and the use of this phrase in Acts 1,4 looks designed to echo the use in Luke 24,49, particularly given that another link between these verses is between "stay in the city" (Luke 24,49) and "do not leave Jerusalem" (Acts 1,4)[111]. The Spirit's coming is described using the Lukanism ἐπέρχομαι[112] (Acts 1,8), a word which has described the Spirit's work in Jesus' conception (Luke 1,35).

The quotation used in Peter's sermon (Acts 2,17-21, quoting Joel 3,1-5 LXX), allied to the programmatic mention of the Spirit in Peter's call for response (2,38), suggests that the Spirit's presence is the distinguishing mark of the renewed people of God[113]. This impression is reinforced when we observe that Peter is the person who claims that Gentiles have received the Spirit καθὼς καὶ ἡμῖν (15,8f) and draws the conclusion that God makes no distinction between Jew and Gentile, so neither should the church. The Pentecostal coming of the Spirit is the model for subsequent comings.

The Spirit's guidance is highlighted in Acts 1–2. The implication of the juxtaposition of the promise of power by the Spirit and the geographical expansion of the church (Acts 1,8) suggests that the development will be guided by the Spirit. The Spirit then equips the young church to speak of God's mighty works in many languages (2,4) and to interpret what has happened as being in line with God's purposes revealed in Scripture (2,17ff). The theme of being "led by the Spirit" (to use a Pauline phrase) is developed in subsequent chapters (e.g. 4,8.31; 5,31f; 6,3f; 8,29.39; 10,19; 11,12; 13,2.4; 15,28; 16,6f;

110. Recently, see R.P. MENZIES, *Empowered for Witness: The Spirit in Luke-Acts* (JPT SS, 6), Sheffield, Academic Press, 1994; W.H. SHEPHERD, *The Narrative Function of the Holy Spirit as a Character in Luke-Acts* (SBL DS, 147), Atlanta, Scholars, 1994; R. STRONSTAD, *The Charismatic Theology of St Luke*, Peabody, Hendrickson, 1984; M. TURNER, *Power from on High: The Spirit in Israel's Restoration and Witness in Luke-Acts* (JPT SS, 9), Sheffield, Academic Press, 1996.
111. PARSONS, *Departure* (n. 4), p. 172.
112. Found 3 times in Luke, 4 times in Acts and only twice elsewhere in the NT.
113. In agreement with JERVELL, *Theology* (n. 58), p. 45.

19,21[114]; 20,22.28). The theme of being guided by the Spirit is, of course, present in the Gospel too: for example, the elderly Simeon comes to the temple ἐν τῷ πνεύματι (Luke 2,27); Jesus understands his mission in terms of the Spirit's anointing for a task drawn from the Scriptures (Luke 4,18ff, quoting Isa 61,1ff); and the disciples are promised the Spirit's guidance what to say (Luke 12,12).

Finally, the confidence (παρρησία, παρρησιάζομαι[115]) which the Spirit produces is notable. Peter can speak with confidence about the deadness of David (Acts 2,29) – presumably not requiring great help from the Spirit to do so! – but the other uses of this word in Acts suggest that we may be meant to hear it as a fulfilment of the promise in Luke 12,12. Peter and John speak boldly when before the Sanhedrin (Acts 4,13). The church prays for boldness of speech when threatened (4,29) – a request which is speedily granted (4,31). Paul preaches boldly about Jesus (9,27f; 13,46; 14,3; 19,8; 26,26), and so does Apollos (18,26). At the end of the book we are left with the portrait of Paul speaking of the Lord Jesus with boldness (28,31).

i. Prayer

Prayer is a key emphasis of Luke's Gospel[116]. Luke portrays Jesus' prayer life more than any other Evangelist, and is often alone in mentioning Jesus praying in stories which he shares with others[117]. Acts 1–2 repeats this emphasis, although in a different situation, showing that the apostolic church continues the concerns of its founder. Thus prayer is an activity in which the waiting group persists (1,14): the church is born out of prayer. They pray before casting lots over Judas' successor (1,24f), and prayer is one of the key markers of the new community (2,42) – again an activity in which they persist[118] – leading to growth of the community (2,47 is clearly consequential upon 2,42).

---

114. So B.M. RAPSKE, *The Book of Acts and Paul in Roman Custody* (BAFCS, 3), Carlisle, Paternoster – Grand Rapids, Eerdmans, 1994, p. 404, noticing the use of δεῖ as implying divine involvement in the decision; *contra* COSGROVE, *The Divine δεῖ* (n. 25), p. 178; H. CONZELMANN, *Acts of the Apostles* (Hermeneia), Philadelphia, Fortress, 1987, p. 164, points to the similar use of δεῖ in 23,11; 27,24.

115. Between them, used 12 times in Acts out of 40 NT uses in total (9 of which are in John).

116. The προσευχή word group is used 22 times in Luke and 25 times in Acts. See further A.A. TRITES, *The Prayer Motif in Luke-Acts*, in C.H. TALBERT (ed.), *Perspectives on Luke-Acts*, Edinburgh, Clark, 1978, pp. 168-186, esp. 169-179; FITZMYER, *Luke I-IX* (n. 86), pp. 244-247; STEIN, *Luke* (n. 99), pp. 51f.

117. Luke 3,21; 6,12; 9,18.28; 11,2; 22,32.39.41; 23,46.

118. The collocation of προσκαρτερέω and προσευχή occurs in one other place in Acts (6,4). Προσκαρτερέω is used only 10 times in the NT, 6 of which are found in Acts (1,14; 2,42.46; 6,4; 8,13; 10,7).

Subsequent chapters of Acts present a rich portrait of the place of prayer in the life of the earliest Christians[119]. Prayer to God is their recourse in persecution or suffering (4,24-30; 16,25). The apostles are set apart for a particular ministry of prayer (6,4). The church commissions those taking responsibility through prayer (6,6; 13,3; 14,23). Prayer precedes the coming of the Spirit or is the means through which the Spirit comes (8,15; 9,11.17f). Dorcas is raised in response to prayer (9,40). Guidance comes as people pray (10,9ff.30). Peter is freed after prayer – although, comically, the church does not expect it (12,5.12-17[120]). Paul prays with the Ephesian elders before departing (20,36) and with the Tyrian Christians (21,5).

3. *Acts 1–2 as Bridge and Overture*

In the light of our studies we may propose three metaphors for understanding the role of these chapters in Luke-Acts.

First, we may see them as a bridge between the story of Jesus and the story of the church. Again and again we have seen Luke highlighting themes in Acts 1–2 which have appeared in the Gospel and which will be developed in Acts, almost always using vocabulary which is focused in Acts 1–2, but which can be mapped throughout the rest of Luke-Acts. Significantly, these themes cluster together in Acts 1–2, so that it is not simply that a few themes which run through the *Doppelwerk* happen to be located in Acts 1–2; rather, there seems to be a very large number grouped together. It is as though a wide road from the Gospel narrows down to a small bridge (Acts 1–2) and then widens out on the other side into Acts.

Second, if we consider ourselves to be standing in Acts 1–2, these themes compel us to be like the two-faced god Janus, both looking back to the Gospel and forward to Acts. The themes we have seen reinforce Blomberg's view[121] that the central section of Luke-Acts is focused on the death and resurrection of Jesus in Jerusalem, with the Gospel moving towards these events in the city and Acts moving away from the city. In both cases the movement is both physical and metaphorical; the former is clear, but the latter is more significant, as the Gospel leads up to the momentous events which make salvation possible, and Acts works out the consequences of these events.

---

119. TRITES, *The Prayer Motif in Luke-Acts* (n. 116), pp. 179-184.
120. See J. GOLDINGAY, *Are They Comic Acts?*, in *EvQ* 69 (1997) 99-107, who discusses other examples of humour in Acts.
121. C.L. BLOMBERG, *Jesus and the Gospels: An Introduction and Survey*, Leicester, Apollos, 1997, pp. 140-145, esp. the diagram on p. 143.

Third, we may see these chapters in relation to the rest of Acts as like the overture to a longer piece of music. It is no exaggeration to say that virtually all of the main themes of Acts are present in these chapters, but often in the briefest form. The development of the themes later in the book offers the expansion of the theme which is characteristic of a musical composer.

If these metaphors express accurate observations about Acts 1–2, we may end by noticing that Luke has not closed the introduction to Acts abruptly. Perhaps, to multiply metaphors further, we ought to see the beginning of Acts as having a "fuzzy" boundary; it seems to slide into the rest of the book without clear announcement.

Where does the beginning of Acts end? That is, what is the end to which the beginning points? The answer seems to be "the ends of the earth" (Acts 1,8), the goal to which Luke looked from the opening verses of his book – and a goal at which he was encouraging the church of his day to aim.

St John's College   Steve WALTON
Chilwell Lane
Bramcote-Nottingham NG9 3DS
England

CHILDREN OF THE PROMISE

ON THE *ΔΙΑΘΗΚΗ*-PROMISE TO ABRAHAM
IN LK 1,72 AND ACTS 3,25

After the healing of a lame, Peter addresses the people witnessing this wonder (Acts 3,12-26). God glorified Jesus, whom they had delivered up. His name and the faith in his name have now healed the lame. Peter proclaims Jesus as the "prophet like Moses", who was announced by Moses and the prophets. He qualifies the Jews he is addressing as the sons of the prophets and of God's promise (διαθήκη[1]) made to Abraham. The motif of God's διαθήκη-promise made to Abraham also occurs in Lk 1,72. Zechariah blesses God, who has raised up a horn of salvation to perform the mercy promised to their fathers and to remember his holy διαθήκη to Abraham. In both cases it is suggested that in Jesus the promise to Abraham is fulfilled. This seems to point at a common theological view. In the present paper I will examine to which extent the promises to Abraham point at a specific Lucan theology which occurs in both the Gospel and Acts. More specifically, it will be argued that the διαθήκη-promises should be seen against the background of Luke's typology of Abraham and the Lucan theme of promises and their fulfilment. Therefore, I will first briefly examine the content and context of the promises to Abraham in Lk 1,72 and Acts 3,25. I will also sketch the place of the promises in Luke's Abraham typology. The perspective will then be extended to the broader theme of divine promises and their fulfilment in Luke-Acts in order to examine how the divine διαθήκη-promises are part of Luke's theology.

1. *The Divine Διαθήκη-Promises to Abraham*

a. Lk 1,72

The Benedictus of Zechariah is both praise and proclamation[2]. This song is divided into two major parts: vv. 68-75 (the praise) and 76-79 (the proclamation with John's function and relation to the saviour). The

---

1. For "promise" as a translation of διαθήκη in Lk 1,72 and Acts 3,25, see E. KUTSCH, *Neues Testament – Neuer Bund? Eine Fehlübersetzung wird korrigiert*, Neukirchen, Neukirchener, 1978, pp. 93-94; and the discussion of both pericopes below.
2. W. CARTER, *Zechariah and the Benedictus (Luke 1,68-79): Practising What He Preaches*, in *Bib* 69 (1988) 239-247, pp. 241-242.

word διαθήκη occurs in the first part, which I will discuss more in detail here.

The ground for Zechariah's blessing (εὐλογητὸς κύριος ὁ θεὸς τοῦ Ἰσραήλ) is God's saving activity, that is expressed by ὅτι + three verbs: ἐπεσκέψατο, ἐποίησεν, ἤγειρεν. God has visited and redeemed his people and raised up a saviour (κέρας σωτηρίας) from the house of David (1,68b-69). The salvation (σωτηρίαν[3]) is taken up again in v. 71 and explained as salvation from the enemies and from all the people who hate them. Verse 70 interprets God's saving act as the fulfilment of the previous promises of the prophets to rescue them from their enemies (1,70-71). Moreover, the purpose of God's actions is mentioned with two infinitives, ποιῆσαι and μνησθῆναι: to perform mercy to the fathers and to remember the διαθήκη concerning Abraham (1,72). The term διαθήκη is explained by the following apposition: the oath (ὅρκον) God swore to Abraham. The content of the διαθήκη or the oath God swore to Abraham is the gift of ongoing service of God, without fear and rescued from the enemies (1,73-75)[4]. This parallel suggests that the διαθήκη to Abraham is in this context a promise confirmed by oath[5] that the people will service God without fear.

Though such a διαθήκη is not mentioned in the Old or the New Testament, Zechariah's song calls to mind several Old Testament texts. That God will act according to His mercy to Abraham in agreement with previous promises, points at Micah 7,20[6]. God's remembering of the διαθήκη to Abraham alludes to several texts, such as Ps 105,8; 106,45[7]; Lev 26,42; Exod 2,24; Exod 6,5. The expression ὅρκον ὃν ὤμοσεν τοῦ δοῦναι is a common one for God's pledge to give Abraham and his descendants the land of Canaan (e.g. Gen 26,3; Jer 11,5; cf. Ps 104,8), which is qualified as a διαθήκη in Gen 15,18 and 17,8. The idea of being rescued by God from the hand of the enemy (ἐκ χειρὸς ἐχθρῶν ῥυσθέντας) occurs throughout the Old Testament (Exod 14,30; 17,1; 21,21; 30,16, etc.).

3. Apposition to κέρας in v. 69, see M. ZERWICK – M. GROSVENOR, *A Grammatical Analysis of the Greek New Testament*, Rome, PIB, [4]1993, p. 175.
4. Against R.L. BRAWLEY, *For Blessing All Families of the Earth: Covenant Traditions in Luke-Acts*, in *Currents in Theology and Mission* 22 (1995) 18-26, p. 23, who states that the διαθήκη has no content in Lk 1,72; and against E. KUTSCH, *Neues Testament – Neuer Bund?* (n. 1), p. 93, who interprets the διαθήκη as a reference to the promise to be a God to Abraham's descendants (Gen 17,7.8b).
5. Cf. E. KUTSCH, *Neues Testament – Neuer Bund?* (n. 1), p. 93.
6. Cf. H. RINGGREN, *Luke's Use of the Old Testament*, in G.W.E. NICKELSBURG – G.W. MACRAE (eds.), *Christians Among Jews and Gentiles*. FS K. Stendahl, Philadelphia, Fortress Press, 1986, pp. 227-235, esp. 232.
7. *Ibid.*

The motif of service to God (λατρεύειν) is typically Lucan[8]. Luke found it in his sources (Lk 4,8 par Mt 4,10, quoting Deut 6,13) and elaborated it. It occurs in Lk 1,74 and in Acts 7,7 as a divine promise. Throughout Luke-Acts, several figures are said to serve (λατρεύειν) God: the prophetess Anna (Lk 2,37); Jesus (Lk 4,8); Paul (Acts 24,14; 27,23); and the twelve tribes of Israel (Acts 26,7). In the Old Testament, the motif that Israel will serve God is both a sign that God sends Moses (Exod 3,12 to which Acts 7,7 alludes) and the purpose of the exodus (Exod 4,23; 7,16.26, etc.), but is never mentioned as the content of a διαθήκη nor as a promise to Abraham. Yet, since it occurs in both Lk 1,73 and Acts 7,7 as a divine promise to Abraham, it is part of Luke's portrayal of Abraham.

Concerning the διαθήκη in Lk 1,68-79 we can conclude that the Benedictus is a song based on a mosaic of Old Testament images, in which the Lucan motif of service to God occurs as the content of a divine διαθήκη-promise to Abraham.

b. Acts 3,25

The promise is mentioned in Peter's speech to the inhabitants of Jerusalem (Acts 3,12-26). After the healing of the lame at the gate of the temple, Peter makes use of the astonishment of the people present to proclaim Jesus. God glorified Jesus, the man they denied. Yet, by his name, the lame is healed (Acts 3,13-16). Peter points at their ignorance and appeals them to repent (3,17.19). It was foretold that the Christ must suffer and all what God predicted by the mouth of his prophets will be accomplished through Jesus in the future (3,18.21). Peter refers to the prophet who would, like Moses, be raised up, as foretold by Moses and the prophets (3,22-24).

Throughout Peter's speech, two views are interwoven. On the one hand, the Jews have delivered and denied Jesus. Moreover, there is a prophecy that those who do not listen to the "prophet like Moses" will be destroyed from the people (Acts 3,13-15.23). On the other hand, the suffering of the Christ has been foretold, which may excuse the Jews if they repent, and the Christ is appointed "for you" (3,18.20). Moses' prophecy also points at a prophet who will be raised "for you" (3,22). Both redemption and destruction of the Jews are possible accomplishments of the divine predictions, depending on the Jewish acceptance or denial of Jesus as their Christ and "prophet like Moses".

---

8. Apart from Luke, it occurs only once in the Gospels (Mt 4,10). Out of 21 occurrences in the NT, 8 are found in Luke-Acts, of which Acts 7,42 refers to the service to the "host of heaven".

The Jews are the children of the prophets and of the διαθήκη-promise (3,25). In the following relative clause, this is explained as the promise which God confirmed to Abraham. The content is introduced by λέγων. God promises Abraham that in his seed all the families of the earth will be blessed. Though the blessing through Abraham's descendants is never called a διαθήκη-promise in the Old Testament[9], Luke quotes Gen 22,18; 26,4 as its content. In Abraham's seed (singular), which means in Jesus, all the families on the earth will be blessed. However, in this quotation, Luke replaced the more universal τὰ ἔθνη, "the nations" by αἱ πατριαί, "the families", which he found in Gen 12,3[10].

The motif of the "children of Abraham", of which the "sons of the διαθήκη-promise" is a variant, occurs several times in Luke-Acts. Luke found it in Q (Lk 3,8 par Mt 3,9) and elaborated it. John the Baptist warns his audience against the false security of relying on the fact that Abraham is their father, by saying that God can make children to Abraham out of stones. Though the motif always refers to Jews in Luke-Acts, I would argue that the possibility that God will make other children for Abraham remains open. The fact that the Jews are the children of Abraham (Lk 3,8; Acts 3,25; 13,26) can be no excuse for not bearing the fruit of repentance (Lk 3,7-9). Moreover, no Jew can be excluded from his inheritance (cf. Lk 13,16 and Lk 19,9). As children of Abraham, the Jews are the prominent and legitimate heirs of the divine promises. Luke emphasises this by altering his quotation of the promise to Abraham. At the same time, the Jews are also the children of the prophets, addressed to and warned by John (Lk 3,7-9), Peter (Acts 3,12-26), and Moses and the Old Testament prophets (Acts 3,22-24).

Remarkable, however, is that the idea of universalism, which was present in Luke's source, is taken up by the word "first" in Acts 3,26. Though Luke portrays the Jews as the prominent heirs of the divine promises, the people to which God has appointed his Christ and his "prophet like Moses", they are not the only ones. The "first" suggests a "thereafter", which must be directed to the Gentiles.

To conclude, Peter's speech with its reference to redemption for the Jews if they repent, refers to the Jews as sons of the διαθήκη. In this way, Luke qualifies an Old Testament promise to Abraham as a διαθήκη, which is to be fulfilled in Jesus.

9. Yet, an act of "making a διαθήκη" is not necessary to refer to a divine promise as a διαθήκη in the Old Testament. Though the promises to David are not called so in 2 Sam 7, David can refer to them as διαθήκη-promises in 2 Sam 23,5.

10. Against H. RINGGREN, *Luke's Use of the Old Testament* (n. 6), p. 233, who thinks this is a free quotation from the LXX.

2. *Divine Promises as Part of Luke's Abraham Typology*

a. The Abraham Typology in Luke-Acts

In the New Testament, several typologies of Abraham can be found. According to N.A. Dahl, Abraham is portrayed as the father of the Christian believers by Paul[11]. James is interested in Abraham's faith, which was at work in his actions, and draws the conclusion that a man is justified by his deeds and not by faith (2,20-24). John considers Abraham to be a witness to Christ before his coming, and to the author of Hebrews he is an example to be imitated (6,11ff). In Dahl's opinion, Luke portrays Abraham as the father of the Jews, never of Christian believers. Abraham is seen as both a historical and an eschatological figure, but to Luke Abraham is mainly the recipient of the divine promises.

The name Abraham occurs 15 times in Luke and 7 times in Acts. Of the occurrences in his Gospel, Luke found this name four times in his sources: once in Mark (Mk 12,26 par Lk 20,37) and three times in Q (Mt 3,9a.9b par Lk 3,8a.8b; Mt 8,11 par Lk 13,28). Abraham is living with God (Lk 20,37) and he will also be seen together with the prophets in the Kingdom of God (Lk 13,28). The characterisation of the living Abraham as an eschatological figure is especially prominent in Lk 16 (vs. 22.23.24.25.29.30). The motif of "the children of Abraham" (Lk 3,8) is taken up in Lk 13,16 and Lk 19,9. In Acts, the motif occurs implicitly in 3,25, where the Jews are called "sons of the διαθήκη-promise" which God made to Abraham, and explicitly in 13,26, where Paul addresses his public as "sons of Abraham". In the remaining texts, there is always some link between Abraham and Jesus. Jesus is a descendant of Abraham (Lk 3,34). The announcement of Jesus' birth is in agreement with God's promises to Abraham (Lk 1,55.73). The God of Abraham, Isaac and Jacob glorified Jesus (Acts 3,13, maybe this is also an allusion to Lk 20,37). Israel's history as described by Stephen (7,2.16.17.32) leads from Abraham to Jesus, whom the Jews have murdered.

Luke's Abraham typology has three main features, two concerning Abraham himself and one concerning his heirs: Abraham is both a living, eschatological and a historical person. As a historical person, he received divine promises, which are eventually connected with Jesus. The motif of "the children of Abraham" raises the question of who are the rightful heirs of Abraham. As far as the διαθήκη-promises are con-

---

11. N.A. DAHL, *The Story of Abraham in Luke-Acts*, in L.E. KECK – J.L. MARTYN (eds.), *Studies in Luke-Acts*. FS P. Schubert, Nashville, TN, Abingdon Press, 1966, pp. 139-158, esp. 139; 142.

cerned, especially the last two ideas are important. The portrayal of Abraham as a historical person and recipient of divine promises is not new. Therefore, the Old Testament background of these promises will be explored in order to examine how Luke adapts the portrayal of Abraham to his own theological interests.

b. Abraham as the Recipient of Divine Promises in the Old Testament

Abraham's father Terach takes him to go to Canaan and settles in Haran (Gen 11,31-32). God orders Abraham to leave his country and to go to a land He will show him. At this moment, He also makes promises: to make a great nation of Abraham; to bless him; and to make his name great (Gen 12,1-3). Abraham obeys and God appears to him, promising that He will give the land to Abraham's descendants (Gen 12,7). The promises of a numerous offspring and of the possession of the land are repeated several times throughout the story of Abraham (Gen 13,14-17; 15,4-7; 17,4.7-8). When Abraham asks God how he will know that he really will get the land, God confirms his promise by ברית (Gen 15,18). The Hebrew term ברית, translated by διαϑήκη in the LXX, points to a very strong commitment[12]. In Gen 15, the ברית is undertaken through a strange ritual. God walks under the image of a smoking fire pot and a flaming torch between the divided parts of animals. This kind of ritual is also known from Jer 34,18-20. By walking between parts of an animal, one invokes a self-curse in case one would not keep his commitment. By performing this ritual, God solemnly pledges to keep his promise to Abraham to give his descendants the land Canaan. Apart from this promise, two other promises are confirmed to Abraham and his descendants in Gen 17,4.8-9: the promise to become a father of a multitude of nations and the promise to become their God. The circumcision is both a duty and the sign of this divine promise. Not his servant Eliezer nor Hagar's son Ismael will be the recipient of God's promises, but Abraham's legitimate heir with his own wife: Sarah's son Isaac (Gen

12. E. Kutsch has argued that the traditional translation "Bund, covenant" does not accurately correspond with the meaning of ברית when used in theological texts. He prefers the meaning "Verpflichtung, obligation", which can be the obligation one takes upon oneself; the obligation somebody else forces you to do; the mutual obligation (only in a 'secular' sense); or the obligation that is forced upon by a third party. See E. KUTSCH, *Verheißung und Gesetz. Untersuchungen zum sogenannten "Bund" im Alten Testament* (BZAW, 131), Berlin – New York, de Gruyter 1973, p. 27. According to F. Crüsemann the focus is not on the one who takes the obligation, but on how the obligation is taken: solemnly and irrevocably. See F. CRÜSEMANN, *Ihnen gehören... die Bundesschlüsse (Röm 9,4): Die alttestamentliche Bundestheologie und der christlich-jüdische Dialog*, in *Kirche und Israel* 9 (1994) 21-38, esp. p. 26. For διαϑήκη in the LXX and in the NT, see E. KUTSCH, *Neues Testament – Neuer Bund?* (n. 1), esp. pp. 47-162.

17,17). In Gen 22,16-18 God pledges to bless Abraham, to multiply his descendants and give the gates of their enemies in their possession. The nations will bless themselves by his descendants because of Abraham's obedience to God.

According to the Old Testament, God's promises to Abraham have greatly influenced the future of Israel. On the one hand, the descendants of Abraham, Isaac and Jacob are heirs of the promises. Thus, God appears in Gen 26,3-5 to Isaac and promises to fulfil the oath He swore to Abraham. God states that He will be with Isaac, will bless him, give the land to him and multiply his descendants. The descendants will receive the land and by them the nations of the earth shall bless themselves, because of Abraham's obedience to God. On the other hand, God remembers his διαθήκη (Exod 2,24; 6,3-5; cf. Ps 105,8; 106,45) and acts accordingly: He delivers his enslaved people. The commitment prevents God of destroying his people in anger (Lev 26,42; 2 Kings 13,25). In 2 Macc 1,2, the motif that God remembers his διαθήκη to Abraham is used to wish the Jews of Egypt well.

Against this Old Testament background, it is easy to understand why it is crucial to be "a child of Abraham". The heirs of Abraham are also the heirs of the divine promises. They are the people to whom God will remember and keep his promises, on which His current salvific acts are based.

c. Luke's Adaptation of the Old Testament Background in Acts 7

In the speech of Stephen, Abraham's history is being recalled. Three adaptations concerning the divine promises are especially remarkable[13]: God's appearance to Abraham; the emphasis on the fact that the promise of the land was not fulfilled in Abraham's own lifetime but in the time of the exodus; and the promise to Abraham that the people, after four hundred years of slavery, will serve God in this place.

In the story of Genesis, God appears to Abraham and makes him promises after he has moved to Haran. According to Acts 7,2, however, God's appearance happens before this migration. This adaptation effects a stronger emphasis on Abraham acting according to God's commandments and promises.

According to Acts 7,5 God gave Abraham no inheritance in the land, not even a foot's length. This is in contradiction with the story of Gen 23. In Gen 23,17-20 it is said stated that Abraham got a field and a cave

---

13. For a more detailed analysis, see N.A. DAHL, *The Story of Abraham* (n. 11), pp. 143-148.

to bury Sarah in his own possession. Luke recalls this story of the burial place in Acts 7,16, though mixing it up with Jacob's purchase of a piece of land at Sechem. By stating in 7,5 that Abraham got no land into his possession, Luke creates a line of promise and fulfilment from Abraham to the time of Moses and the exodus. The exodus with his subsequent entrance in Canaan is presented as the accomplishment of the promise to Abraham. When the people multiplies in Egypt and Moses is born, "the time of the promise that God had granted Abraham grew near" (Acts 7,17). Luke enforces the idea, already present in the Old Testament, that God's salvific acts during the exodus resulted from his remembrance of his promises to Abraham (Exod 2,23-25; 6,5) by presenting the exodus as the explicit fulfilment of the promise of the land.

In Acts 7,7, Luke mentions a promise that was not given to Abraham in the Old Testament: the people will serve (λατρεύσουσιν) God in this place. It is found in the Moses cyclus (Exod 3,12): the promise that the people will serve God upon "this" mountain is the sign that God sent Moses. The alteration into "this place" is probably due to the accusations against Stephen concerning "this place" (Acts 6,13-14). Since Luke presents the exodus as the result of the promises to Abraham, he could easily connect the promise to Moses with Abraham. In this way, the promise is brought forward and the whole exodus comes under the tension of the promise. According to Acts 7,42, however, the people served "the host of heaven" in agreement with the prophecy of Amos 5,25-27. Even the building of the temple did not fulfil this promise to Abraham, since God does not dwell in houses made with hands (Acts 7,48)[14].

Luke's adaptations of the Abraham story emphasise the divine promises, focusing not only at the promise itself, but also at their fulfilment. All of Abraham's migrations are guided by God's plans. The promise of the possession of the land has been fulfilled in Moses' days. Another promise is yet unfulfilled: the people's worship of God.

d. The Promises as Part of Luke's Abraham Typology

The promises to Abraham in Lk 1,72 and Acts 3,25 can solidly be connected with one of the mean features of the Abraham typology of Luke: The historical Abraham is the recipient of divine promises. This portrayal of Abraham was already present in the Old Testament. But the promises of Lk 1,72 and Acts 3,25 do not belong to the διαθήκη-promises to

---

14. Cf. D.P. MOESSNER, *Paul and the Pattern of the Prophet Like Moses in Acts*, in *SBL 1983 Seminar Papers*, pp. 203-212, esp. 205.

Abraham according to the Old Testament. Luke deliberately adapted the promises to build his own image of Abraham which could function in a broader theological line of divine promises and their fulfilment.

This is most clear in Lk 1,72. It was a promise to Moses, not to Abraham, and the purpose of the exodus, that the people will serve God. In Acts 7,7 it is made into a promise to Abraham, which is yet unfulfilled. In Lk 1,68-75 the conception of Jesus is seen as the partial fulfilment of this promise.

In Acts 3,25 the promise to Abraham that in his seed the generations of the earth will be blessed, is referred to as a διαθήκη. It will be fulfilled in Jesus. This again is typically Lucan, which becomes clear from a comparison with a similar text in Gal 3. According to Gal 3,6-7, those who have faith are sons of Abraham who himself had faith. The nations will be blessed in Abraham (v. 8). The sons of Abraham are blessed with him who had faith (v. 9). According to Luke, however, the generations will be blessed, not with Abraham, but through Jesus. Abraham is important, not as the faithful one, but as the recipient of the divine promise which is to be fulfilled in Jesus.

3. *Divine Promises and Their Fulfilment in Luke-Acts*

The theme of God who makes promises and fulfils them occurs on a double level in Luke-Acts. Luke's narrative contains both new and past promises, which are fulfilled through the birth, life, death and resurrection of Jesus and through the mission of his disciples. Luke found some of the promises in his sources. However, he deliberately elaborated the promise and fulfilment scheme[15].

a. "Contemporary" Promises

Some of the promises are made during the lifetime of Jesus and his disciples. These "contemporary" promises are made by heavenly messengers, e.g. by the angel Gabriel (Lk 1,26-38), or by humans, such as Zechariah (Lk 1,68-79), Jesus (Lk 13,33; 6,22-23; 11,47-51), and Paul (Acts 13). Most of them are referring explicitly or implicitly to promises

---

15. For the Lucan adaptations concerning Jesus' predictions of his suffering, death and resurrection, see e.g., B. CURTIN FREIN, *Narrative Predictions, Old Testament Prophecies and Luke's Sense of Fulfilment*, in *NTS* 40 (1994) 22-37, pp. 29-30; for the analysis of Old Testament quotations and allusions in Luke, cf. H. RINGGREN, *Luke's Use of the Old Testament* (n. 6), pp. 227-235; and for the analysis of Luke's language of fulfilment, cf. D. PETERSON, *The Motif of Fulfilment and the Purpose of Luke-Acts*, in B.C. WINTER – A.D. CLARKE (eds.), *The Book of Acts in Its Ancient Literary Setting* (The Book of Acts in Its First Century Setting, 1), Grand Rapids, MI, Eerdmans, 1993, pp. 83-104, esp. 86-88.

of the past. For the infancy narrative B. Curtin Frein distinguishes three functions[16]. The promises set the stage for the upcoming events that are predicted (the birth of John and Jesus). Moreover, they provide the reader with an interpretative framework concerning the ministry of John and Jesus. Lastly, the continuity between the fulfilment of recent prophecies and prophecies made in the past is emphasised: John's actions are the fulfilment of the words of the heavenly messenger (Lk 1,13-17) and of John's father (Lk 1,76-79), but simultaneously also of the prophecy of Malachi to which Lk 1,17 alludes.

As regards the promises outside the infancy narrative, the literary function of setting the stage for events that follow immediately upon it seems to be less prominent. However, from a literary point of view the promises and their fulfilment still function as plot devices in Luke-Acts. Luke constructed the events in such a way that they fulfil both Old Testament and contemporary promises, as Curtin Frein correctly notices[17]. She also remarks that some unfulfilled promises and predictions, especially those concerning eschatological events, are in juxtaposition with other promises that are realised. The actual fulfilment of some of the promises implicitly suggests the reliability of the remaining promises, which are to be accomplished in the future. Hence, Curtin Frein concludes that the main function of the promise/fulfilment theme is the continuity of God's plan of salvation[18]. The continuity of God's saving actions is indeed an important perspective of the promise/fulfilment scheme. However, I think that not only a theological function is at stake, but also a christological and an ecclesiological one.

b. Divine Promises of the Past

The promises of the past also play an important role in the Lucan scheme of promise and fulfilment. According to recent studies, Luke used Old Testament passages as a literary model for his own work[19]. Moreover, the Old Testament provided Luke with a theological framework that could be used for his own purpose. Luke's view on the Old Testament can be described as merely "prophetic"[20]. God's acts of salvation in the past are mirrored and completed in the current events. Luke

16. B. CURTIN FREIN, *Narrative Predictions* (n. 15), p. 26.
17. *Ibid.*, p. 35.
18. *Ibid.*, pp. 35-36.
19. See R.I. DENOVA, *The Things Accomplished Among Us. Prophetic Tradition in the Structural Pattern of Luke-Acts* (JSNT SS, 141), Sheffield, Academic Press, 1997, pp. 81-104: "Literary Device in Luke-Acts: Scripture, Typology and Parallel Patterns".
20. See J.T. SANDERS, *The Prophetic Use of the Scriptures in Luke-Acts*, in C.A. EVANS – W.F. STINESPRING (eds.), *Early Jewish and Christian Exegesis*. FS W.H. Brownlee, Atlanta, GA, Scholars Press, 1987, pp. 191-198.

both explicitly[21] and more typologically[22] refers to Old Testament texts and persons and claims that past promises are being fulfilled in what has happened with Jesus and still happens with his disciples. Apart from a theological function, namely that God keeps his former promises in view of his salvation for Israel and the world, there is a christological and an ecclesiological aim. The main point of Luke's use of the Old Testament is the proclamation of Jesus[23]. The hope of Israel and the messianic expectations have now come to fruition and climax in the life, suffering, death and resurrection of Jesus, who is portrayed as "the prophet like Moses", the Servant, the Davidic Messiah, the Lord[24]. The ecclesiological aim can be discovered in two essential items: the Gentile mission and the rejection by Israel[25]. J.T. Sanders argues for a very radical attitude: "The Jews are out and the Gentiles are in"[26]. Other authors defend a more balanced view. J.A. Weatherly concludes that Luke-Acts does not argue for the complete and general condemnation of the Jews[27]. Only the leaders and the people of Jerusalem are being held responsible for Jesus' crucifixion. In Weatherly's view, Luke-Acts affirm that non-Jews too are responsible to some degree, but there is no consistent attempt to ameliorate the Gentile culpability in order to accentuate the Jewish responsibility.

21. See H. RINGGREN, *Luke's Use of the Old Testament* (n. 6). J.A. Fitzmyer analyses the introductory formula's and the Lucan features of these quotations, cf. J.A. FITZMYER, *The Use of the Old Testament in Luke-Acts*, in *SBL 1992 Seminar Papers*, pp. 524-538.

22. For the idea that Luke not only refers to concrete prophecies but also to "patterns", see esp. D.L. BOCK, *Proclamation from Prophecy and Pattern. Lucan Old Testament Christology* (JSNT SS, 12), Sheffield, Academic Press, 1987.

23. That Luke has in mind "proclamation" rather than pure apologetic "proof from prophecy" has been argued especially by D.L. BOCK, *Proclamation from Prophecy and Pattern*, p. 274; *The Use of the Old Testament in Luke-Acts: Christology and Mission*, in *SBL 1990 Seminar Papers*, pp. 494-511, p. 506; *Proclamation from Prophecy and Pattern: Luke's Use of the Old Testament for Christology and Mission*, in C.A. EVANS – W.R. STEGNER (eds.), *The Gospels and the Scriptures of Israel* (JSNT SS, 102; SSEJC, 3), Sheffield, Academic Press, 1994, pp. 280-307.

24. D.L. BOCK, *The Use of the Old Testament in Luke-Acts*, pp. 496-506. For a thorough study on Jesus as Davidic Messiah in Luke-Acts, see M.L. STRAUSS, *The Davidic Messiah in Luke-Acts. The Promise and Its Fulfilment in Lucan Christology* (JSNT SS, 110), Sheffield, Academic Press, 1995. For the pattern of "the Prophet like Moses" in Acts, see D.P. MOESSNER, *Paul and the Pattern of the Prophet Like Moses* (n. 14), pp. 203-212.

25. On the christological and ecclesiological use of the Old Testament by Luke, see D.L. BOCK, *The Use of the Old Testament* and *Proclamation* (n. 23); J.T. CARROLL, *The Uses of Scripture in Acts*, in *SBL 1990 Seminar Papers*, pp. 512-528; D. PETERSON, *The Motif of Fulfilment* (n. 15); J.T. SANDERS, *The Prophetic Use of the Scriptures* (n. 20); M.L. STRAUSS, *The Davidic Messiah* (n. 24), pp. 348-349.

26. J.T. SANDERS, *The Prophetic Use of the Scriptures* (n. 20), p. 197.

27. J.A. WEATHERLY, *Jewish Responsibility for the Death of Jesus in Luke-Acts* (JSNT SS, 106), Sheffield, Academic Press, 1994, p. 217.

Decisive for possible condemnation is the positive or negative attitude towards Jesus and his gospel. The rejection of Jesus by many Jews is said to mirror the age-old pattern of unbelief of Israel and its rejection of the prophets, whereas the belief of many Gentiles is the fulfilment of the Old Testament view that the eventual salvation of Israel will include salvation for the Gentiles[28].

c. The Divine Promises Yet to Be Fulfilled

Luke's scheme of divine promises and fulfilment through Jesus and his followers has a theological, christological and ecclesiological function. God, who made promises in the past, fulfils them and makes new promises today. In Jesus Christ, the Davidic Messiah, "the prophet like Moses", the announced saviour, many promises are accomplished. Both the current rejection by many Jews and the success among the Gentiles is in agreement with Old Testament prophecy.

Closely connected to the claim of fulfilment of both contemporary and Old Testament promises in what has happened to Jesus and to the disciples, is the matter of the yet unfulfilled promises. As B. Curtin Frein indicates, not all the (contemporary) promises mentioned are yet fulfilled[29]. The fact that some predictions are accomplished provides hope that the remaining promises are reliable too. However, not only some of the "contemporary" promises made by Jesus, but also promises of the past are yet to be fulfilled. The key question is to whom they are addressed. In the Old Testament promises were made to Israel, its ancestors or leaders. In the New Testament the promises are directed to Jesus' followers. Who are the legitimate heirs of the unfulfilled promises? According to M.L. Strauss, eschatological salvation is closely connected with the people of Israel. The eschatological people of God, consisting of the remnant of Israel together with believing Gentiles, is the legitimate heir of the promises made to the fathers[30]. Can the same be said concerning the promises to Abraham?

4. *The Διαϑήκη to Abraham and the Lucan Theme of Promise and Fulfilment*

The promises to Abraham in Lk 1,72 and Acts 3,25 can be situated against the broader background of the Lucan theme of promises and their fulfilment. Zechariah blesses God and meanwhile proclaims Jesus

---

28. See D.L. BOCK, *The Use of the Old Testament*, pp. 506-509; and *Proclamation from Prophecy and Pattern* (n. 23); J.T. CARROLL, *The Uses of Scripture in Acts* (n. 25), pp. 526-528; R.I. DENOVA, *The Things Accomplished Among Us* (n. 19), pp. 37-38.
29. B. CURTIN FREIN, *Narrative Predictions* (n. 15), pp. 35-36.
30. M.L. STRAUSS, *The Davidic Messiah* (n. 24), p. 339.

as the saviour out of the house of David. This is portrayed as the fulfilment of the promises of the prophets (Lk 1,70) and in agreement with
the promise to Abraham. A prophecy from the past is currently being
fulfilled (a saviour has been raised up) and a promise that was once
made to Abraham is now to be accomplished in the near future.
Throughout Luke-Acts, several figures are said to serve God (see above
p. 471). In this way, the promise is gradually being fulfilled. In
Stephen's survey of Israel's history in Acts 7,7, however, the promise is
not said to be fulfilled. Since Stephen compares the rejection of Jesus by
Israel with the acts of their ancestors, true service of God is to be connected with the acceptance of Jesus as the Christ.

In the speech of Peter in Acts 3, the theme of the divine prophecies and
their fulfilment is prominent. Peter proclaims Jesus as the one through
whom blessing has come to the Jews if they repent. Throughout his
speech, he argues that some predictions are fulfilled: the fact that God's
Servant would suffer, the raising up "a prophet like Moses" and the
promise that in the seed of Abraham the families of the earth are blessed.
At the same time, Jesus is announced as the one through whom everything
that God has promised by his prophets will be accomplished (3,20-21).
Peter refers to another prediction that also remains valid: the condemnation of those who do not listen to the prophet. The fulfilment of the
promise through Jesus is connected with the preliminary condition that the
Jews would repent. The reaction to Peter's speech is ambiguous. The leaders of the people arrest Peter but many of the Jews believe him (4,1-4).
The promise is partially fulfilled, which makes it reliable for the future.

5. Conclusion

Twice Luke mentions a διαθήκη-promise to Abraham. In Lk 1,72, he
describes a promise made to Moses as a διαθήκη to Abraham: the people will serve God without fear. In Acts 3,25, Luke qualifies a promise
made to Abraham as a διαθήκη: in Abraham's seed the generations of
the earth will be blessed. Of this promise to Abraham, the Jews are "the
sons". In this way, Luke takes up the motifs of the service to God and of
"the children of Abraham" and uses them in the broader scheme of
divine promises and their fulfilment.

The promises are part of the Abraham typology in Luke-Acts. Luke
creatively built up an image of Abraham, based on the Old Testament
stories. He adapted those stories in function of his own theological interest. Abraham is the recipient of divine (διαθήκη-)promises. Another
main feature of Luke's Abraham typology is the motif of "the children
of Abraham". Luke found the motif in Q (Lk 3,8) and elaborated it. In
Acts 3,25, he connects it with a διαθήκη-promise. As the children of

Abraham are his rightful heirs to whom God will keep his promises according to the Old Testament, the question of who are the legal heirs of Abraham is all-important.

The promises to Abraham play a role within the broader scheme of promise and fulfilment. Some of the predictions are fulfilled and others are being fulfilled gradually or are yet to be accomplished. The gradual accomplishment of the promises provides hope that the remaining promises are reliable too. This has a theological function: the God who made promises in the past, fulfils them and makes new promises today. The main function of the promises, however, is a christological one. Jesus is proclaimed as the one in whom all Israel's hope and expectations have come to fruition. This christological function is closely connected with an ecclesiological aim concerning the rejection of Jesus by many Jews and the belief of many Gentiles. As the fulfilment of the divine promises, both contemporary and past ones, is closely related to Jesus and therefore to the acceptance of Jesus as the Christ, the question arises to whom these promises remain valid.

The promise that the people will serve God (Lk 1,72) is partially fulfilled in Luke-Acts. Every person who is said to serve God, is a Jew. However, in Acts 7, Stephen compares the current actions of the Jews with those of their ancestors. They served "the host of heaven" instead of God. This suggests that the Jews who reject Jesus do not serve God. According to Acts 3,25, the Jews are the sons of the promise, which is in agreement with the overall picture of the children of Abraham in Luke-Acts. Yet, throughout Peter's speech two ways remain open: the Jew who repents will be blessed, the Jew who does not will be destroyed.

Since the promises to serve God and to be children of Abraham are never addressed to non-Jews, I would argue that for Luke the divine διαθήκη-promises are prominently directed to the Jews[31]. However, the fulfilment of the promise is connected with Jesus and with the acceptance of Jesus as the Christ. Therefore, only the Jews who accept Jesus will become heir of the promise. Or, as Luke has Peter say: they are children of both the prophets and the promise.

Elfnovemberlaan 36   Sabine VAN DEN EYNDE
B-3010 Kessel-Lo   Research Fellow FSR-F

---

31. This does not mean that the Gentiles are completely excluded. The fact that God sent Jesus first to the Jews to bless them implies the promise that God will also send Jesus to others. But, the Jews are the first heirs.

DIE BEDEUTUNG DER PROPHETENZITATE
IN LK 4,18-19 UND APG 2,17-21
FÜR DAS DOPPELWERK DES LUKAS

Beobachtungen zu verschiedenen Texten haben mich schon früher zu der Überzeugung gebracht, daß von einer intendierten Einheit der beiden lukanischen Schriften gesprochen werden muß. Dabei sind es gerade Details aus der Evangelientradition, die durch Lukas so bearbeitet wurden, daß sie über das Ev hinausweisen und die Apg als kerygmatischen Orientierungspunkt erscheinen lassen[1].

1. Die Annahme einer intendierten Einheit der beiden lukanischen Schriften wird erhärtet, wenn wir die beiden Zurüstungs- bzw. Salbungszitate aus Lk 4,18f. und Apg 2,17-21 im Zusammenhang mit ihrem jeweiligen Textumfeld auswerten. Diese zwei ausführlichen Zitate haben im Ganzen des lk Werkes einen besonderen Platz und beziehen sich auf zwei Schlüsselereignisse, nämlich die Taufe Jesu und seine Zurüstung durch den Heiligen Geist und die Zurüstung der nachösterlichen Gemeinde durch die Ausgießung des Heiligen Geistes. Beide Zitate sind auch auf besondere Weise durch den Gedanken an die endzeitliche Erfüllung geprägt. Das gilt schon der Form nach. Auf Lk 4,18f. folgt in Kurzform die Predigt Jesu mit dem entscheidenden Satz: »Heute ist diese Schrift vor euren Ohren erfüllt«. Das Verb πληρόω kommt bei Lk sonst nur noch im christologischen Zusammenhang, zumeist in Verbin-

---

1. Ähnliche Verfahren hat Lukas auch innerhalb des Ev angewandt. Erstes Beispiel: in 4,19 hat Lukas Worte über 'das Gnadenjahr des Herrn' aus Jes 61,1 genannt, die dort genannte Ankündigung über den Tag der Vergeltung vorerst ungenannt gelassen, um in 21,22 auf sie hinzuweisen, und zwar mit den bezeichnenden Worten: »daß erfüllt werde *alles,* was geschrieben ist«. Siehe H. BAARLINK, *Ein gnädiges Jahr des Herrn – und Tage der Vergeltung,* in ZNW 73 (1982) 204-220. Zweites Beispiel: In 2,14 besingen die Engel den Frieden auf Erden. In 19,42 klagt Jesus über Jerusalem mit den Worten: Wenn doch auch du erkenntest zu dieser Zeit, was zum Frieden dient. Von ihm als Gottesgabe hier und jetzt (Friede auf Erde) ist denn auch nicht mehr die Rede, sondern von »Friede im Himmel« (19,38). Damit verbindet Jesus dann die Worte: »Wenn diese schweigen werden, so werden die Steine schreien« (v. 40), was deutlich auf Gericht und Friedensentzug weist; vgl. v. 44 und als prophetischen Hintergrund Hab 2,14. Vgl. H. BAARLINK, *Friede im Himmel. Die lukanische Redaktion von Lk 19,38 und ihre Deutung,* in ZNW 76 (1985) 170-186; ID., *Vrede op aarde,* Kampen, 1985, S. 77-93. Ein bemerkenswerter Bogen spannt sich auch von 4,13 zu 22,3 und von 4,19 zu 22,53, ein Sachverhalt, mit dem sich seit H. CONZELMANN, *Die Mitte der Zeit* (BHT, 17), Tübingen, [5]1964, S. 33, der Ausdruck 'satansfreie Zeit' verbindet.

dung mit Jesu Leiden, Sterben und Auferstehung vor (Lk 20,42f.; 22,37; 24,41; Apg 3,18). Daneben können eine kleinere Anzahl Zitate als implizite Erfüllungszitate angedeutet werden. Zu ihnen gehört (neben Lk 2,23f.; 3,4-6; 7,27; 20,17; Apg 8,32f. und 28,25-27) das Joelzitat in Apg 2,17-21. Das gilt nicht oder nicht in dem Maße von anderen Zitaten wie in Lk 4,1-13, in 8,10; 10,27; 13,35; 18,20; 19,38.46; 20,28.38.42f. sowie von größeren Passagen in de Apg in Predigten vor jüdischen Zuhörern in den Kapiteln 3, 4, 7 und 13 sowie für einige andere Stellen wie 1,20; 15,16 und 23,5.

Das besondere der beiden Zitate, die uns beschäftigen, besteht darin, daß sie von der Zurüstung von Mandatsträgern oder Beauftragten Gottes in der Endzeit sprechen. In Lk 4,18f. ist es ein Zitat, vornehmlich aus Jes. 61,1f., angefüllt mit Worten aus 58,6. Es spricht ausdrücklich von der Gabe des Geistes für einen nicht näher bezeichneten eschatologischen Beauftragten. Drei Elemente prägen die Sätze: erstens die Aussage, daß der Geist Gottes auf ihm ist, zweitens eine Umschreibung seines Dienstes, durch den Gott in der Welt Heil schaffen läßt, und drittens die Ankündigung der darauf folgenden Endzeit: »ein gnädiges Jahr des Herrn (und einen Tag der Vergeltung unseres Gottes)«[2]. Dieselben Elemente finden sich in den Worten aus Joel 3,1-15 wieder, die am Pfingsttag in Jerusalem zitiert werden. Erstens die Aussage, daß Gott seinen Geist ausgießen will (und nunmehr ausgegossen hat), zweitens die Umschreibung des prophetischen Dienstes, den die also Zugerüsteten erfüllen werden, und drittens die Ankündigung des jüngsten Tages als Tag des Gerichts und der Rettung.

In beiden Fällen gilt auch, daß nach den betreffenden Geschehnissen (die Taufe Jesu und das Pfingstgeschehen) jeweils ein Hauptbeteiligter und durch den Heiligen Geist Zugerüsteter auftritt und den Anwesenden das Geschehen mit Hilfe dieser Zitate erklärt; im ersten Falle ist es Jesus, im zweiten Fall ist es Petrus als Vertreter der Jüngerschar.

Eine parallel verlaufende Erzählung liegt also auf jeden Fall vor. Läßt sich über das gegenseitige Verhältnis beider Ereignisse, so wie sie durch Lukas geschildert werden, noch mehr sagen? Was Apg 2 betrifft, verfügen wir über keine Parallelen oder Quellen, so daß wir über die redaktionelle Tätigkeit des Verfassers keine schlüssige Auskunft geben können. Anders ist es jedoch im Falle von Lk 3,21f. und 4,18-21. Diese beiden Perikopen sind bei Lukas durch Jesu Stammbaum (3,23-38) und

---

2. Diesen letzten Satzteil läßt Lukas an der Stelle weg, aber er nimmt ihn bezeichnenderweise dort auf, wo Jesus das Gericht Gottes über Jerusalem ankündigt: in 21,22. Siehe Anm. 1.

den Bericht über die Versuchung Jesu (4,1-13) voneinander getrennt. Doch gehören 3,21f. und 4,16-21 genau so eng zusammen wie Mk 1,9-11 und 1,14f.; letzteres wurde in dem Wortlaut von Lukas nicht übernommen, sondern durch die Nazarethperikope ersetzt. Aufschlußreich ist nun aber, daß Lk 3,21f. gegenüber Mk 1,9-11 zwei wichtige Änderungen erfahren hat. Erstens wird nicht mehr direkt über Jesu Taufe berichtet, sondern lediglich, was geschah, nachdem Jesus getauft war. Die Notiz über seine Taufe wird zu einer temporalen Bestimmung, um anzugeben, nach welchem Geschehen und bei welcher Gelegenheit der Heilige Geist auf ihn kam. Der Schwerpunkt liegt also, auch grammatisch, auf der Zurüstung mit dem Heiligen Geist. Zweitens berichtet Lukas kurz über eine bei Markus nicht genannte Handlung: »(als er getauft worden war) und als er betete«. Mit anderen Worten: Der Betende wird mit dem Heiligen Geist beschenkt. Es wäre sinnlos zu fragen, um was Jesus betete. Wer (recht) betet, ist offen für Gottes Wirken an ihm und für seinen Dienst für Gott. Dieselbe Aufeinanderfolge finden wir am Anfang der Apostelgeschichte. Nach der Himmelfahrt Jesu kehren die Jünger nach Jerusalem zurück und sind dort zusammen mit einer Schar Frauen einmütig im Gebet beieinander (1,14). Darauf folgt, unterbrochen durch den Bericht über die Wahl des Matthias anstelle des Judas, die Geschichte der Ausgießung des Heiligen Geistes. Auch in ihrem Fall besteht wegen der Verbindung zu 1,4f. aller Anlaß, das Beten als gläubiges Warten und Offensein für Gottes Wirken zu verstehen.

Der Vollständigkeit halber füge ich hier eine Übersicht hinzu, aus der eine überraschend große Anzahl Parallelismen zwischen beiden Textzusammenhängen erhellt[3].

Lk 3,16 / Apg 1,5	Wassertaufe des Johannes und Geisttaufe durch Jesus.
Lk 3,21b / Apg 1,14	Jesus bzw. die Jünger beteten.
Lk 3,22 / Apg 2,3	Der Heilige Geist kommt herab, sichtbar und hörbar.
Lk 3,21a / Apg 2,4	Jesus wird getauft, die Jünger werden mit dem Geist getauft/ erfüllt.
Lk 4,16ff / Apg 2,14ff	Die gesandten Verkündiger, Jesus bzw. Petrus (als Vertreter der Jünger) erklären den Geistesempfang mit prophetischen Worten: Jes 61,1f., bzw. Joel 2,28-32.

3. Ein gutes Gespür für parallele Reihen bei Lukas verrät C.H. TALBERT in seinem Werk: *Literary Patterns, Theological Themes and the Genre of Luke–Acts*, Missoula, MT, 1974. Ihm verdanke ich auch entscheidende Hinweise auf Parallelen in den hier behandelten Abschnitten.

Lk 4,19 / Apg 2,21	Verkündigung des Gnadenjahres des Herrn bzw. der Rettung für alle, die den Namen des Herrn anrufen.
Lk 4,20f / Apg 2,33	Aller Augen sind auf ihn gerichtet, und die Schrift ist erfüllt vor ihren Ohren / wie ihr hier seht und hört.
Lk 4,22f / Apg 2,22-25	Die Rede über Jesu große Taten bzw. über seine Auferstehung.
Lk 4,24ff / Apg 2,36	Kein Prophet ist geehrt in seiner Vaterstadt / Jesus, den ihr gekreuzigt habt.

Und schließlich als Gegensatz, denn die Geschichte des Leidens und Sterbens Jesu bleibt letztendlich einzigartig; jetzt ist er der erhöhte Herr:

| Lk 4,28-30 / | Zorn, Ablehnung und versuchter Mord bei den Nazarenern; |
| Apg 2,37-41 | Offenheit, Annahme und Taufe bei den Jerusalemern. |

Die Aufeinanderfolge in Apg 1 und 2 macht im Ganzen den Eindruck, ein ungekünstelter Erzählzusammenhang zu sein, auch wenn dieser Erzählung 'theologische' Erwägungen zugrunde liegen. Demgegenüber wirkt Lk 3,20f. eher als beabsichtigte redaktionelle Angleichung. Das bedeutet also auch in diesem Fall, daß alles auf eine intendierte Einheit schließen läßt, wobei die Aufeinanderfolge der Erzählelemente in der Apostelgeschichte das Modell bildet für die Redaktion von Lk 3,20f. und 4,16-20.

2. Die genannten zwei Zurüstungszitate stehen nicht nur thematisch über je einem Teil des lk Doppelwerkes, sondern sie werfen gemeinsam auch ihr Licht auf die Art, wie Lukas über Geschehnisse berichtet und Geschehenszusammenhänge herstellt.

Ich möchte mich hier auf einen Perikopenzusammenhang konzentrieren, den wir allgemein als 'kleine Einschaltung' benennen und von der 'großen Einschaltung' von 9,51–18,14 unterscheiden. Während letztere in der letzten Zeit viel Beachtung gefunden hat[4], beschränken sich die Kommentatoren bis in die jüngste Zeit darauf, den Teil 6,20–8,3 im Rahmen der galiläischen Tätigkeit Jesu auszulegen. Es müßte doch zumindest die Frage gestellt werden, welches Gestaltungsprinzip hier gewaltet hat, nun der Evangelist eine Reihe von Perikopen einander

---

4. Für den Versuch einer Analyse und Strukturbestimmung der großen Einschaltung verweise ich auf meinen Aufsatz: *Die zyklische Struktur von Lukas 9,43b – 19,18*, in *NTS* 38 (1992) 481-506. Auf den letzten Seiten dieses Aufsatzes bin ich bereits kurz auf die Struktur und Bedeutung der kleinen Einschaltung eingegangen.

zuordnet und hier aufnimmt, die nicht aus Mk und nur teilweise aus Q stammen. Eine nähere Betrachtung ergibt, daß er dabei sorgfältig und gut durchdacht vorgegangen ist, darüber hinaus aber auch, daß die beiden Prophetenzitate in Lk 4,18f. und Apg 2,17-21 dabei von entscheidender Bedeutung gewesen sind.

a. In den Perikopen der kleinen Einschaltung zeigt Lukas, auf welche Weise der mit dem Heiligen Geist gesalbte Christus den ihm gegebenen Auftrag erfüllt.

Die Umschreibung der Aufgabe des mit dem Geist begabten Gottesgesandten (4,18f.), der wir uns zuerst zuwenden, kann in drei Aussagen unterteilt werden: a. den Armen das Evangelium verkünden; b. Gefangenen, Unterdrückten und Leidenden zu Hilfe kommen; c. das gnädige Jahr des Herrn verkündigen. Der Evangelist hat daraufhin zuerst Überlieferungsstoff des Mk aufgenommen und ist im großen und ganzen darin auch der Anordnung des Mk treu geblieben (4,31–6,16; vgl. Mk 1,16–3,19). Ab 8,4 bis Ende des 9. Kapitels wird er der mk Überlieferung wieder folgen, um sie dann zum zweiten Mal im Zusammenhang mit der großen Einschaltung zu unterbrechen.

Da Lukas anstelle der Kurzaussage des Markus über die Predigt Jesu (Mk 1,14f.) die ausführlichere Perikope über die Predigt in Nazareth gewählt hat, ist es verständlich, daß er dafür Sorge trug, daß das dort genannte Zitat als Überschrift funktionieren konnte und sein Erfüllungscharakter für den Leser deutlich erkennbar war.

Auf die Auftragsumschreibung, den Armen das Evangelium verkünden, folgt ab 6,20 eine Reihe Seligpreisungen, voran die Aussage: »Selig seid ihr Armen, denn das Reich Gottes gehört euch«. Gewiß enthält dieser Block (6,20-49) auch andere Themen und bildet zusammen mit ihnen eine überlieferte Einheit, die wir hier nicht im Einzelnen zu analysieren haben. Wenn den Armen das Evangelium verkündet und das Reich Gottes zugesprochen wird, dann muß auch all das zur Sprache kommen, was mit dem Kommen und Empfangen des Reiches zusammenhängt. Entscheidend ist für uns hier, daß Jesus dem ihm gegebenen Auftrag gemäß den Armen das Evangelium verkündet hat.

In dem darauf folgenden Teil (7,1-17) erzählt Lukas anhand von zwei Beispielen, wie Jesus seinen Auftrag ausführt, sich tröstend, helfend und genesend der Bedrängten und Leidenden anzunehmen. Die Genesung des Knechtes des Hauptmanns in Kapernaum und die Auferweckung des Jünglings in Nain stehen für viele andere Taten; einige davon waren auch schon in Kap. 5 erzählt worden. Die beiden hier erzählten Geschichten handeln aber nicht nur über die zwei Personen, die genesen bzw. auferweckt wurden, sondern noch mehr über den Hauptmann und die trauernde Witwe und ihre Verlassenheit.

An dritter Stelle hat Jesus den Auftrag, das gnädige Jahr des Herrn auszurufen. Wie wird es gehört, angenommen und erfahren? Zwei widersprüchliche Geschichten stellen sich dieser Frage. Erst die über Johannes den Täufer (7,18-35). Er hatte da seine ernsten Zweifel und äußerte sie in der Frage, ob sie vielleicht auf einen anderen warten und das hieß, ihm den Glauben versagen sollten. Das würde zugleich heißen: das gnädige Jahr des Herrn sei noch nicht angebrochen. Jesus verweist ihn dagegen (v. 21-23) auf seine Taten, in denen die Macht seiner Barmherzigkeit erkennbar war, zitiert dabei Worte aus Jes 29,18 und 35,5f. und ruft dazu auf, nicht an ihm und an der Realität des Gnadenjahres des Herrn irre zu werden.

Anders aber als der zweifelnde Johannes geht eine Frau, die in der Umgebung in schlechtem Ruf steht, ohne irgend ein Zögern davon aus, daß sie bei Jesus Gnade findet. Ihr Tun, die Reaktion der Pharisäer, sowie die Antwort Jesu werden ausführlich erzählt. Der Abschnitt endet mit Jesu Worten zu dieser Frau: »Dein Glaube hat dir geholfen, geh hin mit Frieden!«. Ihre Widersacher werden dort keiner Antwort mehr gewürdigt. Über sie hatte Jesus im vorigen Abschnitt und im Zusammenhang mit der Predigt des Täufers schon gesagt: »Sie verwarfen, was Gott ihnen zugedacht hatte« (V. 30). Und was war das? Inhaltlich kann darauf keine andere Antwort gegeben werden als diese: das Gnadenjahr Gottes.

b. Auf den letzten Abschnitt (8,1-3) fällt eher ein Licht von Apg 2,17-21 her als daß noch von einem direkten Bezug zu 4,18f. gesprochen werden könnte.

Mit den bisher ausgewerteten Abschnitten wäre der Bezug dieser sogenannten kleinen Einschaltung zu dem Prophetenwort aus 4,18f. inhaltlich bereits zur Genüge beschrieben. Und doch sind noch zwei wichtige Punkte außer Betracht geblieben. Erst einmal folgt mit 8,1-3 noch ein abschließender Abschnitt. Es heißt, daß Jesus weiter durch Städte und Dörfer zog, predigte und das Evangelium vom Reich Gottes verkündigte. Es ist bezeichnend, daß Lukas hier die beiden Verben κηρύσσειν und εὐαγγελίζεσθαι benutzt, mit denen in 4,18f. das tätige Sich-erbarmen des Gottesgesandten umschrieben worden war. Weiter wird gesagt, daß ihm dabei die zwölf Jünger folgten, aber nicht nur sie, sondern auch eine Anzahl von Frauen, die nur zum Teil mit Namen genannt werden. Von diesen Versen aus, gefolgt durch die Notizen in 23,49.55 und 24,1.10, besteht eine Brücke hin zu der Zeit, als wieder die zwölf Jünger und die Schar der Frauen beieinander waren, nämlich nach Jesu Himmelfahrt (Apg 1,13f.). In 8,1-3 sind sie beieinander als Zeugen, daß Jesus in der Kraft des Heiligen Geistes seinen Auftrag erfüllt und damit das eschatologische Gnadenjahr Gottes mit Wort und Tat Wirklichkeit hat werden lassen. Inzwischen erfüllen sie alle Vorbedingungen, die nach Apg 1,21f. an die Zeugen der Auferstehung gestellt werden. Dann sind sie wieder beisammen, weil sie darauf warten, daß sie »mit dem Heiligen Geist getauft / erfüllt werden in wenigen Tagen« (Apg 1,5). Durch ihre Anwesenheit in Lk 8,1-3 innerhalb des Geschehenszusammenhanges der kleinen Einschaltung gibt Lukas die heilsgeschichtliche Verbindung zwischen der Zeit Jesu und der Gemeinde an. Er denkt sozusagen von Apg 1 und 2 (!) her. Das Joelzitat über die Zurüstung der Jünger und der Frauen steht ihm nicht weniger vor Augen als das Jesajazitat über die Zurüstung Jesu zu seinem unverwechselbaren und einzigartigen Auftrag.

Daß dies der Fall ist, bestätigt sich, wenn wir auf die systematische Zuordnung von Männern und Frauen bei Lukas achten. Sie bildet auch hier das Rückgrat für die Strukturierung von 6,20–8,3. Nacheinander sind es jeweils drei Paare, die Modell stehen für die Wirklichkeit der Ausführung des messianischen Auftrages. Neben dem Hauptmann steht die Witwe, neben Johannes dem Täufer die Sünderin und neben den Jüngern stehen die Frauen. Die Absichtlichkeit dieser Anordnung geht auch daraus hervor, daß er in diesem Teil, genau wie später in der großen Einschaltung, nacheinander aus verschiedenen Quellen schöpft: 7,1-10 aus Q; 7,11-17 aus dem Sondergut des Lk; 7,18-35 wiederum aus Q; der Abschnitt 7,36-50 hat (nur teilweise) eine Parallele in Mk 14; aber jene Salbung fand nicht im Hause eines Pharisäers statt, sondern im Hause eines Simons des Aussätzigen, auch nicht in Galiläa, sondern in Bethanien, und zwar einige Tage vor Jesu Tod.

Lukas war bereits in den ersten Kapiteln des Evangeliums auf diese Zuordnung bedacht gewesen. Neben dem Lobgesang der Maria in Kap. 1 steht der des Zacharias; in Kap. 2 steht neben Simeon die Prophetin Hanna, auch wenn von ihr kein einziger Satz eines Lobgesanges erwähnt werden konnte. In der großen Einschaltung spielt diese Technik wiederum eine große Rolle: Neben einem Mann mit seinem verlorenen Schaf steht eine Frau mit ihrer verlorenen Drachme (15,4-10); neben den zwei schlafenden Männern werden zwei mahlende Frauen genannt (17,34f.); in Kap. 18 wird erst von einer bittenden Witwe erzählt, danach von einem bittenden Zöllner. Auch in der Kreuzigungsgeschichte kommen Vertreter beider Geschlechter vor: Simon von Kyrene und eine Schar weinender Frauen (23,26f.), und in der Sterbensstunde standen all seine Bekannten etwas entfernt, auch die Frauen, die ihm aus Galiläa gefolgt waren (23,49). In der Apostelgeschichte ist dies formell noch konsequenter durchgeführt; fünfmal wird innerhalb der Berichte ausdrücklich von Männern und Frauen gesprochen (5,14; 8,3.12; 17,4.12). Weiter stehen Ananias und Saphira (5,1-11), der kranke Aeneas und die gestorbene Dorkas (9,32-43), Lydia und der Kerkermeister in Philippi (16,14-30), Dionysios und Damaris (18,2), Aquila und Priscilla (18,18.26), sowie die Töchter des Philippus und Agabus (21,9f.) einander gegenüber[5].

Das alles kann unmöglich auf Zufall beruhen. An sich könnte dem einzig und allein ein persönliches Anliegen des Verfassers zugrunde liegen. Da wir jedoch in dem Joelzitat von Apg 2,17-21 neben dem Jesajazitat in Lk 4,18f ein die Struktur bestimmendes Zurüstungszitat erkannt haben, spricht alles dafür, daß es dieser Text mit dem Nachdruck auf Menschen beiderlei Geschlechts und dem wiederholten Sprechen über Söhne und Töchter bzw. meine Knechte und Mägde gewesen ist, der Lukas zutiefst beeinflußt und dazu motiviert hat, diese partnerschaftliche Nebeneinanderstellung in beiden Teilen seines Werkes, und nun in besonderer Pointierung in der kleinen Einschaltung, zur Geltung zu bringen.

3. Ergebnis. Für die kleine Einschaltung ist es bezeichnend, daß gleich zwei beherrschende Motive aus dem Anfang der Apostelgeschichte den Aufbau und Inhalt dieses Teiles mit bestimmt haben: erstens die Erwähnung derjenigen (Jünger zusammen mit den Frauen), die ab Apg 1 im Brennpunkt des erzählerischen Interesses stehen und am Pfingsttage durch den Heiligen Geist zu ihrem Zeugendienst zugerüstet wurden; zweitens die konsequente und durchgängige Nebeneinanderstellung von Männern und Frauen in beiden Teilen des lk Werkes, die aus dem Wortlaut der Joelprophetie hervorging.

Wir könnten von hieraus der Frage weiter nachgehen, wie beide Grundereignisse, die Zurüstung Jesu sowie die der Jünger(innen), den *discourse* (das Wie der Erzählungen) der Apostelgeschichte prägen. Es wäre nicht schwer, das näher auszuführen. Wir beschränken uns hier auf ein paar kurze Notizen. Einerseits ist Jesus auch in der Apostelgeschichte der machtvoll Handelnde, andererseits sind die Jünger oder Apostel es, die sich durch den Heiligen Geist in Bewegung bringen und

---

5. Siehe auch H. BAARLINK, *Die Eschatologie der synoptischen Evangelien*, Stuttgart, 1986, S. 140-143, oder, sei es weniger vollständig: *Vervulling en voleinding*, Kampen, 1984, S. 184-186.

zum Opfer ihres Lebens bereit machen lassen, wenn auch der Geist in ihnen ein latentes Widerstreben erst noch ausräumen muß (Kap. 10) und die Verkündigung über die Grenzen Judäas hinaus erst durch Verfolgungen in Gang gesetzt wird (8,1; 11,19). Wenn nicht alles trügt, sind die Erhöhung Jesu (Kap. 1) und die Ausgießung des Heiligen Geistes (Kap. 2) die Eckpfeiler, die bis ans Ende des 28. Kapitels für den *discourse* bestimmend sind. Das Buch schließt nämlich mit der bezeichnenden Bemerkung, daß Paulus zwei Jahre in Rom predigte, und zwar mit allem Freimut (παρρησία) und ungehindert (ἀκωλύτως). Die Zurüstung durch den Geist macht ihn freimütig, die wirksame Macht des erhöhten Herrn macht, daß niemand ihn daran hindern kann, »das Reich Gottes zu predigen und von dem Herrn Jesus Christus zu lehren« (28,31)[6].

Aus dieser Untersuchung ergeben sich Erkenntnisse, die bedeutsam sind im Hinblick auf die Einheit des lk Doppelwerkes sowie für die Frage, nach welchen Gesichtspunkten Lukas die beiden Bücher geplant, erstellt und einander zugeordnet hat. Wenn unsere Analyse und ihre Auswertung richtig sind, dürfen wir es als gesichert ansehen, daß Lukas von vornherein die beiden Bücher, die seinen Namen tragen, als ein Doppelwerk geplant hat und daß dabei die theologischen Eckdaten der Apostelgeschichte zugleich die Strukturierung und Darstellung in seinem Evangelium maßgeblich mitbestimmt haben. Das vermindert nicht im geringsten die Bedeutsamkeit der Tatsache, daß auch umgekehrt der durch den Heiligen Geist zugerüstete und nunmehr erhöhte Herr den Gang der Ereignisse nach Pfingsten sowie die Art, wie darüber erzählt wird, bestimmt. Dadurch fällt schließlich auch ein zusätzliches Licht auf den Sinn der einleitenden Sätze von Lk 1,1-4. Aussagen wie »die Geschichten, die unter uns geschehen sind« und »die es von Anfang an selbst gesehen haben« beziehen sich auch auf die Zeugen des Pfingstereignisses und der darauf folgenden Geschehnisse. Denn nur durch den Geist erfüllte Jünger können Zeugen der heilbringenden Geschichte Jesu sein (siehe Apg 2,22-24; 3,13-16; 10,37-43; 13,26-32); und nur durch ihn, der ihnen den Geist geschenkt hat, können sie in ihrer Predigt und nicht weniger auch in ihren (Wunder-)Taten (siehe Apg 3,6.16; 4,7-10) als bevollmächtigte Gesandte auftreten, durch die sich das gnädige Jahr des Herrn weiterhin ereignet.

Wilhelm-Raabe-Str. 529   Heinrich BAARLINK
D-48527 Nordhorn

---

6. Vgl. die eingehendere Darstellung in H. BAARLINK, *Die Eschatologie,* S. 180-183, oder *Vervulling en voleinding,* S. 217-220.

LES VOYAGES À JERUSALEM
(Lc 9,51; Ac 19,21)

Dans son ouvrage sur Lc-Ac, R.C. Tannehill affirme qu'on ne peut pas comparer Lc 9,51 et Ac 19,21 étant donné qu'ils sont si différents. Dans Lc 9,51 Jésus initierait son chemin vers Jérusalem tandis que dans Ac 19,21 il n'y aurait aucun début de voyage[1]. Paul, en effet, après avoir envoyé ses deux collaborateurs, Timothée et Eraste, en Macédoine, reste à Éphèse pendant l'émeute qui s'y fait (Ac 19,23-40) et ce n'est qu'après le tumulte qu'il prend congé des disciples et commence le voyage qu'il avait annoncé. Est-ce donc impensable de proposer une comparaison entre Lc 9,51 et Ac 19,21? Le fait que le voyage de Paul ne commence pas tout de suite, représente-t-il une difficulté insurmontable? D'autre part, est-ce que, dans l'évangile, Jésus commence immédiatement son voyage à Jérusalem? Il n'y aura que l'analyse des textes dans l'ensemble de Lc-Ac qui puisse nous mener à une réponse satisfaisante.

1. Lc 9,51

Dans l'évangile de Luc, le ministère de Jésus en Galilée s'achève sur sa ferme décision de monter vers Jérusalem. La formule utilisée par Luc est grave et solennelle: la section du voyage ou section centrale de l'évangile, initiée en 9,51, se prolongera jusqu'à 19,44. Le voyage de Jésus est conçu comme le résultat d'une détermination personnelle et, en même temps, comme l'accomplissement du dessein de Dieu. Ce double caractère est indiqué par les deux affirmations du v. 51. D'une part, on mentionne les jours de l'enlèvement (ἀναλήμψις) de Jésus: l'heure de la réalisation du plan salvifique de Dieu est sur le point d'arriver avec l'intronisation glorieuse de son Fils. D'autre part, Jésus prend la ferme résolution (τὸ πρόσωπον ἐστήρισεν) de se mettre en chemin vers Jérusalem[2]: il réalise le plan divin avec sa montée vers cette ville. Notons, à

---

1. R.C. TANNEHILL, *The Narrative Unity of Luke-Acts. A Literary Interpretation. Volume 2: The Acts of the Apostles*, Minneapolis, Fortress Press, 1990, p. 240: «Luke 9:51 is the actual beginning of a journey to Jerusalem; Acts 19:21 is not». Par contre, F. Bovon écrit à propos de Lc 9,51: «Luc donnera, dans les Actes, un pendant à cette ouverture: en Ac 19,21, Paul affichera, lui aussi, son projet de monter à Jérusalem avant de devoir visiter Rome»: F. BOVON, *L'Évangile selon saint Luc (9,51–14,35)* (Commentaire du Nouveau Testament, 3b), Genève, Labor et Fides, 1996, p. 32.

2. L'infinitif présent πορεύεσθαι indique une action qui débute et qui va se répéter. L'expression τὸ πρόσωπον ἐστήρισεν, d'origine sémitique (cf. surtout Ez 21,7 LXX),

ce propos, que les deux phrases du v. 51, la première relative au vouloir divin et la deuxième relative à la volonté de Jésus, forment une unité. En effet, l'accomplissement renvoie au dessein de Dieu et reste bien d'accord avec la ferme résolution de Jésus: les deux volontés, celle de Dieu et celle de Jésus, coïncident totalement. Le but du vouloir divin est l'ἀνάλημψις de Jésus et le point essentiel reste la montée vers Jérusalem, lieu de cette ἀνάλημψις. Dans la scène de la transfiguration, on montrait Moïse et Elie parlant avec Jésus de son départ (ἔξοδος) sur le point de s'accomplir (πληροῦν) à Jérusalem (9,31). Or, ce texte justifie l'interprétation proposée en 9,51: les deux affirmations de ce verset doivent être comprises ensemble[3]: Jérusalem est le point géographique et théologique de l'ἀνάλημψις ou ἔξοδος de Jésus. L'ascension ou, mieux, l'enlèvement de Jésus devient ainsi le terme-clé pour caractériser le but du chemin terrestre de Jésus: l'exaltation auprès de Dieu, le Père, est le but de son voyage au ciel. À partir de Lc 9,51 nous nous trouvons au temps («les jours») de l'enlèvement, même si «le jour» de cet enlèvement (Ac 1,2!) n'aura lieu que quarante jours après Pâques et dix jours avant Pentecôte[4]. On entend par là que l'évangile lucanien avance vers l'ascension de Jésus et que celle-ci constitue le point culminant du récit.

Par conséquent, la vie de Jésus, qui va se résoudre dans sa passion/ mort, resurrection et exaltation, consiste en un voyage terrestre (Jérusalem en est le point d'arrivée) mais qui continue, après la résurrection, avec le voyage dirigé vers le ciel (ayant Jérusalem comme point de départ). Dans ce sens, le terme qui indique le point final du voyage (ἀνάλημψις comme enlèvement de Jésus aux cieux) désigne en même temps les événements qui vont y conduire: passion, mort et résurrection[5]. Par contre, le terme ἔξοδος indique le départ ou sortie de ce monde et, par extension, les événements culminants de la vie de Jésus.

---

souligne, comme dit M. Miyoshi, «die feste Absicht etwas zu tun»: M. MIYOSHI, *Der Anfang des Reiseberichts. Lk 9,51-10,24: Eine redaktionsgeschichtliche Untersuchung* (AnBib, 60), Rome, Biblical Institute Press, 1974, p. 9.

3. Les correspondances sont claires: συμπληρόω (9,51) – πληρόω (9,31), ἀνάλημ-ψις (9,51) – ἔξοδος (9,31). Jérusalem est la ville (vv. 31 et 51) où tout devra se passer: le départ de Jésus doit s'y accomplir (ἤμελλεν) et les jours de son enlèvement vont s'y accomplir (ἐν τῷ συμπληροῦσθαι). La nuance temporelle est présente et future.

4. Il n'y a pas d'opposition entre Lc 9,51 («les jours») et Ac 1,2 («le jour»). A.W. Zwiep a montré que dans 9,51 Luc veut exprimer que «the period leading up to the ascension is being (completely) filled up and… this period (will) find its completion in the ascension»: A.W. ZWIEP, *The Ascension of the Messiah in Lukan Christology* (NTSup, 87), Leiden, Brill, 1997, pp. 85-86.

5. Pour le voyage au ciel de Jésus, Luc a utilisé le substantif ἀνάλημψις (9,51) et le verbe ἀναλαμβάνω (Ac 1,2.11.22). En plus, les verbes ἀναφέρω (Lc 24,51), ἐπαίρω (Ac 1,9), ὑπολαμβάνω (Ac 1,9) et πορεύομαι (Ac 1,10).

On peut donc dire que les deux termes, ἀναλήμψις et ἔξοδος, ont dans l'évangile un sens large et inclusif (passion-mort-résurrection-exaltation de Jésus) et un sens plus strict: le départ de cette terre[6] et l'enlèvement au ciel, respectivement les deux aspects du voyage terrestre-céleste réalisé par Jésus.

Il paraît donc que le voyage de Jésus *à* Jérusalem se poursuit par un second voyage *à partir* de Jérusalem. Le verbe πορεύομαι («marcher», «faire son chemin») unifie le parcours de Jésus, terrestre et céleste, et Jérusalem en est comme la plaque tournante. La décision de Jésus de se mettre en marche vers Jérusalem (9,51) est reprise dans 9,53 en une formule grecque de tournure sémitisante du point de vue syntaxique («sa face était en marche vers Jérusalem»): cette formule insiste sur la détermination de Jésus d'aller à Jérusalem[7]. Dans Lc 9,51–19,44 on souligne le fait que Jésus et les disciples continuent leur chemin (9,56.57; 10,38; 13,33; 19,28.36) en direction à Jérusalem (13,22; 17,11): dans tous ces versets cette circonstance est exprimée par le verbe πορεύομαι. Il faut aussi ajouter 18,31; 19,28 («monter à Jérusalem») (ἀναβαίνω) et 19,11 («être proche de Jérusalem») (ἐγγὺς εἶναι). Notons en plus qu'après l'entrée à Jérusalem le verbe πορεύομαι apparaît de nouveau dans la Dernière Cène pour indiquer la marche de Jésus vers la mort (22,22 «le Fils de l'homme s'en va selon ce qui a été fixé»). Encore dans l'épisode de l'Ascension la montée de Jésus au ciel est décrite par les phrases «tandis qu'il s'en allait» (Ac 1,10 πορευομένου αὐτοῦ) et «s'en aller au ciel» (Ac 1,11 πορευόμενον εἰς τὸν οὐρανόν). Par conséquent, le verbe πορεύομαι exprime le voyage de Jésus à Jérusalem, ainsi que le voyage de Jésus vers la mort et vers le ciel. En effet, Jésus va à Jérusalem (Lc 9,51), va à la mort (Lc 22,22) et va au ciel (Ac 1,11). Toute sa vie est un voyage, un chemin (d'où le verbe πορεύομαι), compris comme un enlèvement vers Dieu, prédit par les Écritures, et un accomplissement du plan divin. Ce voyage passe par la mort et trouve sa culmination dans l'exaltation céleste[8].

---

6. Il existe un contraste intéressant entre l'εἴσοδος de Jésus dans ce monde (Ac 13,24) et son ἔξοδος ou départ (Lc 9,31). F. BOVON, *L'Évangile selon saint Luc (1–9)* (Commentaire du Nouveau Testament, 3a), Genève, Labor et Fides, 1991, p. 485, fait noter que Luc parle de l'Ascension de Jésus «comme d'une séparation et un départ» et cite Lc 24,50-51.

7. Quelques auteurs rapprochent la formule lucanienne de 2S 17,11, lue d'après la Septante: par ex. J.A. FITZMYER, *The Gospel according to Luke* (AB, 28), Garden City, NY, Doubleday, 1981, p. 829. Selon I.H. MARSHALL, *The Gospel of Luke. A Commentary on the Greek Text* (NIGTC), Exeter, Paternoster Press, 1978, p. 406, c'est un «example of language that sounds Septuagintal».

8. D'après ZWIEP, *Ascension* (n. 4), p. 86, la deuxième partie de Lc a été écrite «sub specie ascensionis». Certes, on peut dire que Lc 9,51 «organise» 9,51–19,44.

Il est clair que le motif du voyage de Jésus à Jérusalem et, en dernière instance, au ciel, démarre en Lc 9,51 et culmine en Lc 24,50-53 et Ac 1,1-11. Ce voyage est, en fait, le motif central des chapitres 9 à 24 de l'évangile lucanien. Ainsi le dernier texte narratif du voyage à Jérusalem, la parabole des mines, est stratégiquement placé avant l'entrée à la ville; ce texte reprend le thème du chemin en parlant du voyage d'un prétendant à la royauté qui va (19,12 ἐπορεύϑη) dans un pays lointain, c'est-à-dire, au ciel, pour recevoir la dignité royale (βασιλεία), l'investiture messianique. Dans la scène suivante, le jour des Rameaux, c'est Jésus, le Messie, qui est salué par les foules comme «le roi» (19,38) qui visite Jérusalem et reçoit l'intronisation royale. Le voyage de Jésus est orienté vers son Ascension glorieuse[9].

Notons encore que le voyage à Jérusalem qui commence en 9,51 est le troisième des voyages effectués par Jésus à la ville sainte. La première fois que Jésus va à Jérusalem et entre au temple avec sa mère c'est après sa naissance, «lorsque les jours de leur purification s'accomplirent» (2,22 ὅτε ἐπλήσϑησαν αἱ ἡμέραι τοῦ καϑαρισμοῦ αὐτῶν). Jésus est salué par Siméon comme étant «le salut». Celui-ci annonce prophétiquement son ministère controversé, sa passion et sa mort en croix. Anne, la prophétesse, reconnaît dans l'enfant le libérateur d'Israël. Cette première fois, ce sont les parents de Jésus qui l'amènent à Jérusalem. Par contre, la deuxième fois il monte (ἀναβαίνω) à Jérusalem avec eux. En effet, ses parents allaient (πορεύομαι) à Jérusalem chaque année à l'occasion de la fête de Pâque. Or, lorsque Jésus «eut douze ans» (2,42 ὅτε ἐγένετο ἐτῶν δώδεκα), il les accompagna mais il est resté dans le temple, au cœur de Jérusalem, «chez son Père», tandis que tous les autres pèlerins revenaient en Galilée. Les trois jours passés au temple anticipent son ministère public, conçu d'une certaine manière comme une route de trois jours (Lc 13,32-33), ainsi que les trois jours qui séparent sa mort et les apparitions culminées avec l'Ascension (Lc 24,21). Il n'est donc pas hasardeux d'affirmer que Luc propose un schéma de trois voyages de Jésus à Jérusalem, dont les deux premiers (présentation et pèlerinage au temple) anticipent plusieurs des éléments qu'on va retrouver dans le reste de l'évangile, surtout dans le troisième voyage à Jérusalem (9,51–19,44) et les événements qui le suivent, de 19,45 («il entra au temple») jusqu'à 24,51 («il fut emporté au ciel»)[10].

---

9. Cf. I. DE LA POTTERIE, *La parabole du prétendant à la royauté (Lc 19,11-28)*, in *À cause de l'évangile*. FS J. Dupont (LD, 123), Paris, Cerf, 1985, pp. 613-641.

10. La bibliographie sur Lc 9,51-56 est très abondante. Cf. H. SCHÜRMANN, *Das Lukasevangelium. Zweiter Teil. Kommentar zu Kapitel 9,51–11,54* (HTK, 3/2), Freiburg-Basel-Wien, Herder, 1993, pp. 22-23.

2. Les rapports entre Lc 9,51-56 et Ac 19,21-22

Dans Ac 19,21 Paul manifeste sa décision de voyager à Jérusalem et à Rome. Or, ce verset présente des affinités notables avec le début du voyage de Jésus à Jérusalem[11]. La formule ὡς δὲ ἐπληρώθη ταῦτα rappelle la formule plus élaborée et solennelle de Lc 9,51 (où l'on trouve aussi le verbe πληρόω avec un préfixe: συμπληρόω). Il s'agit de deux sentences temporelles, suivies d'un verbe ayant Jésus (καὶ αὐτός) et Paul (ὁ Παῦλος) comme sujet. La différence consiste dans l'orientation de la temporalité: Lc 9,51 vise le futur, l'ἀναλήμψις qui va se réaliser à Jérusalem, tandis que Ac 19,21 envisage le passé. D'après E. Haenchen, Ac 19,21 se rapporte aux événements précédents, les plus immédiats, c'est-à-dire, aux deux ans que Paul a passé à Éphèse, la capitale de l'Asie (Ac 19,10)[12]. Le texte se limiterait donc à certifier l'achèvement de son travail dans cette ville. Mais si l'on considère l'ensemble de Lc-Ac, alors la phrase d'Ac 19,21 prend un relief particulier.

Le verbe πληρόω au passif indique, dans Lc-Ac, l'accomplissement des Écritures (Lc 4,21; 24,44; Ac 1,16; 3,18; 13,27) ou d'un message angélique orienté vers le futur (Lc 1,20). Le futur est envisagé aussi en Lc 9,31 (l'ἔξοδος de Jésus à Jérusalem), 21,24 (la fin de la domination païenne à Jérusalem) et 22,16 (le repas pascal à célébrer dans le Royaume de Dieu instauré): dans tous ces cas on n'est pas loin de l'idée de réalisation du plan divin, soit au présent, soit au futur. Plus strictement, le verbe πληρόω indique l'accomplissement d'une période temporelle qui s'inscrit dans le vouloir divin. Ainsi, dans le discours d'Étienne on mentionne les quarante ans que Moïse avait (πληρόω) lorsqu'il tua l'égyptien et s'enfuit vers Madian (Ac 7,23.29) et les quarante ans qui se sont écoulés (πληρόω) jusqu'à la théophanie de l'Horeb et les événements de l'Exode (7,30). En plus, on mentionne les quarante ans passés par le peuple au désert (Ac 7,36). L'histoire divisée en périodes identiques et l'usage du verbe πληρόω renvoient à l'idée d'accomplissement divin.

Dans le discours de Paul à Antioche de Pisidie, on trouve un autre exemple du verbe πληρόω comme terme rapporté à la réalisation du plan divin (Ac 13,25). Paul souligne que Dieu a envoyé Jésus en tant que Sauveur d'Israël selon la promesse qu'il avait faite. Il est clair que le vouloir divin apparaît derrière la prédication de Jean Baptiste lequel

---

11. Sur l'analogie entre Lc 9,51 et Ac 19,21, voyez W. RADL, *Paulus und Jesus im lukanischen Doppelwerk. Untersuchung zu Parallelmotiven im Lukasevangelium und in der Apostelgeschichte* (EHS, 23/49), Bern-Frankfurt, Lang, 1975, pp. 103-126.

12. E. HAENCHEN, *The Acts of the Apostles. A Commentary*, Philadelphia, PA, Westminster, 1971, p. 568.

anticipe (προκηρύσσω) l'entrée de Jésus dans ce monde (εἴσοδος). Or, à la fin de sa vie, «alors qu'il terminait sa course» (ὡς δὲ ἐπλήρου Ἰωάννης τὸν δρόμον), Jean affirme qu'il n'est pas le Messie. Une formule très proche à celle-ci est mise dans la bouche de Paul lors du discours aux anciens d'Éphèse (Ac 20,24). Paul affirme que le but de sa vie c'est de mener à bien le service que Jésus lui a confié: le témoignage de l'évangile de la grâce de Dieu. Il ne désire rien d'autre, maintenant qu'il termine sa course (ὡς τελειῶσαι τὸν δρόμον μου). La vie de Paul est la réalisation de la volonté du Christ sur lui. Achever sa vie équivaut à terminer la course, accomplir jusqu'au bout ce que le Seigneur a déterminé. Ces deux derniers textes (Ac 13,25; 20,24), fort proches entre eux[13], nous invitent à souligner le parallélisme entre les vies de Jean Baptiste et de Paul. Finir la course est, dans les deux cas, accomplir le vouloir divin: Jean devait être le précurseur du Messie et de Paul, le témoin de l'évangile, d'après le ministère reçu du Seigneur Jésus.

Par conséquent, le choix du verbe πληρόω dans Ac 19,21 n'est pas casuel. On veut identifier l'ensemble de la vie de Paul[14], conçue comme accomplissement du vouloir divin. Le récit indique que la fin de sa course terrestre est arrivée. Paul lui même l'exprime dans le discours de Milet, vrai testament de celui qui a consacré sa vie à la prédication de l'évangile (Ac 20,24). Toujours à Césarée, aux portes de Jérusalem, Paul manifeste être préparé à mourir et ceux qui l'accompagnent exclament: «Que la volonté de Dieu soit faite!» (Ac 21,13-14). À la différence de Lc 9,51 («quand les jours de son enlèvement allaient s'accomplir»), phrase qui se rapporte au présent-futur de l'itinéraire vital de Jésus, la formule utilisée dans Ac 19,21 («quand ceci fut accompli») renvoie au passé de la vie de Paul, depuis l'appel de Damas jusqu'à la mission réussie à Éphèse (Ac 19,10.20). Paul, comme Jean Baptiste, mène à bien sa course sur la terre (δρόμος). Par contre, le programme vital de Jésus, qui avait débuté par l'εἴσοδος (Ac 13,24), conclut par l'ἔξοδος (Lc 9,31) et culmine avec son ἀναλήμψις (Lc 9,51), son enlèvement au ciel.

De toute façon, il faut dire que dans Ac 19,21 on ne se borne pas à regarder vers le passé. Au contraire, le texte est conçu comme le début de ce qui va suivre. J. Dupont affirme: «La notice de 19,21 trace le programme de toute la suite du livre»[15]. Paul, guidé par l'Esprit, prend la

---

13. Le substantif δρόμος n'apparaît que ces deux fois dans Lc-Ac!

14. Il paraît que le pronom ταῦτα d'Ac 19,21 doit être rapporté à l'ensemble de la vie de Paul et non seulement à son ministère éphésien, comme le suppose Haenchen (cf. n. 12). Le poids de l'argumentation repose sur le verbe πληρόω, qui doit être interprété dans un sens fort, et sur le caractère unique de la formule utilisée en Ac 19,21.

15. J. DUPONT, *La question du plan des Actes à la lumière d'un texte de Lucien de*

décision d'aller à Jérusalem, en traversant la Macédoine et l'Achaïe, et finalement, d'après le vouloir divin (δεῖ), il se propose de voir Rome. Même si on peut discuter sur le sens de ἐν τῷ πνεύματι comme référence à l'Esprit Saint dans Ac 19,21[16], les difficultés d'interprétation sont moindres dans Ac 20,22-23. Ici Paul se présente lui même comme «enchaîné par l'Esprit», puisque c'est l'Esprit Saint qui l'avertit des chaînes et détresses qui l'attendent. Encore dans 21,4 et 21,11 on mentionne l'Esprit à propos du projet de Paul de monter à Jérusalem. Par conséquent les trois références à l'Esprit dans la section 19,21–21,16 semblent renforcer l'interprétation proposée pour Ac 19,21. En outre, l'expression unique de Lc 9,51, qui exprime la décision résolue et ferme de Jésus d'aller à Jérusalem lors de son ἀναλήμψις, nous invite à voir en Ac 19,21 une décision aussi ferme de la part de Paul, soutenue par l'assurance et la conviction que seul l'Esprit Saint peut donner.

Paul, comme Jésus, veut se rendre à Jérusalem. En Lc 9,51 on trouve l'expression πορεύεσθαι εἰς Ἰερουσαλήμ. En Ac 19,21 la même phrase se rapporte à Paul, mais le substantif qui désigne la ville sainte est ici Ἱεροσόλυμα. D'emblée, l'auteur de Lc-Ac semble réserver la forme Ἰερουσαλήμ, proche à l'hébreu, pour désigner la ville où le destin de Jesús va s'accomplir[17]. Par contre, dans le cas de Paul, cette dénomination alterne tout à fait avec Ἱεροσόλυμα, un des noms grecs de Jérusalem. Ainsi à partir d'Ac 19,21 et jusqu'à la fin du livre, Ἰερουσαλήμ (14 fois) et Ἱεροσόλυμα (12 fois) sont écrites de façon apparemment indistincte. On assiste ainsi à une dissolution des contours sacrés de la ville, représentés par la forme proche à l'hébreu, qui avaient marqué les débuts de la première communauté: Ἰερουσαλήμ est, en effet, l'endroit où s'enracine l'église apostolique[18]. Maintenant, lors de la dernière étape de la vie de Paul, la ville devient un endroit hostile au christianisme, lieu de persécution du grand annonciateur de l'évangile. L'alternance presque paritaire des deux dénominations contribue à souligner l'échec de Jérusalem, devenue une ville qui tue les messagers de

---

Samosate, in *NT* 21 (1979) 220-231, repr. dans *Nouvelles Études sur les Actes des Apôtres* (LD, 118), Paris, Cerf, 1984, p. 33. De la même façon, Haenchen écrit: «the theme for the finale of this great symphony is sounded for the first time» (*Acts*, p. 569).

16. Plusieurs auteurs, à la suite de Bauer dans son *Wörterbuch* (p. 1616, s.v. τίθημι), veulent y voir une allusion à l'esprit humain. Ils traduisent: «en son esprit (de Paul)».

17. Ainsi FITZMYER, *Luke*, p. 828. En fait, à partir de Lc 9,51, sauf en trois occasions (13,22; 19,28; 23,7), on trouve seulement la forme plus proche à l'hébreu (17 occasions en total dans l'évangile).

18. Entre Ac 1,1 et 8,3, Ἰερουσαλήμ apparaît 12 fois et Ἱεροσόλυμα seulement 2. Entre Ac 8,4 et 19,20, les proportions sont 15 fois pour la forme proche à l'hébreu et 6 pour la forme grecque.

Dieu (comparer Lc 13,34 et Ac 21,13)[19]. Par conséquent, le changement qui se produit, à propos de la dénomination de Jérusalem, entre Lc 9,51 (Ἰερουσαλήμ) et Ac 19,21 (Ἱεροσόλυμα) n'est pas fortuit; il exprime le changement de rôle de la ville. Les couleurs sombres dominent le dessin lucanien de Jérusalem dans les derniers chapitres de Lc-Ac[20]. Jérusalem n'est plus que la ville où Paul sera emprisonné et devra se défendre devant la foule du peuple et devant le sanhédrin d'Israël.

De toute façon, Jérusalem, n'est pas le dernier but du voyage de Paul. A différence de Jésus, qui doit finir sa vie terrestre à Jérusalem, lieu de sa passion-mort et résurrection-exaltation au ciel, Paul, dans Ac 19,21, mentionne deux villes comme but de son voyage: Jérusalem et Rome. Il s'exprime en première personne et explicite la raison qui le pousse vers Rome: «il faut (δεῖ) aussi (καί) que je vois Rome». Sans aucun doute, le voyage à Jérusalem et à Rome est conséquence du plan divin. La forme verbale δεῖ l'explicite très clairement[21]. Comme dans Lc 9,51, la réalisation du plan divin est en cours: l'Esprit guide Paul dans sa décision d'aller à Jérusalem et l'influence divine est décisive dans son projet d'arriver à Rome. L'Esprit et le vouloir divin déterminent la course que Paul va entreprendre à la fin de son ministère apostolique. Toujours, comme dans Lc 9,51, le vouloir divin et la décision humaine se superposent et coïncident. L'Esprit guide Paul vers Jérusalem (21,11) et Paul lui-même se hâte d'y arriver (20,16). Déjà à Jérusalem, Paul aura une apparition nocturne du Seigneur qui est comme la charnière entre les deux étapes de son dernier voyage. Il lui dit: «Tu viens de rendre témoignage à ma cause à Jérusalem, il faut (δεῖ) qu'à Rome aussi (καί) tu

---

19. Jérusalem est le centre où s'accomplit le vouloir divin en Jésus et dans l'Église. Mais à la fin des Actes des Apôtres il se produit un changement radical, déjà annoncé dans Lc 13,33, où Jérusalem est un chiffre pour désigner les dirigeants d'Israël qui s'opposent à Jésus: cf. A. PUIG I TÀRRECH, *La paràbola dels vinyaters homicides (Lc 20,9-19)*, in *RCT* 16 (1991) 39-65. Depuis Ac 21,15 Jérusalem respire menace et persécution contre Paul, hérault de l'évangile, et se manifeste contre le plan divin. Voyez à ce propos les observations de J. ROLOFF dans son Commentaire à Ac 21,15. J. Rius-Camps s'exprime du même: *Comentari als Fets dels Apòstols. Vol. I. «Jerusalem»: configuració de l'església judeocreient, Ac 1,1–5,42* (Collectània Sant Pacià, 43), Barcelona, Herder, 1991.

20. On pourrait faire l'objection que la communauté chrétienne de Jérusalem continue à exister. Ac 21,17-26 raconte l'accueil que Paul reçoit chez Jacques, le leader de cette communauté. Mais par la suite, dès que Paul est arrêté au temple (21,27-36) jusqu'à son départ forcé à Césarée (23,23-33), il reste *seul* dans la prison. La «passio Pauli» rassemble la «passio Jesu». Tous disparaissent et ne sont mentionnés qu'en passant (comparer Lc 23,49 avec Ac 24,23; 27,3; 28,14).

21. Notons que le καί d'Ac 19,21 indique que le vouloir divin affecte de la même façon le voyage de Paul à Jérusalem *et* à Rome. L'interprétation de la forme verbale δεῖ est tout à fait majoritaire. Voyez HAENCHEN, *Acts* (n. 12), p. 568: «the δεῖ... as a reference to the divine will».

témoignes de même». Les ressemblances entre ce verset (Ac 23,11) et Ac 19,21 sont évidentes. Dans les deux cas le vouloir divin et la volonté humaine coopèrent et s'identifient[22]. Le projet de Paul, soutenu par la puissance divine, va se réaliser d'une façon inattendue. Paul arrivera à Rome attaché par les chaînes avec lesquelles les juifs l'ont lié (Ac 21,11). Même dans sa situation de prisonnier à cause de l'évangile, Paul verra (ἰδών) les frères de Rome (Ac 28,15), et ainsi le plan divin s'accomplira: «il faut aussi que je vois (δεῖ ... ἰδεῖν) Rome» (Ac 19,21). De cette façon, l'arrivée-entrée de Paul à Rome est la culmination réussie de son témoignage, lequel dépend du vouloir divin et s'inscrit dans le plan annoncé par Jésus au début du livre des Actes: «vous serez mes témoins à Jérusalem, dans toute la Judée et Samarie et jusqu'aux extrémités de la terre» (Ac 1,8). Dans le cadre de Lc-Ac ces extrémités de la terre ne peuvent correspondre qu'à Rome, la capitale de l'Empire.

Il semble donc évident qu'Ac 19,21 reprend le programme du livre des Actes: la Parole doit se répandre à partir de Jérusalem et elle doit arriver à Rome. Jusqu'à 19,21 la Parole évangélique a été annoncée progressivement dans toutes les régions de Palestine (Samarie, Judée, la côte méditerranéenne), la Syrie (Damas, Antioche), l'Asie Mineure et les régions de l'Égée (Macédoine, Achaïe) pour aboutir finalement à Éphèse (19,1-20). Maintenant, tous les térritoires qui se trouvent sur la voie entre Jérusalem et Rome ont reçu l'évangile. Le récit revient au programme initial et rejoint les deux points géographiques extrêmes de ce qui était proposé: Jérusalem (le point de départ) et Rome (le point d'arrivée). Entre 8,4 et 19,20 l'extension de la Parole se fait à partir de Jérusalem mais avec des retours fréquents à la ville sainte de la part des missionnaires[23]: la mission suit un système de cercles concentriques. Maintenant, après 19,21, le voyage devient linéaire: Paul doit monter à Jérusalem et de là se rendre directement à Rome. C'est le temps prévu par Dieu pour que la Parole arrive jusqu'aux extrémités de la terre, mais dans la plus grande faiblesse: Paul, à Jérusalem, sera rejeté par les juifs et deviendra prisonnier des romains.

22. B. RAPSKE, *The Book of Acts and Paul in Roman Custody* (BAFCS, 3), Grand Rapids, Eerdmans – Carlisle, Paternoster, 1994, p. 420: «Paul's earlier Spirit-inspired conviction of the divine δεῖ of going to Rome (Acts 19:21) receives a direct and emphatic confirmation». De son côté, Cosgrove parle de Paul comme d'un exécuteur créatif du δεῖ divin: C.H. COSGROVE, *The Divine δεῖ in Luke-Acts*, in *NT* 26 (1984) 168-190.

23. Ainsi Paul, après le premier voyage en Asie Mineure, monte à Jérusalem pour l'assemblée apostolique (Ac 15). Après son deuxième voyage en Europe il monte encore une fois à Jérusalem (et non seulement à Césarée! Ac 18,22). Après le troisième voyage, centré à Éphèse, il part vers Jérusalem pour la dernière fois.

Quand même, notons que ce dernier voyage à Jérusalem sera précédée
d'un détour: le voyage d'Éphèse à Jérusalem, vers l'orient, va se faire à
travers deux régions européennes (Macédoine et Achaïe) situées a l'occi-
dent d'Éphèse, dans la direction opposée à Jérusalem! Paul avait visité ces
deux régions au cours de son deuxième voyage après que l'Esprit Saint
l'ait empêché de continuer sa mission en Asie et Bithynie: la porte
d'Europe a été ouverte par Dieu lui-même (Ac 16,6-10). Il paraît donc que
le passage de Paul par les deux régions européennes ait un sens de récapitulation de son travail missionnaire: Éphèse en Asie, et Macédoine et
Achaïe en Europe, résument effectivement l'activité de Paul. Le voyage
décidé en Ac 19,21 se présente comme une synthèse du ministère de Paul:
Éphèse (Asie) comme point de départ, Macédoine et Achaïe (Europe)
comme régions à parcourir, Jérusalem comme but de la première étape du
voyage, et Rome comme point d'arrivée de tout le périple. On peut établir
un certain parallélisme avec le renseignement de Lc 17,11 à propos de la
montée de Jésus vers Jérusalem. Le controverti διὰ μέσον ne devrait pas
détourner notre attention de l'ensemble du verset[24]. Jésus passe (διέρχομαι, le même verbe que dans Ac 19,21) à travers Samarie et Galilée, les
deux régions qui se trouvent près de Judée et qui forment un ensemble
avec elle (cf. Ac 9,31, où l'on cite les trois régions). Or, ceci indique que
le voyage de Jésus à Jérusalem se fait dans l'espace vital des deux uniques
régions possibles[25]. Le ministère de Jésus se développe en forme de
voyage, à cheval entre juifs (galiléens) et non juifs (samaritains). Ces derniers oscillent entre le refus (Lc 9,52.56) et la reconnaissance (Lc 17,18).
Samarie et Galilée, à imitation de Macédoine et Achaïe, sont les régions
parcourues par Jésus et par Paul respectivement, au cours de leur dernière
montée à Jérusalem. Dans Lc 17,11 et Ac 19,21 on constate un certain
désir de récapitulation des ministères de Jésus et de Paul, et, dans le cas de
Jésus, un deuxième sens proleptique: Samarie sera la première région,
hors de Judée, où la Parole va se répandre après la Pentecôte (Ac 8,1.4-
25)[26]. Bref, Ac 19,21 nous invite à considérer ensemble Lc 9,51 et 17,11
et interpréter les deux versets dans une direction semblable[27].

    24. MARSHALL, Luke (n. 7), p. 650 propose de traduire «entre» et d'interpréter
l'expression dans le sens d'un voyage de Jésus tout au long de la frontière entre Samarie
et Galilée. Quoi qu'il en soit, il s'agit d'un voyage orienté, comme Ac 19,21, de façon
inverse: vers l'orient et non vers le sud, la direction de Jérusalem! Notons encore la ressemblance de structures syntactiques entre Lc 9,51 et 17,11.
    25. Luc ignore la Pérée, le territoire de l'autre côté du Jourdain, à la différence de Mt
(19,1) et de Mc (10,1).
    26. Notons le contraste entre le «village de Samaritains» qui refuse Jésus (Lc 9,52-
53) et la «ville de Samarie» qui accepte le Messie (Ac 8,5-6).
    27. Luc semble chercher l'ambiguïté de localisation du voyage de Jésus vers Jérusa-

Les rapports entre Lc 9,51 et Ac 19,21 continuent de façon moins stricte entre Lc 9,52-56 et Ac 19,22. Ce dernier texte mentionne deux collaborateurs de Paul: Timothée et Eraste, envoyés en Macédoine. Paul prolonge son séjour en Asie. De cette façon le récit ouvre une pause pour introduire l'émeute d'Éphèse. Le départ de Paul ne sera effectif qu'après ce tumulte: alors Paul ira finalement en Macédoine (20,1). Si l'on confronte cette séquence narrative (Ac 19,21–20,1) à Lc 9,51-56 on constate tout d'abord que les voyages de Jésus et Paul s'initient de la même manière: quelques messagers / deux collaborateurs sont envoyés à l'avance. La similitude augmente quand on constate qu'après le refus samaritain de Jésus et de ceux qu'il avait envoyés, deux disciples, Jacques et Jean, veulent punir les samaritains et sont réprimandés à cause de cela[28]. Certainement, le texte d'Ac 19, à la différence de Lc 9, ne mentionne pas la tâche des envoyés de Paul mais le lecteur comprend qu'il s'agit de préparer son arrivée (cf. Lc 9,52).

La difficulté principale se trouve dans le refus samaritain de Lc 9,52-56, lequel ne semble avoir aucun parallèle dans le texte des Actes. Mais la comparaison de cet épisode avec l'émeute d'Éphèse (Ac 19,23-40) apporte des éléments intéressants. D'emblée les récits sont très divers, mais les figures de Jésus et Paul sont traités avec un parallélisme notable. Ainsi, l'un et l'autre sont objets d'un refus tranchant de la part des non-juifs: les samaritains rejettent Jésus parce qu'il s'adresse à la ville ennemie de Jérusalem (Lc 9,53) et les éphèsiens accusent Paul d'être un ennemi acharné d'Artémis, puisqu'il ne lui reconnaît pas son statut de déesse (Ac 19,26). Deuxièmement, Jésus et Paul sont empêchés de réaliser leurs projets. Jésus aurait voulu entrer dans un village samaritain et, finalement, il doit s'en aller vers un autre village (Lc 9,52-56). De son côté, Paul, décidé à rejoindre l'assemblée réunie au théâtre, en est empêché par les disciples (μαθηταί) et par quelques amis (φίλοι) qui étaient asiarques (Ac 19,30-31). On trouve un troisième point de comparaison entre les deux textes dans l'épisode des deux compagnons de voyage de Paul, Gaïus et Aristarque, macédoniens, trainés au théâtre par la multitude. On dirait que c'est l'inverse de ce qu'il se passe avec Jacques et Jean, disciples (μαθηταί) de Jésus (Lc 9,54). Dans le livre

lem. On ne peut rien déduire à partir de 9,56: «It is not clear whether the next village to which Jesus and his disciples went was in Samaria or not» (MARSHALL, *Luke*, p. 408). Il n'y a qu'une seule référence géographique qui puisse situer le voyage: celle de 17,11. Et elle reste confuse. Il faut tenir compte de cette ambiguïté, qui est voulue par l'auteur.

28. Notons que dans les deux textes (Lc 9,54 et Ac 19,22) on trouve les noms des deux disciples de Jésus et des deux collaborateurs de Paul. On dirait que l'auteur tient compte de Lc 9,51-96 quand il écrit Ac 19,21-22. Un peu plus tard (19,29) on apprendra le nom de deux autres compagnons de Paul: Gaïus et Aristarque.

des Actes, lorsque Démétrius a fini son discours contre Paul, la foule d'artisans devient furieuse et commence à invoquer la déesse Artémis. Les artisans sont là avec toute la ville: au théâtre, la vie des deux compagnons de Paul est en danger (Ac 19,28-29). Dans l'évangile, lorsque les deux disciples de Jésus apprennent que les samaritains l'ont refusé, deviennent furieux et veulent appeler le feu divin pour qu'il s'abatte sur ceux qui ont rejeté Jésus (Lc 9,54-55). Mais tout va se résoudre: les deux compagnons de Paul resteront en vie et aucun feu du ciel ne fera périr les gens du village samaritain. Bref, dans les séquences narratives de Lc 9 et Ac 19 il y a quelques éléments parallèles[29].

3. Conclusion

On peut constater que dans Lc 9,51 et Ac 19,21, il y a deux programmes, deux itinéraires parallèles, celui de Jésus et celui de Paul. Jésus décide fermement d'aller à Jérusalem parce que la ville doit être le lieu de son ἀνάλημψις, de son ἔξοδος. En effet, Jérusalem est la plaque tournante des deux étapes du voyage de Jésus. Dans une première étape il y a la passion et la mort (voyage terrestre) et dans une seconde étape Jésus est ressuscité et il est exalté (voyage céleste). L'intronisation au ciel de Jésus est l'aboutissement de son voyage à Jérusalem. Jésus monte à Jérusalem mais, en fait, le but final de son voyage est le ciel: il est enlevé, comme Élie, et entre auprès de Dieu. Ces deux étapes du voyage de Jésus (Jérusalem et le ciel) sont déjà exprimées dans Lc 9,51, verset qui fait mention de l'ἀνάλημψις, c'est-à-dire, l'enlèvement au ciel. Dans le cas de Paul, le programme est pareil. Il s'agit d'un voyage en deux étapes, ou, si l'on veut, d'un voyage à Jérusalem qui culmine avec l'arrivée de Paul à Rome. Avec lui, la Parole entre à la capitale de l'Empire, l'extrémité de la terre. Le programme du livre des Actes, annoncé par Jésus ressuscité avant son Ascension, se réalise complètement: la Parole arrive «aux extrémités de la terre» (Ac 1,8). Paul doit monter à Jérusalem mais Rome est le but réel de son voyage. A l'intronisation du Christ au ciel correspond l'arrivée de la Parole et de son hérault, Paul, à Rome. La «vita Christi» s'achève avec son exaltation

29. Lc 9,53 rejet de Jésus   Ac 19,26   rejet de Paul
par les Samaritains   par les Éphésiens
54 menace des deux disciples de   28-29 menace des Éphésiens contre
Jésus contre les Samaritains   les deux collaborateurs de Paul
55 menace sans conséquences: 37 menace sans conséquences:
Jésus l'évite   le chancelier de la ville l'évite
en réprimandant les disciples   en calmant les Éphésiens
56 Jesús change son projet: 30-31 Paul change son projet:
il va dans un autre village   il ne va pas au théâtre

glorieuse au ciel. La «vita Ecclesiae» culmine avec l'arrivée à Rome d'une Parole libre et enchaînée, objet de désaccord chez les uns et accueillie sans réserves par les autres (Ac 28,24.28).

Les programmes de Jésus et Paul s'intègrent dans le plan divin de salut, qui se réalise à travers la Parole évangélique, prêchée d'abord par Jésus et ensuite par la communauté primitive et ses missionnaires. L'exaltation de Jésus, Messie et Seigneur, est la manifestation dernière du vouloir divin de salut: «il n'y a sous le ciel aucun autre nom donné aux hommes par lequel il nous faille être sauvés» (Ac 4,12 δεῖ σωθῆναι ἡμᾶς). L'annonce de la Parole faite par Paul à Rome est la réalisation de la volonté divine exprimée par l'Esprit (Ac 19,21) et par Jésus, le Seigneur: «Tu viens de rendre témoignage à ma cause à Jérusalem, il faut (δεῖ) qu'à Rome aussi tu témoignes de même» (Ac 23,11). Les décisions fermes de Jésus et Paul de monter à Jérusalem rejoignent ainsi le but que Dieu se propose. L'harmonie entre le vouloir divin et les volontés humaines sert à exprimer le programme narratif et théologique de l'auteur de Lc-Ac.

Camí de l'Horta 7   Armand PUIG i TÀRRECH
E-43470 La Selva del Camp
Catalogne

DAS GEBOT DER NÄCHSTENLIEBE
IM LUKANISCHEN DOPPELWERK

Einführung

Fragen wir nach der Auslegung des Gebotes der Nächstenliebe im lukanischen Doppelwerk, dann lassen sich die relevanten Passagen aufgrund der Auslegung von Lev 19,18b sowie der Verwendung von πλησίον und ἀγαπάω in zwei Gruppen unterteilen: zum einen solche Verse und Perikopen, die sich auf »Q« zurückführen lassen (Lk 6,27-36; 7,1-10 und 16,13), zum anderen solche, die zum lukanischen Sondergut gehören (Lk 7,36-50 und 10,25-37). In der ersten Gruppe, die Lukas mit Matthäus gemeinsam hat und die neben Markus auf eine zweite Quelle schließen läßt, findet sich einmal der zweimalige Aufruf zur Feindesliebe (Lk 6,27 und 6,32-35), dann die Perikope über den Hauptmann von Kapernaum, von dem gesagt wird, daß er »unser Volk liebt«, weshalb diese Perikope nicht direkt mit der Nächstenliebe in Verbindung gebracht werden kann (obwohl die Stelle implizit zur Liebe zum jüdischen Volk aufrufen dürfte), sowie zum Schluß die der Gegenüberstellung von Hassen und Lieben (Lk 16,13). Zwei dieser drei Stellen sind insofern thematisch miteinander verwandt, indem sie zum Lieben eines sich nicht in unmittelbarer sozialer Nähe befindlichen Menschen aufrufen, und die Liebe mit ihrem Gegenteil, d.i. dem Haß, konfrontieren. In der zweiten, nur bei Lukas vorkommenden und für unsere Untersuchung besonders interessanten Gruppe geht es um die immer als solche explizit gestellte Frage, wer denn der Nächste sei (Lk 7,36-50 und 10,29-37). Auch hier läßt sich eine thematische Verwandtschaft feststellen, indem die geforderte Nächstenliebe mit einem außerhalb der Gemeinschaft stehenden Menschen verbunden wird.

1. *Lukas 6,27-36; 7,1-10 und 16,13*

In Lk 6,27-28 heißt es: »Aber ich sage euch, die es hören: Liebet eure Feinde, tut wohl denen, die euch hassen, segnet diejenigen, die euch verfluchen, betet für diejenigen, die euch schmähen«. Das Gebot der Feindesliebe ist hier in vier Aufforderungen unterteilt – liebet, tut wohl, segnet und betet –, deren allgemeiner Charakter nun einschränkend auf jeweils vier weitere Gruppen zugespitzt wird: die Feinde, die Hasser, die Verflucher und die Schmäher, deren gemeinsames Merkmal, wiederum einschränkend, ist, daß sie in Beziehung zu den Angesprochenen stehen: denjenigen, die es hören, d.h. entweder den Jüngern (Lk 6,20ff.) oder allen Anwesenden (Lk 6,24ff.). Im Vergleich zu der Parallele Mt 5,44 hat Lukas das Q-Logion (6,27ab.28b) eindeutig erweitert, zum einen durch die Hervorhebung derer, die es hören, zum anderen durch die Hinzufügung der Hasser, Verflucher und Schmäher (wobei Lukas statt von Verfolgern von Schmähern redet). Die Erweiterung ist als eine Konkretisierung aufzufassen: die Feinde werden näher charakterisiert. Ließen sich nun die Angesprochenen identifizieren, dann dürften sich auch die Hasser, Verflucher und Schmäher und damit der Sitz im Leben des Lukasevangeliums näher umschreiben lassen[1].

In Lk 6,29-30 folgen weitere Konkretisierungen, so auch in Lk 6,31-34, dessen letzte Verse aber gleichzeitig aufgrund der »Goldenen Regel« in Vers 31 als Auftakt zur Begründung der Feindesliebe dienen. Nicht die Rückführung auf Q oder die *ipsissima vox* Jesu soll hier Thema sein[2], sondern die Charakterisierung der lukanischen Bearbeitung. In den Versen 29-30 wird der Situation, in der sich die Angesprochenen befinden bzw. wird der historischen Situation der lukanischen Christen – sie werden auf die Backe geschlagen, ihre Mäntel werden weggenommen, sie werden um ihren Besitz gebeten oder er wird ihnen weggenommen – jeweils die rechte Verhaltensweise entgegengestellt: biete auch die andere Backe dar, verweigere auch nicht den Leibrock, gib, aber fordere nicht zurück.

In den Versen 31-34 wird dieser rechten Verhaltensweise, ausgehend von der »Goldenen Regel«, ein sündiges Verhalten entgegengestellt: Der Weg der Sünder ist es, den Menschen gleich zu behandeln, d.h. diejenigen zu lieben, die sie lieben; denjenigen Gutes zu tun, die ihnen Gutes tun; Geld auszuleihen an diejenigen, von denen man hofft, es zurückzubekommen; mit anderen Worten, »ich gebe, damit du gibst«. Die für die Angesprochenen daraus zu ziehende Konsequenz ist, daß man damit den Sündern gleich sein und keinen Dank dafür bekommen wird.

In Lk 6,35 folgt nun die Beschreibung des rechten Lebenswandels und damit der eigentliche Grund, warum man die Feinde lieben sollte, nämlich als »Imitatio Dei«: »Vielmehr, liebet eure Feinde und tut Gutes und leiht Geld aus ohne auf etwas zu hoffen; und euer Lohn wird groß

---

1. Vgl. dazu auch G. LOHFINK, *Der ekklesiale Sitz im Leben der Aufforderung Jesu zum Gewaltverzicht (Mt 5,39b-42/Lk 6,29f)*, in *TQ* 162 (1982) 236-253, S. 236ff.
2. Siehe dazu ausführlich bei D. LÜHRMANN, *Liebet eure Feinde (Lk 6,27-36/Mt 5,39-48)*, in *ZTK* 69 (1972) 412-438, S. 412ff. und vgl. M. SATO, *Q und Prophetie. Studien zur Gattungs- und Traditionsgeschichte der Quelle Q* (WUNT, 2/29), Tübingen, Mohr, 1988, S. 222f. und 394, sowie LOHFINK, *Sitz*, S. 240.

sein, und ihr werdet Kinder des Allerhöchsten sein, denn er ist gütig zu den Undankbaren und den Bösen«.

Bevor wir uns aber der Hermeneutik der Perikope zuwenden, in der der sündigen Verhaltensweise, ihren »Begründungen« und ihren Konsequenzen die rechte Verhaltensweise, ihr Grund und ihr Lohn gegenübergestellt wird, soll das Interesse auf die in den Versen 29-30 implizierte historische Situation gelenkt werden. Die Angesprochenen, über deren Identität sich nichts mit Sicherheit feststellen läßt, befinden sich in einer Situation – nach den Versen 27-28 umgeben von Feinden, Hassern, Verfluchern und Schmähern –, in der sie auf die Backe geschlagen werden, ihre Mäntel weggenommen und sie gebeten werden, ihren Besitz herzugeben oder er ihnen weggenommen wird. Die hier angedeutete Situation weist am meisten Ähnlichkeiten mit den Christenverfolgungen am Ende des 1. Jh.s n.Chr. auf, d.h. in der Zeit nach dem Tod des Paulus (vgl. Apg 20,25.38 und 21,13) und der Zerstörung des Zweiten Tempels (vgl. Lk 21,24), wahrscheinlich um 90 n.Chr. und vielleicht bereits in Rom. Dazu gibt es reichlich Anhaltspunkte inner- und außerhalb des lukanischen Doppelwerks. Innerhalb ist auf die Verfolgung der Gemeinde nach Lk 21,12-19 und z.B. auf die von Stephanus und Paulus erlittenen Verfolgungen nach Apg 6,8ff.; 16,16ff. und 22,22ff. hinzuweisen; außerhalb u.a. auf die Berichte des Tacitus über die Christenverfolgungen[3].

Aus römischer Sicht, und dies dürfte aus den Versen 31-34 hervorgehen, steht die von Lukas geforderte rechte Verhaltensweise diametral der damals herrschenden Ethik gegenüber, die auf *do ut des* beruhte, und daher den Einwohnern des römischen Reiches als »gemeinschaftsfeindliche Gesinnung« (Tacitus, *Annalen* XV 44,4) und als »Torheit« (vgl. 1 Kor 1,18ff.) erscheinen mußte. Aus lukanischer Sicht erscheinen aber nicht nur die damaligen »religiösen« Schranken zwischen Juden und Heiden, sondern auch die politischen und sozialen zwischen Freunden und Feinden oder Reichen und Armen als vollkommen belanglos, wenn es um die kommende Herrschaft Gottes geht. Die Nächstenliebe dürfte sogar einen Schritt in die Richtung dieser Herrschaft darstellen, einen Grund mehr, den Nächsten von ganzem Herzen zu lieben. Es handelt sich um eine Ethik, die jede sozial akzeptierte Handelsweise sprengt, ja, sie aufgrund der Dynamik des in Christus und in der Kirche angebrochenen Gottesreiches umwälzen will.

Zwei weitere Stellen sind kurz zu erwähnen. In Lk 7,5 (7,1-10) bezieht sich die »Liebe« auf die Liebe des Hauptmanns von Kapernaum

---

3. Vgl. H. HOMMEL, *Tacitus und die Christen*, in ID., *Sebasmata. Studien zur antiken Religionsgeschichte und zum frühen Christentum*, II, Tübingen, Mohr, 1984, S. 174-199.

zum jüdischen Volk und kann daher als die Geisteshaltung eines Gottesfürchtigen betrachtet werden[4]. Die Perikope fällt nur deswegen auf, weil
die Erwähnung der Liebe zum jüdischen Volk in der Parallele Mt 8,5-13
(vgl. auch Joh 4,46-53) fehlt. Auch hier hat Lukas bzw. bereits vor ihm
Q-Lukas Q-Stoff erweitert (bes. in 7,4a-6c)[5]. In Lk 16,13 handelt es sich
ebenfalls nicht um die Nächstenliebe im eigentlichen Sinne, wenn es um
die Liebe, hier um die Unterscheidung zwischen dem Dienen zweier
Herren, geht: entweder liebt man den einen und haßt den anderen oder
umgekehrt. Das Logion findet sich fast wörtlich in Mt 6,24. Hier gab es
anscheinend keinen Grund für Lukas, Q-Stoff zu erweitern.

Ist das Gebot der Nächstenliebe im Q-Stoff dem hellenistischen
Judentum zuzuschreiben, von dem es in den Q-Trägerkreis gelang[6], so
wurde es in seiner lukanischen Bearbeitung in einer besonders von Verfolgungen geprägten historischen Situation konkretisiert.

2. *Lukas 7,36-50 und 10,25-37*

Fanden wir bereits in der Übernahme des Q-Stoffes in der lukanischen
Bearbeitung starke Erweiterungstendenzen (Lk 6,27c-28a; 6,33b-35d;
7,4a-6), so ist dies im lukanischen Sondergut (Lk 7,36-50 und 10,29-37)
sogar ausschließlich der Fall. Statt damit jedoch auf eine weitere von
Lukas verwendete Quelle, neben Markus und Q, schließen zu wollen,
soll auch hier auf die Besonderheiten der lukanischen Redaktion hingewiesen werden.

In Lk 7,36-50 geht es, ähnlich wie Lk 10,29-37, um die Beurteilung
des Verhaltens eines Außenstehenden, hier der Sünderin, dort des barmherzigen Samaritaners. Nachdem die Sünderin im Hause eines Pharisäers Jesus gesalbt hat (Lk 7,36-39), sagt Jesus zum Pharisäer:
»Simon, ich habe dir etwas zu sagen. Und er sagte: Meister, sage es. Ein
Gläubiger hatte Zwei Schuldner; der eine schuldete 500 Denarien, der
andere 50. Weil sie nichts hatten um zurückzugeben, schenkte er es den
beiden. Wer von denen nun wird ihn am meisten lieben? Und Simon
antwortete und sagte: Ich vermute, derjenige, dem er am meisten
schenkte. Und er sagte zu ihm: Du hast richtig geurteilt« (Lk 7,40-43).
Dies wird nun auf die konkrete Situation im Hause des Pharisäers bezo-

4. Vgl. B. WANDER, *Gottesfürchtige und Sympathisanten. Studien zum heidnischen Umfeld von Diasporasynagogen* (WUNT, 104), Tübingen, Mohr, 1998.
5. Vgl. SATO, *Q*, S. 55 und 61.
6. Vgl. C. BURCHARD, *Das doppelte Liebesgebot in der frühen christlichen Über-lieferung*, in E. LOHSE *et al.* (eds.), *Der Ruf Jesu und die Antwort der Gemeinde. Exegetische Untersuchungen*. FS J. Jeremias, Göttingen, Vandenhoeck & Ruprecht, 1970, S. 39-62.

gen, dem vorgeworfen wird, er habe Jesus bei weitem nicht so wie die Sünderin geehrt (Lk 7,44-46), wenn es in V. 47 heißt: »Ihre vielen Sünden wurden vergeben, weil sie viel liebte, aber der, dem wenig vergeben wird, liebt wenig«. Abgesehen davon, daß Jesus hier christologisch als derjenige, der Sünden vergeben kann, hervorgehoben wird (Lk 7,48-50), werden zwei Lebensweisen einander gegenübergestellt und mit dem Kriterium der Liebe beurteilt.

Auch hier bedient sich Lukas der Gegenüberstellung, der Kontrastierung zweier ethischer Modelle, das auf Reziprokität beruhende und das in der unermeßlichen Liebe Gottes gründende, in Christus offenbarte und von den Christen geforderte bzw. erwartete. In der Konkretisierung zielt Lukas wiederum auf den Abbau sozial-wirtschaftlicher und religiöser Schranken. Aufgrund der Gleichheit der Menschen vor Gott und seinen Gesalbten ist die auf den bestehenden sozialen Strukturen basierende Ungleichheit der Menschen in der Zeit der Kirche aufzuheben.

In der Lukasparallele zu Mk 12,28-34, Lk 10,25-28, fragt ein Schriftgelehrter Jesus nicht mehr wie bei Markus, was das erste Gebot von allen sei, sondern, was er tun solle, um das ewige Leben zu ererben. Jesus antwortet auch, wie bei Markus, hier mit dem Doppelgebot der Liebe (Dtn 6,5 und Lev 19,18). Auf die Frage des Schriftgelehrten, wer denn der »Nächste« sei, antwortet Jesus in dem lukanischen Sondergut, Lk 10,29-37, mit dem Gleichnis des barmherzigen Samaritaners, dem der Schriftgelehrte die Antwort auf seine Frage entnehmen soll: der Nächste ist immer derjenige, dem man Barmherzigkeit erweisen kann, d.h. dem man selber zum Nächsten wird.

Die nur in Lk 10,25-28 von Markus abhängige und kultkritische Perikope weist in der Ergänzung von Lk 10,29-37 folgende Besonderheiten auf. Erstens geht es hier um die Frage nach dem ewigen Leben, die Christus mit den Worten, »Tue das, so wirst du leben« (Lev 18,5), aufgrund des Gesetzes beantwortet. Und zweitens wird in dem angefügten Gleichnis des barmherzigen Samaritaners (in Analogie zur »Goldenen Regel«) ausgeführt, wie das Gesetz als Ausdruck des Willens Gottes im täglichen Leben konkretisiert werden kann. Hier fällt zunächst die Übereinstimmung mit der zeitgenössisch-jüdischen Deutung des Nächstenliebegebots als das Erweisen von Barmherzigkeit auf (weil auch Gott sich dem Menschen gegenüber als barmherzig erwiesen hat)[7], dennoch endet

---

7. Vgl. auch R.D. AUS, *Weihnachtsgeschichte, Barmherziger Samariter, Verlorener Sohn. Studien zu ihrem jüdischen Hintergrund* (ANTZ, 2), Berlin, Institut Kirche und Judentum, 1988, S. 123-125.

die Perikope damit, daß Jesus zu dem Schriftgelehrten spricht: »Gehe
hin und tue du ebenso« (Lk 10,37). D.h., hier wird auf das Nachahmen
(des Samaritaners) angespielt. Denn es ist erst die Autorität Christi, mit
der denjenigen, die ihm folgen, das Gebot der Nächstenliebe gegeben
wird, und zwar mit der bereits in Lk 10,28 formulierten Begründung:
»Tue dies und du wirst leben«, zwar eine Anspielung an Lev 18,5, aber
auch hier im Munde Jesu. Die Tora, Ausdruck des Willens Gottes, erhält
durch Christus (vgl. Lk 16,16) auch Gültigkeit für das Leben der Kirche.
Dabei stellt das Gebot der Nächstenliebe für Lukas ein besonderes
Gebot dafür dar, wie dem angebrochenen Königreich Gottes, konkretisiert in der jeweiligen historischen Situation, innergemeindlich und nach
außen Ausdruck verliehen werden kann.

Die Frage in Lk 10,29-37, wer denn als Nächster geliebt werden soll,
wird so beantwortet, daß immer derjenige, der liebt, Nächster ist. Der
Nächste ist also in dem Sinne kein Objekt, das man lieben kann, sondern
der Nächste wird hier definiert als der als Subjekt Liebende. Die theologische Begründung dazu ist, daß auch Gott, der Grund unserer Liebe
überhaupt, von sich aus liebt, und zwar alle Menschen ohne Unterschied[8].

Lukas denkt in Begriffen einer weltumfassenden Kirche und will mit
dem nur bei ihm vorkommenden Gleichnis des barmherzigen Samaritaners zeigen, daß »religiöse« Schranken zwischen Juden und Heiden
keine Geltung mehr haben, wenn es um die eine Kirche Jesu Christi
geht. Der Evangelist versteht dies von seiner heilsgeschichtlichen Perspektive aus und betont dabei die ethische Verantwortung der Kirche bis
zur Wiederkunft Christi.

Das Gleichnis des barmherzigen Samaritaners[9] zeigt, daß in der uni-
versell werdenden Kirche zwar auch der Begriff »Nächster« universali-
siert wird, die Frage, wer denn der Nächste sei, aber nicht damit beantwortet werden kann, daß er jeder nur denkbare Mensch sei, sondern daß
man selber – in Nachahmung Gottes und in Nachfolge Christi – von sich
aus, der Nächste seines Nächsten werden soll. Damit wird die Frage (V.
29) eines (christlichen?) Schriftgelehrten (V. 25) von der Schrift aus
beantwortet: auch für die Christen gilt, daß aus Dtn 6,5 und Lev 19,18

8. Zur ganzen Perikope vgl. auch ausführlich bei M. KLINGHARDT, *Gesetz und Volk
Gottes. Das lukanische Verständnis des Gesetzes nach Herkunft, Funktion und seinem
Ort in der Geschichte des Urchristentums* (WUNT, 2/32), Tübingen, Mohr, 1988, S. 136-
155.

9. Zu einer völlig anderen, allegorischen Deutung des Gleichnisses vgl. B. GER-
HARDSSON, *The Good Samaritan – The Good Shepherd?* (Coniectanea Neotestamentica,
16), Lund, Gleerup – Kopenhagen, Munksgaard, 1958, S. 3-31.

(V. 27) vor allem das Erweisen der Barmherzigkeit als Aufgabe menschlichen Daseins folgt.

3. *Apostelgeschichte 15,20 und 29*

In der Apostelgeschichte findet sich weder das Gebot der Nächstenliebe als Zitat von Lev 19,18b noch die »Goldene Regel«, mit Ausnahme von den Ergänzungen zu Apg 15,20 und 29 im sogenannten »westlichen Text«, im Codex Bezae und in einigen Minuskeln, und zwar einmal in der Rede des Jakobus (Apg 15,13-21) und einmal im sogenannten Aposteldekret (Apg 15,22-29): »und was sie/ihr nicht wollen/wollt, daß ihnen/ihr geschieht, sollen/sollt sie/ihr anderen nicht antun«. In beiden Fällen fügen die genannten Handschriften die »Goldene Regel« zu den hier aufgeführten noachidischen Geboten hinzu. Gab es dazu im Text selber einen Anlaß, entweder weil die beiden Verse erklärungsbedürftig wären, oder mit einer damals bekannten Maxime hätten popularisiert werden müssen?

Kapitel 15 der Apostelgeschichte behandelt das sogenannte Aposteldekret und beschreibt die Differenzen zwischen Paulus und Barnabas und der Jerusalemer Gemeinde bezüglich der Frage nach der Beschneidung (1-6), die anschließenden Verhandlungen mit den Reden des Petrus und des Jakobus (7-21) und den daraus resultierenden Beschluß (22-29) samt brieflicher Benachrichtung an die Gemeinde in Antiochien (30-35).

Die mit der »Goldenen Regel« ergänzten Verse 20 und 29 stehen im Kontext der Rede des Jakobus und des Beschlusses, in dem der Vorschlag des Jakobus aufgenommen wird, von allen mosaischen Geboten nur die bezüglich Götzenopfer, Blut und Ersticktem (von D weggelassen) und Unzucht für alle Christen als verbindlich zu erklären. Dabei handelt es sich um drei der sieben noachidischen Gebote, die auch die Gottesfürchtigen und Sympathisanten im Umfeld der Diasporasynagogen aufnahmen, und die alle Juden im Falle von Lebensgefahr nicht bereit sein sollten, aufzugeben (vgl. z.B. tSota 15,17). Dies bedeutet, daß Lukas in einem solchen Kontext spricht, in dem es keine Schranken zwischen Christen, Juden-Christen und Gottesfürchtigen geben sollte oder durfte.

Sind nun aber diese drei noachidischen Gebote, die einen überwiegend rituellen Sinn haben, identisch mit der »Goldenen Regel«, die doch eher sozial-ethisch verstanden wird? Wohl kaum. Ihre Gemeinsamkeit besteht aber darin, daß sie *Zusammenfassungen für die Völker* darstellen: (1) die noachidischen Gebote der ganzen Tora, besonders auch des ersten Gebots bzw. der ersten fünf Worte des Dekalogs; (2) die »Goldene Regel« der einzelnen Gebote, besonders der bezüglich des

Umgangs mit den anderen Mitgliedern der Gemeinschaft bzw. die zweiten fünf Worte des Dekalogs. Beide sind als Minimalforderung für die Völker gedacht.

Somit würden D *et al.* Apg 15,20 und 29 dahingehend verstanden haben wollen, daß wir es einerseits mit dem Doppelgebot der Liebe zu tun haben, andererseits mit einer Minimalforderung der Tora für die Völker. Also haben wir es nicht mit einer Erklärung zu tun, sondern mit einer popularisierenden Ergänzung anhand einer bei Juden, Christen und Heiden bekannten Maxime, die möglicherweise auch den Sinn von Apg 15 trifft.

Eine weitaus wichtigere Frage, die sich aus dem Vorangegangenen ergibt, ist, wie nun die Predigt Jesu vom kommenden Gottesreich und sein Aufruf zur Nächstenliebe im Lukasevangelium sich zum Leben der Gemeinde nach der Apostelgeschichte verhält. Daß es zwischen beiden eine Einheit gibt, d.h. sowohl zwischen beiden Werken als auch zwischen Jesus und der Gemeinde, ist unbestreitbar (vgl. Lk 1,3 mit Apg 1,1-2 sowie Apg 20,18-35). Nur wird die Apostelgeschichte etwas später als das Lukasevangelium entstanden sein, und der Heilige Geist spielt nun eine tragende Rolle (Apg 1,8 und 2,1-13). Die Zielrichtung ist eindeutig von Jerusalem nach Rom und folgt damit den Missionsreisen des Paulus und der Verbreitung der Gemeinde, die auch die von Israel zu den Heiden ist.

4. *Die Rezeption des Gebots der Nächstenliebe*

Den theologischen Zusammenhang zwischen dem Lukasevangelium und der Apostelgeschichte gibt es nun tatsächlich auch im Falle des Gebotes der Nächstenliebe. Wird in Marias Lobgesang (Lk 1,46-55) noch die alttestamentliche Hoffnung ausgesprochen, der Herr fülle »die Hungrigen mit Gütern und lasse die Reichen leer«, und zwar als Ausdruck der den Vätern Israels versprochenen Barmherzigkeit Gottes (Lk 1,53-55), so klingt sie in Jesu Mund bereits als ein nun für seine Jünger und die werdende Kirche geltendes Gebot (Lk 3,11; 6,20-26; 8,14; 9,3.25.46-48; 10,4; 12,13-21.33-34; 14,7-24.33; 16,1-31; 18,18-26), das dann auch gleich befolgt wird (Lk 5,11.28; 8,3; 18,28). Der Aufruf zur Demut und Güterteilung wechselt sich ab mit dem Aufruf zur Nachfolge. In diesem Rahmen muß das Gebot der Nächstenliebe verstanden werden, wobei besonders die Warnung vor Reichtum auffällt.

In der Apostelgeschichte findet sich dann die Beschreibung der Verwirklichung dieses Ideals (Apg 2,45; 4,32.34-37; 11,29-30), wenn auch in idealisierter Form, aber mit dieser Idealisierung wird die Gültigkeit der Forderung auch für die künftige Kirche unterstrichen (Apg 5,4; 20,35). Das Ergebnis dieses von Gott vorgegebenen, von Christus vorgelebten und von der Kirche nachgeahmten ethischen Lebenswandels ist ein Wachsen der Kirche (Apg 17,4; 18,8). Das Gebot der Nächstenliebe und seine historisch bedingte Konkretisierung wird in diesen heilshistorischen Rahmen eingebettet und ist auch selber ein theologischer roter Faden.

Ein weiterer Aspekt ist das Verhältnis zwischen Kirche und Staat. Ist das irdische Leben Jesu noch geprägt vom Widerstand des Herodes (Lk 3,19; 13,32-33), der aber nicht der wahre Grund der Verurteilung Jesu ist (Lk 23,4.14.16.20-22), so gilt für das Leben der Kirche das Gebot der Feindesliebe (Apg 5,29), und ist die historische Situation besonders geprägt von dem Widerstand der Juden (Apg 13,50; 17,5-7.13; 23,10), wobei nur der Schutz der Römer bzw. des römischen Bürgerrechts Schlimmeres verhindert hat (Apg 16,37-40; 22,25-29; 23,27.29; 25,8.25; 26,31; 28,30-31). Aus letzterem Umstand läßt sich eine eindeutig pro-römische Haltung des *Auctor ad Theophilum* ableiten, nicht ungewöhnlich, wenn man diese Haltung doch auch bereits bei Philo und zeitgleich bei Josephus vorfindet[10].

5. *Schlußfolgerungen*

Ausgangspunkt für Lukas ist jeweils das biblische Gebot der Nächstenliebe; charakteristisch für ihn ist, sowohl in der Übernahme des Q-Stoffes als auch im Sondergut, die Erweiterung und Konkretisierung. Dies läßt auf einen besonderen Sitz im Leben schließen: einerseits auf die Gottesfürchtigen in den hellenistisch-jüdischen Gemeinden, was durchaus in Übereinstimmung mit dem Bild der paulinischen Mission nach der Apostelgeschichte ist, andererseits auf die Heidenchristen. Beide Gruppen werden, als Hörer des Evangeliums, mit den Vorbildern der Sünderin und des barmherzigen Samaritaners aufgefordert, eine ähnliche, wahrhaft christliche Lebens- und Geisteshaltung zu entwickeln.

In der Apostelgeschichte findet dieses Ideal nun seine Verwirklichung, und zwar unter Heranziehung zweier Schwerpunkte, die ebenfalls auf eine besondere historische Situation schließen lassen: (1) das Verhältnis zwischen Arm und Reich und (2) das Verhältnis zwischen

---

10. Vgl. G.S. OEGEMA, *Der Gesalbte und sein Volk. Untersuchungen zum Konzeptualisierungsprozeß der messianischen Erwartungen von den Makkabäern bis Bar Koziba* (Schriften des Institutum Judaicum Delitzschianum, 2), Göttingen, Vandenhoeck & Ruprecht, 1994, S. 115-129.

G. OEGEMA

Kirche und Staat. Die damit verbundene Idealisierung ist selber wiederum als Aufforderung zu einem von der Nachfolge Christi geprägten ethischen Lebenswandel für künftige Generationen aufzufassen.

Rathausstraße 7   Gerbern S. OEGEMA
D-72108 Rottenburg

LUKE 10,38-42 AND ACTS 6,1-7

WOMEN AND DISCIPLESHIP
IN THE LITERARY CONTEXT OF LUKE-ACTS

The compositional parallels between Lk 10,38-42 and Acts 6,1-7 have long been remarked on[1]. In order to listen to the word (λόγος) of the Lord, Mary leaves (καταλείπω) the serving (διακονέω) to Martha who complains. Similarly, the apostles assert that they should not have to leave (καταλείπω) the word (λόγος) of God in order to serve (διακονέω) at tables. What is different in a number of more recent studies which deal with either or both of these passages is the emphasis placed on the Lukan composition or redaction of the texts insofar as it reflects issues relating to the ministry of women contemporaneous with the writing of Luke-Acts[2].

My particular interest in the Martha-Mary passage stems from a presentation on women in the Gospel of Luke which I was requested to make for a group of lay parish leaders. At the time E. Schüssler Fiorenza's *But She Said*[3] was recently published, and I included her interpretation among others. Never having had a strong emotional response to the passage myself, I was somewhat taken aback by the intensity of reaction from women and men who told me how angry their mothers had always been when this passage was preached on. I have gradually become more aware that while I had tended to identify with Mary, many, perhaps the majority, of Christian women strongly identify with Martha and resent what is perceived as the unfairness to her portrayed in this passage.

Until fairly recently a comment frequently made about Luke-Acts, and in particular the gospel, was that it was highly favorable in its depic-

---

1. See, e.g., B. REICKE, *Instruction and Discussion in the Travel Narrative*, in *Studia Evangelica*, 4 (TU, 73), Berlin, Akademie Verlag, 1959, pp. 206-216, esp. 212-213; E. LALAND, *Die Martha-Maria Perikope Lukas 10,38-42*, in *Studia Theologica* 13 (1959) 70-85; B. GERHARDSSON, *Memory and Manuscript. Oral Transmission in Rabbinic Judaism and Early Christianity* (ASNU, 22), Uppsala, Almqvist–Wiksell, 1961, pp. 239-242.

2. Not all recent authors, however, are concerned to discuss feminist issues. For example, J.H. NEYREY, *The Social World of Luke-Acts. Models for Interpretation*, Peabody, MA, Hendrickson, 1991, p. 379, asserts that both passages illustrate the perception that serving at table is a subordinate ministry, but that in the Lukan story meals are used as occasions to reverse roles and statuses. However he gives no indication that Martha's "lower" status is reversed.

3. E. SCHÜSSLER FIORENZA, *But She Said. Feminist Practices of Biblical Interpretation*, Boston, MA, Beacon, 1992.

tion of women[4]. At least one scholar has even gone so far as to suggest not only that the gospel author's choice to include so much "pro-woman" material indicates a sympathetic attitude towards women, but that proto-Luke most likely was compiled by a woman[5]. The questioning of this view has been stimulated by some contributions of feminist biblical research; one of the most compelling arguments against the naive assumption of such a perspective in terms of an overall approach to Luke-Acts is that of S. Davies in a chapter within a collection of writings on Jewish women in the Greco-Roman World which describes his initial acceptance of the common view and the reasons which convinced him to abandon it[6]. The articles in this volume reflect a more specific concern on the part of Jewish and Christian scholars that the portrayal of Jesus as a liberator of women within the New Testament should not depict Jewish women of the first century C.E. as being universally dominated by autocratic males, particularly when the New Testament texts themselves provide no support for such a view. In the case of Lk 10,38-42, Davies opposes any interpretation that views the pericope as depicting a liberation of women from domestic servers to diligent listeners. He notes all the presuppositions which such a claim involves:

> one must generalize from a single case to a class and from a single instance to a theme. One must dismiss from serious consideration the fact that it is another woman who objects to Mary's listening role; one must overlook the fact that listening to a man is far from an unusual or liberated role for a woman; and one must regard as irrelevant the fact that in each of the gospels Jesus speaks publicly to crowds of male *and female* listeners. Moreover, one needs to determine whether Luke's Jesus is approving 'listening' or, specifically 'women listening'.... Some have argued that for Jesus, a rabbi, to have taught women would be an exception to traditional and so expected practice. This argument... would hold only if it were also true that Luke portrays Jesus primarily as a rabbi or, in less technical terms, as a teacher and sage. This is not the case. The evangelist depicts Jesus as a wonder-worker (Acts 2,22; 10,38) and a spirit-inspired prophet (Lk 4,14-22). Unless it can be shown that such charismatic individuals normally

4. E.g., A. PLUMMER, *A Critical and Exegetical Commentary on the Gospel according to St. Luke* (ICC), Edinburgh, Clark, 1969 (=1896), p. 528, who refers to the Third Gospel as the "Gospel of Womanhood"; see also R.J. KARRIS, *Women and Discipleship in Luke*, in *CBQ* 56 (1994) 1-20, p. 2, n. 47, and R.M. PRICE, *The Widow Traditions in Luke-Acts. A Feminist-Critical Survey* (SBL DS, 155), Atlanta, GA, Scholars, 1997, pp. xvii-xviii, nn. 30-35.

5. L. SWIDLER, *Biblical Affirmations of Women*, Philadelphia, PA, Westminster, 1979, p. 281.

6. S. DAVIES, *Women in the Third Gospel and the New Testament Apocrypha*, in A.-J. LEVINE (ed.), *"Women Like This". New Perspectives on Jewish Women in the Greco-Roman World* (SBLEJL, 1), Atlanta, GA, Scholars, 1991, pp. 185-197.

refused to instruct women, then the portrait drawn in the corpus simply reflects reality as Luke knew it[7].

Current interpretations resulting from the feminist discussion of Lk 10,38-42 and Acts 6,1-7 basically can be divided into three categories: those which understand the passage, and the author of Luke-Acts, as in some regard favorable to the ministry of women (I); those which employ a hermeneutics of suspicion in regard to the author's view of that ministry (II); those that react to the second approach, either positively, but with qualifications, or more negatively (III). An issue that is explored by several authors in the latter two categories is whether it is possible to actualize the passages in a hopeful manner for women today even if it is determined that the author's view of the ministry of women was less emancipatory than some interpretations of these texts might suggest. Following a presentation which presents selective representatives of these three positions, some critical comments will be offered.

I. FEMINIST APOLOGETIC PERSPECTIVES

A number of studies on early Christian asceticism have demonstrated that consecrated celibacy afforded women an opportunity for the necessary leisure for scholastic study by freeing them from domestic drudgery and subservience to a husband[8]. J.A. McNamara regards Lk 10,38-42 as making precisely this point: "Mary had once chosen the better part in preferring spiritual instruction to domestic duties"[9]. Origen's application of the choice of Mary as reflecting that of contemplative life over active is positively endorsed most recently by R.M. Price, who criticizes Protestant exegetes' dismissal of Origen's view as involving anachronistic readings of the text which tend to devotionalize or psychologize it[10].

---

7. DAVIES, *Women in the Third Gospel*, p. 186. Similarly, SCHÜSSLER FIORENZA, *But She Said*, p. 59. Examples of instances in which Jewish tradition upheld the right of women to study Torah are found in B.E. REID, *Choosing the Better Part? Women in the Gospel of Luke*, Collegeville, MN, Liturgical Press, 1996, pp. 150-153. PRICE, *Widow Traditions*, pp. 179-180, comments in a similar vein, illustrating the way a saying of Rabbi Eliezer ("If any man gives his daughter a knowledge of the Torah, it is as though he taught her lechery") has for the most part been cited with no reference to its context, which offers an entirely different perspective. In fact Eliezer is arguing against a superstitious use of Torah in a test of a daughter's chastity.

8. PRICE, *Widow Traditions*, pp. 180-181. For an extended treatment of the later (500-1500) development of this same idea, see L. ECKENSTEIN, *Woman Under Monasticism*, Cambridge, University Press, 1896.

9. J.A. MCNAMARA, *A New Song. Celibate Women in the First Three Christian Centuries*, New York, Institute for Research in History – Haworth Press, 1983, p. 104.

10. PRICE, *Widow Traditions*, p. 178.

Earlier 20th-century commentators who interpreted the Lukan passage in this vein, including T.W. Manson and J.M. Creed, had remarked on the similarity between Lk 10,38-42 and 1 Cor 7,32-35[11]. D. Wenham seems to view the connection from a somewhat different perspective, proposing that behind 1 Cor 7,32-35 may be the fact that the Corinthian women cited the story of Martha and Mary in Lk 10,38-42[12]. He points out that the Greek verb μεριμνάω, present in the Lukan text, occurs 4 times within 1 Cor 7,32-34, in addition to one use of the cognate adjective, while μεριμνάω is employed only twice elsewhere in Paul's letters. Wenham remarks that Paul's εὐπάρεδρος ("sitting well beside") could recall the story of Mary sitting at the Lord's feet. Further, he notes, the use of ἀπερίσπαστος in 1 Cor 7, as well as that of περισπάομαι in Lk 10, is *hapax legomenon* in the New Testament[13]. Wenham finds it "tempting" to surmise that the Corinthian women had employed this story to argue that the Lord recommended renunciation of Martha-like domestic "worry" in favor of Mary-like undistracted devotion to the Lord. According to Wenham, while Paul agrees that the latter is desirable, he does not therefore also conclude that celibacy is the way to achieve such devotion in every instance. However, as B.E. Reid has pointed out, Paul's use of μεριμνάω conveys a totally opposite sense than the rebuke of Martha's anxiety, since "Paul speaks approvingly of an unmarried woman or virgin who is 'anxious about the things of the Lord'"[14].

11. T.W. MANSON, *The Sayings of Jesus*, London, SCM, 1954 (=1937), p. 263; J.M. CREED, *The Gospel according to St. Luke*, London, Macmillan 1930, p. 154; more recently, in the same vein, M.D. GOULDER, *Luke: A New Paradigm* (JSNT SS, 20), Sheffield, JSOT, 1989, pp. 493-494, even suggests that Luke utilized the written text of 1 Cor 7 in composing his pericope; see pp. 129-146 for a fuller discussion of Luke's familiarity with 1 Corinthians.

12. D. WENHAM, *Paul: Follower of Jesus or Founder of Christianity?*, Grand Rapids, MI, Eerdmans – Cambridge, University Press, 1995, pp. 248-250. PRICE, *Widow Traditions*, p. 182, asserts that the freedom of the virgins in 1 Cor 7,32-35 depends on a church stipend "anachronistic for the era of Paul the Apostle, but not for the later era of 1 Corinthians 7 (which opens a series of pseudonymous addenda to the letter organized with the repeated topical heading 'Now concerning,' just like the chapters of the *Didache*, which probably dates from the same period)". Such a view of the dating of 1 Cor 7 flies in the face of scholarly consensus.

13. T.K. SEIM, *The Double Message. Patterns of Gender in Luke and Acts*, Edinburgh, Clark, 1994, p. 105, n. 22, however, notes some striking differences between the two texts. For a summary of the discussion on the relation between the two passages, see J. BRUTSCHECK, *Die Maria-Marta-Erzählung. Eine redaktionskritische Untersuchung zu Lk 10,38-42* (BBB, 64), Frankfurt – Bonn, Hanstein, 1986, p. 251, n. 64, who accepts a link with some qualifications.

14. REID, *Choosing*, p. 147.

In accepting the view that, at least at one stage, the Martha/Mary story now found in Lk 10,38-42 functioned as "conversion propaganda", inviting women to be more like the contemplative Mary, Price is careful to distinguish his position from a type of feminist apologetic view which expresses a positive appreciation of Jesus' treatment toward women at the expense of Jesus' Israelite heritage[15]. An addition to the examples he provides of such readings is that of A.M. McGrath, who sees Jesus attempting to lift the heavy burden of Martha, and thus chiding not her but the system which burdened her, while praising Mary "for doing that which the religion of Israel did not encourage, and which St. Paul was expressly to forbid (I Cor 14,34-35): she directly approached Christ, the source of spiritual knowledge and power without the mediation of any man"[16].

A variation on this type of interpretation is provided by E.M. Tetlow, who refers to the "domestic" story of Martha and Mary in Lk 10, noting that the entire chapter is concerned with the theme of discipleship and it is not asserted that the two sisters are not disciples. While she still sees Martha's role as that of "serving the men", she contends that Luke was portraying such a role as subordinate to Mary's role of listening, and was going beyond contemporaneous rabbinic Judaism in allowing a woman to learn Torah. Nonetheless, Tetlow notes, Luke does not permit either woman a role of proclamation, and, she suggests: "It is possible that Martha represents the women ministers who were active in Luke's own church. Thus in his composition of this scene the evangelist was attempting to limit and subordinate the ministerial role of such women by appealing to the example of Jesus"[17]. G.P. Corrington holds a similar position, maintaining that the pericope is oppressive to women because the equality of discipleship achieved by Mary comes at the cost of renunciation of female sexuality, as indicated in the *Gospel of Thomas*[18]. Price disagrees with the opinion that the renunciation of female sexuality can be automatically assumed, citing J.E. Salisbury's study of celibate women who by their own accounts indicate that they embraced their sexuality and physicality[19].

15. PRICE, *Widow Traditions*, p. 179.
16. A.M. MCGRATH, *What a Modern Catholic Believes About Women*, Chicago, IL, Thomas More, 1972, pp. 20-21. McGrath displays no awareness of the disputed authenticity of 1 Cor 14,34-35.
17. E.M. TETLOW, *Women and Ministry in the New Testament*, New York, Paulist, 1980, p. 104.
18. G.P. CORRINGTON, *Her Image of Salvation: Female Saviors and Formative Christianity* (Gender and the Biblical Tradition), Louisville, KY, Westminster – John Knox, 1992, p. 89; see also pp. 32-33.
19. PRICE, *Widow Traditions*, p. 181, citing J.E. SALISBURY, *Church Fathers, Independent Virgins*, New York, Verso – London, Routledge, 1991, pp. 111-125.

II. A Feminist Critical Perspective

While Tetlow and Corrington in the previous category are critical of what they perceive as Luke's subordination of Martha's ministry, E. Schüssler Fiorenza goes further in her criticism. She does not view the role of Mary as a positive depiction, and she takes issue with any view that would play off Christianity against Judaism. Schüssler Fiorenza has reflected on Lk 10,38-42 and Acts 6,1-7 in a number of writings. In her 1984 work *In Memory of Her*, she notes that though no women are included within the seven Hellenists appointed to table διακονία in Acts, they are involved in the original conflict depicted in Acts which led to the division of ministry into that of apostles and that of the seven (not actually referred to as διάκονοι). Schüssler Fiorenza maintains that the author of Luke-Acts had a theological-historical motivation for playing down a serious conflict between the Jerusalem apostles and the Hellenists, an attempt that is not wholly successful, since, though Luke-Acts portrays the Hellenists as subordinate to the Jerusalem apostles, to whom the ministry of the word is theoretically reserved, the Hellenists, beginning with Stephen, emerge as powerful preachers and founders of communities. The subordination of one group to the other, Schüssler Fiorenza asserts, clearly reflects Luke's own situation, while the division of the one διακονία into a ministry at table and a ministry of word most likely is indicative of a practice of the Christian missionary movement. Schüssler Fiorenza sees the Martha-Mary pericope in Lk 10 as likewise expressing Luke's interest in subordinating one ministry to another. In this writing she does not go into detail regarding the precise nature of Martha's ministry.

In regard to the widows of Acts 6, Schüssler Fiorenza takes issue with earlier interpretations which understand the situation to be that the "Hebrews" had neglected the impoverished widows of the Hellenists in the daily distribution of food and material goods to the needy. She points out that Acts 6 says nothing to indicate these widows were poor, and the expression "serving at table" has the meaning of table service at a meal, not administration of funds. Citing 1 Cor 10,21, which refers to the table of the Lord, she suggests that table ministry was most likely eucharistic ministry and that it included, in addition to preparation and serving of the meal, purchase and distribution of food and most likely also cleaning up afterwards. According to Acts 2,46, such sharing occurred "day by day". However the context of 2,45, as well as 4,32-37, which refers to distribution of goods, does not employ the terminology "serving at table". Thus it is possible, following a proposal of

H.W. Beyer[20], that the conflict depicted in Acts 6 had to do with the role and even the participation of women at the eucharistic meal. According to Schüssler Fiorenza, Hellenists in both Jerusalem and Antioch most likely took such participation for granted, while "Hebrews" might have had difficulty with the practice[21].

In 1986, Schüssler Fiorenza dealt with the gospel passage in two versions of an article which were later to be included, in expanded and revised form, in *But She Said*. At this point Schüssler Fiorenza concentrates on the nature of the relationship between Jesus and each sister, asserting that while the relationship between Martha and Jesus (host and guest) was one of independent equals, Luke has rejected this equality in favor of a relationship of the kind Jesus has with Mary, who has elected the position of a subordinate student. The Mary-Jesus relationship is likewise descriptive of Luke's idea of what the role of women ought to be, rather than reflecting women's actual place at the time of Jesus. For Luke, according to Schüssler Fiorenza, Martha is actively occupied in preaching the word in the house church, while Mary listens passively. Luke criticizes the active role and attempts to urge the passive model on his readers, some of whom were probably engaged in roles similar to that of Martha[22].

Schüssler Fiorenza devotes a chapter of *But She Said* (1992) to a detailed discussion of Lk 10,38-42 as an illustration of the practice of interpretation she had proposed in an earlier work, *Bread Not Stone*. To this end she employs four interpretive strategies: a hermeneutics of suspicion, which questions not only biblical passages and their interpretations but also imaginative feminist readings; a hermeneutics of remembrance, which attempts to recover all possible remnants of material and textual information in order to construct a more plausible historical picture; a hermeneutics of proclamation, which refuses to affirm or appropriate texts which reinforce patriarchal relations of control and exploitation; and a hermeneutics of liberative vision and imagination, which

20. H.W. BEYER, διακονέω, in *TDNT*, 2, c. 85. Beyer maintains that there is even a question as to whether these women should have been regarded as part of the community.
21. E. SCHÜSSLER FIORENZA, *In Memory of Her: A Feminist Theological Reconstruction of Christian Origins*, New York, Crossroad – London, SCM, 1983-1984, pp. 164-166.
22. E. SCHÜSSLER FIORENZA, *A Feminist Critical Interpretation for Liberation: Martha and Mary: Lk. 10:38-42*, in *Religion and Intellectual Life* 3 (1986) 16-36 and *Theological Criteria and Historical Reconstruction: Martha and Mary (Lk 10:38-42)*, Protocol of the 53rd Colloquy: April 10, 1986, Berkeley, Center for Hermeneutical Studies in Hellenistic and Modern Culture, 1987, pp. 1-12, 41-63. The material in these two publications and in *In Memory of Her* is combined in *Biblische Grundlegung*, in M. KASSEL (ed.), *Feministische Theologie. Perspektiven zur Orientierung*, Stuttgart, Kreuz, 1988, pp. 13-44.

seeks to actualize and enhance the textual remnants of liberating visions[23].

1. *A Hermeneutics of Suspicion*

Schüssler Fiorenza begins by referring to the textual variants in Lk 10,38-42, which basically suggest two different readings, the longer, which assumes a meal setting, and the shorter, in which the one thing probably refers to the activities of the two protagonists. "The climactic word of Jesus then asserts that Mary has chosen the one thing, the good part". She notes that the text does not explicitly refer to a meal or serving at table, and that the reproach of Jesus to Martha does not employ the terms διακονία or διακονέω, but rather chides Martha for being anxious and troubled, similar to the reproach in Lk 12,22.26[24].

Before continuing with her own analysis of the text, Schüssler Fiorenza reviews and critiques a number of other approaches, which she categorizes in two major types: (1) an abstractionist reading, which reduces the sisters to theological principles and types: "justification by works and justification by faith, alms-giving and prayer, Judaism and Christianity, synagogue and church, people who are preoccupied with worldly cares and those who listen to G-d's word and seek spiritual things"; and (2) a "good woman/bad woman" polarization: active and contemplative, laywomen or "nunwomen", secular or religious, serving husbands or serving the Lord[25]. Within this duality she criticizes Protestant interpretations which want to validate Martha's role as a housekeeper; apologetic feminist interpretations which highlight the role of Christian women as disciples at the expense of Jewish women; and psychological and/or eroticizing readings which overlook the view of historical critical exegesis that scripture texts are not concerned with the psychological attitudes and emotions of their protagonists, which perpetuate the stereotype of women as rivals, and which also rely on a negative contrast with Jewish society[26].

Since most interpretations of Lk 10,38-42 emphasize a dualistic antagonism either between Martha and Mary or the principles or lifestyles which they symbolize, Schüssler Fiorenza raises the question of whether this dualistic opposition is present in the text. She decides that it is, for the following reasons: (1) It is absent from the other two

23. *But She Said*, pp. 54-76.
24. *Ibid.*, p. 57.
25. *Ibid.*, p. 58.
26. *Ibid.*, pp. 58-60.

passages in which these two women are present: John 11,1-44 and 12,1-11. (2) Form-critical analysis[27] identifies the passage as an apophthegm, which typically employs antagonistic characterization to make a point and to advocate behavioral norms, here two competing models of discipleship: διακονία-service vs. listening to the word. (3) Linguistic structural analysis[28] identifies a series of oppositions: student/householder, listening/speaking, rest/movement, receptiveness/argument, openness/purposefulness, passivity/agency, better choice/rejection. (4) Narrative analysis: Martha and the Lord are equals at the beginning, while Mary has a subordinate relationship to the Lord. Martha is absorbed with the preoccupations of serving, while Mary's attention is focused on the Lord. Martha's speech, which attempts to change the situation, has both a present (question with two accusations) and a future (imperative sentence with two demands) aspect. By appealing to Jesus, Martha relinquishes the egalitarian relationship of hostess and guest for a dependency relationship, and finds her appeal rejected by the Lord. Thus the Lord, characterized in masculine terms, is the center of the action. Mary is silent and Martha is silenced. Luke intends to make a point regarding his own social-ecclesial situation[29].

2. A Hermeneutics of Remembrance

Schüssler Fiorenza maintains that Lk 10,38-42 addresses a situation in the early church, as evidenced by the use of the title *Kyrios*, which appeals to the authority of the resurrected Lord. She agrees with exegetes who have pointed out that the historical situation is that of the early Christian missionary movement which assembled in house churches, but disagrees with a type of reading which thus contextualizes the narrative in terms of G. Theissen's claim that the Jesus movement was comprised of itinerant (male) missionaries and local households who supported them materially. In such a scenario, Martha is too anxious about hosting itinerant Christian preachers. Schüssler Fiorenza rejects such representations because they reinforce the androcentrism already present in the text[30].

In attempting to recover the memory behind the text, Schüssler Fiorenza makes the following assertions: (1) The text refers to serving,

---

27. Following R. BULTMANN, *History of the Synoptic Tradition*, New York, Harper, 1968, p. 33.
28. Here Schüssler Fiorenza follows BRUTSCHECK, *Die Maria-Marta-Erzählung* (n. 13), pp. 30-49.
29. *But She Said*, pp. 60-62.
30. *Ibid.*, pp. 63-64.

but says nothing of a kitchen or a meal. (2) In Luke's time, διακονία and διακονέω had become a technical term for ecclesial leadership. (3) Both house churches and itinerant missionaries were central to the early Christian missionary movement, and, according to the Pauline writings, both women and men were leaders in house churches as well as missionary endeavors. (4) Διακονία was used in early Christian times to refer to eucharistic table service in the house church, but it also included proclamation of the word, which is evident in Acts 6–8, where the Seven are ostensibly appointed to the διακονία of the tables but nevertheless are depicted as powerful preachers and founders of communities. (5) Unlike in Acts 6,1-7, where the διακονία of table service is subordinated to *preaching*, in the gospel narrative Martha's service is subordinated to *listening* to the word. This reflects the narrator's interest in downplaying the leadership of women. While reflecting that both males and females are members of Jesus' community of disciples, Luke-Acts, despite its numerous male/female parallels, does not pair even one story of a leading male disciple with that of a corresponding female disciple. There is not one account in Acts of a woman preaching, leading a congregation, or presiding over a house church. Thus, Schüssler Fiorenza maintains, "while the Pastorals silence our speech, Acts deforms our historical consciousness… Luke plays down the ministry of those women leaders of the early church whom he has to mention because they were known to his audience. Martha and Mary are a case in point"[31]. This is further substantiated by a review of the placement of the pericope within the context of the Lukan travel narrative, following J. Brutscheck[32], and by a comparison of the treatment of Martha and Mary in the fourth gospel, where the two sisters are not seen in competition with each other and both have important roles[33].

3. *A Hermeneutics of Evaluation and Proclamation*

Here Schüssler Fiorenza explores the implications of her findings for preaching, counseling, individual Bible study, and contemporary feminist readings. She has two major points. First, a hermeneutics of proclamation must critically evaluate the values promulgated by the text,

---

31. *Ibid.*, pp. 64-66; quotation from p. 66. On p. 233, n. 36, Schüssler Fiorenza refers to H.-J. VENETZ, *Die Suche nach dem "einem Notwendigen"*, in *Orientierung* 54 (1990) 185-189, as strongly disagreeing with the position she expresses here.
32. BRUTSCHECK, *Die Maria-Marta-Erzählung* (n. 13), pp. 50-64.
33. *But She Said*, pp. 67-68.

rather than reinforcing its dualistic, oppositional dynamics. This is not to say that Lk 10,38-42 should not be employed in preaching and teaching, but it must be done in such a way as to celebrate the female protagonists as historical and independent apostolic figures in their own right[34].

Second, Schüssler Fiorenza maintains, it is necessary to evaluate the sociopolitical contextualizations that determine how the text is heard today. Here she outlines four possibilities: (1) Instead of stressing Mary's behavior as proper feminine conduct for elite educated women, one might contextualize the narrative in the life of lower and working class women, where "Mary's audacity in taking time out from work to sit idle and relax in good company can have a liberating effect"[35]. (2) Interpretations which depict Martha in terms of sacrificing service run the danger of reinforcing the androcentric tendencies in the text and should be avoided. (3) Theological revalorizations of servanthood which emphasize that it is freely chosen do not take into account that people who are powerless, who are socialized into subservience, are not capable of "freely" choosing servanthood. Biblical concepts of δύναμις/ἐξουσία/σωτηρία need to be explored. (4) Theological speech about ministry as "power for" rather than "power over" runs the danger of obscuring the fact that the church continues to exercise ministry as "power over" so long as it is organized as a hierarchy of power dualisms[36].

4. A Hermeneutics of Imagination

In this stage, which seeks to employ imaginative embellishments and retellings of the text, Schüssler Fiorenza gives several examples of such practices from some of her students[37], one of which involves Jesus in a discussion in Martha and Mary's house of his encounter with the Syrophoenician woman, an incident which is not recorded in Luke's gospel; Schüssler Fiorenza is careful to point out that this is an exercise in a hermeneutics of creative *imagination*, and, in her overall procedure, such techniques are utilized only as the fourth step in a process which begins with exegesis of the text.

34. *Ibid.*, pp. 68-69.
35. *Ibid.*, pp. 69-70; quotation from p. 70.
36. *Ibid.*, pp. 70-72.
37. *Ibid.*, pp. 73-76.

III. REACTIONS TO A FEMINIST CRITICAL PERSPECTIVE

1. A. Reinhartz

A. Reinhartz[38] begins her analysis of Lk 10,38-42 by contrasting the treatment of this pericope by Schüssler Fiorenza with that of B. Witherington[39]. Reinhartz' discussion of Schüssler Fiorenza, published in 1991, is limited to the two 1986 publications referred to above, concluding that each bears the stamp of the agenda of its author[40]. While approving of Schüssler Fiorenza's avoidance of an anti-Jewish interpretation of the text, Reinhartz differs with her on several important points. In particular, she challenges the interpretation of διακονέω as indicating that Martha was engaged in preaching. While acknowledging that this can be one interpretation of διακονέω, she notes that other Lukan passages suggest the broader translation "to serve", and that such service is ascribed to male servants (17,8) and to Jesus (12,37; 22,26-27) as well as to women (4,39; 8,3; 10,40). Reinhartz also notes that Acts 6,2 specifically uses the verb to refer to service at table.

Reinhartz situates the Martha-Mary narrative in the context of the Lukan travel narrative and argues that Martha is to be seen as fulfilling the hospitality described in 10,8. Receiving the disciples by serving them and hearing their word is equivalent to receiving and hearing Jesus, and, to the extent that Martha and Mary do this, they epitomize true belief. "This reading suggests that we have come upon Martha and Mary in the very act of conversion, of turning to Jesus as savior"[41]. The rebuke to Martha possibly indicates that concern for one element of discipleship, taking care of physical needs, should not overshadow the importance of listening to the word. Mary offers to Jesus the opportunity to serve her. Thus the remarks of Jesus are neither intended to limit women's activity to passive listening, as Schüssler Fiorenza maintains, nor do they portray women's new freedom to be disciples, as Witherington would have it; rather they accentuate that "while service to oth-

---

38. A. REINHARTZ, *From Narrative to History: The Resurrection of Mary and Martha*, in A.-J. LEVINE (ed.), *"Women Like This"* (n. 6), pp. 161-185.

39. According to Witherington, Jesus does not attempt to underrate Martha's efforts at hospitality, nor to attack a woman's traditional role, but to defend the right of Mary to learn from him: "this is the crucial thing for those who wish to serve Him". B. WITHERINGTON, *Women in the Ministry of Jesus. A Study of Jesus' Attitudes to Women and Their Roles as Reflected in His Earthly Life*, Cambridge, University Press, 1984, p. 101. Witherington uses the contrast to emphasize the superiority of the Christian over the Jewish milieu for women.

40. *From Narrative to History*, p. 168.

41. *Ibid.*, p. 169.

ers is important, hearing the word for oneself is the essential ingredient of discipleship"[42]. Jesus' words to Martha express the author's attitude toward discipleship in general, not particular views on women.

Further, Reinhartz contends, the fact that Martha and Mary are portrayed only in their relationship to Jesus is not evidence of androcentrism, as Schüssler Fiorenza holds; rather, their characterization should be seen more as christocentric than androcentric, and indeed this is the inescapable focus of the gospel narrative. Additionally, Reinhartz argues that Jesus' seemingly unfair remark to Martha is part of a Lukan literary technique which frustrates the expectations of his implied readership in order to modify them: Mary's act, though seemingly inconsiderate, demonstrates the element of discipleship that Luke considers central: "true service consists not of caring for physical needs but of ingesting, and digesting, the message of the gospel"[43]. While Reinhartz concedes that this does not necessarily acquit Luke of the charge of androcentrism or ignore the later ecclesiastical use of this passage to hinder women from positions of leadership, she nonetheless insists that Luke's use of female figures to express his views on discipleship "at least implicitly attests to a role for women in his view of the church. Further, it suggests the willingness of the male members of his implied audience to derive a lesson from a story in which women are important characters"[44].

Reinhartz then goes on to analyze the two Johannine passages which deal with Martha and Mary. Here she is in general agreement with Schüssler Fiorenza that Martha is presented as making a strong faith confession in chapter 11, and that in both Johannine accounts there is no indication of competitiveness between the sisters. Reinhartz emphasizes somewhat more than Schüssler Fiorenza the elements in the Fourth Gospel narrative which are indicative of the two sisters being both firmly centered in a Jewish community and part of an intimate circle of Jesus' disciples[45]. She concludes by identifying what she perceives as her own two points of bias in treating the Martha-Mary texts: her attraction to the element of imagination in tracking the history of women in a period when their presence has been ignored, and her Jewish background, which makes her more sensitive to readings which pit Christianity against Judaism than to those which use the text for androcentric Christian agendas[46].

42. *Ibid.*, pp. 169-170; quotation from p. 170.
43. *Ibid.*, pp. 170-171.
44. *Ibid.*, pp. 171-172; quotation from p. 172.
45. *Ibid.*, pp. 172-181.
46. *Ibid.*, pp. 182-183.

In *But She Said*, Schüssler Fiorenza notes briefly that she was not able to incorporate much of Reinhartz' reading specifically because of the closeness in publication of the two works, but Schüssler Fiorenza does insist that Reinhartz "overlooks that the rhetoric of kyriocentric texts functions differently with respect to women and men"[47].

2. T.K. Seim

T.K. Seim, in her intensive examination of gender patterns in Luke-Acts, *The Double Message* (1994), disagrees with Schüssler Fiorenza on some issues in the interpretation of Lk 10,38-42, though in relation to the gospel as a whole she does express opinions that are to some degree similar. Seim's reactions to Schüssler Fiorenza are based on the latter's works up to 1988[48].

Though conceding that in the Third Gospel in general the women's service includes more than serving food, Seim contends that the original connotation of the Greek word "to serve food", "to wait at table", is constantly brought into play, including in Lk 10,40. She objects to Schüssler Fiorenza's suggestion that the widows in Acts 6 are being neglected in the area of Eucharistic table ministry as betraying vested theological and political interests[49], tending to associate women's service exclusively with meals, and not making clear what is the role of texts which describe men preparing or distributing food, outside of a redactional interest in suppressing the mention of women[50].

Seim views Lk 10,38-42 as a narrative of hospitality set in the context of the Lukan travel narrative. Martha, who receives Jesus into her home, is an example of a patroness in comfortable circumstances. Nonetheless, Seim asserts in opposition to Schüssler Fiorenza, it cannot be definitively established that such a status involved institutional leadership, and no texts clearly couple functions such as preaching and responsibility for

47. *But She Said*, p. 232, n. 24.
48. Seim seems to be unacquainted with the articles of Reinhartz and Davies.
49. Seim does qualify this by remarking, "It is, of course, no objection in itself to an exegetical result that it may serve as an argument in a theological debate, especially as traditional theological positions and church order are based on androcentric presuppositions" (*The Double Message*, p. 73, n. 150).
50. *Ibid.*, p. 72. It is not clear how Schüssler Fiorenza's remarks on Acts 6 tend to associate women's service exclusively with meals. It appears to me that she rather argues for an attempt by Luke to subordinate the ministry of table to the ministry of the word; her point is precisely that the Seven who are ostensibly called to ministry at table in fact do become powerful preachers of the word (*In Memory of Her*, p. 165). It is Seim who explicitly argues against any connection between a woman being a "patroness" (Schüssler Fiorenza would say "head of a house church") and engaging in preaching.

the Eucharist with the διακον-terminology[51]. The consistent use of κύριος to refer to Jesus characterizes him as authoritative Lord, but does not require a Sitz-im-Leben of a later community which appeals to such authority with no concern for available tradition. Readings such as those of Schüssler Fiorenza which presuppose that the primary aim of the author was to contest Martha's diaconal leadership contain insights into the portrait of Mary, but rest on assumptions of a universally diffused technical usage of the διακον-terms which, according to Seim, are problematic. She maintains that Martha has much in common with typical female figures in Luke-Acts; she is well off, independent, mistress of her own house, and as such is comparable to Tabitha (Acts 9,36ff.), Mary (Acts 12,12), Lydia (Acts 16,15.40), Peter's mother-in-law (Lk 4,38-39), and the women who follow Jesus and provide for him (Lk 8,1-3)[52].

Martha's diaconal activity of practical care for others is set in contrast with that of her sister, who is portrayed in the typical attitude of a student – at the Lord's feet[53]. Seim maintains that this role goes well beyond the usual opportunities for women to hear the word which were available in a worship context. In addition, the text refers to terms which are connected to teaching institutions within the rabbinic traditions[54]. In particular, the term "lot" is used in bBer IV 2b in relation to a pupil at a place of teaching, and it employs a contrast between the lot of the student of the Law with that of the idler. In the gospel narrative, however, the contrast is with studies and a task which in other places in the gospel is stressed as necessary and good. Also, in the gospel narrative, unlike the rabbinic material, it is striking that the student is a woman. Women within Judaism did not have the right or the duty to be taught, Seim asserts, and in the strictest cases were prohibited from doing so, as bKid 29b indicates. Though less data is available on actual practice, "the sources indicate that praxis and theory largely coincided"[55]. The few

51. *The Double Message*, pp. 98-100.
52. *Ibid.*, pp. 100-101. L. SCHOTTROFF, *Lydia's Impatient Sisters. A Feminist Social History of Early Christianity*, Louisville, KY, Westminster – John Knox, 1995, p. 88, suggests that the assumption by most commentators that Lydia is a well-to-do woman is made without exploring "the reality of her work, even though there is plenty of information regarding her vocation". Similarly, p. 244, n. 137: "The text speaks of Tabitha's work, not of her wealth". In general, the section, "The Work of Women in the New Testament" (pp. 79-90) argues that interpreters who often perceive women mentioned in the New Testament as more or less well-to-do are not basing their suppositions on the text, which more often than not makes reference to the work of the women rather than their wealth.
53. In support of this Seim cites Acts 22,3 and *Pirqe' Abot* 1.4.
54. Here Seim cites B. GERHARDSSON, *Memory and Manuscript* (n. 1), pp. 239ff.
55. *The Double Message*, p. 102. No sources are cited in support of this statement.

exceptions usually cited, Beruriah and the servant girl of rabbi Judah, do not contradict this. Women needed knowledge of the Law insofar as it was connected to rules and prohibitions that affected them, but the woman's main task was to give support on the domestic side so that her husband could devote himself to his studies to the greatest possible degree[56]. Seim questions whether the type of argument she brings forth here should *eo ipso* be rejected as "apologetically determined and comparatively anti-Jewish"[57], though she concedes that intensive investigation of Jewish sources from a feminist perspective might alter and significantly nuance the issue.

Seim is in agreement with Schüssler Fiorenza that Martha plays the active role in the narrative, and that her appeal to Jesus alters the relationship between host and guest. She differs somewhat on the significance of the textual variants in 10,41-42, asserting that no matter which variant is chosen, there is at least something to be said in Martha's favor, provided one does not identify "one thing necessary" with "the good part" chosen by Mary. Jesus' rebuke to Martha does not refer to her "serving", but to the fuss and agitation with which it is done, a point also made by Schüssler Fiorenza. Martha's need for help leads her to disregard Mary's choice and to seek Jesus' support in this intrusion, and thus represents a threat that Mary's part can be taken away from her[58].

Though recognizing the conflict present in Lk 10,38-42, Seim asserts that while Jesus confirms the antithesis between the two sisters, he does not initiate it. He defends Mary's role, Seim implies, because Martha's role does not need defending. The διακονία role was taken for granted for women, and only when it is put forward as an ideal for free men and for the leadership does it become necessary to give special and christologically founded reasons[59]. However, despite the strength of Jesus' rebuke to Martha, the fact that the positive adjective ἀγαθή can be used in a comparative sense allows for the understanding that Martha's part can also be good, even if Mary's is better. The positive portrayal of service elsewhere in the gospel makes it difficult to accept that such service should here be viewed as a mistaken choice[60].

---

56. *Ibid.*, pp. 101-103. In support of the last assertion, Seim cites A. GOLDFELD, *Women as Sources of Torah in the Rabbinic Tradition*, in E. KOLTUN (ed.), *The Jewish Woman*, New York, 1976, pp. 257-271, esp. 258.

57. *Ibid.*, p. 102, n. 15. Reference here is made to a critique of such arguments in SCHÜSSLER FIORENZA, *Biblische Grundlegung* (n. 22), p. 33.

58. *The Double Message*, pp. 103-105.

59. Earlier (p. 81), Seim had pointed out that until Lk 12, διακονέω and διακονία are used only of women (4,39; 8,3; 10,40).

60. *Ibid.*, pp. 105-106.

Seim views the relation between the gospel narrative and Acts 6,1-6 in terms of principle and application. Lk 10,38-42 exemplifies a normative regulation, supported by dominical authority, which is applied further in Acts 6. In Acts, it is taken for granted that God would not be pleased if the Twelve abandon the service of the word to serve at table. The conflict of preferences thus takes on an opposite form when it has to do with prominent men. The two passages taken together demonstrate, surprisingly, that the option which the leading men can claim unhesitatingly is valid for women as well, though with the reservation that the relationship between hearing the word of the Lord and the service of the word must be examined more closely. Seim contends that Luke's interest in Acts 6,1-6 is not to make a gender differentiation which involves men taking on responsibility for the word while women busy themselves with charitable activity, but to set a priority so that one service is subordinated to the other[61]. The occasion of the conflict in Acts 6,1, the neglect of the Hellenistic widows in the daily service, is viewed by Seim as of limited significance to the discussion of the gospel pericope. However "the historical fact that the twelve and the seven were men (as is seen from the lists of names) means that the eligibility of women is disallowed, and leadership is defined as the business of men". Nonetheless, passages such as Lk 10,38-42 indicate that relationship to the word is decisive for the discipleship of women and this provides new opportunities for them[62].

In the following sections, Seim goes on to explore how women hear the word in Luke-Acts[63], the context in which they may speak[64], and how they attempt to act on the word even without formal authorization[65]. At the end of the first section, Seim's conclusion is that women are portrayed primarily as recipients of the word, are not entrusted with commissions to preach, and are not depicted as public preachers or witnesses. Near the end of the second section she compares the treatment of women in Luke-Acts with that in the Fourth Gospel, where she notes that women carry out some of the same functions as in Luke-Acts, but that they cross the threshold of the house, being summoned forth, acting in full public view and vis-à-vis men as well as women[66]. The final section acknowledges that though the status of the women as disciples is

---

61. In this respect Seim is in agreement with SCHÜSSLER FIORENZA, In Memory of Her, pp. 165, 315, whom she cites in support.

62. The Double Message, pp. 107-112; quotation from p. 112.

63. Ibid., pp. 112-118.

64. Ibid., pp. 118-147.

65. Ibid., pp. 147-163.

66. Ibid., p. 146.

reaffirmed in the cross and tomb narratives in Luke, they receive no explicit commission to preach, and their attempt to break through the boundaries in proclaiming the resurrection is stillborn. "The effect is that women are withdrawn from the public proclamation and activity as teachers, and the way is laid open for the men's assumption of power in Acts when public testimony to Jesus' resurrection is borne from Jerusalem to Rome"[67].

At the beginning of her final chapter, Seim maintains that she has demonstrated that "it is a preposterous simplification to ask whether Luke's writings are friendly or hostile to women" because the tension in Luke's narrative has become apparent in its ambivalent evidence both of strong traditions about women and of the social and ideological controls that silenced them and promoted male dominance in positions of leadership[68]. This probably illustrates the most fundamental difference between Seim and Schüssler Fiorenza, who certainly acknowledges the tension in Luke-Acts' portrayal of women. Seim seems unwilling to charge the author of Luke-Acts with deliberately setting out to subvert awareness of the leadership role of women in the early church. Though she does not quite come right out and say so, she apparently views Luke as a neutral recorder of both the strong traditions about women and the process of silencing them. Schüssler Fiorenza, on the other hand, has no hesitation in accusing Luke of deliberate attempts to subvert the memory of authoritative women. What Seim views as evidence of "friendly" treatment towards women, such as consistent assertion that women are disciples too, Schüssler Fiorenza regards as so fundamental that Luke could not have questioned it if he wanted to. Schüssler Fiorenza maintains that the function of the women in the cross and tomb accounts and even the names of Martha and Mary are based on historical memory that was so well known at the time Luke-Acts was written that it would have been impossible to totally ignore them.

3. B.E. Reid

B.E. Reid's examination of women in the Third Gospel utilizes elements of historical, literary, and narrative criticism, as well as social study of the New Testament, from a feminist liberation perspective which takes into account the four stages of hermeneutics delineated by Schüssler Fiorenza[69]. In an examination of the meaning of the verb

---

67. *Ibid.*, p. 163.
68. *Ibid.*, p. 249.
69. *Choosing* (n. 7), pp. 2-12.

διακονέω, she deals with Schüssler Fiorenza's argument that the conflict in regard to the Hellenist widows in Acts 6,1-7 had reference to Eucharistic table service, but notes that in general it means to carry out a charge, either from God or some authority within the community. It can refer to waiting on tables, but can also express the epitome of Jesus' mission, as in Lk 22,25-27, where Jesus does not actually serve a meal, but charges his disciples to adopt the attitude of "one who serves"[70].

Reid begins her study of Lk 10,38-42 by raising a number of questions which indicate problems with some earlier approaches. If the Christian ideal is to integrate contemplation and action, why are the two cast dualistically, with one approved and the other impugned? Why is Martha reprimanded for following the directive given by Jesus in Lk 22,27? Why is only hearing the word esteemed here, when the gospel as a whole insists on the importance of both hearing and doing the word? If Mary is such a good listener, why isn't she aware of Martha's problem? Why doesn't Jesus, so compassionate toward the underdog, sympathize with Martha? Further problems are created by the fact that most women identify with Martha, and, feeling they shouldn't be angry with Jesus, direct their resentment toward those sisters who choose the luxury of contemplative sitting.

Interpretations which endeavor either to rescue the text or to defend Jesus from the charge of being unfairly critical of hard-working women assert that Jesus is critical either of Martha's anxiety or of her distraction with "many things", often interpreted as many dishes for a meal. Such readings, Reid maintains, do not take seriously the tensions in the text, which emphasizes only the dimension of hearing, with no hint of how Mary will *act* on the word she hears. Further, the anxiety of Martha is not equivalent to that denounced in other Lukan texts, and it should be noted that Paul in 1 Cor 7,34 speaks with approval about women who are anxious about the things of the Lord. Additionally, διακονέω is not exclusively associated with table service, and the text gives no indication that a meal is involved.

Attempts to pair Luke 10,38-42 with the narrative of the Good Samaritan immediately preceding suggest that, taken together, the two episodes illustrate the hearing and doing of the word. However, Reid points out, there is no evidence that these two episodes were so closely linked in the tradition. In the Johannine accounts of Martha and Mary, Martha goes out to meet Jesus while Mary "sat at home", and Martha

---

70. *Ibid.*, pp. 100-101, with reference to J.J. COLLINS, *Diakonia. Re-interpreting the Ancient Sources*, New York – Oxford, University Press, 1990, pp. 77-95.

complains of Jesus' delay in arriving (with a very different response!), but there is no link with any Good Samaritan incident[71]. The tensions within the text of Lk 10,38-42, Reid suggests, explain the number of textual variants which, in one way or another, attempt to mute the sharp criticism of Martha[72].

Approaches which interpret Jesus' approval of Mary as upholding theological education for women likewise are problematic. If this is what is done for Mary, it occurs at the expense of Martha's service. Observations on how revolutionary Jesus was in instructing a woman reflect stereotyped ideas that social practices were uniform and uniformly observed, and do not take into account that customs were in flux in the first-century Hellenistic world. Likewise, assertions that boundaries between men and women were never crossed flies in the face of biblical evidence from both the Old (Gen 24,10-49; 29,4-14; Exod 2,15-22) and the New Testament (Lk 7,13.48.50; 8,48; 13,12; 23,28-31). Additionally, this type of reading: (1) ignores the fact that formal education of women was becoming more acceptable in the Hellenistic period; (2) quotes Jewish sources in support very selectively, often without regard to their post-New Testament dating; and (3) minimizes the fact that where Jesus is depicted as educating disciples elsewhere in Luke, this is done, as in rabbinic tradition, through dialogue. Mary is a silent audience, not a dialogue partner[73].

The real point of disagreement, Reid maintains, both in the early Church and the contemporary discussion, is not whether women can study theology, but what ministries they may be involved in as a result of such education. The New Testament gives evidence both that women exercised a diversity of ministries, which included leadership, public proclamation, and apostolic work, and also that there was no uniform view regarding the propriety of women exercising such ministries. Reid groups the third evangelist with the author of the Pastorals as being among the group intent on silencing women by placing on the lips of Jesus a strong approval of the silent Mary. Reid argues that, in addition, the textual variants in Lk 10,38 which attest to the reading that Martha welcomed Jesus *into her home* are most likely original, because without them the statement is abrupt and incomplete, and that omissions of them reflect a further stage of develop-

---

71. REID, *Choosing*, pp. 144-148. SEIM, *The Double Message*, p. 14, likewise does not find sufficient evidence to consider these two stories a pair.

72. REID, *Choosing*, p. 149.

73. *Ibid.*, pp. 149-154, with pp. 152-153 focusing on the question of Jewish sources. See also n. 7 above.

ment which attempts to obscure Martha's role as head of a house church[74].

Further, Reid asserts, Lk 10,38-39 does not display tension between the two sisters. The Greek verb ὑπεδέξατο, which expresses Martha's welcome of Jesus, is employed in Luke-Acts not only to denote hospitality in the sense of making a person welcome, but to describe receiving, hearing or understanding the word (Lk 8,13; 18,17; Acts 8,14; 11,1; 17,11). Thus Martha's "welcoming" of Jesus is equivalent to Mary's "listening to him" in that both refer to the act of faith of receiving Jesus and his word[75]. The tension arises over how their respective reception of the word is expressed in ministry. Martha's complaint is not that she has too much work, but that she is being denied her role in ministerial service. In περιεσπᾶτο περὶ πολλὴν διακονίαν, the preposition περί has the sense "about" or "concerning". Her distress is about her works, but not because of them. The verb περισπάω is usually translated "distracted" in this text, but its fundamental meaning is "to be pulled or dragged away"[76], and in this context more likely refers to Martha's being pulled away from diaconal ministry by some who disapprove[77].

The fact that Martha's complaint to Jesus refers to Mary as "my sister", a term which could refer to any Christian woman, may indicate, Reid suggests, that Martha's distress has arisen partially from the fact that her female former companions in ministry have been persuaded to accept a silent listening role. Luke's formulation of Jesus' reply to her in v. 41 omits any reference to διακονία, thus obliterating her diaconal ministry. However the verb θορυβάζω indicates that the "worry" involves a more public matter. While this usage is *hapax* in the New Testament, its cognates θορυβέω and θόρυβος, utilized a total of 11 times in Mk, Mt, and Acts, always occur in the context of a disturbance made by a crowd[78].

Following this analysis of the gospel pericope, Reid goes on to a comparison of the Johannine Martha-Mary texts with results similar to those discussed in the authors above[79]. She then addresses the issue of the contemporary significance of the text, stressing that it is important to recognize that the Lukan approbation of silent, passive women is only one

74. *Ibid.*, pp. 154-155.
75. On this point Reinhartz has expressed a similar opinion in *From Narrative to History*, p. 169.
76. With reference to BAGD, p. 650.
77. REID, *Choosing*, pp. 155-157.
78. *Ibid.*, pp. 157-158.
79. *Ibid.*, pp. 159-160.

side of an early Christian debate, one which was, in fact, rejected by later Christians, particularly in the medieval period[80]. Reid concludes that if today we were to follow the example of creative revisioning of the medieval period in rewriting the second half of the story, such a portrait would perhaps challenge rivalries and hostilities sometimes evident between women who choose different roles, and might cause us to realize that the better part, or the one thing needed, might be different for each person and each community and each age[81].

4. *R.M. Price*

R.M. Price, in *The Widow Traditions in Luke-Acts* (1997)[82], contends that the tensions within the text of Lk 10,38-42 are to be explained by the fact that the present narrative evolved in five distinct stages, each of which offers support for one of the various suggested and often conflicting situations. In the earliest stage of the story, as previously noted by E. Laland[83], the point was appropriate treatment of itinerant missionaries, giving hospitality while avoiding the dangers of overindulging the guest and overburdening the host or hostess. In this early stage, Mary did not appear; the contrast was between potential fellowship with "the Lord" and the failure to realize this potential because of too much fussing. In the first stage, the only historical kernel was the situation of a house-church meal where a considerate missionary spoke to a harried hostess, but their names were not Jesus and Martha[84].

In Stage Two, Price suggests, the addition of the "Mary" subplot reflects a concern to recruit consecrated celibate women by offering them freedom from domestic captivity. A similar concern is exhibited in 1 Cor 7, and, as there, no contrast with any specifically Jewish customs is implied[85]. Stage Three accounts for the addition of "which shall not be taken away from her", a response to the danger that the choice of consecrated celibacy was being discouraged, as evidenced in 1 Tim 5,3-16. From this point, the freedom displayed in Stage Two would only be

---

80. *Ibid.*, pp. 160-161. The medieval examples are taken from E. MOLTMANN-WENDEL, *The Women Around Jesus*, New York, Crossroad, 1987, pp. 14-48.

81. REID, *Choosing*, pp. 161-162.

82. *Widow Traditions* (n. 4), pp. 175-190.

83. LALAND, *Die Martha-Maria Perikope* (n. 1), p. 82.

84. *Widow Traditions*, pp. 177-178. Price considers the suggestion of M.R. D'ANGELO, *Women Partners in the New Testament*, in *Journal of Feminist Studies in Religion* 6 (1990) 65-86, pp. 77-81, that the story reflects a historical Martha and Mary, an early missionary team well known in the early church. He feels that this may have been the reason why a "Mary" was added to this narrative, but that if so this was done at a later stage.

85. *Widow Traditions*, pp. 178-182.

feasible in emerging "heretical" movements such as Montanism or in widows' homes where several women were supported by a wealthy patron, who might also be a widow[86].

It is only in Stage Four that the role of Martha comes into question. At this point the passage has been co-opted by those from whom the previous version endeavored to defend Mary. Price unhesitatingly indicts Luke as the culprit who subtly alters the story mainly by its redactional placement. Like Schüssler Fiorenza, he views the Lukan text as an attempt to abolish the diaconate or gospel ministry of women and reduce them to silent passivity, and takes issue with J.B. Chance[87] and L.T. Johnson[88], who argue against Schüssler Fiorenza's reading of Acts 6,1-7, maintaining that there is no tension between the appointed role of the Seven and their later preaching, because "serving at table" is equivalent to being the greatest in the community and holding apostolic authority, and thus the appointment of the Seven to serve tables symbolizes their receiving the same authority. The problem with such an interpretation, Price points out, is that, since the Twelve expressly aver they will have nothing to do with table service, they would thus seem to be resigning authority rather than sharing it[89]. By dividing ministry into that of the word and that of the table, whether the latter refers to Eucharistic service or food distribution, Lk 10,38-42 appears to prohibit women from exercising either ministry. Martha, who is busy with serving the Lord Jesus, is told not to bother, and Mary is not depicted as doing any ministry other than sitting and keeping still[90].

Regarding the final stage, that of the various textual emendations, Price proposes that such alterations have no relation either to food or to the contrast between the roles of the two sisters. Rather, once the text

86. *Ibid.*, pp. 182-183.

87. J.B. CHANCE, *Jerusalem, the Temple and the New Age in Luke-Acts*, Macon, GA, Mercer, 1988, p. 107.

88. L.T. JOHNSON, *The Literary Function of Possessions in Luke-Acts* (SBL DS, 39), Missoula, MT, Scholars, 1977, pp. 212-213.

89. *Widow Traditions*, pp. 183-185. Elsewhere (pp. 210-216), he suggests that Acts 6,1-6 should be read against Num 11,11-30, where the initial complaint appears to be about food service, but in fact the purpose of the tale is to legitimize the institution of the system of 70 judges. Likewise in Acts, the complaining is simply an occasion for authenticating an ecclesial office: boards of seven men either to supervise food distribution to widows, or, more likely, to arbitrate disputes between widows or listen to their complaints of unfair treatment, thus taking the burden off the Twelve, as the judges did for Moses. Further support of this suggestion can be found in Exod 18,10-27, which Price does not cite. Price points out that in the passage from Acts, Luke has typically added the redactional detail of complaining or murmuring widows to a story which at first lacked it, thus transforming the narrative into a sarcastic put-down of the widows (p. 216).

90. *Widow Traditions*, pp. 185-186.

became regarded as a charter for the widows along the lines of the Synoptic Mission Charge, the variants in Lk 10,38-42 most likely reflect disputes as to what types and what kind of property the widows could own, if any, and what sort of gifts they could receive. The Synoptic parallels display similar inconsistencies among themselves and in their respective textual variants as to whether the missionary may take a staff, no staff, any money, or extra sandals. Thus "we must suspect that the survival of the various significant details in our pericope denotes the addition of 'tradition barnacles'. Had they no purpose, they wouldn't be there"[91].

IV. CRITICAL CONSIDERATIONS

A first remark has to do with the concern of authors like Davies, Schüssler Fiorenza, Reinhartz, Reid, and Price that interpretations which attempt to argue for the superiority of Christian over Jewish treatment of women must be, at the least, viewed with great suspicion. In the case of the passages under consideration, such assumptions are borne out neither by the text nor by supporting argumentation. It is rather surprising that such an approach is still being employed by Seim. Despite her disclaimer, the anti-Jewish bias in her interpretation is problematic. She displays little awareness of the charge of selective citation of Jewish sources, and her statement "the sources indicate that praxis and theory largely coincided"[92] is unsupported.

On the other hand, Reinhartz displays a corresponding lack of awareness, and admits to a lack of interest, of the way interpretations of this passage have disturbed Christian women because of the degree to which they identify with Martha in this passage. It appears to me that Reinhartz overlooks the very real differences between the relations of the two sisters in the Lukan and Johannine narratives. The point is not simply that the Lukan gospel is christocentric, but that Martha is depicted as relating to Jesus not only as a subordinate to the Lord, but in a childish and complaining fashion similar to that of the older brother to his father in Lk 15,11-32. The difference is that the story of the prodigal son does not name either of the two brothers; neither does it contain any likelihood that the reference is to historical persons. In contrast to Luke's use of the two women, Paul employs a reference to two Jewish women, Hagar and Sarah, in Gal 4,21-31, but he limits the point of comparison to the con-

---

91. *Ibid.*, pp. 187-190; quotation from p. 190.
92. *The Double Message*, p. 102.

dition of freedom or servitude which each woman represents, even though in this case the narratives in Gen 16 and 21 to which he alludes do suggest rivalry between the two women.

Additionally, Reinhartz offers little support for her assertions that "while service to others is important, hearing the word for oneself is the essential ingredient of discipleship"[93] and "true service consists not of caring for physical needs but of ingesting, and digesting, the message of the gospel"[94]. One might suggest that acting on the word is also an indispensable ingredient of discipleship, as evidenced in Lk 9,23, where discipleship is portrayed as willingness to take up a daily life of self-denial, or in 9,48, where welcoming a child in Jesus' name is equivalent to welcoming him. Seim, on the other hand, makes a good case for the importance of hearing the word and attempting to act on it[95]; nonetheless, women portrayed in the Third Gospel, as well as in Acts, are restricted in the ways in which they can act out the word[96]. Reinhartz does not deal with the issue pointed out by Schüssler Fiorenza and others that nowhere does the author of Luke-Acts, despite numerous male/female parallels, pair even one story of a leading male disciple with that of a corresponding female disciple and that there is not one account in Acts of a woman preaching, leading a congregation, or presiding over a house church. That the author of Luke-Acts portrays both men and women as disciples is not the issue; what Reinhartz seems to miss is the critique that he consistently presents males in leadership roles in the early Christian community and does not do so for women despite evidence in other New Testament texts that women exercised such roles.

Reinhartz likewise displays no awareness of Schüssler Fiorenza's argument in *In Memory of Her* that in Acts 6 the Seven appointed to table service actually become powerful preachers of the διακονία of the word and that the daily distribution in which the widows were neglected could refer to Eucharistic table service. What perhaps requires further discussion are the assertions about διακονία made by all of these authors in conjunction with the detailed study of διακονία by Collins[97]. Collins contends that the principal meaning of διακονία is that of someone authorized with the task of delivering a message as the representa-

---

93. *From Narrative to History*, p. 170.

94. *Ibid.*, pp. 170-71.

95. *The Double Message*, pp. 112-118.

96. See the detailed treatment of Lukan discipleship in REID, *Choosing*, pp. 21-54.

97. COLLINS, *Diakonia* (see n. 70 above). A more popular version of the argument appears in *Are All Christians Ministers?*, Collegeville, MN, Liturgical Press, 1992; both books have been reviewed by J. D'ARCY MAY, *Ministry Reconsidered*, in *Doctrine and Life* 44 (1994) 150-152.

tive of someone in authority. Likewise pertinent to the discussion are the social historical questions relative to the interpretation of διακονία raised by L. Schottroff[98].

Whether Martha's διακονία involves preaching or practical hospitality, there appears little room for doubt that Luke 10,38-42 in the literary context of Luke-Acts validates a passive role for women rather than an active role, even if the passive role is an apparently sublime one. Seim argues that the passage clearly indicates that Mary's choice is in danger, but is unable to find any other support outside the narrative that this is so[99]. She has finally to admit that in Luke-Acts neither Mary of Bethany nor any other woman is empowered to do anything more than listen, and both Seim and Reinhartz concede that the treatment of Martha and Mary in John's gospel is much more favorable by comparison. Likewise, evidence from the letters of Paul indicates that historically women did have leadership roles in the early church, and there appears to be no evidence in the New Testament that the right of women to be Christian disciples was challenged. It may very well be the case that the reason for this was that, despite the alleged restrictions on Jewish women, it was never questioned that they were part of the people of Israel, the people of God.

Some of Price's suggestions are quite novel, and reconstructing stages of a biblical text is always a risky undertaking, yet his reconstruction does have the virtue of explaining the admittedly contradictory elements in the text which are not dealt with in a completely satisfactory manner in any of the preceding treatments. An effective challenge to his theory of stages would involve an attempt to explain all the contradictory or apparently contradictory elements in the text. As far as procedure is concerned, the major difference between Price and such scholars as Schüssler Fiorenza and Reid is in where they locate precise elements of redactional changes to an original oral or written tradition. Where all three agree is in squarely placing the blame on the author of Luke-Acts for attempting to subvert leadership roles for women that were taken for granted at an earlier period. In this regard the major difference between these three authors in contrast to Reinhartz and Seim is that the latter two view the author of Luke-Acts as

98. *Lydia's Impatient Sisters* (n. 52), pp. 204-233.
99. Price, in discussion of his Stage Three (*Widow Traditions*, pp. 182-183), agrees that Mary's choice was in danger, but has a different interpretation of what constituted Mary's choice.

simply a more or less neutral recorder of this situation of conflict. I would suggest that perhaps this difference is not so critical. None of these scholars, I believe, would deny that Luke 10,38-42 and Acts 6,1-7, in the context of Luke-Acts as a whole, manifests a tension in regard to the proper role of women disciples, a tension which has been mirrored through the centuries in the variety of interpretations of the Lukan text which express some type of polarity[100]. Further, this difference of opinion as to the proper role for women surfaces in the New Testament as a whole.

The more substantive question is, given the fact that these or any other passages of Scripture provide evidence of a difference of opinion in regard to church practice, on what basis should we claim support for contemporary church practice[101]? John Chrysostom believed that the two women mentioned in Phil 4,2, Euodia and Syntyche, were the heads of the church in Philippi, but he clearly did not believe the women of his day to be capable of fulfilling a similar function[102]. Collins leaves open the possibility that women could be ministers today if the church so decided because he reads the New Testament evidence as suggesting that no individual has a right to a particular ministry, but rather that the church has the right to decide who its ministers will be; "what the church declares to be ministry is ministry"[103].

If Luke 10,38-42 and Acts 6,1-7 reflect a division in the early church, this need not be seen as grounds for cynicism. Despite their criticism of the author of Luke-Acts, Schüssler Fiorenza and Reid have offered suggestions about creative ways of reclaiming the history behind the biblical text, a history which Price has attempted to tease out in more detail. Reid in particular has made it her purpose to explore the way in which subsequent tradition can be fruitful in the process of reinterpretation. In his review of Reid's monograph, R.J. Karris praises "the many life-giving and liberative interpretations presented in this book"[104]. As we struggle with our roles in today's church, perhaps it is good to be reminded

---

100. For examples, see SCHÜSSLER FIORENZA, *But She Said*, p. 58.

101. In *Ministry Reconsidered*, p. 152, reviewing Collins' work, D'Arcy May raises the related questions, "Is an exegetical corrective, however persuasive, sufficient to cancel out theological developments which have gone beyond the literal meaning of the text? If not, what are the criteria for the legitimacy of such developments?".

102. Chrysostom views both the men and women of his day as sadly lacking in their living of the Christian life in comparison with the Philippian congregation of Paul's day.

103. *Are All Christians Ministers?* (n. 97), p. 65.

104. R.J. KARRIS, in *JBL* 117 (1998) 539-541.

that those early Christians struggled likewise, and despite their human weakness they succeeded in handing down a portrait of Jesus Christ which still has power to attract.

Barry University   Veronica KOPERSKI
11300 N.E. Second Ave.
Miami Shores, FL 33161-6695
USA

DIE STEPHANUSEPISODE (APG 6,1–8,3)

IHRE BEDEUTUNG FÜR DIE LUKANISCHE SICHT
DES JERUSALEMISCHEN TEMPELS UND DES JUDENTUMS

I

Die Frage, die Charles Kingsley Barrett 1991 in der Bammel-Festschrift stellte und unter Berücksichtigung von Apg 6f.[1] zu beantworten suchte, hat es in sich, die Frage nämlich: »Did the author of Acts... regard the Temple as a good thing, or a bad thing?«[2]. Nicht nur ist sie für das gesamte lukanische Werk relevant, sondern, wie Barrett selbst hervorhob[3], auch für die da überhaupt im Blick auf das Judentum verfochtene Auffassung. Und was dieses umfassendere Problem angeht, so ist es – spätestens – »seit den achtziger Jahren [unseres Jahrhunderts] zu einem Brenn- und Streitpunkt in der Exegese geworden«, um nun eine Formulierung von Daniel Marguerat aufzugreifen[4]. Man gerät, wieder mit seinen Worten ausgedrückt, »mitten in einen exegetischen Konflikt hinein, in dem zwei entgegengesetzte, einander vollkommen widersprechende Interpretationen des lukanischen Doppelwerkes aufeinandertreffen und jeweils mit gleichem Talent entwickelt werden«[5]. Zum einen wird in Fortführung der lange Zeit die Diskussion bestimmenden Position, wie sie zumal Ernst Haenchen vertrat[6], »eine antijüdische Ausrichtung des lukanischen Doppelwerkes«[7] behauptet, so zumal durch Jack T.

1. C.K. BARRETT, *Attitudes to the Temple in the Acts of the Apostles*, in W. HORBURY (ed.), *Templum Amicitiae. Essays on the Second Temple Presented to Ernst Bammel* (JSNT SS, 48), Sheffield, 1991, S. 345-367, 350-352.

2. *Ibid.*, S. 345.

3. *Ibid.*, S. 366: »What Luke allows us to read about the Jewish Temple is parallel to what he says about Jews and Judaism in general«.

4. D. MARGUERAT, *Juden und Christen im lukanischen Doppelwerk*, in EvT 54 (1994) 241-264, S. 241. Vgl. M. RESE, *»Die Juden« im lukanischen Doppelwerk. Ein Bericht über eine längst nötige »neuere« Diskussion*, in C. BUSSMANN – W. RADL (eds.), *Beiträge zum Werk des Lukas*. FS Gerhard Schneider, Freiburg, 1991, S. 61-79, bes. 62, und W. STEGEMANN, *Zur neueren exegetischen Diskussion um die Apostelgeschichte*, in EvErz 46 (1994) 198-219, S. 215(-219).

5. MARGUERAT, *Juden*, S. 242.

6. E. HAENCHEN, *Die Apostelgeschichte* (KEK, 3), Göttingen, ⁴1961; ID., *Judentum und Christentum in der Apostelgeschichte*, in ID., *Die Bibel und wir. Gesammelte Aufsätze*, Bd. 2, Tübingen, 1968, S. 338-374 (zuerst: 1963). S. dazu RESE, *»Die Juden«*, S. 64-66.

7. STEGEMANN, *Diskussion*, S. 216(-217).

Sanders[8]. Auf der anderen Seite wird in Anknüpfung nicht zuletzt an die Lukas-Arbeiten von Jacob Jervell[9] »eine eher projüdische... Position des Lukas«[10] postuliert, z.B. von Robert L. Brawley[11]. Selbst wer die – wie es angesichts dieser Debatte scheint – durch eine gewisse Ambivalenz bestimmten lukanischen Aussagen zu Tempel und Judentum in diesem Miteinander zusammenhalten möchte – und das versuchen etwa Barrett, Marguerat und Wolfgang Stegemann[12] –, wird dabei der Stephanusepisode einige Aufmerksamkeit zu widmen haben. Über die Bedeutung eines solchen Miteinanders entscheidet nämlich das konkrete Detail.

Und hier nun wiederholt sich das Schauspiel der exegetischen Uneinigkeit. Denn daß es in Apg 6,1–8,3 nicht zuletzt um den jerusalemischen Tempel geht, kann zwar wegen der Passage 7,44-50 keinem Zweifel unterliegen. Aber nicht zuletzt dies, *wie* man den salomonischen Tempelbau, von dem in 7,47-50 die Rede ist, zum Vorangehenden – und damit zum Wüstenheiligtum – in Beziehung zu setzen hat, ist selbst bei denjenigen Auslegern umstritten, die hier so etwas wie Tempel-Kritik ausmachen zu können meinen[13]. Es handelt sich bei ihnen wohl um die Mehrheit der Interpreten[14]. Edvin Larsson, der nicht zu ihr gehört, macht demgegenüber nicht nur auf die Möglichkeit aufmerksam, das δέ von V. 47 nicht im adversativen, sondern im enumerativen Sinne zu begreifen[15]. Darüber hinaus verweist er darauf, daß »in Acts 6.11-14 Luke depicts Stephen as *unjustly* accused of temple-criticism«[16]. Und wenn auch gelegentlich die Ansicht vertreten wird, es sei »eine schlichte Identifizierung der Wendung ὁ τόπος οὗτος« von Apg 6,14 »mit dem ἱερόν unangebracht«[17], so ist der Larssonsche Hinweis doch fraglos hilfreich.

---

8. J.T. SANDERS, *The Jews in Luke-Acts*, London, 1987.

9. S. bes. die Aufsatzsammlung: J. JERVELL, *Luke and the People of God. A New Look at Luke-Acts*, Minneapolis, MN, 1972.

10. STEGEMANN, *Diskussion*, S. 217(-219) – bei St. z.T. kursiv.

11. R.L. BRAWLEY, *Luke-Acts and the Jews. Conflict, Apology, and Conciliation* (SBL MS, 33), Atlanta, GA, 1987.

12. BARRETT, *Attitudes*, S. 366f., MARGUERAT, *Juden*, bes. S. 262.264, und STEGEMANN, *Diskussion*, S. 219.

13. S. dazu nur E. LARSSON, *Temple-Criticism and the Jewish Heritage: Some Reflexions on Acts 6-7*, in *NTS* 39 (1993) 379-395, S. 389f.

14. *Ibid.*, S. 388.

15. *Ibid.*, S. 390f. Vgl. K. HAACKER, *Die Stellung des Stephanus in der Geschichte des Urchristentums*, in *ANRW* II.26.2 (1995), S. 1515-1553, 1536 samt Anm. 78.

16. LARSSON, *Temple-Criticism*, S. (382-)384 – Hervorhebung durch mich. Vgl. z.B. HAACKER, *Stephanus*, S. 1543 (doch auch S. 1539 und dazu u. bei Anm. 59). Der Rezipient der an Stephanus gerichteten Frage »εἰ ταῦτα οὕτως ἔχει;« (7,1b) muß schon wegen 6,11.13 dazu tendieren, als Antwort ein »Nein!« zu ergänzen.

17. W. STEGEMANN, *Zwischen Synagoge und Obrigkeit. Zur historischen Situation der lukanischen Christen* (FRLANT, 152), Göttingen, 1991, S. 164(-174).

Für die *lukanische* Sicht des Tempels wäre es in der Tat absurd, anzunehmen, es widerspräche das, was in der Rede des angeklagten »Armen-
pflegers« zum Ausdruck gebracht werden soll, dem, daß der Verfasser
zuvor unmißverständlich von falschen Zeugen (6,14) und – somit – von
falschen Vorwürfen (6,11.14) gesprochen hat[18]. Wenn der Kontext der
Stephanus-»Apologie« unter redaktionsgeschichtlichen Gesichtspunkten
zu berücksichtigen ist, dann jedoch nicht allein der rückwärtige, sondern
auch der nachfolgende, d.h. ebenfalls der Passus 7,54–8,3. Freilich hat
Rudolf Pesch vor über 30 Jahren in einer kleinen Monographie gezeigt,
daß nun gerade die Stephanus-Vision (7,55f.; vgl. 7,59f.) ihrerseits eine
Vielzahl unterschiedlicher Interpretationen erfahren hat[19]. Gegenüber
seiner eigenen, stark durch die sich anschließenden Acta-Kapitel
bestimmten Deutung[20], nach der das Stehen Jesu im Sinne eines Sich-
Erhebens des »sein Volk« anklagenden Menschensohnes zu begreifen
und auf den legitimen »*Fort-Gang* des Evangeliums von den Juden zu
den Heiden« zu beziehen wäre[21], hat Franz Mußner zu Recht auf den
engen Konnex der Visionsschilderung mit der Stephanusrede selbst und
mit der ihr vorangehenden Szene hingewiesen[22].

So wird es sinnvoll sein, die Stephanusrede nun einerseits primär vom
rückwärtigen Zusammenhang (II), andererseits entsprechend vom nachfolgenden Kontext her (III) in den Blick zu fassen, ohne dabei doch auf
diachrone Daten zu verzichten. Im ersten dieser Durchgänge kann ich an
meine – schon ein wenig angestaubte – Dissertation »Jerusalem und der
Tempel« anknüpfen[23], im anderen an die u.a. von Mußner ins Gespräch
gebrachte Vorstellung von der himmlischen »Wohnung Gottes« (und
des Menschensohnes). Nicht zuletzt das m.E. von Pesch nicht sonderlich
glücklich[24] in Betracht gezogene, überdies inzwischen zumal durch die

18. Die Annahme begegnet indes gleichwohl alles andere als selten, wenn auch
zumeist vorsichtig formuliert, z.B. bei Barrett, *Attitudes*, S. 352, und Stegemann,
Synagoge, S. 173.
19. R. Pesch, *Die Vision des Stephanus. Apg 7,55-56 im Rahmen der Apostelgeschichte* (SBS, 12), Stuttgart, 1966, bes. S. 14-23. Vgl. H.-W. Neudorfer, *Der Stephanuskreis in der Forschungsgeschichte seit F.C. Baur* (TVGMS), Gießen – Basel, 1983,
S. 199-207.283-287.313f.
20. S. bes. Pesch, *Vision*, S. 38-42.
21. *Ibid.*, S. 58.
22. F. Mussner, *Wohnung Gottes und Menschensohn nach der Stephanusperikope
(Apg 6,8–8,2)*, in R. Pesch – R. Schnackenburg (eds.), *Jesus und der Menschensohn*. FS
Anton Vögtle, Freiburg, 1975, S. 283-299, bes. 283-288.
23. M. Bachmann, *Jerusalem und der Tempel. Die geographisch-theologischen Elemente in der lukanischen Sicht des jüdischen Kultzentrums* (BWANT, 109), Stuttgart,
1980, bes. S. 238-253 (und 339 Anm. 511). Vgl. (die teils kritischen Anmerkungen dazu
bei) Stegemann, *Synagoge*, S. 164-169.
24. Kritisch dazu schon Mussner, *Wohnung*, S. 291, der insbesondere mit Recht dar-

»Sabbatopferlieder«[25] vermehrte Vergleichsmaterial läßt es angeraten
erscheinen, in einem abschließenden Teil (IV) der Frage nachzugehen,
ob die Vorstellung von der himmlischen Wohnung dazu angetan ist,
eher anti- oder eher projüdisch verstanden zu werden.

II

Es sind fraglos *zwei* Anklagepunkte, welche die Falschzeugen (6,13;
vgl. 6,11) Stephanus gegenüber vorbringen. Nach 6,13 soll er sich
»wider diese heilige Stätte und das Gesetz« gewandt haben. Wenn in
6,14 gesagt wird, er habe Jesus, den Nazoräer, als den geltend gemacht,
der »diese Stätte zerstören und die 'uns' von Mose gegebenen Vor-
schriften ändern« werde, dann sichert die Anspielung auf das – im
Lukasevangelium fehlende! – Tempel-Wort Jesu (Mt 26,61par. Mk
14,58; vgl. Joh 2,19), daß es bei den gegen Stephanus gerichteten Vorwürfen außer um das mosaische Gesetz um den Tempel geht. Daß die
Redeweise von »dieser (heiligen) Stätte« so zu verstehen ist, läßt im
übrigen auch der lukanische Sprachgebrauch erschließen, insbesondere
der Vergleich mit den, 21,28b zufolge, Paulus gegenüber vorgebrachten
ähnlichen Anschuldigungen: er habe allüberall »wider das Volk und das
Gesetz und diese Stätte gelehrt«. Denn die letzte dieser Vorhaltungen
wird dann sogleich (in 21,28c) folgendermaßen substantiiert: »er hat
sogar Griechen in das ἱερόν mitgenommen und diese heilige Stätte ver-
unreinigt«. Die beiden Anklagepunkte von 6,13 werden nicht nur durch
die ausführlicheren Vorwürfe von 6,14 erhellt, sondern offenkundig
auch durch die in 6,11 vorangehende Formulierung, nach der Stephanus
»lästernde Worte in bezug auf Mose und Gott« geäußert haben soll. Wie
bei der Wiederaufnahme in 6,14 wird hier der Bezug zu Mose, zum
mosaischen Gesetz, hergestellt, und darüber hinaus wird deutlich, daß es
bei der den Tempel betreffenden Anklage um den *Gottes*bezug dieser
Institution geht.

Die derart profilierten beiden Anklagepunkte bestimmen nun auch die
Stephanus*rede* (7,2b-53) – ein Sachverhalt, der oft nicht hinreichend
deutlich gesehen wird. Die enge Verbindung der Ansprache mit den
abzuweisenden Vorhaltungen deutet sich u.a. darin an, daß die Rede
sowohl für »das Zelt des Zeugnisses« (V. 44) als auch im Blick auf

auf verweist, daß in Apg 7,55f. nicht vom Aufstehen, sondern vom Stehen des Erhöhten
die Rede ist (vgl. dazu u. bei Anm. 52f.).

25. C. NEWSOM, *Songs of the Sabbath Sacrifice: A Critical Edition* (Harvard Semitic
Studies, 27), Atlanta, GA, 1985.

»das Gesetz« (V. 53) von himmlischer Anordnung spricht (vgl. Gal 3,19, ferner Hebr 2,2), und zwar unter Verwendung von διατάσσειν bzw. von διαταγή, also von gerade auch für das lukanische Werk charakteristischem Vokabular[26]. Sofern dabei die Abschlußformulierung der »Apologie« der Anordnung durch Engel die Nicht-Einhaltung seitens der von Stephanus Angeredeten entgegensetzt, wird die Rolle der himmlischen Gestalten (vgl. V. 38 [und dazu V. 44]) keineswegs im Sinne der Depravation des durch sie Aufgetragenen gewertet. Stephanus erkennt nach diesen Formulierungen vielmehr die Dignität des »Zeltes des Zeugnisses« – und des Tempels – einerseits, des mosaischen Gesetzes andererseits an. Er weist demnach die Anschuldigungen zurück.

Nicht nur das! Die in der zweiten Person Plural nun die Hörer angreifende Schlußpassage der Rede, V. 51-53, wendet den Anklagepunkt der Mißachtung des mosaischen Gesetzes gegen die Ankläger selbst, gegen die Synedristen (s. 6,12). Was sich an diesem Abschnitt immerhin für die *eine* Frage, für die Gesetzesfrage, ablesen läßt, bestimmt nun m.E. ähnlich auch den sozusagen historischen Teil der Rede, die umfassende Partie V. 2b-50, und zwar nun im Blick auf *beide* Anklagepunkte. Ganz im Unterschied zu V. 51-53 begegnet im Geschichtsabriß der Ansprache nach der (natürlich die zweite Person verwendenden) Anrede (V. 2b) von Anbeginn (V. 2c) an die erste Person Plural (V. 11.12.15. 19.38b.39.44.45a.b). Stephanus erscheint so, wenn er z.B. von »unserem Vater Abraham« (V. 2c) und von »unserem Geschlecht« (V. 19) spricht, als in das Volk Israel eingeordnet. An zwei Stellen kommt es aber zu einer Dissoziierung von Redner und Hörern, nämlich in V. 4b und V. 38c. An der ersten dieser beiden Stellen spricht Stephanus von dem »Land…, in dem *ihr* jetzt lebt«, an der zweiten von den »*euch*« zu übermittelnden »Worten des Lebens«. D.h. dort, wo erstmals der lokale Aspekt der Anklage gegen Stephanus berührt wird, und entsprechend bei der ersten Bezugnahme auf den juridischen Vorwurf wird durch jene Dissoziierung angedeutet, daß hier eigentlich nicht des Redners Verhältnis zu Land bzw. Tempel einerseits, mosaischem Gesetz andererseits als fraglich zu gelten hat, sondern das der Hörer.

Dieser rhetorisch raffinierte Zug ist freilich der Beobachtung oft entgangen. Man hat wohl erstens nicht beachtet, daß in der Rede verschiedentlich Zitate und ausschließlich auf die Vergangenheit bezogene Formulierungen ein sozusagen historisches Ihr bieten (V.26.37b.42f.49), das von der Anrede an die Hörer zu unterscheiden ist, und zweitens hat man das in V. 38c u.a. von P[74], Sinaiticus und Vaticanus gebotene ὑμῖν

---

26. S. dazu nur BACHMANN, *Jerusalem*, S. 252 Anm. 231.

nicht als erhellend, sondern insbesondere angesichts des ἡμῶν von V.
38b und V. 39 als störend empfunden und darum, wie die Mehrzahl der
Handschriften, einem ἡμῖν den Vorzug gegeben, damit aber der *lectio
facilior*.

Schaut man indes genauer hin, so kann kaum ein Zweifel daran bestehen, daß in V. 38c nicht anders als in V. 4b dezent angedeutet wird, daß
die Anklagen eher den Hörern als Stephanus gelten müßten. Beim *juridischen Sachverhalt* ist es dann, wie wir schon zu registrieren hatten, im
Schlußteil der Rede mit der Dezenz vorbei, während zuvor »lediglich«
konstatierend von dem Fehlverhalten, der, »unserer«, Vorfahren in
bezug auf Mose und das mosaische Gesetz gesprochen worden war (V.
25.27f.35.39[-43]). Im Zusammenhang damit kommt in V. 40-43 auch
kultisches Fehlverhalten während der Wüstenzeit zur Darstellung; so
wird auf das »(goldene) Kalb« (V. 41) hingewiesen. Bei der *Kult-The-
matik* fehlt freilich ein dem Schlußabschnitt V. 51-53 entsprechender,
die Hörer unmittelbar anklagender Ihr-Passus. Das ist um so auffälliger
und um so erklärungsbedürftiger, als nicht die Frage des Gesetzes, sondern die des Landes und der gottesdienstlichen Stätte den Aufbau des
»historischen« Teils der Rede bestimmt. Was die benannte Leerstelle
angeht, so möchte ich nachher (unter III) eine Erklärung vom nachfolgenden Kontext her versuchen, der m.E. diese Lücke schließt, sofern er
an den himmlischen Tempel denken läßt, dem die Stephanus-Ankläger
durch ihr Verhalten gerade nicht entsprechen.

Jetzt ist erst einmal die These über den Aufbau von V. 2b-50 zu
begründen, die im übrigen so kühn nicht ist, sagt doch z.B. auch Larsson: »the narratives of Abraham, Joseph and Moses all are Israel-cen-
tred«[27]. Zwei Indizien-Gruppen sollen in Betracht gezogen werden: Die
eine hat es mit dem Ausdruck »diese Stätte«, die andere mit Abraham
zu tun, und beide betreffen die dem »Patriarchen«, V. 6f. zufolge, gegebene Zusage, die nach V. 7bβ folgenden Zielpunkt hat: »und sie werden
mich an dieser Stätte verehren«.

Daß hier die Wendung ὁ τόπος οὗτος verwandt wird, ist in doppelter
Hinsicht auffällig. Erstens wird damit ja die Rede des Stephanus mit den
ihm geltenden, wenige Verse vorher dreimal referierten Anklagen
(6,11.13.14) verklammert, insbesondere mit der letzten dieser Formulie-

---

27. LARSSON, *Temple-Criticism*, S. 392 (vgl. S. 386-388), der dabei auf das Land
Israel und gerade auch auf den Tempel abhebt (s. nur S. 385f.388). Anders z.B. (in Aus-
einandersetzung u.a. mit mir) STEGEMANN, *Synagoge*, S. (165-)166 (samt Anm. 50.52):
»Die 'Apologie' des Stephanus kennt keine Verknüpfung von Land(verheißung) *und
Tempel*. Oder anders: Der Bau des Tempels durch Salomo hat nichts mit der Verheißung
des Landbesitzes an Abraham bzw. seinen Samen und deren Erfüllung zu tun«.

rungen (V. 14). Läßt schon das kaum einen Zweifel daran zu, daß nicht anders als in 6,14 auch in 7,7bβ an den jerusalemischen Tempel gedacht ist, so tritt das Zweite stützend hinzu. Die Korrespondenz zwischen rückwärtigem Kontext und Ansprache kommt nur dadurch zustande, daß in V. 7bβ gegenüber dem hier fraglos aufgegriffenen Wortlaut von Ex 3,12eLXX[28] die Vokabel ὄρος durch das Wort τόπος ersetzt wird, vermutlich von Lukas selbst[29]. Wenn hier somit der jerusalemische Tempel als der gottgewollte Ort der Gottesverehrung im Blick ist – und darauf dürfte auch die lukanische Verwendung des Verbs λατρεύειν hindeuten[30] –, so ist offenkundig, daß die Frage der legitimen Gottesverehrung und der gottesdienstlichen Stätte den Verlauf des »historischen« Teils der Stephanusrede bestimmt, der ja im Anschluß an den Hinweis auf die Verfertigung eines »(goldenen) Kalbs« (V. 41) und nach der deswegen von Gott strafend bewirkten Hingabe an ein »dem Himmelsheer« geltendes λατρεύειν (V. 42[-43]) abschließend auf das »Zelt des Zeugnisses« (V. 44) und den Tempelbau (V. 45-50) zu sprechen kommt.

Die Zusage der Gottesverehrung »an dieser Stätte« (V. 7bβ) ist Spitzensatz dessen (V. 6-7; vgl. V. 3), was »unserem Vater Abraham« (V. 2c) »verheißen« (V. 5b) wurde. Auch das ist in doppelter Hinsicht aufschlußreich. Erstens nämlich ist diese alttestamentliche Gestalt im lukanischen Werk auch jenseits der Stephanusrede auffällig eng mit der Frage des »Landes« verbunden, wie ich früher näher zu zeigen versucht habe[31] und wie insbesondere an den Belegen der Apostelgeschichte (s. bes. 3,25f.; 7,2ff.; 13,26f.) leicht verifiziert werden kann. Auch die sich recht eng mit Apg 7,7bβ berührende Formulierung aus dem Benedictus (Lk 1,68-79) des Priesters (s. Lk 1,5) Zacharias (vgl. Lk 1,67 mit Apg 6,5; 7,55) fügt sich hier ein, nach der Gott »Abraham, unserem Vater«, in bezug auf das »Haus seines Knechtes David« (Lk 1,69) geschworen hat, man werde, »aus Feindeshand befreit, λατρεύειν αὐτῷ ἐν ὁσιότητι καὶ δικαιοσύνῃ ἐνώπιον αὐτοῦ« (V. 73f.). Zweitens ist es nicht die Mehrungszusage (s. Apg 7,5b.c; vgl. 7,8.17), sondern die Landzusage an Abraham und sind es die vor die Erfüllung gesetzten, durch Einschränkungen gekennzeichneten Phasen, welche nach dem einleitenden,

---

28. S. dazu nur BACHMANN, *Jerusalem*, S. 246 samt Anm. 209.
29. S. dazu nur *ibid.*, 246f. Vgl. HAACKER, *Stephanus*, S. 1537.
30. Von den sieben Vergleichsstellen haben es zumindest Lk 2,37; Apg 24,14 (s. V. 12.17) und 26,7 (s. V. 4; vgl. nur Lk 2,37 und dazu BACHMANN, *Jerusalem*, S. 337f. Anm. 511) mit einem primär durch den jerusalemischen Tempel geprägten Gottesdienst zu tun. Der Thematik läßt sich wohl auch der (Abraham-)Beleg Lk 1,74 zugesellen (s. V. 69), vielleicht auch der Vers Lk 4,8 (s. V. 9). Und um eine Negativentsprechung handelt es sich bei Apg 7,42.
31. BACHMANN, *Jerusalem*, S. 234-255.

seinerseits durch das Stichwort γῆ (5mal) charakterisierten Abraham-
Abschnitt (V. 2b-8) den daran anschließenden »historischen« Teilen der
Stephanusrede das Gepräge geben. Der Geschichtsüberblick wird insofern durch den Passus V. 5b-7 gegliedert[32], nämlich: in die Zeit der
ägyptischen Gefangenschaft (V. 9-19.20-29; s. V. 6-7a), in die Zeit des
Exodus (V. 30-44 und V. 7bα) und in die Zeit der Erfüllung der Land-
verheißung mit der Inbesitznahme des Landes und mit dem Tempelbau
(V. 45-50; s. V. 6.7bβ). Welch entscheidende Rolle den Zusagen von V.
5b-7 zukommt, läßt sich auch an der Wiederaufnahme der hier verwandten Terminologie in den nachfolgenden Partien der Rede erkennen: Dem
ἐπαγγέλεσθαι von V. 5b korrespondiert in V. 17 die ἐπαγγελία
Gottes, die hier überdies ausdrücklich mit Abraham verknüpft wird (vgl.
V. 32!); auf den Inhalt der Verheißung, der in V. 5b als κατάσχεσις
des »Landes« bezeichnet wird, spielt die Wiederholung der Vokabel in
V. 45 an; daß auch das λατρεύειν von V. 7bβ in V. 42 eine Negativentsprechung findet, wurde schon notiert.

Kurz: Es geht im »historischen« Teil der Stephanusrede um die
Erfüllung der Abraham gegebenen Zusage, es werde zur Inbesitznahme
des »Landes« und am jerusalemischen Tempel zu gottgewolltem Gottesdienst kommen. Da hier ein im Ihr-Stil formulierter, die Hörer der
Stephanusrede anklagender Passus in der Art von V. 51-53 fehlt, ist es
alles andere als wahrscheinlich, daß in V. 47 der salomonische Tempelbau als negativ charakterisiert werden soll. In die gleiche Richtung weisen die schon weiter oben[33] genannten Argumente, daß nämlich mit δέ
hier sehr wohl nur ein weiteres, ein letztes Glied der Erzählung ange-
schlossen werden kann und daß für Lukas die Stephanus geltenden Vorhaltungen, insbesondere die auf den Tempel bezügliche, unzutreffend
sind.

Auf der anderen Seite wird, wie wir ebenfalls bereits konstatierten, in
V. 4b angedeutet, daß die Adressaten ein falsches Verhältnis zum
»Land« – und damit zum gottgewollten jerusalemischen Tempel –
haben könnten. Und diese Andeutung wird durch V. 48-50 noch bekräftigt, sofern hier, einsetzend mit ἀλλά und unter Rückgriff auf Jes 66,1f.,
ein bestimmtes Mißverständnis des Tempels charakterisiert wird: ihn
nämlich für den Wohnort Gottes zu halten – Gottes, der doch dem

---

32. Vgl. dazu nur *ibid.*, S. 238-245, bes. 241, und LARSSON, *Temple-Criticism*, S. 385
samt Anm. 17.

33. S.o. bei Anm. 15f. – Zum nachfolgenden Absatz vgl. bes. HAACKER, *Stephanus*, S.
1535-1540, der insbesondere darauf aufmerksam macht, daß die in der Stephanusrede
abgelehnte Position, nämlich: Gott selbst *wohne* im Tempel, »nach Josephus (Bell 5,459)
... in der Endphase des jüdischen Aufstandes von den Verteidigern Jerusalems vertreten
wurde« (S. 1539; vgl. S. 1543).

himmlischen Bereich zuzuordnen ist. Daß der jerusalemische Tempel wie jeder irdische, mit Händen gemachte Tempel (s. V. 48; vgl. 17,24f.) nicht Wohnort Gottes ist, hätte man der vorangehenden Rede schon entnehmen können; denn in V. 41 und V. 43 wird die Verehrung selbstgefertigter Götzenbilder kritisiert, und beim jerusalemischen Tempel selbst geht es nach V. (5b-)7bβ und noch deutlicher nach V. 46 darum, daß »eine Stätte für das *Haus* Jakob« eingerichtet wird (vgl. 2 Makk 5,19), eine gottesdienstliche Stätte für sich dort andächtig versammelnde Juden (vgl. nochmals Lk 1,74f., ferner Lk 19,45f.). Diese Akzentuierung tritt noch unübersehbarer hervor, wenn man beachtet, daß auch in V. 46 – wie in V. 7bβ – der zugrundeliegende Septuaginta-Wortlaut (von Ps 131[132],5) verändert worden ist, wobei nun οἶκος statt θεός gesetzt wurde[34].

Und daß man für Gottes Wohnen nicht an den jerusalemischen Tempel, sondern eher an den Himmel zu denken hat, klingt ebenfalls schon vor dem Jesaja-Zitat an, nämlich in V. 44, wo von dem Urbild der Stiftshütte die Rede ist, welches Mose »gesehen hatte«. Die Vermutung liegt nahe, daß schon in 6,11.13f. auf die unterschiedlich interpretierbare Beziehung zwischen jerusalemischem Tempel und Gott (bzw. Ort Gottes) angespielt werden soll, wenn die Anklage-Formulierungen, wie wir sahen, statt auf »diese (heilige) Stätte« (V. 13.14) auch – und zuerst – auf »Gott« abheben. So wenig also der jerusalemische Tempel, der Stephanusrede zufolge, als illegitim zu gelten hat, so sehr deutet sich die Möglichkeit an, die Relation zwischen ihm und dem himmlischen Heiligtum nicht zu respektieren.

Der nachfolgende Kontext der Rede, dem wir uns nun zuzuwenden haben, gibt nicht zuletzt mit einer den mosaischen Blick auf jenes Urbild sozusagen aufgreifenden Vision und mit den dadurch ausgelösten Geschehnissen u.a. Folgendes zu verstehen: Jene Möglichkeit ist bei denen, die Stephanus anklagen, realisiert; sie selbst schätzen das himmlische Heiligtum falsch ein, insofern auch den jerusalemischen Tempel. Auch in diesem, auch in dem »Gott« bzw. »diese (heilige) Stätte« betreffenden Punkt fällt die Anklage auf sie zurück.

III

Vielleicht ist es hilfreich, hinsichtlich der Relevanz der Szene Apg 7,54ff. den Passus Barn 16,1-10 zum Vergleich heranzuziehen (vgl.

---

34. S. dazu nur Bachmann, *Jerusalem*, S. 339f. Anm. 511. Vgl. etwa Larsson, *Temple-Criticism*, S. 393 (samt Anm. 35).

auch: Josephus, Bell 5,458f.). Für den jerusalemischen Tempel wird dort die Auffassung derjenigen als irrig charakterisiert, die »auf das Gebäude ihre Hoffnung setzten, als wäre es Gottes Haus, und nicht auf ihren Gott, der sie geschaffen hat« (V. 1). Obwohl dafür – ähnlich wie in Apg 7,49(f.) – auf Jes 66,1 verwiesen wird (V. 2), geht es dann nicht um den doch im Zitat angesprochenen himmlischen Bereich, sondern einerseits um die Zerstörung des irdischen Tempels und Jerusalems (V. 3-5), andererseits (in V. 6-10) um »den unvergänglichen Tempel« (V. 9), der als »der geistliche Tempel« (V. 10) dort ersteht, wo gilt: es »wohnt wahrhaftig in unserer Wohnung Gott in uns« (V. 8)[35].

Lukas verfährt in Apg 7 weithin anders. Er spricht ja weder direkt von einer falschen Einschätzung des jerusalemischen Tempels noch von dessen gottgewollter Zerstörung, noch vom Wohnen Gottes in den Gläubigen. Analog ist aber doch wohl dies, daß der mehr oder weniger deutliche Hinweis auf eine falsche Einschätzung des jerusalemischen Tempels über die Zitation von Jes 66,1f. hinaus noch durch Aussagen gestützt wird, welche eine adäquatere, eine angemessene Sicht des Tempels betreffen.

Daß es dem Verfasser in Apg 7,54ff. darum zu tun ist, legte sich uns ja schon vor diesem Seitenblick auf Barn 16 nahe, und zwar sowohl angesichts der Art, wie die Stephanusrede auf die dem Redner geltenden beiden Vorwürfe Bezug nimmt, als auch aufgrund der Gegenüberstellungen von Himmlischem und Irdischem, wie sie in 7,46-50 in bezug auf das jerusalemische und in 7,44 für das bei der Wüstenwanderung mitgeführte Heiligtum vorgenommen werden, vorbereitet durch das Nebeneinander von »Gott« und »dieser (heiligen) Stätte« in 6,11.13f.

Ein etwas genauerer Blick auf die Formulierungen der Passage 7,54ff. sichert diese Deutung ab, und das bereits dann, wenn man sie lediglich im Rahmen des lukanischen Werks zu verstehen sucht. Kaum anders als in Apg 6,11ff. sind auch in 7,54ff. parallele Umschreibungen von besonderem Interesse: vor allem die der Stephanusvision in 7,55 und in 7,56. Auch der Vergebungsruf von 7,60 darf wohl ähnlich veranschlagt werden, hat er doch eine gewisse Parallele im Wort des sterbenden Jesus von Lk 23,34: »Vater vergib ihnen; denn sie wissen nicht, was sie tun«.

Was nun zunächst die Stephanusvision selbst angeht, so ist schon das angesichts von Apg 7,49 (Jes 66,1) und von Apg 10,11 durchaus erstaunliche Nebeneinander von οὐρανός (V. 55; vgl. Apg 1,10) und

35. Übersetzung: K. WENGST, *Didache (Apostellehre), Barnabasbrief, Zweiter Klemensbrief, Schrift an Diognet* (SUC, 2), Darmstadt, 1984, S. 183.185.187.

36. Vgl. F. LENTZEN-DEIS, *Das Motiv der »Himmelsöffnung« in verschiedenen Gattungen der Umweltliteratur des Neuen Testaments*, in *Bib* 50 (1969) 301-327, S. 313 samt Anm. 3 (und 7).

οὐρανοί (V. 56) aufschlußreich, sofern offenkundig ausgedrückt werden soll, daß der Blick zum Firmament[36] sich als ein Blick in die gegliederte himmlische Welt erweist. Daß Lukas derart zu differenzieren weiß, läßt im Vergleich z.B. mit Lk 24,51 (vgl. ferner Apg 1,10f.; 2,2.5.19) wohl auch Apg 2,34 erkennen, wonach nicht David, sondern Jesus in *die* Himmel aufgenommen worden ist (vgl. noch Lk 12,33 neben Mt 6,20). Wenn dabei in 2,34f. auf Ps 109(110),1 zurückgegriffen wird, so liegt der Ton schwerlich auf Jesu *Sitzen* zur Rechten Gottes, sondern, wie die durch das Zitat abzusichernde Aussage von 2,33 (vgl. 2,25 und Ps 15[16],8) erkennen läßt, allgemeiner auf Jesu Position »zur Rechten Gottes«[37] und auf derart wahrzunehmenden Funktionen, insbesondere auf der Verleihung des von Gott als »Vater« empfangenen Geistes.

Für Jesu Ort im gegliederten Himmel wird in Apg 7,55f. aus Apg 2,33-35 denn auch die zweimal genannte Position zur Rechten Gottes (ἐκ δεξιῶν ... τοῦ θεοῦ) aufgenommen, nicht jedoch ein Sitzen des Erhöhten – obwohl die in 7,56 gegebene Anspielung auf Lk 22,69 das doch nahegelegt hätte, sofern Jesus danach gegenüber den *ihn* Anklagenden von seinem künftigen Sitzen »zur Rechten der Macht Gottes« spricht. Statt dessen ist in Apg 7,55f., ebenfalls zweimal, vom Stehen (je: ἑστῶτα) des Erhöhten die Rede. Die engste Parallele zu diesem Wortlaut ist im lukanischen Werk fraglos bei einer anderen Vision gegeben, und zwar bei der des ἔναντι τοῦ θεοῦ diensttuenden, im ναὸς τοῦ κυρίου (Lk 1,9) befindlichen Priesters Zacharias, mit der die Erzählung des dritten Evangeliums einsetzt (Lk 1,5ff. bzw. 1,8ff.). Da heißt es: »es erschien ihm ein Engel des Herrn, ἑστὼς ἐκ δεξιῶν τοῦ θυσιαστηρίου τοῦ θυμιάματος« (Lk 1,11). Überdies deutet sich auch im dortigen Zusammenhang eine Korrespondenz von irdischem und himmlischem Heiligtum an: schon insofern, als hier, wie auch sonst bei Lukas nicht eben selten[38], der Tempel Stätte einer Vision, Ort einer Offenbarung ist, vor allem jedoch, sofern sich der Engel dann (nach Lk 1,19) vorstellt als ὁ παρεστηκὼς ἐνώπιον τοῦ θεοῦ[39]. Stehen »zur Rechten des Räucheraltars« und »vor Gott« haben für unseren Autor offenkundig etwas miteinander zu tun (vgl. Jub 31,14; TestIsaak 4,45-47; ferner Offb

---

37. Nach *BDR*, [14]1976, §199, wird das τῇ δεξιᾷ von Apg 2,33 und 5,31 »eher lokal als instrumental« gebraucht sein. Vgl. Mussner, *Wohnung*, S. 287 samt Anm. 14 (und u. bei Anm. 46.58).

38. S. bes. Lk 2,22-40 und Apg 22,17-22. Vgl. hierzu und zu weiteren vergleichbaren Szenen Bachmann, *Jerusalem*, S. 161-168 (samt Anm. 99). 346-354 (samt Anm. 536. 542). 363-369.

39. S. dazu und auch zu dem auffälligen Zug, daß hinsichtlich des von Gott zum sich im Tempel aufhaltenden Zacharias gesandten Engels anders als in ähnlichen Szenen (s. nur Lk 1,26.38; 2,9.15) eine Überbrückung einer räumlichen Distanz nicht angedeutet wird, Bachmann, *Jerusalem*, S. 181-186 samt Anm. 34. Vgl. Brawley, *Jews*, S. 130, ferner Mussner, *Wohnung*, S. 291.

8,3f.). Die kultischen Konnotationen des Passus Apg 7,54ff. sind angesichts von zwei weiteren Momenten noch weniger zu leugnen.

Von den Variationen zwischen 7,55 und 7,56 erklärt sich das Nacheinander von »Jesus« und »Menschensohn« wohl sehr einfach: Lukas
knüpft einerseits an den Jesus-Namen von 6,14 und andererseits an Lk
22,69 an. Hingegen ist für unsere Überlegungen – erstens – von einigem
Belang, daß es in 7,55 zunächst, und ohne Parallele in 7,56, heißt, Stephanus habe die δόξα θεοῦ gesehen. Denn nicht nur korrespondiert diese
Voranstellung Gottes bzw. seiner δόξα in gewisser Hinsicht der entsprechenden, bereits für 6,11 konstatierten Vorordnung[40]. Zugleich ist damit,
selbst wenn man lediglich das lukanische Werk in Betracht zieht, angedeutet: Der δόξα-Bereich, dem Jesus aufgrund seiner in Jerusalem
erfüllten ἔξοδος angehört (s. Lk 9,31) – weshalb auch von *Jesu* δόξα
gesprochen werden kann (s. Lk 24,26) –, ist der Bereich eben jenes
Gottes, der nicht erst Stephanus, sondern nach Apg 7,2ff. gerade als
»Gott der *Herrlichkeit*« (V. 2) schon Abraham erschienen war und der
diesem Mann eine künftige Stätte der Gottesverehrung seitens Israels
verheißen hatte (s. Apg 7,7bβ)[41]. Außerdem ist es nach der sogenannten
Weihnachtsgeschichte und nach der lukanischen Fassung der Szene vom
Einzug Jesu in Jerusalem ein Bereich, der von irdischem wie himmlischem Lobpreis bestimmt sein kann, für den aber zumindest gilt: δόξα
ἐν ὑψίστοις (Lk 2,13f.; 19,38)[42].

---

40. Auch zu Lk 22,69 ergibt sich durch den Bezug auf die δόξα θεοῦ eine besonders
enge Relation, sofern der dritte Evangelist dort anders als der erste (Mt 26,64) und anders
als der zweite (Mk 14,62) nicht einfach von ἡ δύναμις, sondern von ἡ δύναμις τοῦ θεοῦ
spricht.
41. Der seltene Ausdruck ὁ θεὸς τῆς δόξης, der durch Gen 12,7 (κύριος) gerade
nicht vorgegeben ist, verdient Beachtung (vgl. HAACKER, *Stephanus*, S. 1538 samt Anm.
82). Insbesondere angesichts der nicht zuletzt durch das Stichwort γῆ (s. bes. Apg 7,3.4b-
5) vermittelten Beziehung zwischen Apg 7,2 und Apg 7,7bβ ist von erheblicher Relevanz,
daß es die auffällige Gottesbezeichnung sowohl in Ps 28(29),3 als auch in 1 Hen 25,7 (vgl.
V. 3) mit dem Tempel zu tun hat. In Ps 28(29),9 heißt es: ἐν τῷ ναῷ αὐτοῦ (nämlich: des
Gottes der Herrlichkeit bzw. des Herrn) πᾶς τις λέγει δόξαν, und in 1 Hen 25,5f. ist von
der »heiligen Stätte« (vgl. Apg 6,13.14; 7,7; 21,28), vom »Haus Gottes, des ewigen
Königs«, und vom (endzeitlichen) Eintreten ins »Heiligtum« die Rede. In diesem Zusammenhang verdient im übrigen Beachtung, daß der »Visionär« Abraham (vgl. nur Gen
15,5.12-20 einerseits, 1QGenAp 21,8; 22,27 andererseits) z.B. nach 2 Bar 4,4f. das himmlische Jerusalem (vgl. Hebr 11,8-10.13) und nach ApkAbr 25,4f. (vgl. 18,1ff.; 29,17) den
himmlischen Tempel schaut. Vgl. u. bei Anm. 51.57 und ferner TestLev 18, wo u.a. von
der »Herrlichkeit des Höchsten« (V. 7; vgl. V. 5: »die Engel der Herrlichkeit des Angesichts des Herrn«) und von der Öffnung der Himmel (V. 6; vgl. V. 10), vom »Tempel der
Herrlichkeit« (V. 6), vom »neuen (nämlich: eschatologischen) Priester« (V. 2) und vom
»Priestertum« (V. 9) gesprochen, überdies auf Abraham (V.6; vgl. V. 14: endzeitlicher
Jubel bei »Abraham und Isaak und Jakob«) Bezug genommen wird.
42. Was das Nebeneinander von οὐρανοί (Apg 7,56) und ὑψίστοι (Lk 2,14; 19,38;
vgl. Apg 2,33; 5,31 und 7,48) angeht, so ist es durch Ps 148,1 und Hi 16,19 vorgegeben

Kultisches ist natürlich – zweitens – auch in 7,60 angesprochen, wenn hier der κύριος, Jesus (s. 7,59), um Nicht-Anrechnung von Sünde gebeten wird. Sofern dabei im Unterschied zum analogen Vergebungswort Jesu von Lk 23,34 nicht *Gott* (»Vater«) angerufen wird, scheint daran gedacht zu sein, daß der zur Rechten Gottes stehende *Jesus* nun am himmlischen Heiligtum ein priesterliches Amt innehat. Man kann darum wohl vom Interzessor reden[43]. Mehrere Indizien sprechen in der Tat dafür, daß ungefähr so zu deuten ist. Nicht nur, daß Jesus, der schon nach Lk 22,31f. fürbittend für Simon (Petrus) eintritt[44] (vgl. V. 24-28.29f.33f., ferner Lk 10,18; 11,20; 12,8), dem reuigen Schächer im Anschluß an jenes Vergebungswort bereits zusagt, mit ihm sogleich im Paradies sein zu werden (Lk 23,40-43) – auch das eine möglicherweise Kultisches einschließende »Ortsbestimmung«[45]; nicht nur, daß das Zerreißen des Tempelvorhangs bei Lukas mit einem vertrauenden Wort Jesu verknüpft wird, nach dem er, ähnlich wie dann Stephanus (Apg 7,59), seinen Geist dem »Vater« anempfiehlt (Lk 23,45f.). Wichtiger noch ist die Parallele Apg 5,31. Gegenüber dem Synedrium heißt es da im Munde der Apostel von Jesus: »Diesen hat Gott als Anführer und Retter zu seiner Rechten[46] erhöht, um Israel Buße und Vergebung der Sünden zu verleihen« (vgl. Apg 13,38; 26,18, ferner Apg 2,25-28). So dürfte es in 7,60 um Jesus als den priesterlichen Interzessor gehen, und daß dabei nicht allein Vergebung hinsichtlich der Steinigung des Stephanus, sondern gerade auch hinsichtlich der Tötung Jesu im Blick ist, läßt der zuletzt berührte Zusammenhang Apg 5,30-33 erkennen und bestimmt auch den rückwärtigen Kontext von 7,60; denn kaum anders als in Kap. 5 kommt es hier im Anschluß einerseits an den kurz vor Ende der Stephanusrede geäußerten Vorwurf der Ermordung Jesu (7,52) und im Anschluß andererseits an den Verweis auf den seinen priesterlichen Platz zur Rechten Gottes einnehmenden Erhöhten (7,55f.) zu einer

---

und findet es in 4Q 400 1 I,20 und II,4 sowie in 4Q 400 2,4 Entsprechungen (vgl. NEWSOM, *Songs*, S. 106).

43. Vgl. H.W. ATTRIDGE, *The Epistle to the Hebrews. A Commentary on the Epistle to the Hebrews* (Hermeneia), Philadelphia, PA, 1989, S. 102 samt Anm. 260, und K. BERGER, *Theologiegeschichte des Urchristentums. Theologie des Neuen Testaments*, Tübingen – Basel, ²1995, S. 163f. (und 404f.). Vgl. u. bei Anm. 53-55; ferner C.H.T. FLETCHER-LOUIS, *Luke-Acts: Angels, Christology and Soteriology* (WUNT, 2/94), Tübingen, 1997, S. 246 (»angelomorphic state« des Erhöhten).

44. Vgl. W. FOERSTER, Art. σατανᾶς *(A. Qumran und die spätjüdische Satanologie, B. Satan im Neuen Testament)*, in *TWNT*, 7 (1964), S. 152-164, 154.156f. (vgl. u. bei Anm. 52).

45. Vgl. nur TestLev 18,(6-)10(-11); 2 Bar 4; TestDan 5,12f.; Offb 2,7 (in Verbindung mit 21,22–22,4, bes. 22,2).

46. S. dazu o. Anm. 37.

massiven ablehnenden Reaktion der auf ihre Vergebungsbedürftigkeit hin Angesprochenen (7,57-59a).

Die These, bei der Stephanusvision sei der himmlische Tempel und in ihm insbesondere Jesus als priesterlicher Interzessor im Blick[47], läßt sich auch durch diachrone Erwägungen stützen[48]. Da Vollständigkeit hier natürlich nicht einmal angestrebt werden kann, müssen einige wenige Hinweise auf die traditionsgeschichtliche Einbettung wichtiger in Apg 7,54ff. begegnender Motive reichen. Daß die Vorstellung von einer Korrespondenz von irdischem und himmlischem Heiligtum nicht unvorbereitet ist[49], läßt der Kontext unserer Passage, läßt die Stephanusrede selbst insofern erkennen, als sie dafür in 7,44 auf Ex 25 (V. 9 und 40) zurückgreift; an weiteren Parallelen für dieses Entsprechungskonzept seien Weish 9,8 und Hebr 9 (bes. V. 24) genannt[50]. Die δόξα Gottes oder doch die auf Gott verweisende δόξα bestimmt z.b. nach 3(1) Kön 8,11 und Hebr 9,5 das irdische, nach Weish 9,10 und Offb 15,8 das himmlische Heiligtum[51]. Einen Platz auf der bevorzugten rechten Seite kann, wie 2 Chr 6,24 zeigt, für Kultpersonal am irdischen Heiligtum genannt werden, und erst recht gilt das nach Ausweis etwa von Ez 10,3 und TestAbr A 12,8.12 dort, wo nicht eigentlich oder nicht nur der irdische Tempel interessiert, sondern die Umgebung Gottes geschaut wird (vgl. Sach 4,3.14; Lk 1,11; AscJes 9,35f.)[52]. Schon die zuletzt erwähnten Stellen lassen erkennen, daß von diensttuenden Priestern gerade ein

---

47. Vgl. Eb. NESTLE, *The Vision of Stephen*, in *ExpT* 22 (1910/11), S. 423; MUSSNER, *Wohnung*, bes. S. 288f. (s. dazu o. bei Anm. 22); A.M. SCHWEMER, *Irdischer und himmlischer König. Beobachtungen zur sogenannten David-Apokalypse in Hekhalot Rabbati §§122-126*, in M. HENGEL – A.M. SCHWEMER (eds.), *Königsherrschaft Gottes und himmlischer Kult im Judentum, Urchristentum und in der hellenistischen Welt* (WUNT, 55), Tübingen, 1991, S. 309-359, 356; ATTRIDGE, *Hebrews*, S. 102 samt Anm. 260.

48. *Ibid.*, S. 97-103.192-195.

49. Vgl. dazu vor allem H. BIETENHARD, *Die himmlische Welt im Urchristentum und Spätjudentum* (WUNT, 2), Tübingen, 1951, bes. S. 123-137.192-204, und B. EGO, *Im Himmel wie auf Erden. Studien zum Verhältnis von himmlischer und irdischer Welt im rabbinischen Judentum* (WUNT, 2/34), Tübingen, 1989, bes. S. 1-16, ferner NEWSOM, *Songs*, bes. S. 23-58.77-80. Was den vorderorientalischen und alttestamentlichen Hintergrund angeht, sei lediglich verwiesen auf M. METZGER, *Himmlische und irdische Wohnstatt Jahwes*, in *Ugarit Forschungen* 2 (1970) 139-158.

50. Vgl. ferner z.B. Offb 11,1.19; 14,17; 15,5 sowie 8,1-3 und 21,2–22,5 – und dazu M. BACHMANN, *Himmlisch: Der 'Tempel Gottes' von Apk 11,1*, in *NTS* 40 (1994) 474-480.

51. Vgl. o. bei Anm. 41.

52. Im rabbinischen Schrifttum kann Michael, hier oft als (fürbittender) himmlischer Hohepriester gezeichnet (s. dazu B. EGO, *Der Diener im Palast des himmlischen Königs. Zur Interpretation einer priesterlichen Tradition im rabbinischen Judentum*, in HENGEL – SCHWEMER, *Königsherrschaft*, S. 361-384, 361-372), zur Rechten des göttlichen Throns plaziert werden; s. dazu nur H.L. STRACK – P. BILLERBECK, *Kommentar zum Neuen Testament aus Talmud und Midrasch*, München, 1922-1928, III, S. 806f.

Stehen ausgesagt wird und auch von in priesterlicher Funktion am
himmlischen Heiligtum wirkenden Gestalten – von Engeln[53]; an weiteren Belegen seien zum einen Dtn 18,7; Jer 35(28),5; Jdt 4,14 und Hebr
10,11 aufgeführt, zum anderen 4Q 401 1-2,3 (vgl. 4Q 400 2,5; 405 23
I,2.6; 405 23 II,7f.); 11Q 13 (Melch) II,10 (vgl. Ps 82,1) und Offb 8,2f.
(vgl. Sach 3,7; Dan 7,10; 12,1). Ähnlich wie der irdische priesterliche
Dienst z.B. nach Lev 16,24 und Hebr 5,3 dem Volk zugutekommt (vgl.
Jes 53,12), kann im Frühjudentum der priesterliche Dienst himmlischer
Gestalten im Sinne der *intercessio*, des Eintretens bei Gott für Menschen, gezeichnet werden[54], so etwa in 2 Makk 15,12(-14); 1 Hen 15,2
und Offb 8,3f.; im Neuen Testament begegnet diese Vorstellung
bekanntlich gerade auch im Blick auf den erhöhten Christus, so zumal in
Röm 8,34; 1 Petr 3,21f.; Hebr 7,25 und 9,24 (vgl. 1 Joh 2,1f.)[55]. Abgeschlossen seien diese fragmentarischen diachronen Bemerkungen mit
der Bezugnahme auf eine Visionsszene, die – abgesehen von der Ortsbestimmung »zur Rechten« (vgl. nochmals den für das Urchristentum
so wichtigen Vers Ps 109[110],1) – alle soeben angesprochenen Züge in
sich vereint, insofern also eine besonders enge Parallele zur Stephanusvision darstellt, zumal hier überdies auch von der Öffnung *der* Himmel
gesprochen wird (TestLev 2,6; vgl. Apg 7,56). Es handelt sich um Test-
Lev 2–5. Levi sieht hier nicht nur im obersten Himmel ἡ μεγάλη δόξα
ἐν ἁγίῳ ἁγίων (3,4; vgl. 5,1) und sich selbst nahe bei Gott stehend und
diensttuend (2,10); außerdem ist auch vom himmlischen Priesterdienst
als einem interzessorischen die Rede (3,5; 5,6f.).

Die Berührungen mit der, wie wir soeben sahen, ohnehin traditionsgeschichtlich alles andere als isolierten Stephanusvision sind so erheb-

---

53. Vgl. G. BERTRAM – B. REICKE, Art. *παρίστημι, παριστάνω* (*B. Septuaginta –
C. Das Neue Testament – D. Die Apostolischen Väter*), in *TWNT*, 5 (1954), S. 836f. 838-
840; W. GRUNDMANN, Art. *ἵστημι*, in *TWNT*, 7 (1964), S. 637-652, bes. 642.645f.649f.;
A.M. SCHWEMER, *Gott als König und seine Königsherrschaft in den Sabbatliedern aus
Qumran*, in HENGEL – SCHWEMER, *Königsherrschaft*, S. 45-118, 83 samt Anm. 114;
sowie EGO, *Diener*, S. 366-375 samt Anm. 71; ferner, was Apg 7,55f. angeht, NESTLE,
Vision, S. 423 (»suggestion that the standing signifies Christ as the priest in the heavenly
temple«). Hinsichtlich des himmlischen Stehens (zur Rechten Gottes) sind auch rabbini-
sche Formulierungen von Interesse, so bHag 15a: s. dazu M. HENGEL, *Psalm 110 und die
Erhöhung des Auferstandenen zur Rechten Gottes*, in C. BREYTENBACH – H. PAULSEN
(eds.), *Anfänge der Christologie. FS Ferdinand Hahn*, Göttingen, 1991, S. 43-73, 64f.
54. S. dazu nur ATTRIDGE, *Hebrews*, S. 99f.102f., und EGO, *Diener*, S. 368-381, wobei
im Blick auf Apg 5,31 der Zug des himmlischen Eintretens Michaels für Israel (S.
371.373; vgl. Dan 12,1) von besonderem Interesse ist und hinsichtlich der Kennzeichnung Jesu, des (dann) visionär Wahrgenommenen, als ὁ δίκαιος in Apg 7,52 und 22,14
(vgl. V. 17f.) festgehalten zu werden verdient, daß Menschen aufgrund von Entrückung
(Henoch, Mose und Elia) bzw. als Gerechte mit dem Kult am oberen Heiligtum verbunden werden (S. 372-381; vgl. Offb 6,9-11; 7,14f.; 11,1).
55. Vgl. o. bei Anm. 43-45.

lich, daß nun aufgrund dieser diachronen und aufgrund der zuvor gesammelten synchronen Daten der Schluß unumgänglich ist: Lukas will in
Apg 7,54ff. tatsächlich von einem Blick ins himmlische Heiligtum und
von Jesus als Priester bzw. Hohempriester[56] reden. Bezogen auf die
gesamte Stephanusepisode, ergibt sich damit zunächst, daß in der Vision
des Märtyrers das zu Ende geführt wird, was in den beiden vorangegangenen Visionen auf den Weg gebracht wurde: nämlich erstens in der das
Land Israel – und damit die jerusalemische Gottesdienststätte – betreffenden, Abraham widerfahrenen Vision von 7,2ff., in der ihm »der Gott
der Herrlichkeit« (und das heißt wohl auch: das himmlische Heiligtum)
sichtbar geworden war, und zweitens in der Mosevision von 7,30-35
(vgl. V. 38), die den Gesetzgeber, 7,44 zufolge, nicht zuletzt das himmlische Urbild des irdischen Heiligtums sehen ließ[57]. Dieser Konnex zeigt
darüber hinaus, wie Lukas den Vorwurf beantwortet wissen will, Stephanus habe gerade auch gegen Gott und »diese (heilige) Stätte« agitiert
(6,11.13f.). Daß die – ja ohnehin als Verleumdung charakterisierte –
Beschuldigung nicht zu halten ist, wird nicht zuletzt mit der in der
Vision zum Ausdruck kommenden Aufnahme der Vorstellung von der
Entsprechung zwischen irdischem und himmlischem Heiligtum verdeut-
licht. Zugleich kann dieser Anklagepunkt nun mit der Stephanusvision –
ähnlich wie in 7,51-53 bereits der auf das Gesetz bezügliche – gegen die
Ankläger selbst gewandt werden[58]. Nicht nur, daß sie, wie schon
während der Rede angedeutet, die von Gott für das »Haus Jakob« berei-
tete (s. nochmals 7,46f.; vgl. V. 4b.7bβ) gottesdienstliche Stätte, den

---

56. In der Visionsszene MartPol 14, deren Formulierung offenkundig an Apg 7,54ff.
anknüpft, spielt denn auch nicht nur die Vorstellung vom Opfer (V. 1f.) und von den Gott
umgebenden himmlischen Gestalten (bes. V. 1) eine Rolle, sondern es heißt da auch im
Munde des zu Gott betenden Märtyrers: σὲ δοξάζω διὰ τοῦ αἰωνίου καὶ ἐπουρανίου
ἀρχιερέως Ἰησοῦ Χριστοῦ (V. 3).
57. Beide Visionen sind im übrigen traditionsgeschichtlich verknüpft, wie insbesondere die o. Anm. 41 (und 45) genannte Stelle 2 Bar 4,4f. schließen läßt, nach der nämlich
Mose eben das in einer Vision gezeigt wurde (vgl. nur Hebr 3,5; 8,5), was schon Abraham offenbart worden war (vgl. nur Hebr 11,10.13)! Der Zusammenhang deutet sich in
der Stephanusrede insofern an, als die Abraham geltende Verheißung in 7,7bβ, wie
erwähnt, gerade mit Worten aus der Geschichte von der Berufung Moses, genauer: mit
Worten aus Ex 3,12, zum Ausdruck gebracht wird.
58. Insofern entspricht die Nachordnung der Stephanusvision recht genau dem, wie in
Mk 14,55ff. (vgl. nochmals Barn 16,1-10, ferner Josephus, Bell 5,458f.) auf den an Jesus
gerichteten – in Lk 22,66ff. fehlenden, jedoch in Apg 6,14 vorausgesetzten – Tempel-
Vorwurf das Wort vom »zur Rechten der Macht« sitzenden Menschensohn folgt (Mk
14,62; vgl. Lk 22,69). Aber daß in Apg 7,55f. (anders auch als in Lk 22,69) vom Stehen
des Erhöhten die Rede ist, bildet doch eine wichtige Differenz. Vermutlich geht für Lukas
im übrigen sachlich und zeitlich das Stehen des Erhöhten seinem Sitzen voraus, ähnlich
wie das in AscJes 9 (bes. V. 27.36f.) und 10 (V. 10) der Fall ist (vgl. 1 Hen 69,[26-]29,
ferner o. bei Anm. 37).

jerusalemischen Tempel, fälschlich für den Wohnort Gottes halten
mögen (s. nochmals 7,48-50); indem sie, die den gerechten Jesus getö-
tet haben (s. 7,52), die Aussage der Stephanusvision über den himmlischen Tempel und den dort priesterlich amtierenden Erhöhten mit der
Steinigung des Visionärs verwerfen, haben sie sogar zum urbildlichen
Heiligtum ein falsches Verhältnis, agieren sie selbst und agitiert eben
nicht Stephanus gegen Gott und Tempel.

IV

Soviel scheint darum gesagt werden zu können: Der jerusalemische
Tempel wird von Lukas einerseits als eine gottgewollte Institution des
jüdischen Gottesdienstes respektiert; andererseits wird die Möglichkeit
des Mißverständnisses dieser Einrichtung und damit ihres Mißbrauchs
zum Ausdruck gebracht[59]. Darüber hinaus ist deutlich, daß der Erhöhte,
der erhöhte Interzessor, ein wichtiges Kriterium des lukanischen Urtei-
lens abgibt.
Ist das Antijudaismus? Kaum[60]! Anders als in Barn 16,1-10 kommt es
gerade nicht zu einer Mißbilligung des jerusalemischen Tempels selbst.
Und wie die Stephanusrede auf dem Hintergrund des deuteronomisti-
schen Schemas vom gewaltsamen Geschick der Propheten (vgl. nur Neh
9,6-37, bes. V. 26) als eine Fortsetzung einer innerjüdischen Argumentation gelesen werden kann[61], ist das auch für 7,54ff. möglich[62]. Wie
analoge Visionstexte, z.B. TestLev 2–5, leistet es nämlich auch die Stephanusvision, innerhalb eines weiteren Spektrums kultischer Auffassungen die spezifische Sicht einer Gruppe zu legitimieren[63]. Das ist jeden-

---

59. Vgl. HAACKER, *Stephanus*, S. 1536-1539, dessen Formulierung, daß »die Stephanusrede... weithin als eine *Bestätigung der Anklage*« (S. 1539) zu begreifen sei, m.E.
indes zu weit geht (vgl. o. bei Anm. 16).

60. Der durch die Vorstellung vom himmlischen Heiligtum ermöglichten Dialektik
entspricht wohl auch Mussners Deutung nicht hinreichend: Es »wird das christliche
Kerygma von der Erhöhung des Menschensohnes Jesus zum himmlischen Throngenossen
Gottes in polemischer Weise gegen den bisherigen 'heiligen Ort' Gottes, den Tempel zu
Jerusalem, eingesetzt, was auch impliziert: Gott hat 'diesen heiligen Ort' endgültig ver-
lassen« (*Wohnung*, S. 288).

61. S. dazu nur M. SALMON, *Insider or Outsider? Luke's Relationship with Judaism*,
in J.B. TYSON (ed.), *Luke-Acts and the Jewish People*, Minneapolis, MN, 1988, S. 76-82,
77f., und HAACKER, *Stephanus*, S. 1540 (samt Anm. 92) sowie 1542-1544, bes. 1544
(samt Anm. 110).

62. Auch hier dürfte – in der Terminologie des in der vorigen Anm. genannten Aufsatzes von Salmon geredet – eher eine insider- als eine outsider-Perspektive vorliegen.
Vgl. zu dieser Fragestellung auch STEGEMANN, *Diskussion*, S. 215-219, bes. 218f.

63. S. dazu B. OTZEN, *Heavenly Visions in Early Judaism: Origin and Function*, in
W.B. BARRICK – J.R. SPENCER (eds.), *In the Shelter of Elyon*. FS Gösta Werner Ahlström

falls so lange kein Antijudaismus, wie es nicht zu einer Bestreitung positiver Perspektiven für die jüdische Gemeinschaft kommt. Neben anderem zeigt der an den Interzessor gerade auch Israels (s. nochmals Apg 5,31 und vgl. TestLev 5,6) gerichtete Vergebungsruf von 7,60 an, daß Lukas von einer solchen Bestreitung weit entfernt ist. Dagegen wird man schwerlich einwenden dürfen, daß in 8,1 Judäa und Samaria genannt werden und daß damit auch Heidenchristen in den Blick gelangen (s. nur 1,8; 8,26ff.; 10,1ff.). Denn »Heiden« spielen wohl auch in TestLev 4,1.4 (vgl. 8,14, auch 2,10) eine Rolle (vgl. Ps 109[110],1ff.), und die in Lk 21,24 gebrauchte Formulierung klingt – zumal wenn man Aussagen wie 2 Bar 6,9 (oder PsSal 17,30f., ferner Offb 11,2; Josephus, Bell 5,19) vergleicht – so, als ob die »Zeiten der ʿHeidenʾ« im Sinne der Bedrückung Jerusalems und der Judenschaft ein Ende haben sollten[64]. In Lk 2,36-38 ist der Tempelgottesdienst denn ja auch ohne Einschränkung mit der Hoffnung auf eine künftige λύτρωσις ʿΙερουσαλήμ und »Israels« (s. Lk 1,68; 2,25) verbunden[65], und nach dem Schlußkapitel des lukanischen Werks trägt der inhaftierte Paulus seine Kette eben »wegen der Hoffnung Israels« (Apg 28,20).

Universität-Gesamthochschule Siegen   Michael BACHMANN
Adolf-Reichwein-Str. 2
D-57068 Siegen

(JSOT SS, 31), Sheffield, 1984, S. 199-215, 206-210, bes. 209, und NEWSOM, *Songs*, S. 65-72, bes. 71. Vgl. auch D.E. AUNE, *The Cultic Setting of Realized Eschatology in Early Christianity* (NTSup, 28), Leiden, 1972, S. 90-95 (bes. 93: »Each of these formal features of Stephen's vision – pneumatic inspiration, the vision of the open heavens, the Son of man as the essential object of the vision and the transformation of the seer – points to the origin of this prophetic vision in a cultic setting«); J. MAIER, *Beobachtungen zum Konfliktpotential in neutestamentlichen Aussagen über den Tempel*, in I. BROER (ed.), *Jesus und das jüdische Gesetz*, Stuttgart, 1992, S. 173-212, 207 (Apg 7,55f. »ist das frühchristliche Bekenntnis kulttheologisch auf den kritischen Punkt gebracht«); BERGER, *Theologiegeschichte*, S. 163 (»Act 6–8 ist... eine Kultätiologie der antiochenischen Christen«).

64. Vgl. dazu J.B. CHANCE, *Jerusalem, the Temple, and the New Age in Luke-Acts*, Macon, GA, 1988, S. 134f. 151; H.-M. DÖPP, *Die Deutung der Zerstörung Jerusalems und des Zweiten Tempels im Jahre 70 in den ersten drei Jahrhunderten n.Chr.* (TANZ, 24), Tübingen, 1998, S. 45f.; H.-J. KLAUCK, *Die heilige Stadt. Jerusalem bei Philo und Lukas*, in ID., *Gemeinde-Amt-Sakrament*, Würzburg, 1989, S. 101-129 (zuerst: 1986), bes. 128 (mit Hinweis auf Act 3,20f.); ferner die 1988 abgeschlossene Heidelberger Dissertation von M. HOFFMANN, *Das eschatologische Heil Israels nach den lukanischen Schriften*, hier bes. S. 72.

65. S. dazu BACHMANN, *Jerusalem*, S. 336-369, bes. 335-340.368.

DU FILS DE L'HOMME ASSIS (LC 22,69)
AU FILS DE L'HOMME DEBOUT (AC 7,56)

ENJEUX THÉOLOGIQUE ET LITTÉRAIRE D'UN
CHANGEMENT SÉMANTIQUE

Le NT nous a habitués à exprimer l'exaltation du Ressuscité à la droite de Dieu en termes de session. Par rapport à cet usage, la double mention[1] de la présence de Jésus (aussi appelé «Fils de l'homme») debout à la droite de Dieu en Ac 7,55-56 est étonnante: Ἰησοῦν ἑστῶτα ἐκ δεξιῶν τοῦ θεοῦ (v. 55); τὸν υἱὸν τοῦ ἀνθρώπου ἐκ δεξιῶν ἑστῶτα τοῦ θεοῦ (v. 56). Elle est reconnue comme une *crux interpretum*. Si l'imagination des exégètes a donné une foison d'interprétations de ce déconcertant ἑστῶτα, de guerre lasse peut-être, plusieurs exégètes récents tendent à décréter insignifiante cette variation dans l'usage habituel.

Il s'agit là d'une solution de désespoir. L'idée a été défendue que la vision du Fils de l'homme debout en Ac 7,56 correspondrait à une interprétation de l'exaltation du Christ antérieure à celle qui est devenue ensuite stéréotypée par utilisation du Ps 110,1 (Fils de l'homme assis)[2]; ceci ne paraît pas fondé si on tient compte de l'ensemble de la double œuvre lucanienne. Luc, en effet, connaît bien le Ps 110 qu'il cite explicitement en Lc 20,42-43 et qu'il utilise à plus d'une reprise, mais notamment lors du procès de Jésus en Lc 22,69 dans une formule inspirée de Mc 14,62. Si, dans le procès parallèle d'Étienne, il passe d'une session à la droite de Dieu à la position debout du Fils de l'homme, ce n'est pas l'effet d'un hasard. Une telle explication ferait fi de l'art du récit lucanien.

L'interprétation d'Ac 7,55-56 s'est peut-être trop orientée dans le passé vers la recherche d'une explication génétique, par le recours à des parallèles bibliques ou issus de la culture de l'époque. Je dresserai un bref inventaire critique des diverses solutions proposées. Après quoi je

---

1. La répétition sur deux versets de cette posture inhabituelle la met particulièrement en valeur, comme le souligne, après bien d'autres, R. PESCH, *Die Apostelgeschichte (Apg 1–12)* (EKK, 5/1), Zürich – Neukirchen-Vluyn, 1986, p. 263.

2. Ainsi, W. GRUNDMANN, *Die Apostel zwischen Jerusalem und Antiochia*, in ZNW 39 (1940) 110-137, voir p. 118. G. SCHILLE, *Die Apostelgeschichte des Lukas* (THNT, 5), Berlin, 1983, p. 188, rappelle qu'à l'époque le Credo n'était pas fermement établi et pense que ce détail déroutant permet peut-être de mesurer l'ancienneté de la tradition reprise par Luc.

risquerai à mon tour une interprétation qui se fondera avant tout sur l'art littéraire de Luc et la conviction que des variations sémantiques de détail dans une structure identique s'expliquent dès lors qu'on resitue tous les éléments de l'œuvre dans la progression au fil du récit et dans la pensée théologique de l'ensemble.

I. HISTOIRE DE L'INTERPRÉTATION

La présentation critique la plus élaborée est celle de R. Pesch[3] qui distingue dix interprétations. Je propose de les ramener à cinq grandes catégories elles-même subdivisées. Selon les deux premières explications, la position «debout» pourrait correspondre à une volonté d'accueillir le martyr ou encore de servir Dieu dans la cour céleste. Un troisième type d'explication recourt à la portée eschatologique du logion. Selon le quatrième, la mention «debout» relèverait du vocabulaire des procédures judiciaires. Enfin, elle pourrait s'avérer sans signification particulière.

1. Debout pour accueillir Étienne le martyr

C'est une des plus anciennes interprétations connues. On la trouve dans les scolies d'Oecumenius sur les homélies de Jean Chrysostome, qui déjà s'étonne: τί οὖν ἑστῶτα καὶ οὐχὶ καθήμενον; ἵνα δείξῃ τὴν ἀντίληψιν τὴν εἰς τὸν μάρτυρα[4]. C'est aussi une des plus couramment reprises par les exégètes[5]. À son encontre, S. Légasse fait remarquer qu'a priori on peut aussi bien accueillir assis que debout[6].

---

3. R. PESCH, *Die Vision der Stephanus* (SBS, 12), Stuttgart, 1966, pp. 13-36. Voir aussi M. SABBE, *The Son of Man Saying in Acts 7,56*, in J. KREMER (ed.), *Les Actes des Apôtres. Traditions, rédaction, théologie* (BETL, 48), Gembloux-Leuven, 1979, pp. 241-279, voir pp. 267-277. J.D.M. DERRETT, *The Son of Man Standing (Acts 7,55-56)*, in *Bibbia e Oriente* 30 (1988) 71-84, voir pp. 75-77, recense pour sa part douze interprétations.

4. Cité dans J.A. CRAMER (ed.), *Catenae Graecorum Patrum in Novum Testamentum*, III. *Catena in Acta SS. Apostolorum e cod. nov. coll.*, Hildesheim, 1967, p. 128.

5. É. JACQUIER, *Les Actes des Apôtres* (ÉB), Paris, 1926, p. 236 (qui cite d'ailleurs le texte de Jean Chrysostome); K. LAKE – H. CADBURY, *The Acts of the Apostles*, in F.J. FOAKES JACKSON – K. LAKE, *The Beginnings of Christianity*, IV, London, 1933, pp. 4 et 84; G. STÄHLIN, *Die Apostelgeschichte* (NTD), Göttingen, 1963, p. 113 (citant la formule de prière «reçois mon esprit» du v. 59 à l'appui de son interprétation); E. GRÄSSER, *Die Parusieerwartung in der Apostelgeschichte*, in J. KREMER (ed.), *Les Actes des Apôtres* (n. 3), pp. 99-127, voir p. 110; J. PLEVNIK, *Son of Man Seated at the Right Hand of God: Luke 22,69 in Lucan Christology*, in *Bib* 72 (1991) 331-347, voir p. 340, n. 31.

6. S. LÉGASSE, *Stephanos. Histoire et discours d'Étienne dans les Actes des Apôtres* (LD, 147), Paris, 1992, p. 137.

2. Debout pour servir Dieu dans la cour céleste

Si l'interprétation précédente est une des plus courantes, celle-ci paraît assez marginale. Quelques auteurs interprètent la station debout du Fils de l'homme à partir de la position d'hommes ou d'anges qui sont debout devant Dieu en signe de respect et de service[7]. C.K. Barrett fait remarquer que, même si tel pouvait être le sens d'une tradition primitive, ce n'est sûrement pas le cas au plan de la rédaction finale, dans le contexte[8]. M. Sabbe note à juste titre le manque de trace d'une christologie angélique[9]. Il est approuvé par S. Légasse, qui ajoute que les anges servants se tiennent normalement devant Dieu et non à sa droite[10].

3. Debout dans un sens eschatologique

Parmi ceux qui estiment que la mention «debout» trouve son sens dans un cadre de pensée eschatologique, il est possible de distinguer trois options:

a. Position intermédiaire entre «assis» et «revenant»

H.P. Owen fonde son opinion sur l'examen de l'ensemble de l'œuvre lucanienne conçue comme un parcours en six étapes[11]. Selon lui, les trois premières, à savoir a. la mort de Jésus comme ἔξοδος (Lc 9,31), départ de ce monde; b. l'entrée dans (εἰσελθεῖν, Lc 24,26) sa gloire lors de la résurrection; c. sa réception au ciel (ἀναλαμβάνεσθαι, Ac 1,2.11.22) quarante jours après sa résurrection, marquent le sommet du ministère terrestre de Jésus. Les trois dernières, par contre, concernent son exaltation et son retour: d. au ciel, il est assis (καθῆσθαι, Lc 20,42; 22,69; Ac 2,34) à la droite de Dieu; e. Étienne le voit debout (ἱστάναι, Ac 7,55-56) à la droite de Dieu; f. il reviendra (ἔρχεσθαι, Lc 9,26; 12,36-38, 18,8; 19,23, 21,27; Ac 1,11) finalement en gloire pour juger le monde. Cela fait apparaître que ἑστῶτα est situé entre καθήμενον

---

7. O. BAUERNFEIND, *Die Apostelgeschichte* (THNT, 5), Leipzig, 1939, p. 120; H.E. TÖDT, *Der Menschensohn in der synoptischen Überlieferung*, Gütersloh, 1959, p. 274. Cette possibilité est évoquée avec deux autres, sans prise de position, par E. HAENCHEN, *Die Apostelgeschichte* (KEK, 3), Göttingen, 1961, p. 243. Dans une perspective proche, H.W. SURKAU, *Martyrien in jüdischer und frühchristlicher Zeit* (FRLANT, 54), Göttingen, 1938, p. 117 n. 50, pense pouvoir déceler dans la position «debout» du Fils de l'homme la trace d'une christologie subordinationiste.

8. C.K. BARRETT, *Stephen and the Son of Man*, in W. ELTESTER – F.H. KETTLER (ed.), *Apophoreta. FS E. Haenchen* (BZNW, 30), Berlin, 1964, p. 33.

9. M. SABBE, *The Son of Man* (n. 3), p. 268.

10. S. LÉGASSE, *Stephanos* (n. 6), p. 137. Sans explication, G. SCHNEIDER, *Die Apostelgeschichte* (n. 16), p. 475, n. 26, estime l'interprétation de Tödt peu vraisemblable.

11. H.P. OWEN, *Stephen's Vision in Acts VII. 55-6*, in *NTS* 1 (1954-55) 224-226.

(d) et ἐρχόμενον (f), ce qui lui donne sa signification particulière: «Christ rises in preparation to his Parousia. The Son of Man in Stephen's vision is the Christ who is about to return»[12]. La vision d'Étienne est donc proleptique: il voit d'avance le Fils de l'homme sur le point de revenir investi de la gloire du Père. Cette vision apporte une réponse au problème du délai de la parousie, puisqu'elle montre que le Fils de l'homme est déjà prêt à revenir. Bien qu'adoptée par quelques auteurs[13], l'hypothèse de H.P. Owen paraît peu probable[14]. Le motif le plus important est que la construction en six étapes ne reflète pas la construction du double récit lucanien, mais une reconstitution à partir de mots isolés puisés en divers endroits de ce récit, sans respecter son ordre. Par ailleurs, cette hypothèse ne semble guère représenter la position eschatologique de Luc[15], chez qui le rôle de juge joué par le Fils de l'homme n'est en tout cas pas accentué[16].

b. Pas encore assis

C'est l'inverse de la proposition d'Owen, pour qui la vision du Fils de l'homme debout préluderait à son retour en gloire. Selon W. Kelly[17], en effet, si le Fils de l'homme est debout, c'est parce qu'il n'est pas encore temps pour lui de s'asseoir. La position assise est celle du juge. Si Jésus ne s'est pas encore assis à la droite de Dieu, mais s'y tient debout, c'est parce qu'un délai de grâce est octroyé aux juifs. Mais Étienne les presse de prendre rapidement leur décision. L'hypothèse de Kelly n'a pas été suivie; elle n'est appuyée par aucun indice textuel au niveau du discours d'Étienne ou du récit de son martyre.

c. Parousie privée en faveur du témoin à sa mort

Cette interprétation a été proposée par C.K. Barrett[18] qui renouvelait ainsi l'interprétation de l'accueil du martyr[19]. Il est parti de deux ques-

---

12. H.P. OWEN, *Stephen* (n. 11), p. 225.
13. M. SIMON, *St. Stephen and the Hellenists in the Primitive Church*, London, 1956, pp. 70-71 (qui concilie l'explication de Owen avec celle de l'accueil du martyr); J. DUPONT, *Études sur les Actes des Apôtres* (LD, 45), Paris, 1967, pp. 293-294.
14. Elle est rejetée par M. GOURGUES, *À la droite de Dieu. Résurrection de Jésus et actualisation du Ps 110,1 dans le Nouveau Testament* (ÉB), Paris, 1978, pour des raisons qui ne me semblent pas totalement convaincantes.
15. C.K. BARRETT, *Stephen* (n. 8), p. 34; A.J.B. HIGGINS, *Jesus and the Son of Man*, London, 1964, pp. 145-146.
16. G. SCHNEIDER, *Die Apostelgeschichte* (HTKNT, 5/1), Freiburg, 1980, p. 475, n. 31.
17. W. KELLY, *An Exposition of the Acts of the Apostles*, London, ³1952, pp. 102-103.
18. C.K. BARRETT, *Stephen* (n. 8), pp. 32-38.
19. Voir ci-dessus la première interprétation.

tions: pourquoi Étienne est-il, dans le NT, le seul personnage en dehors de Jésus à employer l'expression «Fils de l'homme»[20] et pourquoi en parle-t-il comme «debout» et non «assis»? Sa réponse est que dans la perspective lucanienne la mort de chaque chrétien constitue pour cette personne un ἔσχατον individuel. Il est donc normal qu'Étienne, le seul chrétien fidèle dont la mort soit racontée dans les Actes, bénéficie d'une parousie privée, personnelle. Le Fils de l'homme est debout parce qu'il est sur le point de venir à sa rencontre[21]. Cette interprétation n'a guère eu de succès, car la perspective d'une parousie privée en faveur du chrétien mourant n'est pas clairement attestée chez Luc et il n'y a en tout cas aucun indice de son expression en Ac 7,55-56[22]. De plus, on y parle du Fils de l'homme debout et non venant vers son témoin, comme cela s'imposerait dans le cas d'une parousie[23].

4. Debout dans le cadre des procédures judiciaires

Dans le vocabulaire des procédures judiciaires, quatre type d'acteurs peuvent être mentionnés dans la position debout: l'accusé, l'accusateur, le défenseur, le juge. Il est hors de question que Jésus soit debout à la droite de Dieu dans une situation d'accusé. Mais aucun des trois autres rôles n'est a priori exclu.

a. Juge

Le rejet d'Étienne par le peuple juif, et non seulement par le sanhédrin, marque un clivage décisif entre les disciples de Jésus et le peuple juif. À ce titre, le récit d'Étienne occupe une place importante dans le livre des Actes; il se situe à un tournant dans l'histoire du salut, à savoir au moment du passage de l'Évangile des juifs vers les païens. La position «debout» du Fils de l'homme correspond bien à ce tournant, selon R. Pesch[24]. Il avance les textes de Is 3,13-14 et Assomption de Moïse 10,3 pour affirmer que, selon la tradition biblique et juive, le juge divin

---

20. La proposition faite par G.D. KILPATRICK, *Acts vii.56: Son of Man?*, in *BZ* 21 (1965) 209 et *Again Acts vii.56: Son of Man?*, in *BZ* 34 (1978) 232, de lire τοῦ θεοῦ au lieu de τοῦ ἀνθρώπου repose sur une base textuelle trop fragile (P[74] 491 614 et quelques mss coptes ou géorgiens) pour être prise en compte.

21. G. SCHNEIDER, *Die Apostelgeschichte* (n. 16), p. 474, semble séduit par cette interprétation, mais lui préfère finalement celle du Fils de l'homme défenseur de son martyr.

22. J. DUPONT, *L'après-mort dans l'œuvre de Luc*, in *RTL* 3 (1972) 3-21, voir p. 21, n. 66; M. SABBE, *The Son of Man* (n. 3), p. 268.

23. Critique émise par M. SABBE, *The Son of Man* (n. 3), p. 269; S. LÉGASSE, *Stephanos* (n. 6), pp. 137-138.

24. R. PESCH, *Die Vision* (n. 3), pp. 37-58.

est en position assise pour juger les païens, mais debout pour juger les pécheurs de son peuple. Le Fils de l'homme, vu debout par Étienne, est dans cette position parce qu'il juge le peuple juif, suite au réquisitoire que constitue le discours d'Étienne. Si J. Dupont s'est montré favorable à cette opinion[25], elle n'a cependant guère été suivie[26]. Il est, en effet, difficile de parler de tradition à partir des deux seuls textes cités par Pesch, surtout que le sens de l'un des deux n'est pas clair. L'Assomption de Moïse 10,3 présente le Céleste sortant de sa demeure sainte «cum indignationem et iram propter filios suos». Faut-il traduire «propter» par «wegen» ou «gegen» (Pesch[27]) ou par «en faveur de» (Laperrousaz[28])? On peut ajouter qu'en 10,7, Dieu apparaît debout pour juger les nations. D'où l'interprétation de M. Sabbe: «There is no judgment of Israel; God comes with indignation to avenge his own children (10,3) – who preferred to die rather than trespass God's commandments (9,6-7) – upon their enemies (10,2.10) the heathen (10,7)»[29]. Le seul texte clair sur lequel repose l'hypothèse de Pesch est donc Is 3,13-14, ce qui la rend fragile, car dans plusieurs autres textes bibliques Dieu est mentionné debout pour juger les païens[30]. Dans son commentaire ultérieur des Actes[31], R. Pesch est favorable à une solution mixte qui combine cette hypothèse du Fils de l'homme jugeant et condamnant le peuple avec celle du défenseur d'Étienne, selon les deux orientations présentes en Lc 12,8-9.

25. J. DUPONT, «Assis à la droite de Dieu». L'interprétation du Ps 110,1 dans le Nouveau Testament, dans É. DHANIS (ed.), Resurrexit. Actes du Symposium international sur la résurrection de Jésus, Roma, 1974, pp. 340-422, voir pp. 366-368.

26. Contre cette hypothèse, F. MUSSNER, Wohnung Gottes und Menschensohn nach der Stephanusperikope (Apg 6,8–8,2), in R. PESCH – R. SCHNACKENBURG (ed.), Jesus und der Menschensohn. FS A. Vögtle, Freiburg, 1975, pp. 283-299, voir pp. 291-292; M. GOURGUES, À la droite de Dieu (n. 14), pp. 182-183; M. SABBE, The Son of Man (n. 3), pp. 270-272; S. LÉGASSE, Stephanos (n. 6), p. 138.

27. R. PESCH, Die Vision (n. 3), p. 20 traduit «wegen»; mais à la p. 56, il interprète au sens de «gegen».

28. É.-M. LAPERROUSAZ, Le Testament de Moïse, généralement appelé «Assomption de Moïse» (Semitica, 19), Leiden, 1970, p. 127.

29. M. SABBE, The Son of Man (n. 3), p. 271.

30. M. SABBE, The Son of Man (n. 3), p. 271, cite Ps 7,7-9; 9,20; 94,2; 96,13; 98,9; Is 2,19.21; 14,22; 66,15-16. Pour sa part, en conclusion d'une étude approfondie des textes de l'AT, P. BOVATI, Ristabilire la giustizia. Procedure, vocabolario, orientamenti (AnBib, 110), Roma, 1986, pp. 212-218, ne lie pas la position «debout» au jugement soit des juifs, soit des païens. Il pense plutôt que la position «assis» correspond au temps du débat et la position «debout» au moment du verdict. Mais il reconnaît que c'est une interprétation non explicitée par les textes bibliques eux-mêmes.

31. R. PESCH, Die Apostelgeschichte (n. 1), pp. 263-264.

b. Accusateur

Proche de la précédente, cette interprétation[32] accentue le rôle de témoin à charge du Fils de l'homme de préférence à celui de juge. Sur 35 emplois de ἵστημι dans les Actes, 9 mentions apparaissent dans le cadre de procédures judiciaires: 7 pour la comparution d'accusés (4,7; 5,27; 22,30; 24,20; 25,10; 26,6; 27,24) et 2 pour la comparution d'accusateurs (6,13; 25,18). Selon M. Gourgues[33], l'idée du Fils de l'homme comme accusateur correspond bien à Lc 12,9, d'une part; d'autre part, le rôle du Fils de l'homme se situerait alors tout à fait dans la ligne anti-juive du discours d'Étienne. Enfin, cela expliquerait la réaction brutale des auditeurs (7,57). L'hypothèse paraît cependant peu vraisemblable à G. Schneider[34] et Gourgues lui-même préfère la suivante.

c. Avocat de la défense

Le sens du Fils de l'homme avocat céleste, intercesseur, plaidant devant Dieu la cause de son martyr est retenu par de nombreux exégètes[35], d'autant qu'il correspond au rôle du Fils de l'homme en Lc 12,8. L'usage du verbe ἵστημι en ce sens est attesté dans la LXX (Ps 16,8; 109,31; 142,5). On évoque aussi parfois en ce sens l'usage d'une tradition samaritaine[36]. Peu d'objections explicites ont été élevées à l'encontre de cette interprétation[37].

---

32. Elle est affirmée avec force par J.D.M. DERRETT, *The Son of Man* (n. 3), pp. 83-84, en accord avec A. CASALEGNO, *Gesù e il Tempio*, Brescia, 1984, pp. 190-191.

33. M. GOURGUES, *À la droite de Dieu* (n. 14), p. 183.

34. G. SCHNEIDER, *Die Apostelgeschichte* (n. 16), p. 475.

35. GRÉGOIRE LE GRAND: «Sed scitis, fratres, quia sedere judicantis est, stare vero pugnantis vel adjuvantis… Stephanus… in labore certaminis positus stantem vidit quem adjutorem habuit»: cité par É. JACQUIER, *Les Actes des Apôtres* (n. 5), p. 236; T. PREISS, *Life in Christ* (Studies in Biblical Theology, 13), London, 1954, p. 50; O. CULLMANN, *Christologie du Nouveau Testament* (Bibliothèque théologique), Neuchâtel, 1958, p. 136 (témoin à décharge en même temps que juge); E. SCHWEIZER, *Der Menschensohn*, in *ZNW* 50 (1959) 185-209, voir pp. 202-203; A. FEUILLET, *Le triomphe du Fils de l'homme d'après la déclaration du Christ aux Sanhédrites* (Mc., XIV,62; Mt., XXVI,64; Lc., XXII,69), in É. MASSAUX (ed.), *La venue du Messie* (Recherches bibliques, 6), Bruges, 1962, pp. 149-171, voir p. 159, n. 1; C.F.D. MOULE, *From Defendant to Judge and Deliverer. An Enquiry into the Use and Limitations of the them of Vindication in the New Testament*, in *SNTS Bulletin* 3 (1963), pp. 46-47; A.J.B. HIGGINS, *Jesus and the Son of Man* (n. 15), pp. 144-146; M. GOURGUES, *À la droite de Dieu* (n. 14), pp. 183-185 et 193-194; G. SCHNEIDER, *Die Apostelgeschichte* (n. 16), p. 475; T. BAUMEISTER, *Die Anfänge der Theologie des Martyriums* (Münsterische Beiträge zur Theologie, 45), Münster, 1980, p. 128; D.L. BOCK, *Proclamation from Prophecy and Pattern. Lucan Old Testament Christology* (JSNT SS, 12), Sheffield, 1987, p. 224.

36. Voir à ce sujet, par exemple, l'état de la question de M. GOURGUES, *À la droite de Dieu* (n. 14), pp. 183-184.

37. Cependant, C.K. BARRETT, *Stephen* (n. 8), p. 34: «Yet the overall view of Acts

5. «*Debout*» *n'a pas de signification particulière*

De l'avis de nombreux exégètes[38], le participe ἑστῶτα n'aurait pas le sens fort de «debout», mais serait à comprendre au sens faible comme une sorte de synonyme de ὄντα, usage bien attesté dans le grec profane. Quoique tout à fait possible grammaticalement, cette hypothèse se recommande peu, si on tient compte du contexte de la double œuvre lucanienne[39]. D'une part, on peut observer avec Owen[40] que le NT utilise toujours les verbes καθῆσθαι ou καθίζειν ou εἶναι pour parler du Christ à la droite de Dieu et que toutes les allusions au Ps 110,1 ont le verbe καθῆσθαι. Si Luc, le septuagintisant, a évité ce verbe en Ac 7,56, il devait avoir une bonne raison pour ce faire. D'autre part, Luc veut manifestement mettre en parallèle les morts de Jésus et d'Étienne et il aurait été normal qu'il reprenne καθήμενον en Ac 7,56 pour rappeler Lc 22,69[41]. En conclusion, laisser ἑστῶτα sans explication ne fait certainement pas honneur à l'art littéraire de Luc.

II. PROPOSITION SUR BASE DE L'UNITÉ DE L'ŒUVRE LUCANIENNE

À trop chercher l'explication du déconcertant ἑστῶτα de Ac 7,55-56 dans des parallèles bibliques ou extrabibliques, n'a-t-on pas négligé la clé de compréhension essentielle, à savoir la prise en compte de l'unité de la double œuvre lucanienne? Je voudrais explorer celle-ci à partir du parallèle entre les passions de Jésus et d'Étienne. Les questions provenant de cet examen seront éclairées à partir de la théologie lucanienne.

(e.g. 17,31), and of the New Testament generally, is that the Son of man is not witness or advocate but judge». J.D.M. DERRETT, *The Son of Man* (n. 3), pp. 82-83, rejette aussi cette interprétation.

38. G. DALMAN, *Die Worte Jesu*, I, Darmstadt, ²1930, pp. 29-30; C.H. DODD, *According to the Scriptures. The Sub-Structure of New Testament Theology*, London, 1952, p. 35, n. 1; F. MUSSNER, *Wohnung* (n. 26), p. 291; E.J. RICHARD, *Acts 6:1–8:14. The Author's Method of Composition* (SBL DS, 41), Missoula, MT, 1978, pp. 294-299; M. SABBE, *The Son of Man* (n. 3), p. 274; G. SCHILLE, *Die Apostelgeschichte* (n. 2), pp. 188-189; S. LÉGASSE, *Stephanos* (n. 6), pp. 138-140.

39. L'interprétation de M.-É. BOISMARD – A. LAMOUILLE, *Synopse des quatre évangiles en français*, III, Paris, 1977, p. 462, pour qui ἑστῶτα correspondrait à ἀνεστῶτα et signifierait simplement «ressuscité», «vivant» banalise la portée du ἑστῶτα de Ac 7,56. Dans la même ligne qu'eux, voir C. L'ÉPLATTENIER, *Les Actes des Apôtres*, Genève, 1987, p. 99. Une autre interprétation restée marginale est celle de J. BIHLER, *Der Stephanusbericht (Apg 6,8-15 und 7,54–8,2)*, in *BZ* 3 (1959) 252-270, voir pp. 266-267, pour qui le Fils de l'homme serait debout en tant que médiateur, à l'image de Moïse, le médiateur, selon Dt 5,31.

40. H.P. OWEN, *Stephen* (n. 11), p. 224. L'hypothèse de la banalisation de ἑστῶτα est aussi rejetée par A.J.B. HIGGINS, *Jesus* (n. 15), p. 145; C.K. BARRETT, *Stephen* (n. 8), pp. 32-33; G. SCHNEIDER, *Die Apostelgeschichte* (n. 16), p. 474.

41. Dans le même sens, voir J.D.M. DERRETT, *The Son of Man* (n. 3), p. 72.

G. Schneider relève pas moins de 15 parallèles entre Ac 6,10–8,2 et les récits lucaniens et marciens de la passion[42]. Mais il les aligne sans plus. Or, il importe justement d'analyser le fait que les parallèles ne se rapportent pas seulement à Lc, mais aussi à Mc. La comparaison soigneuse établie par Gourgues fait apparaître combien les affinités s'établissent différemment avec les divers récits évangéliques. Je ne peux mieux faire que de reproduire son tableau très précis[43]:

A. Éléments communs à Mt-Mc

1. Faux témoignages contre Jésus (Mt 26,59b.60b; Mc 14,56a.57a).
2. Accusation relative au Temple (Mt 26,61; Mc 14,58).
3. Comportement de l'accusé: silence de Jésus. (Mt 26,63a; Mc 14,61a).
4. Accusation de blasphème (Mt 26,65b; Mc 14,64a).

Parallèles dans Ac

1. Faux témoignages contre Étienne (6,13a).
2. Accusation relative au Temple (6,14a).
3. Comportement de l'accusé: silence extatique d'Étienne (6,15).
4. Accusation de blasphème (6,11b).

B. Éléments communs à Mt-Mc-Lc

1. Déclaration de Jésus:
   a) «Le Fils de l'homme…» (Mt 26,64a; Mc 14,62a; Lc 22,69a).
   b) «…à la droite» (Ps 110,1) (Mt 26,64b; Mc 14,62b; Lc 22,69b).
2. Mort de Jésus: «grand cri» (Mt 27,50a; Mc 15,37a; Lc 23,46a).

Parallèles dans Ac

1. Déclaration d'Étienne:
   a) «Le Fils de l'homme…» (7,56a).
   b) «…à la droite» (Ps 110,1) (7,56b).
2. Mort d'Étienne: «grand cri» (7,60a).

C. Éléments propres à Lc

Mort de Jésus:
1. Invocation au Père (23,46a).
2. Référence au Ps 31,6 (23,46b).
3. Demande de pardon en faveur des bourreaux (23,34a).
4. «ayant dit cela» (τοῦτο εἰπών) (23,46c).

Parallèles dans Ac

Mort d'Étienne:
1. Invocation au Christ (7,59a).
2. Référence au Ps 31,6 (7,59b).
3. Demande de pardon en faveur des bourreaux (7,60b).
4. «ayant dit cela» (τοῦτο εἰπών) (7,60c).

D. Éléments propres à Ac

1. Vision précédant la déclaration (7,55).
2. Réactions des assistants (7,57-58a).
3. Présence et comportement de Saul (7,58b; 8,1).

42. G. SCHNEIDER, *Die Apostelgeschichte* (n. 16), p. 433, n. 6.
43. M. GOURGUES, *À la droite de Dieu* (n. 14), p. 186. J'ai simplement adapté la manière d'écrire les références scripturaires.

Mais Gourgues n'a pas tiré au clair les raisons des affinités variées qu'il a repérées entre évangiles et Actes[44]. C'est pourtant capital pour saisir le sens mis en œuvre dans le passage de la passion de Jésus à celle d'Étienne.

Il saute aux yeux que les parallèles avec Mt-Mc à l'exclusion de Lc (catégorie A) sont liés à l'instruction du procès et plus particulièrement aux accusations: on les retrouve en Ac 6,11-15 et non en Ac 7. Ceci suggère que, pour Luc, qui, dans son évangile, a omis les faux témoignages et les accusations relatives au Temple ou à un blasphème de Jésus, le véritable procès (final) se situe en Ac 6–7. Tout se passe comme si Luc, qui connaissait par Mc les accusations du procès de Jésus, les avait reportées à l'épisode d'Étienne. C'est un bel exemple du procédé narratif lucanien que D. Marguerat appelle «la rétention d'informations»[45]. Pour le reste, en effet, le parallèle entre les deux procès est mis en valeur par de nombreux détails repris des éléments communs à Mt-Mc-Lc (B) ou de ceux qui sont propres à Lc (C).

C'est dans ce cadre que le logion sur le Fils de l'homme peut être comparé dans ses deux versions en Lc 22,69 et Ac 7,56. Encore faut-il auparavant comprendre les différences de Lc 22,69 par rapport au texte parallèle de Mc 14,62 qui constitue sa source. Il y a deux différences importantes: en Lc 22,69, le Fils de l'homme est sujet du verbe ἔσται, tandis que, en Mc 14,62, il est complément d'objet direct du verbe ὄψεσθε; Lc 22,69 ne parle pas de la venue du Fils de l'homme sur les nuées du ciel.

Pourquoi Luc a-t-il sciemment supprimé l'annonce d'une vision collective future du Fils de l'homme, alors qu'il la lisait en Mc? Tout se passe comme si le sens que Luc donnait à cette vision empêchait qu'elle soit promise à ceux qui allaient condamner Jésus. Est-ce plausible? Oui, si l'on se réfère à l'approche lucanienne particulière du thème du Fils de l'homme.

Si on part des passages qui lui sont propres, on constate que, chez Luc, le Fils de l'homme vient en sauveur (Lc 19,10); dans sa condition céleste, il est à la fois juge et avocat des élus (Lc 18,7-8). Par ailleurs, toute décision prise envers Jésus, qu'elle soit de confiance ou de rejet[46],

---

44. Ce n'est pas davantage explicité par les autres exégètes. Tout au plus parle-t-on très généralement de l'imitation du maître par les disciples. Ce n'est pas faux, mais sans doute insuffisant.

45. Voir dans ce volume, D. MARGUERAT, *Luc-Actes: une unité à construire*, p. 62, où il définit comme suit la rétention d'informations: «À plus d'une reprise, l'examen des parallèles synoptiques fait voir que le narrateur a délibérément retenu un motif de l'évangile pour le déplacer en direction des Actes».

46. Avec Mt 10,32-33, contre Mc 8,38 qui n'envisage que le rejet.

a une portée eschatologique, puisqu'elle servira de critère pour le jugement lors de la parousie du Fils de l'homme (Lc 12,8-9). Alors que, en Mc 14,62 et Mt 26,64, la vision du Fils de l'homme pouvait être annoncée aux adversaires de Jésus comme celle du juge eschatologique qui prononcerait leur condamnation, il ne pouvait en être de même en Lc 22,69, car, pour Luc, le Fils de l'homme comme juge eschatologique est d'abord le sauveur des élus.

Par ailleurs, Luc développe une conception particulière du don spirituel. Lorsqu'il est refusé, il revient sur celui qui l'a proposé (Lc 10,5-6). C'est illustré par l'épisode de la prédication à Nazareth (Lc 4,16-30): la bonne nouvelle proposée est refusée et le seul à être sauvé, c'est Jésus qui échappe mystérieusement à la mort. Dans cette logique, la venue du Règne de Dieu annoncée par Jésus est rejetée, ce qui aboutit à la mise en croix; mais la résurrection apparaît comme le retour sur Jésus lui-même du Règne de Dieu qu'il avait proposé et qui a été refusé. Dans leur prédication, les apôtres substitueront d'ailleurs la personne de Jésus ressuscité au Règne de Dieu que Jésus annonçait. Dans une telle perspective, lors de la Parousie, le Fils de l'homme est le salut en personne. Le voir sur les nuées du ciel, c'est voir le salut[47]. On comprend dès lors que Jésus ne pouvait pas promettre cela à ceux qui le rejetaient jusqu'à la mort.

La déclaration de Jésus sur le Fils de l'homme en Lc 22,69 ne déclenche pas, comme dans les parallèles évangéliques, une accusation de blasphème. En fait, il faut attendre Ac 6,11 pour retrouver Étienne accusé de blasphème contre Moïse et contre Dieu. Et, dans le contexte, c'est explicité en reprenant un autre élément de la passion marcienne omis par Lc dans sa relation du procès de Jésus, à savoir l'hostilité contre le Temple: «nous lui avons entendu dire que ce Jésus le Nazôréen détruirait ce Lieu et changerait les règles que Moïse nous a transmises» (Ac 6,14, voir aussi le v. 13). Tout se passe comme si le procès entamé en Lc 22 trouvait ici son aboutissement, son accomplissement.

Cet aboutissement suit le discours d'Étienne qui constitue le sommet d'une prédication apostolique «première manière». Dans cette prédication, il s'agit d'annoncer aux juifs combien le rejet et la crucifixion de Jésus était peccamineux et de les exhorter au repentir et à la conversion

---

47. H.E. TÖDT, *Der Menschensohn* (n. 7), pp. 91, 102, retire au Fils de l'homme eschatologique chez Luc le statut de juge, car lors de la parousie le Fils de l'homme est sauveur des élus. Cela ne provient-il pas d'une identification erronée entre jugement et condamnation? Pour les élus, le jugement consiste dans la vision du Fils de l'homme (leur salut), tandis que le clan du refus ne verra pas ce salut. N'est-ce pas pour cela qu'en Lc 21,26 (verset propre à Lc), les hommes des nations meurent de frayeur avant que ne vienne le Fils de l'homme?

à Dieu qui a ressuscité Jésus. Avec l'espoir d'une conversion générale qui serait associée à des moments de rafraîchissement dans la perspective du rétablissement de tout (Ac 3,19-21).

Malheureusement cette prédication n'a pas abouti. Le discours d'Étienne sanctionne en quelque sorte cet échec: il rappelle la résistance constante du peuple à l'Esprit Saint par le refus des envoyés de Dieu et il situe la mise à mort de Jésus comme le point culminant de la persécution des prophètes. C'est ainsi l'observance de la loi qui a été mise à mal. Quant au Temple, autre objet de l'accusation des adversaires d'Étienne, celui-ci n'hésite pas à rappeler que «le Très-Haut n'habite pas des demeures construites par la main des hommes» (7,48).

Si le discours d'Étienne constitue un climax dans la radicalisation du message apostolique à l'égard des juifs, leur réaction est aussi un sommet dans l'hostilité croissante au kérygme. Jusque là, l'hostilité des chefs du peuple (4,2; 5,33) était compensée par la sympathie du peuple. Mais la lapidation d'Étienne ressemble à un acte de justice populaire; l'opposition devient générale et il s'ensuit d'ailleurs une violente persécution (8,1).

C'est dans ce contexte qu'il faut interpréter la vision d'Étienne, sans omettre le lien avec son discours. Celui-ci est d'ailleurs renforcé par le parallèle verbal de 7,55 avec le début du discours (7,2-3): il y est chaque fois question de la gloire de Dieu. Comme le Dieu de gloire invite Abraham à quitter son pays pour la terre promise, ainsi Étienne voit la gloire de Dieu et le Fils de l'homme debout à sa droite (7,55-56), ce qui lui indique sa nouvelle destination.

Par ailleurs, le discours d'Étienne laisse entendre qu'Israël s'est comporté comme un peuple d'idolâtres. Abraham, le père du peuple a été mené en terre promise pour rendre un culte à Dieu «en ce lieu» (7,7)[48]. Or, en fait de culte, les pères du peuple se sont comportés en idolâtres: ils ont adoré le veau d'or, œuvre de leurs mains (7,41), puis ils ont construit de leurs mains une maison pour Dieu, le Temple, alors que «le Très-Haut n'habite pas des demeures construites par la main des hommes (ἐν χειροποιήτοις)» (7,48). Accusé d'avoir blasphémé contre Moïse (la loi) et contre le Lieu saint (6,11-14), Étienne montre que ses interlocuteurs sont les vrais fautifs sur ces deux plans. D'une part, ils se centrent sur un Temple fait de main d'homme, alors que Dieu n'habite pas dans ce qui est fait de main d'homme (7,48-50). D'autre part, «incirconcis de cœur» (7,51), ils ressemblent à leurs pères que leurs cœurs

48. Les mots «sur cette montagne» de Ex 3,12 sont remplacés par l'expression plus vague «en ce lieu», sans doute à mettre en référence avec le lieu saint de Jérusalem et du Temple (6,13.14; voir aussi 7,47-49).

idolâtres attiraient en Égypte (7,39). Cela les conduit, comme leurs pères qui persécutaient les prophètes, à trahir et assassiner le Juste dont les prophètes eux-mêmes ont annoncé la venue (7,52). Au lieu de constituer le sommet de la vie cultuelle du peuple, le Temple devient un lieu d'idolâtrie[49], dès lors qu'il détourne le peuple de l'Envoyé du Seigneur. La vision d'Étienne retentit alors aussi comme un jugement, une condamnation sévère de ce peuple idolâtre qui a mené jusqu'au bout la persécution des envoyés de Dieu et continue de s'y enfermer après la résurrection du Juste, en persécutant ceux qui l'annoncent. La destruction du Temple est donc bien à l'ordre du jour et le temps des nations, annoncé par Lc 21,24, commence[50].

On voit mieux maintenant les raisons pour lesquelles le titre «Fils de l'homme» est utilisé exceptionnellement par Étienne. Il y a d'abord la volonté de marquer le parallélisme avec le procès de Jésus. Ensuite, pour Luc, c'est exalté à la droite de Dieu au terme de son ἔξοδος que le Christ acquiert enfin sa stature définitive; c'est alors aussi que les juifs peuvent se situer définitivement par rapport à lui. Ce qu'ils vont faire en lapidant Étienne. Cela n'empêchera pas qu'il y ait encore des conversions de juifs par la suite (14,1; 17,11-12; 21,20). Mais la mission chrétienne sera dorénavant globalement tournée vers les païens.

CONCLUSION

En tenant compte du parallèle avec le procès de Jésus, de quelques grands accents de la théologie lucanienne et du discours d'Étienne qui précède immédiatement sa vision, il me semble pouvoir émettre une hypothèse polysémique quant au sens de la position debout du Fils de l'homme. Cette hypothèse conjoint les idées d'accueil, de salut-défense et de jugement. D'une part, sur base du discours d'Étienne, on soupçonne que le Fils de l'homme se trouve à la droite de Dieu, car il est digne de Dieu, lui qui n'est pas fait de main d'homme[51]. Étienne qui le

---

49. Ce Temple, œuvre de leurs mains, ne leur dissimule-t-il pas insidieusement leur idolâtrie, car il les en rend inconscients et les empêche de voir où Dieu est vraiment présent, à savoir dans le Fils de l'homme mort et ressuscité?

50. On retrouve l'idée du tournant dans l'histoire racontée par les Actes tel que l'évoque R. Pesch (voir ci-dessus, n. 24).

51. F. MUSSNER, *Wohnung* (n. 26), p. 288: «Es geht in ihr (= in der Idee von der Wohnung Gottes) vor allem um die Frage nach dem jetzigen 'Ort' Gottes. Dabei wird das christliche Kerygma von der Erhöhung des Menschensohnes Jesus zum himmlischen Throngenossen Gottes in polemischer Weise gegen den bisherigen 'heiligen Ort' Gottes, den Tempel zu Jerusalem, eingesetzt, was auch impliziert: Gott hat 'diesen heiligen Ort' endgültig verlassen und wohnt zusammen mit dem Menschensohn Jesus in der himmlischen Transzendenz».

voit dans la gloire de Dieu va être appelé, comme Abraham, à quitter son pays; ce sera pour rejoindre le Fils de l'homme là où il est possible de rendre à Dieu un culte véritable. D'autre part, en voyant le Fils de l'homme debout à la droite de Dieu, Étienne voit son salut qui coïncide avec le jugement de ses opposants à cause de leur rejet du Juste et de ses disciples. Le don de Dieu qu'Étienne leur proposait revient sur lui après qu'ils l'aient refusé. La vision du Fils de l'homme debout à la droite de Dieu en est le signe.

Rue des Sarts, 2   Camille FOCANT
B-5380 Franc-Waret

EKLEKTISCHE TEXTKONSTITUTION ALS THEOLOGISCHE REKONSTRUKTION

ZUR HEILSBEDEUTUNG DES TODES JESU BEI LUKAS
(LK 22,15-20 UND APG 20,28)

Die Frage, ob im Werk des Autors *ad Theophilum* die Heilsbedeutung des Todes Jesu – insbesondere in der pointierten Form des Theologumenon vom stellvertretenden Sühneleiden – ihren Niederschlag gefunden hat, entzündet sich im wesentlichen an zwei Textpassagen. Dabei handelt es sich zum einen um den Abendmahlsbericht in Lk 22,15-20 und zum anderen um eine kurze Bemerkung in der Milet-Rede Apg 20,28. Der Umstand, daß sich die genannte Frage überhaupt stellt, verdankt sich der schwierigen Textüberlieferung der beiden Passagen. Dies läßt sich an der Bewertung der beiden Textentscheidungen im vom *Greek New Testament* (= *Nestle-Aland*) gebotenen Text ablesen. Bruce Manning Metzger's *Textual Commentary* (1. Aufl.) vergibt in beiden Fällen eine {C}-Bewertung. Das bedeutet: »there is a considerable degree of doubt concerning the reading selected for the text«[1].

In seinem 1993 erschienenen Buch *The Orthodox Corruption of Scripture*[2] hat Bart Ehrman beide Textpassagen einer eingehenden Analyse unterzogen. Dieses Buch entfaltet die These, daß eine Reihe von Lesarten der ntl. Textüberlieferung auf dem Hintergrund altkirchlicher, hauptsächlich christologischer, Auseinandersetzungen zu interpretieren sei. Besondere Aufmerksamkeit gilt denjenigen Lesarten, die später als orthodox geltende Interpretationen einschlägiger Schriftstellen zu unterstützen scheinen. Ehrman unterscheidet dabei vier verschiedene thematische Auseinandersetzungen, denen er die Textlesarten als »Anti-Adop-

* Der vorliegende Beitrag wurde während eines Forschungsaufenthalts am *Netherlands Institute for Advanced Study in the Humanities and Social Sciences* (NIAS) abgeschlossen. Dem Institut und seinen Mitarbeitern sei für alle Unterstützung herzlich gedankt.
1. B.M. METZGER, *A Textual Commentary on the Greek New Testament*, London, 1971, pp. 173-177.480-481, Zitat: Introduction, p. xxviii. Die 2. Aufl. des Textual Commentary von 1994 vergibt nun für Lk 22,17-20 eine {B}-Bewertung (ebd., p. 148). Das bedeutet: »the text is almost certain« (Introduction, p. 14*). Was genau diese Änderung verursacht hat, ist mir nicht ersichtlich.
2. B.D. EHRMAN, *The Orthodox Corruption of Scripture. The Effect of Early Christological Controversies on the Text of the New Testament*, New York – Oxford, 1993. Vgl. auch ID., *The Cup, The Bread, and the Salvific Effect of Jesus' Death in Luke-Acts*, in *SBL 1991 Seminar Papers*, pp. 576-591.

tianist«, »Anti-Separationist«, »Anti-Docetic«, und »Anti-Patripassianist Corruptions of Scripture« zuordnet. Dabei fällt auf, daß Ehrman die für unsere Frage wichtigen Textstellen, nämlich Lk 22,15-20 und Apg 20,28, zwei verschiedenen Auseinandersetzungen zuweist[3]. Diese bloß formale Beobachtung verweist meines Erachtens auf ein materiales Problem, nämlich den tendenziell eklektischen Umgang Ehrmans mit seinem Material. Um Mißverständnissen vorzubeugen, sei gleich hinzugefügt, daß es hier nicht darum geht, eklektische Textrekonstruktionen zu diskreditieren oder gar zu indizieren. Dies wäre allein schon deshalb unsinnig, weil keine einzige neutestamentliche Handschrift an jeder einzelnen Stelle mit dem vermuteten Archetyp der Überlieferung übereinstimmt. Mit anderen Worten: Es besteht prinzipiell die Nötigung zur Auswahl. Die Frage kann allenfalls lauten: Wie und mit welchen heuristischen Verfahren wird die Auswahl unter konkurrierenden Lesarten vorgenommen? Ehrman legt besonderen Nachdruck auf die heuristische Funktion von theologischen Implikationen der jeweils konkurrierenden Lesarten. Diese Matrix hat prinzipiell zwei Bezugspunkte. Der eine Bezugspunkt ist die unterstellte theologische Intention eines neutestamentlichen Autors, in unserem Fall des Autors des lukanischen Doppelwerkes. Der andere Bezugspunkt ist die unterstellte theologische Intention späterer Abschreiber, in unserem Fall späterer Abschreiber des lukanischen Doppelwerkes. Im folgenden wird es nun darum gehen, Ehrmans Umgang mit diesen beiden Bezugspunkten unterstellter theologischer Intention bei der Analyse der genannten lukanischen Passagen aufzuzeigen und auf ihre Kohärenz zu befragen. Ausdrücklich sei darauf hingewiesen, daß die Grundannahme von Ehrmans Buch für sich betrachtet alles andere als unproblematisch ist, die Grundannahme nämlich, daß eine mögliche theologische Interpretation neutestamentlicher Textlesarten auch die Genese dieser Lesarten historisch zuverlässig beschreibt. Es kann im Einzelfall durchaus strittig sein, was genau die Ursache für Alternativlesarten ist, ein schlichter Fehler (Haplographie, Homoioteleuton, etc.), eine sprachliche Verbesserung oder eine theologisch motivierte Änderung. Unabhängig von diesem grundsätzlichen Problem wird sich zweierlei zeigen lassen:

1. Es ist keine einzige griechische Handschrift der lukanischen Texte bekannt, die das Theologumenon von der Sühnebedeutung des Todes Jesu nicht an wenigstens einer Stelle zumindest anklingen läßt. Eine Textrekonstruktion, die dieses Theologumenon bei Lukas gänzlich eliminiert ist darum per se eklektisch.

---

3. Vgl. EHRMAN, *Corruption*, pp. 87-88.198-209.

2. Ehrmans theologische Rekonstruktion der Textüberlieferung von Apg 20,28 ist auch als theologische Rekonstruktion eklektisch. Das bedeutet in diesem konkreten Fall, daß er eine mögliche theologische Alternative gar nicht erst erwägt und sich damit dem Vorwurf aussetzt, in seiner theologischen Rekonstruktion inkonsequent zu sein.

A. Die theologische Textrekonstruktion von Lk 22,15-20 – Theologie des Lukas

Die umstrittene Textentscheidung an dieser Stelle betrifft die Frage »Kurztext oder Langtext in Lk 22,19b-20«; die Frage also, ob im lukanischen Abendmahlsbericht auch Brot- und Kelchwort analog zu der aus 1 Kor 11,24b-25 bekannten Fassung enthalten sind – wie von der überwältigenden Anzahl neutestamentlicher Handschriften geboten –, oder ob diese Worte ursprünglich nicht dazu gehörten – wie es die Textfassungen von Codex Bezae und einigen Altlateinern nahezulegen scheinen. Ehrman sowie auch andere Verfechter[4] des Kurztextes weisen unter anderem darauf hin, daß der Langtext die einzige Passage in Lk wäre, die von der Sühnebedeutung des Todes Jesu spräche. Am lukanischen Umgang mit anderen Stellen seiner angenommenen Markus-Vorlage könne überdies gezeigt werden, daß Lukas dieses Theologumenon geradezu vermeide. Beispielsweise streiche er das λύτρον-Wort von Mk 10,45. Des weiteren vermeide Lukas die unterstellte Anspielung auf die Sühnopferdeutung des Todes Jesu in Mk 15,37-38, wo direkt nach dem Tode Jesu der Tempelvorhang zerreißt[5], indem er, Lukas, das Zerreißen des Tempelvorhangs dem Tod Jesu vorangehen läßt (vgl. Lk 23,45-46). Abgesehen davon, daß es für die mögliche Streichung von Mk 10,45 auch andere Erklärungen gibt[6], ist der Hinweis auf die Deutung des Tempelvorhangs interessant. Codex D 05 nämlich, die einzige bekannte griechische Handschrift, die in der lukanischen Abendmahlsperikope Brot- und Kelchwort nicht bietet, hat wiederum als einzige bekannte griechische Handschrift die Abfolge »Tod Jesu« – »Zerreißen des Tempelvorhangs« auch in Lk 23,45-46! Mit anderen Worten: Die unterstellte Deutung dieser Abfolge auf dem Hintergrund der Sühnopfervorstellung muß darum auch auf den D-Text von Lk angewendet

---

4. *Ibid.*, pp. 200-201. Vgl. z.B. H.J. CADBURY, *The Making of Luke-Acts*, London, 1927, p. 280; M. RESE, *Zur Problematik von Kurz- und Langtext in Luk. xxii. 17ff*, in *NTS* 22 (1976) 15-31, p. 27.

5. »Indicating ... that God now comes to humans (from the Holy of Holies behind the curtain) no longer through temple sacrifice but through the death of Jesus« (EHRMAN, *Corruption*, pp. 200-201)

6. Eine mögliche andere Erklärung findet sich auch bei EHRMAN, *Corruption*, p. 251 n. 83.

werden, auch wenn es sich dabei mit größter Wahrscheinlichkeit um eine »Korrektur« nach den Parallelstellen Mk 15,37-38 (Mt 27,50-51) handelt. Damit wäre unser erster Punkt gezeigt: Es ist in der Tat keine einzige griechische Handschrift der lukanischen Texte bekannt, die die Sühnedeutung des Todes Jesu nicht zumindest anklingen läßt[7]. Auch wenn man für die Entscheidung gegen die D-Lesart von Lk 23,45-46 keine theologischen Deutungen bemühen muß – die Deutung »Parallel-stelleneinfluß« ist völlig ausreichend und viel naheliegender –, so gewinnt man bei der Betrachtung dieser Lesart doch einen Eindruck von der Mehrdeutigkeit konkurrierender Textlesarten. Die in diesem Falle wohl historisch zutreffende Deutung »Parallelstelleneinfluß« für die D-Lesart in Lk 23,45-46 entläßt aus sich noch eine weitere, vermutlich nicht intendierte, theologische Deutung, nämlich die der möglichen Süh-nedeutung des Todes Jesu an dieser Stelle.

Doch nun zurück zu den verschiedenen Fassungen der lukanischen Abendmahlsperikope Lk 22,15-20. Exegeten, die sich für die Langfas-sung mit Brot- und Kelchwort aussprechen[8], entgegnen dem Argument, Lukas vermeide die Sühnedeutung des Todes Jesu, mit dem Hinweis, daß Lukas in Apg 20,28 sehr wohl auf die Sühnevorstellung anspiele. Der lukanische Paulus spricht dort von der »Kirche Gottes, die er sich erworben hat durch sein eigenes Blut (durch das Blut seines eigenen [sc. Sohnes])«[9]. Ehrman, der sich bei seiner Textrekonstruktion von Lk 22,15-20 gerade auch aus der Perspektive lukanischer Theologie für die Kurzfassung ausspricht, interpretiert diese Acta-Stelle folgendermaßen: »The phrasing is enigmatic and, as we have already seen, has led to several interesting textual modifications. [...] But even here, I must point out, the text does not speak of Jesus' self-giving act as an atoning sacrifice for sin, but of God's use of Jesus' blood to acquire (NB, not «redeem») the church. And so, strictly speaking the thrust of the allu-sion is not soteriological...«[10]. Mit dieser Interpretation bestreitet Ehr-man, daß Apg 20,28 für die Sühnedeutung des Todes Jesu bei Lukas in Anschlag gebracht werden kann. Es bleibt dann allein noch die lukani-sche Abendmahlsperikope Lk 22,15-20 übrig. Deren Textüberlieferung ist nicht nur umstritten, sie steht nun auch theologisch isoliert da. Für Vertreter der Kurzfassung ohne Brot- und Kelchwort ist dies ein starkes

---

7. Ehrmans Deutung von Mk 15,37-38 wird hier vorausgesetzt.

8. Vgl. z.B. J. JEREMIAS, *Die Abendmahlsworte Jesu*, Göttingen, ³1960, p. 151.

9. Zur Deutung des absoluten τοῦ ἰδίου als »seines eigenen [sc. Sohnes]« vgl. J.H. MOULTON, *A Grammar of New Testament Greek*, vol. I, *Prolegomena*, Edinburgh, ³1908, p. 90.

10. *Corruption*, p. 202.

Argument, da nun ein kohärentes Bild lukanischer Theologie ohne Bezugnahme auf das Theologumenon von der Sühnedeutung des Todes Jesu entworfen werden kann. Übertragen auf die oben angeführte bipolare Matrix theologischer Textrekonstruktion bedeutet das, daß der Bezugspunkt in diesem Fall die Theologie des neutestamentlichen Autors, also des Lukas ist. Stutzig an diesem kohärenten Bild lukanischer Theologie macht allein der oben zitierte Hinweis Ehrmans, die änigmatische Formulierung von Apg 20,28 hätte zu einigen interessanten »textual modifications« geführt. Um einige dieser Textmodifikationen in Apg 20,28 und ihre theologische Rekonstruktion bei Ehrman soll es nun im folgenden gehen.

B. Die theologische Textrekonstruktion von Apg 20,28 – Theologie der Abschreiber

Vorab sei noch einmal daran erinnert, daß Ehrman die Lesarten von Lk 22,15-20 und Apg 20,28 zwei verschiedenen altkirchlichen Auseinandersetzungen zuordnet. Seine Textrekonstruktion der lukanischen Abendmahlsperikope lokalisiert Ehrman im Zusammenhang anti-doketischer Auseinandersetzungen. Die Sühnedeutung des Todes Jesu gehört seines Erachtens als soteriologische Konsequenz zu denjenigen altkirchlichen Auseinandersetzungen, in denen die Realität des Leidens und Sterbens des Erlösers gegenüber doketischen Bestreitungen verteidigt wird. Die theologische Textrekonstruktion von Apg 20,28 hingegen siedelt Ehrman innnerhalb der adoptianistischen Streitigkeit an, und zwar präzise unter dem Stichwort »Christ as Divine: The Exchange of Predicates«[11]. Der Grund für diese Lokalisierung wird einsichtig, wenn man die konkurrierenden Lesarten in Apg 20,28 betrachtet. Anstelle der Textlesart im *Nestle-Aland* ἐκκλησίαν τοῦ θεοῦ finden sich die Lesarten ἐκκλησίαν τοῦ κυρίου und die Konflation ἐκκλησίαν τοῦ κυρίου καὶ τοῦ θεοῦ. Ehrman schreibt dazu: »... the reading τοῦ κυρίου could refer to Christ as well as to God, making it somewhat more acceptable in the minds of certain Christians who where uncomfortable with the potentially Patripassianist implications of the following phrase, τοῦ αἵματος τοῦ ἰδίου, which may naturally be rendered 'his own blood.' That is to say, orthodox scribes uneasy with the possible interpretation that God the Father shed 'his own blood' appear to have changed the text to make it refer instead to Christ, 'the Lord,' who shed his blood«[12]. Diese Interpretation Ehrmans ermöglicht uns zwei wichtige Beobachtungen:

---

11. *Ibid.*, pp. 87-88.
12. *Ibid.*, p. 88.

1. Es gibt in Apg 20,28 eine konkurrierende Lesart, welche die Sühnebedeutung des Todes Jesu deutlich akzentuiert. Der Text spricht in dieser Version nämlich von der »Kirche des Kyrios, die er sich durch sein eigenes Blut erworben hat«. Der Kyrios, verstanden als Christus, hat demzufolge durch die Selbsthingabe seines Blutes für sich die Kirche erworben. Es ist im übrigen interessant darauf hinzuweisen, daß Codex D 05 hier auch die Lesart »Kirche des Kyrios« bietet. Damit vertritt diese Handschrift wiederum – wie in Lk 23,45-46 (Tod Jesu – Zerreißen des Tempelvorhangs) – einen Text, der für die Sühnedeutung des Todes Jesu in Anspruch genommen werden kann. Wenn wir uns daran erinnern, daß Metzger in seinem *Textual Commentary* der Textlesart »Kirche Gottes« in Apg 20,28 ein beträchtliches Maß an Zweifel bescheinigt, dann kann man an dieser Stelle keinesfalls mit Sicherheit ausschließen, daß nicht doch die Sühnedeutung des Todes Jesu als Konsequenz einer anderen Textentscheidung, nämlich »Kirche des Kyrios«, deutlich angespielt wird. Daß jedenfalls die theologische Rekonstruktion der Textüberlieferung von Apg 20,28 durch Ehrman inkonsequent und reversibel ist, sei noch als weitere Beobachtung angemerkt.

2. Bei seiner Analyse dieser Stelle konzentriert sich Ehrman auf den Bezugspunkt »Theologie eines Abschreibers ntl. Texte«. Die Lesart »Kirche Gottes« sei zu »Kirche des Kyrios« verändert, um ein mögliches patripassianistisches Mißverständnis zu vermeiden. Im selben Abschnitt, »Christ as Divine: The Exchange of Predicates«, bietet Ehrman ein weiteres Beispiel für diese Übertragung von Prädikationen[13]. In 1 Petr 5,1 liest die Mehrheit der Überlieferung den Text »Zeuge der Leiden Christi« und nur eine Handschrift, P[72], liest »Zeuge der Leiden Gottes«. In diesem Fall allerdings optiert Ehrman für die erste Lesart. Die Lesart »Zeuge der Leiden Christi« ist hier nicht Korrektur der patripassianistisch mißverständlichen Lesart »Zeuge der Leiden Gottes«, sondern jene ist antiadoptianische Emphase der ersten Lesart. Verglichen mit dem theologischen Gefälle seiner Textrekonstruktion von Apg 20,28 ist diese Wendung allerdings überraschend, denn dort war es ja genau umgekehrt. Noch erstaunlicher wird diese Umkehrung, wenn man die Belege betrachtet, mit denen Ehrman eine seiner Meinung nach proto-orthodoxe Tendenz bei Schriftstellern des zweiten und dritten Jahrhunderts belegt[14]. Ignatius von Antiochien spricht vom »Blut Gottes« (Eph 1,1), ebenso auch Tertullian (*ad uxorem* 2.3); Tertullian spricht von den »Leiden Gottes« und davon, daß »Gott gekreuzigt«

13. *Ibid.*, p. 88.
14. *Ibid.*, p. 87.

wurde (*de carne Christi* 5); Melito von Sardes sagt, daß »Gott ermordet wurde« (Passa Homilie). Alle diese Belege haben die gemeinsame Tendenz, Christus als Gott zu prädizieren, und zwar in einer hyperbolischen Ausdrucksweise, die die Attribute des Gekreuzigten für Gott in Anspruch nimmt. Wenn man dieser theologischen Tendenz eine für den Verlauf der Textüberlieferung relevante Bedeutung zuschreibt, wie Ehrman das tut, dann weist diese in genau die entgegengesetzte Richtung von Ehrmans theologischer Rekonstruktion für die Lesarten »Kirche Gottes« bzw. »Kirche des Kyrios« in Apg 20,28. Damit ist auch der zweite Punkt gezeigt. Ehrmans theologische Textrekonstruktion ist auch als solche eklektisch. Im Kontext seiner Ausführungen nämlich ist die Abfolge der Lesarten in theologischer Perspektive reversibel. Die Lesart »Kirche Gottes«, die dieser »durch sein eigenes Blut erworben hat«, ließe sich auch als zuspitzende Verdeutlichung des im NT sonst nur noch einmal belegten Ausdrucks »Kirche des Kyrios« (Röm 16,16) interpretieren, entsprechend der von Ehrman für das zweite und dritte Jahrhundert reich belegten Tendenz, Christus als Gott zu prädizieren.

C. Abschließende Bemerkungen

1. Eklektische Textkonstitution basiert immer auf einer Reihe von Kriterien. Die theologische Rekonstruktion sowohl mit Bezug auf den neutestamentlichen Autor als auch mit Bezug auf spätere Abschreiber ist eines davon.

2. Die Schwierigkeit im Umgang mit diesen Kriterien ist nicht nur, die »richtige« Balance untereinander zu finden, sondern auch die möglichst kohärente Anwendung eines Einzelkriteriums im Auge zu behalten. Dies gilt insbesondere für das stark systematisierende Kriterium »Theologische Intention eines Autors bzw. seiner Abschreiber«. Die hier analysierte theologische Textrekonstruktion von Apg 20,28 durch Ehrman zieht sich den Vorwurf zu, das theologische Kriterium selbst eklektisch zu handhaben, zumindest werden die Konsequenzen dieser Form des Eklektizismus nicht bedacht[15].

3. Für die Frage nach Heilsbedeutung des Todes Jesu bei Lukas bedeutet dies: In dieser Form ist die theologische Textrekonstruktion von Apg 20,28 gerade keine Stütze für die Lesart, welche die Sühnedeutung zurücktreten läßt, sondern eher für die gegenteilige Lesart. Läßt

---

15. Ehrmans mangelndes Problembewußtsein bei der Handhabung des Kriteriums »theologische Intention eines Autors bzw. seiner Abschreiber«, hat Klaus Wachtel mit weiteren Beispielen illustriert: K. WACHTEL, *Zur Entstehung und Ausbreitung von Varianten in der handschriftlichen Überlieferung des Neuen Testaments* (erscheint 1999 im *Münsteraner Logbuch für Linguistik*).

sich aber auch mit weiteren Gründen die gegenteilige Lesart als ursprünglich wahrscheinlich machen[16], dann steht der Langtext der lukanischen Abendmahlsperikope (Lk 22,15-20) im lukanischen Doppelwerk nicht mehr theologisch isoliert da.

Kollwitzstr. 13   Ulrich SCHMID
D-33613 Bielefeld

---

16. Stark ins Gewicht fällt meines Erachtens der oben angedeutete Grund, daß der Ausdruck »Kirche des Kyrios« ganz im Gegensatz zu »Kirche Gottes« (vgl. 1 Kor 1,2; 10,32; 11,16.22; 15,9; 2 Kor 1,1; Gal 1,13 u.ö) im NT vergleichsweise untypisch ist. Im Regelfall ersetzen Abschreiber eher einen untypischen Ausdruck durch einen typischen als umgekehrt.

GAMALIEL'S COUNSEL
AND THE APOLOGETIC STRATEGY OF LUKE-ACTS

In a reader-theoretical study, W.J. Lyons recently concluded that Gamaliel's counsel carries a teasing "irony of indeterminacy"[1]. Thus when the illustrious Pharisee declares to the Sanhedrin that "if this initiative or this action[2] is from humans, it will be dissolved, but if it is from God, you cannot dissolve it without rebelling against God" (Acts 5,38f.) – is this an ironically positive statement from the mouth of a Pharisee[3], or is it the opposite: an ironical confirmation of the Pharisaic rejection of the gospel? It all depends on one's reading of Acts and Luke, and that is where exegetes hopelessly differ, reader-response analysts included. Lyons quotes David B. Gowler who views the Pharisees' role in Acts as much more favourable than in Luke and consequently explains Gamaliel's words as a positive statement used by the author to underpin the cause of the gospel. By contrast, John A. Darr considers the image of the Pharisees in Acts to be as bad as in the gospel and hence reads Gamaliel's counsel as a verdict on the Pharisee's own head[4].

However when viewed in its proper contexts, there is more to be made of Gamaliel's clause than ironical indeterminacy[5]. Whatever else

---

1. W.J. LYONS, *The Words of Gamaliel (Acts 5.38-39) and the Irony of Indeterminacy*, in *JSNT* 68 (1997) 23-49.
2. Βουλὴ ἢ ἔργον, see below nn. 42 and 76.
3. If not an ironically crypto-Christian stance! See LYONS, *Words*, pp. 39-43 for the 'Christian career' of Gamaliel.
4. D.B. GOWLER, *Host, Guest, Enemy, and Friend; Portraits of the Pharisees in Luke and in Acts* (Emory Studies in Early Christianity, 1), New York, Lang, 1991; J.A. DARR, *On Character Building. The Reader and the Rhetoric of Characterization in Luke-Acts* (Literary Currents in Biblical Interpretation), Louisville, Westminster – John Knox Press, 1992. Both studies show that modern literary theory does not necessarily help avoiding the traditional pitfalls of confounding the various Jewish movements and leaders into one unknown hostile entity (cf. Darr, p. 118, on Gamaliel and Sanhedrin) and of reading Jesus' critique of specific rules as a "blanket condemnation" of the Pharisees (Gowler on Lk 11). See also nn. 5 and 24.
5. Lyons extrapolates a just rejection of "objectivity" in exegesis into an unjust denial of any foundation to the reclaiming of the "real Paul" by K. Stendahl and others, which consists in taking his relation to Judaism into account instead of viewing him exclusively within a gentile-Christian framework, as did traditional Lutheran and Patristic exegesis. There is a risk here of relapsing into a sceptical permutation of 'meanings' in neglect of the *Wirkungsgeschichte*. The "real" Paul will of course never be known, but some interpretations are more adequate to his cultural surroundings than others. For a more basic thing that tends to be overlooked here is the importance of evidence, especially evidence

one can say about Luke-Acts, its author explicitly announces his as a book about πράγματα, "things that happened" (Lk 1,1)[6]. Hence he invites us to read the Gamaliel episode not only with an eye on its place in the account of Luke-Acts, but also on the socio-political situation the author could have been facing and on elements of contemporary thought he might have had in mind. I submit that if the author used the episode as a major support for his positive image of the Pharisees, he was doing so in the awareness of their position in the political constellation of his day, and that he drew on a tradition insiders would readily recognize as stemming from Gamaliel's own spiritual heritage.

'Apologetic Historiography' and Pharisaism in Josephus and Luke-Acts

Let us begin with the socio-political context. Some years ago, Gregory Sterling convincingly demonstrated the existence in the Hellenistic world of a wide-spread literary genre which he termed "apologetic historiography"[7]. Ever since the days of Manetho's *Aegyptiaca* and Berossus' *Babyloniaca* (3rd cent. BCE), leading non-Greek intellectuals strove to explain the history, culture and religion of their *ethnos* in terms understandable to all Greek-speakers[8]. The importance of this approach is that it explains both the use of historiography, a genre which became typical of the Hellenistic age[9], and its application to the outspoken interests of specific groups and peoples. Sterling focussed on two late first century examples which stand out among the extant sources and both are of prime importance to us: Josephus and Luke-Acts.

hitherto unknown or insufficiently studied such as the Qumran writings or Rabbinic literature. On the relative use of rhetorical analysis for historiography see A. MOMIGLIANO, *The Rhetoric of History and the History of Rhetoric: On Hayden White's Tropes*, in ID., *Settimo contributo alla storia degli studi classici e del mondo antico*, Rome, Edizioni di storia e letteratura, 1984, pp. 49-59; and in the same volume *Classical Studies and Biblical Studies. Simple Reflections upon Historical Method*, pp. 289-296 (also in ID., *On Pagans, Jews, and Christians*, Middletown, CT, Wesleyan UP, 1984, pp. 3-10).

6. Similarly S. MASON, *Chief Priests, Sadducees, Pharisees and Sanhedrin in Acts*, in R. BAUCKHAM (ed.), *The Book of Acts in Its Palestinian Setting*, Carlisle, Paternoster – Grand Rapids, Eerdmans, 1995, pp. 115-177, esp. 151, 158, pointing to the development the Lukan author intends to describe.

7. G.E. STERLING, *Historiography and Self-Definition: Josephos, Luke-Acts and Apologetic Historiography* (NTSup, 64), Leiden, Brill, 1992.

8. Typically expressed by Josephus, Ant. 1.5: ἅπασιν τοῖς Ἕλλησιν... ἐκ τῶν Ἑβραϊκῶν... γραμμάτων; 20.262 εἰς Ἕλληνας.

9. But note the primordial affinities between Jewish and Greek historiography as from the Persian age noted by A. MOMIGLIANO, *Eastern Elements in Post-Exilic Jewish, and Greek, Historiography*, in ID., *Essays in Ancient and Modern Historiography*, Oxford, Blackwell, 1977, pp. 25-35. Moreover, Herodotus and Thucydides well preceded the Hellenistic age proper, just as our two prime examples, Josephus and Luke-Acts, came a century late.

While the striking similarities of Josephus and Luke-Acts have been studied for more than a century[10], many of such common features can be understood from the apologetic character and situation they share. Both authors are writing within the ambit of late first-century Rome, both in Hellenistic fashion preface their works with dedications to dignitaries who hopefully will advance their cause, and both are anxious to demonstrate the antiquity and nobility of their communities on the basis of the most venerable Law of Moses. Within this common framework, they pursue the aims of their own, but even here analogy does not stop. Where Josephus defends the Jewish people as the bearer of an ancient and respectable tradition, the Lukan author offers an apology of Christianity as a legitimate outgrowth of that very same tradition[11]. In this constellation it must be more than coincidental that both authors also give prominence to a movement they portray as being the most dependable and popular representatives of Judaism: the Pharisees. We shall be very interested in their distinct reasons.

If it is laudable by Christian standards, for historians it is unfortunate that the *auctor ad Theophilum* seems to have been less anxious about his personal merit than the one *ad Epaphroditum* and did not bequeath us with an autobiography. In Josephus, the apology of his people after the shameful defeat is intertwined with a rehabilitation of his own conduct. While the Jews have fought bravely, the war had been triggered by extremists and it is fortunate that damage was limited and many could escape unharmed, including the author. Thus the earlier *Jewish War* is patently as apologetic as the *Antiquities*, the *Life*, and *Against Apion*. But there is an interesting shift which recently has been examined anew by Steve Mason[12]. In Josephus' later works, the affirmation of the Jewish Law and of the Pharisees as being the leading and most popular sect is much more outspoken. The first episode of the *Life* even has the author concluding his adolescent *tour d'horizon* as an adherent of their way of life[13]. The question is why. The scruples of old age? Never to be excluded, and who are we to judge? But political factors should not be

---

10. Cf. STERLING, *Historiography* (n. 7), pp. 365-369, our passage being the major case in point (see below n. 65).

11. *Ibid.,* pp. 374-386. The word ἀσφάλεια (Lk 1,4) must be stressed in this connection.

12. S. MASON, *Flavius Josephus on the Pharisees. A Composition-Critical Study* (Studia Post-Biblica, 39), Leiden, Brill, 1991. He concludes that Josephus, while conceding the scribal excellence and popularity of the Pharisees, inwardly remains an unsympathetic priestly aristocrat. This conclusion is very refreshing but may be somewhat overstated (see below n. 21).

13. Life 12.

overlooked either. Josephus is writing in post-war Rome as a client of the imperial house of Flavians, for which reason he came to be called by their patronym, Flavius[14].

Meanwhile, the temple having been destroyed and the Sadducees and Essenes now disappearing from history, spiritual leadership of the Jewish people fell to the Pharisees[15]. So much arises from an analysis of Rabbinic literature, and there is more. Post-war Pharisaism itself was not what it used to be like. Of the two wings comprising the movement, the school of Shammai, apparently the stronger before the war, now was in a minority position. Thus from its post-war centre at Yavne (Jamnia), Pharisaism issued a number of authoritative decrees, at first under the guidance of the outstanding Hillelite, Yohanan ben Zakkai, later under the strong leadership of Gamaliel the Younger, whose rule eventually gained official Roman recognition and who is said to be a descendant of Hillel and grandson of 'our' Gamaliel, i.e. the Elder[16]. Among other innovations, the title of 'rabbi' was now monopolised for ordained law teachers, and henceforth we can speak of Rabbinic Judaism. In sum, the Pharisaic movement had turned into predominant Hillelite Rabbinism.

Hence Josephus' latter-day Pharisaism suffers some interesting specification. Blaming the lost war on the Zealots[17] and labelling himself as a Pharisee comes down to discrediting the Shammaites and supporting the new Hillelite majority. One could almost suspect that the foggy 'fourth philosophy' which he introduces in the *Antiquities* as being fully at one with the Pharisees *except for their nationalistic passion* – not exactly a compliment in his mouth – in fact alludes to the school of Shammai[18].

14. Ant. 20.268; Life 422-429.

15. Characteristically expressed in authority on calendar issues. For this and other items involved here see the syntheses by G. ALON, *The Jews in Their Land in the Talmudic Age (70-640 C.E.)*, vols. 1-2, Jerusalem, Magnes, 1980-84, vol. 1, pp. 86-131; E.M. SMALLWOOD, *The Jews under Roman Rule from Pompey to Diocletian. A Study in Political Relations*, Leiden, Brill, 1981, pp. 331-356; S. SAFRAI, *The Era of the Mishnah and Talmud (70-640)*, in H.H. BEN-SASSON (ed.), *A History of the Jewish People*, London, Weidenfeld and Nicholson, 1976, pp. 305-382, esp. 314-330.

16. The change-over resulted in only a gradual 'Hillelization' of the halakha, in which the Shammaite (!) inclinations of Gamaliel II himself stand out; see S. SAFRAI, *The Decision According to the School of Hillel in Yavneh*, in *Proceedings, World Congress of Jewish Studies* 7:3 (1981) 21-44 (in Hebr.); ID., *Halakha*, in ID. (ed.), *The Literature of the Sages. First Part: Oral Tora, Halakha, Mishna, Tosefta, Talmud, External Tractates* (CRINT, 3/2a), Assen – Maastricht, Van Gorcum – Philadelphia, Fortress, 1987, pp. 185-200.

17. It may be wise to heed the scholars who remind us that Josephus uses the name Zealots only for the years 68-70, and use quotation marks for a more general usage, cf. L.L. GRABBE, *Judaism from Cyrus to Hadrian*, vols. 1-2, Minneapolis, Fortress, 1992, vol. 2, p. 499f.

18. For cautious criticism of this idea see M. GOODMAN, *The Ruling Class of Judaea.*

For this seems to tie in with Rabbinic reports of a bloody confrontation in which the Shammaites imposed a number of anti-foreign decrees on the Hillelites by force of arms, while the protagonist on the occasion, Elazar ben Hananya (ben Hizkia ben Garon), is known from Josephus as one of the main instigators of the Roman war[19]. As to Josephus himself, he interestingly conforms to Hillelite halakha on some prominent issues[20]. But he never became a true supporter of the Hillelite dynasty and maintained an inner reserve. Next to old age scruples, *Realpolitik* must have been a cause of his re-orientation[21].

The role of the Pharisees in Luke-Acts has been the subject of much debate[22]. Following the innovative reading of Jakob Jervell, a growing

The Origins of the Jewish Revolt against Rome A.D. *66-70*, Cambridge, UP, 1987, pp. 93-96, 107f., 209f. The Fourth Philosophy, τετάρτη τῶν φιλοσοφιῶν (Ant 18.23), in War 2.118 is still called the ἴδια αἵρεσις of Judas the Galilean, as distinct from the three 'philosophies'. In contrast to THACKERAY (*ad* War 2.118, *LCL*), FELDMAN (*ad* Ant. 18.23) doubts the 'Zealot' link. But Josephus is explicit that the movement (also lead by Zadok the Pharisee!) inspired the later Zealots (War 2.118, 2.433; 7.253; Ant. 18.4-10). More-over the solemn presentations of the three schools in War 2.119ff. and Ant. 18.12ff. are *both* clearly occasioned by the mention of this 'separate' or 'fourth' movement, which proves its importance, even if Josephus tries to minimize it.

19. mShab 1,4; tShab 1,16; yShab 1, 3c-d; Josephus, War 2.409f; cf. MekhRY yitro 7 (ed. Horovitz-Rabin, p. 229), and MekhRSbY (ed. Epstein-Melamed, p. 148). The iden-tification was made already by H. GRAETZ, *Geschichte der Juden von den ältesten Zeiten bis auf die Gegenwart*, Leipzig, 1888, vol. 3/2, pp. 470-472, 795ff. See also A. GOLD-BERG, *Commentary to the Mishna Shabbat*, Jerusalem, JTS, 1976, pp. 15-22; M. HENGEL, *Die Zeloten. Untersuchungen zur jüdischen Freiheitsbewegung in der Zeit von Herodes I bis 70 n. Chr.*, Leiden, Brill, ²1976, pp. 204-211; P.J. TOMSON, *Paul and the Jewish Law. Halakha in the Letters of the Apostle to the Gentiles* (CRINT, 3/1) Assen – Maastricht, Van Gorcum – Minneapolis, Fortress, 1990, pp. 173-176.

20. Notably divorce and shabbat: Ant. 4.253 (divorce being allowed καϑ' ἁσδηπο-τοῦν αἰτίας, cf. mGit 9,10); Life 426 (Josephus divorcing his wife because of her dis-pleasing behaviour); and 161 (Josephus taking the Sabbath to prohibit carrying weapons if there is no mortal danger, contrast his Shammaite contemporary, R. Eliezer, mShab 6,4).

21. MASON, *Josephus* (n. 12), pp. 357ff. takes it that the pro-Pharisaic words Life 12 are counterbalanced by Shimon ben Gamliel's vicious intrigue to remove Josephus from command in Galilee (Life 189-198). But Life 191 which prefaces that episode is even more flattering about Shimon than War 4.159, and the expression πρὸς ἐμὲ τότε διαφόρως εἶχεν suggests that at the time of writing the disaccord was over. Since Shi-mon appears to have been killed during the war (see ALON and SMALLWOOD, above n. 15), this gives the impression of referring to the post-war Hillelite majority in general.

22. See the contribution by M. Rese in this volume (above pp. 185-201). Some com-ments may be permitted (referring to his paper as read at Leuven). Quite important are two earlier conclusions Rese reiterates: the role of the Jews has to do with the purpose of Luke-Acts, and its meaning must be read from the author's position. Opposing Jervell's approach, Rese sticks to the standard, negative evaluation stated by Overbeck and Haenchen. The frequency difference of Ἰουδαῖος between Luke and Acts he cites as an argument is not to be understood from a shift in genre or chronology, but from the social difference implied by the group appellation 'Jew': whereas the gospel (like Mk and Mt)

number of scholars begin to recognize the positive role the Pharisees play in these works[23]. But many others can only perceive a negative or at most contradictory attitude[24]. A failure common to many of the latter assessments is that in line with the traditional view they neglect social distinctions characteristic of Second Temple Judaism and typically confound the Pharisees as a whole with the priestly temple elite[25].

For a reliable starting point in Luke-Acts, we must take those parts which most directly betray the author's hand, i.e. the infancy[26] and resurrection stories in the gospel and the history of Paul in Acts. In the infancy and resurrection stories, it is not so much the Pharisees as the law that is prominent. Jesus is brought up by pious parents who diligently behave "according to the Law of Moses", and the risen Lord explains the Passover events on the basis of "the law of Moses, the prophets, and the Psalms"[27]. Likewise Paul when defending himself says he has offended "neither against the law of the Jews, nor against the temple, nor against Caesar", and in conversation with the Jewish leaders

stays within a Jewish speech domain, Acts increasingly moves into mixed or non-Jewish speech areas. This does not in itself prejudice the meaning of 'Jew', as is clear from the more positive value of 'Pharisee' many percieve in Acts. The peculiar character of John (in the dominant, final redaction) is that it locates Jesus and his followers within the *alien* surroundings of Jews. See P.J. TOMSON, *The Names Israel and Jew in Ancient Judaism and in the New Testament*, in *Bijdragen* 47 (1986) 120-140, 266-289. Finally, I fail to understand how Rese can both lash out against "historicism" and criticize exegetes of Luke-Acts for overlooking the *Wirkungsgeschichte*.

23. J. JERVELL, *Luke and the People of God. A New Look at Luke-Acts*, Minneapolis, Augsburg, 1972, esp. pp. 41-74 and 133-152; cf. ID., *The Theology of the Acts of the Apostles* (NT Theology), Cambridge, UP, 1996; now also his commentary in the KEK series. See especially the comparison of Luke, Acts and Josephus by MASON (above n. 6). See further J.A. ZIESLER, *Luke and the Pharisees*, in *NTS* 25 (1979) 146-157, stressing the positive image of the Pharisees as compared with the other gospels; R.L. BRAWLEY, *Luke-Acts and the Jews. Conflict, Apology, and Conciliation* (SBL MS, 33), Atlanta, Scholars, 1987, who shows that Luke-Acts gives sustained and respectful attention to the Pharisees, while setting off Jesus and his followers positively from them. On the open-endedness of Acts see below n. 53.

24. J.T. SANDERS, *The Jews in Luke-Acts*, Philadelphia, Fortress, 1987, finds Luke-Acts anti-Jewish while taking the Pharisees to be the stock-in-trade opponents of Jesus. Similarly J.D. KINGSBURY, *The Pharisees in Luke-Acts*, in F. VAN SEGBROECK, *et al.* (eds.), *The Four Gospels* 1992. FS F. Neirynck, Leuven, UP – Peeters, 1992, II, pp. 1497-1512; J.T. CARROLL, *Luke's Portrayal of the Pharisees*, in *CBQ* 50 (1988) 604-621; H. MERKEL, *Israel im lukanischen Werk*, in *NTS* 40 (1994) 371-398. J.B. TYSON, *Images of Judaism in Luke-Acts*, Columbia, UP, 1992, finds Luke-Acts "both pro-Jewish and anti-Jewish and both in profound ways" (p. viii); in *Jews and Judaism in Luke-Acts: Reading as a Godfearer*, in *NTS* 41 (1995) 19-38, he tries to overcome this historical anomaly via Luke's supposed aim of writing for Godfearers.

25. See nn. 4, 5, and 24.

26. TYSON, *Images*, pp. 42-55 recognizes the idealized Jewish piety of the surroundings of infant Jesus.

27. Lk 2,21-28; 24,27.44.

of Rome he is only appealing to "the law of Moses and the prophets"[28]. This signals a fundamental identification with the basics of Judaism, but it does not state that Jesus was a Pharisee, nor Paul in his actual status.

The fact is that the gospel contains some bitter criticisms of the Pharisees. "The Pharisees and law teachers have rejected the plan of God for themselves" by refusing John's baptism, and the Pharisees are "lovers of money". These could still be read as qualifications the author adopted from his sources[29]. But in two passages that appear to be redactional summaries and have no synoptic parallel, "the scribes and Pharisees" as a generalized category keep a watchful eye on Jesus and murmur because he eats with sinners[30]. On the other hand, unlike all other gospels, the Lukan Jesus accepts invitations to a Pharisee home, even up to three times; the Pharisees do *not* plan to kill him for his behaviour on shabbat, but remain in suspense not knowing what to do; indeed, Pharisees try to save his life by warning him for Herod Antipas[31]. And as to Acts, Paul in another of his apologies calls himself "a Pharisee, son of Pharisees"; Pharisees wonder whether an angel had spoken to him; many other Pharisees join the church; and a prominent and popular Pharisee pleads to leave Jesus' followers alone[32].

Clearly, the Lukan author does not idealize the Pharisees and he is not afraid to criticize them. But neither does he come anywhere near the absolutized anti-Pharisaism we find in Matthew, or to the anti-Judaism of John[33]; on the contrary, in Acts he is openly sympathetic. All that his gospel tells us is that Jesus was no Pharisee, and in doing so he seems to give a realistic rendering of conflicts that may have occurred between a non-conformist Galilean teacher and Pharisaic leaders. These stories remind of Rabbinic reports about tension between the Sages and pious

---

28. Acts 28,17.23.

29. Lk 7,30; 16,14.

30. Lk 11,53f; 15,2.

31. The Pharisees' invitations: Lk 7,36; 11,37; 14,1; their doubt as to Sabbath: 6,11 (the optative ποιήσαιεν betraying the hand of the author; contrast Mk 3,6; Mt 12,14; Jn 5,18!); their warning: 13,31. On the latter passage see A. DENAUX, *L'hypocrisie des Pharisiens et le dessein de Dieu: Analyse de Lc., XIII,31-33*, in F. NEIRYNCK (ed.), *L'Évangile de Luc: Problèmes littéraires et théologiques* (BETL, 32) Gembloux, Duculot, 1973, pp. 245-285, and for another reading M. RESE, *Einige Überlegungen zu Lk 13,31-33*, in J. DUPONT (ed.), *Jésus aux origines de la Christologie* (BETL, 40), Gembloux, Duculot, 1975, pp. 201-226.

32. Acts 26,5; 22,9; 15,5; 5,34.

33. The immense significance of this difference tends to be overlooked by those who read Luke-Acts as being anti-Pharisaic (above n. 24). For Matthew and John see P.J. TOMSON, *'Als dit uit de Hemel is...'. Jezus en de schrijvers van het Nieuwe Testament in hun verhouding tot het Jodendom*, Hilversum, Folkertsma Stichting – Zoetermeer, Boekencentrum, ³1997, chaps. 6 and 7 (ET forthcoming).

miracle workers termed "the *hasidim* of old", as well as of ancient traditions preserving inner-Pharisaic criticism of bigotry and hypocrisy[34].
In sum, while the gospel is clear about the differences between Jesus and
the Pharisees and candid in its criticism of the latter, the Lukan author
on the whole displays a remarkable sympathy for them.

Thus we find both Josephus and the Lukan author taking pro-Pharisaic positions which do not quite seem to tally with the contents of their
writings. On the other hand, such a stance must have drawn much attention in a late first century Roman context. Nobody would have forgotten
the Jewish war, and the *fiscus judaicus*, the special tax imposed on the
Jews, was in full swing. Therefore this choice of position can hardly
have been accidental. If it was not the advancement of his own position
or that of the Jewish people as such, what could the motives of the
Lukan author have been? To answer that question we must take a closer
look at the role the Pharisees and especially their leader, Gamaliel, play
in the evolving conflict over the message of Jesus.

Gamaliel's Intervention in the Framework of Luke-Acts

Gamaliel's intervention on behalf of the Apostles has a strategic position in Acts, and thereby in the framework of the two part apologetic history. It forms the last act of the first scene of Luke-Acts which is located
within the holy city, the theologico-geographical centre of the work.
Moreover it is an almost idealized consummation of this first scene[35], in
which glimpses of the growing newborn church alternate with incidents
showing its strained relation with the authorities. The latter are not anonymous but a well-defined power group[36]. In 4,1 it is "the priests, the tem-

---

34. I.e., 7 types of Pharisees, only the last 2 of whom are viewed positively; mTaan
3,8; yBer 9,13b. And cf. critique of "the plague of Pharisees" מכת פרושים, mSot 3,4; its
explanation ySot 3,19a, "this is one who advises inheritors how to avoid paying alimen-
tation to the widow", is a full parallel to Jesus' criticism in Mk 7,9-13. On the ancient
hasidim see S. SAFRAI, *Teaching of Pietists in Mishnaic Literature*, in *JJS* 16 (1965) 15-
33; ID., *Jesus and the Hassidic Movement*, in A. OPPENHEIMER, I. GAFNI, D. SCHWARTZ
(eds.), *The Jews in the Hellenistic-Roman World. Studies in Memory of Menahem Stern*,
Jerusalem, Shazar Center – Historical Society, 1996, pp. 413-436 (in Hebrew).

35. Using this term in its theatrical sense; cf. different usage in R. TANNEHILL, *The
Narrative Unity of Luke-Acts. A Literary Interpretation*, Philadelphia – Minneapolis,
Fortress, 1986-90, vol. 2, p. 43. Not stressing the diaspora element in Acts 6–8, Tannehill places "the climax of the conflict in Jerusalem" in that section (pp. 80ff.). This is
not impossible, 6–8 having an ambiguous character, but precisely so I prefer to distinguish it from 1–5. Also, the election of the seven "Hellenist" deacons signals a new
departure.

36. As correctly noted by BRAWLEY, *Luke-Acts* (n. 23), chap. 7, "Sadducees, Priests,
and Temple".

ple commander[37] and the Sadducees" who come down on Peter and the other Apostles; in 4,5f this alliance is amplified to include "their leaders, elders and scribes who had gathered in Jerusalem, as well as Annas the high priest and Caiaphas and John and Alexander and whoever were of high-priestly birth". However they are unable to arrest them "because of the people" (4,21). Then after another glimpse of the prosperous infant church, the final act is initiated by "the high priest and all those with him, that is, the sect of the Sadducees", alternatively called "the temple commander and the chief priests", who convene "the *synhedrion* and the *gerousia* of the Israelites" (5,17.24). Still, the commander and his officers refrain from using force "out of fear for the people, of being stoned" (5,26). The session, and with it the first scene of Acts, ends with the Apostles being set free at the proposal of the Pharisee Gamaliel.

A comparison with the trial of Jesus in Luke's gospel brings out characteristic parallels[38]. From the start of Jesus' appearance in the temple area, it is "the chief priests, the scribes and the prominent among the people" who confront him but at first cannot take action because of the people, then with the help of Judas succeed in arresting him unseen, and in the end condemn him in their *synhedrion* and hand him over to Pilate[39]. So far the author accords with Mark, which he must at least have had before him[40]. By contrast, in Matthew the brief pericope castigating the wealth-loving scribes known from Mark and Luke is built into a whole chapter attacking "the scribes and Pharisees", thus implicating the Pharisees in the conflict leading up to Jesus' execution[41]. Quite the opposite happens in Luke. Not only does our author add another pericope expressing popular support for Jesus (23,27-31), he also inserts the notice that Joseph from Arimathea, the council member who came to bury Jesus, "did not support their initiative and their action" (23,51) – a phrase that clearly relates to our Acts passage[42]. In short, the Pharisees

---

37. Στρατηγὸς τοῦ ἱεροῦ, i.e. סגן הכהנים, cf. E. SCHÜRER, *The History of the Jewish People in the Age of Jesus Christ (175 B.C. – A.D. 135)*, Edinburgh, T.&T. Clark, 1979, vol. 2, p. 277f.

38. On such parallels see W. RADL, *Paulus und Jesus im lukanischen Doppelwerk: Untersuchungen zu Parallelmotiven im Lukasevangelium und in der Apostelgeschichte* (EHS, 23/49), Bern – Frankfurt/M, Lang, 1975.

39. Lk 19,47f.; 20,1.19; 22,2.4.66; 23,52.

40. V. TAYLOR presents interesting evidence to the effect that Luke follows an independent passion account: *The Passion Narrative of St. Luke. A Critical and Historical Investigation* (SNTS MS, 19), Cambridge, UP, 1972.

41. Mk 12,41-44; Lk 20,45–21,4; Mt 23.

42. Βουλὴ καὶ πρᾶξις. F.J. FOAKES JACKSON – K. LAKE (eds.), *The Beginnings of Christianity*, Part I: *The Acts of the Apostles*, London, Macmillan & Co., 1920-27, vol. 4, p. 62 note the parallel with βουλὴ ἢ ἔργον in Acts 5,38. Cf. below n. 76.

are eloquently absent from the judicial murder, nor do all lay councillors take part in it. Jesus is arrested and executed at the initiative of the same priestly elite who in Acts, precisely in the Gamaliel episode, are denoted as 'the sect of Sadducees'.

Back to Acts and to the second scene, that of Stephen and Philip which stands on the borderline between Jerusalem and the diaspora and also slips in the protagonist of the second half of the book. Stephen and Philip are among the seven deacons appointed on behalf of the "Hellenists" or Greek-speakers[43]. At this stage, it is not the Sadducee elite which troubles Jesus' followers, but diaspora Jews[44] who "stir up the people and the priests and the scribes"; the high priest's role being limited to presiding the *synhedrion*. Stephen is mob-lynched after his violent sermon against the temple authorities while support from *certain* Pharisees is implied, explicitly so in the case of the young law student from Cilicia, Saul[45]. The ensuing persecution of the church occasions not only Philip's preaching to non-Jews but also Saul's conversion. Carrying written mandates from the high priest, he pursues the new sect down to Damascus until he is struck by light from heaven.

We skip the conflicts with diaspora synagogues which now start growing hand in hand with the mission among non-Jews, and jump to the final part of Acts. Paul returns to Jerusalem and agrees to demonstrate his faithfulness to the law in order to pacify the 'zealous' church members. Again, diaspora Jews stir up the crowd, but the Roman commander allows him to address the people. Speaking in "the Hebrew language" (which may have been Aramaic), he reveals his identity: "I am a Jew born at Cilician Tarsus, brought up in this city at the feet of Gamaliel, and trained in the details (ἀκρίβεια)[46] of the ancestral law,

43. Acts 6,5f. See M. HENGEL, *Zwischen Jesus und Paulus. Die "Hellenisten", die "Sieben" und Stephanus (Apg 6,1-15; 7,54–8,3)*, in *ZTK* 72 (1975) 151-206. The diaspora connection is signalled by another of the seven, "Nicolaus, a proselyte from Antioch".

44. Acts 6,9.12. Beza's conjecture Λιβυστίνων (Libyans) for Λιβερτίνων, based on an Armenian variant and next to Cyrenaeans, Alexandrians and those from Cilicia and Asia, deserves serious consideration.

45. Acts 7,58.60. The procedure, described by the Mishna as קנאין פוגעין בו (mSan 9,10) and also supported by Philo, is disapproved of by the later Rabbis. See T. SELAND, *Establishment Violence in Philo and Luke. A Study of Non-Conformity to the Torah and Jewish Vigilante Reactions* (Biblical Interpretation Series, 15), Leiden, Brill, 1995; G. ALON, *On Philo's Halakha*, in ID., *Jews, Judaism, and the Classical World. Studies in Jewish History in the Times of the Second Temple and Talmud*, Jerusalem, Magnes, 1977, pp. 89-137, esp. 112-124.

46. This is another significant term also used by Josephus in this connection, see MASON, *Josephus* (n. 12), *passim*. It parallels Rabbinic דקדוקי סופרים, "niceties of the scribes", which figures in connection with Pharisaic and specifically *havura* particulars:

being zealous for God as you all are today"[47]. Next day Paul is brought before "the chief priests and all the *synhedrion*". When the high priest has him hit in the face, he rebuts with a stroke of Pharisaic ἀκρίβεια which his adversary may well have missed (Acts 23,5). One also wonders whether the author grasped it, but in either case he shows that he disposed of actual Pharisaic traditions, since Paul's pun is understandable only with the help of Rabbinic literature.

Paul says he did not know it was a high priest who had him hit since it is written: "You shall not speak evil of a ruler of your people" (Exod 22,27). What is meant? The answer seems to be found in an anonymous explanation to that verse known from a Rabbinic collection some two centuries younger than Acts: "... A ruler of your people – as long as they observe the custom of your people"[48]. The upshot is that Paul did not *recognize* the man as such because he did not *behave* as a leader of his people. As we shall see, the Pharisees attached great importance to popular custom. This makes us understand even better why Paul now, conscious[49] of the division between Pharisees and Sadducees, provokes uproar by claiming he is being tried as a Pharisee for his belief in resurrection. This time the author comes to the readers' help by pointing out Saducean disbelief on this subject[50], and he concludes by noting that "some of the scribes of the Pharisee party" find nothing wrong in Paul and even allow for the possibility that he spoke on heavenly inspiration (Acts 22,30–23,9).

Thus the author's narrative strategy becomes clear. He locates the hard core of hostility to the message of Jesus at first in the Sadducee power group in Jerusalem, later also in a range of diaspora synagogues[51].

---

tDem 2,5; Sifra, kedoshim 8 (ed. Weiss 91a); cf. bBekh 30b; Tanh wayikra 2 (1b); TanhB wayikra 3 (2a). A.I. BAUMGARTEN, *The Name of the Pharisees*, in *JBL* 102 (1983) 411-428, wishes to explain the name "Pharisees" from this connection: פרושים, "interpreters".

47. Acts 21,15–22,3. The three part "education formula" is a Hellenistic *topos* and signals the author's emphasis, see W.C. VAN UNNIK, *Tarsus or Jerusalem?*, in ID., *Sparsa collecta*, vol. 1 (NTSup, 29), Leiden, Brill, 1973, pp. 259-320.

48. MekhRY mishpatim 19 (Horovitz-Rabin, p. 318), בזמן שהן עושין מנהג עמך, the plural הן suggesting anti-Saducean polemic. I owe this explanation to Shmuel SAFRAI and David FLUSSER. The ignorance of Tora on the part of (Saducean) high priests is proverbial in Rabbinic literature, cf. the expression כהן עם הארץ, bYev 114a etc., and in the Derekh Erets treatises; and cf. the high priest's instruction, mYom 1,6 and concomitant supervision by the (Pharisee) סגן הכהנים = στρατηγός; see SCHÜRER, *History* (n. 37).

49. Γνούς of course not to be taken as an ingressive, as RSV has it.

50. Along with his custom to translate Semitic terms into Greek, this enhances the impression the Lukan author did *not* grasp Paul's midrash on the high priest (and it confirms the tradition that he was a non-Jew).

51. Similarly MASON, *Chief Priests* (n. 6).

The people, as long as they are not mislead, are behind Jesus. Not all Pharisees are laudable, some of them even supporting the persecution of the church, notably young Saul. Yet the overall portrait of the Pharisees is not unsympathetic. They are divided over the message of Jesus, they take no part in his trial, and a number of them would grant Paul the benefit of the doubt. Hence the importance of the earlier moment in the story when Paul's own teacher commends tolerance and restraint by means of a saying of profound wisdom[52]: "A Pharisee in the *synhedrion* named Gamaliel, a law teacher respected by all the people, ... said: ... If this initiative or this action is from humans it will be dissolved, but if it is from God, you cannot dissolve it without rebelling against God" (Acts 5,34.38f.). The well-respected and popular Pharisee does not in fact choose position: he leaves the discussion undetermined. This implies no irony, at least no sarcasm. A similar open-endedness may be discerned in Paul's discussions with synagogue leaders, which despite generally negative reactions sometimes end on a positive note, and in Rome at the very end of Acts are left undecided[53].

In short, we see how the author puts Gamaliel and other Pharisees in a role of permissive tolerance towards Christianity. Comparison with Josephus made us doubt the likelihood of a coincidence; our analysis of Luke-Acts now makes it almost certain the author acted on purpose. We like to speak of his rhetorical "constructions". Yet in announcing a book about "things that happened", he challenges us to take episodes like Gamaliel's to be more than apologetic fiction[54]. How does the episode relate to the actual Pharisees of his day and their tradition, as far as we know it?

---

52. For the positive image of Gamaliel cf. J. MUNCK, *The Acts of the Apostles* (Anchor Bible), Garden City, NY, Doubleday, 1967, *ad loc.*; *The Interpreter's Bible*, vol. 9, New York, Abingdon, 1954, pp. 86f.

53. See the example of Beroea, Acts 17,11: ἐδέξαντο τὸν λόγον μετὰ πάσης προθυμίας. Cf. M. HENGEL, *Zur urchristlichen Geschichtsschreibung*, Stuttgart, Calwer, 1979, p. 58. On Rome, Acts 28,25: ἀσύμφωνοι δὲ ὄντες πρὸς ἀλλήλους. The open-endedness of Acts vis-à-vis the Jews is argued by B.J. KOET, *Five Studies on Interpretation of Scripture in Luke-Acts* (SNTA, 14), Leuven, Peeters, 1989, ch. 5; TANNEHILL, *Narrative Unity* (n. 35), vol. 2, pp. 352f.; F. BOVON, *Studies in Luke-Acts: Retrospect and Prospect*, in *HTR* 85 (1992) 175-196; D. MARGUERAT, *"Et quand nous sommes entrés dans Rome" – l'énigme de la fin du livre des Actes (28,16-31)*, in *RHPR* 73 (1993) 1-21; H. VAN DE SANDT, *Acts 28,28: No Salvation for the People of Israel? An Answer in the Perspective of the LXX*, in *ETL* 70 (1994) 341-358; J.-N. ALETTI, *Quand Luc raconte. Le récit comme théologie* (Lire la Bible, 114), Paris, Cerf, 1998, pp. 167-218.

54. Thus the opinion of E. HAENCHEN, *Die Apostelgeschichte* (KEK), Göttingen, Vandenhoeck & Ruprecht (1956), [7]1977, p. 252; and G. SCHNEIDER, *Die Apostelgeschichte* (HTK, 5), Freiburg, Herder, 1980, p. 388.

Gamaliel and Hillelite Pluralism

If we want to answer this question we must confront the Acts story with external sources informing us about the position and character of the Pharisees at the time of writing.

First, by adding Pharisaic tolerance to popular admiration of Jesus and his message, the Lukan author somehow associates the Pharisees with the populace. This linkage is also found in various other sources. (1) In spite of his inner reserve, Josephus consistently notes massive popular support for the Pharisaic tradition, and since he left Palestine after the Roman war, this must refer primarily to the pre-war situation[55]. He also notes that temple ritual is conducted according to Pharisaic tradition[56]. (2) These statements find chronologically sound confirmation in the Qumran halakhic letter which militates against pressure being exerted on the Jerusalem priests to relinquish ancient priestly traditions shared with the author of the letter – the pressure apparently coming from Pharisaic side[57]. (3) Now this combined information interestingly connects with isolated Rabbinic reports to the effect that Sadducee high priests conformed to Pharisaic custom and had to do so in order to avoid popular outrage. We already heard that Rabbinic tradition explicitly valued popular custom. There also is the story that the prominent Pharisee, Hillel the Elder, expressly went by the standard of popular usage[58]. (4) Finally Rabbinic literature as a whole, which one way or another represents a development from Pharisaic tradition, shows features typical of popular oral literature such as the abundant use of anecdotes and parables. As contrasted with writings like those of Philo and Josephus or those from Qumran, this again suggests that Pharisaic tradition had been in close touch with popular sentiment[59]. When added up, the evidence indicates

---

55. MASON, *Josephus* (n. 12), pp. 372f. Cf. also his conclusion in *Chief Priests* (n. 6), p. 177.

56. Ant. 18.12-17.

57. 4QMMT, see E. QIMRON – J. STRUGNELL, *An Unpublished Halakhic Letter from Qumran*, in *Biblical Archaeology Today*, Jerusalem, 1985, pp. 400-407, and *Discoveries in the Judaean Desert*, vol. 10, Oxford, UP, 1994; Y. SUSSMAN, *The History of Halakha in the Dead Sea Scrolls – A Preliminary to the Publication of 4QMMT*, in *Tarbiz* 59 (1990) 11-76 (in Hebrew).

58. Sadducee (Boethusian) custom being overruled: mSuk 4,9; tSuk 3,16; bSuk 48b (cf. Josephus Ant. 13.372 on the pelting with *etrogim*); Pharisaic control over temple ritual: tPara 3,8; mPara 3,7f; tKipp 1,8; on popular custom above n. 48; Hillel opting for popular custom: tPes 4,14.

59. See S. SAFRAI, *Oral Tora*, in ID., *The Literature of the Sages* (n. 17), pp. 35-199, on the oral and popular character of Pharisaic-rabbinic tradition. The use of parables, a wide-spread popular literary genre absent, e.g., from Qumran, Philo and Josephus, is another important indicator.

that the strong post-war position of the Pharisees was based on the support among the populace they had been enjoying already before the war. To be sure, we should not think here in terms of unequivocal support for a coherent "party line". By all indications, pre-70 Pharisaism was a multiform phenomenon comprising at least the rather different schools of Shammai and Hillel, and popular support for them must at least have varied along similar lines.

Second, the popular character of the Pharisees brings out the historical profile of Gamaliel. A Pharisee bearing that name and being sufficiently important to be mentioned twice in a succinctly written apologetic work about events in the early first century CE, moreover described as being well respected among all the people, can hardly be anyone but Rabban Gamliel the Elder, the Hillelite leader known from Rabbinic literature[60]. He was the father of Shimon ben Gamliel who officiated during the war according to Josephus, who despite personal antipathies also describes him as an eminent and popular Pharisee – to such an extent that one must resist the suspicion that both descriptions are somehow dependent[61].

Third, this brings up the relevance of the Hillelite tradition. As stated, the aftermath of the war against Rome meant not so much the ascendancy of Pharisaism in general as of its specific Hillelite variety. At the time they were writing, Josephus and the Lukan author had to deal with Hillelite Rabbinism. This does not necessarily imply a Hillelite power politics. On the contrary as we saw, if anyone, it were their adversaries of the school of Shammai who had literally tried to enforce their will at the beginning of the war. Hillelite legend typically ascribes peacefulness and tolerance to its founding fathers, Hillel the Elder and Yohanan ben Zakkai.

For in the fourth place Rabbinic literature, precisely in its predominantly Hillelite make-up which originates from the post-70, Yavne period, incorporates a pluralist policy regarding the relation of truth and power. At the level of legend, there is the paradoxical summary of the relation of both traditions *sub specie aeternitatis*: "A heavenly voice came forth at Yavne: Both these and those are the words of the living God, but the halakha is according to the school of Hillel"[62]. While tak-

---

60. According to a *baraita* bShab 15a he was the son of Hillel's otherwise unknown son Shimon, while mAvot 1,16 has him directly succeed Hillel and Shammai. mPea 2,6 mentions him as a leader of the Temple High Court. See A. HYMAN, *Toldoth Tannaim ve'Amoraim*, vol. 1, London, Express Printers, 1910, s.v.

61. War 4.159; Life 190-216 (in the alternative Greek transcriptions Συμεών and Σίμων). For possible dependence of Luke-Acts on Josephus see nn. 11 and 65.

62. yBer 1,3b; bEr 13b; etc. See SAFRAI, *Decision* (n. 16).

ing the Hillelite majority for granted, the saying shows respect for the Shammaite tradition. The same is explicit in a parallel saying which expresses the paradox at the level of practical halakha: "Forever, the halakha is according to the school of Hillel, but... (one must behave) either according to the school of Shammai including their leniencies and stringencies, or to the school of Hillel including their leniencies and stringencies"[63]. This pluralist policy was also expressed in the formulation of the central Rabbinic document, the Mishna. While its overall inclination is towards Hillelite halakha, often the Shammaite tradition is given first, and the question why the minority view is preserved is answered by means of an appeal to respect and to the fundamental open-endedness of tradition[64].

Let us integrate these data in our prior observations. The Lukan author, who at specific points is capable of severe criticism of the Pharisees, nevertheless draws a positive overall picture of them. An important facet of this picture is the moment when Gamaliel, said to be a popular Pharisee leader, convincingly advises the high-priestly circles to leave the movement of Jesus the benefit of the doubt. This advice now seems to accord with the Hillelite strand of Pharisaism of which Gamaliel must have been a prominent representative and which after the Roman war rose to power. We are faced with the intriguing question whether Gamaliel's words as presented by the Lukan author could specifically relate to Hillelite tradition.

As a preliminary, we must face serious doubts as to the authenticity of Gamaliel's speech. The core of his advice is prefaced with two examples. The first concerns Theudas, a messianic pretender who is also mentioned by Josephus, but at a time ten to fifteen years *later* than the presumable date of the Apostles' trial. The second is about Judas the Galilean, who Josephus says was active some twenty years *before* that date[65]. This shows our author used inexact reports and composed

---

63. tSuk 2,3 = tYev 1,13 = tEd 2,3, cf. sources in previous n.; and see Lieberman, ad loc.

64. mEd 1,4-6; tEd 1,3-5.

65. Ant. 20.97-98, followed by a last reference to Judas the Galilean (20.102, because of the crucifixion of his sons). In spite of other similarities, including the same non-chronological order, STERLING, *Historiography* (n. 7), pp. 365f. thinks this no sufficient proof for literary dependence. The opposite has been defended ever since M. KRENKEL, *Josephus und Lucas. Der schriftstellerische Einfluss des jüdischen Geschichtsschreibers auf den christlichen nachgewiesen*, Leipzig, H. Haessel, 1894 (on Gamaliel's intervention, pp. 162-174). I am indebted to Bart-Jan KOET for facilitating access to this work. MASON, *Chief Priests* (n. 6), p. 177 also thinks Luke saw Josephus' later works.

Gamaliel's speech himself, in line with Hellenistic historiography[66]. Hence all appearances are that he also put the saying into Gamaliel's mouth, and that after all the whole speech is mere apologetical fiction[67]. That is, unless we find external evidence to the contrary, presumably from the direction of Pharisaic-Rabbinic tradition. As a matter of fact, we have already seen an important instance where the author uses a tradition he intends to be taken for Pharisaic (whether he fully grasped it or not) and which appears to be preserved in a more explicit form in Rabbinic literature.

The fundamental question is what authorial certainty we can attain to in the case of Pharisaic tradition, which in its formative stage was oral and hence fluid and amorphous[68]. Brevity precludes a full discussion of Rabbinic form criticism, but this much can be stated here. In the framework of an oral tradition, both the exact dating and the authorship of any particular saying tend to be hard to define. There always remains an insuperable margin of uncertainty. But once this 'tolerance' in the technical sense is accepted, what we often *are* able to determine is the saying's belonging to a particular strand of tradition, such as the Hillelite or Shammaite variety, within the span of several generations[69]. Precisely this seems to be the case with Gamaliel's counsel.

The tractate *Avot* which was appended to the Mishna[70] is a collection of wisdom sayings which in its extant form 'proverbially' summarizes oral tradition from time immemorial, through Hillel, Gamliel the Elder ("ours") and the Younger, all the way down to Yehuda ha-Nasi, the redactor of the Mishna, and even to his grandson, Yehuda Nesia[71]. This is the lineage of the Hillelite dynasty, and the tractate patently is meant

66. E. PLÜMACHER, *Lukas als hellenistischer Schriftsteller. Studien zur Apostelgeschichte* (SUNT, 9), Göttingen, Vandenhoeck & Ruprecht, 1972, pp. 10f., 32-38; ID., *Lukas als griechischer Historiker*, in PAULY-WISSOWA, Supplementband 14, 1974, cc. 244-249.
67. See above n. 54.
68. See SAFRAI, *Oral Tora* (n. 59).
69. This is exemplified in sayings attributed both to earlier and later teachers within the same tradition, such as Hillel and his spiritual heirs R. Yoshua and R. Akiva (see TOMSON, *Paul*, p. 246 n. 124), or Shammai and the Shammaite Elazar ben Hananya ben Hizkia ben Garon, MekhRY yitro 7 (ed. Horovitz-Rabin, p. 229), and MekhRSbY (ed. Epstein-Melamed, p. 148).
70. For excellent introductions see M.B. LERNER, *The Tractate Avot* and *The External Tractates*, in SAFRAI, *The Literature of the Sages* (n. 16), pp. 263-276 and pp. 367-402, esp. 369-379.
71. mAv 1,16-2,4, a section not paralleled in ARN and apparently reflecting the final redactional stage. Cf. a similar but much more loosely formulated fragment in ARNa 32 (ed. Schechter 35b-36a).

to record Hillelite tradition. Yet precisely so, not only Hillelite opinions
are preserved. Apart from Hillel, a number of Shammai's sayings are
recorded, just as the proverbs of R. Eliezer ben Hyrcanus, the prominent
Yavnean Shammaite[72], precede those of his eventually more powerful
Hillelite colleague, R. Yoshua ben Hananya[73]. Indeed Rabbinic literature, here apparently again displaying the pluralism typical of Hillelite
tradition, values the discussion between both schools as an indispensable
element. So much is to be gathered from a saying preserved in two variant forms in *Avot* and from the explanatory comments on them contained in *Avot de-Rabbi Natan*, a parallel collection extant in two recensions, the oldest of which is quoted here[74]:

> Every gathering (כנסיה) in the name of Heaven will keep existing in the
> end, but every gathering (that is) not in the name of Heaven will not keep
> existing in the end.
>> What is a gathering in the name of Heaven? You should say: That is
>> the gathering of Israel before Mount Sinai.
> Every dissent (מחלוקת) in the name of Heaven will keep existing in the
> end, but every dissent (that is) not in the name of Heaven will not keep
> existing in the end.
>> What is a dissent in the name of Heaven? You should say: That is the
>> dissent of Shammai and Hillel.

Some comments are in place. These sayings obviously embody a most
tolerant view. Here, Hillelite tradition not just preserves traditions of its
former competitors, but declares the discussion between them to be an
ineluctable feature of truth in the face of Heaven. It is not power that
decides over truth, as the Shammaites thought once at least, but true witness in the long run. This holds true even for the paradigmatic "gather-

---

72. See SAFRAI, *Halakha* (n. 16), pp. 186, 198f.

73. mAv 1,12-15; 2,10-11; ARNb 29-30 (30a-32b). On Shammaite tradition in this
context see LERNER, *Tractate* (n. 70), pp. 265, 372, who also notes (p. 376) that in con-
tradistinction to mAvot 1,12-15; 2,8 and to ARNa 12-15 (24b-31a), the order in ARNb
23-24 (24a-b) is the standard one in Rabbinic literature, i.e., first Shammai, then Hillel.
The same, it may be added, holds for the tradition to be quoted in a moment, where both
Avot and ARNa have the order Hillel-Shammai, while the quoted version, ARNb, has
Shammai-Hillel. Hence Avot and ARNa reflect a later further 'Hillelization' at the redactional level.

74. ARNb 46 (ed. Schechter 64b). The first saying is also found isolated in mAv 4,11
in name of R. Yohanan 'the Alexandrian' (± 150 CE), outstanding disciple of R. Akiva
who was himself the heir to Hillelite tradition; the second anonymous mAv 5,17; both
sayings again together with comments ARNa 40 (ed. Schechter 65a). While undoubtedly
stemming from a single original source, the two sayings appear to derive from independent channels of transmission. Anonymous versions often tend to be the older, but that is
all one can say. On the terminology see below at n. 76.

ing" of the chosen people, Israel before Sinai – an impressively open-minded and even vulnerable statement. Truth remains indeterminate, humanly speaking. Irony? Sure, but good-humoured. When viewed "from above", precisely this modest open-endedness, the maximum humans can attain to, earns divine endorsement. No really serious human conviction may be discarded *a priori*. This is profound wisdom – this is paraphrasing Gamaliel's counsel! Indeed, the material relationship with Acts 5,38f. has long been recognized[75]. Without exaggeration, we can even say that the Rabbinic text offers an excellent elucidation of the illustrious Pharisee's saying.

There may be even more to it. While the two Rabbinic sayings clearly intend to express the same human modesty over against ultimate truth, they differ in only one word, i.e., the term describing the human stance: כנסיה, "gathering", or מחלוקת, "dissent". This makes it the more obvious that these are variants of one basic tradition. One wonders which may be the more original. Or is that a wrong question, and should one look for a single term explaining both variants? The incredible thing is that precisely such a term is found in the Greek βουλή as used in Acts 5,38! I have been translating it in the above as 'initiative' because of the social aspect expressed in the corresponding verb καταλῦσαι[76]. Precisely so, βουλή can be equivalent both to "gathering" and to "dissent", depending on whether the 'initiative' is taken to be centripetal or centrifugal. Hence it covers both Hebrew terms. Food for speculation. Could the saying have once been formulated before a Greek-speaking Jewish audience, using the word βουλή, and subsequently have been translated into two different Hebrew versions? Remarkably, both Gamaliel's saying and the two Rabbinic proverbs have a somewhat odd, binary structure[77].

This much seems certain. In the framework of his positive account of the Pharisees' attitude to nascent Christianity, the Lukan author puts a saying of apparent Hillelite vintage in the mouth of Gamaliel, to the

---

75. H.L. STRACK – P. BILLERBECK, *Kommentar zum NT aus Talmud und Midrasch, ad loc.* cites mAv 4,11 and 5,17. J.J. WETTSTEIN, *H KAINH ΔIAΘHKH, ad loc.* mentions only the more general parallel with Euripides, Bacch. 45.325.1255 and other passages involving the verb θεομαχεῖν. The link with mAv 4,11 is recognized by SCHNEIDER, *Apostelgeschichte* (n. 54), p. 403 (judging the Euripides parallels to be of lesser importance) and J. ZMIJEWSKI, *Die Apostelgeschichte* (RNT), Regensburg, F. Pustet, 1994, p. 271.

76. Ancient English versions have counsel or 'councel', modern translations prefer 'plan' and the like.

77. The slightly uneasy *apodosis* which involves the typically Greek term θεομαχεῖν (above n. 75) may then be read as a (typically Lukan) redactional explanation.

effect that Jewish leaders must leave the ultimate truth about the new movement for Heaven to decide.

Conclusion

Both the author of Luke-Acts and Flavius Josephus in his later works make a remarkable bid for Pharisaic sympathy, before a similar audience and at roughly the same time, i.e. upper class Roman readers some 25 years after the Jewish war. In both cases, this must relate to the make-up of post-war Jewish society which involves the predominance of Hillelite Rabbinism. Their motives differ. Josephus is a priestly aristocrat whose need of personal rehabilitation makes his pro-Pharisaic declarations sound a bit shallow. Much less than a personal career, the Lukan author defends a novel, dissenting interpretation of Jewish Scripture and history. Whilst his rhetorical strategy leads him to put Pharisees including Gamaliel the Elder in a positive light, his supportive citation of the latter does concord with Rabbinic sources. More precisely, his apology of Christianity as a legitimate outgrowth of Judaism makes an intentional appeal to the Hillelite reputation of modesty vis-à-vis religious truth.

This is an exceptional position among early Christian authors. It differs sharply from the other evangelists, notably Matthew and John, as also from early apologetes such as Ignatius, Polycarp, Justin, or Irenaeus. If the Lukan author was a non-Jewish Godfearer, as tradition has it[78], his modest stance also implies criticism of the increasing Judeo-Christian resentment to fellowship with non-Jewish Christians (Acts 15,1.5; cf. Gal 2,11-14). Thus his appeal to Hillelite pluralism is based on more than opportunism: he actually subscribes to it.

What may move a late first-century non-Jewish Christian to sympathize with Hillelite Rabbinism, and not to be impressed by the synagogue ban it issued at about that time[79]? Formally, the project of Luke-Acts seems closest to that of Paul, if it is true that the latter advocates a church consisting both of Jews living 'in the circumcision' and of non-Jews sticking to their 'non-circumcised' ways of life (1 Cor 7,18f). Does

---

78. Eusebius, *Hist. eccl.* 3.4.6. Note the attention Luke-Acts pays to Godfearers. Also, the author at times betrays lack of expertise in matters of halakha and midrash (above at nn. 48, 50).

79. Cf. Jn 9,22; 12,42; 16,2. The ban did probably not have universal validity, see D. FLUSSER, *The Jewish-Christian Schism*, in ID., *Judaism and the Origins of Christianity*, Jerusalem, Magnes, 1988, pp. 617-644, esp. 637-643; and cf. ALON, *The Jews* (n. 15), pp. 288-307. On the restrictive attitude of Gamaliel II in this context see SAFRAI, *Decision* (n. 16).

the Lukan author actually intend to carry on the message of the apostle whom he portrays as a former Pharisee and student of Gamaliel, and that at a time when hardly anyone still believed in it? That interpretation was proposed, of all modern scholars, by Adolf Harnack[80]. I think he was right.

Gen. MacArthurstr. 38/3   Peter J. TOMSON
B-1180 Brussel

---

80. A. HARNACK, *Die Stellung des Apostels Paulus zum Judentum und Judenchristentum nach seinen Briefen; seine jüdischen Schranken*, in ID., *Beiträge zur Einleitung in das Neue Testament*, IV: *Neue Untersuchungen zur Apostelgeschichte und zur Abfassungszeit der synoptischen Evangelien*, Leipzig, Hinrichs, 1911 (involving a very early dating of Luke-Acts). Harnack personally preferred Marcion, the 'ultra-Paulinist': see his *Marcion: das Evangelium vom fremden Gott. Eine Monographie zur Geschichte der Grundlegung der Katholischen Kirche* (TU, 3/15), Leipzig, Hinrichs, 1921, p. 235.

APG 10,1–11,18 IM LICHT DER LUKANISCHEN ERZÄHLUNG
VOM WIRKEN JESU

»Ihr wißt… von Jesus aus Nazaret, wie ihn Gott mit heiligem Geist und Kraft gesalbt hat, der umherzog, Gutes tat und alle heilte, die vom Teufel unterjocht waren, denn Gott war mit ihm. Und wir sind Zeugen all dessen, was er getan hat im Land der Juden und in Jerusalem«. Diese Sätze finden sich mitten in der Rede, die Petrus nach Apg 10 im Haus des Kornelius gehalten hat (vv. 37-39)[1]. Warum stehen sie dort? Die Frage stellt sich schon deshalb, weil *Heiden* in der Apostelgeschichte sonst nicht auf die Taten des Nazareners hingewiesen werden[2]. Sie drängt sich umso mehr auf, als ihr Verfasser die *Apostel* an keiner anderen Stelle so pointiert als Verkünder jener Taten darstellt[3]. Ich möchte daher versuchen zu klären, inwiefern das Wirken Jesu in Galiläa und Judäa für die Begegnung zwischen Petrus, dem Jünger und Apostel, und dem römischen Hauptmann relevant ist.

1. *Das Thema der Erzählung*

Lukas mißt dieser Begegnung zentrale Bedeutung zu: Er widmet ihr die längste Einzelerzählung seines Buches und bringt alle wichtigen Ereignisse mehrfach zur Sprache. Worum es ihm dabei geht, zeigt der als Ausruf der Jerusalemer Judenchristen gestaltete Schlußsatz: »Also auch den Heiden hat Gott die Umkehr zum Leben gegeben« (11,18). Dabei liegt der Ton auf der Wendung »auch die Heiden«, die noch an zwei weiteren Schaltstellen der Erzählung auftaucht: in 10,45 mit Blick

---

1. Im Folgenden beziehen sich bloße Kapitel- und Versangaben auf die Apostelgeschichte bzw. auf deren Kapitel 10–11. – Die Rede des Petrus geht übrigens mit 10,37 keineswegs an der Erzählsituation vorbei; das einleitende »ihr wißt« erklärt sich aus dem – von Lukas betonten – öffentlichen Charakter der Ereignisse um Jesus; cf. 2,22; 26,26, sowie R. PESCH, *Die Apostelgeschichte. 1. Teilband: Apg 1–12* (EKK, 5/1), Zürich, Benziger – Neukirchen-Vluyn, Neukirchener, 1986, p. 343.

2. Cf. 14,15-17; 17,22-31 und 8,30-35; 13,23-31; 26,23. Gegen C.H. DODD, *The Apostolic Preaching and Its Developments*, London, Hodder & Stoughton, [3]1951, p. 28: es sei natürlich, daß gerade Heiden mit den zentralen Fakten des Heilsgeschehens bekannt gemacht würden.

3. Die Pfingstpredigt stellt das vollmächtige Erdenwirken Jesu seiner Hinrichtung gegenüber (2,22-23), und nach 1,21-22; 13,31 ist dessen Kenntnis nur Bedingung für die Einsetzung zum Zeugen der Auferstehung, nicht selbst Gegenstand des Zeugnisses; cf. W. DIETRICH, *Das Petrusbild der lukanischen Schriften* (BWANT, 94), Stuttgart, Kohlhammer, 1972, p. 284.

auf die Ausgießung des Geistes, in 11,1 mit Blick auf die Annahme des Wortes Gottes[4]. Mit dem Geistempfang und der Taufe des Kornelius sind also die Heiden ein für allemal in das Christusgeschehen einbezogen und damit zur Aufnahme in die Kirche als das endzeitlich gesammelte Volk Gottes[5] zugelassen.

Freilich wird mit dieser Zulassung von Heiden zum Heil nur vollzogen, was bereits zu Beginn der lukanischen Jesus-Geschichte durch Simeon angekündigt worden ist (Lk 2,32)[6] und was der Auferstandene den Jüngern von Anfang an aufgetragen hat (Lk 24,47). Jene Zulassung kann deshalb nicht das alleinige Thema der Erzählung von Kornelius und Petrus sein[7]. In der Tat besagen die Stellen, an denen die Wendung »auch die Heiden« begegnet, mehr. Lukas hebt dort ja hervor, daß christusgläubige Juden das heilvolle Handeln Gottes an Heiden wahrnehmen (10,45; 11,1) und anerkennen (11,18). Dabei steht Gottes Handeln in unlösbarer Verbindung mit dem Tun und Reden des Apostels[8]; er ist die eigentliche Hauptperson der Erzählung[9]. Diese soll demnach zeigen: Judenchristen dürfen, ja müssen nach Gottes Willen Heiden den Zugang zu dem in Christus verfügten Heil ermöglichen – durch eigenes Handeln oder zumindest durch überzeugte Zustimmung[10].

Das zentrale Problem solcher Teilgabe am Heil besteht in lukanischer Sicht darin, daß Judenchristen dafür mit Heiden in Kontakt treten müssen. Dabei geht es noch nicht um das Zusammenleben von Juden und Heiden in einer Gemeinde; dieses Thema wird zwar mit 10,23a.48 am Rande erwähnt, aber erst in Kapitel 15 wirklich bearbeitet[11]. In

---

4. Das Gegenstück zu jener Wendung bildet der ebenfalls dreimal benutzte Ausdruck »wie auch wir« bzw. »… uns« in 10,47; 11,15.17. Die nächsten Parallelen im NT bilden Röm 3,29; 9,24; cf. ferner Mt 10,18; Apg 15,17; 26,17.20.23, wo καί jeweils anreihende Bedeutung hat.

5. Zu diesem Kirchenverständnis des Lukas cf. J. ROLOFF, *Die Kirche im Neuen Testament* (GNT, 10), Göttingen, Vandenhoeck & Ruprecht, 1993, pp. 192-206.

6. Cf. ferner Lk 13,19.29; 14,23 und als indirekte Hinweise Lk 4,25-27; 10,13-14; 11,31-32.

7. Gegen A. WEISER, *Die Apostelgeschichte. Kapitel 1–12* (ÖTK, 5/1), Gütersloh, Gütersloher – Würzburg, Echter, 1981, pp. 251-252.

8. Als Petrus noch redet, fällt der heilige Geist auf die heidnischen Zuhörer (10,44; 11,15), und infolge ihrer Begabung mit dem Geist läßt Petrus sie taufen (10,47; 11,17).

9. Cf. M. DIBELIUS, *Die Bekehrung des Cornelius*, in ID., *Aufsätze zur Apostelgeschichte*, ed. H. GREEVEN, Berlin, Evangelische Verlagsanstalt, ²1953, pp. 96-107, hier 104. Man beachte z.B., daß in 10,1–11,18 der Name »Petrus« 19mal begegnet, der Name »Kornelius« nur 8mal.

10. Cf. W. SCHMITHALS, *Die Apostelgeschichte des Lukas* (ZBK, 3/2), Zürich, Theologischer Verlag, 1982, p. 104: »Die Heidenmission ist … Gottes Werk durch die Juden(christen)«.

11. Cf. H.-J. KLAUCK, *Magie und Heidentum in der Apostelgeschichte des Lukas*

10,1–11,18 befaßt sich Lukas primär mit der Frage, ob Petrus als christusgläubiger Jude überhaupt mit Heiden zusammenkommen darf, um ihnen Gottes Wort zu verkündigen[12].

Dreimal wird diese Frage thematisiert, und zwar zunehmend deutlicher: Als Petrus den fremden Boten begegnet, sagen sie ihm, ihr Hauptmann solle – auf Befehl eines Engels – etwas von ihm hören (10,17-22); als er dessen Haus betritt, will Kornelius alles hören, was ihm vom Herrn aufgetragen sei (10,27-33); als dann Judenchristen in Jerusalem Petrus vorhalten, er sei mit Heiden zusammengekommen, stellt er mit den Worten des Hauptmanns klar, daß er jenen Heiden die rettende Botschaft zu predigen hatte (11,2-14).

Man beachte: Für Lukas steht in 11,3 nicht das Thema »Mahlgemeinschaft« im Vordergrund. Petrus geht in 11,4-18 darauf mit keinem Wort ein; daß er mit Heiden gegessen habe, wird zudem in Kapitel 10 nirgends explizit erwähnt; schließlich weist εἰσῆλθες in 11,3 auf 10,25.27 zurück sowie auf 11,12 voraus – und dort ist dem jeweiligen Kontext nach stets eine Kontaktaufnahme im Blick, die der Verkündigung des Wortes Gottes dient. Das Motiv des gemeinsamen Essens veranschaulicht in diesem Zusammenhang, ähnlich wie in 10,41 (cf. 1,3), nur die Gemeinschaft, die bei einer derartigen Unterweisung entsteht[13].

Darf Petrus als Jude mit Heiden zusammenkommen, um ihnen die Heil bringende Christusbotschaft zu verkünden? Diese Frage behandelt Lukas mit der Petrus-Kornelius-Erzählung, und er gibt ihr eine eindeutig positive Antwort: Gott selbst, so heißt es rückblickend in 15,7, hat Petrus für diese Aufgabe »ausgewählt«, hat dessen Bedenken zerstreut und ihn zu Kornelius geführt, hat die Verkündigung an die Heiden durch die Ausgießung des Heiligen Geistes auf sie bekräftigt und damit legitimiert; und durch den Bericht des Petrus wird auch die Gemeinde in Jerusalem davon überzeugt, daß er im Auftrag Gottes gehandelt hat. So macht Lukas deutlich: Gott selbst will die Botschaft, die »zuerst« den Juden verkündigt werden mußte (3,26; 13,46), fortan auch den Heiden zukommen lassen, und zwar durch Juden.

(SBS, 167), Stuttgart, Katholisches Bibelwerk, 1996, pp. 50-51; gegen H. WENDT, *Die Apostelgeschichte* (KEK, 3), Göttingen, Vandenhoeck & Ruprecht, [9]1913, p. 179, der den Eintritt des Apostels in die Tischgemeinschaft mit Heiden als den Kernpunkt der Petrus-Kornelius-Erzählung ansieht.

    12. Cf. R.C. TANNEHILL, *The Narrative Unity of Luke-Acts. A Literary Interpretation. 2: The Acts of the Apostles*, Minneapolis, MN, Fortress, 1990, pp. 135-136.

    13. Cf. dazu K. HAACKER, *Dibelius und Cornelius. Ein Beispiel formgeschichtlicher Überlieferungskritik*, in *BZ* 24 (1980) 234-251, p. 240.

2. Der Aufbau der Erzählung

Von dieser Themabestimmung her erschließt sich, mit welcher Stringenz die sieben Szenen der Erzählung aufeinander folgen und sich zu einer kunstvollen Einheit zusammenfügen[14].

Schon die erste Szene, die Kornelius vorstellt, die Engelserscheinung schildert und seine Reaktion darauf beschreibt (10,1-8), signalisiert: Hier passiert etwas ganz Neues; daß ein Engel Gottes einem *Heiden* erscheint, ist ja in der Ursprungsgeschichte der Kirche, von der Lukas erzählt, ohne Parallele[15].

In Analogie dazu handelt auch die zweite, Petrus einführende Szene (vv. 9-16) von einer radikalen Neuerung: Gott selbst – so die zentrale Botschaft der Vision in v. 15 – habe die Grenze zwischen rein und unrein aufgehoben; daher solle Petrus nun ebenfalls diese Grenze überschreiten[16]. Allerdings bleibt vorerst offen, in welchem Sinn die Vision von »Reinheit« spricht; denn die Möglichkeit, sie wörtlich auf den Verzehr des Fleisches unreiner Tiere zu beziehen, scheidet gemäß v. 17a von vornherein aus[17].

In den folgenden vier Szenen wird Petrus dann Schritt für Schritt dazu angeleitet, den Sinn der Vision zu erkennen und ihr gemäß zu handeln. Zunächst schildern die Verse 17-23, wie die Boten des Kornelius Petrus aufsuchen und ihn nach Cäsarea geleiten. Dabei werden Engelserscheinung und Vision miteinander verknüpft sowie vorläufig gedeutet: Erstere zielt nach v. 22 darauf, daß Kornelius von Petrus etwas hören soll; die Vision aber wird durch den Befehl des Geistes (vv. 19-20) ausgelegt[18]: »Habe keine Scheu vor den heidnischen Männern, denn ich habe sie gesandt«[19].

14. Zu Gliederung und Gedankengang cf. vor allem den Überblick bei F. BOVON, *Tradition et rédaction en Actes 10,1–11,18*, in *TZ* 26 (1970) 22-45, pp. 26-28.

15. Die Besonderheit des Vorgangs wird dadurch unterstrichen, daß die Erzählung ihn noch an drei weiteren Stellen erwähnt; cf. 10,22.30-32; 11,13. Im lukanischen Doppelwerk sprechen Engel als Boten Gottes sonst nur mit jüdischen Personen, die in der Heilsgeschichte eine wichtige Rolle spielen; cf. Lk 1,11-20.26-38; 2,9-15; Apg 5,19-20; 7,30-38; 8,26; 12,7-11.

16. Cf. R. MADDOX, *The Purpose of Luke-Acts* (FRLANT, 126), Göttingen, Vandenhoeck & Ruprecht, 1982, p. 37, der aber zu Unrecht von der Aufhebung des *Gesetzes* spricht (cf. das Folgende).

17. Cf. auch v. 19a. Solch eine Deutung kommt für Lukas, der das Aposteldekret tradiert (15,20.29), nicht in Betracht; E. HAENCHEN, *Die Apostelgeschichte* (KEK, 3), Göttingen, Vandenhoeck & Ruprecht, [13]1961, p. 307. Vielleicht erklärt sich von hieraus, daß in seinem Evangelium das Streitgespräch über Reinheit von Händen und Speisen aus Mk 7,1-23 fehlt.

18. Cf. K. KLIESCH, *Apostelgeschichte* (SKK, 5), Stuttgart, Katholisches Bibelwerk, 1991, p. 86. – G. LÜDEMANN, *Das frühe Christentum nach den Traditionen der Apostelgeschichte. Ein Kommentar*, Göttingen, Vandenhoeck & Ruprecht, 1987, p. 133, bestrei-

Sodann zeigen die Verse 24-33[20], wie der Apostel das Haus des Kornelius betritt und sich auf ein Gespräch mit ihm einläßt. Wiederum werden Vision und Engelserscheinung aufgenommen sowie weitergehend interpretiert. Der Vision entnimmt Petrus nun die göttliche Weisung, »keinen Menschen ... unrein zu nennen« (v. 28c)[21]; Kornelius leitet aus der Engelserscheinung den Wunsch ab, alles zu hören, was der Herr Petrus aufgetragen habe (v. 33). Der Zusammenhang von v. 28 und v. 33 macht dabei endgültig deutlich: Im Sinne des Lukas zielt die Vision weder auf die Aufhebung jüdischer Speiseverbote noch auf die Ermöglichung innergemeindlicher Mahlgemeinschaft mit Heiden[22], sondern darauf, daß Petrus die Heilsbotschaft auch den Heiden ausrichten soll.

In den Versen 34-43 wird daraufhin erzählt, wie Petrus den versammelten Heiden die Christusbotschaft verkündigt. Den Anschluß an die Vision stellt dabei der einleitende Passus vv. 34b-36 her[23]; denn die Erkenntnis des Apostels, von der hier die Rede ist, besagt: Fortan soll jeder Gottesfürchtige, sei er Jude oder Heide, das Wort hören, das den Israeliten ausgerichtet wurde; denn Gott, von dem

tet den Bezug auf die Vision. Die Verse 19-20 knüpfen jedoch auf vierfache Weise daran an: Der Geist spricht zu Petrus, als der über die Vision nachdenkt; die Weisung ἀναστὰς κατάβηθι καὶ πορεύου ist formal dem Aufruf ἀναστὰς ... θῦσον καὶ φάγε (v. 13) nachgebildet; die Wendung μηδὲν διακρινόμενος (dazu s.u. n. 19) weist auf den Protest des Apostels in v. 14 zurück; das Motiv der Sendung durch den Geist erinnert an das Herablassen des Tuchs aus dem Himmel (v. 11).

19. Zwar redet der Geist in 10,20 noch allgemein von etwaigen »Bedenken« des Petrus; nach dessen eigener Aussage in 11,12a aber war damit gemeint, er solle im Umgang mit den heidnischen Boten keinen »Unterschied« machen. Zu dieser Differenzierung zwischen Medium und Aktiv (15,9!) cf. G. DAUTZENBERG, Art. διακρίνω, in EWNT 1, cc. 732-738, hier 733-734.

20. Gegen die Einteilung im Novum Testamentum Graece ist v. 23b mit WEISER, Apostelgeschichte (n. 7), p. 250, als Abschluß der dritten Szene anzusehen, da Petrus erst hier den Befehl des Geistes ausführt; cf. dazu den Konnex zwischen v. 5 und v. 8 in der ersten Szene.

21. Vers 28c wird durch das – von Lukas konsequent in seiner optischen Bedeutung benutzte – Verb δείκνυμι (cf. Lk 4,5; 5,14; 20,24; 22,12; 24,40; Apg 7,3) sowie durch die Aufnahme der Stichworte κοινός und ἀκάθαρτος aus 10,14 als Deutung der Vision ausgewiesen; cf. auch G. SCHNEIDER, Die Apostelgeschichte. 2. Teil: Kommentar zu Kap. 9,1–28,31 (HTK, 5/2), Freiburg, Herder, 1982, p. 73 n. 128.

22. So lautet die Alternative bei J. ROLOFF, Die Apostelgeschichte (NTD, 5), Berlin, Evangelische Verlagsanstalt, 1988 (= Göttingen, Vandenhoeck & Ruprecht, 1981), p. 170.

23. Cf. DIBELIUS, Bekehrung (n. 9), p. 104, der sich freilich nur auf 10,34-35 bezieht. Zum Aufbau der Rede cf. G. SCHNEIDER, Die Petrusrede vor Kornelius. Das Verhältnis von Tradition und Komposition in Apg 10,34-43, in ID., Lukas, Theologe der Heilsgeschichte. Aufsätze zum lukanischen Doppelwerk (BBB, 59), Königstein – Bonn, Hanstein, 1985, pp. 253-279, hier 272-273: Die beiden, jeweils mit dem Hinweis auf »Zeugen« endenden Teile des Korpus (vv. 37-39a.39b-41) werden gerahmt von vv. 34b-36 und vv. 42-43 (dazu s.u. n. 28).

jenes Wort ausgeht, ist unparteiisch, und Jesus Christus, von dem
jenes Wort spricht, ist ein »Herr aller«. Von Ps 106,20 (LXX) her
bezeichnet λόγος in 10,36 nämlich gewiß Gottes eigenes, Heil schaf-
fendes Wort (cf. 13,26); und dieses Wort ergeht nach Lukas in der
Predigt der Zeugen (cf. 15,7 u.ö.)[24]. Daher besteht die einfachste
Lösung für das Problem der grammatischen Zuordnung von 10,36[25]
darin, τὸν λόγον als *accusativus graecus* an v. 35 anzuschließen[26]:
Gott ist jeder Gottesfürchtige »willkommen *in bezug auf* das Wort«.
Diese Verknüpfung von τὸν λόγον mit δεκτός liegt von der Formulierung in 11,1 (τὰ ἔθνη ἐδέξαντο τὸν λόγον τοῦ θεοῦ) her
sprachlich nahe und fügt sich sachlich gut in die Erzählung ein: Was
den Aposteln aufgetragen wurde (10,33), galt zunächst Israel
(vv. 36.42); nun soll es auch Kornelius und seinen Hausgenossen
zukommen, und zwar infolge ihrer in Gebet und Almosen manife-
stierten Gottesfurcht (vv. 2-4.31). Diese führt gewiß nicht selbst die
Rettung herbei[27], wohl aber deren Möglichkeit. Für den Gehalt der
Vision heißt das dann: Die in v. 15 erwähnte »Reinigung« besteht
darin, daß Gott Heiden zum Empfang des Wortes bestimmt hat; prinzipiell ermöglicht wurde sie durch die Einsetzung Jesu zum Richter
und Versöhner (vv. 42-43)[28], aktuelle Realität aber gewann sie in der
Erscheinung des Engels vor Kornelius[29].

Vom letzten Schritt, den Petrus zum Verstehen und Umsetzen der
Vision macht, handeln die Verse 44-48: Weil Gott über die Hörer seiner
Predigt den Geist ausgießt, befiehlt er, sie zu taufen. Von hier aus erhält
die Vision einen Sinn, der auf den Schlußteil der Erzählung (11,1-18)
sowie auf den Bericht vom Apostelkonzil (15,1-35) vorausweist: Wen

---

24. Cf. auch 28,28: »Gottes Heil« sei den Heiden »gesandt«, und diese würden (es)
auch »hören«; gegen C. BURCHARD, *A Note on ῥῆμα in JosAs 17:1f.; Luke 2:15,17; Acts
10:37*, in *NT* 27 (1985) 281-295, p. 291, der 10,36 auf die Botschaft der Engel bei Jesu
Geburt deutet.

25. Cf. dazu den Forschungsüberblick bei F. NEIRYNCK, *Acts 10,36a τὸν λόγον ὄν*, in
ETL 60 (1984) 118-123.

26. Cf. B. WEISS, *Das Neue Testament. Handausgabe 3. Band: Die Apostelgeschichte
– Katholischen Briefe – Apokalypse*, Leipzig, Hinrichs, ²1902, p. 102.

27. So B. WANDER, *Trennungsprozesse zwischen Frühem Christentum und Judentum
im 1. Jahrhundert n. Chr.* (TANZ, 16), Tübingen – Basel, Francke, 1994, p. 189.

28. Der Schlußteil der Rede weist auf die Einleitung zurück; dabei korrespondiert
v. 42 mit v. 36 (Botschaft an Israel, Universalität Christi), v. 43 mit v. 35 (Offenheit des
Heils für alle).

29. Cf. den Rückbezug von v. 35 auf vv. 2-4. Zwar werden Ort und Zeit jener Reinigung nicht explizit benannt; sie lassen sich aber erschließen aus dem Umstand, daß Petrus
den Sinn der Vision erst in der Beschäftigung mit den beiden Berichten von der Engelserscheinung (vv. 22.30-32) zu erkennen vermag: dazu TANNEHILL, *Unity* (n. 12), pp. 130-
132.

Gott mit dem Geist begabt, wessen Herz Gott durch den Glauben »reinigt« (15,9)[30], den sollen Apostel und Gemeinde nicht von der Gemeinschaft des Gottesvolkes fernhalten.

Abschließend wird in 11,1-18 geschildert, wie Petrus sich in Jerusalem für sein Verhalten verantworten muß. Seine Apologie bringt dabei die zentralen Elemente der Begegnung mit Kornelius so zur Sprache, daß ihre prinzipielle Bedeutung hervortritt[31]: Das Vorgehen des Apostels basierte von Anfang bis Ende auf der Führung Gottes (vv. 5-9.12a.13-14.15); was in Cäsarea geschah, bildet gemeinsam mit dem Pfingstwunder die Erfüllung der Geistverheißung Jesu (vv. 15-17); mit der Rettung des gottesfürchtigen Hauptmanns hat Gott demnach allen Heiden den Weg zum Leben geöffnet (v. 18). Auf diese Weise macht die Erzählung deutlich, daß Judenchristen das Wort von Jesus Christus fortan auch den Heiden verkündigen müssen. Eben von solcher Verkündigung wird dann in der Apostelgeschichte ab 11,19 berichtet[32].

3. Der Zusammenhang der Erzählung mit der Jesus-Geschichte

Was hat nun die Begegnung zwischen Petrus und Kornelius mit dem Erdenwirken Jesu zu tun? Der Überblick zu Thema und Aufbau der Erzählung verschärft nur die Dringlichkeit der Frage: Der Rekurs auf jenes Wirken in 10,37-39a findet im übrigen Text weder Parallelen[33] noch explizite Anknüpfungspunkte; das in 11,16 zitierte Jesuswort ist ein Wort des Auferstandenen (cf. 1,5); alle wesentlichen Voraussetzungen des erzählten Geschehens scheinen mit den Ereignissen zwischen Karfreitag und Pfingsten gegeben zu sein.

Dennoch sind die Bemerkungen zum irdischen Jesus für das Verständnis der Erzählung konstitutiv. Es fällt ja auf, daß er hier – in recht einseitiger Manier – als Geistträger und Wundertäter dargestellt wird.

---

30. Zum Konnex Geist/Reinheit cf. C.A. EVANS, *Jesus and the Spirit: On the Origin and Ministry of the Second Son of God*, in ID. – J.A. SANDERS, *Luke and Scripture. The Function of Sacred Tradition in Luke-Acts*, Minneapolis, MN, Fortress, 1993, pp. 26-45, hier 33-34.

31. Cf. H. CONZELMANN, *Die Apostelgeschichte* (HNT, 7), Tübingen, Mohr, 1963, p. 66.

32. Die Frage, welche Tradition(en) Lukas in 10,1–11,18 verarbeitet, kann im Rahmen dieser Studie nicht erörtert werden; cf. dazu die Diskussion bei J. ZMIJEWSKI, *Die Aufnahme der ersten Heiden in die Kirche nach Apg 10,1–11,18. Eine Interpretationsstudie*, in ANRW II.26.2, 1995, pp. 1554-1601, hier 1561-1569. Die vorstehenden Erwägungen legen aber die Annahme nahe, daß sich die Ausrichtung auf die *Verkündigung* an Heiden lukanischer Redaktion verdankt.

33. In 10,36 geht es nicht um die Predigt Jesu, sondern in Analogie zu 10,42 (s.o. n. 28) um die Botschaft der Apostel, durch die Gott den in Christus realisierten Frieden (cf. Lk 2,14; 19,38) verkündigen läßt (s.o. bei n. 24); cf. HAENCHEN, *Apostelgeschichte* (n. 17), p. 297.

Geistträger und Wundertäter aber ist Petrus der Apostelgeschichte zufolge auch[34]. Gewiß stehen er und die anderen Apostel nicht mit Jesus auf einer Stufe: Sie sind Gesandte Jesu Christi (10,41-42) und handeln in seinem Namen (10,43.48). Andererseits wird die Vergebung, die Jesus einzelnen Menschen zusprach, durch ihre Predigt allen Glaubenden zuteil[35]. Man kann also feststellen: In lukanischer Sicht führt Petrus – nebst anderen Aposteln – das Wirken Jesu, dessen Zeuge er war (10,39a), entfaltend fort[36]. Diese Verhältnisdefinition trifft für 10,1–11,18 in spezieller Weise zu; dabei nimmt die Erzählung auf die Geistträgerschaft Jesu ebenso Bezug wie auf seine Wundertätigkeit.

Was das Motiv der *Geistbegabung* angeht, so weist das Stichwort »salben« in 10,38 auf Lk 4,18(-21) zurück[37]. Dort nimmt Jesus für sich in Anspruch, der in Jes 61,1-2 angekündigte endzeitliche Gesalbte zu sein. Die öffentliche Autorisierung zu diesem Amt aber geschah bei seiner Taufe (Lk 3,21-22)[38]. Dem lukanischen Bericht davon ähnelt nun die Darstellung der Petrusvision in hohem Maß. Das Gebet als situativer Rahmen (10,9c; 11,5a), der offene Himmel (10,11), das Herabkommen von etwas Sichtbarem (10,11; 11,5b), das Ergehen einer Stimme (10,13.15; 11,7.9): alle wesentlichen Elemente der Taufszene spiegeln sich in 10,9-16; 11,5-10 wider[39]. So erhält dieser Text nahezu den Charakter eines Einsetzungsberichtes[40]. In Zusammenhang damit gewinnt dann die Bezeichnung »Simon mit dem Beinamen Petrus« aus der

34. Cf. 2,4.17-18; 4,8.31; 5,32; 10,47; 11,15-17; 15,8 und 3,6-8; 4,30; 5,12; 9,34.40.
35. Cf. einerseits Lk 5,20-24; 7,47-50, andererseits Lk 24,47; Apg 2,38; 10,43; u.ö.
36. Zu einem ähnlichen Urteil kommt R.F. O'TOOLE, *Parallels between Jesus and His Disciples in Luke-Acts: A Further Study*, in BZ 27 (1983) 195-212, aufgrund der zahlreichen Analogien zwischen Jesus und seinen Nachfolgern: Mit ihnen wolle Lukas gemäß 1,1 zeigen, »that what God began in Jesus he continues in Jesus' followers« (p. 211).
37. Cf. noch 4,27. SCHNEIDER, *Petrusrede* (n. 23), p. 275, verweist außerdem auf die Kongruenz mit Lk 4,14 im Stichwort δύναμις.
38. M. KORN, *Die Geschichte Jesu in veränderter Zeit. Studien zur bleibenden Bedeutung Jesu im lukanischen Doppelwerk* (WUNT, 2/51), Tübingen, Mohr, 1993, pp. 65-66, deutet die Taufe als öffentliche Bestätigung Jesu in seinem Amt: Das Herabkommen des Geistes mache ihn den Zuschauern offenbar als den, der er von Geburt an sei (Lk 1,35). Demgegenüber gilt es festzuhalten, daß die Taufe als Voraussetzung seines Wirkens (Lk 3,23) auch für Jesus selbst relevant ist: Hier wird er ermächtigt, sein »messianisches« Amt wahrzunehmen, nämlich dem Teufel zu widerstehen (Lk 4,1) und fortan »in der Kraft des Geistes« (Lk 4,14) aufzutreten.
39. Cf. H.-S. KIM, *Die Geisttaufe des Messias. Eine kompositionsgeschichtliche Untersuchung zu einem Leitmotiv des lukanischen Doppelwerks. Ein Beitrag zur Theologie und Intention des Lukas* (Studien zur klassischen Philologie, 81), Frankfurt, Lang, 1993, p. 201.
40. In 15,7 heißt es demgemäß, Gott habe Petrus unter den Aposteln dazu »auserwählt«, »daß durch (s)einen Mund die Heiden das Wort des Evangeliums hören und glauben«.

Erscheinung des Engels vor Kornelius[41] Bedeutung; denn sie erinnert an Lk 6,(13-)14, also an die Wahl des Petrus zum Apostel[42]. Auf diese Weise stellt Lukas klar: Petrus ist bevollmächtigt, das Werk Jesu nun auch unter den Heiden fortzuführen.

Daß der Apostel dabei an die *Wunderheilungen* des Nazareners anknüpft, tritt zunächst in den Verbindungslinien zu Lk 7,1-10 zutage: Wie einst Jesus in Kapernaum, so trifft jetzt Petrus in Cäsarea auf einen »Centurio«, der als Gottesfürchtiger dem jüdischen Volk verbunden ist; in beiden Fällen läßt der Römer den Juden, von dem er Hilfe erhofft, durch eine Gesandtschaft zu sich führen[43]. Neben solchen Entsprechungen aber stehen gewichtige Unterschiede: Jesus hält sich auf Bitten des Hauptmanns von dessen Haus fern, und dessen Glaube führt zur Heilung eines Knechtes; Petrus sucht auf Gottes Weisung hin Kornelius zu Hause auf, und allen dort versammelten Heiden wird durch seine Predigt »Rettung« zuteil[44]. So knüpft das Geschehen in Cäsarea an das Wunder von Kapernaum an, führt aber sachlich – als Eröffnung einer neuen heilsgeschichtlichen Epoche – weit darüber hinaus[45].

Sodann weist das in der Petrus-Vision verankerte Thema »Reinheit« auf die Wundertätigkeit Jesu zurück. Von Reinigung (10,15; 11,9) ist im Lukasevangelium ja überwiegend bei Heilungen von Aussatz die Rede[46]: Jesus geht ohne Sorge um seine eigene Reinheit auf Aussätzige zu und stellt ihre Reinheit wieder her; damit aber wird ihrer Umgebung ermöglicht, ohne Angst vor Verunreinigung mit ihnen zu verkehren. Um ein analoges Geschehen geht es bei Kornelius: Weil Gott Heiden zum Empfang des Heils bestimmt hat, kann Petrus sie aufsuchen und ihnen die Christusbotschaft verkündigen, ohne um seine Reinheit fürchten zu müssen; und weil Gott durch den Glauben ihre Herzen »reinigt« (15,9), können dann auch andere christusgläubige Juden mit ihnen Gemeinschaft pflegen[47]. Im lukanischen Verständnis gehören also Heilung von

---

41. Cf. 10,5; sie wird dann nacheinander von den Boten (10,18), von Kornelius (10,32) und schließlich von Petrus selbst (11,13) aufgegriffen.

42. Cf. dazu R. PESCH, *Art.* Πέτρος, in *EWNT* 3, cc. 193-201, hier 198. Der einzige weitere Beleg für das Nebeneinander beider Namensformen im lukanischen Doppelwerk ist Lk 5,8 – und auch dort ist Lk 5,9-11 zufolge die Berufung zum Apostel im Blick.

43. Cf. Lk 7,2-5 mit 10,1-8; die Zusammensetzung der Gesandtschaft in 10,7 erinnert dabei an Lk 7,8. Ferner weist der Befehl 10,20 auf Lk 7,6a zurück, sofern die Wendung πορεύειν σὺν (αὐτοῖς) im lukanischen Doppelwerk nur an diesen beiden Stellen belegt ist.

44. Cf. Lk 7,6-8 mit 10,27-28; 11,3.12b und Lk 7,9-10 mit 10,44; 11,14-15.

45. Zum Ganzen cf. SCHMITHALS, *Apostelgeschichte* (n. 10), pp. 104-105.

46. Cf. καθαρίζω in Lk 4,27; 5,12-13; 7,22; 17,14.17 (anders Lk 11,39; cf. καθαρός in Lk 11,41) und καθαρισμός in Lk 5,14 (anders Lk 2,22).

47. Zum letztgenannten Zusammenhang cf. M. KLINGHARDT, *Gesetz und Volk Gottes*.

Aussätzigen und Bekehrung von Heiden sachlich zusammen: Hier wie dort überwindet Gott Unreinheit von Menschen, um sie in das endzeitlich gesammelte Gottesvolk zu integrieren[48].

Ferner sind die in 10,38 erwähnten Exorzismen Jesu mit den Ereignissen um Kornelius verknüpft: Wie nämlich Israeliten durch die Austreibung der sie okkupierenden Dämonen und Geister aus der Gewalt des Satans befreit werden, so die Heiden nach 26,18 durch ihre Bekehrung zu Gott[49]. Zudem legt Lukas das Prädikat »unrein« aus 10,14.28; 11,8 in seiner Jesus-Geschichte nur den »unreinen Geistern« bei[50]. Er beschreibt demnach die Mission des Petrus unter Heiden auch als Fortführung des exorzistischen Wirkens Jesu.

Schließlich erinnern zwei weitere wichtige Züge der Erzählung an die Heilungen Jesu überhaupt; denn im Lukasevangelium wird vom Glauben (10,43; 11,17; cf. 15,7.9) oftmals, vom abschließenden Rühmen Gottes (11,18) ganz überwiegend innerhalb von Heilungsgeschichten gesprochen[51].

Überblickt man die genannten Rückbezüge auf das Lukasevangelium, so wird deutlich: Die Notiz zu Geistträgerschaft und Wundertätigkeit Jesu in 10,38 verweist auf die heilsgeschichtliche Kontinuität zwischen seinem Wirken und dem, was durch den Apostel an den Heiden geschieht. In diesem Rahmen verdienen auch die übrigen Punkte Beachtung, an denen sich die Petrus-Kornelius-Erzählung mit der lukanischen Jesus-Geschichte berührt.

Das lukanische Verständnis des Gesetzes nach Herkunft, Funktion und seinem Ort in der Geschichte des Urchristentums (WUNT, 2/32), Tübingen, Mohr, 1988, p. 212.

48. Gewiß ist bei den Aussätzigen von *kultischer*, bei den Heiden im übertragenen Sinn von *innerer* Reinheit die Rede. Für Lukas gehört aber beides zusammen, wie Lk 11,39-41 belegt.

49. Zu 10,38 sind vor allem Lk 10,18-20; 11,17-20; 13,11.16 zu vergleichen. Insofern dürfte es kein Zufall sein, daß die Schilderung der Petrusvision in 10,11 durch das – von Lukas sonst nur in 7,56 auf den Himmel bezogene – Verb θεωρέω auch sprachlich auf die Vision Jesu vom Satanssturz (Lk 10,18) zurückweist. Im übrigen wird die Einbeziehung der Heiden in das Christusgeschehen schon insofern durch Jesu Kampf gegen den Teufel vorbereitet, als dieser nach Lk 4,5-6 über die ganze Welt herrscht; cf. dazu DIETRICH, *Petrusbild* (n. 3), p. 281.

50. Cf. ἀκάθαρτος in Lk 4,33.36; 6,18; 8,29; 9,42; 11,24 (cf. Apg 5,16; 8,7); dabei wird die Nähe der Heiden zu den Dämonen in der Geschichte Lk 8,26-39 anschaulich.

51. Cf. πιστεύω bzw. πίστις in Lk 5,20; 7,9.50; 8,48.50; 17,19; 18,42 sowie δοξάζω τὸν θεόν in Lk 5,25.26; 7,16; 13,13; 17,15; 18,43 (anders Lk 2,20; 23,47) und Apg 4,21 (in 21,19-20 bezieht sich die Wendung wiederum auf Gottes Wirken unter den Heiden). Ferner klingt ἡσυχάζω (11,18) als Ausdruck widerstrebender Anerkennung des Willens Gottes (cf. 21,14) an Lk 14,4 an; cf. dazu T. ZAHN, *Die Apostelgeschichte des Lucas. Erste Hälfte: Kap. 1–12* (Kommentare zum Neuen Testament, 5/1), Leipzig, Deichert – Erlangen, Scholl, ³1922, p. 364 n. 88.

Hier ist zunächst der Konnex mit der Sendungsrede zu nennen: Petrus besucht den Hauptmann in dessen Haus (10,27; 11,12), verkündet ihm den Frieden durch Jesus Christus (10,36), bleibt dann bei ihm (10,48b) und ißt mit ihm (11,3); damit aber setzt er in neuer, veränderter Situation in die Tat um, was Jesus in Lk 10,5-7(.8) den siebzig Jüngern aufgetragen hatte[52].

Sodann bestehen einige einfache Analogien zwischen dem Apostel und seinem Herrn: Von beiden hören Menschen Gottes Wort[53], beide lösen durch die Wirkung ihrer Worte »Bestürzung« aus[54], beide bringen einem Haus, das sie betreten, das »Heil«[55]. Diese Analogien unterstreichen, daß sich das Werk Jesu im Handeln des Petrus fortsetzt.

Weiterhin fallen mehrere Bezüge zu den Gleichnissen vom Verlorenen in Lk 15 ins Auge: Der Vorwurf, Petrus sei mit Heiden zusammengekommen (11,3), spiegelt den fast gleichlautenden Vorwurf aus Lk 15,2 wider, Jesus habe Gemeinschaft mit Sündern[56]; das Motiv »Buße zum Leben« (11,18) weist u.a. auf die Sätze zur – im Himmel Freude auslösenden – Buße in Lk 15,7.10 zurück[57]; der Hinweis auf die einem Juden gebotene Distanz zu Fremden (10,28b) korrespondiert mit dem Bild vom gegensätzlichen Verhalten des verlorenen Sohnes, der in der Fremde bei einem Heiden die Schweine hütet[58]; der Befehl der Himmelsstimme »schlachte und iß« (10,13; 11,7) erinnert an die Einladung zum Fest, die der Vater nach der Heimkehr des Sohnes ausspricht[59]; die entrüstete Entgegnung des Petrus, er habe »niemals« etwas Unreines

52. Für T.J. LANE, *Luke and the Gentile Mission. Gospel Anticipates Acts* (EHS, 23/571), Frankfurt, Lang, 1996, pp. 91-93, ist in Lk 10,7-8 schon die Heidenmission im Blick. Dem steht entgegen, daß die Jünger nach Lk 10,1 Jesus voran, also zu Juden gehen. Die Sendungsrede bereitet daher nicht die Heidenmission vor, sondern weist nur indirekt auf sie voraus.

53. Cf. ἀκούω τὸν λόγον in 10,44 sowie Lk 5,1; 8,13.15; 10,39; 11,28 (ähnlich Lk 6,47).

54. Cf. ἐξίστημι in 10,45 sowie Lk 8,56 (ähnlich Lk 2,47; anders Lk 24,22).

55. Cf. 11,12b.14 mit Lk 19,5.9.

56. Cf. εἰσῆλθες πρὸς ἄνδρας ἀκροβυστίαν ἔχοντας καὶ συνέφαγες αὐτοῖς (11,3) mit οὗτος ἁμαρτωλοὺς προσδέχεται καὶ συνεσθίει αὐτοῖς (Lk 15,2). Übrigens bezieht sich der Vorwurf gegen Jesus nach Lk 15,1 ebenfalls darauf, daß er mit Menschen zusammenkommt, die ihn hören (s.o. bei n. 13); beim Thema »Tischgemeinschaft« hingegen benutzt Lukas nicht συνεσθίω (cf. noch 10,41, im übrigen NT: 1 Kor 5,11; Gal 2,12), sondern ἐσθίω μετά (Lk 5,30; 7,36; 22,11.15).

57. Cf. ferner Lk 5,32 und Lk 24,47; Apg 5,31 u.ö. Zudem klingen in der Wendung εἰς ζωήν (11,18) die Bemerkungen zum »Lebendigwerden« des verlorenen Sohnes an (Lk 15,24.32).

58. Cf. κολλάομαι in Lk 15,15. Ähnlich wird das Verb in 8,29 verwendet; cf. auch 17,34 (anders 5,13; 9,26 sowie Lk 10,11).

59. Cf. Lk 15,23; daneben ist die Kombination von θύω und ἐσθίω bei Lukas nicht belegt.

gegessen (10,14; 11,8), entspricht dem Hinweis des älteren Bruders auf seine absolute Treue gegenüber den Geboten des Vaters[60]. Zudem klingt in dem Hinweis des Apostels, er dürfe Gottes Wirken an den Heiden nicht »hindern« (11,17; cf. 10,47), die Weisung Jesu an, die Jünger sollten Kinder nicht daran hindern, zu ihm zu kommen[61]. Aus all diesen Bezügen geht hervor: Die Heidenmission des Petrus führt konsequent das Werk fort, das Jesus mit seiner Zuwendung zu den religiös Ausgegrenzten innerhalb Israels initiiert hat, das Werk der Liebe Gottes zu den Sündern[62].

4. *Fazit*

Ich komme zum Schluß: Lukas charakterisiert die Begegnung des Petrus mit Kornelius auf vielfältige Weise als Etappe in der Wirkungsgeschichte dessen, was Jesus zu Lebzeiten gesagt und getan hat. Daß im Rahmen dieser Geschichte nun die Grenze zwischen Juden und Heiden überschritten wird, ist im lukanischen Verständnis notwendig. Dies liegt natürlich zum einen in der universalen Bedeutung von Tod und Auferweckung Jesu begründet[63]. Die Grenzüberschreitung ist aber zum anderen schon im Erdenwirken Jesu angelegt. »Gott ist in jedem Volk willkommen, der ihn fürchtet und Gerechtigkeit übt« (10,35) – dieser Satz des Petrus ruft ja in Erinnerung, daß Jesus Qualitäten, die Israel auszeichnen sollten, bei Nichtjuden entdeckt, nämlich Glauben beim Hauptmann von Kapernaum (Lk 7,9), Umkehrbereitschaft bei den Leuten von Tyrus und Sidon (Lk 10,13), Barmherzigkeit und Gotteslob bei Samaritanern (Lk 10,30-37; 17,11-19). Eben solche Eigenschaften schreibt Lukas nun dem Kornelius zu: In seiner Frömmigkeit und Gottesfurcht (10,2) steht er Juden nicht nach[64]; indem er Almosen gibt und beständig betet (10,2b), praktiziert er zugleich, wozu Jesus seine Jünger anhält[65];

---

60. Cf. Lk 15,29; sonst begegnet οὐδέποτε im lukanischen Doppelwerk nur noch 14,8. Hierzu und zu den bei n. 56.59 genannten Bezügen cf. KIM, *Geisttaufe* (n. 39), pp. 202-203.
61. Cf. Lk 18,16; ähnlichen Sinn hat κωλύω in Lk 11,52 (anders Lk 6,29; 9,49.50; 23,2; Apg 16,6; 24,23; 27,43). Zu 10,47 ist vor allem 8,36 zu vergleichen.
62. Cf. 10,43 mit Lk 5,32 und s.o. bei n. 35. EVANS, *Jesus* (n. 30), p. 34, verweist in diesem Zusammenhang auf die Gleichnisse Jesu, die das Eingehen in das Reich Gottes thematisieren.
63. Cf. 10,36.42-43; dazu s.o. nach n. 23.
64. Cf. Lk 1,50; 2,25, sowie TANNEHILL, *Unity* (n. 12), p. 133: »Thus Cornelius is addressed like a Jew by the angel (dazu s.o. bei n. 15) and portrayed like a Jew by the narrator«.
65. Cf. Lk 11,41; 12,33 und Lk 18,1; 21,36. Zur Koinzidenz von Jesus und Schrift im Almosengebot und zu dessen Gewichtung durch den Evangelisten cf. F.W. HORN, *Glaube und Handeln in der Theologie des Lukas* (GTA, 26), Göttingen, Vandenhoeck & Ruprecht, 1983, pp. 58-120.

seine Bereitschaft zu Umkehr und Glaube (11,17-18) geben ihm Anteil an dem in Christus verfügten Heil. Auf diese Weise deckt die Erzählung von Petrus und Kornelius auf, was Jesu Worte über seine Mutter und seine Brüder in Lk 8,19-21; 11,27-28 letztlich bedeuten: Ob Menschen zu Jesus und damit zum endzeitlich gesammelten Gottesvolk gehören, entscheidet sich nicht an ihrer Herkunft, sondern am Hören, Bewahren und Tun des Wortes Gottes. Dazu sind auch Nichtjuden in der Lage. Insofern ist in lukanischer Sicht das Wirken Jesu strukturell offen für die Zulassung von Heiden zum Heil; und um den Vollzug dieser Öffnung geht es bei der Bekehrung des Kornelius[66].

Alexander-Puschkin-Platz 4   Florian WILK
D-07745 Jena

66. Die Hörer meines Vortrags in Leuven und die Mitglieder der neutestamentlichen Arbeitsgemeinschaft Erlangen/Jena haben meine Ausführungen kritisch diskutiert und mir dadurch geholfen, die Gedankenführung zu präzisieren. Frau Angelika Hundertmark hat das Manuskript gesichtet und es von einigen falschen oder mißverständlichen Angaben befreit. Ihnen allen sei für ihre Hilfe herzlich gedankt.

»DAS WORT DES HERRN
GEHT AUS VON JERUSALEM« (JES 2,3)
WARUM WURDE DAS APOSTELKONZIL NACH VORN GEZOGEN?
(APG 15)

1. Die allgemeine Tendenz im lukanischen Doppelwerk

In Jerusalem läßt Lukas das Geschehen seines Evangeliums beginnen
(Lk 1,9), und im Tempel zu Jerusalem endet es, nachdem der Herr zum
Himmel aufgefahren war (Lk 24,53). Schon der Zwölfjährige im Tempel
zu Jerusalem wird uns nur bei Lk geschildert (Lk 2,41-52). Die Visionen
des Auferstandenen in Galiläa fallen bei Lk weg; alles ereignet sich in
und bei Jerusalem. Von Jerusalem sollen die Apostel in alle Welt hin-
ausziehen (Apg 1,4). Nach jeder Reise wird Paulus nach Jerusalem
zurückkommen (vgl. besonders Apg 21,10-17); denn schon von Jesus
war ja – auch nur im LkEv – ein ausführlicher Reisebericht über den
Weg nach Jerusalem gestaltet worden. Die überlieferten drei Versu-
chungsszenen wurden so umgestellt, dass die Versuchung in Jerusalem
am Ende stand (Lk 4,9). So konnte Jesus von Jerusalem nach Galiläa
und von dort direkt zurück nach Jerusalem ziehen. Dabei lässt Lk nicht
nur die gut überlieferte Wanderung ins Gebiet von Sidon und Tyrus (vgl.
Mk 7,24-31par) und die ins Gebiet von Caesarea Philippi (vgl. Lk 9,18)
weg, sondern Lukas allein lässt auch bei der Verklärung die Propheten
mit Jesus über den Ausgang reden, »der sich in Jerusalem erfüllen
sollte« (Lk 9,31). Weitere Beobachtungen innerhalb des *Evangeliums*
brauche ich hier nicht aufzuzählen.

In der *Apostelgeschichte* beginnen die Ereignisse mit der Mahnung
des Herrn, in Jerusalem den heiligen Geist zu erwarten (Apg 1,4). Pfingsten ereignet sich – natürlich wieder nur bei Lukas – in Jerusalem. Und
das Leben der Urkirche in Jerusalem hat vorbildlichen Charakter für alle
Gemeinden. Nach Jerusalem werden alle Paulusreisen, wenigstens kurz,
hinaufführen; und schon früh wird sein Entschluss, den er in Ephesus
fasst, mitgeteilt: »Paulus nahm sich vor, über Mazedonien und Achaia
nach Jerusalem zu reisen. Er sagte: Wenn ich dort gewesen bin, muss
ich auch Rom sehen« (Apg 19,21). Vom Gefangenen in Jerusalem wird
der entscheidende Satz mitgeteilt: »In der folgenden Nacht aber trat der
Herr zu Paulus und sagte: Hab Mut! Denn wie du in Jerusalem meine
Sache bezeugt hast, sollst du auch in Rom Zeugnis ablegen« (Apg

23,11). Die restlichen fünf Kapitel sind dann ausgerichtet auf den neuen Zielpunkt Rom, wie sie vorher alle auf Jerusalem ausgerichtet waren. Wir wollen diese vorausgegangene Entwicklung kurz überfliegen.

Nach der Steinigung des Stephanus bricht eine Verfolgung über Jerusalem herein, »alle wurden zerstreut ... mit Ausnahme der Apostel«, die also in Jerusalem ausharren (Apg 8,1). Kurz darauf werden von Jerusalem Petrus und Johannes nach Samarien ausgesandt (Apg 8,14), und sie kehren nach Jerusalem zurück (Apg 8,25). In Jerusalem verfolgt Saulus die Heiligen (vgl. Apg 9,14), und nach seiner Flucht aus Damaskus lässt Lukas den Saulus sofort nach Jerusalem zurückkehren (Apg 9,26); nach Gal 1,18 lagen dazwischen noch drei Jahre, die er zunächst in der Wüste verbrachte. Petrus entscheidet sich in Cäsarea aufgrund einer Vision vom Himmel, den heidnischen Hauptmann Kornelius taufen zu lassen (Apg 10,18). Trotzdem muss er in Jerusalem (Personen werden dort nicht erwähnt) seine Entscheidung rechtfertigen und gleichsam anerkennen lassen (Apg 11,18). Antiochia fühlt sich mit Jerusalem dankbar verbunden; das wird aufgezeigt durch eine Unterstützung, die man in Antiochia sammelt und »durch Barnabas und Saulus an die Ältesten« in Jerusalem bringen lässt (Apg 11,30). Diese frühe »Kollektenreise« der Apg ums Jahr 42 n.C. wird großzügig vor der Zypernreise eingeschoben. Sie zeigt (und das historisch richtig!) einen Paulus, der sich (später) immer wieder um Kollekten für Jerusalem gekümmert hat; doch wie aus Gal 2,1 hervorgeht ist es historisch falsch, Paulus jetzt schon dorthin gehen zu lassen. Er wird erst »vierzehn Jahre später« nach Jerusalem kommen. Heute dürfte praktisch ein Konsensus darüber bestehen, dass diese Jerusalem-Reise des Paulus noch vor der 1. Missionsreise-Reise, eine geniale dichterische Fiktion des Verfassers der Apg ist. Sie gibt ihm überdies die Möglichkeit, den Johannes Markus von Jerusalem zur bevorstehenden Zypernreise mit nach Antiochia zu bringen (Apg 12,25). Schon hier zeichnet sich ein Schema ab, nach dem vor jeder Missionsreise ein Jerusalem-Aufenthalt eingeschoben wird. Denn von Jerusalem soll das Wort des Evangeliums ausgehen (vgl. Apg 6,7; 12,24f).

Im folgenden soll versucht werden, die Theorie eines solchen vorgezogenen Jerusalem-Aufenthalts auch vor der großen 2. Missionsreise zu erhärten. Am ausführlichsten wurde diese These von Robert Jewett (nach J. Knox) in seiner Chronologie des Pauluslebens behandelt[1]. Dort finden sich auch ausführliche Literaturangaben. Was ich hier vortrage, will nur der Versuch sein, einige zusätzliche, bisher nicht genügend beachtete Argumente anzufügen.

---

1. R. JEWETT, *A Chronology of Paul's Life,* Philadelphia, 1979. Deutsche Übersetzung von G. Köster, *Paulus-Chronologie: ein Versuch,* München, 1982. Der status quaestionis wird klar und übersichtlich geboten von C.B. COUSAR, in *ABD,* III, pp. 766-768.

Es geht also um die Datierung des sogenannten »Apostelkonzils«. Wir haben von einer ersten Theorie gehört: Lukas hat die »Kollektenreise« vorgezogen. Und diese Theorie wird heute praktisch allgemein anerkannt. Ich möchte nun der zweiten Theorie, wonach Lukas auch das »Apostelkonzil« vorgezogen hat, zur selben Anerkennung verhelfen. Denn jene Theorie rechnet zwar mit einer historisch falschen, theologisch und literarisch aber sehr sinnvollen Umstellung.

2. Die These und ihre historischen Argumente

Die These lautet also: Das »Apostelkonzil« muss zeitlich nach der 2. Missionsreise eingeordnet werden.

Argument 1: Paulus ist im Frühjahr 60 in Rom angekommen. Eine etwas spätere Ankunft von Paulus in Rom anzunehmen war bis zum Erscheinen des zweibändigen Werks von Yaakov Meschorer im Jahre 1982[2] noch möglich. Durch die zahlreichen neuen Münzfunde vor allem in Cäsarea ist es inzwischen klar, dass der Wechsel der Prokuratoren Felix und Festus im Jahr 59 stattgefunden hat. Denn die zahlreichen (alle im Jahr 59 geprägten) Münzen tragen ganz verschiedene Typen. Die einen zeigen auf der Vorderseite Speere, die X-förmig überkreuzt sind, und auf der Rückseite einen ganzen Palmbaum. Die anderen zeigen die Buchstaben ΝΕΡΩΝΟΣ in einem Kranz und auf der Rückseite einen einzelnen, immer aufrecht stehenden Palmzweig, daneben die deutlich lesbaren Buchstaben ΚΑΙΣΑΡΟΣ. Offensichtlich sind diese so verschiedenen Münzen von verschiedenen Prokuratoren in demselben Jahr 59 herausgegeben worden. Meshorer selbst hat unter dem Gewicht der Funde seine frühere Ansicht, die er in seinem Werk von 1967 vertrat, geändert[3]. Für uns bedeutet das: Der Ankunftstermin in Rom im Frühsommer 60 ist zu einem unbestreitbaren *Terminus ante quem* für die Pauluschronologie geworden.

Argument 2: Die Gallio-Inschrift stammt unbestritten aus dem Frühsommer des Jahres 52[4]. Zu diesem Zeitpunkt wurde der Brief des Kaisers Klaudius, in dem der Prokonsul von Achaia, Junius Gallio, erwähnt wird, geschrieben. Da Gallio mit seinem Titel genannt wird, war er 51/52 wohl noch im Amt, als er dem Kaiser die Meldung(en) erstattete, auf die der Kaiser in seinem Brief reagierte. Mit dieser Amtszeit muss

---

2. Y. MESHORER, *Ancient Jewish Coinage*, 2 Bände, New York, 1982, hier II, p. 183 und Abb. auf Plate 32 und 33.

3. Y. MESHORER, *Jewish Coins of the Second Temple Period*, Tel Aviv, 1967, hier p. 103.

4. B. SCHWANK, *Der sogenannte Brief an Gallio und die Datierung des 1 Thess*, in *BZ* 15 (1971) 265-266. – Eine Stellungnahme dazu von K. HAACKER, *Die Gallio-Episode und die paulinische Chronologie*, in *BZ* 16 (1972) 252-255.

sich der 18-monatige Aufenthalt des Paulus in Korinth (vgl. Apg 18,11)
überlappen. Und am Anfang seines Korinth-Aufenthalts schrieb er seinen 1 Thess an die Stadt, die er vor kurzem verlassen hatte (vgl. 1 Thess
3,1-6). Rein theoretisch lassen sich daraus für den 1 Thess Abfassungs-
zeiten von 49-52 errechnen. Doch wenn, wie sich aus Punkt 1 notwendig ergibt, der Röm spätestens im Winter 56/57 abgefasst sein muss,
wird man eher zu einem frühen Datum tendieren, um die Ereignisse um
den Gal, den 1 Kor und den 2 Kor und die in ihnen vorausgesetzten Rei-
sewege dazwischen unterbringen zu können. So ist der 1 Thess am
wahrscheinlichsten im Jahr 50 in Korinth abgefasst worden.

Argument 3: Die Entfernungen Jerusalem-Korinth (ca 2100 km Land-
weg und ca 200 km Seeweg) lassen sich zusammen mit den Gemeinde-
gründungen nicht in zwei Jahren (48-50) bewältigen[5]. Im Falle von Paulus kommen überdies Monate hinzu, in denen die Straßen praktisch
unbenutzbar waren. So war eine Überquerung des Taurus-Gebirges in
den Wintermonaten unmöglich. Und vor allem hat Paulus ja unterwegs
Gemeinden nicht nur besucht (Derbe, Lystra, Ikonium, Ankara), sondern
auch neue Gemeinden gegründet, wie Philippi, Thessalonich, Beröa,
Athen, Korinth. Das alles ist zwischen 48 (dem üblichen Datum für das
Apostelkonzil) und dem Jahr 50 einfach nicht unterzubringen.

Argument 4: Nach den Methoden historischer Forschung muss den
Angaben des Gal mehr Gewicht beigemessen werden als denen der Apg.
Wer den Text des Gal unvoreingenommen liest, kommt zu folgendem
Ergebnis: Nach seiner Bekehrung war Paulus zunächst drei Jahre in der
arabischen Wüste, ohne irgend einen Menschen zu Rate zu ziehen (Gal
1,16-18). Dann war er »15 Tage« in Jerusalem, »um Kephas kennenzu-
lernen«. Und erst vierzehn Jahre später kommt er wieder nach Jerusalem
(Gal 2,1). Die drei Jahre sind nicht in den vierzehn Jahren inbegriffen,
sondern müssen zu den vierzehn Jahren hinzugezählt werden, also sieb-
zehn Jahre. Auch bei der Annahme einer sehr frühen Bekehrung des
Paulus vor Damaskus (34) kommt man damit ins Jahr 51, niemals aber
ins Jahr 48.

Die Annahme eines Apostelkonzils im Jahr 48 stellt sich demnach
als Notlösung heraus. Man musste ja danach noch die ganze 2. und
3. Missionsreise (mit den drei Jahren Ephesus-Aufenthalt, vgl. Apg
20,31) unterbringen, konnte aber (vgl. Tabelle!) wegen der Angaben im
Gal nicht noch weiter nach vorn rücken:

---

5. Theoretische Berechnungen haben versucht, das Gegenteil zu beweisen. Doch ich
kann dagegen die Erfahrung setzen. Im Russlandfeldzug (Sommer 1942) sind wir über
1000 km zu Fuß marschiert. Da zeigte sich: Auf Wochen hin gerechnet, ist mehr als eine
Tagesdurchschnitts-Leistung von 25 km einfach physisch nicht möglich.

Nach der Apostelgeschichte:	AD	Nach den Briefen:
	34	(ab Ende) 34 Bekehrung: Gal 1,15
Bekehrung (Apg 9,3)	**35**	drei Jahre Arabien: Gal 1,18
Flucht aus Damaskus	**36**	
1. Reise nach Jerusalem (zum Kennenlernen):Apg 9,26	**37**	frühestens 37, spätestens 39/40 (= Tod von Aretas IV.) Flucht aus Damaskus
	38	**1. Reise nach Jerusalem** (zum Kennenlernen): Gal 1,18
	39	
	40	
	41	
2. Reise nach Jerusalem (bei Hungersnot):Apg 11,30	**42**	
	43	*1. Missionsreise (Zypernreise)* (nichts in Briefen; nach Gal 1,21 nur in Kilikien und Syrien)
	44	
1. Missionsreise (Zypernreise) (Apg 13,4–14,28)	**45**	
	46	*2. Missionsreise (Europareise)* (etwa 46-50 von Antiochia bis Korinth)
	47	
3. Reise nach Jerusalem (»Apostelkonzil«: Apg 15,2)	**48**	
2. Missionsreise (Europareise)	**49**	
	50	um 50 in Korinth: 1 Thess
	51	51/52, »14 Jahre später«: Gal 2,1
4. Reise nach Jerusalem (unmotiviert,vgl. Apg 18,22!)		**2. Reise nach Jerusalem** (»Apostelkonzil«)
	52	
3. Missionsreise (Ephesusreise)	**53**	*3. Missionsreise (Ephesusreise)* dabei Abfassung von Gal, 1 Kor, 2 Kor, Röm
	54	
	55	
	56	Winter 56/57 in Korinth: Röm
5. Reise nach Jerusalem (Kollekte)	**57**	**3. Reise nach Jerusalem** (Kollekte)
Haft in Caesarea	**58**	
Wechsel Felix/Festus	**59**	
Frühsommer: Ankunft in Rom	**60**	

3. Die These und ihre theologische Bedeutung

An sich könnten uns 3-4 Jahre mehr oder weniger nach historischen Grundsätzen unwichtig sein. Doch bei genauerem Zusehen hängt theologisch sehr viel von dieser Weichenstellung ab. Ich will zwei Gesichtspunkte herausgreifen: das Verständnis des 1 Thess und das Verständnis der Apg.

Wie bekannt, enthält der 1 Thess kein einziges Mal die Begriffe »Gesetz«, »Beschneidung«, »Rechtfertigung«, »Gerechtigkeit«, die so bezeichnend sind für den Inhalt der in den nächsten Jahren folgenden Briefe Gal, 1 Kor, 2 Kor, Röm. Man kann versuchen, den Grund dafür bei den Problemen der Gemeinde von Thessalonich zu suchen. Viel überzeugender scheint es mir aber zu sein, den Grund des auffallenden Themenwechsels darin zu sehen, dass zwischen 1 Thess und den übrigen Briefen das sogenannte Apostelkonzil (was auch immer es genau gewesen sein mag) stattgefunden hat. Dort sind diese Begriffe zu grundsätzlichen Problemen geworden.

Noch wichtiger dürfte diese scheinbar rein äußerliche Datierungsfrage für das Verständnis der Apg sein. Für sie ist Jerusalem der Ort, von dem aus das Evangelium in die ganze Welt hinausgetragen wurde, und von wo aus überdies in den ersten Jahrzehnten der Geist Jesu den Aposteln half, die Richtlinien für die ganze Kirche zu finden.

Bezeichnend ist der Beschluss nach Beendigung des Apostelkonzils, einen Brief nach Antiochia zu senden. Er geht nicht vom »Bischof« o.ä. aus, sondern es heißt: »Da beschlossen die Apostel und die Ältesten zusammen mit der ganzen Gemeinde«. Und am Ende dieses Briefes: »Denn der Heilige Geist und wir haben beschlossen, euch keine weitere Last aufzulegen als diese notwendigen Dinge: Götzenopferfleisch, Blut, Ersticktes und Unzucht zu meiden. Wenn ihr euch davor hütet, handelt ihr richtig. Lebt wohl!« (Apg 15,22.28f). Im Brief wird also eindeutig auf die Beschneidung bei der Taufe von Nichtjuden verzichtet, eine Entscheidung, die man nicht hoch genug einschätzen kann. Denn dadurch waren in christlichen Gemeinden, im Unterschied zu jüdischen, auch die getauften Frauen vollgültige Gemeindemitglieder (vgl. Gal 3,27f).

Nach der Darstellung der Apg werden somit in Jerusalem die Richtlinien gegeben. Nachdem sie festliegen, kann Paulus seine große 2. Missionsreise antreten. Sie wird ihn bis nach Europa führen. Jerusalem hat gesprochen, Paulus kann handeln. Doch hat es sich auch wirklich so verhalten? Das ist unwahrscheinlich. Die Heidenmission war eine Initiative des Paulus. Aus *seiner* Initiative entsprang die große Europareise. Und erst nach seiner Rückkehr wurden seine Unternehmungen gutgeheißen.

Diese Gutheißung müsste eigentlich in Apg 18,22 nach der Rückkehr erfolgen. Doch weil schon vorher alles gesagt wurde, ist dort eine peinliche Lücke: »So fuhr er von Ephesus ab, landete in Cäsarea, zog hinauf (sc. nach Jerusalem), begrüßte die Gemeinde und ging dann nach Antiochia hinab (ἀναβὰς καὶ ἀσπασάμενος τὴν ἐκκλησίαν κατέβη εἰς Ἀντιόχειαν)«. Eine Belobigung der Eigeninitiative des Paulus ohne Richtlinie von Jerusalem hätte dem Leitgedanken der Apg nicht entsprochen. Dem Verfasser geht es in erster Linie darum, die Einheit einer Kirche herauszuarbeiten, die begründet ist durch Jesu Tod in diesem Jerusalem. Eine Privatinitiative im kirchlichen Raum würde diesen Gedankengang stören. Im Sinne der großen prophetischen Visionen im Alten Testament soll alles Heil von Jerusalem ausgehen.

So ließ Apg, wie wir hörten, Paulus nach seiner Bekehrung sofort nach Jerusalem kommen, womit der für ihn persönlich so wichtige Arabienaufenthalt wegfiel, bei dem er gerade »keinen Menschen zu Rate« ziehen wollte (Gal 1,16). Und vor der Zypernreise führte der Verfasser Barnabas und Saulus mit Unterstützungsgeldern nach Jerusalem, von wo sie dann Johannes Markus für diese 1. Missionsreise mitbringen konnten.

»Lukas wollte Geschichte schreiben«, hat Claus-Jürgen Thornton[6] erneut und gut in seiner Arbeit *Der Zeuge des Zeugen* dargelegt. Nur darf man bei Lukas den Historiker nicht vom Theologen trennen. Eine dramatische Heilsgeschichte soll vermittelt werden, bei der die theologische Bedeutung der Urkirche von Jerusalem und des dort wirkenden Gottesgeistes betont wird. Wie im Evangelium, so zeigt uns Lukas auch in der Apostelgeschichte: Jerusalem ist der Mittelpunkt der Heilsgeschichte. Und eben dazu hat er auch das sogenannte »Apostelkonzil« vor seine ausführliche Schilderung der Europareise gestellt.

Abteistr. 2   Benedikt SCHWANK
D-88631 Beuron

---

6. C.-J. THORNTON, *Der Zeuge des Zeugen: Lukas als Historiker der Paulusreisen* (WUNT, 56), Tübingen, 1991.

THE UNITY OF PROTO-LUKE

The theory of Proto-Luke is an hypothesis that Luke-Acts first existed in a shorter edition, independently of Mark[1]. As proposed here – in a way which differs from the proposal of M.-É. Boismard[2] – there are essentially three arguments for Proto-Luke:

(1) Distinctive dependence on the LXX. Within Luke-Acts is a stream of texts which has a distinctive dependence on the LXX. This does not prove former separateness, merely distinctiveness. The texts: Lk 1,1–4,22a[3] (except 3,7-9; 4,1-13); 7,1–8,3; 9,51–10,20; 16,1-9.19-31; 17,11–18,8; 19,1-10; chaps. 22–24 (except 22,31-65); Acts 1,1–15,35.

(2) Distinctive unity, especially unity of structure (eight diptychs). The above texts have a unique unity: unity of content and, above all, of structure – a precise structure of eight diptychs. Such unity argues not only for distinctiveness but also for former separateness. (Separateness need not mean two authors. Both editions probably come from one person – Luke the evangelist).

(3) Subsequent verification: the hypothesis solves problems. Once Proto-Luke is so identified (as in the above texts), problems about gospel origins and relationships, including aspects of Mark and Q, come closer to resolution.

Argument (1) – a refinement of the semitic argument of P. Feine[4] – has already been summarized at the 1996 Leuven colloquium[5]. Argument (3) – involving the Mark-related thesis of B.H. Streeter [6] – must wait. In the meantime, the present paper focuses on (2). Accordingly, the purpose here is to indicate briefly that the above-mentioned texts form a

---

1. On the history of Proto-Lukan research, see esp. J.M. HARRINGTON, *The Lukan Passion Narrative. The Markan Material in Luke 22,54–23,25*. Diss. Leuven, 1998, pp. 4-557, esp. 4-45, 98-200, 412-468.
2. See esp. *En quête du Proto-Luc* (ÉB, 37), Paris, Gabalda, 1997.
3. Not 4,30 or 4,27 as indicated in some of the present author's earlier publications.
4. *Eine vorkanonische Überlieferung des Lukas im Evangelium und Apostelgeschichte*, Gotha, Pertha, 1891.
5. T.L. BRODIE, *Intertextuality and Its Use in Tracing Q and Proto-Luke*, in C.M. TUCKETT (ed.), *The Scriptures in the Gospels* (BETL, 131), Leuven, University Press – Peeters, 1997, pp. 469-477, esp. 473-475. On p. 474 n. 16 are listed several articles on the relationship of (Proto-)Luke to the LXX.
6. *The Four Gospels. A Study of Origins,* London, Macmillan, 1924, esp. pp. 207-208.

unity. The unity involves both content and structure. An initial investigation shows that this unity has at least five aspects.

1. Content: The Text Flows Well

The proposed texts (see the list above) flow into one another in a way that corresponds broadly with other biblical narratives. This does not mean that Proto-Luke, as proposed, corresponds to a canonical gospel. For instance, unlike (most of) the gospels, Proto-Luke recounts neither the transfiguration nor a climactic public entry into Jerusalem. To a considerable extent, the gospels are a new genre; but Proto-Luke, despite breaking some new ground, still belongs significantly to an old genre – the genre found in the Elijah-Elisha narrative: two-part, mixed (history and biography), and prophetic. The Elijah-Elisha narrative had provided a skeletal framework, and Proto-Luke expanded that framework in light of other factors, especially in the light of Christian experience. Its unity therefore, while genuine, is something other than that of a gospel. As one goes through the text, this absence of well-known gospel features may seem jolting, but, taken on its own pre-gospel terms, the narrative flows.

From 1,1 to the synagogue scene (1,1–4,22a) Proto-Luke lacks just two canonical passages – John's brood-of-vipers speech (3,7-9), plus Jesus' temptations/testing (4,1-13) – and the absence of these passages still leaves a text that is quite coherent. The viper metaphor is not essential to John's message, and the basic testing of Jesus had already been accomplished in his visit to the temple, especially in his encounter with the temple teachers (Luke 2,41-52).

It bears repeating that this paper is not identifying the contents of Proto-Luke. That has already been done on the basis of a distinctive relationship to the LXX (Argument 1). The issue here is whether the texts thus identified form a unity.

The distinctive use of the LXX stops at the positive response to Jesus' Nazareth speech (4,22a) and resumes in 7,1–8,3. This omits a major section (4,22b–6,49: from rejection in the synagogue to the sermon on the plain), yet the effect, instead of causing the text to be disjointed, leaves a narrative which is smooth and unified: the account of Jesus concluding his words (7,1) refers back not to the sermon on the plain but to the synagogue speech with its positive conclusion (4,16-22a). The transition from the synagogue speech (4,16-22a) to 7,1–8,3 is very understandable: straight from Jesus' references concerning a prophet, healing and remission (4,15-22a) to a prophet-related section (7,1–8,3) which includes episodes of healing and remission. In this section (7,1–8,3) the words said in the synagogue become reality. The positive tone of the synagogue speech is reinforced by the absence of both the vipers speech (3,7-9) and the synagogue rejection (4,22b-30).

The conclusion of 7,1–8,3, with its picture of journeying (8,1-3), provides a very appropriate transition to the next part of Proto-Luke – the death-related journey and mission which begins in 9,51 ("And it happened when the days were fulfilled for his assumption"). The death-related journey and mission (9,51–10,20) forms a unity[7], and – particularly because of its emphasis on heaven, especially the final "your names are written in heaven" (10,20) – also forms an appropriate transition to the subsequent twin stories: the unjust steward (16,1-9) and the rich man and Lazarus (16,19-31).

The culminating emphasis on heaven (10,20 "your names… written in heaven") reappears in varied form at the culmination of the story of the unjust steward (16,9 "receive you into everlasting tents"). And this final verse of the story of the unjust steward (16,9) begins in a way that leads easily to the further story of the rich man: "And I say to you". Thus 16,9 prepares for 16,19: "There was a certain rich man…" – itself a precise echo of the beginning of the story of the unjust steward (16,1).

The end of the story of the rich man (16,31) speaks of resurrection ("even if someone should rise from the dead") – thus matching the earlier stories' climactic references to heaven (10,20; 16,9) and also forming a balancing inclusio with the initial reference to assumption (9,51). So, from assumption (9,51) to resurrection (16,31), the entire body of material (9,51–10,20; 16,1-9.19-31) forms a coherent unity.

The balancing allusion to 9,51, as found in 16,31, prepares in turn for a more obvious echoing of 9,51: Jesus' meeting with the ten lepers begins, "And it happened as he was journeying to Jerusalem" (17,11). Thus begins a block which, apart from 18,9-43 (largely Markan), runs unbroken from the ten lepers (17,11-19) to Zacchaeus (19,1-10). This

7. The unity of 9,51–10,20 needs closer examination. Unlike 7,1–8,3, with its emphasis on prophecy, 9,51–10,20 shifts the focus to journeying, especially to the ultimate journey towards death and beyond (Hades or heaven). At the beginning (9,51-56), as the days are fulfilled for Jesus to be taken up, he sets his face for his destination, towards Jerusalem. Next, during the journey (9,56-62), he warns would-be followers about preoccupation with home and death, and, using the image of a ploughman, he directs them instead to journey singlemindedly towards God. Finally (10,1-20), in a flourish of journeying, the healing mission of the seventy entails orientation towards either hell (10,15) or heaven (10,20). The emphasis on heaven is not only repeated; it is also vivid: it is associated with the descent of destructive fire (9,54), the throwing down of a city (10,14), and, climactically, the fall of Satan, like lightning (10,18). The final note (10,20) is positive: the names of the seventy are "written in heaven".

material too (17,11–18,8; 19,1-10) forms a unity. The lepers' problem of awareness – only one in ten praises God (17,11-19) – exemplifies the ensuing problem concerning awareness of God's kingdom (17,20-37). And the dynamics of that kingdom are then clarified by twin stories – first the account of the unjust judge who, despite his initial attitude, sought justice for the widow (18,1-8), and then the account of rich Zacchaeus restoring ill-gotten wealth (19,1-10). While recalling those who were lost (ἀπόλλυμι) – especially in the flood and the fire (17,27.29; see Genesis 7 and 19) – this entire section (17,11–18,8 and 19,1-10) holds out hope to those who fight diverse odds (the leper, the widow, the tax-collector). The conclusion, at the end of the Zacchaeus story, pulls the section together: "For the Son of Man / Humanity came to seek and save what was lost" (19,10). Furthermore, the Zacchaeus story occurs as Jesus is "passing through" Jericho (19,1), one of the entry points for Jerusalem, thus evoking the end of the journeying which began in 9,51.

Proto-Luke's next event, the Passover plot and preparation (22,1-13), evokes in yet another way the journeying which began in 9,51. The emphasis on the time ("feast"), the death-plot, and the preparation (22,1-13) all recall the initial departure for Jerusalem – the fulfilling of the days; the allusion to death; and the sending of messengers to prepare (9,51-56). Thus at one level the plot and preparation (22,1-13) forms a most appropriate sequence: Jesus' approach to Jerusalem, occurring some time after passing through Jericho, recalls his original departure (9,51-62).

But, unlike 9,51, Jerusalem is not explicitly mentioned (in 22,1-13)[8]. Given the emphasis on Jerusalem both at the original departure and again when meeting the lepers (17,11), narrative coherence would seem to demand an account of the arrival in Jerusalem – and thus the inclusion in Proto-Luke of Jesus' public entry into Jerusalem (19,28-40).

Yet at this point (chap. 22) Proto-Luke's explicit use of the name "Jerusalem" is not necessary. While the name is not given, arrival in the city is clearly implied. There is an analogy for Proto-Luke's procedure: the entire second part of John's gospel (John 13–21), set almost completely in Jerusalem, never uses the name[9]. What is essential for narrative coherence is not that Jerusalem be explicitly named but that Jesus be clearly understood to have arrived there.

---

8. In 22,3, where one might expect the place name "Jerusalem" there is a very different word, Iscariot, a name which, among other things, seems related to a place, the southern town of Kerioth: cf. J.A. FITZMYER, *The Gospel According to Luke X–XXIV* (AB, 28A), Garden City, NY, Doubleday, 1985, p. 620.

9. Whether Luke's omission of the name was theologically motivated, as was John's, is a matter for further research. See T.L. BRODIE, *The Gospel According to John*, New York – Oxford, University Press, 1993, pp. 27-28.

Having recounted the supper (as far as the promise of sitting on thrones "judging the twelve tribes of Israel"), Proto-Luke goes directly to the morning action when Jesus is led to the sanhedrin (22,66) – thus skipping the denials and night action, including the arrest (22,31-65, mostly Markan). This absence of an elaborate arrest account may seem to make the sequence abrupt, but in an analogous case, bringing Stephen before the sanhedrin (Acts 6,12), the sequence is equally compact. Thus the omission of the denials and night action does not deprive Proto-Luke's passion account of narrative coherence.

The second half of Proto-Luke consists of Acts 1,1–15,35, a text which, insofar as it is unbroken, may be regarded as a unity. Overall therefore the designated texts (from Luke 1,1 to Acts 15,35) form a sequence which has basic narrative coherence. The text is not a gospel; but is has unity.

2. Content: Continuity between the Beginning, the Middle and the End

The unity of a text, particularly an ancient text, is generally reflected by the continuity between its beginning, middle and end[10]. In various ways the proposed form of Proto-Luke shows such continuity. Part of this continuity is obvious, especially between Luke 1,1-4 and Acts 1,1-5. But the ending also (Acts 13–15, esp. 15,1-35) is quite fitting. Some aspects of this fittingness are as follows:

– The challenges to various Jews, especially in synagogues, and the Jews' increasingly hostile reactions (Acts 13,4-12; 13,13-43; 13,44-52; 14,1-7; cf. 14,19-20) are a fitting culmination of the tension which had been intimated earlier in Proto-Luke, for instance, in the quiet clash in the house of the Pharisee (Luke 7,36-50).
– The decision of the Jerusalem council (Acts 15,1-21) provides a resolution for a central problem in Proto-Luke – how to move from traditional Judaism to a wider world.
– The final section, the council's decision to write (Acts 15,22-35), contains an elaborate variation on the beginning, on the initial decision to write (Luke 1,1-4; cf. Acts 1,1-5).

3. Structure: The Text's Proportions – Accord with Literary Unity

The proposed text of Proto-Luke is coherent not only in narrative content but also in structure. The first aspect of coherent structure has to do

---

10. See, for instance, V.K. ROBBINS, *The Tapestry of Early Christian Discourse. Rhetoric, Society and Ideology*, London – New York, Routledge, 1996, pp. 50-53.

with general proportions. Like a human body, a unified text has appropriate proportions. If one part of the text is seriously disproportionate,
the whole lacks unity. In the case of Proto-Luke, it may seem at first that
the proposed shape is unbalanced: there are about ten chapters on Jesus,
but virtually fifteen on his disciples. However, this kind of proportion,
this increase in length, accords with basic aspects of biblical narrative. It
corresponds broadly with the way the narrative of Genesis, for instance,
tends to progress from small units to larger blocks; and it accords more
specifically with the proportions of one of Proto-Luke's basic models:
the Elijah-Elisha narrative, a two-part narrative composed of circa eight
chapters and eleven (1 Kings 16,29 – 2 Kings 2; and 2 Kings 3–13).

4. Structure: The Proposed Text Forms Eight Units

The unity of the proposed text of Proto-Luke is indicated by a further
feature of structure: the text falls with relative ease into eight blocks,
two groups of four. Using simplified headings (and subdividing the units
with a double slash, //):

	Luke
Annunciations/Births	1,1-56 // 1,57–2,40.
Ministry: Preaching/Action	3,1-6.10-38; 4,14-22a // 7,1–8,3.
Death-related Journey	9,51–10,20; 16,1-9.19-31 // 17,11– 18,8; 19,1-10.
Death/Resurrection	22,1-30; 22,66–23,49 // 23,50–24,53.

	Acts
Spirit Promised/Given	1 // 2,1-42.
Ministry: Action/Preaching	2,43–4,31 // 4,32–5,42.
Stephen Dies/ Saul Reborn	6,1–8,1a // 8,1b–9,30.
Breakthrough: Peter /Paul	9,31–12,25 // 13,1–15,35.

To some degree, units 1-4 are echoed in units 5-8. For instance,
while unit 1 recounts the infancy of Jesus (his conception, and later his
birth), unit 5 recounts the infancy of the church, its incubation (when
awaiting the Spirit, Acts 1) and its birth (when the Spirit is given, Acts
2,1-42).

This structure of eight blocks/units is not exclusive. A complex text
has many overlapping structures, and this eightfold aspect is just one.
Nor can this proposed division be discussed adequately in this short
paper. Yet it is appropriate, as a matter for further research, to indicate
that such a division exists.

The use of eight as a basis for structure is significant. Eight, comprised of two fours, indicates completeness (cf. four ends of the earth;
four rivers in Eden, Genesis 2; four directions around the tabernacle,

Numbers 2)[11]. Such completeness argues for the independence of these texts and thus for the independence of Proto-Luke.

5. The Diptych Structure of the Eight Blocks

One of the basic features of the eight blocks and one of the indications of their reality, is that each consists, as it were, of two panels; each constitutes a diptych. Thus Proto-Luke consists of eight diptychs.

The basic idea of a diptych is not new to Lukan studies. It is widely recognized that Luke's infancy narrative contains diptychs; first there is a twofold account of annunciation (1,5-25; 1,26-38), and then a twofold account of birth (1,57-80; 2,1-40)[12]. However, the obviousness of these diptychs is but the tip of a much larger phenomenon. The most basic diptych phenomenon in Luke 1–2 is not constituted by the two annunciations, nor by the two birth accounts, but by Luke 1–2 as a whole: the entire first section of the infancy narrative (1,5-56: birth announcements, plus Mary's visit to Elizabeth) is balanced by the entire second section (1,57–2,40: the actual births, plus various visits to the family and to Jerusalem):

John's birth foretold (1,5-25)	John's birth (1,57-80)
Jesus' birth foretold (1,26-38)	Jesus' birth (2,1-14)
Mary visits Elizabeth (1,39-56)	Visits: to the family, and to Jerusalem (2,15-52)

Diptychs vary in nature. Some are short and simple – showing two scenes that are closely similar. Others show two scenes that, instead of mirroring each other, complement one another. When introducing diptychs, (Proto-)Luke does so gradually. He begins with a diptych that is short and simple: the two annunciations with their many similarities of detail (1,5-25, and 1,26-38). Next, in the two births, there is another case, but the degree of similarity is not as great (1,57-80; 2,1-40). Then, when Luke 1–2 is viewed as a whole, there is a further diptych effect, one in which the similarity is of yet another kind: the emphasis is not on parallelism but on complementarity. Thus in dealing with Luke's diptychs, there are two broad principles: relationships between panels vary; and Luke tends to go from simple to more complex.

---

11. On the significance of eight and of (twice) four, see esp. D.N. FREEDMAN, *The Structure of Psalm 119*, in D.P. WRIGHT, *et al.* (eds.), *Pomegranates and Golden Bells. Studies in Biblical, Jewish, and Near Eastern Ritual, Law, and Literature in Honor of Jacob Milgrom*, Winona Lake, IN, Eisenbrauns, 1995, pp. 725-756.

12. See, for instance, C. STUHLMUELLER, *Luke*, in R.E. BROWN, *et al.* (eds.), *Jerome Biblical Commentary*, London, Chapman, 1968, 44:24; R.E. BROWN, *An Introduction to the New Testament*, Garden City, NY, Doubleday, 1997, pp. 230-231.

Part of the increasing complexity is a twofold or spiralling tendency towards greater volume. Thus (counting occasional half verses as units):

In diptychs 1-4: 56 / 70; 44 / 53; 54 / 45; 85 / 60.
In diptychs 5-8: 26 / 42; 62 / 48; 76 / 70; 116 / 105.

Within each half of Proto-Luke, every diptych, except number 2, is longer in total volume than the one which immediately precedes it. In the case of number 2 the decrease in volume may have something to do with the idea that an old order – traditional Judaism and the OT, visibly pervading the infancy narrative, and represented especially in John the Baptist – is fading, diminishing. The opening sequence of the fourth gospel (the seven passages in John 1,1–2,22) also has an initial Baptist-related slump in volume[13].

This entire structure of eight diptychs, in two sets of four, finds a precedent in one of Luke's key sources, namely in the Elijah-Elisha story[14]. There too the second panel is generally longer.

It is useful, without going into detail, to summarize some of the balances and complementarities within the eight diptychs. The subsequent brief analysis follows the outline proposed on p. 632.

1. The Infancy Narrative (1,1-56 // 1,57–2,52)

Complementarity here varies from simple to more complex. The initial instance, between annunciations (1,5-38) and births (1,57–2,14), is easy to see; what is foretold in one becomes reality in the other; the angel's words become flesh. In the case of the visits, however – Mary visits Elizabeth (1,39-56); later, the shepherds visit the baby, and the family visits Jerusalem twice (2,15-52) – the balance is not as obvious. Yet it is genuine. Between Mary's visit, for instance, and the later visit to Jerusalem, complementarities include the following: two ascending journeys to cities of Judea; a stay of three months/days; the return; and, more substantially, the evoking of God's place of abiding: Jesus goes to the Jerusalem temple, and Mary's journey evokes the journey of the ark to Jerusalem – a journey that will eventually lead to the temple (2 Sam 6–7).

2. Ministry: Preaching – Miracles (3,1-6.10-38; 4,14-22a // 7,1–8,3)

The opening panel highlights the first preaching of John and Jesus; and, in broad terms, what is preached in the first panel becomes reality in the

13. BRODIE, John, 1993, p. 73.
14. T.L. BRODIE, The Crucial Bridge: The Elijah-Elisha Narrative as an Interpretive Synthesis of Genesis-Kings and a Literary Model for the Gospels, Collegeville, MN, Liturgical (forthcoming).

second; the word becomes action. This is clearest in the preaching of Jesus: his prophetic synagogue speech, emphasizing miracles and remission (4,16-22a) becomes reality in his role as prophet (7,16.39), in his miracles (7,1-22), and in his remission of the sinful woman (7,36-50). But there are other aspects of balance between the panels[15].

3. To Jerusalem (9,51–10,20; 16,1-9.19-31 // 17,11–18,8; 19,1-10)

There are three main areas of complementarity. First, the headline references to journeying towards Jerusalem through Samaria (9,51-52; 17,11); the balance here, extending into all the journeying in 9,51-62 and 17,11-19, involves other elements, especially: meeting, sending, and awareness of (the kingdom of) God. Second, the announcing of the coming of God's kingdom (by the seventy, 10,1-20; and, in a further form, by Jesus, 17,20-37). Third, two sets of twin stories: The unjust but decisive steward; and the lethargic rich man (16,1-9.19-31). And the unjust but avenging judge; and the decisive rich Zacchaeus (18,1-8; 19,1-10).

The texts on announcing God's kingdom (10,1-20; 17,20-37) share basic elements: a certain unworldliness (no baggage, 10,1-4; the kingdom is "within", 17,1-21); – a double challenge: two places (house and city; 10,5-11); two times: Noah and Lot/Sodom (17,26-30); – final woe (Sodom and woe to the cities, 10,12-16; the taking away of people, 17,31-37); – amid lightning: contrasting emotions (joy, 10,17-20, and frustrated desire, 17,22-25).

Generally, while panel 1 focuses largely on the ultimate heavenly objective, panel 2 seems more concerned with the practicalities of achieving that objective.

4. Death and Resurrection (22,1-30; 22,66–23,49 // 23,50–24,53)

As with Good Friday and Easter Sunday so also with death and resurrection: though apparent opposites, they form a whole. Within this unity some complementarities are basic: two diverse emphases on the body (eucharist, 22,1-30; burial and resurrection, 23,50–24,12); diverse accounts of Jesus' sad fate (the trial, 22,66–23,31; on the Emmaus road,

---

15. Initial emphasis on authorities (Roman and Jewish): rulers (3,1-2); centurion and elders (7,2-3). – John as a prophetic desert preacher (initially, 3,2-6; recalled by Jesus, 7,24-27). – Miracles of nature (3,5) are balanced by miracles in individual lives (7,4-15). – Triple pattern of sayings about what to do (questions, 3,10-14; commands, cf. 7,6-10). – Expecting a prophet; Is this he?; contrast in prophets, and in responses (3,15-20; 7,19.28-30). – Baptism, generation, and a teaching or wisdom which finds a response in all (3,31-38; 4,14-15; 7,29-35). The diptych as a whole is framed by references to Herod and Herod's steward (3,1; 8,3).

24,13-35); final emphasis on forgiveness of sins (before dying, 23,32-49; before ascending, 24,36-53).

5. Spirit Promised and Given (Acts 1 // Acts 2,1-42)

Somewhat like Luke 1–2, most of Acts 1–2 constitutes a diptych of incubation and birth. The birth, however, is that of the church. The incubation occurs in Acts 1: the Spirit is promised; along with the others, Mary is again present in a receptive mode (at prayer); and, with Peter leading, the number of the twelve is restored. But it is only in Acts 2,1-42, when the Spirit is given, that this group comes to birth so to speak. It literally emerges from its enclosed space (from the upper room with the women) into the world, into the presence of a crowd which represents all nations.

There is continuity between the two pictures of the eleven/twelve grouped together – first for prayer (Acts 1,12-14) and later for preaching and prophecy (2,14-21).

Among the various complementarities between Acts 1 and Acts 2,1-42 one of the most important is the contrast in the ways Peter deals with the death of Judas (1,15-26) and the death of Jesus (2,22-42). Both of these death accounts conclude with a heart-searching response and with building up their number (1,23-26; 2,37-42). The final verse, on solidarity with the apostles and in prayer (2,42), dovetails with aspects of the first panel (1,14.26).

6. Peter (2,43–4,31 // 4,32–5,42)

The narrative of Acts 2,43–4,31 centers largely around two decisive actions by Peter – the healing of the lame man (3,1-10), and the punishing of Ananias and Sapphira (5,1-11). The balance or contrast between two actions, however, is but part of a larger balance between two whole panels. First, the panels give summaries of life among the believers (2,43-47; 4,32-37). Then comes Peter's decisive action (3,1-10; 5,1-11). Next there is a focus on Solomon's Porch (3,11-26, Peter's speech; 4,12-16, a summary statement). And finally, there is an appearance before the Sanhedrin – an experience which in no way inhibits the believers (4,1-31; 5,17-42).

7. Stephen's Death – Saul's Conversion (6,1–8,1a // 8,1b–9,30)

There is an obvious continuity between Stephen and Saul; Saul approves of Stephen's killing; the death of one introduces the other

(7,58; 8,1). This explicit link, however, is but part of a larger unity: the accounts of Stephen and Saul form the two panels of a single diptych.

The balance between the panels is often complex and obscure. In simplified terms, there are three major areas of complementarity. First, the persecution which engulfed the wonder-working Stephen (Acts 6) is echoed and intensified in the persecution which led to the evangelization of Samaria (8,1b-13). Second, aspects of Stephen's speech, especially about the role of Moses as an Egyptian (7,1-29) would appear to be echoed in the pictures of Simon and the Ethiopian (8,14-40). Third, and more clearly, the culminating pictures of Moses' call and Stephen's killing (7,30–8,1a) are partly balanced by the pictures of Saul's call and the attempted killing of Saul (9,1-30).

8. Breakthrough: Peter and Paul (9,31–12,25 // 13,1–15,35)

The remainder of Proto-Luke recounts two major breakthroughs: Peter's baptizing of the household of Cornelius (10,1–11,18) and Paul's mission, with its turning towards the Gentiles (13,13-48). The repeated explicit emphasis on the admission of the Gentiles (11,18; 13,46) helps to bind this large body of text into a unity, the last and largest diptych.

There are several balancing features: a general sense of the church, and a journey (9,31-32; 13,1-3); initial miracles (9,33-43, Peter heals; 13,4-12, Paul punishes/blinds); the breakthrough to the Gentiles (10,1–11,18; 13,13-48); and diverse references to persecution, believing, and famine/food (11,27-30; 13,49–14,20). The panels end with a new twist: Peter's angel-led release from shackles (12,1-20); and the strengthened church's Spirit-led move away from the Law (14,21–15,29). Finally there are notes on the word's increase/spread (12,24-25; 15,30-35).

Conclusion

The unity of Proto-Luke is not that of a gospel but of a document which stands halfway between OT narrative and the gospels. Once Proto-Luke is treated thus – on its own terms rather than as a gospel – its unity begins to emerge. The overall effect of the designated gospel texts (from chaps. 1–4, 7–10, 16–19, and 22–24) is to portray Jesus as being like Elijah, a divine prophet, but more so: more divine, and more human. The unity of this portrait of Jesus does not correspond to that found in the later Luke, but, in comparison with the portrait of Elijah, it has its own integrity. The unity of the proposed texts is one of both content and structure. The narrative flows, and it does so both as a whole and in its key areas (beginning, middle and end). The proportions are appropriate. And the structure shows a coherence that is precise and complete. The result is a strong case for unity. And such unity indicates original separateness.

Dominican Studium   Thomas L. BRODIE
Tallaght Village, Dublin 24

THE LUCAN NARRATIVE OF THE "EVANGELIZATION OF THE KINGDOM OF GOD"

A CONTRIBUTION TO THE UNITY OF LUKE-ACTS

INTRODUCTION: THE HERMENEUTICAL ASPECT OF A NARRATIVE APPROACH

This paper tries to approach "the unity of Luke-Acts" by focusing on the concept of βασιλεία τοῦ θεοῦ[1], which seems to give unity to the whole narrative of the Lucan two-volume work, as it is understood from the first to the last time that the narrator uses the aforementioned concept. So, with the logion of Lk 4,43, which gives an overall interpretation of the mission of Jesus, and the last sentence of the colophon in Acts 28,31, the evangelist seems to have placed a framework (or literary inclusion) to the whole of his theological narrative, the inner coherence of which is based on what he understands as the "evangelization of the Kingdom of God". In line with all of this, the narrative of the forty days between Easter and Ascension, which links the two parts of the Lucan work, returns again to the subject of the Basileia (Acts 1,3). Consequently, it is a question of presenting the whole theological project of Luke as a narrative unit with the central theme of the Basileia as its starting point.

Among scholars it is generally agreed nowadays that the notion of Basileia belongs, as a "Leitbegriff"[2], to the core of the theology of Luke. Its interpretation, however, has depended mainly on an exegesis of an existentialist type, highlighting the moment of the personal decision

---

1. Since the presentation of my doctoral thesis, *Evangelizar el Reino de Dios. Estudio redaccional del concepto lucano de Basileia*, in 1979, a number of monographs have been published on this subject, most recently the doctoral thesis of A. PRIEUR, *Die Verkündigung der Gottesherrschaft. Exegetische Studien zum lukanischen Verständnis von βασιλεία τοῦ θεοῦ* (WUNT, 2/89), Tübingen, 1996. All this scholarly research, which has appeared since then, provides me with the opportunity to continue the debate about a main chapter of the theological project of Luke, as well as to complete my earlier exegetical work with a study of the gospels as narratives.

2. M. VÖLKEL, *Zur Deutung des "Reiches Gottes" bei Lukas*, in ZNW 65 (1974) 57-70, p. 61; A. WEISER, *"Reich Gottes" in der Apostelgeschichte*, in C. BUSSMANN & W. RADL (eds.), *Der Treue Gottes trauen. Beiträge zum Werk des Lukas*. FS G. Schneider, Freiburg-Basel-Wien, 1991, pp. 127-135, here 128; M. WOLTER, *'Reich Gottes' bei Lukas*, in NTS 41 (1995) 541-563, p. 541.

of faith through which the believer arrived at that eschatological state (existential). It linked the conception of Luke to an understanding of "Eschatologie als aktuelle Naherwartung"[3], with which the Basileia distanced itself from the original eschatological approach of Luke. For others, the Lucan interpretation of the Basileia does not depend on the objective analysis of the text itself, but on dogmatic prejudices about the "Kingdom of God"[4]. Therefore, it has seemed essential to me to begin this paper with the hermeneutical aspect of the Lucan narrative, the only way to determine the 'form of the content' (semantic categories) of the Lucan narrative and not only the 'form of the expression' (literary models and rhetorical techniques). In other words, it deals with the *narrative model* which allows Luke-Acts to be understood as a double chapter of biblical narrative[5].

1. Lucan Hermeneutics

Many scholars today agree that the hermeneutic key to Luke's theology corresponds to the NT formula "according to the Scriptures" (κατὰ τὰς γραφάς: cf. 1 Cor 15,3f). The Scriptures, in the way that they were interpreted in Jewish and Christian circles of the time, are, therefore, the reference point of the evangelist to understand what God was doing in Christ and in the early church, and, accordingly, the basis of his narrative statements on christology and ecclesiology. The many studies about the OT in Luke's writings[6] have corroborated this, regardless of the lit-

3. H. CONZELMANN, *Die Mitte der Zeit. Studien zur Theologie des Lukas* (BHT, 17), Tübingen, 1954, [6]1977, p. 89.
4. Among the recent studies, M. WOLTER, *'Reich Gottes' bei Lukas* (n. 2), stands out in this respect.
5. Cf. M. BENEITEZ, *"Esta salvación de Dios" (Hch 28,28). Análisis narrativo estructuralista de "Hechos"*, Madrid, 1986, *passim*.
6. For a bibliography about the OT in the work of Luke see F. BOVON, *Luc le théologien. Vingt-cinq ans de recherches (1950-1975)*, Neuchâtel-Paris, 1978, [2]1988, pp. 89-117. For more recent literature, see D.L. BOCK, *Proclamation from Prophecy and Pattern. Lucan Old Testament Christology* (JSNT SS, 12), Sheffield, 1987, pp. 13-53; D.A. CARSON & H.G.M. WILLIAMSON (eds.), *It is Written: Scripture Citing Scripture: Essays in Honor of Barnabas Lindars*, Cambridge, 1988; C.M. TUCKETT (ed.), *The Scriptures in the Gospels* (BETL, 131), Leuven, 1997; C.A. EVANS & W.R. STEGNER (eds.), *The Gospels and the Scriptures of Israel* (JSNT SS, 104; SSEJC, 3), Sheffield, 1994, pp. 280-355. About the OT hermeneutics in Luke's work: C.A. EVANS & J.A. SANDERS, *Luke and Scripture. The Function of Sacred Tradition in Luke-Acts*, Minneapolis, MN, 1993; B.J. KOET, *Five Studies on Interpretation of Scripture in Luke-Acts* (SNTA, 14), Leuven, 1989. About the derashic hermeneutics of the OT in the NT: cf. A. DEL AGUA, *El método midrásico y la exégesis del Nuevo Testamento* (Biblioteca Midrásica, 4), Valencia, 1985; also E.E. ELLIS, *Biblical Interpretation in the New Testament Church*, in M.J. MULDER (ed.), *Mikra. Text, Translation, Reading and Interpretation of the Hebrew Bible in Ancient Judaism and Early Christianity* (CRINT, 2/1), Assen-Maastricht - Minneapolis, MN, 1990, pp. 691-725.

erary models and literary techniques (narrative strategy)[7] that are used by the evangelist. I do not intend to enter in this matter here. However, I would like to make clear from the beginning that the OT is not a mere recourse of literary inspiration for Luke, but the source par excellence for the narrative elaboration of his theological project[8].

The OT appears in the NT in the form of proof texts[9], "but it is becoming clear that early Christians searched the Scripture midrashically to understand why Christ suffered the fate of a criminal ..., why he was crucified"[10]. This semantic functionality of the OT at the service of the event of Jesus of Nazareth[11], which took advantage of the principles and techniques of the contemporary midrashic/derashic Jewish hermeneutics, is what, throughout numerous publications, I have been calling "Christian derash" [12] of the OT. Its objective is to present the

7. A distinction between narrative techniques, narrative strategy, christological elaboration (OT motives), and narrative statement in the Lucan account is to be found in M. COLERIDGE, *The Birth of the Lucan Narrative* (JSNT SS, 88), Sheffield, 1993, *passim*; cf. J.A. FITZMYER, *The Gospel According to Luke I-IX* (AB, 28), Garden City, NY, 1981, p. 35: "He [Luke] is... a writer acquainted with both literary traditions (especially as they are known from the Greek Bible) and Hellenistic literary techniques".

8. A. DEL AGUA, *La interpretación del "relato" en la doble obra lucana*, in *EE* 71 (1996) 169-214, p. 214: "The question of the intellectual influence on Luke's work is not a question of asking about the quantity (which of them is quantitatively larger), but about the *specificity* of each one of them. The affinity of Luke's style and narrative techniques with those of the Hellenistic world affects the literary inculturation of the narrative; on the other hand, the author's profound knowledge of biblical traditions, as well as his expertise in the art of re-applying and updating them for the Christian community, constitutes his theological and hermeneutical world (and implies the Christian derash of the OT). The synthesis between the new cultural elements of Hellenism and the faith in Jesus Christ 'according to the Scriptures' is what represents the originality of Luke's narrative".

9. The Lucan hermeneutics of the OT as "proof-from-prophecy" was initially proposed by P. SCHUBERT, *The Structure and Significance of Luke 24*, in W. ELTESTER (ed.), *Neutestamentliche Studien für R. Bultmann zu seinem siebzigsten Geburtstag am 20. August 1954* (BZNW, 21), Berlin, 1954, pp. 165-186. See also D.L. BOCK, *Proclamation from Prophecy and Pattern* (n. 6); ID., *Proclamation from Prophecy and Pattern: Luke's Use of the Old Testament for Christology and Mission*, in C.A. EVANS & W.R. STEGNER (eds.), *The Gospels and the Scriptures of Israel* (n. 6), pp. 280-307.

10. J.A. SANDERS, *Isaiah in Luke*, in C.A. EVANS & J.A. SANDERS, *Luke and Scripture*. (n. 6), pp. 14-25, p. 15.

11. Cf. A. DEL AGUA, *El "Antiguo" Testamento, primera parte de la Biblia cristiana*, in *EE* 70 (1995) 145-189, pp. 181-182: "The NT made use of the hermeneutical principles and procedures of Judaism. However, all Christian interpretation of the OT starts from the earlier confession that 'Jesus is the Lord', which cannot be arrived at by any exegetical deduction. The semantic change, which Christians introduce into the historical meaning of the OT text, comes from the fact that the NT, depending on an entirely new historical event, Jesus of Nazareth, gives witness of the new in the terms and forms of the old". Cf. J.H. CHARLESWORTH, *What Has the Old Testament to Do with the New?*, in J.H. CHARLESWORTH & W.P. WEAVER (eds.), *The Old and the New Testaments. Their Relationship and the "Intertestamental" Literature*, Valley Forge, PA, 1993, pp. 39-87.

12. A. DEL AGUA, *El método midrásico* (n. 6), *passim*.

person and the work of Jesus as the fulfilment of the promise made by
God to "our ancestors" (cf. Acts 3,12-26; 7,2-53, etc.) and formulated
throughout the OT tradition[13]. It is worth making reference here to two
passages in which the evangelist insists, on the one hand, on the necessity of knowing the Scriptures in order to understand what God was
doing in Christ and the early church, and offers, on the other hand, his
lesson of Christian (derashic) hermeneutics of the OT. In the parable of
Lazarus and the rich man, in Lk 16,19-31, it is said that the rich man,
once he realized why he is in Hades, asks Abraham to send Lazarus
from paradise, where he had gone after his death, to explain to his five
brothers the ultimate truth of his fate. To this Abraham replies that if
they do not read the Scriptures, Moses and the Prophets, using the right
hermeneutics, then they would not be convinced by someone rising from
the dead (16,27-31). Likewise, the last chapter of the gospel (24,13-49)
shares the firm conviction that a proper reading of the Scriptures, Moses,
the Prophets and the Psalms, gives one the ability to see what is happening in the real world; it was the correct hermeneutics of the OT
which helped the disciples on the road to Emmaus and in Jerusalem, to
understand christologically the event of Jesus[14]. Moreover, Luke puts in
the words of the risen Christ the principle which establishes the
hermeneutical function and meaning of the OT, i.e., the meaning of the
OT is Christ himself and its function is that of making intelligible his
own mystery, as it is corroborated by the very word of God (v. 27).
Accordingly, it is not surprising that scholars today see in Luke 24 the
"traces of a Semantic Field of Interpretation"[15] of the Scriptures (= the
Christian derash), because Luke's basic hermeneutics are theocentric[16].

To all of the above-mentioned we must add the consideration that the
gospel of Luke is, as the gospel of Matthew, a "retelling" of the Jesus
story (with respect to Mk and Q). "These retellings have much in common with the general category of 'rewritten Bible'", states C.A. Evans,
which he describes as "the earliest form of reapplication of Scripture",
a phenomenon which takes place within the Bible itself. And he adds:
"they are not retellings of Tanak; they are retellings of the Jesus story.
Like the Jewish retellings of Tanak, however, they do import materials
from the rest of Scripture, and here Tanak appears. The presence of
Tanak ... often provides the cloth out of which an entire pericope is

13. ID., *El "Antiguo" Testamento* (n. 11), *passim*.
14. J.A. SANDERS, *Isaiah in Luke* (n. 10), pp. 18-19.
15. B.J. KOET, *Some Traces of a Semantic Field of Interpretation*, in ID., *Five Studies*
(n. 6), pp. 56-72.
16. J.A. SANDERS, *Isaiah in Luke*, p. 19.

woven". Nevertheless, C.A. Evans goes on, "to conclude that the gospels are midrashim can lead to a great misunderstanding"[17]. Therefore, I agree with Evans when he states that it is better to say that the gospels are derashic/midrashic, and even better that they contain derash/midrash and in some places are midrashically driven. To this end, it is obvious that Luke did not intend to produce a commentary of the Greek OT. Luke rewrote the story of Jesus in order to suit the theological and pastoral needs of the church of his time. Luke's rewriting of this story was greatly influenced by the language and themes of the Scriptures and the way in which the Scriptures were interpreted in Jewish and Christian circles of his time.

2. Our Narrative Model

As regards the model of narrative analysis, I am keeping to the model which I recently presented in a study on the interpretation of the narrative in Luke's work[18]. There, I argued that the narrative study of a gospel is above all a semantic study in search of the meaning, regardless of the style or rhetorical techniques used by the narrator. Consequently, it is not a question of looking for the form of expression but for the form of the content. Therefore, and given that the NT is written in a tradition rather than in a literary form, it is necessary to relate each of the semantic categories of narrative analysis that we used (settings, plot, point of view, character, events, time) with the OT tradition, which is the hermeneutic reference of meaning sought by Luke in his narration[19].

17. C.A. EVANS, *Gospels and Midrash: An Introduction to Luke and Scripture. The Question of Genre*, in C.A. EVANS & J.A. SANDERS, *Luke and Scripture* (n. 6), pp. 1-4, esp. 2-3; ID., *Luke and the Rewritten Bible: Aspects of Lucan Hagiography*, in J.H. CHARLESWORTH & C.A. EVANS (eds.), *The Pseudepigrapha and Early Biblical Interpretation* (JSP SS, 14; SSEJC, 2), Sheffield, 1993, pp. 170-201.

18. A. DEL AGUA, *La interpretación* (n. 8), p. 214: "Although Luke – like the rest of the evangelists – adopted the literary categories of rhetoric, he never makes recourse to argumentation of a logical type, nor is he interested by the old art of argumentation. Luke's biblical premises are always a-logical (based on the Scriptures, which contain a personal revelation), and are, rather, the developments which explain these premises, which occasionally receive through him a logical form"; cf. J. ZUMSTEIN, *Analyse narrative, critique rhétorique et exégèse johannique*, in P. BÜHLER & J.F. HABERMACHER (eds.), *La narration. Quand le récit devient communication*, Genève, 1988, pp. 37-56, p. 51; cf. also W.S. KURZ, *Hellenistic Rhetoric in the Christological Proof of Luke-Acts*, in *CBQ* 42 (1980) 171-195.

19. A. DEL AGUA, *La interpretación* (n. 8), p. 194ff; cf. F. KERMODE, *The Genesis of Secrecy. On the Interpretation of Narrative*, Cambridge, MA, 1979, p. 38: "The modern interpreter argues that the surface of the gospel's narrative conceals a sense that depends on secret allusion to a repertory of OT texts". About the concept of "interpretative narrative", cf. P. RICŒUR, *Interpretative Narrative*, in R. SCHWARTZ (ed.), *The Book and the Text. The Bible and Literary Theory*, Cambridge, MA, pp. 237-257, p. 237: "[In the inter-

And, in fact, each of these narrative categories carries out its semantic function in the text through recourse to the corresponding typological pattern (τύπος)[20] of the OT, be this spatial or temporal (settings), christological, ecclesiological, or theological ("Gottesvorstellungen"[21]).

Our narrative analysis, therefore, is not so much concerned with comparing Luke's narrative with those of his time[22], nor with the literary techniques[23] the evangelist uses in his account, but with his sense of continu-

pretative narrative]... the juncture between exegesis and theology, before being a work of interpretation applied *to* the text, already functions *in* the text if this text is a narrative with an interpretative function"; also cf. A. ALTER, *The Art of Biblical Narrative*, New York, 1981, *passim*.

20. The concept of "pattern", which appears so frequently in the narrative analysis of the gospels and Acts, can have different meanings. Thus, some speak of *narrative patterns* to refer to the rhetorical devices that dominate the composition, i.e., the principles and literary techniques (repetition, contrast, comparison, climax, summarization, inclusio, etc.) which the narrator uses in the organization of his work. See M.A. POWELL, *What is Narrative Criticism?*, Minneapolis, MN, 1990, pp. 32-34. An application of all that is to be found in W.S. KURZ, *Reading Luke-Acts. Dynamics of Biblical Narrative*, Louisville, KY, 1993, *passim*. When the Lucan narrative is compared with the literature of his time, "literary pattern" receives a different meaning: cf. E. PLÜMACHER, *Lukas als hellenistischer Schriftsteller. Studien zur Apostelgeschichte*, Göttingen, 1972; C.H. TALBERT, *Literary Patterns, Theological Themes, and the Genre of Luke-Acts*, Missoula, MT, 1974. For our part, however, we use the narrative notion of "typological pattern" in the sense of what is commonly called "typology" (τύπος), to refer to the different patterns of "theological" type, which, coming from the OT, give meaning to Luke's narrative through each one of the narrative-semantic categories. So, D.L. BOCK, *Proclamation from Prophecy and Pattern* (n. 6), p. 274: "In referring to OT patterns, we refer to what is commonly called typology, while noting that the patterns that occur refer to more than Christology". A definition on the hermeneutical aspect of 'typology' is found recently in M. FISHBANE, *Biblical Interpretation in Ancient Israel*, New York, 1986, p. 350: "As is well known, the term 'typology' and the hermeneutical aspect with which is associated, which sees in persons, events, or places the prototype, pattern, or figure of historical persons, events, or places that follow it in time, are particularly associated with classical Christian exegesis". I have studied the semantic categories of narrative analysis in relation to the OT typology in Lucan account in A. DEL AGUA, *La interpretación* (n. 8), pp. 194-203; also cf. ID., *Die "Erzählung des Evangeliums" im Lichte der derash Methode*, in *Judaica* 47 (1991) 140-154.

21. Cf. A. DEL AGUA, *El derash cristológico*, in *Scripta Theologica* 14 (1982) 203-217; ID., *El método midrásico* (n. 6), p. 235ff; also cf. C.J. DAVIES, *The Name and Way of the Lord. Old Testament Themes, New Testament Christology* (JSNT SS, 129), Sheffield, 1996, *passim*.

22. Cf. above n. 20.

23. An attempt to explain Luke's use of the OT as rhetorical μίμησις has been carried out by T.L. BRODIE, *The Accusing and Stoning of Naboth (1 Kgs 21,8-13) as One Component of the Stephen Text (Acts 6,9-14; 7,58a)*, in *CBQ* 45 (1983) 417-432; *Luke 7,36-50 as an Internalization of 2 Kings 4,1-37: A Study in Luke's Use of Rhetorical Imitation*, in *Bib* 64 (1983) 457-485; *Towards Unravelling Luke's Use of the Old Testament: Luke 7,11-17 as an Imitatio of 1 Kings 17,17-24*, in *NTS* 32 (1986) 247-267, etc. Although he introduces the notion of "internalization", Brodie does not highlight quite enough the hermeneutical role of the OT in Luke's narrative. See the criticism of G. J. STEYN, *Luke's Use of MIMHΣIΣ? Re-opening the Debate*, in C.M. TUCKETT (ed.), *The Scriptures in*

ity and context, "in his understanding of the relationship between the story of Jesus and the church and the story of Israel. Simply put, how does the story of Jesus and the Christian community, ... fit within theological history? The Lucan evangelist grappled with this question, the principal question behind the function of Scripture in his two-volume work" [24].

Thus, my aim in this paper is to prove that "the point of view" of the new story of Jesus undertaken by Luke, and continued in the narrative on the early church, has its main theological pattern of reference in the OT category of βασιλεία τοῦ θεοῦ. Luke has elaborated his christology and ecclesiology in the light of the OT tradition of the Basileia. All this without forgetting that Jesus himself, according to the synthesis of the evangelist Mark (1,14-15), operated within the framework of early Judaism, when he presented his own ministry in the light of the OT tradition of the Messiah-Herald (cf. the hermeneutical function of Isa 61,1-2 in 11QMelch)[25] which proclaims the beginning of the eschatological era as the inauguration of the Kingdom of God: "How beautiful upon the mountains are the feet of the Herald... who says to the community of Zion: 'the Kingdom of your God is revealed'" (TgIsa 52,7).

Since the OT is the real hermeneutic of Luke's narrative, its interpretation cannot depend solely on modern literary fiction[26], a criticism that is sometimes made[27], or on Hellenistic rhetoric, as Güttgemanns[28]

---

the Gospels (n. 6), pp. 551-557, p. 556: "Should a case be made that Luke deliberately copied the structure and style of stories and speeches from his Scriptures in order to create and present the life and work of Jesus, then one must still clearly distinguish between the use of μίμησις by Luke as a literary technique, and the person and character of Jesus as an imitation of outstanding elements from the characters known from Luke's Scriptures". Consequently, when studying Luke's narrative, one must look for a synthesis between the literary aspect and the hermeneutical one, because the literary technique (μίμησις, σύγκρισις...) and 'typology' of the OT are in any case linked in the narrative. Accordingly, it would be better to talk of the typological nature of the synkrisis or of the mimesis in Luke-Acts. So, J.-N. ALETTI, Il Racconto come Teologia. Studio narrativo del terzo Vangelo e del libro degli Atti degli Apostoli, Roma, 1996, pp. 80-86: "Synkrisis e tipologia"; the original text, written in french, has just been published: Quand Luc raconte. Le récit comme théologie (Lire la Bible, 114), Paris, Cerf, 1998; also cf. M. COLERIDGE, The Birth of the Lucan Narrative (n. 7), passim; and A. DEL AGUA, La interpretación (n. 8), pp. 189-191.

24. C.A. EVANS, Gospels and Midrash (n. 17), p. 4.

25. P. MILLER, The function of Is 61,1-2 in 11QMelchizedek, in JBL 88 (1969) 467-469; cf. A. DEL AGUA, El cumplimiento del Reino de Dios en la misión de Jesús: Programa del Evangelio de Lucas (Lk 4,14-44), in EstBíb 38 (1979-80) 269-293, p. 276, n. 28.

26. Cf. J.L. SKA, La "nouvelle critique" et l'exégèse anglo-saxonne, in RSR 80 (1992) 29-53.

27. Cf. M.A. POWELL, What is Narrative Criticism? (n. 20).

28. E. GÜTTGEMANNS, In welchem Sinne ist Lukas "Historiker"? Die Beziehung von Luk 1,1-4 und Papias zur antiken Rhetorik, in Linguistica Biblica 54 (1983) 9-26.

claimed. For this end, the historico-critical method is not sufficient. It is necessary to undertake a more general critical study of the gospels, which deals with the final form of the narration.

I. THE CONCEPT OF "KINGDOM (OF GOD)" IN OT TRADITION

Luke's interpretation of the βασιλεία τοῦ θεοῦ is to be understood in the light of the OT traditions of the Basileia, which all speak of a divine plan of eschatological salvation ("Heilsplan Gottes"). Also, one will understand better Luke's criticism with regard to the way the realization or fulfilment of the Kingdom of God is presented in some of these traditions (cf. Lk 17,20f; 19,11; 24,21; Acts 1,6).

The "Kingdom" is one of the symbols with which Israel expressed its historico-salvific identity as a people of God or of the Covenant[29]. The exegetical tradition which goes back to Exod 19,5f is explicit in this respect[30]. The images which the OT uses to show the special link between Israel and God are many and varied. Thus, together with "possession" (Exod 19,5; Deut 7,6) and "holy nation" (Exod 19,6), "plantation" and "construction" (Jer 49,10 LXX; cf. Jer 24,6), or "house" (Isa 5,7), are found, among others "vine" (Jer 2,21; Isa 5,1-7), "flock" (Isa 40,11; Ps 95,7), "son" (Wis 18,13) and "wife" (cf. Hos 2,18). The NT took these figures as models or patterns (τύποι) to present the church as people of the new and eternal covenant[31]. So, for example, "flock" in Lk 12,32;

A critical reply is found in F. SIEGERT, *Lukas ein Historiker, d.h. ein Rhetor? Freundschaftliche Entgegnung auf E. Güttgemanns*, in *Linguistica Biblica* 55 (1984) 57-60; cf. A. DEL AGUA, *La interpretación* (n. 8), pp. 184-186.

29. Cf. the studies and articles on βασιλεία/Kingdom by G. VON RAD, in *TWNT* 1 (1933), pp. 563-569; K. SEYBOLD, in TWAT 4 (1984), pp. 926-957; E. ZENGER, *Herrschaft Gottes/Reich Gottes* II, in *TRE* 15 (1986), pp. 176-189; N. LOHFINK, *Der Begriff des Gottesreiches vom AT her gesehen*, in J. SCHREINER (ed.), *Unterwegs zur Kirche: Alttestamentliche Konzeptionen* (QDisp, 110), Freiburg, 1987, pp. 33-86; K.G. KUHN, in *TWNT* 1 (1933), pp. 570-573; O. CAMPONOVO, *Königtum, Königsherrschaft und Reich Gottes in den frühjüdischen Schriften*, Göttingen, 1985; A. DÍEZ MACHO, *Introducción general a los Apócrifos del Antiguo Testamento* I, Madrid, 1984, pp. 351-389; B. CHILTON, *Targumic Approaches to the Gospels*, Lanham, MD – London, 1986; E.E. URBACH, *The Sages. Their Concepts and Beliefs* I, Jerusalem, 1970, pp. 400-482; M. HENGEL & A.M. SCHWEMER (eds.), *Königsherrschaft Gottes und himmlischer Kult* (WUNT, 55), Tübingen, 1991; S.A. PANIMOLLE, *Reino de Dios*, in P. ROSSANO, G. RAVASI & A. GIRLANDA (eds.), *Nuevo diccionario de teología bíblica*, Madrid, 1990, pp. 1609-1639.

30. Cf. M. MCNAMARA, *The New Testament and the Palestinian Targum to the Pentateuch*, Rome, 1966, pp. 27-230; R. LE DÉAUT, *Targum du Pentateuque II. Exode et Lévitique*, Paris, 1979, p. 155, n. 10; A. DÍEZ MACHO, *Derás y exégesis del Nuevo Testamento*, in *Sefarad* 35 (1975) 37-89, pp. 70-71; A. DEL AGUA, *El método midrásico* (n. 6), p. 233.

31. On the Matthean concept of "Kingdom of Heaven" in the light of the OT tradition of the Basileia, see A. KRETZER, *Die Herrschaft der Himmel und die Söhne des Reiches. Eine redaktionsgeschichtliche Untersuchung zum Basileiabegriff und Basileiaverständnis im Matthäusevangelium* (SBM, 10), Stuttgart, 1971; also A. DEL AGUA, *Eclesiología como discurso narrado: Mt 13,2-52*, in *EE* 72 (1997) 217-269, pp. 252ff.

"vine" in Jn 15,1ff and Mt 21,33ff; "construction" in Mt 16,16-19 and 1 Cor 3,6ff, etc.

The vocation and the mission of Israel does not prevent it from also recognizing the cosmic and universal dimension of divine Kingship (Pss 22,29; 29; 110,19; Zech 14,9; 1 Chron 16,31; Dan 4,31f...). However, given that the privilege of being the chosen people was conditioned by the faithful loyalty on the part of Israel (Exod 19,5 LXX; 23,22 LXX), Israel ceased to be the Kingdom of God because of its disloyalty to the covenant; but, as OT messianic tradition states, in the eschatological era, the Lord will rebuild his Kingdom, purifying and renewing his people, by means of the Shepherd King, the Davidic Messiah (Ezek 37,23-26; cf. 34).

In the same way that the covenant, the exodus, and the creation are eschatologized and give their name (as soteriological categories) to the future salvation as "the new covenant", "the new exodus", and "the new creation", the apocalyptic tradition also formulates the eschatological salvation as the forthcoming Kingdom of God, which will give rise to the beginning of the new era (Dan 2,44; 7,13ff). Therefore, "in Ancient Judaism there were two expressions for the conception of the Kingdom of God. Just as there are two eras – the present and the future –, they also speak of a (lasting) Kingdom of God in this era and a (future) Kingdom of God in the new era... The lasting Kingdom of God is, for ancient Judaism, *that God has Lordship over Israel...*, but at the end of time this must be recognized by all nations"[32].

In the Hellenistic and Roman period, two very different ways of conceiving the Kingdom are perceived, a political one and a spiritual. On the one hand, a political and earthly conception of the Kingdom of God (as an earthly theocratic reality) is propagated. The popular expectation was orientated towards a nationalist messianism which, together with the defeat of the enemies, predicted the abundance of all good things (1 and 2 Macc). This can be seen in PssSol 17,23-51 or in the *War Scroll* in Qumran (cf. 6,6; 19,5-8); Lk 24,21 and Acts 1,6 also illustrate this view. The heavenly Kingdom, on the other hand, is found in apocalyptic writings (or in writings influenced by these) which illustrate its heavenly dimension. It is not a question of an earthly and inner worldly reality, but of a new order that is introduced by God himself at the end of time, when the Lord delivers justice to his faithful and destroys his enemies (Wis 3,1-10; 5,15f). In Dan 2,44, God is described as the supreme judge who sits on his throne for the final judgement of history (Dan 7,9ff). With this final and supreme intervention, carried out by the Son of man (1 En 45,3; 62,5; 69,27...), God inaugurates his eschatological, eternal and universal Kingdom over all peoples and empires (Dan 7,26ff). After the annihilation of the earthly kings and sovereigns, the righteous will reign in eternal glory (1 En 38,5; 58,3), guided by the Chosen One of God, the Messiah, once the wicked have been destroyed (1 En 45,3.5), condemned to the torments of hell (AsMos 10,8f).

In the *Targum of the Prophets* is found the abstract expression "Kingdom of God", a formula which is not found in the whole of the Hebrew Bible and which implies an important development in the shaping of the tradition of the Basileia. The formula "the Kingdom of God has been/will be revealed" is char-

---

32. J. JEREMIAS, *Teología del Nuevo Testamento* I (Estudios Bíblicos, 2), Salamanca, 1974, pp. 122f.

acteristic for TgIsa 24,23; 31,4; 40,9; 52,7; TgEzek 7,7.10; TgObad 21; TgZech 14,9, and is a clear example of apocalyptic eschatology in the Targum. It deals with a targumism which, besides carrying out the function of an anti-anthropomorphic metonymy, introduces in the translation (by means of a derashic procedure of updating) a new theological element: a reference to the personal and eschatological intervention of God in human history, by which he will carry out his plan of universal redemption or Kingdom of God (the new era). The closeness of the logia of Jesus about the Kingdom of God to the targumic formulation has led biblical scholars to place Jesus in this area of early Judaism, from which he would have taken such expressions[33].

A last significant feature in the liturgy of early Judaism is the link of the Kingdom of God with Sion-Jerusalem and with the temple (Isa 24,23; 33,17-24; 52,1-10; Micah 4,7; 1 En 91,13; Jub 1,28; TgIsa 24,23; 31,4; TgMicah 4,7, etc. Evidence of all this is given by Lk 19,11.

In order to understand the theological project of Luke, it is necessary not to lose sight of the polisemy of the OT traditions of the Basileia. These traditions also form part of Luke's hermeneutical equipment.

II. The Narrative Point of View

The διήγησις περὶ τῶν πεπληροφορημένων ἐν ἡμῖν πραγμάτων (Lk 1,1; cf. Acts 1,1 λόγος), which Luke proposes in the prologue of his gospel, is not an exception to the biblical and Jewish tradition in the art of narrating history[34], although it shows features which come from an Hellenistic milieu (rhetorical techniques and style)[35]. It is a question of presenting the whole narrative of Luke-Acts as a "theological narration" which bases its theological point of view on what its author formulates as εὐαγγελίζεσθαι τὴν βασιλείαν τοῦ θεοῦ in the programmatic introduction to the gospel (Lk 4,43; cf. 8,1; 16,16; Acts 8,12). This section forms an inclusion with the end of Acts, leaving Paul in Rome κηρύσσων τὴν βασιλείαν τοῦ θεοῦ (28,31). Both scenes highlight the narrative unity of the Lucan work and confirm its theological aim. The

33. Cf. G. DALMAN, *Die Worte Jesu* I, Leipzig, 1898, p. 75ff; J. JEREMIAS, *Teología* (n. 32), p. 126; B.D. CHILTON, *Regnum Dei Deus est*, in *SJT* 31 (1978) 261-270; ID., *Targumic Approaches to the Gospels* (n. 29), pp. 85-97.99-107.109-112; ID., *God in Strength. Jesus' Announcement of the Kingdom* (SNTU, B/1), Linz, 1979; K. KOCH, *Offenbaren wird sich das Reich Gottes*, in *NTS* 25 (1979) 158-165; O. CAMPONOVO, *Königtum* (n. 29), pp. 419-432; J. RIBERA FLORIT, *La escatología en el Targum Jonatan y su relación con el Targum palestinense*, in V. COLLADO & V. VILAR (eds.), *II Simposio bíblico español*, Valencia-Córdoba, 1987, pp. 487-499, esp. p. 488.

34. Cf. N.A. DAHL, *The Story of Abraham in Luke-Acts*, in L.E. KECK & J.L. MARTYN (eds.), *Studies in Luke-Acts*, London, 1966, pp. 139-158.

35. Cf. W.S. KURZ, *Hellenistic Rhetoric* (n. 18), *passim*.

βασιλεία τοῦ θεοῦ is the "narrative point of view" from which Luke retells the story of Jesus Christ (Gospel) and the Christian church (Acts)[36].

1. The Plot and Program of a Story in Two Volumes (Lk 4,14-44)

From a narrative "point of view"[37], Jesus' preaching in the synagogue of Nazareth (vv. 14-30) and his work at Capernaum (vv. 31-41) culminate in a summary (vv. 42-44) in which the reader finds the hermeneutical key of the section[38]. It all converges in the *logion* which the evangelist puts in the mouth of Jesus: καὶ ταῖς ἑτέραις πόλεσιν εὐαγγελίσασθαί με δεῖ τὴν βασιλείαν τοῦ θεοῦ, ὅτι ἐπὶ τοῦτο ἀπεστάλην (v. 43). The significance of this expression for the Lucan image of Jesus has taken too long to be adequately dealt with in NT research. A study of the context will lead us to a good understanding and assessment. What Luke wants the readers to understand with the βασιλεία τοῦ θεοῦ must be inferred from the pericope on Jesus' activity at Nazareth and Capernaum.

At the beginning of the section on the messianic selfproclamation of Jesus in Nazareth and the fulfilment of the βασιλεία τοῦ θεοῦ (vv. 16-30)[39], the narrator sets the scene (*setting*) for his (targumizing) reading of Isa 61,1-2a, combined with the phrase "to set free the oppressed" of Isa 58,6; it is the prophetic reading (*haftarah*) of a synagogal service[40].

36. In addition to the commentaries, cf. U. BUSSE, *Die Wunder des Propheten Jesus* (FzB, 24), Würzburg, ²1979, pp. 57-90; ID., *Das Nazareth-Manifest Jesu* (SBS, 91), Stuttgart, 1978, pp. 77-98; U. LUZ, Βασιλεία, in *EWNT* 1, pp. 481-491; O. MERK, *Das Reich Gottes in den lukanischen Schriften*, in E.E. ELLIS & E. GRÄSSER (eds.), *Jesus und Paulus*. FS W.G. Kümmel, Göttingen, 1975, pp. 201-220; W. RADL, *Das Lukas-Evangelium* (EdF, 261), Darmstadt, 1983, pp. 131-133; J. SCHLOSSER, *Le Règne de Dieu dans les dits de Jésus*, Paris, 1980, I, pp. 42-47; A. DEL AGUA, *El cumplimiento del Reino de Dios en la misión de Jesús: programa del evangelio de Lucas (Lc 4,14-44)*, in *EstBíb* 38 (1979-80) 269-294; and the studies by Völkel, Weiser, Wolter, and Prieur (above n. 1 and 2).

37. On Luke-Acts as narration, see esp. R.C. TANNEHILL, *The Narrative Unity of Luke-Acts. A Literary Interpretation*. Vol. I: *The Gospel according to Luke*, Philadelphia, PA, 1986. Vol. II: *The Acts of the Apostles*, Minneapolis, MN, 1990; J.-N. ALETTI, *L'art de raconter Jésus Christ. L'écriture narrative de l'évangile de Luc*, Paris, 1989; ID., *Il Racconto come Teologia* (n. 23); W.S. KURZ, *Reading Luke-Acts* (n. 20); M. COLERIDGE, *The Birth of the Lucan Narrative* (n. 7).

38. In my opinion, the programmatic section of the gospel of Luke includes Lk 4,14-44. So, A. DEL AGUA, *El cumplimiento* (n. 36), *passim*; M. VÖLKEL, *Zur Deutung des "Reiches Gottes" bei Lukas* (n. 2), pp. 63-67; A. WEISER, *"Reich Gottes" in der Apostelgeschichte* (n. 2), p. 129f.

39. For an historico-redactional approach to the section, cf. the commentaries of, among others, H. Schürmann, J.A. Fitzmyer, and F. Bovon.

40. Cf. A. FINKEL, *Jesus' Preaching in the Synagogue on the Sabbath (Luke 4,16-28)*, in C.A. EVANS & W.R. STEGNER (eds.), *The Gospels and the Scriptures of Israel* (n. 6),

The "narrated speech"[41] ("narration of words"[42]), which follows the reading of the book of Isaiah in Lk 4,18f, is presented as a synagogal homily (*derashah*). It puts in the mouth of Jesus a (*derash*) *pesher* through which, identifying himself with the Isaianic tradition of the *mebasser*, he proclaims himself the eschatological "Herald-Prophet" (of the Kingdom of God): σήμερον πεπλήρωται ἡ γραφὴ αὕτη ἐν τοῖς ὠσὶν ὑμῶν. Thus, the Lucan Jesus applies to himself, in an explicit way, a messianic tradition of prophetic typology[43] by which he is characterized as Messiah, Herald of the Kingdom and Anointed by the Spirit (cf. 11QMelch and TgIsa 52,7). The narrator shows himself to be more concerned with teaching the reader about what the βασιλεία τοῦ θεοῦ consists of than with its nearness (diff. Mk 1,14-15). The Kingdom has become visible in Jesus, in whom God fulfils the christological promises made to Israel; hence, christology, narrated as fulfilment of promised salvation, is the direct object of the proclamation of the βασιλεία τοῦ θεοῦ. In Nazareth and Capernaum the reader witnesses a first and programmatic evangelization of the Kingdom of God. Therefore, "die Characterisierung der Basileia als 'überzeitlich-jenseitig' und die einseitige Rede von ihrem 'Wesen' führen dazu, dass die Besonderheit des lucanischen Verständnisses aus dem Blick gerät"[44].

With reference to the content of the evangelization of the βασιλεία τοῦ θεοῦ, the Nazareth pericope, focusing on christology, fulfils a proleptic role. It alludes programmatically to situations which will be made explicit later on. Just as the fulfilment of the Scriptures in Jesus places the Basileia under the sign of fulfilment of the promise, in a later sequence the homiletic development specifies how such a fulfilment is carried out, alluding to the passion by means of the image of the prophet who is not welcome in his home town (v. 24) and of his rejection by the people of Nazareth (vv. 28-30). From the beginning, the Basileia is directed towards the events which will take place in Jerusalem: the death, resurrection and ascension of Jesus. All the rhetoric, culminating in the sentence αὐτὸς δὲ διελθὼν διὰ μέσου αὐτῶν ἐπορεύετο (v. 30) with which the Lucan Jesus is directed programmatically to Jerusalem, is

---

pp. 325-341; C. PERROT, *La lecture de la Bible. Les anciennes lectures palestiniennes du Shabbat et des Fêtes*, Hildesheim, 1973, pp. 194-204; also cf. A. DEL AGUA, *La sinagoga: orígenes, ciclos de lectura y oración*, in *EstBíb* 41 (1983) 341-366; F. MANNS, *Une approche juive du Nouveau Testament* (Initiations bibliques), Paris, 1998.

41. Cf. A. DEL AGUA, *Eclesiología como discurso narrado* (n. 31), pp. 220-237.

42. G. GENETTE, *Figuras III*, Barcelona, 1989, pp. 226-240.

43. Cf. J.-N. ALETTI, *L'art de raconter Jésus Christ* (n. 36), pp. 57f; ID., *Il Racconto come Teologia* (n. 23), pp. 80-86.

44. A. PRIEUR, *Die Verkündigung der Gottesherrschaft* (n. 1), p. 175.

at the service of this understanding ("Verklammerung von Botschaft und Verkündiger"[45]). Due to all this, christology is then thematized theologically in the Lucan narrative as βασιλεία τοῦ θεοῦ.

The Basileia is not confined, however, to christology. The second part of the homily (vv. 23-27) illustrates from the text (*haruzim*) of the OT (1 Kings 17,9 and 2 Kings 5,14) that the messianic salvation which has just begun will not profit Israel. The rejection of Jesus on the part of the people of Nazareth is, therefore, representative of the attitude of all Israel, and anticipates the question of the new structure in the reception of salvation, which will be settled definitively in Acts 28,17-31. Accordingly, the way of the gospel for the gentiles is also thematized as βασιλεία τοῦ θεοῦ, because it is in a church involved in the universal mission that the universal dimension of the Kingdom of God promised in the OT (salvation for the gentiles) is fulfilled.

The apparent lack of unity of the pericope is explained by the double theme Luke has introduced in it, in order to merge in his narrative the two components of his theological conception of the βασιλεία τοῦ θεοῦ, christology und ecclesiology. Both are objects of the Lucan elaboration on the evangelization of the Basileia. Through the divine passive ἐπὶ τοῦτο ἀπεστάλην (Lk 4,43), the narrator invites the reader to consider from a theological perspective the mission of Jesus; it is the establishment of the βασιλεία τοῦ θεοῦ. The Kingdom of God thematizes theologically the event of Jesus. The Lucan narrative point of view is to retell the story of Jesus Christ as αὐτοβασιλεία[46].

At the beginning of a new narrative section, the evangelist again thematizes the activity of Jesus as "evangelization of the Kingdom of God": καὶ ἐγένετο ἐν τῷ καθεξῆς καὶ αὐτὸς διώδευεν κατὰ πόλιν καὶ κώμην κηρύσσων καὶ εὐαγγελιζόμενος τὴν βασιλείαν τοῦ θεοῦ καὶ οἱ δώδεκα σὺν αὐτῷ (Lk 8,1). In fact, this verse goes back to 4,43 and depicts Jesus as an itinerant preacher carrying out the mission given to him by God. Lk 8,1, however, does not only remind the reader of the programmatic saying of Jesus, but also connects, through the linking syntagma βασιλεία τοῦ θεοῦ, with the expression τὰ μυστήρια τῆς βασιλείας τοῦ θεοῦ of the following narrative sequence (the sower: Lk 8,4-15). As regards Luke, the word preached is identified

---

45. M. VÖLKEL, *Zur Deutung des "Reiches Gottes" bei Lukas* (n. 2), p. 66.

46. This expression comes from Origen, *Comm. in Mattheum* XIV,7 (ad Mt 18,23): αὐτὸς [χριστός] γάρ ἐστιν ὁ βασιλεὺς τῶν οὐρανῶν, καὶ ὥσπερ αὐτός ἐστιν ἡ αὐτοσοφία καὶ ἡ αὐτοδικαιοσύνη καὶ ἡ αὐτοαλήθεια, οὕτω μήποτε [δήποτε?] καὶ ἡ αὐτοβασιλεία. The αὐτοβασιλεία of Christ is his *absolute kingship*.

with the proclaimed βασιλεία τοῦ θεοῦ, because the word refers to the fulfilment of the very plan of God in the ministry of Jesus[47].

2. The Journey to Jerusalem

The "interpretative narrative", which puts Jesus on a constant journey to Jerusalem, has, as its main aim, to show that the Kingdom of God and the person of Jesus always go together, so that we cannot talk of the Kingdom of God without Christ nor of Christ without Basileia. This narrative identification between message and messenger is the reason for which John the Baptist does not announce the Kingdom of God, because he is not the Kingdom (Lk 3,3; diff. Mt 3,2). For the same reason, John still belongs to the stage of the law and the prophets, whilst the dynamic fulfilment of the Kingdom of God is only announced with the arrival of Jesus Christ (Lk 16,16), and reaches its culmination in his second coming (Lk 21,31) at the time the Father has established (cf. Acts 3,19-31).

The clarifying process of the messiahship of Jesus, as well as its resulting universal salvific meaning, is a condition for the fulfilment of the Kingdom of God, which demands from the believer conversion, witness and mission (ecclesiological dimension). The narrative development of the Lucan understanding of the Kingdom constitutes an organic body, whose expression needs a framework for the complete development of its universal soteriological virtualities.

The central section of Luke's gospel (Lk 9,51–19,27) represents the most original chapter of the narrative[48]. The aim of the journey is to establish the Kingdom of God in Jerusalem through the passion and the exaltation of Christ. Luke has linked the (formal structure of a) journey to Jerusalem with the christological establishment of the Basileia.

Before the narrative of the journey, there is a prelude in which the narrator returns to his understanding of the Basileia. Thus, as opposed to the apocalyptic representation of the Basileia ἐληλυθυῖαν ἐν δυνάμει (Mk 9,1), Luke simply talks of "seeing" the βασιλεία τοῦ θεοῦ (9,27),

---

47. A. WEISER, *"Reich Gottes" in der Apostelgeschichte* (n. 2), p. 130: "Ähnlich wie Lk 4,43f kennzeichnet er Lk 8,1 zu Beginn eines neuen Abschnitts das Wirken Jesu zusammenfassend als 'Verkündigen des Reiches Gottes'"; A. PRIEUR, *Die Verkündigung der Gottesherrschaft* (n. 1), pp. 181-202.

48. For the current debate about the possibility of a Christian reading of Deuteronomy in the central section of Luke's gospel, cf. C.A. EVANS, *Luke 16,1-18 and the Deuteronomy Hypothesis*, in C.A. EVANS & J.A. SANDERS, *Luke and Scripture* (n. 6), pp. 121-139; and A. DENAUX, *Old Testament Models for the Lucan Travel Narrative: A critical Survey*, in C.M. TUCKETT (ed.), *The Scriptures in the Gospels* (n. 6), pp. 271-299.

alluding to the participation in the Basileia through the forthcoming paschal events. Indeed, the story of the transfiguration (Lk 9,28-36) anticipates, in a prolepsis of the resurrection, the "vision" of the future glory of Jesus (v. 32), which he will reach after suffering the passion and death[49].

The ecclesiological dimension of the Basileia is also present; the path of Jesus is also the path of the disciple to the definite Kingdom (Lk 9,21-27; cf. Acts 14,22). The narration opens with the ecclesiological motives: the following of Jesus (9,57-62) and the mission (10,1-20). The proclamation of the Kingdom is an announcement about Christ. Where he arrives, arrives the Basileia. This is also shown by the signs which he performs (11,14-22), and by the reply of Jesus himself to the Pharisees who ask him when the Kingdom of God is going to come: "The βασιλεία τοῦ θεοῦ is [already active] in the midst of you". The Kingdom of God is already present and active in the person and acts of Jesus, in whom the fulfilment of the salvific plan of God is being carried out[50]. Similarly, the theme of the participation in the eschatological banquet of the Kingdom of God (14,15-24; cf. 13,22-30) illustrates the ecclesiological dimension of the Kingdom of God[51].

3. The End of the Journey: The Arrival in the City

The arrival in Jerusalem and the resulting messianic excitement provides the opportunity for the Lucan definition of the βασιλεία τοῦ θεοῦ. Effectively, the Kingdom of God, closely linked to the city as in nationalist expectations, is going to take place not by appearing suddenly from heaven, but through the royal investiture which the pretender to the throne is going to receive through his death and resurrection (Lk 19,11-27; cf. Acts 1,6-11). The evangelist has joined the βασιλεία τοῦ θεοῦ to the Basileia of Christ (cf. our interpretation of Acts 28,30f);

---

49. Cf. A. DEL AGUA, *The Narrative of the Transfiguration as a Derashic Scenification of a Faith Confession (Mark 9,2-8 par)*, in *NTS* 39 (1993) 340-354.

50. In addition to the commentaries on the passage: B. NOACK, *Das Gottesreich bei Lukas. Eine Studie zu Luk. 17,20-24*, Uppsala, 1948; L. SABOURIN, *The Gospel according to Saint Matthew*, Bombay, 1982, p. 595: "The Kingdom of God is present among men in a form which is not always effective. It is present in Jesus' person, in his deeds, even in his words, but the ministry of Jesus requires a human response"; O. MERK, *Das Reich Gottes in den lukanischen Schriften* (n. 36), p. 216 and p. 219, rightly concludes that the "Gottesherrschaft" is "in der Person Jesu da".

51. Cf. T. SÖDING, *Das Gleichnis vom Festmahl (Lk 14,16-24 par Mt 22,1-10). Zur ekklesiologischen Dimension der Reich-Gottes-Verkündigung Jesu*, in R. KAMPLING & T. SÖDING (eds.), *Ekklesiologie des Neuen Testaments*. FS K. Kertelge, Freiburg-Basel-Wien, 1996, pp. 56-84.

consequently, the royalty of Christ as κύριος of the church, starting from his *sessio ad dexteram*, is not an isolated fact in the general framework in the history of salvation. On the contrary, according to Luke, the βασιλεία τοῦ θεοῦ, as the divine plan of eschatological and universal salvation, is now the framework where the event of Jesus of Nazareth shows all its salvific and universal power. In turn, christology is the place where the fulfilment of the Kingdom of God and its historical realization are revealed to mankind.

When the royal entry of Jesus into Jerusalem has been narrated (Lk 19,28-40) in the light of the anointing of Solomon (1 Kings 1,33-40)[52], the syntagma βασιλεία τοῦ θεοῦ gives way to expressions which make reference to the royalty of Christ. The entry of Jesus into Jerusalem represents an earthly prelude of the forthcoming heavenly enthronement of Jesus (Lk 24,50-52; Acts 1,9-12; cf. 2,32-35) who will establish the βασιλεία τοῦ θεοῦ.

The celebration of the passover, through the institution of the Eucharist (Lk 22,19-20), becomes a sign of the eschatological banquet, in which Jesus is going to take part immediately after his death (22,15-18). The church perpetuates it as an anticipation of the definitive Kingdom of God. The condition for the establishment of the messianic Kingdom is Jesus' passage through death to exaltation (Lk 22,67-70). The passion is the maximum trial which Jesus must overcome in order to show his true messianic condition against nationalist political hopes (Lk 22,28-30; cf. 4,1-13). Jesus promises participation in the eschatological Kingdom which he is going to establish through his death and his immediate exaltation (Lk 23,39-43 μνήσθητί μου ὅταν ἔλθῃς εἰς τὴν βασιλείαν σου... σήμερον μετ᾽ ἐμοῦ ἔσῃ ἐν τῷ παραδείσῳ; compare Lk 1,32-33 with Acts 2,30f).

4. The Narrative of the Way of the Kerygma to the Gentiles as Content of the Evangelization of the βασιλεία τοῦ θεοῦ

In his gospel Luke has consolidated the christological kerygma. The proclamation of the fulfilment of OT promises, which has its core part in the death and resurrection of Jesus, belongs to the present preaching of the βασιλεία τοῦ θεοῦ. Now in a second narrative stage the narrator thematizes the way the gospel reaches the Gentiles. Only when the gospel has reached Rome, can it be said that the fulfilment of the

52. Cf. A. DEL AGUA, *Derash cristológico en el relato lucano de la entrada de Jesús en Jerusalén: Lc 19,28-40*, in A. VARGAS-MACHUCA & G. RUÍZ (eds.), *Palabra y Vida. Homenaje a J. Alonso Díaz*, in *Miscelanea Comillas* 78-79 (1983), pp. 177-188.

universal dimension of the Basileia has been narrated theologically (cf. Acts 1,8 ἕως ἐσχάτου τῆς γῆς)[53].

From a narrative point of view, it is important to emphasize the continuity between the gospel of Luke and the book of Acts with respect to the Basileia. Thus, τὰ περὶ τῆς βασιλείας τοῦ θεοῦ of Acts 1,3, is parallel with τὰ περὶ Ἰησοῦ τοῦ Ναζαρηνοῦ of Lk 24,19 (cf. v. 27). Both formulations, as Acts 28,31 (cf. 28,23) proves, show the thread of the two stages of the story. Likewise, the concluding scene of the book of Acts (28,17-31), which forms an inclusion with Lk 4,14-44, underlines the unity of the Lucan narrative with respect to the βασιλεία τοῦ θεοῦ.

For the narrator, to be a witness of Jesus (Acts 1,8 ἔσεσθέ μου μάρτυρες) is to bear witness of the Basileia (Acts 28,23 διαμαρτυρόμενος τὴν βασιλείαν τοῦ θεοῦ πείθων τε αὐτοὺς περὶ τοῦ Ἰησοῦ ἀπό τε τοῦ νόμου Μωϋσέως καὶ τῶν προφητῶν; cf. 8,12; 19,8), starting from the witness based on the Scriptures. To the first narrative stage of the fulfilment of the Basileia in the death, resurrection and ascension of Christ, now corresponds the stage of command (1,8 ἔσεσθέ μου μάρτυρες ... καὶ ἕως ἐσχάτου τῆς γῆς) and fulfilment (28,17-31), also narrated in the light of the Scriptures. Hence the narrative deals with the "evangelization of the Kingdom of God" to the Gentiles (Acts 8,12; 28,23.31). The universal dimension of the event of Christ is fulfilled in the universal mission of the church. Another aspect of the ecclesiological dimension of the Basileia is linked to this: it is the structure of the reception of the salvation. An almost mechanical conception of salvation is replaced by the necessary personal conversion, which, in its turn, must be gained through a Christian life.

Starting from this standpoint, I proceed with the analysis of the contents of the final scene of Acts with respect to Paul's preaching about the βασιλεία τοῦ θεοῦ (28,17-31).

a. The Proclamation of the Basileia before the Jews (28,23)

At the end of his story, the narrator proceeds to create a suitable scenario for an "evangelization of the Kingdom of God", the theological "point of view" from which the whole of the event of Christ has been told to the reader throughout Luke-Acts. God has fulfilled the universal promises of salvation. Hence, christology becomes the object of the evangelization of the Basileia, which is announced as a present reality.

53. A. DEL AGUA, *Evangelizar el Reino de Dios. Estudio redaccional del concepto lucano de Basileia* (UPCM, IV, 23), Madrid, 1984, pp. 34-48.

To this end, Luke has managed to join together in this last section in Rome all the key elements of the book of Acts.

Three days after his arrival in Rome, Paul summons the "leading Jews" (v. 17a). He delivers a short speech to them in which he makes his own defense (vv. 17c-20). The reply of the Jews to Paul shows that they are ignorant of the Christian message (vv. 21-22). From the narrative point of view, v. 23 constitutes the last chance to offer the Christian kerygma to the Jews. The kerygma is presented in a summary.

> 28,23 Ταξάμενοι δὲ αὐτῷ ἡμέραν
> ἦλθον πρὸς αὐτὸν εἰς τὴν ξενίαν πλείονες
> οἷς ἐξετίθετο
> διαμαρτυρόμενος τὴν βασιλείαν τοῦ θεοῦ,
> πείθων τε αὐτοὺς περὶ τοῦ Ἰησοῦ
> ἀπό τε τοῦ νόμου Μωϋσέως καὶ τῶν προφητῶν,
> ἀπὸ πρωῒ ἕως ἑσπέρας.

The main verb ἐξετίθετο indicates the lasting action of Paul: "he went on explaining to them". On this verb depend the two participles διαμαρτυρόμενος and πείθων. The direct object of διαμαρτυρόμενος is βασιλεία τοῦ θεοῦ, and that of πείθων is περὶ τοῦ Ἰησοῦ. Both direct objects are equally connected to the main verb; moreover, the second one acts as a precise explanation of the first. Therefore, to bear witness to the Basileia is to persuade (them) about Jesus. Christology is the object of the testimony about the Basileia.

This interpretation of v. 23b, which is in line with the interpretation I proposed of Lk 4,43, is corroborated by two very close parallel texts in Acts 8,12 and 28,31. All three give a "summarium" of the message.

> 8,12 ὅτε δὲ ἐπίστευσαν τῷ Φιλίππῳ εὐαγγελιζομένῳ περὶ τῆς βασιλείας τοῦ θεοῦ καὶ τοῦ ὀνόματος Ἰησοῦ Χριστοῦ, ἐβαπτίζοντο ἄνδρες τε καὶ γυναῖκες.
> 28,31 κηρύσσων τὴν βασιλείαν τοῦ θεοῦ καὶ διδάσκων τὰ περὶ τοῦ κυρίου Ἰησοῦ Χριστοῦ μετὰ πάσης παρρησίας ἀκωλύτως.

In the three cases, the same construction appears: verb of speech + βασιλεία τοῦ θεοῦ + christological theme. As is usually admitted, the difficulty of interpretation is found in the first part. However, given that the two parts are connected by what seems to be clearly an explicative καί, it is the second participle which determines the first, except in 8,12 in which the same verb contains the two objects of the sentence. "To convince them about Jesus" indicates the content of the "evangelization of the Kingdom of God". This consists above all of the explanation of the meaning of Christ according to the salvific plan of God predicted in the Scriptures (Acts 13,23.27-29.32-37; 17,3; 26,23...); hence ἀπό τε τοῦ νόμου Μωϋσέως καὶ τῶν προφητῶν also refers to διαμαρτυρόμενος τὴν βασιλείαν τοῦ θεοῦ, since the evangelization of the Kingdom consists in giving witness of the plan of God established in the Scriptures.

The verbs διαμαρτύρεσθαι and πείθειν refer in the book of Acts to the area of Christian preaching in general, and are interchangable, so that διαμαρτύρεσθαι has Jesus as the object and πείθειν in one occasion βασιλεία τοῦ θεοῦ.

8,25 "Now when they had testified (διαμαρτυράμενοι) and spoken the word of the Lord, they returned to Jerusalem, preaching the gospel to many villages of the Samaritans".

18,5 "...Paul was occupied with preaching, testifying (διαμαρτυρόμενος) to the Jews that the Christ was Jesus".

20,21 "...testifying (διαμαρτυρόμενος) both to Jews and to Greeks of repentance to God and of faith in our Lord Jesus Christ".

13,43 "Many Jews and devout converts..., who spoke to them [Paul and Barnabas] and urged them (ἔπειθον) to continue in the grace of God".

This meaning of the verb διαμαρτύρεσθαι, "to bear witness" in favour of Jesus Christ in the light of the Scriptures, corresponds in Acts with μάρτυς, which has Jesus as its object in 1,8. Thus, the command of Acts 1,8 (ἔσεσθέ μου μάρτυρες) corresponds to the fulfilment in Acts 28,23 (διαμαρτυρόμενος τὴν βασιλείαν τοῦ θεοῦ). The testimony about the Basileia is explicity related to christology.

Acts 19,8 "And he entered the synagogue [Ephesus] and for three months spoke boldly, arguing and pleading about the Kingdom of God (πείθων [τὰ] περὶ τῆς βασιλείας τοῦ θεοῦ)".

This last text has as object of πείθειν the βασιλεία τοῦ θεοῦ (compare also Lk 24,19 τὰ περὶ Ἰησοῦ τοῦ Ναζαρηνοῦ with Acts 1,3 τὰ περὶ τῆς βασιλείας τοῦ θεοῦ; cf. Acts 28,31).

Returning to Acts 28,23b, πείθων τε αὐτοὺς περὶ τοῦ Ἰησοῦ is taken as a explanation of διαμαρτυρόμενος τὴν βασιλείαν τοῦ θεοῦ. "To bear witness of the Kingdom of God" is to try to convince (them) that in the event of Christ, particularly his death, resurrection and ascension, God has carried out his salvific plan predicted in the Scriptures. For this reason, I propose the following translation: "He went on expounding the matter to them: from morning till evening testifying to the Kingdom of God, that is to say, trying to convince them about Jesus both from the law of Moses and from the prophets".

b. The Pauline Proclamation of the Basileia to the Gentiles (28,30f)

V. 25-28: obstinacy of the Jews and salvation for the Gentiles. The Jews have a double reaction to the preaching of Paul (v. 24 "some were convinced... while others disbelieved"). Luke then tackles the question of the new structure of the reception of the salvation and, with this, the way of becoming part of the new people (or Kingdom) of God. In this respect, with the definitive opening up to the Gentiles, the expectation of salvation is definitively completed in Acts 28. The emphasis is on personal conversion. This is what some scholars have called "individualized ecclesiology" ("die Ekklesiologie wird individualisiert"[54]). If the two aspects of Luke's understanding of salvation have been concentrated in the concept of the Basileia, the question of the recipients of the salvation cannot be omitted, above all because the salvation as fulfilment applies to the promise and, consequently, to a particular circle of recipients of the promise. This is a question which is dealt with in Acts 28,17ff. The passage presents a structure similar to Acts 13,44ff and 18,1ff. In face of rejection from the Jews, Paul replies: "It was necessary that the word of God should be spoken first to you (ὑμῖν πρῶτον). Since you thrust it from you, and judge yourselves unworthy of eternal life, behold, we turn to the Gentiles" (Acts 13,46; cf. 18,6b). The question of the salvation for Gentiles, alluded to or quoted in the Scriptures, is found from the beginning to the end of the Gospel of Luke (Lk 2,30-32; 3,6; 4,25-27; 24,47). Similarly, in Acts 10–11 there is evidence of the legitimization of the mission to the Gentiles. The biblical proof is found in Acts 15,16-18 with the quotation of Amos 9,10-11.

Personal conversion becomes necessary. This means that only those who believe will enter the Kingdom. In this respect, the quotation from Isa 6,9f represents a derashic *pesher* to justify from the Scripture the situation that was produced, when the Jews rejected the Christian faith. Given that the *pesher* procedure seeks the prophetic meaning of the Scripture, the obstinacy of Israel is presented as "fulfilment" of the said quotation.

V. 30b-31: the evangelization of the Basileia to the Gentiles. In the colophon of the book of Acts, emphasis is again placed on the activity of Paul in Rome and the content of his preaching.

As v. 23b, vv. 30b-31 consist of a main clause and two subordinate participle sentences:

καὶ ἀπεδέχετο πάντας τοὺς εἰσπορευομένους πρὸς αὐτόν,
κηρύσσων τὴν βασιλείαν τοῦ θεοῦ
καὶ διδάσκων τὰ περὶ τοῦ κυρίου Ἰησοῦ Χριστοῦ
μετὰ πάσης παρρησίας ἀκωλύτως.

The main sentence of v. 30b refers to the fact that Paul received everyone who came to him. The narrator, however, thinks above all of

---

54. M. VÖLKEL, *Zur Deutung des "Reiches Gottes" bei Lukas* (n. 2), p. 70.

the Gentiles who, from this point onwards, are the main recipients of the Christian message.

The content of the preaching, in spite of the change of the audience, has not varied in comparison with v. 23: in v. 31 "die Christologie steht im Zentrum der paulinischen Verkündigung der βασιλεία τοῦ θεοῦ"[55]; but in v. 31 the reference to the Scriptures is missing. However, for Luke this announcement of the salvation to the Gentiles is also to be read in the light of the Scriptures. God has been active also among Gentiles. This is made clear by the references to the creation in Acts 14,15b; 17,24-26a. However, there is also a negative side ("[es] findet sich wie bei den Juden so auch bei den Heiden neben der Heilsgeschichte eine Unheilsgeschichte"[56]). God became unknown for the Gentiles (17,23), because they confused the divine with the material things (17,29). In spite of that, "[wird] auch den Heiden jetzt die Herrschaft des ihnen bis dahin unbekannten Gottes verkündigt"[57].

Unlike v. 23, the speech verbs belong less to the line of argument (bear witness, to convince) than to the area of the proclamation and explanation of salvation. In the book of Acts, the object of κηρύσσειν is almost always the Basileia or Christ and his work, whilst the content of διδάσκειν is the word of the Lord. This proclamation includes, again, the question of the new structure in the reception of salvation (ecclesiology).

CONCLUSION

The two volumes respond theologically to the pastoral and theological needs of the church of Luke's time. His narrative shows in fact a church that is very well aware of the focal point which the passion of Jesus occupied in its credo, as well as of its implication in the mission among the Gentiles. Luke has thematized his narrative of the two stages of the kerygma as the realization of the βασιλεία τοῦ θεοῦ. This fulfilment of the plan of God, announced in the OT, becomes present reality through the content of what Luke formulates as "evangelization of the Kingdom", i.e., christology and ecclesiology.

The main implications for his theology can be summarized in the following points:

1. The whole of the Lucan narrative (unity of Lk-Acts) shows a clear theological point of view: the appearance of the βασιλεία τοῦ θεοῦ in

55. A. PRIEUR, *Die Verkündigung der Gottesherrschaft* (n. 1), p. 76.
56. *Ibid.*, p. 77.
57. *Ibid.*, p. 78.

Christ and the opening up of the gospel to the Gentiles through the mission of the church. In other words, Luke has elaborated his christology and ecclesiology in function of and in the light of the Basileia.

2. In order to complete his narrative project, Luke needed the temporal space (narrative time) of the two works. This meant, on the one hand, the story of the passion, death and resurrection of Christ as part of the evangelization of the Kingdom, and, on the other hand, the path of the gospel to the Gentiles. Only in this way does the narrative correspond to the plan of salvation, and to the growing knowledge of the same plan of salvation required on behalf of the disciples. The narrative of the Kingdom follows the path of christology, and this, in its turn, has in the Basileia its authentic theological framework of reference.

3. The Basileia will not begin with the parousia of Christ, but it will have its consummation at the time of the return of the Son of man[58]. The time which it takes between the first and the second coming does not delay the ἔσχατον in the distant future, but receives its eschatological quality from the events through which God has fulfilled his plan of salvation. Consequently, Luke has not historicized the Basileia, but he has eschatologized the salvific act of God undertaken in the history of Jesus and the early Church[59]. The Lucan ἔσχατον is, then, christological and ecclesiological[60].

In this way, Luke has provided an invaluable service to the church of his time and of all times, preparing the way for a change from a concept of Basileia excessively linked to the ἔσχατον and understood exclusively from a chronological point of view, to an eminently historico-salvific concept, which is unfolded from the historical presence of Christ up to the time of the universal restauration established by God (Acts 3,18-21; Lk 21,29-31). Thus, if to the NT ἔσχατον corresponds ἤγγικεν ἡ βασιλεία τοῦ θεοῦ (Lk 10,9.11), to the second coming corresponds ἐγγύς ἐστιν ἡ βασιλεία τοῦ θεοῦ (Lk 21,31). Likewise, to the νεφέλη of the Ascension (Acts 1,9)[61] corresponds the singular ἐν

58. D.L. BOCK, Luke, Gospel of, in J.B. GREEN, S. McKNIGHT & I.H. MARSHALL (eds.), Dictionary of Jesus and the Gospels, Downers Grove, IL – Leicester, 1992, 495-510, p. 504; L. GUY, The Interplay of the Present and Future in the Kingdom of God (Luke 19,11-44), in TyndB 48 (1997) 119-137.

59. A. DEL AGUA, Derás lucano de Mc 13 a la luz de su "teología del Reino", Lc 21,5-36, in EstBíb 39 (1981) 285-313, p. 312. A. PRIEUR, Die Verkündigung der Gottesherrschaft (n. 1), p. 282.

60. Cf. K.H. RENGSTORF, Das Evangelium nach Lukas (NTD, 3), Göttingen, [16]1976, p. 6: "Stärker als Matthäus und Markus und anders als bei Johannes ist die Eschatologie bei Lukas zugleich christologisch und ekklesiologisch bestimmt".

61. D.L. BOCK, Luke (n. 58), p. 505: "The key event at the center of God's provision of salvation is the resurrection/ascension. Among the gospels writers, only Luke mentions and develops the ascension, an event which for him provides the link between Luke 24 and Acts 1".

νεφέλῃ with the return of the Son of man in Lk 21,27 (Mk ἐν νεφέλαις)[62]. The NT ἔσχατον and the parousian ἔσχατον are assimilated as the two poles of one single salvific and dynamic action on the part of God.

4. It is important to underline once again the rich polisemy of the "Kingdom of God". As we have noted, the βασιλεία τοῦ θεοῦ is in the OT tradition also a representation of God, by which is meant the personal eschatological intervention of God in human history: "Regnum Dei Deus est". Luke's derashic approach has given it a christological transposition.

5. The hermeneutical key of the Lucan narrative must be sought in the holy Scriptures and their tradition. The custom of retaining only the purely literary aspect when studying the Lucan narrative (reducing it to style and techniques) should give way to a synthetic study taking into account both aspects the literary and the hermeneutical.

6. Finally, the Church constitutes the eschatological people of God. This should end the reticence of properly relating Kingdom and Church[63]. The Kingdom of God or the divine plan of eschatological salvation is realized, though perhaps not exclusively, in the Church.

Universidad San Pablo-CEU   Agustín DEL AGUA
Isaac Peral, 58
E-28040 Madrid

---

62. A. DEL AGUA, Derás lucano (n. 59), pp. 306-308.
63. Cf. A. PRIEUR, Die Verkündigung der Gottesherrschaft (n. 1), passim.

DER WEG ALS ROTER FADEN DURCH LK–APG

Das Wegmotiv ist im lukanischen Doppelwerk von besonderer Bedeutung. Sowohl sprachlich als auch inhaltlich ist das Aufbrechen, Unterwegs-Sein, Gehen und Zurückkehren durchwegs mehr als nur eine Aneinanderreihung von Ortswechseln. Welche theologischen Schwerpunkte setzt der Verfasser, welches Programm versucht er zu realisieren? Zunächst sollen typisch lukanische Wörter aus dem Wortfeld der Bewegung erläutert werden (1), in der Folge wird eine bibeltheologische Geo- bzw. Topographie versucht (2), schließlich wird der Gebrauch des Begriffs ὁδός im lukanischen Doppelwerk analysiert (3).

1. *Wortfeld Bewegung*

Neben zahlreichen Wörtern der Bewegung wie ἔρχεσθαι, περιπατεῖν, ἀναβαίνειν, καταβαίνειν, ὑπάγειν, die Lukas nicht wesentlich anders verwendet als sonst generell im NT üblich, sind es vor allem fünf Vokabel, die für seinen Stil (und seine Theologie; siehe unten) typisch sind.

a. πορεύεσθαι

Das Wort kommt im NT insgesamt 154mal vor, davon 51mal bei Lk und 38mal in der Apg. Weit mehr als die Hälfte aller neutestamentlichen Belege findet sich also im lukanischen Doppelwerk. Wenigstens 10mal verwendet Lk es diff Mk oder Mt[1], bisweilen (wie auch Mt) als Hebraismus in pleonastischer Verwendung (z.B. Lk 7,22; 11,26). πορεύομαι bedeutet neben den üblichen Ausdrücken der Bewegung (gehen, aufbrechen, reisen, wandeln) bei Lukas auch: weggehen, sich entfernen (z.B. Lk 4,30), jemandem nachgehen, -laufen (z.B. Lk 21,8), mit einem bestimmten Auftrag gesendet werden (z.B. Apg 9,15)[2]. Bei Jesus steht es im Zusammenhang mit dem Weg nach Jerusalem, auch ausdrücklich unter Hinweis auf den göttlichen Auftrag: Lk 13,33 πλὴν δεῖ με σήμερον καὶ αὔριον καὶ τῇ ἐχομένῃ πορεύεσθαι, ὅτι οὐκ ἐνδέχεται προφήτην ἀπολέσθαι ἔξω Ἰερουσαλήμ, obwohl damit der Weg Jesu

---

1. W. RADL, Art. *πορεύομαι*, in *EWNT*, III, c. 326.
2. F. NÖTSCHER, *Gotteswege und Menschenwege in der Bibel und in Qumran*, Bonn, 1958, p. 109: »πορεύεσθαι ist terminus technicus des Sendungs- und Aussendungsbefehls für Jünger und Apostel und bekommt damit auch schon einen geistigen Inhalt«.

noch nicht beendet ist: unterwegs mit den Emmaus-Jüngern (Lk 24,13.28) ist die Himmelfahrt sein letzter Aufbruch: Apg 1,10f. Im gänzlich übertragenen Sinn steht πορεύομαι für das Leben bzw. den Lebensweg in den Tod: Lk 22,22.33. Im Sinn von *schrittweises Wachsen* (der Kirche) steht es in Apg 9,31[3].

b. ὑποστρέφειν

Zurückkehren ist ein typisch lukanisches Wort. Es kommt im NT 35mal vor, außer Gal 1,17; Hebr 7,1 und 2 Petr 2,21, wo es keine tiefere oder übertragene Bedeutung hat, ausschließlich in Lk und Apg. Zunächst fällt auf, daß es weder für umkehren im Sinne von Bekehrung, Reue verwendet wird, noch für die Wiederkunft Jesu in der Parusie. In vielen Fällen steht ὑποστρέφειν für eine Heimkehr, einen Ortswechsel, der signalisiert, daß ein wichtiges Ereignis abgeschlossen ist: Maria kehrt heim (Lk 1,56); die Familie Jesu (Lk 2,43); Abgesandte (Lk 7,10); ein vornehmer Mann (Lk 19,12); der äthiopische Eunuch (Apg 8,28); die anderen Jünger in Milet (Apg 21,6); die Soldaten in die Kaserne (Apg 23,32). Seltener wird angegeben, von wo jemand zurückkehrt (ἀπό: Lk 4,1 Jesus vom Jordan; Lk 24,9 Frauen vom Grab; Apg 1,12 Apostel vom Ölberg); häufiger wird angegeben, wohin (εἰς + Akkusativ) jemand zurückkehrt, z.B. Lk 1,56; 2,45; 4,14; 7,10; 8,39; 11,24; 24,33.52; Apg 1,12; 8,25; 12,25; 13,13.34; 14,21; 21,6; 22,17; 23,32.

Über diese Ortswechsel hinaus hat ὑποστρέφειν einige wichtige Konnotationen, die auf eine ganz bewußte Verwendung durch Lukas schließen lassen. Das Wort markiert einen ausgeführten Auftrag, einen Abschluß und Neubeginn eines wichtigen Ereignisses, eine damit verbundene innere oder äußere Veränderung: der ausgesandten Apostel (Lk 9,10); der 72 Jünger (Lk 10,17); der Apostel (Apg 1,12; 8,25); von Paulus und Barnabas (Apg 12,25) und Paulus allein (Apg 22,17). Auffällig ist, daß achtmal im Doppelwerk das Ziel des Rückkehrens Jerusalem ist: von Josef und Maria (Lk 2,45); der Emmausjünger (Lk 24,33); der Apostel (Lk 24,52; Apg 1,12; 8,25); Barnabas und Saulus (Apg 12,25); Johannes Markus (Apg 13,13); Paulus (Apg 22,17).

Die theologisch wichtigste Tiefenaussage von ὑποστρέφειν ist das Lob Gottes. An fünf Stellen hat das Wort die »Funktion eines Doxologie-Anzeigers«[4]: die Hirten nach dem Besuch beim neugeborenen Jesus

---

3. RADL, *πορεύομαι* (n. 1), c. 327, gegen E. HAENCHEN, *Die Apostelgeschichte* (KEK, 3), Göttingen, [7]1977, p. 321.

4. W. SCHENK, *Die makrosyntaktische Signalfunktion des lukanischen Textems ὑπο-στρέφειν*, in E. LIVINGSTONE (ed.), *Studia Evangelica*, 7, Berlin, 1982, pp. 443-450, hier

(Lk 2,20); der Besessene von Gerasa (Lk 8,39 mit Imperativ!); der geheilte Samariter (Lk 17,15.18); die Apostel (Lk 24,52f). In Apg 1,12 kann dies als Fortsetzung von Lk 24,52 vorausgesetzt werden. In Lk 23,48 schwingt zwar mehr die Betroffenheit der Menge mit, allerdings geht der Rückkehr in V. 47 der Lobpreis des Hauptmanns voraus.

c. διαβῆναι

Dieses Kompositum von βαίνω kommt im NT nur bei Lukas vor. In Lk 16,26 wird damit die (unmögliche) Verbindung zwischen dem Himmel und der Unterwelt beschrieben, in Apg 16,9 die Überfahrt von Paulus von Asien nach Makedonien. Eine wichtige theologische Komponente ist damit aber nicht verbunden.

d. διοδεύω

Dieses Wort kommt im NT nur zweimal – ausschließlich bei Lukas – vor. In Lk 8,1 steht es am Beginn eines Summariums im Imperfekt und zeigt somit eine wiederholte Tätigkeit an, ohne daß damit eine konkrete Ortsangabe verbunden wäre. In Apg 17,1 ist damit nur eine kurze Reisenotiz formuliert, ein Missionsaufenthalt ist nicht mitgemeint[5].

e. διέρχομαι

Das Kompositum von ἔρχομαι findet sich im NT insgesamt 42mal, je nach der Präposition, die darauf folgt, in der Bedeutung von durchwandern, hindurchgehen, hingelangen, erreichen. Drei Viertel der neutestamentlichen Belege stehen im lukanischen Schrifttum. Oft hat es hier die Konnotation »verkündigen«, ja ist geradezu »terminus technicus für das missionarische Wirken Jesu im Judenland, seiner Apostel (Lk 9,6) und Missionare (Apg 20,25)«[6]. Genauso wie Jesus predigend durch die Städte Israels zieht, tun es die Seinen im Römischen Reich.

2. Die wichtigsten Ortsangaben

Die bisherige Untersuchung des lukanischen Sprachgebrauchs hat bereits deutlich gemacht, daß Aufbrechen, Unterwegssein, Zurückkehren beliebte, wichtige Motive sind. Welches Programm ergibt sich aus den Stationsangaben? Daß es sich im lukanischen Doppelwerk nicht nur um eine Aneinanderreihung von Ortsangaben sondern um ein geographi-

---

450: »darf auch dort angenommen werden, wo es ohne die ausdrückliche doxologische Ergänzung steht«.

5. HAENCHEN, *Apostelgeschichte* (n. 3), z.St.

6. U. BUSSE, Art. *διέρχομαι,* in *EWNT*, I, c. 777

sches-theologisches Konzept, um eine durchgängige Linie handelt, zeigt die Formel Lk 23,5 »im ganzen jüdischen Land, von Galiläa bis hierher [i.e. Jerusalem]«, die Apg 10,37-39 wieder aufgenommen wird[7].

a. Jesus

Nach der lukanischen Kindheitsgeschichte ist Jesus schon im Mutterleib unterwegs, weil sich seine Eltern zur Volkszählung nach Betlehem begeben müssen (Lk 2,4). Über Jerusalem (43mal in Lk; erstmals in Lk 2,22) gelangt der Neugeborene nach Nazareth zurück (Lk 2,39). Als Zwölfjähriger ist er wieder in Jerusalem (Lk 2,41-51).

Bemerkenswert ist, daß bei der Taufe, die übrigens erst nach der Gefangennahme des Täufers berichtet wird, keine genaue Ortsangabe gemacht wird: καὶ ἦλθεν εἰς πᾶσαν [τὴν] περίχωρον τοῦ Ἰορδάνου. Vom Jordan kehrt Jesus zurück und wird vom Geist in die Wüste geführt (Lk 4,1), anschließend kommt er wieder nach Galiläa (4,14)[8], 4,16 nach Ναζαρά, 4,31 nach Kafarnaum. 4,44 wird diff Mt 4,23 und Mk 1,39 erwähnt, daß Jesus in den Synagogen Judäas (!) verkündigt – worauf Apg 10,37 ausdrücklich eingeht. Außerdem werden an konkreten Orten noch erwähnt Nain (7,11) und Betsaida (9,10).

Mit 9,51 beginnt der letzte Weg Jesu nach Jerusalem, der dort seinen Höhepunkt, nicht aber seinen endgültigen Abschluß finden wird – das letzte Ziel ist der Himmel, deshalb auch schon an dieser Stelle die Erwähnung der Hinwegnahme (ἀναλήμψις). In 9,53; 13,22; 17,11; 18,31 und 19,28 wird der Hinweis auf diesen Weg jeweils wieder aufgenommen; Jesus begründet dies in Lk 13,33 damit, daß ein Prophet nirgendwo anders als in Jerusalem umkommen darf. Innerhalb dieses großen Reiseberichts kommen zwar nur noch selten Ortsangaben vor (9,52 ein nicht näher genanntes Dorf in Samarien, dessen Bewohner Jesus nicht aufnehmen[9], 10,38 ein Dorf und 18,35 bzw. 19,1 Jericho), aber *daß* Jesus unterwegs ist, wird immer wieder betont: 9,57; 13,22; 14,25; 17,11; 18,31. In 9,57 (par Mt 8,20) wird dieses Unterwegs-Sein Jesu gleichsam als Wesensbestimmung beschrieben: ὁ δὲ υἱὸς τοῦ ἀνθρώπου οὐκ ἔχει ποῦ τὴν κεφαλὴν κλίνῃ.

---

7. W.C. ROBINSON, *Der Weg des Herrn. Studien zur Geschichte und Eschatologie im Lk-Evangelium* (Theologische Forschung, 36), Hamburg, 1964, pp. 30-36.
8. W. BRUNERS, *Die Reinigung der zehn Aussätzigen und die Heilung des Samariters* (FzB, 23), Stuttgart, 1977, p. 154: »Mehr als nur eine Orts- bzw. Landschaftsangabe ist Galiläa dort, wo es den Anfang des Wirkens Jesu markiert«.
9. Worauf sich BRUNERS, *Die Reinigung*, p. 150 stützt, ist nicht einsichtig: »Für das lukanische Doppelwerk ist also einmal die mehrmalige Erwähnung von Samaria und zugleich eine positive Einstellung kennzeichnend«. Allenfalls mag er an die positive Darstellung von Samaritern (Lk 10,37; 17,16) gedacht haben.

Mit dem Einzug Jesu in Jerusalem (19,28) werden die Ortsangaben wieder häufiger, die topographischen Angaben detaillierter: Betfage und Betanien (19,29), Abhang des Ölbergs (19,37), in den Tempel (19,45), das Haus mit dem Obergemach für das Pesachfest (22,10-12), Ölberg (22,39), Haus des Hohenpriesters (22,54), Pilatus (23,1), Herodes (23,8), hinaus (23,26). Auch nach der Auferstehung Jesu ist er weiter unterwegs: mit den Emmausjüngern (24,13-35) und mit den Elf, hinaus nach Betanien (24,50), von wo er in den Himmel emporgehoben wird (24,51).

Bei den meisten Ortsangaben fällt auf, daß Lukas offensichtlich keine genauen Ortskenntnisse besitzt[10].

b. Die Apostel und Jünger

Das Unterwegs-Sein gehört von Anfang an wesentlich zum Selbstverständnis der Apostel bzw. Jünger und Jüngerinnen: nach der Berufung folgen Simon und die Zebedäus-Söhne Jesu nach (Lk 5,11), so auch Levi (Lk 5,28); die 12 Apostel werden auf den *Weg* geschickt (Lk 9,1-6, besonders V. 3), und *kehren* bald wieder zu Jesus *zurück*, parallel dazu die Aussendung und Rückkehr der 72 (Lk 10,1.17). Anders als Mt und Mk zählt Lk 8,1-3 vier Frauen auf, die mit Jesus mitziehen. Das Lk-Evangelium schließt mit der Rückkehr der Elf nach Jerusalem (24,52).

Die Apostel verweilen zunächst längere Zeit in Jerusalem, die erste Missionsreise führt Philippus nach Samaria (Apg 8,4f), es schließt die Taufe des Eunuchen auf der Straße (ὁδός) nach Gaza (8,26-40) an. Barnabas begibt sich nach Samaria (11,22) von wo er wieder – zusammen mit Saulus – nach Jerusalem zurückkehrt (11,30). Petrus scheint eher als ortsfest gezeigt zu werden. Er spielt in den ersten Kapiteln der Apg eine wichtige Rolle, bleibt aber immer in Jerusalem. Erst nach Philippus beginnt auch er, sich auf den Weg zu machen: Lydda (9,32), Joppe (9,36), Cäsarea (Kapitel 10). In 11,1 ist er wieder in Jerusalem zurück. In 12,17 heißt es lapidar, er sei an einen anderen Ort gegangen. Nur einmal wird Petrus noch erwähnt, Apg 15,7 beim Apostelkonvent.

c. Paulus

Schon bei der dritten Erwähnung von Saulus in der Apg (nach 7,58 und 8,3) wird erzählt, daß er unterwegs (nach Damaskus) ist (Apg 9,1). Er kehrt nach Jerusalem (9,26), schließlich nach Tarsus (9,30) zurück. 11,25.30 wird berichtet, daß er neuerdings von Tarsus nach Jerusalem geholt wird. Es folgen die drei Missionsreisen (13,1–15,1;

---

10. Vgl. G. SCHNEIDER, *Das Evangelium nach Lukas* (ÖTK, 3/1), Gütersloh, 1977, p. 32; W.G. KÜMMEL, *Einleitung in das Neue Testament,* Heidelberg, [17]1973, p. 110.

15,36–18,22; 18,23–21,17), die jeweils in Jerusalem enden. Zwischen der zweiten und dritten Missionsreise wird Jerusalem mit ἀναβάς nur indirekt erwähnt, Apg 18,22. Seine letzte Reise, von der Lukas berichtet, führt ihn nach Rom, wo er das Evangelium *ungehindert* (ἀκωλύτως) verkündet[11]. Das göttliche δεῖ, das schon Jesu Weg zum Leiden nach Jerusalem geleitet hat (Lk 2,49; 4,43; 9,22; 13,33; 17,25; 22,37; 24,7.44), gilt auch für Paulus: Apg 9,16; 14,22; 19,21; 23,11; 27,24.26. Es wird in Apg 19,21, wie in Lk 13,33, mit πορεύεσθαι verbunden. Dem Inhalt nach kann wohl auch Apg 20,22 (καὶ νῦν ἰδοὺ δεδεμένος ἐγὼ τῷ πνεύματι πορεύομαι εἰς Ἰερουσαλήμ) zu diesen Stellen dazugezählt werden.

d. Die »Wir«-Berichte

In 16,10-17 (Troas, Neapolis, Philippi); 20,5-15 (Philippi, Troas, Assos, Mytilene, Chios, Samos, Milet); 21,1-18 (Milet, Kos, Rhodos, Patara, Tyrus, Ptolemais, Cäsarea, Jerusalem) und 27,1–28,15 (Cäsarea, Sidon, Myra, Kaloi Limenes, Malta, Syrakus, Rhegion, Puteoli, Rom) ist das nicht durch genauere Angaben präzisierte Subjekt ἡμεῖς, d.h. außer Paulus werden die Reiseteilnehmcr nicht namentlich genannt. Sind diese Wir-Berichte ein Hinweis auf die Authentizität des Verfassers, der Paulus wirklich begleitet hat[12]? Hat der Verfasser der Apg diese Liste als Schiffstagebuch vorgefunden und sie in seine Erzählungen hineinverwoben[13]? Möchte der Verfasser seine Augenzeugenschaft durch das literarische Stilmittel nur unterstellen[14]? Oder will er durch das »Wir« den Leser auf die Reisen des Paulus gleichsam mitnehmen[15]? Als genauer Befund läßt sich jedenfalls festhalten, daß (a) das ἡμεῖς (bzw. ἡμῖν, ἡμᾶς) plötzlich und unvermutet auftritt; (b) die oben genannten Orte aneinandergereiht eine kontinuierliche Reiseroute ergeben, ausgenommen zwischen 21,18 und 27,1 (Cäsarea – Jerusalem); (c) in diesen Perikopen ganz wenige, meist gar keine Einzelszenen (Wunderberichte, Streitgespräche, Heilsereignisse) erzählt werden, die dramaturgisch oder theologisch von besonderer Relevanz wären.

---

11. Vgl. HAENCHEN, *Apostelgeschichte* (n. 3), p. 700: »Er wollte… der Kirche das Martyrium nach Möglichkeit ersparen. Darum hat er die Apg nicht mit dem Märtyrertod des Paulus enden lassen, sondern mit… ἀκωλύτως«.
12. Erstmals Irenäus, Adv. haer. III 1; 10,1; 14,1f.
13. E. HAENCHEN, *Die Wir-Berichte und das Itinerar*, in ID., *Gott und Mensch*, Göttingen, 1965, pp. 227-264.
14. *Ibid.*, p. 263.
15. Dazu grundsätzlich K. HUIZING, *Lukas malt Christus*, Düsseldorf, 1996, p. 28: »die Teilhabe des Lesers am Geschehen des Textes zu zeigen«.

3. Was bedeutet ὁδός?

דֶּרֶךְ steht schon im AT neben der Grundbedeutung »betretener und dadurch festgetretener Weg«[16] öfter im übertragenen Sinn. Ein Mensch geht seinen Weg, ist unterwegs, auf der Reise; das Wort steht aber auch im Sinn von Wegstrecke. Eine typisch deuteronomische Formulierung ist הָלַךְ הַ-דֶּרֶךְ (den Weg gehen, den Gott vorgeschrieben hat): Dtn 1,33; 5,33; 13,6; oder mit סָר, von diesem Weg abweichen: Dtn 9,16; 11,16.28; 17,17; 31,29. Wie aus dem jeweiligen Kontext hervorgeht, könnte dafür auch stehen »die Gebote (des Dekalogs) halten«. In diesem moralischen Sinn steht es allgemein für gottgefälligen Lebenswandel, (bundes)gerechtes Verhalten, besonders häufig in Gen, Dtn, Pss und Spr. An manchen Stellen wird auch vom Weg Gottes selbst gesprochen, womit sein Verhalten gemeint ist, das sich dem Volk zuwendet[17]: Dtn 1,33; Nah 1,3; Jes 55,8f, Hiob 34,27.

Im NT steht ὁδός insgesamt 101mal, »mit deutlichem Schwergewicht…im lukanischen Doppelwerk«[18]: Ähnlich wie im Alten Testament ist auch hier der Übergang von der konkreten Bedeutung für Straße über das Gehen auf diesem Weg bis zum Lebenswandel fließend, vielleicht sogar oft bewußt offengelassen: Es »ist oft kaum zwischen 'eigtl.' und 'übertr.' Gebrauch sauber zu trennen«[19].

Im Lk/Apg lassen sich die Vorkommen von ὁδός in fünf Gruppen einteilen, auch wenn diese Einteilung nicht immer eindeutig ist. Im wörtlichen Sinn von Weg, Straße, Tagesstrecke, Reise wird ὁδός selten gebraucht: Lk 2,44; 8,5.12; 11,6; 12,58; 14,23; 18,35; 19,36; Apg 1,12; 8,26.36.39; 9,17.27. In den letzten vier Stellen ist der Begriff des Weges mehrdeutig und weist auf die Bekehrung, den neuen Lebensweg des Eunuchen bzw. des Paulus hin. »Lukas macht sich hier im übrigen die Doppeldeutigkeit des Begriffs 'Weg' zunutze, um dadurch das folgende Geschehen als die entsprechende 'Wende' zu charakterisieren: Saulus, der 'auf dem Weg' ist (V. 17), um den 'Weg', den er für falsch hält, zu verfolgen, muß sich von der Richtigkeit dieses 'Wegs' überzeugen lassen«[20].

---

16. G. SAUER, Art. דֶּרֶךְ, in TWAT, I, c. 457.
17. Ein Überblick findet sich erstmals bei A. GROS, Le thème de la route dans la Bible, Brussel, 1957. Er weist eine »fortschreitende Spiritualisierung des Weg-Begriffes in der Bibel nach. Gemäß seinen Beobachtungen ist Christus als der neue Mose Vollender des Weges Gottes mit den Menschen, die Kirche als das neue Volk Gottes geht den letzten Exodus.
18. M. VÖLKEL, Art. ὁδός, in EWNT, II, c. 1201.
19. Ibid.
20. J. ZMIJEWSKI, Die Apostelgeschichte (RNT), Regensburg, 1994, p. 378.

Mehrmals in Lk-Apg wird ὁδός im Stil des alttestamentlichen Sprachgebrauchs mit ϑεοῦ oder κυρίου verbunden: Lk 1,76; 3,4f; 7,27; 20,21; Apg 2,28 (mit ζωῆς); 13,10[21]; 16,17 (mit σωτηρίας); 18,26; aber auch Lk 1,76.79 (mit εἰρήνης) gehören zu dieser Gruppe.

Ein durchgehendes Motiv in Lk ist der Weg Jesu, im wesentlichen »nach Jerusalem«: Lk 9,57; 18,35 (?); 19,36; aber auch nach der Auferstehung 24,32.35. Öfter allerdings wird dieser Weg nach Jerusalem mit πορεύεσϑαι gebildet (siehe oben). Es ist auffällig, daß Lk 18,43 ἐν τῇ ὁδῷ von Mk 10,52 durch δοξάζων ersetzt.

Gleichermaßen in Lk und Apg wird damit der individuelle oder gemeinsame Weg der Jünger beschrieben, sei es ihr Lebens- oder Missionsweg: Lk 9,3; 10,4; Apg 25,3; 26,13.

Singulär für die Apg ist der sechsmalige Gebrauch von ὁδός als Umschreibung der christlichen Lehre oder als Selbstbezeichnung[22] der christlichen Gemeinde: 9,2; 19,9.23; 22,4; 24,14.22. (Die deutsche Einheitsübersetzung stellt an allen diesen Stellen das Adjektiv *neu* in Klammer vor *Weg*.) Bis auf die neutrale Formulierung in 24,22 steht diese Bezeichnung immer im Kontext von Konflikt, Auseinandersetzung, Abgrenzung, wenn auch damit das Christentum *nicht* als *wahre* Lehre gegenüber anderen Religionen (im Sinne von »extra ecclesiam nulla salus«) herausgestrichen werden soll[23]. Diese Verwendung von ὁδός hat eine »gewisse Ähnlichkeit mit der Ausdrucksweise von Qumran, ohne daß sich indes die Herkunft des Ausdrucks von dort hinreichend erklären läßt, sondern im breiteren Zusammenhang alttestamentlich-jüdischer und hellenistisch-jüdischer Denk- und Sprechweise zu sehen ist«[24]. Ein ausdrücklicher Bezug zur deuteronomischen Verwendung (»die Gebote halten«; siehe oben), gar eine Ablöse der alttestamentlichen Gebote durch das Christentum ist weder bei Lk noch bei Apg nachzuweisen. Wenn auch Lukas diese Verwendung von ὁδός höchstwahrscheinlich schon vorgefunden hat[25], so paßte sie ihm doch ausgezeichnet in sein Konzept.

---

21. Wege sind »die göttlichen Pläne, besonders die Absichten, die Gott mit der Mission hat«: vgl. W. MICHAELIS, Art. ὁδός, in *TWNT*, V, c. 91.
22. R. PESCH, *Die Apostelgeschichte* (EKK, 5/1), Einsiedeln-Köln, 1986, p. 303: »vielleicht eine der ältesten Selbstbezeichnungen« des Christentums.
23. VÖLKEL, ὁδός (n. 18), c. 1203
24. A. WEISER, *Die Apostelgeschichte* (ÖTK, 5/1), Gütersloh-Würzburg, ²1989, p. 223. Ebenso Völkel, c. 1203. Die von ihm angeführten Stellen (1QS 9,17.19; 10,20; CD 1,13; 2,6) entsprechen aber eher dem allgemeinen biblischen Sprachgebrauch, außer 1QS 9,17: »mit Wissen, Wahrheit und gerechtem Urteil diejenigen zurechtzuweisen, die den Weg wählen«. Vgl. E. REPO, *Der »Weg« als Selbstbezeichnung des Urchristentums*, Helsinki 1964.
25. HAENCHEN, *Apostelgeschichte* (n. 3), p. 308.

Als brennpunktartige Zusammenfassung aller Bedeutungen läßt sich Apg 18,25 verstehen: Apollos ἦν κατηχημένος τὴν ὁδὸν τοῦ κυρίου: mit *Herr* ist hier sowohl Gott als auch Jesus gemeint, die christliche Lehre wird damit eindeutig bezeichnet. »Die christliche Heilslehre ist der Weg schlechthin«[26]. Nur Apg 14,16 (εἴασεν πάντα τὰ ἔθνη πορεύεσθαι ταῖς ὁδοῖς αὐτῶν) läßt sich schwer einer dieser Gruppen zuordnen.

Folgende Linie läßt sich im lukanischen Gebrauch von ὁδός nachzeichnen: Den Weg, den Gott im Ersten Testament sein Volk lehrt und führt, setzt Jesus (durch sein Leiden in Jerusalem) fort. Er nimmt die Jünger mit auf diesen Weg, schickt sie aber weiter, sodaß der Weg Gottes mit den Menschen weder zeitlich noch räumlich begrenzt werden kann. Die Apg endet 28,31 mit dem Adverb ἀκωλύτως.

4. *Folgerungen*

a. Jerusalem

Bei der Menge der Ortsangaben hat Jerusalem in geographischer und inhaltlicher Hinsicht eine Vorrangstellung[27]. Von der Kindheitsgeschichte Jesu angefangen bis zum Beginn der Reise Pauli nach Rom ist die Hauptstadt Israels immer wieder Ziel des Aufbrechens, der Reise, des Weges. Was den Weg Jesu betrifft, hat »Lukas sich durch die Markusvorlage zu seinem Konzept des Weges anregen lassen«[28]. »Beziehungsvoll aber ist, daß das Wegkonzept in der Apostelgeschichte weiterwirkt«[29]. Denn auch in der Apostelgeschichte ist Jerusalem immer wieder jener Ort, zu dem Apostel oder Jünger (zurück)kommen: die Elf in 1,12; Petrus (und Johannes) in 8,25; 11,2; Paulus in 9,26; 15,2 (zusammen mit Barnabas); 18,22; 19,21 und öfter. Jerusalem ist nach Lukas der Angelpunkt, um den sich die Heilsgeschichte dreht, ausdrücklich formuliert im Verbot Jesu, aus Jerusalem vor der Geistsendung fortzugehen (Apg 1,4). Jerusalem ist das (vorletzte) Ziel des Weges Jesu, zugleich Ausgangspunkt für die Weltmission durch die Kirche.

b. Unterwegs

Auf dem Weg zu sein, ist das im Willen Gottes begründete »Schicksal« Jesu und seiner Jünger, der ὑπηρέται γενόμενοι τοῦ λόγου (Lk

---

26. NÖTSCHER, *Gotteswege* (n. 2), p. 122.
27. Vgl. T. BERGHOLZ, *Der Aufbau des lukanischen Doppelwerkes*, Frankfurt/Main, 1995, p. 134.
28. J. GNILKA, *Theologie des Neuen Testaments* (HTKNT Suppl., 5), Freiburg, 1994, p. 197.
29. *Ibid.*

1,2). »Heute und morgen und am folgenden Tag muß ich weiterwandern« (Lk 13,33) – dieses Wort Jesu gilt nicht nur ihm selbst, sondern auch seinen Jüngern. Damit ist der urchristliche Wanderradikalismus, ein »Ethos der Heimatlosigkeit... die Aufgabe der stabilitas loci«[30] widergespiegelt. Lukas hat sich zwar – aufgrund geänderter Umstände – von diesem Radikalismus distanziert[31], auf jeden Fall bleibt die Heilsgeschichte an die Verkündigung gebunden. Selbstredend ist auch mit der Ankunft des Paulus in Rom kein endgültiges Ziel erreicht: ἐνέμεινεν δὲ διετίαν ὅλην ἐν ἰδίῳ μισθώματι. Die Zeitangabe und der Hinweis auf die Mietwohnung deuten auf Vorläufiges hin. Ob sich Lukas bewußt ist, damit die alttestamentliche Zelt-/Lade-Tradition fortzuführen, die dem Tempel gegenüber kritisch war (vgl. nur 2 Sam 7; Ez 37,27) und die sich in den Zeltzitaten des NT (vgl. Joh 1,14; Offb 21,3) fortsetzt, kann nur vermutet werden.

Mit diesem Unterwegs-Sein ist auch ausgedrückt, daß die Heilsgeschichte noch unvollendet ist, bis der Herr wiederkommt. Die Jünger werden daher kritisiert, wenn sie stehen bleiben und zum Himmel hinaufschauen (Apg 1,11). In dieser Zwischenzeit befindet sich die Kirche[32]. D. M. Sweetland hat ausführlich gezeigt, daß dieses Reisemotiv sowohl den einzelnen Jünger als auch die Kirche als ganze betrifft. »In the Gospel, Luke portrays the life of the Christian disciple as a journey. Those who would be followers of Jesus must leave their own way and join Jesus as he travels toward resurrection, ascension and exaltation«[33]. In der Apostelgeschichte, »the early church begins and continues its journey... a church that is in the process of growing and developing as it is guided through history by the Holy Spirit in accordance with the plan of God«[34].

c. Kontinuität und Diskontinuität

Mit dem Weg-Motiv gelingt es Lukas, eine durchgehende Kontinuität der Heilsgeschichte vom Ersten Testament bis in die Gegenwart zu

---

30. G. THEISSEN, *Wanderradikalismus. Literatursoziologische Aspekte der Überlieferung von Worten Jesu im Urchristentum*, in ZTK 70 (1973) 245-271, hier 249.

31. *Ibid.*, p. 270: »In der lukanischen Abschiedsrede widerruft Jesus ausdrücklich seine Gebote für Wandercharismatiker: Die Aussendung ohne Geldbeutel, Tasche und Schuh soll von nun an keine Geltung mehr haben«. Dennoch werden die Zwölf als Wandermissionare gezeigt.

32. H. CONZELMANN, *Grundriß der Theologie des NT,* ed. A. LINDEMANN, Tübingen, [6]1997, p. 160: »Ihr (sc. der Kirche) Ort ist heilsgeschichtlich bestimmt durch ihre Stellung zwischen Auferstehung und Parusie«. Damit hat Conzelmann (bzw. Lindemann) den altbekannten Vorwurf des »Frühkatholizismus« an Lukas deutlich zurückgenommen.

33. D.M. SWEETLAND, *Our Journey with Jesus. Discipleship according to Luke-Acts,* Collegeville, MN, 1990, p. 43

34. *Ibid.*, p. 168.

zeichnen, insbesondere aber den unmittelbaren Zusammenhang von Jesus und der Kirche. »Die Reisen der Umlandmission in Apg 8–10, die in ihrer Zufälligkeit und Planlosigkeit an das Umherziehen Jesu in Lk 4–9 erinnern«[35], sind eine auffallende Parallele. Ist es zu weit hergeholt, die Wanderungen und Reisen der Apostel und Jünger in der Apg formal als Durchführung des Themas, wie es in den Aussendungsreden (Lk 9,1-6.10; 10,1.17) angeschlagen wird, zu sehen; vgl. Apg 9,43; 13,51; 16,15; 17,7; 18,3? Die Missionsreisen, wie sie in der Apg berichtet werden, können durchaus als ausführliche Illustration dafür dienen, daß der Verkündigungsauftrag des Herrn aus dem Evangelium (Lk 9; 10) erfolgreich realisiert worden ist. Diskontinuität besteht allerdings darin, daß nach Lukas das Heil von den Juden auf die Heiden übergeht: »Nazareth, Antioche de Pisidie, Rome: trois jalons d'une même histoire, trois situations permettant des variations sur le même thème: la salut passe des Juifs aux Gentils«[36]. Lukas zeichnet also die »Heilsgeschichte als Lauf oder Weg... der zu den Heiden führt«[37].

d. Der Weg zum Leben

Jesu Weg ist ein Weg der Erlösung, Rettung (Apg, 16,7), des Lebens (2,28), des Friedens (Lk 1,79). Auf diesem Weg ist Jesus der Anführer (Apg 3,15). »Ist Jesu gesamter Weg, einschließlich seines Sterbens, ein rettender, so wird seine Rettertätigkeit durch sein Wirken erläutert und dargestellt... Gutes tuend zog er umher und heilte alle.«[38] Darum zeigt Lukas in der Apg auch immer wieder, daß die Apostel Wunder tun wie Jesus (auf den sie sich immer berufen), wobei die Parallelen zwischen Jesus und Petrus bzw. Paulus bewußt formuliert sind[39].

Aufgabe des Christen ist es daher, wie Jesus und die Apostel der ersten Generation auf diesem Weg zu bleiben und in Wort und Tat an der von Gott kommenden Rettung mitzuarbeiten.

Arsenal 7/4/3   Georg GEIGER
A-1030 Wien

---

35. BERGHOLZ, *Aufbau* (n. 27), p. 100; vgl. auch p. 133.
36. J. DUPONT, *La conclusion des Actes et son rapport à l'ensemble de l'ouvrage de Luc*, in J. KREMER (ed.), *Les Actes des Apôtres* (BETL, 48), Leuven, 1979, p. 401.
37. ROBINSON, *Weg* (n. 7), p. 39.
38. GNILKA, *Theologie* (n. 28), p. 206.
39. A.J. MATTILL, *The Jesus-Paul-Parallels and the Purpose of Luke-Acts*, in *NT* 17 (1975) 15-46.

THE THEOLOGICAL SIGNIFICANCE OF JUDAEA
IN LUKE-ACTS

Modern discussions of Luke's geographical perspective have rightly focused on the importance of Jerusalem as the center-point around which the continuous story of his two-volume work revolves[1]. But Jerusalem is not the only place name mentioned in both volumes of Luke's work. The region designated by the toponym "Judaea" also assumes a prominent place in both narratives[2]. In the Gospel, Judaea serves as one of the key terms in Luke's geographical delineation of Jesus' public ministry[3]. Likewise, in the opening scene of Acts Judaea is singled out by the risen Jesus as the first expanded arena of evangelism outside the city of Jerusalem (see Acts 1,8; cf. 5,16; 8,1.4) In turn, subsequent references in Acts ascribe to the Christians resident in Judaea an

---

1. Just as the Gospel narrative reflects Luke's preoccupation with Jerusalem as the city where Jesus is destined to fulfill his prophetic mission, so in Acts Luke identifies Jerusalem as the place from which the word of God's salvation must spread to the end of the earth. For further discussion of the importance of Jerusalem in Luke's Gospel see, among many others, J. LEAL, *El Plan Literario del III Evangelio y la Geografía*, in *EE* 29 (1955) 197-215; E. LOHMEYER, *Galiläa und Jerusalem bei Lukas*, in G. BRAUMANN (ed.), *Das Lukas-Evangelium* (WdF, 280), Darmstadt, Wissenschaftliche Buchgesellschaft, 1974, pp. 7-12; J.A. FITZMYER, *The Gospel According to Luke* (AB, 28-28A), New York, Doubleday, 1980-1985, pp. 164-171; M. BACHMANN, *Jerusalem und der Tempel. Die geographisch-theologischen Elemente in der lukanischen Sicht des jüdischen Kultzentrums* (BWANT, 109), Stuttgart, Kohlhammer, 1980, pp. 132-170. For a treatment of Jerusalem as a fixed point of orientation in Acts see J.K. ELLIOT, *Jerusalem in Acts and the Gospels*, in *NTS* 23 (1976-77) 462-469; R. PESCH, *Die Apostelgeschichte* (EKK, 5/1-2), Zürich, Benziger – Neukirchen-Vluyn, Neukirchener, 1986, vol. 1, pp. 36-42.
2. Of the 43 instances of ἡ Ἰουδαία in the NT, ten are found in Luke and twelve in Acts. See Luke 1,5.65; 2,4; 3,1; 4,44; 5,17; 6,17; 7,17; 21,21; 23,5; Acts 1,8; 2,9; 8,1; 9,31; 10,37; 11,1.29; 12,19; 15,1; 21,10; 26,20; 28,21.
3. H. CONZELMANN, *The Theology of St. Luke*, New York, Harper and Row, 1961, pp. 18-27, once found reflected in these geographical details Luke's deliberate effort to inscribe the separate periods of salvation-history in the distinguished locales of John and Jesus. While W.C. ROBINSON, *Der Weg des Herrn: Studien zur Geschichte und Eschatologie im Lukas-Evangelium. Ein Gespräch mit Hans Conzelmann* (TF, 36), Hamburg-Bergstedt, H. Reich, 1964, pp. 10-16, has effectively demonstrated that the generic distinction of locales for John and Jesus was already part of the pre-Lucan tradition, this criticism does not invalidate Conzelmann's claim that the term Judaea figures prominently in Luke's own geographical delineation of Jesus' ministry. Further evidence for this may be found in Luke's redaction of Mark's initial summary of Jesus' preaching tour εἰς ὅλην τὴν Γαλιλαίαν (Mark 1,39), in which Luke greatly broadens the scope of the summary by reporting: καὶ ἦν κηρύσσων εἰς τὰς συναγωγὰς τῆς Ἰουδαίας (Luke 4,44). See also the similar geographical summary in Luke 23,5 and in Acts 10,37.

important role in the life and governance of the emerging church (see Acts 9,31; 11,1.29; 15,1; 26,20). As a first step toward exploring the theological significance of this toponym within Luke-Acts, I will examine what Luke intended to signify by the term "Judaea"[4].

The commentary tradition has long identified a puzzling ambiguity in Luke's use of Judaea[5]. In some instances, Luke uses the term to designate a specific district of Palestine clearly distinguished from Galilee and Samaria. In other instances, however, Luke seems to use Judaea to designate a more expansive region. This glaring inconsistency in the literary practice of an author whose terminology often reflects a concern for accuracy and precision poses a problem more easily identified than

---

4. Lexicographers identify the adjective, Ἰουδαῖος, -α, -ov, as a Hellenistic coinage derived from the Aramaic gentilic, יהודי (see LSJ, 9th ed., p. 832, s. v.; BAG, pp. 379-80, s. v.; O. BETZ, Ἰουδαία, in *EDNT*, 1990, vol. 2, p. 191). The first attested use of ἡ Ἰουδαία (sc. γῆ or χώρα) as a toponym for the Jewish homeland is preserved in Josephus' citation from the now lost work of Clearchus, a student of Aristotle, who records Aristotle's recollection of an exchange he once had with a learned Jew: "This man was a Jew (Ἰουδαῖος) of Coele-Syria. These people are descended from the Indian philosophers. These philosophers are in India called Calani, in Syria by the territorial name of Jews; for the district they inhabit is known as Judaea (προσαγορεύεται γὰρ ὃν κατοικοῦσι τόπον Ἰουδαία)" (*C. Apion* 1.179). Similar uses of the term in fragmentary quotations from the works of the third century B.C. historians, Hecataeus of Abdera (*apud* Diodorus Siculus, *Bibl.* 40.3.1-3) and Manetho (*apud* Josephus, *C. Apion* 1.90) demonstrate that ἡ Ἰουδαία was first adopted by Hellenistic authors as the conventional toponym for the ancestral homeland of the Jews. Whereas Greek-speaking Jewish authors tended to avoid the personal use of the adjective (οἱ Ἰουδαῖοι) for self-designation, especially in recorded prayers and liturgical formulae (see K.G. KUHN, Ἰσραήλ, Ἰουδαῖος, Ἑβραῖος *in Jewish Literature after the OT*, in *TDNT*, vol. 3, pp. 359-69), the absolute use of the fem. sing. was generally adopted by Jewish authors and translators of the Hellenistic period as one of the conventional terms used for: (1) the territory assigned to the tribe of Judah (see, e.g., LXX 1 Kgdms 17,1); (2) the southern division of the Davidic kingdom (see, e.g., LXX 2 Chron 11,5; Isa 1,1; Jer 7,2); (3) the post-exilic province within the Persian empire established by Cyrus (see, e.g., Ezra 1,2.3); and (4) the territory liberated from the Seleucids by the Hasmoneans (see 1 Macc 4,35; 5,8; *et passim*).

5. A distinction is commonly made between Luke's use of Judaea in a "narrow" or "specific" sense for the southern district of Palestine immediately adjacent to Jerusalem (e.g., Luke 1,39.65; 2,4; 3,1; 5,17; 21,21; Acts 1,8; 8,1; 9,31) and his use of the same term in a "broad" or "generic" sense for "the entire land of the Jews" (e.g., Luke 1,5; 4,44; 6,17; 7,17; 23,5; Acts 10,37). See A. PLUMMER, *Luke*, 1922, p. 521; J.M. CREED, *Luke*, 1930, p. 73; FITZMYER, *Luke*, pp. 322, 558, 1476; G. SCHNEIDER, *Apostelgeschichte*, 1980, 1982, pp. 203, 254 n. 92, 479; D.L. BOCK, *Luke*, 1994, 1996, pp. 75, 441, 1813 n. 10; J. B. GREEN, *Luke*, 1997, pp. 62 n. 1, 200, 802. Following the earlier suggestion of P. BENOIT (*L'enfance de Jean-Baptiste selon Luc 1*, in *NTS* 3 [1956-57] 169-194, p. 174), H. SCHÜRMANN, *Das Lukasevangelium*, 1969, p. 29 n. 12, contrasts the usage "im engerem Sinn" with what he calls Luke's "Hellenistic" application of the toponym ("unter Hellenisten üblich"). F. BOVON, *Lukas*, 1989, pp. 51 n. 26, 226, claims that Luke always uses Judaea "im hellenistischen Sprachgebrauch" for "das ganzen Judenland". However, Bovon only resolves the ambiguity by ignoring those passages where a more restricted territory is clearly implied.

resolved. Most commentators would have us assume that Luke's allegedly imperfect knowledge of Palestinian geography offers a sufficient explanation for this semantic ambiguity in the text[6].

I. JUDAEA IN JOSEPHUS

Surprisingly, discussions of Luke's problematic usage of the term Judaea have made little use of the writings of Flavius Josephus, whose many references to Judaea reflect a similar ambiguity that can scarcely be attributed to gaps in the author's second-hand knowledge of the area[7]. While prescinding from the question of Luke's possible familiarity with the published works of his fellow historian, I judge it reasonable to find in Josephus' descriptive testimony a representative voice within the literary culture he shared with Luke and Luke's readers[8].

6. Partly in response to the critical evaluation of Acts by members of the *Tübinger Schule* a number of scholars in the late 19th and early 20th century, including A. VON HARNACK (*Acts*, 1909, esp. pp. 49-116) and W.M. RAMSAY (*The Bearing of Recent Discovery on the Trustworthiness of the New Testament*, London, Hodder & Stoughton, ²1915, esp. pp. 39-52), sought to defend the historicity of Acts by adducing external evidence to vindicate the accuracy of Luke's many geographical and topographical references included in his descriptions of Paul's journeys through the eastern Mediterranean. For a modern version of this kind of apologetic scholarship see C. HEMER, *The Book of Acts in the Setting of Hellenistic History*, ed. C. GEMPF, Winona Lake, IN, Eisenbrauns, 1990, esp. pp. 241-243. In contrast, studies of Luke's often puzzling disposition of events and journeys in the Gospel and the early chapters of Acts have tended to call into question Luke's knowledge of Palestinian geography. Whereas many regard as excessively harsh C.C. McCown's charge of "geographical ineptitude" (see C.C. McCOWN, *Gospel Geography: Fiction, Fact, and Truth*, in *JBL* 60 [1941] 1-25, p. 15), most modern commentators have been willing to endorse Conzelmann's claim (*Theology*, pp. 68-73) that Luke had a definite but inaccurate conception of Palestine, which comports with what we find implied in the literary descriptions of other ancient geographers "from abroad". See, for example, E. HAENCHEN, *Acts*, 1971, p. 243 n. 4; J. ROLOFF, *Apostelgeschichte*, 1981, p. 157; SCHNEIDER, *Apostelgeschichte*, vol. 1, p. 479 n. 67; vol. 2, p. 40; M. HENGEL, *Luke the Historian and the Geography of Palestine in the Acts of the Apostles* in his *Between Jesus and Paul. Studies in the Earliest History of Christianity*, London, SCM Press, 1983, pp. 97-128, esp. pp. 97, 99; FITZMYER, *Luke*, pp. 1152-1153; PESCH, *Apostelgeschichte*, vol. 1, p. 314; and C.K. BARRETT, *Acts*, 1994, p. 403. For a more positive estimation of Luke's knowledge of Palestinian geography see I.H. MARSHALL, *Luke*, 1978; and BOVON, *Lukas*, p. 365.

7. While M. BACHMANN, *Der Gebrauch von IOYΔAIA*, in his *Jerusalem und der Temple* (n. 1), pp. 67-131, does allude to Josephus' use of "Judaea" in both a narrow and a general sense, he chooses to leave as an open question whether this evidence can offer an analogue to the ambiguous usage of the toponym in Luke-Acts (see p. 70). For now dated but still useful discussions of Josephus' geographical references see A. SCHLATTER, *Zur Topographie und Geschichte Palästinas*, Stuttgart, Vereinsbuchhandlung, 1893, pp. 348-356; and E. NESTLE, *Judaea bei Josephus*, in *ZDPV* 34 (1911) 65-118. For a more recent historical treatment of individual details see C. MÖLLER and G. SCHMITT, *Siedlungen Palästinas nach Flavius Josephus* (TAVO. B,14), Wiesbaden, Reichert, 1976.

8. A concise review of the scholarship on the long-debated relationship between Luke

a. The apparent ambiguity in Josephus' use of Judaea results from the fact that he employs this term to express not only a topographical concept but also a political and a theological concept. When used in a topographical sense, Judaea denotes one of the four territories of Palestine[9]. This strictly topographical notion of Judaea, as distinct from Galilee, Samaria, and Peraea, is sustained in other sections of the narrative where travel notices involve a traversal of the district's recognized borders[10].

b. Josephus also uses Judaea to express a political concept. In his treatment of Palestine's complex political history under Roman rule, Judaea is often employed to designate an administrative jurisdiction placed under the imperium either of local dynastic rulers or of provincial prefects and procurators sent from Rome. When used as a jurisdictional term, Judaea denotes not a fixed geographical region but a shifting political reality, whose various topographical configurations Josephus is careful to identify and define. Josephus here adopts a Roman custom of nomenclature, whereby the name assigned to a large, composite jurisdiction is taken from the most prominent of the several territorial subdivisions included within it[11]. This practice of naming provincial jurisdictions *a parte potiori* helps to explain why Josephus can use the single term Judaea to designate not only the entire kingdom entrusted first to Herod the Great and then later to his grandson Herod Agrippa[12], but also

and Josephus may be found in G. STERLING, *Historiography and Self-Definition: Josephus, Luke-Acts and Apologetic Historiography* (NTSup, 64), Leiden, Brill, 1992, pp. 365-369. Sterling concludes that, while it is impossible to establish a literary dependence of Luke-Acts on the writings of Josephus, it is reasonable to affirm that both authors not only had access to similar historical traditions but also shared the same historiographical techniques and perspective.

9. In a brief excursus, which gives a fairly detailed topographical description of "the country of the Jews", Josephus identifies the borders and the distinctive topographical features of Galilee, Peraea, Samaria, and Judaea. Concerning Judaea Josephus writes: "On the frontier separating them (sc., Samaria and Judaea) lies the village called Anuath Borcaeus, the northern limit of Judaea; its southern boundary, if one measures the country lengthwise, is marked by a village on the Arabian frontier, which the local Jews call Iardan. In breadth it stretches from the river Jordan to Joppa. The city of Jerusalem lies at its very center, for which reason the town has sometimes, not inaptly, been called the navel (ὀμφαλόν) of the country" (*B.J.* 3.51-52).

10. See Josephus, *Ant.* 14.49; *B.J.* 1.134.

11. For a brief description of Augustus' method of dividing dependencies into provincial jurisdictions see Strabo, *Geogr.* 17.3.25. Strabo never tires of complaining that his work as an historian and geographer is greatly impeded by the "confusion (ἡ σύγχυσις)" caused by the Romans' superimposition of artificial but politically expedient boundaries (see, e.g., *Geogr.* 13.4.12; cf. 12.5.1).

12. For instances of Josephus' use of Ἰουδαία to designate the kingdom of Herod the Great see *Ant.* 15.2; 16.12-13,297. By this point in the narrative of *Ant.* Josephus has made clear that Herod's domain includes not only Judaea proper, Peraea, Samaria, and Galilee, which Herod had received by decree of the Roman Senate in 40 B.C. (see *Ant.*

to the variously configured provincial jurisdictions assigned to a series of Roman governors from A.D. 6 to A.D. 41 and then again from A.D. 44 to A.D. 70[13].

c. As distinct from these strictly topographical and political applications of the term, a theological concept also finds expression in those instances where Josephus uses Judaea as an alternative designation for what he elsewhere calls "the land of the Jews". Obviously anachronistic uses of the term in Josephus' expanded retelling of biblical history from the time when the Israelites first occupied "the land now called Judaea" prepare the reader to recognize the theological connotations attached to subsequent references to Judaea in his later descriptions of the various nationalist movements that emerged during the Seleucid, Hasmonean, and Roman periods[14]. In these contexts, Judaea often signifies what

14.381-389; cf. *B.J.* 1.282-285), but also the coastal cities of Gaza, Authedon, Joppa, and Strato's Tower (later Caesarea), much of the Decapolis, and the northern districts of Trachonitis, Batanaea, and Auranitis, which territories Augustus annexed to Herod's kingdom at various points from 30 to 23 B.C. (see *Ant.* 17.217; 15.342-343; cf. *B.J.* 1.396-398). Josephus' account of the political fortunes of Herod's grandson, Herod Agrippa (I), similarly includes several geographical descriptions of the client kingdom he received from Claudius in A.D. 41 (see *Ant.* 19.274-275; *B.J.* 2.214-217). In his account of the king's final days Josephus reports that Herod Agrippa died τρίτον δὲ ἔτος αὐτῷ βασιλεύοντι τῆς ὅλης Ἰουδαίας (*Ant.* 19.343).

13. According to Josephus, Augustus deposed Archelaeus in A.D. 6 and placed his former ethnarchy, consisting of Judaea proper (including Idumaea), Samaria, and the territory surrounding Joppa and Caesarea Maritima, under the *imperium* of legates from the neighboring province of Syria (see *Ant.* 17.354-355; 18.1-2; *B.J.* 2.117; cf. Strabo, *Geogr.* 16.2.46; Philo, *Leg.* 299). Josephus' use of Ἰουδαία in reference to the prefecture governed first by Coponius (see *Ant.* 18.29) and later by Pontius Pilate (*Ant.* 18.55; *B.J.* 2.169) has been confirmed by a fragmentary Latin inscription found at Caesarea Maritima. For further discussion of this inscription and bibliography see H. VOLKMANN, *Die Pilatus-inschrift von Caesarea Maritima*, in *Gymnasium* 75 (1968) 12-35. After the brief reign of Herod Agrippa, Claudius re-established in A.D. 44 a larger provincial jurisdiction, consisting of Galilee, Peraea, Judaea proper, and Samaria (see *Ant.* 19.363; *B.J.* 2.220; Tacitus, *Hist.* 5). Josephus also attaches the name Ἰουδαία to this new administrative unit governed, *inter alia*, by Cuspus Fadus (see *Ant.* 15.406; 20.97) and Felix (*Ant.* 20.137; 20.142; 20.162; *Vit.* 1.13). For further discussion of the Roman administration of Palestine from A.D. 6 to A.D. 66, see M. SMALLWOOD, *The Jews under Roman Rule* (SJ, 20), Leiden, Brill, 1976, pp. 144-180, 256-292; S. APPLEBAUM, *Judaea as a Roman Province: The Countryside as a Political and Economic Factor*, in ANRW II.8 (1977), pp. 355-396.

14. Josephus' peculiar use of Ἰουδαία to designate the *united* kingdom of David (see *Ant.* 7.101; 8.188) helps to explain his later description of the Assyrian deportation of the ten tribes of the northern kingdom (*Ant.* 9.280; cf. 2 Kings 17,23). In turn, the same toponym is used to designate the remaining Jewish kingdom that was first invaded by the Babylonians (see *Ant.* 10.40,87,110) and then left "desolate" by the second deportation of the remaining two tribes into Babylon (see *Ant.* 10.184). In the post-exilic period the Jewish ἔθνος, according to Josephus, embraced both those who remained in dispersed colonies and those who re-occupied "the home country of Judaea" (see *Ant.* 11.4,60,124; *C. Apion* 1.30-33). For uses of Ἰουδαία in reference to the Jewish domain liberated from the Seleucids by the Hasmoneans see *Ant.* 12.28,245,293,349,416; 13.121.

Josephus and his fellow Jews believe to be the homeland God has appor-
tioned to his chosen people as a lasting inheritance[15].

When Josephus uses Judaea in a theological sense for the ancestral
land now inhabited by the Jewish people, he has in view a territory that
includes the topographical regions of Judaea, Peraea, and Galilee, but
excludes the region of Samaria. Three pieces of evidence may be offered
in support of this claim. First, Josephus' account of the early military
victories in the Maccabean revolt (165-161 B.C.) makes a clear distinction between the battles fought against neighboring foreign nations, such
as the Idumaeans, Nabataeans, and Samaritans, and other engagements,
whose expressed purpose was to liberate Jews resident in Judaea,
Galilee, and Peraea[16]. Second, in his treatment of Pompey's re-organiza-
tion of Palestine in 63 B.C., Josephus makes a clear distinction between
the Samaritans and other non-Jewish inhabitants of the region, whose
cities Pompey liberated from Hasmonean control, and those properly
recognized as Jews, whose nation Pompey now confined "within its
own legitimate borders" by setting up a series of administrative districts
in Judaea proper, Galilee, and Peraea[17]. The third piece of evidence is
found in Josephus' geographical delineation of an uprising of Jewish
nationalists in 4 B.C. Josephus remarks that in reaction to the suppressed
rebellion in Jerusalem "countless new tumults filled Judaea"[18]. What
Judaea signifies in this context is then clarified as Josephus proceeds to
recount a series of representative incidents of violent insurrection not
only in the district around Jerusalem but also in Peraea and Galilee[19].

15. In his Hellenized version of the "Table of Nations" of Gen 10, Josephus presents
Canaan, the fourth son of Ham, as the rightful heir of the land that bore his name before
it was later called "Judaea" (see *Ant.* 1.134). The same toponymic designation is later
used by Josephus to identify the land occupied by Abraham in fulfillment of God's
promise (*Ant.* 1.160).

16. According to Josephus, after first waging war against "the surrounding nations",
Judas Maccabeus sent his brother Simon "to help the Jews in Galilee", while he and his
brother Jonathan crossed the Jordan into Peraea in order to rescue "his fellow countrymen
(τοὺς ὁμοεθνεῖς)", who were being shut up in the fortresses and cities of Galaaditis (see
Ant. 12.327-349).

17. See *Ant.* 14.74-76; *B.J.* 1.155-156. Three of the districts were centered in the
Judaean cities of Jerusalem, Jericho, and Adora; one in Amathus, a city of Peraea; and
the last in the Galilean city of Sepphoris (see *Ant.* 14.91; *B.J.* 1.170). While nothing is
known for certain about these administrative districts, most historians assume that collecting taxes and adjudicating civil suits were among their primary responsibilities. See
further SMALLWOOD, *Jews under Roman Rule* (n. 13), pp. 21-30.

18. See *Ant.* 17.269; *B.J.* 2.55.

19. See the accounts of the insurrections organized by various leaders: (1) Achiab, a
cousin of King Herod, in Idumaea, which Josephus elsewhere considers a toparchy within
Judaea (*Ant.* 17.270; *B.J.* 2.55); (2) Judas, son of Ezekias, in Galilee (*Ant.* 17.271-272;
B.J. 2.56); (3) Simon, the former slave of King Herod, in Peraea (*Ant.* 17.273-277; *B.J.*

Nothing is said of any disturbance in the region of Samaria, whose incorporation within the land of the Jews Josephus is eager to deny[20]. This same geographical delineation is repeated throughout Josephus' account of the quest for Jewish independence in the first century, wherein Judaea is one of the terms used to designate the combined districts of Judaea proper, Peraea, and Galilee, that together make up the ancestral land of the Jews[21].

II. JUDAEA IN LUKE-ACTS

If we are correct in assuming that Josephus' equivocal uses of Judaea were governed by conventions that obtained in the literary culture of the late first century, then it becomes possible to find in Luke's comparable references to the same region not merely an unhappy inconsistency, resulting from an imperfect knowledge of the local geography, but rather a deliberate attempt to accommodate the topographical, political, and theological concepts commonly expressed by the single term, Judaea. A fresh examination of the evidence in Luke-Acts will support the conclusion that, while Luke's topographical and political uses of this toponym are basically consistent with what we find in Josephus, the theological concept conveyed by the term Judaea in Luke-Acts has been decidedly altered in light of the Christ event.

a. Luke marks a transition between two sections of the Acts narrative by stating in Acts 9,31a: "So the church throughout Judaea and Galilee and Samaria had peace and was built up." This sequence of toponyms demonstrates that Luke is capable of using Judaea to signify a topographical district, fully distinguishable from neighboring regions[22]. Fur-

---

2.57-59); and (4) Anthronges, an obscure but charismatic shepherd in the rural districts of Judaea proper (*Ant.* 17.278-284; *B.J.* 2.60-64). What Josephus records in each of these separate accounts is then subsumed within his closing summary statement: ληστηρίων δὲ ἡ Ἰουδαία ἔμπλεως ἦν (*Ant.* 17.285; cf. *B.J.* 2.65).

20. Josephus justifies his anti-Samaritan bias on the grounds that the current residents of Samaria were descendants of the ancient Cuthaeans, a non-Jewish people from Mesopotamia whom the Assyrians had resettled in Samaria after deporting the native Israelites (see *Ant.* 9.277-280; 10.183-184). He portrays the Samaritans as a foreign people who fiercely resisted both the re-establishment of the Jewish nation after the exile (see, e.g., *Ant.* 11.88) and during the Maccabean revolt (see, e.g., *Ant.* 12.257-264). It is scarcely surprising, then, that Josephus fails to mention any disturbance in Samaria during the general uprising of 4 B.C.

21. For examples of open hostility between He Samaritans and the Jews in the decades leading up to the revolt in A.D. 66, see *Ant.* 18.29-30; 20.118-124; *B.J.* 2.232-240.

22. Most commentators identify Acts 9,31 as an editorial summary inserted by Luke. See, e.g., HAENCHEN, *Acts*, p. 333; SCHNEIDER, *Apostelgeschichte*, vol. 2, p. 40; BARRETT, *Acts*, p. 472. For earlier summaries of the church's spirit-directed growth see Acts 2,41.47; 5,12-16; 6,1.7; 11,21-24; 12,24; 14,1.

682 D. BECHARD

ther references in the text allow us to reconstruct the basic outline of this concept. Luke is aware that at the center of Judaea lies the city of Jerusalem, which was surrounded by a number of communities also known to Luke, including the cities of Bethlehem, Jericho, Bethphage, Bethany, Arimathea, and Emmaus[23]. By a consistent use of ἀναβαίνειν in his descriptions of travel to Jerusalem from the coastal city of Caesarea, from Galilee, and from the more proximate city of Jericho, Luke also shows a basic familiarity with Judaea's distinctive topography[24]. On the other hand, in view of Luke's uncertain delineation of Jesus' final journey from Galilee to Jerusalem, especially the problematic travel notice at Luke 17,11, it must be admitted that Luke gives no evidence of having more than a vague concept of Judaea's geographical disposition in relation to Samaria and Galilee[25]. In this respect, Luke's topographi-

23. In his description of those who brought their sick to be healed by the apostles, Luke reports that there gathered in Jerusalem τὸ πλῆθος τῶν πέριξ πόλεων (Acts 5,16). Luke here makes use of a stock expression, attested in later Koine Greek, for a complex of outlying towns and villages that were dependent on a neighboring city. Josephus employs the same formula when he describes the clandestine arrival in Jerusalem of lawless rebels, who were earlier reeking havoc ἐν ταῖς πέριξ κώμαις τε καὶ πόλεσι (B.J. 4.241; cf. 2.505; 3.134). To be included within this circuit of Judaean towns and villages are places Luke not only names but also locates in reference to Jerusalem. While in Jericho Jesus is said to be "near to Jerusalem" (Luke 9,11; cf. 19,28). From Mark (Mark 11,1) Luke knows that, when Jesus and his disciples reach Bethphage and Bethany on the Mount of Olives, they have come very near to Jerusalem. But Luke also knows enough of the local topography to emphasize that upon descending along the western slope one gains a commanding view of the city and the Temple (see Luke 19,37.41). According to FITZMYER, Luke, p. 1526, Luke's singular description of Arimathea as πόλεως τῶν Ἰουδαίων (Luke 23,51) identifies the town as Judaean. The village of Emmaus is said to be "sixty stadia from Jerusalem" (24,13).

24. See his descriptions of journeys to Jerusalem from Galilee (Luke 2,4), Jericho (Luke 19,28), Syrian Antioch (Acts 15,2), and Caesarea Maritima (Acts 11,2; 18,22; 21,12.15; 24,11; 25,19).

25. For a complete list of what an over-demanding geographer would consider Luke's omissions, inexactitudes, and material errors see C.C. McCOWN, The Geography of Luke's Central Section, in JBL 57 (1938) 51-66, pp. 54-56. The crucial evidence for Luke's (mis)understanding of the topographical disposition of the regions of Palestine he distinguishes may be found in the editorial travel notice of Luke 17,11. By construing the peculiar but well-attested phrase διὰ μέσον as a Hellenistic variant for the more conventional idiom διὰ μέσου, most commentators find in this travel note the reference to a journey along the border between Samaria and Galilee. But this creates a problem. It is by no means clear what area "between Samaria and Galilee" Luke wishes to signify. Moreover, a journey along the east-west border of these two regions scarcely befits the itinerary of someone traveling south from Galilee to Jerusalem. CONZELMANN, Theology, pp. 68-73, offers a solution to this problem by suggesting that the itinerary implied by Luke's several travel notices in the "central section" (9,51-53; 10,38; 13,22.33; 14,25; 17,11; 18,35; 19,1.11.28.41) makes sense if we assume that Luke's definite but mistaken conception of Palestine viewed "Galilee as inland, but adjoining Judaea, and Samaria as being to the north of Judaea" (p. 70). MARSHALL, Luke, p. 650, on the other hand, speculates that Luke 17,11 refers to the border between Samaria and Peraea, the latter being

cal concept of Judaea departs from what we find expressed in Josephus' first-hand account, but comports well with the more general and less well-informed descriptions of the region in the works of Strabo and Pliny the Elder[26].

b. If his topographical conception of Judaea is noticeably imprecise, Luke's knowledge of the political geography compares more favorably with what we find in Josephus. Like Josephus, Luke follows the Roman custom of naming an assigned jurisdiction *a parte potiori*. Therefore, Luke's reference to "Herod, king of Judaea" in Luke 1,5, while chrono-logically problematic, employs a fully intelligible designation of the client king's expansive domain, whose constituent parts Luke later delineates in Luke 3,1[27]. Likewise, by referring to Pontius Pilate as "governor of Judaea" in Luke 3,1, Luke adopts the conventional name for the jurisdiction assigned to those prefects who from A.D. 6 to A.D. 41 governed the topographical districts of Judaea proper and Samaria, together with several cities along the coast[28]. This political conception of

reckoned as part of Galilee. This is certainly possible, but it would then be difficult to account for Luke's deliberate omission of Mark 10,1, which portrays Jesus crossing the Jordan (viz, into Peraea).

26. CONZELMANN, *Theology*, p. 69, found supporting evidence for his hypothetical reconstruction of Luke's concept of Palestine in the literary descriptions of the region by Strabo and Pliny. While Strabo's detailed treatment of the interior region of Judaea in *Geogr.* 16.2.34-46 distinguishes οἱ Ἰουδαῖοι from the non-Jewish residents of Idumaea, Galilee, Jericho (!), Philadelphia, and Samaria (see *Geogr.* 16.2.34), he makes no attempt to describe the topographical disposition of the cities and regions thus distinguished. His description of Jerusalem as a city "near the sea" and thus visible from the seaport of Joppa (*Geogr.* 16.2.28.34) betrays the limits of his understanding "from abroad". A similar concept of Palestine finds expression in the later work of Pliny the Elder who identifies Judaea as a wide interior district lying east of the coastal regions of Idumaea and Samaria (*N.H.* 5.15 § 70). The northern subdivision of Judaea, according to Pliny, is called Galilee.

27. The synchronic dating of the beginning of John's ministry (ca. A.D. 28) in Luke 3,1 shows some familiarity with the historical division of Herod the Great's kingdom in 4 B.C. In addition to the ethnarchy of Judaea (and Samaria), over which Archelaeus was allowed to rule until his deposition and exile in A.D. 6, Luke identifies three further divisions. While Trachonitis is included among the territories listed in both of Josephus' variant descriptions of Philip's tetrarchy (see *Ant.* 17.189,319), there is no independent evidence that the northern principality of Ituraea was ever ruled by Herod the Great or his sons. See SMALLWOOD, *Jews under Roman Rule* (n. 13), p. 110. However, as CREED, *Luke*, p. 49 once pointed out, the fact that Panias, a city refounded by Philip as Caesarea Philippi, had once belonged to the Ituraean kingdom partly justifies Luke's description.

28. For evidence in support of the use of "Judaea" as the conventional designation of the jurisdiction assigned to Pilate and his fellow prefects, see above, n. 13. While Luke correctly employs ἐπαρχεία as the *terminus technicus* for the jurisdiction assigned to the procurator Festus (Acts 25,1), he uses ἡγεμών (and its derivatives), the general term for any kind of ruler or governor, in reference not only to Pilate the prefect of Judaea (Luke 3,1; 20,20) but also to the emperor Tiberius (3,1), Quirinius the praetorial governor of Syria (2,2), Felix the procurator of Judaea (see Acts 23,24.26.33; 24,1.10), and his suc-

Judaea finds further expression in Luke's report of Pilate's unsuccessful attempt to recuse himself from the case against Jesus on the grounds that the defendant's status as a Galilean placed him within Herod's jurisdiction[29]. Further references to the political administration of the region may be found in Luke's account of Paul's final arrest in the Temple precincts and his arraignment by the local Roman authorities first in Jerusalem and then in Caesarea, which city Luke clearly identifies as the official residence of Roman governors such as Felix and Festus and the administrative center of the territory placed under their authority[30].

c. These topographical and political applications of Judaea allow us to discern more clearly the third and final use of the term in Luke-Acts. Again following a custom reflected in the writings of Josephus, Luke also uses Judaea to express what may be interpreted as a theological concept. It is generally agreed by commentators that some "general" sense of the term must be assumed in those instances where Luke uses Judaea to delineate the full scope of Jesus' public ministry. For example, in Luke's version of the trial scene, Jesus' accusers seek to arouse Pilate's suspicions by claiming: "He stirs up the people, teaching throughout Judaea, from Galilee even to this place" (23,5)[31]. A similar

cessor in that office, Festus (26,30). Similarly, Josephus' correct use of ἔπαρχος (*Ant.* 18.33) and of ἐπίτροπος (*Ant.* 20.14) does not prevent him from using the non-technical term ἡγεμών in reference to subordinate governors like Pilate and to the Roman Emperor himself (*Ant.* 18.55,33).

29. It is unlikely that ἀναπέμπειν is used in Luke 23,7 in the technical sense of "remanding a prisoner to a higher authority". Herod was not a higher authority, and the same verb is used for Herod's returning Jesus to Pilate in v. 11. While A.N. SHERWIN-WHITE, *Roman Society and Roman Law in the New Testament* (The Sarum Lectures 1960-61), Oxford, Clarendon, 1963, pp. 28-31, presents convincing arguments against finding reflected in this episode the later custom of trying a person in his own province rather than in the province where the crime was committed, CONZELMANN, *Theology*, p. 70, is surely right to discern in this Lucan scene further evidence for the author's concept of the political divisions within Palestine.

30. Luke's narrative account of the legal proceedings against Paul in Caesarea (Acts 23,31–26,32) includes a number of details about the political institutions then established in the capital. When Paul arrives under guard in Caesarea to be tried by the governor, Felix orders him to be guarded ἐν τῷ πραιτωρίῳ τοῦ Ἡρῴδου (23,35). The term πραιτώριον represents a Greek loanword from Latin and refers here to the palace built by Herod the Great in Caesarea (*Ant.* 15.331), which was later used by the Romans first as the headquarters of the military commander and then as the official residence of the governor. For further details see G. SCHNEIDER, πραιτώριον, in *EDNT*, vol. 3, pp. 144-145.

31. This geographical summary of Jesus' public ministry concludes Luke's account of Pilate's first interrogation of Jesus. While much of this scene is derived from Mark 15,1b-5 and, perhaps, a second source (see W. GRUNDMANN, *Lukas*, 1966, p. 421; MARSHALL, *Luke*, p. 852), the summary statement in Luke 23,5 is a clear piece of Lucan composition, whose form and the content well befit the geographical perspective of Luke's theology (CONZELMANN, *Theology*, p. 43 n. 3; FITZMYER, *Luke*, pp. 168, 1473). For further instances of ἄρχομαι ἀπό see Luke 24,27.47; Acts 1,22; 8,35. A similar version of the

notion of Judaea in this wider sense also finds expression in the earlier narrative summaries of the region affected by the public ministry of Jesus[32].

The identity of the territorial districts included in Luke's theological concept of "the land of the Jews" has yet to be clarified. Of special note is the sharp disagreement among commentators over the possible implications of Luke's decision to include three gospel traditions that involve Samaritans[33]. Some find here sure evidence that Luke's depiction of Jesus' journey from Galilee to Jerusalem includes a preaching tour in the region of Samaria[34]. Others insist that the Lucan Jesus avoids Samaria as

summary is repeated in Peter's address to the household of Cornelius in Acts 10,37. The concept expressed by Judaea in the context of Luke 23,5 (and Acts 10,37) is not easily determined. The phraseology of the summary suggests that "Galilee" and "this place" (the Temple or Jerusalem itself) are to be taken as subdivisions of what is here called "Judaea". This would exclude the narrow topographical sense of Judaea. Nor can Judaea here express the broader political concept, which is implied in Luke's earlier reference to Pilate in Luke 3,1. As the immediately following scene makes clear, Galilee lies beyond Pilate's assigned jurisdiction over Judaea. The manner in which Luke uses other geographical markers to specify the scope of Jesus' public ministry strongly suggests that by Judaea Luke wishes in this context to signify the theological concept of "the land of the Jews".

32. The intended meaning of Judaea in Luke 23,5 bears a clear relation to a similar use of the toponym in Luke's first narrative summary of Jesus' ministry in Luke 4,44. The use of Judaea in this context was felt to be a problem from early on. Those manuscripts that replace τῆς Ἰουδαίας with τῆς Γαλιλαίας represent early attempts to harmonize the text with its parallel in Mark 1,39 and with the perceived thrust of the Lucan story.

Modern commentators who assume that Judaea here signifies the topographical district have concluded that Luke 4,44 marks a transition from Jesus' abbreviated ministry in Galilee (Luke 4,14-43) to a more widely conceived mission to the entire Jewish people, beginning at Luke 5,1. See SCHÜRMANN, *Lukas*, p. 260; M. VÖLKEL, *Der Anfang Jesu in Galiläa: Bemerkungen zum Gebrauch und zur Funktion Galiläas in den lukanischen Schriften*, in *ZNW* 64 (1973) 222-232; M. THEOBALD, *Die Anfänge der Kirche: Zur Struktur von Lk. 5.1–6.19*, in *NTS* 30 (1984) 91-108, pp. 91-92. But this interpretation is disconfirmed by the fact that geographical references locate subsequent episodes in or near Galilee: Capernaum (7,1); Nain (7,11); Herod's capital city of Tiberias (implied in 8,1-3; 9,7-9); the region of the Gerasenes "opposite Galilee" (8,26); and Bethsaida (9,10). On the other hand, whereas the Lucan Jesus does not appear to leave Galilee until he begins his final journey to Jerusalem at Luke 9,51, the term Judaea figures prominently in Luke's editorial summaries of the diffusion of Jesus' reputation well beyond the limits of Galilee. In his description of those who witnessed Jesus' healing of the paralytic, Luke replaces Mark's simple πολλοί (Mark 2,1) with a reference to Pharisees and teachers of the law who had gathered ἐκ πάσης κώμης τῆς Γαλιλαίας καὶ Ἰουδαίας καὶ Ἰερουσαλήμ (Luke 5,17; see also 6,17; 7,17). These later geographical references strongly suggest that in the earlier summary of 4,44 Luke substitutes "Judaea" for Mark's "Galilee" in order to express his notion of the full scope and course of Jesus' public ministry, not only in Galilee but throughout the land of the Jews. See further W.C. ROBINSON, *The Theological Context for Interpreting Luke's Travel Narrative (9,51ff.)*, in *JBL* 79 (1960) 20-31, p. 28; FITZMYER, *Luke*, p. 558.

33. See Luke 9,51-55; 10,25-37; 17,11-19.

34. This represents the traditional view, which is still advanced in many modern commentaries. Proponents of this view assume that Luke's interest in Jesus' dealings with the

a hostile territory outside the land of the Jews[35]. Still others demur on the grounds that Luke's geographical imprecision, if not ineptitude, invalidates any such intended distinction[36]. Past attempts to resolve this problem have tended to focus almost exclusively on the travel notices in the "central section" of the Gospel. But if it is true that Luke employs the term "Judaea" in a theological sense in order to situate Jesus' ministry within "the ancestral land of the Jews," then any attempt to determine more precisely the intended scope of this theological concept must also consider analogous uses of the term in Luke's second volume.

In the opening scene of Acts the risen Jesus declares to the assembled apostles: "You shall be my witnesses in Jerusalem, and in all Judaea and Samaria and to the end of the earth" (Acts 1,8)[37]. What this geographical delineation of the apostolic mission implies about the status assigned to Samaria depends upon the intended meaning of Judaea in this context[38]. If Luke here uses Judaea to signify a theological concept,

Samaritans derives from his thematic emphasis on the universality of salvation now made available in Jesus. See, e.g., McCOWN, *Geography of Luke's Central Section* (n. 25), p. 59; M.S. ENSLIN, *Luke and the Samaritans*, in *HTR* 36 (1943) 278-297; FITZMYER, *Luke*, pp. 824, 829; BOVON, *Lukas*, vol. 2, p. 24; GREEN, *Luke*, p. 405.

35. For the classic expression of this view see CONZELMANN, *Theology*, pp. 60-66. Conzelmann finds in Luke 9,52-56 not the inauspicious beginning of a mission in "the other towns" of Samaria but a further illustration of a principle established earlier in the narrative. Just as the Lucan Jesus never returns to those who rejected him at Nazareth (Luke 4,1-30) and in the land of the Gerasenes (8,26-39), so, according to Conzelmann, Jesus here withdraws from the hostile Samaritans: "From now on Jesus avoids these places, thus providing an illustration of the rule which he immediately proceeds to give his disciples in Luke 10,10" (p. 66).

36. See, e.g., K.L. SCHMIDT, *Der Rahmen der Geschichte Jesu. Literarkritische Untersuchungen zur ältesten Jesusüberlieferung* (1919), repr. Darmstadt, Wissenschaftliche Buchgesellschaft, 1964, pp. 246-254, 269; ROBINSON, *Theological Context* (n. 32), esp. pp. 27-29.

37. Luke's failure to mention Galilee in this list of areas to be covered by the mission has been variously explained: (1) Luke had inherited no traditions about the Galilean church (HAENCHEN, *Acts*, p. 333); (2) Luke recognized that the emergence of Christianity in Galilee was prior to and independent of a Jerusalem-centered mission (LOHMEYER, *Galiläa*, pp. 51-54); and (3) Luke was happy to join a general conspiracy of silence about a region where Christianity had failed, surprisingly, to prosper (M. HENGEL, *Acts and the History of Earliest Christianity*, Philadelphia, PA, Fortress, 1979, p. 76; BARRETT, *Acts*, p. 473). In contrast, H. CONZELMANN, *Acts of the Apostles*, 1987, p. 75, proposes a geographical solution. In the sequence of the toponyms mentioned in Acts 9,31 (viz. Judaea and Galilee and Samaria) he finds further evidence for Luke's mistaken conception of Galilee as a region within Judaea which may or may not be mentioned separately.

38. The failure to clarify the meaning of Judaea in Acts 1,8 helps to explain why commentators find different narrative programs summarized in this verse. SCHNEIDER, *Apostelgeschichte*, p. 203, perceives a mission in four distinct zones or stages ("Etappen"), of which the middle two (viz. Judaea and Samaria) are linked closely together. Others discern a three-stage program corresponding more closely with clear divisions in the narrative. In this view, the evangelization of Samaria functions as a transition to the world-

then the separate mention of Samaria must imply its exclusion from "the land of the Jews". If, on the other hand, Judaea here denotes the narrow topographical region around Jerusalem, then we may find in this programmatic statement an instructive example of Luke's use of geographical terms to inscribe a new theological understanding of what constitutes "the land of the Jews" in the Christian dispensation.

In order to resolve this exegetical issue we may reasonably look for clues in those key transitional passages of Acts wherein the geographically delineated stages of the Christian mission are at once distinguished and linked together within the one continuous story. Of special significance for the present study are the suggestive geographical references Luke uses to mark the Cornelius episode in Acts 10 as the opening scene in the Church's Spirit-impelled mission to the Gentiles outside the Jewish homeland. First, Luke signals the beginning of the new narrative sequence involving Peter and Cornelius with the summary statement of Acts 9,31: "And so the church throughout all Judaea and Galilee and Samaria had peace and was built up". This idealized recapitulation of a now completed stage of the mission alerts the reader to the transitional importance of the upcoming event[39]. Second, Luke's account of the Cornelius episode includes a noticeably detailed description of Peter's Spirit-directed journey from the predominantly Jewish towns of Lydda and Joppa to the fully Hellenized city of Caesarea[40]. By explicitly locat-

---

wide mission to the Gentiles. See, e.g., BRUCE, Acts, p. 39; HAENCHEN, Acts, pp. 143-144; G. SCHILLE, Apostelgeschichte, 1983, pp. 72-73. For a persuasive argument in favor of discerning in Acts 1,8 a two-fold movement from a mission in the land of the Jews (i.e., Jerusalem and Judaea and Samaria) to a mission in the wider world, see C. BURCHARD, Der dreizehnte Zeuge (FRLANT, 103), Göttingen, Vandenhoeck & Ruprecht, 1970, p. 134 n. 309. Burchard's thesis is happily supported by a reading of Acts 1,8b preserved in A C* D. The omission of the ἐν before πάσῃ sets off more distinctly the mission in Jerusalem and all Judaea and Samaria from the later progress of the gospel beyond this circumscribed territory.

39. The transitional function of the summary statement in Acts 9,31 is clearly signaled by the ἡ μὲν οὖν, a formula commonly adopted by Luke to mark a new stage in the narrative which is nevertheless connected with what has gone before (cf. Acts 1,6.18; 2,41; 5,41; 8,4.25; 11,19; 12,5; 13,4; 14,3; 15,3.30; 16,5; 17,12.17.30; 19,32.38; 23,18. 22.31; 25,4.11; 26,4.9; 28,5). For further discussion of Luke's use of this classical formula see BDF § 451.1 n. 3; K. LAKE and H. CADBURY, English Translation and Commentary, in F.J. FOAKES JACKSON and K. LAKE (eds.), The Beginnings of Christianity, vol. 4, p. 7. With the earlier period of persecution now brought to a conclusion by the account of Paul's conversion in Acts 9,1-30, Luke here portrays the church at peace and flourishing and so ready for the next stage of expansion, which will begin in the next passage when Peter responds to the Spirit's summons to leave Joppa for Caesarea.

40. Luke's geographical description of these two places as "close together" (Acts 9,38) may also have religious and cultural implications. Both Josephus (B.J. 3.55-56; cf. 2.567) and Pliny the Elder (N.H. 5.14 § 70) identify Lydda and Joppa as the centers of two of the ten (or eleven) toparchies of Judaea. For a discussion of Lydda as a predomi-

ing this first conversion of Gentiles in the city of Caesarea, whose recognized status as the capital of the Roman provincial district only underscores its exclusion from "the ancestral land of the Jews", Luke effectively signals that the Christian mission has now reached the threshold of its last stage of expansion "to the end of the earth"[41]. Third, the geographical perspective assumed by Peter in his remarks addressed to Cornelius' household further confirms Luke's deliberate location of the episode in a non-Jewish sphere of Christian evangelism. It is from this new vantage point that Peter identifies the role assigned to the apostles as witnesses to all that Jesus did "both in the country of the Jews and in Jerusalem"[42].

Insofar as these narrative details clarify the assigned location of the Cornelius episode within Luke's geographical delineation of the apostolic mission, we have sufficient reason to conclude that in the portion of the narrative preceding this turning point Luke intends to depict the successful mission first in Jerusalem and then throughout the land of the Jews. This disposition of the narrative is confirmed by a corresponding shift in Luke's use of the term Judaea in Acts. Prior to the Cornelius episode, Luke uses Judaea to denote the narrow topographical region around Jerusalem[43]. This usage makes sense if Luke's purpose is to

nantly Jewish settlement from the Persian period on see M. AVI-YONAH, *The Holy Land, from the Persian to the Arab Conquests (536 B.C. – A.D. 640): A Historical Geography*, Grand Rapids, MI, Baker Book House, 1966, pp. 226-228. For Joppa see SMALLWOOD, *Jews under Roman Rule* (n. 13), pp. 29, 40, 296, 309.

41. See HENGEL, *Luke the Historian* (n. 6), pp. 117-119.

42. Acts 10,39a. See also Acts 12,19 and 21,10, where, in each case, Luke describes journeys to Caesarea ἀπὸ τῆς Ἰουδαίας. Long ago, A. VON HARNACK, *Acts*, p. 71 found it "noteworthy" that Luke's obvious familiarity with the political disposition of Palestine in the first century did not prevent him from locating Caesarea outside Judaea "in the strict sense". HAENCHEN, *Acts*, pp. 386, 601 solves the problem by claiming that in Acts 12,19 and 21,10 Luke substitutes "Judaea" for "Jerusalem". But this represents a gratuitous solution that ignores the divergent concepts conveyed by the toponym in Luke-Acts.

43. Acts 1,8; 8,1; 9,31. The one exception to this pattern may be found in the appearance of Judaea in the list of peoples and places (Acts 2,9-11a) which further identifies those residents of Jerusalem "from every nation under heaven" (2,5) who witnessed the miracle of Pentecost (2,6-8). The inclusion of Judaea in this list of foreign nations has long been a *crux interpretum*. Most commentators have dealt with this problem by simply excising Ἰουδαίαν from the text, by accepting one of the patristic substitutions, or by proposing a new alternative of their own. For a summary of these suggestions see B. METZGER, *A Textual Commentary on the Greek New Testament*, New York, American Bible Society, ²1994, p. 284. On the other hand, LAKE and CADBURY, *Commentary* (n. 39), p. 19, recognize that Ἰουδαίαν in Acts 2,9 is unanimously attested in all the best Greek MSS. According to their suggestion, if we assume that Luke here intends Judaea in the "prophetic sense" as the "country extending from the Euphrates to the Nile", then we may find in this list an attempt to cover in a methodical order all the districts round the east of the Mediterranean. This reading would comport with what most commentators

emphasize the gradual progress of the early apostolic mission, whose initial stage of expansion reaches its predicted objective in what Luke's summary statement in Acts 9,31 describes as a fully consolidated church "throughout all Judaea and Galilee and Samaria"[44]. On the other hand, once the Cornelius episode marks the inception of a new stage in the apostolic mission, Luke begins to use Judaea in a less restricted sense. Just as Peter is made to defend his dealings with the Gentiles in Caesarea before an objecting group described as "the apostles and brethren who were in Judaea"[45], so Paul's involvement in the last stage of the mission also includes a series of depicted interactions with the Christians resident in Judaea. The famine relief, entrusted to Paul and Barnabas by the church in Antioch, is sent "to the brethren who lived in Judaea"[46]. The

view as the programmatic character of the scene. As such, the exceptional use of Judaea in Acts 2,9 would not seriously challenge our thesis.

44. The use of ἡ ἐκκλησία to designate a single ecclesial community spread throughout (κα9' ὅλης) a large geographical region represents an exceptional, if not unique, application of the term. It is difficult to accept the thesis of K.N. GILES, *Luke's Use of the Term ἐκκλησία with Special Reference to Acts 20.28 and 9.31*, in *NTS* 31 (1985) 135-142, esp. pp. 137-140, who claims that in Acts 9,31 Luke wishes to signify the original church of Jerusalem now dispersed into the regions of Judaea, Galilee, and Samaria. First, Giles' analysis relies on an overly sharp distinction between NT uses of ἐκκλησία which refer to the *ecclesia universalis* and those which signify a local congregation. Second, his interpretation ignores the evangelizing activity Luke explicitly attributes to Philip and other Christians after their dispersal from Jerusalem (see Acts 8,4-40). In the re-appearance of the two toponyms (Judaea and Samaria), both mentioned earlier in the opening commission (Acts 1,8) and in the narrated dispersion of Christians outside Jerusalem (Acts 8,1), SCHNEIDER, *Apostelgeschichte*, vol. 2, p. 40 n. 64, finds a sure indication that Luke intends the summary of Acts 9,31 to signal the completion of the first stage of the apostolic mission.

45. Acts 11,1. This verse represents a Lucan formulation, whose content and some formal features are found also in Acts 8,14 and 11,22. Unless one is willing to accept Haenchen's unsupported claim that here in Acts 11,1, as also in Acts 12,19; 15,1; and 21,10, Luke substitutes Judaea for Jerusalem (*Acts*, pp. 386, 442, 601), the intended sense of Judaea in Acts 11,1 must be determined from the context. The political sense of the toponym can be excluded on the grounds of the implied distinction between Caesarea, where the event occurred, and Judaea as the place where the event was reported. Barrett assumes that Judaea is here used in the topographical sense and so asserts that Luke singles out this region "partly because this is where the church's origin, and no doubt its headquarters, were to be found" (*Acts*, p. 536). But this interpretation raises as many problems as it solves. Jerusalem would have been the more obvious choice for the church's *locus originis*. Moreover, if Luke felt the need to include Christians outside of Jerusalem, then it is difficult to explain the prominence of Judaea to the exclusion of Galilee and Samaria. The best clue to the intended meaning of Judaea in Acts 11,1 may be found in the verse itself. The reported reaction suggests that in his dealings at Caesarea with τὰ ἔθνη Peter had crossed a geographical and religious boundary, which had hitherto been forbidden. This boundary, in Luke's view, had formerly limited the emerging church to the Jewish homeland, which he, from this point on in the narrative, chooses to signify with the term Judaea in the theological sense.

46. Acts 11,29. While commentators sharply disagree over the historical reliability of the sources or traditions upon which Acts 11,27-30 is based, there is general agreement

apostolic council is convened to resolve a dispute that arose in Antioch when Paul and Barnabas were confronted by "some men who came down from Judaea"[47]. And finally, in his defense speech before King Agrippa, Paul's quoted summation of his own career includes a reference to his early work as an evangelist not only in Jerusalem but also "throughout the land of Judaea"[48].

In each of these instances Judaea is used in a specific reference to those who were evangelized during the first stage of the apostolic mission, which, according to Luke's explicit testimony in the early chapters of Acts, includes Christians resident in Galilee, Samaria, and Judaea proper. If we are correct in asserting that in the later chapters of Acts Luke reverts back to his earlier custom of using Judaea in a theological sense so as to situate Jesus' ministry within the ancestral land of the Jews, then we may conclude that Luke's geographical delineation of the

that the passage functions as a further illustration of the harmonious solidarity that existed between the "mother church" and the largely Gentile daughter congregation at Syrian Antioch. See, e.g., HAENCHEN, *Acts*, pp. 375, 379; SCHNEIDER, *Apostelgeschichte*, vol. 2, p. 94; BARRETT, *Acts*, p. 559.

47. Acts 15,1. In view of the later identification of these "agitators" as τινὲς ἐξ ἡμῶν (15,24), many commentators follow Haenchen's suggestion that in Acts 15,1 Luke substitutes "Judaea" for "Jerusalem" in order to avoid creating the impression that the group was an official delegation commissioned by the Jerusalem church. See, e.g., HAENCHEN, *Acts*, p. 442; CONZELMANN, *Acts*, p. 115; SCHNEIDER, *Apostelgeschichte*, vol. 2, p. 177 n. 26. This interpretation, however, rests on the questionable assumption that Luke was consciously seeking to minimize, or even conceal, a perceived tension between the churches of Antioch and Jerusalem. In light of our proposed interpretation of Luke's geographical perspective, it seems more likely that the deliberate insertion of Judaea in Acts 15,1 reflects Luke's conviction that the crucial issue concerning the conditions to be imposed on Gentile converts had to be established by the *entire* mother church, which is here again explicitly located within its proper boundaries.

48. Acts 26,19-20. The placement of the accusative, πᾶσάν τε τὴν Ἰουδαίαν, between two datives represents a solecism, which some early scribes attempted to correct by inserting εἰς before πᾶσαν. While previous sections of the narrative justify Paul's reference to his work in Damascus (Acts 9,19-25) and in Jerusalem (Acts 9,26-29), Acts appears to report nothing of his preaching in Judaea. On the basis of these formal and material considerations, many commentators reject πᾶσάν τε τὴν Ἰουδαίαν as a very old but erroneous gloss, perhaps constructed from a loose reading of Rom 15,19. See, e.g., HAENCHEN, *Acts*, p. 687; SCHNEIDER, *Apostelgeschichte*, vol. 2, p. 375 n. 71; PESCH, *Apostelgeschichte*, vol. 2, p. 278 n. 15. This represents a convenient solution, but it finds no support in any ancient manuscript. An alternative interpretation is also possible. Unless we accept as necessarily valid Haenchen's claim that whenever Luke mentions "Judaea" he really means "Jerusalem", then there is nothing to prevent us from finding in Luke's prior descriptions of Paul's activity within the mother church of Judaea (Acts 11,29 and 15,1) a sufficient basis for the inclusion of Judaea in the geographical delineation of Paul's career in Acts 26,19-20. It can be scarcely coincidental that Paul's spoken summary of his own heaven-directed apostolate in Acts 26,20 explicitly aligns his work with the apostolic mission earlier imposed on the eleven by the risen Jesus in Acts 1,8.

apostolic mission envisions a primitive, and so authoritative, Christian community fully established in the very region earlier encompassed by the public ministry of Jesus. While the testimony of Josephus demonstrates that there is nothing exceptional in Luke's use of Judaea to signify the entire Jewish homeland, Luke's bold inclusion of Samaria represents a remarkable innovation in the theological concept expressed by the term. In Luke's use of Judaea to signify what he understands as the ancestral homeland of the Jewish people, whose status as legitimate heirs of God's ancient promises is now determined not by the quality of their participation in the Temple cult but by the manner of their response to Jesus and his appointed witnesses, we can observe a further instance of Luke's effective use of geography in the service of his theological message.

Fordham University
Bronx, NY 10458
USA

Dean P. BECHARD

OBSERVANT JEWS IN THE STORY OF LUKE AND ACTS

PAUL, JESUS AND OTHER JEWS

1. Unity of Luke-Acts

The unity of Luke-Acts still remains a working assumption within New Testament scholarship. The popularizing of the unity of Luke-Acts goes back over 70 years to the scholarship of Henry Cadbury[1]. Today the view requires little documentation in commentaries and in monographs on the Lukan writings or studies that employ a social scientific or narrative criticism approach to reading of Luke and Acts[2]. In spite of the dominant view having critics, one historian of Acts research concludes "the primary gain of recent criticism of Luke-Acts has been the recognition that the Gospel of Luke and the Book of Acts are really two volumes of one book which must be considered together"[3].

Although the dominant view may still be intact, scholarly debate on the nature of the unity of Luke-Acts is currently very active[4]. Recent studies by scholars have raised a number of serious questions. Queries have related to authorial, canonical, generic, narrative, and theological unity. For example, the issue is raised whether the two documents are a unity: do the Gospel and the Acts share the same genre, and if not, does this violate referring to Luke-Acts as a unity? If the two documents are a unit, how is one to treat gaps or discontinuities of narrative? Or how does one determine theological unity when variables contribute to deciding when the documents are unity? What was the occasion for writing the volumes, and was it the same for both documents? Are the volumes dated in the same period? The fact that current scholarly research had

---

1. H.J. CADBURY, *The Making of Luke-Acts*, London, SPCK, 1961.
2. I.H. MARSHALL, *The Gospel of Luke: A Commentary on the Greek Text*, Grand Rapids, MI, Eerdmans, 1978; J.A. FITZMYER, *The Gospel according to Luke* (AB, 28-28A), Garden City, NY, Doubleday, 1981-1985; J.B. TYSON, *The Death of Jesus in Luke-Acts*, Columbia, SC, University of South Carolina Press, 1986; R.C. TANNEHILL, *The Narrative Unity of Luke-Acts: A Literary Interpretation*, Philadelphia, PA – Minneapolis, MN, Fortress, 2 vols., 1986-1990.
3. W.W. GASQUE, *The History of the Criticism of the Acts of the Apostles*, Peabody, MA, Hendrickson, 1989, p. 309; M. RESE, *Das Lukas-Evangelium. Ein Forschungsbericht*, in *ANRW* II.25.3, p. 2298, considers the unity of Luke and Acts to be the most important development in Lukan studies during the first half of this century.
4. See M.C. PARSONS & R.I. PERVO, *Rethinking the Unity of Luke and Acts*, Minneapolis, MN, Fortress, 1993. F. BOVON, *Studies in Luke-Acts. Retrospect and Prospect*, in *HTR* 85 (1992) 175-196.

raised issues of continuity, coherence, discordant themes, and the potential subordination of one volume or theme to another, suggests the unity of Luke-Acts may not be as secure as once considered. As we seek to clarify "unity" in Luke and Acts, these concerns form part of the broader context.

We propose to consider the theme of unity in Luke-Acts by considering a highly debated topic. It is Luke's perspective on the Jews. Since theological unity forms one critical part of the broader debate and coherence and tensions are a subset of this discussion, the concern over Luke's portrayal of the Jews is a good test case to reflect on unity in the Lukan writings. Luke's mixed and varied perspective on the Jews is one reason theological unity in Luke and Acts is challenged. It is now axiomatic that in his two-volume work Luke portrays the Jews positively and negatively. This perspective has been summarized by J. T. Sanders: "it is incorrect to maintain that Luke is pro-Jewish or simply anti-Jewish. He is both"[5]. He includes both pro-Jewish and anti-Jewish elements in his presentation of the Jews. Even the untrained reader of the two volume work can perceive this multi-dimensional portrayal of the Jews. If one maintains that in some sense Luke depicts the Jews in a coherent way, it requires rethinking his intentions and purpose[6].

2. A Neglected Proposal

The present study will contribute to this overall debate on Luke's treatment of the Jews, but will restrict the discussion to one part of the

5. J.T. SANDERS, *The Jews in Luke-Acts*, London, SCM Press, 1987, p. 317. C.M. TUCKETT, *Luke: New Testament Guides*, Sheffield, Academic Press, 1996, p. 54, summarizes the situation: "there are elements of Luke-Acts that seem extremely positive about Jews and Judaism ... there are elements that seem to betray an intense, almost unrelieved, hostility". See also on Luke on the Jews, M. RESE, *"Die Juden" im lukanischen Doppelwerk. Ein Bericht über eine längst nötige "neuere" Diskussion*, in C. BUSSMANN – W. RADL (eds.), *Der Treue Gottes trauen. Beiträge zum Werk des Lukas*. FS G. Schneider, Freiburg, Herder, 1991, pp. 61-79; D. MARGUERAT, *Juden und Christen im lukanischen Doppelwerk*, in *EvT* 94 (1994) 241-264; = *Juifs et chrétiens selon Luc-Actes. Surmonter le conflit des lectures*, in *Bib* 75 (1994) 126-146; J.B. TYSON (ed.), *Luke-Acts and the Jewish People. Eight Critical Perspectives*, Minneapolis, MN, Ausburg, 1988; F. MUSSNER, *Die Erzählintention des Lukas in der Apostelgeschichte*, in ID., *Dieses Geschlecht wird nicht vergehen. Judentum und Kirche*, Freiburg-Basel-Wien, Herder, 1991, pp. 101-114; J.B. TYSON, *Images of Judaism in Luke-Acts*, Columbia, SC, University Press, 1992; G. WASSERBERG, *Aus Israels Mitte – Heil für die Welt. Eine narrativ-exegetische Studie zur Theologie des Lukas* (BZNW, 92), Berlin – New York, de Gruyter, 1998; H. MERKEL, *Israel im lukanischen Werk*, in *NTS* 40 (1994) 371-398; J. JERVELL, *The Theology of the Acts of the Apostles*, Cambridge, University Press, 1996.
6. Our study will focus on the similarity of perspective between the Gospel and Acts. The case could equally be made that Luke has a different perspective between his two volumes.

equation, i.e. Luke's portrayal of observant Jews. We will ask what traditions he utilizes in presenting his Jewish characters. In particular, we will select three different kinds of evidence: the defense of Paul (Acts 21–26), the infancy narratives (Luke 1–2), and teaching material (Luke 10,25ff)[7].

In order to address our concern we will first make several observations on Judaism as depicted in the late first century from a near contemporary of Luke, namely Josephus. While comparisons between Luke and Josephus have an extensive scholarly history, few have considered Josephus, in particular *Contra Apionem* 2,164-219, in this regard[8]. Second, we will compare this text with Luke's portrayal of Paul as Jew in Acts 21–26, and determine the function and purpose of select examples. While we applaud Brawley's identification with scholars who resist the standard reading of the Lukan writings as a triumph of Gentile Christianity over Judaism, our analysis offers a complementary argumentation to his thesis of appealing to hellenistic rhetorical devices as a means of legitimating Paul, and informs us of the type of Judaism to which Luke accommodates Paul. In our view, if shared Jewish ideals can be isolated from Josephus, and documented within the narrative of the Lukan Paul, this would offer additional evidence as a means to legitimate Paul to the Jews of Luke's day. Third, the picture provided by the Lukan Paul will be tested in the Gospel account where Luke presents observant Jews. We will study examples from Luke 1–2 and Luke 10,25ff. Since Luke portrays some Jews in a positive light, we must determine how accurately

---

7. We will not engage in discussions on the origin of the Samaritans since our concern is simply to suggest that the example of the Good Samaritan reflects ideals of *Contra Apionem* 2.

8. Scholarly comparisons between Luke and Josephus have been investigated by, among others, E. PLÜMACHER, *Lukas als hellenistischer Schriftsteller. Studien zur Apostelgeschichte*, Göttingen, Vandenhoeck & Ruprecht, 1972, pp. 10, 25, 98, 137; H. SCHRECKENBERG, *Flavius Josephus und die lukanischen Schriften*, in W. HAUBECK – M. BACHMANN (eds.), *Wort in der Zeit*. FS K.H. Rengstorf, Leiden, Brill, 1980, pp. 179-209; H. SCHRECKENBERG and F. SCHUBERT, *Jewish Historiography and Iconography in Early and Medieval Christianity*, Assen, Van Gorcum – Minneapolis, Fortress, 1992, pp. 42-49; F.G. DOWNING, *Common Ground with Paganism in Luke and Josephus*, in *NTS* 28 (1982) 546-590; G.E. STERLING, *Historiography and Self-Definition: Josephos, Luke-Acts and Apologetic Historiography*, Leiden, Brill, 1992, pp. 365-389; S. MASON, *Josephus and Luke-Acts*, in ID., *Josephus and the New Testament*, Peabody, MA, Hendrickson, 1992, pp. 185-229. However, these scholars have not considered a comparison of CA with Luke. Reasons for comparing Josephus' CA and Luke: (1) both documents have been dated in the late first century; (2) both have been written by Jews; an increasing number of scholars consider Luke a Jew or at least one closely associated with the synagogue, i.e. a God-fearer; (3) both authors wrote to a mixed audience of Jews and Gentiles; (4) the literary orientation of Josephus and the author of Luke-Acts is influenced by Jewish apologetic.

he depicts observant Jews, and the level of commonality he shared with Jewish ideals of the late first century.

3. The Judaism of Josephus, *Contra Apionem* (CA)

In a forthcoming book[9] we evaluate CA, in particular 2,164-219, to determine whether Josephus' portrayal of Judaism reflects a realistic presentation of Judaism in the late first century. While the material is polemical and apologetical in nature[10], does the summary of Judaism in CA contain elements Jews would consider as critical to their religious perspective? We will not rehearse arguments here but provide several summary conclusions, and focus on some common themes relevant to a comparison with the ideals of observant Jews in the Lukan writings. The importance of CA 2,164-190 is that these paragraphs are considered to be "among the earliest and oldest theological précis compiled by a contemporary of the NT writers"[11]. We have assessed the material by classifying the evidence according to (1) ideas in CA that Josephus shared with the Bible; (2) ideas found in Josephus that are shared by a variety of contemporary Jewish sources; (3) ideas universally shared in antiquity by Jews and non-Jews and included by Josephus in CA; (4) ideas in Josephus attributed to Torah but not found in the Bible; (5) ideas in CA considered uncommon; (6) ideas and formulations peculiar to CA; (7) ideas shared between the Rabbis and CA[12]. Among the relevant Jewish

---

9. G.P. CARRAS, *Josephus and Paul: A Social, Historical, and Theological Comparison of Two Hellenistic Jews* (AGAJU), Leiden, Brill. See also ID., *Dependence or Common Tradition in Philo* Hypothetica *VIII 6.10–7.20 and Josephus* Contra Apionem *2.190-219*, in *SPA* 5 (1993) 24-47. Cf. J.L. DANIEL, *Apologetics in Josephus*, Diss. Rutgers University, 1981.

10. A. KASHER, *Polemic and Apologetic Methods of Writing in* Contra Apionem *in Josephus*, in L.H. FELDMAN & J.R. LEVISON (eds.), *Josephus'* Contra Apionem: *Studies in its Character and Context with a Latin Concordance to the Portion Missing in Greek* (AGAJU, 34), Leiden, Brill, 1996, pp. 142-186; C. GERBER, *Ein Bild des Judentums für Nichtjuden von Flavius Josephus: Untersuchungen zu seiner Schrift* Contra Apionem (AGAJU, 40), Leiden, Brill, 1997, pp. 183-203.

11. G. VERMÈS, *A Summary of the Law by Flavius Josephus*, in *NT* 23 (1982) 289-303, draws our attention to this neglected précis. However, he has not offered a detailed assessment on the importance that this section of CA may have for understanding the NT material (apart from some passing comments on the ethical and religious character of the teachings of Jesus). Cf. E.P. SANDERS, *Judaism and the Grand Christian Abstractions: Love, Mercy and Grace*, in *Int* 39 (1985) 357-372.

12. We maintain that Josephus does present "common Judaism", as he implicitly claims. That is neither so say that all Jews agreed on everything, nor that all ideas were distinctive of Jews: some were shared by Jew and Gentile alike. We have found enough parallels, however, to speak of a common understanding of "Judaism". Jews in general felt that they were, to some extent, a people apart. Josephus states that outsiders, while welcome to a certain degree, were not admitted to the "intimacies" of Jewish life. Jewish

ideals[13] to consider in a study of Luke's understanding of observant Jews include: (1) God is portrayed as monotheistic in nature. He is in control of the world, the sole creator of the universe and its properties, He forbids idolatry, and expects worship by the parctice of virtue in the observance of the Torah (CA, 2,190-193); (2) The Temple is a symbol of Jewish identity: (CA 2,193); (3) The cultus, its existence, practices, and priestly role of authority, are in actual use (CA 2,193-198); (4) Prayer has a central place in the life of the cultic community (CA 2,196); (5) Purity laws are to be observed (CA 2,203.205); (6) Jews are to behave towards each other in a prescribed manner; in particular they must not steal, charge interest or bear false witness, but offer help to the needy and poor (CA 2,207-208); (7) The Jewish religion is to be made accessible to non-Jews (CA 2,209-210); (8) Hope of a future life is affirmed (CA 2,217-219); (9) Obedience and disobedience to the Law bring their own consequences (CA 2,215-218); (10) The foundation of the above injunctions is that Moses is the legislator of the Jewish constitution.

4. Observant Jews in Acts: Paul

a. Critical Context

The proposal and broader context for considering Luke's observant Jews can now be studied from specific examples. We begin with the Lukan Paul. As one means to legitimate Paul as an observant and orthodox Jew, Brawley appeals to hellenistic literary techniques. He maintains that "if Luke legitimates Paul both by portraying him as faithful to the hopes of Israel and by outfitting him with evidence of authenticity in Hellenistic literary terms, then we possess clues that inform us about the type of Judaism toward which Luke accomodates Paul and about the environment in which Luke writes"[14]. Brawley contends that Luke links Hellenistic legitimating devices and his defense of Paul as an authentic Jew. The treatment of these themes together raises the question of what

literature in general and pagan comments about Jews confirm that the insider/outsider distinction was common.

13. E.P. SANDERS has discussed the theme of common Jewish ideals in a study entitled *Judaism: Practice and Brief 63 BCE - 66 CE*, London, SCM Press – Philadelpia, PA, Trinity Press International, 1992. He argues that there was world wide solidarity among Jews on the following: belief in one God, the choice of Israel as God's special people, the giving of the law and the obligation to obey its commands to maintain a covenantal relationship, and God would save his people in the end of time. This "basic" Jewish theology is found in all the sources. While he has not presented a systematic analysis of CA, Sanders' assessment of Josephus on this point concurs with our analysis.

14. R.L. BRAWLEY, *Luke-Acts and the Jews: Conflict, Apology and Conciliation* (SBL MS, 33), Atlanta, 1987, p. 51.

kind of religion Luke envisions as authentic Judaism. Brawley suggests that for Luke Judaism is not culturally exclusive, maintains a belief in the general resurrection and is open to intimate relationships with Gentiles. We suggest that these three characteristics emerge from CA but the list could include other Jewish ideals as a means to legitimate Paul as an authentic Jew.

b. Textual Context

Most agree that Paul is Luke's hero. He devotes over half of the story of the emergence of the early church in Acts to Paul and a quarter of the entire narrative of Acts to an apology for Paul as Jew. Beginning with 21,27 to the end of Acts, a defense of Paul is provided. The charges against and defense of Paul are stated throughout chapters 21–28. Paul is accused of profaning the Temple while he is observing a Jewish purification ritual[15]. Rumors emerged from Asian Jews that Paul is teaching against the Law, people, and the Temple. In response, Luke seeks to demonstrate Paul's fidelity and zeal for the law, and loyalty to Judaism. The charges and refutations can be listed as follows:

21,21   Paul teaches the Jews of the diaspora apostasy from Moses that they should not circumcize their children, and do not need to live according to the customs of the fathers.
21,28   Paul teaches everywhere against the people, the Law, and the Temple; brought Gentiles to undesignated areas of the Temple area and defiled this holy place.
25,8   Paul has neither sinned against the Law nor the Temple.
24,5-6 Paul has tried to profane the Temple.
23,29   The Roman version of the charge is stated that the problem concerns their [the Jews] laws.
28,17   Paul maintains in his refutation that he has nothing against the custom of the fathers and the people.

The charges relate neither to the mission to the Gentiles, nor do they arise from Paul's proposed guilt of political rebellion[16]. Rather, the charges against Paul are that he has sinned against Israel, and is guilty of forsaking the Law and Temple. If these charges were true, Paul would be seriously at odds with distinguishing identity markers of Israel and permit the accusation he is a false teacher in Israel. Luke refutes these

---

15. B. WITHERINGTON, *The Acts of the Apostles: A Socio-Rhetorical Commentary*, Grand Rapids, MI, Eerdmans – Carlisle, Paternoster Press, 1998, p. 652; G. SCHNEIDER, *Die Apostelgeschichte II. Teil: Kommentar zu Kap. 9,1–28,31* (HTK, 5), Freiburg, Herder, 1982, pp. 305-306; R. PESCH, *Die Apostelgeschichte* (EKK, 5), Zürich-Einsiedeln-Köln, Benziger, 1986, pp. 224-227.

16. J. JERVELL, *Theology of Acts* (n. 5), p. 88; ID., *Luke and the People of God*, Minneapolis, MN, Ausburg, 1972, pp. 166-167.

charges in four apologetic speeches whereby the primary purpose is to defend Paul as Jew. The speeches do not consist of missionary kerygma, calls for repentance, scriptural proofs or appeals to eyewitnesses[17]. Rather, Luke defends his hero first by claiming that Paul was and is a Pharisee, and a Jew faithful to the Law (22,3; 23,1.3.5.6; 24,14; 26,4-5). Second, he teaches only what scripture says and believes everything that is written in the law and the prophets (24,14-15; 26,22-23). A third defensive strategy used, although it does not appear as one of the charges against Paul, is that he adheres to the resurrection of the dead, a hope of Pharisaic Israel[18].

c. Temple, Law and People

Central to the charges and refutation is the connection between the people, the Law and the Temple[19]. This interrelationship suggests Paul was perceived as challenging fundamentals of Judaism since the Law is a sign of Israel as the people of God, and the Temple a supreme symbol of Jewish identity. It is suggested by Esler based on scholarship from sociological analysis that we know a great deal about how an ethnic group responds to living within a larger culture. The response ranges from total breakdown of the group's boundaries resulting in complete assimilation, on the one hand, to a tight maintainence of the group's separate identity, on the other. Esler maintains that among diaspora Jews one would expect to find, the latter. Furthermore, he states one finds among diaspora Jews a strong devotion to the Law and the Temple[20]. A Jew such as Paul, who was perceived as teaching against the Law, the people and the Temple, would be a threat to Jewish identity and the social fabric of local Jewish communities, if found guilty. Whatever may have been other reasons for charges against Paul (e.g. taking a Gentile beyond legitimate boundaries of the Temple, attitudes on Gentile law-keeping), Temple and Law observance appear to be central, and are critical in Luke's defense. For our purpose what is important is that these same features, the Law and Temple, are the identity markers Luke appeals to in defense of Paul. In the trial before

17. J. JERVELL, *Theology of Acts*, p. 88.
18. *Ibid.*, p. 87; K. HAACKER, *Das Bekenntnis des Paulus zur Hoffnung Israels nach der Apostelgeschichte des Lukas*, in *NTS* 31 (1985) 437-451. The Jewishness of the refutation is also noted by WITHERINGTON, *Acts of the Apostles*, pp. 659-660.
19. On the Law in the Lukan writings see K. SALO, *Luke's Treatment of the Law: A Redaction-Critical Investigation*, Helsinki, Suomalaien Tiedeakatemia, 1991; S.G. WILSON, *Luke and the Law* (SNTS MS, 50), Cambridge, University Press, 1983.
20. P. ESLER, *Community and Gospel in Luke-Acts: The Social and Political Motivations of Lucan Theology* (SNTS MS, 57), Cambridge, University Press, 1987, p. 146.

Festus (25,8) Paul states that he neither sinned against the Law or the Temple.

It is also these two Jewish descriptors which form a central place in the "Mosaic summary" in CA. In 2,190ff we find Torah-based ideals for Jews described by Josephus as the "precepts and prohibitions" of Torah. It is assumed throughout CA that Torah is to be observed and the consequences for obedience and disobedience can lead to positive and negative results. The "Mosaic legislation" does not consist simply of a list of biblical laws, rather is a "carefully structured exposition" on God, man's relationship to God, and to his fellow creatures[21]. The summary is followed by two appendices: one on punishment awaiting transgressors of the Law, and the other on rewards of the future life awaiting faithful observers of Torah. Throughout the summary are a variety of Jewish ideals, many of which relate to biblical prescriptions and, we have argued, many reflect common Judaism[22]. Regardless of whether some of the ideals are formulated more philosophically, the central place of Torah observance is unmistakable. Because the statements are given in summary format, the lack of explanation may imply the contents are assumed to be central Jewish ideals.

A second descriptor used by Luke in defense of Paul, the Temple, illustrates another common Jewish symbol which also takes an important place in the Lukan account. When Paul defends himself to Felix, he cites his coming to the Temple to bring alms and offering for the Jewish nation. He argues he had not gone to Jerusalem to profane the Temple but to worship God, and the God he was to worship was the God of "our fathers", the God of Israel. Luke also located Paul in the Temple after he had undergone purification. Therefore, where we find Paul is significant as an instrument to defend him against profaning the Temple. Luke places Paul in direct association with a central institution of Judaism, the Temple.

The Temple (CA 2,190-193) also plays a central role as a marker of Jewish identity in Josephus' summary. It is the second topic he considers following his summary on God. Josephus' rationale is that since there is one God and one community, there is one Temple. From this basic premise a sketch is given of the (1) duties of priests; (2) practices to be observed at sacrifices; (3) occasions for purity regulations. It is striking in a work written at the end of the first century that the sanctuary and sacrifices are represented as a present reality. Several explanations are possible: the expectation of a quick restoration of the Jerusalem

21. VERMÈS, *Summary* (n. 11), p. 289.
22. CARRAS, *Josephus and Paul* (n. 9), passim.

Temple, the portrayal is seen as a depiction of a utopian world in which the destruction of the Temple never occurred, or its inclusion reflects the central place of the Temple as a marker of Jewish identity.

In addition to the Law and Temple (recognized symbols of Jewish identity), Luke includes the affirmation of the resurrection of the just and unjust (24,15) in his defense of Paul as a loyal Jew. This idea is considered a common distinguishing feature of Judaism by most Jews in antiquity[23]. Josephus' formulation is belief in "renewed existence" (CA 2,218-219) which although terminologically different is compatible with the concept of future hope in the War (3,374; 7,344-350) and AJ (18,14). The inclusion of the resurrection of the dead in Luke's defense is a further indication of legitimating Paul as a loyal Jew by appeal to a common ideal in Judaism.

In addition to Temple, Torah observance, and hope in a future resurrection, there are several others items shared in Luke's defense of Paul and CA. In Paul's curriculum vitae as a loyal Jew, Luke places on the lips of Paul the affirmation of zeal for God (22,3). This zeal for God was to be expressed in meticulous observance of the Law. In affirming zeal for God, Paul is identifying himself with one of the most fundamental features of the Jewish religion[24]. The point has been made by some scholars that zeal for God is even more fundamental than zeal for God's Law[25].

CA 2,190 begins, as we noted, its summary of Torah with the affirmation of God. He is presented as the sole agent in creation and the one for whom any form of idolatry is prohibited. He is to be worshiped, and the form it should take is by the practice of virtue. God also controls and directs history. The idea of God's providence is tied to the doctrine of creation. As creator of the universe God cares, governs, and sustains it. While the idea of God as one who directs history is assumed in various accounts of Paul's defense (26,6 Paul is on trial because of the hope in the promises made by God), the point is reiterated in the speech at Pisidian Antioch in Acts 13,16ff which gives a historical recital of God's great acts in history. God directs and brings on the stage of history a David, Samuel or Jesus, according to his plan. Similarly, Luke conceives of God as the one who has fixed the time of judgment (Acts 17,30-31). While different aspects of the divine are reflected, we can assume that the monotheistic nature of God is intended by both Luke and Josephus.

23. So SANDERS, *Judaism* (n. 13), p. 279.

24. M. HENGEL, *Die Zeloten*, Leiden, Brill, 1976, pp. 182, 187-188.

25. W.R. FARMER, *Maccabees, Zealots, and Josephus*, New York, Columbia University Press, 1956, p. 49.

This is certainly the case for Luke who often makes reference to the God of Abraham, Isaac and Jacob. This is also the case with Josephus who states that cult is based on the principal of unity.

Another indicator of shared ideals recorded in Luke's defense of Paul and the summary of Jewish virtues is the observance of purity regulations set in relation to the Temple. When we consider Josephus' CA we know that purity regulations were to be observed since he provides three examples. In particular, Josephus states in the following way: "In view of the sacrifices the law has prescribed the purifications for various occasions: after a funeral, after child birth, after conjugal union and for many others" (2,198). These purity laws are found in Lev 12 (child-birth), Lev 15 (emissions from the body), and Num 19 (death). People who were affected by these "changes of status" – life, death and reproduction were to stay away from the sacred (Temple)[26].

If we consider the specific purity regulations relative to Paul, details are absent. What we do find is the Lukan Paul presented as a Jew observing legal custom[27]. In Paul's defense to Felix (24,18), Luke accounts an incident that occurred when Paul arrived in Jerusalem (21,21ff). On the advice of James, Paul was recommended to take a vow to curb rumors that he was against the people, the Law and the Temple. Four men were under a Nazarite vow since they had shaved their heads. At the conclusion of the vow an offering of sacrifice would be given at the Temple. The proposal was that Paul should pay the expenses of the sacrifice. Furthermore, Paul was to undergo purification with the men, accompany them in the Temple and record the time when the purification was complete and the sacifices made. Difficulties surrounding this incident are well-known[28]. The point that can be noted for our purpose is that purification regulations were a sign of loyality in Judaism. Luke associates Paul with legal regulations relative to Temple access.

Restriction of Gentile's association to the Temple is a topic closely related to purification regulations. While the charge that Paul brought a Gentile to the Temple area is denied by Luke, he shows knowledge of the legal regulations regarding this injunction. The denial enables Luke to indicate the implausibility that Paul would engage in such an activity when his purpose for coming to the Temple was for prayer, worship, sacrifice to God, and giving alms to his fellow Jews. It would have been

26. SANDERS, *Judaism* (n. 13), pp. 70-72, 217-219.
27. SALO, *Law* (n. 19), p. 262.
28. *Ibid.*, pp. 260-266; TYSON, *Images* (n. 5), pp. 158-168; ESLER, *Luke-Acts* (n. 20), pp. 125-126.

incredible for a person engaged in religious duty (alms, offering sacrifice) to desecrate the Temple at the same time[29].

One final example to illustrate the shared ideals in Luke's defense and CA. The Jewish religion was not to be kept a private possession of Jews and remain inaccessible to others[30]. In CA 2,210 we read, "To all who desire to come and live under the same laws with us, he gives a gracious welcome". The only restriction is that casual visitors, considered by many to refer to God-fearers[31], should not be permitted to know the intimate details of daily religious practice. This suggests that the offer to non-Jews of membership to the people of God reflects a common Jewish notion and one that was adopted by the early Christians. Beginning with the infancy narrative in Luke's Gospel to the end of Acts, Gentile entry to the people of God is a belief that formed part of the kergyma of early Christian preachers. It is also a notion included at several points in Paul's defense when he tells how and to whom God called him (22,15; 26,17-18).

Several of the common ideals of Judaism documented from CA are appealed to by Luke to legitimate Paul as a loyal Jew of the diaspora. The suggestion being made is not that Luke or Josephus borrowed from each other, or were dependent on each other, but that they shared common Jewish traditions. To whatever extent material in the speeches of Acts are Lukan redaction, the scenes are meant to portray Paul as a loyal Jew by associating him with Jewish ideals and symbols of Jewish self-reference known by many Jews. The legitimation of Paul as a loyal Jew is affirmed by appealing to practices of the Temple, Torah observance, affirmation of future resurrection, belief in the primacy of the Jewish God, regulation of purity, and the openness of the Jewish religion to Gentiles.

Our analysis offers a complementary argument to Brawley's thesis of appealing to hellenistic rhetorical devices as a means of legitimating Paul, and informs us of the type of Judaism to which Luke accommodates Paul. If CA is a reflection of common Judaism, and Luke appeals to these items in his defense and portrayal of the Lukan Paul, it adds force to another legitimating device used by Luke to tell his story.

---

29. I.H. MARSHALL, *The Acts of the Apostles: An Introduction and Commentary*, Leicester, IVP, 1980, p. 379.

30. See S. MASON, *The* Contra Apionem *in Social and Literary Context: An Invitation to Judean Philosophy*, in L.H. FELDMAN & J.R. LEVINSON (eds.), *Josephus'* Contra Apionem (n. 10), pp. 212-214.

31. L. TROIANI, *Commento Storico al "Contro Apione" di Giuseppe: introduzione, commento storico, traduzione e indici*, Pisa, Giardini, p. 192; D. BALCH, *Two Apologetic Encomia: Dionysius on Rome and Josephus on the Jews*, in *JSJ* 13 (1982), p. 119.

5. Observant Jews in Luke 1–2: Zechariah – Elizabeth, Mary – Joseph, and Simeon – Anna

a. Zechariah and Elizabeth

While other common features between CA and Luke's portrayal of Paul could be mentioned, we briefly turn our attention to the infancy narratives to test whether the description of Judaism in CA is reflected in the Gospel. The observation has often been made that Luke's Gospel opens with exemplary Jews in Jerusalem at the Temple. The story begins with Elizabeth and Zechariah who were of priestly descent, Zechariah from the division of Abijah and Elizabeth from the family of Aaron. Both are characterized as righteous before God, and both walked blameless in all the commandments and ordinances of the Lord (1,6)[32]. The combination of commandments and ordinances cover, the individual requirements of the Mosaic law (commandments), and statues in the wider sense including cultic and social obligations. Zechariah was a priest and the narrative states that it fell to him by lot to burn incense in the Temple, a privilege accorded to a priest once in his life. We are also told the priestly couple were barren. This fact stirs in the reader the memory of divine intervention of other Jews, Abraham and Sarah, barren late in life[33]. These brief observations indicate that the themes of Temple, Torah observance, and identification with the priesthood are primary in this opening description of these pious Jews.

b. Mary and Joseph

A second example of exemplary Jews committed to the Law are Mary and Joseph. Their commitment to Torah is best reflected in the presentation of Jesus in the Temple (2,22-39). In the course of eighteen verses Luke records no fewer than five times that Mary and Joseph acted "in accordance with the Law" (2,22.23.24.27.39)[34]. The episode recorded is the Passover visit of Jesus and his parents to Jerusalem. The practice is mentioned but not described in any detail which suggests that the reader is expected to have some familiarity with the content. Circumcision is

---

32. See MARSHALL, *Luke* (n. 2), pp. 50-55 on aspects of the Jewish piety of Elizabeth and Zechariah.

33. M. COLERIDGE, *The Birth of the Lukan Narrative: Narrative as Christology in Luke 1-2* (JSNT SS, 88), Sheffield, Academic Press, 1993, p. 31; MARSHALL, *Luke*, p. 49; J. KREMER, *Lukasevangelium*, Würzburg, Echter, 1988, p. 24.

34. ESLER, *Luke-Acts* (n. 20), p. 112.

mentioned as something regularly done to an eight day old Jewish male (2,21). However, one of the oddities of the episode is the conflation (or confusion) of the purification of the mother after the birth of the male child and the presentation of the child to God[35]. The rite of purification of the mother is in accordance with Lev 12,1-8 and the presentation of the first born with Exod 3,2. We also hear about the modest means of Jesus' parents because they appear to be unable to afford the lamb and bird prescribed for purification. Instead they offer two birds (turtledoves and pigeons) as was allowed for those of modest means (Lev 5,11; 12,8). The narrative presents Joseph and Mary as faithful to the Law given by Moses.

c. Simeon and Anna

A third pair of faithful Jews given in the early chapters of the Gospel are Simeon and Anna. Simeon is described as righteous, one who is obedient to the Law, devout, and waiting for the consolation of Israel (i.e. the Messiah). With Simeon's entry comes a blessing with fulfillment of the divine promise in the coming of Messiah. This fulfillment will bring salvation to the Gentiles. The advent of Simeon will also bring a prophetic warning: the child is destined for the rise and fall of many in Israel. While Anna is not described as devout and righteous, she has a prophetic role and is given the title of prophetess. Her ministry focuses on all who are looking for redemption of Jerusalem. She is depicted as one who fasts and prays day and night and offers thanks to God. In so doing her prophecy is considered theocentric[36].

The six Jewish characters described serve to introduce themes to be developed in later accounts of Luke and Acts. They also portray the world in which the message of Jesus was introduced, "a Jewish world, peopled by characters whose lives are governed by the Hebrew Scriptures and whose center is the Jerusalem Temple"[37]. These personalities represent a Judaism that was Torah observant, Temple based, purity oriented, prophetic-covenantal formulated, and directed under the plan and intention of God. The markers of Jewish identity are replicated in the defense of the Lukan Paul in the Acts and reflect a Judaism consonant with aspects of CA.

---

35. COLERIDGE, *Narrative* (n. 33), p. 159; KREMER, *Lukasevangelium* (n. 33), p. 39.
36. *Ibid.*, p. 181.
37. TYSON, *Images* (n. 5), p. 53.

6. Jewish Virtues in Others: The Good Samaritan

One distinctive of the Jewish religion is the interrelationship between belief and praxis. The indicative of fact and the imperative of action are intertwined. The "love of one's neighbor" involves concrete and specific actions. Luke, in his defense of Paul, indicates that after Paul had been away from Jerusalem for some time he brought alms to his fellow Jews who were in need (Acts 24,17). In a manner common to a pious Jew of the diaspora, Paul brought alms to Jerusalem. We know from Paul's letters (1 Cor 16,1-4; 2 Cor 8–9; Rom 15,23-33) that he brought a substantial sum of money collected from the Gentile churches "for the poor among the saints in Jerusalem" (Rom 15,26).

Care for the needy constitutes genuine faithfulness to Torah and is a virtue of Judaism as described in CA. Josephus devotes a section of his summary of Torah to an exposition on human relationships. Three topics are considered: duties toward parents (2,206), attitudes toward friends or fellow Jews (2,207-208), and behavior toward Gentiles (2,209-214). In addressing his fellow Jews the injunction is given, "he who overlooks one who offers him a petition, and this when he is able to relieve him, he is a guilty person" (2,207). Similar statements are found in a variety of testimonies (Deut 15,7f; Prov 31,20; Sir 4,4-5; Ps.Phoc. 29; Hyp. 7,6).

According to Josephus assistance is to be extended also to Gentiles. The injunction is to give fire, water and food to all in need. Jews are to help all humankind with the basic necessities of life. Equally, Gentiles are to "point out the roads", a rather oblique phrase which may refer to a lost traveler, or the blind (Deut 27,18). The sentiment is probably captured in Ps.Phoc. 26: "Extend your hand to him who falls, and save the helpless one".

Jews are also to care for those who are their enemies, in particular they are to look out for those with whom they have engaged in warfare. Jews are not permitted to destroy orchards where battle has taken place. This general provision is already present in Deut 20,19. A second injunction relating to enemies in warfare is that measures are to be taken to prevent outrage against a prisoner of war, especially women, so Deut 21,19. These examples indicate that Jews are to treat fellow Jews, Gentiles and enemies charitably and in a decent manner, especially those in need.

This emphasis on charitable giving is a dominant theme in the Lukan material. In addition to the example of Cornelius who gave alms generously to the people (Acts 10,2) and Tabitha in Joppa who was devoted to good works and acts of charity (9,36), particular mention should be made to the story of the Good Samaritan (10,29-36)[38]. The account records the exchange between Jesus and a lawyer on how one gains eternal life. Jesus inquires of the lawyer what the Law says, and the legal expert's reply is to love God and love one's neighbor, Deut 6,5 and Lev 19,18. The account proceeds with the question by Jesus as to who is someone's neighbor, and the remainder of the story seeks to answer this question. The story is told of a man in desperate need who is lying by the side of the road, beaten, robbed, and half dead. Three by-passers are given the opportunity to help the man, but two decline to help. A priest and Levite decline to assist, because of the obligation to remain ritually clean. According to Biblical Law priests were strictly forbidden to contact a corpse except for next of kin (Lev 21,1-3). If the man was dead and was touched by the priest or the Levite, they would be considered unclear. For a layperson corpse impurity made one unclean for seven days[39]. The third by-passer, a Samaritan and lay person, showed compassion and mercy toward the man in need. The irony of the story is that the Samaritan would become unclean if the man was dead, yet he is the one who fulfilled the Law prescribed in Lev 19,18 ("love your neighbor as yourself")[40]. The other distinctive feature of this account is that by the Samaritan's action he is fulfilling a law restricted to "Israelites". However, the Samaritan's action shows him to be the real almsgiver, and indicates parameters for helping the needy. Ritual purity and national-religious status are relegated to a lesser role in the interest of showing mercy to the victim in need. From this we can see that the perspective of Paul as a loyal Jew who brought alms to the Jewish people during a time of need is mirrored in the example of the Samaritan as almsgiver. Both reflect a general view documented in Josephus' CA; help for the needy is expected inspite of racial or religious boundaries.

7. Conclusions

This study offers a characterization of observant Jews in Luke-Acts. We considered three different contexts where observant Jews are present: the defense of Paul, the infancy narratives, and the story-parable of

---

38. See D. JUEL, *Luke-Acts*, London, SCM, 1984, 36; W. SCHRAGE, *The Ethics of the New Testament*, Philadelphia, PA, Fortress, 1990, pp. 73-79; D. RAVENS, *Luke and the Restoration of Israel* (JSNT SS, 119), Sheffield, Academic Press, 1995, pp. 83-84; TUCKETT, *Luke* (n. 5), pp. 97-99.

39. RAVENS, *Luke*, p. 83; E.P. SANDERS, *Jewish Law From Jesus to the Mishnah*, London, SCM – Philadelphia, PA, Trinity Press International, 1990, p. 41.

40. Cf. C.A. EVANS, *Luke* (NIBC), Peabody, MA, Hendrickson, 1990, p. 176.

the Good Samaritan. We contextualized this material by comparing the ideals of observant Jews in Lukan writings with Josephus' CA, and to a significant degree found that these two documents held compatible perspectives.

Near Eastern Studies Department   George P. CARRAS
University of California
Berkeley, CA
USA

LUKE-ACTS AND THE TEMPLE

It was for much of the twentieth century a canon of scholarly ortho-
doxy that Luke is the most gentile of New Testament authors[1]. This
position is now a more debated issue in scholarship[2], but the author's
interest in and commitment to the gentile mission is indisputably central
to the narrative of Acts, and the gentile mission is clearly anticipated in
the gospel of Luke[3]. Yet the Jerusalem Temple features prominently in
both volumes of this work. References to the Temple can be explained
neither in terms of widespread Graeco-Roman interest in oriental cults[4]
and the particular reputation of the Temple of Jerusalem[5], nor simply in
terms of the Temple being the location of several of the events recorded.
The Temple may on occasion be incidental to the narrative, or simply a
geographical point of reference, but it is nonetheless significant that
mention should be made of the Temple so frequently, and that key
episodes located elsewhere in Matthew and Mark should be located in
the Temple in Luke[6]. Allusions are never accompanied by detailed
descriptions of the architecture or ritual system which would satisfy the
curiosity of antiquarian or eclectically minded readers[7]. While these factors could indicate that the Temple is of marginal significance for Luke,
there are nevertheless passages where the Temple is integral to the narrative and to his apologetic purpose. References to the Temple in Luke-

1. H. CONZELMANN, *The Theology of Saint Luke*, London, 1982; M. DIBELIUS, *Studies in the Acts of the Apostles*, London, 1956; E. HAENCHEN, *The Acts of the Apostles*, Nashville, 1971; R. MADDOX, *The Purpose of Luke-Acts*, Edinburgh, 1982; J.T. SANDERS, *The Jews in Luke-Acts*, London, 1987; S.G. WILSON, *The Gentiles and the Gentile Mission in Luke-Acts*, Cambridge, 1973; ID., *Luke and the Law*, Cambridge, 1983.
2. See e.g. R.L. BRAWLEY, *Luke-Acts and the Jews*, Atlanta, 1987; B.J. KOET, *Five Studies on Interpretation of Scripture in Luke-Acts* (SNTA, 14), Leuven, 1989; D.L. TIEDE, *Prophecy and History in Luke-Acts*, Philadelphia, 1983.
3. Luke 2,31-32; 4,25-27; 7,2-10; 11,29-32.
4. R.L. FOX, *Pagans and Christians*, London, 1986, pp. 64-101; R. MACMULLEN, *Paganism in the Roman Empire*, London, 1981.
5. Josephus, *CA* 1,198-199; 2,138; S.J.D. COHEN, *Respect for Judaism by Gentiles in the Writings of Josephus*, in *HTR* 80 (1987) 409-30; E. SCHÜRER, *The Jewish People in the Age of Jesus Christ*, II, Edinburgh, 1979, pp. 309-314.
6. This is most conspicuously true of the eschatological discourse, located on the Mount of Olives in Matthew 24 and Mark 13, but in the Temple in Luke 21. The Temple also features in the nativity and post-resurrection narratives more prominently than in the other gospels.
7. For an example of a treatment of Jewish institutions from such a perspective see Pliny, *Nat. Hist.*, 5.

Acts, along with other central and distinctive features of Jewish identity
and culture, serve to define the continuing significance of Jewish institutions in the light of the Christian Gospel, and the relationship of the
Church to Judaism, and therefore merit particular attention[8]. In this
respect at least we need to consider whether Luke-Acts was addressed to
a (Diaspora) Jewish as well as a gentile readership.

In the view of most scholars, Luke wrote his Gospel and its sequel,
the book of Acts, after the Temple in Jerusalem had been destroyed[9]. It
is often assumed on this basis that Luke reinterpreted the traditions he
had received concerning Jerusalem and the Temple in the light of the
events of 70 CE[10]. Whatever the influence of the destruction of Jerusalem
on the transmission of the gospel traditions, Luke wrote at a time when
the Temple was no longer a functioning institution, but one which
nonetheless continued to hold immense conceptual and symbolic value
for at least the majority of the Jewish people[11]. During the last quarter of
the first century CE there would not have been the resignation to the loss
of the Temple that became characteristic of most strands within Judaism
at a later period[12]. Rather, there would have been a general hope and
expectation, at least until the time of Hadrian, that in due time and with
changing political fortunes Jerusalem would be restored as a Jewish city
and the Temple rebuilt, as had been the case after the destruction of
Solomon's Temple by the Babylonians in 587 BCE. It has been argued
that Josephus wrote *De Bello Iudaico* not merely against this background, but in the hope that he would be able to secure the high priesthood in the restored Temple[13]. If a Jew as well connected to the Roman

8. BRAWLEY (n. 2), pp. 107-132; D.A. JUEL, *Luke-Acts*, London, 1983; TIEDE (n. 2).
9. H. CONZELMANN, *Acts of the Apostles*, Philadelphia, 1987; C.A. EVANS, *Luke*,
Peabody, 1990; C.F. EVANS, *Saint Luke*, London, 1990; J.A. FITZMYER, *The Gospel
according to Luke*, New York, 1981-1985; I.H. MARSHALL, *Commentary on Luke*, Grand
Rapids, 1978; G. SCHNEIDER, *Das Evangelium nach Lukas*, Bonn, 1985; *Die Apostelgeschichte*, Freiburg, 1980-1982. Contra, J. MUNCK, *The Acts of the Apostles*, New York,
1967; J.A.T. ROBINSON, *Redating the New Testament*, London, 1976, pp. 86-117.
10. The influence of the events of 70 CE on Lukan composition and redaction is disputed by C.H. DODD, *The Fall of Jerusalem and the Abomination of Desolation*, in *Journal of Roman Studies* 37 (1947) 47-54, who argues that allusions to Old Testament passages account for the differences between Luke 21 and Mark 13. Cf. F.F. BRUCE, *The Acts
of the Apostles*, Grand Rapids, 1990, p. 16; FITZMYER (n. 9), p. 1255; TIEDE (n. 2), p. 67.
11. S.J.D. COHEN, *From the Maccabees to the Mishnah*, Philadelphia, 1989, pp. 214-
231; L.L. GRABBE, *Judaism from Cyrus to Hadrian*, London, 1991, pp. 537-545.592-595.
12. *1 Enoch* 90,28-29; *4 Ezra* 10,25-59; *2 Baruch* 32,2-4; 68,5; *T Ben* 9,2; Josephus,
BJ 5,19. For discussion of Jewish literature of this period see B.W. LONGENECKER, *Eschatology and the Covenant*, Sheffield, 1991, pp. 40-157; G.W.E. NICKELSBURG, *Jewish Literature between the Bible and the Mishnah*, London, 1981, pp. 277-309; SCHÜRER (n. 5).
13. B.D. CHILTON, *The Temple of Jesus*, Philadelphia, 1992, p. 77.

court as Josephus was at this stage in his career could entertain such imminent expectations, then we should expect that those who could only reflect upon the prophetic traditions and pray for the restoration of Jerusalem would expect a less imminent turning away of divine wrath and a redemption perhaps less immediate and less to their personal advantage than that to which Josephus aspired. Nonetheless we should assume that Luke-Acts was written against a background in which the majority of the Jewish people hoped for the restoration of Jerusalem and the Temple in the foreseeable, even if distant, future.

The function of the Temple in Jewish social, economic, political, and cultic life, and consequently its significance in Jewish thought, during the period up to 70 CE was complex[14]. The Temple was, for most Jews, the sole legitimate location of their sacrificial cult, and accordingly a place of pilgrimage particularly at the time of major festivals. The Temple was also the principal centre for the exposition and administration of Torah, and a source of authoritative rulings on all matters of Jewish life and belief, however widely these may have been observed or however vehemently disputed or even quietly ignored[15]. In addition, the Temple and activities located there formed a large part of the economy of Jerusalem and the surrounding areas[16]. Underlying and at the same time being reinforced by these aspects of the Temple system was the symbolic significance of the sanctuary for the Jewish people. The Holy of Holies was the symbolic centre of Judaism, and, in some conceptualisations, of the cosmos[17]. It was also conceived as the earthly residence of God, a notion inextricably linked with that of the election of Israel[18]. The Temple was, in summary, the central institution of religious, political, and cultural identity for the Jewish people. Its destruction therefore precipitated a multi-faceted crisis for the Jewish people, one which went far beyond the discontinuation of the sacrificial cult on Mount Zion. Authority in the exposition of Torah was diffused until reconstructed by

14. J.D.G. DUNN, *The Partings of the Ways*, London, 1991, pp. 31-35; GRABBE (n. 11), pp. 537-545; E.P. SANDERS, *Judaism: Practice and Belief 63 BCE – 66 CE*, London, 1992, pp. 47-72.

15. J. NEUSNER, *Formative Judaism*, Chico, 1983; E.P. SANDERS (n. 14), pp. 190-240; A.J. SALDARINI, *Pharisees, Scribes, and Sadducees in Palestinian Society*, Wilmington, 1988.

16. J. JEREMIAS, *Jerusalem in the Time of Jesus*, London, 1963, pp. 21-27.51-57.

17. Ezek 38,12; *1 Enoch* 26-27; *Jubilees* 8,12. For discussion see J.Z. SMITH, *Map Is Not Territory*, Leiden, 1978; *To Take Place*, Chicago, 1987.

18. However literally or otherwise this was understood, and notwithstanding texts in the tradition which acknowledge the inadequacy of the Temple as a divine residence, the symbolic significance of the sanctuary as a place of divine presence is not to be underestimated. For discussion see E.P. SANDERS (n. 14), pp. 51-54.

the rabbis during a later period[19]. The notion of the Temple as the inviolable earthly residence of God was utterly destroyed[20]. Those Jews who revered the prophetic traditions would have been able to interpret their experience in terms of previous occasions of divine judgement, and thereby to have derived their hopes of eventual restoration[21]. Those who rejected the prophets, and whose power had been derived from the economy of the Temple, were those who failed to re-establish themselves as a force in Jewish society without the Temple, and who ultimately perished[22]. Early Christian attitudes to the Temple, including that reflected in Luke-Acts, must be reconstructed against this background.

Assuming a date during the last quarter of the first century, Luke-Acts must have been written with at least some awareness of the politics of Jewish reconstruction in Palestine, as well as of circumstances in Diaspora Judaism at the time. The prominence of the Temple suggests a conscious presentation of a Christian alternative to the Jewish hope and quest for restoration of the sanctuary and its cult, and to Temple-oriented notions of divine presence, patterns of worship and ordering of daily life. Rather than affirming hopes for the restoration of Temple and cult, Luke expounds a view of the Temple that has been superseded by other manifestations of the divine presence, in the person of Jesus and in the life and expansion of the Church in the power of the Holy Spirit. Before proceeding to develop this point, however, we need to consider whether it is possible to describe a single and coherent Lukan position on the Temple.

Four terms are used of the Jerusalem Temple in Luke-Acts (τὸ ἱερόν, ὁ ναός, ὁ οἶκος, ὁ τόπος ὁ ἅγιος), and Luke is clearly dependent on sources for most references[23]. The question needs to be asked whether

---

19. S.J.D. COHEN, *The Significance of Yavneh*, in *HUCA* 55 (1984) 27-53; NEUSNER (n. 15).

20. Josephus, *BJ* 5,219.439; 6,285-286.

21. GRABBE (n. 11), pp. 561-564; LONGENECKER (n. 12), pp. 40-157.

22. COHEN (n. 19); GRABBE (n. 11), pp. 463-554.592-595; NEUSNER (n. 15); SALDARINI (n. 15).

23. (1) τὸ ἱερόν (Lk 13, Acts 21 occurrences). Luke 19,45.47; 20,1; 21,5; 22,53 have a parallel in Mark. Lk 4,9 probably derives from Q. Lk 2,27.37.46*; 18,10*; 21,37.38; 24,53* all occur in special Lukan material (* possibly Lukan composition). – Acts 2,46*; 3,1.2.3.8.10; 5,20.21.25.42*; 21,26.27.28.29.30; 22,17-18*; 24,6.12.18; 25,8*; 26,21* derive from an unknown source or may be redactional (*).

(2) ὁ ναός (Luke 4, Acts 2 occurrences). Luke 23,45 par. Mark; Luke 1,9.21.22 from a special Lukan source. – Acts 17,24; 19,24 (both with reference to pagan shrines).

(3) ὁ οἶκος (Luke 3 or 4, Acts 3 occurrences). Luke 6,4 and 19,46 par. Mark; 11,51 and 13,35 (?) Q; 2,49 (implied use). – Acts 7,47.48.49 (Lukan composition or derived from a source; v. 49 quotation of Isa 66,1-2).

(4) ὁ τόπος (ὁ ἅγιος). Acts 6,13.14*; 7,7.49; 21,28*bis* (* possibly redactional). For a more detailed discussion, see the commentaries.

we can speak of a single, unified conception and theological position vis-à-vis that institution. The occurrences of ναός all derive from sources rather than from the evangelist, and the same is true of the more allusive, if all but synonymous, term οἶκος. It is, furthermore, unlikely that more than one occurrence of ἱερόν is not derived from sources. Where Luke is drawing on sources, he appears never to change the terminology regarding the Temple, assuming he is using Mark, Q, and further material available only to him. If, however, Luke is dependent on Matthew rather than these sources[24], then he does make some changes, but these are not of major importance. Therefore it could be argued that, at the redactional level, there is no single conception of the Temple. However, some patterns are discernible in the use of these terms, which would suggest at the least that sources have been utilised so as to support the theological position of the evangelist. It has been noted that ναός occurs after the appearance of Gabriel to Zechariah only in contexts where divine residency is denied and the notion thereof derided. Οἶκος similarly appears only in contexts where there is conflict with the Jewish establishment, though the status of the Temple is not necessarily at issue. Ἱερόν tends to refer in more general terms to the Temple precincts rather than specifically to the sanctuary area. While implying a notion of sanctity, ἱερόν is nonetheless theologically the most neutral of the terms employed by Luke, and perhaps conveys a geographical rather than a theological meaning and significance. While we need to proceed with some caution in drawing conclusions on the basis of Luke's use of terminology, it would nevertheless seem that some significance must be attached to the patterns identified in the use of ναός in particular, and also of οἶκος.

Having identified the words used by Luke for the Temple, their sources so far as these can be established, and some aspects of their significance, we need to consider the place of the Temple in the overall narrative of Luke-Acts.

Luke 1,8-22: the appearance of Gabriel to Zechariah in the Temple. — As noted above, this is the only pericope in which ναός is used where the notion of divine residency in earthly Temples is not repudiated. This suggests that, with the events of the Gospel inaugurated in the appearance of Gabriel to Zechariah, Luke understands the special significance of the Temple under the old covenant as having come to an end.

Luke 2,22-39: the presentation of Jesus in the Temple. — While sacrifices would have been offered on such an occasion, ναός is not used. The parents of

---

24. W.R. FARMER, *The Synoptic Problem*, London, 1964; M.D. GOULDER, *Luke – A New Paradigm*, Sheffield, 1989.

Jesus are depicted as Torah-observant, but the emphasis in this narrative is on the fulfilment of eschatological expectations derived from the Isaiah tradition as interpreted by Simeon and Anna, in which the former espouses universalist as well as nationalist hopes.

Luke 2,41-50: the childhood pilgrimage of Jesus to Jerusalem at Passover. — This passage is significant in confirming the Torah-observance of Jesus' family, and also in that Jesus identifies the Temple as his father's house. While Passover would have been an occasion for undergoing purity rituals and partaking of the sacrificial lamb, the emphasis is on Jesus' claim to divine sonship, and by implication to as yet undefined jurisdiction over the Temple.

Luke 4,1-13: the temptation narrative. — Scholars debate the original order of the temptations, with the majority arguing that Matthew follows the sequence of Q. In this case, Luke would be indicating a theological purpose in altering the order of the temptations so that the sequence comes to a climax in the Temple. In this Luke foreshadows the progress of Jesus towards Jerusalem in the gospel narrative, as his vocation is tested in three eschatologically significant locations. Donaldson has drawn particular attention to the progress of the *shekinah* in Ezek 43,2, as the glory of God returns at the restoration, from the wilderness, via the Mount of Olives, to the Temple[25]. This would seem further substantiation of the position taken in this study that Luke presents Jesus as the earthly embodiment of *shekinah* in the gospel, and in Acts the divine presence is portrayed as dispersed with the spread of the Church[26].

Luke 13,34-35: the desolation saying. — As noted above, the allusion to the Temple is disputed. It would seem unlikely, however, that there is no reference to the Temple in this text, though not to the exclusion of a wider range of meanings. While it has been argued that there is no reference to the destruction of Jerusalem in this text[27], it is most unlikely that Luke's original readers would have failed to discern an allusion to this event in this saying. The desolation is not in Luke a consequence of rejection of Jesus himself, which has not yet taken place, but rather the consequence of repeated rejection and persecution of the prophets, in continuity with whose ministry Jesus pronounces judgement[28]. In the prophetic tradition judgement does not necessarily mean inevitable destruction, but hopes rather to evoke repentance[29]. Nevertheless, Luke was writing in the aftermath of the events of 70 CE, and this text could therefore have been interpreted by his original readers only in terms of this judgement having been meted out on Jerusalem, and therefore as having been inevitable were Jerusalem to reject Jesus as it had the prophets before him.

25. T.L. DONALDSON, *Jesus on the Mountain*, Sheffield, 1985, p. 97.

26. Cf. K. BALTZER, *The Meaning of the Temple in the Lukan Writings*, in *HTR* 58 (1965) 263-277.

27. C.H. GIBLIN, *The Destruction of Jerusalem according to Luke's Gospel*, Rome, 1985, p. 42 argues that the abandonment of Jerusalem consists in being without Jesus' ministry. Even if ἔρημος was not in the original text, however, readers would have discerned the allusion to the events of 70 CE, and Luke would have been aware that this inference would have been drawn.

28. *Ibid.*, p. 41.

29. Jer 6,1-8; 26,2-23; Micah 3,1-12; Zeph 3,1-8; 2 Macc 6,12-17.

Luke 19,45–21,38: Jesus' attack on the traders, and subsequent teaching and debating with the authorities in the Temple court. — The emphasis on the Temple as a place of prayer[30] and teaching[31], with the sacrificial cult mentioned rarely[32], with Jesus in frequent conflict with established authority[33], would seem to emphasise continuity with the prophetic tradition of Israel. Unlike Matthew (21,14), Luke makes no mention of healings by Jesus in the Temple. This text includes several pericopae, some of which require separate treatment.

Luke 19,45-46: Jesus' attack on traders in the Temple court. — This is a much briefer account than in Mark (11,15-17) and Matthew (21,12-13), and does not specify the financial transactions taking place. It is notable that the citation of Isa 56,7 omits the reference to all nations, and that Jer 7,11 forms part of a prophecy of the destruction of the Temple. Arguably the omission of reference to all nations from the quotation from Isaiah is because Luke wrote after the Temple had been destroyed, at a time when this text was incapable of fulfilment. However, if, as has been argued in this paper, Luke wrote against a background of expectation of rebuilding of the Temple, then his first readers would not have assumed that (Trito-)Isaiah's prophecy could no longer be fulfilled. Luke's omission of the reference to all nations therefore reflects his own understanding of the Temple as having no eschatological role. He does not anticipate any eschatological fulfilment of Isaiah's prophecy of worshippers from all nations gathering in the Temple.

Luke 21,5-6: the destruction saying, followed by the eschatological discourse. — Whereas in Mark (13,1-2) and Matthew (24,1-2) the destruction saying accompanies Jesus' final departure from the Temple and the eschatological discourse is delivered from the Mount of Olives, in Luke these events take place within the Temple precincts. While the final recorded speech of Jesus in the Temple, the eschatological discourse is not intended as the conclusion to his ministry there, as 21,37-38 suggest a continuing teaching ministry in the Temple after this discourse. The expectation that the Temple would be destroyed is unequivocal, and there is no hint that this could be averted, or that a new Temple might be built.

Luke 21,20-24: the desolation of Jerusalem. — The reference in Mark (13,14) and Matthew (24,15) to the desecration of the Temple through the installation of an idol is replaced with a more general reference to a siege of Jerusalem. The Temple itself is not mentioned, but cannot be separated from the siege and destruction of Jerusalem. Irrespective of whether the differences between Luke in 21,20.24 and the account in Mark and Matthew can be attributed to Luke's knowledge of the events of 70 CE, it is clear that scriptural allusions to the destruction of 587 BCE are employed[34]. While reference is made to captivity and exile of the people, this point is not laboured or embellished with allusions to Titus's carrying the cultic apparatus along with his Jewish captives in triumph to Rome. This, it will be argued below, is to avoid an impression that Rome has

30. Luke 19,46; so also 2,37; 18,9-14; 24,53; Acts 2,46; 3,1; 22,17.
31. Luke 19,47; 21,37.38; so also Acts 3,12-26; 5,19-20.42.
32. (Luke 19,45); cf. Acts 2,46; 3,1.
33. Luke 19,45–20,8.19-40; so also Acts 4,1-21; 5,17-40.
34. Isa 63,18; Dan 8,13; Zech 12,2-3.

become the locus of divine presence in place of Jerusalem. While the concluding phrase ἄχρι οὗ πληρωθῶσιν καιροὶ ἐθνῶν could suggest that Jerusalem might one day be restored when the time comes for the gentiles to be judged[35], it is also open to interpretation as suggesting that the destruction would be complete[36]. As the eschatological discourse proceeds to recount the events immediately antecedent to the parousia (21,25-28), it would seem more likely that any future restoration of Jerusalem and the Temple is precluded[37]. This does not necessarily imply irrevocable judgement on the Jewish people[38], but rather points to a redemption of cosmic proportions which would not include but would transcend the restoration of Jerusalem and its Jewish Temple. For Luke the role of the Temple in salvation history has been completed, and it would therefore not be restored.

Luke 22,66-71: the trial of Jesus before Caiaphas. — Unlike Mark (14,58) and Matthew (26,61), Luke makes no reference to any accusations regarding the threatened destruction of the Temple. This despite the fact that Luke records Jesus' having pronounced this destruction within the Temple and in the hearing of the populace. However, in omitting reference to the Temple here, Luke is able both to avoid the ambiguities of a false charge and to separate the death of Jesus from the destruction of the Temple, as he continues in the crucifixion narrative to be considered below. The accusations surface, in a somewhat mutated form, in the account of the trial of Stephen in Acts (6,14)[39]. Luke presents the christological issues as of central importance to the trial of Jesus, rather than the fate of the Temple. Luke does not link the destruction of Jerusalem directly with Jesus' death, but rather sees the death of Jesus in continuity with those of martyred prophets whose message had been rejected. The judgement aspect of the destruction of the Temple is subordinated to Luke's conviction that divine presence is no longer localised there but disseminated in the expansion of the Church.

Luke 23,26-43: the crucifixion of Jesus. — As with the trial narrative, all reference to Jesus' prophecy of the destruction of the Temple is omitted[40]. Even the address to the women of Jerusalem in 23,28-31 makes no explicit reference to the destruction of the city. Luke's separation of the death of Jesus from the destruction of the Temple becomes most apparent in the account of his death.

Luke 23,44-46: the death of Jesus. — The rending of the sanctuary curtain is reported before Jesus' death, rather than after as in Mark (15,38) and Matthew (27,51). The significance of this event is debated in scholarship. It has been argued that the curtain is torn to open communication between Jesus and God, just as Stephen was to see heaven opened before his death in Acts 7,56[41]. The

35. BRAWLEY (n. 2), p. 125; C.A. EVANS (n. 9), p. 313; MARSHALL (n. 9), pp. 773-774; NOLLAND (n. 9), pp. 1002-1004.
36. FITZMYER (n. 9), p. 1347; J.T. SANDERS (n. 1), p. 218.
37. Cf. C.F. EVANS (n. 9), p. 752.
38. Pace, J.T. SANDERS (n. 1), p. 218.
39. Cf. C.F. EVANS (n. 9), p. 835; MARSHALL (n. 9), pp. 847-848.
40. Cf. Matt 27,40; Mark 15,29.
41. D.D. SYLVA, *The Meaning and Function of Acts 7:46-50*, in *JBL* 106 (1987) 261-275.

rending of the curtain, however, should not be separated from the other recorded portent, that of darkness, which is clearly ominous[42]. There is no indication that Jesus' dying words are addressed to God located in the opened sanctuary. Rather, the torn curtain reveals the emptiness of the ναός, and in placing the exposure of the sanctuary prior to Jesus' death Luke indicates that it had already ceased to be a place where the divine presence was localised. The departure of the *shekinah* from the Temple is not a consequence of Jesus' death, and is therefore not in itself an act of judgement. Rather, the emptiness of the sanctuary reveals that the Temple had already completed its purpose, and the divine presence was already manifested elsewhere, in the purpose of Jesus.

Luke 24,53; Acts 2,46; 3,1; 5,20: the Temple as venue for early Christian worship and teaching. — The indications that early Christian worship in Jerusalem may have on some occasions been synchronised with the sacrificial routine of the Temple (Acts 3,1) is potentially significant, even if this is purely Lukan supposition. However, there is no suggestion of Christians participating directly in the cult until Acts 21,23.24.26.27 when Paul and others underwent a purification ritual. While the Christians are portrayed as not having ceased to regard the Temple as a place of prayer, and they are depicted as continuing Jesus' practice of using the precincts as a place of teaching, this does not mean they regarded the Temple in the same light as did other Jews[43]. Luke has not linked the destruction of the Temple to the death of Jesus, nor has he separated the Temple from the city and people of Jerusalem in his pronouncements of judgement. Christians in Jerusalem are therefore under no obligation to anticipate the destruction of the Temple in their worship or in their teaching. This does not mean that the apostles had forgotten Jesus' proclamation of the destruction of the Temple, but simply that they began to preach the Gospel where Jesus had ended his earthly ministry.

Acts 6,11–7,59: the trial and death of Stephen. — A large number of critical issues surround this text[44]. It is not necessary for the present purpose to rehearse all the debates surrounding the composition of the narrative and its historical background[45]. There is some consensus that Luke has embedded a trial narrative, including Stephen's speech, into a more original account of Stephen's having been murdered by a lynch mob. It is noteworthy that Stephen does not repeat or explicitly refute the charges on which he is arraigned in the narrative frame.

---

42. Cf. *Vitae Proph.* 12, where the tearing of the Temple curtain is an eschatological portent. For discussion see also R.E. BROWN, *The Death of the Messiah*, New York, 1994, pp. 1135-1136.

43. Cf. N.H. TAYLOR, *The Temple in Early Christian Eschatology* (forthcoming); P.W.L. WALKER, *Jesus and the Holy City*, Grand Rapids, 1996, pp. 297-299.

44. For discussion see J. BIHLER, *Die Stephanusgeschichte*, München, 1963; J.J. KIL-GALLEN, *The Stephen Speech*, Rome, 1976; M.H. SCHARLEMANN, *Stephen: A Singular Saint*, Rome, 1968.

45. For discussion see O. CULLMANN, *Von Jesus zum Stephanuskreis und zum Johannesevangelium*, in E.E. ELLIS – E. GRÄSSER (eds.), *Jesus und Paulus*, Göttingen, 1975, pp. 44-56; DUNN (n. 14), pp. 57-74; M. HENGEL, *Between Jesus and Paul*, London, 1983, pp. 1-29; SCHARLEMANN (n. 44); M. SIMON, *St Stephen and the Hellenists in the Jerusalem Church*, London, 1958; É. TROCMÉ, *The Formation of the Gospel According to Mark*, London, ²1975, pp. 215-259.

He is at the very least critical of some conceptions of the Temple[46], although scholars debate as to what precisely the thrust of his critique is. While some scholars draw attention to a dichotomy between the Tabernacle in the wilderness and the Temple[47], the notion of divine residence in earthly structures which Stephen attacks in 7,48 would apply to both, except in that the Temple is immobile and significance is therefore attached to its site[48]. In this respect Stephen stands in continuity with the prophetic tradition, as reflected both in the Deuteronomistic History and in the classical Prophets[49]. Irrespective of whether divine residence was conceptualised in literal terms[50], any challenge to the notion would have been offensive to those who believed the Temple to have been built on a uniquely sacred site, and to those whose economic and political power were derived from the Temple and its cult. Shiloh, the traditional final resting place of the Tabernacle, had been destroyed, as had the Temple built by Solomon; the destruction of the former being cited by Jeremiah in warning of the destruction of the latter[51]. This in principle leaves Herod's Temple vulnerable to divine judgement and destruction, although Stephen makes no mention of the destruction of previous edifices which had been regarded as divine dwelling places[52]. Stephen's speech cannot be understood as a refutation of the charge that he had claimed that Jesus would destroy the Temple, and would be consistent with an implied affirmation that the Temple would be destroyed. Given that the reader is in no doubt that Jesus had proclaimed the destruction of the Temple, there can be little doubt that Stephen's speech, if not a denunciation of the Temple, at the very least rejects the notion of the Temple as a divine residence and prepares for Luke's account of the dissemination of the divine presence with the spread of the Church which follows Stephen's death[53].

Before reaching any conclusions on the significance of the Temple in Luke-Acts, it would be useful to consider it in the context of other theological motifs found in the Gospel and the lukan account of the early Church. The most important of these, perhaps, are divine providence, the manifestation and inspiration of the Holy Spirit and the spread of the Church from Jerusalem to Rome, including gentiles as well as Jews in the process[54]. Rome, however, does not inherit a position forfeited by Jerusalem, and it is arguable that the line of geographical expansion cho-

---

46. DUNN (n. 14), pp. 63-67. For the contrary position see BRAWLEY (n. 2), pp. 121-123; C.C. HILL, *Hellenists and Hebrews*, Minneapolis, 1992, pp. 67-101.

47. C.R. KOESTER *The Dwelling of God*, Wilmington, 1989, p. 80; M. SIMON, *Saint Stephen and the Jerusalem Temple*, in *The Journal of Ecclesiastical History* 2 (1951) 127-142.

48. Cf. SMITH (n. 17). See also BRAWLEY (n. 2), pp. 127-132.

49. 1 Kings 8,27; Isa 66,1-2.

50. For discussion see E.P. SANDERS (n. 14), pp. 51-54.

51. Jer 7,12-15; 26,4-9. Cf. also Ps 78,60.

52. Cf. KILGALLEN (n. 44).

53. Cf. BALTZER (n. 26). See also KOESTER (n. 47), p. 98; SCHARLEMANN (n. 44).

54. CONZELMANN (n. 1); R.F. O'TOOLE, *The Unity of Luke's Theology*, Wilmington, 1984; J.T. SQUIRES, *The Plan of God in Luke-Acts*, Cambridge, 1993; TIEDE (n. 2).

sen by Luke is influenced more by his interest in Paul than by any significance attached to Rome[55]. While Luke focuses on one direction in the spread of Christianity, there is no suggestion that the imperial city becomes the centre of the Church. It is perhaps significant that, by the time Luke wrote the Gospel and Acts, Titus had destroyed Jerusalem and taken such treasures and apparatus of the Temple as could be salvaged from the flames to Rome in triumph[56]. Luke makes no allusion to this, and does not exploit the conveying of cultic apparatus from Jerusalem to Rome to support any central theme of Acts. While the narrative ends some years before these events[57], they would nonetheless have been known to the first readers of the work. Had Luke wished to intimate that Rome had inherited the centrality and symbolic significance of Jerusalem, he could have worked some allusion to the triumph of Titus into his version of the eschatological discourse, and drawn on motifs from the closing chapters of the Deuteronomic History and the prophetic corpus in doing so[58]. However, I would suggest that this is an impression Luke consciously and quite deliberately avoids. The narrative includes two quite emphatic denials of the notion of localised divine presence, delivered by Stephen and Paul, before the latter reaches Rome (Acts 7,48; 17,24). While the narrative of Acts implicitly recognises Rome as the centre of the Empire, and of the world in which the first Christians lived, the notion of divine presence is expressed not in terms of residency and centrality, but is disseminated as the Holy Spirit manifest in the life and growth of the Church. The spread of the Church is not conceived as having been in one direction only[59], even if the narrative focuses on the route from Jerusalem to Rome. A sacred site as the definitive place of communication between humanity and God has become redundant with the ministry of Jesus[60]. Localisation of the divine presence in the narrative of Luke-Acts effectively ends with the appearance of Gabriel to Zechariah at the commencement (Luke 1,8-22), and the negation or termination of divine presence is confirmed through the

55. So BRAWLEY (n. 2), pp. 28-50.

56. Josephus, *BJ* 7,148-152.

57. For discussion of the chronology of Paul's life see R. JEWETT, *Dating Paul's Life*, London, 1979; J. KNOX, *Chapters in a Life of Paul*, London, 1954; N.H. TAYLOR, *Paul, Antioch and Jerusalem*, Sheffield, 1992.

58. Cf. the interpretation of Mark as a response to the triumph of Titus by S.G.F. BRANDON, *The Date of the Markan Gospel*, in *NTS* 7 (1961) 126-141.

59. Luke's interest in the more general expansion of Christianity can be illustrated from the diversity of witnesses at Pentecost (Acts 2,8-11) and the encounter between Philip and the Ethiopian eunuch (Acts 8,26-40).

60. Cf. BRAWLEY (n. 2), pp. 119-120; BALTZER (n. 26).

rending of the sanctuary curtain, exposing the emptiness of the ναός, at
the crucifixion of Jesus, but before his death (Luke 23,45). The ending
of the localisation of the divine presence in the sanctuary with the coming of John the Baptist may be reinforced by his not following his father
in Temple service. Rather, John functions outside the official cult, offering teaching and a ritual system which can in at least some ways be
understood as an alternative to the Temple cult[61]. Furthermore, John's
role is explicitly associated in Luke-Acts with preparation for the coming of Jesus and the manifestation of the Holy Spirit in the Church[62].
Thereafter, both the appearances of the resurrected Jesus and the
empowerment by the Holy Spirit of the followers of Jesus (Acts 2) manifest the dissemination of the divine presence[63]. With the coming of John
the Baptist the Temple ceases to function as the locus of divine presence
on earth. Jesus becomes the primary manifestation of divine presence
during his ministry, but the status of the Temple as divine residence is
not refuted until the moment of Jesus' death. However, it is noteworthy
that, whereas Matthew and Mark record the rending of the veil immediately after the death of Jesus, in Luke it precedes Jesus' death. For Luke
the status of the Temple as divine residence has already ended with the
commencement of the Gospel, and is not brought about by the death of
Jesus.

In conclusion, therefore, I wish to argue that Luke's presentation of
the Temple is to be located in the context of Jewish and Christian reconstruction during the period after the Roman-Jewish war of 66-70 CE. Particularly through his use of ναός, Luke suggests that the divine presence
traditionally associated with the sanctuary of the Temple is no longer
localised in Jerusalem, or for that matter in any other sanctuary. The
shekinah had ceased to be located exclusively in the Temple with the
beginning of the Gospel, and the Jewish sanctuary had accordingly
ceased to fulfil its function long before its destruction; it had been
exposed as an empty shell at the death of Jesus. In Acts, divine presence
has come to be manifested in and through the Holy Spirit in the life of
the Church. The fall of Jerusalem and destruction of the Temple do not

    61. Luke 3,1-20. For discussion see P.J. HOLLENBACH, Social Aspects of John the
Baptizer's Preaching Ministry in the Context of Palestinian Judaism, in ANRW 19, 1979,
pp. 850-875; R.A. HORSLEY – J.S. HANSON, Bandits, Prophets and Messiahs, San Francisco, 1987, pp. 176-181; C.H. KRAELING, John the Baptist, New York, 1951; C.H.H.
SCOBIE, John the Baptist, London, 1964.
    62. Luke 3,16; Acts 1,5.22; 10,37; 11,16; 13,24.25; 19,4.
    63. BALTZER (n. 26).

represent the triumph of paganism and the Roman gods, but simply confirms that the Temple is no longer the locus of divine presence. The restoration of God's presence among the Jewish people is therefore not to be sought through aspiring to rebuild the Temple in Jerusalem, but in receiving Christian baptism and the empowerment of the Holy Spirit, and participating in the dissemination of the Gospel and spread of divine presence throughout the world.

If this hypothesis is correct, it would have implications for what has become a canon of scholarly consensus that Luke-Acts is addressed primarily to gentiles. Even if the author has a primarily gentile readership in mind, he is deeply concerned with the issue of the continuing validity of Jewish institutions, and, by implication at least, posits a path to salvation for the Jewish people apart from the Temple and its cult. Luke is undoubtedly concerned that gentile Christians should recognise their path to salvation as lying outside the boundaries of Judaism, even if deriving therefrom, and may for that reason wish to reassure them that the destruction of the Temple had no implications for them. However, the possibility needs to be considered that Luke may wish to offer to Jewish readers a sense that the Temple had lost its significance before it had been destroyed, and that a new path to salvation had already been established. Rather than seek the restoration of Jerusalem, Jewish readers of Luke-Acts should embrace the diffusion of divine presence throughout the gentile world in the life and mission of the Christian Church.

Faculty of Theology   Nicholas H. TAYLOR
Africa University PO Box 1320
Mutare
Zimbabwe

LK-APG ALS PAULUSAPOLOGIE

Wer das lukanische Doppelwerk (Lk-Apg) *narrativ* als eine Texteinheit begreift und liest[1], dem fällt die prominente Rolle auf, die der Verfasser, im Folgenden der Konvention halber »Lukas« genannt, seiner
Erzählfigur Paulus einräumt. Kann die erste Hälfte der Apostelgeschichte zu Recht als Erzählung über die Jerusalemer Urgemeinde mit
Petrus als ihrem herausragenden apostolischen Vertreter begriffen werden, so beherrscht Paulus ab der zweiten Hälfte der Apostelgeschichte
die narrative Bühne der lukanischen Erzählwelt. Dies ist um so auffälliger, als Lukas sein Doppel-Erzählwerk mit der Ankunft des Paulus in
Rom enden läßt. Lukas liebt es, seine Erzählfiguren je nach Bedarf und
Sachlage auftreten und nach getaner Arbeit auch wieder von der Erzählbühne abtreten zu lassen.

Geschickt führt Lukas seine Erzählfigur Saulus als Augenzeugen der
Steinigung des Stephanus ein (Apg 8,1a). Auf diese Weise wird seine
spätere Verfolgungstätigkeit anschaulich gemacht (V. 3; 9,1-2). In ihr
erweist sich der Pharisäer Saulus als ein überaus konsequenter Eiferer
für die Überlieferungen der Väter (22,3-5). Saulus so darzustellen, ist
aber literarische Absicht. Lukas hat offensichtlich ein großes Interesse
daran, Paulus als den Typ des vorbildlichen Pharisäerchristen auszuwei-
sen. Ausgebildet in Jerusalem zu Füßen Gamaliels (22,3), porträtiert
Lukas seine Erzählfigur Paulus als einen überaus gläubigen Juden pharisäischer Parteizugehörigkeit, dem sich mit dem Glauben an Jesus
Christus die Erfüllung alter Israelhoffnung auf Auferstehung erfüllt hat
(23,6; 28,20; vgl. Lk 2,25; 24,21). Wenn aber der Verfasser des lukanischen Doppelwerkes den christlichen Glauben als die bruchlose Vollen-
dung pharisäischer Glaubenshoffnung darstellt, so deutet das darauf hin,
daß in der Gemeinde, für die Lukas schreibt, das judenchristliche Denken eine viel eindeutigere Rolle spielt als gemeinhin angenommen[2]. Das

---

1. Vgl. hierzu ausführlich G. WASSERBERG, *Aus Israels Mitte – Heil für die Welt. Eine
narrativ-exegetische Studie zur Theologie des Lukas* (BZNW, 92), Berlin – New York,
W. de Gruyter, 1998; R.C. TANNEHILL, *The Narrative Unity of Luke-Acts. A Literary
Interpretation*, Vol. 1 & 2, Philadelphia, Fortress Press, 1986-1990; ID., *Luke* (Abingdon
New Testament Commentaries), Abingdon, Nashville, 1996.

2. Diesen Sachverhalt betont zu Recht J. JERVELL in seinen vielen Aufsätzen zur Apg,
so u.a. *Paulus in der Apostelgeschichte und die Geschichte des Urchristentums*, in NTS
32 (1986) 378-392. Vgl. jetzt auch seine jüngst erschienene Neubearbeitung der Apg in
der Meyerschen Kommentarreihe, *Die Apostelgeschichte* (KEK, 3), Göttingen, Vandenhoeck & Ruprecht, 1998.

Bild einer ausschließlich heidenchristlichen Gemeinde läßt sich nicht aufrechterhalten. Vielmehr nimmt der Verfasser des lukanischen Doppelwerkes augenscheinlich bewußt Rücksicht auf judenchristliche Traditionen und Eigenheiten. So reicht zwar grundsätzlich allein die rechte – christliche – Gottesfurcht, um Zutritt zum Heil Gottes zu erlangen (siehe Cornelius). Dennoch scheinen bestimmte Gebote der Tora weiterhin in Kraft zu sein. Die dreimalige Aufzählung der sogenannten Jakobusklauseln für christusgläubige Nichtjuden (15,20-21.29; 21,25) weist in diese Richtung. Von ihrer Aufhebung wird jedenfalls nirgends berichtet, so daß aus narrativer Sicht ihre Gültigkeit im Zusammenleben der lukanischen Gemeinde angenommen werden kann[3].

In der lk Paulusdarstellung ist es nicht zufällig, daß Paulus dem Antrag pharisäischer Christen auf Beschneidung (15,5), den der Apostelkonvent in Jerusalem abwehrte (V.19), selbst wenig später tatsächlich entspricht, indem er in Derbe seinen nichtjüdischen Begleiter Timotheus beschneidet (16,1-3). Wenn überhaupt, dann müßten christlicherseits die Jerusalemer Apostel Petrus und Jakobus gegen Paulus einschreiten. Aber sie schweigen. Petrus ist nach dem Apostelkonzil, auf dem er ein letztes Mal (für Paulus!) das Wort ergreift, sich – lang, lang ist's her – seiner Vorreiterrolle in der Völkermission erinnert und diese Mission verteidigt (15,7-12), für immer von der lukanischen Erzählbühne verschwunden. Lukas benötigt Petrus nicht weiter für seine Paulusapologie. Vermutlich konnte er mit ihm auch die übrige Petrustradition nicht verbinden, auch nicht in Rom (Apg 28; vgl. 1 Clem 5).

So verbleibt allein der Herrenbruder Jakobus, der den treuen Pharisäerchristen Paulus nach Beendigung seiner dritten Missionsreise in Jerusalem begrüßt. Auffällig ist, daß -ähnlich wie schon bei Jesus und Stephanus – auch in diesem Fall die Gerüchte und Anschuldigungen jüdischerseits gegen Paulus offenkundig falsch sind. Daß Paulus gegen jüdische Gebräuche und Sitten verstoße (22,21), er somit anti-jüdisch[4], d.h. pauschal gegen das jüdische Volk eingestellt sei (V. 28), ist für die lukanischen Leser ein Hohn. Gerade ihr Paulus erweist sich in seinem Christsein doch als ein treuer Jude. Daß aufgebrachte »Juden aus der Asia« (V. 27) die Verhaftung des orthodoxen Jude(nchristen) Paulus

---

3. Selbstverständlich darf nicht unmittelbar von der erzählten auf die historische Welt kurzgeschlossen werden. Dennoch deutet die stark judenchristlich geprägte Erzählweise des Lukas darauf hin, auch mit judenchristlicher Lebensweise im Sinne der sogenannten Jakobusklauseln in der Leserschaft, an die Lukas sich wendet, zu rechnen.

4. Näheres zur Definition von Antijudaismus, s. G. WASSERBERG, *Aus Israels Mitte*, S. 19-30.

ausgerechnet in dem Moment veranlassen, als dieser sich aus Anlaß der Beendigung seines Nasiräatsgelübdes im Tempel aufhält, erscheint daher um so paradoxer.

Dies ist im Vergleich zum Paulusbild, das aus dem Corpus Paulinum zu entschlüsseln ist, eine »jüdische Überzeichnung« des Paulus. Sie ist weniger Hinweis auf eine mangelnde Sachkenntnis des Lukas als vielmehr Ausdruck seiner Überzeugung und bewußt gestaltete Erzählabsicht. Damit paßt Lukas zugleich seine Erzählfigur Paulus – so darf vermutet werden – dem Bedarf seiner Leserschaft an, und das wiederum zeigt an, daß in der lukanischen Leserschaft Judenchristen die Frage nach der Rechtgläubigkeit der Lehre des Paulus gestellt haben dürften: Träfe es zu, daß Paulus, der Christ pharisäischer Prägung, den Abfall von jüdischer Lehre und Tradition lehrte, dann könnten Judenchristen in der lukanischen Christen-Gemeinde nicht länger ihren Ort haben. Ihnen gegenüber zeichnet Lukas ein derart deutliches jüdisches Glaubensprofil seiner Erzählfigur Paulus.

Daß er sich gerade Paulus besonders verbunden weiß, zeigen nicht nur die Wir-Passagen, die – unabhängig von der Frage, ob Lukas historisch ein Paulusbegeleiter gewesen ist[5] – jedenfalls literarisch die besondere Nähe des Verfassers von Lk-Apg zu Paulus ausdrücken sollen. Auffallend ist das Bild, das Lukas vom Zusammenspiel des Paulus und Petrus zeichnet. Wenn Paulus sich selbst primär als Völkerapostel begreift (Gal 1,16), so stimmt diese Grundaussage auch mit dem Ziel der Apostelgeschichte überein (Apg 9,15; 22,21; 26,20.23; *28,28*). Aber daß Petrus die Vorreiterrolle in der Völkermission zukomme (10–11; 15,7), dürfte ein bewußtes lukanisches Stilmittel sein. Denn offenkundig war insbesondere die (der Tora gegenüber liberale) Völkermission strittig – das zeigt nicht nur insgesamt Gal 2, sondern ebenso auch Apg 11,3; 13,44f; 22,21. Deshalb bedurfte die lukanische Leserschaft, um die Völkermission zu legitimieren, einer Autoritätsperson, die für Judenchristen unumstritten war. Paulus kam dafür nicht in Frage, um so mehr aber Petrus (und mit Abstrichen Jakobus). Seine Autorität unter Judenchristen dürfte in den Kreisen der lukanischen Leserschaft – zumindest in dieser Frage – unbestritten gewesen sein. Deshalb kam er als Gewährsmann für die Völkermission in Frage. Seine Toratreue war weniger strittig als die des Paulus. Mit ihm ließ sich bewerkstelligen, was Paulus so nicht möglich war.

5. Pro: C.-J. THORNTON, *Der Zeuge des Zeugen. Lukas als Historiker der Paulusreisen* (WUNT, 56), Tübingen, Mohr, 1991, und contra: J. WEHNERT, *Die Wir-Passagen der Apostelgeschichte. Ein lukanisches Stilmittel aus jüdischer Tradition* (GTA, 40), Göttingen, Vandenhoeck & Ruprecht, 1989.

Geschickt stellt Lukas die Bekehrung seiner Erzählfigur Paulus in Apg 9 der »Bekehrung[6] des Petrus zur Völkermission« in Apg 10–11 voran. Petrus ebnet den Weg, den Paulus dann in seinem Gefolge beschreiten kann. Denn über den Gewinn von Cornelius und dessen Haus für den christlichen Glauben hinaus erfahren wir nichts von einer Völkermission des Petrus. Für ihn scheint diese fast in Vergessenheit geraten zu sein, als er auf dem Apostelkonzil – das aufgrund der erfolgreichen Völkermission des Paulus (und Barnabas) erforderlich wurde (15,1-5) – sich wieder ihrer erinnert (V. 7). So zeichnet Lukas dem Leser nicht nur ein Bild harmonischer Arbeitsteilung in der Missionsarbeit, sondern mehr noch: Der lk Petrus schlüpft in die Rolle des »historischen« Paulus; *er* (Petrus) wird nun zum Paradigma der Völkermission. Dieser Tausch von Urbild und Abbild reicht z.T. bis in die Wortwahl. Der lk Petrus klingt – zumindest andeutungsweise – »paulinisch« (15,7-11).

Während also der lk Petrus nicht allein als erster die Völkermission entdeckt, sondern sie auch gegen judenchristliche Infragestellungen (d.i. Beschneidungsforderungen) verteidigt, bleibt dabei derjenige, der danach vor allem die Völkermission erfolgreich ausführt, auffallend im Hintergrund: der lk Paulus. Und dieser Paulus erscheint dem lukanischen Erzählduktus zufolge eher als »scheiternder Judenmissionar«[7]. Dem von Lukas gezeichneten Paulus ist es primär darum zu tun, »*Juden für Jesus*«[8] zu gewinnen. Seine Mission der Völker schildert Lukas – abgesehen von wenigen Ausnahmen, z.B. in Athen, wo sich der paulinische Erfolg buchstäblich an einer Hand abzählen läßt (17,32-34) – zumindest im Ergebnis immer wieder zwar als überaus erfolgreich (14,27; 15,12; 21,19). Aber die lukanische Erzählweise hebt demgegenüber das Bemühen des Paulus hervor, Juden für den Glauben an Jesus zu gewinnen. Wiederholt folgt Lukas dem Muster: zuerst zu den Juden und erst danach (meist nach jüdischer Zurückweisung) zu den »Heiden«. Dieses Erzählmuster führt Lukas schon auf der ersten Missionsreise nach Zypern (13,5) ein, wiederholt es pointiert u.a. im pisidischen Antiochien (13,13ff), in Korinth (18,1ff) und auch in Ephesus

---

6. Wenn denn schon der Begriff der Bekehrung im Zusammenhang der Corneliusperikope gebraucht wird, so trifft diese Bezeichnung überhaupt nicht auf Cornelius zu, sondern viel eher auf Petrus. Er muß erst mit sanftem und beständigem Druck durch die Tatkraft des Heiligen Geistes von der Rechtmäßigkeit der Völkermission »überzeugt« werden (Apg 10,44-47).

7. Zu dieser Kennzeichnung siehe mein Pauluskapitel in: *Aus Israels Mitte*, S. 306-357.

8. Ich bin mir durchaus des möglichen Mißverständnisses bewußt, den dieser Begriff in der heutigen Zeit auslösen kann. Ich verwende ihn dennoch, nicht um meine eigene Einstellung in dieser heiklen Frage kundzutun – sie ist eindeutig gegen jegliche Form von Judenmission –, sondern um die narrative Erzählweise des Lukas aufzuzeigen.

(19,19), und selbst in Athen begibt sich sein Paulus zunächst in die Synagoge, bevor er auf dem Areopag die Gebildeten der Stadt zu überzeugen sucht (17,17).

Insgesamt zeichnet Lukas somit von Paulus ein Bild, das diesen als unermüdlichen Judenmissionar für Jesus ausweist: Dieser lk Paulus habe ganz und gar nichts unversucht gelassen, seine Treue und Verbundenheit mit jüdischer Glaubens- und Lebenstradition unter Beweis zu stellen. Er ist somit kein Apostat, sondern steht mit seiner Jesus-Verkündigung in nahtloser Kontinuität zu jüdisch-pharisäischer Heilserwartung. Erst in Rom nimmt der von Lukas gezeichnete Paulus seine eigene Berufung zum Völkerapostel vollends an, als er nach (wieder) nur teilweisem Erfolg seiner Jesus-Verkündigung unter den zahlreich anwesenden Juden Roms (28,24) jüdische Heilsverweigerung theologisch als »gottgewollt« deutet (V. 26-27 aus Jes 6,9). Was die Leser schon aus seiner Beauftragung in Apg 9,15 wissen, daß er primär zum Völkerapostel berufen ist — was Paulus auch selbst bewußt ist, wie wir als Leser nachträglich erfahren (22,21; vgl. V. 15) —, das bestätigt sich ihm gerade angesichts jüdischer Ablehnung einerseits und Zustimmung aus dem nichtjüdischen Lager andererseits (28,26-28).

Was uns heutigen Lesern zu Recht Magenschmerzen bereiten muß, nämlich daß Lukas sein Doppelwerk mit dem Verstockungswort des Jesaja (fast)[9] enden läßt, könnte für seine damalige Leserschaft wie die Lösung eines schwerwiegenden innergemeindlichen Problems geklungen haben: Wenn christlicher Glaube die Erfüllung alter Israelhoffnung ist, wieso kommt es, daß gerade Israel sich zu großen Teilen diesem Heilszuspruch im Jesus-Messias verweigert? Zur befriedigenden Beantwortung dieser Frage scheint es für die von Lukas anvisierte Gemeinde von entscheidender Bedeutung gewesen zu sein, daß die Verkündigung des Paulus auch weiterhin mit der jüdisch-pharisäisch-christlichen Lehre übereinstimmt. Paraphrasiert lautet Lukas' Ergebnis für die Judenchristen in seiner Gemeinde: Nicht ihr hier bei uns seid vom rechten jüdischen Heilsglauben abgewichen, sondern diejenigen Juden, die sich christlicher Heilsverkündigung gegenüber verweigern. Insofern ihr der von mir aufgewiesenen Heilslehre des Paulus folgt, seid ihr die den Väterverheißungen treu bleibenden Juden.

---

9. Natürlich ist das Jesajawort nicht das letzte Wort der Apostelgeschichte. Vielmehr muß die Korrelation von V. 26-27 mit V. 28 bedacht werden, und vor allem muß die lk Schlußaussage, daß Paulus »alle« (V. 30) willkommen heißt, die bereit sind, sich der christlichen Heilsverkündigung gegenüber zu öffnen, ernst genommen werden. Lukas trifft keine ontologische Grundaussage über »die Juden«, ihnen steht auch weiterhin die Tür zum Christus-Heil offen, aber der Vorrang Israels in der Heilsverkündigung dürfte vorbei sein.

Das lukanische Doppelwerk ist keine nach außen gerichtete Missions-
schrift[10], auch kein Dialogversuch mit der Synagogengemeinde, sondern
primär nach innen gerichtet, um den Zusammenhalt der Christen jüdischer und »heidnischer« Herkunft zu sichern. Es geht Lukas um die
innere Stabilisierung seiner Gemeinde. In ihr hat Paulus bislang eine
vielleicht im wörtlichen Sinne grund-legende Bedeutung gehabt. Sie
scheint nunmehr gefährdet. So fällt nicht nur die apologetisch angelegte
Art und Weise auf, in der Lukas seine Erzählfigur in völliger Übereinstimmung mit jüdisch-pharisäischer Heilserwartung darstellt – sie ist
kaum in Übereinstimmung zu bringen mit dem Paulus der Briefe. Typi-
scher ist noch, wie eindeutig Paulus das Erzählgeschehen der zweiten
Hälfte der Apostelgeschichte dominiert und daß Lukas darüber hinaus
sein Erzählwerk allein mit dem »Standbild« des einen Paulus enden
läßt, der freimütig und ungehindert das Evangelium verkündigt und
jeden willkommen heißt (Apg 28,30-31)[11]. So zeigt der Erzähler an,
welch herausragende Rolle Paulus im Leben seiner Gemeinde spielt
bzw. spielen soll. Die Botschaft an die Leser lautet: Jetzt ist es an euch,
in der Tradition und Lehre des (von mir nach bestem Wissen gezeichneten) Paulus zu leben.

Gilt somit »die Apostelgeschichte als Paulusgeschichte mit ausführlicher Einleitung«[12], so läßt sich dies dahingehend ausdehnen, daß das
lukanische Doppelwerk insgesamt als Paulusapologie mit ausführlicher
Einleitung angelegt scheint[13]. Schon im Proömium an Theophilus Lk
1,1-4 weist Lukas darauf hin, wie wichtig es ist, das Erzählwerk insgesamt, der Reihe nach, von vorn bis hinten genau zu lesen, um der Ziel-
absicht, nämlich der Glaubenssicherung, seines Erzählwerkes gewiß zu

10. Zur Bestimmung der lukanischen Leserschaft s. G. WASSERBERG, *Aus Israels
Mitte*, S. 41-67.

11. Näheres zur Bedeutung des Erzählschlusses Apg 28 für das Verständnis des lk
Gesamtwerkes siehe G. WASSERBERG, *Aus Israels Mitte*, S. 71-115; 352-357. Vgl. auch
den Beitrag in diesem Band von L. ALEXANDER, *Reading Luke-Acts from Back to Front*
(s. oben S. 419-446).

12. P. LAMPE – U. LUZ, *Nachpaulinisches Christentum und pagane Gesellschaft*, in J.
BECKER *et al.* (eds.), *Die Anfänge des Christentums. Alte Welt und Neue Hoffnung*, Stuttgart, Kohlhammer, 1987, S. 185-216.

13. Damit soll nicht gesagt sein, daß Lk-Apg *ausschließlich* als Paulusapologie zu
verstehen ist. Das wäre viel zu einseitig. Das von Lukas erzählte Heilsgeschehen ist christologisch und theologisch gegründet. Allerdings darf in der Anlage der lk Erzählwelt die
Rolle, die Paulus in ihr einnimmt, nicht unterschätzt werden. Paulus hat für die von Lukas
anvisierte Leserschaft offenkundig eine vergleichbare Bedeutung wie Luther für die
Lutheraner. – Im übrigen wäre es einmal interessant, in einem weiteren Schritt das lk
Jesusbild sowohl in seiner Beziehung zur lk Paulusdarstellung zu untersuchen wie darüber hinaus auch dezidiert danach zu fragen, ob und inwiefern Lukas Paulinismen verwendet. Vgl. hierzu den Beitrag in diesem Band von J. PICHLER, *Das theologische Anliegen
der Paulusrezeption im lukanischen Werk* (S. 731-743).

werden. Erst wer den lk Erzählbogen in seiner Gesamtheit erfaßt, dem erschließt sich vollends die lukanische Tendenz und Erzählabsicht. Daraus folgt: Mit Apg 28 erreicht die lk Erzählung ihr Ziel. Das weist wiederum auf die herausragende Bedeutung des Paulus für die lk Erzählkonzeption hin.

Wird zudem noch die Programmatik der beiden Simeonweissagungen für das lk Gesamtwerk erkannt (Lk 2,29-32.34b-35), so fällt auf, daß hier Begriffe auftauchen, wie z.B. τὸ σωτήριον τοῦ θεοῦ (V. 30; vgl. Apg 28,28) und ἀντιλέγω (Lk 2,34; vgl. Apg 28,22), die besonders im Zusammenhang mit der Verkündigung des Paulus eine große Rolle spielen[14]. Simeon weist schon darauf hin, was sich später an Paulus bewahrheiten wird: Paulus verkündigt nicht nur Israel, sondern dann auch den Völkern das universale Heilsgeschehen in Christus, stößt mit dieser Heilsbotschaft aber vor allem auf jüdischer Seite auf Ablehnung und Widerspruch. Insofern ergibt sich, vom Ende her nach vorn und dann durch das gesamte Erzählwerk gelesen, eine Abfolge von Geschehnissen, die erzählen, wie es dazu kommen mußte, was schließlich kam. Schon der greise Simeon, dieses Urbild alter Israelhoffnung, hat es so prophezeit. Was Paulus und den anderen Heilsverkündigern widerfahren ist, ist kein Unfall in der Heilsgeschichte, sondern von Gott so gewolltes Heilsgeschehen. Durch jüdische Ablehnung kommt das Heil zu den Völkern. Paulus hat dies schmerzlich erfahren und erst in Rom, als sich sein Schicksal fast vollendet hat, vollends begriffen und akzeptiert.

Das ist, grob skizziert, die von Lukas erzählte Welt, in der Paulus eine so herausragende und prominente Rolle einnimmt. Lukas hat offenkundig die Gestalt des Paulus den Bedürfnissen seiner Zeit angepaßt. Seine apologetische Darstellung zeigt an, daß die Völkermission des Paulus der Briefe in vielem so radikal war, daß der Bruch in der Folgezeit nicht nur zwischen Synagoge und Christengemeinde verlief, sondern darüber hinaus auch innergemeindlich zu außerordentlich großen Spannungen führte, so daß eine Generation nach Paulus sich Lukas veranlaßt sah, Paulus derart zu »verzeichnen«, daß es den Judenchristen unter seinen Lesern weiterhin möglich blieb, der christlichen Gemeinde zuzugehören. Insofern zählt diese apologetische Pauluserzählung mit den Deuteropaulinen zu den ersten Zeugnissen der paulinischen Wirkungsgeschichte.

Christian-Albrechts-Universität Kiel   Günter WASSERBERG
Moritz-Schreber-Str. 44
D-24211 Preetz

---

14. Ausführlich hierzu G. WASSERBERG, *Aus Israels Mitte*, S. 71-115; 134-147.

DAS THEOLOGISCHE ANLIEGEN
DER PAULUSREZEPTION IM LUKANISCHEN WERK

Dieser Beitrag stellt ein Thema zur Diskussion, das nicht nur hinsichtlich der Klärung des Begriffs Paulusrezeption geeignet ist, Kontroversen auszulösen, sondern auch in der Fragestellung selbst umstrittenen Charakter hat. Denn die Fragestellung geht implizit bereits von der Einheitlichkeit des dritten Evangeliums und der Apostelgeschichte aus. Damit aber werden zwei Bücher des NT, die selbst wiederum verschiedenen literarischen Gattungen angehören, auf ein sie verbindendes Thema hin befragt. Die Gemeinsamkeit der beiden Bücher wirft möglicherweise ein neues, überraschendes Licht auf die Erzählintention des Autors. Was Overbeck so drastisch negativ gezeichnet hat, daß es nämlich eine Taktlosigkeit von welthistorischem Rang sei, an das Evangelium die Apostelgeschichte folgen zu lassen[1], hat – bei aller Problematik und Richtigkeit des Standpunktes – eine positive Komponente. Diesen erfreulichen Aspekt gilt es im folgenden zu skizzieren. Dabei beschäftigen vor allem die Fragen: (1) Gibt es Kriterien für die Paulusrezeption und wie läßt sich Paulusrezeption nachweisen? (2) Was ist das theologische Problem der Paulusrezeption? (3) In welchem Zusammenhang stehen lukanische Komposition und Paulusrezeption?

1. *Kriterien der Paulusrezeption*

Für den Nachweis der Paulusrezeption im lukanischen Werk bieten sich Kriterien an, die G. Lohfink in zwei Aufsätzen zu den Pastoralbriefen vorgelegt hat[2]. Das gilt unbeschadet der Tatsache, daß im folgenden zunächst nur von der Paulusrezeption in der Apostelgeschichte die Rede ist. Was hier über die Apostelgeschichte gesagt wird, kann auch auf das Lukas-Evangelium übertragen werden. Der Nachweis der Paulusrezeption wird durch die jeweils unterschiedlichen literarischen Genera von

---

1. Zitiert bei J.-C. EMMELIUS, *Tendenzkritik und Formengeschichte. Der Beitrag Franz Overbecks zur Auslegung der Apostelgeschichte im 19. Jahrhundert* (Forschungen zur Kirchen- und Dogmengeschichte, 27), Göttingen, 1975, p. 182.
2. G. LOHFINK, *Die Vermittlung des Paulinismus zu den Pastoralbriefen*, in ID., *Studien zum Neuen Testament* (SBAB, 5), Stuttgart, 1989, pp. 267-289; ID., *Paulinische Theologie in der Rezeption der Pastoralbriefe*, in K. KERTELGE (ed.), *Paulus in den neutestamentlichen Spätschriften. Zur Paulusrezeption im Neuen Testament* (QDisp, 89), Freiburg, 1981, pp. 70-121.

Apostelgeschichte und paulinischen Briefen erschwert. Die deuteropau-
linischen Briefe (Eph, Kol) und die Pastoralbriefe verweisen allein
schon durch ihre Brieffiktion deutlich auf Paulus. Der Apostelgeschichte
stand diese Möglichkeit nicht zur Verfügung, bzw. der Verfasser des
lukanischen Doppelwerkes erachtete für seine Darstellung und Aussage-
absicht ein anderes Genus als vorteilhaft. Dazu kommt, daß die Theologie des Lukas narrativen Charakter hat und sich somit von der des Paulus bereits im Ansatz unterscheidet. Daher können die Kriterien von
Lohfink nur eine grundsätzliche Orientierungshilfe abgeben: (a) semantische Übereinstimmungen und Anklänge. (b) Strukturale Bestimmungen,
die ein ganz spezifisches Wortfeld aufweisen. (c) Wortfeldparallelen, die
durch zusätzliche Bezüge die literarische Abhängigkeit verraten. Für sich
allein vermögen nämlich Wortfeldparallelen zwar die Konstanz der frühchristlichen Sprache in bestimmten Konstellationen aufzuzeigen;
sie erlauben jedoch nicht den Schluß auf eine literarische Abhängigkeit
des Textes. (d) Es muß mit Verkürzungen und Simplifizierungen der
paulinischen Theologie gerechnet werden, weil der Vorgang der Paulusrezeption selbst äußerst komplex verlief. Wenn Lukas Elemente der Paulustradition über Zwischentraditionen vermittelt wurden, liegen Aktua-
lisierungen und entsprechende Nuancierungen nahe, galt es doch in
veränderter Zeit zumindest Elemente der paulinischen Theologie kom-
munikabel zu machen. Kernsätze und Kurzformeln vielleicht auch
Schlagwörter paulinischer Theologie sind denkbar und möglich.
(e) Schließlich können nicht nur Elemente paulinischer Theologie, sondern auch seiner Biographie für die christliche Verkündigung dienstbar
gemacht worden sein. In diesem Rezeptionsvorgang werden bestimmte
Elemente der paulinischen Biographie selektiv herausgegriffen, verstärkt
und literarisch zu sogenannten Patterns konzentriert. Hinter diesem
Rezeptionsvorgang kann der Versuch stehen, in kirchenpolitisch veränderter Zeit, anderen geographischen Räumen und einem veränderten
soziologischen Horizont Paulus als Vorbild und Identifikationsfigur vor
Augen zu stellen, um so eine »lebbare Paulustradition« zu entwickeln[3].
    Die Punkte a-b (bzw. c) würden auf eine *literarische Paulusrezeption*
schließen lassen, während sich die Punkte d-e eher für eine *traditionsgeschichtliche Erklärung* empfehlen. Beide Grundmöglichkeiten der Paulusrezeption können unbehindert von der »Paulinismus-Hypothese«[4]
durchgeführt werden. Sie setzen auch nicht notwendigerweise beim Verfasser der Apostelgeschichte eine Kenntnis der paulinischen Briefe vor-

---

3. Für die Kriterien cf. LOHFINK, *Vermittlung*, p. 275.
4. Cf. P.-G. MÜLLER, *Der »Paulinismus« in der Apostelgeschichte. Ein forschungs-
geschichtlicher Überblick*, in K. KERTELGE (ed.), *Paulus*, pp. 157-201.

aus, sondern würden auf diese offene Frage eine Antwort geben. Die dritte Grundmöglichkeit der Paulusrezeption geht davon aus, daß Lukas die Paulusbriefe gekannt und (zumindest für die Abfassung einzelner Teile der Apostelgeschichte) benutzt hat. Indem Lukas paulinische Ausdrücke und Gedanken übernommen und miteinander verflochten hat (conflation), entstand aus paulinischem Material etwas ganz Neues[5].

2. *Zum Problemhorizont*

Bei der Paulusrezeption der Apostelgeschichte gilt es nicht bloß das sprachlich syntaktische Problem mit zu berücksichtigen, sondern auch und vor allem die theologischen Implikationen. Wenn Lukas in seinem Vorwort die ἀσφάλεια betont (Lk 1,4 als letztes Wort eines kunstvollen Satzes), so muß man wohl fragen, womit die lukanische Gemeinde zu kämpfen hat bzw. wodurch die lukanische Gemeinde verunsichert wird.

Der aufmerksame Beobachter erkennt bei der Paulusdarstellung des Lukas ein Dilemma, das sich nur schwer lösen läßt. Einerseits gibt es das Interesse an Paulus, andererseits vermeidet Lukas in seiner Darstellung bedeutende Kategorien der paulinischen Theologie. Lukas findet es offenbar nicht notwendig, zentrale Punkte des paulinischen Selbstverständnisses aufzugreifen. Sehr massiv zeigt sich diese Differenz zwischen dem originalen Paulus und dem lukanischen Paulus im Begriff des Apostels. Paulus kämpft ein Leben lang um diesen Titel. In der Apostelgeschichte findet sich die ehrenvolle Bezeichnung nur in Relikten (Apg 14,4.14). Dieses Defizit ist hinsichtlich der Frage der Paulusrezeption um so bedauernswerter, als die Verbindung von Apostolat und Evangelium charakteristisch paulinisch ist. Von dieser Verbindung her resultiert erst die Ermächtigung zur gültigen, verbindlichen Interpretation des überlieferten Evangeliums. Durch die Verbindung von Evangelium und Apostolat ist auch schon die Krise gekennzeichnet, die eintreten mußte, wenn die Apostel nicht mehr lebten, und vor allem wenn Paulus nicht mehr lebte. Diese theologische Krise prägt die lukanische Kirche und um diese Krise zu bewältigen, greift Lukas zur Feder.

Die Verbindung von Apostolat und Evangelium inkludiert für die Weitergabe des Glaubens in der nachapostolischen Generation folgenden Arbeitsauftrag: »De facto, angesichts des Todes des Apostels, bedeutet der Anspruch der Kanonizität der apostolischen Auslegung die Historisierung des Evangeliums. Die ursprünglich nicht vorgesehene apostellose Zeit der Kirche wird damit auf die Aufgabe festgelegt, diese

---

5. Cf. L. AEJMELAEUS, *Die Rezeption der Paulusbriefe in der Miletrede (Apg 20,18-35)* (AASF.B, 232), Helsinki, 1987.

Historisierung zu überwinden und dennoch dem Anspruch der Normati-
vität, der die Historisierung de facto bewirkt hat, Rechnung zu tragen«[6].
    Lukas stellt sich diesem Problem, indem er Paulus als Christ der zwei-
ten Generation zeichnet. Als solcher tritt Paulus in theologischen Fragen
in die Fußstapfen des Petrus. Das wird in den Missionsreden[7] der Apostelgeschichte besonders deutlich. Ein aufmerksamer Beobachter
bemerkt rasch, daß die beiden Protagonisten der Apostelgeschichte,
zumindest vor einem ähnlichen Adressatenkreis dasselbe Predigtmuster
verwenden. Dieses Predigtschema der Missionsreden haben vor allem
Dibelius[8], Schweizer[9] und Wilckens[10] herausgearbeitet.
    Fügt man zu dem Predigtschema noch Überlegungen der antiken Rhe-
torik, dann ergibt sich für die Interpretation der Reden eine interessante
theologische Relevanz. Die Missionsreden der Apostelgeschichte stellen
nicht nur die Elemente für das kirchliche Glaubensbekenntis zur Verfügung[11], sondern sie betonen auch die fundamentale Übereinstimmung
von Petrus und Paulus im christlichen Glauben. Das geht besonders aus
der Parallelität der Rede des Paulus in Antiochien in Pisidien mit der
Pfingstpredigt des Petrus hervor. Ein Vergleich zeigt, daß die beiden
großen Gestalten der frühen Kirche im Kerygma eins sind. So weist die
Rede des Paulus im pisidischen Antiochien gleich mehrfach Berührungen zur Pfingstpredigt des Petrus auf[12]. In beiden Reden bedeutet die
Auferweckung Jesu die zentrale Heilstat Gottes, spielt Ps 16,10 für die
Argumentation eine wichtige Rolle (2,27; 13,35), steht David als Typus
Jesus gegenüber, und das Moment der Zeugenschaft wird eigens betont
(2,32; 13,31b). Mit diesen Übereinstimmung ist weiters impliziert, daß
nicht vergangene Kontroversen ausgebreitet werden, sondern die gegenwärtige gemeinsame Überzeugung in wesentlichen Fragen und Diskussi-
onspunkten dargelegt wird. Die Apostelgeschichte liefert somit zu bren-

---

6. P. VON DER OSTEN-SACKEN, *Die Apologie des paulinischen Apostolats*, in ID., *Evangelium und Tora. Aufsätze zu Paulus* (Theologische Bücherei, 77), München, 1987, pp. 131-149, dort 149.
    7. Cf. M.L. SOARDS, *The Speeches in Acts. Their Content, Context, and Concerns*, Louisville, KY, 1994.
    8. M. DIBELIUS, *Die Reden der Apostelgeschichte und die antike Geschichtsschreibung*, Heidelberg, 1949, p. 33.
    9. E. SCHWEIZER, *Zu den Reden der Apostelgesschichte*, in ID., *Neotestamentica*, Zürich – Stuttgart, 1963, pp. 418-428.
    10. U. WILCKENS, *Die Missionsreden der Apostelgeschichte. Form- und traditionskritische Untersuchungen* (WMANT, 5), Neukirchen-Vluyn, [3]1974.
    11. Cf. J. ERNST, *Lukas und das kirchliche Glaubensbekenntnis*, in J. HAINZ (ed.), *Theologie in Werden. Studien zu den theologischen Konzeptionen im Neuen Testament*, Paderborn, 1992, pp. 105-124.
    12. Cf. M.D. GOULDER, *Type and History in Acts*, London, 1964, p. 83.

nenden Fragen der werdenden Kirche Konvergenzerklärungen[13]. Für die lukanische Darstellung hat das zur Folge, daß aus den früheren Kontrahenten (vgl. Gal 2) einmütige Partner geworden sind[14]. Es geht sogar so weit, daß Petrus in der Apostelgeschichte zum Vorreiter für paulinische Positionen wird und der antiochenische Zwischenfall aus diesem Grund gar nicht möglich ist. Diese Aussage unterstreichen auch zahlreiche Parallelmotive in der Petrus- und in der Paulusdarstellung[15]. Insofern der direkte und explizite synkritische Vergleich zwischen den beiden Protagonisten entfällt, muß im Unterschied zu den *Vitae parallelae* des Plutarch gerade an diesem Punkt die entscheidende Aussage gesehen werden. Es geht nicht nur um die Verständigung zwischen beiden, sondern um ihren ungetrübten Konsens in so wichtigen Fragen wie denen des rechten Glaubens, der Ekklesiologie und der gemeinschaftlichen Feier der Eucharistie.

3. *Literarische Paulusrezeption*

Die Beschäftigung mit dem Paulinismus der Apostelgeschichte macht sehr bald deutlich, daß das Paulusbild der Apostelgeschichte ein eigenartiges Doppelgesicht aufweist. Einerseits gibt es das Faktum und das theologische Problem, daß Paulus von jüdischer Seite nicht akzeptiert wurde, so sehr er sich ein Leben lang auch darum bemühte. Ihn verfolgte die Synagoge. Man warf ihm vor, er sei ein jüdischer Häretiker. Diese Vorwürfe gibt es auch in der Apostelgeschichte. Dennoch gibt es auch genau die entgegengesetzte Tendenz, nämlich Paulus von diesen Vorwürfen zu entlasten. Der Völkerapostel steht in engster Verbindung mit Jerusalem, und pflegt zu Petrus und Jakobus engen Kontakt (vgl. z.B. Apg 9,10-18.26-30; 15,1-33). Paulus wird als orthodoxer Pharisäer gezeichnet, der bei seiner Mission den heilsgeschichtlichen Vorrang Israels stets anerkennt. Über ihn wird gesagt, er sei wegen der Hoffnung Israels ein Gefangener. Diese Ambivalenz des lukanischen Paulusbildes vermögen zwar die beiden folgenden Beobachtungen nicht aufzulösen, aber sie möchten zeigen, daß die Frage nach der Paulusrezeption der Apostelgeschichte die benannte Aporetik zu erhellen vermag.

13. Für A. STÖGER, *Jerusalem – Rom. Neuere Kommentare zur Apostelgeschichte*, in *BL* 55 (1982) 102-105, p. 103, sind die brennenden ökumenischen Fragen ein Grund für das besondere Interesse an der Apostelgeschichte.
14. Cf. L. WEHR, *Petrus und Paulus – Kontrahenten und Partner. Die beiden Apostel im Spiegel des Neuen Testaments, der Apostolischen Väter und früher Zeugnisse ihrer Verehrung* (NTAbh, 30), Münster, 1996.
15. Cf. K. BERGER, *Hellenistische Gattungen im Neuen Testament*, in *ANRW* II.25.2, 1984, p. 1176.

a. Zeugenbegriff

Der Zeugenbegriff der Apostelgeschichte muß seiner Grundintention nach als umfassender, autoritativer Legitimationsnachweis gedeutet werden. Dieser Nachweis geschieht hauptsächlich im Rahmen einer ekklesiologischen Fragestellung. Das kommt besonders zum Ausdruck, indem jeweils eine höhere Instanz die entscheidenden Autoritäten der lukanischen Kirche absichert. Aus dem Nachweis bezüglich der Vokabel »bezeugen«[16] fallen jene Stellen heraus, die soviel bedeuten wie »einen guten Ruf haben« (6,3; 10,22; 16,2; 22,12). Bedeutend ist das Verbum μαρτυρεῖν an jenen Stellen, an denen Gott selbst Zeugnis ablegt (13,22; 14,3; 15,8). Wofür sich Gott an diesen Stellen engagiert, ist die *Verkündigung des Evangeliums unter Juden und Heiden.* Genau diesen Inhalt erkennt Paulus als seinen Auftrag und eben diesen Auftrag bezeichnet er in der Abschiedsrede in Milet als seine persönliche Diakonie. Kompliziert wird die Lage in den Verteidigungsreden.

Paulus, der als Angeklagter vor den religiösen und profanen Instanzen steht, erfährt eine neue Rollenbestimmung. Aus dem Angeklagten wird der Zeuge! Diese Formulierung klingt paradox. Die Widersprüchlichkeit macht jedoch auf ein wichtiges Faktum aufmerksam. Die seltsame Transformation des Angeklagten zum Zeugen hat Auswirkungen auf die Bestimmung der literarischen Funktion der Verteidigungsreden. Sie fungieren als Metaebene für die Reflexion der Heidenmission. Während die Ankläger den religiösen Eifer des Paulus bezeugen (22,5; 26,5), tritt Paulus vor »groß und klein« (26,22) bzw. »vor allen Menschen« (22,15) als Zeuge auf. Mit anderen Worten weisen die genannten Belege Paulus als Zeugen jener Kirche aus, die sich aus Juden und Heiden zusammensetzt. Damit wird Paulus den zwölf Aposteln als dreizehnter Zeuge zur Seite gestellt. Nun gibt es aber auch noch den Beleg in 26,16, wo von Paulus gesagt wird, er sei »Diener und Zeuge«. Wie Burchard richtig erkannt hat[17], wird mit der Begrifflichkeit des Zeugen, die Gleichwertigkeit des Paulus gegenüber den Aposteln betont. Was also bewirkt die Verwendung des Begriffs von ὑπηρέτης?

Das Wort kommt bei Paulus und Lukas insgesamt sieben Mal vor, davon entfallen zwei Belege auf das Lukasevangelium, vier Stellen auf die Apostelgeschichte und ein Beleg auf Paulus (Lk 1,2; 4,20; Apg

---

16. Ausführlicher bei J. PICHLER, *Dimensionen des Zeugenbegriffs in der Apostelgeschichte,* in G. LARCHER (ed.), *Gott-Bild. Gebrochen durch die Moderne.* FS K.M. Woschitz, Graz, 1997, pp. 394-403.

17. C. BURCHARD, *Der dreizehnte Zeuge. Traditions- und kompositionsgeschichtliche Untersuchungen zu Lukas' Darstellung der Frühzeit des Paulus* (FRLANT, 105), Göttingen, 1970, pp. 129-136.

5,22.26; 13,5; 26,16; 1 Kor 4,1). Üblicherweise bedeutet die Vokabel »Gehilfe«. Nur in Lk 1,2 und Apg 26,16 hat die Vokabel übertragene Bedeutung. Möchte man die Bedeutung von ὑπηρέτης präzise fassen, kann man zunächst darauf hinweisen, daß die Bezeichnung »Diener« auf die Abschiedsrede des Paulus zurückweist. Dort wurde die Verkündigung des Paulus als diakonische Aufgabe bestimmt. In seiner Verkündigungstätigkeit weiß sich Paulus von seinem Herrn Jesus in den Dienst genommen. Das gilt aber nicht nur für Paulus, sondern auch für die Apostel (Lk 9,24f; Apg 1,2.8; 10,42) und die Funktionsträger der nachapostolischen Zeit (20,28.32).

Der Kontext zeigt, daß an dieser Stelle die *Erwählungsaussage* großes Gewicht besitzt. Die theologische Kategorie der »Erwählung« spielt für die Bestimmung zum Zeugen eine entscheidende Rolle. Es war gerade dieses Argument, das Paulus für sein Apostelamt vorbrachte. Aus diesen Gründen liegt es nahe, den Begriff des Dieners als bewußte Verklammerung von Lk 1,2 und Apg 26,16 aufzufassen. In einer solchen Perspektive bestätigt die Stelle, daß Lukas erst mit Paulus einen umfassenden Nachweis für die Glaubenssicherheit seiner Gemeinde leisten kann. Das bedeutet mit anderen Worten, daß die Theologie des Paulus, insbesondere seine Artikulation und Begründung einer universalen Kirche, für die lukanische Kirche zum *Depositum fidei* gehört. Die Verbindung des Lukas-Evangeliums und der Apostelgeschichte zeigt sich auch durch die Rechtfertigungslehre.

b. Rechtfertigungsterminologie

Lukas verbindet in seinem Doppelwerk die Rechtfertigungsterminologie mit den großen Gestalten seines Werkes. Nach Lukas ist nicht nur Paulus der Theologe der Rechtfertigung, sondern auch Petrus und Jesus selbst benutzen diese Redeweise.

Es empfiehlt sich zunächst in Apg 13,38-39 zu beginnen[18], weil diese Stelle am deutlichsten zeigt, daß Lukas die paulinische Rechtfertigungslehre mit beachtlicher Präzision wiedergibt. Ohne die Stelle allzusehr pressen zu wollen, könnte man behaupten, daß von der antiken Rhetorik her, der Beleg an markanter Stelle steht. Die beiden Verse bilden nämlich die Quintessenz der Argumentatio. Vom Gedankengang der Rede bilden dann die erwählungstheologischen Aussagen der Narratio (vv. 17-25) und die kreuzestheologischen Aussagen der Argumentatio (vv. 26-37) die Wurzeln von der Rechtfertigung des Gottlosen. Das erinnert an

---

18. Cf. J. PICHLER, *Paulusrezeption in der Apostelgeschichte. Untersuchungen zur Rede im pisidischen Antiochien* (Innsbrucker theologische Studien, 50), Innsbruck, 1997, pp. 298-306.

den Galaterbrief. Dort verwendet Paulus die Rechtfertigungsterminologie im Rahmen des Koordinatensystems von Erwählung und Kreuz
Christi zur Auslotung der besonderen Situation in Galatien. Die Rechtfertigungsbotschaft ist damit aktualisierte und transformierte Kreuzes-
theologie[19].

Daß Gott sein Volk erwählt hat, mit dieser Glaubensaussage setzt der
heilsgeschichtliche Überblick in Apg 13 ein und führt dann über die
Aussage des Todes Jesu zur Rechtfertigungsterminologie in vv. 38-39.
Diese beiden Verse haben die Gemüter zahlreicher Interpreten erregt.
Auszugehen ist von der klaren oppositionellen Struktur der beiden
Verse. Immer dann, wenn diese Gegensätzlichkeit nicht klar genug gesehen wurde, neigte man dazu, diese Verse als lukanisches Zeugnis einer
Rechtfertigung auf Raten zu deuten, was wiederum kein gutes Licht auf
Lukas selber warf. Denn der galt in den Augen dieser Exegeten als einer
jener, der mit der paulinischen Theologie einfach überfordert war. Mußner hat allerdings, indem er mit dem Inventar und den Regeln der gene-
rativen Transformationsgrammatik die sogenannten Tiefenstruktursätze
von Gal 2,16 erhob, überzeugend nachgewiesen, daß sich die Aussagen
in Apg 13,38f auf die Grundsätze der Rechtfertigungslehre in Gal 2,16
rücktransformieren lassen[20]. Hinter vv. 38f steht sinngemäß die Aussage: »Gott rechtfertigt jeden, der glaubt. Das Gesetz des Mose kann
nicht rechtfertigen«.

Die nächste Parallele findet sich in Apg 15,9-11. In dieser Rede am
Apostelkonzil kommen die theologisch bedeutsamen Begriffe vor:
»durch die Gnade«, »glauben« und »gerettet werden«. An dieser Stelle
spricht Petrus die paulinische Rechtfertigungslehre aus, um ein damit
zusammenhängendes Problem zu lösen. Kontroversen löst die Behauptung einiger Judenchristen aus, daß mit dem Glauben auch die Beschneidung und das Gesetz heilsnotwendig seien. Dieser irrigen theologischen
Anschauung begegnet der lukanische Petrus mit dem Hinweis auf frühe-
res Wissen (v. 7: ὑμεῖς ἐπίστασθε ὅτι ἀφ' ἡμερῶν ἀρχαίων ἐν ὑμῖν
…). Dieses Wissen ist durch seinen persönlichen Rechenschaftsbericht
gewährleistet und betont seine persönliche Vorreiterrolle bezüglich der
Heidenmission. Damit ist klar, »daß 'paulinisch' kein Unterscheidungs-
kriterium ist gegenüber dem ursprünglich Christlichen«[21]. An diesem
Punkt kommt die synkritische Arbeitsmethode des Lukas mit ihren

19. J. BECKER, *Paulus. Der Apostel der Völker*, Tübingen, ²1992, p. 306.
20. F. MUSSNER, *Petrus und Paulus – Pole der Einheit. Eine Hilfe für die Kirchen* (QDisp, 76), Freiburg, 1976, p. 106.
21. K. LÖNING, *Paulinismus in der Apostelgeschichte*, in K. KERTELGE (ed.), *Paulus* (n. 2), pp. 202-234, dort 227.

impliziten hermeneutischen Konsequenzen voll zur Geltung. Paulus beschreitet Wege, die Petrus persönlich erkämpft und gegenüber der Gemeinde in Jerusalem auch theologisch verantwortet hat. Freilich werden die Wege mit authentisch paulinischen Argumenten beschritten. Durch diese Darstellung wird Petrus zum Prototyp des Heidenmissionars. Er setzt sich mit der Rechtfertigungstheologie und durch die Praxis des συνεσθίειν für paulinische Positionen ein und garantiert deren Rechtgläubigkeit. Weil vor allem Petrus zum Garanten des rechten Glaubens wird, bleibt Paulus als Theologe merkwürdig konturlos.

Nicht genug damit! Bei genauer Betrachtung muß man feststellen, daß die Vokabel »rechtfertigen«[22] bereits im Evangelium vor allem an den Stellen Lk 16,15 und 18,9-14 theologisch bedeutsam ist. Die beiden genannten Stellen scheinen verwandt zu sein. Lk 16,15 lautet: »Ihr seid es, die sich selbst rechtfertigen vor den Menschen, Gott aber kennt eure Herzen«. Durch den Gegensatz »vor den Menschen« und zur Opposition »Gott aber kennt« verlagert sich das Gewicht der Aussage ganz auf die theologische Ebene. Die Erzählung in Lk 18,9-14 modelliert den theologischen Gehalt von δικαιοῦν geradezu plastisch.

Man kann die Perikope als Lehrstück lukanischer narrativer Theologie sehen. In der ganzen Erzählung geht es hauptsächlich um die Frage, wer der Mensch vor Gott sei. Dazu bedient sich der Erzähler zweier oppositioneller Charaktere, die zu zwei verschiedenen sozialen Gruppen gehören und die mit gewissen Vorurteilen leben müssen. Mit der Erzählung über diese beiden Menschen wendet sich Lukas gegen ein falsches Verständnis von Rechtfertigung. Nicht der Mensch rechtfertigt seine eigene Leistung, sondern Gott rechtfertigt den Sünder. Für den, der sein Sündersein erkennt, gibt es bei Gott und von Gott her Hoffnung. Das Adjektiv δίκαιος zielt also von Anfang an auf ein theologisches Geschehen. Lukas entlarvt die menschliche Grundhaltung an einem äußerst sensiblen Punkt, ist es doch gerade das Gebet, in dem der Mensch sein Inneres vor Gott ausbreitet. Die Grundstruktur des Gebetes gibt daher Aufschluß über das menschliche Selbstverständnis. Daher entartet wohl nicht zufällig das Gebet des Selbstgerechten zum Monolog. Die Richtung des Gebets geht πρὸς ἑαυτόν. Das rechte Gebet dagegen ist dialogisch ausgerichtet. Der Sünder wird gerechtfertigt, weil er in seiner Not zu Gott flieht. In diesem Fall weiß der Sünder, daß er aus Gottes Gnade lebt. Lindemann resümiert zu dieser Stelle: »Die Tatsache, daß Lk diese Erzählung enthält ist m.E. ein sehr deutlicher Hin-

---

22. In einem Gerichtswort Mt 12,37 und 11,19 par Lk 7,35. Ferner bei Lk 7,29; 10,29; 16,15; 18,14; Apg 13,38.39.

weis darauf, daß der Verfasser zumindest den Versuch gemacht hat, Tendenzen der paulinischen Theologie auch im Evangelium zu verankern und die Übereinstimmung der Lehre Jesu mit der Rechtfertigungslehre des Paulus zu behaupten«[23].

Den Umstand, daß sowohl Jesus als auch Petrus die Rechtfertigungsterminologie vor Paulus im Mund führen, kann man nicht bloß mit dem Hinweis auf das lukanische Kontinuitätsanliegen erklären. Vielmehr bedient sich Lukas einer literarischen Technik, die sein gesamtes Werk durchzieht, und die sich mit einiger Berechtigung als Legitimationstechnik bezeichnen läßt. Ihr Ziel ist es zu zeigen, daß Paulus in der apostolischen Tradition steht und die Intentionen Jesu sachgerecht interpretiert und verkündet[24]. Damit wird aber klar, daß die Paulusrezeption der Apostelgeschichte nicht als isoliertes Phänomen zu betrachten ist, sondern im Gesamtentwurf des lukanischen Werkes gesehen und gedeutet werden muß.

4. *Paulusrezeption als Verbindungselement der Jesustradition mit der Paulustradition*

Wie die Stelle Eph 2,11-22 legt auch Lukas großen Wert auf die umfassende Einheit von heidenchristlich-paulinischen und palästinisch-judenchristlichen Elementen. Der Epheserbrief mahnt »die Heidenchristen, die (eingeströmten) Judenchristen zu akzeptieren«. Infolge der sozialen und politischen Umwälzung in der Gemeinde muß Lukas das paulinisch-heidenchristliche Erbe den immer stärker werdenden judenchristlichen Traditionen anpassen, um es zu retten[25]. Auf diesem Hintergrund erklärt sich am plausibelsten auch die Ambivalenz des lukanischen Paulusbildes. Lukas möchte in seiner Darstellung Paulus sowohl für Juden- als auch für Heidenchristen akzeptabel machen. Für die Judenchristen betont Lukas vor allem den religiösen Eifer des Paulus und seine Vorbildwirkung in den praktischen Lebensvollzügen. Sie können in Paulus Trost und Hilfe finden, wenn sie das Bild des leidenden

23. A. LINDEMANN, *Paulus im ältesten Christentum. Das Bild des Apostels und die Rezeption der paulinischen Theologie in der frühchristlichen Literatur bis Marcion* (BHT, 58), Tübingen, 1979, p. 163.

24. R.L. BRAWLEY, *Luke-Acts and the Jews. Conflict, Apology, and Conciliation* (SBL MS, 33), Atlanta, 1987, p. 66, führt den Nachweis, daß die von Lukas verwendete Legitimationstechnik auch vom hellenistischen Leser erkannt werden konnte: »A hellenistic audience would have found parallels between Jesus and the protagonist in Acts clues to the true successor of the founder and to the legitimate tradition«.

25. H. SCHÜRMANN, *Das Testament des Paulus für die Kirche Apg 20,18-35*, in ID., *Traditionsgeschichtliche Untersuchungen zu den synoptischen Evangelien*, Düsseldorf, 1968, p. 325 n. 89.

Paulus sehen, der um der Hoffnung Israels willen die Fesseln trägt. Das ist der eine Aspekt der Paulusdarstellung. Der andere Teil der lukanischen Gemeinde sind die alten 'Pauliner', jene also, die Paulus zum Teil wenigstens selbst gekannt haben und wissen, daß Paulus ihre Gemeinde gegründet hat. Könnten sie ihren Paulus nicht in der lukanischen Darstellung entdecken, würde die Apostelgeschichte für ihre religiöse Sozialisation keine Identitätsstütze bedeuten, sondern noch größere Verunsicherung. Von diesen alten Paulinern wird verlangt, daß sie sich mit den Traditionen der Zugezogenen abfinden, indem Paulus als einer gezeichnet wird, »der schon alle Traditionen in sich verkörpert hat, die jene aus Palästina mitgebracht haben«[26]. Andererseits darf der originale Paulus bei diesem Aktualisierungsprozeß nicht domestiziert werden, denn wenn die Mitglieder der paulinischen Gemeinden nicht auch typisch paulinische Positionen in der Darstellung finden könnten, wäre die Darstellung unglaubwürdig. Um originale paulinische Elemente, Spitzensätze und theologische Vorstellungen für den judenchristlichen Teil erträglich und akzeptabel zu machen, werden ursprüngliche theologische Kontroverspunkte bereits in der Petrusdarstellung verankert. Die Paulusdarstellung gewinnt auf dem Hintergrund der Petrusdarstellung an Autorität und darf auf größere judenchristliche Akzeptanz hoffen. Anhand der Petrusfigur ermahnt Lukas seine judenchristlichen Leser und fordert sie auf, wenigstens in kleinen Bissen paulinische Theologie zu kosten, damit sie daran Geschmack finden.

Sieht man, daß der lukanische Petrus theologisch Positionen vertritt, die ursprünglich paulinische waren, und läßt sich nachweisen, daß Lukas paulinische Positionen wenigstens zum Teil in seinem Evangelium verankert, so kann man daraus den Schluß ziehen: Das lukanische Werk bemüht sich um eine bewußte Verbindung bzw. um eine ausgleichende Zuordnung von Jesustradition und Paulustradition. Der Ausgleich wird notwendig, weil Judenchristen, die ursprünglichen Träger der Jesustradition, auf die politischen Umbrüche des Jahres 70 in Israel reagieren: Indem in das Lukas-Evangelium paulinische Positionen einfließen, werden die Judenchristen aufgefordert die theologischen Vorstellungen der vorwiegend heidenchristlichen Bevölkerung in der Provinz Asien[27] zu

---

26. *Ibid.*, p. 325.
27. Juden aus der Provinz Asien hören die Pfingstpredigt des Petrus (Apg 2,9), verwickeln sich in ein Streitgespräch mit Stephanus (6,9) und sind schließlich der Auslöser für die Verhaftung des Paulus im Tempel (21,27). »Die Annahme hat also durchaus nichts Unglaubhaftes, daß in dem Augenblick, wo es zwischen der Jerusalemer Christengemeinde und dem Judentum zum unheilbaren Bruch kam, 62-70, palästinische Christen in Kleinasien ein neues Wirkungsfeld gefunden haben«, urteilt E. HIRSCH, *Studien zum vierten Evangelium. Text – Literarkritik – Entstehungsgeschichte* (BHT, 11),

tolerieren. Diese Toleranz würde rasch an ein Ende kommen, wenn die gesamte paulinische Theologie in das Evangelium einginge. Daher beschränkt sich Lukas auf einige wenige Herzensanliegen.

Die Synthese von Jesustradition und Paulustradition[28] zeigt sich in der Apostelgeschichte vor allem darin, daß Paulus durch seine Berufung in großer Nähe zu Jesus steht und bis ins Extrem bereit ist, den Willen des Herrn zu erfüllen und sein auserwähltes Werkzeug zu sein, und daß in die Abschiedsrede neben anderen Jesusbezügen dessen Mahnung »seid wachsam!« aus Mk 13,37 einfließt (20,21.24.35). Der programmatische Traditionswille des Lukas kommt schließlich auch noch am Ende des lukanischen Werkes voll zur Geltung. Durch die Predigt des Paulus vom Reich Gottes (vgl. 20,25) und die Lehre über den Herrn Jesus Christus in Wahrhaftigkeit und mit Freimut (28,31) knüpft Lukas wohl endgültig die Jesustradition mit der des Paulus so eng zusammen, daß zurecht von einer gegenseitigen Zuordnung gesprochen werden kann.

Indem Lukas beide Traditionsströme miteinander verwebt, macht er klar, daß der Beitrag des paulinischen Offenbarungszeugnisses für die Kirche und die christliche Verkündigung unverzichtbar ist. Mit dieser Position übernimmt Lukas auch zentrale Weisen der Artikulation des heidenchristlichen Kerygmas. Auf der anderen Seite versucht Lukas den so bedeutenden Traditionsstrom der judenchristlichen Jesustradition unverkürzt zu überliefern[29]. Dabei stellt er deutlich heraus, daß das

---

Tübingen, 1936, p. 150. Unter den in das westliche Kleinasien Zugezogenen sollen sich nach dem allerdings relativ späten Zeugnis von Eusebius auch so hervorragende Gestalten wie Philippus und Johannes befunden haben. Daher hat die Anmerkung von SCHÜRMANN, *Testament* (n. 25), p. 325 n. 91, viel für sich, daß besonders die Verteidigungsreden des gefangenen Paulus mit den Augen geflüchteter palästinischer Judenchristen gelesen werden müssen. Zur näheren Begründung, cf. PICHLER, *Paulusrezeption* (n. 18), pp. 348-351.

28. Cf. J. ROLOFF, *Apostolat–Verkündigung–Kirche. Ursprung, Inhalt und Funktion des kirchlichen Apostelamtes nach Paulus, Lukas und den Pastoralbriefen*, Gütersloh, 1965, p. 233: »Wir müssen demnach die Heimat des lukanischen Werkes, wie sich bereits anhand von Apg 20,17-38 nahelegte, am Schnittpunkt jerusalemisch-judenchristlicher und paulinisch-heidenchristlicher Tradition suchen«, F. BOVON, *Studies in Luke-Acts. Retrospect and Prospect*, in *HTR* 85 (1992) 175-196, p. 188: »The Lukan community is mixed and includes a strong Jewish-Christian element«.

29. Gestützt wird diese Vermutung zusätzlich durch die Einheit des lukanischen Werkes, cf. J. GNILKA, *Theologie des Neuen Testaments* (HTK Suppl., 5), Freiburg, 1994, p. 196; A. WEISER, *Theologie des Neuen Testaments. II. Die Theologie der Evangelien*, Stuttgart, 1993, pp. 123f; W. BEILNER & M. ERNST, *Unter dem Wort Gottes. Theologie aus dem Neuen Testament*, Wien – München, 1993, p. 440: »Die Angabe Apg 1,1 'im ersten Buch' verweist eindeutig auf Lk zurück, das also der erste Teil eines zweiteiligen Werkes ist – und dies gilt unabhängig davon, ob der Verfasser bei der Abfassung des Evangeliums schon an sein zweites Buch dachte, was allerdings wahrscheinlich gemacht werden kann«.

christliche Kerygma der Apostel mit dem des Paulus identisch ist. In diesem Sinn ordnet Lukas die Paulustradition der Apostelgeschichte und die Jesustradition des Evangeliums einander zu und versucht gerade dadurch seinen Lesern Glaubenssicherheit zu vermitteln.

Parkstraße 1/II   Josef PICHLER
A-8010 Graz

DIVINE COMMUNICATION IN LUKE-ACTS

In biblical times dreams and visions were important phenomena. It was believed that they could convey messages from God or from the divine realm. It has been suggested that in the New Testament dreaming was far less important than in the OT. In his article about dreams in *TWNT*, A. Oepke argues that, although dreams could be seen as a medium of revelation (Gen 28,11-16; 37,5-11 and 1 Kings 3,4-15), this view was criticised by some prophets (Jer 23,16-32, esp. 25-28; 29,8) and other teachers of wisdom, especially Ben Sirach (34,1-8)[1]. With regard to the NT, Oepke argues that this critical view of dreams is even more important. Although the possibility of divine revelation through dreaming is not out of the question, and although the first Christians were not totally opposed to it, we find, according to Oepke, in the NT a very critical attitude towards dreaming. He suggests that dreams are loosing their importance because in the NT God does not speak in a mysterious way, but in an open one[2]. Although it is true that in the Gospels the Greek word ὄναρ is mentioned only in the Gospel of Matthew and not in the other Gospels, we cannot say that Luke is very critical about dreaming and visions because in the sequel to the Gospel, in Acts, his second book, we do find a lot of night visions.

Because in Acts visions and dreams have an important role and because from the biblical times on dreams and visions have been interchangeable, Oepke's suggestion overstates the case. The question becomes: if it is true that in Acts visions are given an important role and if it is also true that this is in line with some of the OT statements about dreams and visions as an important form of divine revelation, why is this not the case in the Gospels; or to focus our question, in the Gospel of Luke?

The point I will make in this article is that Luke draws upon contemporary Jewish and Hellenistic modes of dream "theories". As we can learn from Acts, Luke sees dreaming as an important medium for the

---

1. A. OEPKE, ὄναρ, in *TWNT*, 5, pp. 220-238, esp. 228-231 (OT). See also A. WIKEN-HAUSER, *Die Traumgesichte des Neuen Testaments in religiongeschichtlicher Sicht*, in T. KLAUSER – A. RÜCKER (eds.), *Pisciculi. Studien zur Religion und Kultur des Altertums. FS. F.J. Dölger*, Münster, 1939, pp. 321-333. For an interesting perspective on dreams, see Job 7,14.
2. OEPKE, ὄναρ, pp. 234-238 (NT), esp. 235.

revelation of God's will. Thus Luke is a child of his age, for the Jewish and Hellenistic world took a great interest in dreams and visions as a form of communication with the divine (within Jewish realm, see e.g. 4Q544, fragm 1; within Hellenistic realm, Apuleius, *Metamorphosis*, 11,1-7.12-13.26, but also 4,27). This fits with the important stream of positive evaluation of dreams in the OT as we mentioned above. For a possible explanation of the fact that in Luke's Gospel dreams or visions are rarely mentioned, we will refer to a special aspect of the divine communication in the OT. Jesus, like Moses, speaks with God "mouth to mouth" (cf. Luke 3,22 and 9,35) and thus he does not need dreams or visions to communicate with God (see Num 12,6-8). Focusing on Luke's vision on dreams and visions will give some insights into the relations between the Gospel and its sequel Acts. In the first part I will describe visions as a means of divine communication in Acts, while in the second I will sketch Jesus' communication with God in Luke's Gospel.

1. *Dreams and Visions in Acts*

In biblical times visions and dreams were interchangeable, as is already clear from Num 12,6[3]. It is also evident from an extended quotation from the prophet Joel in the second chapter of Acts. As argued by R. Maddox such extended quotations are rather rare in Luke-Acts and where they occur they usually underline an important principle or a new phase in the dynamics of Luke's work[4]. In Acts 2,17, Joel 2,28 LXX (or 3,1 MT) is more or less quoted[5]:

> a And it shall come to pass in the last days, saith God,
> b I will pour out of my Spirit upon all flesh:
> c and your sons and your daugthers shall prophesy,
> d and your young men shall see visions (ὁράσεις)
> e and your old men shall dream dreams (ἐνυπνίοις ἐνυπνιασθήσονται)

In line with G.J. Steyn I consider c, d and e as an explanation of b[6]. They are the effects of the outpouring of the Spirit. These verses have a parallel structure, thus showing a close connection between prophecies, dreams and visions. The text from Joel is a programmatic statement for Acts. The events mentioned in the quotation must follow the coming of

---

3. A. JEFFERS, *Magic and Divination in Ancient Palestine and Syria* (Studies in the History and Culture of the Ancient Near East, 8), Leiden, 1996, p. 125.
    4. R. MADDOX, *The Purpose of Luke-Acts* (FRLANT, 126), Göttingen, 1982, p. 44.
    5. For the differences between Joel 2,28-32 (LXX and MT) and Acts 2,17-21, see now G.J. STEYN, *Septuagint Quotations in the Context of the Petrine and Pauline Speeches of the Acta Apostolorum* (CBET, 12), Kampen, 1995, pp. 74-90.
    6. STEYN, *Septuagint Quotations*, pp. 69-73.

the Spirit at Pentecost. The quotation will (partially) be fulfilled in the future. The statement about the daughters who will prophesy is fulfilled in Acts 21,9: Philip's daughters possess the gift of prophecy[7]. The parallel between visions and dreams here is in line with the statement that dreams and visions are complementary. Regarding the fact that dreams and visions are interchangeable, the statement of Joel will also be fulfilled in Acts. Quite a few visions are reported in Acts (see 9,10-16; 10,3-7.11-16; 16,9; 18,9; 23,11; 27,23; cf. 7,55-56). Although there are several levels of visions from the divine realm, all of them are means of divine communication.

The quotation from Joel is the only place in the NT where the word ἐνύπνιον (dream) is used[8]. Like Josephus, Luke is not rigidly consistent with his language in reference to dreams. In his book about dreams and dream reports in the writings of Josephus, R.K. Gnuse argues that it is not easy to define a dream or a dream report[9]. In the ancient Near East and Hellenistic world dream reports encompass a range of phenomena: visual scenes with no oral message, auditions with no visual phenomena, visual scenes with auditions and visual appearances of deities and deceased persons who deliver messages. Gnuse concludes: "One is tempted to view as a dream any experience which communicates a message to a recipient at night or during sleep". But in the ancient world some dream reports give the impression that the recipient was awake to hear an oral message. Later, however, it was said that the recipient awakens, thus implying that the recipient was really asleep throughout the experience. Because the descriptions of dreams differ it is not easy for the modern reader to recognise all kinds of dream reports. Gnuse argues that such terse reports do occur in the writings of Josephus. What applies to Josephus, may also apply to Luke. He does not consistently use one term and some night time and sleeping situations are intended as dream reports. This is in line with the way dreams and visions are described already in the OT. In Gen 15,1 we hear that the word of the Lord came to Abram in a vision, but only from the following (15,5) is it clear that this vision happens during the night: The Lord brings Abram outside and asks him to look at the sky and to count the stars. Gen 20,3-

---

7. G. DAUTZENBERG, *Urchristliche Prophetie: Ihre Erforschung, ihre Voraussetzungen im Judentum und ihre Struktur im ersten Korintherbrief* (BWANT, 104), Stuttgart, 1975, p. 29, refers to the fact that often Acts 2,17-21 is seen as the fulfilment of the promise in Joel about the restoration of prophecy.

8. OEPKE, ὄναρ, pp. 220-221, states that in the NT only Matthew uses ὄναρ, while in the LXX the common word is ἐνύπνιον. Luke especially uses ὅραμα.

9. R.K. GNUSE, *Dream and Dream Reports in the Writings of Josephus* (AGAJU, 39), Leiden, 1997, p. 16.

7 is a comparable situation (God speaks to Abimelech by night), but here it is explicitly mentioned that it is a dream (20,3). Jacob's encounter with the divine One at Bethel in Gen 28,11-19 is also characterised as a dream. It is also possible that a dream or vision situation is meant when only the element of God's appearance is mentioned (see e.g. Gen 12). Surveys of the use of dream and vision language will not reveal exact definitions of dream and visions, but we will find quite a lot of terms to indicate dream experiences[10]. The word most commonly used by Luke is ὅραμα[11]. The texts in which ὅραμα refers to a divine message include both dreams and other general revelations including appearances to people who are clearly awake at the reception of the divine message. A vision can occur during the day, but also during the night. Examples of ὅραμα indicating a vision during the day are Acts 10,3.17.19 and 11,5, and possibly also Acts 9,10.12[12]. Although in Acts 12 ὅραμα occurs in a story which describes an event during the night, this time the whole event seems to be even more than a dream (12,9: "And he went out, and followed him; and wist not that it was true, which was done by the angel; but thought he saw a vision" KJV). It is described, however, as a real confrontation with a spiritual being which can have a physical impact upon an earthly being like Peter. It is remarkable that when Peter is free, he in turn is seen as an angel (12,15). Sometimes the vision occurs during the night, at sleeping time or during sleep (Acts 16,9-10 and 18,9-10). In Acts 22,17 Luke does not use the word ὅραμα, but ἔκστασις[13]. During this trance Paul gets a divine revelation in which he receives the commission to go to the Gentiles. Whereas in 22,17 the divine message comes to Paul in a trance during the day, Acts 23,11 seems to be more like a dream. Although no technical term for a dream or for something similar such as a vision is used, the whole situation suggests a dream: "and the following night the Lord stood by him". In

10. For a lexical summary of the vocabulary used by Josephus, see GNUSE, *Dream and Dream Reports,* pp. 16-20. For dream experiences in Greek literature, see e.g. D. GALLOP, *Aristotle. On Sleep and Dreams. A Text and Translation with Introduction, Notes and Glossary,* Warminster, 1996, pp. 6-10. Cf. WIKENHAUSER, *Die Traumgesichte,* pp. 332-333. For types of visions within apocalyptic literature, see C. ROWLAND, *The Open Heaven. A Study of Apocalyptic in Judaism and Early Christianity,* London, 1981, pp. 52-58.

11. 12x in NT: 1x in Mt 17,9 as a characterisation of what happened at the mountain during the transfiguration scene and 11x in Acts; *TWNT,* 5, *s.v.* ὅραμα, p. 372: "das, was zu sehen ist, Anblick, Schauspiel (seit Xenoph), auch außerbibl schon tt für Vision".

12. Acts 9,12 is text-critically uncertain. Next to the descriptions of visions, seen by some of the disciples, in Acts 7,31 τὸ ὅραμα refers to Moses' encounter with God in the desert; see its use in Exod 3,3 LXX. Stephen, however, tells in his speech that after this vision the voice of the Lord came to Moses.

13. For the connection between ἔκστασις and ὅραμα, see Acts 11,5; cf. 10,10.

Acts 26,12-18 Paul describes, for the second time (and this is the third time that it occurs in Acts), his experience on the way to Damascus. Although the three accounts are quite different, they do complement each other. In 26,19 Luke has Paul declare that he did not disobey the "heavenly vision" (οὐκ ἐγενόμην ἀπειθὴς τῇ οὐρανίῳ ὀπτασίᾳ). As I argued elsewhere, it is in 26,16-18 that Paul's precise mission is revealed to the reader[14]. In the description of this commission there are allusions to prophetic call narratives. By means of these allusions to Scripture Luke depicts the mission to the Gentiles as law-abiding and refutes the charges against Paul (21,27-28). In addition to the argument mentioned there we can add here that this mission is not only based on scriptural arguments, but also depicted as revealed to Paul by the biblical means of divine revelation: God speaks to his prophets through visions and dreams. The last vision is found in Acts 27,24. In this story Paul is shipwrecked on his journey as a prisoner to Rome. During the night an angel of God tells Paul not to fear, because it is ordained that Paul will appear before Caesar.

When Luke mentions vision-like situations in Acts, he shows that in these situations God or his agent communicates with the recipients. Although the form of communication is not always the same, all of them are more or less comparable to a dream-situation in which the divine communicates with the recipient. The messages conveyed during these happenings are important and cannot be challenged, because they come from God.

But what is the content of these messages? In all of these visions the same message is revealed: the Gentile mission is a divine command. In Acts 16,9 Paul is commissioned to go to Macedonia and thus to cross the water and go to Europe and bring the good news there. This commission, a new phase in the Gentile mission, is prepared by the references to the Holy Spirit who prevented Paul and Timothy from preaching in Asia and Bithynia (16,6-7), but instead led them to Troas. In Acts 18,9-10 the vision (this time with three elements: the Lord, the night and a vision) is part of a pericope dealing with the Gentile mission. In the vision Paul is encouraged not to fear when he turns to the Gentiles (18,7)[15]. Paul's vision (now ὀπτασία; for the same word see Luke 1,22 and 24,23) as

14. For this and the following, see my *Prophets and Law: Paul's Change as Interpreter of Scripture in Acts*, in B.J. KOET, *Five Studies on the Interpretation of Scripture in Luke-Acts* (SNTA, 14), Leuven, 1989, pp. 73-96, here 90-91.

15. See my *As Close to the Synagogue as Can Be. Paul in Corinth (Acts 18,1-18)*, in R. BIERINGER (ed.), *The Corinthian Correspondence* (BETL, 125), Leuven, 1996, pp. 397-415.

described in Acts 26,19 and referring to the encounters with God and his messengers, makes it very explicit that Paul is sent to the Gentiles (26,17). Even the vision during the shipwreck (27,24) is a reassurance to Paul that he is an instrument in God's hands for the Gentile mission.

The visions of Paul are in line with the programmatic statement in Acts 2. Peter quotes Joel in such a way that this text can be interpreted as the scriptural proof for the Gentile mission. When the visions, prophesied in Acts 2, occur, they are the channel by which God assures and commands the Gentile mission. We can conclude that Luke chose revelation by dreams and visions as a mode by which he justifies the Gentile mission[16]: Peter, Cornelius, Ananias, but especially Paul, are guided through visions. Dreams and visions are a way of divine communication, as it is in the OT and for many of Luke's contemporaries (e.g., in the writings of Josephus).

2. *Divine Communication in Luke's Gospel*

In contrast with Acts, visions are remarkably rare in Luke's Gospel. What concerns us here is the following: if dreams and visions are an important form of divine revelation, why do they occur so rarely in Luke's Gospel? But does divine communication take place in this Gospel? In the first two chapters Luke tells us how angels, before and shortly after Jesus' birth, convey God's messages: in a vision to Zechariah (Luke 1,11-18; see 1,22), to Mary (1,26-38; cf. 2,21) and to the shepherds (2,9-15). After Jesus' death there are two men in shining garments who tell the women that Jesus is resurrected (compare 24,4 with 24,23)[17]. These divine communications occur both before or after Jesus' public life. During Jesus' public ministry we do not hear that Jesus (or any other person) receives any dream or vision. How then does Jesus communicate with God in Luke's Gospel?

Before focusing on Luke, we have to note that in all the synoptic Gospels there are two moments when a special relation between God and Jesus is at stake: during the baptism and during the transfiguration.

In the three synoptic versions of the baptism there is a voice from heaven[18]. With regard to Luke's version, Fitzmyer states that the main

16. As argued by H. VAN DE SANDT, *The Fate of the Gentiles in Joel and Acts 2: An Intertextual Study*, in *ETL* 66 (1990) 56-77, pp. 59-67, there is a relation between the use of the Joel-text and the proclamation of salvation to the Gentiles.

17. For a list of the divine interventions in Luke-Acts, see J.-N. ALETTI, *Quand Luc raconte* (Lire la Bible, 115), Paris, 1998, pp. 22-24. In the gospel he mentions Luke 1,5-25.26-38; 2,8-14; 3,22; 9,28-36; 22,43 and Luke 24.

18. For a synoptic analysis, see e.g. F. LENTZEN-DEIS, *Die Taufe Jesu nach den Syn-*

purpose of the story about the baptism is to announce the heavenly identification of Jesus as "Son" and indirectly as the Servant of the Lord; it
is in a certain sense a confirmation from God[19]. In my opinion, this is
only half of the truth, because it is also Luke's purpose to depict the special relation between Jesus and his Father as a dual communication. In
this context it suffices to refer to an important element peculiar to Luke:
Jesus' praying.

In Luke's Gospel there is some emphasis on the fact that Jesus prays,
as is clear from the additions in the Lukan redaction of the triple tradition[20]: see Luke 3,21; 5,16 (only Luke adds a remark about Jesus' praying as a conclusion to the story about the healing of a leper); 6,12 (as an
apt introduction to and preparation of the calling of the twelve, Luke
depicts Jesus as praying during the night; see the parallels in Mark 3,13;
Matt 10,1); Luke 9,18 (the introduction to Peter's confession; see Mark
8,27; Matt 16,13); and 9,28.29 (the introduction of the Transfiguration).
The verb is also found in the introduction to the Lord's Prayer. Jesus'
lessons about praying are strongly attached to his own prayer (11,1),
while in Matthew's version it is not mentioned that Jesus prays (cf. Matt
6,9). The only occurrence of "to pray" which Luke has in common with
Mark and Matthew is in Luke 22,41-45[21], but here Luke has a shorter
version[22]. In Luke 3,21, the effect of the mentioning of praying is that
the scene of the baptism is not a one-way but a two-way communication
between God and Jesus.

---

optikern (FTS, 4), Frankfurt, 1970, pp. 30-53. Lentzen-Deis refers to the Markan version
as a "Deute-Vision". J.A. FITZMYER, *The Gospel according to Luke I-IX* (AB, 28), Garden City, NY, 1981, pp. 479-483, esp. p. 481, argues that in Mark this vision is accorded
to Jesus alone. In Mark's Gospel, which lacks an infancy narrative, the scene of Jesus'
baptism is intended to tell the reader who Jesus is. In Matthew the vision has become an
epiphany in a public manifestation. Fitzmyer suggests that Luke's handling of the baptism
scene makes it the least coherent of the three. It is not clearly a "Deute-Vision" and it is
also not a epiphany. Fitzmyer refers to Lentzen-Deis, but does not reflect the nuances in
that book; see LENTZEN-DEIS, *Die Taufe Jesu,* pp. 284-286.

    19. Cf. *Luke*, I, p. 481.
    20. Jesus is also depicted as praying, e.g. in Luke 10,21-24 // Matt 11,25-27.
    21. ALETTI, *Quand Luc raconte*, p. 22, refers to 22,43 as a third communication from
God to Jesus in Luke's Gospel. Within the limits of this article I cannot deal with problems concerning this text. For the opinion that Luke 22,43-44 is no part of the original
text, see J.A. FITZMYER, *The Gospel according to Luke X-XXIV* (AB, 28A), Garden City,
NY, 1985, pp. 1443-1445.
    22. In this context I cannot deal with the relations between Mark and Luke; according
to several scholars Luke is here not dependent upon Mark: see FITZMYER, *Luke*, p. 1438;
cf. J. JEREMIAS, *Perikopen-Umstellungen bei Lukas?*, in ID., *Abba: Studien zur neutestamentlichen Theologie und Zeitgeschichte*, Göttingen, 1966, pp. 93-97 and W.M.A. HEN-
DRIKS, *Zur Kollektionsgeschichte des Markusevangeliums*, in M. SABBE (ed.), *L'évangile
selon Marc. Tradition et rédaction* (BETL, 34), Leuven, ²1988, pp. 35-57.

This element of praying as a direct communication with God reoccurs in the Transfiguration, the second story in which God shows his peculiar relation with Jesus, and even prominently since Luke uses the verb twice. While in the story of the baptism there are no such differences between Mark and Luke, this episode has been composed by Luke with a great deal of freedom.

Although it has been argued that Jesus' metamorphosis is a theme that was borrowed from the Hellenistic religions[23], P. Billerbeck already referred to current Jewish traditions as its background: in literature more or less contemporary to Luke we find the theme of righteous or wise people who will shine like the sun (4 Ezra 7,97) or who will be like angels and be equal to the stars (2 Baruch 51,10)[24]. And already in Daniel we find wise leaders who will shine like the bright vault of Heaven (12,3)[25]. Scholars have also compared Jesus' Transfiguration with the epiphanies to Moses. There are numerous points of contact[26]. Jesus goes up a high mountain after six days (so Mark and Matthew, but eight days in Luke), while Moses went up to mount Sinai and the cloud covered the mountain for six days (Exod 24,16). In Exod 24 Moses is accompanied by three men (24,1.9), and Jesus also brings a group of three men with him. God appears to Moses in a cloud, and speaks from a cloud to Jesus. Moses is covered by the cloud (Exod 24,15-16; see 19,16), and so is Jesus (Matt 17,5/Mark 9,7/Luke 9,34). In Exod 24,16 as well as in Mark 9,7 and parr there is a voice from a cloud. "Hearken to him"(Mark 9,7; see Matt 17,5/Luke 9,35) echoes Deut 18,15 and thus depicts Jesus as a prophet like Moses[27]. After the Transfiguration the crowd comes to meet him, just as Israel waited for Moses.

I will deal with only one element of the biblical traditions that are used in the Transfiguration story: Luke's use of biblical traditions reflecting epiphanies to Moses. A quick look at Luke 9,28-36 and Mark 9,2-10 par Matt 17,1-9 shows that Luke's version is, in several respects, quite different from those of the other synoptics[28]. I will limit myself to

23. See e.g. C.H.T. FLETCHER-LOUIS, *Luke-Acts: Angels, Christology and Soteriology* (WUNT, 2/94), Tübingen, 1997, p. 39, n. 21.

24. BILLERBECK, I, pp. 752-753. He refers also to 1 Enoch 38,4 and 39,7.

25. FLETCHER-LOUIS, *Luke-Acts*, pp. 39-41.

26. B.E. REID, *The Transfiguration. A Source- and Redaction-Critical Study of Lk 9:28-36* (Cahiers RB, 32), Paris, 1993, p. 103; see also M. GOULDER, *Luke. A New Paradigm, I* (JSNT SS, 20), Sheffield, 1989, p. 441 and A. DEL AGUA, *La transfiguración como preludió del 'Exodo' de Jesus en Lc 9,28-36. Estudio derásico y teológico*, in *Salmanticensis* 40 (1993) 5-19.

27. Luke twice quotes from Deut 18,15 (Acts 3,22; 7,37).

28. See e.g. H. SCHÜRMANN, *Das Lukasevangelium* (HTKNT, 3/1), Freiburg, ²1982, p. 563.

those elements which show that Luke stresses the Mosaic features of Jesus in the Transfiguration story. Although in the Markan version there may also be references to Mosaic features of Jesus, Luke's version, especially in the first part[29], gives more emphasis to this similarity with Moses, or more precisely, to the fact that during this encounter Jesus' dialogue with God reminds us of that between God and Moses[30].

a. Mosaic Features of Jesus in Lk 9,28-32.

Already in the beginning of his version Luke changes some important details[31]. He has ἀναβαίνω for ἀναφέρω. In the LXX the former is a key-word in the description of Moses going up to the mountain to communicate with God (cf. Exod 24,1.9.12.12.15.18; 32,30; 33,1; 34,1.1.3.4). It often occurs in combination with εἰς τὸ ὄρος, and it is exactly this combination which reappears here: εἰς τὸ ὄρος (instead of Mark's εἰς ὄρος) supposedly refers to a known mountain. For the readers of the Bible the most important mountain is Sinai. When Luke uses this expression, it reminds the reader of Sinai and of Moses (Exod 9,3; 24,15 and 32–34). The effect of this change is that Jesus in a certain sense is separated from his disciples and that he is even more in the centre whereas the disciples become spectators, rather than participants.

In 9,28.29 Luke adds a reference to Jesus' praying[32], to stress his ability to speak with God. In the Bible and in Jewish tradition Moses is depicted as "the person of prayer" par excellence. This is based on the fact that in Exodus and Deuteronomy Moses speaks with God (Exod 31,18; 32,31-32) and even argues with Him (32,11-13; cf. Deut. 34,10).

In Luke 9,29 μετεμορφώθη (Mark 9,2) is replaced by the paraphrase καὶ ἐγένετο ... τὸ εἶδος τοῦ προσώπου αὐτοῦ ἕτερον. H. Schürmann

29. Luke tends to divide this passage more clearly than Mark and Matthew. After the introduction in 9,28 (introduced by the Septuagintal construction ἐγένετο), there are two parts, both introduced by καὶ ἐγένετο and followed by ἐν τῷ + infinitive. In the first part the emphasis is on Jesus' encounter with the prophets, in the second one we hear about Peter's reaction and God's witness about Jesus to the apostles. See F. NEIRYNCK, *Minor Agreements Matthew-Luke in the Transfiguration Story*, in ID., *Evangelica* (BETL, 60), Leuven, 1982, pp. 797-810, esp. p. 803.

30. D.P. MOESSNER, *Lord of the Banquet. The Literary and Theological Significance of the Lukan Travel Narrative*, Minneapolis, MN, 1989, p. 46, argues that Luke casts the entire public ministry of Jesus in terms of the calling and fate of an eschatological prophet. He lists four features of a Prophet's vocation and this profile fits Jesus (pp. 48-50) as well as the disciples (pp. 51-55). Moessner argues that Jesus is a special Prophet: the anointed Prophet like Moses of Deuteronomy (p. 56). For an evaluation, see A. DENAUX, *Old Testament Models for the Lukan Travel Narrative,* in C.M. TUCKETT (ed.), *The Scriptures in the Gospels* (BETL, 131), Leuven, 1997, pp. 271-305.

31. For ἐγένετο, see NEIRYNCK, *Minor Agreements* (n. 29), p. 802.

32. For the fact that the prayer of Jesus is meant, see *ibid.*, p. 802.

suggested that Luke introduced this sentence under the inspiration of
Exod 34,29-35. Direct communication with God has as its consequence
that the skin of his face shines. By replacing Mark's wording with a
description recalling Moses' "Transfiguration", Luke again places Jesus
in the context of Moses[33].

The conversation between Jesus, Moses and Elijah is unique to Luke
(9,31-33). In 9,31 Luke says that not only Jesus, but also Moses and Elijah "appeared in glory". From this it is clear that not only Jesus, but also
Moses and Elijah are in their heavenly glory. This highlights the position
of these prophets but also shows that Luke thinks it is necessary to link
Jesus with Moses (and Elijah)[34]. In this context it is also said that "they
spoke of Jesus' *exodus* [τὴν ἔξοδον] which he should accomplish in
Jerusalem". Fitzmyer rightly observes that the very word ἔξοδος echoes
the "Exodus" of Israel from Egypt[35]. Jesus' journey to Jerusalem is
compared with Moses' leading Israel. In the second part of Luke's version of the Transfiguration there are again some references to the Moses
tradition of the OT, but now Luke shares them with the other synoptics.

In Mark and Matthew, the Transfiguration story is followed by a discussion about the coming of Elijah (Mark 9,9-13). This is clearly
inspired by the mentioning of this prophet during the encounter on the
mountain. Luke omits it. While in Mark and Matthew there is some balance in the references to Moses and Elijah, Luke omits the discussion
about Elijah but mentions the exodus.

We can conclude that in his version of the Transfiguration story Luke
diminishes the Elijah element and enlarges the Mosaic features of Jesus.
In Luke there is also special emphasis on how Jesus through his prayer
enters in direct communication with God[36].

b. Biblical Traditions about Moses as Background

If we conclude that in the Transfiguration story Jesus gets special
Mosaic features and that Luke stresses this fact, we have to ask if there
is a special text in the background. Commentators often refer to passages
from Exod and also to Deut 18. The Transfiguration story uses elements
from different epiphanies to Moses. Luke does not use these stories as

---

33. For the relation with Mark and Matthew, see again *ibid.*, p. 804.
34. I think that for Luke the connection between Jesus and Elijah is above all eschatological (see e.g. Acts 3,22). He cannot use this aspect here.
35. *Luke I*, p. 794.
36. See also Lk 23,34. Here Jesus adresses the Father and asks for forgiveness for the
Jews, as did Moses in Exod 32–33; see also Num 15,22-31. Cf. G.P. CARRAS, *A Pentateuchal Echo in Jesus' Prayer on the Cross: Intertextuality between Numbers 15,22-31
and Luke 23,34a*, in C.M. TUCKETT (ed.), *The Scriptures in the Gospels*, pp. 605-616.

exact patterns for his description of God's epiphany to Jesus. He rather uses elements from the stories about God's special relation with Moses to colour and to structure his version of the Transfiguration[37].

Exod 24 and 32 are often referred to as backgrounds to the Transfiguration story[38]. In Deut 18,15 the special position of Moses is mentioned: the new prophet is as exclusive as Moses was (see Acts 3,22; cf. 7,37). The Transfiguration story describes Jesus' communication with God against the background of the traditions about epiphanies to Moses: not only those from Exodus, but also the epiphany in Num 12 which specifies Moses unique position and which, to a certain extent, is opposite to the Moses tradition as found in Exodus[39]. This background will give us a possible explanation for the occurrence of dreams in Acts and the absence of them in Luke's gospel.

In Num 12,1 it is told that Aaron and Miriam complain about Moses' wife. But in the following verses it is clear that their complaint is more about his favourite position: "Is Moses the only one through whom the Lord has spoken? Has he not spoken through us as well?" (12,2-3). Moses does not defend himself, but it is God who defends him. Moses, Miriam and Aaron are asked to come to the Tent of Meeting. The Lord descends in a pillar of cloud and summons Aaron and Miriam and says: "Hear now my words; if there be a prophet among you, I, the Lord will make myself known unto him in vision and will speak unto him in a dream" (Num 12,6). This does not apply to Moses, because: "With him I will speak mouth to mouth, even apparently and not in dark speeches" (Num 12,8; but see Exod 33,20).

From this passage we learn two points that are important for Luke's vision of the relation between Jesus and God, and also for Luke's views

---

37. See R.E. BROWN, *The Birth of the Messiah. A Commentary on the Infancy Narratives in Matthew and Luke,* London, 1977, p. 451.

38. See e.g. GOULDER, *Luke,* p. 441. D.A.S. RAVENS, *Luke 9.7-62 and the Prophetic Role of Jesus,* in *NTS* 36 (1990) 119-129, esp. p. 125, refers to Exodus traditions, but he also argues (p. 124): "However, the use of Exodus and, to a lesser degree, Deuteronomy does not rule out other OT influences". Not only traditions about Moses, but also a story like Mk 14,32-42 is rightly seen as a background (see NEIRYNCK, *Minor Agreements,* pp. 802-803). For other possible backgrounds see J. SWETNAM, *Jesus and Isaac. A Study of the Epistle to the Hebrews in the Light of the Aqedah* (AnBib, 94), Rome, 1981, p. 11 and J. POTIN, *La fête juive de la Pentecôte* (LD, 65), Paris, 1971 (Acts 2).

39. DAUTZENBERG, *Urchristliche Prophetie,* p. 176: "Die Stelle [Num 12,6] war eine Art Haftpunkt für Traditionen über Prophetie". For a combination of the Moses from Exodus and the Moses of Num 12, see Philo's *Leg All* III 103 and Pseudo-Philo's *LAB* 11,14 (a reference to Num 12,8 is woven into a paraphrase of Exod 20); cf. *Num R* 14,20 as another text combining several Moses traditions, among them Exod 33,11 and Num 12,8. It is remarkable that Josephus in his Jewish Antiquities omits the narrative of the slanders brought against Moses by Miriam and Aaron (Ant. 3,303-304).

on dreams and visions[40]: (a) God speaks with prophets/prophetesses in dreams and visions (Num 12,6), but (b) God speaks with Moses "mouth to mouth" (12,8; see also Exod 34,5-7 and Deut 34,10: Moses, whom the Lord knew face to face). The first observation teaches us something about biblical prophecy and the second tells us about the special place of Moses (and by implication also about Jesus).

The epiphany to Moses and to his brother and sister takes place at a crucial point, just before the explorers go on their way to the land of Canaan. In Luke the Transfiguration takes place just before Jesus and his twelve apostles turn towards Jerusalem[41]. Another important parallel is the fact that God testifies explicitly to Aaron and Miriam, which can be compared with Peter, John and James (the core group of the apostles) hearing the witness about Jesus. God declares that He has a special relation with the one about whom He bears witness to a select group.

In Numbers Moses is depicted as the only one who is faithful in His house. Moses is part of God's household. He is closer to God than anyone else. A comparable statement is found in Luke 9,34-35. God tells the disciples that Jesus belongs to his household, as his son. "Listen to him" is commonly seen as a reference to Deut 18,15, the famous passage in which Moses proclaims that God will raise a prophet among his people, like him (= Moses). It appears that here God is quoting Moses to testify how much Jesus is resembling Moses, God's servant.

In this passage Jesus is depicted as one who stands very close to God, as his Son, but also as the successor of Moses. More important is his function. This is disclosed in the latter part of God's pronouncement: "Listen to him". Whoever listens to Moses listens to God. And whoever listens to Jesus, hears the New Moses and also listens to God. Jesus' teaching is as trustworthy as Moses' (for the importance of Moses' teaching, see Luke 16,29-31). In Luke 9,28-36 it becomes clear that Jesus, like Moses, belongs to the house of God (Num 12,7). Jesus does not need dreams and visions to communicate with God.

Conclusion

Luke-Acts is a unity, but we learn from the theme of dreams and visions that there is an important difference between the Gospel and its sequel. In the Gospel Jesus is so near to God that he, like Moses, does

---

40. For a summary of Num 12,6-8 in the LXX, the Targums, Rabbinic literature, the writings of Philo, and in 1 Cor 13, see DAUTZENBERG, *Urchristliche Prophetie*, esp. pp. 172-185.

41. For the connection between the twelve apostles and the twelve tribes of Israel, see Luke 22,30.

not need dreams and visions. After Jesus' baptism and before his resurrection Luke tells us only about God's communication with Jesus. Before the baptism and even immediately after the resurrection, Luke refers to divine communication with others. Before Jesus' baptism angelic visits tell us about God's program. In Acts the disciples, like the prophets, do need dreams and visions. After Jesus' resurrection dreams and visions tell the disciples how Jesus' mission is to be followed by their mission and especially the mission among the Gentiles. Dreams and visions in Acts are a proof that the mission to the Gentiles comes from God. Acts is a defence of the Gentile mission. It offers scriptural proof that the Jews remain law-abiding when engaged in the Gentile mission, but the visions also tell us that the Gentile mission is commissioned by divine revelation. These are two sides of the same coin.

Bilderdijkkade 63B   Bart J. KOET
NL-1053 VJ Amsterdam

CICERO UND LUKAS

BEMERKUNGEN ZU STIL UND ZWECK
DER HISTORISCHEN MONOGRAPHIE

Die Frage, welcher literarischen Form bzw. Gattung die Apostelgeschichte zuzurechnen sei, wird in der Actaforschung, wie schon ein
flüchtiger Blick in den 1996 zur Sache erschienenen Forschungsbericht
von Alexander J.M. Wedderburn zeigen kann, nach wie vor intensiv und
vor allem kontrovers diskutiert[1].

An dieser Diskussion habe auch ich mich beteiligt, als ich vor nunmehr bereits über zwei Dezennien vorschlug, die Apostelgeschichte als
eine historische Monographie zu verstehen, in der Lukas einen
bestimmten Teilabschnitt aus dem grösseren Ganzen der Heilsgeschichte, nämlich die »Zeit der Kirche«, dargestellt hat[2]. Da Lukas die
Heilsgeschichte nicht als ein kontinuierlich-einschnittlos verlaufenes,
sondern als ein durch markante Neueinsätze gegliedertes Geschehen
verstand[3], war es ihm von der Sache her durchaus möglich, so zu
verfahren, wie er verfahren ist, d.h. die Apostelgeschichte als eine in
sich geschlossene Erzähleinheit zu konzipieren, in der davon zu
berichten war, wie das Evangelium durch den Zeugendienst der mit
dem πνεῦμα ἅγιον begabten Apostel und Apostelschüler (Paulus!)
heilsplangemäß von Jerusalem nach Rom gelangte und wie dabei zugleich jenes heidenchristlich bestimmte Kirchentum entstand, das die
Gemeinden, für die Lukas gegen Ende des 1. Jahrhunderts schrieb, entscheidend geprägt haben muß. Zur Darstellung dieses historischen Prozesses hat sich Lukas, so meinte ich seinerzeit und meine es noch, der
oben bereits genannten literarischen Form bedient: der der histori-

---

1. A.J.M. WEDDERBURN, *Zur Frage der Gattung der Apostelgeschichte*, in H. CAN-
CIK – H. LICHTENBERGER – P. SCHÄFER (Hg.), *Geschichte, Tradition, Reflexion*. FS M.
Hengel, Tübingen, 1996, Bd. 3, S. 303-322; bei Wedderburn noch nicht berücksichtigt:
C.H. TALBERT, *The Acts of the Apostles: Monograph or 'Bios'?*, in B. WITHERINGTON
(Hg.), *History, Literature, and Society in the Book of Acts*, Cambridge, 1996, S. 58-72,
und K. YAMADA, *A Rhetorical History: The Literary Genre of the Acts of the Apostles*, in
S.E. PORTER – T.H OLBRICHT (Hg.), *Rhetoric, Scripture and Theology. Essays from the
1994 Pretoria Conference* (JSNT SS, 131), Sheffield, 1996, S. 230-250.
2. E. PLÜMACHER, *Die Apostelgeschichte als historische Monographie*, in J. KREMER
(Hg.), *Les Actes des Apôtres. Traditions, rédaction, théologie* (BETL, 48), Gembloux –
Leuven, 1979, S. 457-466; vgl. H. CONZELMANN, *Die Apostelgeschichte* (HNT, 7), Tübingen, ²1972, S. 7.
3. PLÜMACHER, *Apostelgeschichte*, S. 458-460.

schen Monographie[4], die im Bereich der hellenistisch-römischen
Geschichtsschreibung wenn nicht dem Begriff, so doch der Sache nach
wohlbekannt war und die auch Sallust[5] und vor ihm bereits der Verfasser des 2. Makkabäerbuches[6] benutzt haben[7].

4. Der Vorschlag Yamadas, das lukanische Geschichtswerk »as a general history or a
universal history which covers a history of a certain community from descriptions of its origin to its recent events« zu definieren (S. 239 unter Berufung auf D.E. AUNE, *The New Testament in Its Literary Environment*, Philadelphia, PA, 1987), scheitert daran, daß der um das
Jahr 90 schreibende Acta-Verfasser (so u.a. auch Aune, S. 139) kein einziges Ereignis aus
der Zeit nach dem Eintreffen des Paulus in Rom mehr berichtet hat. Den »recent events«
bringt Lukas keinerlei Interesse entgegen. Hinzukommt, daß die Darstellung der Apostelgeschichte ganz auf den Erweis der Legitimität der heidenchristlichen Kirche fixiert ist (dazu
u. S. 770-773) und insofern auch thematisch kaum als »universal history« gelten kann.

5. Vgl. W. STEIDLE, *Sallusts historische Monographien. Themenwahl und Geschichtsbild* (Historia. Einzelschriften, 3), Wiesbaden, 1958, S. 1; A.D. LEEMAN, *Formen sallus-
tianischer Geschichtsschreibung*, in *Gymnasium* 74 (1967) 108-115, dort S. 108f.

6. Vgl. C. HABICHT, *2. Makkabäerbuch*, in *JSHRZ*, I/3, Gütersloh, 1976, S. 189f;
D.W. PALMER, *Acts and the Ancient Historical Monograph*, in B.W. WINTER – A.D.
CLARKE (Hg.), *The Book of Acts in Its Ancient Literary Setting* (BAFCS, 1), Grand
Rapids, MI – Carlisle, 1993, S. 1-29, dort S. 20f.

7. Palmer hat zu zeigen versucht, daß die historischen Monographien zumeist mehr-,
wenn nicht gar vielbändige Werke gewesen seien (S. 5-8.11-14). Dabei sind Palmer allerdings gravierende Interpretationsfehler unterlaufen, die die Stringenz seiner These von der
Mehr- bzw. Vielbändigkeit als dem Normalfall der hellenistischen historischen Monographie einigermassen relativieren. So meint Palmer (S. 6) zu Polybios VII 7: »The accounts
of the fall of Hieronymus (7,7,1), taken as examples, are multi-volume monographs (7,7,7
τὰς βύβλους)«. Das trifft indes nicht zu. Der Plural τὰς βύβλους resultiert an der genannten Stelle nicht daraus, daß die über Hieronymos von Syrakus berichtenden Mono-
graphienverfasser (VII 7,6 οἱ τὰς ἐπὶ μέρους γράφοντες πράξεις) mehrbändige Werke
geschrieben hätten, sondern daraus, daß es mehrere Historiker (VII 7,1 τινὲς τῶν
λογογράφων τῶν ὑπὲρ τῆς καταστροφῆς τῶν Ἱερωνύμου γεγραφότων; VII 7,6 ἔνιοι)
waren, die in ihren Monographien für Polybios' Geschmack zuviel Platz auf den unbedeu-
tenden Hieronymos verschwendet hatten; vgl. die Interpretation von F.W. WALBANK, *A
Historical Commentary on Polybios*, Bd. 2, Oxford, 1967, S. 41: »how much more sensi-
ble indeed would it be, if a writer were to apply that amplification of the narrative, which
fill out the book, to Hiero and Gelo«. Unter ihnen dürfte sich auch Baton von Sinope befunden haben (s. Walbank, S. 39), dessen Monographie nach Ausweis eines bei Athenaeus
befindlichen Testimoniums (VI 251 E = FGH 268, F4) aller Wahrscheinlichkeit nach aus
nur einem Band bestand – was Palmer an anderer Stelle selbst zur Kenntnis gibt (S. 14).
Ebenso mißversteht Palmer eine von Polybios in Buch III 32 gemachte Aussage. Wenn
Polybios hier bemerkt, daß die Werke einer ganzen Reihe von Monographienschreibern (III
32,4 οἱ τῶν κατὰ μέρος γραφόντων συντάξεις) den vielfachen Umfang der – vier-
zigbändigen (32,2) – polybianischen Historien aufwiesen (32,4 τὸ πολλαπλασίοι αὐταὶ
ὑπάρχειν τῶν ἡμετέρων ὑπομνημάτων), dann meint Polybios damit natürlich nicht, daß
der Umfang jeder einzelnen dieser Monographien den des polybianischen Werkes übertraf
(so aber Palmer, S. 6: »His own work stands complete at forty books [3,32,2]; but the particular histories, about which he complains, are many times as long [s. 3,32,4 πολλα-
πλασίους]. Thus, according to Polybius, a 'monograph' may be much longer than a 'universal history'«. Vgl. S. 7: »Since Polybius complains about 'the multitude of the books'
[τῷ πλήθει τῶν βύβλων, (XXIX 12,2)], it is clear that he envisages multi-volume monographs as at 3,32 and 7,7«), sondern behauptet dies nur von der Gesamtheit der mit seinen
Historien konkurrierenden Monographien. Es kann keine Rede davon sein, daß historische
Monographien »*generally* even longer than Polybius's universal history« waren (S. 8; Hervorhebung E.P.).

In diesem Zusammenhang war seinerzeit und ist auch jetzt wieder über den berühmten Brief Ciceros an Lucceius[8] zu handeln, in dem er den ihm befreundeten Historiker im Jahre 56 v.Chr. aufgefordert hatte, seine historiographischen Talente in den Dienst von Ciceros Interessen zu stellen und möglichst bald einmal über jenen die Jahre 66 bis 57 umfassenden Abschnitt der römischen Zeitgeschichte zu schreiben, in dem Cicero zunächst eine überragende Rolle gespielt hatte, dann in äußerste Bedrängnis geraten war, um schließlich erneut zu triumphieren: den Zeitraum vom Beginn der Verschwörung Catilinas bis zu Ciceros Rückkehr aus dem Exil[9]. Hinsichtlich der Form des von Lucceius erbetenen Werkes besaß Cicero sehr genaue Vorstellungen; was er verlangte, war ein in sich geschlossenes Werk von mäßigem Umfang (»modicum quoddam corpus«), eine historische Monographie also[10]. Darüber hinaus hat Cicero aber noch eine ganze Reihe weiterer Forderungen an Lucceius gerichtet, die insbesondere die Frage der »ornatio« des von diesem darzustellenden Stoffes betreffen. Ihnen und ihrer Interpretation möchte ich mich im Folgenden zuwenden.

»Ut ornes me postulem« – Lucceius möge ihn in der geplanten Darstellung der Ereignisse »a principio … coniurationis (sc. Catilinae) usque ad reditum nostrum« ordentlich herausstreichen, so lautet die zentrale Forderung, die Cicero an Lucceius stellt. Wie wichtig ihm solche »ornatio« war, geht daraus hervor, daß er die Forderung alsbald mit gesteigerter Intensität wiederholt: »te plane etiam atque etiam rogo, ut … ornes ea« (»wieder und wieder bitte ich dich nachdrücklich darum, meine Taten herauszustreichen«), wobei es Lucceius sogar erlaubt sein soll, »die Gesetze der Geschichtsschreibung außer acht zu lassen« (»rogo, ut et ornes ea vehementius etiam quam fortasse sentis et in eo leges historiae neglegas«)[11]. Was diese Bitte um Unterordnung der »leges historiae« (sowie eigener Ansichten zur Sache) unter das Ziel der »ornatio« konkret bedeutet, lässt Cicero den Freund wenige Zeilen später wissen: Es geht darum, Cicero in dem geplanten Werk »ein klein wenig mehr, als es die Wahrheit gestattet, zukommen zu lassen« (»plusculum etiam quam concedet veritas largiare«)[12].

8. *Fam.* V 12 = XXII ed. Shackleton Bailey. Nach dessen Ausgabe der *epistulae ad familiares* (Vol. 1, Cambridge, 1977) wird der Brief im folgenden zitiert. Die Übersetzung entspricht in der Regel derjenigen von H. KASTEN, *Marcus Tullius Cicero an seine Freunde*, München, [2]1976, S. 259-267.
9. Vgl. hierzu M. GELZER, *Cicero. Ein biographischer Versuch*, Wiesbaden, 1969, S. 80-166, und C. HABICHT, *Cicero, der Politiker*, München, 1990, S. 43-67.
10. 4,1-3: »a principio enim coniurationis usque ad reditum nostrum videtur mihi modicum quoddam corpus confici posse«.
11. 2,20–3,5.
12. 3,9f.

Natürlich mußte der Leser eine solche »ornatio« auch 'schlucken'.
Hier hat Cicero voll und ganz auf die psychagogische Wirkung einer
dramatischen Darstellung gesetzt, was ihm umso leichter fiel, als er
davon überzeugt war, daß der zur Darstellung anstehende Stoff, die »res
eventusque nostri«, ohnehin die Qualität einer »fabula«, eines Dramas
also, besaß, das mit von gegensätzlichstem Geschehen handelnden
Aufzügen (»varios actus«) und zahlreichen Peripetien (»multasque
mutationes«) ausgestattet war[13]. Von Lucceius literarisch fixiert, würde
die bunte Mannigfaltigkeit von Ciceros Schicksalen ein derart hohes
Maß an Möglichkeit zur Lustempfindung bieten, daß Lucceius' Darstellung kaum verfehlen könne, die Leser in ihren Bann zu ziehen: »multam
etiam casus nostri varietatem ... suppeditabunt plenam cuiusdam volup-
tatis, quae vehementer animos hominum in legendo te (sc. Lucceio)
scriptore tenere possit«. Denn, so fährt Cicero fort, nichts sei ja besser
geeignet, den Leser zu fesseln (»aptius ad delectationem lectoris«), als
der bunte Wechsel von Ereignissen und Schicksalen (»temporum varietates fortunaeque vicissitudines«)[14], wofür Cicero u.a. auf das Schicksal
des Themistokles verweist, von dem niemand lesen könne, ohne auf das
heftigste gepackt zu werden: »cuius studium in legendo non erectum
Themistocli fuga interituque retinetur?«[15]. Und noch ein drittes Mal
schärft Cicero Lucceius ein, worauf es bei der ihm gestellten historiographischen Aufgabe ankomme: darauf, bei der Schilderung der äußerst
wechselhaften und gefährlichen Schicksale eines hervorragenden Mannes an die Gefühle der Leser zu appellieren, damit sie Bewunderung,
Spannung, Freude, Unbehagen, Furcht und Hoffnung empfinden könnten (»viri saepe excellentis ancipites variique casus habent admiratio-
nem, exspectationem, laetitiam, molestiam, spem, timorem«)[16].

Was Cicero Lucceius hier nahelegt, ist nun nichts anderes, als sich bei
der Abfassung des geplanten Werkes der zu dramatischer Darstellung
befähigenden Gestaltungsprinzipien der mimetischen Historiographie zu

13. 6,3-5. – »Fabula ist bei den Römern die offizielle Bezeichnung kunstmäßiger dramatischer Dichtungen jeder Art, sowohl der Tragödie wie der Komödie«: G. Wissowa,
Art. *Fabula* 2, in *PRE* 6, 1909, 1943f, dort Sp. 1943. Vgl. Cicero, *Brut.* 72; *Tusc.* 1,3;
Cato 70. In übertragenem Sinne wie hier: Cicero, *Phil.* 2,34; vgl. Plutarch, *Vita Demetrii*
53,10, wo die soeben beendete vita des Demetrii Poliorketes als Μακεδονικὸν δρᾶμα,
die folgende des Mark Anton als Ῥωμαϊκὸν (δρᾶμα) bezeichnet wird. – Zu »actus« in
der Bedeutung »de fabularum partibus«, s. die Belege TLL I, S. 450f (z.B. Cicero, *Phil.*
2,34 und *Cato* 70).
14. 4,9-13.
15. 5,8-9. Zur Konjektur »interituque« statt des unsinnigen »reditusque«, s. Shackleton Bailey (Anm. 8), S. 321 z.St.
16. 5,11-13. Die Fortsetzung des Satzes (5,13f: »si vero exitu notabili concluduntur,
expletur animus iucundissima lectionis voluptate«) zeigt, daß hier tatsächlich auf die
Gefühle des Lesers spekuliert wird.

bedienen[17], wobei es auch Cicero zuvörderst um das ἐκπλῆξαι καὶ ψυχαγωγῆσαι der Leser ging, das Polybios vordem als das vorrangige Ziel der mimetischen Geschichtsschreiber erkannt und, weil mit den Grundsätzen der – pragmatischen! – Geschichtsschreibung unvereinbar, verworfen hatte. In seinen Augen waren jene nämlich weniger Historiker als vielmehr τραγῳδιογράφοι, Leute, die ihren Lesern Ähnliches zu bieten wünschten wie die Dramatiker ihren Zuschauern und die sich infolgedessen nur allzuoft dazu bereitgefunden hatten, etwas zu tun, was Historikern anders als Dramatikern nicht gestattet war: um einer möglichst spektakulären Darstellung willen auf die gewissenhafte Wiedergabe allein des tatsächlich Geschehenen zu verzichten und stattdessen mittels einer lediglich potentiellen, dafür aber umso packender geschilderten Lebenswahrheit der Darstellung beim Leser Glaubwürdigkeit und Wirkung zu erzielen[18]. Damit hatten die mimetischen Geschichtsschreiber jedoch, wie Polybios empört feststellte, dem Element des Fiktiven Einlaß in die Gefilde der Historiographie gewährt[19], und eben dies verlangte nunmehr auch Cicero von Lucceius, wenn er ihn dazu aufforderte, um der »ornatio« von Ciceros »fabula« willen die Gesetze der Geschichtsschreibung außer acht zu lassen[20].

Das der mimetischen Historiographie entstammende Verständnis von Geschichtsschreibung, das Cicero in seinem Brief an Lucceius offenbart, findet sich in seinem gesamten schriftstellerischen Werk sonst nirgends mehr. Wohl aber finden sich andere Äusserungen zur Geschichtsschreibung, die belegen, daß sich Cicero ohne wenn und aber zur pragmatischen Geschichtsschreibung bekannte, wie sie Polybios einst getrieben hatte und Lukian sie später propagieren sollte[21]. Wie diese wußte auch

17. K.-E. PETZOLD, *Cicero und Historie*, in *Chiron* 2 (1972) 253-276, dort S. 272-274; vgl. A.D. LEEMAN, *Le genre et le style historique à Rome: Théorie et pratique*, in *Revue des études latines* 33 (1955) 183-208, dort S. 190f.

18. Vgl. Polybios II 56,1-12; III 47,6–48,9; XV 34,1f; 36,1-7. Ἐκπλῆξαι καὶ ψυχαγωγῆσαι: II 56,11; τραγῳδιογράφοι: II 56,10; III 48,8; XV 36,7. – Zur mimetischen Geschichtsschreibung s. E. PLÜMACHER, *TEPATEIA. Fiktion und Wunder in der hellenistisch-römischen Geschichtsschreibung und in der Apostelgeschichte*, in *ZNW* 89 (1998) 66-90, dort S. 67-69 und insbesondere die hier genannte Literatur.

19. Polybios II 56,1-12; 58,12; 59,1-3; III 47,6-8.

20. Vgl. M. VON ALBRECHT, *Geschichte der römischen Literatur von Andronicus bis Boethius*, Bern, 1992, Bd. 1, S. 437: »die Bitte, es mit der Wahrheit nicht allzu genau zu nehmen, (klingt) für uns eher peinlich; der antike Leser wird darin die Prinzipien einer 'tragischen' Geschichtsschreibung (gemeint ist die mimetische Historiographie, E.P.) erkannt haben«.

21. PETZOLD, *Cicero und Historie* (Anm. 17), S. 259f.264-272. Vgl. noch P.A. BRUNT, *Cicero and Historiography*, in Φιλίας χάριν. *Miscellanea di studi classici in onore di Eugenio Manni*, Vol. 1, Roma, 1980, S. 309-340, dort S. 318: »Cicero's conceptions of the purpose and substance of history agree well with those of Polybius«.

er: »alias in historia leges observandas putare, alias in poemate«[22], und *de oratore* 2,62 ist zu entnehmen, daß die »prima lex historiae« auch für Cicero darin bestand, nichts Unwahres zu sagen und nichts Wahres zu verschweigen[23]. Wenn Cicero aber, woran kein Zweifel besteht, ernsthaft dieser Ansicht war[24], wie konnte er dann von Lucceius verlangen, die »leges historiae« in der geplanten Darstellung zugunsten von Ciceros »ornatio« zu vernachlässigen?

Zur Beantwortung dieser Frage gilt es zunächst, eine von Cicero gegen Ende des Lucceiusbriefes zweimal benutzte Formulierung genauer zu betrachten. Cicero unterrichtet Lucceius hier von seiner Absicht, die von diesem erbetene Abhandlung im Falle von dessen Weigerung eventuell selbst schreiben zu wollen. Die Notwendigkeit, sich dann selbst loben zu müssen, mißfällt Cicero allerdings sehr; dem Zwang zum Eigenlob sei er indes enthoben, fährt Cicero fort, »si recipis causam nostram« (»wenn du meine Sache übernimmst«[25]) – eine Formulierung, die Cicero im letzten Absatz des Briefes noch einmal, leicht variiert, aufgreift: Lucceius werde von ihm eine Zusammenstellung aller einschlägigen Fakten erhalten, »si enim suscipis causam« (»falls du die Sache übernimmst«)[26].

Die Wendung »causam recipere« bzw. »suscipere« begegnet bei Cicero auch sonst; sie entstammt dem juristischen Bereich und bedeutet fast stets »als Anwalt einer Prozeßpartei einen Fall übernehmen«, dies entweder aufgrund einer Verpflichtung oder Bitte (»recipere«) oder aufgrund eigenen freien Entschlusses (»suscipere«)[27]. Cicero bittet Luc-

---

22. *Leg.* 1,5. Vgl. Lukian, *hist. conscr.* 8: ποιητικῆς μὲν καὶ ποιημάτων ἄλλαι ὑποσχέσεις καὶ κανόνες ἴδιοι, ἱστορίας δὲ ἄλλοι (Homeyer, S. 102,17-19) und μέγα ... κακόν, εἰ μὴ εἰδείη τις χωρίζειν τὰ ἱστορίας καὶ τὰ ποιητικῆς, ἀλλ᾽ ἐπεισάγοι τῇ ἱστορίᾳ τὰ τῆς ἑτέρας κομμώματα (S. 104,13-16).

23. »Quis nescit primam esse historiae legem, ne quid falsi dicere audeat? Deinde ne quid veri non audeat?«. Vgl. Polybios I 14,6: ὥσπερ γὰρ ζῴου τῶν ὄψεων ἀφαιρεθεισῶν ἀχρειοῦται τὸ ὅλον, οὕτως ἐξ ἱστορίας ἀναιρεθείσης τῆς ἀληθείας τὸ καταλειπόμενον αὐτῆς ἀνωφελὲς γίνεται διήγημα, und Lukian, *hist. conscr.* 39: ἓν γὰρ ... τοῦτο ἴδιον ἱστορίας, καὶ μόνη θυτέον τῇ ἀληθείᾳ, εἴ τις ἱστορίαν γράφων ἴῃ, τῶν δὲ ἄλλων ἁπάντων ἀμελητέον αὐτῷ (S. 146,3-6 Homeyer).

24. Dazu vgl. z.B. die in Anm. 17 und 21 genannten Arbeiten von Petzold und Brunt. Zur Beteuerung historiographischer Wahrheitsliebe als reinem Lippenbekenntnis s. die Belege bei G. AVENARIUS, *Lukians Schrift zur Geschichtsschreibung*, Meisenheim, 1956, S. 43f.

25. 8,1–9,1.

26. 10,1f.

27. *Recipere* in Verbindung mit *suscipere*: *Verr.* 1,34; *div. in Caec.* 26; *de orat.* 2,101; vgl. auch *fam.* V 8,1.5; *recipere*: *Brut.* 155; *Att.* XIII 54,1; vgl. noch *Att.* XV 26,3; *suscipere*: *Cluent.* 43f. Zur – nicht stets genau gegeneinander abgrenzbaren (A.S. WILKINS, *M. Tulli Ciceronis de oratore libri tres*, Oxford, 1892, S. 279) – Bedeutung von *recipere* und *suscipere*, s. A.D. LEEMAN – H. PINKSTER – E. RABBIE, *M. Tullius Cicero, de oratore libri III. Kommentar*, Bd. 3, Heidelberg, 1989, S. 39, sowie OLD s.v. *recipio* 10a und *suscipio* 8c.

ceius hier also nicht nur erneut darum, eine seine Taten preisende Darstellung zu verfassen, sondern auch darum, bei der Erledigung der ihm angetragenen Aufgabe gewissermaßen als Anwalt zu verfahren, der einen Fall übernommen hat. Die Identität des Vokabulars, in dem Cicero seine Bitte vorträgt, mit demjenigen, das gewöhnlich zur Bezeichnung der Übernahme eines Prozesses dient, macht diesen Schluß unausweichlich. Auf Bitten der Sizilier hatte Cicero einst deren Fall – den Prozeß gegen Verres – übernommen: »hanc causam Siculorum rogatu recepissem«[28]; nun bittet er mit denselben Worten Lucceius, das entsprechende für ihn zu tun: »idque – sc. recipere causam nostram – ut facias rogamus«[29]. Selbst die in Ciceros Prozessreden so häufig zu beobachtende feine Differenzierung zwischen »recipere« und »suscipere« kehrt im Brief an Lucceius wieder; aus Gründen der Höflichkeit muß es ihm geraten erschienen sein, die im Schlußabschnitt des Briefes Lucceius letztmalig vorgetragene Bitte um Abfassung der in Rede stehenden Darstellung so zu formulieren, als könne dieser Ciceros 'Fall' noch allein aus eigener Initiative übernehmen (»causam suscipere«) – ganz so, als ob ihn Cicero nicht längst wie z.B. in 2,5-14 darum gebeten hätte, »causam illam totam« zu vertreten, in der es um die angemessene Würdigung von Ciceros Taten im Horizont der catilinarischen Verschwörung ging[30]. Wozu Cicero, der zum Zeitpunkt der Abfassung des Lucceius-

28. *Verr.* 1,34.

29. 9,1f.

30. In ganz ähnlicher Weise wie im Lucceiusbrief hat Cicero die Begriffe *recipere* und *suscipere* auch in *fam.* V 8 (XXV ed. Shackleton Bailey) benutzt, einem an M. Licinius Crassus gerichteten Brief, in dem er sich dem nach Syrien abgereisten Konsular als Anwalt von dessen Interessen anbot. Wie im Brief an Lucceius geht es auch hier nicht um die Führung von Prozessen, sondern um Interessenwahrung im weiteren Sinne. In seinem Schreiben lässt Cicero Crassus zunächst wissen, mit welch großem Einsatz er sich bereits für dessen »dignitas« eingesetzt habe (»quanta numquam antea ulla in causa«), um ihm im Anschluß daran zu versichern, daß er es »auf sich genommen« habe »ein für alle Mal für die Erhaltung aller deiner Ehren zu kämpfen« (1,1-8: »suscepique mihi perpetuam propugnationem pro omnibus ornamentis tuis«). Da die Initiative hierzu von ihm selbst ausgeht, wählt Cicero zur Bezeichnung der Tatsache, daß er die Vertretung von Crassus' Interessen zu übernehmen gedenkt, das Verb *suscipere*. Am Schluß des Briefes schlägt Cicero Crassus dann vor, den Brief als förmlichen Vertrag (»foedus«) anzusehen, der Cicero dazu verpflichte, »das, was ich dir verspreche und auf mich nehme, unverbrüchlich einzuhalten und gewissenhaft auszuführen« (5,1-4). Hiernach resultiert die von Cicero übernommene Wahrung der Interessen des Crassus aus einer vertraglichen Verpflichtung, und infolgedessen formuliert Cicero jetzt: »meque ea quae tibi promitto ac *recipio* sanctissime esse observaturum diligentissimeque esse facturum«. Da diese Verpflichtung jedoch eine Selbstverpflichtung Ciceros darstellt (vgl. 5,9f: »mea sponte id esse facturum«), kann er in 5,4f mit gleichem Recht auch formulieren: »quae a me *suscepta* defensio est te absente dignitatis tuae«. Summa: Cicero verspricht hier, für Crassus das zu tun, was er *fam.* V 12 von Lucceius für sich selbst verlangt, und verwendet in beiden Fällen auch das gleiche Vokabular.

briefes ganz unter dem Eindruck seiner als katastrophal empfundenen politischen Lage stand[31], Lucceius veranlassen wollte, war also dies: sich in seiner Eigenschaft als Historiker zugleich auch als Anwalt Ciceros zu betätigen, was bedeutete, das ins Auge gefasste Geschichtswerk über den Zeitraum »a principio coniurationis usque ad reditum nostrum« als apologetisches Plädoyer in Sachen Cicero zu gestalten[32] und diesem auch dadurch zu dienen, daß er »das perfide, intrigante, verräterische Treiben vieler« gegen ihn, wie es Pflicht des plädierenden Prozessredners war, »mit allem Freimut (*liberius*[33]) anprangerte«[34].

Es ist leicht zu verstehen, daß bei solchen Absichten die verpönte Vernachlässigung der »leges historiae« kaum zu vermeiden war. Wenn sich Lucceius aber, wie von Cicero erbeten, den Anwaltstalar überzog und sich der »res nostra« nicht nur als Historiker, sondern auch als einer 'causa Ciceronis' annahm, in der es durchaus parteilich zu plädieren galt, brauchte er wegen der damit verbundenen Verstöße gegen die »leges historiae« keinerlei Vorwürfe zu befürchten. Nach Ciceros Überzeugung würde Lucceius nämlich, wenn er wie gebeten verfuhr, nur etwas tun, was ihm – nicht als Historiker, wohl aber als Anwalt, der er nach Ciceros Willen ja auch sein sollte – schlicht zustand. Mit aller Klarheit geht dies aus einer Aussage Ciceros hervor, die er in seinem von der Entwicklung der römischen Redekunst handelnden Dialog *Brutus* gemacht hat. Cicero kommt in der betreffenden Passage zunächst auf das Ende Coriolans zu sprechen und dichtet diesem um der Schlüssigkeit seiner Argumentation willen einen Tod an, den er in Wirklichkeit nicht gestorben war. Zu diesem – vorsätzlichen – Verstoß gegen die historischen Fakten lässt Cicero dann den Dialogpartner Atticus, der sich in seinem *liber annalis*[35] offenbar korrekt über Coriolans Ende geäußert hatte, folgendermaßen Stellung nehmen: »concessum est rhetoribus ementiri in historiis, ut aliquid dicere possint argutius«[36], den Rhetoren

---

31. Siehe *Att.* IV 7,1f: »quid foedius nostra vita, praecipue mea? ... ego vero, qui, si loquor de re publica, quod oportet, insanus, si, quod opus est, servus existimor, si taceo, oppressus et captus, quo dolore esse debeo?«, und 4 (Erwähnung des Briefes an Lucceius); vgl. GELZER, *Cicero* (Anm. 9), S. 171-173; HABICHT, *Cicero* (Anm. 9), S. 70.
32. Vgl. O. LENDLE, *Ciceros ὑπόμνημα περὶ τῆς ὑπατείας*, in *Hermes* 95 (1967) 90-109, der S. 105 von der »apologetischen Konsulatsschriftstellerei« Ciceros spricht (ebenso S. 103).
33. Vgl. Cicero, *Cluent.* 142: »honeste hanc causam et libere defendere«; *Sest.* 4, sowie Forcellini s.v. *libere* = μετὰ παρρησίας (wie Demosthenes, *or.* 6,31; 9,3).
34. 4,7-9: »... et, si liberius, ut consuesti, agendum putabis, multorum in nos perfidiam, insidias, proditionem notabis«.
35. Dazu M. FLECK, *Cicero als Historiker* (Beiträge zur Altertumskunde, 39), Stuttgart, 1993, S. 162-178.
36. *Brut.* 42.

– die im Rom Ciceros ausschließlich ihrer Anwaltstätigkeit sowie der Politik zu leben pflegten[37] – stehe die Freiheit zu, im Kontext ihrer Plädoyers historische Fakten zu manipulieren (oder gar: zu erdichten), um auf solche Weise pointierter argumentieren zu können[38]. Cicero hat seine oben skizzierten Ansichten zur Geschichtsschreibung, die ihn als Anhänger der pragmatischen Historiographie ausweisen, im Lucceiusbrief also keineswegs desavouiert; allerdings war er zugleich der Auffassung, daß eine plädierende Geschichtsschreibung, wie er sie sich von Lucceius erhoffte, den strengen Regeln, die etwa Polybios in der Historiographie angewandt wissen wollte, nicht zu gehorchen brauchte und um ihrer apologetischen Ziele willen stattdessen von den zur Psychagogie tauglichen schriftstellerischen Mitteln und Lizenzen der mimetischen Geschichtsschreibung Gebrauch machen durfte.

Die zur Psychagogie fähige Darstellungskunst der mimetischen Geschichtsschreibung ist für Cicero nun aber auf das engste mit der Form der historischen Monographie verknüpft gewesen. Das ergibt sich zunächst aus dem zweiten Abschnitt des Lucceiusbriefes. Hier bittet Cicero den Freund darum, seine Taten nicht im Kontext von dessen gerade im Entstehen begriffenen und einen längeren Zeitraum behandelnden Werk zu schildern (»coniuncte … cum reliquis rebus nostra [res] contexere«), sondern lieber nach dem Vorbild einiger griechischer Historiker zu verfahren und so, wie diese bestimmte historische Sachkomplexe außerhalb ihrer »perpetuae historiae« behandelt hatten (»separaverunt«), auch den Stoff, um dessen Darstellung es Cicero ging, die »civilis coniuratio«, von den sonstigen Geschehnissen der Zeit, namentlich den auswärtigen Kriegen, getrennt zu behandeln (»seiungere«)[39]. Wenige Zeilen später gibt Cicero dann zu erkennen, weshalb er für die Darstellung seiner »causa«[40] einzig die zweite Möglichkeit als geeignet ansieht: Bei der Konzentration der Darstellung auf ein Thema (»uno in argumento«) und eine Person (»unaque in persona«), in einer historischen Monographie also, werde sich alles – d.h. alles, was Cicero

37. Vgl. *de orat.* 2,55: »nemo enim studet eloquentiae nostrorum hominum, nisi ut in causis atque in foro eluceat«.
38. Die Lizenz »in historiis ementiri« bezieht sich also nicht auf die Geschichtsschreibung, sondern auf die historischen *exempla*, die die Rhetoren in ihre Argumentation einflechten konnten (PETZOLD, *Cicero*, S. 258; vgl. Cicero, *orat.* 120: »commemoratio autem antiquitatis exemplorumque prolatio summa cum delectatione et auctoritatem orationi affert et fidem« und *de orat.* 1,18), wobei ihnen, wie natürlich auch sonst, im Rahmen des »amplificare rem ornando« (*de orat.* 3,104) die »augendi minuendive causa veritatis supralatio atque traiectio« gestattet war (*de orat.* 3,203; vgl. *orat.* 139).
39. 2,5-11.
40. 2,14: »causa illa tota et tempus«, »jene Epoche und der Verlauf der Sache in ihrer Gesamtheit« (Übersetzung KASTEN, S. 261).

am Herzen lag, nämlich die Schilderung seiner Taten und Schicksale im
Horizont der catilinarischen Verschwörung – viel reicher und schöner,
»uberiora atque ornatiora«, ausnehmen[41]. Mit den Worten »omnia uberiora atque ornatiora« kann sich Cicero nun kaum auf etwas anderes
beziehen als auf das Ergebnis der im weiteren Text des Briefes so
nachdrücklich eingeforderten »ornatio« des von Lucceius zu behandelnden Stoffes, einer »ornatio«, die, wie oben dargelegt, mit Hilfe der von
der mimetischen Geschichtsschreibung gebotenen Stilmittel und Lizenzen erreicht werden sollte. Deren Wirkung würde sich jedoch, so möchte
Cicero dem Freund hier durch den Gebrauch der Komparative »uberiora« und »ornatiora« signalisieren, am besten in einer historischen
Monographie entfalten können[42].

Diese Sicht der Dinge lässt sich durch einen Blick auf die Abschnitte
4 bis 6 des Briefes bestätigen. Im Anschluß an eine längere Ausführung
über das psychagogische Wirkungspotential, das bestimmten Stoffen –
denjenigen, die von den »temporum varietates fortunaeque vicissitudines« handeln – innewohne[43], kommt Cicero erneut auf die Frage zu
sprechen, welche äußere Form das Werk haben sollte, in dem Lucceius
als Historiograph Ciceros ein Beispiel für solche »temporum varietates
fortunaeque vicissitudines« schildern würde. Nunmehr geht es auch
expressis verbis darum, in welcher historiographischen Form das psychagogische Potential jener Stoffe am besten zur Wirkung gebracht und
zur Erregung der Affekte der Leser benutzt werden könne. Eine Aufreih-
ung von Fakten in annalistischer Manier vermöge, so bemerkt Cicero
zunächst, gleich einer kalendarischen Tabelle nur mäßig zu fesseln:
»etenim ordo ipse annalium mediocriter nos retinet quasi enumeratione
fastorum«[44]. Die »viri saepe excellentis ancipites variique casus«, deren
Schilderung im Leser so viele – von Cicero einzeln benannte – Affekte
wachrufen könne, erfordern, so ist zu schließen, einen anderen literarischen Rahmen. Und in der Tat bittet Cicero im Folgenden Lucceius
dann ein weiteres Mal ausdrücklich darum, das Drama seiner Erlebnisse
und Schicksale, die »fabula rerum eventorumque nostrorum«, nicht in
»continentibus tuis scriptis, in quibus perpetuam rerum gestarum historiam complecteris«, »nicht in deiner zusammenhängenden Darstellung,

---

41. 2,14-17: »si uno in argumento unaque in persona mens tua versabitur, cerno iam
animo quanto omnia uberiora atque ornatiora futura sint«.
42. Der Umstand, daß die historischen Monographien in hellenistischer Zeit in der
Regel Kriege behandelt haben (so PALMER, *Acts*, S. 14), hat jedenfalls Cicero nicht davon
abgehalten, diese literarische Form auch für die Darstellung der »civilis coniuratio«
(2,10) als äußerst geeignet anzusehen.
43. 4,12–5,9.
44. 5,9-11.

in der du die geschichtlichen Ereignisse fortlaufend wiedergibst«, zu
behandeln, sondern jenes Drama, das von mannigfaltigstem Geschehen
geprägt sei und so viele Peripetien aufweise[45], unbedingt von seiner
»perpetua historia« getrennt darzustellen (»secernere«), und das kann
nur heißen: in einer historischen Monographie zu schildern[46]. Auch hier
zeigt sich also, wie fest Cicero davon überzeugt war, daß die auf die
Affekte der Leser zielende mimetische Historiographie am ehesten im
Rahmen einer historischen Monographie jene durchschlagende psychagogische Wirkung würde erzielen können, deren es seiner Meinung nach
bedurfte, um die apologetischen Zwecke, denen die geplante Darstellung
seiner Taten und Schicksale dienen sollte, auch voll und ganz zu erreichen[47]. Zieht man zudem die Tatsache ins Kalkül, »dass sich in der hellenistischen Zeit mit dem Bestreben, die Historie der Dichtung ...
anzunähern, eine Tendenz auf in sich geschlossene monographische
Darstellungen von Ab- und Ausschnitten der Geschichte« herausgebil-
det hatte, »da nur so die dramatische Konzentration auf Höhepunkte und
Peripetien hin erreicht werden konnte«[48], darf man Cicero wohl sogar
die Überzeugung unterstellen, eine historische Monographie sei überhaupt nur im Stile der mimetischen Historiographie zu schreiben[49].

Von der Lucceius abverlangten Monographie ist nichts überliefert,
und so bleibt ungewiß, ob er sie tatsächlich so, wie von Cicero
gewünscht, gestaltet hat. Doch gibt es zumindest zwei Schriften, deren
literarische Gestalt ganz der von Cicero im Lucceiusbrief skizzierten
entspricht und die beide ebenfalls apologetischen Zwecken dienen. Die
eine, von Ciceros eigener Hand stammend, ist das griechische

---

45. 6,4f: »(fabula) habet enim varios actus multasque mutationes et consiliorum et
temporum«.
46. 6,1-5.
47. Cicero empfand die historische Monographie als die für ein Produkt der mimetischen Historiographie bestmögliche äußere Form. Vor allem deswegen hat Cicero sie
Lucceius als Rahmen für die Darstellung der 'causa Ciceronis' empfohlen. Der Wunsch,
sich so bald wie möglich gefeiert zu lesen, spielt demgegenüber, obwohl wiederholt ausgesprochen (1,9-14; 9,3-8), eine eher untergeordnete Rolle, dies auch deshalb, weil Lucceius in seiner »perpetua historia« von der Behandlung des Cicero interessierenden Zeit-
raumes nicht mehr allzuweit entfernt war (vgl. 2,3-5).
48. K. VON FRITZ, *Die Bedeutung des Aristoteles für die Geschichtsschreibung*, in
Histoire et historiens dans l'antiquité (EnAC, 4), Genève, 1958, S. 83-128, dort S. 126.
Vgl. VON ALBRECHT, *Geschichte* (Anm. 20), S. 291: in die historische Monographie
»wirkt eine auf Affekterregung ausgehende Darstellungsweise herein, die sich zum Teil
an der aristotelischen Tragödientheorie orientiert«.
49. Dies gilt insbesondere dann, wenn Cicero im Lucceiusbrief »eine hellenistische
Theorie der historischen Monographie überliefert« hätte, wie dies LEEMAN, *Formen*
(Anm. 5), S. 109 meint. So auch schon R. REITZENSTEIN, *Hellenistische Wundererzählungen*, Leipzig, 1906 (Darmstadt, [3]1974), S. 84-86.

ὑπόμνημα über die Ereignisse seines Konsulatsjahres[50], das er einige
Jahre zuvor mit der Bitte, »ut ornatius de iisdem rebus scriberet«, an
Poseidonios von Apameia geschickt hatte[51], und das durchaus kein der
schriftstellerischen »ornatio« noch entbehrender Rohentwurf im Sinne
Lukians[52] war, sondern eine bereits nach allen Regeln der Kunst ausge-
schmückte historische Monographie darstellte[53]. Da Plutarch das als solches nicht erhaltene ὑπόμνημα in seiner Cicerovita intensiv ausge-
schrieben hat[54], läßt sich noch erkennen, daß sich Cicero bei dessen
Abfassung ganz an das historiographische Programm gehalten hat, das
er später Lucceius zur Anwendung empfahl[55]. Wir finden hier die für die
mimetische Geschichtsschreibung so charakteristischen dramatisch
komponierten, psychagogischen Szenen[56], und wir finden hier auch die
für jene nicht minder bezeichnende Manipulation mit historischen Fakten[57], das eine wie das andere dem Zweck dienend, Ciceros Handeln im
Konsulatsjahr ins rechte Licht zu rücken und dadurch zu rechtfertigen
sowie den in jenem Jahr gewonnenen Ruhm festzuhalten[58].

Die zweite Schrift ist die Apostelgeschichte des Lukas. Auch sie
ist eine historische Monographie, und auch sie dient apologetischen
Zwecken. Wie Lucceius einen bestimmten Abschnitt der römischen
Zeitgeschichte zum Zweck der politischen Rechtfertigung und Glorifi-
zierung desjenigen schildern sollte, der in diesem Zeitraum eine herausragende, aber von seinen Gegnern immer wieder heftig kritisierte Rolle

50. *Att.* I 19,10: »commentarius consulatus mei Graece compositus«; II 1,2: »nostrum illud ὑπόμνημα«.
51. Warum sich Cicero mit diesem Anliegen gerade an Poseidonios wandte, ist
unbekannt. Eine plausible Annahme wäre, daß sich Poseidonios dem Römer durch seine
den Usancen der mimetischen Geschichtsschreibung verpflichteten Historien (dazu
F. JACOBY, FGH II C, S. 159, und O. LENDLE, *Einführung in die griechische Geschichtsschreibung von Hekataios bis Zosimos*, Darmstadt, 1992, S. 236) empfohlen hätte, doch
ist eine Bekanntschaft Ciceros mit den Historien nirgends nachweisbar: vgl. J. MALITZ,
Die Historien des Poseidonios (Zet. 79), München, 1983, S. 28. Poseidonios hat Ciceros
Wunsch nicht erfüllt (*Att.* II 1,2).
52. *Hist. conscr.* 48; dazu AVENARIUS, *Lukians Schrift zur Geschichtsschreibung*
(Anm. 24), S. 85-104.
53. Vgl. *Att.* II 1,1: »meus ... liber totum Isocrati myrothecium atque omnes eius dis-
cipulorum arculas ac non nihil etiam Aristotelia pigmenta consumpsit«.
54. C. 10-23; dazu LENDLE, *Ciceros ὑπόμνημα περὶ τῆς ὑπατείας* (Anm. 32).
55. *Ibid.*, S. 93f.
56. Etwa c. 15; 22,1-4; 5-7; vgl. Lendle, S. 101f.
57. S. die zeitliche Raffung des Geschehens in c. 19,4 / 20,4, deren Zweck nicht nur
darin besteht, durch die Herstellung einer größeren dramatischen Konsequenz der Handlung den Leser verstärkt zu fesseln, sondern vor allem darin, nicht über für Cicero peinliche Umstände berichten zu müssen; vgl. Lendle, S. 101.
58. Mit Recht bezeichnet LEEMAN, *Genre* (Anm. 17), S. 185, das ὑπόμνημα darum
als »un ouvrage de tendance nettement propagandiste«.

gespielt hatte, so unternahm es auch Lukas, einen bestimmten Abschnitt der Kirchen- und darüber hinaus der Heilsgeschichte zu dem Zweck zu schildern, seine Leser – gewissermaßen seine Klienten – von einem entweder von ihnen selbst empfundenen oder ihnen von anderer Seite vorgehaltenen Makel zu befreien: dem Verdacht, daß es mit der Legitimität ihres Heidenchristentums aufgrund mangelnder Kontinuität zu den judenchristlichen Anfängen der Kirche und darüber hinaus zu Israel nicht zum besten stehe[59]. Cicero hatte sich der an ihm geübten Kritik im ὑπόμνημα dadurch zu erwehren gesucht, daß er die Großtaten seines Konsulats als seinerzeit von den Optimaten vorbehaltlos anerkannt, vom Volke gefeiert und vom 'consensus omnium bonorum' getragen darstellte[60]. Lukas gelingt sein apologetisches Vorhaben ebenfalls durch die Interpretation von Geschichte, nämlich durch die Interpretation der Geschichte der beiden ersten christlichen Generationen als eines Geschehens, in dem der seine Leser beunruhigende Zustand ihrer Kirche als einer Kirche ohne Juden von niemand anderem als der *providentia* selbst herbeigeführt worden war und somit legitim sein musste[61].

Vor allem aber: um seine Leser von der Legitimität der heidenchristlichen Kirche zu überzeugen, hat Lukas in seiner historischen Monographie auch zu den gleichen schriftstellerischen Mitteln gegriffen, die Cicero »in explicandis causis rerum novarum« Lucceius empfohlen[62] und zuvor im ὑπόμνημα selbst genutzt hatte – zu den für ein apologetisches Plädoyer unbedingt notwendigen psychagogischen Darstellungs-

---

59. Aus Raumgründen kann diese Thematik hier nicht im einzelnen entfaltet werden; Literatur zum Thema bei E. PLÜMACHER, Art. *Apostelgeschichte*, in *TRE* 3 (1978) 483-528, dort S. 518-520; ID., *Acta-Forschung 1974-1982*, in *TR* 48 (1983) 1-56, dort S. 45-51, und M. RESE, *Die »Juden« im lukanischen Doppelwerk. Ein Bericht über eine längst nötige »neuere« Diskussion*, in C. BUSSMANN – W. RADL (Hg.), *Der Treue Gottes trauen.* FS G. Schneider, Freiburg-Basel-Wien, 1991, S. 61-79. Besondere Beachtung verdienen L. GASTON, *Anti-Judaism and the Passion Narrative in Luke and Acts*, in P. RICHARDSON – D. GRANSKOU (Hg.), *Anti-Judaism in Early Christianity*, Waterloo, Ont., 1986, Vol. 1, S. 127-153; K. LÖNING, *Das Verhältnis zum Judentum als Identitätsproblem der Kirche nach der Apostelgeschichte*, in *»Ihr alle aber seid Brüder«*. FS A.T. Khoury, Würzburg-Altenberge, 1990, S. 304-319; W. STEGEMANN, *Zwischen Synagoge und Obrigkeit. Zur historischen Situation der lukanischen Christen* (FRLANT, 152), Göttingen, 1991, insbes. S. 271f.; H. MERKEL, *Israel im lukanischen Werk*, in NTS 40 (1994) 371-398; D. MARGUERAT, *Juden und Christen im lukanischen Doppelwerk*, in *EvT* 54 (1994) 241-264; R. VON BENDEMANN, *Paulus und Israel in der Apostelgeschichte des Lukas*, in K. WENGST – G. SASS (Hg.), *Ja und nein. Christliche Theologie im Angesicht Israels.* FS W. Schrage, Neukirchen-Vluyn, 1998, S. 291-303, und M. WOLTER, *Die Juden und die Obrigkeit bei Lukas, ibid.*, S. 277-290.

60. LENDLE, *Ciceros* ὑπόμνημα περὶ τῆς ὑπατείας (Anm. 32), S. 106.

61. Vgl. die in Anm. 59 genannte Literatur.

62. Lucceius soll ein »modicum quoddam corpus« schreiben, »in quo ... illa poteris uti civilium commutationum scientia vel in explicandis causis rerum novarum vel in remediis incommodorum« (4,3-5).

mitteln, wie sie die mimetische Geschichtsschreibung bereit hielt. In Gestalt des dramatischen Episodenstils, der die Erzählung der Apostelgeschichte weithin prägt, hat sich Lukas die Darstellungsweise jenes Zweiges der Historiographie kongenial zu eigen gemacht[63] und dabei gerade in den für seine apologetischen Absichten zentralen Episoden wie z.B. Apg 10,1–11,18 oder 15,1-33 Kabinettstücke dramatisch-psychagogischer Erzählkunst geliefert[64]. Beide Passagen (und nicht nur sie) zeugen zudem von der Bereitschaft des Acta-Verfassers, um seiner apologetischen Zielsetzung willen – ganz so, wie Cicero dies von Lucceius verlangt hatte – auch von jener in der mimetischen Geschichtsschreibung gern genutzten Lizenz Gebrauch zu machen, derzufolge die Beachtung der auf die Wiedergabe allein der historischen Fakten dringenden »leges historiae« gegebenenfalls zugunsten lebenswahr geschilderter Fiktion hintangestellt werden konnte. In Apg 10–11 beschreibt Lukas kein auch nur im entferntesten so wie geschildert abgelaufenes historisches Ereignis[65], sondern trägt seinen Lesern »im Gewand der Historie« (E. Haenchen) ein die Legitimität der Heidenkirche sicherndes Argument vor: sie sollen wissen, daß sich die Heidenmission (und damit deren Resultat, die heidenchristliche Kirche) ganz und gar dem alles lenkenden Willen Gottes verdankt. Dasselbe apologetische Interesse leitet Lukas in Apg 15; auch hier geht es ihm nicht um eine korrekte Schilderung historischer Vorgänge, sondern wiederum um die dramatische Inszenierung einer für den Erweis der heidenchristlichen Legitimität fundamentalen Aussage: die Leser der Apostelgeschichte sollen aus der lukanischen Schilderung des Apostelkonzils entnehmen, daß die – beschneidungsfreie – Heidenmission bereits von den judenchristlichen Autoritäten Jerusalems gebilligt worden ist[66].

---

63. Dazu E. PLÜMACHER, *Lukas als hellenistischer Schriftsteller. Studien zur Apostelgeschichte* (SUNT, 9), Göttingen, 1972, S. 80-136; ID., *Apostelgeschichte* (Anm. 59), S. 509-513.
64. Dazu PLÜMACHER, *Lukas*, S. 86-89; LÖNING, *Verhältnis* (Anm. 59), S. 315-318; J. WEHNERT, *Die Reinheit des »christlichen Gottesvolkes« aus Juden und Heiden. Studien zum historischen und theologischen Hintergrund des sogenannten Aposteldekrets* (FRLANT, 173), Göttingen, 1997, S. 55-58.
65. E. HAENCHEN, *Die Apostelgeschichte* (KEK, 3), Göttingen, [7]1977, S. 349: Lukas »beschreibt nicht unmittelbar ein wirkliches Geschehen, sondern stellt eine Glaubensüberzeugung (Gott hat die Heidenmission herbeigeführt) im Gewand der Historie dar«.
66. *Ibid.*, S. 446f: »Die Konzeption, mit der Lukas die Legitimität der gesetzesfreien Heidenmission (und d.h. für ihn: ihre Anerkennung durch Jerusalem!) und das Ringen der Antiochener um die Anerkennung dieser ihrer Heidenmission versöhnt, ist eine imaginäre Konstruktion und entspricht keiner geschichtlichen Wirklichkeit«. Das gilt völlig unabhängig davon, ob Lukas bestimmte Textbausteine in der Tradition vorgefunden hat oder nicht. Lukas formt überliefertes Gut gegebenenfalls in seinem Sinne um. Zur Traditionsgrundlage von Apg 10–11 und 15 s. G. LÜDEMANN, *Das frühe Christentum nach den Traditionen der Apostelgeschichte. Ein Kommentar*, Göttingen, 1987, S. 136-138 und 176f.

Der Vorschlag, in der Apostelgeschichte eine historische Monographie zu sehen, wie sie Cicero in seinem Brief an Lucceius konzipiert und, was gemeinhin übersehen wird, im ὑπόμνημα auch selbst gestaltet hat, ist nicht mehr neu. Im Mittelpunkt der hier vorgelegten Erwägungen stand etwas anderes, nämlich die Interpretation der Äußerungen Ciceros über die Art und Weise, in der Lucceius in dem von Cicero projektierten Werk dessen Taten und Schicksale in den Jahren 66 bis 57 schildern sollte. Wie bereits Karl-Ernst Petzold erkannt hat, empfahl Cicero Lucceius, sich dabei der auf psychagogische Wirkung angelegten Stilmittel der mimetischen Historiographie zu bedienen, um mit ihrer Hilfe ein die Leser rundum überzeugendes historisches Plädoyer in Sachen Cicero zu verfassen. Von der Bitte um ein solches in mimetischer Manier gestaltetes Plädoyer ist nun freilich die weitere Bitte Ciceros an Lucceius, für die Schilderung seiner Taten und Schicksale unbedingt die Form der historischen Monographie zu wählen, nicht abzutrennen – dies deshalb nicht, weil Cicero in ihr diejenige literarische Form sah, in der sich das der mimetischen Geschichtsschreibung inhärente und Lucceius zu einschlägiger Nutzung empfohlene psychagogische Potential am eindrücklichsten zur Wirkung bringen lassen würde.

In Stil und Programm der mimetischen Geschichtsschreibung sowie der ihr verpflichteten historischen Monographie hat Cicero freilich keineswegs seine historischen Ideale gesehen; seine Vorstellungen davon, wie man Geschichte zu schreiben habe, waren, wie wir gesehen haben, andere. Wenn der römische Anwalt und Politiker für die Schilderung seines Tuns und Ergehens »a principio coniurationis usque ad reditum nostrum« von Lucceius dennoch die Abfassung einer im psychagogischen Stil der mimetischen Geschichtsschreibung gestalteten historischen Monographie verlangt hat, dann resultiert dies aus den speziellen Zwecken, denen jene Schilderung dienen sollte: den Zwecken einer Cicero-Apologie. Für deren Zwecke – aber eben nur für sie! – ist Cicero die in mimetischer Manier geschriebene historische Monographie als die am meisten taugliche literarische Form erschienen.

Die Eignung der den psychagogischen Darstellungsmitteln der mimetischen Geschichtsschreibung eng verbundenen, wenn nicht gar substantiell verpflichteten historischen Monographie[67] für apologetische

---

67. Auch Sallusts Monographien bezeugen den psychagogischen Charakter der historischen Monographie. Vgl. LEEMAN, *Formen* (Anm. 5), S. 114: Sallust versteht es, »φόβος und ἔλεος zu erregen, nicht im Dienste eines sensationellen Pathos ..., sondern im Dienste einer κάθαρσις, die dem Leser den einzigen Weg zur Freiheit zeigen kann«; s. außerdem H.A. GÄRTNER, *Erzählformen bei Sallust*, in *Historia* 35 (1986) 449-473. Schließlich sei hier noch auf das 2. Makkabäerbuch verwiesen, dessen Verfasser das ψυχαγωγεῖν gleichfalls zu seinen Zielen zählt (s. 2 Makk 2,25).

Zwecke hat nun genauso wie Cicero auch Lukas, der Anwalt der Legitimität eines sich von seinen jüdischen Wurzeln immer weiter entfernenden Heidenchristentums, erkannt[68]. Das literarische Resultat dieser Erkenntnis liegt in der Apostelgeschichte vor[69], einem Werk, das auch auf andere Weise noch von der Neigung und der Fähigkeit des Lukas zeugt, zur Beförderung seiner apologetischen Absichten bei der hellenistisch-römischen Historiographie Anleihen zu machen. Ein charakteristisches Beispiel hierfür sei genannt: die Konzeption von den (Missions-) Reden als die (Kirchen-)Geschichte lenkenden Faktoren, die sich (mutatis mutandis) genauso wie in der Apostelgeschichte auch bei Dionys von Halikarnass und Livius findet, und die Lukas dazu benutzt hat, um aufzuweisen, daß bei den zur Entstehung der heidenchristlichen Kirche führenden Geschehnissen das in den Missionsreden der Apostel und des Paulus zu Wort kommende – Legitimität spendende! – Jesuszeugnis selbst das entscheidende Movens der auch sonst von Gott gelenkten Ereignisse war[70].

Schließlich: man kann fragen, ob es sich denn überhaupt lohnt, in Erfahrung bringen zu wollen, welcher literarischen Form die Apostelgeschichte zuzurechnen sei. Auf diese Frage kann ich nicht treffender antworten als mit dem folgenden Zitat: »Nur durch die Form wird die Geschichte faßbar, und nur durch die Sprache dieser Form wird sie mitteilbar. Die Form eines Geschichtswerkes verstehen heißt also das Wesentliche seines 'Inhalts' verstehen«. Mit dieser Einsicht hat Anton Daniel Leeman den einleitenden Absatz eines dem »Großmeister ... der historischen Monographie in Rom« gewidmeten und »Formen sallustia-

---

68. Entsprechend ist meine 1979 publizierte Äußerung zum Grund für das lukanische Interesse an der Form der historischen Monographie (s.o. Anm. 2, S. 463) zu ergänzen.

69. Um nicht mißverstanden zu werden: ich behaupte natürlich nicht, daß die weitgehende formale Kongruenz, die zwischen der Apostelgeschichte einerseits und Ciceros im Lucceiusbrief niedergelegten Vorstellungen von einer historischen Monographie sowie seinem ὑπόμνημα andererseits besteht, aus lukanischer Cicero-Kenntnis resultiert. Mehr, als daß Lukas hier aus den Traditionen der hellenistisch-römischen Historiographie geschöpft hat, lässt sich – wie im Falle des 2. Makkabäerbuches auch – nicht feststellen. Immerhin sei vermerkt, daß das von Atticus in Griechenland verbreitete ὑπόμνημα (Att. II 1,2) noch Lukas' Zeitgenossen Plutarch vorgelegen hat (s.o. S. 770) und der Lucceiusbrief von einem weiteren Zeitgenossen des Acta-Verfassers, dem jüngeren Plinius, in einem Brief an Tacitus nachgeahmt worden ist (epist. VII 33):, vgl. H.W. TRAUB, Pliny's Treatment of History in Epistolary Form, in Transactions and Proceedings of the American Philological Association 86 (1955) 213-232, dort S. 226-229; selbst im griechischen Roman hat er Spuren hinterlassen, vgl. Achilles Tatius VIII 4,4: ἔπειτα τῶν ἔργων παρελθόντων ἡ διήγησις τὸν οὐκέτι πάσχοντα ψυχαγωγεῖ μᾶλλον ἢ λυπεῖ mit fam. XXII 4,15–5,1: »habet enim praeteriti doloris secura recordatio delectationem«.

70. Vgl. E. PLÜMACHER, Die Missionsreden der Apostelgeschichte und Dionys von Halikarnass, in NTS 39 (1993) 161-177.

nischer Geschichtsschreibung« betitelten Aufsatzes beschlossen[71]. Es kann nicht falsch sein, Leemans Einsicht auch im Blick auf die lukanische Schriftstellerei gelten zu lassen.

Fuggerstr. 19   Eckhard PLÜMACHER
D-10777 Berlin

---

71. LEEMAN, *Formen* (Anm. 5), S. 108. So auch WEDDERBURN, *Frage* (Anm. 1), S. 304: »Die Frage der Gattung eines Werkes ist deswegen besonders wichtig, weil die richtige Wahrnehmung der Gattung eines Textes unentbehrlich ist für das Verstehen dieses Textes ... In der Frage nach der Gattung der Apg geht es also um den Versuch, zu verstehen, was der Verfasser der Apg wollte und beabsichtigte, als er sein Werk schrieb«.

INDEXES

LIST OF ABBREVIATIONS

AASF	Annales Academiae Scientiarum Fennicae
AB	Anchor Bible
AfrTJ	Africa Theological Journal
AGAJU	Arbeiten zur Geschichte des antiken Judentums und des Urchristentums
AJBI	Annual of the Japanese Biblical Institute
AnASU	Annales Academiae R. Scientiarum Upsaliensis
AnBib	Analecta Biblica
AnGreg	Analecta Gregoriana
ANRW	Aufstieg und Niedergang der römischen Welt
ANTZ	Arbeiten zur neutestamentlichen Theologie und Zeitgeschichte
ASNU	Acta Seminarii Neotestamentici Upsaliensis
ATANT	Abhandlungen zur Theologie des Alten und Neuen Testaments
BAFCS	The Book of Acts in Its First Century Setting
BBB	Bonner biblische Beiträge
BBR	Bibliographies for Biblical Research
BCH	Bulletin de correspondance hellénique
BETL	Bibliotheca Ephemeridum Theologicarum Lovaniensium
BGBE	Beiträge zur Geschichte der biblischen Exegese
BHT	Beiträge zur historischen Theologie
Bib	Biblica
BibTod	The Bible Today
BJRL	Bulletin of the John Rylands Library
BL	Bibel und Liturgie
BN	Biblische Notizen
BTB	Biblical Theology Bulletin
BTS	Biblisch-theologische Studien
BU	Biblische Untersuchungen
BWANT	Beiträge zur Wissenschaft vom Alten und Neuen Testament
BZ	Biblische Zeitschrift
BZNW	Beihefte zur ZNW
CBET	Contributions to Biblical Exegesis and Theology
CBFV	Cahiers bibliques. Foi & Vie
CBQ	The Catholic Biblical Quarterly
CNT	Commentaire du Nouveau Testament
ComViat	Communio Viatorum
ConBibNT	Coniectanea Biblica. New Testament Series
CRINT	Compendium Rerum Iudaicarum ad Novum Testamentum
CurrTMiss	Currents in Theology and Mission
DBS	Dictionnaire de la Bible. Supplément

ÉB	Études bibliques
EdF	Erträge der Forschung
EDNT	Exegetical Dictionary of the New Testament
EE	Estudios eclesiásticos
EHPR	Études d'histoire et de philosophie religieuses
EHS	Europäische Hochschulschriften
EKK	Evangelisch-katholischer Kommentar zum Neuen Testament
EstBíb	Estudios bíblicos
ETL	Ephemerides Theologicae Lovanienses
ETR	Études théologiques et religieuses
ETS	Erfurter theologische Studien
EvErz	Der evangelische Erzieher
EvQ	Evangelical Quarterly
EvT	Evangelische Theologie
EWNT	Exegetisches Wörterbuch zum Neuen Testament
Exp	The Expositor
ExpT	The Expository Times
FRLANT	Forschungen zur Religion und Literatur des Alten und Neuen Testaments
FTS	Frankfurter theologische Studien
FzB	Forschung zur Bibel
GNS	Good News Studies
GNT	Grundrisse zum Neuen Testament
GTA	Göttinger theologische Arbeiten
HBS	Herders Biblische Studien
HCNT	Hand-Commentar zum Neuen Testament
HNT	Handbuch zum Neuen Testament
HSS	Harvard Semitic Studies
HTK	Herders theologischer Kommentar zum Neuen Testament
HTR	Harvard Theological Review
HTS	Harvard Theological Studies
HUCA	Hebrew Union College Annual
IBS	Irish Biblical Studies
ICC	International Critical Commentary
Int	Interpretation
JBL	Journal of Biblical Literature
JPT (SS)	Journal of Pentecostal Theology (Supplement Series)
JSHRZ	Jüdische Schriften aus hellenistisch-römischer Zeit
JSJ	Journal for the Study of Judaism in the Persian, Hellenistic and Roman Period
JSNT (SS)	Journal for the Study of the New Testament (Supplement Series)
JSP (SS)	Journal for the Study of the Pseudepigrapha (Supplement Series)
JTS	The Journal of Theological Studies

KEK   Kritisch-exegetischer Kommentar über das Neue Testament

LD   Lectio Divina

NCBC   New Century Bible Commentaries
NEB   Neue Echter Bibel
NICNT   New International Commentary on the New Testament
NIGTC   New International Greek Testament Commentary
NJBC   New Jerome Biblical Commentary
NKZ   Neue kirchliche Zeitschrift
NRT   Nouvelle revue théologique
NT   Novum Testamentum
NTAbh   Neutestamentliche Abhandlungen
NTD   Das Neue Testament Deutsch
NTOA   Novum Testamentum et Orbis Antiquus
NTS   New Testament Studies
NTSup   Supplements to Novum Testamentum
NTT   Nederlands theologisch tijdschrift
NTTS   New Testament Tools and Studies

ÖBS   Österreichische biblische Studien
ÖTK   Ökumenischer Taschenbuchkommentar zum Neuen Testament
OTP   Old Testament Pseudepigrapha

ParSpirV   Parola, spirito e vita. Quaderni di lettura biblica
PerspRelSt Perspectives in Religious Studies
PIBA   Proceedings of the Irish Biblical Association
PRE   Pauly's Real-Encyclopädie der classischen Altertumswissenschaft

QDisp   Quaestiones Disputatae

RB   Revue biblique
RCT   Revista catalana de teologia
RestQ   Restoration Quarterly
RevSR   Revue des sciences religieuses
RHPR   Revue d'histoire et de philosophie religieuses
RivBib   Rivista biblica
RNT   Regensburger Neues Testament
RSR   Recherches de science religieuse
RTP   Revue de théologie et de philosophie
RTR   Reformed Theological Review

SANT   Studien zum Alten und Neuen Testament
SBAB   Stuttgarter biblische Aufsatzbände
SBL DS   Society of Biblical Literature. Dissertation Series
SBL EJL   Society of Biblical Literature. Early Judaism and Its Literature
SBL MS   Society of Biblical Literature. Monograph Series
SBM   Stuttgarter biblische Monographien
SBS   Stuttgarter Bibelstudien

SBT	Studies in Biblical Theology
SC	La Scuola cattolica
SE	Science et esprit
SJT	Scottish Journal of Theology
SKK	Stuttgarter kleiner Kommentar zum Neuen Testament
SNT	Studien zum Neuen Testament
SNTA	Studiorum Novi Testamenti Auxilia
SNTS MS	Society for New Testament Studies. Monograph Series
SNTU	Studien zum Neuen Testament und seiner Umwelt
SPB	Studia Postbiblica
ST	Studia Theologica
SUC	Schriften des Urchristentums
SUNT	Studien zur Umwelt des Neuen Testaments
TANZ	Texte und Arbeiten zum neutestamentlichen Zeitalter
TB	Theologische Beiträge
TDNT	Theological Dictionary of the New Testament
TF	Theologische Forschung
TGeg	Theologie der Gegenwart
THNT	Theologischer Handkommentar zum Neuen Testament
TLZ	Theologische Literaturzeitung
TQ	Theologische Quartalschrift
TRE	Theologische Realenzyklopädie
TS	Theological Studies
TSAJ	Texte und Studien zum antiken Judentum
TSK	Theologische Studien und Kritiken
TR	Theologische Rundschau
TRev	Theologische Revue
TrinJ	Trinity Journal
TTZ	Trierer theologische Zeitschrift
TU	Texte und Untersuchungen zur Geschichte der altchristlichen Literatur
TViat	Theologia Viatorum
TWNT	Theologisches Wörterbuch zum Neuen Testament
TyndB	Tyndale Bulletin
TZ	Theologische Zeitschrift
WBC	Word Biblical Commentary
WdF	Wege der Forschung
WMANT	Wissenschaftliche Monographien zum Alten und Neuen Testament
WuD	Wort und Dienst
WUNT	Wissenschaftliche Untersuchungen zum Neuen Testament
ZBK	Zürcher Bibelkommentare. Neues Testament
ZDPV	Zeitschrift des deutschen Palästina-Vereins
ZNW	Zeitschrift für die neutestamentliche Wissenschaft und die Kunde der älteren Kirche
ZTK	Zeitschrift für Theologie und Kirche

INDEX OF AUTHORS

STEINER, A. 421[5] 423[12] 441[57.58]
STENDAHL, K. 434[45] 585[5]
STENSCHKE, C. 461[89]
STEPP, P.L. 46[211]
STERLING, G.E. 47[216] 586[7] 587[10.11] 599[65] 677[8] 695[8]
STEYN, G.J. 374[76] 378[94] 383[112] 644[23] 746[5.6]
STINESPRING, W.G. 37[169] 478[20]
STÖGER, A. 314[4] 735[613]
STONEMAN, R. 440[54]
STRAATMAN, J.W. 212[23]
STRACK, H.L. 228[17] 558[52] 602[75]
STRANGE, W.A. xv 51[237] 84[5] 91[33] 97 104[70] 105
STRAUSS, M.L. xvi 10[25]43[197] 55[257] 133[2] 137[13] 145[43.46] 148[53] 149[60] 151[65.66] 152[68] 158[92] 159[96] 160[97] 161[102.104.105] 162[107] 163[108.111] 314[3] 479[24.25] 480[30]
STREETER, B.H. 49[230] 84[4] 627[6]
STRONSTAD, R. 165[3] 464[110]
STRUGNELL, J. 597[57]
STUHLMACHER, P. 387[130]
STUHLMUELLER, C. 32[149] 633[12]
SUGGS, M.J. 143[34]
SURKAU, H.W. 565[7]
SUSSMAN, Y. 597[57]
SWEETLAND, D.M. 9[23] 31[146] 31[148] 672[33.34]
SWELLENGREBEL, J.L. 368[48]
SWETNAM, J. 755[38]
SWIDLER, L. 518[5]
SYLVA, D.D. 9[24] 40[184] 43[196] 44[203] 128[64] 189[12] 716[41]
SYREENI, K. 51[238]

TAEGER, J.W. 33[153]
TAJRA, H.W. 204[3]
TALBERT, C.A. 8[22] 9[23] 9[24] 15[64] 30[144] 31[146] 31[148] 32[151] 36[167] 37[171] 40[181.184] 43[197] 44[200] 46[211.212] 52[240.241.243] 53[245] 54[252] 71[41] 306[26] 376[81] 449[11] 465[116] 485[3] 644[20] 759[1]
TANGHE, V. 123[42.43]
TANNEHILL, R.C. 8[22] 40[182] 51[238] 111[6] 112[9] 118[30] 124[48.49] 128[65.66] 135[7] 234[44] 302[12] 304[18] 309[35] 372[66] 374[74] 390[144] 393 394[165] 395[169] 442[59] 448[9.10] 455[70] 457[78] 463[104] 493[1] 592[35] 596[53] 607[12] 610[29] 616[64] 649[37] 693[2] 723[1]

TATUM, W.A. 165[3] 180[49]
TAVERDON, P. xv 84[5] 95[49] 100[53]
TAYLOR, J. xx xxi 8[22] 49[231] 282[2.3] 283[4.5] 284[8] 361[14.18] 363[24] 364[27.29] 365[36] 367 369[52]
TAYLOR, N.H. 717[43] 719[57]
TAYLOR, V. 593[40]
TETLOW, E.M. 521[17] 522
THACKERAY, H.S.J. 588[18]
THEISSEN, G. 672[30.31]
THEOBALD, M. 685[32]
THISELTON, A.C. 138[18.19]
THOMPSON, R.P. 9[24] 189[12]
THOMPSON, S. 264[27]
THORNTON, C.-J. 49[229] 625[6] 725[5]
TIEDE, D.L. xviii 8[22] 39[179.180] 189[12] 194[33-35] 376[82] 390[144] 709[2] 710[8.10] 718[54]
TISCHENDORF, C. 360[10]
TÖDT, H.E. 565[7.10] 573[47]
TOMSON, P.J. 589[19] 589[22] 591[33] 600[69]
TORREY, C.C. 4
TRAUB, H.W. 774[69]
TRAVIS, S. 448[7]
TRITES, A.A. 30[144] 465[116] 466[119]
TROCMÉ, É. 20[95] 165[3] 717[45]
TROIANI, L. 703[31]
TUCKETT, C.M. xvi xvii 5[9] 9[23] 9[24] 30[143] 36[167] 39[178] 43[197] 45[205] 49[231] 55[256] 69[34] 136[9] 141[27] 142[32.33] 143[35.37] 145[41.46] 146[48] 161[103] 163[108] 189[12] 338[9] 358[5.7] 380[102.104] 381[105-107] 382[108.109] 383[111.115] 384[116] 385[122] 386[123-128] 387[129.131] 391[149] 392[151] 426[23] 627[5] 640[6] 644[23] 652[48] 694[5] 707[38] 753[30] 754[36]
TUILIER, A. 285[11]
TURNER, M.M.B. 29[142] 41[185] 42[192.194] 138[18] 143[38] 154[77] 155[83] 165[3] 173[28] 380[104] 382[108] 383[111] 385[122] 448[7] 464[110]
TUTTLE, G.A. 43[197]
TYSON, J.B. xviii 9[24] 11[26] 14[51] 28[138] 29[142] 39[177.180] 40[181-183] 46[211] 189[12] 191[18.19] 192[23.24] 193[25-27] 199[51.53] 373[72] 374[73.74] 389[140] 423[14] 438[51] 440[52] 443[62] 561[61] 590[24.26] 693[2] 694[5] 702[28] 705[37]

ÜBELACKER, W. 17[73]
UNTERGASSMAIR, F.G. 29[142]
URBACH, E.E. 646[29]
USPENSKY, B. 440[52]

INDEX OF BIBLICAL REFERENCES

OLD TESTAMENT

25,6-7	258[15]
31,20	706

WISDOM

1,7	169 179[46]
2–5	160[98]
3,1-10	647
3,7	272
3,9	272
4,15	272
5,15-16	647
9,1-6	291
9,8	558
9,10	558
9,17	169
14,11	272
18,13	646
19,15	272[41]

SIRACH

1,14	176
4,4-5	706
15,3	291
18,20	272
23,24	272
24,8	114
24,11-12	114
24,19-22	291
24,20	114
24,23	115
34,1-8	745
36,10	115
37,26	115
44,19-21	115 127[62]
44,20	113
44,21	115
45,25	115
46,8	115
48,12	179
50,20	350

ISAIAH

1,1	676[4]
2,3	619
2,19	568[30]
2,21	568[30]
3,13-14	567 568
5,1-7	646
5,7	646
6,9-10	63 64 176 199 308 390 658
6,9	727
6,10	381
7,14	321
8,9	463[108]
9,1	343
9,6-7	112[9]
10,3	272
10,12	272
11,1-5	170
11,1-2	xxii 320
11,2	169
14,9	305[20]
14,18	305[20]
14,22	463[108] 568[30]
14,32	305[20]
15,1	120[36]
23,17	272
24,22	272
24,23	648
28,26-27	19
29,6	272
29,18	488
32,15	180 323
33,17-24	648
35,5-6	488
35,5	381[106]
40–55	158-160
40,1	301[8]
40,5	63 304 395 436
40,11	646
41,8-9	159
41,14	301[8]
42,1	xxii 169 314 315
42,6-7	306
42,6	115 305
42,7	336 339 435
42,16	339
43,14	301[8]
44,1	159
44,3	169
44,24	301[8]
45,4	159
46,13	306
48,16	169
48,20	463[108]
49,1	342
49,3	159
49,6	115 304 305 374[76] 395 435 463[108]
49,9	306
49,13	301[8]
51,17-23	310[38]
52,1-10	648
52,9	301[8]
52,10	304 306
52,13	140[25]
53	140 159 160
53,12	559
55,3	129 130
55,8-9	669
56,1	306
56,7	715
57,19	377[90] 462[100]
58,6	144[39] 229 381-383 461[90] 484 649
59,21	169
60,1-9	306
60,1	305
60,12	305[20] 353
60,19-22	306
60,19	305
61,1-2	xviii 143 144 159[93] 180 181 229 380 382 383 434 465 484 612 645 649
61,1	xxiv 144[39] 169 172 336 381 384 387 461[90] 483[1]
62,11	463[108]
63,10-11	169
63,18	715[34]
66,1-2	552 554 712[23] 718[49]
66,1	459

New Testament

Matthew		Matthew (cont.)		Mark (cont.)	
1,1	437	23,2	229[23]	1,39	226[6] 249[111]
3,2	652	23,37-39	208		386 666
3,9	473	23,38	310		675[3] 685[32]
4,10	471	24,1-2	715	1,40-45	238 248[106]
4,23-25	249[111]	24,15	715	2,1-12	241[66]
4,23	666	25,36	275[46] 278	2,1	685[32]
5,4	143[37]	25,43	275[46] 278	2,6-7	238
5,25	309[31]	26,26	281 292	2,7-11	239
5,44	508	26,29	292[23]	2,12	239
6,9	751	26,31	289	2,13-17	238
6,20	555	26,59-60	571	2,17	136[9]
6,24	510	26,61	548 571 716	2,18	299
7,11	173[29]	26,63	571	3,1	366
7,28	225[5]	26,64	556[40] 571	3,6	222[62] 591[31]
8,5-13	510		573	3,7-12	249
8,10	435[48]	26,65	571	3,8	249[112]
8,11	473	27,11	198[48]	3,11	248
9,2	238[58]	27,19	206[11]	3,13	751
9,7	239[59]	27,24-25	206[11]	3,19	226[6]
9,24	243[76]	27,26	207	4,1-9	226[6]
9,36	290	27,29	198[48]	4,12	63 429
10,1	751	27,37	198[48]	5,22-24	243
10,18	606[4]	27,40	716[40]	5,35-43	243
10,32-33	572[46]	27,50-51	580	5,35	243[75] 247
10,40	262	27,50	571	5,38	243[75]
11,19	739[22]	27,51	716	5,38-40	247
11,25-27	751[20]			5,39-40	243[76]
12,14	591[31]	Mark		5,40	246[98]
12,37	739[22]			5,41	244
13,14-15	429	1,1	165[6] 437	5,42	241[66]
14,19-20	281	1,2-3	434	6,1-6	227[13] 235
15,1	229[23]	1,9-11	485		236[47] 359
15,29	290	1,10	384[117]	6,5	249[110]
15,36-37	281	1,11	150	6,14-29	208[17] 219
16,13	751	1,14-15	165[6] 227	6,16	208
17,1-9	752		485 487 645	6,30-44	252
17,5	752		650	6,34	283 290
17,9	748[11]	1,16–3,19	487	6,41	252 281
19,1	502[25]	1,20	136[9]	6,43	281
19,28	435[48]	1,21-28	226[6]	6,48	269
21,11	385[121]	1,21-22	235 386	7,1-23	63 608[17]
21,12-13	715	1,21	366	7,3	198
21,14	715	1,28	386	7,9-13	592[34]
21,23	457[77]	1,29-31	248[106] 250[117]	7,24-31	619
21,33	647	1,32-34	145[41] 248	7,24-30	237
22,16	222	1,33	248[107]	8,1-10	252
		1,35-39	248[106]	8,6	281

1,16	111 435⁴⁸	1,53-55	514	1,79	456 670 673
	461⁹⁴	1,54-55	112 122	1,80	171²³ 435⁴⁸
1,17	66 156 386	1,54	434 435⁴⁸	2,1-20	298
1,18	269³⁶ 334		461⁹⁴	2,1-14	633
1,19	273 555	1,55	124 303¹⁶	2,2	177 683²⁸
1,20	497		434 473	2,4	158 228
1,21-22	712²³	1,56	664		245⁸⁹ 297
1,22	749 750	1,57–2,52	634		298 666
1,23	21	1,57–2,40	632 633		675² 676⁵
1,25	180⁴⁸	1,57–2,14	634		682²⁴
1,26-38	xx 273 274	1,57-80	437 633	2,8-15	456
	456 477	1,58	269³⁶	2,8-14	750¹⁷
	608¹⁵ 633	1,65	675² 676⁵	2,9-15	608¹⁵ 750
	750	1,66	117	2,9	555³⁹
1,26-28	272	1,67-79	437	2,10	303¹⁶
1,26	555³⁹	1,67	172 179 437	2,11	151 158 277
1,27	158 273		454⁶⁰		297 461
1,28-38	333	1,68-79	471 477 551	2,13-14	556⁴²
1,28-29	273	1,68-75	477	2,13	338
1,29	309	1,68-69	434 470	2,14	277 303¹⁶
1,30	274	1,68	xx 113 245⁸⁷		483¹ 611³³
1,31	321 437		257 261 275	2,15-52	633 634
1,32-35	38¹⁷³ 321		277⁴⁸ 435⁴⁸	2,15	555³⁹
1,32-33	xv 111 126⁶¹		461⁹⁴ 562	2,20	614⁵¹ 665
	158 321 325	1,69-75	275	2,21-28	590²⁷
	326 654	1,69	158 303¹⁶	2,21	298 456 705
1,32	112 129		461 470³		750
	303¹⁶		551³⁰	2,22-40	555³⁸
1,34	273 322	1,70-71	470	2,22-39	xxi 297-312
	334	1,70	454⁶⁰ 481		425²¹ 432
1,35	xvii xxii 38	1,72-73	113		704 713
	66 179 230²⁶	1,72	276 469-471	2,22-24	75 298
	276⁴⁷ 313-		476 477 481	2,22	496 613⁴⁶
	327 386 464		482		666
	612³⁸	1,73-75	470	2,23-24	484
1,37	xv 112 117	1,73-74	551	2,25-35	299
	123 269³⁶	1,73	124 434 471	2,25-28	115
1,38	273 555³⁹		473	2,25-27	299
1,39-56	633 634	1,74	471 551³⁰	2,25-26	xxi 302 437
1,39	458 676⁵	1,76-79	437 478	2,25	172 301 434
1,41-45	325⁴⁰ 437	1,76-78	275		435⁴⁸ 461⁹⁴
1,41	172 179 437	1,76	454⁶⁰ 460⁸⁶		562 616⁶⁴
1,43	142 460⁸⁶		670		723
1,45	273	1,77	303¹⁶ 382	2,26-27	230²⁶
1,46-55	514		434 436⁴⁹	2,26	158 298
1,47	171²³ 434		461 461⁹¹	2,27	172 465
	461	1,78	xx 257 261		712²³
1,48	112		275⁴⁶ 276	2,28	303
1,50	113¹⁴ 616⁶⁴		277⁴⁸	2,29-34	38

LIST OF CONTRIBUTORS

BIBLIOTHECA EPHEMERIDUM THEOLOGICARUM LOVANIENSIUM

SERIES I

* = Out of print

*1. *Miscellanea dogmatica in honorem Eximii Domini J. Bittremieux*, 1947.
*2-3. *Miscellanea moralia in honorem Eximii Domini A. Janssen*, 1948.
*4. G. PHILIPS, *La grâce des justes de l'Ancien Testament*, 1948.
*5. G. PHILIPS, *De ratione instituendi tractatum de gratia nostrae sanctificationis*, 1953.
6-7. *Recueil Lucien Cerfaux. Études d'exégèse et d'histoire religieuse*, 1954. 504 et 577 p. FB 1000 par tome. Cf. *infra*, nᵒˢ 18 et 71 (t. III).
8. G. THILS, *Histoire doctrinale du mouvement œcuménique*, 1955. Nouvelle édition, 1963. 338 p. FB 135.
*9. *Études sur l'Immaculée Conception*, 1955.
*10. J.A. O'DONOHOE, *Tridentine Seminary Legislation*, 1957.
*11. G. THILS, *Orientations de la théologie*, 1958.
*12-13. J. COPPENS, A. DESCAMPS, É. MASSAUX (ed.), *Sacra Pagina. Miscellanea Biblica Congressus Internationalis Catholici de Re Biblica*, 1959.
*14. *Adrien VI, le premier Pape de la contre-réforme*, 1959.
*15. F. CLAEYS BOUUAERT, *Les déclarations et serments imposés par la loi civile aux membres du clergé belge sous le Directoire (1795-1801)*, 1960.
*16. G. THILS, *La «Théologie œcuménique». Notion-Formes-Démarches*, 1960.
17. G. THILS, *Primauté pontificale et prérogatives épiscopales. «Potestas ordinaria» au Concile du Vatican*, 1961. 103 p. FB 50.
*18. *Recueil Lucien Cerfaux*, t. III, 1962. Cf. *infra*, n° 71.
*19. *Foi et réflexion philosophique. Mélanges F. Grégoire*, 1961.
*20. *Mélanges G. Ryckmans*, 1963.
21. G. THILS, *L'infaillibilité du peuple chrétien «in credendo»*, 1963. 67 p. FB 50.
*22. J. FÉRIN & L. JANSSENS, *Progestogènes et morale conjugale*, 1963.
*23. *Collectanea Moralia in honorem Eximii Domini A. Janssen*, 1964.
24. H. CAZELLES (ed.), *De Mari à Qumrân. L'Ancien Testament. Son milieu. Ses écrits. Ses relectures juives* (Hommage J. Coppens, I), 1969. 158*-370 p. FB 900.
*25. I. DE LA POTTERIE (ed.), *De Jésus aux évangiles. Tradition et rédaction dans les évangiles synoptiques* (Hommage J. Coppens, II), 1967.
26. G. THILS & R.E. BROWN (ed.), *Exégèse et théologie* (Hommage J. Coppens, III), 1968. 328 p. FB 700.
27. J. COPPENS (ed.), *Ecclesia a Spiritu sancto edocta. Hommage à Mgr G. Philips*, 1970. 640 p. FB 1000.
28. J. COPPENS (ed.), *Sacerdoce et célibat. Études historiques et théologiques*, 1971. 740 p. FB 700.

29. M. DIDIER (ed.), *L'évangile selon Matthieu. Rédaction et théologie*, 1972. 432 p. FB 1000.
*30. J. KEMPENEERS, *Le Cardinal van Roey en son temps*, 1971.

SERIES II

31. F. NEIRYNCK, *Duality in Mark. Contributions to the Study of the Markan Redaction*, 1972. Revised edition with Supplementary Notes, 1988. 252 p. FB 1200.
32. F. NEIRYNCK (ed.), *L'évangile de Luc. Problèmes littéraires et théologiques*, 1973. *L'évangile de Luc – The Gospel of Luke*. Revised and enlarged edition, 1989. x-590 p. FB 2200.
33. C. BREKELMANS (ed.), *Questions disputées d'Ancien Testament. Méthode et théologie*, 1974. *Continuing Questions in Old Testament Method and Theology*. Revised and enlarged edition by M. VERVENNE, 1989. 245 p. FB 1200.
34. M. SABBE (ed.), *L'évangile selon Marc. Tradition et rédaction*, 1974. Nouvelle édition augmentée, 1988. 601 p. FB 2400.
35. B. WILLAERT (ed.), *Philosophie de la religion – Godsdienstfilosofie. Miscellanea Albert Dondeyne*, 1974. Nouvelle édition, 1987. 458 p. FB 1600.
36. G. PHILIPS, *L'union personnelle avec le Dieu vivant. Essai sur l'origine et le sens de la grâce créée*, 1974. Édition révisée, 1989. 299 p. FB 1000.
37. F. NEIRYNCK, in collaboration with T. HANSEN and F. VAN SEGBROECK, *The Minor Agreements of Matthew and Luke against Mark with a Cumulative List*, 1974. 330 p. FB 900.
38. J. COPPENS, *Le messianisme et sa relève prophétique. Les anticipations vétérotestamentaires. Leur accomplissement en Jésus*, 1974. Édition révisée, 1989. XIII-265 p. FB 1000.
39. D. SENIOR, *The Passion Narrative according to Matthew. A Redactional Study*, 1975. New impression, 1982. 440 p. FB 1000.
40. J. DUPONT (ed.), *Jésus aux origines de la christologie*, 1975. Nouvelle édition augmentée, 1989. 458 p. FB 1500.
41. J. COPPENS (ed.), *La notion biblique de Dieu*, 1976. Réimpression, 1985. 519 p. FB 1600.
42. J. LINDEMANS & H. DEMEESTER (ed.), *Liber Amicorum Monseigneur W. Onclin*, 1976. XXII-396 p. FB 1000.
43. R.E. HOECKMAN (ed.), *Pluralisme et œcuménisme en recherches théologiques. Mélanges offerts au R.P. Dockx, O.P.*, 1976. 316 p. FB 1000.
44. M. DE JONGE (ed.), *L'évangile de Jean. Sources, rédaction, théologie*, 1977. Réimpression, 1987. 416 p. FB 1500.
45. E.J.M. VAN EIJL (ed.), *Facultas S. Theologiae Lovaniensis 1432-1797. Bijdragen tot haar geschiedenis. Contributions to its History. Contributions à son histoire*, 1977. 570 p. FB 1700.
46. M. DELCOR (ed.), *Qumrân. Sa piété, sa théologie et son milieu*, 1978. 432 p. FB 1700.
47. M. CAUDRON (ed.), *Faith and Society. Foi et société. Geloof en maatschappij. Acta Congressus Internationalis Theologici Lovaniensis 1976*, 1978. 304 p. FB 1150.

48. J. KREMER (ed.), *Les Actes des Apôtres. Traditions, rédaction, théologie,* 1979. 590 p. FB 1700.
49. F. NEIRYNCK, avec la collaboration de J. DELOBEL, T. SNOY, G. VAN BELLE, F. VAN SEGBROECK, *Jean et les Synoptiques. Examen critique de l'exégèse de M.-É. Boismard,* 1979. XII-428 p. FB 1000.
50. J. COPPENS, *La relève apocalyptique du messianisme royal. I. La royauté – Le règne – Le royaume de Dieu. Cadre de la relève apocalyptique,* 1979. 325 p. FB 1000.
51. M. GILBERT (ed.), *La Sagesse de l'Ancien Testament,* 1979. Nouvelle édition mise à jour, 1990. 455 p. FB 1500.
52. B. DEHANDSCHUTTER, *Martyrium Polycarpi. Een literair-kritische studie,* 1979. 296 p. FB 1000.
53. J. LAMBRECHT (ed.), *L'Apocalypse johannique et l'Apocalyptique dans le Nouveau Testament,* 1980. 458 p. FB 1400.
54. P.-M. BOGAERT (ed.), *Le livre de Jérémie. Le prophète et son milieu. Les oracles et leur transmission,* 1981. *Nouvelle édition mise à jour,* 1997. 448 p. FB 1800.
55. J. COPPENS, *La relève apocalyptique du messianisme royal. III. Le Fils de l'homme néotestamentaire.* Édition posthume par F. NEIRYNCK, 1981. XIV-192 p. FB 800.
56. J. VAN BAVEL & M. SCHRAMA (ed.), *Jansénius et le Jansénisme dans les Pays-Bas. Mélanges Lucien Ceyssens,* 1982. 247 p. FB 1000.
57. J.H. WALGRAVE, *Selected Writings – Thematische geschriften. Thomas Aquinas, J.H. Newman, Theologia Fundamentalis.* Edited by G. DE SCHRIJVER & J.J. KELLY, 1982. XLIII-425 p. FB 1000.
58. F. NEIRYNCK & F. VAN SEGBROECK, avec la collaboration de E. MANNING, *Ephemerides Theologicae Lovanienses 1924-1981. Tables générales. (Bibliotheca Ephemeridum Theologicarum Lovaniensium 1947-1981),* 1982. 400 p. FB 1600.
59. J. DELOBEL (ed.), *Logia. Les paroles de Jésus – The Sayings of Jesus. Mémorial Joseph Coppens,* 1982. 647 p. FB 2000.
60. F. NEIRYNCK, *Evangelica. Gospel Studies – Études d'évangile. Collected Essays.* Edited by F. VAN SEGBROECK, 1982. XIX-1036 p. FB 2000.
61. J. COPPENS, *La relève apocalyptique du messianisme royal. II. Le Fils d'homme vétéro- et intertestamentaire.* Édition posthume par J. LUST, 1983. XVII-272 p. FB 1000.
62. J.J. KELLY, *Baron Friedrich von Hügel's Philosophy of Religion,* 1983. 232 p. FB 1500.
63. G. DE SCHRIJVER, *Le merveilleux accord de l'homme et de Dieu. Étude de l'analogie de l'être chez Hans Urs von Balthasar,* 1983. 344 p. FB 1500.
64. J. GROOTAERS & J.A. SELLING, *The 1980 Synod of Bishops: «On the Role of the Family». An Exposition of the Event and an Analysis of its Texts.* Preface by Prof. emeritus L. JANSSENS, 1983. 375 p. FB 1500.
65. F. NEIRYNCK & F. VAN SEGBROECK, *New Testament Vocabulary. A Companion Volume to the Concordance,* 1984. XVI-494 p. FB 2000.
66. R.F. COLLINS, *Studies on the First Letter to the Thessalonians,* 1984. XI-415 p. FB 1500.
67. A. PLUMMER, *Conversations with Dr. Döllinger 1870-1890.* Edited with Introduction and Notes by R. BOUDENS, with the collaboration of L. KENIS, 1985. LIV-360 p. FB 1800.

68. N. Lohfink (ed.), *Das Deuteronomium. Entstehung, Gestalt und Botschaft / Deuteronomy: Origin, Form and Message*, 1985. XI-382 p. FB 2000.

69. P.F. Fransen, *Hermeneutics of the Councils and Other Studies*. Collected by H.E. Mertens & F. De Graeve, 1985. 543 p. FB 1800.

70. J. Dupont, *Études sur les Évangiles synoptiques*. Présentées par F. Neirynck, 1985. 2 tomes, XXI-IX-1210 p. FB 2800.

71. *Recueil Lucien Cerfaux*, t. III, 1962. Nouvelle édition revue et complétée, 1985. LXXX-458 p. FB 1600.

72. J. Grootaers, *Primauté et collégialité. Le dossier de Gérard Philips sur la Nota Explicativa Praevia (Lumen gentium, Chap. III)*. Présenté avec introduction historique, annotations et annexes. Préface de G. Thils, 1986. 222 p. FB 1000.

73. A. Vanhoye (ed.), *L'apôtre Paul. Personnalité, style et conception du ministère*, 1986. XIII-470 p. FB 2600.

74. J. Lust (ed.), *Ezekiel and His Book. Textual and Literary Criticism and their Interrelation*, 1986. X-387 p. FB 2700.

75. É. Massaux, *Influence de l'Évangile de saint Matthieu sur la littérature chrétienne avant saint Irénée*. Réimpression anastatique présentée par F. Neirynck. *Supplément: Bibliographie 1950-1985*, par B. Dehand-schutter, 1986. XXVII-850 p. FB 2500.

76. L. Ceyssens & J.A.G. Tans, *Autour de l'Unigenitus. Recherches sur la genèse de la Constitution*, 1987. XXVI-845 p. FB 2500.

77. A. Descamps, *Jésus et l'Église. Études d'exégèse et de théologie*. Préface de Mgr A. Houssiau, 1987. XLV-641 p. FB 2500.

78. J. Duplacy, *Études de critique textuelle du Nouveau Testament*. Présentées par J. Delobel, 1987. XXVII-431 p. FB 1800.

79. E.J.M. van Eijl (ed.), *L'image de C. Jansénius jusqu'à la fin du XVIIIᵉ siècle*, 1987. 258 p. FB 1250.

80. E. Brito, *La Création selon Schelling. Universum*, 1987. XXXV-646 p. FB 2980.

81. J. Vermeylen (ed.), *The Book of Isaiah – Le livre d'Isaïe. Les oracles et leurs relectures. Unité et complexité de l'ouvrage*, 1989. X-472 p. FB 2700.

82. G. Van Belle, *Johannine Bibliography 1966-1985. A Cumulative Bibliography on the Fourth Gospel*, 1988. XVII-563 p. FB 2700.

83. J.A. Selling (ed.), *Personalist Morals. Essays in Honor of Professor Louis Janssens*, 1988. VIII-344 p. FB 1200.

84. M.-É. Boismard, *Moïse ou Jésus. Essai de christologie johannique*, 1988. XVI-241 p. FB 1000.

84ᴬ. M.-É. Boismard, *Moses or Jesus: An Essay in Johannine Christology*. Translated by B.T. Viviano, 1993, XVI-144 p. FB 1000.

85. J.A. Dick, *The Malines Conversations Revisited*, 1989. 278 p. FB 1500.

86. J.-M. Sevrin (ed.), *The New Testament in Early Christianity – La réception des écrits néotestamentaires dans le christianisme primitif*, 1989. XVI-406 p. FB 2500.

87. R.F. Collins (ed.), *The Thessalonian Correspondence*, 1990. XV-546 p. FB 3000.

88. F. Van Segbroeck, *The Gospel of Luke. A Cumulative Bibliography 1973-1988*, 1989. 241 p. FB 1200.

89. G. THILS, *Primauté et infaillibilité du Pontife Romain à Vatican I et autres études d'ecclésiologie*, 1989. XI-422 p. FB 1850.
90. A. VERGOTE, *Explorations de l'espace théologique. Études de théologie et de philosophie de la religion*, 1990. XVI-709 p. FB 2000.
91. J.C. DE MOOR, *The Rise of Yahwism: The Roots of Israelite Monotheism*, 1990. *Revised and Enlarged Edition*, 1997. XV-445 p. FB 1400.
92. B. BRUNING, M. LAMBERIGTS & J. VAN HOUTEM (eds.), *Collectanea Augustiniana. Mélanges T.J. van Bavel*, 1990. 2 tomes, XXXVIII-VIII-1074 p. FB 3000.
93. A. DE HALLEUX, *Patrologie et œcuménisme. Recueil d'études*, 1990. XVI-887 p. FB 3000.
94. C. BREKELMANS & J. LUST (eds.), *Pentateuchal and Deuteronomistic Studies: Papers Read at the XIIIth IOSOT Congress Leuven 1989*, 1990. 307 p. FB 1500.
95. D.L. DUNGAN (ed.), *The Interrelations of the Gospels. A Symposium Led by M.-É. Boismard – W.R. Farmer – F. Neirynck, Jerusalem 1984*, 1990. XXXI-672 p. FB 3000.
96. G.D. KILPATRICK, *The Principles and Practice of New Testament Textual Criticism. Collected Essays*. Edited by J.K. ELLIOTT, 1990. XXXVIII-489 p. FB 3000.
97. G. ALBERIGO (ed.), *Christian Unity. The Council of Ferrara-Florence: 1438/39 – 1989*, 1991. X-681 p. FB 3000.
98. M. SABBE, *Studia Neotestamentica. Collected Essays*, 1991. XVI-573 p. FB 2000.
99. F. NEIRYNCK, *Evangelica II: 1982-1991. Collected Essays*. Edited by F. VAN SEGBROECK, 1991. XIX-874 p. FB 2800.
100. F. VAN SEGBROECK, C.M. TUCKETT, G. VAN BELLE & J. VERHEYDEN (eds.), *The Four Gospels 1992. Festschrift Frans Neirynck*, 1992. 3 volumes, XVII-X-X-2668 p. FB 5000.

SERIES III

101. A. DENAUX (ed.), *John and the Synoptics*, 1992. XXII-696 p. FB 3000.
102. F. NEIRYNCK, J. VERHEYDEN, F. VAN SEGBROECK, G. VAN OYEN & R. CORSTJENS, *The Gospel of Mark. A Cumulative Bibliography: 1950-1990*, 1992. XII-717 p. FB 2700.
103. M. SIMON, *Un catéchisme universel pour l'Église catholique. Du Concile de Trente à nos jours*, 1992. XIV-461 p. FB 2200.
104. L. CEYSSENS, *Le sort de la bulle Unigenitus. Recueil d'études offert à Lucien Ceyssens à l'occasion de son 90ᵉ anniversaire*. Présenté par M. LAMBERIGTS, 1992. XXVI-641 p. FB 2000.
105. R.J. DALY (ed.), *Origeniana Quinta. Papers of the 5th International Origen Congress, Boston College, 14-18 August 1989*, 1992. XVII-635 p. FB 2700.
106. A.S. VAN DER WOUDE (ed.), *The Book of Daniel in the Light of New Findings*, 1993. XVIII-574 p. FB 3000.
107. J. FAMERÉE, *L'ecclésiologie d'Yves Congar avant Vatican II: Histoire et Église. Analyse et reprise critique*, 1992. 497 p. FB 2600.

108. C. BEGG, *Josephus' Account of the Early Divided Monarchy (AJ 8, 212-420). Rewriting the Bible*, 1993. IX-377 p. FB 2400.
109. J. BULCKENS & H. LOMBAERTS (eds.), *L'enseignement de la religion catholique à l'école secondaire. Enjeux pour la nouvelle Europe*, 1993. XII-264 p. FB 1250.
110. C. FOCANT (ed.), *The Synoptic Gospels. Source Criticism and the New Literary Criticism*, 1993. XXXIX-670 p. FB 3000.
111. M. LAMBERIGTS (ed.), avec la collaboration de L. KENIS, *L'augustinisme à l'ancienne Faculté de théologie de Louvain*, 1994. VII-455 p. FB 2400.
112. R. BIERINGER & J. LAMBRECHT, *Studies on 2 Corinthians*, 1994. XX-632 p. FB 3000.
113. E. BRITO, *La pneumatologie de Schleiermacher*, 1994. XII-649 p. FB 3000.
114. W.A.M. BEUKEN (ed.), *The Book of Job*, 1994. X-462 p. FB 2400.
115. J. LAMBRECHT, *Pauline Studies: Collected Essays*, 1994. XIV-465 p. FB 2500.
116. G. VAN BELLE, *The Signs Source in the Fourth Gospel: Historical Survey and Critical Evaluation of the Semeia Hypothesis*, 1994. XIV-503 p. FB 2500.
117. M. LAMBERIGTS & P. VAN DEUN (eds.), *Martyrium in Multidisciplinary Perspective. Memorial L. Reekmans*, 1995. X-435 p. FB 3000.
118. G. DORIVAL & A. LE BOULLUEC (eds.), *Origeniana Sexta. Origène et la Bible/Origen and the Bible. Actes du Colloquium Origenianum Sextum, Chantilly, 30 août – 3 septembre 1993*, 1995. XII-865 p. FB 3900.
119. É. GAZIAUX, *Morale de la foi et morale autonome. Confrontation entre P. Delhaye et J. Fuchs*, 1995. XXII-545 p. FB 2700.
120. T.A. SALZMAN, *Deontology and Teleology: An Investigation of the Normative Debate in Roman Catholic Moral Theology*, 1995. XVII-555 p. FB 2700.
121. G.R. EVANS & M. GOURGUES (eds.), *Communion et Réunion. Mélanges Jean-Marie Roger Tillard*, 1995. XI-431 p. FB 2400.
122. H.T. FLEDDERMANN, *Mark and Q: A Study of the Overlap Texts*. With an *Assessment* by F. NEIRYNCK, 1995. XI-307 p. FB 1800.
123. R. BOUDENS, *Two Cardinals: John Henry Newman, Désiré-Joseph Mercier*. Edited by L. GEVERS with the collaboration of B. DOYLE, 1995. 362 p. FB 1800.
124. A. THOMASSET, *Paul Ricœur. Une poétique de la morale. Aux fondements d'une éthique herméneutique et narrative dans une perspective chrétienne*, 1996. XVI-706 p. FB 3000.
125. R. BIERINGER (ed.), *The Corinthian Correspondence*, 1996. XXVII-793 p. FB 2400.
126. M. VERVENNE (ed.), *Studies in the Book of Exodus: Redaction – Reception – Interpretation*, 1996. XI-660 p. FB 2400.
127. A. VANNESTE, *Nature et grâce dans la théologie occidentale. Dialogue avec H. de Lubac*, 1996. 312 p. FB 1800.
128. A. CURTIS & T. RÖMER (eds.), *The Book of Jeremiah and its Reception – Le livre de Jérémie et sa réception*, 1997. 332 p. FB 2400.
129. E. LANNE, *Tradition et Communion des Églises. Recueil d'études*, 1997. XXV-703 p. FB 3000.